Edward III and the Triumph of England

RICHARD BARBER

Edward III and the Triumph of England

The Battle of Crécy and the Company of the Garter

ALLEN LANE
an imprint of
PENGUIN BOOKS

ALLEN LANE

Published by the Penguin Group
Penguin Books Ltd, 80 Strand, London WC2R ORL, England
Penguin Group (USA) Inc., 375 Hudson Street, New York, New York 10014, USA
Penguin Group (Canada), 90 Eglinton Avenue East, Suite 700, Toronto, Ontario, Canada M4P 2Y3
(a division of Pearson Penguin Canada Inc.)
Penguin Ireland, 25 St Stephen's Green, Dublin 2, Ireland (a division of Penguin Books Ltd)
Penguin Group (Australia), 707 Collins Street, Melbourne, Victoria 3008, Australia
(a division of Pearson Australia Group Pty Ltd)
Penguin Books India Pvt Ltd, 11 Community Centre,
Panchsheel Park, New Delhi – 110 017, India
Penguin Group (NZ), 67 Apollo Drive, Rosedale, Auckland 0632, New Zealand
(a division of Pearson New Zealand Ltd)
Penguin Books (South Africa) (Pty) Ltd, Block D, Rosebank Office Park,
181 Jan Smuts Avenue, Parktown North, Gauteng 2193, South Africa

Penguin Books Ltd, Registered Offices: 80 Strand, London WC2R ORL, England

www.penguin.com

First published 2013
002

Set in 10.2/13.875pt Sabon LT Std
Typeset by Jouve (UK), Milton Keynes
Printed in Great Britain by Clays Ltd, St Ives plc

ISBN: 978-0-713-99838-2

For Helen
16 August 1942–17 February 2013

Contents

List of Illustrations   ix

Maps and Diagrams   xiii

A Note on Terms   xv

Companions of the Garter Elected 1349–1361   xvii

Preface and Acknowledgements   xix

Different Voices: Reading the Evidence   3

PART ONE
The Rise of English Power

Prologue: The Political Background   33

1 Edward, Philippa and their Comrades 1327–1330   44

2 'A jolly young life': Tournaments, Festivals, Display   67

3 Apprenticeship in War: Scotland and Flanders 1332–1340   97

4 The Kingdom of France   123

5 'As it was in the days of King Arthur'   149

6 The Crécy Campaign   178

7 The Battle at Crécy   213

PART TWO
The Company of the Garter

8 The Royal Chapels and the College of
  St George at Windsor   259

9 'The company of the knights of Saint George
  de la gartiere'   293

PART THREE

The World of the Garter Companions

10 Knightly Associations: Orders, Companies, Fraternities   343

11 Knights in their Own Words   366

12 Laws of War and the Reality of Warfare   391

PART FOUR

A Question of Honour

13 The Garter Companions at War   415

14 The Most Noble Order of the Garter   464

Epilogue: The Legends   483

Appendix 1. *The English Battle Formation at Crécy: A Hypothetical Reconstruction*   493

Appendix 2. *Eustace (Sauchet) d'Auberchicourt*   499

Appendix 3. *Sources for Biographical Material on the Companions of the Garter Elected before 1361*   511

Appendix 4. *Chronological List of Royal Tournaments of Edward III*   520

Appendix 5. *The Statutes of the Garter*   525

Abbreviations   539

Bibliography   541

Notes   569

Index   611

List of Illustrations

1. Edward III, on the lion of England, is given a sword by Philip V of France, while Philip VI cowers beneath. From a manuscript of *c.* 1360–70 (© The British Library Board, MS Egerton 3277, fo. 68ᵛ).

2. Edward III gives the charter for the principality of Aquitaine to Edward prince of Wales. From the original charter of 1362 (© The British Library Board, MS Cotton Nero DVI, fo. 31).

3. Philippa of Hainault, from the manuscript she gave to Edward at the time of their wedding (Bibliothèque Nationale, Paris, MS français 571, fo. 6).

4. Four-wheeled cart of type used by Edward's army in 1346. From the *Roman d'Alexandre, c.* 1344 (The Bodleian Library, University of Oxford, MS 264, fo. 83ᵛ).

5. Archery practice, from the Luttrell Psalter, *c.* 1335 (© The British Library Board, Add. MS 42150, fo. 147ᵛ).

6. An early bombard, from the treatise presented by Walter de Milemete to Edward III in 1327–8 (The Governing Body of Christ Church College, Oxford, MS 92, fo. 70b).

7. Tents, from the *Roman d'Alexandre, c.* 1344 (The Bodleian Library, University of Oxford, MS 264, fo. 83ᵛ).

8. A reconstruction of the Garter pavise of *c.* 1350 (John Roberts).

9. An army on the march from a manuscript of *c.* 1350–75 (© The British Library Board, MS Egerton 1894, fo. 8ᵛ).

10. St George in Garter robes, with the duke of Bedford kneeling before him. From the Bedford Hours, 1423 (© The British Library Board, Add. MS 18850, fo. 256ᵛ).

11. St George's chapel in the 1430s (Eton College, Windsor, MS 213).

12. William Bruges, Garter king at arms, with St George, from his Garter Book of *c.* 1430 (© The British Library Board, MS Stowe 594, fo. 7ᵛ).

13. A figure from the Luttrell Psalter (© The British Library Board, Add. MS 42150, fo. 158ᵛ).

14. A knight wearing the Garter, from an Italian fresco of *c.* 1370 (detail from Andrea di Boniauto, *The Way of Salvation*, Chiesa di Santa Maria Novella, Florence).

15. Dancers and musicians, from a French manuscript of *c.* 1275–1300 (Bibliothèque Nationale, Paris, MS français 146, fo. 34).

16. The Chichester-Constable chasuble. Made in England *c.* 1330–50 (©The Metropolitan Museum of Art/Art Resource/Scala, Florence, 27.162.1).

17–18. Miniatures from the works of Gilles li Muisit, showing fashionable dress at Tournai, about 1352–3. (Bibliothèque Royale, Brussels, MS IV 119, fos. 168 and 213).

19. Two groups of fashionable courtiers, dancing and conversing. From the *Roman d'Alexandre*, *c.* 1344 (The Bodleian Library, University of Oxford, MS 264, fo. 181ᵛ).

20. Feast given at St Denis in 1378 by Charles V. The miniature dates from the following year (Bibliothèque Nationale, Paris, MS français 2813, fo. 47ᵛ).

21. Embroidered purse, French, second half of the fourteenth century (©RMN-Grand Palais (Musée de Cluny – Musée National du Moyen-Âge)/Jean-Gilles Berizzi).

22. Leopards from a horse trapper, English, fourteenth century (©RMN-Grand Palais (Musée de Cluny – Musée National du Moyen-Âge) / Franck Raux).

23. Tapestry of the Scrope of Masham arms, fifteenth century (Dean and Chapter of York Cathedral).

24. Carriage from the Luttrell Psalter. (© The British Library Board, British Library Add. MS 42150, fos. 181ᵛ–182ʳ).

25. A tournament *mêlée*, from an Italian manuscript of 1352–62. (© The British Library Board, British Library Add. MS 12228, fos. 150ᵛ–151).

26. The chest made to contain the documents regarding the confirmation of the treaty of Brétigny at Crécy in October 1360 (The National Archives, E27/8).

27. Replicas of the heraldic achievements of Edward prince of Wales (Dean and Chapter of Canterbury Cathedral).

Maps and Diagrams

Maps

1. France in the fourteenth century — 37
2. The Low Countries — 115
3. Windsor Castle, showing the site of the Round Table building of 1344 (Jill Atherton) — 166
4. The Crécy campaign, 5 July 1346 to 3 September 1346 — 195
5. The siege of Caen, 26–30 July 1346 — 201
6. Cassini's map of the mouth of the Somme, 1790, showing Blanchetaque — 207
7. Cassini's map of Crécy, 1790 — 231
8. Windsor Castle, showing the original site of St George's chapel (Jill Atherton) — 285
9. Prince Edward's raid into Languedoc, 1355 — 425
10. The Poitiers campaign, 1356 — 429

Diagrams

A. The rival claimants to the French throne: a family tree laid out in such a way that Edward appears visually as the first claimant — 124
B. Conjectural reconstruction of English battle formation at Crécy — 495

A Note on Terms

Writing about medieval history always poses problems of terminology, and there are two particularly difficult concepts at the heart of the present book. The first is that of knighthood and chivalry, for which we have two words in English; in all other European languages there is only one, and the subtle distinction between the status of being a knight and the ideology of that status is lost. I have used knighthood for both, as chivalry has – thanks to Sir Walter Scott and the Victorians – acquired romantic overtones which are only occasionally appropriate.

'Man at arms' presents another problem; it is a term used generally and quite vaguely in medieval texts. I have used it to denote any soldier wearing metal armour, which means that they could be armoured infantry or the most heavily armed knights; it is not a rank but a classification. It excludes archers, who would have been lightly armed, and infantry with short lances or daggers who might have leather armour or heavy quilted jerkins as protection.

For reasons which will appear in the course of the book, I have followed the usage of the royal accountants of Edward III, and called what we know today as 'the Order of the Garter' 'the Company of the Garter', except for references to the body of Garter knights after 1415, when the contemporary sources begin to use the word 'Order'.

In order not to confuse the reader, I have used what might be called the personal name for nobility: Henry of Grosmont is successively earl of Derby, earl of Lancaster and duke of Lancaster, for example, and I have simply called him Henry of Grosmont throughout. Full titles can be found in the index.

Countries and regions are generally given their modern names; in some cases this is anachronistic or slightly misleading, but, again, it simplifies an already complicated text.

Currency is normally in sterling, as pounds, shillings (20 to the pound) and pence (12 to the shilling); the mark is two-thirds of a pound, or 13*s*. 4*d*. The French *livres tournois* were usually exchanged at five to the pound.

All unattributed translations are by the author. In these cases, the original source is cited for reference.

Companions of the
Garter Elected 1349–1361

This list covers all the traditional founding knights listed in the statutes, together with those appointed subsequently, again according to the traditional lists, down to 1361. The uncertainities and problems surrounding these lists are discussed on pp. 299–300.

Edward III
Edward prince of Wales

Henry of Grosmont, earl of Derby and Leicester, later duke of Lancaster
Thomas Beauchamp, earl of Warwick
Roger Mortimer, later earl of March
William Montagu, second earl of Salisbury
Thomas Holland, later earl of Kent
Robert Ufford, earl of Suffolk
William Bohun, earl of Northampton
Jean de Grailly, captal de Buch

Ralph Stafford, later earl of Stafford
John, Lord Lisle, of Rougemont
John, Lord Beauchamp
John, Lord Mohun
John, Lord Grey, of Rotherfield
Reginald, Lord Cobham
Thomas, Lord Ughtred

Bartholomew Burghersh the younger
Hugh Courtenay
Richard Fitzsimon
Miles Stapleton, of Bedale
Thomas Wale
Hugh Wrottesley

Nigel Loring
John Chandos
James Audley
Otho Holland
Henry Eam (Oem)
Eustace ('Sanchet') d'Auberchicourt
Walter Pavely
William Fitzwarin
Walter Mauny
Frank van Hale
Richard de la Vache
Thomas Ufford
Edward, Lord Despenser
John Sully

In addition, the king's three sons, Lionel, John and Edmund, were appointed in April 1361.

Preface and Acknowledgements

This book arose out of a conversation with Henry Summerson, medieval editor for the *Oxford Dictionary of National Biography*, for whom I had written a number of entries on the knights of the Garter. At that point, the first group biographies were being added to *ODNB*, and my offer of an article on the original knights of the Garter was warmly accepted. However, I was not entirely happy with the result, which summarized existing scholarship; I felt there was more to be discovered, and my suggestion for a full-scale book on the question was encouraged by Simon Winder at Allen Lane. What follows is not what I expected to write, and has taken much longer into the bargain; I hope Simon feels that his patience has been rewarded. It has been a particularly difficult book to structure, tracing as it does the careers of individual knights as well as the world in which 'the Company of the Garter' came into being and the events which shaped it, and his advice has been particularly welcome. I also owe a great debt to Fionnuala Jervis, who read the text with particular attention to non sequiturs and obscurities, and to Lisa Barber, who challenged me on numerous points of scholarship from her considerable expertise on the early documents concerning the Company of the Garter: in both cases, the book was considerably improved.

In the narrative which follows, I have tried to avoid the temptation to speculate, the great lure of writing medieval history. There are therefore two discussions which I have put into appendices. These are both fascinating and potentially controversial questions. The nature of the English battle formation at Crécy will aways be a hypothesis, and in order to present the evidence as clearly as possible, I have tried to restrict the account of the battle in the main text to an analysis of the varied versions offered by the chroniclers. However, that analysis also points to a possible solution to the problem of how Edward drew up his army, and it is this which forms Appendix 1. I am deeply indebted to Sir Philip Preston for his contribution to the result, since he knows the topography of Crécy and the theories about the battlefield far better than I do, and he can also draw much better plans than I.

Appendix 2 discusses the identity of the mysterious 'Sanchet d'Auberchicourt' among the early knights of the Garter. Here I am grateful for the comments and references of Professor Michael Jones and Professor Michael Prestwich, and particularly for the sustained criticism of my argument by Lisa Barber; we have agreed to differ, but the argument has much improved my presentation of the case.

The other people to whom I owe a great debt are Mark Ormrod, who knows far more about Edward III than I do, for his encouragement and help, and for reading the draft version; and Paul Dryburgh and Jonathan Mackman, who have patiently hunted down references in the National Archives, and sent transcriptions and photographs, from which much of the detail in the book derives. Andrew Ayton helped to point me in the right direction at an early stage, and has also kindly read a draft version. Adrian Ailes greatly improved Chapter 14 on the evolution of the office of herald.

I have shamelessly questioned other scholars about specific points, and doubtless bored them with my latest speculations on obscure details. I am grateful to those who have listened patiently and read parts of the book, particularly Jonathan Boulton, Michael Jones, Chris Given-Wilson, Christopher Allmand and Kelly DeVries. Maurizio Campanelli, whose paper at the Leeds Conference some years ago led me to the dramatic account of the battle of Crécy in an anonymous Roman chronicle which had been overlooked by historians for more than two centuries since it was first printed, has been generous in letting me publish before his own account has appeared in print. Others who have helped on linguistic matters are Michael Lapidge and Bart Besamusca, while Werner Paravicini, whose account of the Prussian crusaders has been a basic text, has also contributed his extensive knowledge of Continental heraldry. Linne Mooney, when the book was almost complete, explained that the poem about the Garter knights which was attributed to Chaucer was in fact by Thomas Hoccleve. My thanks go also to Elizabeth Archibald, Christopher Berard and Nigel Saul for discussions on points ranging from heralds in fifteenth-century plays to the relationship between Arthurian romance and chronicles and the early form of the company itself.

I discussed modern military matters with Jamie Lowther-Pinkerton, and medieval seamanship with the late Alan Gurney, whose friendship and nautical knowledge are sorely missed. My sister Philippa Lane shared her knowledge of harvests, chalky soil and the decreasing height of corn. On more obviously relevant topics, I am grateful to Thomas Woodcock and Hubert Chesshyre at the College of Arms, and particularly to Tim Tatton-Brown on Windsor Castle: it was his knowledge of the building accounts there which inspired the book on Edward III's Round Table building while we worked with Time Team on its excavation in August 2006.

As to books, the London Library's resources account for most of the titles quoted in the bibliography: their staff as always have responded impeccably to innumerable requests. Cambridge University Library provided many of the remainder, together with the British Library, the Society of Antiquaries and the Bodleian Library. Finally, I am grateful for the help of Clare Rider, archivist of St George's Windsor; Robert Yorke, librarian at the College of Arms, and to Elisabeth A. Stuart at the Duchy of Cornwall office for the loan of a manuscript translation of Henxteworth's journal.

I am grateful to the copy-editor, Elizabeth Stratford, for her close reading of the text, and particularly for detecting the points where I had contradicted myself over dates and facts; and to the proofreader, Stephen Ryan, for his thorough work. Similarly, the work of the indexer, Auriol Griffith–Jones, helped to uncover problems over the treatment of names and a number of actual errors. Keeping control of often very disparate material is always difficult, and their work has eliminated most, if not all, of the resulting vagaries.

I am aware that, despite all this expert advice, errors and omissions undoubtedly remain, for which I am unwittingly responsible. I am, however, entirely aware of my responsibility for the revisionist view both of the tactics of the battle of Crécy and of the nature of the Company of the Garter itself, and regard this simply as a contribution to an ongoing scholarly debate. I may well be wrong on both counts, but would be disappointed if I have not made at least a reasonable case to be answered, and encouraged other scholars to look again at the evidence.

EDWARD III AND THE TRIUMPH OF ENGLAND

Different Voices: Reading the Evidence

Only twice in English history has a full-scale seaborne invasion of France been attempted. On both occasions, at the height of summer, a huge invasion fleet appeared off the Normandy coast south-west of Cherbourg. D-Day in 1944 was an unparalleled operation, with a huge range of ships of all sizes, and involved landings on a wide front along the Baie de la Seine. Six hundred years earlier, Edward III's fleet in 1346 landed from ships more similar in size to those of the armada of 'little ships' that rescued the survivors of Dunkirk in 1940. They moored in the anchorage of the Grande Rade off St Vaast-la-Hougue, close to Cherbourg itself, the safest place in the Baie, which offers shelter from the prevailing south-westerlies that blow up the Channel.[1]

Edward had led armies into France before, and would do so again, in pursuit of his claim to the French crown. Since the twelfth century, English expeditions which had been sent to Gascony had landed at the port of Bordeaux, held by Gascons loyal to their English masters. The estuary of the Gironde offered safe harbour for hundreds of ships; on the north coast of France, by contrast, there was little choice. The Breton ports, sometimes but by no means always in friendly hands, were far too small for a naval force of more than 1,200 ships. To the east of Cherbourg, all the ports were securely in French hands, and the only possible landing places were well defended.

Like D-Day, Edward's invasion in 1346 was shrouded in secrecy. The French were aware of his intentions, but had little hard information about his plans, with the result that the landing was unopposed. The campaign which followed was to lead to the first great victory of the English army over French forces, and to the capture of the key port of Calais, the most desirable foothold for the English on the north coast of France, with ready communication with Dover. It gave plausibility to

3

Edward III's dream of enforcing his claim to the French crown, and transformed England's reputation from that of an unimportant offshore island to that of a major military power with new methods of fighting which aroused dread and admiration among Continental princes.

This book examines the men to whom this achievement can be attributed. The central figure is of course Edward III, but it is his comrades in arms who were the crucial element in the English success, seasoned campaigners who had a decade and more of experience in the harshest kind of warfare, and who had learnt the lesson which so often evaded medieval commanders, that of a genuine comradeship and *esprit de corps*. It is a study of a group of men and their culture – culture in the widest sense, from their places in society and politics to their attitudes and beliefs, their dynastic ambitions and their role models and ideals.

Edward III achieved the almost unique feat of retaining the loyalty of the great lords of England throughout his long reign from 1327 to 1377. There were of course doubtful moments, and times when relations between king and magnates were uneasy, but by and large it was an era of exceptional loyalty to the sovereign. Many of Edward's comrades in arms fought at his side for thirty years or more, and his most intimate friends were a close-knit group. The ties that bound them were a critical element in Edward's success, and found their outward expression in the creation of the Company of the Garter, which we know today as the Order of the Garter. The nature of that company, and the way in which it attained its unparalleled reputation in the world of knighthood, are central to the theme of this book.

Who were the original members of the Company of the Garter? First and foremost, they were the men who led the expedition of 1346, the men who changed England's military reputation with their victory at Crécy, and took the town of Calais in the following year. We know the names of forty-nine of the commanders of Edward's army, and of these fourteen were to become knights of the Company of the Garter. A further seven individual knights who fought on the campaign were also among the probable founder members. It is for this reason that the Crécy campaign is crucial to our understanding of the company. Although the common military experience of the earliest Garter companions was much wider than this one expedition, it was in Normandy in 1346 that the bonds between them were fully forged.

There is a basic assumption behind the study of a group of this kind which also needs to be declared. This book starts from the idea that individuals can make a very considerable difference to the course of history, and that economic and social movements are only part of the story. Edward III is a supreme example of this: his political skills and his relations with the men around him largely account for the exceptional degree of co-operation between crown and magnates during his reign. The men he selected as companions of the Garter shared his ideals and tastes, and, although their personal history is often fragmentary and disjointed, we can in most cases form a good idea of their different characters and origins.

A great deal has been written about the military history of the year 1346, and the outlines of what happened are well established. But as soon as we begin to ask more detailed questions, it becomes clear that, behind the confident narratives of the nineteenth-century historians and the more critical commentaries of recent writers, there is a basic issue which is rarely addressed, and problems which need to be declared before we investigate this small group of men and their individual biographies, let alone try to assess them as a group.

My starting point is therefore the question 'How do we know what we think we know?', and I begin by looking at the writers and sources who can shed light on the history of England and France in the mid-fourteenth century. It produces important and sometimes surprising results; and the question of evidence is a theme which recurs throughout the book. This is particularly true in relation to the early history of the Company of the Garter itself; despite its subsequent fame, we cannot even be sure of the names of the original knights. To listen carefully to these different voices and what they have to tell us, we must first discover who they were, and what lies behind the documents they have left for us.

The medieval past comes down to us through a range of different voices, and the nature of these is an essential part of our story. It is possible to write the history of the fourteenth century from the dry entries in the public records; or it can be done from the vivid story-telling of Jean Froissart, whose highly individual view of the warfare of the period was the chief source for historians until the twentieth century. Neither of these sources is quite what it seems, and between the two extremes is a whole range of further texts and documents.

Before the fourteenth century, chronicles had largely been created by monks or clergy as a record of institutional and national history, and secular writers were very unusual. For Edward III's reign we have a much wider range of authors, writing out of personal enthusiasm and sometimes personal involvement in the events they describe. Their immediacy is gained at the expense of the measured consideration of the cloistered chronicler, but it is unjust to dismiss the majority of them as 'episodic, prejudiced, inaccurate and late'.[2] The public records can give us dates, names and places, but little of what people thought and felt. The chronicles may fall down on precise details; yet they alone can give us the material to understand something of the times. Precisely because they are 'different voices', however, we need to have a sense of the original audience for each text if we are to understand what it is telling us, and how we can use it to assemble the evidence.

Let us begin with the dramatic and picturesque. Jean Froissart's chronicles, written from the viewpoint of someone who travelled between the English and French courts and owed allegiance to both (or neither) at different times, should be a wonderful resource. However, although historians have been admirers of his work for centuries, they have also been baffled and infuriated by it: we have to confront its origins and nature and try to understand this essential text which has so dominated the history of Edward III and the exploits of his knights. Even a historian as rigorous as Jonathan Sumption has to refer to Froissart frequently in his magisterial work on the Hundred Years War, but we have to remember that Froissart was writing towards the end of the fourteenth century, as much as fifty years after the events he describes. For the early years of his chronicle, with which we are largely concerned, he too was listening to the same voices as us and interpreting them as best he could.

Froissart's model, as he himself tells us, was the chronicle of Jean le Bel, canon of Liège, who had written his work at the request of Jean de Hainault, uncle of Edward's wife Philippa.[3] We have a pen-portrait of Le Bel by a man who knew him personally, Jacques d'Hemricourt: tall and handsome, he dressed in rich knightly clothing, and was attended by a following of sixteen to twenty people when he went to church on weekdays. On Sundays and festivals, his entourage, fifty strong, was as grand as that of the bishop himself: and the bishop of Liège was a prince who ruled his own diocese as a state within the Holy Roman Empire. Le Bel's men dined at his table and received robes from him annually, forty sets for his squires, three for his canons and two for his knights. He him-self had been trained as a knight in his youth, had fought in tournaments and had been in the household of Jean de Hainault. Jean de Hainault accompanied Edward III on his Scottish expedition in 1327, and Le Bel served under him. He had twin sons by his mistress, one of whom became a knight and the other followed him as a canon at St Martin's.[4]

Writing chronicles was essentially a literary occupation; the idea of a professional historian does not appear until much later, and all the histories, chronicles and annals on which we shall draw have a strong literary background, whether secular or religious. Le Bel's approach is distinctly on the secular side: he 'knew how to write songs and *virelais*', according to Hemricourt. However, he makes no pretensions to a high style: his great virtues as a writer are directness and clarity, and he is an accomplished and orderly narrator.[5] His account of the warfare in Scotland is exceptionally vivid, and makes him one of the very few writers of the period who actually experienced a campaign.[6] He wrote the chronicle in stages: the first part, covering up to 1340, was written some time between 1352 and 1356; the second part, to 1358, was finished that year, and the final chapters are contemporary with the events they record.[7]

Le Bel sets out his objectives in the prologue to his chronicle, chiefly in terms of presenting a riposte in plain prose to the puffery of a large book in verse which has lately appeared claiming to present the history of the recent wars between the French and English kings. He will offer a short, accurate account of events – though the result is far from brief – and he is particularly concerned to do justice to all those who took part in 'such cruel and dangerous battles' without exaggeration or 'attributing to someone incredible prowess which the human body could not achieve'. It should be enough to say that a particular knight had performed best in such and such a battle, and that other knights had done well, 'and to name the knight and the battle'. But he acknowledges that he is partisan: Edward III is his hero, and it is the story of the 'gallant and noble king' that he sets out to tell.[8] His hero has one fatal flaw; Le Bel is reluctant to believe the story which shames the king, but, because he believes it to be true, he resolves to include it. This is the legend of Edward III's rape of the countess of Salisbury, which almost certainly originated in French propaganda designed to defame the king's knightly reputation.[9]

The events which particularly interest him are the knightly episodes, within the context of a narrative which is very much focused on personalities rather than the details of diplomatic documents. And his only possible source for these knightly deeds is the knights themselves and their personal memories. Jean de Hainault himself was a prime source, and Le Bel therefore has a first-hand account of the battle of Crécy from the French side, which he must have recorded no later than nine years after the event (Jean died early in 1356); he had information not only from Jean himself but also from ten or twelve of his household knights, and from several English and German knights who were present.[10] The romantic account which he gives of Walter Mauny, a knight from Jean de Hainault's circle, at the siege of Hennebon in Brittany was also first-hand, though very different in tone. Mauny was with an English force to help Jeanne de Montfort, countess of Brittany, and when they landed she entertained them lavishly. After the entertainment he looked out of the window, and swore he would destroy the huge siege machine which was pounding the town. Taking 300 men, he destroyed it and retreated, pursued by the enemy: he turned and faced them, crying, 'May I never be embraced by my dear love if I return to the fortress without unhorsing one of these attackers, or being unhorsed by them.' This is warfare overlaid by knightly convention: the countess, an accomplished military leader herself, as a lady in distress; an encounter with the enemy as a knightly adventure complete with knightly vow.[11] The truth, as we shall see, was probably much more prosaic, but this was how Mauny wanted the event to be remembered; it may well be how he did indeed recall it after the event.

Jacques d'Hemricourt records that Le Bel's squires were under instructions to invite any 'valiant stranger' to dine with their master, so that he could talk with him. But Le Bel was quick to admit when he was unable to find an informant. He writes in his account of the year 1340 that he has not described the conflict between the English and the Scots at that time because he does not know enough about it. 'And certainly in what I have written above, I have kept as close to the truth as I could, according to what I personally have seen and remembered, and also what I have heard from those who were there, telling me what they really knew, when I was not present; and if I am mistaken about anything, may I be forgiven for it.'[12] More than any other chronicler of the period, he admits openly to his ignorance, refuses to write about matters of which he knows nothing, and tries to distinguish between rumours and information of which he is sure.[13]

Le Bel's presentation of what he has learnt, observed and researched remains literary; he is writing history with heroes and villains, with moral lessons in mind. This may influence his selection of facts, yet he tries to be a conscientious recorder, and largely succeeds in his aim of writing a 'true history'.

Another writer with even closer links to the court of Hainault was Jean Bernier, the provost of Hainault and one of William I of Hainault's most trusted officials. His memoirs are not really a chronicle, as they open with a series of episodes from his career, and other notable events from the history of Valenciennes, where he lived. What he offers is a wonderful insight into the life of wealthy Flemish merchants and their peers, and a rather less important narrative of the history of Flanders, which was evidently continued by other members of his family. In 1334, at his house near the St Pol bridge in Valenciennes, he gave a feast for about seventy people, including the kings of Bohemia and Navarre, the count of Flanders and the bishop of Liège, as well as his master William I and Jean de Hainault. He gives us the seating plan, the menu and the wines they drank; he even tells us that the lampreys came from the royal fishmonger in Paris.[14] Like Le Bel, he was in a position to learn a great deal at first hand from the nobility of Flanders, but only occasional insights appear in the chronicle which follows. The impulse to write history is secondary to his (and his descendants') desire to justify his career, particularly as he was in disgrace after William I's death, and only exonerated some time later.

Le Bel's follower Jean Froissart was of humbler origins; like Jean Bernier, he seems to have been from Valenciennes, but his life before his departure for England in 1361 is obscure. Nor do we know how he managed to get an introduction to Queen Philippa, and to present her with a chronicle of the Anglo-French wars of the previous decade. This sudden appearance at the heart of the English court must have been due to an introduction from someone in Hainault of knightly rank who knew Philippa well, and it was probably due to his literary genius that he obtained this introduction. For we may remember Froissart as a chronicler today, but he had a reputation as a poet and writer of romances before he turned his hand to history. He was famous for his lyrics, and, while he was writing the first version of his chronicles, he was also composing a long Arthurian romance, *Meliador*. For much of his life, he was more famous as a poet than as a historian; and, just as episodes in *Meliador* are drawn from real life, so there is a strong element of knightly romance in his history. He may not have aspired to the knightly lifestyle of Le Bel, but he certainly felt that he belonged to the same knightly milieu.

Froissart sets out a grander scheme at the beginning of his chronicle:

> In order that the great deeds of arms which have come about through the wars of France and England may be suitably recorded and held in perpetual remembrance so that good men may take them as an example, I wish to undertake to set them down in prose. Indeed Sir Jehan le Bel, formerly canon of Saint Lambert at Liège chronicled in his time something of these matters. Now I have augmented this book and this history by careful enquiry as I travelled throughout the world, asking the valiant men and knights, and the squires who helped them, to add to the truth of what happened; and also asking several kings of arms and their marshals, both in France and England, in order to establish the truth of the matter. For such men are rightly the investigators and reporters of such affairs, and I believe that their honour is such that they would not dare to lie.[15]

For the events of this book, Froissart is a second-generation historian. He was probably not yet twenty when the battle of Poitiers was fought in 1356; his information is not contemporary with the events, which means that, were he an ordinary chronicler, he would be piecing together his story from earlier writers. Instead, Froissart tries to discover the truth largely through oral evidence from the participants. While a modern historian will be much more sceptical than he is about their veracity, there are two very valuable elements in his work. Firstly, like Le Bel, he offers us a direct insight into the attitudes of these participants, and sometimes into their individual character. Talking to Froissart, who was known as a chronicler from his earliest days at the English court, the knights could ensure that their version of events was recorded, even if their voices come down to us with a literary veneer added by the writer rather than a verbally accurate report. Froissart often tells us, unconsciously, how such men wished to be remembered. Secondly, this is an age when personal memory was much more highly regarded than it is today: we demand written records or eyewitness accounts contemporary with the event in question. But in the fourteenth century an entire lawsuit could be built round the memory of knights, squires and clergymen: the case of Scrope versus Grosvenor in the Court of Chivalry in 1386 consists solely of the sworn statements of men who had seen one or other of the knights in question bearing the arms which were in dispute. Memory is of course fallible, but Froissart sometimes manages to be surprisingly accurate with very little apparent recourse to written documents. For instance, describing the English naval campaign of 1387, he notes the part played by Piers du Bois of Ghent; this man's presence on the expedition is confirmed by the official records, and makes it likely that Froissart's account of his influence on strategy is probably correct.[16]

Froissart has been called 'the ancestor of our great reporters ... in whose investigations the sensational and the unusual have pride of place'.[17] His work is closer to that of a journalist than of an orthodox historian of the period, and we can watch him at work on his journey to Foix in the winter of 1388-9, where he was anxious to find out more about one of the most famous princes of the age, Gaston III, lord of Foix-Béarn in the Pyrenees, nicknamed Phoebus. He also hoped for news of the affairs of Spain and Portugal from members of his court, 'since there had been no great deeds of arms in Picardy or Flanders for a long time'. On the last stage of his journey, he spent three days at Pamiers waiting for someone else who was going to Béarn and knew the roads, because a lone traveller was very much at risk. He found a talkative Gascon squire in the service of Gaston, Espan du Lion, who was the ideal companion, and also very knowledgeable about the count's affairs. Froissart's account of their conversations on the way show him using sophisticated interviewing techniques, gaining the confidence of his fellow-traveller and offering his own news stories in return for the information he obtains from him. He finds knights from Aragon and members of the household of John of Gaunt from England, and gets the latest situation in Castile, Navarre and Portugal from them; and he manages to learn a good deal about Gaston Phoebus himself from Espan du Lion, who talks with some hesitation about Gaston's murder of his only son and of his cousin. It is brilliant journalism, vivid and racily told; but Froissart was never one to check his facts, and the cousin in question was actually very much alive when Espan told his story.[18] In contrast, the Bascot de Mauleon, a Gascon knight whom he met on the same journey, provided him with what seems to be a straightforward and factual account of his career: where he first fought a battle, and his campaigns thereafter, all described in considerable detail.[19] Much of what he says is supported by other evidence, and, apart from the story of how he and his men captured the castle of Thurie disguised as women, the tone of the narrative is realistic.

Froissart is a man with a mission, and he is not afraid of revising his work. There are at least four versions of the first book of his history, and he returned to it again and again throughout his life in order to recast it and get closer to what he believed to be the truth. The version written in the last years of his life, after his visit to England in 1395, is the considered work of a man who has spent nearly fifty years in search of his vision of a true account of the events of Edward III's reign, when 'prowess reigned for a long time in England, through the deeds of King Edward III and of the prince of Wales, his son'.[20] The earliest versions are largely reworkings of Le Bel's chronicle. To these Froissart adds details from his frequent conversations with the knights who had taken part in the Crécy and Poitiers campaigns, expanding the text very considerably.

At the very end of his life, however, he set down a shorter version of these stories, as if he was attempting a real overview of the events which had fascinated him for so long. This version survives in just one manuscript, now in Rome. Here he showed that he could do more than tell a good story; his reflections and revisions produced a work which takes a much more thoughtful and sometimes philosophical view than his exuberant first attempts. And Froissart is distinctly less romantic about knighthood: there is a new cynicism about the kings and nobles and their politics which balances his account of their heroic deeds.[21] He had always adopted something of the high moral tone of the monastic chroniclers in his treatment of the three kings of England about whose reigns he writes: returning in 1395 from an England in the throes of a political crisis pitting the king against the nobility, he remembered the disasters of Edward II's reign seventy years earlier, and, by the time he finished the longest version of his chronicle, Richard II had met the same fate as his grandfather. In this last, short, version, Froissart reassesses Edward III in the light of experience, and, instead of treating him – as Le Bel had done – as a heroic figure from the start, tries to give some account of how he came to learn statesmanship. At the end of the book, Edward III and Philippa are presented as the most glorious sovereigns in the world; but they have earned this place by the king's wisdom, the queen's devotion and the wise counsel of men such as Walter Mauny.[22]

The Rome manuscript shows how Edward was remembered thirty years after his death; in terms of actual new evidence, there is very little, and it is sometimes most interesting for what it omits rather than for what it includes. We can test Froissart's own opinion of his earlier account against this text; obviously, the rejected stories have to be treated with more scepticism than those he repeats in his final, considered version.

Where we have to be cautious from the historical point of view is in respect of Froissart's literary quality. Froissart writes for effect, and his effects can be striking; when his material falls into a recognized literary pattern, he cannot resist moulding it to fit that formula. He may write pure fiction at times, and if we rely on Froissart for facts it can be very dangerous. His account of the treachery of Robert d'Artois is largely imaginary in terms of times and places.[23] Yet by using his superb literary skills, he can draw out Robert's motives and character by using this combination of a well-organized and integrated, if fictional, narrative. If we read him first and foremost for the mindset of the princes and magnates of the period, he is invaluable.

In the later middle ages Froissart was read as much for entertainment as for instruction, and in the sixteenth century his work was regarded as an adventure story like the romances. When the French translator of the hugely popular Spanish romance *Amadis de Gaula*, Herberay des Essarts, published the fourth volume of the work, he included a puff for his work from an anonymous poet which claimed that, now *Amadis* was available in French, there was no need for the 'Lancelots, Tristans and Froissarts'.[24]

As an antidote to Froissart, we turn to another canon, Gilles li Muisit of Tournai. Like Le Bel, he was a canon for most of his life, while Froissart's post as canon of Chimay was probably a reward for good service in the secular world. Like Le Bel and Froissart, he wrote poetry, much of which survives. But Li Muisit was a regular canon, that is, he was a monk subject to the Benedictine rule, and hence he was a less worldly figure than the other two. He lived within the monastery at Tournai for most of his life, apart from three years studying in Paris, and was abbot from 1331 until his death in 1352. His poems are moral and religious, and he wrote on the history of his abbey. The original manuscript of this survives, and at the end of it is Li Muisit's chronicle, his last work. In Paris, he had been nicknamed 'Pluma', quill pen, and it seems that for much of his life he noted down important events and information.[25]

In 1345 he began to go blind, and it was at this point that he started to write, unable to lead his previously active life. The notes he had accumulated over the years were read to him; he dictated a text based on them to his scribe, but was unable to read the result and correct it. Even though he recovered his sight in 1352 after an operation, he never revised the text, because he died soon afterwards. He completed the chronicle proper in 1348; this he then continued in what he called annals, and both these and the later years of the chronicle are therefore more or less contemporary with the events of Edward III's reign, which makes him a valuable source. His style is dry, and there are none of the picturesque details found in Froissart and Le Bel, but he is well informed and thoughtful. In particular, he is very cautious about figures, and tries to give accurate estimates wherever he can, perhaps because he had an interest in mathematics and in astronomy.[26]

Li Muisit does use written sources quite extensively, but only names one or two. Likewise, he draws on oral testimony, but reveals the identity of just two of his informants, a papal chaplain with much experience of the papal court at Avignon, and his cousin, a councillor in the French parlement. Tournai, although almost surrounded by Flemish territory, was an important French stronghold, besieged by Edward III in 1340, and Li Muisit is, like the inhabitants in general, very much pro-French. He describes how, during the siege of Tournai, the French forces defending the town managed their relations with the inhabitants so well that 'there was never a disagreement or strife between them; but they were like blood brothers together'.[27] His abbey received many distinguished guests, and it is from them that much of his information must have come. But he protests that he is a severe critic of what he hears: 'People in general believe easily, and even more easily repeat and spread what they have heard, so that what they say is partly false, partly true: I do not approve of such talk and put no trust in it, particularly because if I write down things about which I may not be certain, my whole work will be in disrepute, and I will not be believed in other matters.'[28] This leads him to give an account of the outcome of the battle of Crécy very different from that of other chroniclers. Yet for all his protestations, he is happy to repeat horror stories of the atrocities of English troops in 1338,[29] while the French forces can do no wrong. He is a dour but largely realistic counterweight to the narratives of chivalrous exploits in Le Bel and Froissart. And his voice speaks not for the nobility, for whom war represented glory and profit, but for the defenceless and weak who were the main sufferers.

Jean de Venette was, like Gilles li Muisit, a highly placed cleric, prior of the Paris convent of Carmelite friars, and eventually head of the order in France.[30] The work of the Carmelites put them in close touch with the lay world; Venette himself was of peasant origin. He was very probably writing as events happened from 1360 onwards, and has much detail of the disasters which overtook ordinary citizens and countrymen after the battle of Poitiers, in the time of the popular uprising known as the *Jacquerie*, a violent reaction to the failure of government after the capture of John II of France. He is less inclined to blame the English exclusively for the horrors of war, and sees events from the standpoint of the classic definition of the orders of society: for the well-being of all, the peasant should work, the clergy should pray and labour at spiritual matters, and the knight should defend all three orders. His theme is that the knights have failed in their duty, and that the disturbances are the result of this failure, particularly as they now extort payments in return for this non-existent protection. Jean de Venette is another voice to set against those of the aristocratic chroniclers. He, like Gilles li Muisit, is moved to set down what he has seen and heard as a record of the disasters of the times.

Le Bel, Li Muisit and Venette all seem to have been stimulated to write their histories because of their own personal experience of the war and its consequences. In England, there is only one comparable author, Thomas Gray, whose background, like Le Bel's, was the Scottish wars.[31] His family came from near Berwick, where an ancestor had been mayor in 1253. Thomas was probably born soon after 1310, and first appears in the records in 1331 accused of poaching, and in 1332 he was involved in the abduction and ransom of a citizen of Berwick. His first experience of warfare may have been at the battle of Dupplin Moor in the same year; six years later he was certainly in the retinue of William Montagu, first earl of Salisbury, when Edward III sailed for Flanders. He returned from Flanders in 1340, possibly after Montagu had been captured by the French, and his movements thereafter are not clear. He may well have been the Thomas Gray, 'knight of the prince's household', who was presented with £20 when he was given leave to go to visit his friends in 1344–5.[32] This was about the time his father died, and his career henceforth was in the north: he inherited his father's estates and played an increasingly important military role. He was at the battle of Neville's Cross in 1346, when the Scottish king David II was captured, but he himself was captured by a Franco-Scottish force in 1355, and found himself in prison for a year. Here, like the more famous knight-prisoner Thomas Malory, he occupied his enforced leisure by starting his chronicle. He was released by autumn 1356, and continued to write until 1362, seven years before his death.

Gray's chronicle is therefore largely the work of a contemporary, often an eyewitness, and of a man highly experienced in war. Le Bel's brief service as a squire gave him something of the same authority, but his is a more literary creation. Gray is practical, direct and independent: he is openly critical of William Montagu, his leader in Flanders, saying that he was captured due to his own folly in undertaking 'a foolhardy *chevauchée*'* and he accuses him and Edward III of wasting the army's time for fifteen months, jousting and devoting himself to pleasure, after they arrived at Antwerp in 1338. He has little time for the niceties of knighthood: warfare on the Scottish border was a harsher and more brutal affair altogether. He began his work by drawing on two chronicles written in the north, and on the popular history of the time, the so-called *Brut*,[33] and used these to bring his work up to the point where his own career began. His style is straightforward but often vivid in its descriptions, and it is a great pity that his account of the years 1340 to 1356 is missing from the unique manuscript.[34]

There is another knightly chronicle, which is the work of someone who was an eyewitness of the Spanish campaign of 1366–7. This is *The Life of the Black Prince*, by the herald of John Chandos:[35] a personal herald was known by his master's name, so he names himself 'Chandos Herald'. We know nothing about him apart from the evidence of his work: the language reveals that he was probably from Hainault, like Froissart, and indeed Froissart obtained much information from him.

---

* A *chevauchée* is an expedition on horseback, usually a raid into enemy territory.

Chandos Herald was a participant in many of the episodes he describes. He was probably the man who carried money to John Chandos from the king of Navarre in 1363.[36] However, his description of the battle of Poitiers implies that he was not in John's service at that time, and therefore was not an eyewitness, since he says at one point, 'The book and the story tell . . .'[37]

Chandos Herald writes in verse, perhaps because this was the traditional way of memorizing history in an oral culture; there are accounts of tournaments by heralds in the thirteenth century which use similar verse forms. It is an awkward form for a factual history such as his and was old-fashioned even when he composed his poem, and he admits as much in the opening lines. However, 'people . . . should not give up writing poems about good deeds, if they know how to, but should write them in a book, so that when they are dead there is an honest record'.[38] As to his purpose, he wishes to record the names of the participants and the feats of arms which they accomplished; shameful deeds are not on the agenda, and he pointedly refuses to list the French knights who fled from the field of Crécy: 'three kings left the field, many others fled – how many I do not know, and it is not right to count them.'[39]

Nearly half his chronicle is taken up by the Spanish campaign of 1367, at which he was present, and his role as a herald shapes his account: his lists of names can be checked against record sources and are very accurate, and he is our best source for the sequence of military events. Yet this factual record is overlaid with some of the conventions of romance, such as the scene of Edward prince of Wales's parting from his wife. And warfare is a matter for his heroes: when the Spanish ambush the army, they send 'men at arms riding mules and other ruffians to attack them'. The hardships of the crossing of the Pyrenees and the horrors of war are glossed over.[40] If, as is possible, the poem was written for Richard II in the 1380s, this is how a knightly audience wished to see itself reflected in the mirror of history.

The battle of Nájera is the only occasion when we have a detailed eyewitness account from the other side. Pero López de Ayala was definitely a grandee, and he writes in the same vein as Froissart. Born into the Castilian aristocracy, he had a distinguished career as a soldier, diplomat and finally grand chancellor of Castile. He fought at Nájera, and was captured by the English forces, becoming a prisoner of the prince of Wales. He was also a poet and a writer; his *Rhyme of the Palace* is both

a satire on the life of the royal court and a confessional.[41] The foreword
to his history of Pedro's reign declares:

> The memory of men is weak and they cannot recall everything that hap-
> pened in the past. For this reason, the wise men of ancient times invented
> letters and ways of writing so that the sciences and great deeds of
> the world were recorded and kept so that men knew of them, and learnt
> from them to do good and to avoid evil, and to keep them in lasting
> remembrance. And books were later made in which such things were
> written and recorded ... And thence it became the custom that princes
> and kings should order that books be made, called chronicles and histo-
> ries, where deeds of knighthood and any other actions of the princes of
> old were recorded, so that those who came after them, when they read
> of their deeds, would make greater efforts to do good and to avoid doing
> evil ...
>
> And therefore from now on I, Pero López de Ayala, with God's help,
> intend to continue recording, as truthfully as possible, what I have seen,
> and I intend to tell nothing but the truth; with all possible diligence I will
> also record other events which happen in my age and time in places where
> I was not present, if I hear of them by truthful report and witness from
> gentlemen and others worthy of belief.[42]

López sees history as an example to his contemporaries, reflecting his
unusually intellectual education under his uncle, Cardinal Gómez Barroso; and he insists on the veracity of his sources. He sees the 'truthful
report and witness' of reliable informants as the key to writing his
chronicle, echoing the approach of Le Bel and Froissart: history should
be reported by those who were present, and deeds are the mainspring of
the action.

The insistence on reportage and eyewitness evidence does not surprise
us today; indeed, it seems entirely normal. But the writers we have met
so far are outside the tradition of the historians of the early middle ages.
Since, before the fourteenth century, chroniclers were generally members of the clergy, and most commonly monks who were technically
confined to their monasteries, they were entirely reliant on second-hand
reports of events outside their walls. However, the great monasteries
often had good contacts with the royal court: in England, this was true
of St Albans in the thirteenth century. In France, the great French official

chronicle, the *Grandes chroniques*, was the work of the monks of St
Denis, the royal monastery to the north of Paris where the kings
of France were buried and the *oriflamme* or banner of France was
kept. This was both a history of the reigns of each king and also a general history of France. The continuation of this, dealing with John II
and Charles V,[43] begins in the monastic style, but seems to have
been written from 1350 onwards by someone close to Charles V. It is
not far from being propaganda, and is much more interested in putting
across official business and the official viewpoint on current affairs than
in the details of campaigns, let alone of knightly exploits. But it is
important for our understanding of the French side and of the king
whose new tactics effectively held the English at bay throughout his
reign.

Paris never became a great centre for the recording of history;
London, by contrast, had a number of important authors in the mid-
fourteenth century.[44] These men, like Le Bel and Froissart, were secular
clerics, usually canons; they went about the king's business or the business of their cathedral or church among the populace at large, and had
the opportunity of seeing events at first hand as well as access to official
records and men of standing who could give them information. The
canons of St Paul's were frequently also royal officials, and three sets of
annals written at or near St Paul's in the early years of Edward III's
reign give us a view of the king and his business from the heart of the
capital.[45] The anonymous author of the first annals (up to 1337) gives
us vivid descriptions of Edward's early royal tournaments in London,
and details of government activity in the city. He was followed by Adam
Murimuth, a diplomat who carried out a number of missions for
Edward II to the papal court. His work is relatively brief and selective –
he often comments that nothing important happened in a particular
year – and it ends in 1347. His approach is unusual for the time, but
also what one might expect from a senior government official. Much of
what he tells us has to do with diplomatic work; his experiences make
him anti-papal and anti-French. He gives us in great detail an assessment of Edward III's claim to the French crown, and information about
several attempts to negotiate peace between the two kingdoms. But for
our purposes the most valuable part is the descriptions of the skirmishes
and battles, by land and sea, of the early years of the Hundred Years
War. In some cases he summarizes what may have been a written report,

but he also preserves the full text of several documents which were effectively royal circulars on the progress of the campaigns in France.[46] And he shows us government propaganda at work during the Crécy campaign, in the sermon of Archbishop Stratford in August 1346 at St Paul's, at which the archbishop read out a French plan for the conquest of England which had been found when the city of Caen was captured. He was not an unstinting admirer of Edward, however, and criticized his conduct of the war in Flanders. Like Thomas Gray, he attacked William Montagu for the 'senseless audacity' which led to his capture. On the other hand, he gives an admiring account of the great festival at Windsor in 1344, which he either witnessed or heard about from one of the many citizens of London invited to the occasion by the king.[47]

Robert of Avesbury was a legal official serving the archbishop of Canterbury, and lived near St Paul's. His chronicle is boldly entitled 'The wonderful deeds of the magnificent king of England ... and his peers'.[48] When Edward shakes off the rule of Isabella and Mortimer, Avesbury declares that 'from henceforth the said lord Edward the Third held the sun of his majesty and reigned as a magnificent king, wishing to exercise himself and his men in deeds of arms'.[49] The 'wonderful deeds' alert us to expect a narrative which sees Edward in knightly terms, and this is indeed what we get. However, Avesbury's sources, like Murimuth's, are the official reports of the fighting in France, many of which he quotes, including two from the St Paul's archives: others come from the Canterbury archives. Almost half his text is taken up with copies of such documents, which he obviously took great pains to collect: he is able to quote a letter to the king of France from the captain of Calais found in a ship captured by the English during the siege of 1347. Occasionally he finds an eyewitness who has a tale to tell, as in the episode at Calais in 1350 when Edward and the prince of Wales personally fought off a surprise attack by French forces: this was related to him by one of the captured French knights. This episode becomes a set piece in several chronicles, and, if there is an element of hero-worship in all this, it gives us a good idea of how the first half of Edward's reign was viewed by his supporters.[50]

The untitled chronicle written in French in London in the 1330s offers a very different perspective on the events of the time. It is much more direct, as if we were listening to someone telling of his experiences, though the stories may well have been at second or third hand. The chronicle is sometimes cast in a conventional literary style: Edward is made to voice remarks such as 'Because Christ died for us on a Friday, we will not attack the enemy today', or to exhort his troops with: 'Fair lords and my brothers, do not be dismayed, but be of good comfort, and he who enters the battle for me today and fights for the good cause will have God's blessing.'[51] Edward is called 'our king', alongside 'our archers' and 'our engineers', which implies that an oral narrative underlies the text: and episodes such as that of Edward's sudden return in 1340 to chastise the officials at home for their failure to send money to him in Flanders seem to be told by eyewitnesses of scenes in London and at St Albans. This is the talk of the London merchants, deeply concerned about the troubled times in which they lived, and eager for news.

Men were just as avid for news outside London, even if it was scarcer and less reliable than in the capital. One chronicle stands out as a history with many different continuations, rather like the *Anglo-Saxon Chronicle* four centuries earlier. This is the *Brut*, so called from Brutus, the supposed founder of Britain, with whose exploits it begins. It survives in French, Latin and English versions, in more than 300 manuscripts, and was aimed particularly at a knightly readership. The material on Edward II and Edward III in the original French version is often very vivid and evidently well informed, particularly about the events from Isabella's landing in England to the battle of Halidon Hill in 1333. This part of it (and perhaps the earlier sections as well) was written at the behest of two particular families of powerful magnates, the earls of Lancaster and the Bohuns; it certainly represents a view of England different from that of the capital. For these years, it has a vivid directness that implies that the author had access to good oral sources, for example for Edward III's coup against Mortimer in 1330.[52] Although the original version ended in 1333, it was continued by other hands. Most of these continuations are brief and rather dull; just occasionally we encounter a well-informed writer who has original material not found elsewhere.[53]

The best of the chroniclers outside London is Geoffrey le Baker, who was in a way a country equivalent of Adam Murimuth; although the latter's career was largely in London, the two men probably knew each other, and Baker started his chronicle using Murimuth as a basis.[54] He seems to have had connections in Oxford, possibly through the house of

Carmelite friars there, and came from nearby Swinbrook. One of his sources of information, and perhaps his patron, was Thomas de la More, a local magnate and member of parliament for Oxfordshire between 1340 and 1351, who was also nephew of Archbishop John Stratford, who played a central part in the government up to 1341. Baker also seems to have had a connection to the Bohun family, the king's cousins, earls of Hereford and Northampton. He must have been friendly with men who had seen service in Edward III's campaigns, both as soldiers and as clerks, because he has eyewitness accounts of the fighting as well as detailed notes of the routes taken by the armies which must come from official records. He gives a view of the war as seen by the provincial knights who were the backbone of the royal armies. As his chronicle ends in 1356, it was almost certainly written very shortly after this and is therefore a contemporary voice.

The chronicles from France which cover this period are largely written, like Froissart's final version, with hindsight. The best of them is the *Chronicle of the First Four Valois Kings*, whose author may have been a cleric in the Norman administration at Rouen, and which dates from the 1380s; it takes a strongly nationalist view, and reflects the changing attitudes at the end of the century, when the divisions of nationality outweighed the old common culture of knightly aristocracy. In some ways, it is the French equivalent of Geoffrey le Baker, a provincial voice; it gives a different, local perspective on many events: we hear of the heroic resistance of the Normans at the battle of Sluys, which appears in the earlier chronicles as a much more one-sided affair; and the English are very clearly the enemy. But accounts of deeds of arms and knightly episodes persist, such as that of the invasion of Guernsey, when the local girls gave chaplets of flowers and violets to their admirers, telling the men that with such lovers they should fight for them all the harder.[55] The author is also, like his predecessors in monasteries who wrote chronicles, partial to gossip which must have come from passing travellers. Examples are the story of the man who was commanded by a voice from the air to go and tell Charles V that he was not fighting hard enough against his enemies, and the rumours about the marriage of Edward prince of Wales and Joan of Kent, which was said to have roused Edward III to fury, because his son might have made a brilliant alliance with a foreign princess.[56] The myths are beginning to accumulate: this is not Froissart's measured reconsideration of the history of the English years of triumph. Instead, it looks forward to a world where there is a black and white contrast between English and French, and national identity is the overriding force.

The same is true of the *Norman Chronicle*, written in Normandy between 1369 and 1372 by a fierce supporter of Charles V just at the point where events were turning in favour of the Valois kings.[57] It is markedly different from most of our sources in being generally unenthusiastic about warfare, accepting it wearily as a fact of life rather than condemning it passionately. The author is difficult to place, but may have been a town-dweller: he is a record-keeper rather than a chronicler, and his work reads as a series of disjointed episodes. There are no heroes here, and he is more taken by a story of how a garrison was nearly lured out of a town when their herd of pigs was let loose by the enemy than by any knightly exploits. It is a different, rather incoherent view of the war, and where the author gained his information is unclear; perhaps from other towns, as we know that towns corresponded with each other during this period, sending warnings of imminent attack and other vital information on a regular basis.[58] Rodez in central France communicated with nearly sixty other towns in the period 1358–86, and recorded the costs in its accounts under 'Messengers and Spies'. If this suggestion is correct, the *Norman Chronicle* may preserve firsthand accounts of the events of the late 1360s; for the earlier years, it may tell us something of the resigned weariness of the citizens of France in the face of disaster.

We still have original copies of some of the town letters, and letters in general, whether original or, as so often, copied into chronicles or into official records, are a vital source of our knowledge of events. The French and English letters that survive are very different in character, but almost all of them are factual records which tell us little about the men who wrote them, reflecting only their immediate preoccupations. The purposes of the letters diverge sharply. The English letters are for the most part propaganda designed to encourage the war effort at home, while the French correspondence is part of a network of self-help against the unpredictable marauders at large in the countryside, whether it is an English army on a raid or freebooting adventurers in search of plunder – not that there was always much of a distinction between the two.

Communication between English forces on the Continent and the government at home must have been a problem from the campaigns of Henry II in the twelfth century onwards. The important messages may often have been oral, but from the late thirteenth century there are surviving letters about the progress of the English armies. Letters were often sent out before a campaign to the archbishops and bishops of England and Wales requesting prayers, masses, sermons and processions in support of the king and his army, and these letters usually included a brief statement of the reasons for the king's actions.[59] Other letters are formal government documents, and really belong with the official records: the most important example is a letter sent by Edward III to his council in London on 29 July 1346, just after he had taken the city of Caen on his campaign in Normandy. He relates the fortunes of the campaign, giving details of the castles and towns taken, and requests that letters be sent to the prelates and clergy, and to the City of London, telling them of these events, so that they are reassured, and so that prayers may be said for his future success. Then he turns to practical matters, requests for money and supplies, particularly bows, arrows and bowstrings. Other letters are sent with this one, to be forwarded to his allies in Flanders and to the archbishop of York and the lords in the north of England: these were presumably about military affairs, as he planned to join up with the Flemish army, and there was a threat of Scottish invasion.[60]

At the next level, there were semi-official communiqués which reported a victory. After the sea-fight at Sluys, Edward sent out a letter ordering public thanksgiving for the victory, but the details of the battle were very brief.[61] The short chronicle known as *The Acts of War of Edward III* may have been prepared for Bartholomew Burghersh the elder to read to parliament in late 1346;[62] its style is not unlike that of Edward's own letter, but it is much more extensive and detailed. For the battle of Poitiers, we have the letters of Edward prince of Wales: that describing the Poitiers campaign was taken by the prince's chamberlain, Nigel Loring, to the mayor and officials of London, and clearly had some status as an official document.[63]

There are also a large number of letters which are highly personal, but were clearly intended to be shared as widely as possible or summarized for other readers. The most personal of these is Edward prince of Wales's letter to Joan of Kent after the battle of Najéra: Joan had given birth to their first son, Edward, while he was away on campaign, and he writes to reassure her that all is well; he begins: 'My dearest and truest sweetheart and beloved companion, as to news,' and concludes after giving his account of the victory, 'You will be glad to know, dearest companion, that we, our brother Lancaster and all the nobles of our army are well, thank God, except only Sir John Ferrers, who did much fighting.'[64] This is the only time that we get any glimpse of the prince's character from his own hand, and is clearly written in the heat of the moment. If there were other official letters, they have not survived, but the news of the victory would have been copied and passed on.

The same is true of the much larger number of campaign letters which were sent by members of the army to their friends and contacts at home. Many of them are from the clerks who were responsible for the administration of the army, and therefore had writing materials to hand. Such letters often went from one royal official to another, but not as a formal report; Adam Murimuth and Robert of Avesbury, because they were part of this circle, copied a dozen or so of these documents into their chronicles. Indeed, it is possible that two letters from a clerk with the royal army, Michael Northburgh, may have actually been addressed to them; these cover the whole of the campaign, with a gap of about seventeen days between the events in the first and second letters, perhaps because a third letter is lost. This is real reporting, an attempt to give a systematic account of events.[65]

Other letters are more personal: the best example of this is a letter to Richard Stafford, who had been sent back to England from Gascony in 1355, from his friend and colleague John Wingfield, bringing him up to date with events in Gascony early in 1356. He reassures Stafford that his men, who are with John Chandos and James Audley, are at Castelsagrat, 'and have enough of all kinds of supplies to last until midsummer, except only for fresh fish and greens, according to their letters'. He adds that a strong French contingent under Marshal Boucicaut has arrived nearby, and that 'there will be a good company there for each to try his comrades' worth'.[66] It is a rare glimpse of the concern of commanders for their men.

The reports sent home at the time of the campaign often resurface in a number of fourteenth-century chronicles which describe the king's march in some detail. Northburgh's letters and *The Acts of War of Edward III* are among half a dozen such documents which seem to have existed for the events of 1346, and by analysing the details which the chroniclers give we can see which 'campaign diary' they used. Similarly, two campaign reports survive for the Poitiers campaign, one of them apparently quoted verbatim by Geoffrey le Baker. Sometimes these diaries are simply a list of places at which the army halted, copied out as a separate text. In one instance, the so-called 'Kitchen Journal', the diary is part of a set of accounts kept by Walter Wetewang, in charge of the army's finances, which notes this information at the end of each day's entries.

The existence of other letters, now lost, can be detected in passages from the English chronicles which are clearly paraphrases of them. These represent one 'news network'; but there were other networks beyond that of the English government's propaganda. Across Europe, the great Italian trading companies maintained a detailed correspondence, for the latest and most accurate information was vital to their business; and mercenaries and knights fighting far from home also passed on news of their military adventures.

The Italian companies based in Florence were so deeply involved in the financing of the wars and commerce of the first half of the fourteenth century that by 1350 the major lenders, Bardi, Peruzzi and Acciaioli, had all been bankrupted. They were remarkably like modern firms, with shareholders and speculative capital, but because they did not operate for long, and had no direct successors, very little of their archives has survived.[67] We can only guess at the extent of their correspondence from chance survivals of later merchants' letters, such as those of the Datini company used by Iris Origo in *The Merchant of Prato*, which gives an extraordinary picture of one merchant's network. Up to 1357, each of the Italian companies seems to have run its own, highly expensive couriers; the need for retrenchment meant that in that year seventeen companies co-operated to set up a common service. The Datini records show the dispatch and receipt of 320,000 items over two decades, averaging almost fifty items a day. Much of this was purely commercial, bills and financial documents, but there was also vital market intelligence, which included political reports.

Giovanni Villani, who was still writing his *New Chronicle* when he died of the plague in 1348, was at the heart of this commercial world.[68] In 1324 he was head of the international company of the Buonaccorsi, while his brothers worked for the Peruzzi. The Buonaccorsi were a second-rank company, but nonetheless were active in England, and employed a former agent of the Bardi. They were soon involved in banking in France and Flanders as well, with branches in Bruges, Antwerp, London, Paris, Reims and Laon, all with agents who would report regularly on current affairs to the head office in Florence. The company failed in 1341, brought down like the others by huge loans to sovereigns – in effect, government bonds – and speculation in commercial activities. Both these activities required fast and accurate intelligence; for the last twenty years of his life Villani assembled the political information from his records into his chronicle day by day. He used both oral reports from Florentines returning from foreign countries, and above all the mercantile letters which flowed into Florence; sometimes he writes as if he is an eyewitness, but he is in fact quoting from a letter, while the final chapter is a letter on an earthquake in the Alps, copied verbatim. This final chapter provides extremely accurate information, confirmed by other accounts of the earthquake, and shows how the merchants' news network was generally very reliable.[69] Villani's evidence is therefore of prime importance, often less biased and sometimes better informed than that of English and French records.[70] His brother Matteo, who continued the chronicle down to 1363, is less well informed about English affairs, perhaps reflecting the declining commercial contacts between Florence and England after the Black Death.[71]

As to men who actually fought in the battles, their experiences usually come down to us at second hand in chronicles such as those of Jean le Bel and Geoffrey le Baker; and when we do have their own words, as in the case of a German knight writing to his lord about his part in the battle of Crécy,[72] they are often very general. The question of how much we can ever know, even from eyewitnesses, of what went on in a battle, is one to which we shall return. The English victories at Crécy, Poitiers and to a lesser extent Nájera, resounded across Europe, and we can watch the way in which the reports of these events changed over the years. After Poitiers, first news of the battle claimed that King John himself had been killed by a Navarrese squire, while other letters related accurately that he had been captured; the French emphasized the bravery of the king and his youngest son, while the English had only to underline the scale of their victory. By the end of the century, chroniclers are diligently sifting through the varying stories to try to arrive at a considered view of what had happened.[73] And they embellish their accounts:

Geoffrey le Baker and Matteo Villani give the prince of Wales a speech in which he rallies his men; Baker's is an exercise in rhetoric, while Villani uses it to outline the prince's dire straits, unable to escape and vastly outnumbered by the enemy.

There is one chronicle which seems to preserve in passing eyewitness accounts of the battle of Crécy from two viewpoints. One is that of a Genoese crossbowman hired by the French, who may be the source for parts of Giovanni Villani's story; the other view of the battle is very probably from a Bohemian or German knight in the company of King John. The combined description is preserved in an anonymous Roman chronicle which gives a dramatic account of the republican politics of Rome in the 1350s, and the information on Crécy was not of interest to the Italian historians who originally edited it.[74] It is a difficult text to analyse: written by a well-educated author, it is in a broad Roman dialect, and has many aspects of popular oral literature, particularly the repetition of key phrases, in the manner of a ballad singer. The content, however, is another matter. The striking aspect of this account is that it is in parts very detailed, in a way that would be difficult to invent. To take a single instance: the attack by the crossbowmen failed, and Villani attributes this to the crossbow strings being wet. He is right about the battle being fought in showery weather, but the Roman chronicle tells us that the rain had made the ground so slippery that the crossbowmen could not draw their bows, because when they put their foot in the stirrup, which had to be planted firmly on the ground so that the string could be wound upwards and tensioned, it was impossible to hold the bow still. Now, the land at Crécy is chalk, with a thin covering of topsoil, and, like all chalk hills, is 'slick as silk' after rain.[75] There are other aspects of the Roman account which are wildly off the mark, but these concern matters which a member of the army would only have known by hearsay. I believe this is one of those moments when, for once, we can actually see the reality of medieval battle: a man at arms struggling with his weapon in adverse conditions.

At the other extreme from this dramatic silhouette of the reality of battle lies the sophisticated art of propaganda, all too familiar today, but equally one of the weapons in the armoury of medieval kings. One of the greatest financial and military powers in Europe had been destroyed only decades earlier by skilful propaganda on the part of the French kings. The Order of Knights Templar, the bankers of Europe, had been brought down by Philip the Fair, who was seeking an excuse to confiscate their vast wealth, by accusations of heresy and black magic. Indirectly, this contributed to the emergence of the secular orders of knighthood; but the skills learnt during this episode were deployed by the French in the early years of the war between France and England. It is possible that the belief that Edward II escaped to the Continent rather than being murdered at Berkeley Castle originated in documents forged in France, reported to Edward III by his agent at the papal court. At a critical juncture in Edward's relations with his nobles, he was accused of raping the wife of his closest friend, a story which only appears in French chronicles. A satirical poem attributing the beginning of the war to a dissatisfied French nobleman who goads Edward into action at a feast to which he brings a heron, a symbol of cowardice, was another example of the attempts to undermine Edward's reputation. The English riposte was far less subtle: the mocking poems of Laurence Minot are little more than invective, and the whole emphasis of English propaganda efforts is directed at maintaining public support for the war. Edward was assiduous in reporting his successes back to the administration in England; the letters he wrote also went to the English bishops, bailiffs and sheriffs, and the clergy were urgently requested to pray for success.[76] The knights of England and Hainault were also expert at telling their stories to chroniclers such as Jean le Bel and Froissart, and building up their image as knightly heroes. The result is war, not as reality, but as heroic autobiography.

This, then, is the material from which the picture which follows is built up: hugely variable in origin and quality, often a minefield of contradictions, a range of voices so different that it is hard to weigh one against another. Sometimes the focus eludes us altogether, and then suddenly the picture is sharp and clear for a moment. We can usually map out the sequence of events, but, as we shall see, character and motive are much more speculative. By looking in detail at the 'Company of the Garter', a group of men with close ties to each other and similar backgrounds, there is perhaps a chance that their lives will illuminate each other, and that their communal activity will emerge more clearly.

The Rise of English Power

Prologue: The Political Background

When Edward came to the throne of England in 1327 at the age of four-teen, he faced three major issues. The most immediate was the war with Scotland, which had begun at the end of his grandfather Edward I's reign. The second was the political legacy of his father, Edward II, which had left the magnates deeply divided and power in the hands of Queen Isabella and her close adviser and probable lover, Roger Mortimer. Fur-thermore, the dramatic events surrounding his father's deposition and death were far from resolved. And thirdly, after the accession of Philip of Valois, Edward's cousin, to the French throne in 1328, Edward had a strong claim to be the rightful heir to the French crown.

The rivalry between the kings of England and France was an ancient one. When the forebears of the English kings, Viking raiders from Nor-way led by Rollo, invaded France at the beginning of the tenth century, the French were unable to drive them out, and attempted to restrain them by granting them the land around Rouen in 911. By 933 the Vikings had pressured the French king Raoul into conceding almost all the territory that became the medieval duchy of Normandy.

Much of medieval history is concerned with the tension between kings and their great vassals, and the duke of Normandy was to prove the most troublesome of all the lords who owed homage to the French king. With Duke William's conquest of England, the Norman dukes commanded resources at least equal to those of the French king, whose own domains were centred round Paris, and whose control over the more distant lordships such as Aquitaine was often tenuous. When, in 1137, Louis VII of France married Eleanor, who was duchess of Aqui-taine in her own right, the problem of Aquitaine seemed to have been resolved: it was a huge territory, stretching from Poitiers to the Pyren-ees, but intrinsically weak, since the ducal government at Poitiers had in turn little control over its own distant vassals. However, Eleanor failed to bear Louis a son, and, desperate for an heir, he divorced her in 1152, only to see the duke of Normandy and future King Henry II of England carry her off within a few weeks. Henry and Eleanor's marriage created a network of vassal territories far more powerful than that of the kings of France, since Henry had inherited Anjou and Maine from his father, and his lands now extended from the Channel continuously down almost to the Mediterranean. In addition, he was of course the king of England. Historians often refer to it as the 'Angevin empire', but it would be more truthful to call it 'Henry II's empire'; it was he who was its linchpin, and it was very much his personal creation.

But the contest was not as unequal as it might have seemed, since Louis VII was king of the Franks, and could use his status as overlord to restrain his overmighty vassal. Henry's position, as sovereign in his own right in England and vassal of another sovereign for much of his territory, was a complete anomaly in the feudal system, which needed a strictly pyramidal structure to function effectively. Henry was on the second tier of the French feudal pyramid, and at the head of the English feudal pyramid. As far as French affairs were concerned, however, he was simply a 'tenant-in-chief' holding his lands directly from Louis.

Henry II held his 'empire' together largely by the force of his personality and the effectiveness of the Norman administration. He fought not only the French kings, the Scots, Welsh and Irish, and the unruly barons of the south of France, but his own sons, all of whom in turn rebelled against him. It was therefore no surprise that after his death in 1189, the temporary union of these lands quickly unravelled, but what was unexpected was that the heartland from which the Norman expansion had begun, Normandy itself, was lost within fifteen years in the face of a determined onslaught from Louis VII's successor, Philip Augustus.

Kingship at this period was an institution in process of evolution. In the seventh and eighth centuries, kings were often elected, and not always formally crowned in a religious ceremony. Election by acclamation remained, if only as a formality, as part of the English medieval coronation ceremony. In the ninth century Charlemagne had replaced kingship in France with a revival of Roman imperial authority, and, when his empire broke up in the century after his death, the French lands became a kingdom once more. The crucial difference was that it became a feudal kingdom, in which the great lords held their lands from the king in return for military service in his army; they were also his councillors and his means of government in their respective regions. Furthermore, from 816 onwards the sacred nature of kingship was underlined by the use of a coronation ceremony which included both the crowning and anointing with holy oil; and this consecration came to be carried out in a specific place by the spiritual leader of the nation – Reims in France, Canterbury in England and Cologne for Germany.

Philip Augustus and his successors were able to challenge the Angevin threat by emphasizing their royal status, which gave them an authority outside that of the feudal system. In the tenth century, kings were generally described as leaders of a people, rather than rulers of a territory: Athelstan was the first ruler in the west to change his title, partly because he claimed overlordship of several nations as 'king of all Britain'. Philip Augustus styled himself 'king of France', though he continued to use the title 'king of the Franks' as well. Kingship was an important propaganda weapon in the struggle against over-mighty subjects; but, in the case of France, it was also to be an Achilles heel.

Under the leadership of Philip Augustus, the French held their own against the Angevins, fomenting rebellion among Henry II's ambitious sons. When Richard I, the most able of them, was mortally wounded in Poitou trying to bring one of his own fractious lords to heel, his younger brother John was no match for Philip, and a combination of manoeuvres under feudal law and force of arms led to the loss of Normandy to the French in 1204. Over the next century, particularly during the reign of Henry III, other Angevin territories fell away, until only the duchy of Aquitaine itself was left, an area which in itself was often ill-defined and subject to the wavering allegiances of local lords; it included not only Gascony to the south-west, but also provinces nearer Paris such as Poitou and the Limousin. The French kings were always on the alert for reasons to intervene, and in 1293–4 a feud between the sailors of England and Gascony and those of Normandy developed into a full-scale naval war. The fact that Edward I tried to stop his subjects from attacking the French was ignored, Philip IV declared that the breach of feudal loyalty warranted the confiscation of the duchy and war ensued. The French were able to seize large parts of Gascony, and Edward was only able to force Philip IV to negotiate by creating a large and expensive, but ultimately effective, alliance with the princes on France's eastern border. Threatened with a joint Anglo-Flemish attack, Philip agreed to mediation by the pope.

The papal settlement of this dispute, intended to reconcile the two kingdoms, was to have wholly unexpected consequences. One of its chief features was a proposed marriage alliance between the French and English royal families: Edward I's only surviving son, Edward of Caernarvon, was to marry Philip's daughter Isabella. Edward of Caernarvon was to become duke of Aquitaine.

The war with France was always in a sense a personal one, waged in the name of the English king as duke of Normandy or of Aquitaine. The English possessions in France did not belong to the realm of England, but to the king of England as an individual. How then did the English nobility and gentry regard their king's involvement in French affairs? Edward I had been forced to fight to defend his rights in Gascony back in 1294 by the French king's refusal to negotiate seriously. To raise an army, he issued a feudal summons to the great lords of England to send troops to Portsmouth with orders to embark for France. Their response seems to have been that war overseas, which was patently not in defence of the realm of England, could not be the reason for such a summons: it was above and beyond the duty they owed to the king as their feudal lord. The army that eventually sailed did not contain any contingents serving on feudal terms. The following year, Edward tried a different tactic, and offered wages to the magnates he asked to accompany him, but this was still unattractive. It was only by reminding the lords of their unpaid debts at the exchequer, and ordering his officials to collect these immediately, that he obtained the troops he needed. In the end, the expedition of 1295 took so long to organize that it never left England.[1] Yet in the end – and despite heavy taxation – Edward seemed to have carried public opinion with him, and the war with France was not openly opposed. Careful propaganda, portraying the French as a threat to England itself and even bent on destroying the English nation, may have helped.

The problem was not resolved, however, as the much more dramatic reaction in 1297 was to show. Personal grievances on the part of men such as Roger Bigod, earl of Norfolk, and Humphrey Bohun, earl of Hereford, combined with resistance from the clergy to the payment of

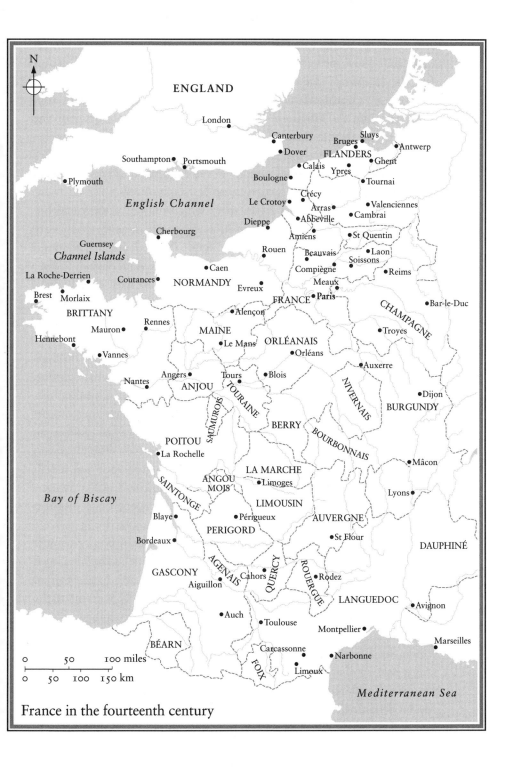

France in the fourteenth century

further taxes, led to a major crisis. Robert Winchelsey, archbishop of Canterbury, saw the demand for funds for the king's French war as outside the legitimate framework within which the king could tax the clergy; it was not a matter of defence of the realm, or an urgent situation affecting the kingdom which would permit him to override the general principle that the clergy should not pay taxes to secular governments. The same view was put forward by the magnates in respect of their requirement to serve the king, adding that England was in danger from the Scots and that it was folly to send men overseas in such circumstances. One chronicler has a story which may be apocryphal but which sums up the heated confrontation in the parliament of February 1297. Edward is reputed to have told Bigod: 'By God, sir earl, either go or hang,' only to get the retort, 'By the same oath, O king, I shall neither go nor hang.' In the end, Edward had to make do with a very small army, fewer than 1,000 mounted men and around 8,000 infantry. It was only by creating an expensive network of alliances that he was able to persuade Philip IV to negotiate a truce.

Opposition to the war was real enough among the men who mattered, and who provided the most resources for such expeditions, whether in men or money. But there was no overall motive for their dissatisfaction, which was often as much to do with their personal relations with Edward as with broader principles. Essentially, it was a failure on Edward I's part to manage them with sufficient skill, even though he won through in the end. But the element that was decided once and for all was that the feudal summons did not apply to the king's war in France.

Hostilities between France and England broke out once more in 1324, largely because Edward II had prevaricated about doing homage to Charles IV, who had become king two years earlier. A border dispute in Gascony in 1323 in which a French official was lynched by men loyal to the English crown triggered a swift reaction leading to the formal confiscation of the duchy of Aquitaine in June 1324. By September, the area from Agen, where the lynching had taken place, along the Garonne valley to La Réole, a key fortress outside Bordeaux, was in French hands; La Réole itself was surrendered by Edmund earl of Kent, the king's half brother, recently appointed lieutenant of Gascony, in return for a six-month truce. As always, the English territories in France could not be defended by relying on the local levies, and no troops had been sent to Gascony yet. In October a council was summoned in London to discuss the situation, with a view to raising an army to be led by Edward himself for the following summer. Edward was careful to act in conjunction with a small group of advisers selected by the council, and a date of March 1325 was set for the expedition's departure, to be led by the king himself. However, there was a change of plan at the last minute, and the earl of Surrey led this force; the king was to follow in May.

There was little opposition to this plan, though the advisers warned that its departure might leave the kingdom without sufficient defences. It was not Edward's handling of the recruitment of the Gascon expedition that led to his downfall, but the continuing anger aroused by his attitude towards the magnates, exemplified by his blatant favouritism. Early in his reign, Piers Gaveston had been showered with honours and had appalled the rest of the court by his arrogant behaviour. Edward ignored this, and a civil war ensued, in the course of which Gaveston was seized by the magnates and executed. Edward did not learn his lesson: he seemed to have a need for a close confidant, and within a few years Hugh Despenser the younger occupied the same position. Neither of these relationships was necessarily, on the evidence we have, homosexual; they were, however, friendships intense enough to blind the king to the enmity that such favouritism aroused. Both favourites were described by contemporary chroniclers as 'second kings'.[2] Edward was victorious in a second civil war in 1321–2, and set out to crush his opponents by confiscating their lands and imprisoning or executing them. One of them, Roger Mortimer, whose lordship was centred on Wigmore on the Welsh borders, escaped from prison in 1323 and fled to France, where he acted as a focus for the opposition to the king.

The reaction of Edward and his council to the military situation in 1324 was hesitant, and their diplomatic efforts were little better. Charles IV was in no hurry to reach a settlement, and, when English envoys arrived in Paris in December, the French raised new objections, accusing the English of treason and now rejecting the truce arranged by the earl of Kent. They did however propose that Queen Isabella and her son the young Prince Edward should come to Paris, and that Prince Edward should perform the homage which was the prime cause of the stand-off. In a sense, this was part of what the marriage alliance between the two royal families was intended to do: to create an atmosphere where personal relations might overcome diplomatic disagreements. Charles's motives, however, were probably more devious: he was on good terms with his sister, and knew of her intense dislike of Despenser; she had also been offended at being treated as a potential enemy alien, as her estates and household had been taken into the king's hands at the outbreak of war.

Edward and his council were aware of the potential conflict of loyalties if they allowed Isabella to go, but they had no obvious alternatives: they could not raise a new army for Aquitaine quickly enough to prevent the French making new conquests if the truce was not renewed, and there was no obvious way out of the diplomatic impasse. On 9 March 1325 Isabella left England, without her son; she was to return under very different circumstances. At first, matters went reasonably smoothly, though the new truce drawn up on 13 June was on harsh terms; there was now an additional threat, that a French army would be sent to Scotland to assist the Scottish king in an attack on England's northern border. Edward was therefore highly reluctant to leave England in order to perform homage for Aquitaine, and on 5 July he and his council proposed to the French that the duchy should be granted to Prince Edward, who would then be able to carry out the necessary ceremony on his own account.

This proposal was not immediately set in motion. Edward decided, despite all his reservations, to go to Beauvais on 29 August for the ceremony of homage, but then had second thoughts. The official version was that he was taken ill on his journey near Dover; in fact, a council seems to have been hastily assembled there on 15 August, at which he finally abandoned the idea. Instead, the alternative plan was quickly put in place: Prince Edward was granted Aquitaine on 10 September, and crossed the Channel two days later. He joined his mother in Paris, and performed homage at the French royal palace of Vincennes on 24 September. The prince was twelve, and this was his first major political act.

Edward and his council now expected Isabella and the prince to return to England, but they obviously doubted that this would happen without some persuasion. Walter Stapledon, bishop of Exeter, was given this task, but Isabella is said to have openly declared that she would only return when the person who was trying to break the bond between her and her husband – meaning Hugh Despenser the younger – was removed from the scene. Stapledon was so dismayed that he fled back to England at the first opportunity. About this time, it seems that Isabella first made contact with Roger Mortimer, whom she would have known at least slightly since her arrival in England. If Edward would not get rid of Despenser, she was now determined to do so herself. Her relationship with Mortimer at this point was probably simply a question of making common cause against a hated enemy. Early in 1326 the archbishop of Canterbury wrote to reassure her that Hugh Despenser bore no ill will against her; she replied that she was astonished he could say this, because it was for this reason that she had left Edward, since he had entire control over the king and kingdom; she protested her love for and loyalty to her husband, but declared that she was in danger of her life because of Despenser.[3]

Isabella and Mortimer were not alone in their opposition to Despenser; indeed, Mortimer may not necessarily have been the ring-leader, though it was Mortimer's activities which were of the greatest interest to the English government. Edmund earl of Kent, the earl of Richmond and the bishop of Norwich were all part of the group, in self-imposed exile. Their activities, and particularly those of Isabella, became a diplomatic embarrassment to Charles IV; by June 1326 she was using the revenues from Ponthieu, of which Prince Edward was count,[4] to hire an invasion fleet to be supplied by the count of Hainault, William I. Rumours of an alliance between Isabella and the count had been circulating in England since the beginning of the year, and it was said that Charles IV was behind this. The French king may well have suggested Isabella's next move, which was a marriage alliance between Hainault and England; Prince Edward would marry one of the count's daughters. On 27 August 1326 the prince was formally betrothed to Philippa, William's third daughter.

Isabella, the earl of Kent and Roger Mortimer now moved the centre of their operations to Holland, also ruled by the counts of Hainault, where Jean de Hainault, the count's younger brother, joined them in their plans to invade England. Within a month, Jean had raised a force of 700 mercenaries, and the English exiles probably contributed a similar number of men. They were all, however, experienced soldiers, and the majority were mounted troops: it was a small but formidable army. They sailed in ninety-five ships to the haven of the river Orwell, and landed on the north bank, in Colneis hundred, on 24 September. By the time they had marched across Suffolk and Cambridgeshire, and had halted at Dunstable in Bedfordshire, they had gathered many supporters, including the earl of Norfolk, Thomas of Brotherton. At Dunstable, they were met by Henry earl of Lancaster, Prince Edward's distant cousin, and at least four of the bishops. How far this was due to contacts before the invasion took place, and how far to a simple dissatisfaction with the king's conduct which only needed a spark to transform it into open rebellion, is hard to say. The hostility to the king was such that he abandoned London just over a week later, and headed for Wales, where he hoped to find men who were prepared to rally to his cause.

Edward II's efforts to raise an army in the Welsh borders came to nothing. Because he was so uncertain of the response to his summons, he moved on from Gloucester, the mustering place for his forces, before the date when they were due to appear. He very quickly found himself moving from place to place with no real plan, and sought refuge on Lundy Island, accompanied by Hugh Despenser and a handful of men. He may have intended to retreat to Ireland, where the administration would have been sympathetic, but in the event contrary winds drove the ships back to Cardiff. He retreated to Despenser's fortress at Caerphilly, and once again tried to summon a non-existent army; even though the fortress could have resisted a long siege, he moved on at the beginning of November, since without support outside the walls his fate would have been sealed anyway. A fortnight later, after seemingly aimless wanderings in south Wales, he was betrayed and captured, and taken to Henry of Lancaster, while his followers were imprisoned at Hereford. Kenilworth, Henry of Lancaster's strongest castle, was to be Edward II's place of imprisonment.

On 13 January, a carefully orchestrated council at Westminster heard Roger Mortimer and Thomas Wake, Lancaster's son-in-law, speak for the magnates, giving reasons why Edward II should be replaced by his son. The bishop of Hereford described a recent interview with Edward II at Kenilworth, in which he claimed that Edward had annulled the oaths of loyalty sworn to him by the great lords; and the bishop of Winchester preached on the theme that the weakness of the kingdom was caused by the king's own weakness. Then the proposal that Prince Edward should replace his father was put to the assembly, and acclaimed by all present. Finally, Edward III was presented as king with the words 'Behold your king'.

The actions of the assembly were duly reported to Edward II at Kenilworth, and, according to those present, he abdicated in favour of his son. The whole business of deposing an English monarch was such

a novelty that there were inevitable doubts and obscurities about procedures and about the validity of the deposition and abdication. The fact
of the matter was that Edward III was nominal head of the new government, and his father was a prisoner. But there were men who still
supported Edward II, and plots were made to free him. Who was behind
these plots is hard to tell, as the actual participants seem to have been
mainly a group of Dominican friars who 'had little or no idea of what
they expected to happen if they succeeded in freeing Edward'.[5] As a
security measure, Edward II was moved from place to place, ending up
in Berkeley Castle, which belonged to Thomas, Lord Berkeley, a close
ally of Mortimer.

It was here that the last act of the drama was played out. A further
conspiracy, said to have the backing of the Welsh prince Rhys ap Gruffudd, was discovered in September, possibly by Mortimer himself, who
was in Wales at the time. It seems to have been his personal decision to
eliminate Edward II, and, although we cannot be completely certain of
what happened, he died on 21 September, probably at the hands of
Thomas Gurney and William Ockley and their men, who were his
guards at Berkeley. Gruesome tales of his treatment circulated in later
years, possibly with some truth; equally, and, much less reliably, he was
said to have escaped and survived on the Continent until the middle of
the following decade. It is of course possible that this story derives from
the rumours spread by Mortimer to entrap the earl of Kent in 1330,
which could have been picked up in France. Whatever the exact circumstances, Edward III was now undoubted king of England, but its real
rulers were Isabella and Mortimer.

I

Edward, Philippa and
their Comrades 1327–1330

We know remarkably little about the early years of Edward III's life. Apart from the occasional appearance at a great occasion of state, there are few records of his activities.[1] He did not even play a nominal part in the government, and was never named as keeper of the realm if his father was absent abroad, as was customary for the heir to the throne. He does appear once, in September 1322, presiding at a royal feast at York in honour of a visiting French nobleman while his father was in Scotland; but this is virtually the only mention of state duties.

As heir to the throne, he had his own household establishment from the outset, and this is where we can see a little of the men who looked after his affairs and the first companions of his own age. Richard Damory was 'keeper of the body' of the young prince by 1318, but he is the only figure we can name from these early years. By 1320, his household included his younger brother John and his sisters Eleanor and Joan; in that year, John in turn was given his own household, and one of the queen's ladies was appointed to look after his sisters, with a separate establishment. From 1323 onwards, William of Cusance, who had been clerk to the Despensers, was keeper of Prince Edward's household, and other Despenser retainers were placed in the queen's household and that of John of Eltham, evidence of the family's ambition to control all aspects of the king's life, and of the king's acquiescence in their domination. In 1324, John and Eleanor were placed in the care of Hugh Despenser's wife Eleanor; Prince Edward does not seem to have been so closely controlled. There are very few records of the prince and his father being in the same place, and this is underlined by the survival of letters which show him communicating with his father by letter rather than in person.[2] He was nominally required to attend the king as part of his duties as a peer of the realm, as in formal summonses to parliament, and the personal writ to him to serve with the army in August 1322. However, it is unlikely that he attended such occasions, or, if he did, he would have appeared at the ceremonial opening of parliament but not at the business sessions.

It is possible that Isabella succeeded in keeping him out of the inner circle of the court after Hugh Despenser became the king's favourite and her estrangement from her husband began. After the feast in York in September 1322, the king's Scottish campaign had ended disastrously: the king was nearly captured by a Scottish raiding party in north Yorkshire, well south of the border, and the queen had to escape from Tynemouth by sea. Prince Edward was, if only for a few days, in serious danger at York, with few if any troops present. After this, apart from a single account entry which shows him dining at the Tower of London with his mother in February 1323, the trail goes cold.

It is only through a fragment of his accounts used as part of the binding of a later manuscript that we get a glimpse of his household just before he left for France in August 1325.[3] Perhaps the most important figure is that of Henry of Beaumont. Five entries record Prince Edward gambling at dice with Henry, evidently losing as much as four shillings on one occasion. Henry of Beaumont was in fact a French nobleman whose grandfather had become emperor of Constantinople after crusaders seized the city in 1204. His sister had married an English lord in 1279, possibly because she was a distant cousin of Eleanor of Castile, then queen of England, and Henry may have come to England as a result. At the age of seventeen, he was one of Edward I's household knights, and was close to Edward II, who made him joint warden of Scotland in 1308, and gave him the Isle of Man, then a separate kingdom. He married the heiress of the earldom of Buchan in 1310. He had fought with Edward I in Flanders in 1297, and had been on the disastrous 1322 campaign in Scotland, and was a highly experienced soldier. On 2 September, as the process of granting Prince Edward the duchy of Aquitaine began, Beaumont was formally appointed his guardian, with Walter Stapledon, the bishop of Exeter. Unlike Stapledon, Beaumont joined Isabella in her opposition to Edward, and was with the prince during the whole of the period in exile and during the invasion of 1326.

Apart from Beaumont, a few other names appear, but none of them are the close knightly associates of the king who emerge in the course of the next five years. Gilbert Talbot, his chamberlain from 1327 to 1334, appears as a banneret in 1325, and Thomas Lucy rises from squire in 1325 to knight of the household in 1334.[4]

Just as the Despensers had placed their men in Prince Edward's household, so Mortimer ensured that the new king's rather larger household contained men who owed loyalty to him rather than to the royal family. Edward was still only fourteen at the time of his accession, and does not appear to have had any young men of his own age who were consistently with him during the upheavals of the last years of his father's reign. At his coronation on 1 February 1327, after he himself received knighthood from his cousin Henry earl of Lancaster,[5] Edward knighted Edward Chandos, who may have been the father of one of his closest friends of later years, John Chandos. Three years later, Chandos was further rewarded specifically for his loyalty, having stayed with the king 'continually by his side' without pay.[6] Edward also dubbed a number of other knights, some from his household; but most of these do not reappear in the records, with the single exception of Ralph Stafford.[7] Lancaster also knighted Edward Bohun and the three sons of Roger Mortimer. It was in Roger Mortimer's circle that he was to receive his first experiences of knighthood, and perhaps also to show the first signs of rebellion.

Within three months of Edward's crowning, preparations for war were under way. There had been an uneasy truce with Scotland since 1323, and this was now breaking down. Isabella and Mortimer, anxious to strengthen the alliance against Edward II, had made vague promises that Scotland should be independent if they succeeded. In January 1327, however, one of the reasons given for Edward II's deposition had been that he had lost Scotland through default of good governance, and this was taken by the Scots as an indication that attempts were going to be made to reimpose English overlordship. A renewal of the 1323 truce in March was little more than cover for military preparations on both sides, and by 18 May an English army was supposed to have gathered at Newcastle. As usual, the troops were not there on the appointed day, and the king himself did not arrive until the end of June.

Much of the army assembled at York before going north, and among the contingents were a group of men from Hainault, led by Jean de Hainault, who had played such an important part in the invasion of

1326. Among them was Jean le Bel, who later described the campaign in his chronicle. The venture started badly, with a quarrel between English archers and the Hainaulters over a game of dice, during a royal feast to celebrate Trinity Sunday. It was the knights of Hainault who quelled the riot, which left scores of English dead. From then on there was a persistent tension between the two groups in the camp, but interestingly, given that the episode occurred so early in the reign, any potential xenophobia did not recur once the campaign was over.

Le Bel gives a vivid portrait of the discomforts of the army in the field in the weeks that followed, unable to keep up with the highly mobile Scottish troops. They were often bewildered as to their whereabouts, while suffering from shortages of provisions and torrential rain. The armies spent days drawn up in battle order at a place called Stanhope Park on either side of the swollen river Wear, made impassable by huge rocks and raging waters. And he gives us an equally striking portrait of Edward himself. Edward was Le Bel's hero; how much of this is the chronicler seeing him in the golden light of his subsequent reputation, and how much is his genuine admiration at the time which fired his enthusiasm for Edward, is difficult to say. It does seem to be the case that this was a formative experience for the fourteen-year-old king. It is quite possible that the exclusive use of the cross of St George on this campaign for the pennons and banners of the army was his own idea: as far as we know, his father and grandfather had always carried the arms of St Edmund and St Edward as well.[8]

The leaders of the army were three earls: Edward named as captain in July his cousin, Henry of Lancaster, aged about forty-six, the most experienced soldier of the three, who had fought in Flanders, Wales and Scotland. The other two were much younger: his uncles Edmund of Woodstock, aged twenty-five, and Thomas of Brotherton, aged twenty-seven. Mortimer, their senior by more than a decade, held no official command, but was generally blamed for the failure of the campaign.[9] Mortimer and the three earls seem to have disagreed about tactics: one chronicler says that Thomas of Brotherton, as marshal, forbade Lancaster to attack, acting on Mortimer's instructions. Edward was little more than a figurehead, as a complete novice in the art of war. When the Scottish army was first sighted, and the English had formed up in battle order, 'some of the English lords led the young king to ride along our lines, to hearten the troops; he graciously appealed to each man to strive to fight well and preserve his honour; and he gave orders that no one, on pain of death, should go ahead of the banners or make any move until the command was given'.[10] But instead of a glorious victory, the encounter at Stanhope Park was nearly a disaster: the Scots under James Douglas made a surprise night attack on the English camp and rode through it in bright moonlight 'until they came to the king's pavilion and killed the men in their beds, crying "Douglas! Douglas!", at which the king, who was in his pavilion, and many other people were very frightened; but – blessed be Almighty God! – the king was not captured; and the realm of England was in great peril'. The Scots retreated, but it was a humiliating episode.

Edward returned to York, the temporary centre of government, by way of Durham, reaching the city on 13 August. His first experience of warfare had been harsh and frustrating; he himself was still inexperienced in the use of arms. At the end of the year, after his father's funeral on 20 December, he held a series of tournaments in a chain of festivities which lasted from Christmas until after his marriage to Philippa of Hainault at the end of January.[11] These began at Worcester on 23 December, continued with events at the royal hunting lodges at Clipstone in Sherwood Forest and ended at Rothwell in Yorkshire in mid-January, before the festivities at York on 25–8 January. This was the first series of the magnificent court occasions which were to be a major feature of Edward's reign.

Tournaments, since their inception in the twelfth century, had been both a serious method of training knights in the skills of handling their horses and weapons, particularly the specialized expertise with the lance, and important festivals, social gatherings which brought together many of the great nobles and their retinues. In peaceable times, such gatherings posed no danger to the kingdom at large; but if the nobles were disaffected with royal government, the tournament could either be deliberate cover for the assembly of an army, or could develop spontaneously into an armed rebellion. Tourneying had been subject to royal control since 1194, when Richard I restricted tournaments to just five sites in the whole of England, the reason being that such occasions, which were after all gatherings of armed men, could lead to rebellion and civil war. It was therefore rare for the ruler himself to enter the lists. Richard I and Edward I had jousted in their youth, but ceased once they came to the throne.

A series of English tournaments in the mid-thirteenth century which led to violence underlined the need for regulation, and in 1292, at the request of the magnates of the realm, Edward I ratified a code of conduct for tourneyers, which effectively limited full participation to great lords. Even in this legislation, the tournament was still a rough-and-tumble affair: each lord was allowed three squires, who could legitimately enter the fray and pull another participant from his horse, which then became their prize.[12] Both the lord's squires and his other attendants could wear only partial armour, and they and the onlookers were forbidden on pain of imprisonment to carry arms. Even in peace-time, there was always a danger that personal feuds could be settled under cover of a tournament.

At the beginning of Edward II's reign, Piers Gaveston had held a tournament at Wallingford in December 1307 to celebrate his marriage. He appeared with three times the number of knights he had said he would bring, and thus had roundly defeated the earls who attended. He also defeated them at a tournament at Faversham in honour of Edward's marriage to Isabella, and aroused such hatred that he himself asked the king to cancel a third tournament at Stepney planned as part of the cor-onation festivities.[13] Edward II held only one tournament during his reign, which he personally organized, at Kennington in September 1308. Despite lavish expenditure, memories of the troubles earlier in the year led the barons to stay away – 'wisely', adds the chronicler – and an unknown knight knocked down the tentpoles of several of the pavilions under cover of darkness.[14] Thereafter Edward II issued a series of edicts banning tournaments, and there are few instances of licensed tourna-ments: that at Northampton in 1323, at which the king was present, is a rare example, and was at one of the five sites named in Richard I's statute. The effectiveness of royal control is underlined by the fact that most important tournaments were fought at these places until the mid-fourteenth century, with the one exception of London.

The prohibitions continued during Edward III's minority, since at times of crisis Mortimer and Isabella were well aware of the dangers of armed assemblies, however apparently sportsmanlike. In 1328 a pro-posed tournament at Northampton was prohibited on the grounds that magnates might go to the tournament rather than to the parliament sum-moned in the same place, but the underlying purpose was to prevent a possible assembly of armed men who might disrupt the proceedings.

At the local level, prohibitions were designed to deal with the kind of local disturbance which is reflected in the activities of John Daniers, one of the prince of Wales's knights, in 1352. In the course of a feud with the local parson, he proclaimed a tournament at Warrington, near the parish, and seized the torches from the parson's house to burn 'at his revelry there'; the stands were built using the parson's timber stored in the church.[15]

For an example of a serious challenge to royal authority there is the tournament at Toulouse in 1343. Here, the king of Majorca, who claimed the county of Toulouse, entered the town in the absence of the French royal officials, and held a tournament in defiance of a ban in force in French territories, as a way of marking his right to hold Toulouse as an independent principality. To make matters worse, his knights entered the lists shouting the English war cry of 'Guyenne, St George'.[16]

The difference between the early tournaments of Edward II and those of Edward III could not be more marked. Instead of a king at loggerheads with his nobles, and a reluctant participant in tournaments, Edward III's enthusiasm, fostered by Isabella and Mortimer, was shared by his nobles, and his investment in rich displays of armour and clothing was far from wasted, since it created a new comradeship between the king and his lords. We have the detailed accounts for some of his equipment, such as the two suits of armour covered in purple velvet made for the Clipstone tournament, embroidered with 21,800 gold threads in a pattern of crowns and oak leaves at a cost of £8 3s. 4d. Clipstone is the first recorded instance of the very rare practice of jousting at night; there is one other known example in England, later in Edward's reign, at Bristol on New Year's Day 1358.[17] The image of the young king riding out into the night, the torchlight glinting on the gold of his armour, is a harbinger of the highly visual nature of Edward's later knightly celebrations.

The series of four tournaments in quick succession leading up to Edward's marriage to Philippa in January 1328, which seem to have passed off without any political repercussions, was unprecedented in England. Tourneying activity continued at a very high level for the next three years. In 1328 Roger Mortimer gave two great tournaments. His family had a long tradition of enthusiasm for tournaments: as long ago as 1195, the Mortimer of the day had had his lands confiscated for tourneying without licence;[18] and his grandfather had held a round table of 100 knights and 100 ladies at Kenilworth in 1279, partly paid for by wine barrels filled with gold presented to him by Blanche queen of Navarre, wife of Edmund of Lancaster, the lord of Kenilworth. Roger Mortimer's first tournament was at Hereford in June, to celebrate the marriage of his two daughters, and was attended by the king and Isabella.[19] This was followed in the autumn by tournaments at Wigmore to commemorate his creation as earl of March in the parliament of October 1328, an extraordinary title since it did not correspond to any territorial boundaries. The display he put on there, and the title he had assumed, was one of the reasons that led one chronicler to comment that Mortimer and Isabella had usurped royal power and had gathered up the contents of the royal treasury.[20] The chronicle of Wigmore priory had a different take on it: the king had swept into Mortimer's domains, and had spent a fortune at his castles and in his parks on tournaments and other entertainments, handing out generous presents – all at Mortimer's expense, since (so rumour had it) the king did not repay him.[21] If this was so, Mortimer was probably spending the king's own money in any case.

There is a very curious entry in the royal accounts for this period which may hint at a distinct coolness between Edward and his mother, the result of the affair between her and Mortimer. One of the entitlements of members of the king's household was a new suit of summer and winter clothing each year. Among the entries for the summer of 1328 are three entries that are not concerned with the regular issue of livery, which read as follows:

> ... red cloth for the king and his 12 knights for the performance of a game which is called the game of the society of Craddok, and coloured cloth for half-tunics for 14 valets, servants to the knights at the said game.

> ... for lining 13 tunics for the king and 12 knights of the society of Craddok ...

The date would seem to connect it with the festivities at Hereford at the end of May 1328. But 'Craddok' has a peculiar relevance to the situation. It is probably a reference to the Arthurian story of Caradoc, an episode attacking the morals of Arthur's court, which first appears around 1300. In the *Lay of Mantel*, Arthur is holding a high festival, and tradition demands that he does not dine until some new adventure has happened at court. A young man appears and produces a splendid mantle, which will detect any ladies who have been unfaithful. He asks the king to get the ladies of the court to try it on without saying what the results will show. Guinevere, told that the mantle will be hers, tries it on, but it is too short; and all the other ladies of the court try and fail, finding it too long or shrinking revealingly until they are almost naked. Finally, Caradoc's lady, who was absent at the beginning, comes in, and the mantle fits her perfectly. The original seems to have been a Welsh tale, and the story was certainly known on the English border with Wales in the fourteenth century; it was incorporated into a continuation of the romance of *Perceval* by Chrétien de Troyes, where a drinking horn rather than a mantle is the test.

It is not unreasonable to assume that this little episode is related to the increasingly scandalous relationship between Mortimer and Isabella. A later report claims that there was a rumour that 'the Queen Mother was pregnant, and Lord Mortimer more than anyone else was suspected of being the father. The rumour spread like wildfire until the young king was made fully aware of it . . .'[23] Was the 'game of Craddok' a re-enactment of the romance episode aimed at the lovers? If so, was it performed in front of them, or was it a private affair between the king and the twelve knights for whom costumes were made?[24]

Whatever this was about, it is the first instance of a theme which was to recur throughout Edward's reign: the team or group of knights led by the king in tournaments or games. At this stage, the twelve knights were very probably drawn from the king's household bannerets, knights and squires. The bannerets were knights who would have had retinues of their own and ranked above the ordinary knights, and it was they who were most likely to have been part of such a group. Of the names we have from 1328, there are men who either were related to the king, or were later among his confidants: Edward Bohun, his cousin, William Clinton, later earl of Huntingdon, Walter Mauny, who came over from Hainault with Queen Philippa,[25] and William Montagu, later first earl of Salisbury. Ralph Stafford, who had fought in Scotland the previous year, was probably also there, but whether Mortimer's three sons were with the king is harder to say. That their friendship with Edward survived their father's disgrace we do know, from Roger Mortimer the younger's subsequent career.[26]

We have left until last the queen and her entourage, a vital element in the culture of the Edwardian court in general, and important in the history of the Garter. Philippa came from a family whose cultivation of dynastic history and enthusiasm for chivalrous sports were as strong as those of Edward. Her entourage included a handful of knights from Hainault, and the Hainault connection remained an important one until her death in 1369, not least because she had a good claim to be countess of Hainault. Edward, preoccupied with his own claim to France, was not in a position to pursue this seriously; it was consistently opposed by a large section of the Hainault nobility, who, like the French with regard to Edward, saw Philippa's rule as leading to domination by a foreign power. In 1362 a scheme was put forward for a marriage between Edmund of Langley, their fourth son, and the daughter of the count of Flanders, the idea being that Edmund would inherit the claim to Hainault and the count would support him in enforcing it. This came to nothing because the pope refused to allow the marriage, on the grounds of consanguinity, though papal officials admitted that it was in fact because it would give Edward a dominant position against France.

When English kings had married abroad in the past, the influence of their wives' fellow-countrymen at court had often been a serious problem, most notably under Henry III. In Philippa's case, the Hainault contingent seem to have merged into the English court without difficulty, apart from the problems at York on the Scottish campaign of 1327, which had no later repercussions.

This absence of friction was probably due to Philippa's personal popularity. Thomas Walsingham remembered her in the 1390s as 'a most noble woman and a most constant lover of the English people'.[27] She emerges from both chronicles and records as a compassionate and warm-hearted person; when in 1331 she narrowly escaped death or injury in the collapse of a stand at a tournament in Cheapside, she asked for mercy for the carpenters whose negligence had caused the accident.[28] The scene in Froissart where she begs for mercy for the six citizens of Calais after the town's surrender in 1347 has passed into legend; it is entirely in harmony with what we know of her character, and there are several petitions in the English records where her intervention on behalf of young girls or pregnant women secured a pardon for them.[29]

Her father, William I of Hainault, and her brother, later William II, were also welcome visitors at court, and participated in Edward's tournaments.[30] Jean de Hainault, who had accompanied her to England when she went there to be married, returned several times; his military support, both in the invasion of 1326 and in the Scottish campaign of 1327, was much valued by Edward, but was also quite expensive: his full claim was for more than £14,000 in wages, though he settled for rather less.[31] It is perhaps precisely because he had been welcome at Edward's court that when Jean de Hainault fought on the French side at Crécy, the Rochester chronicler calls him 'traitor to the king of England'. Philippa was also in constant touch with her mother, who paid several visits to England in the 1330s: in 1333, Philippa paid for seven ships to bring her mother and her companions and 250 horses from Wissant to Dover on 23 September, returning the same way on 13 October.[32] During Edward's wars in Flanders she was with him for much of the time. However, after hostilities resumed in 1342, visits from Philippa's family became less frequent, particularly since William II was absent from Hainault for much of the time from 1342 until his death at the battle of Staveren in 1345.

The connection with Hainault seems to have been an influential one in knightly terms. William I jousted at the tournament held for Philippa's wedding to Edward in 1328, and the Hainault knights were also present at a tournament held by Edward in Brussels in 1339. Walter Mauny figures largely in the pages of his fellow-Hainaulter Jean le Bel, while Jean Froissart, also from Hainault, was in England in Philippa's household in the 1360s.

William II seems to have been almost obsessed by knightly ideals. At the beginning of his career, there had been a round table at Haarlem on the occasion when he was created titular count of Zeeland on 28 September 1333. He was the official sponsor of the event, at which his father gave a supper for the 'knights of the round table'[33] and their ladies, on the evening before the ceremony.[34] There were other jousts immediately afterwards, at 's-Gravenzande.[35]

In 1343–5 his career seems to have been almost exclusively concerned with such matters. In 1343 he went to Prussia, to crusade with the Teutonic Knights against the heathen, and was still there in early 1344.[36] He returned to Holland on 8 April, and almost immediately set in hand preparations for a lavish round table at The Hague. This was held, from Sunday to Thursday, and was on a considerable scale; the count's officers referred to it as the 'great feast' in their accounts:[37] the total expenditure came to £791 11s. 8½d., a very substantial sum.[38] The count rode straight from The Hague on the Thursday to another tournament. Tournaments, combined with another journey to Prussia, seem to have occupied most of his time in the years 1344–5.[39] In the spring and summer of 1344 he took part in 'festivals' involving jousting on seven occasions, beginning with the events at The Hague and Beauvais. In June he fought at Brussels; in July he was at Bergen, Laon and Gertuidenberg; and in September he was at Metz. The following year there were two tournaments in April, at Nijvel and Mechelen, and in August he returned to the favourite tourneying site of Haarlem. His death at the battle of Staveren in the following month brought to an end a knightly career which surpassed in enthusiasm even Edward's most spectacular efforts.

On William II's death, it appears that two of his squires made their way to the English court rather than risk the uncertainties following the loss of not only the count but many of the nobility of Hainault. Besides these two, Henry Eam and Eustace d'Auberchicourt, there may well have been others. Auberchicourt's father had received Edward and his mother in 1326 on their way to invade England, and had served Edward in Scotland, so he was assured of a warm welcome. The links with Hainault were also extremely useful in terms of providing a bridge to the politics of the Low Countries; the death of William I in 1337 was a major blow to Edward, as he was an astute, if not always predictable, politician, and his son was not in the same mould. William II joined Edward's alliance against France in 1338, but went over to the French side in 1343–4. On a different scale, the presence of the Hainault contingent in the English army, and especially that of Walter Mauny, seems to have smoothed the way for negotiations with the besieged inhabitants of Calais in 1347, who would have been more likely to trust them rather than the English invaders.

Philippa came from a family which included a number of women who had been patrons of the arts and particularly of literature. She ordered two books of hours for herself in 1331 from Robert of Oxford, 'with diverse images and large and small letters of gold', one of which may be the volume known as the Taymouth Hours; and she later had an illuminator called Master Robert.[40] Her wedding present to Edward was a lavishly presented manuscript, on whose opening page a young woman holds a book, evidently the volume itself, which she presents to the figure on the far side of the text, a young man with a surcoat embroidered with the arms of England. It seems to have been written in Flanders and illuminated by an English artist (Plate 3). This manuscript, like those presented to the king by one of his clerks, Walter Milemete,[41] concentrates on good advice for a future king, and indeed contains a French text, *The Secret of Secrets*, which was also presented by Milemete. Besides this, Philippa's manuscript includes an encyclopedia, *The Book of Treasures*, which ranges across world history, natural sciences, rhetoric and statesmanship. And there is a satirical poem on the ways of the world, the *Romance of Fauveyn* or *Fauvel*, a moral tale on the treachery of mankind. The hero is the horse Fauvel, who personifies deceit; the text is short and heavily illustrated in the manner of a comic strip. Illustrations also abound in *The Book of Treasures*; this is clearly a volume designed to entice the viewer, through its visual splendour, into reading the improving tales it contains; as such it does not reflect Philippa's own personal tastes, but has been designed as an appropriate formal gift for the occasion.[42]

Last but by no means least, the marriage of Philippa and Edward seems to have been one of enduring affection. There are hints of an affair in 1347 at Calais, and of some kind of attempt by John Stratford, archbishop of Canterbury, to stir up trouble between the king and his wife in 1340. The first depends on the interpretation of an obscure allegorical commentary on Edward's reign by a Yorkshire friar, which speaks of a lecherous 'Diana' who tempts Edward; Edward neglects the war with France as a result, and England is punished with the Black Death.[43] All this reads like the kind of monastic reasoning which later attributed the great storm of 1362 to plans for a tournament in which the knights would be disguised as the seven deadly sins; it is difficult to take it seriously, particularly as Philippa was present at the siege for at least part of the time. The second occurs in a letter to the pope which was written by Edward when he was furious with the archbishop over his political opposition to Edward's wishes.[44] Neither of these is a substantial charge, and it is only at the end of the marriage, when Philippa was ailing, that Edward took a mistress, the notorious Alice Perrers. Perrers was one of Philippa's attendants, ambitious and a shrewd businesswoman, who was determined to use her charms on the elderly king and to make her fortune. Although she bore Edward a son in 1364, it was not until after Philippa's death in 1369 that she played a major part in the court. But her activities in the last years of Edward's reign were to be remembered, and were to give Edward a lascivious reputation at odds with that of his prime.[45] For most of his reign, the image of the royal marriage was one of happiness and prosperity; his insistence on spending long periods with Philippa during her first pregnancies speaks of his devotion. And their sons, healthy and energetic warriors, outshone their French counterparts. Philip's only son, John, suffered serious illness in his youth, and his life was in danger in one of these episodes.

Since June 1328, Henry of Lancaster had taken offence at Roger Mortimer's control of the king, and his increasing usurpation of royal powers. The stand-off came to a head after Mortimer's creation as earl of March at Salisbury the following October, and armed conflict was narrowly avoided at Winchester in November 1328 and again at Bedford in January 1329. Henry of Lancaster and his followers submitted to arbitration, but they were forced to give sureties for the future, and a number of leading lords were excluded from the agreement. These included Henry of Beaumont, Edward's guardian in 1325, who with several other magnates went into exile. Nonetheless, perhaps to distract the king from Mortimer's secure hold over the government, tournaments continued throughout 1329; and the king was not the only promoter of such occasions, because the records of Thomas, Lord Berkeley note a number of occasions when he was jousting and the king is known to have been elsewhere. These were usually local affairs in the west country, at Bristol and Exeter for example, and on a much smaller scale; the fact that they were not prohibited says something for Mortimer's confidence in his control of this region, since, in the days of Gaveston and the Despensers, such events had been focal points for the opposition.

Berkeley was present at some royal tournaments, at Coventry on 2 January and Guildford on 6 March (with Thomas Bradeston, one of his retainers), where another of Mortimer's supporters, Geoffrey Scrope, was also a participant.[46] This was a court festival, because 7 March was Shrovetide, a day of carnival before the Lenten fast began, and 'false visages' or masks were provided for the occasion. In June, when Edward went to Amiens to perform homage to Philip of Valois for Aquitaine and Ponthieu, a tournament was on the agenda;[47] and it is possible that both kings entered the lists. There was more jousting on the return journey, at Canterbury and Dartford:[48] at Canterbury the king evidently fought fiercely, as an armourer had to be summoned to mend his armour on the spot, before the Dartford tournament a few days later.[49]

Mortimer then organized a series of tournaments to entertain the king on the Welsh borders, and perhaps to keep him out of the increasingly threatening political scene. These began with an event at Gloucester at the end of August, and then another at Hereford in September. There were jousts at both Hereford and Wigmore, but the king appears to have stayed at Hereford, and avoided Mortimer's home ground. The jousting fraternity then moved on to Worcester;[50] ailettes or shoulder-plates were made for this occasion quartered with the arms of William Montagu and Bartholomew Burghersh the elder, probably because they were the leaders of the king's tournament team. Geoffrey Mortimer, Roger Mortimer's eldest son, was given a suit of armour. The grand finale of the season was at Dunstable on 12 October; witnesses in two different cases in the Court of Chivalry in Richard II's reign still remembered it, and one of them, William Penbrugge, had taken part as one of Robert Morley's squires.[51] No fewer than 400 pairs of shoulder-plates were made for the Dunstable tournament, 200 with the arms of Maurice Berkeley and John Neville quartered and 200 with the arms of St George.

We have detailed records for these tournaments, from which we can build something of a picture of the proceedings; the style of Edward's jousts varied little for the rest of the reign, even if they were not always as visually striking as in the early years. These were occasions in splendid style; Mortimer and Isabella were renowned for their extravagance, and they held the purse-strings. Philippa, whose love of clothes was later to lead to serious financial problems with her household, was allowed to place her own orders, and Edward was doubtless delighted with what his armourers and clothiers produced. He evidently loved the Hainault fashions: there was a suit of armour with blue angels and gold letters 'in the style of a suit of armour given to the king by the count of Hainault' and saddles 'decorated with various beasts and images in the style of Hainault' in honour of Edward's bride and her entourage. Letters, whose meaning we can rarely guess at, figure prominently: crowned silver letters P, I and E on costumes probably made for Dunstable stood for Philippa, Isabella and Edward, but the silver-crowned Ms at Guildford, and twelve tunics with the letters K and E at Worcester, are a mystery. The latter, which had silver chains as well as the letters, required 400 peacock feathers, and, with four tunics for the king's squires decorated with eagles' heads, caused so much work for the painter Francolin of Murkirk and his men who were employed to make them that large quantities of candles had to be bought so that they could work on them at night to get them ready in time. The Wigmore accoutrements included two sets of armour patterned with gold and quartered with silver, decorated with birds and beasts, and a banner to match, with birds and 'babbewyns' or grotesques. Highly decorated lances were made by Peter of Bruges: an order for twelve lances, 'well ornamented', ranged from blue lances with green rosebushes and red roses, to black lances with silver pommels and green lances with silver shields and red vamplates. At Worcester, an eagle crest was supplied, almost certainly for the king, matching the eagles on the squires' tunics. Masks are recorded for the same tournament. The joust at Dartford seems to have been on the theme of Richard the Lionheart's famous encounter (*passus*) with Saladin, an image found on medieval English tiles and embroideries, and taken from the romance written about him in the thirteenth century: there is a hat for the king with the 'passus Saladin' embroidered on it, and thirteen lances and swords finished in silver for the knights of 'the same passus Saladin'.[52] One of the royal treasures was a Saracen helmet 'lately of the Sultan Saladin' complete with silver-gilt circlet recorded on 30 April 1327, just three months after Edward came to the throne; and images of the encounter recur throughout his reign, ending with the will of Edward prince of Wales in 1376.[53]

By the end of 1329, it was generally known at court that Philippa was expecting her first child. Yet her status as queen had not been officially recognized, since she had not been crowned. Arrangements for her coronation were made in some haste, and the ceremony was carried out on 18 February. There seems to have been a major tournament in connection with the celebrations; according to Jean le Bel, the contingent from Hainault was led by her brother Jean de Hainault.[54] Once again, Hainault fashion was the favoured style: in the bills from the king's armourer, Thomas Copham, among the standard pieces of armour and tunics, there are items for decorating 'tunics in the Hainault and other fashions'.[55] Philippa's household may well have contributed a number of jousters at this time. We only know for certain at this point that Walter

Mauny, who came over with Philippa, was a squire in the royal household.

In the spring of 1330 the ominous political atmosphere precluded such lightweight events as tournaments. Despite the official announcement of Edward II's death, and his state funeral at Gloucester, rumours now began to circulate about his survival. Mortimer, aiming to consolidate his control of Edward III and therefore of the government, seems to have been behind these rumours as a means of ensnaring his enemies. He succeeded in deceiving such high-ranking men as William Melton, archbishop of York, and even Edward II's half-brother, Edmund earl of Kent. Edmund and the king's other uncle Thomas of Brotherton, earl of Norfolk, had kept a wary distance from the court since Mortimer was created earl of March, but they had also dissociated themselves from Henry of Lancaster's rebellion. Mortimer regarded the earl of Kent as an opponent and feared that he might gain the young king's confidence and turn him against Mortimer. It seems that his machinations successfully ensnared the unwary Edmund into a plot to restore the king's father, said to be imprisoned at Corfe. Mortimer was already highly unpopular because of the treaty made with Scotland in 1328 after the debacle at Stanhope Park.

At a parliament at Winchester in March 1330, Mortimer was also blamed for the inability of the government to pay for the sending of troops to defend Gascony, which was once more under threat from the French because Edward had only partially performed homage for the duchy at Amiens in 1329. The royal treasury was known to have been well funded before Edward II abdicated, and the suspicion was that Mortimer (and Isabella) had appropriated the money to pay for their extravagant lifestyle and to reward their followers lavishly. Mortimer distracted attention from these complaints by having the earl of Kent arrested on charges of treason, a turn of events which was completely unexpected by the king. The charge was supported by a letter from Edmund to the keeper of Corfe Castle, encouraging an attempt to place Edward II on the throne again. Kent was found guilty; and, according to the *Brut* chronicle, Mortimer went at once to the king, whom he found at dinner, and told him of the verdict. But Mortimer feared that the king would pardon his uncle, and arranged for Kent's immediate death; it was Isabella who ordered the bailiffs of Winchester to have him executed. 'And when the king learnt of it, he was exceedingly sorry, and had his body buried at the Greyfriars church at Winchester.'[56] The earl's estates were treated by Mortimer as his personal spoils and given to his eldest son, Geoffrey, and several of the leading knights who were loyal to him.

Edward retreated into his personal affairs; he went to Woodstock within a week of the end of the parliament, and spent the next three months there, awaiting the birth of Philippa's first child and hunting in the neighbouring forests. His son Edward, later famous as 'the Black Prince', was born on 15 June, and a few days later the king left the palace, returning at intervals during July and holding a tournament there for Philippa's 'churching', the service at which the medieval Church exorcized the superstitious taboos surrounding female fertility and readmitted the mother of the newborn child to its rituals. Such 'churching' festivals were to be a regular part of the life of the royal court.[57] As befitted such an occasion, the queen was provided with the most magnificent of robes, in purple velvet embroidered with golden squirrels – perhaps a reference to her favourite pet – at a cost of just over £200; a third of the cost was for the embroiderers' work.[58]

Quite apart from Edward's revulsion at the judicial murder of the earl of Kent, there were strong signs that he was chafing under the hold which Mortimer had over him through the liaison with his mother. It was now no longer a matter for satire, as in the episode of the 'society of Craddok' (if we have read that rightly), but of his own self-preservation. His friends among his household knights and fellow-tourneyers had little experience of politics, and his household was partly staffed by Mortimer's henchmen. John Maltravers, an associate of Mortimer's since 1322, was appointed steward of the king's household in February 1328, despite the fact that he was widely said to have been one of the men responsible for the death of Edward II. In May 1330 he was among a group of knights loyal to Mortimer who were to be 'always with the king'; the others provided a bodyguard of 230 men at arms, of whom the vast majority were under the command of Simon Bereford.[59] Edward Bohun, though a supporter of Mortimer, was also the king's cousin, while Maurice Berkeley was a tournament companion of the prince. The Berkeleys were relatives of Mortimer, and Thomas Berkeley, lord of Berkeley Castle, was Mortimer's brother-in-law, part of the west-country network which was Mortimer's power base. And Mortimer also had his spies in place: 'he put John Wyard and others around the king to spy on his actions and words, so that he was unable to do as he wished, so that he was like a man in custody.'[60]

Nonetheless, Edward had found means to circumvent Mortimer's attempts to prevent him from independent action. Richard of Bury, later bishop of Durham, had been chamberlain of his earldom of Chester from 1320 to 1323, and was later constable of Bordeaux when Edward was created duke of Aquitaine in 1326: in 1328–9 he was keeper of the king's wardrobe, and then keeper of the privy seal, the office responsible for the king's private correspondence. At the time when Mortimer was encircling Edward with his own men, it was Richard of Bury who helped to arrange for a secret sign by which the pope could distinguish those messages which were genuinely from the king personally from official messages, the implication being that the latter would be dictated by Mortimer. The king's personal letters were to bear the words 'pater sancte', 'Holy Father', written in the king's own hand. This scheme had been set in motion by William Montagu, one of Edward's household knights, during an embassy to Avignon in late 1329. He had explained to the pope Edward's frustration with his inability to act on his own account, and his wish to throw off the dominance of Mortimer. The original letter was carefully filed in the Vatican archives, with the specimen of the king's handwriting: but no other letters to the pope from Edward have come to light. The existence of this one letter, however, tells us that Edward was building a network of his own to counter Mortimer's ambitions as early as September 1329, when Montagu left England.

Mortimer's reputed involvement in the death of Edward II, his certain role in the execution of the earl of Kent, and his imperious manner – he always walked beside the king or in front of him, never behind him[61] – made it seem that he was bent on seizing the throne for himself and Isabella. Years later, Jean le Bel recorded a rumour that Isabella was pregnant by him, though it does not seem to have been current at the time.[62] Even without this, Mortimer had put himself in the same position as the ill-famed favourites of Edward II. But he was only the favourite of the queen regent, not of the king himself: and therein lay his weakness.

The spy Wyard did his job well, and got wind of a conspiracy. Mortimer knew that he was up against formidable problems, and when he and Isabella went to Nottingham in October 1330 for a great council (ostensibly to discuss the crisis in Gascony) he betrayed his nervousness.

He and Isabella arrived first, and Isabella took personal possession of the keys of the castle. The king arrived in the town, to be told that if he wanted to enter the castle he could only do so with three or four servants; his household knights and companions would have to lodge elsewhere.

What we know about the events that followed comes not from the chronicles of officials like Adam Murimuth, but from the anonymous writer of the *Brut* chronicle and from Thomas Gray's *Scalacronica*. Gray, as we have seen, was a member of Montagu's retinue in 1338, eight years later, and probably heard his version from Montagu himself: but he was writing thirty years after the events. We know less about the sources of the *Brut*, but the style in which the episode is told also implies eyewitness information, and was probably written around 1334, very shortly after the event.[63] The *Brut* names the ringleaders of Edward's party as William Montagu, Humphrey Bohun, William his brother,[64] Ralph Stafford, Robert Ufford, William Clinton and John Neville, 'and many others who agreed with them'. Thomas Gray says that the plot was discovered, and they were examined by Mortimer and the ruling council: all of them denied it, and Montagu openly defied the council to say that he had done anything improper, with the result that they only replied in general terms. Once the council was over, Montagu 'said to the king that it was better to eat the dog than to let the dog eat them',[65] and advised him to send someone to speak to the constable of the castle, telling him to keep the plan secret, and leave a postern gate* open that night. According to Thomas Gray, most of the conspirators missed their rendezvous in the castle park that night, and only Montagu and John Neville went in through the gate, with twenty-four men. The constable met them and led them through an underground passage into the castle. When they made their way to the chamber where Mortimer and the queen were discussing what to do next, the steward of the household, Hugh Turplington, saw them as they approached the room, and cried: 'Traitors! You have come here for nothing. You will all die a foul death!' He was killed at once, stabbed by Neville. Mortimer pulled on his armour at the door of the tower, but was seized, and Isabella cried out, 'Fair sirs, I beg you not to hurt him: he is a worthy knight, our

---

* A 'postern gate' often meant an escape route, and therefore does not contradict the story of the underground tunnels.

well-beloved friend and dear cousin!'[66] Mortimer was taken to the king, and orders were given for his close confinement; the king made arrangements for Isabella's safety, in reality a guarded exile from court that was to last until her death in 1358. Mortimer's supporters fled for their lives, and Edward's companions took charge of the government in his name. Mortimer's crimes were declared 'notorious' at a parliament in London in November, and he was therefore condemned without being allowed to defend himself. He was executed on 29 November at Tyburn, 'the common gallows of thieves'.[67]

In all, we have the names of sixteen men who were definitely involved in the attack at Nottingham, because they were specifically given pardons for the murder or rewarded for their actions that night. Seven of the knights are named in the *Brut*, as well as William Eland, keeper of the castle; in addition to these, there are eight other men. Three were knights, Thomas West, William Latimer and Thomas Thornham.[68] West and John Molyns, a squire at the time, were close companions of Montagu. Latimer's father and grandfather had distinguished themselves in royal service; his father had died three years earlier, and he became a knight of the king's household around the time of the coup. This promising career was cut short when he died in 1335, aged about thirty-five. Latimer brought at least four retainers with him, including one man, John Maunsell, who was a squire in the king's household. Finally, two other men about whom we know very little, Robert Walkefare and John Crombek, were also pardoned.

The men named are associates of Montagu and Neville, and this implies that Thomas Gray's statement that only Montagu and Neville and their retinues actually entered the castle is correct. It follows that Edward himself, who is usually said to have been present, is unlikely to have been there, particularly as the *Brut* tells us that those who seized Mortimer 'went thence', i.e. out of the chamber, 'and brought the Mortimer and presented him to King Edward'.[69] Thomas Gray makes no mention of Edward during the entry to the castle and the attack on Mortimer. The traditional scene of Isabella pleading with her son for Mortimer's life which Baker portrays so dramatically is therefore untrue; and he admits that Isabella could not in fact see the king.[70]

The moving spirit behind the plot was William Montagu, but he was acting with the king's full confidence. Edward was still learning the craft of managing men, and Montagu seems to have been an excellent tutor. In the parliament held a month later at Westminster, the bishops and magnates present asked the king to reward him because 'the said William had worked nobly concerning the arrest of the said Roger and his accomplices, for the peace and quiet of all the people of the realm'; and he was duly showered with lands and honours, much of it Mortimer's own territory.

Edward was fully aware of his powers as king, but, perhaps all too mindful of his father's disastrous handling of his favourites, seems instinctively to have regarded himself as first among equals, part of a group or team, rather than insisting on his superior rank. Montagu may have been his closest companion, and even his brother in arms;[71] but he never became more than that in the world at large, and his political influence was limited to advising Edward confidentially on government business. His seal might be used on royal letters, and he might convey the decisions of the royal council to the clerks in chancery, but Edward never went so far as to let him exercise power on his own, as the Despensers and Mortimer had done. Equally, Montagu was not ambitious: he never tried to outshine the other magnates, the fatal flaw which had led to Gaveston's downfall.

The social culture of the court continued to revolve around tournaments and festivals, and in both the king appears as one of the participants, sometimes dazzlingly arrayed as the sovereign, but at other times clothed in a team uniform. We have already met such uniforms in the case of the 'society of Craddok'; there is a particularly splendid set recorded in 1330, which has been associated with the coup of that year. These are aketons, which were basically padded jackets which went under armour to prevent chain mail or plates from chafing: they were worn over a linen shirt. In principle, they were invisible, since they were designed as an under-garment, but during a tournament there would be times when a knight would not be wearing his armour, and his quilted cotton jacket would be visible. The aketon replaced the heavier woollen or linen gambeson in the early fourteenth century, and first appears in Edward II's specifications for the arms to be borne by the wealthier members of the troops levied in the 1320s for feudal service.[72] The king and William Montagu had jackets of this kind made in the summer of 1330, and a further seven were made in November 1330; the materials were velvet, silk and linen, the colours purple, green and red, and the embroidery silver and gold. However, it is difficult to fathom the choice of the men who went resplendent in this costume. It has been suggested that they were all participants in the coup of October 1330, and the timing would certainly suggest this, as would the presence of John Neville, Robert Ufford and William Clinton, whom we know to have been involved. Thomas Bradeston and Maurice Berkeley are highly likely candidates for involvement. But the addition of the king's physician, Master Pancio, and the bishop of Salisbury means that this is not just a group of knights. Indeed, the bishop, Robert Wyville, is a real puzzle. He had been made bishop only months before, and the chronicler Adam Murimuth gives a hostile account of him: 'he wrote the queen's special letters, an illiterate and uncouth personage, whom, had the pope seen him, I believe he would never have promoted to such heights'. He had been arrested at Nottingham as one of Mortimer's supporters, but was soon released.[73]

This kind of puzzle is typical of the problems we face when trying to get closer to the men among whom the king was at ease and who shared his courtly life. Even if they were all involved in the coup, what did the wearing of these gaudy costumes convey, unless it was perhaps a whim of princely magnificence to a random group of followers? Where the same names recur as the recipients of magnificent costumes, we can be more certain that these are the king's intimates: Montagu, Ufford, the Bohun twins and Ralph Neville, John Neville's nephew. On one occasion Montagu and the king appeared in identical red surcoats embroidered with birds and mottoes.[74] But this apparently frivolous context was an important part of the life of the court, and can tell us much about the king and his relationship with his courtiers. It is a theme which tends to be submerged in the politics and military history of Edward's reign, appearing intermittently in the intervals of peace. Yet it probably occupied, together with hunting, as much time in Edward's life as the great affairs of state.

2

'A jolly young life': Tournaments, Festivals, Display

Thomas Gray tells us that, once the king had removed the controlling hand of Mortimer, he embarked on his favourite pleasures, and that it was William Montagu who aided and abetted him: 'At this time and for a long while after, the king was advised by William de Montague, who always encouraged him to virtue and honour, and to a love of arms, and they led a jolly young life, awaiting a greater season for greater affairs.'[1] A list of armour issued to the king for tournaments for 1330–31, ending on 24 January, shows four tournaments, beginning at Clarendon on 13 November, moving to Westminster later that month and then to Guildford for the beginning of the Christmas festivities, and Westminster again on 20 January.[2]

Edward III took to jousting with immense enthusiasm. What had once been a subversive activity, tolerated rather than encouraged, and rarely patronized by the crown, became the official sport of the English court. We have seen how Edward learnt to love tournaments and festivals while he was under the tutelage of Isabella and Mortimer, yet he was shrewd enough to see that such display could arouse enmity as well as admiration. By his extravagant display on these occasions, Mortimer was declaring himself as the dominant player in the English political scene, with power and wealth to rival the king. There is only a handful of tournaments in 1330 before Mortimer's arrest and execution in November of that year. Once Edward had dispatched his erstwhile master and mentor, he gathered round him a group of magnates and knights who were to be the core of his administration and household. These men were at the heart of the renewed festivities of the winter of 1330–31, and William Montagu, leader of the coup against Mortimer, was Edward's new fellow-enthusiast. The king, however, was now in charge, and Montagu was no more than an adviser.

The attitude towards tournaments was changing, perhaps because of the king's personal enjoyment of them. In 1331 three general prohibitions were issued, an indication that the political situation was still volatile. But in later years such bans were rare and were usually put in place when the king was going abroad or there was a military campaign in progress. Compared with France, where royal bans were largely directed at gatherings of great lords whose relations with the king were often hostile, the English magnates were now generally allowed to hold jousts in the king's absence. Few of their household accounts survive; most of the records of local jousts that survive come from the fourteenth-century accounts of Thomas, Lord Berkeley, which have remained at Berkeley Castle since they were written. And chroniclers from the religious houses of which the magnates were patrons took an interest in their lords' doings: the priory at Wigmore described the tournaments of the earls of March, and Henry Knighton at Leicester kept track of the activities of Henry of Grosmont, the king's cousin and heir to the earldom of Leicester. The king might also use a prohibition to eliminate events which clashed with his own: a royal ban was issued in February 1341 to the sheriff of Kent because the king was holding jousts at Norwich and did not want local competition which might reduce the attendance at his festival.

The distinction between *hastiludium*, literally 'game with the spear', usually translated as joust, and *torneamentum*, 'tournament', a word whose origins and meaning are less obvious, is difficult to define, but in the records of Edward's reign it is reasonably clear that *hastiludia* usually take place in a confined space, and are therefore more likely to have been single combats, while the tournament was the traditional mock-warfare (*mêlée*) as practised since the early twelfth century, which required open spaces and a large area for an encounter between groups of knights (Plate 25).[3] The French word *joute*, which is the equivalent of *hastiludia*, also appears in the Latin records as *justa*, and there is also the *burdeicium* (*bohort* in French, 'burdis' in English), which was usually a kind of practice tournament restricted to squires. A major event could include all three forms of fighting; the *bohort* is usually only mentioned in the chronicles when there is an accident or a disturbance, and is almost totally absent from the exchequer records.

In April 1331 Edward travelled secretly to France to swear conditional fealty to Philip, who was pressing for a complete oath of fealty to complete the homage made in 1329. It was a move which could have caused problems at home if it had become public. As if to mask his brief absence, he celebrated a tournament at Dartford as soon as he returned. The writer of the St Paul's chronicle evidently had an eyewitness account of this occasion: the defending team, including the king, fought under the banner of William Clinton, and the king, 'though he was of a tender age, performed very well, battered by heavy blows and enduring them strongly'. At the end of the tournament, his horse played up, and he called for a palfrey* to be brought; but one of his knights protested that it was not fitting for him to change horses on the field. The king ignored this and rode safely back to his lodgings; meanwhile, the first horse bolted with his new rider, and plunged into the river, nearly drowning the knight: 'the horse was so overheated by the tournament that it wanted to bathe in the water'. If the fully armed king had been riding it, he would almost certainly have perished.[4]

The king, undeterred, spent much of the spring and summer jousting. In early May, there was a tournament at Havering, a royal manor belonging to the queen which had been remodelled on a lavish scale under Henry III, with a chamber, chapel and two wardrobes for Eleanor of Provence.[5] The event seems to have had an Arthurian theme, since the king had a suit of armour decorated with 'a castle with the flags of the arms of Lancelot issuing from it' made for the occasion.[6] The tourneyers moved on to Newmarket at the end of the month; Walter Mauny was present on both occasions, and suits of armour were bought for eight of the king's household knights. Two further jousts were held, at Lichfield and Bedford, some time during the summer and autumn.[7]

The major events, however, were held in the capital. The Dartford jousts were the first of three which attracted the attention of the London chroniclers in 1331. Edward had held tournaments at Westminster, but not in and around the City until this year. Perhaps the memory of the disaster of Gaveston's cancelled Stepney jousts in 1309 still lingered: if so, it was a memory triumphantly expunged at the same place in June. This was as much festival as tournament, showing off the regal style of the new regime as if to counter any possible rumours of the king's

---

* An ordinary riding horse, as opposed to the larger tournament charger.

submission to France. The organizer was ostensibly Robert Morley, a member of the king's inner circle; it was paid for by the king, and marked the first birthday of his son Edward. The king fought under Morley's banner, together with his uncle, Thomas of Brotherton, and twenty-three other knights. The event began with a procession to St Paul's, where they all made offerings at the high altar. The knights were in uniform costumes of green tunics and mantles with red hoods, the mantles embroidered with golden arrows; their fifty squires were dressed in white with green right sleeves also with golden arrows, and green hoods. To conceal the king's identity, they were all masked.[8]

William Montagu was the leader in the even more splendid occasion held within the City itself , in Cheapside from 22 to 25 September. The writer of the St Paul's chronicle watched the event:

> The whole market area, between the conduit and the cross of the queen [Eleanor] where they were to ride was enclosed with stout timber and planks, and the whole pavement was strewn with sand. At the bishop's palace, where William was the host, there was great plenty of provisions and many marvellous things. At the time for which the tournament was arranged, the king, earls and barons and all the knights in the kingdom gathered in London, and on the Sunday, the eve of St Matthew the apostle, William, who was captain of this solemn occasion, appeared with the king and other chosen knights in splendid clothing, with masks like Tartars. There came with them the same number of the most noble and beautiful ladies of the kingdom, all wearing red velvet tunics and caps of white camel's hair cloth; and each knight had on his right-hand side a lady whom he led with a silver chain. The king had at his side the lady Eleanor his sister, a most beautiful girl. All of them, both knights and ladies, came at the hour of vespers, riding in pairs down the middle of Cheapside, preceded by more than sixty squires all dressed in the same uniform; and they were followed by their jousting horses covered with fine horsecloths; and thus, to the sound of trumpets and a variety of other instruments, they rode to their lodgings. On the following days, that is, Monday, Tuesday and Wednesday, the sixteen knights who were the keepers defended themselves from early morning to evening against all comers, both native and foreign. On the first day of the jousts there was an extraordinary accident: the balcony which ran across the street, in which the queen and all the other ladies were sitting to watch the spectacle, suddenly

collapsed; and many ladies as well as knights were seriously hurt, and scarcely escaped with their lives.[9]

The citizens were duly impressed: 'never were such solemn jousts seen in England', noted one of them.[10] The king's armourer, John of Cologne, was paid the huge sum of £356 3s. 7d. for his work on costumes, saddles and suits of armour supplied for these occasions.[11]

Behind the games and the spectacle, the apparent indulgence in idle pursuits and lavish expenditure, there was a deeper purpose. These events brought the aristocratic world of the court and the equally rich world of the City together, and we shall see how this is one of the key elements of Edward's success. The court moved round the country from one royal residence to another, and could seem remote to the citizens of London. Even when the king was at Westminster, this was outside the city walls, and except for the rare occasions when he was at the Tower of London, a fortress rather than a place for courtly pageant, he was not seen in London itself. The ties between court and the City could be of great political importance, and we shall find a consistent pattern of jousts in London and even invitations to the citizens to attend jousts elsewhere that seem to indicate that the king was using these occasions as a way of forging a relationship between the two.[12] This is knightly prowess as visual entertainment, even theatre, of a kind which was to become very familiar down to the seventeenth century; it is the direct ancestor of the 'magnificence' of Renaissance princes.[13] The Stepney and Cheapside jousts of 1331 are among the earliest known examples of the tournament as royal pageant, though Philip of Valois had staged jousts on his formal entry into Paris in 1328 which may have been in the same vein.[14] There were similar occasions in Flanders: it is possible that jousts at Tournai in 1331, for which we have a detailed record of the jousters' performance, included a parade of knights through the streets and possibly a dramatic scenario, though no record of this part of the proceedings survives.[15]

A grand occasion like the Cheapside 'tournament' in 1331 would begin with the traditional *mêlée*, in which all the knights took part. In the *mêlée*, the knights would fight as teams, and the same teams, usually called 'those inside' (*intrinseci*) or defenders and 'those outside' (*extrinseci*) or challengers, would then fight individual jousts against all members of the opposing team. Performance in the *mêlée* was hard to judge, though the romances of the period make great play of the heroic feats of individual knights in such combats, one of whom is then acclaimed by the heralds and the assembled company as the victor. What actually went on in the *mêlée* was hard to describe; even the writers of romances found it difficult to invent a detailed account of their imaginary tournaments, and are very vague as to the details of what was happening: 'Then Sir Gawain and his brother Sir Gaheriet began to perform such splendid feats of arms that anyone who saw them would have deemed them the best knights in the world: they spurred up the field and down, felling knights and horses, and doing so much by their valor that their enemies were defeated by their might . . .'[16]

Minstrels or public criers, the forerunners of heralds, provided a commentary on the action in twelfth-century tournaments so that spectators could identify the knights and understand what was happening. By the fourteenth century it is more likely that some kind of scoring system, such as is found on Tudor jousting 'cheques', was emerging, and that a knight such as Thomas Beauchamp, the victor of the jousts at Smithfield in 1343, was the winner of the largest number of individual jousts. The other problem with the *mêlée* was that most accidents in the sport happened in this type of combat: although tournaments were probably no more dangerous than rugby or American football today, there were some spectacular fatalities, including John of Beaumont, brother-in-law of Henry of Grosmont, at Northampton in 1342.

A knight who excelled in the lists was the equivalent of a modern sporting hero, and the small group of tourneyers whose names appear alongside that of the king himself were made up of such star performers. As with all tourneying records, the details are very sketchy – there is no equivalent to the lists of knights in a lord's retinue when he went on campaign – but certain names stand out. First and foremost is Henry of Grosmont, whose close friendship with his cousin Edward was partly based on their shared enthusiasm for jousting. Henry was responsible for the grant of a licence in 1344 to a company of knights at Lincoln who proposed to hold an annual tournament, of which he was to be the captain in perpetuity. In the charter Edward declares that he has made the grant because of Henry's 'delight in warlike deeds', and 'having studied the deeds of our forefathers, and bearing in mind how much the practice of knightly skills and the love of arms exalts the name and glory of men, and how much the royal throne is strengthened by the number of men expert in arms, as well as the confusion and danger which often arises from laziness'.[17]

The role of captain appears in other tournament records. William Montagu, the nearest to a favourite in Edward's court, was another, and Edward fought under his leadership as *capitaneus* at the tournament at Cheapside in 1331; in the same year he also appeared under William Clinton, at Dartford, and Robert Morley, at Stepney. Morley was certainly one of the most experienced jousters, as he was present on at least ten occasions over a twenty-year period. Twelve years later, in 1343, the king was again in the lists with Morley as captain. He also fought as a 'simple knight' at Dunstable in 1342, and in 1348 wore the arms of Thomas Bradeston, who was evidently captain for the occasion, at Lichfield. Such occasions must have created a strong sense of fellowship, yet none of these captains were to become companions of the Garter.

Jousts and tournaments took place almost entirely in peacetime. The records of such occasions show a clear pattern which confirms this. There are jousts in 1328–9, 1331–2, 1334, 1339–40, a major series in 1341–4, and another in 1348.[18] In the 1350s there were only brief intervals when there was no threat of hostilities or actual war, and, by the end of the decade, Edward was fifty, and his enthusiasm for the sport was diminishing. The Garter companions would therefore have experienced a court culture in which the art of performance was a major factor, very much in contrast with the opening and closing decades of the century. The younger knights, such as Edward prince of Wales, would have regarded tournaments and festive jousts as a natural and integral part of their lives; the older knights were among those who helped Edward III to revive and develop his grandfather's traditions.

Knightly gatherings may have fulfilled another function. Jousts were usually court events, and would have had an important influence on creating an *esprit de corps* among the household knights and those usually in attendance on the king. The degree to which the knights who took part in tournaments overlapped with those who served on royal campaigns is well illustrated by the event at Dunstable in 1334,[19] for which we have a list of 134 knights who took part. Of these, 89 can be identified as members of the household in the 1330s and/or participants in the campaign of 1346 which culminated in the battle of Crécy.

Tournaments held outside the capital were very probably useful to the king as a way of sounding out local opinion and impressing his subjects with his 'magnificence'. The series of tournaments held in 1328–9 looks very much like a royal tour by the new king, doing the equivalent of the later royal progress; just as Elizabeth I paraded herself and her court before her subjects, so Edward may have used these events both to introduce himself to his people, and to impress them with his martial skills, particularly as his father was said to have had a very unregal love of 'the art of rowing and driving carts, of digging ditches and thatching houses'.[20] The king also used such tours to celebrate his military successes, and his return from a campaign would often be marked with a tournament, as in 1334, at the end of the Scottish expedition which included the victory at Halidon Hill. The tournaments of 1348 are similar, in that they mark – on a much grander scale – the victories at Crécy and Calais. There were also tournaments at the end of rather less successful military activities: in Flanders in 1339–40, the first foray into France and the unsuccessful siege of Tournai, which ended in the truce of Esplechin, were celebrated with jousts, perhaps as a distraction from pressing problems of finance and as a way of raising the army's morale.

During a campaign, even if the king was not present, there was a continual flow of communication with important magnates and the captains of the army. In peacetime, there was no mechanism for discovering the mood of the nobility outside the court, other than through the formal summoning of a parliament – which was, as its name (from *parler*, to talk) implies, a place where discussion took place. The tournaments from 1341 to 1344 look like an informal way of keeping in touch with local magnates, particularly since they correspond to the low point of Edward's rule, following the opposition to his policies in the spring of 1341 after which he had had to accept terms imposed by Archbishop Stratford and his allies. This was possibly a deliberate way of regaining the confidence of the disaffected shire knights.

From the outset, the tournament had been governed by rules, designed to prevent injuries as far as possible and the degeneration of such events into private warfare. The nearest contemporary set of jousting regulations are those issued by Alfonso XI of Castile for the knights of the Sash, founded in 1330, and thus exactly contemporary with Edward III's tourneying activities. This is a severely practical document, which is concerned to prevent accidents or outright cheating, and to restrict any possibility that quarrels might arise, or be settled, in the thick of the fight. For the mass combat of the tournament proper, bugles and kettle-drums signalled the start of the fighting, as well as its ending. Swords were to be blunted, and armour should not have any sharpened points. A blow with the point of a sword, or with the flat of the blade in the face, was prohibited. If a knight lost his helmet or fell to the ground, he was not to be attacked or trampled on. If knights lost their horses, they were to be impounded until the fighting finished; but they were then returned to their owners. In the twelfth and thirteenth centuries it had been possible to make a fortune by capturing horses in tournaments, as if in war itself; but this no longer held good. The prizes were to be awarded to the knights who had performed best in each team: a large tournament of fifty knights on either side would have twelve judges for each side, and the judges would confer with the squires and ladies present before coming to a decision.

For single combat, which seems at this period to have been almost exclusively a contest with lances, the critical objective was to break a lance on the body of the opposing knight. A specified number of courses were to be run, and the winner was the knight who had broken most lances. If a knight succeeded in unhorsing his opponent, that counted for two lances. If two knights unseated each other, a knight whose horse fell with him was declared the winner of that course, on the grounds that his fall was the fault of his horse. If a knight dropped his lance, his opponent was to raise his lance and not strike him.[21]

The actual combats were only part of the tournament. From their inception in the twelfth century tournaments were major social occasions. It is possible that the rapid development of heraldry was due to the spectators' interest in the individual knights and their exploits, for which clear visual identification was required; and the mystique of the early heralds depended on the knowledge and skill with which they were able to pick out the champions of the day. As the tournament moved away from mass encounters to the joust between two participants, so the length of the proceedings increased: fifteenth-century descriptions make them sound rather less exciting than the most protracted of cricket matches, with only one or two encounters an hour. This in turn increased their potential as social occasions, combined with the opportunity for display, not only of horsemanship and knightly skills, but also of opulent costume and elaborate heraldic trappings.

Tournaments were held entirely at the king's will, though there were certain royal occasions where a tournament became part of the ritual of the royal court. There is a consistent series for the baptism of royal children and the churching of the queen: of Philippa's twelve children, on only one occasion can we be certain that there was no baptismal tournament, because Margaret of Windsor was born on 20 July 1346, a week after Edward had landed in France. Otherwise there are definite or possible records for all of the others. Betrothals and marriages of royal children were also occasions for tournaments: Lionel's betrothal in 1342, John of Gaunt's marriage, held at the same time as that of his sister Margaret in 1359, and Mary's wedding to the earl of Richmond in 1361, were all accompanied by jousting. However, the wedding which should have been the grandest of all, that of Edward prince of Wales to Joan of Kent, was treated as a largely private affair;[22] and that of his younger brother Edmund, marrying his sister-in-law's half-sister in 1372, also seems to have been low key, though jousts had by then faded from the court's rituals.

There was a widespread tradition of tournaments at Shrovetide and on Midsummer Day throughout Europe, but these are almost entirely absent from the records of Edward's tournaments. The major feast of the year was Christmas and Epiphany, a time of year generally unsuitable for the sport. By far the greatest number of tournaments after Edward threw off the tutelage of his mother and Mortimer, and after the halcyon interlude of his 'jolly young life', have to do with recent victories, or with political campaigns to rally public opinion. We have already looked at the jousts on his return from doing homage in France in 1331 up to the beginning of the Scottish campaigns. The jousts in 1334 were a celebration of Edward's first great military success; during the Flemish campaigns, the brief periods of military action were followed by jousts in Brussels and Ghent. The great tournament at Dunstable was definitely for the betrothal of Lionel; how far it was also a celebration of the recent Anglo-Scots truce as well is doubtful. Subsequent tournaments in 1342–3 seem to revolve round the political and military problems of renewing the war in France as Edward's grand alliance gradually dissolved and he determined to rely in future on his own military resources, a process which culminated in the tournament at which the Round Table was announced in January 1344. The jousts of 1348 were undoubtedly a kind of Roman triumph, proclaiming the king as victor of Crécy and Calais. These were in the same style as those of the early 1330s, with Edward jousting in the arms of Thomas Bradeston and Stephen Cosington to emphasize his role as fellow-knight rather than sovereign, and with highly decorative costumes throughout. Thereafter the list of tournaments is sparse: on average, we have definite knowledge of only one a year until 1363, and only two in the last fourteen years of the reign. This is partly because the highly informative and detailed chronicles available for the early years peter out in the early 1350s and partly because the royal accounts which tell us so much about the king's activities in the lists are missing. Such glimpses as we have fail to reveal any sustained periods of jousting, and offer instead only the ceremonial marriage tournaments or political spectacles, such as the occasion in 1358 when three kings were present at Windsor for St George's Day.

THE KING'S GAMES

Tournaments were not only occasions for the display of royal splendour. Equally important were the royal entertainments at great court festivals. Jousting is recorded in the official records as *hastiludia*; it is almost as if the clerks wished to classify it with the other royal frivolities, called simply *ludi*, the king's games. Jousts had military and political overtones; the royal games were pure entertainment, overlaid only by a deliberate display of splendour and an often elaborate – and now usually indecipherable – use of images and mottoes. The games were almost always associated with Christmas or with baptisms and weddings; they included music, dancing and the use of masks and disguises, possibly with some dramatic theme or simple play-acting, though this has left no positive traces. The word *ludi* covered a wide range of activities, from gambling through entertainments to actual plays; even the religious mystery plays were called *ludi*.

Ludi and *hastiludia* could overlap: there are several occasions when a joust had a theme, and the participants were disguised, or where masks were used. The costumes were used on these occasions for the preliminary parade, not in the jousting itself: the account of the 1331

THE RISE OF ENGLISH POWER

tournament at Cheapside gives a very clear picture of the proceedings, and specifies that in this case the participants were *ad similitudinem Tartarorum larvati*, 'masked like Tartars'. *Larvati* is a word generally associated with hideous or devilish masks; the Tartars were obviously represented as nightmarish figures of pagans. It is difficult to associate the use of this disguise with an obvious political event, but the Tartars were a powerful and menacing force on the borders of Christendom at this period, raiding the Byzantine Empire and controlling Russian affairs. Masks ('false faces') were also used at Worcester, Guildford, Canterbury, Reigate and Hereford in 1329.[23] Fourteen years later at Smithfield, Edward's team appeared dressed as the pope and twelve cardinals, an allusion to the dispute over the use of papal taxes raised in England to help the French cause, about which Edward was protesting at the time.[24] In 1359, again at Smithfield, both teams, including the king and four of his sons, dressed as the mayor of London and the twenty-four aldermen of the City; in this case, it was probably a compliment to their hosts.

In 1362 a tournament was planned in Cheapside to mark the wedding of Edward prince of Wales. Two days before the event, one of the greatest storms ever to occur in England in recorded times struck, cutting a devastating swathe across the country: the unfinished choir of Vale Royal Abbey in Cheshire was blown down, and London was a scene of havoc and devastation. The tournament did not take place, but monks at Reading and Canterbury recorded that the prince and his knights had planned to dress as the seven deadly sins, and the hurricane was a divine judgement on this blasphemy. Reading between the lines, it seems more likely that the extreme violence of the storm demanded an exceptional act of impiety to explain it, and that the idea of this disguise was a figment of the imagination on the part of one or other of the monks.[25] Tournaments with religious disguises were not unknown, and in Spain in 1428 the king of Castile and his knights dressed as God and the twelve apostles:[26] but no dire consequences followed on this occasion.

Masks and costumes were an essential part of the king's Christmas entertainments. There are numerous records of expenditure on 'vizors' and on 'heads', and for two occasions we have detailed descriptions of what was ordered. For the king's revels at Guildford in 1347, the original bill from John of Cologne survives, giving more detail than the summary on the annual account roll. This battered sheet of parchment lists a series of different disguises: fourteen heads and busts of girls, fourteen heads of bearded men, fourteen silver angels' heads with curly hair, fourteen silver-plated dragons' heads with a black mane, fourteen heads of swans. To go with these there are tunics decorated with the eyes of peacocks and gleaming with stars.[27] At Otford the following year, there are twelve heads each of lion cubs, elephants, men with bats' wings, wild men and twenty-seven heads of virgins. The inclusion of busts and bats' wings implies that the 'heads' covered the upper part of the body, and were not simply masks, but something nearer to hoods, which came down over the shoulders. In some cases, there are tunics associated with the heads. Usually the disguises are decorative or fabulous, and no theme emerges: for Christmas games at Merton in 1349, there were simply masks of dragons' heads and crowned heads of men. At Windsor in 1352, however, we find thirteen devils and thirteen friars in black with white scapulars, a clear reference to the Dominicans.[28] This must refer to some contemporary event or dispute; but whether the Dominicans drove off the devils, or the Dominicans themselves were demonized, we cannot tell. Sadly, no actual costumes or even fragments of costumes survive (Plate 15).

Scenery was certainly used on these occasions, but is rarely specified: there are often extensive entries for payments to painters, but we are not told what they were doing. One exception is the Christmas feast in 1337, at Guildford, for which timber and canvas were provided and painted to resemble 'a wood with various trees', seemingly inhabited by the fifteen baboons for whom heads, tunics, hose and gloves were made.*[29] In 1331, canvas and wool were used to make hides for both wild men and deer, implying an overall costume.[30]

The puzzling thing about these entries is the consistent numbers, usually twelve, thirteen or fourteen (and sometimes multiples of this, for instance forty-two), for the quantity of heads or tunics or other items which are ordered. We have no account of a royal entertainment which would begin to explain this. The only reasonable assumptions are that we are looking at either some form of team game, or some form of dance. If the entertainments were in the context of a tournament, the teams might have been the two sides in the jousting, the defenders and

---

* The king kept real baboons: in May 1340, Hugh, 'keeper of the king's baboons', received a gift from the king.

attackers. But they are consistently called *ludi*, not *hastiludi*, so the most likely explanation is some kind of dance. This is supported by images in two illuminated manuscripts, the *Romance of Fauvel* and the *Romance of Alexander.*[31] In the *Romance of Fauvel*, a wide-ranging satire on Church and State written about 1314, there is a theatrical interlude at Fauvel's wedding in which actors appear with both masks and heads. The *Romance of Alexander*, written in Tournai in 1344 and therefore exactly contemporary with Edward's festivals, has an illustration which shows exactly what we are looking for: courtiers – identifiable by their expensive parti-coloured clothes – dancing in animal heads. A few pages earlier, there is a similar group with extravagant beards, unlike the neat beards which Edward III and the prince of Wales wear in surviving miniatures and effigies. These are probably examples of the fourteen bearded men's heads provided for the Guildford entertainment in 1347.

We are still left with the problem of why groups of about a dozen are evidently a key element in the proceedings. This is not an idle question, because when we come to the Company of the Garter, it is made up of two sides, the king's side and the prince's side, each with twelve knights. Most of the orders for sets of twelve items relate to tournaments, though at one point, in 1334, William Standerwyk provided twelve standards and banners with the king's arms, and twelve with the arms of St George and St Edmund for the Scottish wars, which might imply that the army was organized into twelve units of some kind; but the figure does not reappear. Twelve and thirteen are standard numbers in tourneying terms, with either the king in different clothing and his knights dressed alike, or both king and knights in one style. The idea of a uniform was relatively new in medieval armies: the earliest English records come from the mid-thirteenth century. Guilds in London adopted specific costumes by 1347, when Henry Knighton notes that, when David II of Scotland was brought to the Tower as a prisoner, the guilds paraded, each 'honourably arrayed in its own distinctive livery'.[32]

Edward's use of livery to mark out a smaller group may have been something of an innovation, and it appears at the very beginning of his reign, specifically in the context of a *ludus* or game, the 'game of the society of Craddok' which we have already looked at, and which seems to have a specific political context. Here we have both the figure of twelve costumes for the knights 'of the same pattern', and a further fourteen for the squires. Furthermore, the meaning of *ludus* here is not simply that of dancing, which seems to be one of the contexts for the use of masks and heads. Something is being acted out, which is neither a joust nor a dance; but beyond this we have little idea. We can only point to rare episodes which are reflected in the accounts: two squires compensated for the burns they suffered while 'playing' before Edward II in 1325, or Bernard the fool and fifty-four of his fellows dancing naked for him in 1313.[33]

An episode from the French court in 1393 is perhaps the best indication of how the masks and disguises were used. Charles VI and a group of nobles dressed as wodewoses or wild men, and danced at a court festival; an inquisitive onlooker (said by Froissart to be the duke of Orléans, the king's brother) put a torch too close to their costumes, which contained pitch, and several of them were burnt to death. The king himself was not with the dancers at the time, and this stroke of luck saved his life. The monk of St Denis who recorded this tragedy waxed eloquent on the iniquities of such wanton revelries.[34] However, the accounts of the so-called 'Bal des ardents' are clear evidence that it was not necessarily actors or minstrels who used these elaborate and expensive costumes, but that the performers and dancers could be the courtiers themselves.

The masks and costumes ordered by the king often seem to have some specific meaning in mind, as if there is a kind of programme behind both these and the decoration of the clothing. Occasionally, we also have mottoes, and the Garter motto itself may well have originated in the context of an entertainment. There are only three recorded mottoes which appear in the accounts: 'It is as it is', 'Sure as the woodbine' and 'Hey, hey, the white swan, by God I am the king's man'. Two mottoes appear for Philippa, 'Ich wrude muche' and 'Myn biddenye'.[35]

We may be able to decipher these mottoes, although with some hesitation. The woodbine is the modern honeysuckle,[36] and this is an old motif in Arthurian romance: in the twelfth century, Marie de France wrote a poem of Tristan and Iseult meeting in the forest, beneath a hazel branch along which honeysuckle was entwined, symbolizing the inseparable nature of their love. The most likely explanation is that this was a declaration of Edward's love for Philippa. Philippa's mottoes appear to be in a dialect of medieval German. 'Ich wrude' might be 'ich vreude', 'I rejoice', and the first motto could be 'I rejoice greatly'. 'Myn biddenye' is connected to 'beten' or praying, perhaps 'the answer to my prayer'. 'It is as it is' appears in 1342 in conjunction with the Dunstable tournament in honour of the wedding of the king's second son, Lionel. It was used on the white borders of a set of twelve green doublets, embroidered with the motto in jewels and pearls and with clouds and vines in gold. It also appeared prominently on the lavish hangings and resplendent state bed made for Edward on this occasion. Twelve hangings six yards long and three yards wide were made up, embroidered with the king's words 'It is as it is'. These presumably lined the walls of the room where the state bed was set up, and the top sheet of the bed was worked with a pattern of five circlets: the four corner circlets contained angels, and the central circlet the royal helmet and crest. The background was embroidered with the repeated motto, as on the hangings. Lionel was also provided with a similar state bed, without the motto and to a different design. In 1349, for the king's Epiphany games at Merton, a single doublet was made up, in white with a green border, which seems to indicate that it was more than an ephemeral choice of motto. It is a curiously stoical statement and is no clearer to us today than Philippa's mottoes.[37]

As to the swan motto, there are even wider possibilities. The legend of the Swan knight, made familiar to us by the story of Lohengrin, was known on the Continent, and various English families could claim descent from this hero of romance. The knighting of Edward II in 1306 was followed by the 'feast of the swans', at which the king and others swore oaths on the swans connected with the imminent campaign in Scotland. The swan badge was later to be associated particularly with Thomas of Woodstock, Edward's youngest son.[38]

At the end of it all, however, we are no nearer the meaning of the figures and mottoes: as the Elizabethan courtier Sir Henry Wotton said of the *imprese* or visual mottoes of Gloriana's tournaments, 'some were so dark that their meaning is not yet understood, unless perchance that were their meaning, not to be understood'.[39]

Occasionally, we get a glimpse of increasingly elaborate scenarios based loosely on the characters of Arthur's court rather than on the actual events of the romances. Both at a tournament at Le Hem in 1278 and in a Dutch account of an undated round table of Edward I, the emphasis is on role-playing. The characters are limited to the central figures of Arthur's court; at least, there is no mention of minor roles: we have evidence for knights playing Lancelot, Tristan, Palamedes, Yvain, Gawain, Kay, Perceval, Agravain, Gareth, Bors and even Arthur's treacherous nephew, Mordred. Ladies played Guinevere and Soredamors. There appear to have been scripts written for the occasion, with a reasonable amount of detail in them, and evidence from the century following the Windsor festival of 1344 shows an increasing literary element in later tournaments, often departing entirely from an Arthurian framework.

If play-acting seems an unexpected activity for a fourteenth-century royal court, we have only to turn to a contemporary historian's description of the elaborate theatrical staging at a French royal feast in Paris in 1378 (Plate 20).[40] The theme was probably inspired by Charles V's interest in leading a new crusade, and centred on the story of Godefroi de Bouillon and the conquest of Jerusalem in 1099. The first scene represented a ship carrying Godfrey to Palestine, which was moved by men inside it in such a way that 'it seemed like a ship floating on the water'; this was followed by a representation of Jerusalem itself, including the lifelike touch of 'a Saracen making the call to prayers, in the Arabic tongue'. Chaucer describes such an occasion in 'The Franklin's Tale', apparently the work of specialists in this kind of entertainment, whom he calls 'tregetours', and whose skills seem to have included the use of candles and glasses filled with water to create illusions.

These *ludi* or knightly charades took place within the framework of a great feast. In the romances, Arthur traditionally refused to dine on high days and holidays until some adventure had taken place, such as the arrival of a mysterious messenger asking for help or offering a challenge. Imitating this in real life would give the perfect cue for an Arthurian interlude to become part of the occasion. This line of thought leads us to the opening of the greatest of all English Arthurian poems, *Sir Gawain and the Green Knight*, written towards the end of Edward's reign or early in that of Richard II:

> This king lay at Camelot one Christmastide
> With many mighty lords, manly liegemen,

Members rightly reckoned of the Round Table,
In splendid celebration, seemly and carefree.
There tussling in tournament time and again
Jousted in jollity these gentle knights,
Then in court carnival sang catches and danced;
For fifteen days the feasting there was full in like measure
With all the meat and merry-making men could devise,
Gladly ringing glee, glorious to hear,
A noble din by day, dancing at night![41]

The poet goes on to describe the richness of the setting, the courtesy of knights and ladies, and the character of Arthur himself, who announced

that he never would eat
On such a fair feast-day till informed in full
Of some unusual adventure, as yet untold,
Of some momentous marvel that he might believe,
About ancestors, or arms or other high theme;
Or till a stranger should seek out a strong knight of his,
To join with him in jousting, in jeopardy to lay
Life against life . . .[42]

The stranger who arrives to lay life against life is hardly what Arthur expects: a knight green from head to foot, bearing a great axe and a holly branch, a warrior as courteous as any of his knights but carrying the symbols of an earlier age. The Green Knight offers not a joust, but a bargain: one of Arthur's knights is to behead him, and must seek him out in a year's time to stand a return blow. All that he proposes, says the Green Knight, is an entertainment:

So I crave in this court a Christmas game,
For it is Yuletide and New Year, and young men abound here.[43]

It is not difficult to imagine this scene being acted out at Edward's court; indeed, a 'head' with a special framework could easily be constructed which would allow the Green Knight to be decapitated in full view of the audience. The poem is generally dated to after 1360, although its authorship and origins have been much debated. But its cultural context is firmly within the milieu of Edwardian court life, and the unique manuscript ends with a version of the Garter motto, 'Hony soyt qui mal pence', though the reason for its presence here is unexplained.

The results of the massive expenditure recorded so carefully by the clerks of the exchequer must have been an extraordinary splendour. Sadly, little of the opulent fabrics and costumes survives, and we have to rely on illuminations in manuscripts. The most vivid pictures of jousting costume are from Germany, in the famous Manesse manuscript of the love songs of the thirteenth century. The fashions may be different to those of Edward's court, but the ideas are the same. The fantastic heraldic crests, figures or emblems surmounting the helmets, shown on the stall plates of the Garter companions in the 1420s, appear in even more extravagant form in the Manesse miniatures. Whereas the Garter heraldry confines itself to the more orthodox heraldic bestiary, heads of boars, lions and so on, the Manesse images include such strange sights as the inverted legs and claws of an eagle, a pair of hunting horns forming a crescent, Venus goddess of love, two battleaxes trimmed with peacock feathers, and a pair of carp trimmed with black cock's feathers.[44] The knights wear long surcoats, matching their horses' trappings, which are patterned or emblazoned with their arms. The manuscript was probably completed in the first years of the fourteenth century, two decades before Edward III's first appearance in the lists.[45] The style of armour had changed in the intervening years, and the chain mail shown in the German miniatures had been replaced by plate armour. Numerous entries in the accounts refer to 'pairs' of plates (breastplate and backplate) being covered with material: usually this is velvet, as in the prince of Wales's list of items given to his friends in the years up to 1358. Interestingly, three of the pairs of plates are covered with black velvet, one 'powdered with feathers', the prince's ostrich feather badge;[46] others are in blue or red velvet. For a grand occasion, the richest cloth was used: Edward III, presiding over a meeting with King Peter of Cyprus at which David Bruce, king of Scotland, was also present, ordered a complete suit of armour covered in gold 'baldekyn of Lucca', as well as a set of clothes in the same material.[47]

A sumptuous appearance in the lists, where all eyes were on the individual knights, was highly important, but the real splendours were reserved for the social occasions, feasting, dancing and games, which formed the setting of the tournament. Edward III was spending lavishly at the beginning of his reign. The 'great wardrobe' which dealt with his personal and household expenses had outgoings of £2,427 in the last year of his father's reign. This immediately doubled to £4,574, partly because of administrative changes, but five years later, in 1332–3, it had risen to £10,083.[48] A fair proportion of this was going on clothing, and this was to increase to the point where 'the Great Wardrobe was almost certainly the major purchaser and employer in the City of London'.[49]

There were four elements in the richness and splendour of the clothing: the materials from which it was made, the embroidery, the pictorial designs on it, and the fashionable style. Merchants from Flanders, Paris and Italy provided an immense range of fabrics, both the cloths woven from English wool and more exotic materials in silk and linen traded by merchants from throughout Europe and from the near east. They acted as wholesalers, and supplied most of the expensive materials used in England. The best cloth was woven at Brussels; light and of a fine weave, it was dyed using highly expensive ingredients: scarlet dye came from the Mediterranean, and was such a byword for luxury that any costly cloth was known as a 'scarlet' cloth, and 'scarlets' ranging from black to peacock blue are entered in the accounts. Linen came from Paris and Reims, and, most costly of all, velvet and silk were imported from Italy and the east. Chinese damask has been found in London in a context which dates it to 1325–50; it exemplifies the culture of luxury represented by Edward's court.[50] Silk was also imported as thread for weaving and embroidery, and some plain silk cloth was brought in for dyeing. Patterned velvet was the most expensive of the fabrics, to be used without the addition of embroidery. In 1343 the accounts give prices for a wide range of materials. (As a measure of relative values, the annual wage for William Fitzwarin as knight of the queen's chamber in 1333 was £6 13s. 4d.)[51] Velvet with gold stripes bought in Bruges cost about £7 for a piece nine yards long, while other velvets bought in London were never less than half that price. Cloth of gold silks cost the same as ordinary velvet, and plain silks went for £1 for nine yards; interestingly, good quality woollen cloth was much the same price. Silks were usually patterned, and occasionally the design was so impressive that it was specified in the bill, as with the cloth of gold on which dragons and serpents writhed on a blue background provided for the marriage of

Edward's daughter Joan in 1348.[52] And still the search for even richer effects went on: the finishing touch might be gold leaf stamped onto the garments, which could be used to pattern them with heraldic arms. Finally, gold could be hammered into thin pieces to be sewn onto the material; we find examples of besants (gold coins) or even the badge of the Garter itself being added in this way.

For winter clothing, furs were needed, sometimes to make whole garments, but more often to trim the clothes, and sourced from the Baltic and from Russia. Miniver, made from the winter belly-fur of red squirrels, trimmed down so that only the white was used, and sewn together into large pieces, was bought in large quantities, while the most luxurious fur was ermine, the white winter fur of the stoat with a black tip to the tail. Furs supplied by the royal tailor in 1347–8 included more than 20,000 pieces of miniver, but only 20 of ermine: it was in effect reserved for the king and queen.

Many of the costumes described above would have looked very like the famous medieval embroidery known as *opus anglicanum*, 'English work', which was in great demand for religious apparel from the thirteenth century onwards: the best examples often survive in the treasuries of churches and cathedrals (Plate 16). John of Cologne, the most important of Edward's armourers, had a workshop with a large number of embroiderers; he is sometimes described as working in the Tower, but the armourers in the Tower actually date from the beginning of Richard II's reign.[53] Rather, he would have been an independent merchant with a large establishment, possibly in the Steelyard, the home of the north German merchants from the towns of the Hanseatic league. It is his bills submitted to the king's great wardrobe which are the main source of information about royal expenditure on clothing. Designs were probably drawn up by the king's painters, and sketched by draughtsmen on the linen base for the embroiderers to start work.

The king's tailor was responsible for the less elaborate clothing, and for the provision of the 'livery' provided in summer and winter for members of the household. His team was also involved in the manufacture of clothes for special events, notably for the Round Table festivities in 1344.[54] In 1352, the wages for the workers employed to make garments for the king's daughter Isabella for St George's Day and for her forthcoming wedding show that the draughtsmen were paid twelve pence a day, and the most skilled embroiderers nine pence a day, for a total of eighty-four working days. The bills for the court's ceremonial clothes were now on a par with those for the king's armour.

Banners, tents and standards were also needed for jousts and outdoor events. The simpler banners, such as those with the cross of St George, were produced by appliqué sewing. If detailed heraldry or other patterns were involved, draughtsmen would need to be employed. In 1351, one draughtsman appears to have spent six days supervising the manufacture of twenty-four clouds of gold, silver and silk, made by six men and two women, and using an ounce of gold. These were evidently exceptional decorations on a large scale, rather than items to be sewn on a costume. Streamers, the huge masthead flags with bold heraldic or figurative devices designed to be visible from a distance to identify the king's ships, were produced in relatively small quantities; manuscript illuminations give some idea of how impressive they must have been.

For tents in the same period, draughtsmen were employed for a total of 158 working days: the most spectacular of these were a round blue linen tent with stars on the outside and crowns on the inside, and a green tent whose interior had gold eagles on a red buckram lining. In the inventory of the keeper of the Tower in 1341, the clerks note 'two houses of canvas, called pavilions', and although there do not seem to be detailed accounts from Edward III's tentmaker, we have an idea of the scale of such royal tents from those taken by Edward I on campaign in Scotland in 1303.[55] These included what we would call a marquee, 'a great hall with six posts'. Tents were certainly used at tournaments and ceremonial occasions such as coronations; the usual term for them, pavilions, is derived from the Latin *papilio*, a butterfly, which implies that they were highly coloured, as much for display as for practical use (Plate 7). This may have been in contrast to the leather tents used for the royal chambers and the financial office. Canvas tents had to be dried at intervals, as they were only moderately waterproof. The scale of the tents was substantial: the 1303 inventory for the siege of Berwick describes an ensemble of tents with two halls, ten chambers, four chapels, and forty-nine 'houses', about half of them round tents. One of the halls was 140 feet long, and the king's chamber was 80 feet long.

Other technical processes included staining and painting: both were the province of the painter-stainers of London, who first appear as a company in 1268. Painting was used for scenery and hangings for the royal festivals as well as for military equipment.[56] Hugh of St Albans, in charge of the murals at St Stephen's Chapel, Westminster, also worked on the streamers of the royal ships, which were sealed with wax to make them waterproof. He was doubtless responsible for designs for clothing and for the king's entertainments, though we have no specific evidence of payments to him in this respect.

One of the most dramatic manuscript images of the period is the illustration of a royal carriage in the famous Luttrell Psalter (Plate 24).[57] A number of such carriages were probably made for Philippa and other members of the royal household: it is possible that the Luttrell picture actually represents Philippa, as the figure at the front is crowned and holding a squirrel: Philippa is known to have had these as pets. There is a detailed account of the cloth used for the carriage made for Edward's sister Eleanor in 1332, when she left England for her marriage to Reginald count of Guelders. The outer canvas had two alternative covers, one green and one scarlet; inside there was a purple velvet cloth studded with glass stars, as a canopy inside the canvas. Pillows and mattresses in red and green offered some comfort to the occupants, and there were silk loops to hold on to when the roads were particularly rough. The outside of the carriage was a display of heraldry, presumably of the arms of England and Guelders, which also appeared on the saddles of the horses. Similar details are visible in the Luttrell Psalter, and five horses were evidently the norm for such a vehicle, as the illustration corresponds to the accounts, which specify that number.[58]

FASHION

When Philippa and her entourage came to the English court in 1328, they brought with them fashions in dress and armour sufficiently distinctive to be noted by the king's armourer and tailor; we have already noted entries for armour and saddles in the Hainault style, and, in an entry under the year 1344, the *Brut* and John of Reading's chronicle both record that

> At this time, Englishmen so followed and clung to the madness and folly of foreigners, that from the time of the arrival of the Hainaulters some eighteen years before, they changed the shape and style of their clothing every year, abandoning the old honest and good style of large, long and

wide clothes, in favour of short, narrow-waisted clothes, cut with jagged edges, slit and buttoned, with sleeves and tippets on the surcoats, and great long hoods which hung down too far. To tell the truth, they looked more like tormentors and devils in their clothes and appearance than men. And the women copied the men in even more curious ways: for their clothes were so tight that they sewed foxtails beneath their clothes to hang down and protect and hide their arses . . .[59]

The period between 1330 and 1365 was a time when fashions changed substantially and rapidly. The novelties were such that a number of monastic chroniclers attacked the new fashions as immoral and described them as the cause of various natural disasters visited on the people at large because of the wantonness and decadence of the ruling class.[60] Although such tirades against court fashions can be found as far back as the reign of William Rufus in the eleventh century, the detailed descriptions given in the fourteenth-century chronicles are evidence that a real change was afoot.

Thirteenth-century clothes were loose-fitting, and the way in which they hung on the body was the most important element in tailoring them. The cloth was used economically, in long lengths, and the desired effect was a restrained elegance; the fastenings were girdles and strips of tied cloth. The outer clothes were loose, cloaks and gowns, while the tunic beneath consisted of two T-shaped pieces sewn back to back.

Early in the fourteenth century, dress became much more complex in structure. The T-shaped tunic gave way to a garment with armholes and sleeves, and the sleeves in turn could be loose or tight-fitting. It has been suggested that this style was following the development in armour at the time, the change from chain mail to the new plate armour which fitted the body more closely. Buttons are first mentioned in the early fourteenth century as an important feature of dress, and with them came the need for carefully stitched buttonholes. Tailoring became a highly specialized, and highly paid, skill; and where the splendour of the material – rich silks rather than woollen cloth, perhaps – had earlier been the only thing that distinguished the wealth and prestige of the wearer, the new style depended on the skill of the cutting and sewing.

Once the idea of designing clothes to fit the body had been accepted, tailors were quick to see that a huge range of variations was possible, and from 1330 onwards 'high fashion' began to develop. John of Reading's dating of the new style to around 1328 is supported by evidence from manuscripts from Paris and Tournai which can be dated to around 1330. In one, a man is shown wearing a buttoned tunic with inset sleeves, and in the other a lover wears buttoned sleeves (Plates 17–19).[61]

From a simple attempt to follow the natural lines of the body, features were unnaturally exaggerated: the low-slung waist of the 1330s, with a hipster belt and close-fitting doublet, the conspicuous waste of cutting clothes with jagged edges, and the visual distraction of parti-coloured garments were just a few of the variations that rapidly developed. Jean de Venette, writing in 1359–60, remembers 1340 as the year when appearances changed:

> Men were now beginning to wear disfiguring costumes. This was especially true of noblemen, knights, squires and their followers; but it was true in some measure of burgesses and of almost all servants. Garments were short to the point of indecency, which was surprising in a people who had up to this time conducted themselves becomingly. Everyone also began to grow long beards. This fashion which nearly everyone in France, except those of royal blood, adopted gave rise to no little mockery on the part of the common people.[62]

The new ideas travelled rapidly, because fashion was international, and the dress of the aristocracy was broadly similar throughout western Europe. Attitudes of moralizing monks were also similar: French chroniclers saw the military disaster at Crécy as punishment for the equally extravagant dress of the French nobility. According to them, short clothing was again at the root of the problem, and many of the details they give are the same. Some tunics, however, were gathered at the back like women's dresses, while others were so tight that the wearer had to be peeled rather than undressed. Giovanni Villani makes similar comments about the dress of the French companions of Walter de Brienne, who was appointed commander of the Florentine armies in 1342. The French and Italians seem to have loved magnificent hats: two extreme examples are the symbolic headgear worn by the republican Cola di Rienzo in Rome in 1347, on which a silver sword cut a golden coronet in half, and the 'parade' hat made for John II of France for the wedding of his daughter Blanche de Bourbon in 1352, on which gold figures of children keeping pigs under oak-trees 'as if they were alive' formed the main theme, with flowers, pearls and other ornaments.[63] The English milliners were much more sober, judging by the surviving records of simple beaver hats with the occasional jewel.

The best visual evidence for the new fashions is from a wonderful illuminated version of the romance account of the life of Alexander the Great, now in the Bodleian Library. Just as Arthur, a warrior king, became the focal point of romances from the twelfth century onwards, so the great conqueror of antiquity re-emerged in the guise of a medieval king, surrounded by a court with contemporary ceremonials and costumes. We know that this manuscript of the *Romance of Alexander* was made in Tournai in 1344. There has been much debate about the patron for whom it was made, as such a hugely expensive volume would not have been created without a commission. Tournai was fiercely loyal to the French during the warfare of the late 1330s, and this has been put forward as the reason why Philip VI is the most likely patron.[64] On the other hand, it was a trading city, with strong links to the other towns in the Low Countries, and lay between Hainault and Flanders. Edward's youngest son, Thomas duke of Gloucester, probably owned the manuscript in the latter half of the fourteenth century; it corresponds to a book described in the inventory of his goods after his death. There can be no definitive answer to the puzzle, but I would suggest that it was commissioned by Philippa; we have already seen that she is believed to have had other manuscripts made for Edward. The commission must have been placed by the beginning of 1338, as the scribe finished work on 18 December of that year. The work of illuminating the text was not completed until April 1344, and even allowing for the amazing array of pictures which are the book's glory, it implies that there was a considerable pause in the production process. If the *Romance of Alexander* was being produced for Philippa, work may have been suspended when Tournai was besieged by Edward and his allies in 1339; hostilities only ended with the switch of the theatre of war to Brittany in 1341.

Furthermore, the romances contained in the book include Jacques de Longuyon's *The Vows of the Peacock*, probably written about 1310 for the bishop of Liège. This was a highly popular work, which formed a self-contained episode within the framework of the Alexander story; it related the adventures which followed vows made by knights on a peacock at a feast. *The Vows of the Peacock* is itself continued in *The Restoration of the Peacock* of around 1335 by Jean Brisebarre and Jean de la Mote's *Perfection of the Peacock* of 1340.[65] For the counts of

Hainault, Alexander seems to be their specific hero, just as Arthur occupied the same place in the dynastic mythology of the later Plantagenets, particularly Edward I, Edward III and Edward IV. Just as Edward I had a personal interest in Arthurian legend, William I of Hainault was evidently an Alexander enthusiast. In 1319, Watriquet de Couvin wrote of him, 'As long as the count lives, Alexander will not come to an end,' and in 1330 his provost, Jean Bernier, provided a peacock for a civic festival at which the winning entry was twenty-two men bearing the shields of 'the most valiant of King Alexander's followers'.[66] After William I's death, Jean de la Mote compared him at length to Alexander, in an elegy addressed to his daughter Philippa.[67] The *Romance of Alexander* manuscript is the only one to contain the music for a poem in *The Restoration of the Peacock*, which would imply a close connection to Hainault where the text originated. It links, too, with the romance of *Perceforest*, a work which is presented as being 'found' by William I himself, and which was certainly written either in Hainault or in England.

Whether or not the manuscript was destined for England or France, artists working in Tournai, on the borders of Hainault and distant from Paris, would in any case be more likely to reflect the dress of Hainault. As with most medieval manuscripts, the pictures consist of large formal full pages or half pages and marginal decorations, usually at the foot of the page. Here we meet the world of Edward's court face to face. For the *Peacock* poems celebrate Alexander not simply as a conqueror, but as a model of princely courtesy. Their authors draw on a wide range of sources to transform Alexander from a great military leader into the leader of a cultured and resplendent court, the model which the counts of Hainault and Edward III all aspired to. The pages containing the *Peacock* poems present illuminations which are the nearest we shall get to a vision of Edward's court. A feast is held in honour of the peacock and the visual narrative in the bottom margin shows the feast being prepared, the queen going to the feast with her attendants and musicians, ladies dancing with a bearded man and others, ladies dancing a carol or round dance, and a whole orchestra of musicians. In another dance, six ladies face six knights before they start; this is repeated with five men in 'heads' and six women. The opening of *The Vows of the Peacock* is marked by ladies dancing with men in 'heads'. The margins only fill with dancers when court festivities are described in the text. These figures are small: to get a better idea of the costume and fabrics, in fabulous colours and patterns, from silks with fine foliage designs to bold diagonal stripes, we have to look at the miniatures, the largest of which occupy a whole page, divided into panels. Here are the elongated figures, the men's fashions which would have suited the slim, imposing, tall figures of Edward and the prince of Wales so well, and the bare shoulders of the ladies and their increasingly elaborate hairstyles. The book itself is one of the few physical relics we have of this astonishing world.[68]

The lavish style of the English court made a wide impression. In the aftermath of the victory in France, the new wealth that the veterans of the campaign brought back apparently resulted in a wild imitation of court magnificence by some of the less savoury elements connected with the court. Henry Knighton describes a troop of camp followers who appeared regularly at tournaments in 1348:

> In those days a rumour arose and great excitement amongst the people because, when tournaments were held, at almost every place a troop of ladies would appear, as though they were a company of players, dressed in men's clothes of striking richness and variety, to the number of forty or sometimes fifty such damsels, all very eye-catching and beautiful, though hardly of the kingdom's better sort. They were dressed in parti-coloured tunics, of one colour on one side and a different one on the other, with short hoods, and liripipes wound about their heads like strings, with belts of gold and silver clasped about them, and even with the kind of knives commonly called daggers slung low across their bellies, in pouches. And thus they paraded themselves at tournaments on fine chargers and other well-arrayed horses, and consumed and spent their substance, and wantonly and with disgraceful lubricity displayed their bodies, as the rumour ran.[69]

Knighton is writing half a century later, but probably using a contemporary source; this might well be the description of a particular disguising adapted to make a moral story, for he records that, wherever they went, God punished them with dreadful thunderstorms and cloudbursts. The costume, with the long tubular liripipes wound round the dancers' heads and the parti-coloured tunics, fits the 1340s accurately.

Not surprisingly, no exact examples of this clothing survive, but there are two *pourpoints* from the 1370s, also called *jaques*, which are immediately recognizable as the forerunner of the jacket of today. That in the museum at Lyons belonged to Charles de Blois; it is cut from six pieces of silk brocaded with gold, with twenty-four buttons, and is very much a tailored and designed garment, the sharpest possible contrast to the draped clothing of the beginning of the century. These exaggerated figure-hugging garments were for men only; women's clothing was generally more modest, hence the scandal caused by the amazons described by Knighton.

The abiding image of Edward's court, reading the accounts and these outsiders' views of it, is of a society with a fondness for splendour and display as a mark of rank and as a way of impressing the onlookers, and also of a world where that display could be competitive, in terms both of richness and of style. It was another area where knights would strive to excel, and where the king could use his patronage to single out his favourite companions. We begin with the king and William Montagu in the same costume and progress through the aketons given to the conspirators, to the appearance of teams with heraldic epaulettes or even heraldic suits of armour who take part in the king's games.

The members of the household and court of these first years of Edward's personal rule were of course beneficiaries of royal largesse, particularly those involved in the coup of 1330. The 'new men' who had in effect brought Edward to power were given considerable estates in the course of the next seven years, and, if Montagu was the most prominent among them, it was a broad group whose only allegiance was to the new king. Edward was careful to present these grants as the results of deliberations with his advisers and even with parliament, so that they were not seen as arbitrary awards made on a personal whim to favourites: the writs in favour of Ufford, Clinton and Montagu emphasize their part in Mortimer's overthrow, and other writs were made out with the agreement of parliament.[70] Edward was fortunate in that there was no obvious focal point for political dissent; he was on good terms with Henry of Lancaster, the only powerful nobleman surviving from his father's generation, who was in any case blind and prematurely aged. Lancaster's son, Henry of Grosmont, two years older than the king, was rapidly becoming one of Edward's closest friends.[71]

Edward, however, was careful not to be vengeful against those who had supported Mortimer and Isabella; if he kept them at arm's length for a time, this was a sensible precaution, but he was astute in not creating the kind of resentment which had been his father's downfall. Mortimer was the only great lord to be executed throughout his entire reign, and the nobility in general remained loyal to the king for the next half-century. This was in stark contrast to the relations of his father and grandson with their nobility. Edward retained many of his existing officers and household; this was not unusual, but those who had served Mortimer rather than him in the preceding three years were only briefly in disgrace, and figures such as Henry Burghersh, bishop of Lincoln, quickly returned to favour and played a vital part in the new administration. Lands and moveable property including jewels, which were in fact a form of cash rather than for pure ornament and display, were confiscated. The jewels would be retained by the treasury, but personal belongings, even in Mortimer's case, were soon returned to the heirs: Edmund Mortimer got back his father's armour and items which may have been his own property from the castle at Wigmore, including white hangings showing small children chasing butterflies, a year after his father's execution.[72] The lands might be granted to other lords, but usually on the basis that tenure was for a limited term, or was revocable at the king's will if he provided an alternative source of income, and in any case would revert to the king on the death of the holder. It was through measures like these that he was able to reinstate such men as Mortimer's grandson, also called Roger, and give them back their ancestral estates, if he deemed them worthy of it. When the younger Roger rose to prominence in the wars in France in the 1340s and 1350s, Edward rewarded him with the return of his ancestral lands and the revival of the title of earl of March which had caused such consternation when it was given to his grandfather. By such means, Edward ensured that his court was remarkably free of factions until the very last years of his reign.

3

Apprenticeship in War: Scotland and Flanders 1332–1340

By the end of 1331, the series of tournaments had drawn to a close, and the 'greater season for greater affairs' had come. The priority was the situation in Scotland, where the uneasy relationship between the two kingdoms – a close parallel to the problems of feudal lordship between France and England – had once more come to a head. Robert Bruce had died in 1329, having secured a treaty with Isabella and Mortimer at Northampton in 1328 which was regarded by the English nobles as a shameful surrender, and which contributed greatly to the couple's unpopularity. He was succeeded by his son David II, a five-year-old, who was married to Edward's seven-year-old sister Joan under the terms of the Northampton treaty. Another clause in the treaty had agreed that three English lords should have their lands in Scotland restored.

Among these lords was the man who had been Edward's informal guardian in 1325–7, Henry of Beaumont. He had gone into exile in 1329, in protest at Mortimer's behaviour, and returned in 1330. His claim was to the earldom of Buchan; and he and the other lords petitioned Edward for help in recovering their inheritance. Edward and his advisers, unwilling to mount a full-scale royal campaign against the Scots after the stalemate of 1327, instead turned a blind eye to a private invasion which the 'disinherited' organized. Edward was careful to denounce it in public; it is one of a series of unofficial or unexpected 'adventures' which recur during the first two decades of Edward's reign. No documents survive, but the military preparations went ahead despite writs to the contrary sent to the sheriffs. Thomas Gray has a curious story that Edward actually sent the petition to the earl of Moray, who was guardian of Scotland during David II's minority, for his reaction, and received the reply that he should 'let the ball roll'.[1]

The ball rolled with deadly effect. Henry of Beaumont strengthened his cause by enlisting the support of Edward Balliol, who was the son of the king whom Edward I had placed on the Scottish throne thirty years earlier. Several of Edward's household joined him, including Ralph Stafford and Walter Mauny, as well as veterans of Edward II's Scottish campaigns such as Thomas Ughtred, who had fought at Bannockburn with Beaumont. They landed with 400 men at arms in Fife at the beginning of August 1332, and were almost immediately confronted by the Scots, who could see how small the force was. The earl of Mar, commanding half of the Scottish army, surrounded them, and Beaumont decided on a bold night attack to escape from a desperate situation. His men succeeded in overrunning the Scottish footsoldiers, but when they regrouped they realized that not only were the mounted troops unscathed, but the other half of the Scottish army, led by the earl of Dunbar,[2] was only a short distance away. Beaumont seems to have been responsible for the disposition of the English, at the head of a narrow glen; he placed archers on each flank, and ordered his men at arms to dismount.[3] The Scottish leaders quarrelled as the battle began, because the earl of Mar was accused by one of the Bruce clan of being in league with the enemy. Bruce swore to be the first to attack, and led a disorganized charge against the English. The Scots, despite heavy losses due to the English archers, came up against the English spearmen, and were gaining the upper hand when, according to a Scottish chronicler, Ralph Stafford shouted 'Shoulders to your lances, not your chests', in other words, to stand sideways so that they presented a smaller target to the enemy; and the English line held.[4] The Scots broke up in confusion, only to become entangled with the troops led by Mar trying to force their way up the glen. In such circumstances, the archery fire was deadly, and the Scottish casualties included most of the leading nobles; Mar, Bruce and Moray all perished.[5]

Although the army of the earl of Dunbar was at large, and at one point besieged Balliol and Beaumont in Perth, Balliol succeeded in having himself crowned at the abbey of Scone as tradition demanded. But his triumph was brief, and at the year's end, lulled into a false sense of security, he went with only a small guard to his castle at Annan to celebrate Christmas. There he was surprised in a sudden attack by his enemies, and he and his supporters, including Beaumont, were once more driven out of Scotland.

Edward himself had spent May and June at Woodstock, where Philippa gave birth to her first daughter, Isabella, on 16 June. A tournament was held for her churching in mid-July. Henry of Grosmont was present, as were the king's household knights, including Gilbert Talbot and Thomas Bradeston.[6] The king's household accounts for 19 July record an expenditure of £292 3s. 11¾d., evidence of a major celebration.[7]

By the beginning of 1333, Edward and his advisers had decided to make a major attempt to settle the Scottish problem, and the centre of government had been moved to York, as it had been during his grandfather's wars in the north. The 'disinherited' returned, with the formal backing of the king, in March 1333, and proceeded to besiege the one Scottish stronghold on the border, the port of Berwick, which was also the wealthiest town in Scotland. This small force under Edward Balliol and Henry of Beaumont included William Montagu, John Neville[8] and Henry of Grosmont. Edward himself joined them on 17 May. When the army was fully assembled, it contained a number of familiar faces from the halcyon tournament days of 1330–31: William Clinton, the twins Edward and William Bohun, Thomas and Maurice Berkeley, Reginald Cobham, William Fitzwarin and Thomas Ughtred.[9]

The Scots, led by Archibald Douglas, tried to distract the English army from the siege by a series of raids; but forces from Carlisle won several small victories, and the raids merely gave Edward the formal pretext for declaring that the treaty of 1328 had been broken, and he was now free to make war on Scotland in person. By the end of June, Alexander Seton, the warden of Berwick, was forced to agree to a fifteen-day truce, at the end of which, if the town had not been relieved by a Scottish army, the inhabitants would surrender. This forced Douglas to do what he least wished: to confront the English directly, and abandon his tactic of drawing them away from the town. On the last day of the truce, a Scottish raiding party crossed into English territory and attempted to enter the town from the south: William Montagu intercepted them with a small band of English cavalry, but failed to prevent William Keith from getting into Berwick. Keith took over as warden, and claimed that the town had been relieved. Edward, however, had laid down precise terms for the relief of Berwick: the Scots had to approach from the north. He refused to acknowledge the relief, and hanged two of the hostages whom he held as guarantees for the truce. The Scots were in no position to rescue the remaining hostages, and swiftly agreed to a new truce, set out in writing and sealed, which gave them a further five days before they surrendered: if they did so, their lives and property would be safe.

The Scottish army was forty miles away; it was much larger than the English forces, but much of it was a crowd of infantry, better adapted for raids than for pitched battles. And since Edward knew the army could not reach him in less than two days, he had time to select the ground on which to fight. He chose Halidon Hill, high ground to the south of the town, which could be reached only across marshes and a steep valley, and positioned his men so that the covering fire of the archers would reach the enemy as they struggled across these obstacles. His men were rested and in good order, while the Scots had had three hard days' march. Henry of Beaumont was the commander of the first of the three divisions into which the army was organized, and may have been Edward's chief adviser as to tactics, given his victory of the previous year. The other two divisions were led by Edward himself and by Edward Balliol, each consisting of men at arms in the centre and archers on either flank.

The Scots advanced, a huge host that dismayed the English at first; but as soon as they came within range of the archers, it was clear where the advantage lay. When the Scottish schiltrons, squadrons of spearmen in close order, reached the English line, they were already decimated and in some disorder, and the battle was remarkably brief. Two of the three schiltrons turned and fled soon after they engaged the English men at arms; the third, which consisted of men whose job was to break the siege of Berwick once the English were defeated, was locked in combat with Henry of Beaumont's division for much longer, but in the end gave way. By this time, the rest of the English army was in pursuit of the fleeing Scots; it was during this part of the engagement that the majority of the Scottish casualties occurred.

Halidon Hill was the battle which founded the reputation of Edward as a commander, and of the English army as a formidable, if not invincible, body of men. The key elements recur in the later English triumphs: a well-chosen defensive position, established in good time, usually on a hill and preferably with physical obstacles which the enemy had to surmount; the use of flanking fire from the English archers, who were the only troops at this period to use the longbow; and a well-ordered and well-disciplined body of men at arms commanded by men who were less concerned with personal glory than with working together to achieve victory. Edward himself seems to have had one particular virtue as a commander, and the same applies to his son: because he was working with men whom he knew well and respected, he listened to their views and acted on their advice. We have little direct evidence about the English councils of war; all that can be said is that, in all the battles the English fought, there is no trace of the violent disagreements that afflicted the Scots at Dupplin Moor and the French at Crécy and Poitiers.

The threat to Berwick had been averted, and the Scottish defeat meant that, for the moment, Scotland seemed secure, and Edward returned south in September. He spent the autumn at leisure, hunting in Savernake forest near Marlborough in November and December, going on pilgrimage, visiting his mother at Castle Rising. A tournament was held at Dunstable in January 1334, about the time that the queen gave birth to her second daughter, Joan.[10] It is possible that this was one of the jousts organized by another member of the king's entourage, as the timing is improbable if Edward was responsible for it. There is a roll of arms listing the knights at the tournament which does not include him as one of the participants. However, next to the name of William Montagu is an entry for 'monsieur Lionel'. The arms are given as *argent a quarter gules*, in other words, white and red. We can be sure that this was the king, because a suit of white armour quartered in red was made for him for this occasion.[11] In addition, four horse-trappers in the same colours were provided, as well as one great 'harness for the joust' and four smaller harnesses with the same arms and pennants for lances; the king evidently had four attendants in matching livery. Eight years later, again at Dunstable, Edward was to fight as a 'simple knight'; but by then he had named his third son Lionel and, once again, a suit of armour with Lionel's arms was made for him.[12]

Why should Edward wish to identify himself as 'Lionel'? The usual reaction from scholars has been to refer to the Arthurian legends: Lionel is the cousin of Lancelot, the supreme hero of Arthur's court, and his chief function in the *Prose Lancelot* is to search for Lancelot, whose endless adventures always mean that he disappears just as Lionel is about to find him. He acts as go-between for Lancelot and Queen Guinevere, and his chief characteristic is an impulsive and disobedient nature:

his nickname is 'Unbridled Heart'.[13] All in all, he is not a figure to be emulated. In the *Quest of the Holy Grail*, he attempts to kill his saintly brother Bors, in a test of Bors' character: will Bors lift his sword against his brother or not? He will not, even when Lionel slaughters a hermit who tries to restrain him. This is not a model for a would-be knightly king.[14]

The best answer comes from the heraldic world: Edward is playing the part of 'England's little lion', as his most recent biographer puts it.[15] 'Leonellus' is used in heraldry, and the 'lion shield', *l'écu lionel*, is referred to in twelfth-century poems.[16] The identification of Edward as the 'little lion' may go back to a nickname given to him by Mortimer and Isabella: at the tournament at Wigmore on 6 September 1329 he was given a golden goblet with 'four escutcheons bearing the arms of *leonell*'', and for the Dunstable tournament the following month, October 1329, he was provided with a suit of armour covered in white muslin and red velvet: this ties in with the arms of Lionel as specified in the tournament roll for Dunstable in 1334.

The arms of 'Lionel' are in fact those of the earl of Chester, Edward III's title before he came to the throne; although they now technically belonged to his eldest son, created earl in March 1333, the combination of 'leonellus', his nickname, and these youthful arms takes us back to Edward's boyhood: there are no specific records of his jousting in the royal arms before this date, so it could simply be that he continued to use the Chester 'badge', as the heralds called it, after he became king. 'Lionel' is simply an earlier avatar of Edward himself, not a pale imitation of a hero of romance.[17]

The arms of '*leonell*'', little lions, are therefore different from the arms of Lionel, but both refer to the same person, the king himself. And why should it be tournaments at Dunstable which centre on Lionel? Three major assemblies took place there – in 1334 there were 135 knights, in 1342 around 230 knights – and on each occasion the king is disguised in the same way. It is a nice puzzle, but not one that we can ever hope to solve exactly.

The 'four entire suits of armour' were evidently well used in the following months. Edward's tournaments tend to be grouped within short periods, and 1334 was typical: three, at Dunstable, Woodstock and Newmarket between 16 January and 9 February; two in summer, at Burstwick and Nottingham; and two in September, at Guildford and

Smithfield. The whole year could be read as a celebration of the battle at Halidon Hill, Edward's first great victory: this was the equivalent of the Roman triumph accorded to a victorious general. And it cemented the bonds between Edward and his commanders.

It was one thing to win such a victory as Halidon Hill, and quite another to follow up the advantage and secure the long-term objective of con- quest or control. This again was to be the pattern of the English campaigns, as Edward learnt for the first time in Scotland in 1334–6. The apparent disappearance of opposition in Scotland had enabled Edward Balliol to reinstate himself as king, but the English government seriously underestimated the forces required to support the new admin- istration. By the end of July 1334 Balliol had fled back to England, betrayed by even his closest supporters and robbed of his treasure. Even then, it was not until September that serious preparations were made for a new invasion of Scotland on the requisite scale. The army that marched north to Roxburgh in December 1334 was a mixture ranging from two companies of a hundred pardoned felons to the king's house- hold knights and the retinues of the magnates; there were archers from Cheshire and south Wales, but the bulk of the army came from York- shire, Lancashire, Cumberland and Westmorland. This was normal practice, since the summoning of large bodies of troops from the distant south would take time and would be much more costly, as they would have to be paid on the march to Scotland. Because Edward himself was leading the expedition, the household knights and magnates were drawn from throughout the kingdom. In later years, however, when war could break out either in Scotland or France, or indeed in both simultane- ously, a distinctive group of northern knights and magnates emerged who served as the commanders of the northern army; few of them appear in the court records or as household knights. Only two of these north- ern lords became members of the Company of the Garter in Edward's reign, Henry Percy in about 1365, and John Neville of Raby in 1369.

For the 1334 campaign, Edward had the same familiar group with him, since the composition of his household knights changed relatively slowly. The bannerets included Thomas Beauchamp, Henry of Gros- mont, John Grey of Rotherfield and Thomas Ughtred, while among the household knights were William Montagu, William Bohun, William Clinton, Robert Ufford and William Fitzwarin, as well as Thomas

Bradeston, Maurice Berkeley and Reginald Cobham.[18] The campaign was not a success: a winter expedition was always hazardous, and the Scots were elusive. The Rochester chronicler recorded that

> Other than the youths of the realm and the magnates, he [i.e. Edward] had few people with him. No one bore the hardships and the harshness [of the winter] or laboured more willingly than he; and all the time he greatly comforted his army by words, gifts and deeds, saying that they would all drink from the same cup. And thus he inspired their resolve.[19]

What victories there were went to the Scots, and minor sieges and skirmishes often had a serious impact, such as the capture of Henry of Beaumont at Dundarg in late December. All that the English army could do was to ravage the Scottish territories; the savagery of these activities merely drove the inhabitants into the arms of the nationalists. Furthermore, the contracts for service were only for three months, and expired in February 1335, at the height of the hard weather. Few men chose to stay on, and new recruits were scarce, so Edward's army was effectively disbanded. Edward moved south, leaving only a handful of men under his brother John of Eltham and under Maurice Berkeley to counter any Scottish activity.

To make matters worse, there were new diplomatic complications. Since 1326 there had been an alliance between France and Scotland, which up till now had been of little practical effect; but in the course of the usual tortuous attempts to settle the dispute over Aquitaine, Philip VI had decided to use the Scottish situation to bring further pressure to bear on Edward. He had given refuge to David II in May 1334, and made it clear that any settlement would have to include the Scots. Negotiations moved very slowly, complicated by Philip's long-standing wish to go on a crusade in which Edward would participate. The ambitions of Philip and Edward were in a sense very similar: Edward admitted that Scotland was a kingdom in its own right, but claimed that it was held as a fief of the English king, while Philip equally admitted that Aquitaine was a duchy in its own right, and wished to enforce the homage of the English king in the latter's capacity of duke of Aquitaine.

On the ground in Scotland, a brief truce followed, which expired at midsummer. This suited Edward, who used the interval to raise a much larger army, which was to divide into two to invade Scotland, Edward taking the western route while Balliol moved up the east coast. The same group of men who had been on the winter campaign reassembled; there were more household knights than before, and, in response to the appeal for more troops, William Montagu distinguished himself by raising a very large retinue and appearing – unusually – at the appointed rendezvous at Newcastle on the day arranged, 11 June 1335. Soon after the campaign began, Edward honoured him by granting him the right to bear the eagle crest which was his own personal symbol, and giving him a charger with the Montagu arms on its trappings.

The two armies swept unopposed through Scotland, and met at Perth in mid-August, having laid waste much of the country, sparing only the lands loyal to Edward Balliol in Galloway. By the end of the month, Edward told Philip that the war in Scotland was over.[20] He seems to have believed that, faced with the military reality of the English domination of Scotland, Philip's desire for a crusade would outweigh his loyalty to David II. In this, Edward misjudged Philip; and Philip in turn misjudged Edward's determination to reach a settlement with the Scots on his own terms. Balliol's opponents had had a minor victory at Culblean in September, when the earl of Atholl, an ally of Balliol, was killed. This boosted their morale, and was later remembered as the turning point in the war; but the real turning point was the result of the diplomatic impasse early in 1336. Edward had named his closest confidants among his household, William Montagu, Robert Ufford and Ralph Neville, to negotiate a peace settlement with the French and the supporters of David II, with the help of mediators sent by the pope. Following meetings at Newcastle in January 1336, a draft treaty was agreed, and was sent to the Scots for ratification. The idea was that the difference in age between Edward Balliol and David II could form the basis for peace, David becoming Balliol's successor since the latter had no heir. But under this arrangement, Scotland would remain an English fief, subject to Edward III; and the Bruce party rejected the terms outright.

For the first time, serious French intervention in the Scottish war now seemed possible. Philip made major preparations to invade England in support of David II, and Edward sent another army to Scotland under Henry of Grosmont. Edward Balliol covered the lowlands, while Henry was to operate in the Highlands against a guerrilla force led by William Douglas. It proved a fast-moving campaign, not least for the king himself. The objective, as always, was to bring the main body of the Scottish forces to battle; but, in imitation of Scottish tactics, isolated fortresses were relieved by bold and decisive strikes, and even the main army moved extremely rapidly. The commander of Edinburgh Castle took thirty-two small boats across the Firth of Forth to Cupar Castle in Stirling, under siege from a strong Scottish contingent led by three earls, and with 200 men panicked them into flight and the abandonment of the siege along with all their equipment. Edward himself was at Northampton, for the approaching opening of a great council. On 6 June he left on a wild ride north with just fifty men at arms, reaching Newcastle five days later and Perth a week after that. Here he found the two armies, who had just rebuilt the town's defences, recently destroyed by the Scots. They were astonished by the king's sudden appearance, and greatly encouraged: 'seeing the king, they were amazed at his boldness, and wept for joy'.[21] Among the knights there were Henry of Beaumont, Thomas Beauchamp, William Montagu, Robert Ufford, Thomas Ughtred and William Bohun.[22]

Since the battle of Culblean the previous year, Henry of Beaumont's daughter Catherine, countess of Atholl, had been at Lochindorb Castle, unable to escape and now besieged by Andrew Murray, guardian of Scotland, and his men. They were seventy miles away, and Edward saw a chance of forcing a battle, as well as a splendid knightly rescue of a damsel in distress. He selected a highly mobile force, probably consisting of 500 men at arms and knights, and set out to challenge the besiegers. It was a calculated risk, since others had suffered on similar bold forays into enemy territory. Guy count of Namur had been captured on a raid the previous year, with a smaller escort, when he had been forced to take refuge in the ruins of Edinburgh Castle.

Edward covered the seventy miles and confronted the Scots in four days. He found the main army before he reached the castle and very nearly succeeded in surprising his enemy. Andrew Murray was at mass when his scouts recognized the English army, but none of them dared interrupt him. When the English came up, the Scots were just in formation, and had to retreat: one of them knew a rocky side path down which they were able to escape successfully. Baulked of his prey at the last minute, Edward was nonetheless able to ride on and lift the siege of Lochindorb, in itself an important strategic fortress, and release his old mentor's daughter.

This might be the knightly and romantic side of warfare; Edward sent a letter back to Philippa at the end of the campaign. It described his heroic exploits at Lochindorb but went on to outline the second part of the operations, a black devastation of the east coast of Scotland, where the French fleet was expected to land. Aberdeen, the largest port available to the fleet, was left in ashes, and the lands around were reduced to a desert. The king returned south in September, though various alarms in the autumn brought him temporarily back to Berwick and the lowlands.

Although Edward returned to Scotland at intervals until 1345, none of these occasions were major campaigns. In the autumn of 1336 much work was done on the defences of various castles, and this might have been a prelude to the creation of the kind of network of fortresses which had enabled his grandfather to subdue the Welsh. But the Welsh castles formed much more of an interlocking pattern, particularly the compact group along the north coast, and even the most isolated castle was not more than a few days' march from the English border. The Scottish castles were another matter: it is impossible to imagine a pattern of fortresses which would be viable in terms of supply and mutual support, and Edward never seems to have seriously envisaged such a plan. Without it, however, he had to reach a political settlement, and this was to elude him for another ten years. In the end, the fate of Scotland was determined by the chances of war, as, in a sense, he had always hoped it would be.

For the moment, he had to leave the defence of the English interest in Scotland to the lords of the north of England. The 'disinherited' remained disinherited. Henry of Beaumont abandoned his claim to the earldom of Buchan, and followed Edward on his French expeditions, as did William Montagu. Montagu had been promised considerable lands in Scotland at the beginning of the Scottish wars, and during the time in Scotland had been given the Isle of Man, the one conquest from the Scots which was to prove permanent; with it he acquired the title of king of Man. Thomas Gray has a curious story that Montagu, 'one of the most intimate of the king's council at that time', left Flanders when he 'realized that their support for their German alliance did not seem to be drawing to a profitable conclusion' and 'put his complaint before parliament rather than the king and took himself to Scotland', to the siege of Dunbar.[23] The chronology does not work, as the unsuccessful English siege of Dunbar, led by Montagu and the earl of Arundel, ended before the Flanders expedition left; but it is probably a rare glimpse into the attitudes of Edward's councillors at this period, as well as Montagu's relationship with Edward. The Scottish wars were not necessarily seen as a less important challenge than the coming war with France.

The most powerful card in Philip VI's hand in the Scottish negotiations was Edward's status as duke of Aquitaine. The exact terms of Edward's personal status as the liege man of Philip, the ruler who was potentially his greatest enemy, had not been resolved, either at Amiens in 1329, or after the secret and conditional homage of 1331. It would in any case have been difficult for Philip to claim that Edward was bound by the terms of any homage not to attack a king who was linked to Philip by a treaty of allegiance, but there were other ways in which the French could cause problems for Edward. When Edward offered Philip's enemy Robert d'Artois refuge in England in 1334, he unintentionally played into Philip's hands. Robert d'Artois had supported Philip's accession to the French throne, and in return expected the king's support over his claim to inherit his grandfather's territory, the county of Artois. However, Philip refused to back him, and, after an episode in which Robert tried to forge a letter to prove his claim, he fled France in 1332 to avoid trial and probable execution. He went first to Namur and then to Brabant, but both were fiefs of the French king, and Philip threatened to invade in order to seize Robert.[24] By seeking refuge in England, he placed himself beyond Philip's reach. On the other hand, this gave Philip the chance to use Edward's harbouring of a criminal as a new reason to confiscate the duchy of Aquitaine.

A series of diplomatic missions had failed to make any headway with Philip. Philip, for his part, was eager to go on crusade: but he could not go while hostilities with England were a real possibility, and needed Edward's participation to guarantee peace. If both kings were absent, there could be no war. When Geoffrey Scrope, an experienced lawyer, returned from France in July 1334, he had met such obstructive tactics from the French that he demanded that he should not be sent on any further such missions,[25] and his instinct was correct: when William Montagu and William Clinton, accompanying the new archbishop of Canterbury, John Stratford, went the following winter, they were treated to a lecture from Philip which ended with the declaration that peace 'will never be established among Christians until the king of France sits on the judgment seat in the middle of England and is judge and ruler over the kingdoms of France, England and Scotland'.[26] Two years later, Philip seized on Edward's protection of Robert d'Artois as the reason for the formal confiscation of Aquitaine, and proclaimed the territory forfeit on 24 May 1337.

When in February 1337 Edward created six new earldoms, four of which went to the comrades who had helped him to carry out his coup, he was careful to justify his action as being for the good of the nation as a whole:

> Among the signs of royalty we considered it to be the most important that, through a suitable distribution of ranks, dignities and offices, the king is sustained by the wise counsels and protected by the many powers of formidable men. Yet because the hereditary ranks in our king-dom ... through a failure of issue and various other events have returned into the hand of the king, this realm has experienced for a long time a sub-stantial loss in the names, honours and ranks of dignity.[27]

The new earls were William Montagu, first earl of Salisbury, William Clinton, earl of Huntingdon, Robert Ufford, earl of Suffolk, William Bohun, earl of Northampton, participants in the events of October 1330; and Henry of Grosmont, earl of Derby, and Hugh Audley, earl of Gloucester. Not everyone agreed that the nation benefited from these promotions: Thomas Gray once more gives a dissident view, looking back on the distribution of lands following the creation of the new earl-doms as the cause of the king's heavy taxation in later years: 'So generously did the king distribute his estates to these earls and to his other favourites, that he scarcely retained for himself any of the lands pertaining to his crown, and was obliged to live off windfalls and sub-sidies at great cost to people.'[28] But there were few such dissenting voices, and in fact many of the grants were made from estates forfeited to the crown by nobles condemned as a result of the disturbances of the first years of Edward's reign up to 1330, notably the lands of the Despensers and Mortimers. And no one could deny the earls' excep-tional service to the king at the most critical juncture of his reign; if this was favouritism, it was in return for favours received. Furthermore, by increasing the number of great lords, Edward was avoiding the situ-ation that had prevailed in his father's reign, where one or two families wielded exceptional influence. And as in the first years of his personal rule, he was careful not to grant the lands in perpetuity, but either for a term of years or under conditions which meant that there was the possibility of reversion – a reversion which he might want to grant back to the original family if they were restored to favour, as happened with Roger Mortimer's grandson.

There was a further motive in the creation of new earls in 1337: a war was in the offing, and the earls were the traditional leaders of the army. Throughout the previous year, war of some kind had been regarded as inevitable, and the appointment of the new earls should be seen in the context of a council of the great lords at Nottingham in January 1337, when preparations for a campaign against the French began in earnest. Such a war was not a novelty. Over the past two centuries, the pattern had been that after a brief spell of open warfare, the two sides would come to a new compromise. The English had generally come off worse, because the resources to fight a war across the Channel were difficult to muster, and their kings could no longer draw on the resources of the vast domains bequeathed by Henry II. Normandy, homeland of the English dynasty and the most accessible point for an invasion, was now the fiefdom of the eldest son of the king of France, while Aquitaine barely had the resources to keep its turbulent lords loyal and obedient to the English crown, let alone contribute to an attack on the ruler of France.

Edward's remarks about the diminishing numbers of great lords when he justified his creation of the new earls were entirely true. Three of the existing earls died in the years 1336–8, and had either no successors or heirs who were not fit for military service.[29] Two others were invalids: the earl of Lancaster had been blind since 1328, and the earl of Devon, restored to his title in 1335, was elderly and seems to have confined his soldiering after this date to the defence of Devon and Cornwall. This left just three active earls, rather than the dozen or more who might usually be expected to lead the king's armies, and by creating the additional earls he was doing no more than making good the losses. For example, Humphrey Bohun, earl of Hereford, was one of the heirs who was an invalid, and in 1338 he transferred his hereditary office of constable of the royal army to his brother William, newly created earl of Northampton.[30] These men would serve with substantial retinues: the nine earls who took part in the Brittany campaigns in 1342–3 raised about 900 men at arms between them, against about 1,100 from all other sources.[31]

Edward saw the interest of king and magnates as essentially one and the same in this pronouncement. The highly structured state created by the Normans in the eleventh century had been modified gradually over the succeeding three hundred years, but it was still recognizably a unified system, in which the barons had a crucial role. The 'magnates' were a relatively small group,[32] ranging from figures such as Richard Fitzalan, earl of Arundel, capable of lending huge sums to his fellow-lords, to knights banneret who had made their way up the social ladder in the king's service, and who owed their status to grants made by their master. Like the king, the greatest of them lived off their estates, and maintained splendid households; and their power, if united against the king, could be fatal to royal ambitions, as Henry III and Edward II had discovered to their cost. In peace, they looked to the king to govern justly and maintain a suitably magnificent court; in war, they wanted a leader who would bring military success and the enrichment that went with the spoils of war. As K. B. McFarlane puts it,

> the real politics of the reign were not confined to the short if frequent parliaments; they were inherent rather in Edward's daily personal relations with his magnates. The king's service was profitable . . . men went to court and to the royal camp, not to express unacceptable views, but for what they could get. Under a ruler who knew his job they were amply rewarded.[33]

Among the magnates there were smaller groups, the knights of the royal household who (as we have already seen) were most closely associated with the king and were under his personal command, and the earls and barons who frequented the court in various official and unofficial roles. The knights of the household were hugely important in Edward's wars, and provided a large proportion of the troops who sailed for Flanders in 1338. Because this was not an army assembled for duty under a feudal summons, Edward was free to choose his followers more widely, and the result was a very varied group, including minor nobility from old families, newcomers to England – often from his father-in-law's county of Hainault – and professional soldiers of obscure origin who had won their place by their military skills. This harked back to his grandfather's days, when the household knights played a similar role in Edward I's

Scottish campaigns, and it was a commonplace that warfare should be waged by a group of men close to the king, an idea that had its origins in the war-bands of Celtic and Germanic tribal society. A 'household knight' was retained by the king, and would receive robes at the new year. The list of the distribution of robes, given the often erratic payment of fees to royal retainers, is perhaps the best way of identifying the household. They in turn would recruit men to serve in the royal army, so that sixty such knights in Flanders in 1338 had almost 800 men at arms in their own retinues.[34] In peacetime, the household knights had been as prominent in royal tournaments as the great magnates.

Other magnates, such as the marcher lords of the north, rarely came to court, and lived largely in their own country, preoccupied with their own interests. However, if the king's rule started to falter, they were often the first to show signs of rebellion, being independent-minded and wary of the central powers. A successful king had therefore to balance the aspirations of these different groups against his own ambitions; Edward I had done so with great skill for much of his reign, appearing at various times as a knightly hero and as a great lawgiver. Edward II's failure was a stark warning to his son.

Edward believed that England alone could not take on the armies of the vastly wealthier kingdom of France. So in 1337–8 he set about constructing a grand alliance based on Flanders, where Philip had been trying to enforce his rights over the Flemish towns and where there was considerable hostility to the French. In this he was imitating his grandfather, who had built a great alliance in very similar circumstances in 1297, when the English possession of Gascony was threatened. Edward's diplomacy was apparently successful, and, during the next three years, he established a substantial power base in north-western Europe: the count of Flanders, an ally of Philip, was forced out, and Edward was given authority over Germany and the Low Countries as the deputy of the German emperor. The new earls and members of his household were prominent in the negotiations for these alliances. Typically, a diplomatic mission would consist of an experienced royal official and his secretariat alongside a member of court who in a sense represented the king, and was assumed to have his confidence. William Clinton went on such missions to France in 1332 and 1334, and, at the beginning of the Flemish project of 1337, we find Montagu and Clinton sent with Henry

Burghersh, bishop of Lincoln, in April 1337 to negotiate the necessary treaties; they were in many ways the chief architects of the scheme. However, in order to achieve an active military alliance, Edward's negotiators had to adopt a policy of promising huge sums to his allies for the costs of bringing their troops to join his army. This in turn meant that the king would have to show quick results in order to balance his books. In November 1337, Walter Mauny provided him with a brief success; as admiral of the north, he escorted the English fleet taking wool to Flanders and on the way launched an attack on the Flemish port of Sluys, since the count of Flanders was a vassal of Philip VI. He was repulsed, but in an ensuing battle on the neighbouring island of Cadsand he captured the count's half-brother, and was able to sell his prisoner to the king for £8,000. The only long-term effect of this episode, however, was to give Mauny the foundation of his subsequent fortune.

In the midst of this vastly ambitious financial and political scheme, and at a time when the king was trying to raise huge sums of money, Edward typically put on a magnificent display at his Christmas feast at Guildford in 1337. Against a canvas background painted with a rabbit warren and a wood, a pillory and ducking stool were set up; fifteen baboons were the centrepiece of the action, while other actors wore white surcoats with red sleeves decorated with gold leaves. The king himself appeared in a dramatic piece of headgear, a hood covered in gold and silver ornaments, embroidered with 'tigers holding court made from pearls and embossed with silver and gold, and decorated on another edge with the image of a certain castle made of pearls with a mounted man riding towards the castle on a horse made of pearls, and, moreover, between each tiger a tree of pearls and a tree of gold . . .'[35] Eight pairs of shields were made of gold and silver and varicoloured silk, for the king, Henry of Grosmont, Richard Fitzalan, William Montagu, Henry Ferrers, Thomas Poynings and the newly rich Walter Mauny. Seven less elaborate pairs were given to the Beauchamp brothers, Maurice Berkeley, Thomas Bradeston, John Molyns, and the Ufford brothers, Robert and Ralph. And three fantastic costumes were provided for the king, Henry of Grosmont and William Montagu,

> decorated with the image of a castle made of silk and trimmed with gold, displaying towers, halls, chambers, walls and other pertinent things around it, and within the walls divers trees of gold, while on the breast of

each tunic an embroidered figure in gold standing under a canopy on the battlements, whereas the hems of these tunics are designed in such a way in green cloth as to resemble the moats and ditches of this castle surrounded by a green field.[36]

The tunics and mantles of the king and queen and of William Montagu were trimmed with 228 golden clouds. If splendour equalled power, Edward was staking his claim to be one of the most powerful rulers in Europe.

Time was not on Edward's side, and as a result the grand alliance proved to be no more real than the golden clouds. His allies were more than happy to take his money, but much less happy about actually providing the resources for the kind of campaign that Edward had in mind. Other than the financial rewards, the rulers whom Edward had signed up – the lords of the various counties and duchies in the Low Countries and the German emperor, Louis IV – had little real interest in taking the war into France; the lords of the Netherlands were chiefly concerned to keep Philip out of their affairs, while Edward needed a considerable military victory if he was to enforce the restitution of the duchy of Aquitaine. Moreover, the allies knew that Edward was thinking of making public his claim to the French throne, at which point the rights of the French king would pass to him, and they would merely have exchanged the threat which Philip posed for a vastly more powerful ruler of France.

Edward arrived in Antwerp in July 1338. This was to be his base, and, just as when he had moved his court to York for the duration of the Scottish wars, Philippa and his two daughters accompanied him: the eight-year-old prince of Wales was left in England as regent, the nominal head of a regency council which included William Clinton. But the administration had to remain in England, whereas for the Scottish wars it too had moved north. Communication across the Channel was not always easy, and the king's plans were putting enormous strains on the government, with repeated demands for large sums of money. The allies were slow to commit troops to the planned campaign against France, while demanding the payments they had been promised, and Edward spent a frustrating year trying to bring them together as an army. He had a moment of diplomatic triumph at Koblenz on 5 September, when he was appointed as imperial vicar-general in a magnificent ceremony, for which Edward had fifteen tunics and mantles made in red and gold

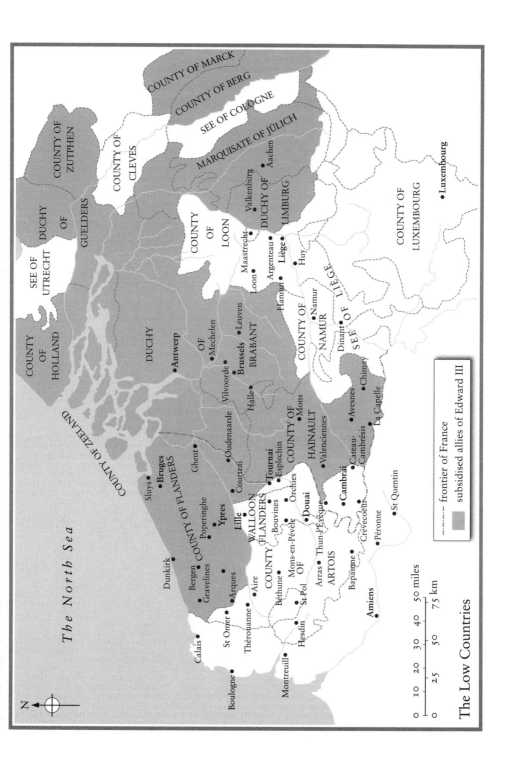

The Low Countries

The North Sea

COUNTY OF ZEELAND

COUNTY OF HOLLAND

SEE OF UTRECHT

DUCHY OF GUELDERS

COUNTY OF ZUTPHEN

COUNTY OF CLEVES

COUNTY OF MARCK

COUNTY OF BERG

SEE OF COLOGNE

MARQUISATE OF JÜLICH

Aachen

DUCHY OF LIMBURG

Valkenburg

COUNTY OF LOON

Maastrecht

Loon

Argenteau

Liège

Huy

Hannut

SEE OF LIÈGE

COUNTY OF NAMUR

Namur

Dinant

COUNTY OF LUXEMBOURG

Luxembourg

DUCHY OF BRABANT

Antwerp

Mechelen

Leuven

Brussels

Vilvoorde

Halle

Oudenaarde

Ghent

Bruges

Sluys

Dunkirk

COUNTY OF FLANDERS

Bergen

Gravelines

Arques

Aire

Ypres

Poperinghe

Lille

WALLOON FLANDERS

Courtrai

Tournai

Esplechin

COUNTY OF HAINAULT

Mons

Valenciennes

Cateau-Cambrésis

Avesnes

Chimay

La Capelle

Orchies

Douai

Bouvines

Mons-en-Pévèle

Thun-l'Évêque

Crèvecoeur

Cambrai

St Quentin

Péronne

Bapaume

Arras

St-Pol

COUNTY OF ARTOIS

Béthune

Hesdin

Montreuil

Thérouanne

St Omer

Calais

Boulogne

Amiens

N

frontier of France

subsidised allies of Edward III

0   10   20   30   40   50 miles

0   25   50   75 km

for himself, the emperor and other magnates of England and Germany.[37] And at Antwerp in the second week of January 1339 he celebrated the birth of his second son, Lionel, and the churching of Queen Philippa with the traditional tournament. The participants would have been his household knights, the earls and possibly some of the local knights.

It was not until September 1339 that Edward finally cajoled his allies into joining him in the field; the promised subsidies had only been partly paid, and there was little money coming from England. He had to persuade his companions to sign a document by which eight of them would become hostages for the payment of the sums due to the duke of Brabant if the king defaulted. The document survives, signed and sealed by the king and twenty-five of his magnates: all the English earls, as well as Henry of Beaumont as earl of Buchan, and thirteen other lords, including the bannerets of the king's household.[38] After which – though not without some further hesitation until Edward himself set out with just the English army – the allies invaded the territory of the bishop of Cambrai, outside the borders of France, but like the count of Flanders a vassal of the French king. The object was to force Philip to come to the rescue of the bishop; he did so grudgingly, at first pretending that he thought the English king was still at Antwerp. We have a detailed diary of the campaign, which notes the raids carried out during the next fortnight, devastating the lands round Cambrai: William Montagu's brother Edward took two castles in a raid on 10 October, and Walter Mauny captured Thun l'Évêque, while Thomas Poynings, another household knight, was killed trying to take the castle at Honicourt. A larger raid, under Henry of Grosmont, William Bohun and William Montagu, followed. This was not enough to force Philip to challenge Edward's army, and on 9 October Edward invaded France itself. His brother-in-law, William II of Hainault, refused to accompany him, since he was a vassal of King Philip; but many of his men stayed with the English, as did his uncle, Jean de Hainault. On the first day of the invasion, Laurence Hastings, the heir to the earldom of Pembroke, was given his full title even though he was still under age; sixty-seven squires from the English army were knighted on the same and following days.

Philip had at last responded to the English threat, and was not far from the invading army. For the first time since the reign of Richard I, there was a real likelihood that the kings of France and England would meet on the battlefield. Edward encamped eighteen miles from Philip's position, at Péronne on the Somme, and his raiders burnt a village only two miles from the French camp; Walter Mauny and Wulfart Ghistels, a Flemish knight from Ostend, actually raided the outposts of the French position. Philip still refused to move, and appeared to be prepared to sit out the invasion until the English were forced to retreat for want of money and supplies. But the French lords with him were eager to engage, and he sent a challenge to Edward naming a day for the battle, with the result that the two armies came face to face at Buironfosse, on the border with Hainault, on 21 October. Edward followed the pattern of Halidon Hill in drawing up the army, dismounting his knights and men at arms, and placing archers, guarded by Welsh spearmen, on the flanks. The king's battalion formed the vanguard, and included Henry Burghersh, bishop of Lincoln, and Jean de Hainault, with Thomas Bradeston, William Fitzwarin, Reginald Cobham, Walter Mauny, Thomas Holland and Maurice Berkeley among the household knights. The right wing was under Henry of Grosmont and Robert Ufford, and the left under William Bohun and William Montagu, as well as Laurence Hastings taking his first command.[39] Edward's Continental allies were in the centre, with Robert Ufford's brother William evidently as a liaison officer. Almost all the English commanders were veterans of the Scottish wars, and had been comrades in arms on numerous occasions over the previous six years. The English army was a much smaller force than that commanded by Philip; yet when Philip came in sight of the enemy battle array, he ordered the vanguard to halt, and a defensive position to be prepared.

A fierce argument broke out among the French lords. Some argued that the king would be disgraced if he did not attack the enemy – exactly the reaction that Edward wished to provoke. Others urged caution, partly because of a fear of treachery on their own side, and partly because they were uncertain of the outcome of a battle with the English and their allies.[40] If Edward was unsure of his allies, he was at least confident that the English magnates would never betray him; Philip was in a worse position, because it was his own lords who were the source of his problems. Both sides withdrew after facing each other for a day; Edward could not afford to stay in a position where he had no supplies, Philip because he did not want to risk a battle. In terms of reputation, Edward had enhanced his fame: not only had he defeated the Scots in the open field, but the French had not dared to take him on. Philip was seen as

having retreated out of fear or cowardice, although some French chroniclers tried to claim that it was the English who had withdrawn silently in
the night when they saw the size of the French army. Philip had done the
right thing in tactical terms, but that did not stop his nobles from wearing
fox-fur hats mocking Philip's cowardly behaviour, like the fox in
folklore.

But Edward had nonetheless failed in his objective. Military failure
meant that the costs of maintaining the alliance could not be defrayed
by the spoils of war, and what had been intended as a swift campaign
dragged on with no end in sight. This war had to be financed out of taxation: and the result was one of the heaviest periods of taxation ever
seen in England. In the spring of 1340 he had to return home to use
such persuasion as he could muster on an increasingly recalcitrant country, and to explain that he had now declared his hand and had, in a
ceremony in the marketplace at Ghent on 8 January, publicly laid claim
to the French throne by assuming the title 'king of England and France'.
The announcement was followed by jousts in celebration the occassion.[41]

In his absence, William Montagu and Robert Ufford mounted an
expedition with the aim of capturing Lille, in advance of a major campaign planned for the summer. Three divisions, two from Flanders and
one from Hainault, were to join forces for the siege; Montagu and
Ufford, in charge of one of the Flemish divisions, seem to have ridden
forward with no more than forty men at arms to reconnoitre the
defences of Lille, and were captured when the French garrison sallied
out against them. According to Le Bel, they found themselves trapped in
the earthworks outside the town; another French chronicle says that
Montagu was seriously wounded. The English chroniclers blamed them
for their 'foolish audacity', and this was probably correct: overconfidence in the superiority of the mounted horseman over infantry was
more often the downfall of the French, and, combined with Montagu's
evident liking for bold action, proved disastrous in this instance.[42] News
of Montagu and Ufford's capture reached the king at Windsor in early
April, where he was holding an Easter tournament,[43] and must have cast
a shadow over proceedings. It was the most serious loss that the English
had suffered since the beginning of Edward's reign: Philip, triumphant,
put them in a cart like ordinary criminals and locked them up in the
Châtelet, a common prison in Paris, rather than in the honourable captivity which they might have expected. Montagu had already lost an eye

in a skirmish in Scotland in 1337, and it is possible that his health was now permanently impaired.

The sheer power of the French military machine was now at its most daunting, even though Philip's counter-raid into Hainault achieved relatively little. At the same time as mustering a substantial army for this purpose, Philip also threatened to cut communications between England and Flanders by assembling a powerful fleet of 202 ships, which arrived in the Swijn estuary controlling the entrance to the port of Sluys about 8 June. Word of this quickly reached England. If Edward wanted to continue his French campaigns, he had to destroy the French fleet, but the stakes were high: defeat and the loss of his army would leave England open to French invasion. Archbishop Stratford, as head of the regency council, advised him not to go, and, when he appealed to the commanders of his fleet, both highly experienced seamen, they supported the archbishop. Robert of Avesbury, who was close to Stratford, claims that Edward declared: 'I will cross the sea in spite of you. You are frightened when there is nothing to be afraid of, and can stay at home.'[44] He continued to recruit men and ships with renewed energy.

Edward's fleet sailed from the Orwell estuary in Suffolk on 22 June, with a fleet slightly smaller than the French armada, but with more fighting men and smaller crews. They reached the Flemish coast near Sluys on the evening of 23 June, and Reginald Cobham was sent ashore to report on the French positions; Walter Mauny knew the area, and was able to provide additional intelligence. The French ships had been idle for a fortnight, and their captains were quarrelling; the vessels were chained together to prevent the English breaking through the line, but in so doing lost all means of control. The next day, early in the day, the English fleet set out to fight. The English were good seamen, and it is probable that they manoeuvred so that they approached the French from the south, anchoring once they were in sight of the fleet to wait for the tide. Once it had turned, about midday, the three admirals in charge of the fleet, Robert Morley, admiral of the north, William Clinton, admiral of the west, and John Crabbe, once admiral of Flanders and since 1333 employed by the English, hoisted anchor and moved towards the French, and then changed tack as if they were about to retreat. The French hastily broke their chains, and tried to pursue them.

At this point both fleets were attempting to sail into the wind, moving very slowly: when the English turned to attack, they had the impetus of both wind and tide with them. The first shots were from siege engines mounted on the ships, followed by the classic English use of archers. As on land, they had a deadly effect, driving the enemy from the decks of the ships. As the ships closed, the English men at arms clambered onto the French vessels, where their superior numbers made short work of the few French troops and of the crossbowmen and sailors. Edward himself was wounded in the thigh, but there were almost no English casualties, and a horrific slaughter of the French which shocked contemporaries. A contingent of Genoese galleys escaped in the early evening, but more than 150 French ships were taken back to England. The real heroes of the hour were the naval commanders, whose skilful handling of their squadrons had been crucial to the victory. Edward, however, claimed the victory as his personally; and in a sense it was, because he knew that he was not an expert in war at sea, and was prepared to hand over the fleet to those who were. Once again, the contrast is between collaboration and common sense among Edward and his men, and pride, distrust and quarrels among their adversaries.[45] However, the French still had considerable naval resources, including the Genoese galleys that had escaped at Sluys and which were often used to raid English ports, and they were accustomed to hiring their ships from Genoa and Castile, whereas Edward had to rely on English resources only.

Edward, as always desperate for money to pay his allies, turned his victory to good use. A parliament was hastily convened to hear the news of the king's great victory, and in the general enthusiasm the taxes voted for the next two years were converted into an immediate lump sum. With this reassurance, he embarked on his planned campaign: Tournai, the most important French fortress near the Flemish border, was to be besieged. If it was taken, it would be a major achievement; but the real objective was to try once more to lure Philip to the battlefield. In the event, Tournai held out, and there was no battle. When the two armies were apparently on the point of engaging in early September, Jeanne, dowager countess of Hainault, mother of Queen Philippa and sister of Philip of Valois, emerged from the convent where she was living in retirement to plead for a truce. With a suitable show of reluctance, Philip agreed to negotiate; and the duke of Brabant, Edward's most important ally, forced Edward, who was still hoping for a quick victory, to send Henry Burghersh, William Clinton and Geoffrey Scrope to open the talks. Within two days, a truce was agreed at Esplechin on 25 September 1340. One of its provisions was that Montagu and Ufford should be released on parole, though the ransoms were heavy. Philip VI was fully aware of Edward's close dependence on Montagu, and made it a condition of his parole that he would never fight in France again. However, in June 1342 this condition was removed in exchange for the release of two important French prisoners.[46] But he only fought briefly in Brittany late in 1342, and possibly at the siege of Algeciras in 1343, and his capture outside Lille effectively marked the end of Montagu's career as Edward's right-hand man in the English command.

Although the usual jousts were held to celebrate the end of the campaign, the absence of military victory was a disaster for Edward, who blamed his failure on the administration in England. The new taxation he had been granted by parliament in June yielded only 15 per cent of what had been expected. His closest advisers in England were now thoroughly opposed to the war, and at the end of November Edward sailed back to London, furious with what he saw as their lack of support, and suspicious that their reports were false. His response to the situation was to attempt to repeat the coup with which his personal rule had begun in 1330. His action was as dramatic as it had been at Northampton: he arrived secretly by night

and entered the Tower of London by torchlight, and no one knew he had come. He at once asked for Sir Nicholas de la Beche, the constable of the Tower and guardian of the duke, son of the king of England. And the under-constable fell on his knees at the king's feet, and said, 'Sire, he is out of the town.' This put the king into a rage and he ordered all the chests to be opened for him so that he could see for himself what was in the Tower. And when he had looked at these, he sent urgently for Andrew Aubrey, then mayor of London.[47]

Aubrey was ordered to arrest leading members of the administration, even though he had no official post, and despite the fact that William Bohun and Walter Mauny were with the king. Even the official records note the king's midnight arrival,[48] but, despite the surprise, the results were not what he had hoped. The king had had secret information that the administration were cheating him: yet the truth was that his demands had been excessive in the extreme. Archbishop Stratford, who had been president of the regency council since 1330, withdrew to Canterbury, and waged an effective propaganda war against the king, knowing that right was on his side; he refused to answer for his actions except before parliament. When parliament met in April 1341, Edward tried to exclude him, but the other lords forced him to admit the archbishop and to come to terms with him. It was a tremendous blow for a king who had hoped to avoid the troubles of his father's reign; echoes of the fall of Edward II were particularly strong, since Stratford had been a leader of the opposition in the 1320s. The king had to agree to legislation which gave parliament a large role in selecting the royal officials, and to an audit of his finances; and the lords insisted that none of them should be imprisoned without a trial before his peers in parliament. Edward was perilously close to the kind of political crisis that had repeatedly marred his father's reign.

4

The Kingdom of France

If we are to understand the history of Edward's wars against France, we have to define the enemy – the king, nobles and people of the kingdom of France. They were Edward's opponents, and their strengths and weaknesses were as critical to the events which followed Edward III's declaration of war on France in 1337 as were those of the English leaders. Furthermore, the relationship between the kingdoms of France and England and the kings of the two countries were different in nature. The two kingdoms were separate political entities: there was no question of an English claim to France because that kingdom was a vassal state (or vice versa). It was the kings personally who were at war, rival claimants to the French throne. On Philip V's death in 1328 without direct male heirs, the law on the succession was not clear, since the last time that this situation had arisen was three centuries earlier, in 987. Philip VI claimed the throne as the nearest male descendant of Philip V's grandfather, Philip III, through a male line. Edward III claimed the throne as the nearest male relative of the late king through the female line, because his mother was the daughter of Philip IV. The question as to whether a claim to the throne could be inherited through a daughter was put to the lawyers of the university of Paris, who declared that such a claim was not valid; but there was enough doubt about the matter for Edward III to play the ultimate card in the rivalry between the French and English kings, and declare himself king of France as grandson of Philip IV. Edward's view of the matter is neatly demonstrated in a family tree, carefully laid out in the 1350s to show why his was the best claim.

The rival claimants to the French throne: a family tree from Geoffrey le Baker's chronicler, set out in such a way that Edward appears visually as the first claimant.

Philip, called 'the conqueror', king of France, begat

Philip, the Fair, king of France, who begat

Isabella, queen of England, who gave birth to

Edward the king of England, the third since the Conquest

Charles the Brown, count of Marche and later king of France and Navarre, the third to be born

Philip the Tall, count of Poitou and later king of France and Navarre, the second to be born

Louis, the first born, king of France and Navarre, who begat

John, his son, who lived exactly eight days

Joanna, his daughter, queen of Navarre and countess of Auxerre

Charles, count of Valois, who begat

Philip, count of Valois, later king of France, who begat

John of Valois, crowned of the French, captured at the battle of Poitiers

Charles, count of Alençon

Louis, count of Evreux, who begat

Charles, count of Evreux and king of Navarre by right of his wife

Joanna, queen of France, married to Charles, king of France

LANGUAGE, CULTURE AND
ANGLO-FRENCH RELATIONS

Edward's decision to make war had been entirely personal, in pursuit of his personal right to the French throne. Behind it lay the legacy of the ambitions of the Angevin kings. The two countries were Siamese twins, joined and yet separate; the English kings had at times ruled more land in France than the French kings themselves. Edward III himself was more than half French, since Henry III and Edward II had both married French wives. So there was an element of civil war about the conflict; the enemy were the inhabitants of a country with which the English aristocracy had close links, personal, cultural and historical. Only six generations separated them from forebears who had held lands in both Normandy and England, and there were continuing administrative links with Aquitaine and north-eastern France: Bartholomew Burghersh the elder had served as seneschal of Ponthieu in the early years of Edward's reign.

But the dreams of empire and memories of the former greatness of the English kings remained. The English nobility, many of whom retained lands in France, regarded the English presence across the Channel as part of their birthright. The kings of France and England might be at loggerheads over territorial claims; on the other hand, England and France were intertwined in ways which would seem unimaginable to us today. First and foremost, they shared a common language. Until the mid-fourteenth century, all those educated in England spoke French, not as an alternative language, but as their native tongue. They would probably know a little Latin, for the purposes of royal business. And they would also speak English if necessary. That it was not familiar is shown by the Anglo-French glossary compiled by Walter of Bibbesworth in the 1250s for the use of local gentry in managing their estates and talking to their stewards.[1]

The whole of north-west Europe was French-speaking to a greater or lesser degree as far as the landowning knightly classes were concerned. There was a shared body of literature, particularly in terms of the romances, which also reflected a shared ethos among the knights. Knighthood had always been an international movement, from the early tournaments of the twelfth century onwards, and knights continued to travel long distances in pursuit of their favourite sport. From this came a set of ideals broadly accepted by knights throughout Europe: the most popular book on knighthood, Ramon Llull's *Book of the Order of Knighthood*, was written in Catalan at the end of the thirteenth century, but was translated into Spanish, and into French in the fourteenth century; Caxton made an English version in 1484. The language of heraldry, too, was international; pride in ancestry was not merely a local affair, but something to be paraded abroad. We shall come across knights who left their coats of arms in churches they visited in the near east as a memento of their crusading journeys there.

The merchants were likewise an international community, though French was less of a unifying factor, since many of them came from German-speaking countries. The Hansa, the great league of north German traders, had a massive presence in London at the Steelyard, its fortified warehouse on the north bank of the Thames. And a succession of Italian bankers sought their fortune in England by lending to the king, only to be ruined by him. Their network of mercantile and political intelligence was highly sophisticated, and the great events of European affairs were swiftly reported to their headquarters in Italy. English merchants in the fourteenth century were rapidly growing in wealth and status; the prime example is William de la Pole of Hull, who replaced the Italian bankers as the leading creditor of the king in the 1340s, and whose son became earl of Suffolk in 1370. London merchants such as Andrew Aubrey and John Pountney were similarly wealthy. Their world overlapped with that of the royal court in many ways: they were its chief suppliers, especially of the hugely expensive textiles produced in Flanders, which cost the king as much as his purchases of jewels. Within London they played a sometimes crucial political role. We have seen how, in the most serious crisis of his reign, in 1340/41, Edward had to call on Andrew Aubrey to get his opponents arrested. Equally, merchants and their wives were spectators – though never participants – at the great displays of jousting in the City and at Windsor. They read much of the same literature, and shared the social values of the knights. And through their international contacts they were in touch with the latest fashions in the arts and particularly in clothing.

In terms of trade and business, there were of course numerous Englishmen working as administrators in the English-held territories, who would not necessarily return home when these lands were taken over by the French. Perhaps the most famous example of this is the man who guided Edward III across a crucial ford over the Somme in 1346; the abbot of Meaux near Beverley in Yorkshire records that he was 'an Englishman born at Ruston near Nafferton, who had lived in those parts for sixteen years'.[2] In 1330 this part of France, known as Ponthieu, had been under English control, and it changed hands during the war of 1338–40. So he had been there for almost as long under French rule as he had been under English rule, and there must have been many with similar experiences.

The clergy were international in a different way. Most of the English clergy were born in England, younger sons of noble families, who had entered the Church because the family lands were inherited by the eldest son; or they were the clever children of tradesmen or of the English managers of great estates. A few of the great princes of the Church were foreign, 'provided' to their bishoprics by the pope: the right to do this was fiercely resisted by the English kings, who wanted to place their own men in positions which were as much about secular power as religious devotion. All clergy, however, were acutely conscious of their loyalty to the pope, and many of the senior clergy had direct knowledge of the papal court at Avignon, because this was where appeals in cases involving Church law were determined, and there was a constant stream of English travellers to and from the city. During the whole of Edward III's reign, the papacy was here, in exile from Rome, and often heavily biased towards the French view of politics.

But for the bulk of the population, the native English speakers of the villages and small towns, the world of the wealthy was alien, not only in lifestyle, but in language and customs. England was still to some extent an occupied country. Although the Anglo-Norman nobility occasionally intermarried with their Anglo-Saxon predecessors, it was primarily a case of Norman lords marrying Englishwomen. The English rarely appear as more than freemen, with modest estates, parish priests and small traders, though able Englishmen might well rise to high rank within the Church. English was the language of communication for the parish priest teaching his parishioners and for the bailiff giving orders to the men in the fields. It survived as a literary language in monasteries, since entering a monastic order was an attractive prospect for a talented Englishman; alongside the manuals for preachers produced in

English, a handful of writers continued the literary tradition of the Anglo-Saxons.

When ordinary English soldiers went to France they did not find any points of cultural contact: this was a strange land, and a strange language. For most of the thirteenth century, there had been little military action, and it was only in the last years of Edward I that the English sent troops to Aquitaine in any numbers. The Flemish campaign was the first time that a major English force had ever engaged with the French on French soil; and the invasion of 1346 was the first time that an army almost entirely composed of English troops had campaigned there. It was here that the common soldiers discovered an alien enemy, with whom they could not communicate, a very different view of the world to that of their commanders.

PHILIP OF VALOIS

When Philip of Valois confiscated Aquitaine in 1337, he was venturing into territory which had never in practice been directly ruled from Paris, unlike Normandy, where there had been a full-blown French administration since the early thirteenth century.[3] Loyalty to the English as heirs to the dukes of Aquitaine was strong, at least in part because the fiercely independent local lords preferred a distant king in London to one whose army was only a few days' march away.

Edward faced three kings of France during his reign, three very different characters, with different political backgrounds. His quarrel was personal, and only indirectly a matter for the English state: the French territories under English rule were his personal fiefs, not land conquered by the English. His claim to the French throne was entirely personal, through his mother Isabella, and the personal enmity between him and Philip of Valois was reflected in the diplomatic insults in their correspondence after 1337: 'you who call yourself king of France' is a favourite line of Edward's, and it is interesting that he never uses this epithet to either of Philip's successors.[4]

Philip, unlike Edward, had never expected to be king. Edward himself had been heir to the English throne since his birth in 1312. Philip, nineteen years older than Edward, was no more than a first cousin of Louis X, some way down the line of succession. When Louis X died in

1316, he had no surviving sons, but his wife was pregnant, and another son was born two months later; but he lived for only a few days, and Louis's brother claimed the throne as Philip V. Louis had a daughter, Jeanne, but no woman had ever succeeded to the French throne, and Philip was crowned. A challenge to this on behalf of Jeanne was overruled by an assembly of lords, clergy and citizens in Paris, advised by the lawyers of the university, which declared that women could not succeed to the French throne.

Philip of Valois was brought up simply as heir to the county of Valois, son of a royal peer of France, no more than the eldest of a string of distant relatives of the king. Philip V's son Philip was born in 1313, and it was only on his death in 1321 that the twenty-eight-year old Philip of Valois became second in line to the succession. Philip V died in 1322, again without an heir; his younger brother Charles IV died in 1328, leaving his wife pregnant: the child proved to be a daughter, and only at that point did Philip of Valois become a claimant to the French throne. He rested his claim on the idea that a woman could inherit private property but not public office, which had emerged in discussions on the conflict between Roman law and the teaching of the Church.[5] But it was not clear whether despite this a claim could still pass down through the female side, as Edward argued. To make sure of his title, Philip was chosen as king by a council of the French magnates, the 'twelve peers' of France: outside the council, he was supported by other important lords, including Robert d'Artois, Guy count of Blois and William I of Hainault.[6] The leading royal officials, anxious for continuity, supported Philip's claim.

Philip of Valois's upbringing had therefore never been that of the confirmed heir to the throne; furthermore, he had been largely overshadowed by his father, who died in 1325, and he had only been lord of Valois for three years. He was merely a member of the French peerage, whereas Edward had been at the centre of the English royal household since his birth. Moreover, the troubled history of the French monarchy since 1316 meant that there was a great deal of political manoeuvring in the uncertain situation, and Philip had no personal entourage among the men at the centre of power. On the other hand, he had at his disposal a well-organized administration, developed since the late thirteenth century under Philip IV and Philip V. One of the aims of these kings had been to continue the attack on English power in France that had begun in the late twelfth century under Philip Augustus. Philip of Valois continued this process, with the added incentive that by so doing he was weakening his rival for the throne.

However, because to some extent he owed his throne to the other princes and prelates, Philip was restricted in his ability to impose his power in the same way as his predecessors had done. The French kingship had tended to be more absolutist than that in England, with less reference to the consensus of the nobility which in England developed into a parliamentary structure. Philip admitted in negotiations with Edward in 1329 that, even if he wanted to restore all Edward's estates in France, he was not in a position to make sure that such an order would be carried out.[7] In the early years of his reign, while Edward was under the tutelage of Isabella and Mortimer, their personal relations seem to have been cordial, and they may have jousted together when Edward performed homage at Amiens in 1329. Once Edward was free of his mother's influence, however, the good relationship quickly evaporated.

Philip was an experienced soldier, having campaigned in Italy in 1320 and in Aquitaine with his father and brother in 1324,[8] and early in his reign had won a crushing victory against the Flemish, who were resisting his claims to be their overlord, at Cassel in 1328. It was a victory that had nearly been a disastrous defeat: there had been a stand-off between the two armies for three days, as Philip rightly refused to attack the Flemish, who had a strong position on a hilltop. Instead, he besieged them, and tried to provoke them into an attack by burning the surrounding countryside. The Flemish finally decided to attempt a surprise onslaught in the heat of the day; one chronicler says that the king was taking his accustomed nap.[9] Gilles li Muisit claims that the Flemish were aiming to kill the king himself, and they certainly reached his part of the encampment.[10] But the French rallied just in time, the king was armed and part of the French army quickly regrouped. Once the royal banners were raised, and the king appeared with the host, the Flemish footsoldiers, who had broken ranks to infiltrate the French camp, were driven out; they made a last stand on unfavourable ground and were overwhelmed by the French cavalry.

Despite the narrow escape, Philip's strategy, in not attacking an infantry force entrenched on a powerful defensive site, had been entirely correct. His subsequent tactics at Buironfosse in 1339 and outside Calais in 1347 were exactly the same, attempting to persuade his enemy to attack; but Edward was a different sort of opponent, as calculating as Philip, and even more disciplined. The decision to attack at Crécy was not characteristic of Philip – if it was indeed a conscious decision. The problem was that a defensive policy, which was eventually to break the English power later in the century, was not what the knightly attitude to war encouraged: and the knightly ideals of the time were an essentially French construct, even more powerful in the mindset of French leaders than in that of the English army. Furthermore, the French armies were consistently larger, grander and more confident of victory.

Philip does not come across as a sharply defined character. His father, Charles of Valois, had been a distinguished soldier, but Philip, despite his victory over the Flemish at Cassel in 1328, was not a natural commander. His weakness was his inability to surround himself with sound advisers; he himself was serious and committed, but the men he chose to serve him were often of a very different calibre. He seems to have been indecisive on the battlefield, but he was a determined opponent on the diplomatic front. He had none of Edward's panache, and contemporary poets and writers blamed him severely for his failure to attack Edward in Flanders in 1338, and equally severely for doing so at Crécy in 1346 and suffering a catastrophic defeat. And he did not get on with his fellow-lords.

TREACHERY

Philip's greatest difficulty, which was to remain a major problem for the next two decades, was that of maintaining the loyalty of his subjects. Partly because he himself had not been a particularly prominent member of the nobility before his accession, and partly through bad luck, he suffered from the kind of baronial rebellions that had brought down Edward II, though these arose less out of supposed favouritism and maladministration than out of the pursuit of claims to great principalities. Robert d'Artois, who was reported as saying that Philip 'was made king by me', felt that he was rightfully count of Artois on the death of his aunt, Mahaut; it was another claim involving rights through the female line, but complicated by the fact that Philip was married to Jeanne d'Artois, whose title to the county was probably better than Robert's.

There were now two claimants to the kingdom of France. The solution for peers of France discontented with Philip was simply to switch sides. In the French king's view, this was treason; in Edward's view, recognition of his just cause. Treason was the nightmare of the French monarchy, and is a recurrent theme in the reigns of Philip and of his son. Robert d'Artois was the most influential figure to change sides, and was seen by some chroniclers as the prime mover of Edward's war against France. A French poem satirizing Edward's claim to France, *The Vows of the Heron*, casts Robert in this role.[11] Robert is at Edward's court and goes hawking; he returns with a heron, which is served at a feast. Now, the heron was regarded as the most cowardly of birds, and Robert accuses Edward of cowardice because he will not attack the French to enforce his claim to the throne. Stung by his reproaches, the king and the assembled company take increasingly absurd vows to fight. By mocking the knightly idea of vowing to pursue a quest, the poet puts Edward's pursuit of his title into the same potentially ridiculous category. Furthermore, from the French standpoint, the accusation of faint-heartedness was made by a man who was himself a traitor, branding Edward's whole enterprise with both treachery and cowardice, the two cardinal sins of the knightly world.

But treachery was a real and present danger to Philip and his successors. Once Robert d'Artois had defected, traitors might be lurking anywhere. Le Bel says that at Buironfosse in 1339, when Philip and his advisers discussed whether or not to attack the English,

> there was much debate and quarrelling over this: some of the French lords said it would be a great disgrace and dishonour if the king didn't fight when he knew that his enemies, who'd been burning and ravaging his kingdom before his very eyes, were now so near and still in his own land; but others declared that on the contrary it would be a great folly to do battle, for there was no way of knowing what everyone was thinking and if there was any danger of betrayal . . .[12]

In 1342 there was a dispute over the inheritance of another great fief of the French crown, the duchy of Brittany. The rivals were Charles de Blois, son of another of Philip's supporters at his accession, and the English claimant, Jean de Montfort. One of the great Breton lords, Olivier Clisson, decided that it would be to his advantage to change sides; he was close to the French court and had indeed been with Philip in Italy and had been knighted by him. In the autumn of 1342 he made a secret treaty with Edward which seems to have included recognition of his title to France, and fought briefly on the English side before a truce was proclaimed in January 1343.[13] The following July, during another truce in the fighting in Brittany, he rashly attended a tournament in Paris, perhaps relying on the terms of the truce for immunity. He was arrested by Philip's officers, charged with dealings with the king's enemies – which he seems to have admitted – and executed as a traitor, with all the attendant spectacle of horrors.

Clisson was a man of considerable influence, and his continuing presence on the English side would have changed the balance of power in Brittany. In his wake, and before his downfall, other, lesser lords followed, notably Godefroy d'Harcourt, who was to become Edward's adviser on the Crécy campaign. He was lord of the great castle at St Sauveur-le-Vicomte, south of Cherbourg, which was to pass to two Garter companions in succession twenty years later,[14] and his defection arose out of a purely local quarrel with a neighbouring lord, Robert Bertrand, over the marriage of a heiress. Bertrand, however, was a royal servant, and was both wealthy and powerful. When Harcourt and Bertrand drew their swords over the quarrel in the king's presence, they were both summoned before the parlement in Paris. Harcourt, realizing that Bertrand was much more influential, refused to appear and began a private war against Bertrand and his brother, the bishop of Bayeux, which he comprehensively lost: St Sauveur was taken and razed to the ground, and Harcourt fled the country, eventually finding his way to England.

If the actual damage done by this treachery was relatively limited, the author of the *Grandes chroniques*, writing only a few years later, points to the psychological effect on the king:

> The king, seeing so many treacherous acts done by so many people in so many parts of his kingdom, was greatly troubled, and began to consider and wonder – not without good cause – how such things might be happening; because he saw that almost everyone in the duchies of Brittany and Normandy was in revolt, especially the very noblemen who had promised to serve him loyally until their dying day. He therefore summoned an assembly of the princes and barons of his kingdom to consider how he could avoid such great fraud and inquity, and how this enmity could be entirely removed from his kingdom, so that it was once more a reliable and loyal country.[15]

Treachery was not yet widespread, as the author claims, but related much more to local opportunism in the wake of the English involvement in Brittany. After the campaign of 1346 this was to change for the worse.

At Crécy itself, divided loyalties meant that the shadow of treachery was present. In many cases, there were genuine difficulties: the Rochester chronicler calls Jean de Hainault 'a traitor to the king of England',[16] even though he owed no formal allegiance to Edward, and the only tie was that he was uncle of Queen Philippa. The story in the anonymous Roman chronicle of the capture of the prince of Wales at Crécy may have some ground in fact;[17] the aftermath, however, in which the prince is set free by Philip's brother, Louis count of Alençon, is not really credible:

> Louis count of Flanders saw all this [i.e. the capture of Edward]; he had been chased out of his county and had been in Paris in the pay of the French king for a long time. He was an old man, a good and honest person. He loved King Philip and the king's honour. He saw this treachery in the midst of the French lords. He raised his voice and said: 'Ah, count of Alençon, this is not the loyalty and faithfulness with which you should serve the crown. The war was won and you have lost it.' When the count of Alençon heard this, he did not want to hear any more. He turned the head of his destrier and with the same mace gave the old count of Flanders such a blow that he killed him. What an evil thing that leads to a man being killed for telling the truth and reproving the wicked! Not one of the company of the count of Flanders was moved to do something about this deed. Only a close member of his household, a servant and footsoldier of common lineage, seeing such cruelty, unsheathed his dagger and ran it right through the count of Alençon's belly, so that the count of Alençon, who had betrayed his brother [i.e. Philip], died on the spot. This servant who killed the count of Alençon then went to King Philip and told him he had killed his brother to avenge his master, and proved this by good witnesses. When King Philip heard this he pardoned him and did not take vengeance on him.[18]

This picturesque episode, like many of Froissart's little set pieces, may have no real basis in fact, but it gives a vivid impression of the confusion of the battle, the claims of different loyalties and the possibility of betrayal for whatever reason.

Edward's victory at Crécy meant that there was a real possibility in men's minds that the English might become, if not rulers of France, then a major political and military force throughout French lands. The effect was immediate. Edward marched from Crécy to lay siege to Calais, and, as Jonathan Sumption says, 'Edward III had never received as many offers of support from well-placed French noblemen as he did during the eleven months when his army stood immobile outside Calais.'[19] Rebels from Burgundy came to him for help, and were given a generous subsidy; in consequence, the forces of the duke of Burgundy, Philip's brother-in-law, were tied up for most of 1347 dealing with the uprising. Opportunists tried to seize towns and go over to the English side; the most notable case was at Laon, on the edge of the county of Champagne, an area which a decade later was to fall into anarchy.

The most dramatic case of an accusation of treachery occurred in the first weeks of the reign of John II, Philip's successor, in November 1350. Raoul count of Eu, who had been constable of France in 1346 and was captured by Thomas Holland at Caen, came to Paris on parole to raise his ransom. Jean le Bel captures the mood of the events which followed, a bolt from the blue which no one seemed to understand:

> When he arrived back in France he went to see King John, expecting a fond welcome – he'd loved the count well enough before he became king. The count bowed to him in humble greeting, and expected to be warmly and joyfully received after five years as a prisoner in exile. King John led him into a chamber alone and said:
>
> 'Look at this letter. Familiar, is it?'
>
> They say the Constable was utterly dumbstruck when he saw it; and seeing his shock, the king cried:
>
> 'Ah, wicked traitor! Death is what you deserve, and you'll have it, by my father's soul!'
>
> And he ordered his guards to seize him there and then and imprison him in the tower at the Louvre in Paris, where the Count of Montfort had been held – and had died, so it's said. Everyone was distressed that the worthy Constable should be so treated, for he was much loved, and no one could understand the king's motives. And next day the king swore to all the Constable's friends who were pleading on his behalf that before he ever slept again he would have him beheaded, and no one would persuade him otherwise. And indeed it was done that very night, in the tower

of the Louvre,[20] without any trial or judgement, much to the grief and anger of everyone, and it earned the king great reproach and cost him much love. No one but the king's innermost circle knew why it had happened, but some guessed that the king had been informed of some liaison that had either occurred or been planned between his wife the lady Bonne and the worthy Constable. I don't know if there was any truth in this, but the way in which it happened made many people suspect it.[21]

The wild rumours were probably very wide of the mark: Matteo Villani reports a violent argument between the English and French ambassadors at the papal court a little later, in which it emerged that the count of Eu had arranged to sell the castle of Guines near Calais to Edward to settle his ransom, which he was otherwise unable to pay. It was his property, but it was also a French fief, and a key fortress on the French border. It was almost certainly this that John II regarded as treachery; the King's fury meant that there was no trial and a summary execution.[22]

It was a disastrous move, and one which unsettled and alienated his supporters. The morale of the French nobility, already damaged by Crécy, was now further lowered by this arbitrary act of tyranny. John was widely condemned, and it is possible that Edward may have enacted the Statute of Treasons in the parliament of 1352 partly in response to this dramatic episode. The statute strictly defined treason and limited it to physical attacks on the royal family or plots against them, making war against the king or helping his enemies, forgery of royal documents or counterfeiting money or killing senior royal officials. As in France, treason had begun to mean in English law an infringement of the king's rights as well as the direct actions defined in the statute. The charge of treason had also been widely – and often, but not always, correctly – used in his father's reign. The 1352 statute reassured the English nobility that they were not going to be exposed to the instant and unjust judgement of a furious king, as seemed to be the case in France, and reinforced the trust between Edward III and his magnates.[23]

The case of the count of Eu is made all the more dramatic because John II was much admired by his contemporaries; he is generally portrayed as benevolent and merciful. However, he was subject to sudden rages, and the extremely sensitive threat of treachery evidently roused this devastating anger. Petrarch admired him, and he is described as dignified and intelligent, a lover of luxury (though too liberal in his gifts) and a great hunter, an enthusiasm which Petrarch counts as one of his faults. His health was not good, and he was seriously ill in 1335 and 1344; doctors and surgeons were always near at hand. Perhaps because of this, he was not skilful with weapons: at the marriage feast of his younger brother, Philip duke of Orléans, he was unseated in the first joust by the lord of St Venant. His courage at Poitiers was perhaps unexpected: he was a relatively seasoned campaigner, but had never fought in a major battle. He was intellectually curious, a great reader and very interested in music: it was he who was the real founder of the great royal library usually connected with his son Charles V.[24]

John II was not the only man in France to mete out summary justice – or perhaps injustice. French politics, already complicated enough by Edward III's challenge to the throne, were made even more fraught by the activities of Charles king of Navarre, who (as if by contrast to John II, nicknamed 'the Good') has gone down in history as 'the Bad'. He too had a claim to the French throne. He had inherited the kingdom of Navarre through his mother, who was the daughter of Louis X. As daughter of the eldest son, if the French throne too could pass through the female line as Edward argued, she gave Charles a better claim than Edward. But the resources of Navarre were nothing like those of England, and Charles vented his frustration by muddying the turbulent waters of French politics throughout his lifetime. Unfortunately for John II, he inherited the kingdom of Navarre a year before John himself came to the throne, along with a handful of fiefs in Normandy. His mother should have inherited Champagne while she was still a child, a huge territory in eastern France, but her uncle, Philip V, had deprived her of it, and the Norman estates were a poor compensation.

None of this would have been serious had not Charles been the ultimate self-seeking politician, charming, witty and eloquent, a small, highly ambitious man, with the ability to win over great nobles or the common people to his cause. Soon after inheriting Navarre, he married John II's daughter and thus became part of the inner circle of John's court. But he had no great estates to keep him occupied – he visited Navarre only for his coronation, and thereafter avoided it for the next decade – and neither power nor position at court. His mother's loss of Champagne still rankled, and he was too ambitious to be content with anything less than a major and powerful role in French political life.

John was generous, to the despair of his treasury, but not always in the right way. Charles desperately needed money and estates and was promised both by John; but neither the lordships which were rightfully his nor the cash was forthcoming.

Furthermore, John was lavishing gifts on his favourite, a Spaniard called Charles de la Cerda, great-grandson of Alfonso X of Castile. His father had been the rightful heir to the Spanish throne, but had never been able to make good his claim against his brother, Sancho IV. Charles himself was a good soldier, and was making his way in the world as a commander: he seems to have been in charge of the Castilian galleys at the battle off Winchelsea in 1350. In 1352, among John's lavish gifts to him was the county of Angoulême, which had been exchanged by Charles of Navarre's mother for the lands they had never received in Normandy. Charles of Navarre's quarrel with Charles de la Cerda dates from this point; these two proud and arrogant characters were obvious rivals. The court quickly divided into two factions, and Charles of Navarre began to bring in Navarrese troops: if Navarre was poor in revenues, it had a high population, and was a natural source of hardy soldiers, who sought their fortunes elsewhere. He was intent on recovering the Norman lands to which he was entitled, and by 1353 there was a serious threat of civil war. But Charles of Navarre's first objective was to remove the man he saw as the obstacle to his advancement, and his brother Philip deliberately picked a quarrel with de la Cerda at the royal court at Christmas, during which weapons were drawn and insults exchanged. Barely two weeks later, Charles de la Cerda was assassinated by mercenaries led by Philip of Navarre, who trapped him in his bedroom in an inn in southern Normandy.

It was the beginning of a career of treachery, double-crossing and alliances and treaties made and broken which was to last for thirty years. Charles of Navarre seriously damaged John II's ability to rebuild the French military effort in the years before Poitiers; the exasperated king finally seized him in April 1356, and he was held in prison until he escaped in the chaos after the defeat at Poitiers. Once again his activities undermined attempts to restore some sort of order to the French kingdom. He was still actively scheming during the prince of Wales's expedition to Spain in 1367.

THE FRENCH ROYAL COUNCIL AND THE KING'S ADMINISTRATION

Charles of Navarre in himself would have been a serious obstacle to French success, but he was a symbol of the deeper weakness of the French kings. The emergence of a strong administration led by a council largely drawn from its ranks was theoretically an ideal structure for supporting the French royal power; but it largely sidelined the aristocracy who had until then been the king's advisers, separated the military and civil leadership, and meant that the court had become a largely ceremonial affair. In the face of defeat, it was the nobles who were blamed for military disaster, not only by the populace at large, but also by the civil servants in Paris. The atmosphere surrounding John II was poisoned with accusations and suspicions, and the king himself was far from immune from them.

When John II was captured at Poitiers, the dauphin Charles attempted to act as regent in the turbulent aftermath. He faced the hostility of the citizens of Paris during three years of violence in which the city fell variously under the control of the reforming 'Council of Eighty', the partisans of the king of Navarre, and the provost, Étienne Marcel. After the latter's death at the hands of the mob he had once encouraged, Charles managed to rebuild, slowly, a semblance of orderly governance; but he himself was tainted by his flight from the battlefield at Poitiers. Just as he was beginning the work of reconstruction, he was taken ill, an illness which left him too weak to wield a weapon; ten years later he was unable to ride a horse, and the sickness recurred at intervals for the rest of his life. But he was far more astute than his father and grandfather, and had one great ambition: to drive the English out of France. He pursued this single-mindedly for the whole of his reign, ignoring all the tenets of knightly superiority, and recruiting like-minded advisers, shrewd political operators who formed the new administration. Soon after he came to the throne, he sent one of his council to the count of Foix. They met at a small village on the northern border of the count's territories, and talked privately in a garden by the river. It so happened that one of the prince of Wales's agents was in the neighbouring garden, and overheard the entire conversation, which set out Charles's strategy in detail, and wrote at once to report it to his master. In summary, the councillor declared, Charles would respond favourably to English proposals until he had recovered all the hostages for John's ransom who were still in England, and then 'he would make war everywhere on the English and on the principality [of Aquitaine], because . . . King Charles will be emperor and will recover everything lost to the English and finally he will destroy them'.[25]

In England, Edward's inner circle of advisers was consistent throughout his reign, the only dramatic changes being in the crisis of 1340/41; even then, Archbishop Stratford, who was dismissed as leader of the regency council, was on good terms with the king two years later, and there was an orderly succession to the great offices of state. In France, the king's council and the great officers of state who might have provided some degree of continuity between the reigns of Philip, John and Charles failed to do so. A handful of loyal servants remained in office for long periods, but the membership of the council was often as much a political plaything as the composition of the royal court.

Part of the problem was that the French royal family was much more numerous. Edward III had only one brother, John of Eltham, who died without children in 1336, and two sisters, both of whom married abroad. By 1340, his only surviving cousins were the Bohun brothers Humphrey and William, the earls of Hereford and Northampton, both good friends of the king and staunchly loyal to him. By contrast, the French king had numerous close relatives, as we have seen in the convoluted history of the claims to the French throne. Even if they were not in a position to claim the throne, the royal peers pursued their own agenda. On a personal level, they regarded Philip VI as 'first among equals'; he had been one of them before he became king, whereas Edward had always been heir to the throne, and thus set apart. Geographically, the problems of ruling distant provinces were obviously much greater in France, and the structure of the kingdom was that of a tightly held centre, the ancient royal domains around Paris, with a loose ring of semi-independent territories extending outwards from that centre.

The twelve peerages of France went back to Charlemagne's time, and the 'twelve peers' appear in the epic *Song of Roland* as the leaders of his army and his councillors. When Louis X had died in 1316, there were six ecclesiastical peers, and six dukes and counts who were lay peers, holding the great fiefs of Burgundy, Aquitaine, Flanders, Brittany, Artois and Anjou. In the troubled succession of the next decade, a further eight peerages were created, and this process continued until 1360, when the total of lay peerages reached twenty-four. Many of these peerages were territorially as large as or larger than the duchy of Lancaster, the greatest of the English lordships, and far more independent.

The leading figures in the French royal council under Philip were, at the outset, those peers who had backed his claim to the throne together with the leading crown servants from his predecessor's day, who included Pierre Roger, later to become Pope Clement VI. By 1335, the dominant figure was Mile de Noyers, an elder statesman among the French administrators. Born in 1270, he had a distinguished military career, and had fought in the Flemish wars from 1302 onwards: he was marshal of France from 1303 onwards. At Mons-en-Pévèle, he had saved the sacred French standard, the *oriflamme*, and it was he who alerted Philip to the surprise attack by the Flemish at Cassel in 1328. He was one of Louis X's executors, and a valued councillor under his two successors. Charles de la Cerda had been brought up under his tutelage. He was from northern Burgundy, and was close to the duke, Eudes IV; the Burgundian influence on Philip's council was resented by the other peers, but Noyers was astute enough to keep a relatively low profile, and never to appear to be the sole author of royal policy, though at times this was in fact true. He is said to have warned Philip against engaging the English at Crécy. Noyers was one of the very few figures in the administration who offered some kind of continuity.

After the disaster at Crécy, the royal council began to meet with much greater frequency, and there was an attempt to set up a commission of reform to deal with the causes of the defeat and the weakness of the government. However, after the fall of Calais, the three abbots who had been charged with this task were replaced by career civil servants, because the reforms had not produced results quickly enough to avert Philip's humiliating withdrawal. The council continued to meet very regularly, and from 1348 onwards John II, then duke of Normandy, was in effective charge of the government. It was at this point that Charles de la Cerda first appears as John's closest confidant. However, the council was to prove a weakness rather than a strength: it was more powerful than the informal English council, and nearer to those in Castile and Hungary, ruled by French dynasties.[26]

THE FRENCH COMMANDERS
AND THE FRENCH ARMY

In England, the royal household knights formed an influential group, not because of their specific office, but because they were the close companions of the king and were, so to speak, the pool of talent from which his commanders (and councillors) were drawn. In France, the *chevaliers du roi* were much less important, and were simply a royal bodyguard. This was mainly due to the far greater number of high-ranking magnates in France, who expected to hold high office under the king. Edward, on the other hand, had to create magnates in order to lead his armies. However, military offices were often held by lesser lords: the counts of Eu, both named Raoul, constables in succession from 1329 to 1350, had relatively modest estates in north-eastern France, and the large ransom demanded for the second of them after he was captured at Caen in 1346 reflected his military importance rather than his wealth. Charles de la Cerda and Jacques de Bourbon, their successors, were both members of the royal family, but were able commanders who had earned a good reputation before their appointment. Neither had had experience of a major campaign or a major battle. After Poitiers, where Walter de Brienne, appointed constable earlier that year, was killed, the post went to Robert Moreau de Fiennes, about whom relatively little is known, other than a minor role in the counter-attacks on Calais in 1347. He held the post until 1370, when he resigned in favour of Bertrand du Guesclin, the nemesis of the English armies in the last years of Edward III.

Bertrand du Guesclin is the most successful figure among the French commanders, accorded heroic status in the epic poem written about him by Cuvelier shortly after his death in 1380. He came from the kind of family which, on both sides of the Channel, often produced distinguished soldiers: a knightly family of small resources, where an ambitious young man could only make his way in the world by winning a reputation in the field. His forebears played their part in local politics and local campaigns, and most of them were knights: Bertrand himself was knighted at the relatively advanced age of thirty-four. The first trace of his military career is only a year earlier, in the Breton war between Charles de Blois and Jean de Montfort, but it was he who in 1356 inflicted a major defeat on Henry of Grosmont by his successful defence of the city of Rennes, the first reverse that the English commander had ever suffered. It was this that made his reputation: rewarded with £200 for his 'loyal and profitable services to the king in the war and in the defence of Rennes',[27] he was made captain of Mont-Saint-Michel. He fought against the English in the Reims campaign of 1359–60, and then returned to his home territory as the king's lieutenant in southern Normandy; in 1364 he defeated the English at Cocherel, taking the Anglo-Gascon leader the captal de Buch prisoner: the French fought with the war cry 'Notre-Dame, Guesclin',[28] the count of Auxerre's son, who was nominally in charge, having declined the honour. The tables were turned in the autumn of 1364, when he was defeated, and Charles de Blois killed, at the battle of Auray. Here he was taken prisoner for the third time by the English. He was leader of the free companies who deposed Pedro in 1366, and fought against the prince of Wales and Pedro the following year at Najéra, where he was taken prisoner for the fourth time. In 1370 he became constable, and took charge of the war of attrition which was to lead to serious losses on the part of the English; at his death he was accorded the honour of burial in St Denis near Paris, alongside the French kings.

The constable was overall commander; below him were the marshals; there were four at the time of both Crécy and Poitiers, but there were sometimes as many as six. They often acted as leaders of a campaign or of local forces: Robert Bertrand, who was in charge of the militia who briefly opposed the English landing at La Hogue in 1346, had been deputed to guard the Norman coast, with wholly inadequate resources. His campaigning experience was limited to the French manoeuvres in response to Edward's attack on the Flemish border in 1339–40, but he had commanded successful raids in the Channel, and had taken Guernsey in 1338; he was given the lordship of the Channel Islands, and returned to attempt to take Jersey in 1339. The galleys he was employing were needed for a raid on Gascony, and he had to withdraw in the face of a very small English garrison.

Three marshals stand out: Arnoul d'Audrehem, Jean de Clermont and Jean le Meingre, known as Boucicaut. Audrehem was marshal from 1351 to 1370, and fought at both Poitiers and Najéra. Froissart describes him as serving in Scotland with a contingent sent to reinforce the Scots under the count of Eu in 1332, and returning there in 1340 and 1341.

He fought in Brittany in 1342, and in Aquitaine with John II when he was duke of Normandy in 1346. He became the royal captain at Angoulême in 1349, and was captured in a skirmish with the English in 1351. He was appointed marshal in that year, and played a very active role in the next five years, firstly in the south-west and then in Normandy, where du Guesclin served under him, and was knighted in his presence; but he was also among the party who arrested Charles of Navarre in April 1356. He was given custody of him, and rewarded with an annual income of 1,000 *livres tournois*.

Poitiers was his first major battle, and the disagreement between him and Jean de Clermont, the other marshal, was one of the major factors in the French defeat. Clermont argued for caution, realizing that, if the English were prevented from moving south towards their own territory, shortage of supplies might force them to surrender. Audrehem's wish for an immediate attack was fulfilled, and he was captured, while Clermont fought to the death. Audrehem remained for the most part in England until agreement was reached on his ransom, which was to be paid by John II, in 1362; Edward evidently admired him, since he was granted a pension on his departure. He spent the next five years trying to control the free companies in Languedoc, but became commander, with du Guesclin, of these very same men on the Spanish expedition of 1366 in support of Henry of Trastamara.

Jean le Meingre also had experience of English captivity; he was taken prisoner three times, the third being at Romorantin in the month before the battle of Poitiers, in the year that he was appointed marshal. He had fought in Gascony from 1349 to 1352, and had been captured in minor engagements at Lusignan and Agen. In 1355 he was still on parole for ransom, and was unable to take up arms against Edward when the king made a foray from Calais in November of that year, but he was able to enter the English camp freely, and to report on the strength of the English army. Neither side, however, was strong enough to risk a battle. Despite a great reputation for prowess and knightly exploits, his military record lacks any notable campaigns or successes.

The French constables and marshals were not without experience in the field; indeed, they were often under arms for long periods, but they had never had the chance to learn hard lessons on the battlefield similar to Edward's ventures in Scotland in the 1330s, and, because few of them fought more than once in a formal battle, they failed to get the measure of the English tactics. John II used the technique of dismounting his knights at Poitiers on the advice of the Scottish knight William Douglas, but that in itself was not enough: the English commanders in a similar situation would have known that to attack an army which had entrenched itself in a reasonably strong position on a hillside was to invite disaster, particularly with knights unused to entering the action on foot. By comparison with the English leaders, those in charge of the French army were mostly – through no fault of their own – lacking in military skills.

The English army after 1342 had a strong and resilient structure, based on the recruitment of retinues by the knights, bannerets and lords who were to fight with them. In effect, the leaders of the units of the army were able to choose their men. The French still relied heavily on the *arrière-ban*, a summons invoking the general duty of all able-bodied men to fight in the defence of the kingdom: it was proclaimed seven times between 1338 and 1356. (It is fair to say, that in the same circumstances, faced with an invading French army, the English kings might also have used the feudal summons.) The problem was that these generalized summonses were much less effective: the structure of the army was much looser, and with the *arrière-ban* it was more difficult to exercise control over the disparate levies that arrived in response to the summons. For a start, service could be commuted by payment of what was a kind of war tax; this was particularly true of the non-noble participants, who would be assessed at so many men at arms for a number of hearths. They could – but rarely did – recruit the men at arms themselves and send them off to the army; or they could pay a set rate per man at arms. The results of the *arrière-ban* were therefore to some extent unpredictable, and matters were further complicated by those communities which chose to send their own men. The militia from the towns were unreliable into the bargain: at Crécy, only the men from Orléans stayed with the army for the actual battle. The towns also had their own crossbowmen, for the purposes of defence; these troops were much more valuable than the infantry, and continued to be sent once the attempt to get some military value out of the town militias had been abandoned.

It was primarily on the great nobles – as in England – that the core of recruitment depended. The use of the *arrière-ban* did not cover the feudal obligations of the nobles, but the feudal summons was always used alongside it. The system of written contracts (letters of retinue) was used in France in similar form to that in England, but because the French were fighting a defensive war, it was rare for the length of service to be specified: there was a period for which a first payment was made (the *prêt*) followed by an indefinite time served for wages (*caissement*). The actual rates of pay were not dissimilar, but the *prêt* was less generous than the *regard* paid in England. Furthermore, wages in France were not payable by the leader of a retinue or company, but were left to the king's war treasurers, who were renowned for the slowness of their payments;[29] the English system meant that the war was funded by a number of relatively wealthy individuals, who were either able to use their influence to get payment, or could afford to help the king by waiting for settlement.

In England, the recruitment areas were a very simple division between north and south, those who fought in Scotland and those who fought on the Continent. The French had a number of fronts on which they might be fighting, and recruited accordingly. In 1340 Philip had three theatres of war: Flanders, the Norman coast and Gascony, and later in the reign Brittany became another area of engagement. Recruitment was much more local, and even in the main army that assembled at Bouvines in 1340, the majority of the French contingent, 60 per cent of the troops, were from the north of the Loire. What was more striking was that one-third of the whole army consisted of knights from outside France – mostly from the borders of the German-speaking lands nearest to France. The French were used to using mercenaries, and had done regularly since the twelfth century: the large groups of Genoese crossbowmen and galley crews were the most prominent of these. The lords and the knights of the Holy Roman Empire came in smaller groups, but some of these came from families with a long tradition of service in France.

The cohesion of the French armies was undoubtedly weaker than that of the English in the two major battles of the period. The French army that fought at Crécy in 1346 consisted of four elements: the French feudal nobility and their retinues, the troops from the Holy Roman Empire, including Philip's allies and the traditional hired knights, the infantry from the towns summoned under the *arrière-ban*, and the Genoese crossbowmen. Philip had gathered his forces as best he could on hearing of the English landing, but there seems to have been little organization beforehand. The first gathering point was Rouen at the end of July, by which time the English had been in the field for three weeks; one of the reasons that Philip was not prepared to give battle in early August was that his full complement of men had not yet arrived, and some had come reluctantly, 'amazingly ill-armed'.[30] When Philip withdrew towards Paris, he was still receiving reinforcements, and the final rendezvous point was on the march north, at Amiens. Even so, large contingents had not reached the army by the time of the battle; they arrived in disorderly fashion on the day after the main action and were in turn overcome by superior English forces.

The leaders of the French army were the king and three great lords, his brother Charles d'Alençon, his nephew Louis de Blois and his cousin Louis de Nevers, count of Flanders. The largest foreign contingent was led by King John of Bohemia and his son Charles. The constable of France, Raoul count of Eu, who should have been the overall commander of the army, was not present for the simple reason that he had been captured earlier in the campaign. In his absence, his duties on the field were fulfilled by the marshals, of whom there were four at the time: Robert Bertrand, the commander who had failed to prevent the English landing at La Hogue, and three others, who may or may not have been there: Charles de Montmorency, Robert de Waurin and Guy de Nesle. The core of the French army had gathered in Paris about three weeks earlier, but the bulk of the army that arrived on the battlefield had only been together since Amiens, which it had left on 23 August, and reinforcements had probably arrived during the march. There had been no time for proper organization, or for an array of troops on the day of the battle itself, and the undisciplined nature of the French attack implies that this was not a coherent fighting force, but a loosely grouped set of units. The size of the French armies, consistently larger than the English, and the fact that there were ten separate battalions to control, required a far stronger command structure and left little room for improvisation if matters were not to get out of hand. The issue was further complicated by the way in which men were allocated to the different battalions: on arrival at the assembly point for the army, their mounts and equipment would be inspected, and they would then be told which battalion to join. As the bulk of the army were often individual knights, there were none of the links that existed within an English retinue, and very little *esprit de corps.*

At Poitiers a decade later, the problems were of a different nature. The large size of the army was possibly less of a disadvantage, but the army had again assembled in an ad hoc fashion, and only moved as a body on 6 September, when the king left Chartres. The results of three months of effort, with the *arrière-ban* proclaimed no less than three times, were unimpressive; the treasury was empty, and the knights knew that they might well serve for a very delayed reward. The shortage of money also meant that there was little hope of attracting the imperial knights who had been present in large numbers at Crécy. There were far too many infantry, largely of poor quality, and not enough mounted troops. A planned campaign in Gascony against the prince of Wales by the count of Poitiers had been cancelled, and his army, such as it was, was instructed to move northwards to hold the Loire against the prince until such time as the king's army could join it. The two armies met on 10 September, and therefore fought the battle only nine days after they had first come together, and only a fortnight after the royal army had moved off from Chartres. The morale of the French was an important factor in the battle; most of the troops led by Philip duke of Orléans and other battalions left the field without striking a blow, perhaps because they had seen the dauphin Charles being escorted to safety. An army with better cohesion would not have done this.

The English army had become skilled on the battlefield, and the lessons learnt at Crécy and Poitiers would be remembered at Agincourt; but battles alone did not win wars, and the English triumphs were countered, after terrible civil disturbances, by a system which used the vast resources of the French monarchy to deploy proper defences and to ensure good government. The English were unable to follow up their great victories in 1346 and 1356 by establishing themselves across wide areas in France which would recognize Edward's rule. The Reims campaign of 1359–60 was intended to produce a *coup d'état*, the coronation of Edward III as king of France, rather than a conquest, but the French defeated Edward by strengthening their towns and stubbornly refusing the lure of knightly glory on the battlefield.

5

'As it was in the days of King Arthur'

We left Edward at the low point of his career in the spring of 1341, his unjustified attacks on the regency administration set aside, and apparently facing serious resistance to his plans. However, by the autumn of that year all the restrictions imposed by parliament had been reversed. On 1 October Edward boldly annulled the legislation, on the grounds that he had been coerced into signing it. Behind this lay a swift personal campaign by Edward to regain the allegiance of the great magnates who had ranged themselves against him. It says much for his personality that he was able to do this, in the face of the record of military failure over the previous three years.

An element in this, which has not previously been noted, seems to have been a series of tournaments held during 1341; the records are almost certainly incomplete, but at least four tournaments are known to have taken place. They began shortly after Edward's return, before the crisis had come to a head. The king celebrated Christmas at Guildford, in Henry III's palace, which had belonged to the queens of England since 1273, and had reverted to the crown after 1330. It was still magnificent, though in need of repairs, with elaborate decoration and glazed windows, and a series of separate apartments for the king, the queen and their son; many rooms had fireplaces, and there were two chapels and a garden with a cloister.[1] He then held a tournament at Reading, followed by another at King's Langley on 2 February, where he knighted a number of Gascon nobles, who had probably come over with Oliver Ingham, the seneschal of Aquitaine, at the end of January. The next tournament was planned while Edward was at King's Langley, and was the traditional Shrovetide occasion to mark the beginning of Lent; it was to be held at Norwich on 20 February and no other tournaments were to be fought in the mean while.[2] The tournament was fought outside the gates of Norwich priory, and Robert Morley, who had contributed so much to the victory at Sluys, was among the participants. The parson of Scole remembered half a century later that he had seen the hero of the hour at those jousts.[3] And another traditional joust was held to mark the churching of Queen Philippa at King's Langley, after the birth of Edmund, her fifth son. This may well have been the first occasion on which William Montagu and Robert Ufford reappeared in the lists after their captivity in France, since the king's team fought bearing shields with the arms of Montagu and Ufford quartered.[4] The king was frequently at King's Langley during the year, and it is difficult to pinpoint the exact date, particularly as he seems to have been hunting there and at Woodstock as well as jousting. The accounts for the year record magnificent hunting costumes, all of green or mulberry Turkish cloth. These were seemingly for just one occasion, the 'king's hunting expedition', on which Edward was accompanied by eleven earls and knights, fifteen royal squires, Queen Isabella, Queen Philippa and four countesses.[5]

The following year, 1342, saw three major festivals.[6] The first was held at Dunstable at Shrovetide, and was specifically to mark the betrothal of Lionel of Antwerp, Edward's third son (at the tender age of three), to the heiress of the earl of Ulster. It may also have been intended to celebrate the recent truce with the Scots, as it was announced as soon as the truce was agreed. The king fought as a simple knight, alongside 'all the younger earls of the kingdom'. The earls of Gloucester, Devon and Surrey excused themselves on the grounds of age, while Richard Fitzalan and William Clinton were ill. Knights came from not only the south, but all parts of England, though no foreign knights were present; the total was more than 200, which was probably why proceedings did not start until it was almost nightfall, 'hindering the whole business so that ten horses were killed or injured'. [7]

This was followed two months later by an event at Northampton on 10 April. The tournament was on a smaller scale, but was marred by the death of John, Lord Beaumont, brother-in-law of Henry of Grosmont; fatalities in Edward's tournaments were rare, but something evidently went badly wrong, since many other nobles were seriously injured and maimed, and many horses were lost. Two months later, in July, the visit to England of Edward's brother-in-law, William II, count of Hainault, was marked by a tournament at Eltham Palace near London. Unfortunately, it was William himself who was injured on this occasion, breaking his arm.[8]

All these tournaments were good publicity, a means of rallying the great lords and the wealthy citizens behind him; and this harmony between the king and his magnates was to last until the very end of his reign. Edward's frequent appearances as *miles simplex*, a simple knight, emphasized his solidarity with the leading lords of the kingdom, fighting alongside them on equal terms. The king had not only made himself the chief promoter of the sport of jousting, once a potential rallying point for dissenting barons, but had made it one of his best methods of keeping the nobles on his side. And there was now the prospect of a new and more promising strategy in France. Instead of a full-scale invasion of France, Edward preferred for the moment to achieve his ends by stirring up trouble between Philip VI and his vassals. In a sense, this had already begun when Edward sheltered Robert d'Artois; Edward's proclamation of himself as rightful king of France meant that anyone who went over to his side was simply recognizing his claim. Any disgruntled vassal could offer his allegiance to Edward if he felt it was worth his while.

Although the truce of Esplechin was extended until June 1342, Edward was not going to miss any opportunities, and Adam Murimuth noted that, at the same time as the extension was negotiated, 'Edward and some of his earls were nonetheless making great arrangements for ships and victuals for an overseas expedition'.[9] Edward, acting in his right as king of France, backed the young heir of Brittany, Jean de Montfort, in his claim to the duchy, in opposition to Philip's candidate, his nephew Charles de Blois. There was little to choose between the rivals, because the previous duke of Brittany, Jean III, had tried to disinherit Jean de Montfort, who was his half-brother, in favour of his niece Jeanne, married to Philip's nephew, only to change his mind shortly before he died. Philip regarded this as an internal affair, though he knew that military action would provoke English intervention, and undeclared war followed in Brittany in 1341. Philip did all he could to prise Brittany from the English grasp without actually mounting a campaign. Edward recruited important allies among the French nobility, Olivier Clisson and Godefroy d'Harcourt, and was able to recruit disaffected nobles in Gascony, while his Breton allies continued a guerrilla war against the French. Jean de Montfort was himself an English magnate, since he was heir to the earldom of Richmond.

Although military aid was agreed in the autumn of 1341, Jean de Montfort himself was captured in late November, and it was left to the countess, his wife Jeanne de Montfort, to rally his supporters. It was the following year before a small force under Walter Mauny sailed to support the Montfortists, with instructions to secure the westernmost ports for the two expeditions which were to follow later in the year. He landed at Brest; his troops consisted of 128 knights and squires, and 200 mounted archers,[10] while Charles de Blois had a substantial army in the field, and had already taken the eastern cities of Nantes and Rennes. The countess had established her headquarters at Hennebont, and shortly after Mauny's arrival was besieged by the French army. The French started to skirmish with the garrison, but were driven back, at which point a full-scale, disorderly assault on the town was ordered. This ended with a counter-attack by the garrison, who burnt the French camp, but the French returned soon afterwards. The siege became a series of intermittent attacks and eventually simply an attempt to starve out the defenders. Jean le Bel (and Froissart after him) devotes his account of the campaign of 1342 largely to an account of Walter Mauny's exploits. These are certainly splendid embroideries of the real facts: while there is no evidence to counter the idea that he appeared at Hennebont to encourage the countess in her resistance, it is unlikely that he got into the castle and led sorties against the French as a kind of pre-dinner entertainment, as Le Bel would have us believe. His activities were low key, given his small resources, but did include an enterprising raid to capture one of the leading French supporters of Charles de Blois, Hervé lord of Léon. Mauny handed him over to Edward III, who gave him to Montagu to guard, and then used him, along with the captured Scottish regent, Andrew Murray, to secure Montagu's release from his oath never to fight again in France.

Mauny returned home in July to report that the Montfortist cause was in serious trouble. Charles de Blois had recruited reinforcements, who reached Brittany early in July, and forced the countess to abandon Hennebont and flee to Brest, where she was besieged by them from mid-August onwards. She had some English soldiers with her, led by Hugh Despenser (son of Edward II's notorious favourite), who had come into one of the Breton ports on his way to Gascony with Oliver Ingham, and had found the situation so desperate that he decided to stay. A month later, a second, much-delayed English expedition under William Bohun,

Ralph Stafford and Robert d'Artois sailed into the great harbour at Brest and surprised the fourteen Genoese galleys at anchor there. Eleven were burnt, and three escaped upstream where the English ships could not follow.[11] Bohun's fleet was large for the number of men it carried: almost half the ships were intended for naval actions. So the French grossly overestimated the army he led, and at once raised the siege, retreating to the north and east, and leaving the Montfort party in control of western Brittany.

It was the only real success of the year. Bohun attempted to follow it up by securing a port which would be more accessible from England, on the northern coast of Brittany: to reach Brest, the fleet had had to round cape Finisterre, heading south into the Atlantic and then east into the harbour. Morlaix, thirty miles away, could be reached without this difficult passage, as it lay north-east of the cape. But the defenders were on the alert by the time Bohun moved against the town, and he had to settle down to a long siege while he waited for the third expedition, under Edward himself, to arrive.

On 29 September Bohun's scouts reported the arrival of a French army. Charles de Blois had come to raise the siege, and Bohun risked being caught between troops sallying out of the town and the advancing enemy. That night, he moved his men to a site near a wood. His men dismounted, and fought in a solid phalanx with their backs to the trees. Bohun, a veteran of the Scottish wars, does not seem to have used the usual tactic of placing archers on the flanks, as he had too few men; instead, he dug pits in front of the line, and camouflaged them with greenery from the woods behind his position. The French vanguard, led by Geoffroy de Charny, were unable to reach the English line in good order because of these traps, and were thrown back; a second charge met with the same fate, and the French fled. Fifty French knights were killed, and about 150 captured. The fight at Morlaix was the fiercest encounter with the French before the battle of Poitiers, according to Geoffrey le Baker.[12] The result was indecisive: although the French cavalry were driven off, the English had to take refuge in the forest to avoid the large numbers of enemy troops in the area.

There had been huge problems in gathering the fleet for the king's expedition, and Edward had been at Sandwich since the end of August. He was hoping to employ the ships that had returned from transporting

Bohun's army, but half of these deserted, and a desperate search for boats, even small ones, ensued. When Edward finally sailed on 3 October, his luck in crossing the Channel for once deserted him. He later claimed that whenever he sailed for his kingdom of France the wind was always with him; it was only when he tried to return that he met storms and gales. But this time it took him three weeks, and some of his troops had to be marched to Portsmouth to embark.[13]

When he at last reached Brittany at the end of October, his plan was to retake Vannes, on the south coast of Brittany, which, like Brest, had a good harbour, and was in the centre of the territories where support for the Montforts was strong. Walter Mauny was sent to reconnoitre, and reported that there were potential faults in the defences which looked promising. However, by the time Edward arrived in late November, the defenders were very much on the alert. Edward had left the English fleet under the command of Robert d'Artois, the man who had been one of the key factors in triggering the Anglo-French war. He took the ships south, sailing past Vannes, and attacked the galleys from Castile and Genoa whose services the French had engaged. He was driven off, losing both large numbers of ships and many of his men; but undeterred he headed back to Vannes and, again entirely on his own initiative, attempted a surprise attack, which proved fatal both to him and to Edward's plans. At first it almost succeeded, but he did not have enough men to follow up his advantage, and was wounded in the fray. He encamped nearby, caught dysentery and died, cursed by the French and not greatly loved by the English.

The foray by Artois meant that any hope of surprising Vannes was lost, and Edward had to settle in for a winter siege. The small size of his force, no more than 5,000 men, meant that his options were limited, but Bohun's men operated as raiders and attacked Nantes itself with the help of Thomas Beauchamp and his retinue in December, while Montagu led a handful of men to raid the area round Dinan in the north-east. The English had made their presence felt the length and breadth of Brittany, but desperately needed reinforcements if they were to hold their gains, since a French army under John duke of Normandy was on its way. But the bad weather and difficulties of recruitment which had hampered the year's operations continued: the army which was meant to leave Plymouth on 3 November failed to do so because of a lack of ships, and was then driven ashore on the Scilly Isles. Hugh Audley and

Laurence Hastings managed to cross with their personal retinues, but in the interval 400 Welsh troops had come to the end of their contracted term and had returned home.

When the French forces eventually reached Brittany in January 1343, they came within twenty miles of Edward's army, but then refused to commit themselves to a battle. The pope had sent two cardinals to Brittany the previous summer in an attempt to secure a truce, and both sides were now prepared to talk to them. Edward was able to conceal the weakness of his position, and managed to retain all the lands he had taken during the year; Vannes was to be neutral for the duration of the truce; and Jean de Montfort was to be released by the French. The truce was intended to last until 29 September 1346.

Edward never returned to Brittany, and the war there was largely carried on by a series of commanders of lesser rank, who became specialists in Breton affairs, men such as John Hardreshull, William Latimer and Thomas Dagworth; William Bohun was to return in the summer of 1345, and in 1354–58 Thomas Holland and Henry of Grosmont were named as the king's lieutenants in Brittany. It remained an important but rather separate theatre of war, and after the war of 1341–3 the only other member of Edward's inner circle of commanders to appear there was John Chandos.

Edward did not take seriously the avowed reason for the truce, which was to enable a peace conference to take place at Avignon. At the end of 1343, although there were no specific plans for a campaign in France, Edward was anticipating renewed fighting; he refused to take the peace talks seriously, sending junior government clerks to meet the French princes of the realm, while supporting the partisans in Brittany. He sent Bartholomew Burghersh the elder to the parliament of May 1343 to explain the situation: and when parliament reconvened in June, the grant of a subsidy specifically stated that 'the many things attempted on the part of the enemy ... were declared in full parliament: and how his said enemy strives as much as he can to destroy our said lord the king, his allies and subjects, lands and places, and the English language'. Edward had neatly extended what was once a dispute over rival claims to the throne of France to cover the very existence of Englishness itself.[14]

Although the next two years brought very mixed success, the effect on French politics was considerable. Philip's relations with his great lords were much less congenial than Edward's; and he reacted violently.

It was at this point that Olivier Clisson was seized on a visit to Paris and summarily executed. His execution may have been politically expedient, but the manner in which it was carried out sent the wrong message to other French nobles who might have a quarrel with Philip: the king was not to be trusted. By 1343, Edward could see the prospect of being able to renew the French war with the aid of disaffected French lords rather than expensive, non-committal foreign allies.

It was clear that the task of gathering an army would not be easy. He had to persuade parliament to vote yet another tax for the purposes of the war, and he had only Flanders on his side on the Continent, which meant that his army would have to be raised almost entirely from within England. The Breton situation was too confused to expect any substantial force from his supporters there, and Gascony needed all the troops he could spare, whether local or English. A measure of the problems he faced is that in 1345, when the Crécy campaign was being planned, he introduced a special bonus for the English men at arms who fought overseas, while on the other hand he introduced a new method of assessing the military liabilities of landowners by relating it to their income.

All this implies deep concern about the levels of recruiting, and Edward enlisted knightly ideals as a means of solving the problem, announcing a great tournament at Windsor in January 1344. At the end of the festival, he declared that he would create a new knightly institution on the model of King Arthur's Round Table, which would also serve as a body of knights personally loyal to him, just as the members of the legendary order owed loyalty to Arthur. This was a strikingly original move, since the idea of a permanent association of knights was almost unknown, and Edward himself had not sought to identify himself with the legendary king until this point.

Contrary to general belief, there is little in the early part of Edward's reign to indicate that he was deeply interested in the Arthurian legend. His grandfather, Edward I, has been described as an 'Arthurian enthusiast',[15] and his involvement in the conquest of Wales was the driving force behind this idea. His Arthurian tournaments and the creation of the Round Table at Winchester all date from the period when he finally defeated Llywelyn the Great. The knighting ceremonies and tournament at Winchester in September 1285, which were the occasion for the making of the Round Table which still hangs in the castle hall, were a direct response to the aftermath of the Welsh wars, designed to impress his subjects and justify the heavy taxes they had paid to support the king's armies.[16] (Ironically, it was on this occasion that Hugh Despenser, the bane of Edward III's youth, was knighted.) After an earlier victory over Llywelyn in 1278, he went to Glastonbury and had the supposed remains of Arthur and Guinevere reinterred before the high altar, 'while the heads and knee-joints of both were kept out for the people's devotion'.[17] In 1284, before his return to England after the final conquest of Wales, he had held a tournament at Nefyn, once a court of the Welsh princes, where the prophecies of Merlin were said to have been found. In 1285, he presented Arthur's crown, which had been surrendered to him by the Welsh when they submitted to him, to Westminster abbey.[18] And he had used Arthur's supposed overlordship of Scotland when arguing his claim for sovereignty over the Scots in a personal letter to the pope in 1301.[19]

Edward III's association with Arthur is much slighter. He went to Glastonbury in 1331, accompanied by Philippa: we have two eyewitness accounts of their visit, but neither makes any mention of the relics of Arthur. He was there again in May 1344; although a royal writ was issued a year later for a certain John Blome of London to search at Glastonbury for the remains of Joseph of Arimathea, there is no evidence to connect the licence with the king's visit to Glastonbury.[20] And he seems to have played no part in the repositioning of Arthur's tomb by Abbot Monington in 1368.[21] Indeed, the supposed Arthurian enthusiasms of Edward III fit better, for the most part, into an effort to emulate his grandfather rather than something he himself felt keenly. It was the chroniclers who were eager to see him as the reincarnation of King Arthur: Jean le Bel compares him to Arthur at the end of the Scottish wars, not because of his military achievements but for the social life he led: 'these great feasts and tourneys and jousts and assemblies of ladies earned him such universal esteem that everyone said he was the second King Arthur.' And he repeats this a few lines below: 'he was so loved and honoured by all his people, great and small alike, for the high nobility of his deeds and words and for his great heart and glorious festivities and assemblies of ladies and damsels, that everyone said he was King Arthur.'[22]

Edward III is assumed to have been a great enthusiast for all things Arthurian, largely on the strength of references to him as the 'new Arthur', and his foundation of a Round Table in 1344. However, what interested him was the Arthur of history portrayed in the chronicles, not the heroes of the Arthurian romances. When we look carefully at the evidence for ownership and readership of Arthurian romances at Edward III's court, it is his mother Isabella who is the most enthusiastic collector and reader of such books.[23] There is a list of issues and receipts from the privy wardrobe during the keepership of John Flete, from 1322 to 1341, including many loans of books.[24] Nine books were issued to Isabella on 5 March 1327; of these, one is a copy of the romance of Perceval. At her death in 1358, Isabella possessed books in French on the deeds of Arthur, on Tristan and Iseult, on Perceval and Gawain, and on the Holy Grail (mistranslated as *de sanguine regali*, 'on the royal blood', because the clerk, unfamiliar with the book, read its title as *sang real*).[25] She also borrowed Arthurian romances from John II of France when he was a captive in England in 1357. Thomas of Woodstock, duke of Gloucester, whose huge collection of books is well documented, possessed two romances of the history of Troy, two of that of Alexander (including the copy written in Tournai in 1344 discussed above), a *Merlin*, a *Lancelot* and a book '*of the Tretys of king Arthur*'.[26] This is a relatively modest element in his collection. It has been argued that John Flete's list, which notes a stock of fifty-nine *libri de romanciis*, indicates widespread reading of romances at Edward's court in his youth and in the early years of his reign.[27] However, *romancia* means a book in a romance language, typically French,[28] as well as what we would now call a romance, and, looking at some of the surviving titles, this figure clearly includes histories in French, French versions of Latin treatises and even a 'romance' Old Testament. The only book of romances actually identifiable as Arthurian is the romance of Perceval. It is suggested that the 160 'various books' in John Flete's accounts represent a royal library, but, remembering that this account covers nearly twenty years, this is too small a number. Furthermore, there is very little evidence that books were sent out and returned; in only one case are books delivered into the great wardrobe, by the keeper of the king's chamber, as part of a miscellaneous collection of items.[29] The list is an incidental accumulation of items which have passed through the hands of the keeper of the great wardrobe, not an organized collection of any kind. Many of the Arthurian books can be connected to Isabella, whose interest in Arthurian romance may have been purely personal, and part of her French cultural background.

The second important list which could be evidence for Edward's reading is a list of books which apparently belonged to him at his death, which were in the care of John Bacon, commissioned to deal with his personal property.[30] Isabella's books officially passed to the king, but he gave away at least one to his sister Joan, queen of Scotland, and Bacon's list includes just three Arthurian books, one of which is probably Isabella's romance of Perceval, described as a romance of Perceval and Gawain.[31] Another is a romance of King Arthur, which could be her French prose romance of the death of Arthur, but equally might be a retelling of the historical story of Arthur in French; and the third is 'a book called Galaath [Galahad]', probably the Grail book belonging to Isabella mistitled '*de sanguine regali*'. Of the remaining nine books, two definitely appear on Isabella's list. Edward's interest in Arthurian romance, such as it was, does not seem to have extended to buying or commissioning manuscripts for his own use.

While Arthurian stories and heroes were very much part of Edward's cultural background, they are not a prominent part of the books that he or his descendants owned. Furthermore, ownership of such books is found mainly among the ladies of the court; the Arthurian romances are specifically part of the cultural heritage of his mother and of his wife. Philippa gave him in 1333 as a new year's gift a ewer with figures of heroes: Julius Caesar, Judas Maccabeus, Charlemagne (with Roland and Oliver) and Arthur, Gawain and Lancelot du Lac. And two items in an inventory of 1369 may have come from her household after her death, a cup with Tristan apparently in the forest, and a ewer decorated with the knights of the Round Table.[32]

Edward need not have owned or even read the romances of Arthur to have learnt about the Round Table and its reputation. There is still much debate as to how common what we would call 'reading' today was in the middle ages. Reading silently to oneself in private may have been the least common way in which manuscripts were used. There is a famous miniature of Chaucer reading his poetry to the court of Richard II, and a century earlier Alfonso X of Castile had prescribed that books of knightly deeds should be read aloud at meals at his court, to encourage the practice of arms and knighthood.[33] Such readings, to larger or smaller groups, would have been the most likely source of Edward's knowledge of the romances. Many more general books on history or on the heroes of the past would mention Arthur in passing, as part of the cultural background of the period. Only once do we find evidence of a more particular interest in Arthur on Edward's part, and we have already discussed it: the curious episode of the 'society of Craddok'. Nor were his tournaments Arthurian, in the way that his grandfather's tournaments appear to have been. There are two occasions when we know that Edward's tournaments had themes: in 1343 he and his knights fought disguised as the pope and twelve cardinals; in 1359 they appeared as the mayor and aldermen.[34] Masks were also frequently provided, though whether these were worn in the lists or at the festivities surrounding the jousting is not clear. There is no sign of Arthurian disguises, only the usual exotic figures such as Tartars and wild men.

This does not mean that Arthurian romances and heroes were absent from Edward's cultural background, but there is no question that they figure only occasionally after he became king. His direct knowledge of Arthur was almost certainly very different. In the romances, Arthur is portrayed as a grand but inert figure, who presides over the court but does not take part in the adventures. For most educated men in the fourteenth century he was quite simply the greatest of the kings of Britain. Edward's image of Arthur was that created by Geoffrey of Monmouth in the first part of the twelfth century, a fiction cheerfully copied into sober histories by chroniclers during the intervening period, and very rarely questioned by other scholars. The closest literary representation of Edward's image of Arthur is that of the alliterative *Morte Arthure*, written in the late fourteenth century when memories of his victories and of the bloody slaughter at Crécy were still fresh. It echoes episodes from his wars, but is by no means a *roman-à-clef*. Arthur's campaigns are not modelled on Edward's – or indeed on anyone else's; its real value is in the very different view of the nature of war from that found in the *Lancelot-Grail* and the romances based on it. War is bloodthirsty, and a means to political ambitions which hardly figure in the world of fiction. Edward would also have been aware at second hand of the Arthurian romances, and of the great Arthurian characters such as Lancelot and Guinevere, perhaps through hearing the stories read or told; this aspect of the Arthurian story, however, was something for a disguise at a tournament or a passing reference in one of his *ludi* at court, not for the serious matter of the king's royal image.

Beyond the specific records of book ownership, we can point to a long family tradition of involvement with Arthurian romance before his grandfather's day, stretching back to the first appearance of the stories in the twelfth century. Henry II was said to have been involved in the discovery of Arthur's tomb at Glastonbury in 1189; Richard I gave a sword said to be Excalibur to Tancred of Sicily in 1191.[35] Edward I, according to Rusticiano of Pisa, who wrote an Italian version of the story of Tristan, took a volume of Arthurian romance to Palestine with him when he went on crusade, and it was from this copy that Rusticiano made his translation.[36] And romances could be heirlooms: Edward II rewarded a minstrel who brought him a book of romance which had belonged to Eleanor of Provence, his grandmother, and had been bequeathed by her to Edward I.[37]

We are fortunate in having what may be a first-hand account of the great festival at Windsor in January 1344. Edward deliberately invited not only knights, but also wealthy citizens from London. It is Adam Murimuth who describes the occasion for us; he was probably either one of the London contingent, or heard about it from a friend who had been there. What he has to say is this:

> In this year the lord king ordered a most noble tournament or joust to be held in his birthplace, that is, at Windsor Castle, on 19 January, which he caused to be announced a suitable time in advance both abroad and in England. He sent invitations to all the ladies of the southern part of England and to the wives of the citizens of London. When the earls, barons, knights and a great number of ladies had gathered on the Sunday, 19 January, the king gave a solemn feast, and the great hall of the castle was filled by the ladies, with just two knights among them, the only ones to have come from France to the occasion. At this gathering there were two queens, nine countesses, the wives of the barons, knights and citizens, whom they could not easily count, and to whom the king himself personally allocated their seats according to their rank. The prince of Wales, duke of Cornwall, earls, barons and knights ate with all the other people in tents and other places, where food and all other necessities had been prepared; everything was on a generous scale and served unstintingly. In the evening dancing and various entertainments were laid on in a magnificent fashion. For the three days following, the king with nineteen other knights held jousts against all comers; and the king himself, not because of his kingly rank but because of his great exertions and the good fortune

that he had during the three days, was held to be the best of the defenders. Of the challengers, Sir Miles Stapleton on the first day, Sir Philip Despenser on the second, and Sir John Blount on the third, were awarded the prize.

Another writer, using Murimuth's account as his base, continues with a detailed description of the elaborate founding ceremony for the Round Table:

This feast lasted from Sunday to Wednesday. That night, after the end of the jousts, the king had it proclaimed that no lord or lady should presume to depart, but should stay until morning, to learn the king's pleasure. When the morning of Thursday came, at about nine o'clock the king caused himself to be solemnly arrayed in his most royal and festive attire; his outer mantle was of very precious velvet and the royal crown was placed upon his head. The queen was likewise dressed in most noble fashion. The earls and barons, and the rest of the lords and ladies, prepared themselves in appropriate fashion to go with the king to the chapel in the castle of Windsor and hear mass, as he commanded them to do. When mass had been celebrated, the king left the chapel; Henry earl of Derby, as steward of England, and William earl of Salisbury, as marshal of England, went before him, each carrying the staff of his office in his hand, and the king himself holding the royal sceptre in his hand. There followed him the young queen, and the queen-mother, the prince of Wales, the earls, barons, knights and nobles, with the ladies and all the people flocking to see such an extraordinary spectacle, to the place appointed for the assembly. There the king and all the others at the same time stood up. The king was presented with the Bible, and laying his hand on the Gospels, swore a solemn oath that he himself at a certain time, provided that he had the necessary means, would begin a Round Table, in the same manner and condition as Arthur, formerly king of England, established it, namely to the number of 300 knights, and would cherish it and maintain it according to his power, always adding to the number of knights. The earls of Derby, Salisbury, Warwick, Arundel, Pembroke and Suffolk, the other barons and very many praiseworthy knights of probity and renown likewise made an oath to observe, sustain, and promote the Round Table with all its appendages. When this was done, trumpets and drums sounded together, and the guests hastened to a feast . . .[38]

The spectacular nature of this occasion was duly relayed to Edward's arch-enemy, Philip of France, and a continuation of the official chronicle of the French court gives us the reaction to it. This ends in 1348, so it is almost contemporary with the event:

> When the king was in England again, he proclaimed very great jousts at a castle of his named Windsor. Knights came from all countries to win praise there. He commanded that the Round Table and the adventures of chivalry which had ceased since the days of King Arthur should be revived; but in his heart he was thinking of very different things, which he did not show outwardly. For all this time he was preparing great ships and gathering great provisions at a port of his called Portsmouth.[39]

For the French, this knightly gathering was simply a smokescreen for Edward's active preparation for the renewal of war, though in fact it was not until March that any active steps were taken towards a new campaign.

Most of the other chroniclers who report the event do so much more briefly, and give us only a few additional details. The author of the English version of the *Brut* chronicle, who like Murimuth had London connections, claims that 'of divers lands beyond the sea, were many strangers'. Edward's letter of protection issued before the feasts and addressed to his officials throughout the kingdom makes no mention of overseas participants, referring only to knights and others 'of whatever region or place', but it does seem from the evidence of the *Brut* and St Omer chronicles that there was a large contingent of visitors from the Continent. Few other chroniclers mention the event; only those close to the court would have regarded it as special, more than just another lavish court spectacle.[40]

A much more valuable source of information is the royal accounts. There is relatively little in the records about the preparation for this great gathering, but two telling details do emerge from the archives. Edward had pawned his great crown, his second crown and Queen Philippa's crown in 1339 when he was desperate for money to pay his allies in Flanders. Such transactions were not uncommon, as jewellery was a form of ready cash or security, but to pawn the great crown as well as two others indicates the seriousness of his situation. In 1343 negotiations had begun for its redemption from the archbishop of Treves and Edward's son-in-law the duke of Guelders, although the principal finance had actually been provided by Vivelin Rufus, a Jew from Strasbourg. It seems to have cost around £8,000 to redeem them all.[41] At the end of 1343 the great crown was still in pawn, but by 16 January of the new year Edward had his second crown back, just in time to wear it at the festivities at Windsor, and he paid the negotiators handsomely for their efforts.

It seems that the preparations for the festival were also made in a hurry, as if the decision to hold the festival had been made on the spur of the moment. Major tournaments usually involved lavish expenditure on costumes designed for the occasion, as well as gifts of robes. However, special costumes are not mentioned in the accounts, and any gifts of robes were probably included in the traditional Christmas handout of robes to courtiers a week or two earlier. We do learn that Edward wore two very expensive suits of red velvet, an exotic import, one long and one short, and consisting of six garments in all. An ermine cloak, for which 369 skins were used, and a smaller mantle of 67 skins, may also have been made for the occasion. At the same time as the suits, 118 tunics for the king's squires, men at arms and minstrels were made. The accountants note that seven furriers worked at great speed for three days to complete these.[42]

Despite the haste, these sound like clothes designed to present an image of majesty rather than the theatricality of earlier tournament clothes, embroidered with mottoes and elaborate pictorial designs. Edward was no longer playing the knight errant but was staking his claim to be regarded as a knightly monarch on a par with Arthur himself. And he proposed to create a building of unparalleled size as the home for his new institution. Thomas Walsingham, writing forty years later at St Albans, a monastery which kept a kind of official royal chronicle in the thirteenth and fourteenth centuries, does not actually mention the festival, although he knows the exact dimension of the house of the Round Table:

> In the year of grace 1344, which is the eighteenth year of Edward's reign, King Edward summoned many workers to Windsor Castle and began to build a house which was called 'The Round Table'. Its size from the centre to the circumference, the radius, was 100 feet, and its diameter was therefore 200 feet. The weekly expenses were at first £100, but afterwards, because of news which the king received from France, this was cut back to £9 because he needed a great deal of money for other business.

At the same time, Philip of Valois, king of France, spurred on by what the king of England had done, began to build a round table in his own country, in order to attract the knights of Germany and Italy, in case they set out for the table of the king of England.[43]

What exactly did Edward have in mind when he proclaimed his Round Table in imitation of King Arthur's original? One possibility is that he was thinking of the Arthurian tournaments of his grandfather, such as the Winchester tournament of 1285, which were called 'round tables'. These may have involved some kind of ceremonial and the formation of a temporary society for the purposes of the jousts. These were relatively common from 1220 to 1330, but rare thereafter, perhaps because they were too closely associated with the Mortimer family for comfort, and indeed the antics of Geoffrey Mortimer just after Edward came to the throne may have brought them into disrepute. The author of the *Brut* chronicle writes:

And about the same time, Sir Geoffrey Mortimer the younger, Mortimer's son, called himself the King of Folly; and he did indeed become the king of folly afterwards, for he was so full of pride and evil ways that he held a round table in Wales for all comers, and imitated the manner and customs of King Arthur's table, but totally failed in his intention, for the noble king Arthur (unlike him) was the most worthy and famous lord in the whole world in his day.[44]

As to the original Round Table, it is so inseparably linked to Arthur in our ideas about the Arthurian legend today that it comes as a surprise to find that the Round Table is not part of the earliest accounts of Arthur. It does not appear in the Welsh stories, nor in Geoffrey of Monmouth, whose *History of the Kings of Britain* created an international audience for Arthur. Geoffrey's Arthur is the archetypal king as conqueror, who wins an empire for himself, and was immediately seen as the greatest figure in the line of British kings: but he has no Round Table of knights.

The Round Table is first mentioned in about 1155 in a free translation of Geoffrey of Monmouth's work into Norman French, some twenty years after the original had appeared. The poet, Robert Wace, came from the Channel Islands, and wrote the *Romance of Brut* for Henry II's court. Wace tells us how Arthur established a new type of seating arrangement at his court which was intended to avoid the

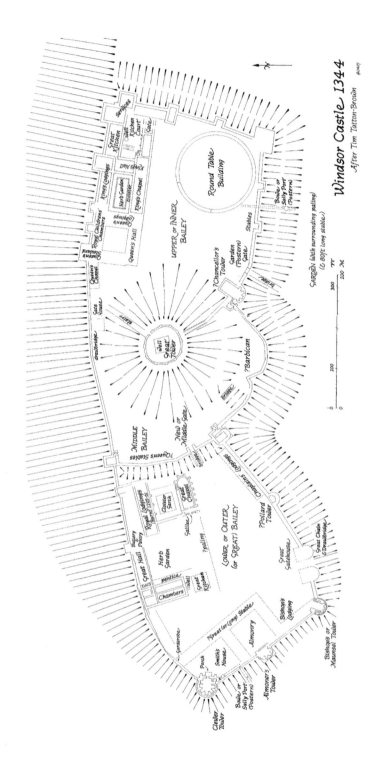

Windsor Castle 1344

After Tim Tatton-Brown

UPPER or INNER BAILEY

Round Table Building

Services
Great Kitchen
Small Kitchen Court
Gate
King's Hall
King's Chapel
Herb Garden
King's Lodgings
Royal Children's Chambers
Queen's Lodgings
Queen's Hall
Queen's Lodgings

Boale or Sally Port (Postern)
Garden (Postern) Gate
Stables
Garden (with surrounding pailing)
(c. 80ft long stable)

Bridge

?Chancellor's Tower

Gate House
Drawbridge

Well
Great Tower

?Barbican

MIDDLE BAILEY

New or Middle Gate
?Queen's Stables

Coolings
Bridge

LOWER or OUTER (or GREAT) BAILEY

Royal Lodgings (rebuilt 1354-6)
Cloister Garth
Great Chapel
Galilee
Buttery Pantry
Great Hall
Herb Garden
Penlice
DAIS
Well
Great Kitchen
Chambers
Gardrobe
Porch
Smith's House
?Great (or Long) Stable
Almonry
Almoner's Tower
Boale or Sally Port (Postern)
Clewer Tower

Coolings
?Pollard Tower
Great Gatehouse
Great Chain & Drawbridge
Bishop's Lodging
Bishop's or Maunsel Tower

100
300 ft
100 M

quarrels which arose when there was a clear place of honour, at the king's right hand, and the status of an individual was judged by how closely he was placed to the king. Arthur withdraws from the main table in his own hall, and replaces it by the Round Table:

> Never did one hear of a knight who was in any way considered to be praiseworthy, who would not belong to his household, if it were possible to have him. If he wished to serve for recompense, nonetheless he never left to gain recompense. For the noble barons he had, each of whom felt that he was superior [to the rest] – each one believed himself to be the best, and nobody could tell the worst – King Arthur, of whom the Britons tell many stories, established the Round Table. There sat the vassals, all of them at the head of the table, and all equal. They took their places at the table as equals. None of them could boast that he was seated higher than his peer. All were seated in the place of honour, and none was at the far end. At this table sat Britons, Frenchmen, Normans, men from Anjou, Flanders, Burgundy and Lorraine. There were knights who held land of the king, from the furthest marches of the west to the hill of St Bernard.[45]

At the outset, the Round Table was therefore the answer to a political problem, and Wace's depiction of it reflected the difficulties that Henry II had had at the beginning of his reign. He had inherited a kingdom torn apart by civil war and the rivalry of great lords, and had imposed order on it.

It is easy for us to forget that Arthur's fame in the middle ages took two distinct forms. Wace was writing a chronicle in verse, and thought of himself as a historian. Despite the severe doubts about Arthur's place in history expressed by some sceptical writers in the twelfth century, Arthur became an accepted part of the history of Britain until the sixteenth century, when questions were once more raised about the story presented by Geoffrey of Monmouth. We cannot read Edward III's mind in January 1344 to discover what he intended by the establishment of the Round Table, but I believe that the weight of the evidence is in favour of the idea that this was all part of his campaign to establish his rights in France, and that, just as his grandfather had used Arthur in support of his claim to overlordship of Scotland, so Edward was invoking the idea of Arthur to be found in the chronicles of the time as conqueror of France. There is nothing to indicate that at this stage he was founding any formal order of knighthood, a concept which emerges in the second half of the fourteenth century. The king says nothing about the formal constitution of the Round Table in his announcement; in the chronicles it is simply an alliance or fraternity of knights under the king.

Arthur's fame came in the end, not from his place in the supposed history of Britain, but from his image as a paragon of the new ideas of knighthood, and the Round Table too was transformed into the home of the best knights in the world. It is mentioned by all the early writers of romance; it begins as an incidental part of Arthur's court, as in the writings of Chrétien de Troyes, where Arthur is the central but rather nebulous figure around whom the world of his heroes revolves. Here, as in Wace's *Brut*, the knights of Arthur's court are referred to as 'ces de la Table Reonde' – those of the Round Table – on three occasions, and there is a similar reference in the poems of Marie de France, a contemporary of Chrétien. In these early romances, the Round Table is no more than a synonym for Arthur's court, with no idea of specific membership or specific rules; it is Arthur's court, rather than the Round Table itself, which is home to the best knights in the world.

As the Arthurian romances were expanded and grew more complex, the Round Table becomes a society or company with a limited and defined membership and at the same time the physical object where those members assemble. The number of knights is repeatedly given as 150, and they are called members or companions of the Round Table.[46] They are bound to each other by certain conditions; there is evidently an oath which they swear on admission to the company, though the terms of it are never precisely spelled out, and we only gather from passing references what these conditions might be. They seem incidental beside the much more prominent insistence on the importance of the relations between the members of the Round Table. First and foremost, the companions are bound by oath to help each other. When Gawain is fighting Hector, another knight reproaches him fiercely for attacking a fellow-member of the Round Table, and succeeds in stopping the combat: 'As for Sir Hector, your companion, by the oath of the Round Table you are bound to him and to all the others who are companions of the Round Table, so that you can't kill them except in self-defence without becoming the falsest and most foresworn knight of all.'[47]

Indeed, the members of the Round Table are bound to help each other, to the extent of avenging any defeat suffered by another of the companions: 'the custom of the Round Table is such that if I see my companion defeated or killed, I must avenge him before I leave and must kill with my own hands the man who fought him, unless both are companions of the Round Table.'[48] This became more than a mere custom: it appears that there was now an oath which all knights had to swear, though we never learn its exact wording. By the late thirteenth century, writers thought of it as involving an oath of brotherhood ('Remember the oath and pledge of the Round Table, in which we are brothers and companions ...'[49]), and it also included an oath of obedience to the king.

Some of these ideas could have been part of Edward's thinking, but it was not the prime reason for his appeal to the past: he was staking a claim to the identity which he had already been given by the more enthusiastic chroniclers, a reincarnation of Arthur as ruler of Europe, and more specifically of France.

Let us look again at Murimuth's account and see what the details tell about Edward's agenda in making his announcement in January 1344, ignoring all the splendour surrounding the occasion and concentrating on what the king had in mind for the future.

First of all, the founding of the Round Table is not part of the festival itself, but a separate occasion after the jousts and feasting had concluded. The ceremony takes place with all the formal pomp that can be mustered, and Edward wears his crown, a symbolic act which normally happened only on certain specified occasions. He also carries the royal sceptre, which would indeed have been a highly unusual act even at a major court feast, and the chief royal officers of the court, the steward and marshal, also carry their ceremonial staffs. The assembly takes place, not in the chapel as might be expected, but in what appears to have been an outdoor environment. The staging of the occasion, as we have seen from the accounts, was carefully choreographed. The king had one of his most splendid sets of robes made for the occasion, an item which stands out even among the vast sums recorded in his accounts with his tailor. The crown, even though it was only his second-best crown, was also highly symbolic, since it had been in pawn for the previous four years. This may well have been the first time since 1337 that Edward appeared in full state regalia; it is likely that he did so in that year when his eldest son was created duke of Cornwall, and six of his closest associates were raised to the rank of earl. If so, it implies that the founding of the Round Table was intended, not as a simple adjunct to a joust, but as a moment of great political significance.

Perhaps the most curious aspect of this is the opening of the solemn oath sworn by the king. Instead of declaring outright his intention to found the Round Table, Edward prefaces his words with 'provided that he had the means'. In 1344 these words would have had a very specific resonance. The greatest crisis of Edward's reign had been three years earlier, when his extravagant plans for buying himself an alliance of German princes for his campaign against France had led him to near-bankruptcy and to a rift with the council charged with ruling England in his absence. The royal finances were only just on the mend, as witnessed by the recent redemption of the crown, and this was an undertaking that was likely to cost a great deal. Already the expenditure on feasting alone for this week amounted to £1,954 18s. 3¼d.[50] To put this in perspective, without attempting a false analogy with modern currency, it was approximately three months of normal kitchen expenditure for the king's household, and, although the feast in 1337 when the duke and earls were created cost £439 2s. 8¼d., there were no other festivities at that time. In comparison with the costs of mounting a military campaign, the kitchen expenditure for the Windsor festival would have paid the wages for Edward's army on the Crécy campaign two years later for seventeen days. Obviously the inaugural occasion was a special one, but to provide for an assembly of 300 knights on a regular annual basis was not going to be cheap if it was to be done in high royal style.

This number is the next detail which the writer gives us. The way in which he explains the membership of the Round Table is not entirely clear: I read it to mean that the total number of knights was to be 300, but that it would begin with a smaller number, and that Edward undertook to continually recruit knights until it reached that number. Otherwise, the membership would effectively have no limit. An institution as large as this would have been something quite exceptional, in terms of the size of the group, the scale of the building and the scale of expenditure on the inauguration. As a one-off event, it was manageable, but with the costs of providing a building for it and with annual gatherings, even Edward seems to have realized that this was going to stretch his resources.

Immediately after the feast, Edward gave his instructions for the building works to begin. Thomas Walsingham's account of the dimensions proved exactly right when excavations took place in the upper ward at Windsor Castle in 2006, and the foundations of the house of the Round Table were uncovered. It was a huge undertaking, and the number of men required for the workforce meant that building work on sites throughout south-east England came to a halt. At its peak, in the first week of March 1344, 720 men were employed. However, by April there was a real prospect of a renewal of open war with France, and the work almost ceased after this one month of hectic activity. The king's means were insufficient to support the anticipated building expenses, which amounted to £509 12s. 11¾d. by the time work stopped altogether at the end of the year. The peak rate of monthly expenditure was four times as much as the average for the whole of the work done when Windsor Castle was remodelled by William of Wykeham in 1356–61.[51] Wykeham's work was funded by the profits of the war with France; in 1344 there were no profits as yet, and a huge debit in prospect for the costs of the new campaign.

Given the lavish scale of the inaugural feast, what was Edward's objective in all this? The nearest we can get to Edward's intentions in this respect is from the response of the barons to Edward's promise to 'begin a Round Table, in the same manner and condition as Arthur, formerly king of England, established it'. The barons reply by swearing to 'observe, sustain and promote' the new institution. This implies that there was to be something which had to be 'observed'; but do we have any idea what this might have been? In the chronicles, and in particular in the poem *Morte Arthure*, which is almost entirely based on the supposed history of the real Arthur, the Round Table takes on a different aspect, and becomes the equivalent of the group of knights at the English royal court known as the household knights. The *Morte Arthure*, which is entirely concerned with Arthur's French wars, and was written around the end of Edward III's reign, depicts the Round Table as follows:

> ... I'll tell you a tale both noble and true
> of the royal ranks of the Round Table
> who were champion knights and chivalrous chieftains,
> both worldly wise and brave in battle,
> daring in their deeds, always dreading shame,
> kind, courteous men, courtly in their manners.
> How they won in war the worship of many ...[52]

It is conceivable, given the large membership proposed by Edward, that the Round Table was to be an extension of the institution of household knights, providing the king with even larger resources of manpower under his own direct control. The pomp and ceremony attached to it would then have been largely aimed at recruiting additional knights; if the core was to be the existing knights of the household, Edward's remarks about continually adding to the number make sense. There may be an echo of Edward's ideas in John Lydgate, writing eighty years later about the institution of the Round Table, who makes one of its roles a 'martial academy' where young knights could learn to bear arms, and avoid 'the idleness of youth'.

If this view is possible, the Round Table becomes both a training ground and a serious military grouping. Such an organization might justify the creation of a *domus*, but what we know of the building indicates that it was intended not as the headquarters of a permanently staffed organization, but as a place for feasting and knightly ceremony. A large enclosed space open to the sky – if that was indeed what the *domus* was to have been – would have its uses as a training ground, but few advantages over the usual jousting areas annexed to castles. We know that the upper ward was used for jousting, as there is a reference in the accounts to the special chamber provided for the king when he armed himself for jousts there.[53] Huge though the building was, the space outside it in the upper ward would still have been larger and better able to accommodate the lists. However, it is worth pointing out that the area required for lists was specified by Thomas duke of Gloucester in the fifteenth century as '60 pace long and 40 pace broad . . . and that the listes be strongly barred about'. A pace is about three feet, perhaps slightly less, so this area would just fit within the Round Table building with its diameter of 200 feet, even allowing for seats, table and arcade around the outside. The problem is that Gloucester is discussing trial by combat, which was usually on foot, and this specification would not therefore allow for jousting. And the shape of the building would be wrong for a jousting arena, even though an Elizabethan writer, John Ferne, in *The Blazon of Gentrie*, talks of lists as 'a place circular and rounde, compassed in with lowe rayles or pales of wood, painted with red'.[54] There are no surviving documents which give the measurements for a fourteenth-century jousting arena, and the style of fighting at tournaments was in the process of changing from the old-fashioned *mêlée* involving a large number of knights, to the joust in which one knight challenged a single opponent.

This may lead to one possible explanation of the function of the Round Table building. In the magnificent treatise on tournaments by René of Anjou, king of Naples, in the mid-fifteenth century, he illustrates the start of a *mêlée*. The opening ceremony takes place within a set of barriers, where the two sides are ranged against each other, with banners displayed. At a signal from the heralds, the barriers are opened, the knights ride out into an open space and the fighting starts, using swords only. Given the disposition of the House of the Round Table in the upper ward, we could envisage the knights assembling within the open space at the centre of the building for the opening ceremony. At the signal from the heralds, the great doors would be opened, and the fighting would continue in the larger space of the upper ward. This can only be a hypothesis, but it fits well with what we know of the organization of the events known as 'Round Tables'.

There is a second possible use for an arena of this size. Any discussion of the fourteenth-century concept of an Arthurian Round Table leads us back to the series of festivals called 'round tables' which are documented from 1232 onwards, when Henry III refers in an official document to knights assembling *ad rotundam tabulam*, 'for a round table'.[55] At the knighting of the sons of John of Ibelin in Cyprus in 1223 the chronicler records that the knights imitated 'the adventures of Britain and the Round Table'.[56] There are a number of events across Europe in the thirteenth century which are recorded as 'round tables', usually with no further information. The *domus* could have been the setting for the king's *ludi*, and these could have been re-enactments of the romances of the Round Table. Because we know so little about the content and context of the *ludi*, this can only be a speculation.

The Round Table building at Windsor does seem to have inspired the author of an Arthurian romance, the mysterious and dramatic *Perceforest*, which appears to be from these years, even though the version that has come down to us is definitely from the fifteenth century. *Perceforest* tells the pagan prehistory of the Round Table, and unites the legends of Alexander, much admired by the counts of Hainault, with the legend of Arthur. One of the central scenes is the moment when Perceforest, to whom Alexander has given the land of Britain, discovers a tower which has magically appeared in his castle. Within is a vast hall, with seats for 300 knights. When Perceforest sees the hall of the Franc-Palais for the first time, there are only twelve shields hanging on the walls, those of the band of knights who have undertaken a vow which provides the main framework of the action. The next day, when they re-enter the hall, the king's shield is above his seat at the high table; and next to it, in the place of honour on his right, 'there hung a golden shield with a red lion, and it belonged to Lyonnel du Glat'.[57] I believe this is a flattering reference to Edward in his character of Lionel; and the hall is modelled on the Round Table *domus*. Its dimensions are exactly those specified by Thomas Walsingham and confirmed by the 2006 excavations, a diameter of 200 feet. No other circular building of this period approached this size, and it seems highly unlikely that the measurement is a coincidence.[58]

The Round Table project looks backwards to a golden age of knighthood, and romanticizes the present by attempting to revive the ancient glories of Arthur's court. It is, however, typical of the time: Jean Froissart, whose imaginative version of the Hundred Years War still colours our vision of the harsh warfare of the times, makes ordinary knights and mercenary captains into men governed by knightly ideals. The patronage of knightly ideals by the courts of Europe, which had made them a kind of lingua franca of the knightly class, reached its apogee in the late fourteenth and early fifteenth centuries; but it was patronage with a purpose. The Emperor Frederick II had built great castles to impress his subjects with their power, castles which were not always strategically necessary but were highly visible, as at Enna in Sicily and Castel del Monte in Apulia; and Edward I's Welsh castles fulfilled the same role, and also evoked Britain's imperial past as recorded in Welsh legend.[59] Now monarchs turned to knightly festivals for the same purpose. It is the beginning of a tradition which led to the great pageants of the Renaissance and to the court entertainments of the Italian princes, the age when 'the art of festival was harnessed to the emergent modern state as an instrument of rule'.[60] I would argue that this process first emerges much earlier than has usually been acknowledged, particularly as we find one of the first examples of a 'royal entry' with a symbolic programme in London in 1357, when the prince of Wales brought King John of France to the city as a captive after Poitiers. Edward III's agenda at Windsor had moved beyond the conspicuous consumption enjoined by the romantic virtue of *largesse* to a novel use of knighthood. Note that the ceremony of inauguration of the Round Table was carefully orchestrated, and that Murimuth records that all the people flocked to see the spectacle. This is knightly display as public relations.

The Round Table failed, however. It was too ambitious, too extravagant. There was no intrinsic obstacle to its revival in 1347; the half-finished buildings were still in place. But the events of the ensuing months had dramatically changed the king's priorities. If the Round Table was to be a new focus for recruiting the king's armies for overseas campaigns, Edward had effectively solved that problem in 1344–6, and the system of raising an army by means of commanders with individual contracts and special payments of bonuses to captains and common soldiers alike was to remain in place for the rest of his reign.

Although the breakdown of the 1343 truce was expected as early as April 1344, it was a long time before the storm actually broke. Half-hearted peace talks at Avignon meandered on for twelve months. Edward wanted Jean de Montfort released from French custody before negotiating seriously, and in any case he was absolutely determined to pursue his claim to the throne of France. The pomp and ceremony of the Round Table festival was only one aspect of a propaganda campaign to present Edward as a monarch of the first rank: a new gold coinage was issued within weeks of the ceremony, and Edward made a point of using it when presenting the traditional Maundy money at Marlborough at Easter 1344. Documents given to the negotiators at Avignon contained the idea that 'since the king of France was sovereign in his lands, no earthly authority was empowered to arbitrate upon the title', which could be decided only by the divine judgement implicit in the outcome of war.[61] Since this blatantly ran contrary to the pope's claim to be God's vicar on earth, there was not the remotest possibility of the talks succeeding if this approach was mentioned. It can only have been a counter in the diplomatic dealings: there are hints that Edward would have settled for an independent Aquitaine and the restoration of the lands lost since the settlement of 1259.

About the time that the talks collapsed, Edward had formulated the strategy for his next move against France. The moribund Flemish alliance had collapsed, and even his brother-in-law William II of Hainault had gone over to the French side: only the Flemish towns led by Jacob van Artevelde remained loyal to the English alliance. William II's French allegiance was relatively brief, as he was killed in an abortive attempt to put down a revolt by the independent-minded Frisians at Staveren in 1345.[62]

Edward was seeking an alliance with Castile to secure the seas against the Castilian ships, which had fought on the French side, but, in terms of an attack on France, he was now going to rely on his own resources, and on his allies in Brittany and western Normandy. Fortunately for him, Jean de Montfort escaped from Paris and reached England in March 1345, and both local quarrels and the French nobility's fear of Philip after the summary execution of Olivier Clisson played into his hands: his most useful new ally in this area was Godefroy d'Harcourt, whose lordship lay in the Cotentin peninsula, south of Cherbourg.

Edward's plans for the campaign of 1345 were on a grand scale. William Bohun would go to Brittany, Henry of Grosmont to Gascony, and he himself would invade French territory somewhere on the Channel coast. In June Bohun arrived in Brittany, and by August Henry of Grosmont was in Bordeaux: at the end of that month he, Walter Mauny and Ralph Stafford, together with Laurence Hastings, earl of Pembroke, had taken Bergerac, a key stronghold on the Dordogne fifty miles east of Bordeaux, and with it important hostages and much of the wealth of the town. Henry then advanced south-east to La Réole in Périgord, having defeated the French at Auberoche in October, and taken prisoners estimated by Villani to be worth £50,000.[63] He recaptured the town in January 1346, and this success was followed up by Stafford's capture of Aiguillon, south-east of Bordeaux. But this was not much to set against the problems in Brittany. Jean de Montfort died on 26 September 1345, leaving his five-year-old son as heir to his cause, and all that Bohun could do was ensure that as many of Montfort's supporters as possible remained loyal. Edward himself had to make a hasty voyage to Flanders to salvage his alliance with the towns when the Flemish leader van Artevelde was assassinated in July. When he was finally able to set sail with his army, one of the most violent storms he ever encountered in the Channel blew his fleet apart, some of them limping back from the North Sea once it was all over. The army was in no fit state to re-embark and undertake a campaign, and he reluctantly called off the expedition. The invasion fleet was to reconvene at Portsmouth on 15 May 1346.

6

The Crécy Campaign

The fleet which assembled at Portsmouth in May and June of 1346 had long been planned. Its destination was secret, and precautions were taken to prevent any information about its objective from reaching the French. Yet the new expedition could only have been intended for Brittany or Normandy. The reason that we know the destination of any given expedition from England is simple. Medieval ships could not sail to windward, that is, into the prevailing wind. If the wind was south-westerly – and south-west is the prevailing wind direction in the English Channel – they can head north-west, through north and east, to south-east. Their range, so to speak, is only 180° or half of the compass. By contrast, a modern yacht, under the same conditions, can head within 30° of the wind direction and use 300°, five-sixths of the compass, from south of west through north, east and south to west of south. So expeditions for Gascony left from Plymouth, in the hope of catching at least a north-westerly wind; even so, they would need a wind in the east to clear the Breton peninsula. To get to Brittany from Portsmouth a westerly or north-westerly was needed, and Normandy could just about be reached in a westerly. Anything from the north or east made these journeys easy, but these are not the usual Channel winds. Because the timing of the crossing was so uncertain, tides could be used to certain advantage only at the outset of the voyage: going to Normandy from the Solent, to get as far to windward as possible. This would mean leaving at the beginning of the ebb for a west wind, the beginning of the flood for an east wind, since the tides flood towards Dover and ebb away from it.

Assembling a fleet was an elaborate operation, because there was no permanent royal navy.[1] The king owned a number of ships, but they were not organized in any way. At the beginning of his reign, Edward had only two ships of his own, and this number was not increased for a decade, because his chief preoccupation was with the wars in Scotland. As soon as France became the target, he set about building ships, and by 1342 there were ten available for an expedition to Brittany. The next four years saw a major effort to improve the situation, and twenty-five royal vessels were among those at Portsmouth. Technically, the men of the Cinque Ports, the five ports on the south coast which enjoyed special privileges in return for providing fifty-seven vessels for the king when he went to war, should have been the next major source of ships, but just as feudal service was commuted to money payments in the 1340s, so this obligation had become obsolete. The bulk of the fleet was therefore created by summoning ordinary trading and fishing vessels from the ports around the country, to serve at the king's wages. The total for the 1346 flotilla was more than 1,000 ships, the largest seen in England before the sixteenth century.[2]

In the absence of a royal navy, there was instead an admiralty, a highly efficient government department whose task it was to gather this enormous quantity of shipping. There were usually two admirals, and the country was divided into the admiralty of the north and the admiralty of the west; the dividing line was Dover, so the admiral of the north was in effect in charge of the ports on the east coast, and the admiral of the west covered everything from London round to Cornwall. These posts had largely been in abeyance up to 1335; thereafter, Robert Morley was admiral of the north until 1360, except in the decade after 1344, when he was replaced by leading military commanders. In 1344–7, the admiral of the north was Robert Ufford.[3] The admiralty of the west changed more frequently, and names such as Bartholomew Burghersh the elder and William Clinton appear up to 1344; from 1344 to 1347, Robert Ufford's colleague was Richard Fitzalan.

The admirals had overall responsibility for the operation: their lieutenants oversaw a substantial staff devoted to the task of organizing the requisition of ships, and the coast was subdivided into smaller sections for this purpose. Officials would be sent to individual ports to 'arrest' ships for the king's service, and to contract the shipmaster to be at Portsmouth at the agreed time. The pay offered was obviously acceptable, as we do not hear of the refusals to serve which had plagued the efforts to raise fleets under Edward II. Substantial payments were made in advance once the ships reached the appointed rendezvous: one official paid out more than £1,600 in two months.[4] The names of the shipmaster and crew, and the name of the ship, would be recorded and sent to Westminster, and we have full payrolls for several of Edward III's campaigns, though unfortunately not for the 1346 fleet.[5] However, contracting for a ship to be at Portsmouth was one thing; getting it there, particularly from the admiralty of the north, was another matter. The prevailing westerly winds meant that the voyage from major ports north of Dover through the straits of Dover was likely to be much slower than a voyage from the south-western ports, and distances were greater.

Despite generally excellent organization, there was an inevitable delay in assembling the ships. The summons for the fleet was issued rather hopefully for the end of February, and then postponed to the end of March. The equinoctial gales, usual at that time of year, again forced a delay, and it was the end of April before the first ships began to appear in the Solent. Once they arrived at Portsmouth, they were under the admiral's command, and they were provisioned and allocated a mooring, while they waited for the rest of the fleet to assemble. The process of gathering the ships was as usual a long affair; the king would have known that the earliest that he could expect to sail would be in April, in time for a spring campaign. In the event, it was the end of June before the ships were ready.

An even more formidable bureaucratic effort had been in process on land, to assemble the troops and to purchase the necessary provisions and cart them to Portsmouth. If we have little detail for the naval accounts[6] we have a great deal for the provisioning and supplies, the army retinues and the actual accounts for the king's kitchen during the months in Portsmouth and in France. Tantalizingly, the rolls for the army retinues probably survived until the early eighteenth century, when they were destroyed along with other papers after the death of a scholar who was working on them.[7]

Edward was setting out to fight a campaign where he would have no territories of his own to draw on, as would have been the case in Gascony, and no allies, however unreliable, as in the earlier expeditions to Flanders. In his Scottish wars he could call on supplies to be brought up overland, and he was not totally dependent on his fleet. In the summer of 1346, everything had to be loaded onto the ships, and he was relying on the same ships to bring him back, whatever the outcome of the fighting. Weapons and horses formed the bulk of the military supplies, but in addition the necessary equipment for the army's engineers was part of the freight, and even items such as coracles for the king's fishermen are to be found in the accounts.

First and foremost, huge numbers of bows and arrows were needed. Although numerous orders to the local sheriffs survive, we lack any secure idea of what sort of total number was involved. We can work backwards from the figure of about 7,500 archers in the army to arrive at a figure; one suggestion is that at the rate of seventy per man, half a million arrows weighing four ounces each would be the kind of quantity involved, and that they would weigh fifty-five tons, which in turn required fifty to sixty carts to carry them – and the carts also had to be shipped from England. Orders for 5,500 sheaves, or 132,000 arrows, are known to have been issued, along with 2,100 bows, giving a ratio of sixty arrows per bow.[8] Such huge quantities had to be divided out among the shires which were skilled in making them, and even then they were often delivered in stages, and there were often considerable shortfalls on the numbers requested: sometimes only a third of the order was supplied by the sheriff responsible. At the end of the day the archers in the field would be permanently reliant on being able to retrieve spent shafts, and on a regular further supply of arrows made en route. Each man would have his own bow, but reserve bowstaves and stores of bow-strings would be needed. Spare arrowheads and finished bows corded in bundles were shipped in barrels, as staves could be cut when the army was in the field: it was harder to set up forges, but there were undoubt-edly a number of portable smithies with the army, essential for reshoeing horses and repairing armour and swords, as well as making arrowheads.

The other field weapons were the swords and lances of the mounted knights and men at arms, and the smaller swords and knives carried by the archers and other footsoldiers. These were not issued by the king, but were the responsibility of the individuals. There was one innovation in terms of weapons: the use of guns. The treatise which Walter Milem-ete presented to Edward at the beginning of his reign illustrates a simple bombard, a bulbous cannon about three or four feet long; the guns at Crécy are likely to have been smaller, since bombards were heavy and unreliable, and mostly used in sieges (Plate 6). It is possible that sieges were what the Crécy guns were intended for, and they were brought into play only as a means of terrorizing the enemy, and particularly their horses. Instructions were sent to the head of the Tower armouries in 1345 to supply a hundred 'ribalds', small multi-barrelled guns firing lead shot. These were experimental weapons, at the cutting edge of a new technology: even so, Edward seems to have had with him some 'guns', i.e. cannons, and as much as 2,000 pounds of gunpowder, a substantial amount.[9] Edward might love the antique trappings of knightly display, but he was also an innovator, interested in new techniques and ingenious devices, as illustrated by the great clock he had installed at Windsor, a novelty in England at the time. The guns might have been bought in Flanders or made at the armouries in the Tower of London. The Tower served as a collection centre for many of the military stores, and for naval supplies such as ropes and sailcloth. It was also a major factory for all kinds of weapons, and the shortfall in arrows supplied by the shires was usually made up by employing extra workmen at the Tower.

Alongside the archers and the handful of gunners there were forty carpenters, the engineers of the army, led by William of Winchelsea. Although there is no surviving record of what materials were supplied for their use, in Brittany three years earlier enough timber for three complete bridges had been shipped, the medieval equivalent of the Bailey Bridge of the Second World War. The engineers played a vital role in the progress of the army when they succeeded in repairing the bridge at Poissy near Paris, which had been deliberately broken. The gap was sixty feet, and they threw a single beam, a foot wide, across it. This was sufficient for enough archers and men at arms to cross and drive off the enemy harassing from the other side. They then used the beam as a base from which to build up a roadway strong enough for the rest of the army to cross to the north bank of the Seine.[10]

Another vital element in the army's composition does not appear separately in the accounts. A huge number of carts must have been needed to convey the stores overland once the army reached Normandy.[11] Quite apart from the fifty or sixty carts carrying bows and arrows, there were the vital provisions which the army needed to supplement what it could find by foraging. A medieval army on the march did not consist of serried ranks of horsemen and footsoldiers marching in tight formation: it was more like a huge straggling merchant caravanserai (Plate 9). It included live beasts and birds, who were slaughtered for food en route. The kitchen accounts differentiate between beasts taken from the stock brought from England and those captured in foraging raids. The latter are listed as 'kept from spoils'; if the accounts are right, there were still cattle listed as simply 'kept' as late as 30 August, as if they had been brought from England.[12] Relatively exotic birds as well as ordinary poultry were brought for the king's table, probably in cages on the carts, and there are regular entries for food for them throughout the campaign; the stocks of poultry were evidently replenished by the foragers.[13]

When the army encamped for the night, the image that immediately comes to mind is of a busy scene of pitching tents, organizing the camp, lighting fires and settling down to a night under canvas. There is actually little trace of this in the accounts, and we know very little about the art of the medieval tent-maker. That there were tents for the king, and that some were mended for the expedition, is about all that can be said.[14] If we trace the army's progress, there are many occasions when quarters for the king and magnates were requisitioned in a town or monastery. Encampment was an emergency procedure at best, and the army would often split up in order to find sufficient shelter. Between leaving La Hogue on 18 July and the encounter with the French army on 26 August, a total of thirty-nine nights, the halts were in small towns or villages on twenty-five occasions, in cities (Caen and Lisieux) for seven nights, and at abbeys for three nights, leaving four occasions when the army was almost certainly under canvas for lack of a suitable settlement nearby, as on the day when they laboriously crossed the marshes to the east of Caen. On five occasions, usually when the king was staying at an abbey, the forces were split, and the prince of Wales found lodging elsewhere. Some of the troops would have found shelter in these settlements as well; despite the king's initial proclamation that the inhabitants of his new kingdom were to be spared, what normally seems to have happened is that the local population were driven out – if they had not already fled – and the troops took over the houses before burning them as they left.[15]

Feeding the army was probably the greatest concern after the levying of the troops. The operation to provision the forces on this campaign was huge, on an unprecedented scale, because, once the army was on French soil, opportunities for sending further provisions would depend on the weather and the whereabouts of the king and his men, and would therefore be highly unreliable. When Edward's armies fought in Scotland, provisioning by land was possible, and the initial supplies were therefore less crucial. In effect, an English force fighting in France had to take as large a supply as it could, because the availability of local provisions was uncertain in the extreme. Foraging was a constant preoccupation, but deliberate burning of crops and slaughter of cattle was a recognized defensive technique for starving out a raiding force and ensuring that it would not remain in the area for long.

The system of obtaining the necessary food depended heavily on the royal purveyancers, who had the power to seize food and buy it at fixed, but not necessarily fair, prices. Not surprisingly, they were extremely unpopular, but it is possibly an indication of popular support for the campaign that in this case not only did the raising of supplies pass off relatively peacefully, but the required stocks were also raised. Getting provisions to Portsmouth was the most elaborate of all the bureaucratic operations for the expedition. We have the full receipts for some counties which detail all the stages involved.[16] Firstly, empty barrels had to be bought, usually tuns, which stood about six feet high and three feet in diameter. The flour sent from Yorkshire required eighty of these, and there were about forty more for oats, pork, peas and beans. Ten men had ridden round the country for a fortnight purchasing and arranging for the transport of these supplies, paying for them with wooden tallies which could be redeemed at the exchequer later. Boats and carts were requisitioned, and the supplies were taken by road and river to seven depots. They were then shipped to Hull, where the corn was ground. It took seven men a week to unload the wheat and reload the flour. At all stages, clerks had to record the transactions, and men were appointed to guard the goods. Everyone in the county must have been aware of the king's men at work, and the aftermath would be shortages and rising prices because of the extra demand.

The provisions raised in this way tell us what the army lived on. The common soldiers ate very much what they were accustomed to at home, mainly peas and beans or oats made into pottage with such meat and other vegetables as were available. The royal kitchen accounts are at the other extreme, and show the royal household also enjoying its customary, but much more luxurious, diet. The households of the great magnates would have eaten in a similar, but less elaborate style; there might have been between five and seventeen such groups within the army, each with their own supplies.[17] The menu for the king and his immediate companions was very varied. Mutton, pork and beef were all provided, but much of it was salted or cured, so it is not surprising to find a large expenditure on the ingredients for sauces: verjuice,* vinegar, mustard, garlic, onions and parsley. Fresh meat, as we have seen, was derived partly from the small herd that travelled with the army, and partly from the results of foraging. There are regular payments throughout the journey to the kitchen boys who 'pursue and kill oxen and sheep'.[18] Poultry came from stock, and was almost certainly foraged as well. Rabbit was also on the menu, as the king's ferreters were in the contingent. More important were the fishermen, since fish was regularly eaten on Friday, as prescribed by the medieval Church. The range of fish is surprising: in addition to the salt cod, or stockfish, which was a staple of medieval diet for Fridays, there was salmon, which must have been dried or even cured, rather like smoked salmon,[19] eels of varying sizes, spiced herring (the rollmops of today). The lamprey, a parasitic eel-like creature, was a great delicacy in the middle ages, since it tastes more like meat than any other fish: four were served on 12 July at a cost of sixteen shillings.[20] Again, fish from the original provisions, fish bought in the market and fish caught by the king's fishermen are sometimes noted separately. Other items include carp, pike and crayfish: the king at least enjoyed a rich and varied menu. Wine was also supplied in large quantities: nearly 300 tuns, or 130,000 gallons; but before we think of this in modern terms, wine and ale were the customary drinks, because of the poor quality of the water available. It was simply not advisable to drink water unless absolutely necessary, so this was no luxury, but an essential part of the supplies.

The provisioning and shipping of an expedition was a mammoth task even without the raising of the army itself. Edward had a great deal of experience of bringing together an army, but an invasion of the kind that he now had in mind was a novelty. In Scotland in the 1330s he had used tried and trusted methods of recruitment, which harked back to the old duties of defence of the realm, part of the duties of all who held land by feudal service. In the campaigns in Flanders and Brittany from 1337 to 1342, he had relied heavily on local allies, particularly in Flanders, which had not served him well. He had tried to recruit princes like mercenaries, for pay, and they had failed to deliver when their political interests outweighed the money on offer.

* Sour fruit juice, often used instead of the more expensive vinegar.

By 1346, Edward had determined to rely exclusively on his own resources. To do this, he had begun to move towards a new system, since the traditional feudal service did not carry the obligation to serve outside England. We have seen how the Round Table could have been part of an exploration of new methods of recruiting an army. The deliberations which may have been going on in early 1344 resulted in a royal commission, for which Edward did not have the specific agreement of parliament, but which he justified on the basis that parliament had given general assent to the war, and he was merely exercising his executive prerogative and responding to a threat of invasion. The commission was asked to provide a list of everyone in the country with an annual income of 100s. up to £1,000, and to assess how many troops they should provide on a scale related to their income from lands. However, the data provided were used by Edward to order a muster of troops at Portsmouth by Easter 1346, with the purpose of taking them abroad to serve at the king's wages. Because the operation had a financial basis, the obligation to provide troops was quickly commuted in many cases to a money payment, effectively a tax to subsidize the war in France. The rates were set by the rank of soldier to be provided. An income of 100s. meant that a mounted archer had to be sent; twice that, and a hobelar or lightly armed horseman was required. Over £25, a man at arms was to be provided and from then on the scale was in proportion to income: a lord with an income of £1,000 would provide forty men at arms. The cost to the landowners was either that of hiring men to serve, or losing the value of their own men's labour for the duration of the campaign. The men themselves would be paid the king's wages, and would either be led by their lord or attached to another lord's retinue if their own lord was not serving in person.

In addition to the men serving because of the military assessments, there were commissions of array, the traditional method of raising foot-soldiers.[21] The commissions were sent to the local officials, and requested specific numbers of archers or spearmen. They in turn would raise these troops from local towns and landowners. For example, on 10 February 1346 orders for the array of troops went to 142 towns in the southern half of England, requesting just under 2,000 men. We know how many men were requested under these commissions, but it was unusual for such requests to be fulfilled completely, and we do not have the necessary records to tell us the result. So we have to rely on estimates, and the best guess from a recent study of the problem is a total of 8,000 men, of whom 5,000 were archers.[22]

We then have to add to these the great lords and their retinues, which consisted in broad terms of equal numbers of men at arms and knights, and mounted and foot archers. Again, we have to use estimates, and the best guess is 2,800 men at arms and knights, and the same number of archers. If this is correct, we are looking at a total of 13,600 men who boarded ship at Portsmouth. The driving force behind this army was the retinues raised by the king himself, his great magnates and the lesser barons and bannerets. It was around these retinues that the three divisions of the army were arranged, and they were in effect the building blocks of the force.

The records of wages for the campaign do not define the king's retinue, which is listed as separate retinues for his household knights and officers; Walter Wetewang, the treasurer, whose accounts tell us so much about the personnel, was a banneret and had his own retinue of three knights, twenty-five squires and thirty-five archers.[23] The largest single retinue was that of the prince of Wales, with 11 bannerets, 102 knights, 264 esquires, 384 mounted archers and 69 archers on foot. He also had more than 500 Welsh infantry, organized under five standard bearers and twenty-five vintenars (commanders of units of twenty men), with their own chaplain and doctor, and a 'proclamator' or crier. Elsewhere we learn that the prince's Welshmen had their own green-and-white uniform, 'a short coat and a hat of both colours', which had its origins in the wars of the prince's great-grandfather.[24] This was normal for companies of archers, as the troops raised by array were to be clothed 'all in the same cloth'.

Next in rank below the prince were the earls, whose military function dated back to Anglo-Saxon times. They were crucial to the organization of any English army, and Edward had created six new earls in 1337, with the specific objective of strengthening the military structure of his kingdom. Three of these new earls were on the campaign: at the end of it (when Edward was besieging Calais), Huntingdon, Northampton and Suffolk brought 685 men between them, while the four hereditary earls, Arundel, Oxford, Warwick and Pembroke, provided almost double that number, 1,140 men. The new earls were not as rich as the established families, relying largely for their income on lands granted to them by the king since their promotion. Henry of Grosmont, who was in Gascony and only joined the army at the siege of Calais, had a retinue even larger than that of the prince of Wales.

A group of seven great lords each raised retinues of between 100 and 300 men, of whom about a third were archers. In total, these lords' retinues were almost as great as those of the seven earls. Below them were a large number of bannerets with around fifty to sixty men, and then knights who were not attached to a larger retinue.

This last group of men were largely raised from the estates of their lords, and therefore shared the same background and loyalty. In modern terms, the nearest equivalent would be the private regiments raised in the First World War, such as the Lovat Scouts, which came from the estates of one particular landowner, Lord Lovat, or the Sandringham company of the Royal Norfolk Regiment, recruited from the royal estate. It is a commonplace of military psychology that the soldier does not fight for the abstract 'king and country' but for his comrades and friends, and local groupings of this kind contributed greatly to the morale of the army as a whole.

The earl of Northampton's retinue has been studied in detail, and a further important factor in the shaping of these bodies of men emerges. This was not an ad hoc collection of soldiers who happened to be available in 1346, but a group who had fought alongside their lord for as much as a decade, going back to the Scottish campaign of 1336, and the days before he had become an earl. In the 1340s Northampton had fought at Sluys and in Brittany, and there is good evidence that the majority of his men had already been through a full-scale battle under his command.[25] There were of course men who many years later remembered that they had been 'first armed' when they landed in Normandy in 1346, and others who joined different retinues for this campaign, but there is a remarkable degree of cohesion and stability in this sample.

A 'retinue' was after all a group of 'retained' men, bound by a specific contract to serve their lord, and this core, who would in turn have their own loyal servants, is at the heart of the system. The knights and squires relate to the lord in terms of long service just as their lord relates to the king himself. A good example of such contracts is that between the prince of Wales and Henry Eam in January 1348:

> Grant for life to Sir Henry Eam of a yearly rent of 100 marks payable by
> equal portions at Easter and Michaelmas out of the prince's manor of

Bradenash, co. Devon, with power of distraint in the manor if the rent be in arrear: as the said Sir Henry, when he received the order of knighthood from the prince's hands, freely offered and promised to be attentive to the prince's service for life, and to go with him on sufficient warning wherever he might wish, whether for peace or for war, and to be with him armed against all manner of persons, except only the duke of Brabant, his liege lord, when fighting in defence of his own lands; and the prince wishes to grant him such a reward as will bind him the more to his service, and enable him the better to support the advancement of his estate.[26]

Eam does not hold land of the prince as a reward for his service, but is paid in cash from a specified source so that he can maintain himself in suitable style. More particularly, the yearly rent of 100 marks is intended to cover the cost of maintaining horses, armour, squires and other followers needed to make him an effective warrior and contributor to the prince's retinue. On Eam's death in 1353, he was replaced by John Sully, who was retained by the prince of Wales on slightly more generous terms (£40 instead of £33 13s. 4d. from the revenues of the same manor), but he was required to provide the services of one esquire as well.[27]

Indentures 'for peace or war' applied only to a small number of retainers, the leading figures in the household of a magnate.[28] We have only chance survivals of the original documents, and the overall composition of the household retinue is difficult to assess. In the case of Henry of Grosmont, there are five surviving indentures, of which the most important is with Edmund Ufford (younger brother of Robert Ufford, earl of Suffolk). Edmund was steward of one of Henry of Grosmont's major estates, and he would have been expected to be on hand to deal with his lord's business and act as escort when required; he would almost certainly have been a member of Grosmont's household council. Edmund was to provide three men at arms in war; they were to wear the earl's livery. He was also required to have ten horses and pages to look after them, and a chamberlain; all his men were to dine in the earl's hall. In peace, the numbers were reduced by more than half.[29] In the case of another of Henry of Grosmont's retainers, Ralph Hastings, there is a document relating to one of his followers, John Kirkby, retained for life in 1362, which deals with the conditions under which Kirkby can be dismissed – the nearest we come to a modern contract of employment. Duties in peacetime in older contracts had often included attendance at tournaments, but this ceases to appear after about 1340. The commonest type of contract of retinue was an agreement for service either for a specified length of time or for the duration of a campaign. It was a system which was highly flexible, and which could apply to the greatest lords as well as to individual knights. In the largest contracts of this kind, the king agreed terms with his commanders which covered the numbers of troops they were to provide, the conditions on which they would serve and the division of any spoils or 'profits of war'. Since the king himself was the commander of the expedition of 1346, much of this did not apply, and we do not have surviving documents which tell us what the arrangements were. At the next level were the contracts directly between the king and individual lords, which set out rates of pay and expenses, and when payments would be made. It became the practice in the 1340s to pay *regard* to the captains of retinues, a sum additional to the customary rate of pay, which was related to the number of men they actually had serving under them at the beginning of the campaign and was designed to encourage them to produce the number of troops they had contracted for.[30] There would be a further series of contracts between the captain and his men, so that the whole system would form a legal basis for the recruitment and payment of the retained troops. Similar arrangements were made with the masters of the ships involved in the campaign.

This elaborate administrative edifice evolved as the solution to a problem which had dogged the English kings ever since their French domains had come under attack in the early thirteenth century. While they were in control of these domains, they could raise men and money for their defence in the territory in question; but once they had been lost to the French crown, the problem was one of reconquering them, and they had to use resources from England or from other parts of France. The war was no longer defensive in the eyes of those whom the English king wanted to fight for him, and there was therefore no obligation to serve, their argument ran. In the thirteenth and early fourteenth centuries, a series of uneasy compromises resulted, and Edward's solution was to prove strikingly successful in the short term.

However, not all the soldiers were covered by contracts or by the summons of array. A large number of them seem to have served for simple pay, without specific contracts, but with the hope of additional rewards if the expedition was a success. Taking Henry of Grosmont as an example once more, among the men named as serving him on military expeditions and diplomatic business abroad, about 10 per cent received grants of lands or annuities. Sometimes these were rewards for individual actions in war; on other occasions they could be a kind of pension for long service; and they might also be for 'past and future good service', both reward and retainer at the same time.

One factor which did not play any great part in the calculations of men who signed up for the Crécy expedition was that of the 'profits of war'. Apart from Henry of Grosmont's victory at Auberoche, previous English expeditions abroad had not produced any notable spoils, and there was no reason to think that this occasion would be any different. One view of the situation was that Edward was attempting to establish his right to France, and this was not therefore a war of conquest, but a question of winning over the inhabitants to support his cause. The proclamation made at the beginning of hostilities in France emphasizes this:

> the English king, feeling for the sufferings of the poor people of the country, issued an edict ... that no house or manor was to be burnt, no church or holy place sacked, and no old people, children or women in his kingdom of France were to be harmed or molested; nor were they to threaten any other people except men who resisted them, or do any kind of wrong, on pain of life or limb.[31]

If there was resistance, there might be spoils of war and ransoms. Anyone who captured and ransomed important prisoners was obliged to pay a substantial proportion of the money he received to his commanding officer or to the king; but such ransoms were always few and far between, a lottery win rather than a regular source of wartime income. Profits of war, ranging from casual trophies taken from a farm or village to the sacking of a rich town, hardly figured in the mindset of the ordinary knight in the early wars of Edward's reign. Scotland was a poor country, and the towns small and few. When Edward declared in 1327 and again in 1334 that anyone setting out to fight the Scots could keep any booty he gained, it looks more like revenge for the Scottish raids on the English border counties than a serious prospective source of income.[32] The campaigns in the Low Countries had been largely a stalemate, and little had been captured, while in Brittany the English forces were supporting the claimant to the duchy, and opportunities for plunder were entirely unofficial. The campaign of 1346 marks a watershed, as we shall see. The 'profits of war' were such that they became a regular part of the contracts for service, and after 1350 the pattern of granting the one-third of both booty and ransoms appears to be well established. Before that, the only evidence for a system of this kind is in the warfare on the borders of Wales and Scotland, though much older laws in Wales reserved one-third of all plunder to the king.[33] At sea, however, the rule seems to have been that income from ransoms and sale of plundered goods was to be divided equally between the crown and the master and crew.[34] The reason for this was that compensation was not paid for loss of ships in the royal service; and, interestingly, as the king began to claim a similar share in land warfare, the elaborate system for paying compensation for lost or injured horses to knights and men at arms was gradually abandoned.[35]

What is less easy to see is how this huge disparate mass of men was organized, both on the march and on the battlefield. There were three divisions in the army, and it seems that these may have been used as an organizational scheme from the start of the journey. The problem was that there was no clear chain of command. At one extreme, men from the towns were under the command of a relatively humble leader, whose authority was probably not very strong; at the other, there were the battle-hardened and reliable men at the heart of the noblemen's retinues. How all these were welded into an effective fighting force is also something we know almost nothing about. The *Acts of War of Edward III* tells us that, as the army was disembarking at St Vaast-la-Hougue, 'the English king appointed the earl of Northampton constable, and the earl of Warwick marshal of the army, to check the rashness of the troops. Then they divided the army into three divisions: the vanguard under the prince of Wales, the centre under the king, and the rearguard under the bishop of Durham.'[36] The author goes on to name the leaders of retinues who 'raised their banners' in each division, so we have a picture of three separate bodies of men with the banners as visual rallying points and rendezvous for the members of the retinues within each division. 'With the army divided in this way by the king's counsel, and with everything prepared in the correct fashion', they were able to set out. Discipline was in the hands of the leaders of the retinues, but ultimately lay with the constable of the army, while the marshal was responsible for assembling the army in good order, and organizing its encampment at night, whether in lodgings or under canvas.

All of these troops brought their own weapons, armour and personal equipment, but the men at arms and knights also brought horses; many knights would have two or more horses, so the total was probably well over 5,000 for these two elements of the army. We have to add another 3,000 or so for mounted archers, so something in the region of 10,000 horses would have needed transport. Shipping horses presented a huge number of problems, from getting them on board ship to making sure that they were rested after the voyage and in good condition for the arduous life of the campaign. The ships which had been collected were similar in type, but each would have to be adapted individually for transporting horses. The hold was divided into stalls by hurdles, and thousands of these were ordered as part of the supplies, as well as feed racks and barrels of water. It seems that relatively small ships were used: we have detailed specifications for the building of horse-transports used in the kingdom of Sicily in the late thirteenth century, which carried thirty horses each in specially constructed stalls.

Moving horses by sea was a skilled and specialist operation, commensurate with the value of the horses and the vital role they played in the expedition.[37] Obviously the adaptation of existing ships was a less satisfactory method, but the Channel crossing was usually quite rapid. When in 1344 Reginald Cobham raised a fleet for an expedition to Brittany, the smaller ships were specifically reserved for horse-transport. In similar circumstances in 1303, the number of horses ranged from ten to thirty-two per ship; if we allow twenty horses on average per ship, this would mean that there were 500 ships to be loaded and unloaded, an immensely slow process even when each of the great warhorses might have its own groom.[38] Methods of loading were cumbersome: each horse had to be led up a gangplank, either over the full height of the side of the ship or through a loading door specially cut in the stern, which would then be sealed for the voyage. Sometimes the horses had to be put in a sling and winched aboard using a crane.[39] Once the horse was on board, it would have to be manoeuvred in a confined space into its stall.

Fortunately, the voyage in 1346 was relatively brief, though even the horses were on board for a week or more from loading to unloading. Often horses had to be rested for several days before the army could begin its march: when Richard I landed in Cyprus in 1190, 'the horses were walked about, because they were all stiff and lame and dazed after being at a sea for a month, standing the whole time, unable to lie down. The next day, without giving them any more rest than they had had (although they deserved more), the king ... mounted.'[40]

The fleet was ready to sail on 5 July, and got as far as the Needles, off the western end of the Isle of Wight, but contrary winds made it impossible to proceed further, and the king ordered the ships back to Portsmouth. He said in a letter of 7 July from Yarmouth to John Offord, his chancellor, and William Edington, his treasurer, that he and his companions had agreed to set out on the next tide, and to go wherever the wind took them; but the second half of the letter warns against spies in London, and the vagueness may have been a precaution in case the letter fell into their hands.[41] Bartholomew Burghersh the elder, writing ten days later, was positive that the king had intended to go to Gascony. It is difficult to gainsay this first-hand evidence, particularly when the information was no longer of use as a deception, but the difficulties of a passage from Portsmouth to Gascony and the king's apparent indecision ten days earlier must count against it.[42] The weather changed for the better by 10 July, and on 11 July the expedition set sail for Normandy.

On Edward's arrival off the Norman coast on 12 July the length of time it took to unload the ships seems to have been determined by the sheer amount of material that was involved. The day-by-day diaries of the clerks of the army all agree that five nights were spent at La Hogue, which would mean that around 200 ships were unloaded each day. It is unlikely that they were all taken into the small harbour at St Vaast-la-Hougue for the purpose, which even today is about 550 yards by 220 yards overall. In the medieval period there would probably have been little more than a small jetty, to allow four or five ships at most to moor alongside. The shallowness of the bays to the north and south of St Vaast, protected from the westerly wind which had probably brought the fleet across, meant that a good number of ships could be moored so that they dried out at low tide. High water was at about 11 a.m. on 12 July, and the first ships would have been moored inshore at that point, and unloaded in the afternoon. The same pattern would apply to the following days, with the time of high tide moving on by about an hour

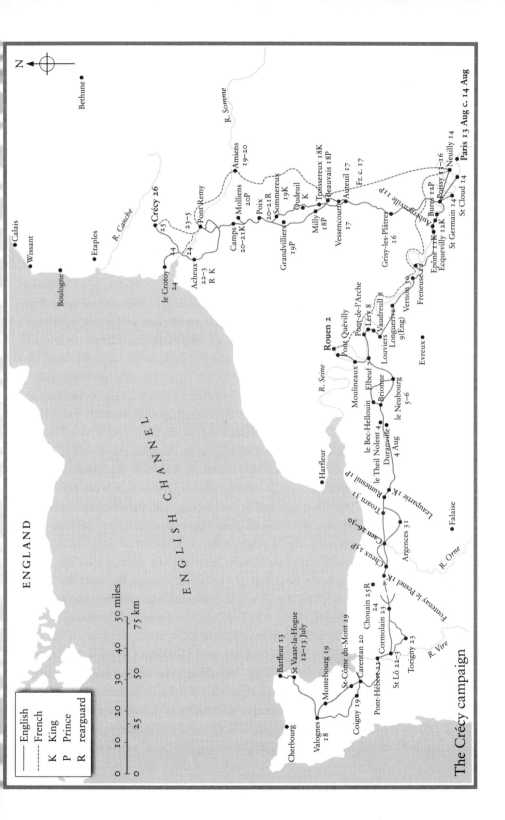

The Crécy campaign

ENGLAND

ENGLISH CHANNEL

N

	50 miles			
0	10	20	30	40	50
0	25	50	75 km		

English
French
K — King
P — Prince
R — rearguard

Bethune

Calais

Wissant

Boulogne

Etaples

R. Canche

Crécy 26

25

le Crotoy 24

24

23–5

Acheux 22–3 R K

Pont Remy

R. Somme

Amiens 19–20

Camps 20–21K

Molliens 20P

Poix 20–21R

Sommereux 19K

Oudeuil K

Grandvilliers 19P

Milly 18P

Troissereux 18K
Beauvais 18P

Vessencourt 17

Auteuil 17 [Fr. c. 17]

Grisy-les-Plâtres 16

Buré 12P

St Germain 14

Epône 11K
Ecquevilly 12K

Aubergenville 11P

Freneuse

Vernon 10

Longueville 9(Eng)

Vaudreuil 8

Léri 8

Pont-de-l'Arche

Pont Quévilly

Rouen 2

R. Seine

Harfleur

Moulineaux

le Bec-Hellouin

Elbeuf 7

Brionne

le Neubourg 5–6

le Theil Nolent 4

Duranville 4 Aug

le Rumesnil 11P

Troarn 31

Leauparte 1K

Argences 31

Caen 26–30

Cheux 25P

Fontenay le Pesnel 1K

Chouain 23

Cormolain 24

Pont-Hébert 24

St Lô 22–3

Torigny 23

Evreux

Falaise

R. Orne

R. Vire

Barfleur 13

St Vaast-la-Hogue 12–13 July

Montebourg 19

St-Côme-du-Mont 19

Carentan 20

Coigny 19

Chouain 25R

Valognes 18

Cherbourg

Paris 13 Aug c. 14 Aug

Neuilly 14

Poissy 13–16

St Cloud 14

a day.[43] The tidal range is on average around sixteen feet, and the beach is largely sand with smooth rocks. Unloading could then have been done across the beach, with plenty of space to work on a number of ships at the same time. The selection of this landing place, ideal for a large fleet, points to good local knowledge, and thus almost certainly to the advice of Godefroy d'Harcourt and his companions, since the Harcourt lands lay only a short distance away: his base was the great castle at St Sauveur-le-Vicomte.

The English fleet came into the bay in the morning, at low water, and the leaders of the army only disembarked when the tide was nearly high, at noon. The first action of the campaign was a traditional ceremony: in anticipation of battle, it was customary to create new knights, and to mark the beginning of the invasion the prince of Wales, aged sixteen, was dubbed by his father, together with several of his companions. The *Acts of War* names William Montagu, heir to the earldom of Salisbury and son of the king's closest friend, as well as Roger Mortimer, son of the earl of March, William le Ros, Roger de la Warre and Richard de Vere 'and various others'. Other nobles knighted men in their retinues.

The expedition had achieved its first objective: complete surprise. It was only at the end of June that the French government in Paris had realized what the destination of the English force was likely to be. Preparations for raising a fleet to challenge any seaborne invasion had been made as early as March, but this relied on hiring galleys from Genoa, which had to make the long Atlantic sea voyage to reach the Channel: in early July they had got as far as Lisbon, and there was no French force at sea because the local shipping (including seventy-eight galleys built in Normandy) was to be under the command of the absent Genoese.[44] The French should have been able to deduce that the only likely objectives were Brittany or Normandy, since the fleet had assembled at Portsmouth, but no real provision had been made for the defence of the north. This was because the French armies were fully occupied elsewhere: in Brittany, Thomas Dagworth had defeated the troops of Charles de Blois on 9 June, and Henry of Grosmont was harassing the French besiegers of the great fortress at Aiguillon on the river Lot. As soon as it became apparent that the English fleet was ready to move, the constable of France, Raoul count of Eu, was ordered to return from the army in Gascony to take command of Harfleur, the port at the mouth of the Seine.[45] The garrisons along the coast to the north of Har-

fleur were reinforced; from all this, it is clear that the French believed
that the landing would take place in the Seine estuary. The Cherbourg
peninsula, more than 100 miles away, was defended only by local militias and a handful of mercenaries. At St Vaast itself, the only troops in
the neighbourhood, 500 Genoese crossbowmen, had withdrawn because
they had not been paid. A handful of local men attempted to ambush
Thomas Beauchamp and his party, but were quickly driven off. Robert
Bertrand, one of the two marshals of France, who had summoned the
militia to resist the English landing, withdrew once he saw the overwhelming size of the English force. He must have done so reluctantly,
because it was a personal quarrel between him, his brother the bishop
of Bayeux and Godefroy d'Harcourt that had led to the latter joining
the English king.

Edward was thus able, as his clerk Michael Northburgh reported
later in the month, 'to disembark the horses, to rest himself and his men
and to bake bread until the following Tuesday'.[46] Raids were carried out
on nearby towns and villages on the first night after landing, after which
Edward issued his proclamation that the inhabitants of his new kingdom were not to be harmed, unless they resisted him. However, this did
not prevent further raids across the peninsula, and an attack on the port
of Barfleur, which was burnt: this was a legitimate target, as the port
contained 'seven curiously fitted-out warships'. Destruction of shipping
along the coast, to prevent its being used in naval operations, was a regular feature of operations while the army was within reach of the sea.

When the army set out on 18 July, they marched in the three divisions
which had already been organized.[47] Much ink has been spilt over what
Edward III had in mind as his army marched into the hills and woods
of the Cotentin peninsula. There was certainly a deeper strategy at
work, given the scale of the expedition, and a strategy which operated
on several levels: the overall English engagement with the French, the
immediate objective of the raid into Normandy, the day-to-day effect of
the army's destructive actions on the French populace, and the ultimate
exit plan for the operation. One objective was to relieve the pressure on
the two much smaller English armies already operating in France, and
in this he succeeded before he had even landed, drawing the constable
and marshals of France away from the siege of Aiguillon to defend the
Normandy coast. A second aim was probably to attempt to force Philip VI
to face him in battle. Philip had preferred a defensive strategy in Flanders

in the late 1330s, and, despite moments when an encounter seemed imminent, had always backed away from engaging with the English army. There is always a danger of reading intentions after the outcome is known, but the argument that a battle was the purpose of Edward's invasion is hard to resist. This in turn dictated his day-to-day conduct: he had to show that the French king was unable to protect the inhabitants of Normandy, so that Philip was forced to prove that he was equal to the task of taking on the invaders. Edward was 'seeking battle' from the outset, and his behaviour was therefore provocative: but he chose his targets carefully, to secure maximum damage with minimum risk to himself. And it is also reasonably clear that his exit plan, whether in victory or defeat, was to join up with the small English force under Hugh Hastings operating in alliance with the Flemish on France's north-eastern border, either to continue the campaign or to re-embark from Flanders.[48]

Edward's hope was that by marching close to Paris, preferably on the north bank of the Seine, he would draw Philip's army to a battlefield of his own choosing. Philip's obvious choice of a rendezvous for his troops would be Rouen, the capital of Normandy, and Edward's route was designed to bring him close to that city, but without any intention of attacking it. He did not intend to besiege any towns, as he would then lose the manoeuvrability which was essential if he was to be able to choose the best site for a battle. The early stages of the march took the army through a series of small towns in the Cotentin: Valognes was taken on the first night, and set on fire as the troops left the following morning. The next day presented a real obstacle: the road eastwards led through Carentan, approached by bridges and causeways across extensive marshes stretching down to the sea on the north and reaching far inland to the south. Fugitives had warned the townsmen of the approaching enemy, and the main bridge was broken to prevent their passage. The army had to encamp at the hilltop village of St Côme-du-Mont while a task force was sent down to repair the damage. The carpenters, guarded by Reginald Cobham, Roger Mortimer, Hugh Despenser, Bartholomew Burghersh the younger, John Stirling and their men, worked through the night, and the army crossed the next morning to Carentan. After a brief resistance, the garrison surrendered and the commanders went over to the English side. It seems that at this stage Edward still envisaged holding the territory which he had invaded, as the commanders were left in charge of the castle in his name. However, it was retaken by the French soon after Edward left, and they were executed for treason.[49] The town itself was sacked by the footsoldiers, who rampaged out of control, wasting wine and food; and local chronicles record that more than a thousand of the inhabitants were killed. Edward had to repeat his edict about the need for discipline, and emphasized 'that no one should waste more food than he needed'.[50] On Friday, 21 July, having crossed the bridges and causeway across the marshes beyond Carentan, scouts found that the next key bridge, in the valley below Pont-Hébert, had again been broken. The prince of Wales's men repaired it the following day, and the army moved on to the town of St Lô. Here Edward signalled his support for Godefroy d'Harcourt and his own status as king of France by burying the heads of three of Harcourt's supporters which had been displayed in the town since their execution for treason in 1343.[51]

Robert Bertrand had retreated in the direction of Caen after his abortive attempt to resist the English landing, and it was reported that he and the constable of France, Raoul count of Eu, had only left St Lô the previous day. Edward was now on the alert for the appearance of the French forces, but they had regrouped within the defences of Caen. Caen lay on the river Orne, and seagoing vessels could come up to the town. It was a rich merchant town, with good defences and a powerful castle, and Edward's tactic was to avoid any fortified place which might delay him or involve the risk of casualties. The presence of the French forces threatened to block his route or at the very least cut off his line of retreat to the ships along the coast. Edward was anxious to keep in touch with his fleet, both as a source of supplies and as a possible means of escape if matters went seriously wrong.

Despite his reluctance to attack a place as strong as Caen, there were therefore good reasons why the army could not simply continue on its way. So Edward encamped in the villages around the town and sent a monk, Geoffrey of Maldon, to offer terms to the citizens, by which their goods would be spared if they surrendered. But Geoffrey did not return. The bishop of Bayeux, Godefroy d'Harcourt's old enemy and now commander of the garrison in the castle, threw him in prison, as a challenge to the English. It was a challenge which was quickly taken up. At dawn the next day, the prince's division and the king's division approached the town, and met with no armed resistance when they entered the landward gates. Half the town was quickly secured, including the twin abbeys for monks and nuns founded by William the Conqueror and his wife: the prince of Wales took up his quarters in the Abbaye aux Dames. The French were hugely outnumbered, as they had only managed to raise 200 armed men and 100 crossbowmen; they had therefore retreated towards the fortified part of the town, the *grand bourg*, around the harbour and the castle, which was separated from the rest of the town by a bridge and a ford. They were backed up by thirty ships in the port, which were positioned to prevent the English from crossing over to the *grand bourg*.

A fierce and undisciplined attack on the bridge, which was guarded by a tower at the entrance, began, and met with equally fierce resistance. Welsh archers fought the Genoese crossbowmen at the ford; it was low tide,[52] and they managed to get at the ships and burn two of them. They then found small boats, and made a landing, while at the same time the English at the bridge overwhelmed the defenders and forced them to retreat and take refuge in nearby buildings. Despite impromptu resistance by the inhabitants, who built barriers using doors and windows from the houses, the English quickly flushed out their enemies, though some found refuge in the castle. Many important captives were taken. Thomas Holland captured the constable, Raoul count of Eu,[53] and a knight in the prince's service, Thomas Daniel, took the count of Tancarville, one of the marshals, prisoner. Nearly a hundred prisoners were taken in all, though in the confusion and lack of discipline, the English footsoldiers killed a number of French noblemen. More than 2,500 men were slain, which implies that a large number of townsmen were among the victims. Edward had his edict against indiscriminate slaughter repeated, but it was clear that the army could not be tightly controlled, and there was in any case a well-established understanding that, under the laws of war, any town taken by storm was open to ravaging by the victors.

The booty taken at Caen quickly became a legend. The *Acts of War* describes how, once the fighting was over, 'the English eagerly returned to the work of despoiling the town, only taking jewels, clothing or precious ornaments because of the abundance. The English sent their booty to their ships . . . [which] followed them along the shore . . . They found such a mass of goods sent to them that they could not transport all the spoils from Caen and elsewhere.'[54] A seventeenth-century French author

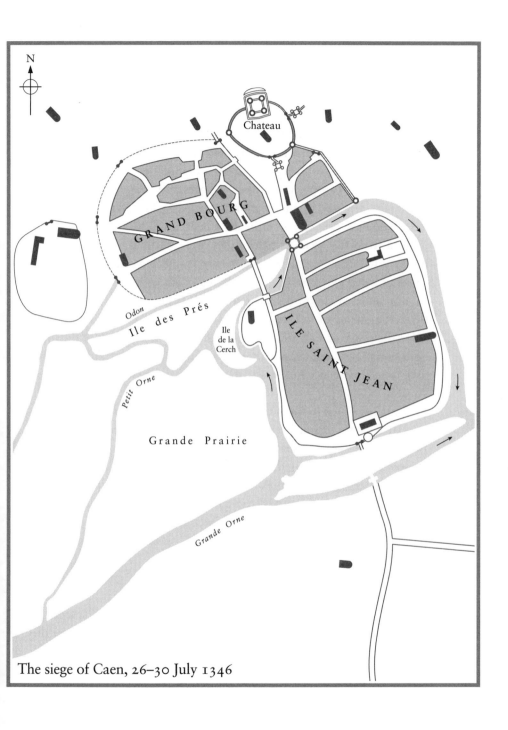

N

Chateau

GRAND BOURG

Odon

Ile des Prés

Ile
de la
Cerch

Petit Orne

ILE SAINT JEAN

Grande Prairie

Grande Orne

The siege of Caen, 26–30 July 1346

believed that 40,000 pieces of cloth were taken from the town, while in the eighteenth century Thomas Warton dated the rise of certain English families from the sack of Caen and the riches that it brought to them.[55] William Clinton, earl of Huntingdon, returned to England 'because of his grave and perilous sickness, although he was very unwilling to go back', taking the prisoners with him; he was instructed by the king to tell the whole story to the royal council.[56]

Part of William Clinton's report was a splendid propaganda coup for Edward. In the town archives at Caen, a detailed plan for the invasion of England in 1339 by John duke of Normandy was found. This was almost certainly due to information provided by Godefroy d'Harcourt, who would have known about the document. It must have been carefully removed from the archives before they were burnt, and it was sent at once to London, where the archbishop of Canterbury read it out on 14 August at a service of prayers for the king's success in France.[57] Edward was now able to claim that his expedition was not only to secure his title to the throne of France, but was an essential pre-emptive strike to ensure the peace of England. This, together with the reports of the huge prizes taken at Caen, changed the attitude of the nation at large from reluctant acquiescence in the war to positive enthusiasm.

The army remained in Caen for five days, during which time the inhabitants of Bayeux, terrified by the fate of Caen, surrendered to the king. They were probably extremely concerned because it was the bishop of Bayeux who had mistreated Geoffrey of Maldon, and was now holding out in the castle at Caen. According to a local chronicle, Edward arranged for a garrison of 1,500 men to be left in the town, and instructed them to besiege the castle. Once again, this implies an intention to hold the conquered territory on a permanent basis. But a combination of a popular uprising and a sortie by the bishop and Robert Bertrand led to the slaughter of the English garrison shortly afterwards.[58]

On 31 July the English forces moved a few miles outside the town to the great abbey at Troarn, overlooking another natural obstacle, the wide marshlands of the river Dives. A long day's march brought them to Léaupartie, the first village on dry ground on the far side of the valley. They then turned south towards the cathedral city of Lisieux, where Edward met two cardinals sent by the pope from Avignon, who

1. Edward III, on the lion of England, is given a sword by
Philip V of France, as a symbol of his inheritance of the
French throne, while Philip VI cowers beneath. From a
manuscript of *c*. 1360–70.

2. (*above*) Edward III gives the charter for the principality of Aquitaine to Edward prince of Wales. From the original charter of 1362.

3. (*left*) Philippa of Hainault, from the manuscript she gave to Edward at the time of their wedding.

4. Four-wheeled cart of type used by Edward's army in
1346. From a manuscript of *c.* 1344.

5. Archery practice, from the Luttrell Psalter, *c.* 1330.

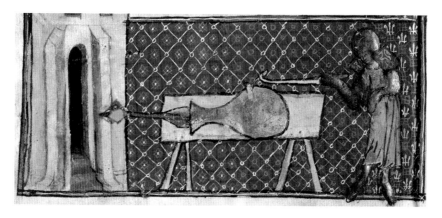

6. An early bombard, from the treatise presented by Walter de
Milemete to Edward III in 1327–8.

7. Tents, from the *Roman d'Alexandre*, c. 1344.

8 (*above right*) A reconstruction of the Garter pavise of c. 1350.

9 (*below*) An army on the march, with prisoners and oxen, from a manuscript of c. 1350–75.

10. (*above*) St George in Garter robes, with the duke of Bedford kneeling before him. From the Bedford Hours, 1423.

11. (*below*) St George's chapel in the 1430s. It is the building with three windows to the right of centre, near the outer wall.

12. William Bruges, Garter King of Arms, with St George, from his Garter Book of *c*. 1430.

13. The earliest known representation of garters: a figure from the Luttrell Psalter, *c.* 1330.

14. A knight wearing the Garter, possibly Sir Edward Despenser, from an Italian fresco of *c.* 1370.

15. Dancers and musicians with 'vizors' or masks covering head and shoulders. From a French manuscript of 1275–1300.

attempted to negotiate a peace between the English and French kings. They had come from an interview with Philip, who was urgently gathering an army at Rouen forty miles away. They offered Edward the duchy of Aquitaine, to be held on the terms that his father had enjoyed, and with the restoration of the same lands, but 'the king thought that their mission was a waste of time',[59] and sent the cardinals back to the papal court after restoring twenty horses which his Welsh soldiers had seized from them.

When the English army set out again on 4 August, the Flemish allies led by Hugh Hastings had invaded French territory south of Calais. France was now under attack in Normandy, Aquitaine and Artois; Philip could only let matters take their course in Aquitaine and summon local militias to deal with the Flemish army, while he concentrated on plans to destroy Edward's forces. On 6 August Godefroy d'Harcourt was sent to reconnoitre Rouen, and was able to report that Philip and his army were now in the castle and city; ditches had been dug in addition to the existing defences, and the main bridges had been broken. Edward was south of the Seine, and urgently needed to cross the river northwards, in order to be able to regain the coast. In a letter of 27 July, he had asked for the ships which had returned to England after Caen with the earl of Huntingdon to be sent back to Le Crotoy, a port on the north bank of the river Somme, with such money and men as the council in England could raise, as well as bows, bowstrings and arrows.[60] If he could not force a battle with Philip, he would at least be able to join up with his Flemish allies.

But Le Crotoy was due north, and for the next nine days he was forced to march down the south bank of the Seine, attempting a crossing wherever he thought it might be feasible, while Philip watched and waited on the other side. There was a marked change in the conditions in which the troops were operating from the first weeks of the campaign. As far as Lisieux, there had been opportunities for replenishing supplies by raiding small undefended towns and villages, and there had been little time for the French to organize the withdrawal of stores into fortified safe places. The terrain was good agricultural land, for the most part. Now, along the Seine valley, the army was repeatedly faced with strongly defended towns, garrisoned and well organized, which they could not take without considerable delay. And delay was not an option: Edward knew that he had to keep one step ahead of Philip, and find a way to cross the Seine before the French army was in position on the other bank. So the troops moved on, testing the defences of the bridges and the towns as they went, from Le Neubourg to Elbeuf, where the Welsh troops managed to cross the Seine by swimming, and brought back a number of small boats after driving off the French who met them on the far bank. Possibly because of the presence of these French soldiers, no attempt was made to mend the broken bridge.

Rather than follow the meandering course of the river, Edward cut across country, 'taking his whole army across country where no one had ever travelled before',[61] and went direct to Vernon to see if he could cross there. However, the town was vigorously defended, and he was unable to gain access to the bridge. The castles at Gaillon, north of Vernon, and at La Roche-Guyon to the east of the town were both attacked, and the first was burnt. The raid on La Roche-Guyon was daring: Robert Ferrers took his men across the Seine in small boats and forced their way into the castle, which surrendered. The *Acts of War* claims that the castle was full of noble ladies, who were released unharmed on promising to raise ransoms for the knights and squires who had been captured. No attempt was made to hold the castle, and the exercise seems to have been a piece of bravado, as there was no question of the army crossing at this point. Edward Attewode[62] was killed here, and either at this castle or at Gaillon Richard Talbot and Thomas Holland were wounded.[63] The following day, 10 August, the army tested the defences at Mantes, and the next day at Meulan, and found them both too strong. At Meulan, the bridge was defended by a tower filled with men at arms and crossbowmen, and there was no quick way of seizing it.

Philip continued to track Edward's movements, and realized that his next target would be Poissy, a major crossing-place ten miles to the west of Paris. The French broke down the bridge because the defensive wall around it had not been reinforced, and evacuated the town, including the convent of which Philip's sister was the prioress. This was Edward's last chance: the march from Lisieux had been arduous, and supplies had been hard to come by, particularly in the deserted country north of Vernon. He could not hope to attack Paris itself, and, if he failed to cross the river, he would be forced to turn back and retrace his steps: he had already requested urgent reinforcements and supplies to be landed on the Normandy coast, and his situation was perilous. The king arrived at Poissy on 13 August, and took up his quarters in the new royal palace, while the prince of Wales installed himself in the old palace, and ordered the carpenters to set about repairing the bridge. That afternoon, the workmen had succeeded in laying a sixty-foot-long beam across the gap when a small French force was seen in the distance. Although the beam was only a foot wide, sufficient English men at arms and archers, led by the earl of Northampton, managed to cross it in time to drive off the French, inflicting heavy casualties. They found twenty-one carts loaded with stone shot and crossbow bolts, evidently intended for an attack on the team repairing the bridge.

This was the most critical moment of the campaign; Edward now needed to gain time for a full repair of the bridge, so he sent out raiding parties to ravage the outskirts of Paris, targeting in particular the royal properties which ringed the city: the castle of Montjoie, Philip's new palace at St Germain-en-Laye and St Cloud were all burnt. Surprisingly, there was no immediate response from the French king, who gathered his army at St Germain-des-Prés on 13 August, and moved the next day to St Denis, to the north of Paris. The 15th of August was one of the great feast days of the Church, the Assumption of the Blessed Virgin Mary, and neither army moved on that day. Despite the reports of English activity on the bridge at Poissy, Philip seems to have believed that the English were heading either for Gascony or for Tournai on the Flemish border, and that, whichever route they chose, they would remain south of Paris. He therefore moved to a position fifteen miles to the south-east of Poissy on 16 August.

The carpenters had had three days in which to work on the bridge unhindered by French attacks. Using timbers from nearby woods and hedgerows, as well as two large pieces fished out of the river,[64] they built a replacement bridge around the sixty-foot beam. As Philip waited for the English to move southwards, the entire force marched north across the newly repaired structure that day. When news of this feat was brought to Philip VI's court, the author of the *Grandes chroniques* was present, and saw the nobles and knights who advised the king mock the messenger, and call him a liar, because they simply could not believe that it was feasible.[65]

Edward was now on the right course for the intended rendezvous with his ships at Le Crotoy at the mouth of the Somme, and Philip was in the position of having to pursue his enemy, rather than wait at a spot of his own choosing to intercept him. On 14 August, he had issued a challenge to Edward to fight him outside the walls of Paris on the south bank of the Seine, or to the north of Paris. These letters reached Edward three days later, when he was already at Auteuil near Beauvais, forty miles from Paris, and he replied saying that Philip had prevented him from giving battle by breaking down the bridges, and that 'at whatever hour you approach, you will find us ready to meet you in the field', but not on the terms and conditions dictated by his opponent.[66] If Edward moved fast, Philip was even swifter, and by Sunday, 20 August he was in Amiens, where he had given orders for troops to assemble at the beginning of the month: they had been gathering there since 4 August, and for once the French king had his men in exactly the right place. He had brought a contingent under the command of King John of Bohemia with him in the rapid march from Paris.

Edward was only ten miles away, and his men were suffering from shortages of food: on the previous Friday they had had to eat meat instead of fish, and bread was sold in the army for five shillings a loaf. Only the royal household was exempt from eating meat, because the king's fishermen had caught an abundance of fish in the local rivers. Furthermore, there were problems with discipline: Edward gave orders to press on as quickly as possible, but a rebellious detachment, possibly the Welsh archers of the prince of Wales, led by the Flemish knight Wulfart Ghistels, attacked the strongly fortified town of Poix, even though the king twice sent sergeants to order them to halt their activities. The army's progress was hindered by the local militia, and by some Bohemian troops who rode out from Amiens: in both skirmishes, the English were able to beat off the assault, but at the cost of further delays.

Once again, Edward was faced with the problem of escaping from a French army which was closing in on him by finding a way across a major river: Le Crotoy, his objective, was on the north bank of the Somme. According to Jean le Bel, the king waited at Airaines, risking a full-scale attack by the French, because he wished to find an easy passage across the river.[67] He organized a diversionary attack on the town of Oisemont to try to deceive Philip, as it lay in the opposite direction to his intended route; it was taken and set on fire so that the French king's scouts would see it. He sent Thomas Beauchamp and Godefroy d'Harcourt to the nearby town of Pont-Rémy, but found it heavily defended, and they were beaten off before they could capture the bridge. The same thing happened at the bridge at Long-en-Ponthieu, and three

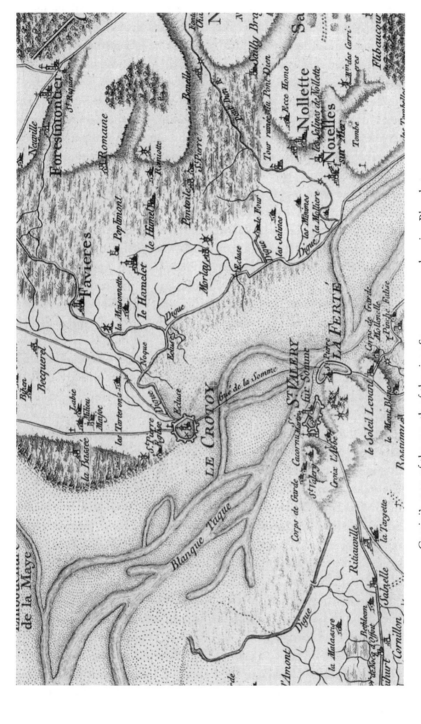

Cassini's map of the mouth of the river Somme, 1790, showing Blanchetaque.

other possible crossings were investigated without challenging the French troops which guarded them. Thomas Beauchamp had ridden thirty miles and fought two skirmishes, but he had nothing to offer the king. However, this was country well known to a number of the English army: Ponthieu had been in English possession until 1338 and Edward himself had been at the castle of Crécy a few miles to the north in 1329. The Somme estuary was shallow and marshy, and there were a number of crossing-places known to the locals, though most of them were quite unsuitable for an army with heavy carts which would require a large ford. The existence of a good ford, known as the 'white spot' or Blanchetaque, was rumoured, but the English had to find it.

The chroniclers give the impression that although the existence of the ford at Blanchetaque was known, its exact nature was a problem. Edward had moved north again, towards Abbeville, the most important town in the area, which his troops had reconnoitred, hoping perhaps to surprise the garrison of this well-defended place. Instead, they had met the French outside the walls, because they had sallied out to meet them. They were victorious in the ensuing skirmish, but the possibility of capturing the bridge was gone.

That evening, encamped at Acheux, Edward sent out scouts to look for the ford. The most probable account of its discovery is given by the Bernier family's chronicle of Valenciennes, a generally reliable source. A squire from the retinue of Wulfart Ghistels came back to the camp and told the king that he had found a good way across: 'and it has a good bottom, because I crossed it several times on horseback when the tide had gone down a little.' Philip was also aware of the crossings in the seven miles of marsh and river between Abbeville and the sea, and had sent Godemar du Fay with three other knights, 500 men at arms and 3,000 of the local militia, to guard these crossings. From the north bank, any movement on the other side of the river would have been clearly visible. By the time the English army was in place at the ford, Godemar had found them, and drew up his men on the north bank. He had Genoese crossbowmen with him. Meanwhile, Philip had set out from Abbeville with his main army in the hope of catching the English before they crossed the ford, and forcing them to engage hemmed in by the river, without being able to choose their field of battle.

The story of the passage of the English army and its dramatic escape from the pursuing French army became the stuff of legend very quickly.

The most reliable accounts, as always, are those brief passages in the English newsletters written within days of the event. They agree that this was not a narrow ford, but a crossing on a broad front: Richard Wynkeley, the king's confessor, wrote on 2 September:

> our lord the king was unable to find a way across except in the tidal reach between Crotoy and Abbeville; here the whole army crossed unharmed at a place which none of the local people knew to be a safe ford except for six or ten people at a time. Our men crossed almost everywhere, as if it were a safe ford, much to the amazement of those who knew the place.[68]

Edward III gives a similar description:

> When we came to the river Somme, we found the bridges broken, so we went towards St Valery to cross at a ford where the sea ebbs and flows ... By God's grace a thousand men crossed abreast where before this barely three or four used to cross, and so we and all our army crossed safely in an hour and a half.[69]

The idea of 1,000 men in line abreast is obviously an exaggeration, as this would need an area nearly half a mile wide, yet it was clearly a broad crossing place. This is confirmed by the account of the Valenciennes chronicle. When the army reached the river bank, the squire

> spurred his horse and went into the water, and he rode down river and up river in the presence of the king and his men. And when he had tested the bottom down river and up river, he came out, and said to the king, 'Did I tell you the truth?' And the king agreed, and at once gave him a hundred écus.[70]

The squire does not ride *across* the river, but goes up and down to show that the troops can cross abreast.

The St Omer chronicle describes the ford as being near St Valéry, a place 'where the cattle of the region were accustomed to cross when the tide was out', which would again indicate a broad passage.[71] And Jean le Bel says that Edward was told that a dozen men abreast could cross; 'and carts can cross there safely, too, because there's a bed of good, firm chalk, which is why it's called Blanchetaque.'[72] Henry Knighton records that 'no regular passage there was known to the men of those lands, and so they crossed a wash of the sea about a league wide'.[73] It is quite clear from these descriptions that this is not a river ford, but in the estuary itself. The estuary is sand, but the chalk cliffs at St Valéry indicate that there is a band of chalk on the river bed which reappears at Le Crotoy. Even so, this would be a treacherous crossing without a guide, as the sands would drift over the chalk base. Today there are organized guided walks across the estuary from St Valéry to Le Crotoy,[74] and, although the estuary has silted considerably since the river was turned into a canal in the eighteenth century a couple of miles inland, the basic geology would of course have been the same. The chronicle of Meaux abbey in east Yorkshire says that

> King Edward, instructed by a certain Englishman born at Ruston near Nafferton, who had lived in those parts for sixteen years, went to a ford on the aforesaid river [the Somme] at the towns of St Valéry and Le Crotoy, where the sea flows and ebbs. He crossed there with his men, where previously the local inhabitants had never crossed more than six or four at once.[75]

Nafferton was one of the abbey's larger estates, and this is possibly first-hand information. If the crossing was indeed there, Edward's informant may well have shown the king the way across the difficult sands, which required a knowledgeable guide: the distance was about two miles, and involved the crossing of at least one channel. Similar sand-crossings, for example at Morecambe Bay in England, were crossed by coaches in the eighteenth century, and would easily have borne the weight of carts if the right track could be found.

It was high water during the night, at 3 a.m., and the army left Acheux at dawn, which would have been at 5.30 a.m., and reached St Valéry at low water. The sands would have been passable around 7.30 a.m. It was three days after spring tides, so there would have been little or no tidal water at this point, and only a narrow flow from the river Somme. It was an ideal moment for a mass of men to cross: Edward's luck had held. The English formed up in battle order on the south bank, and moved across ready for action. The archers were in front, as they would normally be on the battlefield, since their range was considerably greater than the crossbowmen they were expecting to encounter. They were followed by the Welsh spearmen, and a contingent led by Thomas Beauchamp and Godefroy d'Harcourt; then came the carts carrying provisions and supplies, and the main divisions of the army led by the king, the prince of Wales and the bishop of Durham. The advance party were detailed to fight off the French defending the north shore. It seems that they did this without any help from the rest of the army. Godemar du Fay, who was a distinguished commander, simply did not have enough men to resist the English onslaught, and was forced to flee after a bitter fight, having lost a large number of his men.

Soon after the crossing was completed, the French army came into sight on the south shore. Philip had hoped to find the English delayed by Godemar du Fay, and at his mercy, but he had already been told by his scouts that they were crossing successfully. He probably arrived at Blanchetaque after 9.30 a.m., when the tide would have turned, and it was dangerous to attempt the crossing when the water was rising if he was to get his whole army safely across.[76] According to Edward's newsletter,

> That same day, soon after we had crossed the river, our adversary appeared on the other bank with a very large force. He arrived so suddenly that we were not in the least ready; so we waited there and took up battle positions, and stayed like this the whole day and the next day, until the afternoon. Finally, when we saw that he did not want to cross but turned back towards Abbeville, we marched towards Crécy to meet him on the other side of the forest.[77]

Edward was now on familiar ground. He had been at Crécy in 1329, and had hunted there; one of his commanders, Bartholomew Burghersh the elder, had been seneschal of Ponthieu at the time, and is likely to have visited the castle of Crécy, while Gawan Corder, a knight in the royal household, had held a manor nearby. The accounts of the clerk of the kitchen record that the army camped that night 'below the forest of Crécy', but this does not imply that the men were in a thickly wooded area. The medieval forest was a place where forest law applied, and, as with the New Forest in England today, it included areas of heathland or open scrub. It appears that the forest area stretched down to the river bank, with the wooded area, which still exists today, to the north.

Edward's move the next day took him out of sight of any French scouts watching from the south bank, and to a site which he quickly identified as an ideal ground on which to meet Philip's army. It has been argued that Edward had considered this as a possible battleground from early in the campaign, and that the request for provisions and men to be sent to Le Crotoy relates to the idea that he could lure the French to

Crécy. This seems unlikely; one of the skills of the medieval general was to choose the right terrain swiftly and under pressure, as the vagaries of any campaign were far too great to allow for much planning. But once Edward was at Crécy, he and his commanders saw the potential of the land to the east of the forest as terrain on which the military techniques they had learnt in Scotland could be deployed to advantage.

The exact site of the battle, generally thought to have been the fields to the east of the village of Crécy, cannot be identified for certain.[78] The greatest problem is that there is absolutely no solid archaeological evidence to indicate that a battle was fought on the area now generally accepted as the battlefield. Added to this is general confusion among the chroniclers as to the description of the site; but it is open rolling country and it is extremely difficult to characterize a given place or even an area. One prominent physical contour on the hillside, a steep bank called the Vallée des Clercs with a drop of sixteen feet, is not mentioned by any of the chroniclers, but would certainly have played a major part in determining the direction of the French attack. All we can say for certain is that the slopes running down from the ridge to the north of the village to the little river Maye, and bounded on the south-west by the bank, are the most likely position for the battlefield. The river may have been wider, and the water table higher, in the fourteenth century, and therefore more of an obstacle to the advance – or retreat – of an army.

The ground is thin soil over chalk, which may account for the lack of archaeological finds. Some of this would have been cultivated land, in the traditional medieval form of strip farming: between the crops there would have been strips of grazing. It was a landscape of small and varied agricultural activities, with no particular features to help or hinder the movement of an army. Edward's defensive positions were evidently towards the top of the hill, as was usual: the uphill slope would slow both the attacking infantry and cavalry. The only prominent object mentioned by a small number of chroniclers is a windmill at the top of the slope, from which Edward is said to have directed his troops.

We can describe the setting of the battle with reasonable confidence. When it comes to the action, the task is much harder.

7

The Battle at Crécy

What happened at Crécy in the following days became an instant sensation: word of this astonishing event spread rapidly through Europe, and its mythical status survives even today. English families will claim with pride that they had an ancestor who fought at Crécy; though these claims are all too often unfounded, deriving from Victorian patriotism rather than any genuine tradition, the battle is an event which still resounds.

The problems of retrieving any real picture of the events leading up to the battle or of the battle itself are extremely difficult. Chroniclers faced with describing such a battle, with little hard information to go on, either tended to rely on the testimony of individuals, or retreated to a summary of the reasons why the English won or the French lost, depending on their viewpoint. Even within a decade of the battle, we can detect these two tendencies at work, and there is a third difficulty: the sheer impossibility of any one single observer being able to know what was actually happening on the ground. What the chroniclers managed to record is the individual impressions of soldiers which were very largely determined by their position within the battle array. The only people who might have been able to give a more coherent account would have been the king himself and his commanders, if the story that the king stationed himself on a windmill to the rear of the battlefield is true, as it very probably is: ten years later, at Poitiers, the prince of Wales established himself on a high point which gave him an overview of the fighting. A handful of men with the king at Crécy might have had some idea of the sequence of events, but would have known little of the details.

The battle of Crécy has been endlessly analysed by military historians with their neat diagrams of oblong blocks of troops, arrows indicating movement, and precise maps of the terrain. Their concern is with military strategy and organization, but none of the chroniclers on whom they have to rely have more than a rudimentary grasp of such matters. They rarely agree as to the number and position of the battalions, their commanders or their manoeuvres. Instead of beginning with the overall picture, it is far more realistic to listen to the witnesses as carefully as we can, and see what conclusions we may draw.

The idea that no one could really know what went on in a medieval battle was admirably summed up by Gilles li Muisit, the abbot of Tournai, writing his account of the battle of Crécy five years later. Anticipating John Keegan's classic account of the difficulty of using eyewitness accounts for the events of Waterloo by six hundred years,[1] Li Muisit roundly declared that, in the heat of the fighting, no one was aware of more than his immediate surroundings:

> Since the events of war are uncertain, and seeing that the conflict is between deadly enemies, each fighting man intent on conquering rather than being conquered, and no one can take account of all those fighting around him, nor can those present form a good judgement of these matters, only the result of their deeds can be judged. Therefore, because many men say and record many things about this conflict, and on the side of the French king and his men some maintain things which cannot be known for certain, and others on the part of the English king also maintain things about which the truth is not known, because of these varying opinions I will not enquire after the event about what cannot be proved, but have tried to satisfy the understanding of those who come after me by setting down only those things which I have heard from certain people worthy of belief, even if I cannot be totally sure that they are what happened.[2]

The only direct eyewitnesses for the events of the battle are from the English side. They are from Edward himself and his administrative staff, in the newsletters sent back to England within days of the battle. What they have to tell us is meagre and disappointing, but the writers were probably well aware that, although they were almost the only people to have any kind of overview of the battle, even they could not describe the action with any precision. The accounts of the capture of Caen had been more detailed, because the stages of the struggle were marked by buildings which could be readily identified and remembered. But here at

Crécy, there had been a mass of men in hand-to-hand combat in the open field. Edward himself is extremely terse as to the action: 'The battle was very fierce and long drawn out, lasting from mid-afternoon until the evening. The enemy bore themselves nobly, and often rallied, but in the end, praise be to God, they were defeated and our adversary fled.'[3] When it comes to the aftermath, he is on surer ground; he has the names of the kings who were killed, and knows that many other nobles died, who have not been identified at the time of writing. And he has seen that in the 'small area' where the first attack took place, 'more than 1,500 knights and squires died'.

Michael Northburgh simply echoes the king's phrases, saying that the battle was 'very stubborn, and endured a long while, because the enemy bore themselves very nobly'. Richard Wynkeley, in contrast, does have some details: 'The adversary himself [i.e. Philip], intending to attack the king personally, stationed himself in the front line; and he was opposed by the prince, who was in our front line. After a fierce and prolonged conflict, the adversary was twice driven off, and a third time, having gathered his men, the fighting was fiercely renewed.'[4] Wynkeley does not say that the battle was won, but lists the kings and nobles who died, and claims that the French king, wounded in the face by an arrow, barely escaped, and that the French standard, the *oriflamme*, was torn to pieces and its bearer killed. He concludes by giving thanks for the escape of Edward and his army 'from great danger'.

These were the immediate messages home. Was there an official account, at greater length, which recorded the battle in more vivid terms? The *Acts of War* is incomplete, and looks very much like an official record of the campaign. It opens with pomp and ceremony: 'These are the acts of war of the most illustrious prince lord Edward, by grace of God king of England and France and of Edward the eldest son of that king, prince of Wales, duke of Cornwall and earl of Chester, which they did at sea and in the kingdom of France, from the last day of June 1346 onwards.'[5] What is striking is that the timespan of the campaign is left in the air: where one would expect a triumphant mention of Crécy and Calais, there is nothing, no ending. There is the question of whether the *Acts* was ever completed. We have no way of knowing, except by looking for traces of it in the contemporary English chronicles. If it was finished in late 1346, Adam Murimuth and Robert of Avesbury, with good access to official records, would almost certainly have used it. Instead, they have only the newsletters. This means that it is unlikely to have been – as has been suggested – the same as the report that Bartholomew Burghersh the elder presented to parliament at Westminster on 13 September 1346, in which he

> declared the graces which God had given our lord the king and others of his company since their arrival at la Hogue in Normandy, such as good towns, castles, and prisons, takings of war, both at Caen and in many other places, and also the victory which God gave them at Crécy, where the enemy was defeated with all his great host . . .

Burghersh went on to outline the king's intention to take Calais, where the siege had just begun, and then to go in pursuit of his enemy and not to return to England before he had brought an end to his war overseas. He then produced the plan for the invasion of Normandy found at Caen, and used this and the king's achievements as a basis for a request for new taxes.[6]

The purpose of the *Acts of War* is therefore not clear. All we can say is that the writer was a clerk deeply involved in the campaign, with access to documents such as Philip's challenge to battle sent to Edward and Edward's reply. What we have is probably written up from notes made at the time, but this could have been done a year or two after the campaign. Judging from his accounts of other military actions, the writer is relying on what he sees himself, and on the immediate talk within the camp. His account of Crécy, if it ever existed, would have been similar: it would have been detailed and immensely valuable, but it would have been gathered from individuals rather than edited as an official history.

There may have been other such documents; indeed, given that we know that a number of letters were sent home, and that some of them were addressed to individuals rather than sent for official circulation, it is virtually certain that the surviving letters are only a portion of those which contained descriptions of the battle. Details that are found in later English chronicles may be from eyewitness accounts. On the other hand, there are no narratives of the battle in the English chronicles which immediately stand out as coming from a single comprehensive version of the events at Crécy. With one exception, Adam Murimuth, whose work ends in 1347, the chroniclers are writing at the distance of a decade or more, most of them after the second great English victory, at Poitiers in 1356; they are inevitably influenced by the stories, true or otherwise, that grew up around the earlier spectacular victory in the interval. But the English historians do not tell those stories; instead, we have a detail here and there which sheds a little light on the events of the battle.

It is less surprising that the French chroniclers have relatively little to tell us about the events of 26 August 1346. Defeat always figures less largely in the history books than victory, and this is no exception. Furthermore, the earliest major chronicle from France that survives today was written more than thirty years after the event. The Flemish chronicles, however, are much more informative, and seem to have drawn on the experiences of knights from Hainault, who fought on both sides. Jean de Hainault, Philippa's uncle, was one of the French leaders, while there was a strong contingent of Hainault knights and squires in the English ranks. Jean le Bel tells us specifically that his information came from Jean de Hainault personally before his death in November 1356; the chronicle of Valenciennes seems to have drawn on English informants. But neither these nor the other Flemish chronicles give us a rounded account of the sequence of manoeuvres. All we have is a series of snapshots, or collections of snapshots, of episodes within the battle, around which the chroniclers attempt to make sense of the stories they have heard.

For the best contemporary overview of the battle, we have to turn, surprisingly, to an Italian source: the chronicle of Giovanni Villani, writing in Florence. Villani specifically tells us that his information came from several sources; in accounting for the casualties, he prefaces his estimates with the words, 'In the said grievous and unfortunate battle most of those who write about it say . . .' Given that he is writing not later than 1348 – he died of the plague that year – his sources cannot have been other chroniclers, but must have been newsletters reaching the great merchant houses of Florence. He seems to have had news from the French side, and possibly from Genoa, since he has details which appear to come from the crossbowmen themselves, and names both their commanders. Equally, he has good information on the English side, and we know that his contacts with England were very close. His account of the battle tells us a great deal about the disposition of the troops, and particularly about the situation to the rear of the army. Whoever provided the original information knew how the English forces had been organized and placed, and it is tempting to think that it might have been a clerk or administrator who witnessed the fighting from the rearguard.

This is Villani's picture of the battle and the events following the crossing of the Somme at Blanchetaque:

> Then they went on their way, hungry and with great discomfort, march-ing on Friday, 25 August almost twelve Picard leagues by day and night, without rest, with much anxiety and hunger, and arrived six leagues from Amiens at a place and village beside a forest which was called Crécy. And they had to cross a small river, which was deep, and could only go through it one or two abreast as they came out of the ford, which they had not reckoned on. And hearing that the king of France was following them, they encamped in the place outside Crécy on a hill between Crécy and Abbeville in Ponthieu; and to strengthen their position, feeling that they were very few in number compared with the French, and to increase their safety, they enclosed the army with carts, of which they had plenty, both of their own and from the country.[7] They deliberately left an entrance, and, unable to avoid a battle, they made ready to fight and to die in battle rather than die of hunger, because they could not flee. And the king of England arranged his archers, of whom he had a great many, on top of the carts and underneath them, with guns[8] which fired iron shot,[9] to frighten and destroy the French horses. And the next day he organized his knights into three battalions within the carts.[10] The king's son was the captain of the first, the earl of Arundel of the second, and the king of England of the third. All the riders dismounted with their horse to their right to save their energy and to comfort themselves with food and drink.

Villani's focus then moves to the pursuing French army, hard on the heels of their exhausted prey, and full of self-confidence:

> And they felt that they had plenty of good men at arms and knights, because the king of France had a good 12,000 knights, and almost num-berless men at arms on foot, while the king of England had hardly 4,000 knights and 30,000 English and Welsh archers, and some men with Welsh axes and short lances. When they came close enough to the English camp to charge them on horseback, on a Saturday after noon, on 26 August 1346, the king of France arranged his men in three groups, called battles. In the first there were a good 6,000 Genoese and Italian crossbowmen led

by Carlo Grimaldi and Anton Doria, and with the crossbowmen was King John of Bohemia and his son Charles, elected king of the Romans, with some other barons and knights, 3,000 horsemen in all. The next battle was led by Charles count of Alençon, brother of the king of France, with several counts and barons, 4,000 horsemen and a good number of men at arms on foot. The third battle was led by the king of France with the other kings we have named and earls and barons, and the rest of his army, a countless number of men on horse and on foot. As soon as the battle began, there appeared above the armies two great ravens, crying and croaking; and then there was a little shower of rain; and when it stopped, the battle began. The first division with the crossbowmen attacked the carts of the king of England and began to fire with their bows; but they were soon rebuffed, because on the carts and under the carts under cover of the canvas and drapes which protected them from the crossbow bolts, and in the battalions of the king of England, which were inside the array of carts drawn up in good order as battalions of knights, were 30,000 archers, as already mentioned, both English and Welsh, who, when the Genoese fired one round of crossbow bolts, fired three arrows with their bows, like a cloud in the air. They did not fall in vain, but wounded men and horses; there were also shots from the bombards, which made such a roaring and tumult that it seems as if God himself was thundering, with great slaughter of men and bringing down of horses. But what was worse for the French army, because the entrance to the array of carts of the English king was such a narrow place,[11] the second battle led by the count of Alençon pressed the crossbowmen so close against the carts that they could not move or fire with their crossbows, so that many were wounded or killed. Because of this the said crossbowmen could not hold their ground, crowded in and pressed against the carts by their own horsemen; so they turned and fled. The French knights and men at arms, seeing them flee, thought they had been betrayed; they themselves killed them, and few of them escaped. Seeing the first division of crossbowmen of the king of France take to flight, Edward the fourth,[12] son of the English king, prince of Wales, who led the first battalion of his knights, 1,000 in number with 6,000 Welsh archers, mounted his horse and they all rode out of the array of carts to attack the French king's cavalry, with the king of Bohemia and his son in the first battle, and the count of Alençon, brother of the king of France, the count of Flanders, the count of Blois, the count of Harcourt, Sir Jean de Hainault and several other counts and great lords. The encounter was bitter and hard, but the second battalion of the king of England followed after him, led by the earl of Arundel, and they put the first and second battles of the French to flight, mainly through the flight of the Genoese. And in this turmoil were killed the king of Bohemia and the count of Alençon, with many counts and barons and knights and men at arms. The king of France, seeing his people flee, charged the array of carts of King Edward with his third battalion, and did such great deeds of arms himself that he forced the English back inside the carts. And they would all have been defeated if King Edward and his third battalion had not left the array of carts by another opening, which they made so that they could attack the enemy from behind and come to the rescue of their comrades, fiercely attacking the enemy from the flank, with his Welsh and English footmen with bows and Welsh lances, whose only purpose was to disembowel the horses. But what most confused the French was that a multitude of their men, who were both on horse and on foot, who intended to charge the English and break their ranks, piled up on top of one another as had happened at Courtrai with the Flemish; and the dead Genoese hindered them particularly, as they lay on the ground from the rout of the first battalion with exhausted and dying horses; and they were attacked by bombards and arrows so that there were no French horses which were not wounded, and innumerable dead. This grievous battle lasted from vespers to two hours after nightfall. In the end the French could not endure it any longer, and fled; and the king of France fled wounded to Amiens that night . . .

Villani then describes the action on the following day, in the course of which some French troops who had remained on the battlefield made a stand, and were put to flight by Thomas Beauchamp and William Bohun. Further levies then arrived from Amiens, and were likewise defeated, leaving the English in control of the battlefield. He concludes with a list of the dead, and with the moral to be drawn from this disaster:

> Among the notable lords who died there were King John of Bohemia with five counts of Germany who were in his company, and the king of Majorca, the count of Alençon, brother of the king of France, the count of Flanders, the count of Blois, the duke of 'Renno', the count of Sancerre, the count of Harcourt, the count of 'Albamala' and his son, the count of Salm in Germany who was with the king of Bohemia, Sir Carlo Grimaldi

and Anton Doria of Genoa, and many other lords, for we do not know the names of all of them. King Edward remained on the field for two days, and had the mass of the Holy Spirit sung, thanking God for his victory, and for the dead; he had the place consecrated and buried the dead, both enemy and friend, and had the wounded carried from among the dead and cared for by doctors. The common soldiers were given money and dismissed. The lords who were found among the dead he had buried most nobly there at an abbey, and among the rest he held a most grand and honourable funeral for the king of Bohemia, as befitted a king's corpse, and wept for love of him because of his death. He and many of his barons dressed in black, and sent his body with an honourable escort to Charles his son, who was at the abbey of 'Riscampo', and from there his son took it to Luxembourg. And this done, the said King Edward, after his most fortunate victory, in which few of his people died in comparison with the French, left Crécy and went to Montreuil.

O *sanctus sanctus dominus deus Sabaoth*, runs the Latin, 'holy, holy, holy, Lord God, lord of hosts', great is Your power in heaven and on earth, and especially in battles. Sometimes and often He makes the smaller number and force conquer the greater army to demonstrate His power, and to beat down pride and pomp, and cleanse the sin of the king and lords and people. And in this defeat He showed His power, because the French were three times as many as the English. But it was not without good reason that this disaster befell the king of France, who among his other sins – quite apart from the wrong done to the king of England and his other lords by occupying their heritage and lordships – had ten years before taken the cross and sworn to Pope John, promising to go overseas within two years to reconquer the Holy Land, and had taken the tenths and subsidies from his whole realm, and made war with them unjustly against Christian lords. As a result of this, 100,000 Armenians and other Christians who had begun a war against the Saracens of Syria expecting his help were killed or enslaved: and that is enough to explain it all.[13]

Villani is a good historian, and this is a historian's account of the battle, the first of many attempts to create some kind of order out of the turmoil of the fighting. His final paragraph shows that he is trying to set out his history in the widest context, that of morality and divine judgement, but at the same time he is a master of detail and analysis. There are obvious errors: numbers, as so often in medieval chronicles, are wild overestimates, because very few people ever saw a large gathering of men. And other points can be corrected either from records or from writers with better sources of information. He is writing before the stories had begun to grow up and before writers like Baker and Froissart made the event into a kind of set piece – for Baker, it is an opportunity for a display of Latin rhetoric, for Froissart, a chance to write it up as a series of scenes from a contemporary romance. Both are in their way deeply serious historians; yet Villani's mixture of businesslike analysis and moral judgement is probably the most accurate of the early chronicles.

The story of Crécy was written and rewritten for the next half-century, using the accounts of men who had been there, quickly becoming a legend rather than history. Villani was probably working entirely from written sources, and had a sound grasp of French geography as well as an instinctive distrust of the personal reminiscence. The anonymous author of a chronicle written in Rome a decade after Villani is principally concerned with the dramatic events that led to the declaration of the Roman republic in 1347. It is a very personal document: the author declares that he has told it from the experiences of himself and of men he knows, but he also gives us 'certain information, in brief, about happenings which were concurrent with these' from written sources.[14] All we know about the author is that he had studied medicine at Bologna in his youth, and that he had read classical authors such as Livy and St Isidore's great medieval encyclopedia called the *Etymologies*. He records in the course of his Roman history other 'novelties' which took place at the same time elsewhere in Europe, one of them being the battle of Crécy. His account seems to rely on at least one contemporary newsletter, from which he got some of his figures for the strength of the armies and the number of those killed, and on oral accounts by Genoese and Bohemian soldiers who took part in the battle. These are supplemented by ideas about battle tactics derived from Livy.[15] The result is a strange but very striking document, by turns very detailed and vivid as to events on the battlefield, and hopelessly confused about geography: he seems to believe that Paris lay close to the battlefield. This is what he has to say:

> King Philip had promised to take the field; he knew well that his barons were not loyal to him. He knew well that his barons had bargained with

the English and put them in the midst of France. He grieved greatly to see his enemy wander freely through France unopposed. However, he provided himself with many good men. He had 100,000 knights and 12,000 men on foot. He had the king of Bohemia, named John, with 1,000 Germans. This John liked to fight as a mercenary. He also had the king of Majorca – his name was Jaime – who had been chased out of his kingdom. He too took the king's wages. And there was Louis count of Flanders, who had been chased out of his county. And there were Sir Otto Doria and Sir Carlo Grimaldi with 5,000 Genoese crossbowmen. There were many counts and barons and a good number of soldiers. Now I look at the king of England who encamped for the night in a very broad valley which was eight leagues from Paris. This valley lay below a castle which was called Mount Crécy. On the other side there was a town with more than 5,000 inhabitants called Abbeville. Between these two places, in the open fields at the foot of the slope of Crécy he placed all his men and drew up his host.

The chronicler describes the activity in Paris and the arrival of the news that the English had pitched camp. Armour was in such short supply that a complete suit cost 200 florins:

Day dawned. King Philip's pleasure was that the king of Bohemia was to be his captain-general and should set out in safety; and so it was. John, king of Bohemia, son of the Emperor Henry, Jaime king of Majorca, Louis count of Flanders and all the other barons set out from Paris. As they set out, the English watched the direct road from Paris from a distance, for they had a good view of it. They watched the French setting out and coming towards their camp. They could tell where they were by the flashing of the polished helmets and by the fluttering of the banners lit by the rays of the rising sun.[16] King Edward watched them and knew for certain that he could not escape giving battle. And considering the number of the French it is not surprising that he was a little afraid. He was doubtful and said aloud, 'God help me!' Then quickly, in a small space of time, he surrounded his host with good iron chains with many iron stakes stuck in the ground. This surround was made in the shape of a horseshoe, closed all round, except for a larger space behind like a gateway for the entrance and exit. Then he had deep ditches dug where there were weak places. All the English were set to work. Then this chain was surrounded by carts which they had brought with them. They put one cart beside the next

with the shafts up in the air. It looked very like a good walled city and
the carts stood in a dense row. Then the king arranged his troops in this
fashion. On the left flank, on the side towards Crécy, there was a little hill.
On this was a piece of woodland. The corn was also standing, which had
not been harvested. It was the month of September, the third day.[17]
Because it had been very cold in that country, the corn only ripened in
September. In that wood and in the cornfield he arranged 10,000 English
archers in hiding. Then he placed in each cart a barrel of arrows. He allocated two archers to each barrel.[18] Then he chose from his army 500
well-equipped horsemen. Their captain was Edward prince of Wales,
his son. This was the first battalion. Behind these 500 he placed two
wings each of 500 knights, one on the right and one on the left. Behind this
500 he placed 1,000 knights, who were the third battalion. Behind these
1,000 he placed himself with all the other knights, behind the host and
behind the chains. When he had done this he comforted his men and com-
mended himself to God and said: 'Ah God, defend and help the righteous
cause!'

On the French side, the king of Bohemia was briefed about the English
dispositions, and sent a message to Philip that the battle could not be
won; but when Philip accused him of being afraid, he denied it, and
drew up his army:

Then he ordered the battalions which had been drawn up to advance. For
in the meanwhile he had drawn up nine battalions. But three were the
famous ones, the principal ones. The first battalion was that of Sir Otto
Doria and Sir Carlo Grimaldi, captains of 5,000 Genoese crossbowmen
on foot. The second was that of the king of Majorca and the count of
Flanders with 3,000 knights. Then there were many individual groups
of soldiers. Then there was the battalion of the king of Bohemia with
1,000 Germans and 4,000 Frenchmen and with his son Charles. The first
battalion which came into the field in the morning was the Genoese crossbowmen, 5,000 in number. They were ordered to climb the slope at Crécy
to take up a position above[19] the English; but this was not done, because
the English had occupied the hill and placed obstacles in the corn. So they
placed themselves on another hillock further off. Then there was a shower;
they could not fire their crossbows, because they could not load them.
There had been a little rain. The ground was waterlogged and soft. When

they wanted to load their crossbows, each man put his foot on the stirrup. His foot slipped. They could not fix the foot of the crossbow in the earth. Then there was a murmuring among the French and they were afraid that the Genoese had betrayed them because they had not received their pay. They said: 'These men are not firing their crossbows, and if they do fire them they are using wooden shafts without iron tips. Let the Genoese die.' Saying this, the French grew angry with their soldiers. They roughly drew their swords and lances. The Genoese were killed to the last man. Sir Otto complained about the death of his men to the king, who replied, 'We do not need footsoldiers. We have enough men.' This was the first exchange of blows. Five thousand Genoese were killed in an hour. Now the scene of conflict changed to the clash of the battalion of the king of Majorca with Edward duke of Wales. When they came together, the shock was so great, the noise and the clash of spears, that it seemed as if mountains were colliding. One man gave a blow, another took it. They sounded numbers of trumpets and bagpipes . . .

While this was going on, the English archers came down the hill through the corn, and fired continually on the cavalry. They drew their bows and fired arrows – thud, thud, thud. They put everyone in danger. On the left side the horses fell, so that half the army was missing. The wounded knights began to flee. The horses fell dead. The English followed. This battalion was lost.

There are many problems with this account, and it would be easy to dismiss the whole story out of hand. Against this, there are some very striking details, in terms of the general description of the landscape, and the realistic reason given for the failure of the crossbowmen to respond to English fire. What he has to say about the carts corresponds closely with Villani, but is plainly drawn from a different source.

Few of the writers, however, tell us how the English army was drawn up, because most of the French and English chroniclers were concerned to record the battalion in which the great nobles served, and were interested in the honour and deeds of individuals rather than the broader – and much more elusive – question of deployment and tactics. Modern military historians have taken radically different views as to what Edward's battle preparations were, faced with the absence of any real description in the French and English sources. The most striking example of the variation in chroniclers' attitudes is perhaps that of the *Chronicles of*

Flanders, a relatively late compendium which includes early material, and the St Omer chronicle, which is a variant version of it. The writer of the *Chronicles of Flanders* is only interested in the way in which the army was drawn up:

> Edward had the trumpets sounded and the alarm raised throughout the army; he ordered his battalions as we will describe. He made three of them. The first was led by the prince of Wales, son of the English king. This battalion was on a slope leading up to a mill, and behind it there was a wood. The second was led by the king of England but he was not armed in his full arms, and had a surcoat of green velvet with gold letters. And this battalion was behind the other one, and they made a great hedge of their carts, so they could not be surprised. The third battalion was led by the earl of Arundel . . .[20]

The St Omer chronicle, by contrast, wants to tell us about the personnel, omitting all reference to tactics and giving lists of names of those in each battalion instead, though the framework is identical:

> Edward had the trumpets sounded and the alarm raised throughout the army; he ordered his battalions as we will describe. He made three of them, and we will name the banners in the three battalions. The first was led by the prince of Wales, son of the English king, and with him the bannerets who followed him: that is, the earl of Northampton, the earl of Warwick, Sir Roger Mortimer, the Lord Fitzwalter, Sir William Kerdeston, Sir William Carswell, Sir Bartholomew Burghersh and Sir Bartholomew his son, the lord of Man, Lord Say, Sir William Cantilupe, Sir Thomas Dashwood, Sir Aymery de St Amant, Lord Scales, Sir Thomas Ughtred, Sir Robert Bourchier and Sir Robert Verdon. The second was led by the king of England but he was not armed in his full arms, and with him were the earl of Oxford, the son of the earl Warenne, Sir Richard Talbot the king's seneschal, Sir John Darcy and Sir John his son, Sir Reginald Cobham, Sir Maurice Berkeley, Sir John Stirling, Sir John Chevereston, the Lord Poynings, Sir John Lisle, Sir Robert Causton, Sir John Grey, Sir William Fitzwarin, Sir Thomas de Braose, Sir Thomas Bradeston, Sir John Montgomery, Sir Robert Ferrers. And this battalion was behind the other one, and they made a defence out of their carts behind them. The third battalion was led by the earl of Suffolk, the earl of Arundel, the earl of Huntingdon, Sir Hugh Despenser, Sir Robert

Morley, the lord of 'Tringas' and the lord of 'Baruf'. This battalion was the rearguard and guarded the tents and the carts.[21]

The author of the St Omer chronicle, in his enthusiasm to show his knowledge of the lords serving in the English army, has suppressed information which we would find much more valuable. His list is fairly garbled in terms of who served in which division, but shows some knowledge of the leading figures. It probably came direct from one of the clerks with the English army. It was easier to describe the battle in terms of people and personal stories than to give an overview, and we have to build up any picture of the sequence of events from scraps of information.

Returning to the issue of the formation used by Edward, the idea of an array or fence of carts is confirmed by several other chronicles. The Rochester chronicler says: 'The English placed the first battalion, in which were the prince of Wales, the king's son, the earl of Northampton, constable, the earl of Warwick, marshal, to meet the French. They quickly took up their places, and, putting their carts in front of them, fought strenuously and manfully.'[22] The *Norman Chronicle* is particularly valuable as it is not one of the semi-official French histories of the period,[23] which not surprisingly tend to gloss over the whole disaster. The writer makes the carts reinforcements for natural features and other unspecified obstructions:

> and the English were well shielded by their carts and by strong hedges and other obstacles and fired many arrows. And particularly when they saw that the rate of fire of the Genoese diminished, they fired so thickly that the Genoese started to flee and many were killed or wounded. And when the French men at arms saw them turn, many of them charged them and killed more of them. And when the English saw this confusion, they sallied out of their carts and attacked the French and did much harm, more with the arrows than with anything else, for the French horses, when they felt themselves wounded by the arrows, started to break ranks, and many were killed. Then king Edward left the carts . . .[24]

The *Chronicles of Flanders* say that the English made 'a great hedge of their carts',[25] and Mathias von Nuewenburg, who got his information from the Bohemian knights led by King John, makes the most interesting comment of all: he says that 'The English hid all their horses with their attendants near a wood and fought on foot, surrounding them-selves with carts so that the French horsemen could not attack them anywhere except the front wing of the army.'[26] This corresponds to the other accounts which describe an opening in the circle of carts, and to the conjectural reconstruction offered in Appendix 1.

This gives us a radically different version of the tactics from that to be found in most military history textbooks, which depend far too much on later accounts. There is a reluctance to admit Edward's use of the carts as a defensive laager, carts drawn up to form a defensive wall, though the evidence for it is consistent in the early documents, particu-larly those from non-knightly sources.[27] There may be a reason for this, though it can only be conjecture. For Froissart and Le Bel, steeped in the traditions of knightly ideals, the carts reminded them too uncomfort-ably of one of the great moments of Arthurian romance, when Lancelot, in pursuit of Guinevere's captors, and deprived of his horse, mounts a passing cart, and is known for ever afterwards as 'the knight of the cart', because a knight would only be seen in a cart on his way to a shameful death by execution. Consciously or unconsciously, they suppressed the role of carts in the actual fighting. In 1340, when William Montagu and Robert Ufford were captured, according to Geoffrey le Baker, they 'were callously treated by the arrogant and angry Frenchmen. Although they had given their word not to escape when they surrendered, they were actually shackled in irons and carried, not on horseback, but in a cart like robbers.'[28]

Given that there is good evidence from Italian, English and Norman writers soon after the battle that carts were used, there seems to be a plausible case for a defensive structure of this kind used by the English army at Crécy. Is this then a complete innovation by Edward, or some-thing which was known and used, albeit in different ways, at earlier periods? The idea of using wagons as a means of constructing a defence is found in classical times in Vegetius' famous treatise on warfare; this was the standard textbook in the middle ages: an Anglo-Norman trans-lation was dedicated to Edward I before he came to the throne, and nearly three hundred manuscripts survive of the Latin and French ver-sions. Vegetius notes that 'all the barbarians arrange their carts connected together in a ring like a fort at night, secure against anyone who may approach them'.[29] The Byzantine treatise *Taktika*, written by or for the Emperor Leo VI in the tenth century, also discusses the use of wagons as defensive structures. And in the extraordinary technical treatise *Bellifortis* by Conrad Kyeser, written in 1405, there is an illustration of a square of wagons used as a defence.

The strategy of forming a defensive wagon-fort was the hallmark of the followers of John Hus, the religious reformer, against the imperial armies in the fifteenth century. We have the specifications for the manning of a Silesian battle wagon in 1429, which shows that the idea of fighting from carts was well established by then: it was manned by eighteen men under a captain, six of whom were crossbowmen, two were handgunners and eight were infantry with chain flails and pikes. The supplies for each cart included chains to fasten the wagons when necessary, and each cart was drawn by four strong horses, or six less powerful horses.[30] The wagon-forts were regarded as extremely dangerous to attacking armies: in 1427 an agent of Frederick von Brandenburg advised that such formations should not be attacked until a meeting had been held with two unnamed men, probably Czech anti-Hussite nobles; and another agent wrote that it was better to attack a walled city than a wagon-fort.[31]

The idea of positioning the carts to the rear of the army is a common theme in accounts of medieval battles, often as a kind of wagon park with soldiers detached to guard the valuable contents and vital supplies they contained. Alternatively, they are used in line to prevent an attack from the rear, and simply ranged in a row. However, the further possibilities of such a defensive use of carts had been amply demonstrated some forty years earlier, at the battle of Mons-en-Pévèle, when the French army led by Philip IV was confronted by the Flemish infantry levies led by William of Juliers.[32] The battle was chiefly remembered because William of Juliers was captured and surrendered himself to the count of Dammartin, offering a ransom: the count refused, because his father had been killed at Courtrai two years earlier, and he stabbed William to death. It was therefore an event which was widely recorded in contemporary chronicle accounts. We have four apparently independent accounts written within a decade of the battle which describe the Flemish cart-wall.[33] When the Flemish took up their battle position, they deliberately emptied their carts and deposited the contents elsewhere under guard. The carts were then positioned to the rear of the Flemish army; one wheel of each cart was removed, and they were chained together, so that it was impossible to move the carts quickly and break through the line. One version claims that the carts were in staggered rows, three deep, to make it impossible to break through the line even if horsemen jumped the chains.[34] The French did indeed attack the rear, but were unable to remove any carts and force their way through before the Flemish infantry drove them off.

The length of the battle front at Mons-en-Pévèle is said to have been 1,000 yards; if we assume a space of 6 feet for each cart, a single line would require 500 carts, and a triple line 1,500 carts. Are these numbers feasible? The most recent study of the logistics of supplying a medieval army estimates the ratio of carts to combatants as 1 : 20,[35] which, given an estimate for Edward's army at Crécy of around 14,000 men, gives 700 carts. Hard data on the military use of carts is minimal. The anonymous Roman chronicler says that Edward embarked with 3,000 carts in 1346,[36] while Jean le Bel claims that Edward III had 'six thousand handsomely fitted wagons, all brought over from England', which stretched for four miles, for his expedition in 1359, the most elaborate of his French campaigns.[37] Given that each cart could carry around a ton, the anonymous Roman chronicler's figure implies 3,000 tons of supplies and equipment for the Crécy campaign, but, as with most such figures in chronicles, it is probably exaggerated. Taking the calculation already quoted that implies that the arrows alone required fifty to sixty carts,[38] a figure of 500 carts would be an absolute minimum (Plate 4).

Edward was fighting a defensive battle, and the terrain at Crécy offered few natural defences. The wood offered some protection to one side, and there were one or two hedges. The Vallée des Clercs, a deep natural bank running down the hillside, was an obstacle, hindering the enemy's approach, but did not offer shelter of the kind he needed. He had to create his defences artificially, and the carts seem to have been central to his strategy. They were an ideal answer on an open site of this kind, and there was no problem in manoeuvring them on the firm ground. The defences were also strengthened with holes a foot square to break any cavalry charge which reached the first line;[39] even though it would be difficult to dig these in the hard chalk, there was more than enough time to do so, since the English army was encamped in the area for two nights before the actual battle.

The position of the archers has been hotly debated, though earlier discussions have largely ignored the evidence about the use of carts. However, not all the archers were stationed on the carts, and there were

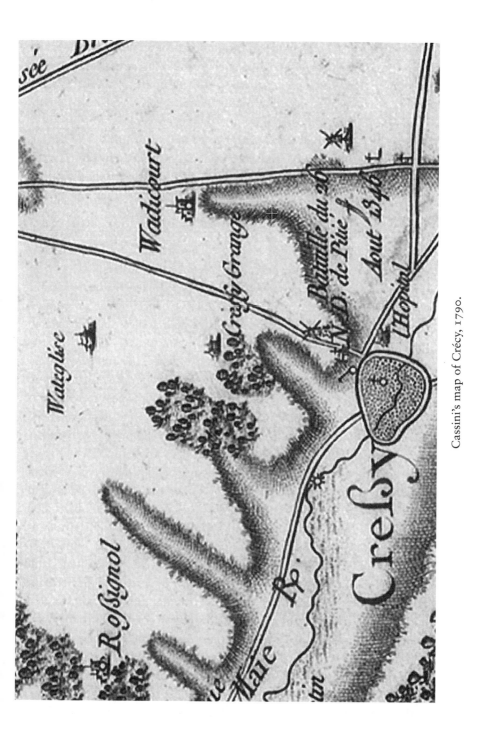

Cassini's map of Crécy, 1790.

certainly formations of archers outside the cart fortress. Robert Hardy, in *The Great Warbow*, makes the good point that if the archers were on the wings, firing across the front of the vanguard, as would be logical, they could not be much more than 500 yards apart from each other to give proper coverage of the ground.[40] Geoffrey le Baker describes the archers as stationed 'almost like wings on the flanks of the king's army',[41] and specifies that they were not among the men at arms. The archers lying in ambush on the edge of the woodland mentioned by the anonymous Roman chronicler are also found in the *Chronicle of the First Four Valois Kings* and in the *Norman Chronicle*, where they lie in wait 'among the hedges'; again, they would be on the wing of the army. There is also the mysterious remark in Froissart about the archers' disposition 'in the manner of a *herse*'.[42] This word is derived, not from the Latin for a harrow or an ecclesiastical frame for candles, but from *ericius*, as the French scholar du Cange recognized in the eighteenth century. The original meaning of the word is 'hedgehog' or 'porcupine'; this could well describe the array of carts with archers on them, shooting arrows like quills.

To echo Gilles li Muisit again, there is no sure evidence as to the disposition of the army, and each modern writer is in effect 'setting down only those things which I have heard from certain people worthy of belief, even if I cannot be totally sure that they are what happened'. Any reconstruction of the English battle formation is bound to be hypothetical; this also applies to the possible solution in Appendix 1, which takes into account what the chroniclers tell us, but ultimately is as much informed imagination as fact. The broad sequence of events is indeed all that we can 'set down' with any confidence. To recapitulate: before the battle, the English army was drawn up in good order, in three divisions, in a position strengthened by improvised defences, which almost certainly included the use of carts, and possibly shallow ditches and wooden or iron stakes. There was little natural cover, but they seem to have set ambushes using the cover of woodland, hedges or standing corn. The personnel in the three divisions of the army prior to the battle is clearly recorded by the author of the *Acts of War*, who very probably had access to official records. He gives us the organization of the English forces at the outset of the campaign on 15–17 July, and this corresponds at several points with the St Omer chronicle, the only other early chronicle to report the names of the leaders of each division. Most of the chroniclers are describing a medieval battle as it was traditionally fought: if the suggestions above are correct, Edward was using highly unusual and innovative tactics, as well as the novel weapons of the longbow and of artillery, which would have made it even more difficult for eyewitnesses to be sure what they were seeing.

The organization of the French army is less clear. There is no doubt that the attack was led by the Genoese crossbowmen; after that, the situation becomes chaotic. According to the Valenciennes chronicler, the second division was the militia from Reims, followed by three battalions of knights and men at arms. The first of these was led by King John of Bohemia, his son Charles and the counts of Alençon, Flanders and Blois. The next was under the command of the duke of Lorraine, with the count of Beaumont, German troops under the count of Salm, and the prior of the Knights Hospitaller of France. The rearguard was led by the king, Jean de Hainault and the members of the king's council and household. Villani claims that the French army was in three divisions, like the English army, and this would be true if he was only counting the knights and excluding the crossbowmen and militia. The anonymous Roman writer makes the first clash of arms after the retreat of the Genoese between a division led by the king of Majorca and the prince of Wales, and seems to imply that the king of Bohemia was to the rear of the army. He is shown as the last to attack, in a futile knightly gesture when the French had fled. This is confirmed by the chronicle of Matthias Nuewenburg which says that 'the Germans remained in the conflict for a long time, and many thousands were killed as a result'.[43]

Since there is general agreement that the French attacked in disorder, it is not surprising that the divisions are harder to disentangle. The usual ordered sequence of attacks, by the vanguard first, followed by the centre, with the rearguard only engaging towards the end of the battle, does not seem to apply to the French manoeuvres. It is fair to say that, once the Genoese onslaught failed, the French forces were more or less out of the king's control. Indeed, if we are to believe Le Bel's persuasive account, King Philip's attempt to check an army which was already raring to attack what they regarded as an easy prey was the moment at which the ranks of the French, already in some disarray because of their hasty arrival on the battlefield, began to disintegrate.

In the circumstances, it is hardly surprising that the survivors' memories of the battle were of isolated moments of drama centred on individual prowess or disaster. The confusion and rage of the contest are reflected by the fact that the sacred *oriflamme*, the French king's standard and the banner of the prince of Wales all went down during the fighting. The *oriflamme* was borne by Mile de Noyers, who wrapped it round his body to prevent its capture; the English claimed that 'it could no longer be venerated as a relic' after this, meaning that it had lost its magical effect, though they failed to capture it. The French king's standard-bearer was killed and the banner torn to pieces. The prince of Wales's banner went down during a fierce attack on the prince himself: Richard Fitzsimon laid it down, and stood over it while he defended the prince, and both he and Thomas Daniel, who raised it again, were richly rewarded once the crisis was over. If banners such as these went down the psychological effect was enormous: it implied that adversaries had penetrated to the core of the army and had either killed the owner of the banner or had managed to destroy the banner itself. The banner acted as the marker for a point where the men fighting in that contingent should regroup; without it, recovery from an attack which had forced them to disperse would be very difficult.

We do know something of the actions of the leaders of the armies, simply because they were the focal points of everyone's attention. On the English side, the fortunes of war of the prince of Wales were recorded in several chronicles, evidently from a number of different witnesses, while, on the French side, dramatic stories about the fate of the king of Bohemia quickly circulated. If we are being rigorous about the evidence, all that we really know is that the prince's battalion bore the brunt of the French assault, as would be expected given that he was leading the vanguard. We also know that the king of Bohemia was killed, probably in the closing stages of the battle.

Only the broadest sketch of the prince of Wales in action survives in the English chronicles: Geoffrey le Baker's rhetorical account of the action gives a glorious but totally imprecise account, describing him as 'showing his mettle to the amazement of the French, running through horses, striking down knights, crushing helms, cutting lances short, skilfully avoiding missiles, commanding his men, defending himself, raising his friends who had been overcome, and setting a good example to all his men'.[44]

At the other extreme, there is a persistent rumour in the Continental chronicles that the prince of Wales was captured at some point by the count of Flanders. This developed into a strange legend, recorded by the anonymous Roman chronicler, that he was only released by the count of Alençon – the implication being that it was not the fighting power of the English but the knightly stupidity of the French which lost the battle. And it underlines the theme of treachery which would later decay into total paranoia on the part of John II himself.

In this battle something unusual happened. The prince of Wales spurred his horse deep into the midst of the enemy. He did great harm by himself. A count called the count of Valentinois[45] saw him and recognized him, and thought that he would win a fortune. He determined to catch this big fish. He rode alongside him and threw his arms around Edward prince of Wales. Then he took him by the fastenings of his breastplate[46] and said, 'You are my prisoner.' Then he stopped and drew him by force out of the conflict and took him into his power. While the count of Valentinois led the son of the king of England thus, the count of Alençon came up, who was the half-brother of King Philip, and saw that young Edward[47] was lost, tied up like a lamb, and said angrily, 'Count of Valentinois, how dare you take my cousin prisoner!' He did not wait for an answer but raised his mace studded with iron which he had in his hand, and struck the count of Valentinois on the head. And he repeated the blows one after another until the count of Valentinois was unconscious. He let go of the bridle and armour of young Edward and fell dead to the ground from his horse. Then young Edward spurred his horse and, not a little joyful, rejoined his company, who had begun to waver.[48]

We are on firm ground with the story that the prince's banner was struck down, and there is no question that the action did centre round the prince. The supporting evidence for the capture of the prince, however, is not very strong, but has perhaps been underestimated. According to the Norman Chronicle, which seems generally well informed, 'the prince of Wales, son of King Edward, and Godefroy d'Harcourt rode so far forward to attack the French that it is said that the count of Flanders captured the prince of Wales, but he was soon rescued.'[49] The Valenciennes chronicler confirms that the prince was in the thick of the fighting in his description of this detail of the action:

And the prince of Wales was so hard pressed that he was forced to his knees twice, and Sir Richard Fitzsimon, who bore his standard, took the standard and placed it under his feet and stepped on it to guard it and to rescue his master, taking his sword in both hands and beginning to defend the prince and to shout: 'Edward, St George, to the king's son!' And to his rescue there came the bishop of Durham and many valiant knights who rescued the prince, and Sir Richard raised his standard again.[50]

The prince is shown as fighting on foot, and this would fit the early part of the action. The other detail here is that a contingent from the rearguard, under the bishop of Durham, was involved in the intense fighting around the prince's position, apparently in answer to Fitzsimon's shouts for help. Geoffrey le Baker confirms this, but depicts the episode on a much smaller scale:

> Indeed their non-stop attacks kept the prince and his comrades so busy, that the prince was compelled to fight kneeling down against the masses of the enemy who poured around him. Then someone ran or rode to the king his father, explained the danger threatening his first-born son, and asked for help. The bishop of Durham was sent with twenty knights to the help of the prince, but the bishop found the prince and his men leaning on their lances and swords, drawing breath and taking a moment's rest over long mountains of the dead, as they waited for the enemy to return from his retreat.[51]

This rescue is in turn embroidered by Froissart in his usual novelistic style into a refusal of help which enhances the prince's heroic stature – as the king, in Froissart's view, must intend. The sheer vivacity of his story-telling has made this into the 'standard' version of events for generations of readers, and for many historians. A knight named Thomas Norwich was sent to the king to summon help:

> On the knight's arrival, he said, 'Sir, the earl of Warwick, the Lord Stafford, the Lord Reginald Cobham and the others who are about your son, are vigorously attacked by the French; and they entreat that you would come to their assistance with your battalion, for, if their numbers should increase, they fear he will have too much to do.' The king replied, 'Is my son dead, unhorsed, or so badly wounded that he cannot support himself?' 'Nothing of the sort, thank God,' rejoined the knight; 'but he is in so hot an engagement that he has great need of your help.' The king answered, 'Now, Sir Thomas, return back to those that sent you, and tell them from me, not to send again for me this day, or expect that I shall

come, let what will happen, as long as my son has life; and say, that I command them to let the boy win his spurs; for I am determined, if it please God, that all the glory and honour of this day shall be given to him, and to those into whose care I have intrusted him.'[52]

This episode is probably distinct from the manoeuvre described by Villani; he depicts Edward's army, as we have seen, fighting from within a laager of carts. At the critical moment, the array is opened at the back and the entire rearguard, which included the bishop of Durham and his men, comes to the relief of the hard-pressed vanguard, in a classic encircling manoeuvre which anticipates Poitiers. The battle of Poitiers had not been fought when Villani was writing, so there is no question of accounts of the later encounter influencing what he wrote. A classic tactical manoeuvre has been transformed by other writers, who focus on the characters involved rather than the sweep of the action, into a personal rescue of the prince of Wales.

For the readers of Villani and many of the other chronicles, detached from the Anglo-French courts, it was the mechanics of the great disaster which had overtaken the French that were of the highest interest; personal exploits were far less meaningful. For the French chroniclers nearer to home, on the other hand, the knightly aspects of the battle were paramount; Froissart represents the culmination of this trend. There is, however, one chronicle which, even in this context of heroic deeds, goes against the expected grain. Describing the aftermath of the battle, the Valenciennes chronicler remarks:

> The king of England remained at Crécy for four days with his son the prince of Wales and the other barons who had won the battle on the Saturday. And the king asked the prince of Wales, his son, what he thought of going into battle and being in the midst of it, and whether it was a fine game, and the prince said nothing and hung his head.[53]

The realities and horrors of war fleetingly cast a shadow over the glory of knightly prowess.

The other heroic action in the battle, ending in tragedy rather than glory, was the death of the king of Bohemia. Here the anonymous Roman chronicler has a detailed account, which seems to be based on the first-hand experience of someone in his entourage: the details of the disposal of the bodies after the battle seem to come from someone involved in the operation:

[After the French had fled] the king of Bohemia asked his men how matters stood on the battlefield. The reply was that no one was left alive except him and his men. All the French had been cut to pieces. The English stood strong and firm, with their standard raised. Then the king of Bohemia commanded two of his greatest barons, who were related to him, to make ready to strike. They said to him: 'What do you want to do? All the French have been put out of action. The English are in a strong position. We are not foolish. It would be mad to attack so many men.' The king replied, 'You aren't the sons of my two friends, who were the most valiant in all Germany.' The two barons replied: 'It isn't a question of courage, because we aren't engaged with the enemy.' The king said, 'I wish us to go forward. Let us go forward and die with honour.' The barons said, 'What will you gain from your death and ours?' The king said, 'In good faith, what I say I am saying because I believe we are fighting for the truth.' At this the two barons were convinced. They lowered their voices like lambs and said: 'King, do as you please.'

The king summoned his barons and commanded them to obey his son Charles as they would have obeyed him, and honour him as their king and lord; they were also to rescue him from the battle.

Then he ordered the barons, who were before him, that they should put him directly in front of the English, so that, if there was an encounter, he could not return. Then he chained himself between the two barons and tied the fastenings of their breastplates together, because a common death would be an honour for them. The first squadron was 1,000 Germans from Luxemburg, good troops, Bohemians and gentlemen from Prague. They were followed by 4,000 Frenchmen, Burgundians and Picards. His son Charles served in the rear. Then the trumpets and bagpipes sounded on both sides. Then they lowered their spears and spurred their horses, and fought without mercy. The English had two powerful stratagems: the first was 500 knights reinforced by 1,000 to the rear, the second was two wings of 500 and 500 to the right and left, ranged along the top of the slope. When the Germans engaged with the English in the first line of the centre, the two wings, who had taken up their positions, attacked from the side on each flank. The king of Bohemia was attacked from behind, on his flank and on his side. The king's horse fell. The king was unhorsed and was killed by the horses of the two lords attached to him. The first to fall was a noble French knight who carried the king's banner.[54] He was unhorsed and killed in the first charge. The Germans did not turn their backs but put up a good fight, given that they had neither king nor standard. Many English died. In the end the squadron of the king of Bohemia was broken like salt pounded with a pestle.

Charles wanted to avenge his father's death, but was surrounded by his lords, who seized the reins of his horse and turned him towards Paris:

[The English gathered the bodies from the battlefield.] . . . The 1,000 Germans were taken to Paris on carts. The greater part of the king of Bohemia's body was taken; much of it had been destroyed. These bodies were taken naked from the field to Paris for burial. The other bodies were not collected then but remained for four days on the earth in full view of everyone.[55]

Once again, this is the stuff of popular history, though with more truth in it than the tale of Edward's refusal to help his son. John of Bohemia was closely related to the French royal family by his marriage to King Philip's niece and that of his son to Philip's daughter Blanche, and he was far more at home in the knightly culture of France than in Bohemia itself, where he was regarded as a foreigner: apart from anything else, his efforts to introduce tournaments and knightly ceremonies there had been a failure. The desperate gesture of flinging himself, blind as he was, into the fray, led by two of his lords, gave him the immortal knightly reputation he seems to have craved, and is noticed not only by the likes of Froissart, but even by the Bohemian chroniclers. Beneš z Weitmile, writing about 1374, declares that, when his lords tried to retreat from the battle with him, he declared: 'Be it far from the king of Bohemia to flee! Lead me into the thick of the fray and God be with us. Let us not be afraid, as long as you guard my son carefully.'[56] Weitmile attributes his death to the archers – 'he died pierced by many arrows' – whereas the western chroniclers such as St Omer portray his end in more knightly terms:

And when the valiant king of Bohemia heard this, he ordered Le Moine de Basle [Heinrich Münch], a very valiant man who held his bridle, to lead him straight to the king of England so that he could fight him. And

Le Moine de Basle led him a long way into the press, striking to right and left at friend and enemy alike, for his sight was poor. His enemies all rushed on him at once, and beat him to the ground, and mortally wounded him; and Le Moine was killed in front of him.[57]

Even Froissart cannot improve on these accounts of John's death, adding only the story that the bodies were found with the horses tied together beside them. And the impact of John's action is probably reflected in the adoption of the black ostrich feather by the prince of Wales. John Arderne, who may have been the prince's doctor, recorded in a medical treatise written about the time of the prince's death that 'Edward the eldest son of Edward the king of England bore a similar feather above his helmet, and he obtained the feather from the king of Bohemia, whom he killed at Cresse in France. And so he assumed the feather which is called "ostrich fether" which that most noble king used to carry above his helmet.'[58]

These were the heroes of Crécy. King Philip, who is the only other figure about whom anecdotes survive, is the subject of a wide variety of stories. There are very divergent opinions about his responsibility for the rash attack on the English while his forces were not yet properly arrayed. Le Bel claims that Le Moine de Basle advised him strongly against any onslaught until the following day; Philip agreed willingly to this, but 'none of the lords wanted to turn back unless those in front of them turned back, because otherwise they would be shamed; so they stood still and did not move, and the others behind them continued to advance, and it was through pride and jealousy that they were destroyed'.[59] We have already quoted the version of the anonymous Roman chronicle, which has a similar but rather more elaborate story attributing the advice to the king of Bohemia instead of one of his knights. The Valenciennes chronicler, who, like Jean le Bel, quotes Jean de Hainault as an authority, contradicts Le Bel's story and, like the Italian chronicler, blames the king himself:

> When the king of France had taken up his position and saw the host of the king of England, he realized that the king of England would not challenge him to a battle because he was so close to him; and he told Jean de Hainault and his men that he wanted to give battle because his enemies were in sight. Some praised, others not, because it was Saturday.[60] And all

the same Sir John and the other barons said: 'Sir, do as you will: we will follow you.'[61]

The *Norman Chronicle* broadly agrees with this, adding that Philip did not wait for the whole of his army to arrive on the battlefield, but attacked with those forces who were with him. This is confirmed by the aftermath of the conflict, when French troops arrived in quite substantial contingents, which were picked off by the English as they came onto the scene.

We would expect to find stories of the exploits of the two kings. Both were experienced warriors: Philip had been in the fray when he defeated the Flemish at Cassel in 1328, and Edward had likewise fought in several battles in Scotland. Jean de Hainault was at Philip's side from the start of the battle, and talked to Jean le Bel afterwards. His story is that the king took no part in the action, and had to be led away by his companions after the defeat, going first to the nearby village of La Broye and then on to Amiens. Edward certainly took no part in the early stages of the battle, and there is the strong possibility that during most of the action he was directing operations from the windmill which stood at the top of the slope.[62] It is mentioned in the *Chronicle of Flanders* and the St Omer chronicle; eighty years later, a Norman chronicle described how the king had a windmill filled with wood and set on fire to illuminate the battlefield when the fighting had ended.[63] This is not implausible; and, just as carts may have been excluded from the 'knightly' accounts of the battle, the idea of the king in a windmill is not something that would have fitted the scene that Froissart or Le Bel wished to portray.

We therefore know nothing of Edward's personal role in the fighting, and, if Le Bel is right, there is nothing to say on Philip's part either. The Flemish chronicles are ambiguous: they report that Philip reproved his men as they fled, yet it is not clear whether he is simply in the rearguard, 'on the field, facing the enemy', or actually in the thick of the fighting. But the other chroniclers give him an active part in the battle: Richard Wynkeley, reporting to England immediately after the battle, says that he was hit in the face by an arrow, and Villani confirms that he was wounded; later English and Italian writers describe two or three wounds. The French sources, which would have been better informed, say nothing. He was also said to have had two horses killed under him.[64]

Perhaps the entry which is nearest to the truth is that in the *Chronicle of the First Four Valois Kings*: the French lost the battle through haste and disarray, yet 'the French king ... bore himself that day as a very good knight, but fortune went against him'.[65]

The aftermath of the battle was as dramatic as the fighting itself. The English army remained on the field all night, in battle array, and on the following day isolated groups of French troops, coming up and expecting to join their victorious king, were attacked and defeated. As soon as the main action ended, and in the intervals between these sporadic actions, the horrific task of searching out the wounded and identifying the dead began; the operation lasted four days. The English knew that a large number of French nobles had been killed, because both sides had unfurled their most significant banners to indicate that it was a fight to the death, and that no prisoners were to be taken. The French displayed the *oriflamme*, the sacred banner of the abbey of St Denis, probably red with gold flames, while the English, according to Geoffrey le Baker, flew a standard 'showing a dragon clothed in the king's arms'; the leopards and lilies of Edward III's heraldic device, tempering ferocity with mildness, were changed into the cruelty of the dragon.

According to the St Omer chronicle, the small contingent of German knights on the English side, who were fighting as mercenaries and therefore were keenly interested in the profits of war, remonstrated with Edward, saying that they were astonished that he was allowing so much noble blood to be spilt. If they were taken prisoner, the French command would be weakened and large ransoms could be obtained. The king's answer was that these were his orders, and it was the right course of action.[66] It was a sound military decision: he could not afford to have knights taken out of action as they attended to securing prisoners, when the English were heavily outnumbered and in danger of being overwhelmed. And Baker implies that Edward had the banner unfurled in response to the French declaration that no prisoners were to be taken.

The full picture of the resulting slaughter only emerged gradually. Le Bel says that

> The king then ordered Sir Reginald Cobham, a most worthy knight, to take a herald well versed in arms, and some of the lords and the other heralds, and to go among the dead and record the names of all the knights they could identify, and to have all the princes and magnates carried to

one side with each man's name written down and laid upon him. Sir Reginald did as commanded; and it was found that there were nine great princes lying on the field and around twelve hundred knights, and fully fifteen or sixteen thousand others, squires and Genoese and the rest, while the bodies of only three hundred English knights were found.[67]

Other sources say that the king, Godefroy d'Harcourt and other lords led the search of the bodies; they were stripped of their surcoats or other identifying marks, and only three of the greatest of the French leaders – the king of Bohemia, the count of Alençon and the count of Harcourt – were singled out for special burial. The surcoats, arms and mantlings[68] were taken to the king's tent, where the French heralds later came to help to identify them. In total, 2,200 such items were said to have been collected from the battlefield.[69] The bodies were put in mass graves specially consecrated for the purpose, though the site of these has never been found, while the remaining armour was destroyed.

Godefroy d'Harcourt suffered the most personal loss: both his brother the count of Harcourt and his nephew were among the casualties; it was said that he had tried to protect them, but had been unable to do so in the thick of the fighting. His brother, and the count of Alençon, Edward's cousin, were buried in a chapel near Crécy. Many of the other French nobles would have been known to the English, and there were men in the retinue of Jean de Hainault who would have fought alongside them in Scotland only a decade earlier. As a result of the battle Godefroy seems to have bitterly repented his part in Edward's campaign, and, during the siege of Calais, found an excuse to repudiate his allegiance with Edward and return to the French side, which he did before the year was out.*[70]

The death of the king of Bohemia resounded throughout Europe: it is the one fact which is almost universally picked up by writers who mention Crécy. The death of a king in battle was extremely rare in the period of feudal cavalry warfare, and the circumstances in which it took place, his blindness and the determination – or sheer folly – which led him into the fray, heightened the drama. The uncertainty about the casualties and the problems of identifying them is highlighted by the widely differing versions of his end. Most chronicles confirm that he died in the

---

* He went back to the English side in July 1356, but was ambushed and killed by French troops in November of that year.

fighting, but, according to the St Omer chronicle, which is generally well informed,

> some knights came to the king who said that they had found the king of Bohemia lying on the battlefield and that he was not yet dead. The king ordered that he should be sought out and brought to his tent; and when he saw him he was very sorry for him. He ordered his surgeons to attend to him diligently. And when his wounds were dressed and he was laid in a bed, he gave up his spirit to God.[71]

At the other extreme, the anonymous Roman chronicler claims that 'the greater part of the king of Bohemia's body was taken [to Paris]; much of it had been destroyed'.[72] Edward was deeply moved by his death, and, as Villani says, 'held a most grand and honourable funeral for the king of Bohemia, as befitted a king's corpse, and wept for love of him because of his death. He and many of his barons dressed in black, and sent his body with an honourable escort to Charles his son.'[73] The funeral and requiem mass were conducted by the bishop of Durham, taking up his spiritual role after playing his part in the battle itself. The setting was not a great cathedral, or even the modest church in the village of Crécy or a nearby abbey; it seems to have in the open air, on the battlefield itself.[74]

It is this moment, rather than the heroics of the fighting, which defined the foundation of the Garter. This was the moment of Edward's triumph, when for the first time he had proved himself against the French, and established through trial by battle that he was the rightful king; but it is also a moment of intense tragedy and deep religious feeling. We shall see how the Garter commemorates both the triumph and the tragedy, in that it is a religious confraternity dedicated to remembering the departed and to honouring Edward and his family.

Crécy caused a sensation throughout western Europe. Chroniclers who rarely reported events outside their own country included a brief account of the battle and of the unexpected triumph of the English army. But such victories could be short-lived: a similar disaster had befallen the French at Courtrai in 1302 at the hands of the Flemish militia, when so many noblemen and knights had been killed that it was known as the 'battle of the golden spurs', from the heap of spurs which were gathered from the dead after the conflict. Yet two years later the French were able to overcome the Flemish armies at Mons-en-Pévèle, and, although Flanders gained a great measure of independence after Courtrai, a further defeat at the hands of Philip of Valois at Cassel in 1328 meant that within a quarter of a century French influence was very largely restored. The victory at Courtrai had in large measure been due to the bravery and skill of the two princes in command of the militia, William of Juliers and Guy of Namur, who fought in the front rank armed with the long pikes[75] used by the footsoldiers of the Flemish militia, and to the fact that the commanders of the French army were killed in the attack on the Flemish line. The defeat at Mons-en-Pévèle was equally due to the ability of Philip the Fair to rally the French when their attack began to fail. Tactics alone were not enough: morale and leadership were the deciding factors. The ability of the English armies to repeat their successes in the following decades, at Poitiers and Najéra, was due as much to their commanders and the morale of the army as to the military skills of the troops.

The English army that marched north from Crécy at the end of August was in serious need of help from the other side of the Channel. Edward wrote on 3 September:

> And we have now moved towards the sea to get reinforcements and supplies from England, both of men at arms and equipment and other necessaries, because our marches have been long and continuous. But we do not expect to leave the kingdom of France until we have made an end of our war, with God's help.[76]

The next day, Michael Northburgh hints at Edward's plans for the continuation of the campaign, as well as emphasizing the dire state of the army:

> From what I have heard, he [the king] intends to besiege Calais. For this reason the king has sent to you for supplies, to be sent as quickly as possible; because since we left Caen we have lived off the countryside with great difficulty and much harm to our men, but, thanks be to God, without losses. But we are now in such a plight that part of our needs must be met by supplies.[77]

Fortunately, supplies were close to hand; an English fleet which had been dispatched a week or two earlier, and which was meant to have made a rendezvous with Edward at Le Crotoy, finally caught up with him at Calais, having tried and failed to force its way into Boulogne on the day Michael Northburgh wrote. Calais harbour was in the hands of the French, so the English established themselves to the south-east of the town, on the road to Gravelines, which had a small harbour. As at St Vaast-la-Hougue at the beginning of the campaign, ships could also be brought ashore and unloaded on the long sandy beaches closer to the camp. Edward secured the support of parliament for the continuation of the fighting when it met on 13 September; a combination of the heady success at Crécy and a repeat of the reading of the French invasion plan found at Caen was enough to persuade the commons to vote for war taxes for both the present and following year. Letters proclaiming the victory at Crécy, and ordering proclamations to be made that traders should bring their goods and supplies for the proposed siege to Calais, had already been sent to the bailiffs of the major ports and to the sheriffs of the counties on 6 September, almost as soon as the news of the battle reached England. Reinforcements of men and materials were raised, and, in addition, supplies were bought in Flanders and carried in along the coast road. It was another huge logistical effort, coming hard on the heels of the efforts required only a few months earlier to prepare the invasion fleet. Vast quantities of food and building materials were landed over the next few weeks, not without difficulty, since there was a strong French fleet including Genoese galleys now operating in the Channel: twenty-five English ships were attacked and destroyed on 17 September within sight of the coast. After this initial disaster, the English ships were better armed, and the French lost the service of the Genoese galleys when their contract finished at the end of the year. Even before then, houses had been built for the king and the leading commanders, either of timber or of brushwood, and by Michaelmas the encampment, which was christened 'Villeneuve le Hardi', the bold new town, was deemed sufficiently safe and comfortable for Queen Philippa to join her husband. Eventually, the settlement grew to such a size that its market rivalled that of Arras or Amiens, and the Flemish merchants were quick to exploit this opportunity; Villeneuve was after all home to more than 30,000 inhabitants.

Edward had two objectives in besieging Calais, and it is hard to say which was uppermost in his mind. The size of his army suggests strongly that he was hoping to lure Philip into another battle. He could have cut off the town and denied it supplies from the landward side with far

fewer men, and he fortified the camp very strongly as if he expected
such a challenge. Calais was a great prize, and Philip could ill afford to
lose it, since it would give the English a safe port and stronghold on the
Continent from which to mount repeated attacks on France. This, too,
was undoubtedly part of Edward's calculations. If he did not succeed in
making an end of his war, as he had said in his letter of 3 September, he
could at least secure a superb base for its continuation.

Even with the huge resources that Edward succeeded in raising for
the siege, it was a bold, almost foolhardy, undertaking. Calais was a
strongly fortified town, and its defences had been repaired and reinforced throughout the summer, beginning as soon as news of Edward's
invasion had been confirmed. It had a double wall, in itself unusual,
and in addition to that a double moat. The height of the walls was
legendary – they were said to have been built by Julius Caesar – and two
of the main methods of attacking a besieged town were impractical. The
marshy ground meant that neither undermining the walls nor building
huge siege engines was possible, because any mines would be flooded
and the siege engines needed firm foundations. The only means of success would be the long, slow process of starving the town out. The
citizens were well supplied, and it took some time to secure the harbour
so that no ships could enter. It was only with the withdrawal of the
Genoese galleys during the winter that the English could be sure of controlling the sea approaches.

Early in October there was a period when it seemed that Philip might
rise to the bait, and attempt to relieve the town by attacking the besiegers. Edward sent for reinforcements, though on a modest scale; he and
the prince of Wales requested about 400 men at arms and 1,000 archers,
the prince ordering the justice of Chester 'not to be so negligent or tardy
as he was in the last array'.[78] Neither the French army nor the reinforcements had materialized by the beginning of November, and the request
for more men was repeated in mid-November, and again at the end of
the month. Edward had concocted an ingenious but somewhat hazardous scheme for getting small boats into the moat surrounding Calais.
Scaling ladders would be placed on their decks against the walls, while
small wooden siege engines and cannon kept up a bombardment. Fifty
boats were requisitioned from Dover as well as hurdles and mattresses
to place against the walls, and carpenters were enlisted to make ladders
up to forty feet in length. There seem to have been repeated attempts

from the end of November onwards to mount a successful assault, until the idea was abandoned the following February.

Sieges were never particularly good for an army's morale, particularly when they threatened to last over the winter, so news of a new victory in England was more than welcome. David II of Scotland had taken the opportunity of Edward's long absence in France to reopen Anglo-Scottish hostilities in support of his French allies. He crossed the border and moved on Durham in mid-October, but William Zouche, the archbishop of York, and the northern nobles were already in the field, and intercepted them at Neville's Cross on 17 October. The fight was fierce, and seems to have been largely an old-fashioned struggle on foot, in which archers played little part. The Scots eventually gave way, and David II himself was captured.[79]

News of the capture of David of Scotland had reached Calais around the beginning of November, and Thomas Bradwardine, chancellor of St Paul's cathedral, who had been with the army since the beginning of the campaign, preached a victory sermon to raise morale and to celebrate the double triumph of English arms. The king had asked for the Church's prayers for divine aid; and Bradwardine took as his text 'Now thanks be unto God, which always causeth us to triumph'.[80] He then explained that those who sought causes other than God's will were in error: some said it was in the stars, or in the workings of fortune or fate, while others said it was their superior numbers (which was patently untrue anyway). Even their military expertise was not responsible, while those who managed to argue that it was all down to the goddess of love, who favoured bold men and lusty lovers, were no better than pagans. Bradwardine, who had written a treatise *On God as Cause* some years earlier, saw only one reason for the English victory: God had willed it.[81] The Church had prayed, and God had answered.

More serious than the lethargic efforts of the French to counter-attack were the conditions in Villeneuve le Hardi: sieges were notorious for the onset of disease, and the marshes were unhealthy places, damp and occasionally flooded by a spring tide. In November there was an epidemic of some sort, which led in turn to desertions from the army. Camp sickness of various kinds continued throughout the winter, as did the desertions. In England, sheriffs and other local officials were warned to look out for deserters, but usually found that they were too weak or too badly wounded to be sent back to the fray. Fire, another hazard in a wooden town of flimsy buildings, also became evident: one chronicle claims that a fire destroyed the king's privy wardrobe, where the jewels, armour and other valuables were kept.[82]

The tedium of the siege did not help, though a series of minor raids helped to occupy the troops: William Bohun, earl of Northampton, led an attack on the nearby town of Thérouanne, and the Flemish attempted an (unsuccessful) assault on St Omer. The chronicler from that town recorded that at Christmas Edward held a great feast, and a solemn crown-wearing, and there were evidently attempts to keep up morale among the knights by holding courtly festivals: at Easter, the king had the rich altar furniture from his private chapel sent over from London for use at Calais.[83] Winter now set in with a vengeance, and the marsh dykes froze over. Thomas Beauchamp seized the opportunity to attack the castle of Hammes, three miles from Calais, by crossing the ice on the moat; it was captured and burnt. Froissart later recorded 'great adventures and fine deeds of arms on one side and the other', but this is his usual highly romantic gloss on affairs. In reality, a series of skirmishes were initiated by the French, written up in detail in the St Omer chronicle, while the English raided the local French fortresses and towns: Marck and Guines were also burnt.[84]

Philip had not been idle during the winter. He had signed a contract with the Castilians to supply galleys to replace the Genoese, but nothing came of this. However, the galleys were to have fought alongside the French naval forces, and the latter were now pressed into service. A major effort was made to assemble supplies and to load them onto convoys sailing out of Boulogne, and twelve galleys from the French naval base at Rouen accompanied the merchant ships. These successfully landed a large quantity of stores and supplies in March and April. But supplies on this scale were needed on a regular basis, and at the end of April the English succeeded in completing the blockade of the town by building a palisade on the sand dune which protected the harbour to the north, and erecting a large wooden fort on the very end of it with a permanent garrison of more than 200 men, archers and men at arms, and with cannon and catapults installed. This was a deadly blow to the hopes of those holding out in Calais. In May, an attempt to run the gauntlet of this fortification failed, and it was not until the end of June that another convoy sailed from the mouth of the Seine. A substantial English fleet was now lying off Calais, under the command of the two

English admirals, John Montgomery and John Howard, the earl of Pembroke and the earl of Northampton. When they approached the convoy on 25 June, the crews of the merchant vessels first threw their cargo overboard in an attempt to lighten their ships and make a quick exit, and then jumped into the shallow water themselves; the escort of galleys turned tail and fled.

Philip matched these naval operations with a plan to raise a new army to challenge Edward. The *oriflamme* was taken from the treasury at St Denis on 18 March, marking the formal start of the campaign. Usually, the administrative skills of the French regime meant that there was little difficulty in raising an army; but the mood of the country after the disaster of the previous year was deeply hostile to the nobility who were the linchpin of any effort to muster troops. Poems circulated accusing them of treachery and of failure to do their duty to protect the realm, and raising taxes had proved extremely difficult during the previous winter. The king was therefore short of money to pay for his army, and the nobles were in even worse case. Many of them had only recently inherited their positions as a result of the death toll at Crécy, and found that their predecessors had incurred heavy debts to equip themselves, quite apart from the problems of a lavish lifestyle. The debts of the Italian bankers had been seized by the crown, so the king was in the position of both asking them for further expenditure and looking for repayment of the existing loans. It was hardly surprising that the response to the summons was lukewarm: and, when the army did assemble at Arras in June, Philip had a further problem. There had been continuous skirmishes and fighting along the border with Flanders during the past year, as the young count of Flanders supported the French, while the towns, mindful of their dependence on the raw wool they imported from England, favoured the English. The French had been unable to deal with the rash of minor assaults and the entrenchment of garrisons in the region, and there was always the danger that, if the army marched against the English, the Flemish would take the opportunity to increase their attacks or even join forces with Edward's troops.

Philip therefore dispatched two divisions, forming the bulk of the assembled army, to deal with this problem. Neither succeeded: one division under Charles de la Cerda, the king's cousin, attacked the Flemish at Cassel, a natural stronghold built on a dramatic hill, and was driven off with considerable losses, while the other, under the lord of St Venant, one of the marshals of France, and Jacques de Bourbon, fought a battle at Béthune which resulted in heavy casualties on both sides and an indecisive result. The Flemish were damaged, but were still free to create problems for the French as they reassembled and marched towards Calais in the second half of June. The royal headquarters were set up at Hesdin, fifty miles south of Calais.

Almost as soon as Philip had established himself at Hesdin, word came of the disaster that had befallen the French attempt to supply Calais on 25 June. On the morning of the 26th, the English saw two small boats trying to leave the harbour as dawn broke. They gave chase, and, as they did so, they saw one of the officers in the French boats tie something to an axe and hurl it into the shallow water as near the shore as he could. The boats were captured, and at low tide the English were able to retrieve the axe. There was a letter attached to it, a dramatic appeal for help written by the commander of Calais, Jean de Vienne, addressed to the French king. Edward read it, and forwarded it to Philip with his personal seal attached, to show that he knew exactly how weak the garrison's position was:

> The town is in desperate need of corn, wine and meat. There is nothing in the place which has not been eaten, no dogs, cats or horses, and nothing to keep us alive unless we eat human flesh. You wrote before this that I should hold the town as long as we had something to eat. Now we are at the point where we have nothing to keep us alive. We have therefore agreed that, if no help comes within a short time, we will make a sortie from the town into the fields, to fight to the death. For it is better to die honourably in battle than to eat one another.[85]

Edward knew that he was now close to his goal of either forcing Philip to give battle, or taking Calais. He had received considerable reinforcements during the spring, including William Clinton, earl of Huntingdon, somewhat recovered from his illness of the previous summer, who brought a contingent with him. More important, Henry of Grosmont, who had until now taken no part in the campaign in northern France because of his military activities in Gascony, arrived in late May with further reinforcements. Almost every important military figure from England was now gathered at Villeneuve le Hardi.

A further sign of the garrison's desperation was the appearance of 500 inhabitants of the town outside the walls, driven out in order to save provisions for the able-bodied survivors who could fight in its defence. Le Bel, who always gives a favourable gloss to Edward's actions, claims that he gave them food and drink and money, and sent them on their way: Henry Knighton, who may have drawn on the memories of the retinue of Henry of Grosmont, says that they perished miserably of cold and hunger in the ground between the town walls and the English army.[86]

On 18 July, Edward sent Henry of Grosmont to ravage the country within thirty miles of Calais, and he returned on 20 July with 2,000 cattle and 5,000 sheep. He also had news of the whereabouts of Philip and his army: they were marching towards Calais, and were now near Wissant. Conflict was close enough for both kings to organize prayers for their success: Edward's letters asking for prayers for his victory went to England on 23 July; the day before, there had been a procession in Paris bearing the relics of St Genevieve for the same purpose. By 27 July Philip had arrived in sight of Calais, and had occupied a position at Sangatte, the hill to the west of the town, which overlooked it and the English camp beyond. He could see the defensive barricade of boats drawn up on the sand, manned by archers and artillery, which formed an immovable rampart barring the passage across the dune to the north of Villeneuve le Hardi. The other flank of the camp, which had been very strongly fortified against a frontal attack, was on the road leading eastwards into Flanders. Here Edward had positioned a formidable force under the command of Henry of Grosmont.

According to Jean le Bel, the two marshals of the French army, the lords of Beaujeu and St Venant, were sent by Philip to survey the English positions and returned to inform him that there was no way of attacking them 'unless he wanted to expose his men to greater losses than those at Crécy'.[87] Philip, to save face, sent letters to Edward asking him to allow him to cross the river defending the English position so that they could fight; Edward, knowing that he had the upper hand, refused. There was nothing that Philip could do except open negotiations, and for three days, under a truce, two delegations explored the possibilities of peace. Henry of Grosmont, William Bohun, the margrave of Juliers, Walter Mauny, Reginald Cobham and Bartholomew Burghersh the elder represented the English; the duke of Bourbon, the duke of Athens, the royal chancellor Guillaume Flote and Geoffroy de Charny spoke for the French. But the negotiations ended in deadlock: Edward was not going to forgo his prize, and was not afraid of a French attack.

By this time, the garrison was desperate, and on the night of 1 August they signalled to the French that they were going to surrender. Geoffrey le Baker says that, when the French army first appeared, they had raised the royal standard of France on the tower of the castle, with those of the king's commanders, and had lit a great fire at dusk to illuminate them: they also sounded trumpets and beat drums for half an hour. The next night they lit a smaller fire and made less noise. When they could no longer hold out, they made a fire that could scarcely be seen from the French camp, and lamented pitifully for almost an hour before cutting down the standards and letting them fall into the ditch.[88] When the French royal army saw this, they burnt any equipment that they could not take with them and destroyed their stores, to make a quick retreat, and left before dawn: the rearguard was harried by Henry of Grosmont and William Bohun as they departed. Philip had done his best, but it was not enough, and his retreat was held to be even more shameful than his departure from the battlefield at Crécy.

The surrender of Calais is one of the famous scenes of English history, immortalized in Rodin's sculpture as well as in numerous popular accounts. Geoffrey le Baker, writing a decade after the event, presents a sober and practical ceremony. Jean de Vienne, riding a little horse[89] so that his feet touched the ground, with a rope round his neck, came into the king's presence, followed by other knights and citizens on foot, bareheaded and barefoot, also with ropes round their necks. Vienne offered the king his sword of war, as befitted a ruler who had won the town from the greatest power in Christendom. Then he handed over the keys of the town. Finally, he offered the king the sword of peace, symbol of the king's righteous justice. Taking this, Edward ordered Vienne, fifteen knights and fifteen burgesses to be sent to England. The other knights and burgesses were allowed to go free and take their money with them, while he ordered the common people to be taken unharmed to the nearby French fortress of Guines.

This orderly scene becomes much more dramatic in the hands of Le Bel (and later of Froissart, who merely retells Le Bel's story). Le Bel tells us that, when Jean de Vienne signalled that he wished to parley, the earl of Northampton, Walter Mauny, Reginald Cobham and Thomas Holland were sent to him. Vienne asked for mercy and to be allowed to leave in peace, as they had only been doing their duty as subjects of Philip, but Mauny, speaking for the king, replied that Edward was so infuriated by their resistance and the harm they had done him that they must all put themselves at his mercy: some would be killed and some ransomed. Vienne asked Mauny to take his request to the king, who at first refused to listen. But, so Le Bel tells us, Mauny himself took Vienne's part, saying that it would be a bad precedent, and that he and other knights in Edward's service could find themselves in the same predicament. At this Edward modified his demand, and asked only that six leading citizens should be brought to him to be at his mercy, for him to do with them 'exactly what I please'. Mauny again pleaded for them, but it was only when Philippa, expecting her eleventh child, fell at her husband's feet, that he relented and granted them to the queen, who spared their lives, and ordered that they should be 'freshly clothed and made comfortable'.[90]

Has Mauny, who was clearly Le Bel's informant, taken this opportunity to write himself into history as he would like to be remembered? It is probably the outstanding example of the way that oral testimony is used by the knights to create their own history – or myth, if you prefer it – with the chronicler's connivance. The story fits Le Bel's knightly agenda perfectly, and the arguments put forward by Mauny and the queen's intervention are all plausible; yet in the end we may be reading a romance.

The campaign of 1346–7 ended in the traditional fashion. Negotiations for a truce were set in hand, and as usual dragged on for a couple of years. Meanwhile Edward landed in England on 12 October, and celebrated his return home with a series of festivals and tournaments. This time, however, the jousts were more in the nature of a Roman triumph than a display of pageantry; and the king's popularity needed no reinforcement among either the great lords or the common people. Edward had ensured that his victories were well publicized; he now made his appearance as the victor of the French campaign, after an absence from England of just over fifteen months, the longest period he was to spend abroad. He celebrated Christmas at Guildford, in the palace there, one of Henry III's most attractive residences, and one of Edward's favourite places for that feast: he was there in 1330, 1337 and 1340. The usual elaborate masks and painted tunics were ordered, in sets of fourteen: six sets of buckram tunics, a set of masks of girls' faces, a set of masks of bearded men, another set of silver angels' heads; there were two sets of crests, one with reversed legs with shoes and the other with hills and rabbits. Peacock costumes, tunics painted with peacocks' eyes, head masks and wings, formed another set, as did white costumes for swans with similar masks and wings and a third set with dragons' heads. It was the most extensive wardrobe for Christmas games of his reign, though the similar list for the following Christmas at Otford runs it close: the centrepiece of this was a complete set of buckram armour for the king and his charger, spangled with silver, and with the king's motto 'Hey hey the white swan, by God I am the king's man'.[91] Fourteen buckram tunics with heads of men, virgins, lions and various other beasts were also provided.[92]

The series of tournaments which followed were at Reading and Bury St Edmunds in February, which seem to have been on a relatively modest scale. At Reading, the king wore blue armour, tunic and doublet. The king's crest was made of pheasant feathers, mounted with copper on stiffened linen, in the manner of the elaborate German crests seen in thirteenth-century manuscripts.[93] The most ostentatious display was reserved for a series of four jousts between 4 May and 14 July, at Lichfield, Eltham, Windsor and Canterbury.[94] The account for the Lichfield event is one of the most detailed that we have, and gives a long list of names; as in earlier years, the jousting circus seems to have moved on en bloc from one site to the next. This would explain why Lichfield has by far the greatest expenditure, while little additional cost was incurred for the other two: 288 masks for ladies and their attendants as against 44 for men and women alike at Canterbury. The king had two sets of armour and horse-trappings. One was of blue velvet decorated with flowers and branches of columbine, bears and lions; the other was white silk stamped with the arms of Thomas Bradeston. Blue was the dominant colour of the event, as blue robes with white hoods were made for the king, his household knights and his squires, and for Henry of Grosmont. The ladies of the court were dressed in blue gowns trimmed with fur, also with white hoods. The king wore blue and white again at the last jousts of the season, at Canterbury on 14 July, whereas the ladies were now dressed in green. The numbers here may have been small, but the costumes for the entry into the city required eight pounds of Cyprus gold thread, five pounds of scarlet silk and 3,000 gold leaves. At Windsor, the king's younger sons made their first appearance in the lists, Lionel, aged nine, in a grey and azure doublet; he, John of Gaunt (aged eight) and Edmund of Langley (aged six) all had armour covered in green velvet. It was an occasion when the scale of Edward's victories was made plain by the appearance of the captives he had taken during the previous two years: David, king of Scotland, the count of Eu, the count of Tancarville and Charles de Blois, 'and many other captives' were present.[95] Suits of armour were provided for the Scottish king and Charles de Blois as the most eminent of the prisoners.

Shortly after the jousts at Canterbury, Prince William, in honour of whose baptism the jousts at Windsor had been held, died, and the court was in mourning for some time after his burial at Westminster on 5 September.[96] In early June the most notorious plague of the middle ages, the Black Death, arrived in England, when an infected ship landed at Weymouth. It spread, largely by sea, first to the west country and then to the ports around the south and east coasts, reaching London around the beginning of October. Its fearsome reputation had preceded it, and men watched its progress with the greatest concern. It was against this background of impending doom that the foundation of a new college of priests at Windsor was announced on 6 August. There were no further tournaments that year.

PART TWO

The Company of the Garter

8

The Royal Chapels and the College of St George at Windsor

It was almost exactly a year after Calais fell, on 6 August 1348, that Edward issued letters patent re-establishing the private royal chapels of St Stephen at the Palace of Westminster and of St Edward at Windsor Castle, his two chief residences.[1] The two chapels were evidently intended as twin foundations. The preambles to the letters use the same phrases, and, thirty years later, Richard II issued letters settling their affairs on the same day.[2] Both were to become secular colleges, that is, colleges whose religious members were bound not by monastic rules, but by a set of ordinances which regulated their life and the organization of the institution. Monks took vows of obedience after a period as novices; members of a college merely undertook to live according to the common rules of their establishment. Secular colleges were rare in England before 1348.[3] Most were the early colleges of Oxford and Cambridge, where the function was entirely different, while others were almshouses, caring for the poor and sick.[4] Edward's two newly founded colleges were intended to be his personal contribution to the prayer and worship which was the essential communal activity of the Church as a whole.

When Edward's letters were issued, the buildings of both establishments were in disrepair. The chapel of St Stephen was said to have been founded by King Stephen,[5] and was certainly in existence at the beginning of the thirteenth century. Henry III, who largely rebuilt the Palace of Westminster, left the building untouched, but spent considerable amounts of money on furnishings and vestments for it. It may have been damaged in a major fire in 1263, which would explain why Edward I set about rebuilding it in 1292. Work progressed erratically, with frequent pauses of several years, until 1331, when one of Edward III's first acts after he had shaken off the tutelage of his mother and Roger Mortimer was to order the work to be resumed. It took another seventeen years, with a three-year pause during the Scottish wars due to shortage of money, for the building itself to be completed. But in 1348, St Stephen's chapel was still an empty shell, awaiting its furniture, glass and decoration.

At Windsor, the chapel dedicated to St Edward the Confessor had been built by Henry III. It was on a new site in the lower ward of the castle, and was begun in 1240, replacing a smaller chapel about which we know little, and which was part of the buildings around the great hall. The chapel was completed and furnished by the end of the decade. We know from the order to start the work that it was seventy feet long and twenty-eight feet wide, and lay in the middle part of the upper part of the lower ward, with space for a grassed area between it and the royal lodgings. By the end of the century, because Edward I rarely used Windsor, and because of a fire in the royal lodgings nearby in 1295–6, the chapel was in decay, its windows broken by gales, and little was done during Edward II's reign beyond necessary repairs. However, the chapel must have been in a reasonable state in November 1312 when Edward III was born in the upper ward of the castle and baptized in the chapel. Fifteen years later, repairs were again urgently needed: the wind had damaged the windows yet again, and the great joists of the vault were rotten. But there were more urgent claims on the royal income, and nothing seems to have been done. In 1348 St Edward's chapel was in serious disrepair.

Edward's letters patent give no hint of the fact that the chapels in the king's two noblest residences were both in need of work. Rather, the text lays emphasis on the king's personal involvement with them: both had been begun by his ancestors, and he had completed the building at St Stephen's, while he recalled that he had been 'washed in the holy water of baptism' at St Edward's. He then went on to create two new foundations which rededicated the chapels: St Stephen's was to be in honour of the Virgin Mary and St Stephen, while St Edward's received a triple dedication, to the Virgin Mary, St George and St Edward. Edward's personal devotion to the Virgin is recorded by chroniclers on a number of occasions, and is confirmed by the records of his almsgivings and pilgrimages.[6] The famous shrine of the Virgin at Walsingham in Norfolk was at the head of the list, alongside her statue in St Paul's and Our Lady in the Undercroft at Canterbury cathedral. The latter were relatively easy for him to visit, but Walsingham entailed a special journey of more than 200 miles from London. He would offer alms in person at statues of the Virgin which he passed on his travels, but would also instruct members of his household to make such offerings on his behalf to more distant shrines. Most notably, Edward, who was renowned for his bad luck with the weather when attempting to cross the Channel, founded the monastery of St Mary Graces near the Tower in Mary's honour, saying that through her mediation he had escaped from many perils by land and sea.[7] The chroniclers record two occasions when he vowed to found a monastery dedicated to her during a stormy Channel crossing. In March 1343 he returned from Brittany in an Atlantic storm, at the height of which he knelt before a relic of the True Cross 'which had long been with the kings of England' and implored the Virgin not to let him perish in the watery depths of the sea. If he were saved, he would found a monastery in her honour.[8] Similarly, he had prayed to the Virgin during a storm on his return from Calais in early October 1347, saying, 'O my lady Mary, what does it mean that when I set sail for France all goes in my favour, the sea is smooth and my affairs prosper, but when I return to England I always meet with adversity?'[9] While devotion to Mary was commonplace in the fourteenth century, Edward's worship of the Virgin was particularly intense, and this would explain the addition of her name to the royal chapels which he was refounding.

We know a good deal about the decoration, furnishing and layout of St Stephen's chapel, which survived, much altered but with fragments of the original still in place, until the fire of 1834.[10] It was on two storeys, with the lower chapel dedicated to the Virgin and the upper chapel as the private royal family chapel, to which distinguished visitors might also be admitted on state occasions such as baptisms or weddings. There are also references to pilgrims, probably visiting the golden statue of the Virgin in the lower chapel, who were only to be admitted as far as the threshold; but a charter of the canons recorded that they should have access 'without let or hindrance of the King's ministers of the palace'. The upper chapel may possibly have been visible as well.[11] Its decor was certainly such as to imply that it was intended for some degree of public display: it was a carefully planned and elaborate programme laid out in such a way that it portrayed the royal family in parallel with the Holy

Family, interweaving other themes of their personal devotion. The east end had two tiers of paintings, the upper tier showing the Three Kings presenting their offerings to the Christ child to the left. In the centre Mary presented Christ to the High Priest in the Temple, while to the right the shepherds worshipped the new-born child. Linked to these scenes, on the left of the lower tier, were the figures of the king and his sons, with St George drawing their attention to the scenes above them, while the right-hand side showed the queen and her daughters. Between these two sets of portraits stood the high altar.

The emphasis on the Virgin is explained by the dedication of the chapel, but St George seems to be present as Edward's personal patron. The figure of the saint, whose gestures indicate that he is presenting the king to the Virgin and Child in the tier above, is unparalleled in contemporary art: donors often appear in paintings, but their patron saint is usually portrayed as standing over them protectively rather than actively promoting their cause. The Magi or Three Kings, who figure prominently in the upper tier above Edward and his sons, were also the object of the king's personal devotion. He made offerings at their shrine in Cologne in 1338, and continued to give gifts of gold, frankincense and myrrh on the Feast of the Epiphany. Contemporary writers believed that he planned to be buried at their shrine, unlikely as this may seem, and the poet of *Winner and Waster* seems to envisage that, having conquered Paris, Edward would go to Cologne to give thanks for his victory at the Three Kings' Shrine.[12] A mazer made for Edward III with the arms of the Three Kings of Cologne on it was part of the royal treasure at the death of Richard II.[13]

The king's best painters and craftsmen worked at St Stephen's for at least a decade. As many as forty painters were at work there in 1350, and a substantial team of stained-glass makers was also on the site; they were to provide the glass for the Windsor chapel as well. The importance attached to the work is underlined by the problems encountered when the stalls were being designed. The original seating was a two-tiered Purbeck marble bench running round the outer wall,[14] and changing this to the stalls required by a collegiate church proved difficult. In July 1351, after work had been going on for two years, the stalls were removed, and the carpenters were ordered to work on 'raising various panels for the reredos of the said stalls in order to show and exhibit the form and design of the said stalls to the treasurer and other members of the king's council'.[15] In 1355 work was still continuing, and a new carver, Master Edmund of St Andrew, was brought from Newstead abbey, where he was a canon. As well as the thirty-eight stalls, the private 'closets' for the king and queen and their children were built at the eastern end of the nave: the royal family 'would have had an exceptionally good view of the altar murals which, in characteristically medieval illusionistic play, depicted themselves similarly "closeted" in perpetual prayer'.[16]

The murals were hidden behind panelling and forgotten for many centuries. In 1800, the Act for Union with Ireland was passed, which meant that an additional 100 MPs would join the House of Commons. Extra space was urgently needed, and a major refurbishment of St Stephen's chapel was put in hand which led to the destruction of what remained of Edward III's chapel. John Topham, introducing a series of engravings which recorded the paintings in 1795, described the effect of the chapel from the fragments which were still visible:

> It is necessary to observe that the whole of the architecture, and its enrichments, on the inside, are in gilding and colours, appearing extremely fresh; and what is remarkable and singular, the columns are decorated with a sort of patera, and several of the mouldings are filled with ornaments so very minute, that those on the spandrels and grand entablature, could hardly be perceived by the eye from the pavement of the chapel; but the artist designed that the whole of the work should have the same attention paid it, and that one universal blaze of magnificence and splendour should shine around, making this chapel the *ne plus ultra* of the art . . .[17]

To understand the purpose behind Edward's magnificent refurbishment of St Stephen's, we have to look to the Sainte-Chapelle in Paris, the religious focus of St Louis's palace on the Île de la Cité, with a similar relationship to king and government to that of St Stephen's at Westminster.[18] There was a tradition of establishing 'saintes-chapelles' in the French royal family. If we count Edward as part of that family (as he indeed was), his is a relatively early successor to St Louis's foundation: the bulk of such foundations in France are later in the fourteenth century. For England, this was a major innovation on Edward's part; but, as so often with his new ideas, he was looking over his shoulder at his supposed kingdom of France.[19]

The provision for clergy at St Stephen's in the letters patent of

8 December 1355 is identical with that at the Sainte-Chapelle in Paris, the magnificent housing created by St Louis for the relic of the Crown of Thorns which he had acquired from Baldwin II, emperor of Byzantium, in 1239 at exorbitant expense.[20] The architecture of St Stephen's echoed that common to the French royal private chapels, which were similarly buildings on two levels. However, Edward was working with an existing structure, and did not attempt to rival the soaring architecture and dazzling windows of the upper chapel of the Sainte-Chapelle. Nor did he have a relic to match the Crown of Thorns. The result was splendour of a very different kind, and with a different focus.

For the prime purpose of St Stephen's was introspective: it was a dynastic chapel where prayers were to be said for past, present and future members of the royal family, and which was designed to reinforce the idea of kingship as a divine calling, setting kings apart from their subjects. Many of the objects within the chapel were emblazoned with the royal arms, and the arms of the great baronial families were also worked into the decoration. The commemoration of family connections on tombs was becoming a commonplace at this period, with arms and figures of important relatives or colleagues incorporated in the design; but at St Stephen's, Edward is celebrating his living family, looking at themselves as if in a mirror. The paintings were completed during a decade when Edward was consciously creating an elaborate family settlement, involving marriage alliances which could have led to English princes ruling in Flanders and Brittany. And by the end of the decade, all but one of his sons had taken part in the campaigns in France.[21] There is nothing of the past here, no ancestral portraits: it is a bold statement of the power and wealth of the present generation, of their recent military triumph and their hoped-for dynastic success in France.

THE COLLEGE OF ST GEORGE

The letters patent founding the College of St George at Windsor provided for the same number of clergy, fifteen canons, as at St Stephen's. St Stephen's was the larger building, some ninety feet by thirty feet, against seventy feet by twenty-eight feet at Windsor,[22] but the two establishments were clearly intended to rank equally in importance. If Westminster was the pre-eminent royal palace and centre of government, Edward was in the process of making Windsor the pre-eminent castle of his realm. His personal attachment to the place was underlined in the document of 1348; this was his birthplace, from which he got his name, Edward of Windsor, and he had already used the castle for the greatest festival of his reign, in 1344. Windsor had always been the castle which he used most frequently; he was at Westminster more often, but this was due to the requirements of government. Woodstock, his other favoured residence, was a hunting lodge on a palatial scale with a park and pleasure gardens, a private place with no military or political significance; Edward's first three children had been born there, and its atmosphere is best summed up in the payment in 1354 for building a balcony for Princess Isabella so that she should have a view of the park.[23] He took up residence there for months at a time in the 1330s, but visited it only briefly and occasionally after 1340.

On the face of it, a more likely candidate as the home of a new institution might have been Winchester Castle. Winchester had been much patronized by his grandfather, and had strong Arthurian connotations, but the castle had been partially destroyed in a fire in 1302 in which the king and queen narrowly escaped with their lives. The damage does not seem to have been repaired until the 1330s.[24] Edward stayed there very rarely, though the great hall was repaired in 1348–9. It has been suggested that the Round Table was first mounted on the wall of the great hall during these repairs, and that there is a link with the supposedly Arthurian Company of the Garter at Windsor. However, we shall see that the Company of the Garter is in no way Arthurian, and there would be no point in these elaborate exercises in Arthurian propaganda at precisely the moment when Edward was moving away from the Arthurian imagery of the years prior to the Crécy campaign.[25]

The underlying question remains, however: why did Edward choose to found two new colleges rather than just one at Westminster? St Stephen's celebrated his dynasty and his military prowess in terms of princely magnificence. What else did he want to celebrate or commemorate? Much of the answer lies in the nature of the foundation, which we can only understand if we read it in conjunction with the religious provisions of his new institution. St Stephen's was at the heart of the seat of government, while St George's was established in the castle which best typified the king's military power.

Dedications to St George were relatively rare in England; most church dedications date from the twelfth century or earlier, and only 120 instances of St George as patron are recorded.[26] Despite the fact that the first dedication of the chapel at Windsor is to the Virgin Mary, it is as St George's chapel that it is remembered. It crystallizes the long process by which St George is identified with the triumph of the English armies. The red cross of St George, the great patron of military endeavour and of the crusades, had been adopted by Edward I in 1277 on his Welsh campaign, and was used again in 1290.[27] In the Scottish wars, his banner, alongside those of Edward the Confessor and St Edmund, was displayed by Edward I at the siege of Caerlaverock in 1300. The king's personal devotion to St George led him to present a gold statue of him, together with one of St Edward, to the shrine of Thomas Becket at Canterbury in 1285, at the very substantial cost of £374.[28] Edward III was very conscious of his grandfather's military reputation, and consciously took up many of the themes of his reign.

St George seems to have been established as a royal symbol of power and good government by the end of Edward I's reign, and this may be the message behind two magnificent manuscripts produced in the 1320s. In the margin of a devotional book, the Douce Book of Hours, two knights face each other: one is St George, while scholars believe that the other represents Thomas of Lancaster, cousin of Edward II and his bitter opponent, leader of the baronial opposition which had seized power in 1312 after Edward's favourite Piers Gaveston had been executed.[29] By the end of Edward II's reign, when this image was painted, Thomas of Lancaster had become a symbol of good government, and a popular cult had grown up around his tomb, even though he had died as a rebel fighting against the king. The image may therefore show St George as the representative of rightful royal government which Thomas of Lancaster had attempted to uphold.

The other manuscript was very probably presented to the young Edward III around the time of his accession to the throne. St George stands facing a young man whose surcoat bears the three leopards of England. He is about to hand him a shield bearing the same device, to complete his arming. This image is from a lavish manuscript apparently intended for Edward II, but hastily adapted for presentation to Edward III just as he became king. The book had been started in the dark years of his father's reign, when Edward was in his early teens. The text is a treatise on 'the nobility, wisdom and prudence of kings', and it is intended as a book of advice to a king, a king whom the author addresses in the most flattering terms. If it was addressed to his father, it would have been a reproof, for much of the counsel that it offers runs exactly contrary to Edward II's behaviour in real life. For Edward III, on the other hand, the text as much as the image of St George foreshadows his future achievements.

The treatise was composed by a clerk in royal employment, Walter Milemete, as a companion volume to another work of the period which was celebrated for its section on kingship; it also contained a great deal of medical advice, and this curious miscellany, known as *The Secret of Secrets*, supposedly written for Alexander the Great by his tutor, was very popular in the thirteenth and fourteenth centuries. When the great expert on manuscripts, M. R. James, produced a lavish facsimile of Milemete's treatise, he dismissed the text as 'second-hand book-learning'.[30] But in recent years scholars have looked at Milemete's work more closely, and found a text which is rather more interesting than James suggested. The advice that Milemete offers is designed to encourage a partnership between the king and his great lords; and it was exactly this collaboration that had been so singularly lacking in Edward II's reign.[31]

So far St George had been a saint to whom the king had a special relationship. In the late 1330s, with the advent of the war against France, his red cross on a white ground becomes a nationalist symbol, emblem of the English nation as well as the English king. When the constable of Bordeaux in 1338–9 was fighting to recover territories lost to the French in the previous decades, he ordered standards to be flown in the fortresses and towns he reconquered. Nine of these bore the arms of St George, and six bore the king's arms. The French enemy were evidently expected to recognize that St George was the emblem of English power, in opposition to St Denis. And in the satirical poem about the French wars, *The Vows of the Heron*, Edward's vow to fight for the French throne is sworn by 'St George and St Denis', seen as the patron saints of England and France.

The triple dedication to Mary, St George and St Edward may also have further resonances. In late fourteenth-century English popular poetry, St George appears as 'Our Lady's knight', a title that draws on stories about St George being raised from the dead and armed by the Virgin. This story seems to arise from the legend of St Mercurius (sometimes said to be St George's cousin) being confused with that of

St George. In the great repertory of saints' lives, *The Golden Legend*, St Mercurius is raised from the dead by the Virgin to kill the apostate Emperor Julian, and this episode is illustrated in the Lambeth Apocalypse in the mid-thirteenth century, where St Mercurius bears arms similar to those of St George. The version of the same episode in Queen Mary's Psalter is unambiguous: the arms are those of St George. Two manuscripts close in date to Milemete's treatise also have this miracle as a marginal illustration: the Smithfield Decretals (*c.* 1330–40) and the Taymouth Hours (*c.* 1325–35).[32] It would seem that the link between St George and the Virgin was established by the beginning of Edward's reign, though it is only in the chorus to the famous Agincourt carol, nearly a century later, that the phrase appears in literature: 'Enforce we us with all our might / To love Saint George, Our Lady's knight'.[33] It is tempting to speculate that Edward, a devotee of the Virgin with a victorious campaign behind him, might identify himself as 'Our Lady's knight', and thus also with St George. Furthermore, the Virgin had a special meaning in connection with his claim to the French throne. The French kings claimed the favour and protection of Our Lady, and the lilies which Edward now quartered with the English arms were her flower.

THE GARTER BADGE AND THE PLANNING OF THE COMPANY OF THE GARTER

The early history of the Company of the Garter has long baffled historians, because we no longer have the records of its foundation and of its early years. There are a handful of chronicle entries, mostly from the end of the fourteenth century, that mention the founding, and we have to fall back on the highly problematic evidence in the royal accounts. The garter first appears as a badge, with an associated blue-and-white colour scheme, on garments ordered for the king and his companions: yet even here there is a mystery.

Garters are an uncommon item of clothing, and in the fourteenth century the word is very rare except in connection with the Company of the Garter: there are perhaps half a dozen instances of it simply as an item of clothing. It derives from the Latin *garetta* and French *garet*, the crook of the knee, and was a piece of material tied round a man's leg to keep up stockings, usually called hose. Garters were so simple that purchases would not have warranted an entry in the royal accounts. However, garters as expensive decorative items do appear: they are recorded as early as 1307, in the accounts of Edward II as prince of Wales, who was provided with 'four garters for the prince's person decorated with silver silk' by his armourer Hugh of Bungay, who also provided eight pairs of gilded shoes.[34] In 1322 there is a entry for garters decorated with silver and red enamel.[35] Both these records imply that the garters were visible, and this may mean that the general assumption that male hemlines were below the knee until the 1330s is incorrect.[36] The first record of garters belonging to Edward III is in 1332, when the king's armourer and supplier of costumes John of Cologne makes a pair of pearl garters for the king for the tournament at Woodstock on 16 June. These may be the same as the 'pearl garters encrusted with gold' listed in the treasurer's accounts in 1334.[37] About five years later, 'a pair of garters the band of which is of red velvet' were bought for the eight-year-old Edward prince of Wales.[38] There is another account entry for two pairs of silver garters in 1341.[39] We know that the king's close friend Henry of Grosmont was fond of garters: in his treatise *The Book of Holy Medicines*, he confesses to his pride in his appearance as a young man. In the convoluted imagery used by writers of such texts, he describes how pride attacked him through various points of his body; it entered him through his feet, which, it seemed to him, 'look good in the stirrup, or in hose or in armour, or as I dance with a light foot; and garters suit me well, in my opinion'.[40] The use of garters was a relatively new and unusual fashion; Walter of Bibbesworth's Anglo-French glossary in about 1250 describes the garter as an item of apparel used by fashionable squires, but it is another fifty years before we have a definite record of them. When a new fashion for 'paltoks', a very short padded garment which came down to just below the hips, appeared in the 1360s, the chroniclers noted that hose were now laced to the pal-toks,[41] which must have made garters superfluous.

The Luttrell Psalter, famous for its illuminations of everyday life and the grotesques which inhabit its borders, has a little scene in which one of the figures is clearly wearing garters, tied with a decorative end hanging down (Plate 13). It seems to display a curious game, or perhaps a symbolic group, in which one man is trying to lift a pole over a molehill, and is prevented by his companions who are standing on the ends. The verses above from Psalm 88 lament the loss of friends; the dress of the gartered figure is in the latest fashion, and, together with the apparent game, seems to imply that the scene represents lost youth, a distant echo of Henry of Grosmont's self-portrait as a young man.[42]

Garters do not appear as part of women's dress until the fifteenth century: about 1400, a writer claimed that 'from the men [i.e. knights] of the garter came the use of the garter', and the first reference to women wearing garters is about the same date.[43] Men's garters were of course visible, and women would have worn a gown over their hose, so it may be that they were simply not mentioned, though, if women did indeed use them, one would expect to find silk garters in the detailed accounts for Queen Philippa's often extravagant apparel. Garter robes were issued for the ladies of the royal family from the beginning of Richard II's reign onwards,[44] but there is no specific mention of garters being issued to them. Until the end of the fourteenth century, the badge is therefore a strictly male emblem.

After 1341 there are no further references to garters in a context which implies that they are simply items of clothing. They emerge gradually as a badge around 1348, again in the accounts of the king's armourer, John of Cologne. These records show the extent to which he was responsible for supplying not only armour, but also many items of clothing and furniture, often with heraldic insignia. The details are found in three main documents, two of which are copies.[45] The first is an indenture between John of Cologne, the king's armourer, and Thomas Rolleston, clerk of the privy wardrobe, 'attesting to the delivery between 25 March, 19 Edward III [1345] and 22 June, 23 Edward III [1349] of divers garments and equipment made by John for the king within this period'. The second is a copy of this indenture on Thomas Rolleston's account roll for the period, and the third is a copy on the general account roll, or pipe roll, for 1349. The list seems to have been made up from notes of the king's purchases kept in John of Cologne's shop, and the dating and sequence of the material is a real problem, given that it covers four years. Sometimes a year is given; very rarely, there is an actual date. We can place some items by what we glean from other documents. A further complication is that the original is fragmentary, and the copy on the account roll is a version written up by Rolleston's clerks. The masks for an entertainment at Guildford which

John of Cologne describes as 'fourteen girls' faces with *bosettis*' evidently baffled the copyist, and remains a mystery today. 'Fourteen angels' heads' a line or two later become 'fourteen Englishmen's heads', the old confusion between *angeli* and *angli*.[46] John of Cologne's accounts were next made up in 1351, for the period 1349–51; the long period of the previous account is probably due to the king's absence abroad. John of Cologne first appears in the royal accounts in 1328–9; he seems to have died about 1367, when he is described as a merchant and citizen of London, and his executor, William of Cologne, is trying to collect long overdue debts.[47] John would have commissioned the making of a wide variety of armour and clothing, rather than manufacturing it himself, though he may have had a workshop for finishing such items. The supplies were probably authorized by a letter under the privy seal and individual items would then be ordered by the clerk of the wardrobe as and when needed.

Our next piece of evidence is even more confused than John of Cologne's records. It is in the register of Edward prince of Wales, the official copy of documents issued by his council, and is an account submitted in 1352 by William Northwell, who had been keeper of the prince's wardrobe between June 1345 and January 1349.[48] This is therefore a copy of Northwell's account, which in turn had been made up from notes relating to transactions going back to at least 1345.[49] Here there is a different problem. There are a number of dates, but many of the entries simply say 'bought the same day' when it seems highly improbable that these were the actual dates of purchase: if we are to believe the records, the prince of Wales bought all his new year's gifts – the traditional day for gift-giving at court – on 24 June the previous year; and furs, also a traditional winter gift, were bought on 28 June. The dates do not seem to relate to the actual transactions.

This may seem a rather long-winded disquistion on medieval accounting: but these entries are the most tangible evidence of the Company of the Garter in the course of formation. Another way of looking at the entries is to see how they are grouped. In the case of John of Cologne's accounts, there is some kind of pattern: he puts together all the entries relating to William of Windsor, the king's son, born in May 1348, who died in September 1348. The entries for his funeral precede those for the celebration of the churching of the queen after his birth, in June 1348. Similarly, there is a series of entries for the items made for the king's entertainments, and another series for the purchases for the king's jousts. It is therefore no surprise that there is a group of entries which relate to the use of the symbol of the Garter on royal and other clothing, armour and furnishings. The groupings are not absolute: there are stray entries elsewhere, but, as far as there is any principle in the drawing up of the account, it appears to be by topic.

The first items in the sequence as we have it are two worsted streamers, one with the image of St Lawrence with a white *pale* or stripe powdered* with blue garters. This is for a ship and there are a number of ships in the records called the *Lawrence*. Streamers could be prepared for diplomatic journeys abroad by the king as well as for military expeditions: in 1338 the accounts show streamers being prepared for his crossing on his way to Cologne to meet the emperor, in a very similar style.[50] The most likely dating is that the streamers were prepared for Edward III's journey to Calais to meet the count of Flanders in 1348.[51]

The streamers are followed by a blue silk bed, on which the garters carry the motto 'Hony soit qui mal y pense'. (The motto is frequently cited in the accounts without the word 'y': this changes the meaning from 'Shame on him who thinks evil of it' to 'Shame on him who thinks evil', but is probably just a scribal error.) Then there are items of clothing, beginning with a blue cloth *chlamys* or short military cloak: this classical word is very rare in English sources before its use for the Garter costume, and is a deliberate echo of the costume of Roman knights. It is only in the fifteenth century that it is found in more general use.[52] Two silk jupons or close-fitting tunics of different kinds complete the list: on both the *chlamys* and the jupons, the garters have buckles and pendants of silver-gilt. These items, apart from the streamer of St Lawrence, may have been made for the Eltham tournament of 1348, at which the king appeared in a robe powdered with twelve blue garters with the motto 'Hony soit qui mal pense'. Three sets of armour were made for the king for the Windsor jousts at midsummer that year, worked with blue garters and wild men or wodewoses, also in blue.[53] At Canterbury a month or so later, blue velvet was used for a *lappekyn* or cloth covering the helmet and leg-armour all decorated with garters, as well as for eight tunics and hoods for the king, and twelve gowns for

---

* Decorated with an irregular pattern.

their ladies. There is also a cloak and hood with no less than 100 silver garters with buckles and pendants.

Blue is suddenly the colour of the month, and the significance of the costumes for the tournaments of 1348 which we noted earlier becomes clear.[54] The heavy emphasis on it this year is evidently related to the imagery of the Garter. Apart from blue cloth, there are blue hands on white velvet armour, and dancing blue men embroidered on white hoods. Probably at the end of the year, Henry of Grosmont was given a set of armour and horse-trappings in blue and white silk.

So far, the symbol of the Garter and its colour might simply be one of the many decorative schemes adopted by Edward at various times during his reign. It has been suggested that it might have originated as a tournament badge; against this, there is no sign of the use of such badges in tournaments, and there must be some kind of reason behind the adoption of the symbol.

There is no reference in the royal accounts for 1348 to any form of company or order called 'of the Garter'. However, when we turn to the prince of Wales's account as recorded by Northwell, we find the phrase 'de societate Garteri',[55] of the Company of the Garter, used twice, and two other references which must be to decorative garters:

> A plate, gilt and enamelled, of the company of the Garter, with a hatchment, made for a herald of arms, bought the same day, to William de Stafford, herald of arms of Alvan'.

> Twenty-four garters made for the prince and bought the same day; to the knights of the company of the Garter.

> Thirty buckles, sixty girdle-tips and sixty bars, bought the same day; to sir John Chaundos for his robes, of the prince's livery.

> Sixty buckles, sixty girdle-tips and a hundred and twenty bars, bought the same day; to the knights of the prince's company for the tournament of Windsor.[56]

The only certainty about Northwell's account is that it ends in January 1349; the problems over the phrase 'bought the same day' make it impossible to be more precise about the date of the Windsor tournament. However, the preceding entries do give some clue. Two entries above the gift of a plate to William Stafford is an item which seems to conclude a list of gifts to ambassadors who came to England in the autumn of 1347 in an unsuccessful attempt to persuade Edward III to stand for election as Holy Roman Emperor: it is a gift to the notary who accompanied the ambassadors. The next entry consists of presents to the nurse and attendants of William of Windsor, in honour of whose baptism the midsummer 1348 tournament appears to have been held. It therefore looks as if these entries are copied from a new list, which should have been given a new date.

The gifts to Chandos and the prince's knights are for making up garters to attach to their clothing or armour, and we know that armour decorated with garters was worn by the king. The key item, however, is the reference to the twenty-four garters given to the 'knights of the company of the Garter', as this is the first time that we meet the Garter as a formal institution. This does not mean that the Company of the Garter was fully functioning at midsummer 1348. It seems most likely that the members had been chosen, and that the statutes at least drafted, and that the decision to make it an adjunct of the new College of St George at Windsor had been taken.

This tangled web of evidence therefore shows us little more than that the idea of the company was in the air in 1348 and possibly earlier; but this is hardly surprising, since Edward created the College of St George on 6 August 1348. This may have been the occasion when both the college and the company were set in motion. Neither were questions of great moment; indeed, the huge half-finished shell of the Round Table building in the upper ward of the castle was a reminder to the king not to overreach himself with ambitious plans. The membership of the company may well have been settled between April 1348 and New Year 1349, and the wording of the entry in the prince's account, made in 1352, reflects the situation at the time of writing. The items in question were perhaps given to the *future* companions at the end of 1348, who became knights of the companionship of the Garter at the first annual assembly on St George's Day, 23 April 1349. This is borne out by two payments to John of Cologne, which were modest advances against the costs of the first Garter robes; he received £30 on 11 January 1349, and a further £30 on 2 March, 'for various works for the king's person and for his companionship of the Garter', and for 'robes and garters for the king'.[57] A date of 23 April 1349 is therefore the most likely moment for the initial meeting, which implies the selection of the members well before then.

Another way in which we may be able to find clues as to how the Garter companions were chosen is to look at what we know of the actual creation of the company. The statutes place its institution firmly in 'the twenty-third year' of Edward's reign, that is, between 25 January 1349 and 24 January 1350, which would point to 23 April 1349 as the most likely date for its inception. The only historian writing within a decade of the foundation who gives a detailed account of it is Geoffrey le Baker, and he dates it firmly to 1350. Chronology is not his strong point: he places the Windsor tournament of 1348 a year later, and in the earlier part of his work uses a system of starting the new year at Michaelmas, taken over from Adam Murimuth, on whose chronicle he bases this part of the narrative. He also merges the institution of the college with that of the company, and it is clear that he has good information about both, except for the question of the timing. If he is right about the two institutions being founded at the same time, which would be logical, that evidence would support a date of 23 April 1349 as the moment when both schemes were set in motion. The college was the first to be officially confirmed, while the company's statutes had to wait for the approval of the first gathering of the knights a year later. On balance, this is the best reconstruction of the sequence of events that can be offered.

What then is the significance of the adoption of the garter as an emblem, and of the motto 'Hony soit qui mal y pense'? The first appearances of the garter in the royal accounts are within a few months of the probable foundation date, so it is likely that it was always intended as a knightly symbol for the planned company: garters embroidered with the motto appear very early on, and the two are virtually inseparable. William Camden, the great antiquary of the early seventeenth century, whose *Britannia* is one of the classics of the period, makes a remark which seems to have been overlooked by modern writers. He tells us in suitably rhetorical prose in his entry for Windsor: 'In this place, king *Edward* the third, for to adorne martiall prowesse, with honors, the guerdon of vertue, ordained that most noble order and society of knights, whom (as some report) for his owne garter given forth as signall of a battaile that sped fortunately, hee called knights of the Garter . . .'[58] This would be a strong possibility if we knew that garters were used in this way, as a kind of coded badge in a battle. Juliet Vale has suggested that the garter could have been adopted as a general emblem for the invasion of France in 1346; it is an attractive suggestion, but again, there is no evidence of such usage and the mystery remains.[59] The motto is now generally accepted as a reference to Edward III's claim to the French throne, a defiant challenge to those who denied or opposed his right. However, if it were a propaganda statement as part of the general campaign to present Edward III as the true king of France after his assumption of the title in 1340, it should really appear at a much earlier date. I would suggest that the motto also has a particular resonance *after* the battle of Crécy. The French were not only defeated, but their nobility were shamed, a shame and loss of honour which went like a shock wave through France, and is expressed in surviving poems. *Honi* is literally 'shamed' rather than 'shame', *honte*, and the usual English translation is misleading: it should be 'Shamed be he who thinks evil of it'. It is a motto which fits perfectly the situation after Crécy, when Edward had shamed his opponents.

There is a third aspect to it: like all good mottoes of this kind, it has multiple meanings. One of these was directed at the critics of the war in England, who, though largely silenced in the aftermath of the events of 1346–7, were still a force to be reckoned with. In particular, the parliaments of January and March–April 1348 were dominated by the commons' attempt to restrain the king's efforts to raise new war taxation, and to bring such exactions under their control. From this point of view, the war was highly unpopular. The commons carefully avoided any formal opposition to the war in principle – 'as regards your war and the array of the same, we are so ignorant and simple that we neither know nor are able to give counsel thereon' – but had a great deal to say on the question of the resulting taxes, which they called 'a very great charge from his poor commonalty'. The king got his money, but the commons did their best to hedge the grant, 'made to their great misfortune', with as many conditions as possible.[60] The complaints and unspoken hostility to the war were, in Edward's view, shameful, when he had just won such a glorious victory.

The blue and gold of the garter are the French colours, and the form of the garter – not a simple tie, but a minute version of the knight's belt, the *cingulum militare*, which was a central part of the knighting ceremony, and which was used to gird on the new knight's sword – proclaims its military intent. The choice of the garter as emblem is also practical, since it could be displayed over armour without difficulty, like the Spanish Order of the Sash, founded in 1330, and which William Montagu and Henry of Grosmont would have known from their mission to Spain in 1343.[61] The statutes of the institution focus on commemoration and religious ceremony; the badge reminds us that the company is, in its original form, a memorial to a great victory, which also looks forward to the continuation of the spirit which had made that triumph possible, and the pursuit of the ultimate goal, Edward's coronation as king of France.

The closest that we can get to Edward's own concept of the new institution is by looking once again at the royal accounts. From the earliest mention of the knights of the Garter until the end of his reign, the clerks of the great wardrobe and of the prince of Wales consistently call it a *societas* or company.[62] Only at the end of Richard II's reign is it called a *fraternitas* or brotherhood by the clerks, although Geoffrey le Baker describes it as such around 1360.[63] It is not called an order in the exchequer records until the end of Henry V's reign, though in 1403 the parliamentary clerks refer to it as 'an order of knighthood'. There is one exception to this, when in 1353 John Buckingham records the alms given by the king for masses for 'the deceased brothers of the said order [i.e. of St George]'. Here the Company of the Garter is seen in religious terms as an organization within the Church; it is not being portrayed as a secular order of knighthood. If it were, the text would read 'the deceased *knights*' instead of 'the deceased brothers'.[64]

The surviving copies of the early statutes are all later than 1415, and some of them refer to the 'company or order of knighthood' of the Garter; these probably reflect usage at the time the copies were made rather than the original lost text. The absence of any straightforward copy of the original statutes means that the texts have to be used with caution. It seems that modifications were made in Richard II's reign and again in Henry IV's reign, and the extent of those changes is not clear.

The twin victories of Crécy and Calais lie at the heart of the function of St George's chapel. The statutes of the Company of the Garter lay a stronger emphasis on the religious duties of the knights than on anything military or knightly.[65] Only two clauses deal with secular matters: the requirement that the knights are of good behaviour and noble birth, and the stipulation that knights shall be given preference when sum-moning forces for a campaign: and it is not impossible that the second is a later addition. As portrayed in the statutes, the Company of the Garter was a religious confraternity, and the chief duty of its members was to attend the annual service at Windsor on St George's Day.[66] Penal-ties for non-attendance at the services, without permission of the king, were severe. A knight who failed to appear was to be publicly shamed the following year, and, if he missed two such occasions without excuse, he had to offer a jewel worth twenty marks on the altar, a fine which was doubled for each consecutive repeated absence. The day after the St George's festival all knights had to attend a requiem mass before departing. Even if a knight had permission to be absent, he had to observe the feast wherever he might be.

On the death of a knight the king was to have 1,000 masses said for the knight's soul, and other members were required to provide masses according to their rank, ranging from 700 from the prince of Wales down to 100 from a simple knight. In effect, at least 5,000 masses would be said within three months of a knight's death. Even by medieval stand-ards, this is a very large number. Furthermore, in common with other religious confraternities of this type, it meant that, if a knight died on campaign without leaving a will which made provision for such masses, his soul would not be left to languish in purgatory. Since the majority of knights do not appear to have made wills before they departed on cam-paign, this was 'a type of insurance policy for the soul'. In the case of John Chandos, who died intestate in 1370, 'his fellow companions in the order paid for at least 5,300 masses to be said to speed his soul through purgatory'.[67] In 1372 John of Gaunt paid for 500 masses to be said for the soul of Walter Mauny, 'our most dear companion, one of the knights of the Garter', at a cost of 41s. 8d., so the total expenditure by members of the company on the death of one of the knights would have been around £23, the equivalent of the annual fee of a banneret in the king's household.[68]

Given this emphasis in the company's statutes on the observance of St George's Day and on the remembrance of the dead, it is clear that the prime object of both company and college is commemoration. Founded a year after the end of the Crécy–Calais campaign, possibly on the anni-versary itself of Edward's entry into the conquered town, it is a memorial to the triumph of England. Anniversaries were hugely important in the medieval Church: on the anniversary of the death of anyone of rank, lay or clerical, masses would be said for their soul. And those masses, in the case of the company, would include not only the handful of dead on the English side, but the vastly more numerous souls of the enemy casualties, included as part of the Christian world at large in the annual requiem mass 'for the souls of all those companions who have died and all Christians'[69] held on the morrow of St George's Day. Crécy had been a great victory; but it had also been a massacre on an almost unprecedented scale, not simply of a faceless enemy, but of men who were close friends and relatives of the members of the company.

The statutes of St George's College are carefully designed to prevent that scourge of many religious institutions of the time, the absentee holder of a sinecure. Edward III therefore provided that a canon who failed to reside at Windsor received only 40s. a year, while a resident could receive as much as £20 5s., since a payment of 1s. was made each day to those canons present at services in chapel.[70] The king's concern for continuous celebration of masses is further evidence of the commemorative aims of the foundation: he 'wanted the flow of intercession to be unceasing'.[71] And it was to continue, of course, beyond his death, particularly for himself: in 1416, apart from the general requirements for masses contained in the company's statutes, specific obits were observed for Edward III, Philippa and Edward prince of Wales, Henry of Grosmont, Thomas Beauchamp and William Bohun.[72]

The only official of the company recorded before the fifteenth century was William Whitehorse, the usher or verger of the company, who seems to have been appointed before 1352. In 1352–3, the building accounts have entries for his lodging, a half-timbered building which was not part of the college, but probably stood in the middle ward.[73] Whitehorse was one of the king's yeomen, and in 1353 he was granted permission to have a substitute for an office he held in York because he 'stays continually in the king's service at his side'.[74] He had been in the king's service since 1343, and in 1347 was made constable of Conisbrough Castle; he had evidently been with the king at Calais and possibly also at Crécy, and was described as 'the king's beloved squire'. In 1360 he was again rewarded for 'his sedulous service at the king's side', and the next year he retired to Wenlock abbey to be maintained by the abbey. In 1366 he went abroad, possibly on pilgrimage.[75] He was evidently one of the king's personal attendants, and seems to have had charge of the king's jewels, perhaps as receiver of the chamber.[76] As such, he would have been familiar with the knights of the Garter even before the company was established. They in turn gave him gifts and lands: he received £5 from Prince Edward in 1355 and later a grant of lands, and Thomas Holland also granted him lands.[77] His role as usher was largely ceremonial, and fitted in with his duties about the king's person: he was 'to bear the rod in [the king's] presence before the college of the chapel in processions on feast days'.[78] The post of usher was merged with that of the verger of the College of St George when Thomas Sy was appointed by Henry IV in 1399; Sy was also keeper of the knights' robes and black rod of the Company of the Garter.[79] This seems to have been the first move in Henry's reappraisal of the Company of the Garter.

The biggest question about the nature of the Company of the Garter under Edward III is that of the supposed tournaments which, according to many historians, were a central part of its ceremonies. If we look carefully at the records, we have only two positive records of jousts at Windsor after the St George's Day ceremonies, those of 1349 and 1358. The 1358 occasion was certainly impressive, but it was not a customary occasion, despite the claim of Thomas Gray in his *Scalacronica*, apropos of these jousts, that 'At that place of Windsor, the said King Edward held his great feast with jousts and revelry on St George's Day, as was customary'.[80] It seems to have been on a similar scale to the Round Table of 1344, a tournament 'open to all wishing to compete within their degree'. At the beginning of March, heralds were sent to France, Germany, Brabant and Flanders to proclaim the jousts; personal letters were sent to English lords, and countesses and other ladies were similarly summoned.[81] The jousts were proclaimed by Roger Mortimer, earl of March, who borrowed £1,000 from the prince of Wales on 17 February, probably to finance his part in the tournament. The prince himself gave no less than £100 to the attendant heralds and minstrels.[82] Edward and his prisoner King John were present, as were Isabella, Philippa and Joan queen of Scotland, and as usual the chroniclers declared that it was 'a solemn banquet and round table such as had never been held in England since the time of King Arthur'.[83] It was also a diplomatic occasion, since John himself wrote to the citizens of Nîmes a week or two later saying that at this splendid festival he had been given assurances that full peace negotiations would soon be under way.[84] Matteo Villani describes it as a 'solemn and vain festival of knights errant in the city of London', where, 'renewing the ancient fables of the Round Table, twenty-four knights errant were created, who, in imitation of the fallacious romances which were spoken of in olden times, challenged and were challenged to joust for the love of ladies'. The knights do not seem to have assumed Arthurian identities, but merely to have echoed the proceedings in the romances: 'the ladies and knights came before the king with pretended claims of grave misdeeds' which were settled by jousts between the lady's champion and the supposed offender. Villani's repeated description of the event as 'vain and pompous and full of stupidities', with few specific details, shows that he is more concerned to make a moral point than to record the event accurately; he ends with the notion that it all ended in tears, because soon afterwards the king's sons fell ill of the plague, though he fails to note that Henry of Grosmont was wounded in the crotch in the tournament itself.[85] King John is said to have remarked that he had never seen 'so royal and costly a feast made with wooden tallies, without paying in gold and silver', a reference to the English exchequer's system of issuing promissory notes in the form of a stick split in half; the creditor's half had to be matched to the exchequer half before payment could be made.*[86]

Much has been made in recent years of the idea that the company might have been based on two tournament teams. Juliet Vale wrote in 1982: 'It is immediately apparent that the seating arrangement [i.e. in the chapel] also provided two potential tournament teams.'[87] She sees the selection of the king's and prince's companions in the company as being driven by this idea: 'Age and experience seem very carefully matched in the two sides, who would evidently provide an evenly balanced encounter. In itself this parity strongly suggests that Edward's distribution of the knights was influenced by the need to compose two fairly matched tournament teams.'[88] Ian Mortimer claims that 'Geoffrey le Baker ... states that Edward founded it *at* (not before) this tournament on St George's Day 1349 ... The implication of le Baker's description

---

* It was a highly unpopular system: in the late 1330s the poem 'Against the King's Taxes' complains that it would be better for the king 'to eat from wooden platters and pay in coin for food, than to serve the body with silver and give pledges of wood'.

is that the founder members were defined by their being there that day: *they took part.*[89] Baker actually dates the event to 1350, but this is a different question. Whether he is talking about 1349 or 1350, the event he describes is a *convivium*, which has the specific meaning of feast, particularly a feast in terms of an ecclesiastical festival or celebration: mass is sometimes referred to as *sacrum convivium*. If Baker says nothing at all about a tournament, the accounts of Thomas Rolleston do indicate that there was a tournament at the same time as the first Garter feast, because, after a list of items for the chapel of St George for the 1349 Garter feast, he accounts for 'cloth of Dest, canvas and satin bought and used to make four suits of armour of cloth of Dest at the same time'.[90] This is the only moment at which there is evidence of a possible tournament in connection with the Garter feast. The issue of robes for subsequent feasts is never connected to the gifts of arms which are typically found for major tournaments, and the 1358 event is the exception, rather than the rule.

Furthermore, if we look at other contemporary knightly companies or orders, discussed in Chapter 12, we find that tournaments are specifically mentioned in their statutes. The oldest known order is the Hungarian Fraternal Society of St George, founded in 1326.[91] Here the statutes specifically required participation in tournaments if the king was one of the jousters: the fifty knights of the order were required to 'follow the king in every recreation and especially in the military games'.[92] The members of this Hungarian order hold a position nearer to that of the English household knights, but are organized, like the Garter, as a fraternity.

The Castilian Order of the Sash was unique among the early knightly orders in making the tournament a central element in the order's proceedings. The knights were to gather at Whitsun each year for the specific purpose of tourneying, 'if the king should have time for this'.[93] If at any time there was a tournament within thirty miles of wherever they happened to be, they were bound by their oath as members of the order to take part in it, 'so that it shall seem that wherever knightly deeds are performed, some knights of the Sash will always be there'.[94] There were complex rules for gaining admission to the order by challenging current knights of the order to joust, and this was a dominant feature of membership. The contrast between the statutes of this Castilian order and those of the Garter is therefore very striking, and reinforces the idea that the Garter is essentially distanced from purely knightly displays.

The Company of the Garter is much closer to the proposed Company of the Virgin and St George in France, a project which antedated it by five years. The letters patent of Clement VI, giving John II, who was at the time duke of Normandy, licence to found a church and college of 200 knights in 1344, specify that the knights shall, on the feast days of St George and of the Assumption of the Blessed Virgin, meet 'not for jousts or tournaments or any other deed of arms, but only for the purpose of devotion to the said church ... assembl[ing] there annually in person'.[95] The Company of the Garter and the proposed French Company of the Virgin and St George are both centred on an actual ecclesiastical establishment, with a royal chapel as their focal point. And in the French case it is specifically stated that tournaments are not to have any place in the company's proceedings.

It is not therefore surprising to find that the tournament element of the Garter is probably a mirage: the surviving evidence consists of Thomas Gray's throwaway remark that the king did this every year. He may well have meant to say that the king held a great annual festival on St George's Day, and assumed that 'jousts and revelry' were automatically part of such an occasion: given his remoteness from court life at this time, his information is by no means conclusive. It is much more likely that tournaments, however largely they figured in knightly ideals and in the mindset of Edward and his companions, were not part of the religious festival at the heart of the Company of the Garter.

St George's Day was undoubtedly transformed into one of the major court festivals, on a par with the four great Church festivals on which the king and his household traditionally gathered.[96] It is not unreasonable to see the ceremonies at Windsor on the feast of St George as the medieval equivalent of Remembrance Day. In 1353 the expenditure on food during this period was the highest of any of the year's festivals, and the reunion may have extended beyond the royal family to a larger group, whom we can only occasionally discern.[97] In 1357, during a session of parliament at Westminster from 17 to 30 April, the king appears to have declared a recess in order to go to Windsor.[98]

The bishop of Winchester was also present as the prelate of the company. It has been claimed that Winchester was chosen as prelate, despite the fact that Windsor is in the diocese of Salisbury, because of its Arthurian associations, being traditionally identified as Camelot. In fact, there were just three prelates for the first century of the Garter's existence: William Edington, Edward's right-hand man during the period of the Crécy campaign, William of Wykeham, the rebuilder of Windsor, and Henry Beaufort, son of John of Gaunt and a major figure in early fifteenth-century politics. These men were all part of the inner royal circle, and what may have been intended as an appointment at the king's will became a tradition (that the prelate was from Winchester) because of their longevity: Beaufort died two years before the centenary of the foundation of the Company of the Garter. Again, the evidence tends to point to this being a reunion each year of a small group, the king's family and intimates, rather than a gathering with wider resonances.

The requirements for the celebration of large numbers of masses may have encouraged the striking development of St George's into one of the major centres of the new polyphonic music from 1360 onwards. The records of the chapel are much fuller than for most other centres, so it is not easy to compare with other cathedrals, while we know very little about St Stephen's. What we can say is that St George's was home to John Aleyn, composer of the motet in praise of Edward entitled *Sub Arcturo plebs vallata*,[99] 'one of the most complex and remarkable ... motets ... to have survived from anywhere in Europe' from this period. Aleyn was a canon from 1362 to 1373, and the implication is that from the start St George's was one of the major musical centres of England,[100] and that the Garter services were performances of a rare quality.

If we know a great deal about the St George's music and almost nothing about that at St Stephen's, the reverse is true about the architecture and decoration of the chapels. Henry III's chapel at Windsor was superseded by Edward IV's new chapel in the 1470s, though the former was left standing.[101] Most of the original chapel was demolished when Henry VII's Lady Chapel was added to Edward IV's chapel in 1494–8, and we have no images of the interior. A small fifteenth-century sketch of the outside does survive in a drawing of the whole of Windsor Castle, and we know the dimensions of the chapel and its general architecture from the original writs of Henry III commissioning the building. It was twenty-eight feet wide and seventy feet long, and it was to have 'a high wooden roof . . . in the manner of the new work at Lichfield, so that it resembles stonework'; there was to be a turret in front of it with three or four bells (Plate 11).

Something of this original chapel remains. The masonry of the north wall of the original chapel is the south wall of the dean's cloister, with its blind arcades; it survived because in order to replace it the cloister would have had to be rebuilt. It is the narthex or west porch of Henry III's chapel which is the most important survival, forming an ambulatory between the east end of Edward IV's chapel and the chapel beyond. Henry VII made this into a Lady Chapel, and it was remodelled in Victoria's reign as the Albert Memorial chapel. Again, there are blind arcades with fine Purbeck marble columns: in the centre of the wall is a magnificent pair of wooden doors decorated with iron patterns, the original entrance to both Henry III's chapel and Edward III's remodelled

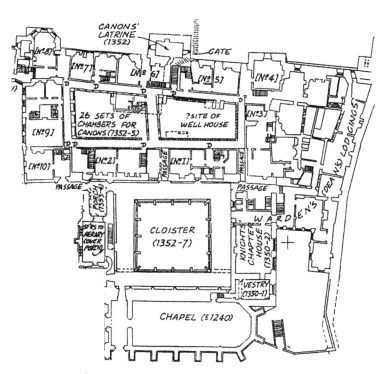

Windsor Castle, showing the original site of St George's chapel.

Garter chapel. These seem to have been the work of a goldsmith named Gilbert Bonington, one of the moneyers responsible for minting the new silver pennies issued in 1247; his mark, '+ Gilebertus', is stamped on the metal, the only example of marked English medieval ironwork.[102]

The interior of the chapel was filled with elaborate furnishings, relics and statuary, and the glass was made by the glaziers working at Westminster. Work started in 1352, and seems to have been complete by November; the glass was put aside and stored for the winter, before being sent to Windsor the following spring, in boxes packed with hay and straw, and installed in time for the Garter festival of 1353. The glass was therefore similar in style to St Stephen's, but nothing survives from either set of windows.[103]

The nearest approach to what the glass of the original Garter chapel might have been like is the great east window at Gloucester cathedral, a work on a monumental scale which is the largest surviving example from the fourteenth century. At the foot of the serried ranks of the hierarchy of heaven, there is a row of shields. Some have come here by chance, but there is a core of the original heraldry, and the owners of these shields can be placed at Crécy and Calais: Richard Fitzalan, Thomas Berkeley, Thomas Beauchamp, William Bohun, Laurence Hastings, Richard Talbot, Maurice Berkeley, Thomas Bradeston. Higher up there are the shields of Prince Edward and Henry of Grosmont. The window is dated in the most recent study to 1350–60, and seems beyond reasonable doubt to celebrate the campaign of 1346–7. The windows at St George's chapel would almost certainly have contained this mixture of religious themes and topical heraldry, and would have commemorated the same events.[104]

Although there had been extensive painting by Brother William of Westminster in 1248–56 in the original chapel, there is no record of painting being carried out at St George's during Edward III's remodelling of the interior. However, it is possible that there was no space for an ambitious iconographic programme like that at Westminster. If a fifteenth-century sketch of Windsor Castle, done before Edward IV's chapel was built, is reasonably in proportion, the walls must have been about thirty feet high, with a series of substantial windows whose sills were fifteen feet above the floor; and we know that below these windows were the elaborate stalls of the knights and canons.[105] There are no real parallels for a chapel with seating for both laymen and clergy, and any reconstruction must be conjectural. We do have surviving choirstalls from a set made in the 1360s for the chapel of the hospital of St Katharine's by the Tower, under the patronage of Queen Philippa.[106] These are probably in the same style as those for St Stephen's and for Windsor, and measure approximately twenty-seven inches across. The knights' stalls must have occupied a space of about twenty-seven feet on each side, and, assuming that the canons also had stalls against the walls, the total run of stalls would have been fifty-four feet. However, the placing of these presents some problems. The king and the prince of Wales had separate seats, which were likely to have been in a place of honour close to and facing the altar, and it would be logical for the knights' stalls to be adjacent to these. A second but less likely possibility is that the canons may have been close to the altar, with the king, prince and knights further down the choir. If we look at the arrangements when Edward IV's new chapel came into use in the late fifteenth century, it seems that the knights and canons sat either in the two higher rows or in alternate seats.[107] In front of the stalls were cloth-covered benches.[108] Here the choristers sat: if a knight was late for the service on the eve of St George's Day, he was not allowed to enter his stall, but had to sit 'lower down, in front of their stall, in the choristers' place'.[109] At the end of the stalls, presumably forming a return running across the end of the choir against the pulpitum, was a pew for the queen.[110] As there was a doorway to the vestry on the north side, this pew would have been to the south.[111] In addition to the high altar, there were two other altars at the east end. One was behind the high altar, for the use of the priest celebrating mass. The other, against the north wall, was probably dedicated to St George, as it had on it a wooden board with brass plaques illustrating the saint's life.[112]

The main visual feature of the choir must have been the tracery and carving of the stalls, on which a great deal of time and money was expended in 1351–3. Between twelve and fifteen carpenters worked on the stalls for sixty-four weeks, and the turning of the capitals for the stalls took the king's master carpenter, William Hurley, and his assistant about forty weeks, quite apart from the carving of figures on the misericords, carried out by Robert Burwell and Robert Kynebell, and the production of pinnacles and other ornaments for the upper part.[113]

Above each stall was a fitting on which the knights' swords were hung. Twenty-four such 'crooks' were bought 'for the stalls in the choir of the chapel'.[114] This tells us that the knights were within the choir, a highly unusual arrangement. Normally the choir was reserved for the clergy, and this placing may underline the religious connotations of the new company. It also suggests that the number of knights had not yet been increased to twenty-six. The problem of the difference in numbers, here as elsewhere, may be that the king and prince of Wales are not treated as knights in the strictest sense, but have a different status.[115]

On the pulpitum or stone choir screen were the organs, an altar and a desk from which the Gospel and Epistle were sung. Beyond it lay the antechapel, with two altars on either side of the doorway to the choir: one of these was dedicated to the Virgin. The font was probably in the antechapel: it was described in the seventeenth century, in a list of items taken by the Puritan army in 1642, as a 'Great Brasse Bason or Font for Christenings given by the founder Edward III', and would have resembled the brass fonts which survive at Rostock, Schwerin and Wismar in eastern Europe. It may have come from Flanders, where there was a long tradition of highly skilled metalwork of this kind.[116] William of Windsor was probably baptized here in 1348.

Statues of St George and the Virgin stood on either side of the altar; St George was in wood, and was carved in 1352, possibly by William Herland.[117] The reredos was not installed until 1367, but it had probably been in the making for some time. It was of alabaster, and cost the huge sum of £166 13s. 4d. Even more surprising is the fact that it needed ten carts, each pulled by eight horses managed by two men, to transport it from Nottingham to Windsor. English alabasters of this kind were just coming into their own at this date. Although the stone had been used locally for effigies for some decades, the first document referring to alabaster from Tutbury, the main quarry in the medieval period, is dated 1362, and the first reference to an alabasterman in Nottingham is in fact that for the making of the St George's reredos.[118] As in the case of the music to be heard in the chapel, St George's was at the cutting edge of the art of the period. The largest surviving alabaster reredos recorded seems to be that at St Seurin in Bordeaux, consisting of fourteen panels in three rows, and that at St George's would have been on a similar scale.[119] Like most medieval sculpture, alabaster was painted; it was a good surface for the purpose, and the effect was as powerful as frescoes, but with the added depth given by the three-dimensional carving. It was this reredos that provided the main pictorial element in the chapel, but it did not survive the demolition of the original building.

The reredos had both carved and painted panels and blank niches, where jewels and relics could be displayed, and it had two wings which could be closed to form a cupboard.[120] An inventory of 1384 lists twenty-one items on the reredos shelves, most of which are jewels. On the altar stood a reliquary in the shape of an arm, containing part of the arm of St George, while the total number of relics possessed by the chapel was around two dozen. The most important was the Neith Cross, containing a fragment of the True Cross. This was presented to Edward I by the Welsh in 1283 at Conway following his defeat of Dafydd of Gwynedd and the final subjugation of Wales. It was paraded through the streets of London in 1285 at the head of a procession which included the king and his family and many of his magnates, as a visible symbol of his victory. It was therefore an important talisman, and was presented to St George's by Edward III as the principal relic of the chapel, a reminder of his ancestor's military triumph.

From the beginning, St George's seems to have possessed an outstanding collection of vestments. Earlier in the century, Canterbury cathedral owned sixty-nine sets of vestments and forty-nine copes; St George's, a much smaller establishment, owned twenty-five sets of vestments and no fewer than forty-three copes,[121] including such items as a vestment of cloth of gold 'powdered with various birds', in which Joan countess of Kent was married to Edward prince of Wales and Aquitaine, and two vestments with stars and eagles and a golden cope given by her husband.[122] Many of the items were evidently either made of cloth intended for secular purposes or are reused from secular garments: the cope given by Edward prince of Wales is an exception, showing 'various martyrdoms of various saints'.

A number of the furnishings listed in the inventory of 1384 proclaimed that the chapel was home to the Company of the Garter. There are two cushions embroidered with garters and the arms of St George; and the veil used to cover the altar during Lent is 'powdered with Garters and golden eagles'. Carpets with heraldic designs covered the floor of the choir: six of these had the king's and prince's arms, or those of Garter companions (Thomas Beauchamp and Pembroke).[123] Six other carpets had garters on them, on blue or red backgrounds. Only four plain carpets are listed.

Finally, there are the swords and helms above the stalls. We have seen how 'crooks' were provided for the swords, and the inventory of 1384 lists eight helms and three of the swords, so the helms were part of the original scheme. We shall see that the stall plates are likely to have been an innovation on the part of Henry V, as part of the attempt to recover the lost early history of the company. The practice of hanging helms and swords over a knight's tomb is particularly English, and there is little evidence of it before the mid-fourteenth century. There are wills in which the horse and armour used at a knightly funeral are left to the church in which the knight is buried, but these are probably donations in kind rather than items for display in the church.[124] There was certainly a tradition of knightly splendour at such funerals, to the extent that other wills specifically prohibit such demonstrations of worldly status. An alternative reading of the presence of the swords in St George's would be as a kind of ex-voto for victory.[125] It is possible that the helms and swords in St George's chapel may represent the beginning of this fashion for heraldic display in churches, particularly since the most spectacular of all funerary monuments of this kind is the tomb of Edward prince of Wales in Canterbury cathedral, dating from the late 1370s. Here, not only the helm and sword are preserved, but also his shield, gauntlets and heraldic surcoat.

The external appearance of the college was relatively modest, in line with its status as the king's personal foundation within the castle. A visitor to Windsor in 1360 would have found a broad open space inside the great gatehouse, with buildings on the far side. Crossing this area to the great hall, the major state room of the castle, he would have seen to his right, at the top of the slope of the lower bailey, an elegant two-storey porch. The walls on either side ran from the chapel to the buildings against the outer wall of the castle, forming a self-contained space within the castle, which proclaimed that this was a separate entity. The porch itself was in the latest architectural style, related to the great porch of the twin establishment at St Stephen's.[126] Its elaborate and ingenious vaulting and decoration formed the entrance to the cloisters within. The buildings (particularly the cloister) have largely survived, buried in later constructions, but the enclosed nature of the college has been lost.

Within the college, the accommodation was mainly for the canons and vicars. The twenty-six poor knights, elderly or disabled men supported out of charity as specified in the college's foundation charter, were a negligible element in the establishment until long after the Reformation; owing to Edward III's failure to provide adequate endowments after his initial grants to the college, there were never more than three of them in the medieval period, instead of the twenty-six envisaged in the charter. The knights themselves were only occasional visitors to Windsor, and did not require permanent quarters, and the one building associated with their gatherings was the chapter house of the company.[127] The annual chapters of the knights and the elections were not attended by the canons, though one of the latter would probably have acted as registrar. How formal this appointment was in the early years we cannot tell, but, before the creation of the post of Garter king at arms under Henry V, such records as the company had were certainly kept in the college.[128] Architecturally, the chapter house is modest. Although it is quite large, it has a ceiling rather than a vault; built of stone, it was originally thirty-eight feet by twenty-three feet. The dominant feature is the elaborately traceried windows, one of which still survives, though without the stained glass.[129] The chapter house glass must have been magnificent: it was made at the same time as the glass for the chapel itself, at Westminster, and was shipped up the Thames in the same fashion. There is a reference to the drawing of 'images' in the windows, and to a wide range of colours of glass: there is no record as to whether the images were of knights or saints, or both. The knights would have used the room for elections as well as their annual chapter; but it was an occasional meeting-place rather than a central element in the company's life.

The worshipper in St Stephen's was surrounded by a dazzling display of the power and wealth of Edward's dynasty, lavishly executed in the latest style of painting. St George's, by contrast, uses a rich interior and rich apparel to focus on the religious purpose of the chapel, while the helms, swords and carpets proclaim the high reputation in arms of the knights, who are accorded higher status than the clergy in the choirstalls. Here the king and his sons appear in a different context, that of their military prowess, seated as the leaders of the victorious English army, whose commanders fill the stalls. The focus is equally commemorative and religious; even the helms and swords, and later the stall plates, are not displays of secular grandeur, but memorials of victories granted by the grace of God. And the detailed provisions in the statutes for the penalties for neglecting the annual Garter services reinforce the religious aspect of the company.

9

'The company of the knights of Saint George *de la gartiere*'

The earliest surviving version of the statutes of the Company of the Garter dates from the reign of Henry V, and was probably issued in a chapter of the company on 22 April 1415, about sixty-five years after the company's first gathering.[1] The opening of the statutes declares:

> 1. In honour of Almighty God, of St Mary the glorious Virgin, and of St George the martyr, our supreme lord, Edward III, king of England, in the twenty-third year of his reign ordained, established and founded a certain company or knightly order within his castle of Windsor, in this manner: Firstly, he decreed himself to be the sovereign of the said company or order, his eldest son the prince of Wales, the duke of Lancaster, the earl of Warwick, the captal de Buch, the earl of Stafford, the earl of Salisbury, Lord Mortimer, Sir John Lisle, Sir Bartholomew Burghersh the younger, Sir John Beauchamp, Lord Mohun, Sir Hugh Courtenay, Sir Thomas Holland, Sir John Grey, Sir Richard Fitzsimon, Sir Miles Stapleton, Sir Thomas Wale, Sir Hugh Wrottesley, Sir Nigel Loring, Sir John Chandos, Sir James Audley, Sir Otho Holland, Sir Henry Eam, Sir 'Sanchet d'Abridgecourt', Sir Walter Pavely.
>
> 2. It was agreed that the king of England, whoever it shall be at the time, shall in perpetuity be the sovereign of this Order of St George or Society of the Garter.[2]

In other early copies of the statutes, variations occur in the spelling of names, which is common in medieval manuscripts, but apart from this the list is consistent. The wording implies that these are the first founders. However, the opening sentence itself and the first clause listing the founders do not really connect. Edward establishes a company 'in the following manner' in the preamble, and the text which follows should describe the regulation of the company, as indeed it does from the second clause onwards. The fourth clause simply says that 'the aforesaid twenty-six ... shall wear the mantles and garter as ordained at the said castle as often as they shall be present there' for the ceremonies of the company. It is only in the next clause that there is a reference to 'the aforenamed founders'. Later in the statutes, there are references to the 'first founders'; when any member of the company dies, his successor shall have the same stall in the chapel, even if he is not of the same rank. An earl's stall may be taken by a simple knight, and vice versa: there is to be no precedence by status within the company, with the exception of the king and the prince. 'And this is ordained so that it shall be known who were the first founders.' Again, clause 24 reads as if it were drafted after some of the 'first founders' had died; it provides for the famous stall plates to be mounted on the back of the deceased knight's stall, but also says that any subsequent plates are to be placed below those of the 'first founders'.

A further possible problem is clause 10, which provides that, if St George's Day falls within the fourteen days after Easter, the actual ceremonies shall be deferred to the second Sunday after Easter, so that the knights are not obliged to travel during the Easter period. This would mean that the ceremonies should have been deferred in 1351, 1356, 1359, 1362 and 1367. In 1356 and 1359, the new dates would have been on 6 and 3 May respectively, and the king was definitely at Windsor. In 1351 and 1362, he could have been at Windsor, but there is no evidence either way.[3] And in 1367, when the date was 1 May, he was at Sheen. Against this, he was consistently at Windsor on 23 April each year, unless he was abroad. It is difficult to judge from the slim evidence, but his presence elsewhere in 1367 might imply that this clause was not introduced until after the end of Edward's reign.

Taken together, these minor discrepancies might simply be the result of hurried copying, the omission of a sentence at the beginning of the first clause saying that these are the names of the first founders. But they are consistent across a large number of copies, and therefore may indicate something more serious: that the statutes are a reconstruction, from a somewhat damaged or fragmentary text, of the company's rules. The text itself does not have the clarity one would expect from Edward III's highly experienced clerks, and there is no question that this earliest version of the statutes dates from the reign of Henry V; they must have been written from copies of documents which no longer survive and which certainly went back to the early days of the company.

It has long been known that the records of the succession of the knights in the early years is a major problem, and that the tidy lists of knights produced by heralds in the sixteenth century are difficult to support from any other evidence. Henry V's motives in producing this set of statutes have been described as follows: 'it might have been brought to his notice that there were no actual formal statutes for his Order to be found. More likely there existed a series of documents containing Edward III's original regulations for the Order and numbers of subsequent chapter ordinances.'[4] This idea is supported by a document from 1378, when a visitation of the College of St George was made. As an ecclesiastical establishment, it was liable to regular inspections by its superior, the bishop of Winchester, and one of the defects found during the visitation was that the deeds and records of the college, which are likely to have included those of the companions of the Garter, were 'remissly and negligently kept'. The prior of the college was ordered to obtain a proper chest in which to keep the papers, and to maintain his records in a more regular fashion.[5] There was no proper provision for a registrar for the company itself until the early fifteenth century, and the lack of such regulations combined with the general disorder of the college records would adequately account for the disappearance of the original statutes.

In 1400, when Henry IV had come to the throne and there was renewed interest in the Garter – his grandfather Henry of Grosmont had of course been a founding member – two tables listing the knights were made for display in the chapter house of the company. Such tables were used elsewhere as a way of informing visitors of the history of a church, the best surviving example being the 'great table' at Glastonbury, now in the Bodleian Library.[6] This consists of three boards, just over three feet high, which, when unfolded, form a hinged screen three feet wide. They are mounted in a wooden box, which was positioned in a prominent place inside the abbey church, where visitors could consult them. There are two similar examples at York, with general historical information; another, specifically relating to the life and miracles of St William of York, was kept near his shrine. There are records of similar tables in five other English cathedrals, and in five monasteries. The earliest known examples are a table at Seaford in Sussex, recorded in the late eleventh century, and the late twelfth-century tables which were at Bury St Edmunds. There seems to have been a vogue for such tables from the late fourteenth century onwards, as the vast majority date from this period, the Windsor tables among them.

There is a considerable amount of material in the Glastonbury tables, and they are not intended as a kind of placard of the sort that is found at historic sites today, with perhaps two or three hundred words in all, to be read easily and quickly. The modern edition of the contents runs to fifty pages, and the impression is of a collection of texts for reference, where the curious visitor can look up the answer to a question. They may well have been used by the monks themselves, to save them looking up a passage in one of the monastery's manuscripts. The Windsor tables were simply a list of the knights, rather like the last page of the Glastonbury tables, which gives 'a brief listing' of all the saints buried at Glastonbury.[7]

We first learn of the existence of the Windsor tables listing the Garter knights in the entries in the precentor's rolls at St George's in 1400–1401, when John Page was paid fourpence for 'writing the names, that is, of the king, prince and other companions of the Garter in the tables'.[8] A new table was probably written in 1416–17, because parchment costing sixpence was bought for Henry Bourne to 'make the tables' in 1416, and he was paid twenty pence for writing the responses for the feast of the exaltation of the Holy Cross and entering the names of the Garter companions on the tables in September 1417.[9] The feast of the Holy Cross was an important date in the calendar of St George's, because the chapel's chief relic was the Neith Cross, containing a fragment of the True Cross, and the table may have been prepared for that occasion.

After the Restoration, Elias Ashmole, one of the great antiquaries of the period – founder of the Ashmolean Museum as well as Garter king at arms – produced a full account of the Company of the Garter, and printed as an appendix the text he found on the two tables 'remaining in the Chapter-house at Windesor'. The list gives the division of the knights into the 'king's side' and the 'prince's side', information which is not in the fifteenth-century statutes, and it probably derives from John Page's original table of 1400. However, in the form in which Ashmole saw them, the tables date from Edward IV's building of the new chapel in the 1470s, as the names down to that date are all written in the same hand, with additions up to 1495. The information on the tables does not always correspond with the contemporary records of knights' names, which are reasonably full and consistent, and a number of names are simply omitted. It appears from this that the tables, which should be a prime witness, were obviously not prepared with a great deal of care, and so cannot be relied upon in our exploration of the founder knights.[10] The tables were last seen in the eighteenth century, and were probably destroyed.

A further source of information should be the stall plates, which were taken from the original Garter chapel when it was demolished, and placed in the new chapel when it was furnished. Again, these are a highly fallible guide. William St John Hope, who studied the architecture of Windsor Castle in the late nineteenth century, examined the stall plates carefully, and found that the majority of them had not been made until the time of Henry V, in Ashmole's words 'that happy restorer of the honor of the Order, having (at his entrance to the Royal Throne) found its glory upon abatement, not only raised it to its former lustre, but very much increased the honor thereof'.[11] The same error occurs both in the Windsor tables and on the stall plates, where the captal de Buch, Jean de Grailly, is called 'mons. Piers', and the style and size of the plates show that the majority of them were made in one batch. Only one plate, that of Ralph Bassett, actually dates from before 1400, and even this appears to have been adapted from a memorial brass.[12]

There is therefore nothing in the Windsor records which we can securely date to before the end of the fourteenth century – statutes, tables or stall plates – but there is an earlier list, dating from around 1360, and this may well be the most reliable witness to the identity of the founder members, though it gives us only thirteen names. It is in Geoffrey le Baker's chronicle, and the date of the list that he had in front of him can be fixed, because Roger Mortimer is described as a simple knight, with the added comment that he is now earl of March. He was restored to his father's earldom in 1354, so the original list predates that year. Geoffrey le Baker's account reads in full:

In that year on St George's Day the king held a great feast in his castle at Windsor. During it he instituted a chapel of twelve priests and founded an almshouse in which impoverished knights whose own resources were inadequate could obtain sufficient assistance from the perpetual alms of the founders of that college. The other people who contributed to the founding of that almshouse besides the king were of course the firstborn of the king, the earls of Northampton, Warwick, Suffolk and Salisbury, other barons and also some who were merely knights, namely Roger Mortimer who is now earl of March, Sir Walter Mauny, Sir William Fitz-warin, Sir John Lisle, Sir John Mohun, Sir John Beauchamp, Sir Walter Pavely, Sir Thomas Wale and Sir Hugh Wrottesley. These men who were merely knights were linked with the richest earls because their worth had been tested and tried.

All these together with the king were clothed in russet gowns, spangled with gold, and with armbands of Indian blue. They also had similar garters on their right legs, and they wore a mantle of blue with the escutcheons of St George. Dressed like this and with bare heads they solemnly heard a ceremonial mass sung by the prelates of Canterbury, Winchester and Exeter, and then in due order seated themselves at a common table in honour of the holy martyr to whom they specially dedicated this noble fraternity, calling it the companionship of the knights of Saint George *de la gartiere*.[13]

The names of the founding knights given by Baker correspond with the record of the statutes and the Windsor table, with three exceptions: Robert Ufford, earl of Suffolk, William Bohun, earl of Northampton, and Walter Mauny. All of these are given in the Windsor records as subsequent appointments to the company: Ufford and Bohun succeeded to the stalls of Richard Fitzsimon and Hugh Courtenay, both of whom are said to have died in 1348–9, while Mauny took the place of John, Lord Grey, as late as 1359. If the list which Baker was using predates 1354, then there is a serious conflict of evidence with the Windsor records. But it is also possible that Baker was simply confused about which of those knights who were members of the company at the time when he was writing had been among the founders. On the other hand, the three knights he names who are not in the Windsor list are obvious candidates as 'first founders'.

Baker's summary follows the sequence of the statutes of 1415, which mention the priests in clause 5, followed by the poor knights in clause 7. The qualification for the poor knights is given in similar terms: the statutes say that 'it is ordained that twenty-six veteran knights, who have no means of sustenance, shall have there in the honour of God and of the blessed George a sufficient maintenance', in the new foundation. There is reason to believe that he was working from a document rather than an oral report. He also describes the robes correctly,[14] which are not given in the 1415 version of the statutes; clause 4 simply speaks of the 'mantle and garter as ordained', but does not specify them, although clause 8 is precise about the mantles for the poor knights.

It is impossible to determine whether Baker is right and the surviving Windsor records are wrong. But it is very important to realize that the names of the original twenty-six knights are by no means certain, and the succession is even more open to challenge; we shall look at instances where there is new evidence that may disturb the accepted lists in a moment.

Historians have commented on the uncertainty of the lists; Nicolas Harris Nicolas wrote in 1842 that

the deficiency of materials for the ancient History of the Order renders it more than probable that many knights may have been elected whose names are not recorded; and it is not impossible that a few are errone-ously supposed to have received its honours . . . The precise date of the elections of many of the companions is very doubtful . . . [the effect] of numbering the knights, and calling any one of them the 'twentieth' or 'the hundred and second knight of the Garter', is to mislead.[15]

Yet numbered lists continue to appear, as though we were as sure of the succession of knights as of the kings of England. In fact, the evidence as to the identity of the original knights and as to the succession before 1400 is very much open to question, even if it is difficult to propose an alternative list of members of the company.

We can get a little further by looking more closely at the Windsor list in terms of who the knights were, when they died, and their successors in the stalls. The sequence of admission to the company derives from the Windsor tables, and, for most of the knights, the dating is not a prob-lem. However, the early admissions do present serious issues. Three of the original twenty-six knights are said to have died before the end of 1349, and to have been replaced. These are 'Sauchet' d'Auberchicourt, Richard Fitzsimon and Hugh Courtenay. It is very probable that 'Sau-chet' d'Auberchicourt is actually Eustace d'Auberchicourt, who died in 1372.[16] We have no definite date for Richard Fitzsimon's death, as, apart from his appearance in Henry of Grosmont's retinue in Aquitaine in 1345 and as the prince of Wales's standard-bearer at Crécy, there is nothing further in the military records about him. We can be certain about Hugh Courtenay's death, as the queen paid for a cloth to be laid on his tomb on 2 September 1349.

If Eustace d'Auberchicourt is one of the founding knights, the succession to his stall presents serious problems. William Fitzwarin, who is said to have succeeded him, died in 1361, eleven years before the stall became vacant. We know that Fitzwarin was definitely a companion of the Garter, as his tomb effigy shows him wearing a garter over his armour on his right leg. There is a similar problem with Henry Eam, or Oem, whose death can certainly be ascribed to 1353;[17] his successor is supposed to have been Thomas Ughtred, on the basis that Oem died in 1358. The succession list is based solely on the sequence of supposed dates of death of the knights, and assumes that the rule providing for prompt election of successors was often disregarded.[18] It would make logical sense for Eam's successor to be John Sully, who took over Eam's position as the prince of Wales's household knight shortly after his death.

Confusion over the succession of knights may well be due to the high rate of mortality among the knights in 1359–61, when no less than nine companions of the Garter died. This was partly due to the second great plague of Edward's reign, in 1361, which, as the chroniclers noted, caused a great mortality among the nobility, who had largely escaped the Black Death. Henry of Grosmont was the most notable victim, but Thomas Holland, earl of Kent, William Bohun, earl of Northampton, Reginald, Lord Cobham and William Fitzwarin also died between September 1360 and October 1361.[19] It was probably the death of Henry of Grosmont in March 1361 that was the reason for the issue of black cloth for Garter robes in this year.[20] A further spate of deaths occurred in 1368–9, when seven knights died in fourteen months. If – and this can only be a hypothesis – in such periods of rapid turnover, the sketchy record-keeping of the company broke down, this would account for the difficulties in reconciling the succession recorded in the Windsor tables with what we know of the knights from other sources. The very strict provisions in the statutes that elections are to take place within six weeks of the certification of the death of a knight by the sovereign, and that a knight must be installed within a year of his election or the election is void, may well be a later addition, as a result of problems in earlier years.[21]

THE FIRST GARTER KNIGHTS: A CLOSE-KNIT GROUP

For present purposes, we shall look at the first thirty-seven names in the list of Garter companions as generally accepted, which takes us down to 1360, a group we shall call the 'companions to 1360'. In that year three of the king's sons were elected, and over a quarter of the knights were from the king's immediate family, changing the nature of the company away from knights of lesser rank but greater military accomplishment.[22]

If we look first at the 'traditional' list of twenty-six founders from the statutes, including the king and the prince, they fall into four groups by age. Four of them are under twenty, contemporaries of the eighteen-year-old prince of Wales, and a further ten are between twenty and thirty, knights with up to fifteen years' experience of warfare. Nine are between thirty and forty; some are experienced commanders, the king's contemporaries, while others are not yet bannerets. Finally, there are three men senior in age to the king, but interestingly not in the first rank of the leaders of the army. The eleven knights appointed after the foundation and before the king's three sons in 1360 have a rather different profile. Five of them are found either as in command of a division in a major battle or as acting as independent commanders, four are older knights, and only two are under thirty. The average age for this additional group is forty-three, compared with thirty for the first group.

Overall, the average age of the companions to 1360 is thirty-three. The companions of the Garter are the new men of Edward III's reign, with little involvement in the convoluted politics of his father's time. Three of them had served as young knights in 1324–5, mostly abroad, and only Thomas Ughtred, the oldest member of the group, had had any serious political engagement in the 1320s. He had sided with the king against Thomas of Lancaster in the civil war that led to the latter's execution; Thomas of Lancaster came to symbolize the baronial and popular resistance to Edward II's rule, and his tomb became a place of pilgrimage. Ughtred was only elected to the company around 1358, when he was sixty-seven and his solid record of military and political achievement under Edward III outweighed any memories of his youthful activities; he was one of the oldest men serving in the army on the Reims campaign of 1359–60.

The overriding common factor among the companions to 1360 is that all save two were present at the siege of Calais, the exceptions being the Gascon lord Jean de Grailly, captal de Buch, and Thomas, son of Robert Ufford, earl of Suffolk, who was only twelve at the time. The majority of them had also served on the Crécy campaign; the exceptions were those who had been fighting in Gascony at the time: Henry of Grosmont, Walter Mauny and Frank van Hale. We do not have direct proof for Henry Eam, but he had been knighted by the prince of Wales before January 1348, and thus was almost certainly with him at Calais, if not earlier in the campaign.

If the list of founder knights in the statutes is correct, only one of the commanders at Crécy was included when the company began: this was Thomas Beauchamp, marshal of the army and commander of the prince's division, which bore the brunt of the fighting. Two other commanders may have been founders, or were appointed shortly afterwards: these were William Bohun, earl of Northampton, also a commander in the prince's division, and Robert Ufford, earl of Suffolk, commander of the rearguard. Six of the list in the statutes – John Beauchamp, Lisle, Burghersh the younger, Mohun, Grey and Audley – fought as bannerets at Crécy, with their own retinues; two more bannerets were among the companions to 1360, William Fitzwarin, who may have been a founder, and Reginald, Lord Cobham. Eleven of the group were mere knights at the time of the battle. Of the total of twenty-five men who fought in the battle as ordinary knights, twelve had fought in the king's division, ten in the prince's division and three in the rearguard.

For the most part, we can only conjecture about the reasons for selecting these particular men. In one case, that of Richard Fitzsimon, there is an individual act of heroism, the defence of the prince's banner, which would account for his choice. William Montagu the younger had been knighted with the prince at La Hogue, and several of the knights later closely associated with the prince – John Chandos, James Audley, Nigel Loring and Bartholomew Burghersh, son of the master of his household – were chosen. Henry Eam and Auberchicourt, like Walter Mauny, were part of the 'Hainault connection'. Another group of knights are part of the king's entourage, and there are members of a key group of men who had been involved in the overthrow of Mortimer in 1330. Where members of the conspiracy had died, their heirs or relatives were elected to the company. William Montagu, first earl of

Salisbury, Edward's closest friend, had died in 1344, but his son was among the prince's companions at Crécy, and there was hence a double reason for his inclusion among the founders. There was a similar double reason for the inclusion of William Bohun, earl of Hereford and Northampton; he and his twin brother Edward Bohun had both been among the plotters, but Edward had drowned while trying to rescue his squire from a wild beast in Scotland in 1334. Robert Ufford, earl of Suffolk, also comes within this group; like Bohun, he was elected in the first years of the company, by 1350. The namesake and heir of one of the plotters, William, Lord Latimer, was, like the young William Montagu, with the prince at Crécy, but was not elected until much later, in 1361.

Another way of trying to define the qualities of the Garter companions or the reasons for their election is to look at those prominent figures who might have been expected to appear among them, but who were left out. Of the six earls created by Edward in 1337, three were members of the company. William Montagu the elder's son, the second earl of Salisbury, was included. Hugh Audley, earl of Gloucester, died in 1347; he left no sons, but Ralph Stafford, his son-in-law, was one of the first knights. This leaves one surprising omission: William Clinton, earl of Huntingdon. Clinton had set out on the Crécy campaign, but was forced to return home because of a 'most serious and grievous illness',[23] and did not take part in the battle. He did return to the siege of Calais in the spring of 1347. In 1350, he petitioned the pope for a private chapel at his castle at Maxstoke, on the grounds that he and his wife spent much time there and had difficulty in getting to the parish church in bad weather; this, together with his virtual disappearance from the public records after 1347, suggests that the illness he had contracted was the cause of his retirement. If this is correct, it implies that the company was intended not simply as a gathering of participants in the Crécy–Calais war to commemorate the momentous events of those months, but as a group united by their common recollections and by their service to the king, who were going to build on those achievements. In other words, these were the men who were going to take forward Edward's plans for the conquest of France.

We can account, therefore, for the new earls of 1337; there were six other earls who might also have qualified,[24] but of these the earls of Hereford and Lancaster were permanently incapacitated by sickness and blindness, and John de Vere, who had fought in the king's division at Crécy, was, like Clinton, the victim of long-term illness, though he resumed his career in 1355.[25] The earl of Devon, Hugh Courtenay, never seems to have been active outside his own lands, but his son was briefly elected to the company, dying in 1349.[26] Of the two remaining earls, Thomas Beauchamp was a prominent member of the company, but the absence of the earl of Arundel from the list is a real puzzle. Richard Fitzalan was an ambitious and energetic man, who rebuilt the family fortunes from a very low ebb at Edward III's accession.[27] His father was a supporter of Edward II when Isabella and Mortimer invaded England in 1326, and was summarily executed as a traitor in November 1326. His lands were forfeited, and Richard, aged thirteen, fled abroad, having been involved in a plot against Mortimer. He returned in 1330, and petitioned for the restoration of his inheritance, which was granted in parliament in 1331. He and Edward had been brought up at the royal court together, and Edward regarded him as a trusted servant of the crown. His career was wide-ranging: from 1343 onwards, he was one of the leading diplomats in English embassies abroad. He was something of a financial wizard: as one of the most active administrators in Edward's government, he was well rewarded for his work, but he chose to use his money shrewdly rather than indulging in spectactular displays of wealth. If he bought jewels, they were as a form of ready cash;[28] he lent huge sums to both the king and the prince of Wales, and the record of his transactions in royal writs makes it seem that he was banker to most of the leading captains of the time. He was also prepared to speculate: we find him lending money to London merchants 'to trade therewith to the earl's profit'. Moreover, he himself was a highly experienced captain, and was on five campaigns in Scotland between 1333 and 1342; he fought at Sluys and Winchelsea, and on the Reims campaign. Most important for our purpose, he was on the Crécy campaign, and commanded the rearguard with Robert Ufford. Why then might he have been excluded? There are three possible explanations: one is that, in the financial and political crisis of 1341, Arundel had spoken his mind against the king (as had Huntingdon), and that Edward had never forgiven him for this. Yet his continued active employment in the royal service argues against this, and the king and queen were present at his scandalous marriage to Eleanor, sister of Henry of Grosmont, in February 1345: Arundel was already married to Isabella, daughter of Edward II's favourite, Hugh Despenser the younger, but his wife was now a political liability. A month later, the first marriage was annulled by the pope, on dubious grounds.[29] And in 1351 Edward specifically confirmed Arundel's title to his lands, in case there was any doubt because his father had forfeited them. There is no reason to believe that Edward was harbouring a grudge against him.

The second explanation is that Arundel's banking activities were seen as unchivalrous, and not suitable for a member of a company designed to celebrate knightly and religious ideals. The curious nickname 'Copped Hat' which has been attached to him[30] has an obscure origin. 'Copped' means peaked or pointed, and these pointed hats were a new fashion. When John II entered Paris after his coronation at Reims in 1351, the Parisian trade guilds each wore their own livery. Among them were the Lombard bankers, dressed in cloth of gold and 'tall pointed hats'.[31] These are the only costumes described, which suggests that they were novel and unfamiliar. Arundel was famous for his banking activities in Europe as well as England: in 1364 the abbot of Cluny commented on his extraordinary wealth. He was also descended from a Lombard family, his grandmother being the daughter of the marquess of Saluzzo in Piedmont; a chronicler noted this, saying that his father was descended from 'the impious Lombards'. The tension between the old knightly nobility and the rising merchant class is reflected in 1381 in the statutes for the Order of the Ship in Naples, which forbid the membership of bankers,[32] and in the next century in Germany by regulations banning anyone who partook in trade from entering tournaments. Could a similar prejudice be at work here?

The third alternative raises the question of how seriously the third of the statutes of the company was taken: it provides that no one shall be elected to the company unless he qualifies both by descent and by reputation. Candidates must be 'of noble birth and a knight without reproach'. Arundel's bloodline amply qualified him for election, and it therefore comes down to whether he would not have been seen as 'a knight without reproach'. His remarriage, and the attendant lawsuits, were in process at exactly the time when the first knights were being chosen, and it would seem that it was this that was the stumbling block. His honour and fame were in dispute, and, given the consistent importance attached to these in the evidence in the Court of Chivalry, the idea that a newly proclaimed company which specifically required good repute could admit him seems unlikely. There is nothing in the record of any of the Garter companions prior to the foundation of the company which is as notorious as Arundel's behaviour; it is only in subsequent years that renegades like Auberchicourt and Wrottesley indulge in profitable lawlessness. This, then, is the most likely reason for his exclusion, though his behaviour generally with regard to trade speaks of a character with an eye to the main chance, ambitious in the extreme and not given to consideration of the finer points of honour.[33]

The other aspect of warfare reflected in the Company of the Garter was the close companionship of men who had fought side by side for as many as fourteen months, from the beginning of the campaign on 11 July 1346 to the return from Calais in September 1347. This service formed a strong bond, as the great majority of the founding knights had taken part in the campaign, the exceptions being the leading commanders in Gascony at this period. The hardships and difficulties of the months in camp and the dramatic moment of victory meant that this was a group with a very large degree of common experience.

The victory at Crécy and the taking of Calais had transformed Edward's situation with regard to recruitment, because the lure of profits of war was now a real one. Accounts of the taking of Caen in 1346 emphasize the riches that could be won if a town was taken:

> And those who could carry away booty came back with a vast amount of treasure from the houses ... The English eagerly returned to the work of despoiling the town, only taking jewels, clothing or precious ornaments because of the abundance. The English sent their booty to their ships ... [which] found such a mass of goods sent to them that they could not transport all the spoils from Caen and elsewhere.[34]

If the Round Table festivities had been aimed at attracting a wide range of knights who were likely to bring retinues to an army, the Company of the Garter included those likely to provide the largest retinues as well as potential captains who might build up a following. One of the Garter statutes provides that 'if some knightly expedition arise, or anything else which may be perceived to result in knightly honour, the sovereign of the order shall be obliged to prefer by his grace the companions of the order to all others in such knightly actions'. The original companions of the Garter had been chosen because of their military prowess, and their successors were expected to be the elite commanders of the future.

FAMILY NETWORKS:
THE ROYAL FAMILY

Companionship in war was one bond. There was another, almost as important. The families of the companions of the Garter were a very closely linked group, even by comparison with the royal houses of Europe and the aristocracy of England, who continually intermarried in pursuit of political or economic goals. Marriage between members of such groups, who were very often already related, was not a secular matter. It was controlled not in the king's courts, but in the ecclesiastical courts, and the result was a complicated interplay between politics and religion. Canon law forbade marriages within the prohibited degrees, and the degree of consanguinity specified – the so-called third degree of kinship – meant that any couple who had one great-great grandparent in common required papal dispensation in order to marry. Usually this dispensation was forthcoming for second or third cousins, but grew more difficult as the relationship became closer. In terms of aristocratic and royal matches, it was all too often less about the pair in question than about the political and dynastic implications: during the papacy of Clement VI, whose earlier career had been in the French administration, the political matches made by Edward III in pursuit of Continental alliances were usually disallowed if they did not suit the interests of the French kings. It gave the pope a considerable degree of control over this aspect of European politics.

There were other complications to marriage as well, because, although it was a sacrament of the Church, there was no requirement that a priest should be present if a marriage was to be valid. Spousals, as opposed to marriage, were valid in the eyes of the Church, and a couple could wed by declaring that they would take each other as man and wife, either at the present time or at some future date, in the presence of witnesses, provided there were no impediments of relationship or previous marriage. If a promise of future spousal was followed by consummation, then it automatically became a de facto marriage. The priest's function was to bless the spousal, and thus to turn it into a sacrament. Even in a church wedding, these aspects were kept firmly separate: in the *Canterbury Tales*, the Wife of Bath declares that she has had five husbands 'at the church door', because the contractual part of the wedding, the spousals, were a public ceremony before the couple actually entered the church for the liturgical blessing.

Of all the women who married Garter companions, the most famous case is that of Joan of Kent. She was married to three Garter companions in turn and her connections among the knights include five brothers-in-law[35] and three sons. Joan was the eldest child of Edmund earl of Kent, half-brother to Edward II, and Margaret Wake, sister of Thomas, Lord Wake. Thomas Wake, although married to the sister of Henry of Grosmont, had no children, and Joan was (through her mother) heiress in her own right to his lands.

Her father was executed for treason when she was two, and Joan was subsequently adopted by Queen Philippa, spending much of her childhood in the royal household. In 1337 Joan may have gone with the rest of the royal family to Flanders. By the time they returned to England Joan was twelve and already seems to have had a reputation for beauty and gaiety: later generations were to remember her as 'the Fair Maid of Kent', though contemporaries ironically called her 'the virgin of Kent' because of her marital record. At this early age, she had attracted the attention of Thomas Holland, a dozen years older than herself and at that time a knight of the royal household. They married in the spring of 1340 in conditions of utmost secrecy: Joan, although her prospects of inheritance were far from certain, was a member of the royal family. The marriage was a spousal – the recognized term was *per verba de praesentis*, in front of witnesses – and the match was duly consummated. Holland was with the English army all that summer, and set out for Prussia in late 1340, remaining there until the middle of the following year. In the meanwhile, Joan's marriage seems to have remained a secret, because her mother arranged for her to wed William Montagu, the son of the first earl of Salisbury. She was married to Montagu, this time with due ecclesiastical ceremony, in the winter of 1340–41, and remained with her new husband even after Thomas Holland's return in 1341. The latter became steward to the young couple shortly after the younger Montagu succeeded to the earldom in 1344, an appointment which implies that Montagu knew nothing of the past history of Thomas and Joan.

It was almost certainly lack of funds, and perhaps also his financial dependence on Montagu as his steward, that had prevented Holland from reclaiming his wife before 1346. Following the sale of the rights in the ransom of the count of Eu to Edward for 12,000 florins, he was now in a position to proceed; furthermore, as steward to the Montagu household, he knew that they were short of money, the revenues from the young earl's inheritance being in the king's hands because he was still under age.[36] Within a few months of the king's grant of the purchase money in June 1347, he began proceedings at Avignon for the return of Joan, declaring that he and Joan had been lawfully wedded and that the marriage had been consummated. Later, 'not daring to contradict the wishes of her relatives and friends', she had been married to the earl 'by their arrangement' in Holland's absence.[37] The earl, aided and abetted by Joan's mother, refused to acknowledge Thomas's claim, who had therefore brought the present case.

It was a case which would not normally have been heard in a papal court, but the pope, either feeling that Holland would not get a fair hearing in England, or seeing it as an opportunity to cause trouble for Edward, authorized its hearing and summoned William Montagu to put in an appearance, as well as Joan. However, the papal envoys were unable to get the earl to plead before the court, and Holland, in a subsequent petition, alleged that the earl and his accomplices were holding Joan against her will and in seclusion. The pope intervened on Joan's behalf in May 1348, but a further eighteen months elapsed, largely through the delaying tactics of the earl and his attorney, before a papal bull, dated 13 November 1349, declared Joan's marriage to Montagu void, and ordered that her marriage to Holland be properly celebrated in a church ceremony, which took place shortly afterwards. At about the same time Joan became heiress to the Wake estates when her uncle died without children.

Joan and Holland had five children in the next few years; both the eldest, named Thomas after his father, and the second son, John, were later companions of the Garter. Otho, Holland's younger brother, was one of the original members of the company. In 1352 Joan's younger brother, John, died unexpectedly, and she became countess of Kent in her own right. Thomas, her husband, also died unexpectedly, in Normandy on 28 December 1360. Joan's widowhood was, however, brief. At some time in the spring or early summer of 1361, Edward prince of Wales asked for her hand in marriage. She accepted him and they contracted a clandestine marriage, just as she had done with Thomas Holland twenty-one years earlier. The betrothal seems to have been an entirely private affair, and in view of Joan's previous marital history and her status, this was a surprising turn of events. In addition, the pair were related within the prohibited degrees – they were cousins, and the prince was godfather to Joan's eldest son. The match has given rise to much speculation. At the time of his betrothal to Joan there were plans for the prince to marry Margaret of Flanders. Matteo Villani says that everyone who knew the prince was surprised by the marriage.[38] One French chronicler produced a fanciful romance telling of the unspoken love of Joan for the prince of Wales, and of the prince for Joan, and of the king's subsequent fury.[39] According to the *Chronicle of the First Four Valois Kings*, one of his knights, the sieur de Brocas,[40] asked the prince of Wales to approach the newly widowed Joan on his behalf. The prince went gladly to see Joan, whose beauty and poise 'pleased him marvellously', but his representations were in vain; and, after repeated visits, the prince declared that, if they were not related, 'there is no lady under heaven whom I would hold so dear'. The countess, portrayed as mistress of every feminine wile, declared that she would never marry because she was in love with 'the man of most prowess under the sky'. The prince insisted on being told who it was, and, after a suitable show of reluctance, Joan told him that he was the object of her affections. They were married, and Joan insisted that she must leave England 'because the king of England would put her to death' if she stayed; and so the prince of Wales and his wife went to Aquitaine. It is a wonderful little set piece – the editor goes as far as to call it 'a masterpiece' – but it is a masterpiece of fiction. In fact it seems unlikely that the king was outraged, since Edward III, as well as his son, petitioned for a papal dispensation, which was granted on 7 September 1361. It is from this document that we learn that there had been a clandestine marriage, and that the couple were to endow two chapels as penance for it.[41]

On 6 October Joan publicly plighted her troth to the prince of Wales in the presence of the archbishop of Canterbury, and four days later, in the presence of most, if not all, of the royal family, including the king, and a large congregation, the wedding was celebrated at Windsor. The prince was thirty-one, and Joan probably two years older. They spent Christmas at Berkhamsted, one of the prince's favourite residences, where the king and queen visited them. Joan's style of living, which had once been restricted by her lack of income, had improved when she became countess of Kent and also inherited the lands of her uncle, Lord

Wake; now it seems to have become positively extravagant. The prince, already renowned for his lavish gifts, spent large sums of money on clothes and jewellery for her early in 1362.[42] She brought to his household her two sons and two daughters, one child having died in infancy. When the prince of Wales set sail for Aquitaine from Plymouth on 9 June 1362, the whole family accompanied him.

During the nine years that they spent in Aquitaine the couple had two sons. The elder, Edward, was born in 1365, but died five years later. His younger brother, the future Richard II, was born in January 1367. Relatively little is known about Joan's life in Aquitaine; she seems to have spent most of the time at Angoulême or Bordeaux. It was at Angoulême in April 1365 that the prince of Wales held the most magnificent tournament of his time in France, to celebrate Joan's churching after the birth of their first son, and the scale of the festivities gave rise to stories about the princess's love of luxury and the latest fashions. As early as 1363 French visitors to the prince's court had reported that the princess and her ladies wore furred gowns with slit coats and great fringes; in the French view, these were copied from the mistresses of English freebooters, and were unsuitable for courtly society. The prince's affection for Joan is evident in his letter to her after the battle of Nájera; and on his return from Spain she met him at the cathedral at Bordeaux with his eldest son: he dismounted, and 'they walked together holding hands' to the bishop's palace, where they were staying.[43]

On the prince's death in 1376 Joan became guardian of the person of the young Richard, and received his allowance, while one-third of the revenues of Wales were reserved to her once he became prince of Wales. For the second Garter feast of his reign, in 1379, she and eleven other ladies were issued with the Garter robes, an innovation which was to become a regular occurrence under the new king.[44] Apart from administering the estates that had once belonged to her husband, Joan seems to have had considerable influence with the king: a large number of pardons and grants in the years 1377–85 are recorded as being 'at the request of the king's mother', and it is probable that the idea of the issue of robes to the so-called 'ladies of the Garter' was hers. The ladies so honoured, however, had no part in the fraternity itself; the robes were an ad hoc recognition of their standing, and conferred no formal title or association with the Garter knights themselves.[45]

Joan became ill and very overweight in her last years, and died, probably at Wallingford Castle, in 1385. The St Albans chronicler believed that it was out of grief because her second son, John Holland, earl of Huntingdon and companion of the Garter, had murdered Ralph Stafford, whose grandfather had been one of the original companions, in cold blood in the course of a feud, and Richard, swearing to see that justice was done, had refused to listen to his mother's pleas for mercy for his half-brother, and had him executed. She asked to be buried, not with the prince of Wales at Canterbury, but near the monument of Thomas Holland in the Minorite church at Stamford. She left to the king her new bed, decorated with golden leopards and with the silver ostrich feather badge of his father.

By 1376 no fewer than eight members of the company were also members of the royal family. Apart from Edward and three of his surviving sons,[46] the king's first cousin once removed, Humphrey Bohun, and the three royal sons-in-law, the earls of Pembroke, Richmond and Bedford, were all Garter companions. Other knights of royal blood already deceased included the king's second son, Lionel, his cousins Hugh Courtenay and William Bohun, and his second cousin Henry of Grosmont. Two of the knights from Hainault were linked to the royal family by marriage: Walter Mauny's bride was Margaret of Brotherton, the king's cousin, and Eustace d'Auberchicourt had married Philippa's niece, Elizabeth of Juliers. Approximately a quarter of the sixty-three knights belonging to the company before Edward's death were thus family members.[47] The company founded to celebrate Edward and his dynasty became a way of binding that dynasty together.

FAMILY NETWORKS: THE GREAT LORDS

But there were other networks present within the company as well as that of the royal family itself. The most extensive of these linked John Mohun with the Burghersh, Montagu and Mortimer families. John had been the ward of Bartholomew Burghersh the elder, and was married to Burghersh's daughter Joan. Their daughter Elizabeth married William Montagu, after his supposed marriage to Joan of Kent had been dissolved, and William Montagu's sister Philippa married Roger Mortimer. Another set of marriages linked Thomas Beauchamp, Ralph Stafford and Henry of Grosmont, through Ralph Stafford's sons: the eldest, also called Ralph, who predeceased his father, married Grosmont's daughter Maud, while the second, Hugh, who inherited the title, married Beauchamp's daughter Philippa.

In both cases, this was largely a question of social advancement: the Burghershes and Staffords were from a relatively modest background. Ralph Stafford himself was highly ambitious, as his own marriage to Margaret Audley, daughter and heiress of the earl of Gloucester, shows. Bartholomew Burghersh the elder and his brother, Henry Burghersh, bishop of Lincoln, were key figures in Edward's administration: Bartholomew Burghersh the younger, John Mohun's brother-in-law, married money rather than rank: both his wives were from the city of London, and the second was the heiress of one great merchant and the widow of another. These were unusual matches for a companion of the Garter, but perhaps less unexpected given the family's background. His sister's match balanced this with an alliance to a family very close to the king.

At the other extreme, there were five knights who appear to have remained bachelors. John Chandos and James Audley were the most prominent of these; both definitely died unmarried, whether by inclination or simply because they were so continuously engaged in warfare. Other knights married locally: this was true of men such as Nigel Loring, Hugh Wrottesley and even Robert Ufford, earl of Suffolk. And for a handful of knights, we have simply the name of their wife or the fact that they were married, and nothing more.

THE WOMEN OF THE GARTER FAMILIES

Not all marriages were for dynastic reasons: and the most important exceptions come from members of the royal family themselves. The majority of Edward's children were swept up as pawns in the endless game of diplomatic alliances sealed by betrothals. The recital of Edward's failed attempts to use marriage as a tool in such negotiations would cover at least twenty years of his reign. John of Gaunt did in fact marry the heiress of Castile, with dire consequences for both English and Spanish politics, and Mary married the son of Jean de Montfort, who succeeded to the duchy of Brittany. Edward's sister Joan had married David II of Scotland, an unhappy match both politically and personally. Lionel duke of Clarence died in Italy just after his marriage to Violante Visconti, daughter of the duke of Milan, while Joan, Edward's second daughter, died of the plague in Bordeaux on her way to marry the son of the king of Castile.

However, Edward's two eldest children, the prince of Wales and Isabella, both chose their own partners. We have already looked at the prince of Wales's sudden marriage to the newly widowed Joan of Kent. Four years later, Isabella married, at the relatively late age of thirty-three, a French nobleman, Enguerrand de Coucy; again, this seems to have been a love match. Coucy was one of the hostages for John II, and had been at the English court for four and a half years; Froissart said that he was 'much in favour with both French and English', and he was partly of English descent. Furthermore, as we have seen, the king's cousin Eleanor also made a love match, in more scandalous circumstances. After her first husband died, she had become the mistress of Richard Fitzalan, earl of Arundel, the wealthiest man in England. He was married to the daughter of Hugh Despenser the younger, executed as a traitor at the overthrow of Edward II; it had been a good match politically at the time, but in 1344 it was of no consequence, following her father's disgrace. If the king's cousin as mistress of a great magnate was a scandal, the divorce proceedings were even worse. The petition sent to the pope stated that 'Richard earl of Arundel and Isabel, daughter of Hugh Despenser ... at the respective ages of 7 and 8, not by mutual consent, but by fear of their relations contracted espousals, and on coming to years of puberty expressly renounced them, but were forced by blows to cohabit, so that a son was born',[48] and asked for the dissolution of the marriage. The fact that two daughters were also born of the marriage was not mentioned. The son, Edmund, was formally declared a bastard and disinherited, though he retained a place at court and married the sister of William Montagu, second earl of Salisbury, in 1349.

Independence of choice of husband among royal women was unusual; and Eleanor was fortunate to get off so lightly for her affair with the earl of Arundel. Edward's mother Isabella, who might have continued as regent and as a power in the land during Edward's younger years, was fatally weakened by her association with Mortimer, and after the coup of 1330 her life was passed in enforced retirement – a genteel captivity similar to that of a royal prisoner being held for ransom, with some freedom of movement and a suitable but not luxurious lifestyle. Far worse was the penalty for clandestine adultery if detected: the affair of the tour de Nesle in France in 1314 showed what could happen to errant royal spouses. Isabella had three sisters-in-law, all daughters of the dukes of Burgundy. In April 1314, while Isabella was visiting her father in Paris, a scandal erupted at the French court. Margaret and Blanche, the wives of Philip the Fair's sons Charles and Louis, were accused of adultery with two household knights from Normandy, and arrested. Their sister Jeanne was accused of knowing of the affair, and aiding and abetting them. They had apparently been in the habit of meeting in a guard tower called the tour de Nesle, overlooking the Seine. The knights were executed by breaking on the wheel, and Margaret and Blanche were found guilty of adultery, and sentenced to life imprisonment. Jeanne was confined to the castle of Dourdan, and released in 1315 after a trial in which she was found innocent.[49]

Thomas Gray, writing fifty years later, claims that 'common gossip had it that this scandal was revealed to the king of France by his daughter Isabella, queen of England, though many considered this was not true'.[50] His account of the affair is highly coloured, as with his other stories from Continental Europe, but the tradition survived in later chronicles, with elaborate details explaining that Isabella suspected the knights when she saw them wearing purses which she had given to her sisters the previous year. There may be a reference to the affair in a verse chronicle written close to the time of the events. The author praises Isabella's beauty and wisdom, and says that 'through her many things were later disclosed and revealed in France' which later proved to be true, 'which we will speak of when we come to the next year'; the promised entry does not materialize. There is no way of telling whether the accusation against Isabella is true; the scandal itself was real enough, and extremely serious for the French royal house. Later writers attributed the affair to a curse placed on Philip the Fair and his family by the master of the Order of the Knights Templar, burnt at the stake on the king's orders in March 1314, a month before the affair came to light.

Adultery by a queen consort had the most serious of implications, in that it might cast doubt over the legitimacy of her children and lead to disputes as to the succession to the throne. For the other aspect of the role of women in marriage was that of landed wealth and inheritance of estates. It was this that lay behind the child marriage of Richard Fitzalan and the daring coup by Ralph Stafford in carrying off Margaret Audley: in the first instance, the Despensers, as newcomers to the nobility, were anxious to make an alliance with a wealthy and old-established family; in the second, Stafford, as an ambitious newcomer with little property of his own, was securing a marriage to an heiress who would bring valuable lands with her.

Interestingly, there is only one other example of marriage to a great heiress among the Garter companions, that of Walter Mauny to Margaret of Brotherton, the king's cousin and heiress to half the lands of the earldom of Norfolk, and widow of John Seagrave, who died in 1353. Again, the marriage was made without permission, in this case in defiance of the king himself. There was obviously more to this than a merely political match. At some time in 1350, Margaret seems to have set off for Avignon to seek a divorce while her first husband was still alive, despite a royal prohibition against direct appeals to the pope.[51] She crossed the Channel, where a servant of Mauny's met her at night to help her on her journey. Unfortunately he broke his lantern, apparently by treading on it; the pair were caught and arrested as they tried to escape in the dark. In 1354, soon after her second marriage, both she and Mauny were summoned to explain the breach of the prohibition four years earlier, which implies that this was a love match. Mauny had some links with her father's household; Thomas of Brotherton had appointed him marshal of the king's Marshalsea prison in 1331, and he had therefore probably known Margaret for some twenty years.[52] She was briefly restricted to Somerton Castle in Lincolnshire (imprisonment is perhaps too severe a term), but was soon at liberty again. Margaret was a strong-minded and determined character, and this must have been very much a marriage of equals; she was indefatigable in pursuit of her rights and inheritance, in which Mauny aided and abetted her. That she was the prime mover is shown by her claim in 1382, after Mauny's death, to the title of earl marshal, which had belonged to her father, and to a debt of £2,000, outstanding since the time of Edward II. She was treated, as she expected to be, as a magnate in her own right, exchanging new year's gifts on equal terms with John of Gaunt. When she died, she left money for new choirstalls to the church of the Greyfriars in London, and asked to be buried there.

At the other end of the scale, those Garter companions who never rose to the peerage tended to make marriages which reinforced their local standing. We have looked at the marriage links within the company, which show that some of the knights saw their natural allegiance as being with other families represented among the order's members. Of those who married outside, and setting aside the possible love matches discussed above, there was occasionally a match with the daughter of a powerful lord: Reginald Cobham's wife was daughter of Thomas Berkeley of Berkeley Castle, of whose household he had been a member. Berkeley's retinue included other distinguished knights: his cousin Maurice Berkeley and Thomas Bradeston would both have been candidates for the Company of the Garter. Maurice died in February 1347, however, and Bradeston was relatively old, having served in Edward's Scottish wars.[53] Age may have been the reason why he was not chosen, as he would otherwise seem to be a prime candidate, having been involved in the capture of Mortimer in 1330, and a close companion of Edward in the tournament field.

Miles Stapleton's marriage to Joan Ingham was a similar alliance to that of Reginald Cobham. Though Joan's father, Oliver Ingham, had served much of his life in Bordeaux and did not have a following in England, he was a powerful and respected figure, and it is interesting that Stapleton moved the centre of his estates from Yorkshire to Joan Ingham's home territory on the Norfolk coast, and that he founded a priory and chantry at Ingham rather than at Bedale, where his father's estates had been.

Marriages such as Hugh Wrottesley's to Isabel Arderne, daughter of a neighbouring landowner, and those of John Grey to Katharine Fitzalan of Bedale, and to Avice Marmion, were probably part of a network of local friendships and alliances, perhaps involving modest inheritances. That of Robert Ufford to the daughter of William Norwich may reflect an attempt to extend the Ufford estates in East Anglia. In one case, we know the specific reason for a marriage: when William Bohun married Elizabeth Badlesmere, the widowed daughter-in-law of Roger Mortimer, in 1335, it was made known that the match was taking place to help the reconciliation between the Mortimer and Bohun families, who were neighbours on the Welsh borders.

CASTLES

Five of the Garter companions came from well-established families, whose estates centred on a castle built by their ancestors. Of these, only Thomas Beauchamp undertook extensive building works, at Warwick Castle, part of a programme of reconstruction which lasted into the 1390s. He used the wealth he had garnered in the wars in France to remodel the eastern defences, beginning with the gatehouse and what is now called 'Caesar's Tower', and including the watergate. Caesar's Tower and the watergate are both unusual in plan; the inspiration seems to have been from local architecture rather than from abroad, particularly in the layout of the interior spaces – a trefoil plan in the tower, and a polygonal entrance in the watergate, which also has striking octagonal towers. Thomas Beauchamp spent much of his life abroad, as the most energetic and most feared of Edward's commanders, and he may have left the construction in the hands of his household officers, which might explain why the work drew on local styles rather than the international fashions which might have been expected.[54]

Other Garter companions had been granted estates which included castles, but, in at least one instance, a knight, Ralph Stafford, had risen to new eminence, but had no castle. However wealthy he had become, he could not simply build one: he needed a 'licence to crenellate', broadly speaking royal planning permission to build a castle or convert an existing manor into a fortress. Originally devised to give the king control over potentially dissident barons who might raise castles which could be used against him, by the second half of the fourteenth century this was largely a mark of status.

When Ralph Stafford started his new castle at Stafford in 1348, he, like Thomas Beauchamp, drew on local styles; the contract with his mason, John of Burchester, specifies that John is to work to plans provided by the earl. It was a stylish building, again with polygonal towers, and reflects his sudden rise to fortune in 1347. He had married in 1336 Margaret, daughter of Hugh Audley, earl of Gloucester, against her father's wishes; he seems to have been reconciled with his father-in-law, and certainly enjoyed the king's favour. In 1341, during the king's dispute with Archbishop Stratford, he had played a key role, and as steward of the royal household had tried to prevent the archbishop from attending parliament in April. This angered the fiercely independent peers, and one of the most senior of them, John, Earl Warenne, had turned to the king and said, 'Everything is turned upside down: those who should be the principals are shut out, and hired servants sit here in parliament who should not belong to your counsel.'[55] It was, however, Stafford who had the last laugh. When his wife came into her inheritance in 1347, he actually commissioned the castle a few weeks before having the necessary licence to do so: he was confident that he was now recognized as one of the leading men of the realm, in the light of a decade of military success combined with loyal service to the king. The new building also anticipated his creation as an earl in 1351, and is very much a visual statement of his social rank. A description of it in 1521 speaks admiringly of its excellent design and position, so it would evidently have succeeded in making a suitable impression on his contemporaries.[56]

Men with less substantial estates, often scattered across the country, might have to make do with older castles, such as the timber castle at Rougemont by which John Lisle 'of Rougemont' was distinguished from other men of the same name. This was an enlarged twelfth-century castle, with the necessary buildings from which to administer his manor of Harewood. Bartholomew Burghersh the younger, who spent most of his life in the service of Edward prince of Wales, held the castle of Ewyas Harold in Herefordshire, which appears to have been the most important building on his estates. However, it remained ruinous at the time; his absence on the prince's business and his close links with the City of London meant that he lived elsewhere.

And about half of the members of the company were household knights, who were not in a position to aspire to more than the grant of a comfortable income paid by the king or the prince. Men like John Chandos, one of the prince's closest councillors, might find themselves granted a castle in Normandy, in his case that of St Sauveur-le-Vicomte, formerly the property of Godefroy d'Harcourt and retained by the English after he returned to the French side. Chandos was put in charge of the garrison there in 1360,[57] and the grant was made by Edward III in 1361 after the treaty of Brétigny. It was ratified by the French king, and Chandos held it until his death.

We know little about how any of the Garter companions ran their estates, with one striking exception: that of Hugh Wrottesley.[58] This

takes us away from the court and the world of great military victories
to the murky local politics and feuds of ordinary life and the darker side
of the Anglo-French wars. Wrottesley came from Shropshire, from a
family without obvious connections to the court. His first appearance in
the records is in the patent rolls in 1334, when he was twenty, and was
proposing to join the crusade planned by Philip of Valois; he was
granted letters of attorney to cover the management of his affairs in his
absence. The crusade came to nothing; in the same year, deeds relating
to the feuds over property which were to occupy him for the rest of his
life appear. Since the original archive survives, there is a welter of detail,
and we can trace the interminable progress of his main quarrel, beginning, in 1337, with the Perton family. He accused them of an armed raid
in August 1336, when twenty-nine men carried off his harvest, to the
value of £20. This was followed by counter-accusations and counter-
attacks, and the king was forced to issue a special commission to inquire
into the disturbances, which had resulted in the death of John Perton, to
be headed by William Shareshull. Shareshull was a neighbour of Wrottesley's; it is suspicious that Wrottesley, about the time the commission was
set up, departed for Scotland with William Montagu, taking with him all
his supporters who were named in the inquiry; they duly got letters protecting them from prosecution during their absence on military service,
and it may be that Shareshull warned him of what was afoot.

Almost as soon as he returned from Scotland in June 1338, he
departed, again with letters of protection, to serve under Montagu in
Flanders. By the end of the year, he had distinguished himself sufficiently
to get a full pardon for the death of John Perton because of his good
service. But he lost another lawsuit brought by his father-in-law, to
whom he had mortgaged the rents from his estate, which Wrottesley
had then attempted to collect himself. This left him very short of ready
money, and he solved the problem by confiscating twenty-seven and a
half sacks of wool which the tenants at Wrottesley had hidden from the
official collectors; the wool had been granted to the king by parliament,
because he too was short of ready cash to pay for his expedition.
Wrottesley's export of the wool without paying dues was noticed, and
entered as a debt in the exchequer records, but in 1348 the money was
written off. His next move was to eject his mother and stepfather from
lands to which they seem to have been entitled under his father's will,
with the help of a dubious judgement from William Shareshull.

In 1342 he was in the retinue of Ralph Stafford in Brittany, where he remained until 1343. During the summer of that year, there was an uneasy truce, complicated by the fact that, although Philip of Valois had promised to release Jean de Montfort, the claimant to the duchy supported by the English, he had failed to do so. In October 1343 the pope wrote to Edward to complain that a man named Hugh Wrottesley with others from the English army had seized Ralph de Montfort and his companions from their beds and abducted them from the French camp, robbing them as they did so. Ralph and the others were still captive, and the pope demanded their release. It seems that this was a case of mistaken identity, or perhaps an attempt to obtain a bargaining counter, the object being to release Jean de Montfort from captivity rather than seizing his namesake Ralph. Somewhere along the line, Hugh Wrottesley appears to have collected a considerable ransom, since on his return to England he repaid his very substantial borrowings in the course of the next year.

He served in the prince's division at Crécy and Calais, and evidently distinguished himself, because in 1350 he became a knight of the king's chamber. At the same time, his debts at the exchequer dating back to 1337 were written off over a period of time by order of the king: they may have totalled as much as £2,000. Hugh was now a reasonably wealthy man, and held an important post at court; but disaster was at hand. A new sheriff was appointed in 1352, who evidently intended to collect the debts which had not yet been notified to him as forgiven; moreover, he was the brother-in-law of John Perton, killed by Hugh in 1337. The posse raised by the sheriff was met by Wrottesley and his men at dawn on 29 November, and in the ensuing affray the sheriff and his clerk were killed, and a third man died soon afterwards. Two of the widows charged Wrottesley with the murders in the court of king's bench in spring 1353, and Wrottesley was imprisoned in the Marshalsea. He and his companions proceeded to escape at some point later that year, and in 1354 a sentence of outlawry was pronounced. Wrottesley had made his way to Brittany and had joined the English army there. Here his luck ran out: he was captured, and had no means of raising a ransom or even of getting funds for his maintenance while in enemy hands. How he obtained his release is unclear, but, when proceedings against him were renewed in October 1355, he was able to get the outlawry lifted because he was not in England at the time sentence was

THE COMPANY OF THE GARTER

pronounced. Furthermore, he was able to produce the king's pardon for his part in the murders and for breaking out of prison, granted on 5 March 1355. His lands were restored to him in November, and in the following April he arranged to rent his lands for a fixed sum, implying that he was planning to leave England again. He probably served with the prince of Wales at Poitiers, since he does not reappear in the English legal records until November 1357. He was with the king as a household knight on the Reims campaign in 1359–60, evidently fully restored to favour. He appeared at the Garter feasts with some regularity: robes were issued to him in 1363 and 1364, and again in 1372. In 1366 he made a settlement of his property which may imply that he was about to go abroad again: since the next entry in the legal records is in April 1368, it seems likely that he went with the prince on his Spanish venture, and may have fought at Nájera. Evidence of the same sort would place him on the abortive expedition of 1372 to Aquitaine, when the king's fleet was driven back by storms in September. He attended all the Garter feasts from 1374 to 1379.

The absence of military activity in the late 1370s meant that Wrottesley was back in England, terrorizing his neighbours once again. A dispute with Adam Peshall led to a petition to Richard II, in which Adam described how, when he was returning from the king's coronation, 'Hugh de Wrottesley, designing his death, had made various ambushes of men ... on the high roads between London and the country, and he had himself laid in wait with many armed men at a place called Foxhunte Ledegate ... with a view of killing and murdering the said Adam.'[59] Hugh's answer to this was a series of counter-charges, though at first he hoped to get away with mere bluster, only to find that the council were no longer in a mood to favour lawless knights, however well connected. There is no further word of the suit; Wrottesley died in January 1381, aged sixty-seven.

His career is typical of many of the knights of the period: valuable as warriors, they were almost as lawless as their freebooting counterparts in France: to take just one example, James Audley of Heighley, namesake and distant relative of the James Audley who was a knight of the Garter, was also one of the prince's military commanders. The prince's domain of Cheshire was a palatine county, not subject to royal authority, and was renowned for its lawlessness. James Audley of Heighley was accused of corrupting the prince's officials in the course of his crimes and was outlawed, with an additional fine of 700 marks for his extortionate behaviour while serjeant of the peace. Three years later, he fought at the prince's side at Poitiers.[60] Ironically it is only through the sporadic efforts of their victims and of the law courts to bring them to book that we know about this other side of the coin. Even more notorious were the activities of the Coterel and Folville gangs, in the Peak District and in Leicester, at the beginning of Edward's reign, whose activities in the years between 1327 and 1332 went as far as issuing forged royal writs for fines, which they collected with menaces and the often complete suborning of the local and even national justices and judges. In both cases, some semblance of order was restored when the ringleaders took up service in Edward's Scottish wars: the king's armies may have included criminals and evildoers, but, by recruiting them, the royal officials and local lords solved the problems of local society, for a time at least. The lawbreaker, often with a grievance over their treatment by the law, and the respected knight on campaign, were often one and the same.[61]

BACHELORS

A smaller group of Garter companions were younger sons and knights who remained bachelors. Such men had modest estates of their own and were career soldiers: three of the prince's retainers, Loring, Audley and Chandos, who appear together in a writ of 1351, had highly distinguished careers. Perhaps partly because they were not in the king's service but in the prince's household, they were less richly rewarded than other comparable commanders. Nigel Loring's estates, apart from his own lands in Bedford, were mostly in the earldom of Cornwall, given for his service by the prince. James Audley had an income of £400 a year from the Cornish tin mines and estates in France and was lord of the Île d'Oléron near La Rochelle; apart from these grants, he had only his father's manor at Stratton Audley in Oxfordshire. John Chandos likewise had both gifts and grants of estates from the prince; his career was almost entirely in France, and he spent the last ten years of his life in Aquitaine, Spain and Normandy.

Two of the original knights came from Hainault, in the wake of the death of William II at the battle of Staveren in 1345, and depended entirely on what they could earn as household knights, in effect transferring from William's household to that of the prince of Wales. Both Eustace d'Auberchicourt and Henry Eam have mystified historians of the early years of the Company of the Garter.[62]

Curiously, the key evidence about Henry Eam has been in print since 1931 but has not previously been noticed. It was known that he was a foreigner, because when he became one of the prince's household knights in 1348 he pledged obedience to the prince of Wales, saving only his duty to his liege lord, the duke of Brabant. In 1351 he was given letters of protection by the prince when he went to Flanders, since anyone from Brabant was liable to be arrested there. There is a further document in the prince's register addressed to his aunt, Margaret countess of Hainault, which gives his Dutch name, Oem. Although there is no absolute proof of this, he is almost certainly the squire called Heinken (Heynric) Oem who accompanied William II, the prince's uncle, to Prussia in 1343-4.

For his career at the court of Hainault, we have the detailed accounts of the count's household for 1343-5, and Heinken Oem first appears in July 1343, when the count paid his farrier for tournament armour which the latter had supplied for Heinken's use.[63] As a serving squire, who had completed his basic training in arms, he is likely to have been between fourteen and sixteen, which gives a probable birth date of around 1330. This would make him a similar age to the prince of Wales. Later in the same year, he accompanied William II on a pilgrimage to the Holy Sepulchre. William had originally intended to go to Granada, but instead, on 8 August, he set out for Palestine.[64] On 11 August Heinken offered five 'angels of Luxemburg' on behalf of the count at a church at Kaisersberg, south-west of Strasbourg. The same day, a bay tournament horse was bought for Heinken by the count at Colmar.[65]

Four weeks later, the count and his entourage had evidently travelled to Venice, and taken a ship to Ragusa, now Dubrovnik, on the Dalmatian coast, where the count instructed Heinken to give alms to two monks who had come from Mount Sinai.[66] By December, the accounts show that they had returned from Palestine and had reached Vienna: the duchess of Austria gave the count a fur cap, a girdle and a purse, and the bearer was rewarded by Heinken with six gulden; the minstrels of the town of Vienna performed for the count while he was there, and received seven gulden from Heinken. The duke presented the count with a black horse, and the man who brought it was given six gulden by Heinken; the count rode the horse at Vienna, but with suitable lordly generosity then gave it to one of the local knights.[67] The party went on to Prussia, but the success or otherwise of their crusading is not recorded; by 8 April 1344 they were back in The Hague. Apart from acting as the count's go-between when it came to rewarding messengers and minstrels, Heinken seems to have occasionally bought horses for the count, in particular during their return to Prussia from December 1344 to the end of March 1345. While they waited for the winter campaign to begin, William II won 600 gulden at dice from Louis of Hungary, who was very angry that he had lost so much. William made matters worse by saying, 'Money that I win at gambling, I don't hold on to', and threw his winnings to his followers.[68] William did not have the same luck with the campaign, which proved to be fruitless. Heinken is the most frequently mentioned of the squires who accompanied the count during this period, and it may be that he was something of a favourite.

We do not know whether he was on the fateful expedition to Friesland in September 1345. All that we can say is that his career in Hainault ended some time between 1345 and 1348, when we learn that he had been knighted by the prince of Wales and was a member of his household. The best explanation would be that he had sought another master on William II's death, and had not unnaturally turned to the latter's nephew, who had an equally knightly reputation. It is tempting, and probably plausible, to fill the gap by making him one of the 264 esquires who accompanied the prince on the Crécy campaign; we might also assume that he was knighted in the course of the English march from La Hogue to Calais. In January 1348 letters patent from the king confirmed a grant to Henry Eam, as he was now known, of an annuity of 100 marks to support the estate of knighthood. He became 'the prince's bachelor', one of the household knights, while retaining his connections in Brabant.

The final notice of him in the prince's records was also missed in earlier accounts of his life. On 12 March 1353, 'the prince, on the death of Henry Eam, who ... had 100 marks yearly as his fee by the prince's grant out of the issues of the manor of Bradenynche, has retained Sir John [Sully] at a yearly fee of £40 out of the same issues'.

The most plausible reason for Henry Eam's presence among the Garter knights is a personal friendship between himself and the prince of

Wales, based both on his connection with the prince's uncle, and on a shared love of jousting and the knightly world; there may well have been military accomplishments to his credit as well, but of those we know nothing.

RELIGION AND RELIGIOUS FOUNDATIONS

The Company of the Garter was a religious confraternity, in an age when religion loomed very large in personal lives. We know something of the attitudes of individual knights to religion, though the private devotions of the middle ages come down to us largely by chance: an inscription in a book of hours, a gift recorded in the royal accounts, an anecdote recorded in a chronicle. Very rarely we have a book written by a layman of high rank, and there is sometimes a personal element that can be disentangled from the formal piety of the foundation of chantries and monasteries or the commissioning of tombs. There is no narrative of knightly piety, only a fragmentary mosaic.

The most valuable evidence that we have for the religious attitudes of the Garter companions is *The Book of Holy Medicines* by Henry of Grosmont.[69] He wrote this in 1354, not long after the foundation of the Company of the Garter, but, more importantly, while the memory of the Black Death was fresh in men's minds. It may have been undertaken on his confessor's instructions as a penitential task. The text as a whole is hard to read with any great enthusiasm today, unless one is steeped in the devotional literature and imagery of the fourteenth century. It is allegorical and confessional in tone, and tells how the author – perhaps one should say simply the sinner – has been invaded by the seven deadly sins through each of his five senses, which have even penetrated to his heart, the keep of the castle, so that the fortress of his body is infected by evil. He prays to Christ as physician of the soul, through the 'sweet lady' his Mother, to provide remedies for the infection in all its manifestations, remedies which he himself suggests.

If this was all the book contained, it would have been just another devotional treatise of the kind that were produced for pious laymen by the clergy. What gives it its colour and interest, particularly for a modern reader, is the way in which the religious allegory is continually reinforced by reference to Henry's own life and experiences. From the image of his body as a castle, the similes extend outwards, from military operations to hunting, travel and everyday life. His similes are like the illuminations at the foot of the page of the psalter or book of hours: the scenes of foxes and hounds, of carriages full of ladies, of marketplaces and cookery which we look at today for our amusement are really there as yet another piece in the great jigsaw of God's design of the world for our spiritual instruction. Here in literary form is a version of the rich vein of medieval preaching which used examples from everyday life as a basis for sermons that spoke more directly to a congregation; but the difference is that these pieces are written from experience.

The castle, Henry observes, is as often taken over the walls as through the gates, because men guard the former less carefully; the seven deadly sins undermine the walls, and can then enter as easily as through a gate. He links this to his underlying image of the body by comparing the walls of the castle to his feet:

> pride has entered me through my feet when I have advised myself badly, for it seems to me – and to no one else – that my feet look good in the stirrup, or in hose or in armour, or as I dance with a light foot; and garters suit me well, in my opinion: all of which is worthless, and if I dare to say so, my mad joy in this was greater than all else, and quite without restraint.[70]

The vividness of the scenes from everyday life which Henry cites contrasts with the repetitive and conventional piety of his self-reproaches for his sins, which to a modern reader are unrealistic and difficult to take seriously. Yet these are just as much Henry's own words as those of the descriptive passages; this is how devout laymen would have expressed themselves, echoing the words of their confessors and the sermons of the preachers they listened to, using a vocabulary which no longer speaks directly to us. The penitential attitudes which underlie this deliberate rejection of worldly pleasures by a man who nonetheless indulged in them point us towards the confessional wills of the later fourteenth century, where the writer emphasizes his spiritual unworthiness, and demands an ascetic funeral without the least trace of worldly glory.

There are occasional glimpses of aspects of personal devotion in other Garter companions, but they are few and far between. Miles Stapleton's reputation for being 'wonderfully devoted to the blessed Virgin' is a throwaway remark by the chronicler Geoffrey le Baker, sandwiched between his trustworthiness and his unusual experience in the business of war. But his religious faith is confirmed by the evidence of a witness in the case of Lovell versus Morley in the Court of Chivalry, who records that, when Robert Morley died on Edward III's ill-fated expedition in 1359–60, 'Miles Stapleton preached to him of the faith of Holy Church and the mercy of God shortly before his death.'[71]

One of the permanent concerns of medieval knights was the possibility that they would die unconfessed in battle; there were few clergy with the army, though Geoffrey le Baker notes at Bannockburn in 1314 that the king had 'his bishops and other men of religion' with him in his division in the battle. The solution for those who could afford it was to have a private confessor and a portable altar at which mass could be said regularly, or, in rare cases usually affecting those of the highest rank, to petition for plenary remission for their sins at the hour of their death. Successful petitions for this privilege in 1343 before the renewal of war in Brittany included Henry of Grosmont, William Bohun and Thomas Beauchamp; during the preparations for the Calais campaign, Ralph Stafford and John Beauchamp also obtained it. Portable altars and private confessors were often combined with the right to celebrate mass before daybreak, otherwise contrary to canon law, but often essential on a fast-moving expedition, or on the morning of a battle. William Montagu was granted a portable altar and a confessor in October 1333, a licence renewed for him and Henry of Grosmont when they went to Algeciras in 1343. And during the troubles in Aquitaine from 1365 onwards, Nigel Loring, Walter Pavely and John Chandos from the prince's household were granted the same privilege; furthermore John Lyons, Chandos's chaplain, was granted the faculty to hear the confessions of English soldiers, because, in the past, 'being ignorant of the language, [they] have died imperfectly confessed'.[72]

As to the personal worship of the members of the confraternity, the prince of Wales's devotion to the cult of the Trinity is the best documented. He and Joan of Kent founded a chantry chapel at Canterbury on their marriage, and in the foundation charter the prince mentions his especial worship of the Trinity. This is reiterated by several chroniclers, and confirmed by three works of art: a lead badge showing the prince kneeling before the Trinity, of which two examples survive,[73] the frontispiece of a manuscript of Chandos Herald's life of the prince with a similar composition, and the magnificent painting on the tester or headboard of his tomb at Canterbury. The same particular form of the Trinity, the so-called 'Throne of Grace', is used in all three, so that the kneeling prince is praying for God's mercy in these images. The cult of the Trinity had been established at Canterbury in 1162 by Thomas Becket, and the cathedral was rededicated to the Holy Trinity. It was only in 1333 that the festival of the Holy Trinity was generally adopted by the Church as a whole on the instructions of John XXII. The earliest evidence of the prince's devotion to the Trinity is in a letter of Bishop Grandisson of Exeter to his clergy in the autumn of 1356, announcing the news of the victory at Poitiers, as the king had requested; Grandisson adds instructions that particular thanks should be offered to the Trinity and that the mass for Trinity Sunday should be celebrated. The following Trinity Sunday, the prince ordered sixteen swans for a feast on that day. The prince had undoubtedly made frequent visits to Canterbury, though the only pilgrimages that are recorded are those in 1343 and 1346 when he accompanied his father. He also went to the chief shrine of the Virgin Mary in England, Walsingham, before his two major expeditions to France, in 1346 and 1355; in 1346 he was with his father, and, on the second occasion, he may have been accompanied by Bartholomew Burghersh the younger.[74]

The prince's choice of devotions overlapped to some extent with that of his father, but Edward himself was a staunch and traditional worshipper of Our Lady, the first-named of the three patrons of the Company of the Garter, and he does not seem to have had any interest in the cult of the Trinity. His preferred shrines were those of the Virgin, not only at major centres of pilgrimage such as Walsingham, but also any local sites where she was worshipped which he passed on his travels. For instance, he may have visited the shrine of Our Lady of Grace at Ipswich in 1340 before he embarked to engage the French fleet at Sluys, as he sent an offering there 'out of special devotion' in 1342, and this may explain the choice of St Mary Graces as the dedication of his London foundation in her honour.[75]

The king was also a very frequent visitor to Canterbury. He was of course a worshipper at the Lady Chapel, and he also made offerings at the tomb of Becket, as the English kings had done since Henry II, in expiation of his murder at Henry's behest: he was now considered one of the patron saints of England. Edward also honoured St Edmund, the royal martyr, and St Edward the Confessor, his name-saint, his predecessors as king before the Norman Conquest and also revered as national patrons. He had been baptized in the castle chapel at Windsor dedicated to St Edward, on St Edward's feast day, in the great bronze font which later stood in St George's chapel. These were the traditional royal saints, who had been invoked in support of royal ambitions since the mid-thirteenth century.

We have already mentioned his other enthusiasm, which was rather more unexpected: the shrine of the Three Kings at Cologne Cathedral.[76] This was linked to his appointment as vicar-general of the Holy Roman Empire in 1338 as part of his alliance with the Emperor Louis, and his relations with the cathedral were a reflection of his imperial connections and ambitions. However, this did not last; it was reported that in 1359, before the Reims expedition, Edward had said that, although people thought that he was to be buried between the Three Kings there, this was not true, because Westminster was far more beautiful. The three kings among whom he wished to lie were all buried there: Edward the Confessor, Henry III and Edward I, 'a most noble king and my ancestor, who in all his life was the most illustrious and daring in deeds of arms, and in the commanding of armies'.[77]

Pilgrimage figures in the biographies of other Garter companions, for all of whom it was probably a common experience, with varying degrees of enthusiasm. Bartholomew Burghersh the younger was actually buried before the high altar in the pilgrimage church of Our Lady at Walsingham, in 1369; he had projected a pilgrimage to Jerusalem with his father and Walter Pavely in 1354. Henry Eam probably went to Jerusalem with William II of Hainault as a squire. In 1350 William Fitzwarin was the leader of a group of no less than 168 named pilgrims[78] who were given permission to leave England on pilgrimage to Rome, embarking from Dover. William took with him six yeomen and seven horses, and there are a number of other illustrious names in the company, so it must have be a troop of at least 350 people, all on horseback. If there were any pilgrims on foot they would have made their way separately once they landed.

The list of pilgrims who went with Fitzwarin shows that they were mostly nobles, knights and clerics. Two widows of great magnates were in the party, and had the most substantial retinues. Blanche, widow of

Thomas, Lord Wake of Liddell, was the sister of Henry of Grosmont, and brought thirty attendants and three damsels with her. Ida, Lady Neville, daughter of Robert, Lord Fitzwalter and widow of John, Lord Neville, two of the great families of Essex, travelled with an escort of twenty attendants, male and female. There was one other widow, six married couples and three apparently single women. Beatrice Luttrell, daughter-in-law of the Geoffrey Luttrell who commissioned the Luttrell Psalter, came without her husband Andrew. Seventeen of the men are identified as knights or men at arms, but others were certainly of knightly standing. The largest group were, not unexpectedly, the thirty-seven clergy; the foremost of these was the prior of Worcester, travelling with two of his fellow-monks.

How this group was assembled is hard to say. It may be that Fitz-warin had been named as leader, and that anyone who wished to go on pilgrimage had been told to assemble in London at the beginning of September. Despite Fitzwarin's service with the queen, there is no obvious link to the queen's household, but there are a number of men from the Welsh marches, and another group from Lincolnshire. This would imply that Fitzwarin's group was simply one of several such companies for whom a record has survived; but it was almost as diverse a collection of people as Chaucer's famous pilgrims to Canterbury.

The reason for this particular expedition was that 1350 had been declared a jubilee or holy year by Pope Clement, when exceptional privileges would be granted for those who came to Rome. The jubilee year, which is still one of the major celebrations of the Roman Catholic Church, had never before been officially declared in advance. Its origin was curious, although the idea of the jubilee, originally a time when salvation was especially near for the faithful, had entered the language of preachers from Jewish tradition in the twelfth century and the first jubilee seems to have happened spontaneously.[79] The end of the century was always a moment when apocalyptic predictions of the return of Christ were rife, and in 1299 this led to rumours that exceptional indulgences[80] would be granted for those in Rome on 1 January 1300. Pope Boniface VIII validated this belief retrospectively on 22 February, and extended it for the whole year, declaring that such a jubilee would be held every hundred years. However, in 1343, Clement VI, partly for financial reasons, and partly appealing again to the Jewish tradition which specified a fifty-year interval, changed the interval to fifty years, and thus gave notice that 1350 would be a jubilee. Despite the ravages of the Black Death, which had not quite died out in the northern parts of Europe, the event was a huge success, and, although the records imply that William Fitzwarin's party was the largest by far to leave England, many other Englishmen at a humbler level took part in the pilgrimage that year, alongside a throng of travellers from the rest of Europe.

We know that the party crossed from Dover. Given that Englishmen were not welcome in France during the uneasy truce that existed between the two countries, and the political turmoil there, it is unlikely that they followed the old pilgrim road through eastern France. Instead, they probably took a route to Rome through the Low Countries, Germany and Switzerland to Milan, via the St Gotthard pass, which had been opened up in the thirteenth century.[81] It took them through a series of substantial towns and cities, where accommodation for such a large party would have been possible, such as Bruges, Ghent, Cologne, Koblenz, Speyer, Strasbourg and Basle. The difficult part was the journey over the St Gotthard itself on the steep and narrow Alpine roads. Since William Fitzwarin and his companions were on horseback, they should have averaged around twenty miles a day,[82] which would have brought them to Basle around 10 October, and to the pass before the first snowfall. The route through Italy would again take the group through large cities, accustomed to dealing with sizeable groups of travellers. Once in Rome, they spent only a few days in the city, because of the huge crowds; the Romans, in order to extract the maximum profit from their visitors, had initially put word about that to obtain the sought-after indulgences, the main churches had to be visited repeatedly. But this abuse was ended when the papal legate issued an edict that pilgrims should only spend six days in the city.

The return journey is much more difficult to assess, as we do not know when they landed in England again; the group would not have reached the Alps until late November at the earliest. This meant that they would have to struggle through snow and ice: pilgrims did cross the passes in winter, but only at great personal hazard. The cost of staying in Italy until the spring would have been considerable. For such a journey, it was clearly vital to have a trusted leader, and someone like William Fitzwarin, with military experience, was almost essential if a pilgrimage on this scale was to be successfully completed.

Elsewhere, we have to rely on records of royal, princely and knightly charity for an idea of the religious enthusiasm of the Garter companions. The foundation of religious establishments, particularly in the later years of life, was a common theme among the magnates of the time, and the Garter companions were no exception. In addition to the chapels of St Stephen and St George and the abbey of St Mary Graces, Edward founded a nunnery at Dartford. The prince of Wales re-founded the house of canons at Ashridge in Hertfordshire which his predecessor as earl of Cornwall had established as a house of the *Boni Homines*, or Brothers of Penitence; and he also gave them Edington college in Wiltshire, and a rector was appointed there from the brethren at Ashridge.[83]

Other collegiate and monastic institutions founded by Garter companions included the college of canons at Newark of which Henry of Grosmont was the patron, and the London Charterhouse, which Walter Mauny sponsored. The Newark college, established in 1356, was on much the same scale as St George's itself, as one might expect from someone of the rank and devoutness of the duke of Lancaster. There was a dean and twelve canons, with thirteen vicars, and it was actually more substantially endowed than St George's, which Edward neglected somewhat after the first flush of enthusiasm. It was a re-foundation of the hospital at Newark which Henry's father had begun twenty-five years earlier, and the fifty poor folk it housed were the equivalent of the twenty-six poor knights at Windsor. Many of the statutes of the college concerned the commemoration of Henry's family, just as St George's focused on Edward and his dynasty; while neither were chantries, whose prime purpose was the celebration of masses for the departed, they were novelties in their time, colleges which were neither monastic nor a group of secular clergy based on a cathedral.

Walter Mauny's Charterhouse (as Carthusian abbeys were called) in London stemmed from his lease of a plot of thirteen acres from St Bartholomew's Hospital in Smithfield, outside the city's walls, for the burial of victims of the Black Death in 1349.[84] This was next to a plot purchased by the bishop of London, Ralph Stratford, which had already been filled by the end of 1348. At the dedication, on the feast of the Annunciation, the bishop of London preached on the first word spoken by the angel Gabriel to the Virgin, 'Hail'. The Charterhouse, when it came into being, was known as the House of the Salutation of the Mother of God. Mauny's first intention was to set up a college similar to that of Henry of Grosmont at Newark, but in the end a modest hermitage was built instead, with two occupants whose duty was to pray continually for the dead.[85]

The idea of offering the unused part of the plague burial site to the Carthusians appears to have been the work of Michael Northburgh, bishop of London from 1355; on his travels as a diplomat he had seen the new Charterhouse at Paris. The Carthusians had originally sought out remote and desolate places for their monasteries, but had recently adopted a policy of creating secluded communities within the bounds of great cities, as an example of holy living in the midst of the temptations of the metropolis. Mauny may have seen those at Liège and Bruges; when Northburgh approached him, he readily agreed to the new plan, and it was supported by the priors of the two leading Carthusian foundations in England. Unfortunately both died shortly afterwards, and the plan was not revived until the late 1360s. Mauny agreed once more to proceed, and the terms were agreed with the order in 1370. The foundation charter was issued in 1371, and Mauny gave the house rich endowments. When he died the following year he was buried at the altar of the old graveyard chapel, which was to become the church of the new Charterhouse. But his gifts were rendered ineffective by his death: one of the estates was seized by other claimants, and the £4,000 which the king owed him – perhaps from the loan in the Netherlands thirty years earlier – was never repaid. If he had been alive to claim the debt, he would probably have obtained at least some of the money as a personal favour from the king. The Charterhouse was built and the community came into being, but at times it led a hand-to-mouth existence rather than the secure living that its founder had intended.

Walter Mauny also played a small part in the foundation, or at least the early years, of two Cambridge colleges. In 1347–8, shortly after his return from Calais, he helped Edmund Gonville, a member of an old Norfolk family who had some connection with Henry of Grosmont, to found the college that bears his name, dedicated to the Annunciation of the Blessed Virgin (like his cemetery and proposed college of canons in London). The charter, dated 28 January 1348, states that Gonville's petition had been supported by Mauny. A few years later, he and his family were enrolled in the Guild of Corpus Christi around the time that the College of Corpus Christi and the Blessed Virgin Mary obtained its charter in 1352. The college was unusual in that it was a creation of the united guilds of St Mary, whose history goes back to the late thirteenth century, and that of Corpus Christi, instituted in 1350. Like Gonville College (now Gonville and Caius), the new college was a response to the urgent need for more clergy, in the light of the huge death toll of the Black Death. Henry of Grosmont, as alderman of the Guild of Corpus Christi, petitioned for the grant of the charter. A further link is the figure of William Bateman, bishop of Norwich, and fellow-diplomat of both Henry of Grosmont and Walter Mauny on an embassy to the papal court at Avignon in September 1348: he founded Trinity Hall in 1350, and took up the affairs of Gonville College after Gonville's death in 1351 with the work only partly completed. Mauny and Grosmont had been companions in arms in 1345–6 in Gascony, and again at Calais, so knew each other well, but how their common interest in the new foundations in Cambridge came about is a mystery. Equally, Mauny's relations with Gonville are a mystery, though Gonville seems to have been a manager of landed estates, and Mauny was an equally business-minded character.[86]

It is possible that we can trace the way in which Henry of Grosmont himself was drawn into the foundation of Corpus Christi. The records of the Guild of Corpus Christi note that John Clement of Tamworth 'was and is the best councillor and helper in London in all the business of the Guild and college'.[87] Tamworth lies to the west of Leicester, the centre of Grosmont's lands; at Leicester, Grosmont was well acquainted with the townspeople, and a popular figure with their leaders; there are records of friendly exchanges between the duke and the corporation, and he sent them news of his progress in Aquitaine in 1346. On his return they gave a dinner in his honour, which indicates a degree of warmth unusual in the relations between a town and a neighbouring lord. John Clement may well have had some connection with Grosmont, perhaps through John Gynewell, who was Grosmont's steward from 1343 to 1345 and held a prebend in Tamworth as well as at St Mary's in Leicester Castle. And, given Grosmont's known openness towards townsfolk, Clement may have regarded him as both approachable and extremely prestigious. It is no more than a speculation, but no other figure in courtly circles had the same kind of civic reputation.

These were major foundations: other companions of the Garter worked on a humbler scale. The commonest examples are extensions or rebuildings of churches already associated with their families, whether to create a new chantry chapel or even a modest religious house associated with the church. At Ingham in Norfolk, Miles Stapleton rebuilt the parish church with an impressive tower and spacious nave, out of scale with the small village which it still dominates. In 1360, after the work was completed, it was attached to the Trinitarian priory which he founded, part of whose purpose was to ensure that the necessary masses were said for himself and his wife, and her father, Oliver Ingham. The Trinitarians as an order were particularly concerned with the redemption of captives, especially captives who had fallen into the hands of infidels, and one-third of its income was set aside for this purpose. At this period, there was relatively little warfare which involved this kind of transaction; in Prussia, where Stapleton had fought, ransoms appear to have been unknown, and it is possible that Stapleton's choice could have been influenced by the prince's enthusiasm for the Trinity.

Only one other Garter companion is recorded as founding a priory or monastery; Ralph Stafford created an Augustinian priory at Stafford in 1344, in memory of his first wife. She and her family were to be remembered with prayers, as was the king. Although this preceded the building of his castle and his earldom, it was undoubtedly intended as part of a building plan appropriate to his new status. He later founded a chantry at Cold Norton priory for himself and his second wife. William Fitzwarin, soon after he returned from his pilgrimage to Rome, obtained a licence in 1351 to give lands and rent to support three chaplains at the parish of Wantage. He also included the king as a beneficiary: the chaplains were to celebrate masses 'for the good estate of the king, Queen Philippa and him, and for their souls when they are dead'. Nigel Loring, though he did not found a new establishment, was a benefactor of Dunstable priory, added a chantry chapel to his parish church at Chalgrave where he is buried, and is commemorated in the book of benefactors of St Albans abbey for his gift towards the building of the cloister there. The miniature of him in the abbey's book of benefactors, painted about 1380, is the earliest representation of a Garter companion, and shows him in a white robe powdered with blue garters.[88]

At Warwick, Thomas Beauchamp began the rebuilding of St Mary's, the largest parish church of the town, which was still incomplete when he was buried there in 1369. Reginald Cobham was buried in the parish church at Lingfield in 1361, but after his death the church was rebuilt and enlarged, and the college there was only founded in the fifteenth century. Other Garter companions were simply buried in churches which were already family mausoleums, and which did not undergo any rebuilding in honour of their distinguished occupants: this is true of William Montagu, second earl of Salisbury, at Montacute priory at Bisham, of William Bohun, earl of Northampton, at Walden priory in Essex, and of Roger Mortimer, earl of March, at Wigmore priory.

FUNERALS

Funerals were great ceremonial occasions and in most cases remained so for the nobility, despite the preaching of the reformist Lollards against such worldly pomp and show in the setting of a church service. The prince of Wales specified very precisely in his will in 1376 what the procession and its heraldry should be:

> And we wish that at the hour when our corpse is taken through the town of Canterbury to the priory that two warhorses covered in our arms, and two men armed in our arms and helms go in front of our corpse, that is to say, one equipped for war with our whole arms quartered, and the other equipped for peace with our badges of ostrich feathers with four banners of the same, and that each of those who carry the said banners shall have on his head a hat with our arms. And the man who is armed for war shall have an armed man carrying near him a black pennon with ostrich feathers. And the hearse shall be built between the high altar and the choir, on which we wish our corpse to be placed while the vigils, masses and divine services are performed; and when those services are performed, our corpse shall be carried to the chapel of Our Lady and buried there.[89]

He also gave very precise instructions for the design and imagery of his tomb, and the epitaph to be used on it, which was a traditional text contrasting the glory of this world and the state to which his body was reduced.

The prince's instructions were largely carried out, though his tomb is in fact near the chapel of the Trinity rather than in the Lady Chapel. Walter Mauny told his executors to bury him in a style befitting his rank, without 'worldly show, and without too much expense, but in a reasonable style, according to current fashion'. The tomb was to be in the middle of the choir of the Charterhouse he had founded at Smith-field, and was to be of alabaster, with 'a knightly effigy with my arms, like that made for John Beauchamp at St Paul's in London, in remem-brance of me and so that men may pray for me'.[90] Froissart claims that the burial was attended by the king, prelates and nobles, but there is no supporting evidence: he is (not for the first time) describing what he thinks should have happened.[91]

The only other funeral of an early Garter companion of which we have any record is that of James Audley at Poitiers in 1369: Froissart, who was in Brabant at the time, can tell us only that the prince of Wales attended in person.[92]

MONUMENTS

Most of the tomb effigies of the first Garter companions did not survive the ravages of the Reformation. The earliest surviving effigy, that of Wil-liam Fitzwarin at Wantage, is much damaged; the Garter can be seen as a raised band on his leg, but no details or painting remain. In many cases, there may not have been an effigy, particularly where there were no surviving family members; in other cases, the memorial may have been a brass. None of the brasses survive, but we do have a drawing of that of Miles Stapleton. Surprisingly, there is no sign of the Garter, per-haps because it had worn away; but the drawing appears to have been done from a brass in good condition. Alternatively, the absence of the Garter may be because the brass was a relatively standard one, bought from a workshop in London.

The three great monuments relating to the Garter which do survive largely intact are the tomb of Reginald Cobham at Lingfield, a chest tomb with a series of shields around the base, the effigy of Thomas Beauchamp at Warwick, and the brass of Hugh Hastings at Elsing in Norfolk: although Hastings was not a companion of the Garter, it includes images of several members of the company.

And it is from tombs that we get our shadowy glimpse of the physical appearance of the members of the company. On two occasions, the tombs of Garter companions have been excavated. Walter Mauny's rest-ing place was found before the high altar during an exploration of the remains of his Charterhouse in 1947, following its destruction in an air raid in 1941. His coffin was opened, and revealed the remains of a man a little over 5 feet 7 inches tall, with most of his hair and a full beard but lacking most of his teeth. He was strongly built with a large round head and broad face, and appears to have been fit, with little signs of disease or arthritis. It seems that a papal bull had been hung round his neck; the ribbon and lead seal survived, and it may have been the licence granted to him by Clement VI in 1351 to choose a confessor who would give him full remission of sins at the hour of death.[93]

Bartholomew Burghersh the younger's tomb at Walsingham was found in 1961, during an excavation of the chapel of the Holy House.[94] This had held the replica of the house in which the Annunciation had taken place, built in the eleventh century by Richeldis, after a vision of the Virgin Mary had appeared to her. Burghersh was buried in front of the high altar, with the image of the Virgin, as he had specified. He was around fifty when he died, and his skeleton showed him to have been a little under six feet tall, with a strong physique, and only slight evidence of wounds given his long career in the field: a damaged ankle and broken ribs. His face was narrow, with the eyes set high; he had a full set of teeth, though much worn by the coarse medieval diet.

PART THREE

The World of the Garter Companions

10
Knightly Associations: Orders, Companies, Fraternities

The idea of an 'order' of knighthood springs from two sources. The first is in a religious context, of knighthood as one of the three 'orders' of society: those who pray, those who labour and those who fight to defend the other two. This was the rationalization of society made and preached by the Church, a background to the way knighthood was seen rather than a direct inspiration for the actual orders. The Church had a second and more precise meaning for 'order', a group of men living under a common rule, as in the orders of monks which evolved within Christian society from the third century onwards, and of which the most influential model was that of the Benedictines, whose rule dates from the first half of the sixth century. From this monastic ideal evolved the idea of an order as that of a select group of knights living according to a common rule which became the 'military orders' of the Church, the monastic knightly orders of the twelfth century designed as a bulwark against the heathen, both defending Christendom and its holy places and aggressively expanding its boundaries by conquest.

The idea of such orders was a direct result of the crusades: the original orders were groups of knights who vowed to protect and care for pilgrims to Jerusalem, and who lived according to a religious rule; they were in effect the 'monks of war'. From their humble beginnings, these military and religious orders grew immensely wealthy, as the kings and nobility of western Europe gave them lands to provide them with the income they needed for their work. This gradually extended from the protection of pilgrims to cover the defence of the kingdom of Jerusalem and the other western principalities in the near east. By the end of the thirteenth century the orders were huge and complex international organizations. The Knights Templar and the Knights Hospitaller remained in Palestine, while the Teutonic Knights had transferred their attentions to the pagans on the eastern borders of the Holy Roman Empire. But the Templars and Hospitallers had failed in their objective of maintaining a Christian presence in the east, when the last crusader stronghold fell to the Arabs in 1291.

If the war in the Holy Land had ended in defeat for the two great orders, the struggle against the infidel continued elsewhere. In Prussia, the Teutonic Knights were lords of a secular state of their own, a situation which had never arisen in the Holy Land. However, by the mid-fourteenth century the Hospitallers were in a similar position as rulers of the island of Rhodes. The Templars had been the scapegoats for the loss of Palestine, and had been disbanded on trumped-up charges in 1311; those of their leaders who protested their innocence were burnt at the stake. The two surviving orders were therefore both political and territorial powers, and the monastic and religious element had sharply diminished.

Both Templars and Hospitallers had played a major part in the *reconquista*, the wars which attempted to destroy the power of the Muslim kingdoms which had been established in the south of Spain since the eighth century. From this base, the Muslims had nearly succeeded in overrunning the peninsula by the mid-tenth century. There had been no international crusades in Spain after the eleventh century, and the religious zeal to be found in Palestine was muddied in Spain by the shifting allegiances of local lords, as well as a considerable degree of religious tolerance on both sides. But there was a proliferation of knightly orders in the Spanish peninsula. The Order of Santiago, founded about 1170, is particularly interesting, as it arose out of a peculiarly Spanish phenomenon, the *hermandad* or confraternity of knights. These were at first informal associations in which knights would come together to choose a leader and fight against the Muslims. The knights of Santiago were not technically a religious order; their members could marry, and their role was that of a secular religious fraternity whose purpose was the defence of the kingdom as well as the crusade against the Muslim princes of southern Spain. By the early thirteenth century the Order of Santiago had an established constitution and an elected master, and it was envisaged as a permanent foundation. The members of the order fought alongside the king's troops, and it quickly became a vital element in the royal armies. By 1254 the king expected to have a say in elections;

five years later the order's statutes were amended to insist on noble birth for anyone wishing to become a knight, and its secular aspect became more prominent. When the order was in crisis after most of its knights had been killed in a disastrous battle near Granada in 1280, Alfonso X of Castile merged Santiago with another order which he had recently helped to establish, but retained the name of the senior order.

The disappearance of the Templars left a gap in the defences of Spain. In 1307, Philip the Fair of France seized the goods of the Order of Knights Templar in his kingdom, and persuaded the pope to suppress the order on charges of heresy. Their real fault was the acquisition of a political and financial power in the west which went hand in hand with the decline of the crusading presence in the east. They had become bankers on a large scale, originally in order to transfer money from western Europe to the Holy Land, as well as diplomats and administrators, often carrying out royal commissions. The complex story of the trial of the Templars is outside our present subject; but much of the property belonging to the Templars passed, at least temporarily, into the control of the kings and princes of Europe. Some of it ended up in royal treasuries; much of it went to the Hospitallers.

However, in Portugal and Aragon, the kings were anxious to maintain the armed support which the Templars had supplied. So, instead of simply letting the Hospitallers take over, as happened elsewhere in Europe, they set about establishing replacement orders on the lines of the Order of Santiago. The first of these was the Order of Christ in Portugal, set up in 1317 by King Dinis, and approved by the pope; similarly, in Aragon, King Robert set up the Order of Montesa two years later, and papal bulls were issued in March 1320. The exact power wielded by the kings over the two orders is not defined in their statutes, but there is clear evidence in their subsequent history that, like the Castilian orders, they were a hybrid of religious and secular orders of knighthood, with a large element of royal influence that had been totally lacking in the days of the Templars. Furthermore, these were no longer international orders, but had a specifically national base. However, Alfonso XI of Castile was slower off the mark, and, after long negotiations over the fate of the Templar lands and castles, he asked for the establishment of a new order in 1331 to take over these estates, only to be told that it was too late to do this, as the pope had given the lands to the Hospitallers.[1]

*

Five years earlier, in 1326, the Hungarian king, Károly I, founded an entirely new type of institution to which he gave the title of 'fraternal society': its full title was 'The Fraternal Society of St George',[2] echoing the Latin title used for the Knights Templar, 'brothers of the knighthood of the Temple'. St George was widely regarded as patron of knighthood by this time, and, although there was to be a strong knightly element in the statutes, the preamble to the charter of 1326[3] establishing the society defines its purpose in terms which imply that it is a direct descendant of the military religious orders:

> since the kingdom touches everywhere on the borders of the infidels and pagans, and therefore the government of the kingdom is entirely given over lest the pagans have the upper hand; and the lord of the same kingdom shall benefit from such a friendly society by which his life and body shall be made safe and the kingdom shall be defended from the infidel.[4]

The one problem with this statement is that the reality of Hungarian politics was rather different. Károly's energies were directed not against Hungary's external enemies, but against the independent-minded oligarchs within his kingdom. Károly came from the Angevin royal house of Naples, who had wide estates in both southern Italy and Provence, and therefore had a Franco-Italian background. His claim to the throne, through his grandmother, was only recognized by a small minority of the nobles, and, when he appeared with a handful of knights at Esztergom early in 1301, it was only the support of the pope and of the archbishop-elect of Esztergom that led to his coronation. Almost immediately he was forced to surrender the throne to a rival claimant, the king of Bohemia, and it was not until 1309 that Károly was able to win back the throne, if not the kingdom. He was now in a position to start to enforce royal authority, demanding the return of lands usurped from the crown, and forbidding the oligarchs to conscript the local nobles into their service. This met with fierce resistance, and only after a series of victories over the various rebellious oligarchs, particularly in the long-drawn-out war against Matthew Csák, which ended in 1321, was he in effective control of his lands. His ultimate victory was as much due to the failure of the oligarchs to unite in resistance to the king as to outside support. It is at this point, when the court was moved from Timişoara on the western border of the kingdom to Visegrád near Buda, in the centre of his lands, and the internal battles seemed to be at an end, that the Fraternal Society of St George was established to emphasize his sovereignty, a point also made by the new gold coinage issued in 1325.

Károly's strategy was to ensure that the representatives of the old families were given posts which removed them from the centre of power, and to bring forward a new aristocracy drawn from the next tier down in the feudal hierarchy, the lords who had been subject to the princes. By 1333 only one of the numerous counts, who had previously been barons and members of the royal council, was still entitled to a place on the council. Károly also created a royal household on the model of the French court, and we find knights of the household from 1324 onwards.[5] Károly also reorganized the royal domain, using the castles which had been usurped from the crown by the princes and were now once more under royal control. They became administrative centres, controlling the lands of the royal domain, collecting taxes and meting out royal justice. The counts were deprived of their automatic right to carry a banner, in other words to command a retinue similar to that of a banneret in the English army; instead, the bannerets were appointed by the king. Under the previous regime, the oligarchs had maintained troops in each of their castles as part of their power base, and these also disappeared, to be replaced by a more general royal levy.[6] These made up the royal army in a way very similar to that of the armies of Edward III. By the end of his reign, royal power in Hungary was firmly established thanks to measures of this sort, and the princes or 'true barons of the kingdom' no longer challenged the king's authority.

It was to these new bannerets that the Fraternal Society of St George was addressed. Károly's institution was designed to strengthen the ties of these new men to the king's person. Although on a strict interpretation the king had no direct authority over the society, it is clear that he was the driving force behind it. He harnessed the ideals of knighthood to a political end, just as the military orders had harnessed religious ideals for the same purpose, but it is interesting that he felt the need to appeal to the old crusading concepts to justify his creation of the society. This is particularly striking because the content of the rest of the statutes labels the society as a firmly knightly institution but with distinctive features which are not found in any similar organization. These look like the work of Károly I himself, a practical and far-sighted ruler, in touch – like his contemporary John of Bohemia – with the ideas current among the nobility of western Europe. In the early 1320s, John was attempting to arouse enthusiasm for tournaments among the knights of Prague; when he met with little success, he went off to France to fight in tournaments there. John's exploits were highly personal, but they are evidence of the strong cultural influence of French knighthood in central Europe at this period. Coats of arms and crests were granted by the king for the first time in 1324. Károly's upbringing would have been that of a French prince, and he was hoping that the new lords whom he was installing in positions of power would take their cue from him.

This is the context in which the Fraternal Society of St George was founded. We know nothing of it apart from the charter of 1326, which repeats the text of the foundation charter and adds an amendment. From this we can get a clear idea of what was proposed, but we have little idea how it worked in practice. The constitution is striking: the members were limited to fifty, and the society was under the control of two judges, one lay and one clerical, elected by the members themselves. The original members must have been nominated, presumably by the king; anyone could offer himself for membership, subject to election, again by the existing members. If this is a hint of the egalitarian streak found elsewhere in knightly culture – the round table at which all are seated equally or the custom of kings and heroes fighting incognito – this is counterbalanced by the stated purpose of the society, to protect the king's person.

The political purpose of the society is reflected in the extraordinary status which the members enjoyed. They could be tried only by the two judges of the society, and were exempt from normal jurisdiction; and they could request the judges to intervene in cases in the ordinary courts in which they were involved. No subsequent order of knighthood contained such sweeping privileges for its members; but in return there were sweeping, though often vague, obligations. There is a wide duty to protect the king and his interests, including the requirement that knights should report any rumours hostile to the king. When the knights are at court, they are to meet monthly, and to dine together each Monday, so that they form a distinct and close-knit group; they are also to take part in the three general assemblies each year. There are detailed provisions about relations between the members, but these are not very different from those found in other lay confraternities of this period. Once a month at their weekly assembly, if the judge requires it, the knights are to discuss the welfare of the king and the kingdom and practical matters concerning them. This makes them a kind of royal council, rather larger than a privy council, and similar to the 'continual council' of the kings of England in the fourteenth century.[7] If all the prescribed meetings were held, they amounted to fifty-five days a year, a demanding schedule.[8]

The knights were required to follow the king in all his knightly pursuits and tournaments, and there was a strong social element to the fraternity. Károly himself was evidently an enthusiastic tourneyer, since in his funeral procession three knights carried his armour, one his decorated tournament armour, the second his armour for jousting and the third his armour for war.[9] The first known tournament in Hungary had been held in 1319: the king knocked out three of a knight's teeth, and granted him three villages by way of compensation. Furthermore, he decreed that knights in royal service should have heraldic arms, because in the royal service, 'namely in the army, in tournaments and other military processes and expeditions', they needed to be distinguished from one another; the first grant dates from 1324.[10] When the friar Walter atte More was sent on an embassy to Hungary by Edward III in 1346, his account for expenses submitted on his return included a payment of 3s. 9d. for 'painting the shields of the Hungarians', presumably as a manuscript roll recording their arms, information which was not known to those expert in heraldry in the west.[11] The knights of the fraternity themselves had a uniform, a black hooded mantle embroidered on the back with the words 'In truth I am a rightful member of this society'. No later secular order had a habit of this kind; we shall see that they all relied on a device or badge instead, and this too marks a transitional stage between the military religious orders and their new secular successors.

We know nothing of the Fraternal Society of St George after the issue of the charter and amendments in April 1326. It may well have been no more than a project which failed to prosper, and there is no evidence, therefore, that it was active in 1346 when Walter atte More went to Hungary, but there would certainly have been members of the court who remembered the attempt to create it. Given More's apparent interest in Hungarian heraldry, it is tempting to conjecture that he carried some information about the society back to Edward III. But apart from the dedication to St George, the restricted number of knights and the obligations of confraternity in both orders, the Fraternal Society of St George has very little in common with the 'Company' or Order of St George founded by Edward III shortly after More's return.

THE ORDER OF ST CATHERINE

At some time in the 1330s, statutes for an Order of St Catherine were drawn up in the principality of Viennois (today called the Dauphiné) in south-east France, whose ruler was Humbert II.[12] The statutes are a very curious document. The preamble states that in the present troubled times, 'new counsel' is needed, particularly in view of the wars, dissensions and other similar pestilences which might disrupt the good faith and affection between the dauphin and 'the good people of his country'. The purpose is to create an order, which is to be named 'of St Catherine', to guard the honour and estate of the dauphin, his people and his country. The lords responsible for the document – whose names are evidently missing – protest that if anything is written in the ordinances which displeases the dauphin, they will amend them as he desires.

This is therefore – at least in theory – a voluntary association of nobles in support of their ruler, though this may simply be a fiction. The preamble is followed by a fairly simple set of rules. The badge of the order is to be an image of St Catherine in red, holding a white sword in her right hand and in the left hand a motto 'To be more worthy', on an azure ground: each knight is to have such a shield made as soon as possible. The knights are to meet once a year (unless sick or more than three days' journey away) on the eve of the feast of St Catherine (25 November) at La Côte St André between Vienne and Grenoble, the meeting-place of the estates of Vienne, where a chapel in honour of St Catherine is to be founded. The lord of Anjou and Guillaume Alamans are to be captains of the order, with two captains from each of the three 'marches' of the principality. These captains are to deal with any 'riots, dissensions or disagreements' between companions of the order and are empowered to expel them if they are disobedient; they can also summon them to assemble for the good of the dauphin, the order and the country. Companions are always to have their arms and armour in readiness for the dauphin's service. They are to do their best to dispel or counter any rumours to the detriment of the dauphin or the order, and are to help the clergy, widows and orphans if so requested. Only one provision relates to tournaments: if at a joust one of the companions is without a horse, the others must lend him one, and are not entitled to refuse the request.

On the evidence of this document, the Order of St Catherine was similar to the confraternities of knights which came together to fight on the Spanish frontier, in that it appears to have been a spontaneous creation among the nobles, troubled by the prospect of civil strife. Humbert was an unsatisfactory ruler, more interested in the idea of a renewed crusade in the east than in the good government of his domains, and after 1335 he was actively trying to sell his principality, first to the pope, and then successfully in 1349 to Philip VI of France. The only hint that the order might have had something to do with him is the dedication to St Catherine, who was associated with the monastery of Sinai, and hence appropriate for a would-be crusader. On the other hand, given that Humbert was related to Károly I of Hungary, the parallels with the Fraternal Society of St George, also charged with supporting the sovereign and with a network of members across the country, may be more relevant. Whether the order ever came into existence is not known, but it is valuable evidence of the way in which princes and nobles regarded such institutions. Here we have a knightly brotherhood, with some religious commitments, but also with obvious political reasons for its existence.

What these shadowy 'orders', 'societies' and 'fraternities' tell us is that the idea of a group of knights coming together for secular or religious purposes was something that was very much in the air in the decades after the sudden decline in prestige of the great military orders after the loss of Palestine. Groups like this do not appear to have existed in the thirteenth century, and this is a real change in knightly attitudes. In France and England, the greatest centres of knightly culture of the mid-fourteenth century, no fewer than five proposed or actual groups emerged between 1344 and 1352, in a more fully developed form than any of those which we have already described. These were Edward's proposed Order of the Round Table of January 1344, the Congregation of the Virgin and St George of John duke of Normandy (later John II) later the same year, Edward's Company of the Garter in 1348–9, John

II's Company of Knights of Our Lady or of the Noble House, or Company of the Star, in 1351, and Louis of Taranto's Company of the Holy Spirit in Naples also in 1352.

Edward's proposed Round Table, the nebulous nature of which we have already explored, survives as little more than a curiosity, with the remains of a building destroyed soon after it was created as the only tangible evidence of its existence, and with only the vaguest indications of what was in Edward's mind in the accounts of very well-informed chroniclers. For the second of these orders, we have a full-scale written proposal.

THE CONGREGATION OF THE VIRGIN AND ST GEORGE

At some time in 1344, John duke of Normandy, heir to the French throne, applied to Pope Clement VI for letters granting religious privileges to the order which he was proposing to found. Károly I's fraternal society had had the approval of the Hungarian bishops, but this was the first occasion that full ecclesiastical authority for the creation of an order to be headed by a prince or monarch had been sought. The scheme for which John sought and obtained approval was centred on the foundation of a new church in honour of the Trinity and the Virgin Mary, in the names of the Virgin and of St George. The pope's letters tell us that it was to be a collegiate church of twelve secular canons and twelve resident priests, and it fitted broadly into the pattern of 'saintes-chapelles' founded by members of the French royal family. John's father, Philip VI, had founded a chapel of this kind near Le Mans in 1329,[13] and the clergy of John's chapel were to celebrate their offices 'according to the manner that has been and is used in the royal palace chapel',[14] the Sainte-Chapelle in Paris, making the link between the two quite explicit: the act of foundation of the 'sainte-chapelle' at Bourges in 1405 specifies that the offices shall be celebrated 'in the manner and style that one does so in the chapel of the lord king in his royal palace in Paris'.[15] The distinctive feature of the scheme for the new company, however, is the presence of a

communion or congregation of two hundred knights, and these knights shall gather in person each year on the feast of the Assumption of the Blessed Virgin Mary [in August] and the feast of the Blessed George the

Martyr in the month of April, not for jousts or tournaments or any deeds of arms, but solely out of devotion to the said church, including both those usually absent as well as those of them who through pious and charitable arrangements and right intent shall reside there through the goodwill and desire of the said duke of Normandy.[16]

The knights of this 'Congregation of the Virgin and St George' were granted ecclesiastical privileges in the papal letters relating to confession and absolution. John's intention seems to have been to found a specifically religious confraternity of knights attached to his new college, but beyond that we cannot say what particular circumstances may have given rise to the project. The other qualifications for a 'sainte-chapelle' were physical: it had to be a palace or castle chapel, its architecture had to be modelled on that of the Paris building and it had to contain relics of the Passion. The scheme never went beyond the stage of papal approval to actual planning and construction, and there is therefore no evidence on these points. Indeed, John's proposals could simply have been intended to provide similar lay support for a 'sainte-chapelle'.

The reasons for the suspension of activity after the papal letters of 1344 are not far to seek: from mid-1344 onwards, the renewal of warfare between England and France was imminent, even though the truce negotiated at Malestroit between the two kingdoms was due to run until 1346. By the autumn of 1344 it was increasingly evident that Edward intended to repudiate the truce, and he did so in February 1345. The Crécy campaign and its disastrous consequences for Normandy and France as a whole were followed by the Black Death, and the projected foundation faded into oblivion. There are no traces of it in French chronicles or records.

THE COMPANY OR SOCIETY OF KNIGHTS OF OUR LADY OF THE NOBLE HOUSE OF ST OUEN

Historians have tended to treat the 'Congregation of the Virgin and St George' of 1344 as the same institution as the knightly company which John II founded soon after he came to the throne in 1350. The distinction is that the congregation was designed by its founder as a religious institution, whereas the new company was definitely secular.

It seems that John II never abandoned the idea of some kind of knightly fraternity. He succeeded his father in 1350, and in 1351–2 he put new plans into effect. The document which tells us most about his thinking is a charter of 1352 in favour of the newly founded 'Noble House' and collegiate chapel at the royal manor of St Ouen, outside Paris. It is a splendid piece of rhetoric, but beneath the flowery prose is an acute perception of the realities of power: a well-motivated knightly class is essential to the peace and power of the kingdom. In the background looms the French defeat at Crécy, a defeat which John saw as humiliating, partly because his father had fled from the battlefield. He also concurred in the wave of criticism launched against the French nobles for their pride, ineffectiveness in battle and quarrelling between themselves. The prologue to the charter was probably written by a royal clerk, but we can probably detect in it the king's own concept of the place of knighthood in the state. It starts from the premise that the ancient high ideals of knighthood in France, which had assured the kingdom's peace and security, are in sharp decline, and by appealing to those 'faithful knights' who remain and bringing them into a 'perfect union', the desperate state of the kingdom may be redeemed.[17]

The company is to be in honour of the Virgin alone, instead of the Virgin and St George in the scheme of 1344. The change may be an indication that St George was now becoming the accepted patron saint of England. It is to be called 'the Company or Society of Knights of Our Lady of the Noble House of St Ouen' and there is to be an associated college of canons to celebrate the divine offices. The king hopes that, through the intercession of the Virgin, Christ will so inspire the knights that they, 'starved of honour and glory, will henceforth bear themselves with such concord and valour that the flower of knighthood, which for the reasons we have already described has, so to speak, wilted in the shade, will flourish under our sceptre and shine again in perfect harmony to the honour and glory of our kingdom and our faithful subjects'. This is a clear reference to John's continuing dismay over the behaviour of the French nobles at Crécy and in its aftermath. The charter itself is concerned with the financing of the new college of canons, and tells us nothing more about the company as a whole.

In November of the previous year, he had sent out letters to the knights whom he had chosen as the founder members. The only surviving copy of these letters is addressed to his 'beau cousin', a term which could apply to a large number of kinsmen of the royal house, and gives an out-line of the rules of the new institution. The king explains that 'in honour of God and Our Lady, and to encourage chivalry and increase honour, we have ordained that a company of knights shall be made who will be called the Knights of Our Lady or of the Noble House.'[18] This letter is to inform the addressee of his election to the company, and to summon him to its first gathering. The badge of the company is to be a white star with a blue circle in the middle, in which was a golden sun: Jean le Bel called it 'the Company of the Star', and this is its usual but incorrect title. The knights are to swear to give 'loyal counsel' to the king in mat-ters of arms and other affairs, and are obliged to resign from any other company. If they cannot honourably do this, the present company is to take precedence. If any knight leaves the battlefield or otherwise disobeys orders, he is to be suspended from the company. They are to attend the annual festival on 15 August, the Assumption of the Blessed Virgin, if they reasonably can, and are to celebrate it wherever they might be.

John II's view of the company as founded on knighthood rather than religious devotion or fraternity emerges in the subsequent paragraphs:

> It is ordained that in the Noble House there shall be a table named the table of honour, at which there shall be seated on the eve and on the day of the first feast the three most excellent princes, the three most excellent bannerets and the three most excellent knights bachelor present at the feast who are to be received into the said company; and on each eve and festival of mid-August each year following there shall be seated at the said table of honour the three princes, three bannerets and the three knights bachelor who during the year shall have done the most in deeds of war, because deeds of peace shall not be counted for this.
>
> And it is also ordained that everyone shall bring his arms and his badge painted on a sheet of paper or parchment so that the painters may put them promptly and correctly in the place where they belong in the Noble House.

The knights are to be 500 in number, and the king, as 'inventor and founder' of the company, is to be its prince, as are his successors. We learn a little more of the details of the statutes from Jean le Bel, who has his own ideas about the name and origins of the order:

In the year of grace 1352* King John of France founded a splendid company, great and noble, modelled upon the Round Table that existed of old
in the days of King Arthur. It was to be a company of three hundred of
the outstanding knights in the kingdom of France and was to be called
the Company of the Star; each knight was to wear at all times a star of
gold or gilded silver or pearls as a badge of membership. And the king
promised to build a great and handsome house near Saint Denis, where
all the companions and brothers who were in the land and had no reasonable impediment would meet at all the most solemn festivals of the year;
it was to be called the Noble House of the Star. At least once a year the
king would hold a plenary court which all the companions would attend,
and where each would recount all the adventures – the shameful as well
as the glorious – that had befallen him since he'd last been at the noble
court; and the king would appoint two or three clerks who would listen
to these adventures and record them all in a book, so that they could
annually be brought before the companions to decide which had been
most worthy, that the most deserving might be honoured. None could
enter this company without the consent of the king and the majority of
the companions present, and unless he was worthy and free of reproach.

Moreover, they had to vow never knowingly to retreat more than three
hundred yards[20] from a battle: they would either fight to the death or
yield as prisoners. They vowed also to help and support each other in all
combats, and there were a number of other statutes and ordinances to
which they all swore, too. The Noble House was almost built; the idea
was that when a knight became too old to travel the land, he would make
his home there at the house, with two servants, for the rest of his days if
he wished, so that the company would be better maintained.[19]

The Round Table may be the inspiration for the Noble House, but the
parallel is not that close; any description of a knightly event in the fourteenth century tends to invoke Arthur's name as a kind of benchmark. The
idea of a book in which the knights' deeds should be recorded is an obvious
echo of Arthur's command at the end of the romance of the Holy Grail:

> the king made great clerks to come before him, for cause that they should
> chronicle of the high adventures of the good knights. So when Sir Bors
> had told him of the high adventures of the Holy Grail such as had befallen

* In fact, November 1351.

him and his three fellows, which were Sir Lancelot, Perceval and Sir Gala-
had and himself, then Sir Lancelot told the adventures of the Holy Grail
that he had seen. And all this was made in great books which were stored
in cupboards at Salisbury.[21]

Likewise, Alfonso the Wise had recommended in his laws that 'the
ancients' had established the custom that 'narratives of great deeds of
arms performed by others should be read to knights while they ate, as
well as accounts of their wisdom and power by means of which they
were able to conquer, and accomplish what they wished . . .'[22] Knightly
ideals were something to be recorded in books and debated among
knights, a sentiment which Froissart and López de Ayala would reiter-
ate when they came to write their chronicles later in the century.

Like the Company of the Garter, the Company of the Star had nothing to do with secular activities such as tournaments. The royal letters
notifying knights of their election have no mention of jousting; the
badge of the company is to be worn on secular clothing or on war
armour only.[23]

The first assembly and feast of the Company of the Noble House was
held on 6 January 1352, and we can glimpse some of its splendours
from the royal accounts.[24] Edward might put up a good display of
wealth in his great festivals, but the wealth of the French court made it
hard to compete with them. Thousands of ermine furs were used for the
knights' clothing; three great embroidered stars for the king's chamber
had to be made 'in great haste, working night and day', by his armourer
Nicolas Vaquier; red sendal and velvet and silver damask were provided
for the king's use. Haste and confusion appear elsewhere in the records:
cloths of azure sendal scattered with gold stars were put aside unused,
in favour of cloth of gold and silver. The king's throne was set up on a
dais surrounded by clouds made of cloth of silver, each containing a
star. There was an exceptional display of jewellery, much of it sewn onto
clothing or worked into the stars. The dauphin's armourer produced a
tapestry of the oceans, in which there were people like angels, 'made of
Cyprus gold'.[25]

The Company of the Star evidently included the majority of the great
nobles of the realm. We have no official lists of the members, but the
accounts name twenty of them. The largest single group is that of the
younger members of the royal family. All four of John II's sons were

included, from the future Charles V, aged fifteen, to the youngest, aged nine, who was to become known as Philip the Bold, duke of Burgundy; and the king's younger brother and four of the king's cousins were also named. Knighthood was conferred on five of them on this occasion, the other four presumably already being knights. The core of the company was therefore the royal family itself, and it was seen as the forum for their knightly upbringing. This is in line with the tone of John's preface to the charter, in which he looks forward to the future of knighthood in France: how many of the knights and lords who had so signally failed to defend the kingdom at Sluys and Crécy were given the badge of the star, we cannot tell, but among the remaining names the great majority are the household officers of the king and of the dauphin Charles, reinforcing the idea that this is a tightly knit group centred on the royal family. There are three outsiders, all notable in their own way. Humbert II of Vienne, who had sold the Dauphiné to the French crown in 1349, was obsessed by the idea of reviving the crusades, and, after an abortive attempt in the 1330s, had been appointed leader of a papal fleet directed against a Turkish prince in 1345. He had left the expedition before it achieved anything, and, when he had sold his principality, he took holy orders and became patriarch of Alexandria.[26] Despite this he returned to France and appeared at the knightly gathering at St Ouen as a knight and seems to have been admitted to the company. One foreigner was present, a knight from Naples named Giacomo Bozzuto, whose grave in the cathedral at Naples records that he 'was of the Company of the Star of the illustrious lord John king of France' and was also a councillor of the king of Naples. And finally, although he is not noted as being given the insignia of the company, the name of Geoffroy de Charny, famous for his prowess and his expertise in knighthood, appears in the records. As he was certainly a member of the company very soon afterwards, he is likely to have been one of the founders.

The splendid inauguration of the Company of the Noble House might have led to great things, if it had not been for the continuing misfortune of the French armies and of the French royal family. Jean le Bel records the disaster which almost immediately befell a large number of the lesser, anonymous members of the company at the battle of Mauron:

But in the year 1353* a large English force of men-at-arms came to Brittany to aid and support the valiant Countess of Montfort and to lay waste the region that had sided with lord Charles of Blois. As soon as the King of France heard the news he sent a great body of men-at-arms to oppose them, including knights from the Company of the Star. But the English, on learning of their approach, sprang such a brilliant trap[27] that all those French who rushed to engage too soon and too recklessly were routed and slaughtered. No fewer than eighty-nine knights of the Star were killed there, and all because of their vow about not retreating: had it not been for that vow, they would have been perfectly able to withdraw. Many others died, too, on their account: men they might well have saved had it not been for this vow of theirs and their fear of reproach by the company.

This noble order was never spoken of again, and I think it has come to nothing and their house has been left empty. So I'll leave this now and tell of another matter.[28]

Le Bel was writing in 1358, and he was correct in saying that the Company of the Noble House was effectively extinct by then. There is no trace of any meeting after the initial festivities, although John kept the project alive, and continued to give grants to the college until his capture at Poitiers in 1356. Thereafter the problem of raising the huge ransom demanded by the English precluded any further expenditure on the company. The star briefly became a royal badge in the reign of Charles V, but then disappeared altogether.

However, the legacy of the company, shortlived as it was, was not insignificant. It served as the model for the Company of the Holy Spirit in the kingdom of Naples, founded by Louis of Taranto and which first met in May 1352.[29] The statutes are more elaborate and less practical, and read like excerpts from a romance. Here the table of honour is reserved for those who have fought in a full-scale battle, and were therefore entitled to wear their knots untied. There was also a table of disgrace, for knights who had left a battle or were otherwise in dereliction of their military duty. Like the Company of the Noble House, the Company of the Holy Spirit did not survive for long: it was too

---

* In fact, August 1352.

elaborate and overlaid with romantic ideas to be taken very seriously, and Louis of Taranto himself was characterized by his contemporaries as a 'lord of little weight and even less authority ... He took little trouble about feats of arms ... He was eager to make money, administered justice softly, and made himself little feared by his barons.'[30] The order was almost certainly devised by his chief councillor and *éminence grise*, the Florentine Niccolò Acciaioli, as a somewhat desperate attempt to create a body of knights loyal to his rather dubious master and to bring an end to the civil war within the kingdom. He overlaid a fairly severe list of commitments to the king's service with a scenario drawn from the Arthurian romances in an attempt to restore 'the tarnished glory of his master's kingdom, house and person ... by performing great deeds of honour and knighthood'. Such deeds were supposed to be written in a book to be kept by the company, and this does seem to have existed, because Giovanni Boccaccio, who could have seen it when he stayed with Acciaioli in Naples in 1362, mocked it in a letter to a friend, saying that Acciaioli had written it 'in the style in which certain others in the past wrote of the Round Table. What laughable and entirely false matters were set down, he himself knows.'[31]

The idea of a secular order of knighthood which emerged in the first half of the fourteenth century starts from the model of the military religious orders. The binding force in the great crusading orders was religion, and a belief in the spiritual righteousness of warfare against the heathen. Philip the Fair's opportunistic attack on the Templars in their moment of weakness did not destroy this ideal, but opened up the idea that such orders should be under royal rather than ecclesiastical control. The creation by the kings of Portugal and Aragon of new, smaller orders to continue the work of the Templars and take over their possessions was possible only because of the continuing wars against the Moorish kingdoms of southern Spain. Castile might well have followed suit, but Alfonso XI was too late to secure the lands of the Templars for the use of such an order. Instead, we have the first purely secular and monarchical order, the Order of the Sash, which has no religious element whatsoever. The Fraternal Society of St George in Hungary represents another approach, in a different context. Károly I paid lip-service to the idea that such an order has a function in the wars against the heathen, but seems, from the sparse documentation that survives, to have provided himself with a group of selected retainers bound by special ties to the crown. This body was entirely devoted to the service of the king, despite the invocation of the religious aspect of warfare in the prologue to the foundation charter, and the inclusion of religious duties as part of the order's statutes, together with a dedication to a patron saint.

THE ORDER OF THE SASH

We have already seen how Alfonso XI had applied to the pope to create a new religious order to replace the Templars and take over their lands. In the same year that he wrote to the pope, and, very probably knowing that the request would be declined, he established his own secular order. Compared with the Fraternal Society of St George, we know far more about the Order of the Sash,[32] which is the first secular order on record to be headed by a monarch. In the *Chronicle of Alfonso XI*, we are told that in 1330 the king established a uniform of white clothing with a dark sash that was 'as broad as a man's hand, and was worn over cloaks and other garments from the left shoulder to the waist' which he gave to selected knights and squires of his household. This was to encourage knightly deeds, and other knights could join the order by challenging those who wore the sash or performing suitable knightly exploits.[33]

Although the qualification for membership was thus relatively loosely defined, the group quickly developed into a formal order, whose statutes survive in a copy whose elaborate decoration implies that it was prepared for use by the order itself.[34] The preamble lays heavy stress on knighthood: '[the king] ordered this book to be made of the Order of the Sash, which is founded on two principles: chivalry and loyalty . . .' The most obvious difference between the Order of the Sash and the other fourteenth-century orders is that it has no spiritual element, and the only religious stipulation is that knights shall attend mass each day. Given Alfonso's rebuff from the pope over the foundation of a new order using the assets of the Templars – a new order which would have been largely religious – his purely secular society could be seen as a riposte. This secular approach also distinguished it from the Order of Santiago, which, as we have seen, was partially under royal control.

The statutes seem to aim at a distinctive *corps d'élite*, set apart both by their way of life as the most polished of courtiers and by their special oaths of loyalty, as well as their function as the royal bodyguard in war. Two things stand out: the knight of the Sash is obliged to be a vassal of the king or one of the king's sons for the rest of his life: if he should leave their service, he is to surrender the insignia. This implies that many of the knights would be retained for a fee rather than holding lands from the king, since the landholders could only switch allegiance if there were two claimants to the throne. The knight is also obliged to treat the other knights as brothers. In most fraternal orders, there is a clause of this kind, but here it is strongly worded.

The ritual for admission then follows: both knights and squires are eligible for admission, and that the procedures of admission to the order are unusual. All other orders require the candidates to be knights, whereas Alfonso envisages the possibility that squires might become members. There was a good reason for this, because, when the order was founded, Alfonso himself had not yet been knighted: his knighting and coronation took place later in 1332. As was the custom when one of the royal family was knighted, other squires were knighted with him. Of the 110 participants in this mass ceremony, a handful were already members of the order, so the provision about squires was not a special exception made for the king.

As to admission to the order, when we look at the names of those known to have been knights, it is clear that Alfonso controlled the appointments fairly closely. Lists of the early members of the order survive attached to the two versions of the statutes, and over half of these can be identified.[35] Of the thirty-six knights whose names are recorded, six were of the highest rank: two cousins of the king, two magnates and two of the foremost royal officers. Next came four of the men in charge of the households of the king's sons. About the remainder, we have no information; the Castilian records for this period are relatively sparse. But, on the basis of their surnames, only ten families are represented, so it is a tightly knit group which probably represents the major aristocratic dynasties of the period.

The clauses which follow are surprisingly detailed, obliging them to hear mass each morning, prescribing the arms and armour they should possess, forbidding them to boast, complain or gamble, and regulating their clothing and table manners. Some of these passages reflect a traditional view of knighthood set out by Alfonso's grandfather, Alfonso X, known as 'the Wise'. Alfonso X's *Las siete partidas* is one of the great law codes of western civilization, not merely a list of legal enactments but a veritable encyclopedia of the medieval way of life.[36] The behaviour of the knights is regulated by the statutes, and these sections are a much abbreviated version of the laws on knighthood in *Las siete partidas*. Alfonso the Wise writes at length, giving the history of the practices he prescribes; in the statutes, there is none of this elaborate background.

The real purpose of the Order of the Sash emerges in the statutes following those on weddings and funerals. The knights are to form a single squadron when the royal army is on campaign, and it is clear that the order was intended to be the elite corps. Throughout the statutes, there is an emphasis on excellence, whether of arms and armour or of skill in arms. The knights are to meet once a year at Whitsun,[37] for a tournament, and to hear *The Book of the Sash* read to them. The implication is that this book may contain the deeds of the knights as well as the statutes of the order, for rewards and punishments are to be meted out by the king accordingly. A mass is to be said in honour of St James, the patron of the Spanish armies in the war against the Muslims, and also patron saint of the release of the captives taken in warfare and in raids on Christian territory: each knight was to give enough alms to release seven captives.[38]

Tournaments are as much of a driving force behind the workings of the order as the role of the knights in the royal squadron in warfare. Knights of the Sash are required to attend any tournament within thirty miles of the place where they are staying, 'so that it shall seem that, wherever knightly deeds are performed, some knights of the Sash will always be there'. Refusal to go is a punishable offence: the offender is banned from wearing the sash for a month, and is required, dangerously, to run three courses with another knight of the order without having a lance himself.

Alfonso had particular reason to value loyalty to his person and peace among his knights. He had come to the throne before he was two, and a troubled regency of thirteen years had followed. Continual revolts and intrigues had seriously weakened the kingdom, and much territory was lost to the Moors. Though Alfonso's first campaigns in 1327 and 1330 regained some of this, his domestic troubles continued. He had one of the former regents assassinated in 1326, but another former regent was still rebellious in 1332, and became a vassal of the king of Aragon at about this time. So the Order of the Sash may have been an attempt to bind the nobles in personal loyalty to himself, improve the royal army for campaigns against the Moors and provide an alternative to the existing military orders.

The Order of the Sash, unlike the Fraternal Society of St George, survived and flourished for nearly forty years. At the battle of Nájera in 1367, Pero López de Ayala carried the 'banner of the Sash' in the vanguard of Henry's forces; 'and those on the side of King Pedro and the prince of Wales wore as their badge white shields and surcoats with red crosses, for St George; and all those on King Henry's side wore that day sashes on their surcoats'.[39] Here, however, it is not a question of the Order of the Sash, but of using the sash as one of the royal emblems. There are other examples where the badge of an order is displayed on battle standards and pennants, as the king's symbol, rather as the badge of the Garter was displayed on English pavises. Henry and his son are shown in a contemporary painting wearing the Sash in the approved fashion. Henry's son Juan II minted gold coins from 1406 onwards showing a plain shield with the sash, held at each end by lions' heads. It seems as if the order itself ceased to exist after the death of Pedro in 1369, and it was thereafter simply a royal badge or device.

The Order of the Sash was purely knightly and military. Its purpose was to provide a body of knights closely associated with the king, skilled in arms, who would fight with him in the continuing battles of the *reconquista*, and who would also play a political role as a group of vassals with a particular sworn loyalty to the king's person. If Alfonso knew of the existence of the Fraternal Society of St George, he may have taken these ideas from Károly I's creation. It is more likely that these concepts were more broadly current in European courts at the time, particularly in the context of the decline of the religious military orders, but Alfonso's solution is more extreme, in that it ignores all religious elements and the Order of the Sash is entirely secular.

With the exception of the Order of the Sash, the groups of knights formed or proposed up to 1350 are therefore not knightly orders in the later sense of the word. However, they have one central element, which is that they focus on the monarch as their leader, even when they are specifically religious in purpose, as with the Company of the Garter and the Company of the Noble House. The way forward was to be that foreshadowed by the Company of the Knot, where the honour of the individual knight was paramount; the fully fledged knightly orders of the fifteenth century were essentially honorific, and the only one of the early companies to survive into the next century did so by moving with the times. Membership of the Company of the Garter, originally based on fellowship and a common religious celebration, became an election in which the final choice lay with the monarch. Reputation was everything; one such victory as Crécy, however tremendous, could easily have been eclipsed by subsequent defeat. Instead, the companions of the Garter were to become famous for their remarkable series of successes on the battlefield.

II
Knights in their Own Words

The first manual on knighthood to be written by a knight – in this case, a former knight turned philosopher and missionary – is *The Book of the Order of Knighthood*, by Ramon Llull. Llull was one of the greatest intellectual figures of his age, born in Catalonia in the 1230s into a knightly family. His career was as a knight and courtier, until, in 1265, so he tells us himself, he was composing a song to a lady he loved when he had five visions of the crucified Christ. He went on pilgrimage to Santiago de Compostela, and then devoted himself to planning a great crusade to north Africa in imitation of that of St Louis, and to writing religious and philosophical treatises. He was deeply concerned about the conversion of the Arabs, whether by force or persuasion, and proposed that schools should be established where missionaries could learn Arabic so that they could preach more effectively. He taught at Paris and Montpellier universities, and led an extraordinarily active life. He wrote more than 250 works, and managed also to make a series of visits to north Africa to debate with Jewish and Muslim philosophers, and then to preach to the Muslims when he was in his late fifties. In the course of one of these journeys he was nearly stoned to death by his infuriated listeners.

Despite his formidable reputation as a philosopher, Llull was well aware of the requirements of his audience in *The Book of the Order of Knighthood*. He did not expect knights to settle down to read a dry treatise, and dressed his text up in the trappings of a romance, so that it is told by a knight who has retreated to a hermitage after a lifetime of activity: he 'had long sustained the order of knighthood and ... by his nobility and strength and high courage and wisdom, and by risking his life, had been through wars, jousts and tournaments, and had had many noble and glorious victories in battle'.[1] His teaching is addressed to a young squire who fell asleep while on his way to the king's court, and whose horse carried him to the hermit's door. On learning that he seeks to be knighted by the king, the hermit offers him a little book, which will tell him all he needs to know about knighthood – which is of course the book that Llull has written.

Llull is not concerned with the practice of knighthood, but with its place in a philosophical world-view. What follows is cast in the form of a reminder to knights that their true calling is the defence of society: he calls for them to 'return to the devotion, loyalty and obedience which they owe to their order'. This is typical of medieval thinking: the appeal is always to the authority of the past, and not to a new ideal. 'Order' in this case refers to knighthood in general as one of the three orders of society, and it is from this general concept that the idea of specific named 'orders of knighthood', whether religious or secular, comes. Llull sets his treatise firmly in this context: knights have a specific place in the hierarchy of society, below the authority of the prince and with authority over the people, and a specific task, to defend both society and the Church. Llull particularly emphasizes the defence of the people and the maintenance of justice; for this purpose, the knight must appear terrifying, his mere appearance a deterrent to evildoers. Bodily strength, boldness and armour are the outward signs of this, but these are no help unless the knight is inspired by the right motives, and has 'true courage':

> Seek not noble courage in speech, for speech is not always truth; seek it not in rich clothes, for many a fine habit conceals cowardice, treachery and evil; seek it not in your horse, for he cannot speak to you; seek it not in fine harness and equipment, for they too often conceal an evil and cowardly heart. Seek noble courage in faith, hope, charity, justice, strength, moderation and loyalty . . .[2]

This is the stuff of sermons, and knights were doubtless used to such exhortations; but Llull, a knight himself, has a sharp sense of the knight's psychology, his enthusiasms and weaknesses. He is happy for knights to 'ride great horses, joust, go to tournaments, hold round tables, hunt stags and rabbits, boars, lions and similar creatures'[3] because such exercises make him a better horseman and more adept at handling his weapons. He is also aware that knights have a role to play within the hierarchy of the state: they not only support and enforce justice by their power, they are also a key part of the administration of society, and should 'love the common good' by serving as royal officials, as he himself had done when he was a knight.

Underlying Llull's portrait of the ideal knight is a call for reform, a sense that in real life the conduct of knights is all too often the reverse of the picture he paints.[4] For each knightly virtue that he describes, he is all too aware that the opposite may well prevail, as in the passage above, where the splendid appearance of the knight only acts to conceal the vices within. Ultimately, *The Book of the Order of Knighthood* may more often have been found in the hands of preachers and confessors who needed to address a knightly audience than actually read by the knights themselves.

When Ramon Llull wrote his little treatise, his days as a knight were past, and he speaks from the point of view of a philosopher rather than that of a practical man at arms. Geoffroy de Charny, writing seventy years later, was in the thick of the fighting in the Anglo-French wars, and never claimed to be other than a warrior. That is not to say that he was not a devout man, and he is today most famous as the first recorded owner of what is now called the Shroud of Turin. His books were written in the context of the years after Crécy, and particularly in relation to the founding of the Company of the Star. And they were written while he was in his prime; they are not the admonitions of the retired expert, looking backwards, but are very much concerned with the here and now.

Geoffroy de Charny was the younger son of a younger son, and from a minor knightly family in Burgundy; his grandfather was Jean de Joinville, companion and biographer of St Louis, but none of the wealth or prestige of his ancestor had come down to him.[5] The connection may have been useful in obtaining service under the count of Eu, constable of France, with whom he had a distant link by marriage. His first appearance in the records was in Raoul count of Eu's retinue in Gascony in 1337, accompanied by five squires; he had some small means of his own, probably through his marriage. He was still with Raoul count of Eu when Tournai was besieged in 1340, and was among the successful defenders. His next venture, in the wars which began in Brittany in 1341, was in the service of John II, then duke of Normandy, who was attempting to enforce Charles de Blois's claim to the duchy. He had evidently distinguished himself in action by 1342, when he was put in command of the vanguard at the attempt to relieve Morlaix. After the French army were repulsed, a number of prisoners were taken: Adam Murimuth tells us that 'among them was Geoffroy de Charny, who was reputed to be one of the best and wisest knights in the French king's army; he was captured by Richard Talbot, and sent to Castle Goodrich on the borders of Wales'.[6] It seems that he was purchased from Talbot by the earl of Northampton as commander of the expedition, the usual practice with important prisoners, for in 1343 it was the earl who appointed attorneys to receive Charny back into captivity when he returned from a journey to France to raise his ransom.

Despite being still on parole, Charny seems to have been back in action against the English in Brittany in late 1342,[7] just before a truce was arranged. We next hear of him on crusade, with Humbert dauphin of Viennois, in 1345, sailing to support the fleet of galleys raised by Pope Clement which had just seized Izmir (Smyrna) on the Anatolian coast. Humbert was more of a scholar and idealist than a military leader, and nothing was achieved; Charny returned in 1346, while Humbert resigned his position in 1347 prior to abdicating and becoming a monk. Charny rejoined the duke of Normandy's army, and fought in Gascony in 1346 until the army returned to Paris in haste on hearing the news of the defeat at Crécy. Charny was named standard-bearer of the *oriflamme* when Philip took his army to the relief of Calais in July 1347, only to retreat in humiliating circumstances. Charny was one of the French negotiators of the truce of September 1347.

Criticism of the king and of the French knights was rife at this time: there are a number of surviving poems attacking them for their disastrous failure at Crécy. Philip responded by appointing new advisers, and Charny became a member of the royal council in January 1348, with a house in Paris in acknowledgement of his services. Valued though he was as diplomat and councillor, Charny preferred action, and it was he who dreamt up the scheme to recover Calais by bribing the mercenary whom Edward had appointed as master of the king's galleys, Aimeric di Pavia, to open the gates to a small French force which he was to lead.[8] The plot led to his defeat by Edward's household knights under the king and the prince of Wales in person, and his capture by John Potenhale after he was wounded. He began his second English captivity as the king's prisoner, Potenhale having been given 100 marks for his good service in taking Charny. This time the ransom was substantial, and, soon after the duke of Normandy came to the throne in 1350 as John II, he is said to have paid 12,000 *écus* towards Charny's ransom. He was back in France by June 1351, and defended Ardres near Calais against an English attack: he was now the commander for Picardy and the Norman frontier, and he used this post to settle scores with Aimeric di Pavia, whom he regarded as having broken his word, and with the captain of Guines, who had sold his fortress to the English. Both were seized and summarily executed: Charny regarded treachery as one of the cardinal sins of knighthood.

Charny was one of the founder members of the Company of the Star in 1352, and it is possible that he had been connected with the plans for this order since John II originally proposed it in 1344, as he had been in John's service in Brittany prior to that. He certainly wrote one of his works specifically for the order, the *Questions on Jousts, Tournaments and War*, and it is possible that his *Book of Chivalry* was also intended for the knights. He also wrote a *Book of Charny*, a personal account of his life; it is tempting to suggest that this was the product of his enforced leisure in England in 1349–50, since we can point to a number of knights who wrote while in captivity: Thomas Gray, author of the *Scalacronica*, the poems of Charles of Orléans, and, most famously, Thomas Malory's *Le Morte Darthur*.

In June 1355, as preparations for the renewal of the war began, John II again appointed Charny bearer of the *oriflamme*, and he carried the sacred banner at the battle of Poitiers the following year. Here Charny was killed in the final moments of the battle, in the small knot of knights who made a last stand in defence of the king and of the standard. Geoffrey le Baker wrote of him that he was 'more practised in military matters than any other French knight, and that, besides his long experience of war, he had been given the excellent gift of the quick wits of a lively nature',[9] while Froissart simply called him 'the most worthy and valiant of all'.

The *Book of Chivalry* is therefore the work of a central figure in the knightly world of the mid-fourteenth century, well known in both France and England, and with experience of both countries. It is as close as we shall come to understanding the mindset of the companions of the Garter, belonging as it does to the common culture of knighthood which transcended the political divisions between England and France.

Charny begins by defining a scale of prowess, and here we immediately encounter a vital element in knightly ideas of the mid-fourteenth century. It is that much of knightly life is competitive: the focus is on the individual, not on the team aspects of warfare. The objective towards which knights strive is personal fame and reputation, their model the heroes of romance rather than the great commanders of history. This cult of the individual is underlined in heraldry, where the coat of arms is unique and personal, and cannot be borne by anyone other than the rightful holder. The first cases concerning unauthorized use of arms in the Court of Chivalry date from this period, notably from the siege of Calais in 1346–7, when Robert Morley and Nicholas Burnell both laid claim to the same arms, and a similar case was heard between John Warbleton and Theobald Russell.[10] Charny is in search of the superlative individual, as his introduction makes clear: 'And always the noblest way rises above all others, and those who have the greatest heart for it go constantly forward to reach and achieve the highest honor.'[11] He discusses knightly activities in terms of this 'scale of prowess', with deeds of arms in tournaments at the bottom, then deeds of arms in local wars, and finally deeds of arms in full warfare: 'it is from good battles that great honors arise and are increased'. The reputation of the individual Garter companions arose from their 'good battles', and together their fame became that of the company as a whole.

He then looks at other activities which can enhance a knight's reputation, in a series of short discussions on travels to distant places, serving for pay and performing feats of arms for the love of a lady; each ends with a variation on the refrain, 'I therefore say: whoever does best, is most worthy.' He gives us a series of character sketches: the knight who spends extravagantly on 'great state and outward show', but cannot afford to keep up his expenditure for long enough to wait for the action in which he might distinguish himself; the men whose deeds are undertaken in remote places, and which nobody knows about; the men who are too eager for plunder and then lose both their booty and their reputation. He sketches his ideal knight, an enthusiast who listens carefully in his youth to men of experience talking about deeds of arms or weapons, armour and horses, learning all he can about the skills of a knight, and about how a knight should conduct himself. He learns how to handle arms, first through jousting, 'the first exercise in the use of arms which he can encounter', and then through tournaments, from which he progresses to real warfare 'in order to achieve the highest honor in prowess'. In order to take part in warfare, he observes the techniques of managing an expedition and deploying troops, whether attacking or withdrawing, as well as siegecraft against castles and walled towns. He seeks out places where sieges are in progress and, stationing himself there as observer, watches all the different siege machines and techniques of mining, bombardment and scaling walls. He then travels to find countries that are at war, so that he can take part in a battle, and so his career begins. Charny recognizes that the best way to advancement is through service with a great lord, because his retinue will be larger, and will be a better milieu for learning knightly skills; the lord will be able to choose the best men at arms and is more likely to be a good leader.

Having won high renown in the field, the knight must look to his reputation, 'for there will be much greater talk and notoriety about their shortcomings than there would be concerning someone without such a great reputation'. And, in order to ensure that scandal does not touch the ambitious knight, he must adopt the right kind of lifestyle from the outset. So Charny becomes a kind of medieval life coach, and launches into a detailed discussion of the vices and virtues involved, with vivid glimpses of contemporary manners. He condemns drunkenness and gluttony, and even being a gourmet is forbidden: 'do not concern yourself with being knowledgeable about good dishes and fine sauces nor spend too much time deciding which wines are the best . . .'[12] Gambling is another besetting sin, and the evidence from the royal accounts shows that this was a very frequent failing. More curiously, he condemns real tennis, a specialist game with a small but avid following; but this is because of the wagers which were placed on the outcome. Jousting and dancing naturally meet with approval, as do conversation and singing; these are social pastimes and always to be recommended in good company. 'Yet fine games are good where there is no anger, but when tempers rise, it is no longer play';[13] so the choice of companions is important, and lords whose entourage includes men who are a bad influence are to be avoided.

Above all, the ambitious knight needs to be single-minded in his pursuit of honour. Charny would have been horrified by Falstaff's view of honour: 'What is honour? A word. What is in that word honour? What is that honour? Air – a trim reckoning!' Honour is a word Charny cannot use often enough, and his sermon on honour is the central part of his teaching, in the course of which he moves on from the almost fanatical pursuit of honour earned to the inspiration for such deeds. Here his book takes up the traditional theme of love as the fount of honourable deeds: it is perhaps the least original part of his text, rather as if he himself is repeating a lesson learnt, a convention that is beginning to outwear its time.

Having paid his respects to courtly love, Charny quickly returns to instructing his knight in less ethereal matters. In the section on physical strength and courage, he gives a splendid list of the terrors that await a knight who loves comfort too much once he is in the field. He lives in fear of walls that might fall on him, rivers that can drown him, bridges that might collapse; he will go miles out of his way not to cross a boggy patch, is frightened by the least illness and cannot stand the sight of blood. He cannot sleep at night in case the wind brings down the house he is sheltering in.

The closing sections of Charny's book return to the conventional religious view of society and knighthood; there is less about the practicalities of knighthood in this theoretical section, and his ideas are largely derived from Ramon Llull and the concept of the three orders, though he turns aside to discuss the virtues relevant to a good man at arms, condemning those who are outwardly devout but harbour secret vices, those who are too clever to take practical decisions because they are always seeing subtle complications, the rash, those who avoid responsibility and will not lead. And in his final pages, he gives a sermon against richness of dress in men which runs counter to the personal extravagances of both the English and French kings. But it is the presence of this section, however stereotyped, which is important: Charny is trying to mould his knight to be both practical and effective, and with a strong spiritual background, understanding where his power comes from and how it should best be used.

Charny's other works illustrate knightly life in different ways. The *Book of Charny*, written in simple verse, covers some of the same ground as the *Book of Chivalry*, but the images that Charny provides of the knight's actual experience in the field are intriguing. Here he is on the subject of what might happen in the course of a siege:

> If they are attacking a castle or tower, be there to take part in the assault.
> You will have to suffer great blows, and often fall to the ground; rocks

will be thrown at you from mangonels,* arrows and crossbow bolts will fly around you and some will strike you and wound you, of course. Now you are up to the walls, and the blows are so hard that I am not sure you will come back. Everyone is looking out for a chance to wound you, and nothing can protect you any more, I know this for a fact, unless God shields his own, finding some good in them; then he will be gracious to them and let them escape, and hide them under his mantle; at least so it seems to me when men often escape from such great danger.

Now the scaling ladder is against the wall, be the first man up; but you will come down badly, head first. Lances and swords will attack you, and very heavy stones will fall on you. Then you will have to be picked up and carried to your lodgings on a shield. They will shout in your ear, and you will not say a word. It will be a great miracle if you are alive. Your eyes are closed, your face is pale and your blood is everywhere. If you are alive, thank the Son of the Virgin Mary with all your heart. If He wishes, He can rescue you but you cannot do anything without Him. So you see that an ass that munches thistles or a beast harnessed to a cart are not as unfortunate as he who learns to be a knight.[14]

Charny paints similarly gloomy vignettes of the battlefield and of sea voyages in search of adventures in the east. But doing nothing is not an option: if the knight gives up, he will become like a horse crowded into a stable for a long time and badly looked after, that loses all its qualities. Faced with danger, he should trust in God, and continue to strive to do his best: he will win honour and praise when he returns home. The last section of the poem deals with the education of the aspiring knight, with a strong emphasis on religious observance, and a discussion of the seven deadly sins, before Charny concludes very much in the same vein as in the *Book of Chivalry*.

The last of Charny's works, *Questions on Jousts, Tournaments and War*, is the only one definitely associated with the Company of the Star. It consists of a series of problems to be put to the knights for their decision, acting as a kind of court of knightly behaviour. We have only the questions: Charny probably never wrote the answers, and genuinely intended them as matters for the knights of the Star to discuss, after which decisions might have been recorded. There are three sections, on

---

* A type of siege engine.

jousts, tournaments and warfare. In the sections on jousts and warfare, the main topic is the booty to be acquired, how title to a defeated knight's horse in a joust or to a prisoner for ransom can be established. The questions on ransom and the conditions connected with the terms of captivity are his main concern, forming a third of the text. The section on warfare is detailed, and includes two items on the status of the standard-bearer, the position that Charny himself held. There are occasional mentions of honour and prowess, but by and large these are matters which reflect the business of war, and much of it seems more appropriate to matters of trade than matters of knighthood. Occasionally the purely romantic ideals intervene, as in question 88, which pits two companies of fifty knights against each other: one company has just come from seeing their ladies, while the others are on their way to their paramours: which, asks Charny, will fight the better? Sadly, we shall never know the answers.

The importance of these books is that, unlike earlier treatises, which belong on the bookshelves of preachers or clergy in a great household, these do seem to be books whose readership is genuinely envisaged as the knights themselves. However, Charny's desire to reach an audience of his peers was to be disappointed: perhaps because of his death at Poitiers, the books never reached a wide circulation, and survive only in two manuscripts, with little evidence that they were known to other readers.

Knights and books did not mix, on the whole. If reading was widespread among knights, we would expect to find a larger number of manuscripts on knightly matters surviving, even allowing for the massive destruction of medieval books in succeeding centuries. Major works often survive in unique manuscript copies, whether historical texts such as Jean le Bel's chronicle, Thomas Gray's *Scalacronica*, or romances such as *Sir Gawain and the Green Knight* or Thomas Malory's *Le Morte Darthur*. We may know something about lost works through references to them by other writers or from medieval library catalogues and inventories, but there is little to suggest that what we have seriously under-represents the ownership of such books by knights. Literacy was largely a matter of rank. The great magnates were the most likely to own, and probably therefore to read, chronicles and romances and works on knighthood. It is not until the fifteenth century that we find aspiring knights like John Paston collecting texts about knighthood as part of their efforts to improve their social standing.[15] In France, where warfare affected almost every part of the kingdom in the second half of the fourteenth century, there was a lively debate on knights and the conduct of military affairs, which only appears in England once the English war effort faltered at the beginning of the fifteenth century.[16]

How then did the majority of knights know about the content of these books, and about romances? Ideas about knightly ideals, and about the knights' place in society, were mediated through preachers; sermons are full of exemplary stories about how knights should behave, and the dire fate that awaits knights who succumb to the sins of pride and luxury, to which they are supposedly exceptionally prone. The same ideas would be mediated through tutors in the households of great lords, which acted in a sense as schools of knighthood; it was common practice for knights to send their sons to such a household to serve as squires, and they would be taught, it seems, alongside the lord's own sons. And at court the idea of discussions on knighthood was encouraged; Alfonso IX of Castile decreed that texts concerned with knighthood should be read during mealtimes, just as monks might have the Scriptures read to them at dinner. The household ordinances of Edward IV provide for discussion of knightly matters after supper. And finally, there were always a small number of knights who were interested in books and learning, such as Charny and Henry of Grosmont, as well as the 'knight-prisoners' like Thomas Malory, Thomas Gray or Charles duke of Orléans who turned to writing to relieve the tedium of captivity.

In short, the world of the romances and treatises may reflect the ideals of knighthood and the theory of the place of the knight in society. But we cannot assume any very direct link or any very great influence of books on the everyday attitudes and thinking of the majority of knights. To learn something of their mindset, we have to turn to legal records.

THE COURT OF CHIVALRY

Chivalry, we have to remind ourselves, is one of those English words which makes a distinction which is not present in other languages. Chivalry and knighthood are united in the French word *chevalerie*, which Charny uses, and he does not recognize the division of the ideals and practice of knighthood found in the English vocabulary. This is well illustrated by the so-called 'Court of Chivalry', as it is now generally called in legal textbooks. It was originally the military court, *curia militaris*, which dealt with army discipline in the field. Its French name was *court de chivalrie*, and it was this name that persisted, rather than the 'Court of the Knighthode of Engeland' which appears in the late fourteenth-century documents.[17] The Court of Chivalry appears for the first time in the records during the siege of Calais, though it had existed before then in a less formal way. It was effectively a system of military justice, administered by the constable and marshal of England, the two officers responsible for the discipline of the army. By 1390 the court was important enough for parliament to be alarmed by its activities, and to petition the king that it should not interfere in 'any kind of contract made within the kingdom of England which may be tried by the common law, unless solely concerning [heraldic] arms, which cannot be tried by the common law'.[18] This was granted; the implication is that the constable and marshal and their court still have jurisdiction over matters outside England, such as the questions of ransoms for prisoners taken in France. We shall return to the ransoms, but for the moment it is their authority over disputes about arms that interests us.

The organization of the army depended on small units grouped around a knight or banneret, who in turn answered to a commander; that commander might be in the pay of a great lord. The visual signs which identified the groups and sub-groups were the banners and coats of arms of the various levels of leaders. It was therefore important in any large army that there was no duplication of the arms borne by leading knights, and from the beginning of the fourteenth century we have pictorial records of the coats of arms displayed in some of the campaigns, either as a commemoration of the event, or as a fair copy of working notes used in the field.

It is significant that the first recorded disputes about the right to bear particular arms arise out of the Crécy campaign, the largest English army to have fought abroad up to that date. An engraving of a lost document settling a dispute at Calais describes the group of lords who issued the decision as appointed to 'try and judge all manner of debates over arms and helms in the army and in the siege before Calais'.[19] The implication is that the two cases at Calais which have come down to us are only a small remnant of a good number of such claims, and that this was a serious issue. The judges are of the highest rank: Henry of Grosmont, duke of Lancaster, as steward of England, William Clinton, earl of Huntingdon, Reginald Cobham, Walter Mauny, William Lovel and Stephen Cosington.

Confusion over arms could have practical repercussions in the field, and the only authorities who could settle the matter were those responsible for army discipline. It was not the heralds who were called in, because their jurisdiction in such matters was not recognized until the early fifteenth century. Nor were they called as witnesses in such cases; all the testimony in the records that have come down to us is from fellow-knights, with the single exception of John Suffolk, herald to Robert Ufford, earl of Suffolk, in the case between John, Lord Lovell and Thomas, Lord Morley, in 1386–7.[20] Knowledge of arms was something which every knight was expected to acquire, as we shall see from other evidence in this case.[21] Arms, and the reputation attached to those arms by virtue of the deeds of the men who had used them in the past, were an essential part of knightly morale. This is best illustrated by cases where shaming a knight by displaying his arms upside down was used as a means of trying to get him to pay up on a ransom on which he had defaulted. Henry Pomfret did this to the count of Tancarville in the 1360s, though the count denied that Pomfret had taken him prisoner according to the laws of war; and Lord Scales suffered the same treatment at the hands of a French captain in the 1430s.[22] And for a knight convicted of treachery, the surcoat of his arms would be torn from his body and replaced by one of his arms reversed.

A claim by a rival knight to a coat of arms which another family believed was theirs by right challenged the very roots of their existence. But part of the reason why these disputes arose at Calais was that coats of arms would only be seen together in a large army. The arms disputed by Richard, Lord Scrope, and Robert Grosvenor were also borne by an obscure Cornish family, who, despite the duplication with Scrope, had already been permitted to use them.

The cases in the Court of Chivalry are the most immediate witnesses we possess to the real world of medieval knighthood. Detailed records survive for just two cases, that of Scrope versus Grosvenor and the case of Lovell versus Morley; actions at law of this kind were highly unusual. The cases were heard by commissioners, who recorded the actual words of the witnesses – or something very close to them – in their reports. These report rolls were then written up in more formal style as a statement of the case. From the reports, we learn at the outset the bare outlines of the witness's career, his name, status and age. There are three types of evidence: occasions on which the plaintiff or defendant was seen wearing the disputed arms, descriptions of items on which the arms appeared, and a more general assessment of whether the party for whom the witness was speaking was believed to be entitled to these arms.

What do these witnesses have to tell us about the world of the knight at the time of the founding of the Company of the Garter? The picture that emerges is of an England where regional loyalties are gradually giving way to a national view, and where there is an increasing emphasis on the fame and honour of individuals and families. There is little evidence that arms were regarded as exclusive to one lineage before the beginning of Edward III's reign, simply because the lives of knights in Cornwall and Yorkshire were unlikely to overlap. The armies of Edward I in Scotland were still substantially regional, drawn – for good practical reasons – from the north of England and reinforced by the king's household troops and those of the great magnates. This remained true in Edward III's reign, and it is very striking that the first northern knight to become a member of the Company of the Garter is Henry Percy in 1365, sixteen years after the company's foundation. In turn, this meant that reputations were local, and confined to a fairly small circle, that of the magnates of the area. The Grosvenors were long established in Cheshire, and, for a Cheshire man at arms, his arms would be part of the knightly tradition of that county. The Scropes were known and honoured for the same arms in Yorkshire, but had entered royal service and were therefore recognized in London and at court as the rightful bearers of those arms.[23]

The personal reminiscences recorded in the Court of Chivalry cases are very striking, and the memories of the witnesses stretch back for a surprisingly long timespan. John Sully, a companion of the Garter, claimed to be 102 when he was interviewed, and his squire was 84. In the 1380s there were men like Richard Fyfield who could remember the battle of Bannockburn in 1314, in which he had taken part. The length of military service is surprising: Nicholas Sabraham had been with William Bohun at Lochmaben in 1335 and went to Spain with the prince of

Wales in 1367; he had been 'armed thirty-nine years'.[24] The witnesses in support of Lovell's claim are even more remarkable: forty-eight of them claimed over forty years in arms.[25] Because men who could remember what might be the earliest evidence for use of the arms were particularly sought out, this length of service must be treated as exceptional; but it overturns the popular image of medieval life as 'nasty, brutish and short'. It also underlines the sheer experience of Edward's armies: many of the men who had fought in Scotland in the 1330s were still active on his Reims campaign of 1359–60. Most of the witnesses recollect their 'first arming', a crucial moment in the military career of knights and squires, in a similar way; sometimes it refers to the actual knighting ceremony, as at La Hogue in 1346, at other times it simply means 'the first battle in which I fought'. And there is much detail in many of the depositions which allows us to get a general idea of the pattern of military careers in Edward III's reign, though it has to be treated with caution because the evidence concerns a limited number of engagements. Furthermore, the range of witnesses indicates the increasing role played by the esquires – the gentlemen of later centuries – who were not knights. More than two-thirds of those in the Lovell–Morley case belonged to this rank, and were treated with the same respect as their knightly superiors.[26]

Much of the evidence is concerned with the use of the disputed arms on a campaign, and all the great battles of Edward's reign are frequently recalled, as well as many lesser encounters. A number of witnesses also recall seeing the knights in their arms at tournaments of which we have no other record. Ralph Ferrers told the court that 'tournaments are where arms are taught and studied'; heraldic arms had in large part originated at twelfth-century tournaments, and they were still essential to the spectator at such an event two centuries later.[27] These glimpses can be a real window into the past, as in the case of Nicholas Sabraham's account of Stephen Scrope, dressed in the gold and blue of the disputed arms, receiving knighthood from King Peter of Cyprus on the crusade of 1365, at the siege of Alexandria.[28] Geoffrey Chaucer remembered walking down a London street, and seeing what he believed to be Scrope's arms above the door of lodgings; on enquiry, he was told that these were the arms, not of Scrope, but of a member of the Grosvenor family. This, he said, was the first time he had ever heard of the Grosvenors' claim to the arms.[29]

The visual evidence reveals a world where arms were displayed, not merely in the grey remnants of heraldry we see on tombs today, but seemingly everywhere – on silver, on the walls of great chambers, on embroidered vestments presented to churches, in church windows, on church walls, and in vivid colours on monuments. The expensive accoutrements of the knight, surcoat, shield and horse-trappings, were only a small part of this (Plates 22–3, 26–7). On the other hand, this impressive catalogue of images rarely includes armorial displays in churches similar to those on the Garter stalls or on the prince's tomb at Canterbury, where helms, swords and surcoats were preserved as heraldic memorials. The only such memorials recalled by witnesses are the banners set up to commemorate Robert Morley's death on the Reims campaign, and the heraldic armour of William Morley at Somerton.[30]

Another test was 'public fame': was it generally acknowledged that the family in question had the right to the arms? This brings us into the elusive problems of reputation and honour, the remembrance of the great deeds of arms done by knights wearing the disputed coat of arms. Occasionally, old chronicles and documents are quoted, usually by clerics, as supporting evidence, but this was principally a matter of word of mouth, the stories attached to the family and sometimes evidence of their activities abroad. The more battles at which a knight had displayed his banner, the greater was the honour attaching to that coat of arms; and battles against the heathen had a particular value. Hugh Hastings II, unfurling his banner for the first time in a battle against the Saracens, had done 'special honour' to those arms; and the same idea was echoed by Anne Mauny, daughter of Walter Mauny and married to John Hastings, earl of Pembroke, when she thanked Hugh Hastings III 'for the honour you have done to the arms of Hastings in the past', and hoped that he would continue to do so in his own forthcoming journey to the east. And to ensure his reputation, Hastings duly left little shields with his arms at the places to which his travels took him.[31]

CRUSADING

Most of the evidence for the participation of English knights in the Prussian crusades in the mid-fourteenth century comes from the Court of Chivalry proceedings. In this international setting, knights were eager that their arms should be recorded as participants in the wars against the heathen, and the expeditions to the lands of the Teutonic Order combined both the quest for honour and the spiritual rewards of going on crusade. What may seem false and unreal to us, the attempted conversion by force to Christianity of the pagan tribes living on the eastern borders of the Holy Roman Empire, and the elaborate conventions of the 'table of honour', were eagerly sought after by knights from all over Christian Europe in times of truce or peace. They could gain spiritual merit, earthly glory and practice in arms and warfare through the 'Prussian journey'.

With the fall of Acre in 1291, the first series of crusades, grandiose expeditions aiming to recover Jerusalem from the infidel, had come to an end; there was no longer a base on the mainland from which to mount a campaign in Palestine. The idea of a great crusading expedition persisted, however, and one of the objectives of the popes at Avignon for much of the period of the Anglo-French wars was to persuade the two sides to make peace so that a new crusade could begin. However, it was not until 1395 that these efforts were successful and a new crusade was launched; but the disaster that befell the Christian army at Nicopolis in that year effectively marks the end of the eastern crusades.

Crusading in the mid-fourteenth century meant a rather different kind of activity. Since the mid-twelfth century, there had been an ongoing war on the eastern frontier of the Holy Roman Empire against the heathens in Poland, Lithuania and Latvia, led by an order of knights which had begun life in Palestine as guardians of a hostel for German pilgrims. Like the other crusading orders, the Teutonic Knights, as they are usually called in English, had developed a belligerent life of their own, carrying the attack to the invading Muslim armies. But towards the end of the twelfth century the order acquired lands in eastern Germany, particularly in what became Prussia, and began to campaign there with the object of converting the pagan tribes by force to Christianity, and settling their land with German inhabitants.

The Teutonic Knights were fighting a different kind of warfare to that in Palestine. The latter was a war of conquest and counter-conquest, as huge Muslim forces swept in and were confronted with varying degrees of success. The war in Prussia was a war of attrition, punctuated by occasional moments when the heathen tribes united under a single leader. It was fought in a landscape even more hostile than the Palestinian desert, a trackless wilderness of swamps and waterways with islands of habitable land, which was impenetrable for much of the year: it was sometimes passable in a dry summer, but the majority of campaigns (called *reysen,* 'journeys') were fought in the winter, when the swamps would freeze hard and horses and baggage trains could cross. One of the most famous encounters – in which the Teutonic Knights were defeated by an army from Novgorod led by Alexander Nevsky – was the 'battle on the ice' on lake Peipus in 1242.

The Teutonic Knights were a small order, though relatively wealthy. They were a sovereign power, and, under the leadership of their best masters, they encouraged trade and settlement, and were able to supplement their revenues from their extensive landholdings in Germany, given to them by pious supporters. But their resources of manpower were relatively slender, and like their fellow-knights in the great crusading orders in the east, they needed reinforcements from the west. Large armies were a liability in the terrain in which they had to fight, and they developed a system by which small groups of knights, or even individual knights, were encouraged to come to their headquarters at Marienburg, for a *reyse,* a summer or winter expedition.

The Teutonic Knights were not slow to see the possibility of using the pent-up desire to go on crusade as a means of furthering their own conquests, and they were able to offer all the spiritual benefits that would have derived from participation in a crusade to the Holy Land. Despite a dubious reputation for ferocity and high-handed behaviour in the lands they ruled, they were still regarded in most western European courts with the same respect that had been accorded to the Templars and Hospitallers in the previous century.

Small numbers of knights had been recruited by the Teutonic Order in Germany for specific campaigns in the thirteenth century, but it was from 1328 onwards that the Prussian crusades became part of the international knightly scene. King John of Bohemia, an impractical ruler but an inspirational figure in terms of knightly enterprises, led a group of Bohemians to Prussia in that year, and returned twice in 1344–5. A Prussian chronicler notes that 'many nobles from England and Germany' also came in 1328, and this expedition seems to have set a fashion that was to last for almost a century, until the order's disastrous defeat by Vladislav II of Poland at Tannenberg in 1410.

Knights from France and Hainault joined the crusades in the mid-

1330s, but the peak of enthusiasm for crusading was during the truce of Esplechin, which suspended fighting in France more effectively than during the truces after 1346. The crusading seasons of 1343–5 saw, in addition to the king of Bohemia's two journeys, two similar expeditions from Hainault and numerous knights from France.[32] A year of victories in 1348, similar to the English *annus mirabilis* of 1346, saw three successful expeditions against the Russians, Lithuanians and Samogitians. The grand master elected in 1352, Winrich von Kniprode, presided over the most glorious period of the order's history. In the next century the chronicle of the order would look back to this period nostalgically as a time when 'many lords, knights and squires from Christendom desired to see the order, and came with their forces to Prussia, and stayed at Königsberg with great provisions, many waiting for a whole year for a *reyse* against the enemy'.[33]

Surviving records name more than sixty English knights, about a hundred from Holland and Hainault, and more than a hundred from France who went to Prussia during Edward III's reign. Because of the order's close connection with Germany, the numbers from the Holy Roman Empire probably exceeded all the rest put together. Most of these names come from the accounts of great lords, and are of knights and squires serving with them. For the smaller retinues, there is no documentation, and only a few individual names of leaders of such retinues have come down to us; any records of the order which might have named the guests of the grand master have disappeared, so we are only able to identify a small proportion of those who reached Prussia.

Typically, the number of men in a group was very similar to that of a lord's or banneret's retinue in one of Edward III's armies. They would rarely stay for more than a year, and there was a constant traffic to and fro from Prussia; the journey was not a lengthy one, like the overland route or the sea voyage to Palestine, and it was possible to travel from England or France in a little more than a month. In 1344, William II of Hainault, Edward III's brother-in-law, took thirty-six days to reach Marienburg starting from Haarlem in Holland, leaving on 14 December. The count and his retinue arrived back at Valenciennes on 30 May 1345, having taken part in the *winterreyse*.[34] Henry Bolingbroke (later Henry IV), who led the largest English expedition to Prussia in 1390–91, left Boston in Lincolnshire on 22 July 1390; the journey was quicker by sea, and took twenty-six days outwards and thirty days on the return voyage, reaching Hull on 30 April the following year.

Knights arriving at Königsberg found themselves in an atmosphere which was very like that of a great lord's castle in their homeland. There were, of course, the monastic observances of the order; but alongside these, there was a knightly existence on a grand scale. Because the *reyse* depended so much on the right weather, there were long periods when Königsberg was crowded with would-be crusaders: such waiting time was a regular occurrence, and a tradition of feasting, courtly gatherings and display evolved. This knightly culture was not deliberately encouraged by the order, but seems to have arisen spontaneously from the numbers of knights present at Königsberg.

However, the order saw the possibilities of using knightly pride to assist it in recruiting those who were interested in joining its crusades. It was probably the grand master Winrich von Kniprode who created the focal point of social life during this enforced idleness, the table of honour, an idea which he almost certainly took from the short-lived Company of the Star, announced by John II in 1351.[35] The *Ehrentisch*, to give it its German name, is famous from Chaucer's portrait of the Knight in the *Canterbury Tales* who 'had often sat at the head of the table above all the other nations in Prussia'; in other words, had been chosen as the most distinguished of the guests.[36] This was not a metaphorical honour, but literally a table at which the chosen knights sat. In 1413, Gilbert de Lannoy saw 'the arms, the place and the table of honour' in Königsberg, implying that it was set apart, possibly in the main refectory of the order's castle there, and that the walls were hung with the shields of those who had sat at it. Other accounts indicate that twelve or fourteen knights sat at the table, and that only those who had come at their own expense were eligible: in 1400, knights paid by the duke of Lorraine as part of his retinue were disqualified, even though they were regarded as worthy of the honour in all other respects. The ceremonial dinner took place in winter, often before the *winterreyse* began, in late January or early February, and the choice of knights was therefore based on their reputation and not on their performance on the *reyse*. Furthermore, the choice of knights seems to have been made by the heralds who had accompanied the crusaders to Prussia. Occasionally there is a hint in the texts of why a knight was chosen: he might simply be 'a good knight', or have shed his blood 'in many countries'. Another was honoured as standard-bearer of the order's banner of St George on a previous *reyse*.

As to the dinner itself, we have a description of that held in 1375 according to an eyewitness:

> The grand master ... wished twelve knights from different kingdoms to be seated at the table of honour. And from France Sir Hutin de Vermelles and Sir Tristan de Maignelay sat at the high table, whom all men called good knights, and from other countries two from each up to a total of twelve, in the places specified by the master; and they were served in accordance with the glory of the day. And after grace was said, these twelve were told about the institution of the table and how it had been established. And then one of the brethren of the order pinned a word written in golden letters onto their shoulders, 'Honour conquers all'.[37]

The idea of the table of honour is found in two contemporary orders of knighthood in western Europe, those of the Star and the Knot, which predate the first recorded appearance of the table of honour in Prussia by twenty-five years. Both were orders relating to kingdoms, or monarchical orders. The statutes of the Company of the Star of 1351 include a provision that at the annual feast of the order,

> there shall be a table called the table of honour, at which shall be seated on the eve and the day of the first festival the three most distinguished princes, three most distinguished bannerets and three most distinguished knights among those who shall be members of the said company and who are present at the said feast; and at each eve and festival in mid-August, every subsequent year, the three princes, three bannerets and three knights who have performed the greatest deeds in war shall be seated there, for no deeds in arms of a peaceful nature shall count towards it.[38]

The idea of a table of honour was less impressive within the context of an order whose knights had already been chosen because they were supposedly outstanding in knighthood. In Prussia, where a different group of knights assembled each year, there was more purpose in such a table; it formed a focal point for the knightly ambitions of the crusaders, while the ordering by nations made it an international body which also served to unify the temporary army which arrived for a single campaigning season. It does not seem to have survived beyond the end of the century.

Any knight who came to Königsberg towards the end of Edward III's reign would be instantly reminded of the enthusiasm with which his predecessors had made the journey to Prussia. The cathedral was filled with knightly paraphernalia, massive quantities of painted shields recording the arms of the crusaders; the inns where they had lodged had similar displays, as did other castles in the territory. The accounts of Jean count of Blois in 1369 show huge expenditure on painting his arms and those of his companions, and the concern for accurate recording of exactly who was with him. He set out on the *reyse* with forty-three knights, but seven others joined him in the field, and their arms had to be added when the campaign ended. More ominously, the arms he had put up on his first visit in 1363 had to be replaced 'because the English had torn them down'.[39] Arms of this kind were to be found as mementoes of pilgrimage, at Santiago de Compostela and on the road to Jerusalem and in the Holy City itself, but there was no display elsewhere remotely on this scale.

THE *REYSE*

The hardship of the *reyse* must have seemed a direct contrast to the glories and festivities of Königsberg. But only a small number of knights actually experienced warfare in Prussia. There were on average three *reysen* a year from 1305 to 1409, but less than a third of these had a contingent of foreign knights. And on many occasions, the weather prevented any expedition taking place while a crusader was in Prussia. The duke of Geldern went on crusade seven times, but only once was he able to take part in a *reyse*.[40] Often the winter was too mild for the ice to form, so that the swamps remained impassable, or there was a sudden thaw, as in 1344, when floods from melting snow and ice forced a hasty retreat. In 1352 heavy rain nearly destroyed the army: knights had to make their way back on foot because their horses starved to death, or both knights and horses drowned in swollen streams. On the other hand, in 1364, there was such a hard winter, lasting three months, that numerous forays were possible.

Prussia was not therefore a place where encounters with the enemy were frequent. Even if the army entered pagan territory, there was often no resistance and little fighting. However, if a knight was fortunate (or perhaps unfortunate) enough to go on a *reyse*, the experience of campaigning in harsh and unfamiliar territory was a swift initiation into the hardships of life in the field, given the extremes of weather and the lack of obvious routes into the wilderness which sheltered the enemy. When Edward III unexpectedly launched a winter campaign in France in late October 1359, many of the leaders of retinues in the army had had experience of winter warfare in Prussia.

Almost half of the founding Garter companions made the journey to Prussia. The earliest who can be traced precisely is Thomas Holland, who travelled there for the *winterreyse* in 1340–41, and probably took part in an attack on Livonia, which was abandoned because of humidity: the warm air produced fogs and thawed the ground. Reginald Cobham and William Fitzwarin seem to have gone on one of the expeditions led by nobles from the Low Countries in 1340–45.[41] Their arms are included in the records of the herald Claes Heynenzoon, which seem to be based on a list of crusaders from that period, and the link between them, perhaps begun on this journey, continued as late as the 1360s.

In the absence of fighting in France in 1351, Henry of Grosmont led a major expedition to Prussia. His company included four members of the order: the young earl of Salisbury, William Montagu, and three knights, Nigel Loring, Walter Pavely and Miles Stapleton.[42] The advance party of his army were guarding the duke's treasure as it was taken across northern Germany, when it was attacked by men led by two local magnates, and the treasure seized. Henry and his men were captured, and forced to pay a ransom of 3,000 gold crowns. Despite this setback, Henry and his men reached Prussia, only to find that they were too late for the *reyse* and that a truce was now in force. It seems that he continued to Poland, in the hope that the king of Poland might need his help against the Tartars, but found that they had just retreated.[43] Henry later accused Otto duke of Brunswick of having arranged the ambush in order to take him prisoner and hand him over to King John of France, and the affair ended in a judicial duel between Henry and Otto at the French court. As so often, the participants were prevented from fighting and were reconciled by the king.

With the exception of a Prussian journey by Jean de Grailly (and probably James Audley and Miles Stapleton as well) in 1357–8,[44] English knights did not return to Prussia until after the treaty of Brétigny. Of the Garter companions, Humphrey Bohun, who had just succeeded his uncle as earl of Hereford and Northampton, was there in the winter of 1362–3, a year before his election to the order, with four squires and several other knights. Thomas Beauchamp, earl of Warwick, spent both the summer of 1365 and the winter of 1365–6 on crusade. Both earls returned for a further crusade in 1367–8. They very probably took part in one or more campaigns, as numerous expeditions are recorded by the historians of the Teutonic Order in this period, and none of them seemed to have encountered adverse weather.[45]

The majority of those who went to Prussia were in their twenties; some of them were already experienced soldiers, while for others it was their first experience of war. But the journey to the headquarters of the Teutonic Knights at Königsberg was for many an introduction to the international world of knightly display and festivities, particularly for squires in a lord's retinue. It was in this role that Henry Eam and Eustace d'Auberchicourt saw Prussia, in the retinue of William II of Hainault in 1344–5. This was the place where the rivalry for knightly fame and honour was probably most evident; in the 1350s and 1360s tournaments, the usual outlet for this competitive spirit, were rare in England and the Low Countries, and almost unknown in France, during the most destructive phase of the Anglo-French wars. Equally, it was the one place where the English and French knights met on largely friendly terms and made common cause against a very different enemy. Many of the leaders of the French armies were veterans of the Prussian crusades: the count of Eu surrendered at Caen in 1346 to a fellow-crusader, Thomas Holland. A very large contingent of about a hundred French nobles, knights and squires came to Prussia at the time of Humphrey Bohun's visit in 1362–3. After 1370, however, the French continued to appear in Prussia regularly, while there is only one recorded English crusader between 1369 and 1383.

Just as the secular orders of knighthood sprang up in the vacuum created by the decline of the military religious orders, so the crusade itself in Prussia had acquired a heavily secular veneer. It was less demanding in terms both of time and of actual warfare than the eastern crusades, and the customs of secular war in the west had extended to such matters as ransoming. In the thirteenth century, the knights of the Teutonic Order rarely took prisoners, and were usually killed by the pagans if they were captured. With the appearance of the first western crusaders, customs began to change, and by the mid-fourteenth century ransoms were commonplace, to the extent that, under Winrich von

Kniprode, the order guaranteed to ransom any captured crusader, though the ransom had to be repaid once he was freed.

The predominantly winter campaigns meant that a knight could fight in France during the larger part of the spring and summer, go to Prussia and be back in time for the next season's warfare in the west. Like Jean Boucicaut at the end of the fourteenth century, he probably went 'because it seemed to him that there was a great lack of warfare in France at that time . . . he returned to Prussia for the second time because he had been told that there was bound to be fine fighting there that season'.[46] In peacetime, such a crusader might occupy the summer in tournaments. The best example of this is William II of Hainault, whose brief reign ended in a burst of knightly activity, with two expeditions to Prussia in 1343–5, punctuated by a series of festivals and tournaments (as well as a pilgrimage to Jerusalem) before his death in the disaster at Staveren, where knightly overconfidence was no match for the determination and numbers of the enemy. His crusades had involved little action – two abortive raids and a brief siege had scarcely added to his military experience.[47] Prussia was not the place to learn about the larger issues of strategy and tactics, and the handling of an army in battle.

12

Laws of War and the Reality of Warfare

What was medieval warfare really like? Most descriptions of medieval warfare that have come down to us are by poets or chroniclers who (like modern historians) have never been in a battle. The images which Geoffroy de Charny conjures up are at the opposite pole from the rhetoric of Froissart or Baker: blunt, direct and pulling no punches about the possible outcome.

Jean le Bel also wrote from direct experience about the hardships of a campaign in enemy territory. He vividly remembered Edward's first expedition into Scotland in 1327, with both sides in equally dire straits:

As soon as they [the enemy] had been found we were told to strike camp and take ourselves and all our gear to another mountain directly facing them. Then we formed our battle line and made as if to advance, but as soon as they saw us coming they left their shelters and smartly planted themselves close to the opposite bank of the river; but they wouldn't cross to meet us, and attacking them was impossible: we would all have been miserably slaughtered or captured.

So there we encamped, confronting them on that second mountain, for eighteen days in all. Every day we'd draw up our lines to face them, and they to face us; but they wouldn't cross the river to meet us, or give ground on their side to allow us to deploy, or accept our offer of ground on our side where they could do the same. And all the while they had no bread, no wine, no salt, and no leather or material to make hose or shoes: instead they made shoes out of raw cowhide, the hair still attached. Not that we were much better off: we had nowhere to lodge or shelter, and nowhere to forage but moor and heath. I can't tell you how frustrated we were about our tents and tools and baggage-carts: we'd brought them to make our lives easier and then had left them in a wood, unguarded, with no way of recovering them – we didn't even know where the wood was! We spent a month in this abject, miserable state, with all our supplies missing when we needed them most. It's true that provisions were daily brought for sale from all directions throughout the time we were besieging the Scots and were stuck there facing them – but at what a price! A badly baked loaf (of low-grade grain) cost three pence when it would have been worth just a *parisis* in the town, and a gallon of warm, poor-quality wine cost twelve when a barrelful would have been worth but three. We had to feed ourselves and our pages very sparingly, constantly fearing greater hunger still and that our money would run out if we had to stay much longer.[1]

Edward's armies rarely found themselves in such dire straits again, but any long campaign would mean problems of supply, serious wear and tear on armour, clothing and shoes, and horses with patched-up harness who were often unshod. The English army at Crécy was the worse for wear after six weeks in the field, even though their baggage train was intact, and they were reasonably well provisioned. But there were also benefits from time spent on campaign in a well-disciplined army, notably the growth of *esprit de corps* and a mutual trust between the commanders and their men.

As to the battles themselves, the terror and chaos of the action itself is never evoked in the chronicles, which generally resort to clichés and to vague overall descriptions. We have no descriptions of what it was like to be met by a hail of arrows from the English archers, or to withstand a French cavalry charge on foot. Only at one moment do we get some feeling of what participation in a battle might have been like, in the descriptions of Prince Edward and his men at Crécy. Prince Edward was 'compelled to fight kneeling down against the masses of the enemy who poured around him', and when the bishop of Durham arrived with reinforcements, he 'found the prince and his men leaning on their lances and swords, drawing breath and taking a moment's rest over long mountains of the dead, as they waited for the enemy to return from his retreat'. The dead, of course, had not been slain by Edward and his companions alone; most would have died at the hands of the archers or simply been crushed against the bodies of men and horses which blocked their way.[2] And in the aftermath, the king asked his son 'what he thought of going into battle and being in the midst of it, and why it was a fine game and the prince said nothing and hung his head.'³

The most controversial and sometimes the most gratuitously violent moments of Edward's campaigns came during the raids into France, which were intended to demonstrate to the populace at large that the French kings could not defend them, and were therefore not the true rulers of the country. At the same time, they were intended to provoke the French to put an army in the field and fight a pitched battle. Despite Edward's claim at the outset of the Crécy campaign that he intended to protect the civilian population, there were excesses from the start, largely because it was extremely difficult to control an army in which there were undoubtedly men out for pillaging and rape. As early as the siege of Caen, in the second week of the Crécy raid, there were severe problems of this kind. And there was official brutality, the burning of towns and destruction of crops and property, in the name of economic warfare.

None of this was as bad, however, as the lawlessness which followed the French defeat at Poitiers, banditry over which neither the French nor English king had control, though Edward undoubtedly exploited it when he could, as did Charles of Navarre. Only one of the Garter knights, Eustace d'Auberchicourt, seems to have been involved, and that fairly briefly. This brigandage, however, stemmed from the troops made unemployed by the truce between England and France, and led to the formation of the 'great companies', whose organized depredations were the most terrifying of all. The narrow border between these ex-brigands and the royal armies was underlined when they were incorporated into both the French and English expeditions to Spain in 1366–7.

THE FINANCES OF WARFARE

For the English knights, and for some fortunate footsoldiers, there were fortunes to be won (and sometimes lost) on the battlefield and on campaign. The Garter companions occupy a very wide spectrum in this respect, from men who had only just been knighted to the greatest magnates of the realm. A man like Henry Eam would have had at most half a dozen men in his retinue, and possibly just a squire. His main expense would have been his horses and armour; an adequate warhorse cost between £15 and £30, and he would need one or two lesser horses besides as reserves, or for riding if he wished to rest his best horse.[4] His armour would cost somewhere around the same amount: a helmet could cost £5, and a pair of plates (the coverings for chest and back) as much again. The knight's basic equipment represented a substantial investment, and the ongoing expense of maintaining even a modest retinue required the income from a small manor at least: the grant to Sir Henry Eam when he took service with the prince of Wales was for £66 13s. 4d. to be paid out of the revenues of the manor of Bradninch. This was in fact an honour, or group of manors, and therefore an important source of income for the prince, and only from such a source could fees on this scale be paid. Sometimes the grants were in the form of annuities to be paid until a suitable holding was free, which would provide the equivalent in income.

The system under which the companions of the Garter and other knights of similar rank served was relatively new; it had been introduced in the 1340s after Edward's bitter experience with hiring foreign troops in Flanders. Because the feudal obligation to serve the king could be directly invoked only if there was a threat of invasion, a new system was needed, and rates of pay were critical. Men had to be paid to fight abroad; Edward paid a *regard* or retainer to the leaders of retinues, whether knights or bannerets, and then wages, again payable to the leader, which were quickly doubled for the overseas campaigns. The problem was that the king was always short of ready cash, and at the end of the campaign the knight might be owed a substantial sum because he had had to pay his men out of his own pocket. Typically, the wages owed by the king to the leaders of retinues were paid in part during the campaign, and the settlement of the balance might take as much as twenty years. Some knights evidently could not afford to finance their men: in the record of payments for the 1355 Gascon campaign kept by John Henxteworth, John Mohun is paid a series of small sums at regular intervals, while his fellow-knights are paid large lump sums occasionally.[5] The explanation for this seems to be that Mohun lacked the cash resources to which the others had access, and his financial problems are indeed documented in the law cases in which he was involved at the time.

Many knights would resort to borrowing for a major campaign.

Quite apart from the direct and unavoidable costs they had to meet, there was the temptation to spend money on display; Charny observes that there are men who commit themselves to 'great state and outward show', the cost of which exhausts their resources. Visual display was part of military life, and it was always tempting for an ambitious knight to make a brilliant appearance in terms of fine warhorses, elaborate trappings and the best armour. A case in point is Walter Mauny: in 1342–3 he led a small force to Brittany, and the accounts for payments for horses lost show that his retinue had horses of much higher than average value, while he himself rode a *destrier* worth £100, the highest valuation in the record. Mauny was a great polisher of his knightly image, and turning up on campaign on the equivalent of a Rolls-Royce may have all been part of this, along with the splendid stories he told to Jean le Bel and later to Froissart. His squadron, also on fine horses, would have made a strong impression and enhanced his reputation.[6] Mauny had already made money from ransoms and was in a position to lend the king £4,000 in 1340, so could clearly afford such a display.

For those who could not, raising money was not difficult. A lease could be sold on an estate or the revenues pledged for a loan; Hugh Wrottesley's tangled finances included several transactions of this kind. Many knights resorted to straight borrowing from magnates or merchants. A number of these transactions were recorded at the exchequer, and we can trace the fortunes of individual knights. The greatest lender in the country was Richard Fitzalan, earl of Arundel. We have already noted his absence from the Company of the Garter, despite his military record, with the suggestion that it might be this financial record that was the reason. In the decade between 1350 and 1359, he lent sums varying between 200 marks and £2,000 to five different Garter companions. The last transaction is one of a class of somewhat mysterious dealings on the eve of military campaigns. In this case William Bohun, earl of Northampton, lends Richard Fitzalan, earl of Arundel, £2,000; and Arundel lends Northampton £2,000. Such back-to-back loans are often found in connection with performance of a contract, such as an engagement between the heirs of two families; if there is a default, then the defaulting party loses his money. But in the context of imminent departure on an expedition, this must have a different function. Until we find an example of one of these loans which was actually called in, the most likely explanation is that it is some kind of mutual insurance, against a ransom perhaps, or simply shortage of cash: if for example Northampton could not pay his men, he could go to Arundel and draw on the pre-arranged loan for ready money.

For lesser men, the entries at the exchequer are of a series of more modest debts – modest in comparison, but a heavy burden for knights with small resources. John Mohun appears with five debts between 1350 and 1355 totalling £468, of which only £9 13s. 4d. is shown as repaid: the lenders include John Beauchamp, the bishop of Worcester and the king. William Fitzwarin borrows £100 from his patron Queen Philippa in 1345. Knights whose careers are largely abroad appear less frequently in these lists: there are only a handful of entries for Audley, Chandos, the younger Burghersh and Loring.

Against this, we have to set the income from warfare. Firstly, there are the king's wages and the *regards* paid to the leaders of retinues. For the ordinary knight, it was only the wages that counted, and these were paid at the standard rate of two shillings per day.[7] This was twice that for an ordinary man at arms, and half that for a banneret. The responsibility for feeding the troops lay with the commander of the retinue to which they belonged; the Garter companions, unless they were magnates, were attached either to the prince's or to the king's household. We know a great deal about the king's household and its provisioning on campaign, for the detailed accounts of the Crécy campaign survive. The quantities involved indicate that the supplies were for the king's personal entourage only, rather than feeding his whole retinue. There are episodes in the chronicles where, describing acute food shortages during a campaign, the writer says that bread or other food was sold very expensively, which implies that there was some purchasing of supplies within the army. In the circumstances two shillings a day, which was the equivalent of £36 p.a., was in itself enough to make a cautious man reasonably wealthy simply by his presence in the army.

The real money was to be made where there was booty to be had, and particularly where there were ransoms to be secured. After the sack of Caen, writers say that an astonishing amount of loot was sent back to England. Once it was unloaded from the ships which had been sent back to fetch more supplies, we hear nothing more of it; it may have been quickly sold on to London merchants, or it may have gone to adorn manors up and down the country. But booty is cited only in general terms as a profit of war; it is difficult to quantify from the records we have. The principles, however, were established by the laws of war, by contract and by custom.[8] For the most part, the knights with whom we are concerned were fighting either in the king's name or under his command. This meant that they were fighting in a 'just war', a war declared by a sovereign or a great prince. Under these conditions, there was no doubt as to the legality of their spoils; the activities of English captains in France after 1356, when the official truce after Poitiers degenerated into a free-for-all, were much more questionable in terms of the law of arms. In the case of a siege, the loot was entirely the king's property, and this would have been the case at Caen. But the king had already agreed terms with his commanders, and they in turn had contracted with the knights in their service as to the division of spoils. The English custom was generous: for most of the campaigns of Edward III's reign, the spoils were divided evenly between the captain and the soldier who had taken the booty.[9] In France, the captains had only a tenth; the incentive to loot was therefore much greater for the English, even though it was directly at odds with Edward's sporadic efforts to win over, rather than terrify, the French people he claimed to rule.

Even if we cannot put figures on the total of booty taken – the king's share was treated as his private income, and did not pass through the exchequer records – the real concern of soldiers about its acquisition and distribution is reflected in Charny's *Questions on Jousts, Tournaments and War*. There are fifteen headings for discussion, which deal with the problems that might arise, such as the case where part of a troop of soldiers have fled from the action and the remainder have fought on and won substantial booty: are they all entitled to a share, or do those who have left the battle forfeit all right to booty?[10] Charny's basic premise in all the discussion points is that booty is taken for the common good of the whole force engaged in the combat, and is only divided afterwards: there is no question of individual profit. Furthermore, the division of spoils is after an individual engagement, rather than at the end of a campaign. Beyond this, we know little of how the actual goods were handled, transported or sold to merchants. Records of the sharing out of ordinary spoils are extremely rare: I have found only one specific payment for booty, when Chandos and his men were paid £118 16s. for 215 cattle on 22 June 1356 near Périgueux.[11] At the other extreme, where individual objects of great value are concerned, we know that the prince of Wales acquired the crown, badge of the

Company of the Star and a silver table centrepiece in the form of a boat found in John II's tent at Poitiers; he promptly pawned the last two items to the earl of Arundel in return for a loan.

Ransoms were quite another matter.[12] If the right captive fell into a knight's hands, it was like winning the lottery; and precisely because large sums and important political figures could be involved, there was a considerable body of law about the capture of prisoners, the way in which they should surrender and how the rights of the captor could be enforced. In the tumult of a medieval battle, it is extraordinary that a transaction of this kind could be carried out in a way which ensured that both captor and captive recognized its legitimacy, and which in turn was acknowledged by the rest of the army. For the lawyers in the calm of their chambers, the capture of a prisoner established a contract in law, sealed by an oath: the prisoner literally became his captor's property, and could be inherited, subject to the terms of his ransom, like any other asset. In return for surrendering his liberty, the captive gained the protection of his captor. In the heat of battle, there had to be a good deal of trust: the ransom could not be settled on the spot, and the initial duty of the captor was to ensure his prisoner's safety. In practice, the prisoner would have been taken out of the battle by a squire to the rear of the army, where he would be guarded until the action had ended. If the captor's side was defeated, that did not mean that prisoners necessarily gained their liberty, as they would usually remain with the retreating losers.

The most famous case is that of the count of Dammartin, whose case was entered as a matter of public record in the prince of Wales's register, three years after his capture at the battle of Poitiers. Thomas Beauchamp, earl of Warwick, and Reginald Cobham, as constable and marshal at the time, and therefore the highest authorities of the army in terms of military law, testified that the prince had made an ordinance, publicly proclaimed before the battle, that 'no man should linger over his prisoner on pain of forfeiting him, but that each man without hindrance or dispute should have the prisoner to whom he should first be pledged'. The count himself then declared before the prince's council and his notary the events of his capture. The first to approach him to surrender – by implication he was clearly in no fit state to resist – was a squire who identified himself as John Trailly, of the prince's household. 'He called on me to surrender,' recalled Dammartin, 'and I gave him my fealty in such wise that he should save me.' Trailly took off his prisoner's helmet, and, when he protested, said that he would be quite safe. He also took off his gauntlets, and someone else cut off his sword, which Trailly collected. Trailly put him on his own horse, and gave him to one of his retainers to guard. But the retainer went off, and left him. A Gascon appeared, and demanded that Dammartin should surrender to him. 'I answered that I was already a prisoner, but all the same I gave him my fealty, simply so that he should save me.' He took a badge from his armour, and left: as the Gascon went, Dammartin said that if anyone else came up and asked him to surrender to him, he would do so. 'Save yourself, if you can,' was the answer. The next to appear was one of John de Blankmouster's retainers. Dammartin explained that he had already been taken prisoner twice, but surrendered yet again. 'This man stayed with me, guarded me and brought me to the earl of Salisbury, and I gave my fealty to the earl at the wish and consent of my last captor.'[13]

This must have been typical of the chaos surrounding the taking of prisoners; it usually happened in the last and most confused stages of the battle. Presumably Trailly, his retainer and the Gascon either felt themselves to be in danger or went off in search of more profitable booty; even if they understood who their captive was, they might well have little idea of his importance unless his armour and arms made it clear that he was someone of the highest rank. This takes us back to ransoms as a contract: in return for the prisoner's surrender, the captor was guaranteeing his safety. If he wandered off and left him, and failed to guard him, the contract was valueless, and the process could begin again. The prince of Wales claimed Dammartin as his prisoner, because his squire was the first to take him, but the court adjudged that this contract was broken, as was that with the anonymous Gascon, and that Dammartin was the prisoner of William Montagu, earl of Salisbury. A charter was duly drawn up, putting in writing the conditions of the ransom. The prisoner had to promise to obey and be loyal to his captor, and to renounce any attempt to dispute his captor's right to ransom once he had signed the document. If he failed to carry out these obligations, he was to suffer the penalties, both spiritual and secular, for perjury, and his captor could disgrace him by displaying his arms reversed[14] as a traitor.

Further documents would set out the terms of captivity, and the arrangements for paying the ransom. Even if the prisoner was rescued by his own side, he was still bound by the agreements, and, while he was subject to ransom, he could not fight against his captor or his allies. The conditions of his captivity were specified, which varied from actual imprisonment to the requirement that he should return to the place of captivity each evening. As to raising the ransom, this was the most difficult point of all. The price had to be set, and was in principle a sum which the prisoner would be able to raise, though this was not always the case. There are many instances of ransoms not being paid in full, as with John II after Poitiers, either by agreement or because the knight in question absconded after a substantial payment had been made. In the end, of the huge sum of thirty million gold crowns demanded as John II's ransom, between 45 and 55 per cent of it was paid; as much of it went directly to the king's private treasury, we do not have exact accounts.[15] Other prisoners spent much of their life in prison awaiting ransom; and exceptionally a prisoner might be so important that his release was forbidden. Henry V forbade the release of Charles duke of Orléans after Agincourt, because he was head of the Armagnac family, rival claimants to the throne of France; and Charles's son, born after his release in 1440, did indeed become Louis XII of France.

More typically, a reasonable ransom would be set, and the prisoner would be allowed to travel on licence to his home to set about raising it: his status was in effect that of a non-combatant. He would have to find men, usually from his own retinue, to act as sureties for him and remain with his captor while he was away. Charny does outline a case where a prisoner, on the advice of his surety, passes all his estates to his heirs, and fails to return or pay up; the surety then excuses himself on the grounds that the prisoner has no assets. In real life, legal manoeuvres of this sort seem to have been very rare, and Charny is probably asking a rhetorical question.[16] If the prisoner failed to reappear, the sureties would be liable for the ransom themselves; there was little effective recourse against escaped prisoners in these circumstances, since their assets were in enemy territory and a lawsuit would be almost impossible. The only real recourse was that of dishonour, which was said to be taken extremely seriously: the aggrieved captor could display the escaped prisoner's arms in a public place, but just as important was to spread the word that the captive had broken his word.

In 1360, the treaty of Brétigny had stipulated that, if John II travelled to France to organize his ransom, his younger son, Louis duke of Anjou, should go to England as one of his sureties. Anjou went in 1361, very reluctantly: on his arrival, he was fêted by the English court, particularly by Queen Philippa, along with the other dukes who were John's sureties. The usual state occasions and feasts were laid on, and also many informal social gatherings.[17] It must have been about this time that Louis was presented with the only Garter badge from Edward III's reign of which a record survives:

> Another brooch, made in the manner of a garter, and it is enamelled in blue. And on it is written: *honny soit qui mal y pense*. And in the middle a little boar which is on a green ground. And to one side there is a balas ruby. And above its back there are six little diamonds. And around the said boar there is also a white rose, on the leaves of which are six little escutcheons in the midst of which is a diamond. And the whole of the brooch is surrounded with pearls, and there is a little escutcheon of St George.[18]

The symbolism of this is difficult to disentangle. Both Edward and the prince of Wales were referred to as 'boars' in the symbolism of political poems and in chronicles. As the boar is a 'pourcel', literally piglet, it may refer to the prince of Wales rather than his father, and Geoffrey le Baker calls him the 'boar of Cornwall' in the context of the victory at Poitiers.[19] But why was such a symbol of English victory and French humiliation handed to Louis of Anjou?

Despite the lavish festivals, Louis chafed at his captivity, and contrived to escape in September 1363; he was being held by the English in Calais, and was allowed to leave on parole for three days at a time to visit his wife, whom he had married in 1360, at the nearby castle of Guise. After one such visit, he simply failed to come back, and, when his father tried to persuade him to return, he flatly refused. It was an act with huge consequences: a private treaty between John II's sureties in England and Edward III which would have settled the problem of the ransom payments became valueless, and Anjou's escape was one – but not the only – reason for John II's return to England and death there in 1364. This was the most dramatic breach of faith over a ransom; but there were other, more marginal cases, particularly those of Arnoul d'Audrehem and Bertrand du Guesclin after the battle of Najéra in 1367. Both had been captured by the English and ransomed, Audrehem at Poitiers and du Guesclin at Auray in 1364. Both had only paid part of their ransoms, Audrehem to the prince of Wales and du Guesclin to John Chandos. Both therefore faced the same accusation: that they had fought against their captors in breach of their oaths. According to the Spanish chronicler Pero López de Ayala, who may have been present, the prince called Audrehem 'a false traitor'. Audrehem replied, 'Sire, you are a king's son and I do not answer you as respectfully as I should: but I am neither a traitor, nor false.' The prince agreed to a trial by twelve knights from his army, four from England, four from Aquitaine and four from Brittany. He made a speech outlining the charges. Audrehem asked if he might defend himself without incurring the prince's wrath, and the prince told him to speak freely since it was a matter 'of knights and of war'. Audrehem then came up with a convincing argument: in response to the prince's charge, he pointed out that he was not fighting the prince, but Pedro of Castile; they were both hired swords, serving other masters, and he had not therefore attacked the prince's interests. Ayala, preferring the chivalrous rather than the practical view of such matters, claims that 'the prince and the other knights were very pleased that the marshal had found such a good reason to excuse himself, because he was a good knight'.[20] Even allowing for Ayala's knightly attitude to the matter, this shows how the 'laws of war' operated in reality. There was nothing to prevent the prince of Wales from taking justice into his own hands, as Philip VI might have done, and simply executing Audrehem; the court of law which tried the case was one which he had himself created, and the authority was that of the common interests and ideals of knighthood. Ayala's account is confirmed by a judgement in a similar case involving du Guesclin in 1390 before the highest court in France, the parlement of Paris; the defendant cited Audrehem's argument that the prince was merely a 'soudoier' or mercenary in Pedro's service.[21]

After Najéra, du Guesclin was apparently challenged to set his own ransom by the prince: as a man of relatively humble estate, he was in no position to pay a high price himself, and the prince of Wales knew that he was the most skilful of the French commanders. Indeed, his advisers were aghast when the prince made the offer, as they would have preferred to see him safely out of the way for as long as possible. Du Guesclin named a high sum, of around £20,000, which placed him on the same level as most great magnates,[22] and, as soon as it was agreed, obtained financial help from Charles V and was released a few months later.

Getting ransom money, for the ordinary knight, was a matter of luck. The commanders, however, were entitled to a share of any payments arranged with men in their retinue; just as with the knights, this was income used to defray their expenses, and to make a profit, though it would be difficult to judge what contribution it made to the huge outgoings involved. With individual knights, we can see the effects of ransoms on their fortunes much more clearly.

Many minor ransoms have left no trace in the records, so, when we look at the prisoners taken by the Garter companions personally, it is not surprising that we can find only eight of the thirty-six knights who are known to have profited from such transactions. Of the seven named captives, the majority are of the highest rank, as the list below shows. There were also eight other unnamed knights or groups of knights for whom Garter companions received ransoms on recorded occasions, but there must have been a far larger number of transactions of this kind which were on a small scale. For instance, Hugh Wrottesley's improvement in fortunes in 1343, after his rather dubious seizure of prisoners in Brittany, is almost certainly due to ransom money. At the bottom end of the scale is the income that Eustace d'Auberchicourt made from freebooting in 1358–9 in Champagne, less a question of ransoms than of extortion from the local populace in best Mafia style.

Prisoner:	*Captor*:	*Battle*:
Jacques de Bourbon	Captal de Buch	Poitiers 1356
Archbishop of Sens	Thomas Beauchamp	Poitiers 1356
Count of Longueville	Reginald Cobham	Poitiers 1356
Bertrand du Guesclin	John Chandos	Auray 1364
Raoul count of Eu	Thomas Holland	Caen 1346
Guy of Flanders	Walter Mauny	Cadzand 1337
John Crabbe	Walter Mauny	Roxburgh Bridge 1332

Poitiers was unusual for the high number of captives taken: the prince's edict before the battle seems to have worked well, in that the large-scale ransom operations did not interfere with the course of the battle. At Crécy, where both sides had signalled that no quarter was to be given, we know of very few prisoners, and none of any rank. At Poitiers, the captives were about 40 per cent of the total of enemy losses, while at Agincourt the ratio was 25 per cent; far more were killed in proportion to those captured.

Ransoms worked both ways, of course. Six Garter companions had to be ransomed during their career, from Robert Ufford, captured with William Montagu in 1340 due to a rash escapade in enemy territory, to Jean de Grailly, taken prisoner at Cocherel in 1364, and again at Soubise in 1372, dying in prison in Paris in 1377 because he refused to abandon his allegiance to the English. Eustace d'Auberchicourt was also captured twice in the course of his career as a freebooter, and on one occasion narrowly escaped being put to death on the spot. Wrottesley was captured in Brittany in 1354; his finances were always poor, and this was a serious matter, since he was outlawed in England and had no means of raising money. How he escaped and regained the king's favour is something of an enigma. John Beauchamp was taken in similar circumstances to those of Robert Ufford and William Montagu, leading a raid out of Calais, where he was captain of the town, in 1351. Thomas Ughtred was ransomed with help from Edward II early in his career, after the battle of Byland in 1322, when the Scots raided as far as north Yorkshire; ransoms in Scotland were usually modest compared with those demanded in France, because of the poverty of the country. For the English knights in general, the debit side of the ransoms, however, was very much smaller than the credit side.

Ransoms proved an excellent safeguard against death in battle, as long as you were on the winning side. It is astonishing how light were the English casualties in the early decades of the Hundred Years War. The French lost many more knights at Crécy alone than the English did in the whole period up to the end of Edward III's reign. Only two Garter companions fell in battle. John Lisle died, in what may have been an accident, early on the prince's raid towards Toulouse in 1355: in John Wingfield's words, he was killed 'very strangely, by a crossbow bolt'. Fifteen years later, John Chandos was killed on the bridge at Lussac. Froissart tells us that he slipped on the ice, because he was wearing a long surcoat embroidered with his arms, and that his attacker was on his blind side, as he had lost an eye many years earlier, so that he did not see the fatal blow. His great comrade, James Audley, narrowly escaped death at Poitiers, while Miles Stapleton probably died of wounds received at Auray. Most of the deaths recorded on campaign were due to other causes: Roger Mortimer died, much to Edward's grief, on the ill-fated Reims campaign, and it is surprising that no other Garter companions appear to have died in the field or at sieges, as the mortality rate at the siege of Calais far exceeded that for the battle of Crécy. Of the illnesses brought on by years of the harsh life of the camp and battlefield we know little. Three other knights who had been on the 1359–60 campaign died in the following two years: Henry of Grosmont, William Bohun and John Beauchamp, but this was due to the outbreak of plague in 1361 which, in comparison with that of 1349–50, took a far greater toll of the nobility. By the end of 1361, half the original founders were dead.

LAWS OF WAR

The existence of a system of ransoms depended on the laws of war. Behind the confusion of battle, the *chevauchées*, sieges and skirmishes of the official campaigns, and even behind the activities of the brigands of the companies there was a concept of a set of laws which applied to all warfare. The moral justification for any kind of warfare was a huge problem for theologians: Christianity – strange though this would have seemed to the Garter companions – is in theory an essentially pacific religion, and warfare posed all kinds of difficulties when it had to be reconciled to the teaching of the Gospels. In practice, theology was supplemented by a system which was more in tune with the harsh realities of life, the so-called law of arms, which tried to regulate the conditions of combat, appealing to the idea of the 'law of the nations' found in Roman legal writing. This rather vague concept was based on the idea that there was a 'natural' law, to which all men, whether Christian or heathen, were subject, and it therefore enabled the lawyers to deal with cases in which both believers and infidels were involved, even if the latter did not recognize the 'law of nations'; it was a legal fiction which attempted to solve an intractable problem, but at the same time it provided some kind of framework which meant that there were generally understood principles behind the waging of war.

Few, if any, of the knights fighting with Edward's armies would have troubled themselves with these high-minded ideas. What would have been familiar to them were the rules of engagement, the limits which both sides generally observed, either from a sense of honour or out of an instinct for self-preservation. The treatment meted out to their victims or captives might be what they themselves would face if the fortunes of war went against them. Their concept of these rules would have derived, not from the legal texts, but from the ideals promoted in the romances or sermons which we have already looked at. One stumbling block was that these ideals present the knight as a *defender*, and have little to say about his role as aggressor. This was where the 'laws of war' came into play: they restrained the aggressor from overstepping certain limits, and provided some relief to those who were on the losing side.

The 'laws of war' do not seem to have existed as a formal written legal code, but as a set of customs; when it came to a lawsuit, these customs would be taken into account, but the higher principles of the 'law of nations' might override such customary law. There is a tantalizing mention in an early fifteenth-century French chronicle whose author may have met Henry of Grosmont's grandson, the future Henry IV, during his exile in France in 1399.[23] Speaking of Henry of Grosmont, he tells us: 'Henry the duke of Lancaster, earl of Derby, who was so skilled in the law of arms and other matters, and who for the instruction of nobles made the book of the laws of war . . .'[24] Henry of Grosmont was certainly capable of writing such a book on the evidence of his authorship of *The Book of Holy Medicines*; but there is no trace of this book.

In legal terms, a case brought under the 'laws of war' was likely to be inconclusive, and difficult to enforce; as a result, such matters as ransoms were dealt with by contract. So the 'laws of war' are really an extension of mutually accepted conventions in warfare. For example, to display a banner implied that a state of war existed, whether it was a royal banner or that of a banneret. The unfurling of such a banner was a declaration that the rules of war now applied, and that a formal challenge to fight had been issued. In skirmishes, the only display might be of knights' pennons, even though a man of high enough rank to display a banner was present; in this case there was no formal engagement between the combatants. At the other extreme was the display of a specific banner which indicated that it was war to the death, *guerre mortelle*, and that no prisoners were to be taken: the banner for such occasions usually had a red background, and would be displayed by the king: the *oriflamme* unfurled at Crécy and Poitiers by the French, and the dragon banner attributed to Edward III at Crécy, are examples of this.

Outside the major campaigns, and particularly in periods when a truce was in force, much of the fighting was in fact outside the scope of the 'laws of war'. A knight was entitled to wage private war against an individual, provided he had good and lawful reason to do so, and had sent a defiance to his opponent. The cat-and-mouse fighting on the Gascon border might occasionally have qualified as private war, but was usually a simple breach of the truce when one side saw an opportunity to seize a fortress or capture an important opponent. Technically, the operations of men like John Chandos and James Audley were sometimes on the wrong side of the 'law of arms', but both sides were equally guilty in this respect. More serious were the activities of Eustace d'Auberchicourt as a leader of a private company in Champagne; not only was he in breach of the truce, but he actually defied a specific order from Edward III to desist from his activities.

A display of banners clearly identified the leader in whose name the action was being fought. The war cry could also be used as a means of proclaiming the army's nationality or allegiance. This took various forms: the early war cries were national ones, 'Montjoie St Denis' for France and 'St George' for England. These could be coupled with other words indicating allegiance, as in the cry 'Guyenne, St George', used at Poitiers ten years later, Guyenne being another name for the English domains in Aquitaine. Individual war cries were later attributed to families: if an army attacked using the cry of a great lord, it was assumed that they were acting either under his personal leadership or on his instructions. At Cocherel in 1364, according to Froissart, the count of Auxerre, technically the senior officer in the French force, declined to have his cry used, and ordered that du Guesclin's name should be the signal, as the latter already had a great reputation: so the cry became 'Notre Dame, Guesclin'.[25]

SAFE CONDUCTS

In wartime, certain of the enemy were automatically granted safe conduct: messengers, heralds and ambassadors. For the ordinary knight, safe conduct usually only applied under strict conditions; if he was taken prisoner, he might travel home under safe conduct in order to raise his ransom. He would also need safe conduct if he was not involved in the war, and needed to travel through hostile territory. This was all well and good if that territory was under the control of a recognized authority; the king's safe conduct was generally effective, but in the periods when the free companies were operating, safe conducts might be needed from a number of captains active along the route the traveller was taking. And such freebooters would not necessarily respect the safe conducts given by their allies.[26] One of the most famous cases involved Walter Mauny. In 1346 he was one of the captains at Aiguillon in Gascony when it was besieged by John duke of Normandy. In the course of the siege, he captured one of John's knights, and ransomed him in return for a safe conduct from the duke to travel through French territory to Hainault. When he tried to use it, however, he was captured and imprisoned; he escaped, but was caught again and sent to Paris. Here, John's first attempt to persuade his father the king to release him was refused, and, according to Jean le Bel, John was 'so upset by this that for as long as [Mauny] remained imprisoned he refused to be part of his father's household', and in the end he secured Mauny's release.[27] To disregard the duke of Normandy's safe conducts was to dishonour him, and Henry V decreed towards the end of his reign that anyone who defied a royal safe conduct should meet the same fate as a traitor: he would be hanged and drawn. But as with so many other legal aspects of war, what happened in the field had little relation to what custom and royal decrees might dictate.

SIEGES

The most striking application of the laws of war was at the end of a siege. Sieges could end in three ways: the castle, town or city could be taken by storm, the besieged could surrender unconditionally, or the two sides could reach an agreement as to the terms on which the siege would end. In addition, there was of course the not uncommon possibility of treason.

For a fortified place to be taken by storm was a disaster of the first magnitude. The laws and customs of war were stark: the goods and chattels of the citizens were at the disposal of the conquerors, and they themselves, with the exception of women, children and priests, were fair game, particularly if they offered resistance to the seizure of their worldly wealth. In the heat of the fighting, however, murder, rape and assault were regarded by the chroniclers as to be expected. Caen in 1346 is a prime example of the scenes which followed a victorious assault by the besiegers; even the high-ranking leaders of the French garrison narrowly escaped with their lives. The garrison, as frequently happened, was able to retreat to the castle keep, and to hold it until the English army had moved on. It was therefore almost always the civilian population that bore the brunt of the siege. Behind the scenes of devastation lay Edward's decision to make an example of Caen, and to show that resistance to his authority on the part of his French subjects would not be tolerated. From the point of view of his men, the booty and ransom from Caen became a legendary moment in the war, when the possibility of profits of war was realized for the first time. As we have seen, it also influenced popular opinion in England in favour of Edward's campaigns.

At Calais, the surrender was negotiated, but was unconditional. The town was therefore at Edward's mercy just as if it had been taken by storm. It was, however, unusual for a brutal pillaging of a town to follow such a capitulation. Instead, the goods would be taken on the king's behalf in a systematic and orderly fashion, and would be divided out as spoils according to the terms of the agreements he had made with his captains. The famous scene of the surrender of Calais, as described by Jean le Bel, makes absolutely clear that Edward was within his rights to put everyone in the town to death; the alternative was to punish the leaders of the resistance to his authority, and in practice this was the norm. Cold-blooded massacres of an entire population are unknown, though on occasion all the occupants of a castle that surrendered might be killed. The likelihood that Edward would order the execution of the six burghers who came to surrender to him is what makes the tension of Le Bel's narrative so acute, and the drama of the intervention, first by

Walter Mauny and then by the queen herself, so vivid. Le Bel makes Edward's action one of simple mercy.[28] When Froissart came to rewrite Le Bel for the first time, he made it a more pragmatic deed: Mauny, he says, argued that, if the leaders of Calais were executed, the same might happen to English commanders under such circumstances.[29]

The most notorious siege of the period was that of Limoges in 1370. It was surrendered to the French without resistance by its lord, the bishop of Limoges, who was godfather to the prince of Wales's eldest son. According to Froissart the prince retook the city by storm, and, furious at the bishop's betrayal of him, threatened to execute him. The city was then pillaged and the inhabitants slaughtered to a man. The English chronicler Thomas Walsingham seems to confirm this, claiming that 'the prince almost totally destroyed it and killed all those he found there, a few only being spared their lives'. However, the city's own chronicle merely says that the inhabitants were taken prisoner, including the bishop, while a note in the chronicles of the monastery of St Martial of Limoges written very soon after the event put the death toll at 300. A careful study of the tax records before and after the siege by a local historian arrived at a similar figure, perhaps 10 per cent of the population. These were probably casualties of the fighting, and the 'massacre' is very unlikely to have taken place. What the episode reveals is not the prince's cruelty – it is sometimes cited as having given rise to his nickname 'the Black Prince' – but what chroniclers expected to happen at a siege where the ruler's honour had been seriously slighted by treachery.[30]

For a complex arrangement for the ending of a siege, Edward III's capture of Berwick just before the battle of Halidon Hill in 1333 is an excellent example. It specifies the time by which the relief force must reach the city if the surrender is not to take place, and even the direction from which it must approach. The relief force did not have to enter the town, but merely to encamp near it. In this case, a small army appeared, but from the wrong direction: they entered English territory, and attempted to attack from the south, so the agreement was null and void. Calais is another case where a relief agreement was made and failed, even though Philip VI had raised a huge army and brought it to within a few miles of the town. His retreat was held to have dishonoured him, and the question of honour recurs again and again in relation to sieges. Even the precise specifications for relief are part of this: the two armies were not regarded as fighting a campaign when these details were drawn up, but rather participating in a formal judicial combat. If the garrison refused to surrender a fortress when they should have done so under an agreement, any hostages given by the besieged were liable to be executed; and they often were, the death of Alexander Seton's son at Berwick being an example. It was a symbolic penalty for the treason of the besieged, and treason was above all a crime against honour.[31]

PART FOUR

A Question of Honour

13

The Garter Companions at War

Sixteen months after Calais had been taken, in December 1349, Geoffroy de Charny approached a Genoese mercenary, Aimeric di Pavia, who was stationed there as master of the king's galleys, to see if he would betray the town to the French for a suitable fee. Charny may well have known Aimeric from the days when he was in French service, because he had been in the French garrison during the siege, and had changed to the English side when the town was captured. The price agreed was 20,000 gold pieces,[1] and the date of the operation was set for the very end of the year. Aimeric was to obtain the keys to one of the towers, and would admit Charny and his comrades by night. Aimeric, however, decided to play a double game, and wrote to Edward revealing the entire plot: Baker claims that he had pangs of conscience, but as a mercenary Aimeric had probably simply weighed up the situation and decided that Edward was likely to reward him better for the information.

The news reached the king at Havering on Christmas Eve, and he hastily assembled a small group of knights from his household, including the prince of Wales and Roger Mortimer, with a number of men at arms and archers. They reached Calais just before the town was due to be betrayed, and set up an ambush for the French. Baker describes in great detail how the knights were hidden by a specially constructed dry wall, which could be pushed down at the right moment, and how the drawbridge was partly sawn through so that it could be broken by a stone toppled from the parapet above. This is probably an elaboration: he claims that the knights were concealed there for three days, 'like hermits'. It is more likely that the trap involved the double walls and moats surrounding the town, and that a special arrangement for bringing up the outer drawbridge, supplementing the usual mechanism and invisible to the scouts, was put in place.[2] When Charny arrived before dawn on 4 January, unaware of the double-dealing that had taken place, he was certainly cautious. The French standard was flying over the gate by which he was to be admitted, but he sent in scouts to ensure that the entrance was safe and that there were no suspicious signs. He demanded Aimeric's brother as hostage, and sent him as a prisoner to the nearby castle of Guines. Only when he was reassured that all was well did he hand over the first payment to Aimeric. Charny ordered the advance guard to move into the town, and as soon as the first body of men had crossed the bridge, it was raised. Since the inner drawbridge was not yet lowered, they were trapped between the inner and outer walls; the English knights emerged from their hiding places and captured them. The French standard was replaced by that of England, and Charny and his men realized that they had been betrayed. They started to withdraw across the narrow causeway through the marshes, but the king led a handful of men out of the gate and pursued them.

When the French realized how few the king's companions were, they turned to fight, and for a moment it seemed that Edward had put himself in serious danger; he later rewarded his standard-bearer, Guy Brian, for his bravery in carrying the standard and defending it in the fighting. However, the king had sent archers to find dry places in the marsh where they could station themselves, and the prince of Wales brought reinforcements out of another gate. A brief but fierce fight ensued, ending with the capture of Charny and Eustace de Ribemont, the other French commander. The archers probably accounted for the majority of the 200 French killed in the encounter. Le Bel has a typical romantic story of the aftermath. According to him, when the French commanders were brought before Edward, he reproached Charny, the supposed model of knighthood, for his treachery in trying to take Calais by deceit and sent him to England as a prisoner; but set Ribemont free: the king crowned him with a chaplet of pearls in honour of his bravery, and released him on condition that he wore it for a year whenever he was in the company of ladies. In fact, Ribemont was sent by Edward on parole to Philip of Valois to tell him what had happened, after which he went to England as a prisoner. Two years later Charny, having paid a substantial ransom for his freedom, had his revenge on Aimeric di Pavia, whom he captured in the course of an attack on Guines, now in English hands, and the outposts of Calais. He took his prisoner to St Omer, where he was tortured and executed.[3]

The truce was supposed to include the Castilians who had supplied ships to fight with the French navy, but the Castilian seamen had continued to harass English shipping in the Channel on their own account, combining this with trading with the Flemish ports. Their activities became so alarming in the summer of 1350 that Edward decided to take action against them. The Castilian ships were armed merchantmen, considerably larger than cogs or galleys; these were busses, with high 'castles' forward and aft. A buss was less manoeuvrable than the smaller ships, but had the advantage in a sea-battle, because missiles could be dropped on a cog or galley which came alongside to grapple it. Edward requisitioned ships to assemble at Sandwich, ordering them to have similar wooden castles fitted, and raised a small army with which to man them. A major attack on the Castilians was intended, as the whole fleet was under his command, and the prince of Wales, Henry of Grosmont, William Bohun, William Montagu, Richard Fitzalan, William Clinton, Hugh Audley and Thomas Beauchamp were given squadrons.[4] Reginald Cobham, Walter Mauny, Robert of Namur and John Chandos were also present, as well as John Lisle, Lord Basset, Thomas Holland and Guy Brian.[5]

The Castilians had previously attacked a wine convoy from Gascony, and appear to have been cruising close to the English coast looking for places where they could land and loot the ports. This would explain why Edward was able to intercept them without difficulty off Winchelsea. It would have been hard to find such a fleet if it was even as close as mid-Channel; by the time a small vessel, however fast, had found the fleet and reported its whereabouts, pursuing ships would have been unable to catch up. It seems more likely that coastal watchers were able to sight it and send word by land to Sandwich so that the English ships would be well out to sea before the Castilian fleet passed. The Spaniards had twenty-four great ships, loaded with valuable Flemish cloth, which towered over the English ships, in Geoffrey le Baker's vivid phrase, 'like castles over cottages', as well as other smaller ships. When the fleets engaged, the English archers were able to open fire out of range of the Spanish crossbows. However, they were unable to clear the decks and when the English engaged at close range and tried to board the ships, they suffered heavy casualties alongside because of the shower of missiles which rained down on them. Once the English boarded, they were able to overcome the lightly armed Castilian crews; in several cases they had to take refuge in the captured ships because their own vessels had been sunk while grappled to the Spanish. The battle ended at dusk, and, when the English prepared to renew the conflict the next day, twenty-seven ships had escaped, leaving seventeen in their hands. To celebrate the victory, the king knighted eighty squires.

Shortly afterwards 1,000 pavises, shields used to protect archers on ships and to shelter men involved in siege works, were delivered to Robert Mildenhale, keeper of the armoury at the Tower: they were painted white, with the royal arms encircled by a blue garter; a further 100 were of burnished silver-gilt, with a garter above the king's arms. Pavises such as these were a novelty in England at the time and these would have made a dramatic display, very probably in a naval battle. Although we cannot associate them with a particular event, they were a powerful statement of the place of the Company of the Garter at the heart of the English military effort.[6]

The pavises also remind us how little we know about display of arms on the battlefield. The debate in the contemporary poem *Winner and Waster* takes place before a king who is clearly identifiable as Edward: Winner argues for austerity and saving, while Waster advocates expenditure – 'with our feasts and prosperity we feed the poor' – and argues that money 'huddled and hidden and hoarded in coffers' does no good to the people at large.[7] The poem is often said to be a satire on Edward's expenditure, but the debate is balanced, and, at the end of the argument, the king pronounces an even-handed judgement; the views of the protagonists have a strong echo today. The poet sets the scene on a battlefield where the opposing armies of Winner and Waster are drawn up, and depicts the king's camp on the cliff above, a scarlet tent decorated with gold ornaments encircled by blue garters: between them were woven the words 'Hething have the hathel that any harm thinketh!', a paraphrase in English of the Garter motto. Its guardian has a magnificent helm with a golden leopard crest, and a cloth with the arms of England and France quartered. The king sits nearby on a silken bench, in a brown mantle embroidered with ducks so realistic that they seemed to tremble in fear of the falcons who threatened them. This is an allusion to Edward's love of falconry, but the interest for us lies in the image of the tent resplendent with garters. We have no details of the decorations of Edward's war pavilions; perhaps the poet had indeed seen one of them, and, as with the pavises, the Garter was the dominant theme in the 1350s, the decade to which the poem is usually attributed. If the French associated the Garter with the English victory at Crécy, it would have been a potent and threatening visual symbol.

But was the sea-fight off Winchelsea a victory? Geoffrey le Baker, whose account we have quoted, certainly thought it was, and many other writers agreed with him. Gilles li Muisit, writing from Tournai, and relying on news brought back to Flanders, was more doubtful; although he could not really decide what could be said about the occasion, he thought the king of England had suffered greater losses than the Spaniards, because his forces were the flower of his army, and the Castilians were a ragbag collection of merchants and mercenaries from Flanders.[8] The majority of the Castilian fleet had escaped, and he had simply ended up with less than half their cargo – and it was this which the English were really interested in. This cynical account is somewhat contradicted by the fact that a formal truce for twenty years was signed with Castile very shortly afterwards, because the Spaniards realized that they could not overcome the English; and since, quite apart from the raid on the wine fleet, Edward had made considerable arrangements for the militia to defend the English coast that summer, the Spaniards were clearly the aggressors.

Le Bel, for once, is silent about this occasion; Froissart has a very full account, probably from his patron Robert of Namur, who was one of the commanders. If we reduce it to the basic information, what he has to say is credible: the fight was very severe, because of the Spanish advantage of the height of their castles. The king's ship rammed and dismasted one Spanish ship, the mast destroying the Spanish after-castle as it fell, but the force of the collision made the English ship spring a leak. Despite this, the king grappled another Spaniard, and eventually abandoned his own ship and boarded and took the Spaniard. The prince of Wales had a similar adventure, but was in danger of losing his victim and sinking with his ship when Henry of Grosmont grappled the Spaniard on the other side. As soon as the prince's men were able to storm the Spaniard, their own ship sank. Robert of Namur, in a ship called *Salle du Roi*, was grappled by a Spanish vessel which towed him away from the battle; one of his sailors got aboard and cut the main-mast stays, bringing it to a halt, and Robert and his men were able to conquer it.

The general pattern of the fight, the sinking of the English ships and the capture of the Spanish vessels is plausible enough. Froissart turns it into a much more knightly occasion than it is likely to have been in real-ity. Before the battle begins he presents us with this scene:

> The king posted himself in the fore part of his own ship: he was dressed in a black velvet jacket, and wore a small black beaver hat which suited him well, and he was, as I was told by those who were there, as joyful that day as they had ever seen him. He made his minstrels play for him a German dance which Sir John Chandos, who was present, had recently brought back. For his amusement, he made the said knight sing with his minstrels, and took great pleasure in it. And from time to time he looked up at the forecastle, where he had placed a lookout to tell him when the Spanish hove into view. And as the king took his pleasure and all the knights were happy to see him, so full of joy, the lookout, who had seen the Spanish fleet coming, running before the wind, cried: 'Ahoy! I see a ship coming, and I think it is from Spain!' Then the minstrels ceased . . .⁹

The king knew that it was at best a partial victory, because on 8 Septem-ber he wrote to the citizens of Bayonne, his southernmost city in Gascony, whose sailors were deadly rivals of the Castilian seamen and more or less permanently at loggerheads with them, that the Castilian fleet was on its way home and that they should arm themselves against a possible attack: in October, the Bordeaux wine fleet was given a pro-tective escort. On the other hand, the discipline and co-ordination of the English had been impressive, against considerable odds; for once, they were fighting at a disadvantage, and their commanders had been able to keep up the morale of their men amid the unfamiliar and difficult situ-ation of a battle at sea.

For a decade or more, the main theatre of the war between England and France had been northern France, from Brittany to Flanders. Gascony, where the French had taken substantial territory from the English, had been the scene of continuous skirmishes, but only one major campaign, that of Henry of Grosmont in 1345–6. When it became clear in early 1355 that the series of truces and peace negotiations which had maintained an uneasy calm for eight years was finally exhausted, Gascony became the focus of attention. The French lieutenant-general, Jean d'Armagnac, appointed in 1352, had successfully extended the area under French control, particularly along the valley of the river Lot, and was now continuing his successes closer to Bordeaux. Ralph Stafford, the commander in Gascony, had failed to prevent this creeping erosion of English authority, and Jean de Grailly, captal de Buch, and the lords of Lesparre and Mussidan came to England to meet the king and his council. At first the plan was to send Thomas Beauchamp to Gascony, and orders to requisition ships for him were made on 10 March. At the end of March, Henry of Grosmont returned from the failed peace nego-tiations at Avignon, and, at a great council in April, it was decided that the prince of Wales should lead the expedition. According to Chandos Herald, whose biography of the prince in verse was probably written around 1380, the prince told his father that 'one of his sons' should be sent to Gascony because the nobles there needed encouragement. As Lionel, the second son, was only sixteen and had no experience of war-fare, it was obvious that he was asking to be given the command himself. The prince himself, in a writ to his steward in Cornwall on 24 April, says that he 'has prayed the king to grant him leave to be the first to pass beyond [the] sea', ahead of the troops being sent to Normandy at much the same time.[10]

The formal indenture between Edward and the prince of Wales setting out the terms of his appointment as royal lieutenant in Gascony was drawn up on 10 July, and names Thomas Beauchamp, Robert Ufford, John de Vere, William Montagu the younger, John Lisle and Reginald Cobham as his companions. The prince was given full powers to act 'as if the king were there in person' in all matters concerning the government of the province, and in making truces and armistices. There was a safety clause as well: 'the king has ... promised that, if it shall happen that the prince is besieged or beset by so great a force that he cannot help himself unless he be rescued by the king's power, then the king will rescue him in one way or another.'[11] The principal means of such a rescue would have been the expeditionary force which was sent at the same time to Normandy under the command of Henry of Gros-mont, and the leaders of this army swore to undertake such a mission if required.

The prince of Wales was by now an experienced soldier, but, despite his nominal command of the vanguard at Crécy, he had never undertaken a campaign alone before this. The men who accompanied him were also highly experienced, and among them were the leaders of the 1346 campaign, who, like the prince, had been part of Edward's council of war. If the ultimate authority rested with the king, the evidence – though we have no formal record of how decisions were made – suggests that Edward listened to the opinions and advice of his commanders, and that the great strength of the English high command was the closeness and trust between the group who led the army from the landing at La Hogue in July 1346 to the departure from Calais in October 1347, a very long time for an army to be in the field in the middle ages. As we have seen, the majority of this group became companions of the Garter, and, of the twenty-six members of the company, fourteen were definitely with the prince in 1355–6. Five were engaged in military activity elsewhere, and for the remaining seven we have no definite information. The commanders of the divisions during the raid and at the battle of Poitiers were all Garter knights, with the single exception of the earl of Oxford, who never became a member of the order. The prince's companions were therefore old comrades in arms and accustomed to working together. Robert Ufford, titular head of the prince's council since the latter's coming of age in 1337, was the oldest of the group, aged fifty-seven, while there were two contemporaries of the king, in their forties: Thomas Beauchamp, marshal of the army on that expedition and commander of the prince's division, and John de Vere, both veterans of Edward's Scottish and Flemish wars. Of the other lords who brought retinues, Reginald Cobham had fought in Flanders, and was the same age as Robert Ufford, while William Montagu the younger was the prince's contemporary, and had been knighted with him at La Hogue. John Lisle had fought in Gascony in the 1340s.

Among the Garter companions with the prince of Wales, several had been in Gascony before, with Henry of Grosmont in 1345–6; these were the prince's chamberlain, Nigel Loring and James Audley. John Chandos had been a companion of the prince's since 1339, and he and Audley seem to have been the prince's personal advisers. Other knights, such as Bartholomew Burghersh the younger and Eustace d'Auberchicourt, had probably been in the prince's household since Crécy. Edward Despenser, who became a Garter companion in 1361, was on his first military expedition.[12] There was a mixture of great military experience and youthful enthusiasm, and a strong sense of loyalty to the prince – already a heroic figure after Crécy – which, taken together, contributed greatly to the success of the subsequent campaigns.

As usual with an expedition on this scale, the departure for Gascony, planned for early July, was delayed by weather and logistics. Everything was ready on land by the end of July, but a steady south-westerly throughout August prevented ships from coming down the Channel, and as the bulk of those requisitioned came from the east and south coast, with relatively few from Devon and Cornwall, this meant that the whole expedition was delayed. Plymouth was always the most difficult port from which to move an army to the Continent, but it was also the only practical option if a fleet was destined for the south-west of France.

The fleet finally disembarked at Bordeaux on 20 September, and the prince's council, having consulted the chief supporters of the English cause in Gascony, decided on immediate action. In the remarkably short time of a fortnight, the army was on the move. The aim was to take the war into the lands of the man who had done the most damage to the English in the past decade, Jean d'Armagnac, the king's lieutenant in Gascony; these territories lay south-east of Bordeaux. This was to be a raid or *chevauchée* like that in Normandy ten years before, through much more difficult terrain, and with the objective of causing as much damage as possible. This was partly in order to draw d'Armagnac into battle if he would rise to the bait, but also to weaken the economic base of his power. On 7 October the army entered d'Armagnac's territory, twenty miles from Bordeaux. The vanguard was under the command of Thomas Beauchamp, as it had been at Crécy, with Reginald Cobham. The prince of Wales took the king's role, in charge of the second column, with John de Vere, Bartholomew Burghersh the younger, John Lisle and the Gascon Jean de Grailly, the chief supporter of the English in the region. The rearguard was under the relatively inexperienced William Montagu the younger. Very early in the campaign, at the town of Monclar, fire broke out while the prince was lodging in the town; as a result, for the rest of the campaign he insisted on sleeping in tents pitched in the open countryside, because of the risk of fire and surprise attacks. John Lisle was the first serious casualty of the raid, wounded by a crossbow bolt at a village near Monclar; he died the next day. The only major town to be sacked in the first fortnight was Plaisance, on the river Adour, whose inhabitants had deserted; on two occasions, possible targets were spared because they were Church property. The general impression is of much greater discipline than on the Crécy raid, though one village, Seissan, was later burnt in direct contradiction of the prince's instructions. This was unknown territory, and John Henxteworth's day-book of expenses includes payments to guides on several occasions: the substantial sum of 22s. 6d. was paid to two men who showed the prince the way on 6 October from Castets-en-Dorthe to Bazas, 'a hard day of marching through the woods'. Arnaud Bernard was the prince's chief guide, and was even more highly paid, receiving £9 for his services on 28 November. Even at the very end of the expedition, guides were needed near the border of the English lands in Gascony. [13]

By 26 October the English army was approaching Toulouse, head-quarters of Jean d'Armagnac. Preparations had been made for a possible invasion even before there was definite news of any attack: the local nobles and militia had been summoned, and their followers were instructed to wear a white cross badge for identification. Stocks of provisions were to be laid in, and those living in the countryside were told to be ready to take refuge in the nearest fortified castle. These tactics point to a decision to fight a defensive war; in addition, Jean d'Armagnac had a fairly mixed force at his disposal. There were a small number of royal soldiers under the constable of France, Jacques de Bourbon, and the marshal of France Jean de Clermont, the local nobles and their reti-nues, and a number of hired crossbowmen. He could not be sure of the quality of his men, and knew that, if he was besieged, he was unlikely to receive any help from distant Paris.

The prince of Wales did not know that Jean d'Armagnac was actually in Toulouse until he had passed the city. To besiege Toulouse was impos-sible, since the army had no siege train. If he continued, he could find his way back blocked. If he went north, he knew that the countryside had been stripped in preparation for a possible invasion. It was late in the year, and the weather was worsening, but he decided on a bold stroke: to continue to the east, where the towns and cities felt they were safe from marauders, because any raiding army would not risk penetrating so deep into enemy territory. Furthermore, the terrain was difficult, and the Garonne and the Ariège had to be crossed, swollen with rain, and an unknown ford had to be found – 'yet by God's grace we found it', wrote John Wingfield, the prince's steward. [14] The expedition was now, in le Baker's phrase, 'in lands where the fury of war had never been seen

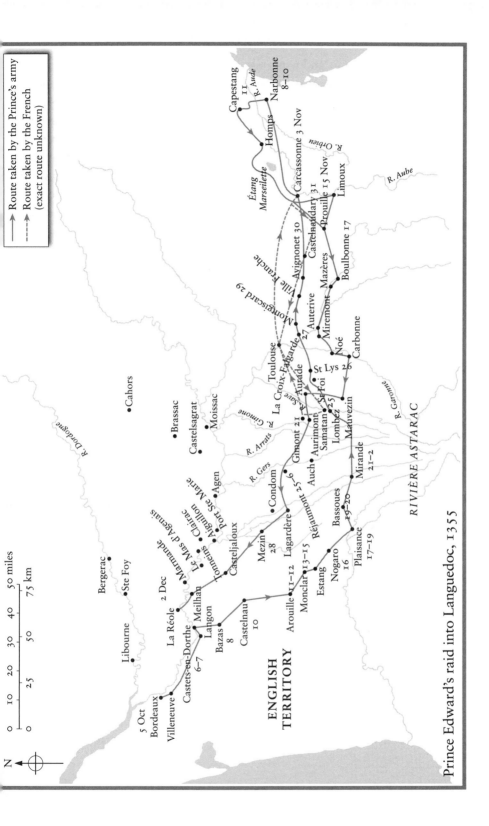

Capestang 11
R. Aude
Narbonne 8–10
Homps
Carcassonne 3 Nov
R. Orbieu
R. Aube
Étang Marseilette
Castelnaudary 31
Prouille 15 Nov
Limoux
Boulbonne 17
Avignonet 30
Mazères
Montgiscard 29
Auterive
Miremont
Ville Franche
Noé
Carbonne
Toulouse
La Croix-Falgarde
27
St Lys 26
Auade
R. Save
St Foi
Aurimont
25
Samatan
Lombez
Gimont 21
Mauvezin
Auch
Mirande 21–2
R. Arrats
R. Gers
Condom
Réjaumont 25–6
Bassoues 19–20
Lagardère
Plaisance 17–19
Mézin 28
Monclar 13–15
Estang
Nogaro 16
Casteljaloux
Arouille 11–12
Castelnau 10
Aiguillon
Port Ste Marie
Clairac
Tonneins
Le Mas d'Agenais
Agen
Moissac
Castelsagrat
Brassac
Cahors
R. Gimone
R. Garonne
R. Dordogne

RIVIÈRE ASTARAC

Marmande
La Réole 2 Dec
Meilhan
Langon
Bazas 8
Castets-en-Dorthe 6–7
Villeneuve
Bordeaux 5 Oct
Ste Foy
Bergerac
Libourne

ENGLISH TERRITORY

N

0 10 20 30 40 50 miles
0 25 50 75 km

Prince Edward's raid into Languedoc, 1355

before'.[15] Towns and windmills were burnt; at Carcassonne, the citizens offered 25,000 gold crowns but refused to renounce their allegiance to King John. The lower town, or *bourg*, was occupied by the English, and an attempt was made to besiege the strongly fortified citadel itself, but the defenders used flaming arrows to set the wooden houses beneath them on fire, and the prince's men had to withdraw. Much damage had been done, but the French were a force to be reckoned with now that they were fighting a defensive war. Pressing on to Narbonne, the army again met with serious resistance, since word of the prince's activities had led to rapid defensive preparations. The town was burnt by using flaming arrows, but the castle held out.

News now came that Jean d'Armagnac had left Toulouse, with the intention of finding the prince of Wales to do battle with him. Soon after leaving Narbonne, the prince, as he later wrote, was expecting 'a battle within the next three days',[16] but by 15 November he realized that Armagnac had retreated, and the army, which had been in close order in case of battle, resumed its formation as three divisions. The prince's division crossed three rivers in one day, a feat which earned them a day's rest 'in calm and delightful weather',[17] but this enabled Armagnac to come within six miles of the rearguard, evidently hoping to surprise them. The prince drew up his men in battle order, and, when the French scouts discovered this, Armagnac once more withdrew, but not before most of the forty knights who had been observing the English were captured by Burghersh, Chandos and Audley and their men.

We have no contemporary French version of the events of the next few days, and the prince of Wales's report on the campaign puts a positive spin on what happened. According to him, the capture of their scouts

> made the enemy retreat in great fear to their camp, and they marched to the towns of Lombez and Sauveterre, which are only two miles apart. We encamped outside the towns that same night, so close that we could see their campfires. But there was between us a very large deep river,[18] and that night, before we came, they had broken the bridges, so that we could only cross the next day after we had got our men to repair the bridges. From there the enemy moved to the town of Gimont, which we reached on the same day as them, and before they could enter the town our men captured or killed many of them. That same night we encamped outside

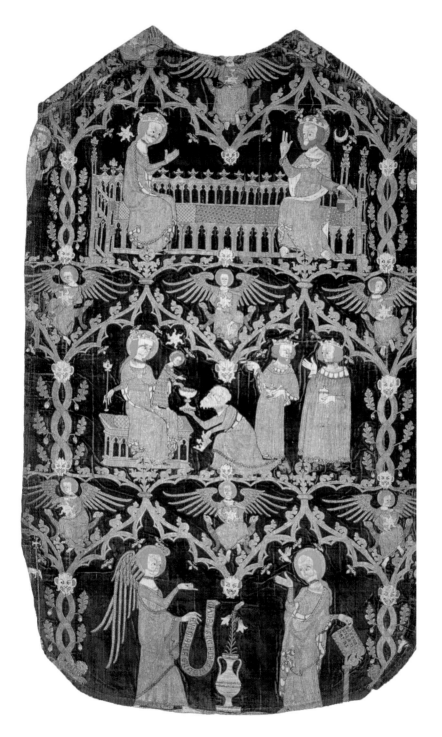

16. The Butler-Bowdon cope, a magnificent example of *opus anglicanum* embroidery. The colours of the silks have faded. Made in England *c.* 1330–50.

17–18. Gilles li Muisit, poet, historian and monk of Tournai, complains in his poems of the lavish dress of the gentry and of the women of Tournai. The miniatures date from the end of his life, 1352–3, and represent accurately the high fashion of the period.

19. (*above*) A group of fashionable courtiers dancing.

(*below*) men wearing vizors and dancing
From the *Roman d'Alexandre c.* 1344.

20. (*above*) Feast given at St Denis in 1378 by Charles V: the siege of Jerusalem and the ship at sea were both dramatic interludes staged in the hall. The miniature dates from the following year.

21. (*left*) Embroidered purse, French, second half of the fourteenth century.

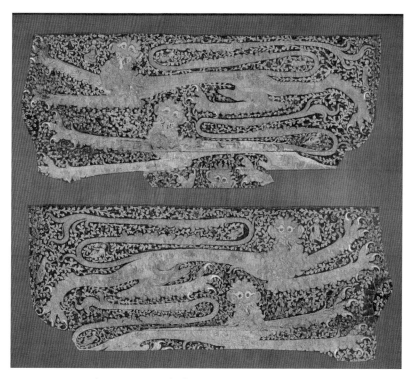

22. (*above*) Leopards from a horse trapper, English, fourteenth century.

23. (*below*) Tapestry of Scrope arms (*azure a bend or*), differenced here for an eldest son, fifteenth century.

24. Carriage from the Luttrell Psalter, showing the elaborate decoration. The figure at the front with a squirrel may well represent Philippa.

25. A tournament *mêlée*, from a North Italian manuscript of 1352. Edward's son Lionel married the daughter of the duke of Milan, and the costumes and armour are not very different from those in England.

26. (*above*) The chest made to contain the documents regarding the truce at Crécy in 1347, with the arms of some of the signatories.

27. (*below*) Replicas of the heraldic achievements of Edward prince of Wales at Canterbury Cathedral.

the town, and waited there the whole of the next day, hoping that a battle might take place. And the following day we and the whole army were in battle order before sunrise, when news came that before daybreak most of the enemy had left.[19]

The prince held a council of war, and decided that, since the enemy did not want a battle, they should turn for home. What he does not say is that the French had successfully obstructed his progress, and had gained their objective, which was to see him safely back in English territory as soon as possible. Without their manoeuvres, he would have continued to ravage the countryside and destroy the smaller towns, even if he now knew that the large towns and cities were too heavily defended. Nor could he afford to continue such a game of cat and mouse well away from his supply bases, against an enemy who only had to retreat to nearby Toulouse for new supplies and reinforcements. It was a foretaste of the defensive tactics which were eventually to nullify the glories of the English triumphs on the battlefield: but Jean d'Armagnac's caution was not to the liking of the constable of France, Jacques de Bourbon, his fellow-commander. In the spirit of the overconfident knighthood that had helped to destroy the French at Crécy, he roundly condemned Armagnac's tactics, and returned to Paris to resign his post.[20]

Nonetheless, the prince could claim a notable military achievement, chiefly in terms of damage to the economic base on which the French relied for the continuation of the war. John Wingfield, the prince's steward, wrote home to England to report the destruction that had been wrought with the eye of a man used to assessing revenues and estates:

It seems certain that since the war against the French king began, there has never been such destruction in a region as in this raid. For the countryside and towns which have been destroyed in this raid produced more revenue for the king of France in aid of his wars than half his kingdom; and that is without the profits of recoinage and the profits and customs which he takes from those of Poitou, as I could prove from authentic documents found in various towns in the tax-collectors' houses. For Carcassonne and Limoux, which is as large as Carcassonne, and two other towns near there, produce for the king of France each year the wages of a thousand men at arms and 100,000 old crowns towards the costs of the war. According to the records which we found, the towns around

427

Toulouse, Carcassonne and Narbonne which we destroyed, together with
Narbonne itself, produced each year, over and above this, 400,000 old
crowns as war subsidies.[21]

Matteo Villani estimated the booty at 1,000 carts loaded with the possessions of the inhabitants, and 5,000 prisoners; but given that there is
little mention of either booty or prisoners in the English letters home,
and looking at the march which the army undertook, it seems unlikely
that anything on this scale had been taken.[22] If the result in military
terms had been a stalemate, in that the two armies both returned to base
with minimal casualties, the propaganda advantage was definitely on
the prince's side: in the view of the French public at large, Jean
d'Armagnac had failed to protect the population of the territory for
which he was responsible, and had shown himself a coward by not
attacking the English army. The prince, on the other hand, had shown
that the military skills of the English enabled them to raid at will deep
into lands which had been regarded as impregnable, demonstrating that
no Frenchman could safely rely on being protected by John II. Yet when
forced to choose between the two sides, John was still regarded as the
better bet, as the refusal of the inhabitants of Carcassonne to renounce
their allegiance showed.

The winter of 1355–6 was passed in skirmishes and raids of the kind
that had been endemic in Gascony ever since the official seizure of the
English territories there by the French king in 1324. The English had
not deployed so many troops or such skilled commanders since Henry
of Grosmont's activities in 1345–6, and a satisfying amount of territory
was recovered. In the spring of 1356, an ambitious war plan was
developed: reinforcements were to be sent to Gascony so that the prince
of Wales could continue his activities, and in Brittany Henry of Grosmont was also to be reinforced. Edward himself was planning, it seems,
a third army which was to join up with Henry of Grosmont and then
draw the French into battle west of Paris, while the prince moved up
from Gascony to cut them off from the city and attack them from the
rear. By July, troops had been sent to Gascony and Brittany, but Edward's
own role had not yet been decided.

The French knew that such plans were afoot, but had no idea of their
nature. As far as the prince of Wales was concerned, they assumed he

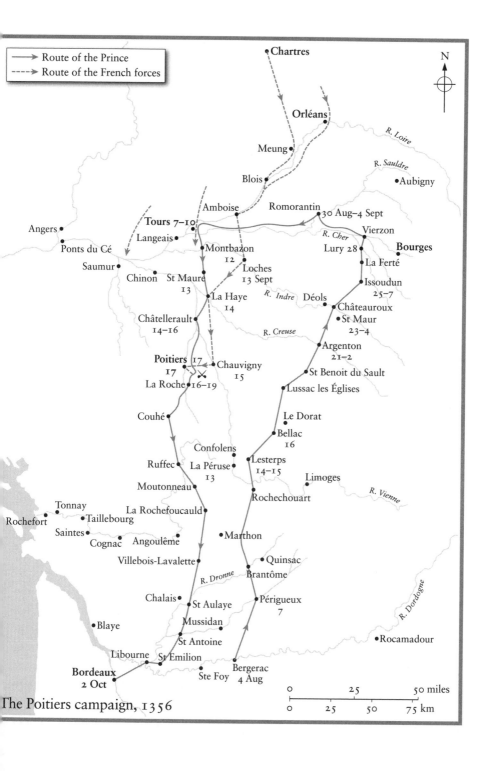

Route of the Prince
Route of the French forces

• Chartres

• Orléans

Meung •

R. Loire

R. Sauldre

Blois •

• Aubigny

Amboise •   Romorantin

Angers •   **Tours** 7–10   30 Aug–4 Sept

Langeais •   Vierzon

Ponts du Cé   • Montbazon   R. Cher

Saumur •   12   Lury 28   **Bourges**

Chinon • St Maure   Loches   • La Ferté

13   13 Sept   Issoudun

• La Haye   R. Indre   Déols   25–7

14   R. Creuse   • Châteauroux

Châtellerault •   • St Maur

14–16   23–4

Poitiers 17   Argenton

17   • Chauvigny   21–2

La Roche • 16–19   15   • St Benoit du Sault

Lussac les Églises

Couhé •   • Le Dorat

Confolens   • Bellac

Ruffec • La Péruse •   16

13   • Lesterps

Moutonneau •   14–15   • Limoges

          • Rochechouart   R. Vienne

Tonnay •

Rochefort • • Taillebourg   La Rochefoucauld

Saintes •

Cognac • Angoulême   • Marthon

Villebois-Lavalette •   • Quinsac

          R. Dronne Brantôme •   R. Dordogne

Chalais • St Aulaye   • Périgueux

          Mussidan   7

• Blaye   • Rocamadour

St Antoine

Libourne •   St Emilion

Bordeaux   Bergerac

2 Oct   Ste Foy 4 Aug

          0   25   50 miles

          0   25   50   75 km

The Poitiers campaign, 1356

would simply return in greater strength to Languedoc, and, when he gathered his army at La Réole, thirty miles south-east of Bordeaux, in early July, Jean d'Armagnac summoned the feudal militia of Languedoc, and ordered that the countryside should be cleared and anything movable, particularly stores, should be taken to the nearest walled town. John II sent the count of Poitiers to Bourges to assemble another army, since he was tied down by Grosmont's activities in Normandy. The French had failed to second-guess the prince's intentions. Instead of moving south, he moved north-east to Bergerac on the Dordogne, and spent the last weeks of July and the beginning of August preparing to march into Périgord and Poitou, the old heartland of Eleanor of Aquitaine's territories. Firstly, however, he had to provide against the possibility that Jean d'Armagnac might use the defensive force he had just summoned to mount an attack on the southern border of English Gascony, and appointed Gascon lords to lead a force of 2,000 or 3,000 men in that direction.

The pressure on the French was increased by the news that Edward had given orders on 20 July for a third army to be gathered at Southampton, to invade Normandy. John II was still engaged in Brittany, even though Grosmont had retreated to his base near Cherbourg on 12 July, and the count of Poitiers had only managed to raise a small army at Bourges, which was still intended for the south. The prince of Wales moved quickly to the old border between English territory and lands which had always been French, at the river Vienne, which he crossed on 14 August to the east of Limoges, unfurling the standards of his army as he did so. The usual campaign of destruction now began, and the prince was heading towards Bourges; this was, he later wrote, 'where we expected to find the king's son, the count of Poitiers. The chief reason for our going there was that we expected to hear that the king had crossed . . .'[23]

The tactical situation was fast-moving: in the following week, the prince must have received news that the expedition planned by his father had been completely disrupted by the arrival of a fleet of galleys from Aragon which the French had hired, and which were preventing ships from reaching Sandwich: all shipping was ordered into port for fear of attacks. Also about this time, he probably learnt that John II was retreating from Brittany, and was likely to move down to Touraine to confront him. This was indeed the French plan, and the count of Poitiers was to join the king's army. The prince of Wales still hoped that Grosmont would be able to reinforce him. He therefore moved towards the Loire, where John Audley and John Chandos captured some French prisoners, who told him that the French were uncertain of his whereabouts, and that groups of French, under the lord of Craon, Jean Boucicaut, and the marshal of France Clermont, were searching for him. On 30 August the prince discovered that Craon and Boucicaut were in the castle at Romorantin: they were a tempting prize, and he attacked the fortress. It cost him five days to secure it and the two French commanders, and by that time the bridges over the Loire had been broken on John II's orders. The prince therefore marched to Tours, where the bridge was still intact, but it was too heavily defended, as both the count of Anjou and Clermont were in the city, and hasty repairs to the dilapidated walls combined with a fierce resistance were sufficient to hold off an assault force led by Bartholomew Burghersh the younger. The prince could not afford to commit his entire army to a siege, as he needed to maintain his mobility at all costs; he was far from his base, and living off the land, and was in jeopardy even if he had been able to join up with Grosmont, who was said to be on his way. There was a further adversary in play: the weather. The Loire, a sluggish and broad stream, was very variable in its flow: in a dry summer, it was possible to cross at a number of places, apart from the bridges, but continuous wet weather had made the river valley into a huge marsh, as Burghersh found when he tried to attack Tours. The only bridge available to Grosmont, at Ponts-de-Cé, south of Angers, had been broken; we know so little of his actual movements that it is not certain that he even advanced that far.

The prince of Wales left Tours on 10 September, heading back towards the safety of Gascony if all else failed. His prime objective was to engage the French in battle. He knew that John was now south of the Loire. John had had great difficulty in recruiting his forces, and there were a large number of relatively poorly equipped footsoldiers. He had paid many of them off in order to match the mobility of the prince's army, and, once he joined forces with the count of Poitiers and crossed the Loire at Blois, he moved swiftly. Furthermore, the dauphin Charles was now at Tours with another 1,000 men from Normandy, and joined the main French army soon after it reached the area. The prince was held up for a day at Montbazon by two cardinals, ambassadors from the pope: he told them bluntly that he was not empowered to make either truce or peace, and that anyway John was nearby and spoiling for a battle. He then spent two days halted at Châtellerault, hoping against hope that Grosmont was on his way, while his scouts failed to find the French, and the French army was ahead of him by 15 September. However, John had ridden ahead with the best-mounted men at arms, and now had to wait in turn for the rest of his army to catch up. The prince now outmarched him, and came to Chauvigny, ten miles to the east of Poitiers, on 17 September, having encountered part of the French rear-guard on the way. The French found an English detachment four miles from Poitiers, who retreated in the face of superior numbers, but the pursuit led them to the main English forces, where they were overcome and the counts of Auxerre and Joigny were captured. The prince had to halt at Chauvigny to allow the army to regroup. John had likewise halted to regroup, and, when the prince moved on the next day, he found the French army drawn up in battle order outside Poitiers, across his route southward to Bordeaux.

As the prince of Wales turned away in search of a suitable place in which to fight a defensive battle with the French, the two cardinals reappeared, urging a truce. The prince's reply was that it was not a time for sermons, but for a battle, and they had better be brief. Despite this, the cardinals did manage to secure a day's pause in hostilities. Both sides claimed that the other took advantage of this: the French were said to have brought up reinforcements, while the English were accused of for-tifying their position. This position was on a hillside south of Poitiers, overlooking the abbey of Nouaillé; the valley of the small river Miosson was below. It was a site not unlike Crécy, but much more heavily wooded, and with substantial hedges. The negotiations on Sunday, 18 September came to nothing. When the cardinals returned to the prince's camp the next day, the prince was prepared to extend the truce, but the French, sure that they had their prey at their mercy, refused. The cardi-nals withdrew, and both sides prepared to fight.

This was an encounter on a much smaller scale than that at Crécy. John had an army composed mainly of noble retinues: if the count of eighty-seven banners said to have been reported by the English scouts is correct, there were fewer than 100 men at arms in each of these, as the best estimate of the total is around 8,000 in all, with 2,000 crossbow-men and an uncertain number of light infantry in moderate disorder. The English had a smaller force, of around 6,000 men, of whom half were men at arms and the rest were archers. John's army of reluctant lords, recalcitrant levies and professional crossbowmen had gathered less than a fortnight earlier; the English had been in the field for more than six weeks, and in any case the prince's army was battle-hardened from the previous autumn's campaigns. Many of them were veterans of the Crécy–Calais campaign of ten years earlier. But, as at Crécy, they were short of supplies and water, and had been in battle array all night.

Jonathan Sumption, in his masterly if somewhat indigestible account of the Hundred Years War, finds himself puzzled by one particular aspect of the battle:

> However, the most striking contrast between the two armies was at the level of command. Manoeuvring large bodies of men-at-arms who had never trained together was one of the perennial problems of medieval battlefields. Orders were generally transmitted to section commanders by trumpet, occasionally by messenger, and thence by shouting. Signals could be complex, and hard to hear inside a visored helmet. Yet the Prince and his adjutants had shown a remarkable ability to control the movements of their men in the midst of the fighting, far superior to anything that the King of France's staff had been able to achieve. The French divisional commanders had been given their orders before the battle, and they carried them out with grim persistence regardless of what was happening elsewhere. By contrast, the Prince had been able to improvise plans in the heat of the action and to communicate them quickly to those who had to act on them in the line.[24]

The answer to this, it seems to me, must lie in the interaction of the leaders of the two armies, both among themselves and between them and their men. This is something about which no historian and no set of documents can tell us, so I turned for advice to someone who had served in conditions which seem as near to this kind of warfare as possible in today's circumstances, a former officer in the British SAS. His comments were very interesting to a novice in such matters: he cited modern examples of manoeuvres with minimal communication. He explained the concept of a mission goal, where the point of departure and the ultimate objective were set, and logistics and support were provided, but the commander was left to achieve the desired result by his own means. He emphasized too the huge value of charisma in an officer, in terms of his relationship with his men: the officer in the Falklands War who could say to his men, 'Follow the black bobble hat if in doubt, and you'll be OK,' is very like the banneret with his group of men at arms: if the banneret was a knight renowned for his prowess in tournaments or war, his men would follow his banner with confidence.

The fact that the prince's men had been marching and fighting together for three months in the previous year, and had assembled again two months before the battle, meant that they knew each other and their commanders well. Medieval armies generally do not appear – as far as we can tell – to have had any kind of group training, and fighting on raids was an excellent substitute. By contrast, the French army had been thrown together scarcely more than a fortnight before. But there are two ways of training an army: my source of military wisdom suggested that the British way in modern times has been to train from the ranks up, and to spend much less time on co-ordinated training of the officer groups; the German approach has historically been the reverse, to concentrate on the brigade-level staff, and to ensure a tight and well-trained central commanding machine. I would argue that the prince's army had just such a coherent general staff, and that it was largely made up of the knights of the Garter.

In order to answer Jonathan Sumption's puzzle, let us try to look at the actions of the Garter knights leading the various divisions at Poitiers. Accounts of Poitiers are a great deal more consistent as to the sequence of events than the multiple and contradictory stories about Crécy. Geoffrey le Baker was writing within three years of the battle, and had undoubtedly spoken to the participants; the other accounts vary in details, and there are the usual problems of interpretation of the battle order, but the evidence gives far less scope for debate about what happened. Interpretation of the evidence is complicated by partisan views of French and English historians; as an extreme example, a classic French account of the battle published in 1940 offers us an engagement in which the course of events was largely determined by the prince's Gascon allies rather than the English forces or even the prince's advisers.[25] It is also worth reminding ourselves of the nature of a medieval army; H. J. Hewitt's vivid sketch is a good likeness:

> A feudal army had not a well-defined hierarchy of command ... nor was it a military machine the parts or whole of which responded immediately

and unfailingly to the will of the commander-in-chief. It was an assembly of groups of men with their leaders whom they recognized by their shields or banners, and a 'battle' was nothing more than a temporary combination of small groups into a larger group.[26]

The leaders of these groups were therefore critical to the functioning of the army as a unit; if the leaders failed to co-operate or to understand each other's likely reaction in the face of unexpected problems, the army was likely to disintegrate into these smaller units.

King John, advised by the two marshals, Audrehem and Clermont, and by the Scottish knight William Douglas, who had long experience of fighting the English in his homeland, decided to start with a preliminary cavalry charge to destroy the English archers, followed by an attack on foot by the French knights. The cavalry would draw back as soon as the archers were in disarray, and there would be less risk of the slaughter of horses which had brought the French charges to a halt at Crécy. The French attack was to be led by the marshals, and this was to be followed by three divisions of knights under the dauphin Charles, the duke of Orléans (the king's brother) and the king himself.

The prince's position on the hillside was a strong one, and his archers were well entrenched, using hedges with ditches dug in front of them. The divisions of knights seem to have been drawn up with relatively little defensive work around them. The first division was under Thomas Beauchamp and John de Vere, both of whom had fought at Crécy. Beauchamp, at forty-two, had fought in all of Edward III's campaigns, and had a formidable reputation: in 1344 the abbot of Abingdon addressed him as a 'magnificent and powerful man and most energetic warrior'.[27] The central division was that of the prince, corresponding to the king's division at Crécy, with the prince's closest friends, Chandos, the younger Burghersh, Audley and Cobham. William Montagu the younger and Robert Ufford, more than thirty years older, were given the rearguard, the position in which Ufford had fought at Crécy.

We may know the sequence of events, but the very first move in the fighting is difficult to interpret, and the puzzle has never been clearly resolved. The best evidence is that of the prince of Wales himself, in his report home: 'Because we were short of supplies and for other reasons, it was agreed that we should take a path traversing their front, so that if they wanted to attack or to approach us in a position which was not in any way greatly to our disadvantage we would give battle.' The general consensus is that this manoeuvre, carried out by Thomas Beauchamp and the vanguard accompanying the baggage train, was a tentative attempt at a retreat, to see if the French would stay in their defensive position, because at that point the French 'refused to yield any advantage by being the first to attack'. If the prince could lure the French from their positions, and persuade them to pursue the vanguard, the battle would have opened as he wished; if the French remained immobile, he would be able to continue on his way southward. A retreat would not have solved his problems, as the French would have followed him closely, but the one thing he wanted to avoid was being manoeuvred into a position where he had to commit his troops to an attack.

The opening gambit, whatever its precise intention, worked far better than the prince of Wales could have hoped. Neither side, at this point, was sure what was going on in the enemy camp. The English sent out scouts under Eustace d'Auberchicourt, but he was captured. However, the French scouts quickly reported the movement of Thomas Beauchamp's troops to the marshals; Audrehem seems to have assumed that the retreat had begun, but Clermont was suspicious and advised caution. Audrehem insulted him, and led his men forward, while Clermont did not move. The result was a classic illustration of the point just made about the absolute necessity for understanding between the army's leaders. The narrow bridge at Nouaillé was blocked by carts, and the vanguard under Thomas Beauchamp were returning to report this by way of a ford a mile or so to the west. Audrehem's men charged, and at long range the archers were unable to make any impact on the horses, which were armoured on their heads and fronts. When Clermont at last moved forward, the next English commander came into play: Montagu, who was in charge of the third division, brought his men up to cover the flank of Beauchamp's men, now heavily engaged with Audrehem's men. This seems to have been both good fortune and quick thinking by Montagu, who found himself within striking distance of Clermont at the critical moment, and realized what was happening. At twenty-eight, only two years older than the Black Prince, Montagu had seen service at Crécy, in the sea-battle at Winchelsea and in Prussia. The expedition of 1355–6 was his first opportunity for major command. The combat was indecisive, until John de Vere took a body of archers to a position in the marshes of the river Miosson from which they could fire at the flanks and rumps of the horses. The effect was dramatic: the charge quickly turned into the same mass of injured horses and men that had marked the opening stages of Crécy. Clermont meanwhile had tried to mount a flank attack on William Montagu in the rearguard through a gap in the hedge, but Montagu moved the archers to cover the gap with their fire, with devastating effect: Clermont himself was killed, and a large number of his men died with him.

The first stage of the action had been decided by quick tactical thinking and an understanding of what would have appeared as a very confused struggle to the other English commanders. At this stage the prince of Wales was positioned higher up the hill so that he could get an overview of the action, again like Crécy, where Edward probably had the advantage of a windmill. His standard-bearer, Walter Woodland, and his bodyguard and war council were around him: Nigel Loring, William Trussell, Alan Cheyne and others from his household, and his friends Chandos, Audley and Burghersh. John de Vere was the senior figure present, with Baldwin Botetourt and Edmund Wauncy. The prince may have been able to send messengers with the necessary instructions; yet there was no guarantee that a messenger could reach any of the commanders in person. If no message was received, the prince and his advisers could rely on their friends to keep to the 'mission goal' while improvising their immediate responses.

There was now a pause, since the French battle plan had gone badly wrong: the charge which was meant to open the way for the dismounted knights had happened in the wrong place, and King John probably could not see what had befallen the marshals. The English had time to reposition themselves, and to improve their defensive position before the first division of knights reached them, and the vanguard under Thomas Beauchamp now joined the prince's battalion in the maze of hedges and vineyards. The prince, taking overall command in a battle for the first time, was evidently anxious to gather his forces and use the superior weight of numbers which this would give him. As the French climbed the hill – no easy task for a fully armed knight – the archers tried to pick them off. However, only a lucky shot which found a joint in the armour or a vizor slit would cause casualties, as plate armour was strong enough to deflect an arrow fired at long range. On they came, banners displayed, shouting their war cry 'St Denis', answered by the English 'St George'. This was an encounter in slow motion, as hundreds of individual hand combats were engaged and fought out along the length of the English position. The only English troops not yet committed were a reserve of some 400 horsemen.

As the prince of Wales and his companions watched, they saw the French attack falter, and then the French knights drifting away in ones and twos back to the main army; Geoffrey le Baker echoes the taunt thrown at Philip of Valois after Crécy, that he made a fair retreat, in describing the French withdrawal.[28] The dauphin's standard had been lost, and his standard-bearer, Tristan de Maignelay, captured. When they returned to the main army, the dauphin and the other royal princes left the field in search of a place of safety, since the outcome of the battle was now beginning to be in doubt. This was possibly on the king's orders; however politically advisable it was, it seems to have had an immediate and disastrous effect on French morale. No sooner was the dauphin on his way than the next division, led by the duke of Orléans, moved up to attack and a large part of it promptly retreated, without having struck a blow. The official line after the battle was that this was all done on purpose: 'Monsieur the duke of Normandy, messieurs of Anjou and Poitou, and the duke of Orléans retreated on the command of monsieur the king,'[29] wrote Jean d'Armagnac to the inhabitants of Nîmes a fortnight later. But the confusion it caused implies that Matteo Villani's scathing comments may have been at least in part deserved: he calls the dauphin and the duke of Orléans 'most vile and cowardly ... such fear had entered their timid and vile hearts that, although they could have retrieved the situation, they did not have the heart to face the enemy, and were not ashamed to abandon the king'.[30] The dauphin and his brothers left for Chauvigny in good order, with a strong escort, so Froissart tells us, and it may be that the removal of troops for the escort was the real problem. There is some suggestion that the remainder of Orléans' division may have made some sort of attack before retiring to join the remainder of the army, which was now regrouping round the king himself and preparing to charge the English.

John's assault might well have succeeded. He still had a contingent of crossbowmen, and the English archers were not only very tired, but running out of ammunition, even though they had been able to move forward during the lull and retrieve as many arrows as they could find. The English men at arms, short of water and sleep, had already fought for some hours. Geoffrey le Baker indicates that some of them were beginning to despair when King John launched his attack, blaming the prince for leaving so many men away from the army to defend the rest of Aquitaine. Although the remaining French contingent was smaller, they were fresh, well rested and fed. In terms of armament, the sides were equally matched. Matters were made worse by the fact that some of Beauchamp's men had set out in pursuit of the fleeing enemy, not realizing that the decisive action was yet to come. The prince and his commanders seem to have rallied their men successfully in this desperate situation.

The English, however, were battle-hardened in a way that few of the French troops were; and the prince of Wales and his advisers were much more experienced strategists. The French, although much of their battle plan had failed, stuck resolutely to it, while the prince and his commanders improvised brilliantly. One move, the dispatch of a small mounted reserve under Jean de Grailly, captal de Buch, to attack the French from the rear, was straight from the textbooks; but de Grailly, a Gascon who had fought with the prince for the last year, carried it out expertly. As few as sixty knights and a hundred archers left the English army, rode over the hill to the north and round the wood at Nouaillé: they were able to keep out of sight of the enemy until they reappeared behind them on the crest of the hill to the west of Nouaillé and charged down the valley of the Miosson. When they signalled their presence by unfurling their banners, the prince and a small number of men would mount and the French would be charged simultaneously from front and rear. The unexpected moves were those of the prince and Beauchamp: the prince, in face of the advancing French, ordered his banners to *advance* to meet the French, which both strengthened the morale and commitment of his men and surprised the enemy, who were expecting to attack a defensive line. Equally important was the improvised attack by Beauchamp, who succeeded in rallying enough of his scattered troops to mount an assault on the French flank before de Grailly was even in sight. This cannot have been a premeditated move on the prince's instructions, because the prince was in the thick of the fight, with other Garter knights such as Sir John Chandos and Sir James Audley. The double assault of Beauchamp and de Grailly, a classic if unplanned pincer movement, combined with the forward movement of the prince's division, was enough to decide the day.

The French, by now severely depleted, were driven towards the river: here, tradition has it, the final action took place in the *champ alexandre*, 'the field of Alexander', probably so called because of the heroic scenes that followed. John was as passionate about knighthood as his Plantagenet rivals, and he and his bodyguard made a last stand here. His standard-bearer, Geoffroy de Charny, was killed defending the *oriflamme*. John himself, and his youngest son, Philip, who had rejoined his father when his elder brothers departed, were taken prisoner. Philip, unarmed, had stood by his father in the last moments of the battle, warning him of assailants, crying 'Father, look to the right, and to the left' as they attacked.[31]

The English commanders had worked together with one aim in mind and had understood each other's tactics in an exemplary fashion. By contrast, the French had hampered each other: they had adhered rigidly to a battle plan, and had failed to co-operate. From the outset, when Clermont and Audrehem quarrelled, they were convinced of their ability to defeat the English easily, and therefore did not concentrate on what was actually happening, and what supporting action was needed. The departure of much of the second division was similarly due to poor co-ordination of the command, in that if John II did indeed order his sons to leave the battlefield, as he later claimed, he failed to get the message to his commanders, and they in turn failed to realize the purpose of what he was doing.

I would argue that the English success at Poitiers owes something – though by no means everything – to the spirit of teamwork reflected in Edward III's creation of the Company of the Garter. These were men who knew each other well, who had fought together, in real warfare and mock warfare, and who in a tight corner instinctively realized how the others might react. The prince may indeed have managed to convey his commands to them in the heat and confusion of battle: but he would not necessarily have known how matters stood with them. Much of what happened on the battlefield was like a 'mission goal': the commanders knew the objective, and were free to use any means they chose in order to achieve it, if orders did not reach them, or did not correspond to what was happening on the ground. The prince inevitably had to rely as much on their judgement as on his own, and he knew them well enough to trust them implicitly.

Describing the events of the evening after the battle, Baker tells us that, while the prince of Wales and his royal captive were at dinner, James Audley was found severely wounded on the battlefield. Baker gives a vivid picture of how the prince 'brought him back to life by his praiseworthy attention ... and comforted him by telling him that he had captured the king, which the wounded man would hardly have believed'. The prince then returned to dinner, where Audley's heroism was praised by John, and the king replied to the prince's efforts to comfort him by saying that at least he had been captured in fair fight. All this sounds plausible enough, but Baker dresses it up in rhetorical Latin, just as he invents a splendid speech for the prince before the battle, based on a classical model.[32] Le Bel, too, cannot resist a set piece for the prince: he tells us that the prince waited personally on his captive and indeed all the other diners, as a squire would wait on his lord, and in reply to the king's request that he would sit with him, declared:

> Don't feel humbled, sire, if God has chosen not to favour you today. I assure you, my father the king will treat you as honourably and as amicably as he can and will agree sensible terms: you will make a lasting friendship. It seems to me you should be of good cheer, even though the battle has gone against you, for you have earned a reputation for high prowess and surpassed the finest of your army in the way you fought today. I'm not saying this to flatter you! All your companions agree with me in awarding you the prize and the laurels if you'll accept them.[33]

And with that, King John was led into captivity in England by the prince of Wales.

For the moment, it seemed as if Edward and his son had the inheritance of France within their grasp. The history of King John's captivity, the long search for peace, the tortuous negotiations, the disastrous effects of the English victory on almost the whole of France, are not part of our subject. There were truces between France and England, but there were no truces and no mercy shown in the desperate civil war that now broke out in France, a war between ambitious great lords such as Charles king of Navarre, known to French history as Charles the Bad for his endless scheming, and at the same time a war between the peasantry, desperate from hunger and oppression by freebooters, and anyone with wealth or power. That France survived at all was due to the dauphin Charles, who succeeded in rebuilding the French state and re-establishing the order necessary if the threat from England was to be countered. Unlike his father and grandfather, his approach to war was political: it was not a theatre for military glory or high hopes of victory, but a question of patient defence and quiet diplomacy which would nullify the English predominance in military matters.

Even knights who had followed an orthodox military career until now found themselves unemployed. If, as in the case of Eustace d'Auberchicourt, they were younger sons, with little in the way of lands, they found that the truce signed in Bordeaux in 1357 had brought their military careers and hence their income to a temporary end. Eustace acted as a freebooter alongside other English captains in Champagne on his own account, but he and the other captains seem to have been acting in concert with Charles of Navarre: Peter Audley certainly attempted to take Chalons with Navarrese help,[34] and when the Navarrese stronghold of Melun was besieged by the French, 'Eustache d'Auberchicourt and Peter Audley were kept informed of the day [when the relief expedition was to set out] and were to be there with all their men'.[35] This seems to have been the first connection between Auberchicourt and the king of Navarre; he was later to spend a decade in his service.

There seems little doubt that Edward III covertly used the wayward king of Navarre – and was exploited in turn by him – during the truce of Bordeaux.[36] French chroniclers were convinced of this, and Matteo Villani, writing in Florence but with good contacts in the mercantile towns of eastern France, says repeatedly that the English and Navarrese acted in concert: the king of England 'concealed himself behind the shield of the king of Navarre, whose forces were all Englishmen'.[37] It was not a consistent policy. Edward had an interest in raising the huge ransom demanded for the release of John II, which required stable government and efficient tax-collection in France. Equally, a weak French state would be easier to conquer if he were to mount a new invasion. In effect, it was a 'dirty war', and like all such ventures was opportunistic and often muddled in its application. And it was hard to control the freebooters once they had been let loose; official denunciations by the English of their behaviour meant little to them. Jean le Bel sums up the situation neatly: the king 'let these brigands terrorise and wreck the whole kingdom ... in the hope that it would either bring the war to a successful end or peace on his own terms'.[38]

Against this chaotic background, diplomatic efforts to find a solution continued. Edward negotiated with his prisoner, King John, in London; and John in turn negotiated with the government led by his son Charles in Paris. But it was impossible to get agreement between three parties with very different interests. In 1359 a treaty which was to provide for the release of John II and the re-establishment of the English presence in almost half of France was negotiated in London, subject to its acceptance in Paris by the dauphin and the estates-general of France. Ratification was intended to take place on 24 June. In return for Edward's renunciation of the French throne, it would have re-created an empire similar to that of Henry II, who had ruled from Scotland to Toulouse, and in whose time the kingdom of France was confined to the Paris basin and the eastern side of France. Not only Gascony, the inheritance of Eleanor of Aquitaine, was to be largely restored, but the lands of William the Conqueror, Normandy, Anjou, Maine, Touraine, as well as Brittany, were to be held by the English king again. For King John and his entourage, eager to return home after nearly four years in captivity, it seemed harsh but possible. For the dauphin and his advisers, it seemed an impossible folly, even if the alternative was a huge struggle to fund a war from an impoverished and disordered kingdom. They refused to put their names to the treaty, and on 24 June, instead of peace, the war was instantly renewed.

Edward's last great military adventure in France was also the most ambitious. He proposed to aim for the ultimate confirmation of his right to rule France: he was going to march on Reims, take the city and have himself crowned in the cathedral, where French kings had held their coronations (with one or two exceptions) since 1179. The archbishop of Reims was the senior member of the French clergy, and, like the archbishop of Canterbury in England, had the right to crown a new monarch: Edward had some reason to think he might be favourable to his cause. To achieve this, Edward would need a massive force, capable of besieging a large town; it was a bigger undertaking than the siege of Calais. Furthermore, he genuinely seems to have hoped that the French would accept the proposed treaty, because, although some degree of preparation and planning was in place by June, it was only on 24 June that the English war-machine swung into full action. The army that had taken Calais had gathered over a period of time, and had included the original expeditionary force and also many of those who had been fighting in Gascony under Henry of Grosmont, as well as reinforcements from England. Edward now proposed to raise 12,000 men, the largest single force ever to sail from England. But half the year had gone: the king reached Sandwich about 16 September, and did not sail until 27 October. He was hazarding everything on being able to fight a winter campaign. He had indeed carried out the siege of Calais through the winter, and Reims was well to the south: but the continental climate inland would be more extreme than that of the sea-coast. The preparations were thorough, and the result was an impressive but unwieldy mass which had to be moved slowly from Calais southwards to Reims. Jean le Bel describes it vividly:

> he set out from Calais next day, with the finest supply train ever seen: it was said there were 6,000 handsomely fitted wagons, all brought over from England. And he ordered his battalions so splendidly that they were a pleasure to behold: he commanded his Constable, whose title was the Earl of March [Roger Mortimer], to ride half a league ahead of him with 600 heavy cavalry, the most splendidly accoutred in the army, and 1,000 archers; next he formed his own battalion with 3,000 cavalry and 5,000 archers, and followed his marshal in battle array, ever ready to fight if the need arose; behind this great battalion came the baggage train, stretching fully four miles, carrying everything needed for camp or combat, including hand-mills and ovens for baking bread in case they found that all the ovens and mills in the country had been destroyed; and behind the train rode the Prince of Wales and his brother the Earl of Richmond [John of Gaunt] (recently married to the Duke of Lancaster's daughter): in their battalion they had 2,500 heavy cavalry, superbly mounted and richly armed, and 4,000 archers and as many brigandines forming the rearguard. They didn't allow a single fellow to fall behind: they'd wait for any straggler; so they couldn't cover more than three leagues in a day.[39]

Much of Le Bel's description is borne out by English records. The 1,000 carts requisitioned for the expedition were to carry everything from the portable boats for the king's fishermen and the portable mills and ovens which Le Bel describes to a mass of raw materials, lime for siegeworks, iron for horseshoes, and of course provisions. It was these last that were to be the Achilles heel of the unwieldy enterprise. In France, the harvest had been gathered and stored for the winter, and when the dauphin Charles, regent in place of his captive father, ordered these stores to be moved into the towns or destroyed, the task was relatively easy, particularly since the planned English incursion had been long expected.

The main invasion was preceded by two raids. The first, led by Henry of Grosmont, was formed of his own personal retinue and German mercenaries, recruited by Walter Mauny and led by the margrave of Meissen. Part of the reason for the raid foreshadowed the problem of provisioning: the mercenaries had been waiting so long in Calais that they had used up a significant part of the stores sent there for the main army, and Grosmont was effectively told to get them out of the town and take them on a raid down to Arras and along the Somme. He was followed by Roger Mortimer, who raided along the Channel coast, and met up with Grosmont as they returned to Calais. Apart from getting the German mercenaries out of Calais, the raids do not seem to have served any strategic purpose. It seems, reading Le Bel closely, as if they set out with minimal provisions: they took four days to reach the abbey of Mont-Saint-Éloi, near Arras, 'where they stayed for four days to rest and recover, for they found the place well provisioned and they certainly needed sustenance, having tasted neither bread nor wine for the previous four days'.[40] If this is true, their last square meal was in Calais itself. In order to get provisions, they had to attack towns; and they found almost everywhere that the townsmen, having suffered for years at the hands of the English and of freebooting companies in the lawlessness following the French defeat at Poitiers, had protected themselves by renewing their fortifications or raising new ones. Grosmont tried to take Bray-sur-Somme, probably to get provisions, and was driven off, and it was only after three weeks on the march that he succeeded in getting stores by storming Cerisy; at which point he was summoned back to Calais.

From the outset, therefore, the army that left Calais in mid-November was divided into three, specifically, according to John of Reading, 'on account of provisions'. At times they were as much as fifty miles apart, and communications were a further problem. If there was a broad swathe of devastation as a result, it was less as a matter of policy than a desperate search for the wherewithal to feed the men: the towns were not only well fortified, but well defended, with commanders whose instructions were in effect to batten down the hatches until the storm had passed. The chronicler at St Mary's abbey, York, seems to have had access to a detailed letter about the campaign; if his account reflects it accurately, there are no claims that serious economic damage has been inflicted on the French regime, as in the case of the prince's raid of 1355, but simply the endless repetition of the phrase 'destroying and wasting the country'. There was little engagement with the enemy, and no heroic actions worth reporting. Worse, if we are to believe Froissart, the weather was raw and rainy; the rain fell almost every day and every night, and, even though Edward had heard of the dearth of provisions in France, he had not been able to bring enough fodder for the horses with him: 'the horses got by as best they could', Froissart comments, stating the obvious.[41]

The three divisions were commanded by the king, the prince of Wales and Henry of Grosmont. The veteran leaders of Crécy and Poitiers were with the king – Thomas Beauchamp, Robert Ufford, William Montagu the younger and John de Vere, but there were also new faces: his sons Lionel of Clarence and Edmund of Cambridge were with him, as well as Jean, the young claimant to the dukedom of Brittany. The prince was accompanied by his old companions William Bohun and Richard Stafford, and by his brother John of Gaunt, who had already fought in three campaigns with the king. Edward's forces took the most easterly route, Grosmont was in the centre, and the prince took a longer path, first south-west to Montreuil, then back to the valley of the upper Somme before all three divisions met at a small village twenty miles from Laon and thirty miles north of Reims. They met apparently by chance, because 'one division did not know where the others were' until 28 November; and a council of war was held at which it was decided that, despite the problem with communications, they should continue in three separate divisions, but 'in such a way that each would know where the others were'.[42] The king went direct to Reims and set up camp there at the abbey of St Basle near Verzy; the prince, probably in search of a good store of provisions, marched away from Reims to Rethel, which he attacked unsuccessfully before rejoining the king and establishing himself at the monastery of St Thierry, north-west of the town; and Mortimer and Grosmont took up residence at Bétheny, to the north-east.

The siege of Reims was a largely non-military affair. What Edward seems to have hoped is that the show of force outside their walls, and the non-appearance of any relieving army, would persuade the citizens, and particularly their archbishop, Jean de Craon, said to favour the English cause, to open their gates and welcome him in. Villani says that he promised to make it 'the most magnificent and important town in France if he could be crowned there, and to treat the inhabitants kindly',[43] though there is no actual record of any English overtures to the city. Strict injunctions against any kind of harmful activity were issued, and the army settled in as best it could to blockade the town; the weather was poor, and provisions short. Edward could see that the fortifications were in excellent repair, but he probably did not know that the dauphin had warned the citizens of the English plans as early as 10 July. Furthermore, under the leadership of the captain appointed by the dauphin to guard the town, Gaucher de Châtillon, the archbishop had been treated as suspect, and had been forced to move to his palace in the heart of the city from his house near one of the city gates because he refused to allow defence works there; the low garden wall was replaced by a new enclosure, which joined the fortifications on either side. The archbishop had not made himself popular with the citizens, and in reality had little support. As elsewhere, all grain and other foodstuffs from the surrounding countryside had been brought into the city; anything which could not be removed had been spoiled. The citizens were armed and trained in organized bands, and the streets were equipped with chains which could be used to block the way in case the enemy penetrated the defences. Gaucher knew that he could hold out for a very long time against a blockade, and that the English would starve sooner than the inhabitants of Reims. Reims would not share the fate of Calais. The only alternative was a full-scale assault, and Edward knew that both politically and practically this would not succeed.[44]

At Christmas, Edward and his companions were said to have celebrated the festival in style: 'every lord made merry with others as though he were on his own estates in England.' The celebrations may have been improved if Froissart's information is correct. He says that soon after their arrival before the city, Eustace d'Auberchicourt, who had been operating as a freebooter in the area before they arrived, seized the nearby town of Attigny and found 3,000 barrels of wine there, much of which was sent as a present to the king and prince. Soon after the festival, chiefly because more supplies were urgently needed, but also to satisfy an increasingly bored army, a raiding party was sent out to the east, under Grosmont, John of Gaunt and James Audley. They took the town of Cernay, which was razed to the ground, and two smaller fortresses, which were entrusted to Eustace d'Auberchicourt; and

Bartholomew Burghersh the younger and his men scaled the walls of Cormicy. But this was only a diversion. The army could not stay in one place any longer, and on 11 January, after six weeks outside Reims, the English raised the siege. They left in good order during the night.

The problem now was where to go next. Edward does not seem to have had any real alternative master plan as to what his objective was. For the moment, his problem was still that of finding supplies, and the solution proposed was that the army should keep on the move, foraging for whatever it could recover from a countryside deliberately stripped of provisions, until a new supply fleet could be sent from England to Honfleur in Normandy. The timing of the arrival of supplies was uncertain, particularly in the depth of winter, when storms could keep ships in harbour for weeks at a time.

Edward could not return north the way he had come, because he had already exhausted any supplies there; so he headed southwards, and negotiated a large ransom from the men of the county of Bar to spare them from the passage of his troops. And less than a month later Edward presented a similar demand to the Burgundians if they wanted to prevent the English from entering their duchy, which was much less well defended than the countryside round Reims. The negotiations took a month, at Pontigny, where Thomas Becket had once been in exile two centuries before. While Edward negotiated, the prince of Wales rode south-westwards to Auxerre, where the freebooters were still active, and suffered the first real losses of the campaign, to nocturnal marauders who killed knights and squires in their quarters, and to attacks on his foraging parties. It was during this march from Reims that Geoffrey Chaucer was taken prisoner and ransomed; his friend the Italian poet Petrarch, travelling through the area later in the year, wrote to his friends at home that he did not recognize the thriving countryside he had seen on previous visits to Paris.

Edward now decided to threaten Paris, and to see what might happen as a result. He turned to the tactics of previous raids, and authorized burning and looting in a way that had not characterized the campaign until this point. Jean de Venette, who was in Paris at the time, has left vivid descriptions of what went on. For six days after the king's arrival, 'his troops, dispersed throughout the vicinity, wasted and burned everything so thoroughly that not a man nor a woman was left in any of the villages near Paris, from the Seine to Étampes'. On Good Friday, the smoke and flames rising from the towns to the heavens were visible at Paris in innumerable places. Thither a great part of the rural population had fled. It was lamentable to see men, women and children desolate. On Easter Day, I myself saw priests of ten country parishes communicating their people and keeping Easter in various chapels or any spot they could find in the monastery of the Carmelite friars at Paris. On the following day, the nobles and burgesses of Paris ordered the suburbs of Saint-Germain, Notre-Dame-des-Champs and Saint-Marceau to be burnt.[45]

Other mansions and manor houses near the city were destroyed to prevent their use by the English, while in some places the churches were fortified. At Châtres, a quarrel between the captain and leaders and the rest of the village led to the church being set alight by the captain's men, and the death of 1,200 people in the ensuing inferno. The mere presence of the English was enough to bring disaster on anyone living outside the city walls. As in the past, Edward hoped that the scale of the damage and the chaos within Paris would force the dauphin to act and bring his army out to drive off the enemy.

He had already met papal envoys who were seeking a peace settlement, and John had succeeded in tightening his grip on the Paris administration: he too was anxious to make peace and regain his liberty, while the dauphin was unwilling to pay the price that would be demanded in any peace treaty. A meeting of the peace negotiators was held on Good Friday, 3 April; the English were represented by Grosmont, William Bohun, Thomas Beauchamp, Chandos and Walter Mauny. Nothing came of it. The French blamed 'the excessive demands of the enemy'.[46] Although Paris was in turmoil and short of provisions, Edward could not afford to attempt a siege. Instead, he made one last attempt to draw out the dauphin by parading his army in battle array on the morning of 12 April, just outside the walls of Paris. But the dauphin made no move, and Edward gave orders for the army to move south-west towards Chartres in search of forage, setting out on the following day.

Natural disaster overwhelmed the army as it moved off. The persistent rain of the winter was followed by a huge hailstorm, which caught the army on the move and therefore at its most vulnerable. Jean de Venette says that 'the strength of the horses failed. They could not pull their loads, and the wagons, soaked with rain, remained stationary on the roads and highways. Many horses and their drivers were pitiably drowned by the hail and torrential rain.'[47] The English remembered it as Black Monday,[48] and it became a legend: a hundred years later, a London chronicler described it as 'a foul dark day of mist and of hail, and so bitter cold, that sitting on horseback men died'.[49] Henry Knighton claims that the army's supply train was almost entirely destroyed, with the loss of 6,000 horses, 'and they had to return to England'.[50]

Knighton was in a sense right: the losses were not dire enough to stop the campaign there and then, and supplies did reach them from Honfleur immediately after the disaster. Nonetheless Edward halted five days later near Orléans. Froissart reports that Henry of Grosmont argued that they should bring the fighting to an end. As so often, the chronicler presents his own summary of the situation as direct speech and attributes it to an appropriate figure. The choice before Edward was either to continue fighting with an uncertain outcome, much expenditure and the danger that he could lose all his gains, or to accept peace on honourable terms – though these would be much less favourable than they might have been a fortnight earlier. The king's choice was peace, a peace which, wrote Jean de Venette, eased 'the anguish of the French people, who had borne for twenty-four years and more the burdens and disasters of the wars waged by the English', and which was agreed upon 'by the inspiration of the Holy Spirit and to the joy of the angels'.[51] Terms were worked out at Brétigny, near Chartres, on 1 May. Edward was to have Aquitaine in full sovereignty, free of any French overlordship, but he had to give up his claim to the overlordship of Brittany and his more shadowy claims to Normandy and the provinces on its southern border. King John's ransom, originally set at four million gold florins, was reduced to three million. All this was to be worked out in detail at a conference at Calais beginning on 15 July. A preliminary agreement was ratified by both the prince of Wales and the dauphin by 15 May. Three days later Edward and his son were back in London, leaving the army to follow over the next few weeks. It had been an expensive seven months, not only in terms of cash, but also in terms of losses among the commanders: Roger Mortimer, earl of March, only two years older than Edward and his childhood friend, died of fever in February 1360 while the army was between Reims and Paris; the king 'mourned him greatly', according to Froissart, and his body was later brought back to England and buried at Wigmore. Other victims were Thomas Beauchamp's eldest son Guy, and Robert Morley, a highly experienced commander and administrator who had spent many years in charge of the English fleet.[52]

The dauphin continued his policy of defensive warfare when he came to the throne as Charles V in 1364, after John II's death in captivity in London. When the war had started, it had been the French whose tactics were outmoded, derived from an old-fashioned romantic view of the value of the mounted knight as chivalrous hero, descendant of the heavily armed warriors whom three centuries earlier the Byzantine princess Anna Comnena described as capable of piercing the walls of her city with their cavalry charge. Charles V, faced with the unquestioned superiority of English arms and English tactics on the battlefield, discarded the knightly idea that an army must be met by an army, if honour was to be preserved, and that battle was the decisive mode of warfare. Instead, his policy was to fortify, raise militias and target the enemy's sources of supply, the weakest point of any invading force, by withdrawing the provisions available into heavily defended towns and leaving the countryside empty of resources. It was a remedy which worked superbly against the English army: Charles had applied the English tactic of always trying to fight a battle from a defensive position to the strategy of the war as a whole.

The coming of peace with England had one consequence which Jean de Venette did not foresee in his celebration of the new order: the hordes of mercenaries who were let loose on the French countryside when their employment ceased in 1360 with the treaty of Brétigny. Both sides had employed them, officially and unofficially; now they were turned loose to find their own ways of making a living. This had happened in the years immediately after Poitiers, but not on a grand scale; individuals had held communities to ransom and fought private wars; after the treaty of Brétigny, the mercenaries worked out the advantages of co-operation, and fought as the so-called 'free companies'. When several of these companies collaborated, they could field a formidable army: at Brignais near Lyons in 1362, they annihilated a French royal army under Jean de Tancarville and Jacques de Bourbon, experienced commanders who totally failed to realize that they were faced by superior numbers and hardened fighters.

In November 1361, Edward actually sent commissioners to France to round up any English subjects who were engaged in this sort of warfare, order them to leave France within a limited time, and arrest them if they refused. The writ states that the king is taking this action because of a complaint by 'our brother of France' about the English depredations, and it is clearly a diplomatic attempt to satisfy John rather than a serious proposal for the removal of the English, as it begs all kinds of questions about how the two commissioners were going to enforce the king's demands.[53]

Edward III's attitude to these freelances was at best ambivalent, and there is some evidence that he covertly supported them: their operations were doing a great deal of harm to his opponents. A case in point is that of Eustace d'Auberchicourt. As a companion of the Garter, he was closely aligned with Edward, even though as a foreigner he was not technically one of the king's subjects. He had been one of the commissioners who confirmed the treaty of Brétigny at Calais on 4 October 1360. Five days earlier, he had made a prestigious marriage to the lady whose love affair with him Froissart describes, Queen Philippa's niece, the former countess of Kent, Elizabeth of Juliers. His military service for Edward had come to an end in 1363: he was supposed to go to Brittany that spring, but instead he took a substantial force, of 350 mounted soldiers, to Ireland.[54] However, in 1364, he contracted with Charles of Navarre to be 'guardian for my lord of Navarre of the lands which he holds in France, Normandy and Burgundy'.[55] His first recorded act was to sign a truce in respect of Normandy on 13 March, his co-signatory being the king's brother, Louis of Navarre.[56] On 7 June he sealed a charter of liege homage to Charles of Navarre: he was to serve in peace and war against everyone except the king of England and his children, most especially in the wars which that king had at present in the kingdom of France. He was specially charged with keeping the castle of Carentan.

One of his first actions in this capacity was also one of the most dramatic. Charles of Navarre believed that there was an opportunity to regain his lost lands in Normandy, and sent a force of about 400 men by sea from Bayonne under the command of Auberchicourt and a Navarrese knight to invade the duchy. They embarked at the end of July, and soon after their arrival news came that the long-standing civil war in Brittany between Jean de Montfort, backed by the English, and the French claimant, Charles de Blois, had flared up again. In September, Auberchicourt led his men to join an Anglo-Breton army led by John

Chandos[57] which was trying to prevent Charles de Blois from raising the siege of the town of Auray. The commanders on the French side were Charles de Blois himself, Jean de Chalon, whom Auberchicourt had fought in Champagne, and the young Breton captain Bertrand du Guesclin, who was later to prove the scourge of the English armies. The battle was fought entirely on foot: Chandos had a strong defensive position, on a hillside above a river. There were negotiations before the battle, and the Bretons with Charles de Blois were apparently ready to accept Jean de Montfort's terms. But the English soldiers and the French under du Guesclin were determined to fight: their livelihood depended on the spoils of war, whereas the Bretons had a vested interest in peace. As soon as negotiations failed, the Bretons on the French side began to desert, and in the opening moments Jean de Chalon was captured. The French formation broke, and more Bretons deserted Charles de Blois: his knights were overwhelmed, he himself was killed, and du Guesclin captured.[58] The latter was freed before the end of the year on promise of payment of a ransom of 100,000 francs to John Chandos.

Auberchicourt now returned to his original purpose, that of regaining the lands claimed by Charles of Navarre. He and his men joined the army under the command of Louis of Navarre, which invaded lower Normandy in mid-October: and it was at this point, on 14 November 1364, that Edward III addressed a fiercely worded writ to him and two other captains, Hugh Calveley and Robert Scot: he had recently heard, he declared, that, under colour of the war which the king of Navarre was waging on the king of France, they had invaded French territory with a large force and were waging open war, pillaging, robbing, burning, raping and causing much damage. This was in breach of the peace, and very damaging to the king's reputation; on receipt of the letters they were to cease their activities forthwith. These letters were also addressed to the prince of Wales, John Chandos and all French and English officials in France.[59] It was a public disavowal of the covert policies of the previous seven years: why Edward should have taken such action at this moment is obscure, because he had no obvious reason to wish to show favour to the king of France; it runs counter to his diplomatic attempts to outflank him by creating a major alliance with the count of Flanders. Whether Auberchicourt actually took much notice of the letter we do not know; but he remained in the king of Navarre's service.

*

By 1365, after much head-scratching by the French and by the pope, whose territories round Avignon had been subject to the raids of the companies, a scheme for getting them out of France had been devised. It hinged on the situation in Castile, where the autocratic rule of Pedro I, the son of Alfonso XI, was being challenged by a baronial revolt led by Henry of Trastamara, his illegitimate half-brother. Both the French and the Castilians' neighbours in Aragon were eager to see a change of regime, and, with the pope's connivance, an expedition to depose Pedro was launched in November 1365 under the guise of a crusade to drive the Muslims out of southern Spain. The leaders were to be Arnoul d'Audrehem, the marshal of France who had fought at Poitiers, and two younger commanders: Bertrand du Guesclin had made his name fighting against the companies in Brittany, while Hugh Calveley, a knight from the prince of Wales's lands in Cheshire, had been a leader of those same companies. This improbable plan was put into effect by the promise of huge sums to the mercenaries, and by September they were heading south. Alongside the French and English companies who had fought at Auray and elsewhere in Brittany were a much wider range of soldiers, freebooters from Burgundy and southern France and a variety of French knights seeking to retrieve their fortunes. This massive group of soldiers was quickly nicknamed the 'Great Company'.

The problem was that Pedro had recently signed a treaty with the prince of Wales in Aquitaine: part of the point of putting together the Great Company was to undermine English power there by transferring the allegiance of Castile from England to France. Pedro invoked the treaty; but all that he got in the way of support was a proclamation from Edward III on 6 December 1365 addressed to John Chandos as constable of Aquitaine, Hugh Calveley and two other captains who were actually part of the invading army. Edward instructed them to find any English forces intending to join the Great Company and to stop them; disobedience would be severely punished, and would extend to their friends and relatives.[60] Hugh Calveley ignored the letters, and continued as du Guesclin's second in command.

Auberchicourt played a more ambiguous role. He was in Navarre on 20–24 January 1366,[61] when he renewed his liege homage in the name of himself and his eldest son, excepting only his allegiance and duty to Edward III and his eldest son, in return for an annual pension of 1,000 *livres tournois* and a payment of 65,000 gold florins for past service, the price of loyalty in difficult times.[62] Records show him in Navarre at intervals until mid-March, and it is entirely possible that he had separated himself from the expedition and was working for Charles of Navarre instead.[63] An order was given to the castellan at St Jean Pied du Port, at the foot of the Pyrenees, who had detained Auberchicourt's siege engines; they were to be allowed through on 22 February, for the defence of the Navarrese town of Peña, as part of the defensive precautions taken by Charles before the invasion of Castile began. Intriguingly, a safe conduct was issued on the same date for Geoffrey Chaucer and three companions to travel freely through Navarre, and to talk to anyone they pleased.[64] It is not impossible that this was arranged by Auberchicourt, and was part of the covert English activities in Navarre.

On New Year's Day, the leaders of the companies feasted with Pere IV, king of Aragon, in Barcelona. They left for Castile a week later, and met little resistance, but then Calveley marched across the Navarrese border on his way to the Castilian capital at Burgos. His move was probably purely strategic, in that the main road to Burgos ran through Navarrese territory, and, although some towns were secured as a precaution, Calveley's troops recrossed into Castile a day or two later.[65] The campaign was very brief: Pedro's supporters deserted him when du Guesclin approached, and Henry was crowned king at Burgos on 29 March 1366. Pedro fled south to Seville, and then to Portugal. Five days earlier, du Guesclin and Auberchicourt had dined with the king of Navarre at San Vicente.[66] Following the unexpectedly sudden end to the expedition, Auberchicourt recruited a number of English knights who were with du Guesclin's expedition to Charles's service, and writs were issued in evidence of this: in one case, his own seal was used for a knight who did not have a seal of his own.[67] Stephen Cosington, one of the prince of Wales's household knights, was recruited on 6 April, and it seems clear that there was a broad strategy of placing men in Navarrese service in case of some future political development.

The prince of Wales and his advisers had not anticipated a swift victory by the companies. Their intelligence about Pedro seems to have been poor. Pedro's character was suspect: Thomas Gray has a long and highly inaccurate anti-Semitic story of how his love for his Jewish mistress led to his inclusion of Jews among the knights of the royal order of knighthood, the Order of the Sash. This, according to Gray, led many of his men to support Henry of Trastamara. Though the tale is not true, it indicates Pedro's poor reputation outside Spain.[68] Pedro's ambassadors at Westminster in November 1365 had had to work to counter such tales, and the prince's entourage at Bordeaux was also, according to Froissart, very reluctant to support this supposedly unchivalrous monarch. But the politics of the situation were now such that the prince had little choice in the matter: if Aquitaine was not to be threatened by a hostile power on its southern border, Pedro had to be supported. He consulted with his father in England, and seems to have been told firmly that diplomacy must take precedence over any hesitation about Pedro's character. An agreement was reached on 23 September 1366, and signed at a great meeting at Libourne near Bordeaux. The prince was to provide a great army for an invasion the following year, in return for the Basque province of Vizcaya, which would become part of Aquitaine, and the reimbursement of all his expenses. Pedro had only some valuable jewels, and no source of ready money until his kingdom was back in his hands, so the prince had to advance all the wages as well as a bribe to Charles of Navarre for free passage through his territory.

The stakes for the prince of Wales were therefore high: his five years as ruler of Aquitaine had shown that his skill on the battlefield was not matched by his skill as a ruler and diplomat. It may be that the scheme promised an attractive diversion from the everyday problems of administration and negotiation with dissident nobles, and that the lure of new military glory weighed heavily in his mind in favour of the expedition. Details such as the problems of obtaining the promised payments were a secondary question. From the outset, however, there was a degree of distrust between the prince and the ousted king of Castile.

Recruiting men for the army was not difficult: late in the proceedings, Froissart says, the prince of Wales tried to reduce the contingent to be provided by the Gascon lord of Albret, a noted leader of the companies, only to be told that these men had forgone opportunities for lucrative work elsewhere, and must be included. Under a leader of the prince's calibre, there were likely to be good opportunities for ransoms and other profits of war, and the largely mercenary army was quickly assembled. The core was the knights of the prince's household together with a contingent under John of Gaunt, who sailed from England to Cherbourg in December 1366 and marched down the west coast of

France, gathering on the way a force of Breton and English mercenaries recruited by Robert Knolles, another leader of the free companies. The bulk of the army was Gascon, with two or three other groups centred on commanders who had been freebooters in Brittany and eastern France such as John Cresswell and Robert Briquet. Auberchicourt returned to Gascony in early December with the other English members of the Great Company under the leadership of John Chandos to join the prince's army.[69] Only a handful of Castilians were present when the army marched from Dax at the foot of the Pyrenees at the end of January 1367.

Meanwhile, Henry of Trastamara, who had obtained the backing of Pere IV of Aragon, had also signed a treaty of alliance with Charles of Navarre, who was anxious to insure himself against the possibility of Henry's victory. This was a serious mistake, as Charles was notorious for duplicity, and Henry believed that he had genuinely achieved a diplomatic success. The king of Aragon thought the same, and even supposed that the prince of Wales had cancelled his plans because of this development.[70] In confident mood, Henry released du Guesclin and Calveley from his service, and allowed them to withdraw from Castile. But the prince, far from cancelling his plans, took advantage of his opponent's mistake, and promptly instructed Calveley – who had disobeyed specific instructions when he took Henry's side, and was probably anxious to make good his position – to invade Navarre immediately. This drove Charles to hasten to Gascony and reaffirm his commitment to the prince.

The journey into Spain was arduous, across the famous pass of Roncesvalles where, so the epic legend had it, Roland had lost his life fighting off an attack on the rearguard of Charlemagne's army. It was a daring move to take troops over the mountains in the winter snows; Henry's belief that the expedition would be abandoned offered the possibility of a tactical surprise which was too good an opportunity to miss. When the news of the prince's arrival in Navarre reached the Castilian capital, Burgos, there was indeed consternation, and a number of minor rebellions in favour of Pedro broke out. Henry was able to get word to du Guesclin, and to balance Calveley's defection to the prince's side by retaining his erstwhile French colleague. He set up his headquarters at Santo Domingo, near the border with Navarre, while the prince of Wales advanced through Navarre to the capital, Pamplona. Here he sent out a reconnaissance party under Thomas Felton, including Hugh Stafford and Thomas Ufford,[71] who were able to cross into Castile and meet supporters of Pedro at Logroño, which had never surrendered to Henry. They told him that the usurper's army was thirty miles to the west, and that his movements indicated that he was working on the assumption that the prince would cross the river Ebro into Castilian territory at Logroño; given that the city was in friendly hands, this was the obvious route. But the prince chose instead to take a more difficult and unexpected route, through the mountains to Salvatierra, entering Castile further to the north. If he had been able to do so quickly, he would have achieved a considerable tactical advantage, but the route proved harder than expected, and the army was short of provisions as it made its way through the difficult terrain. Six days' rest at Salvatierra were needed before the prince could move forward again, and the element of surprise was lost.

At this point there was a serious disagreement between Henry's Spanish advisers and their French allies. Du Guesclin and Audrehem argued strongly that all that was required was to guard the passes on the Salvatierra road that led to Miranda in Castile, and the prince's army would be so deprived of provisions that it would have to withdraw. Henry, on the other hand, instinctively wished to fight: his reputation as a chivalrous and heroic leader as against Pedro's calculating and cold approach was at stake, and furthermore there was news of increasing defections by his supporters now that the legitimate king was back in the region. But at first he heeded the advice he was given, which had been backed up by a letter from Charles V cautioning him against committing himself to a battle. Henry moved forward so that he was in a position to harry the English, particularly their foraging parties, using the light cavalry which were a Castilian speciality.

His success in doing this encouraged him to attempt a more serious action. Don Tello, Henry's second in command, and Audrehem were sent to make a dawn raid on the English encampment. Don Tello found Hugh Calveley's men just as they were getting up, and many of them were killed in their beds; their baggage train was badly damaged. Don Tello then attacked the encampment of the vanguard, but John of Gaunt, alerted by the noise of the attack on Calveley, gathered his forces in battle order and summoned help from the prince; the raiders were quickly driven off. Audrehem attacked an outpost manned by William

Felton on a nearby hill, some 400 men at arms and archers, including squires from the prince's household. Felton was killed, with many of his men, and the rest taken prisoner, after a fierce resistance: they were finally overcome by a combination of dismounted knights and cavalry, the tactic which had failed at Poitiers. Here, however, there were only a handful of archers to deal with the cavalry. It seems as if the prince of Wales had forgotten the standard precaution of keeping an adequate watch at night, perhaps because he did not think that an enemy assault was likely. And he also assumed that the whole enemy army was about to attack, and so did not immediately go to the help of Felton and his men.

The prince of Wales now retreated into Navarre, in order to take the alternative road into Castile by way of Logroño; the countryside was more welcoming, and forage would be easier to find, but the march back through the mountains was harsh, and Walter of Peterborough, one of Edward's clerks, describes in his history of the expedition how he spent the night sleeping in a small copse in the bitter cold. On 1 April the army at last reached Logroño and crossed the river Ebro. At this point the prince replied to a formal challenge to battle which Henry had sent a month before, by calling on him to give up the throne which he had usurped. Henry replied in an openly insulting and angry tone, accusing the prince of being much attached to vainglory (a comment not entirely wide of the mark) and suggesting that two or three knights from either side should choose a suitable battlefield. The prince curtly dismissed the idea.

The next day the prince of Wales advanced to Navarrete, a small fortress nearby, which Thomas Felton had reconnoitred the previous month. This was no longer the terrain for guerrilla warfare, and Henry was in any case more inclined to take up the challenge of a battle than to sit out a long campaign of attrition. The defections were continuing, and he and his council felt it was imperative to strike quickly. Henry had established a defensive position along the bank of a small tributary which fed the river at Nájera, and the prince's scouts had made him aware of this. The English were not prepared to attempt a frontal attack, so just before dawn they set out on a track which was concealed from the Castilians, leading behind a ridge which rose some 600 feet high to the north. Henry's scouts failed to find the prince's men, and their appearance from the north-east took the Castilians entirely by surprise.

They quickly attempted to realign their formation, but the defensive advantage had been lost.

The vanguard of Henry's army was largely made up of experienced troops under two war-hardened commanders, du Guesclin and Audrehem. But at both Crécy and Poitiers, the best commanders had been kept in the centre, where they could direct tactics. Here the two French knights were subordinate to Henry himself, and had little chance of influencing the course of the battle except as fighting men. The elite of the Castilian knights were also in the vanguard, among them the knights of the Sash, whose banner was carried by Pero López de Ayala, who later included an account of the battle in his *Chronicle of King Pedro*. They fought dismounted, since they had expected to be holding a defensive position. Henry commanded the central division, and there were two troops of light cavalry on the wings. The Castilian army seems to have lacked crossbowmen and archers.

Against them were ranged a force equal or possibly larger in size. The vanguard was commanded by John Chandos and John of Gaunt, with a large body of archers. The prince of Wales was in the next division, where the Castilians were placed for fear of possible defections; there were also Navarrese troops and Gascons under the command of Jean de Grailly, captal de Buch, and the lord of Albret. All these were dismounted; in the rear was a mounted division under Jaime of Majorca, Hugh Calveley and Jean d'Armagnac. This could be used as a highly mobile squadron if an encircling movement, as at Crécy and Poitiers, was called for.

The first defections occurred before the battle started. It was a bad omen for Henry of Trastamara, even though the group of light horse which changed sides was small. The actual fighting began with an English attack, John of Gaunt's men advancing with shortened spears shouting 'Guyenne, St George', to engage with du Guesclin's vanguard who answered with their war cry 'Castile, Santiago'. The hand-to-hand fighting was indecisive, and the prince of Wales engaged his main battalion, the centre of which was to support John of Gaunt. Two detachments were sent to deal with Don Tello and the count of Denia, who led the troops of light cavalry. However, on the approach of the English, all the light cavalry deserted, though the count of Denia himself entered the action and was captured fighting with the vanguard. The Castilian division was faced by the whole English army, and Henry called his main

460

battalion forward. He himself rode into the thick of the fight, to the place where López de Ayala held the banner of the Order of the Sash. But very few of his men followed him into the fray, because the English clearly had the upper hand. Most of them fled, and the battle was effectively over. The English mounted knights pursued the fugitives, and many of the leaders were either killed or captured, mainly along the banks of the river Ebro as they attempted to cross. But Henry himself managed to escape.

The tally of captives was impressive, and included many of Henry's leading supporters, his brother among them. More important to the English was the capture of both du Guesclin and Audrehem, both familiar to the prince of Wales since they had previously been in English hands. Du Guesclin had been captured at Auray in 1364 by John Chandos's men, but had paid his ransom; Audrehem, on the other hand, still owed money to the prince for his ransom after Poitiers eleven years earlier. Worse, he had sworn not to fight against the prince until the ransom had been paid in full. The prince angrily reminded him of this, and is said to have threatened him with execution as a traitor.[72] Audrehem stood his ground, and pointed out that he was not fighting the prince, but Pedro, and both he and the prince were merely captains under the command of the Castilian rivals – both mercenaries, in effect. The prince pardoned him, though he was not forgiven the ransom due.

The victory was due to the prince of Wales's skill in manoeuvring his army rapidly in response to a changing situation: if his attempt to march into Castile by an unexpected route failed, the repositioning of his men at Najéra unseen by the enemy was a great success. Once the actual fighting began, his success was at least partly due to the defections from Henry of Trastamara's army. The failure of the usurper's division to engage with the enemy was very similar to the failure of the French second division to move forward at Poitiers. The tight-knit English command in the vanguard, combined with the use of archers, meant that the fighting was already strongly in their favour by the time enemy reinforcements came into play, and any hesitation that those reinforcements may have had – at Poitiers, the removal of the king's sons from the field, at Najéra the uncertain loyalty to the recently crowned Henry – was at once magnified. Morale once again was critical, and ultimately morale depended on loyalty, not only to comrades, but to those leading the army.

The aftermath of the battle was disastrous for the prince, both financially and personally. It rapidly became plain that Pedro could not meet the costs of the campaign, which were almost as large as the ransom paid by King John of France, because Castile was not a rich country, and any attempt to raise such a sum would have simply alienated his already dissatisfied subjects. The prince of Wales lingered in Castile in the hope that his presence might pressure Pedro into action, but only a fraction of the total due was ever paid: the most tangible part of it was a great balas ruby[73] which still adorns the imperial state crown of England. Distrust quickly set in, and even grants of land were subtly blocked: the prince was told firmly by the Basques that Vizcaya was not Pedro's to give away, since they chose their own rulers, which was indeed strictly true. At the end of August, the prince gave up and returned to Gascony. By then he had contracted the unexplained malady which was to recur for the rest of his life, and to lead to his early death. Military might had failed to outweigh French diplomacy, the more so since Henry of Trastamara returned two years later, defeated Pedro at the battle of Montiel, lured him to his tent afterwards, and murdered him in cold blood with the connivance of Olivier Mauny, Walter Mauny's cousin, and Bertrand du Guesclin. It was not the end of English involvement in Spain: John of Gaunt married Pedro's daughter Constanza in 1371, two years after her father's death, and became the claimant to the throne of Castile, a position he maintained for the next sixteen years. His efforts to establish himself in Castile were to end in humiliation after a disastrous attempt to invade his kingdom with Portuguese help in 1387. Henry of Trastamara's son Juan was recognized as king in return for a payment to Gaunt which once again nearly bankrupted the kingdom.

An enduring victory in Castile would have had a considerable effect on the war between France and England, as Castilian ships continued to pose a serious threat to English shipping, and were responsible for the critical defeat of the English fleet at La Rochelle in 1372, in which the ships commanded by John Hastings, who had become a companion of the Garter three years earlier, were trapped among the sandbanks of the harbour entrance and overwhelmed. The Spaniards had no time for chivalrous niceties, and Hastings was tied up like a dog on a leash in a Spanish prison for the next two years, and died soon after he was released. Even when there was peace in France, the Castilians were not bound by it: three years later, they destroyed thirty-nine English merchant vessels off La Rochelle, seriously weakening the English naval resources, and the following summer they participated in the galley fleet that ravaged the south coast of England.

Ultimately, the leadership of the founding knights of the Company of the Garter was at its best on the battlefield. Their skills, which had evolved in the wars against the Scots, were essentially those of an attacking army in hostile territory, with the ability to win battles in difficult circumstances; but they were invaders, not conquerors. Both the logistics and the temperament for successful conquest were lacking; Edward III's own ability to weld together the lords of England into a loyal and effective high command was not shared by the prince, whose rule in Aquitaine was more of a precursor of his son's reign in England than a parallel to his father's. Haughty and insensitive to the concerns and local pride of the Gascon lords, his splendid court at Bordeaux failed to foster friendship and loyalty in the way that the festivities of Edward and Philippa had succeeded in doing. Yet England, regarded as almost irrelevant in terms of military power when Edward came to the throne, had enjoyed twenty years when its armies were the most consistent and most feared in Europe; and that triumph was due in large part to the companions of the Garter.

14

The Most Noble Order of the Garter

The closing decades of the fourteenth century saw a sharp decline in the military fortunes of the English in France, and the days of Edward III began to seem like a golden past, with the first companions of the Garter as heroic figures. This coincided with an increasing emphasis on knightly honour, of which Geoffroy de Charny was one of the first exponents, and which permeates the pages of Jean Froissart; his prologue declares his intention to record past deeds so that they can be 'viewed and known' now and in the future. Froissart's various introductions to the different versions of his work all return to the theme of great exploits and the glory to be gained from them.

The Company of the Garter at Edward III's death consisted of a core of members of the royal family by birth, a number of descendants of the original founders, knights chosen from the current military commanders (among them a group of courtiers including the chamberlain, William Latimer) and two men who held lands in both France and England, both sons-in-law of the late king. Clause 19 of the statutes provided that at an election each knight present 'shall nominate nine qualified persons, whom he shall believe to be free from all ignominy or shame, who shall be subjects of the sovereign of the order or others, foreigners not subject to him but who yet shall not favour or uphold any party opposed to the said sovereign'. Men like Walter Mauny, owning great estates in England and Hainault, would not have been troubled by this stipulation. But any foreigners and those who held lands from the king of France or one of his allies in the Low Countries could be in danger of a conflict of loyalties. There was no specific clause requiring allegiance to the king of England in the statutes of the Garter, and, during the period of English military ascendance, this requirement not to 'favour or uphold' the enemy had not been an issue.

But the increasing success of the French changed this. Within four months of Edward III's death, Enguerrand de Coucy, earl of Bedford and lord of Coucy, married to Edward's daughter Isabella, resigned from the Company of the Garter. He sent a letter to Richard II, which was carefully endorsed by one of the royal clerks to the effect that it was delivered by Jean Pieres to the king at Hatton Grange near Hounslow on 30 October 1377, and that Jean Pieres spoke in English. In it, Coucy declares that, since war has been renewed between his 'natural and sovereign lord the king of France' and the king of England, he feels obliged to resign from 'the company and order of the Garter' to which his father-in-law Edward III had appointed him.[1]

In more ways than one, this letter marks the end of the original company which Edward founded. In this case, the prospect of the coming war makes Coucy fear that he will be required to fight against Richard II, a fellow-companion of the Garter, which is forbidden by an article in the statutes: he is anticipating a position where he will be disqualified from the company. There is a similar concern in the dealings of Eustace d'Auberchicourt with Charles of Navarre, where he specifies in his contract that he shall not be required to fight against Edward III because he is his liege lord.[2]

Coucy's letter is the first occasion I can trace where the company is called an 'order'. Religious orders of knighthood were a familiar concept, and the alternative title is partly a reflection of the past history of groups of knights: it was easy to apply it to the Garter company, which had a strong religious element through its connection to the College of St George. However, it also reflects a parallel development of secular orders of knighthood, which, like the military religious orders, had statutes which prescribed elaborate rules for the knights' conduct and usually an oath of allegiance to the sovereign or prince. In contrast to these formal orders, we have seen that these fraternities, societies and companies of knights were usually more loosely regulated, and often very short-lived. Dozens of ephemeral knightly groups, usually called 'societies', appeared and disappeared in Germany during the late fourteenth and fifteenth centuries.

The first society of knights to call itself specifically an 'order' was that of the Sash in Spain, which did include an oath of loyalty to the sovereign and an elaborate set of rules. It stands alone in the period up to 1377, since the other early knightly organizations which call themselves 'orders' had a different purpose. The Order of the Collar founded by Amadeus of Savoy in 1364 and the shadowy Order of the Sword founded by Peter I of Cyprus in about 1347 were both intended to form the core of a crusading army, and are therefore not secular orders in the usual sense.

The next purely knightly society to be called an order is the Order of the Ship, established at Naples in 1381 by Charles of Durazzo, successor to Louis of Taranto. The original statutes survive in two copies evidently made for individual knights in the brief four-year existence of the order. It is specifically called an 'order of knighthood', the earliest instance of the usage in connection with a royal foundation of this kind, in the prologue to the statutes; but in the statutes themselves it is still called a 'company'.[3] Nine founder knights were named in the statutes, which are highly elaborate, and include detailed ceremonials for the admission of new members and for the holding of chapters of the order. The spiritual obligations of the companions are specified, and there are provisions for masses for deceased companions. However, the companions also undertook secular obligations to the prince, ranging from loyalty to the avenging of any offence against him and revealing anything which might tend to his harm or dishonour. An annual court was to be held at which such matters were to be discussed, and at which the companions' adventures during the year were to be recounted and set down in writing. The Order of the Ship never seems to have met after the founding ceremony and Charles was murdered in Hungary in 1386 shortly after he won that kingdom. Its regulations, and particularly those regarding the annual court, foreshadow those of the Order of the Golden Fleece.

By the end of the fourteenth century, therefore, there had been a number of attempts to set up confraternities, companies and even orders of knighthood, but none of them had survived for long, with the sole exception of the Company of the Garter. The reasons were diverse, but they were usually linked to the fate of the sovereign or prince who founded them. The Company of the Garter had survived into the next generation, but in 1399, with the deposition of Richard II, it might well have gone the way of the other institutions. However, partly because it had an established reputation and was seen as part of the English kingship, and partly because of the personal connections of Henry IV,

Richard's nemesis, the Garter was not suppressed: instead, it led the way for subsequent knightly orders, and showed how a relatively informal company could evolve into an institution with proper officers and records.

Henry IV was Edward III's grandson, and also grandson of his closest friend and cousin, Henry of Grosmont, who had played a large part in the formation of the Company of the Garter. Furthermore, he seems to have deliberately emulated his namesake in knightly exploits, going on crusade in Prussia in 1391, forty years after Henry of Grosmont. He himself had been made a knight of the company at the same time as Richard II, at the beginning of April 1377, two months before Edward III died. The complex story of Henry's overthrow of Richard is not our present subject. Suffice to say that Henry badly needed to show himself as a legitimate ruler, as, even if Richard freely resigned, Henry was not the nearest heir to the throne. His cousin, Edmund earl of March, was senior in descent from Edward III; and Henry's claim was distinctly dubious. By reinforcing the status of the Company of the Garter, with which he had such strong connections, he was also reinforcing, in a small way, his legitimacy as king. Furthermore, Richard had appointed his boon companions, 'new men', to the company, whereas Henry's supporters were the old aristocracy, in many cases descendants of the original Garter knights.

At Richard's accession, the companions of the order were still largely Edward's military commanders; even courtiers like the unpopular lord chamberlain, William Latimer, and the group associated with him, Richard Pembridge, Ralph Neville and Alan Buxhull, had reasonably distinguished careers as fighting men. Others were the sons of earlier holders, such as the younger Thomas Beauchamp and William Ufford, but again the military tradition was strong, and the household knights still provided the leaders of the English armies as well as most of the companions of the Garter. During Richard's minority, the new companions were for the most part men from his father's household. Richard seems to have been at Windsor quite frequently for St George's Day.[4] However, once he came to power in 1381, the Garter was one of the favours he bestowed on his close friends, the group of courtiers who came to represent everything that the older generation of nobles detested: Robert de Vere and Thomas Mowbray were his contemporaries and had very little military experience when they were elected in

1383–4. De Vere was the most notorious of Richard's favourites, and was impeached for treason when the lords had the upper hand over the king in 1387–8; he became the first Garter knight to be expelled from the company. Richard Fitzalan, son of the earl of the same name and elected immediately after de Vere, was one of these lords, and was charged with treason by the vengeful king ten years later. This was all of a piece with Richard's failure to understand the unspoken principle behind the Company of the Garter: that it represented the king in harmony with his great lords, working towards a common purpose. It was partly Richard's own character which brought about these dissensions, the other element being the withdrawal from the war with France, the common purpose which had until then brought the knights together.

The turbulence of Richard's last years meant that, when Henry IV became king, there were a large number of vacancies, partly due to the execution of four earls by the mob in the course of the so-called 'earls' rebellion' in January 1400. Ten new companions were therefore chosen within the first year of his reign: five of these were Henry's sons and brother-in-law, and among the others were one duke and three earls. Traditional appointments, such as that of the veteran campaigner Thomas Erpingham in 1401, continued to be made.

The real change under the new reign was the approach to the administration of the company. Apart from the activities of the College of St George relating to the Company of the Garter, largely to do with the St George's Day feast, no records from Windsor for the company from the fourteenth century survive, and it is fairly clear that even when Henry IV came to the throne there was a distinct lack of systematic documentation. It is just after his accession that the Windsor tables, evidently displayed in the Garter chapel or the knights' chapter house, were drawn up by John Page, which implies a determined attempt to record the company's past history.[5] The earliest records of chapter meetings and elections to survive date from the reign of Henry V; the 'Black Book' of the Garter compiled in the mid-sixteenth century notes for the reigns of Edward III and Richard II that there is nothing on record except items gleaned from other sources.

The company itself was evolving and slowly changing in character. Although tournaments had never been part of the feast of St George, the presence of so many knights famed for their skill in the lists among its members seems to have led to the idea that there was a link between the company and jousting. However, the first occasion on which we can document such a connection is at the Smithfield jousts of May 1390.[6] If only Geoffrey Chaucer, who was responsible for the building of the scaffolds for the onlookers, had put pen to paper;[7] but there is only a single witness, the author of the *Brut* chronicle for the period, writing thirty years later, who claims that the knights defending the lists in the king's name were the twenty-four knights of the Garter. He was perhaps confused into thinking this was a Garter festival because, at the end of the celebrations, Richard made the count of Ostrevant a knight of the Garter; the duke of Guelders may have been appointed at the same time.[8] These have sometimes been treated as the first elections of foreigners to the company for diplomatic reasons; in fact, like Jean IV of Brittany, Edward's son-in-law, they were relatives of the royal family. Guelders was Richard's second cousin through his great-aunt Eleanor, and William of Ostrevant was the son of the count of Holland and his second cousin once removed through his grandmother Philippa. However, their inclusion was probably more to do with their part in the jousts of St Inglevert, a celebrated tournament which had been held near Calais earlier in the year, and Richard's desire to outshine these with his Smithfield tournament.

The idea of the Garter as a company of knights who might be challenged as a group to a tournament makes its first documented appearance in 1408. In that year, Jean de Werchin, seneschal of Hainault, issued a general challenge to the Garter companions, couched in highly romantic terms, in which he recalled the deeds of the knights of the Round Table and Edward's foundation of the Garter, and challenged them, as successors to the knights of the Round Table, to meet him in single combat, on horseback and on foot, with lances, swords and axes. Since he was young and inexperienced, the companions of the Garter should look favourably on this knightly enterprise. Henry IV acknowledged that 'following the memory of the said order [of the Round Table] one of our predecessors as king ordained another order of knights which still exists and which is called the garter'; however, he politely pointed out that this one-sided challenge was 'very strange with regard to the said order [of the Garter], because we never read in the old histories of the round table that all the knights of that order went out to fight against one single foreign knight', and as sovereign of the order refused his request.[9] Instead, he offered John Cornwall as representative of the order; the affair dragged on, and it is not even clear whether the proposed encounter took place, although Werchin was granted a safe conduct in February 1410 to come to England with a large company of men. This seems to be the only example of a challenge to the knights of the Garter all together, and the surprise expressed by Henry IV is strong evidence that the company never regarded itself as a tourneying society.

The letter also tells us that, by 1408, the erroneous connection made by Froissart between Edward III's Arthurian Round Table and the Garter was widely accepted. The Round Table was never represented as an *order* of knights in any accepted sense of the word, and even Thomas Malory in the late fifteenth century does not depict it as such: when Arthur learns of Lancelot's rebellion at the end of *Le Morte Darthur*, he laments that he has 'lost the fairest fellowship of noble knights that ever a Christian king held together', not that the order that he has created has been broken apart.

The honorific element in Garter appointments, which began with Richard's appointment of de Vere and Mowbray, comes into play under Henry V. Although the original companions seem to have been chosen on the basis of their personal relationship to Edward III and the prince of Wales, they could for the most part be deemed to have merited their membership of the company by their military careers; and those of whom we know little probably qualified in this respect as well. When de Vere and Mowbray were elected, they had done nothing to merit election, and their membership therefore honoured them rather than rewarded them for past actions. This honorific element also applies in a different way with the election of Sigismund emperor of Germany in 1416, followed by that of Philip the Good of Burgundy in 1422. These were the first of a series of elections of foreign princes which gathered pace under Henry VI, and which spread the fame of the Garter throughout Europe. A dozen princes were members of the order during his reign, and a further nine were elected by Edward IV. Frequently, the election was a kind of reciprocal exchange of honours, and the English kings gathered the insignia of the corresponding foreign orders.

The reputation of the Garter in the later fourteenth and early fifteenth centuries outside the company itself and the court is hard to trace. In about 1400, Walter of Bibbesworth's little Anglo-French glossary was translated into English verse, and the author knew so little about 'garters' that he said rather vaguely 'from those men of the garters came the usage of the garters', i.e. garters were invented for the Company of the Garter.[10] There are no specific literary mentions of the Company of the Garter, even though Geoffrey Chaucer was clerk of the works at Windsor and responsible, however indirectly – he may have worked through a deputy – for the repair of St George's chapel: it was a separate and specific commission, and not a sinecure.[11] One great literary work has an apparent Garter connection, but the link is elusive. At the end of the unique manuscript of *Sir Gawain and the Green Knight*, the Garter motto has been written, as if to make this a comment on the poem itself. Scholars are still in two minds as to when the motto was written, but, even if it was not the work of the original scribe, it could be to do with ownership of the manuscript, and attempts have been made to link it to specific Garter knights, even to Henry of Grosmont, but these must remain speculative.[12] Alternatively, the writer may have felt that the content of the poem could reflect in some way on the Company of the Garter, and the more fantastic theories of this kind try to use it to authenticate the fifteenth-century stories of the foundation of the Garter and to link the 'shame' in the motto to the supposed rape of the countess of Salisbury by Edward III. It is a pity that we cannot define a link between the greatest knightly poem in English and what later came to be seen as the greatest English knightly institution. All we can say is that, if it is not an ownership inscription, it must date from a time when the memory of Edward's original confraternity was starting to fade, and it was beginning to be reinterpreted as a society with different ideals; but this would mean dating the inscription to the second quarter of the fifteenth century or later.

The emergence of the Garter as a 'knightly order' takes place in the reign of Henry V. In 1414, when the first St George's Day feast under the new king was held, Henry was much concerned with the threat posed by the Lollard heresy to the authority of the crown. Sir John Oldcastle, a leading Lollard, had rebelled in January, and, at the parliament at Leicester at the end of April, the chancellor, Henry Beaufort, who as bishop of Winchester was prelate of the Company of the Garter, made an impassioned attack on the Lollards. Probably to coincide with the Garter feast on 23 April, the poet Thomas Hoccleve addressed two poems to the king and the 'most honourable company of the Garter'.[13]

Men call them 'the flower of chivalry', but his appeal is not for any secular knightly prowess. Instead he praises Henry as the true upholder of the faith, and 'warrior against heresy's bitter gall', and asks that he should ban the kind of open discussion of matters of faith beloved of the Lollards. The 'company of the Garter' are by implication suitable champions to support such action, and the second poem speaks to them directly: their motto says 'that they are enemies of shame' – a free interpretation of the Garter motto – and 'you, my lords . . . shall quench all this nuisance', a deed of high prowess, and suited to men 'of St George's livery'. He concludes with an appeal to both king and lords of the Garter to remember the Trinity, whose virtue gives them heart and strength 'in faithful unity'.

It is a surprising poem, until we remember Henry V's reputation as a devout monarch, and his opposition to the Lollards. Hoccleve seems to hope that the Garter knights, as a religious confraternity, might be persuaded to enlarge their commemorative role to the active defence of religion, and to the suppression of heresy. As one of the four clerks in the office of the privy seal and therefore a senior member of the administration, he was aware of Henry's strong views on heresy as a threat to the authority of the crown.[14] He certainly knew some of the Garter knights, but whether he is appealing to them as the king's closest companions or was aware of their personal views we cannot tell.

It is possible that Henry's undoubted enthusiasm for the Garter after Agincourt might have made it more rather than less of a religious institution, but he died before the renewal of the Company of the Garter was complete. Henry IV had called the Company of the Garter an 'order' in his response to the challenge from Jean de Werchin in 1408. Nonetheless, it was under Henry V that the company was formally transformed into an order, not perhaps as a deliberate act, but by a process of evolution. Henry added a number of new clauses to the statutes, and may have revised others; the earliest statutes of the company that we possess date from his reign. In 1415, at the trial of Henry, Lord Scrope, for treason, he is described as 'a knight of that distinguished and excellent knightly order of the Garter'.[15] A letter survives in which, the king being absent in France, his deputy requests one of the Garter knights to have masses said for two recently deceased fellow-companions. This probably dates from the autumn of 1420: Walter Hungerford and Lewis Robessart died in October and November of that year. In it, the writer speaks of 'the knightly order of Saint George the martyr of the company of the Garter', a designation which reconciles the new idea of the Garter as a knightly order with that of the original company.[16]

It was Henry who created the office of Garter king at arms, and installed his own personal herald, William Bruges, as its first holder. He had been appointed by letters patent from Richard II as Chester Herald in 1398 as part of the administration of his new principality of Chester. His father, Richard Bruges, had been Lancaster Herald, and William was the personal herald of Henry of Derby, before he became Henry V; he also held the title of Aquitaine king of arms. William's appointment in 1398 was one of the first to be made on a formal legal basis. He was appointed Garter king at arms between May 1417, when he is still referred to as Guyenne king of arms, and September 1417, when he is named as Garter king at arms for the first time.* This coincided with general regulations for the heralds of England.

Bruges' greatest work was the re-creation of the Company of the Garter to reflect the changing times. The old title of 'company' survived in the statutes, but it was now commonly referred to as an order. Bruges created two armorial records of the knights. One was a stained-glass window at Stamford in Lincolnshire, where he was buried in 1450; sadly, this is lost, but seventeenth-century drawings survive. The other is his Garter Book, which displays portraits of the knights in their robes and with their arms, the finest of the early armorials which gradually replaced the rolls of arms. These were the result of Bruges' considerable activity in tracing the history of the companions from the foundation, much of which seems to have been lost or forgotten. It was he who appears to have been responsible for the making of missing stall plates in the period after 1420. There are renewed references to provision for record-keeping and the updating of the tables in the accounts of the College of St George; we can only surmise that the records of the company had been kept by one of the clerks of the college, as a secondary duty. Now the organization and administration of the company were put in the hands of the company's own officer, a dramatic departure from earlier practice.

The appointment of Bruges, taken with the other reforms, was part of a movement towards the modern secular orders of knighthood, which

---

* His present-day successor ranks as the senior member of the College of Arms.

focus on honour rather than prowess, and in which heralds play a prominent part. Around 1400, the French heralds were formally organized, possibly the inspiration for the English College of Arms established in 1420. Until this point, there is very little evidence of a permanent official role for heralds, and the evolution of the 'king at arms' is even more obscure. What the early records reveal is that 'herald' in the thirteenth and fourteenth centuries means little more than a man expert in heraldic identification, who may well earn his living as a minstrel[17] or musician, or even as a barber.[18] The original role of these experts, back in the twelfth century, had been to do with tournaments, and the identification of knights' coats of arms as they fought in the confusion of the *mêlée*. They seem to have been commentators, announcing the names of the contestants to the audience, and perhaps adding comments, but they had no official status.

There is plenty of evidence that the public announcers at twelfth-century tournaments also doubled as minstrels and entertainers; in the biography of William Marshal, who rose to fame in the early thirteenth century through his prowess in tournaments, the waiting crowd at a tournament was entertained by 'a singer who was a new herald of arms', implying that there was some kind of recognition of his expertise in identifying the participants. Other references in the Marshal's biography suggest that heralds, although they might also be minstrels, did have a distinct function: we certainly find them as messengers at an early date. A satirical poem by Bertran de Born describes Eleanor of Aquitaine as sending a tax receipt on the torn-up tabard of a 'king of arms'; this is a joking reference, and cannot really be taken as evidence for such an official in her household. The point was that the queen's receipt was worthless, as if it had been written on any scrap of material to hand, and that it did not save the taxpayer from the knives of his creditors.[19] If such officials had existed, we would expect to meet them again in the succeeding years; but there is no sign of anything resembling an officially appointed herald for another two centuries.

There is, however, good evidence for kings of heralds. At the English court between 1272 and 1307, we have the names of at least fifteen possible kings of heralds. Typically, they appear to be in charge of a group of minstrels, or of all the minstrels at a particular occasion; 'king Baisescu' and 'king Caupeny' share out royal gifts between the minstrels at the great feast for the knighting of Edward II when he was prince of

Wales, in 1306. Such men are also called heralds, yet they are definitely minstrels, because in the same year 'king Caupenny' is paid with other minstrels 'for performing plays and making their minstrelsies in the presence of the Queen'.[20] 'Caupenny' was from Scotland, and is given the title 'king Caupenny of Scotland': we also hear of the 'king of Champagne', the leader of the minstrels from Champagne.[21] Interestingly, a king of heralds is paid for making a proclamation about the prohibition of tournaments in England at Northampton on Christmas Day 1300, underlining the idea that one of their functions was as public criers.[22] And from 1282 to 1320, two 'kings of heralds' appear on the royal payroll: Robert Little and Nicholas Morel. Andrew Norrois, apparently Nicholas Morel's successor, drew war wages in 1311–12, and was still at court in 1338.[23] They received summer and winter liveries with the rest of the court servants, presumably with a permanent responsibility for the minstrels at court. They were clearly minstrels themselves, as Robert is paid for 'making his minstrelsy' on New Year's Day 1303, and is probably the same as 'Robert the king's trumpeter' on the Scottish campaign of 1301.

There are traces of a tradition of heraldic titles which may stretch back into the late twelfth century. Bruiant appears as a herald in the Marshal's biography, in a poem about the tournament at Chauvency in 1285, and again in the accounts of Edward II; and 'bruyant' means loud or noisy: in modern French, 'un homme bruyant' is a loud talker. This, and the comment – again from the Marshal's biography – that knights have to have three or four heralds in tow, seems to suggest that heralds acted as cheerleaders. The Marshal himself was accused of creating a false reputation by having a certain Henry le Norrois with him, who cried 'God is with the Marshal' whenever he appeared in the lists.[24] It is possible that the name Norrois, like Bruiant, became a traditional one among heralds, and may have been handed down to Andrew Norrois a century later. His name is believed to be the origin of today's Norroy Herald at the College of Arms.[25]

Kings of arms are still grouped with minstrels in the statute regulating tournaments issued by Edward I in 1292, the *Statuta armorum*;[26] and it was only gradually, during the following century, that they began to acquire authority in questions of coats of arms. Visual collections of coats of arms began in the 1230s, and include the famous shields in Matthew Paris's great chronicle in the 1250s; the first known roll of arms, Glover's Roll, dates from about 1255. Many rolls of arms are clearly intended as a record of knights' arms which is to be used to identify shields, and the earliest examples – such as Glover's Roll – often survive only in copies, the originals presumably having been worn out with use. It is at the end of the thirteenth century that we find these rolls of arms being created as records of the knights present at a given military event: after the battle of Falkirk in 1298, a roll was created recording 'the great lords with banners who king Edward the first since the conquest had with him in Scotland in the twenty-sixth year of his reign at the battle of Falkirk on St Mary Magdalene's day'. Similar documents exist for the siege of Caerlaverock near Dumfries in 1300, for an expedition into Galloway in the same year, and the siege of Stirling in 1304. Only the Caerlaverock roll survives in the original, so we cannot tell whether these were all the work of the same herald travelling with the army or not.[27]

There is no doubt, however, that this is firm evidence that men with heraldic knowledge were now part of the real military world, as opposed to figures in the mock warfare of the tournament. But they were not employed as professional heralds, with a definite office: they were freelances who had other parts to play in the army. They probably performed multiple roles, like Robert Little at the court of Edward II. Little was certainly in Scotland in the year following Caerlaverock as one of the royal trumpeters. The correct identification of banners could be critical; Simon de Montfort's lookout (who doubled as his barber) wrongly identified the enemy's banners as those of Montfort's men at the battle of Evesham in 1265, with disastrous consequences.[28] Rolls of arms would help to avoid such errors, and it is possible that they were shown to the knights so that they could identify their friends in battle. But they are unlikely to have been the work of specialists whose sole job was to deal with heraldic matters: they are much more akin to the paintings done by the friar Walter atte More in the course of his diplomatic mission to Hungary in 1346. Walter atte More was not a herald, but he recognized the usefulness of the heraldic information and either painted it himself or, more probably, commissioned someone else to do it.

The status of the heralds is still unclear by the beginning of Edward III's reign. There are payments to William Volaunt, king of heralds, in 1354.[29] Andrew Clarenceux is entitled herald and king of arms in a wardrobe account of 1334, in his capacity as leader of a group of minstrels playing to the king on the day the king of Scotland did homage.[30] John Musshon, herald, was in the service of the prince of Wales in 1353, and appears several times in the prince's household records.[31] John Suffolk, herald, was in the service of Robert Ufford, earl of Suffolk, from at least 1340 to after 1359; his is the only testimony from a herald in the records of the Court of Chivalry.[32] After 1350, an increasing number of personal heralds appear, and even the *routier* captains had their own pursuivants. Heralds were sent out by Edward in their traditional role as criers of public events in January 1344 to announce the great tournament at Windsor. The accounts of the count of Holland show heralds coming and going in the 1330s, from the king of Cyprus or conveying invitations from neighbouring princes.[33]

The scattered mentions, taken together, seem to indicate that it was in the later 1340s that heralds acquired a more distinguished status and a definite place in royal and baronial households, but they were still largely messengers, conveying information by letters from their masters or by word of mouth. As such, they enjoyed immunity from war, in the same way as men in holy orders, and this immunity seems to have been invariably respected in the fourteenth century. One of the earliest pieces of firm evidence of their role in warfare is a letter from Henry of Grosmont describing his raid into Normandy in 1356: heralds were sent on 8 July by John II to challenge him to a battle at Verneuil.[34] They are still most in evidence at feasts, as masters of ceremonies organizing the entertainments and controlling the possibly unruly performers. Edward increased the number of his heralds in the 1350s for the long series of Garter feasts in the latter part of his reign.[35]

When it comes to written records, such as the list of the dead after Crécy, such items were far more likely to be the work of clerks in the army's administration; the freelance heralds were called in to help with the identification of arms, and indeed there is no reason why the clerks themselves would not have had some knowledge of heraldry. Le Bel tells us that Reginald Cobham was told by the king to take with him 'a herald who knew arms' to seek out the dead French nobles at Crécy, implying that not all heralds were expert in the subject.[36] The critical evidence for the heralds' lack of official recognition as authorities on coats of arms in the mid-fourteenth century comes from the proceedings of the Court of Chivalry which we discussed earlier. The evidence, carefully and laboriously assembled both in the court itself and by commissioners sent to obtain statements from outside the capital, who spent a good deal of time and energy on the process, never once involves a herald. If the court's proceedings had been informal and oral, we might argue that the records merely failed to mention the heralds' evidence. However, it is absolutely clear that only the evidence of fellow-knights and sometimes of clergy of similar standing is admissible, the sole exception being that of the earl of Suffolk's herald mentioned above. Written records such as the rolls of arms are never referred to, though painted heraldry in tombs, churches and great houses is endlessly cited. The knights themselves sometimes recall their training in heraldry, as in the case of Robert Laton, giving evidence in the Court of Chivalry in 1386, who testified that his father taught him to write down in a schedule (probably meaning a roll) all the arms that he had learnt from his ancestors.[37] Another knight, however, does remember a herald announcing the decision in an earlier case in the Court of Chivalry, presided over by Henry of Grosmont, at Calais in 1347; but the man in question was acting as Grosmont's public crier, rather than as an expert in arms.

Towards the end of the fourteenth century, Froissart could call heralds 'rightly the investigators and reporters of such affairs, and I believe that their honour is such that they would not dare to lie'.[38] He places a herald at the centre of the scene which is effectively the opening of the Hundred Years War: the much-travelled Carlisle Herald returns to Edward III's court at Westminster in April 1338 after five years wandering abroad, coming post-haste with letters from the Anglophile lords of Gascony that war had broken out with the French in their region, which he supplements with an oral report.[39] I would argue that Froissart is re-creating the scene as he thought it should have happened, looking back from the 1370s; heralds had gained considerably in stature in the intervening forty years. It is a neat way of outlining the beginning of hostilities to his audience, by creating a scene with which they would have been familiar. His declaration that he had got much of his information from heralds is certainly true, but that does not mean – particularly in the first book of the chronicle – that every scene containing a herald is genuine. Froissart often succumbs to the temptation to create a vision of heralds and heroes, history seen through a technicolor prism of shining deeds and brilliant colours.

In England, the heralds probably acquired their formal authority over the question of entitlement to arms and to the regulation of their use as a result of the increasing reluctance of men of knightly status to take up arms in the last quarter of the fourteenth century. If men who claimed a coat of arms were no longer seen on campaign, the proceedings in the Court of Chivalry, based on the testimony of their fellow-knights, could not be used as a method of establishing such a claim. Instead of the memory of fellow-knights, records were needed and written documents: and in respect of the Company of the Garter itself, such records were sadly lacking, as we have seen. Henry IV started the work of re-creating the lists of knights and may have amended the statutes in respect of holding the feast on alternative dates if St George's Day clashed with other religious festivals.

There are traces of some kind of territorial authority over heralds and minstrels which go back into the thirteenth century, and, although this evidence poses as many questions as it solves, there does seem to have been some kind of loose organization, whether founded on royal authority or simply by a mutual guild of performers choosing a spokesman. All we have to go on are titles; apart from the kings of arms whose names seem to recur – as in the examples already quoted of Bruiant and Norrois – there are records naming a minstrel or herald as king of a region. The name Norrois ('of the north') might link to 'Peter king of the heralds beyond the Trent on the northern side', who appears in a deed of 1276, or to William Morley, king's minstrel, called 'Roi de North' in 1322. The wording of Peter's deed complicates the issue, as it includes an extraordinary clause specifying that he is paying his creditor for his debts 'owed to him from the beginning of the world down to March 18 1276': is it another minstrel's joke? The document itself looks real enough.[40]

What seems to have happened in the first quarter of the fifteenth century is that all these informal traditions of the heralds, as well as their scattered records, were gradually brought together into a regulated and organized framework. The old reliance on the oral tradition and memory of knights was replaced by visual and written records, and the celebration of deeds of arms moved from the minstrels and poets to the chroniclers, Jean le Bel, Froissart and Pero López de Ayala, who believed that they should be held in writing. These new full-time heralds, appointed officially by kings and princes, seem to have appeared first in Froissart's home territory of the Low Countries; at the very beginning of the fifteenth century we have Claes Heynenzoon, king of heralds of the Rhine, who had begun as herald of the duke of Guelders and was later herald to the duke of Bavaria.[41] His activities were wide-ranging, and he left us two splendid armorials, *The Book of Arms of Guelders* and *The Book of Arms of Bavaria*, as well as his *Lobdichten*, poetic portraits of the great knights of his time. These volumes, as well as the extensive depictions of arms by skilled artists, include historical texts, among them two chronicles. The arms are arranged systematically by rank, beginning with the German emperor and working through the kings of Europe, each with the arms of those who owed allegiance to him. And while he was employed by the duke of Guelders, he was responsible for buying heraldic flags when the duke sailed to England. In the first quarter of the fifteenth century, the herald was increasingly the representative of the person whose name he bore: his status moved from that of a freelance whose skills were rewarded with the occasional gift to someone who had a definite diplomatic, legal and armorial function.

The appointment of William Bruges marks the starting point of the process by which the Company of the Garter, whose original members were Edward III's friends and comrades in arms, became the Order of the Garter, a symbol of honour. It was part of a wider transformation of knightly life in the fifteenth century, seen at its most striking in the rituals and festivals of the Burgundian court. Edward's court may have had its splendour of dress and its myriad tournaments; but these were only marginally political, and organized ritual played relatively little part. Under Richard II, ceremonial became much more central, and the handful of tournaments in the 1380s and 1390s were not held because of the king's enthusiasm for the sport but to enhance his prestige. The appearance of the heralds in regular positions of authority marked the point at which knighthood was institutionalized and absorbed into court rituals and ceremonies, and the royal orders of knighthood began to flourish.[42] And the fifteenth century was the moment when the modern concept of honour came to the fore, replacing the old emphasis on prowess, which was to survive in the ideals of the gentleman.

Furthermore, the English triumphs came to an end with Nájera, and the deaths of Edward III, Edward prince of Wales and John II mark the end of an era when the English and French rulers saw knighthood as a military virtue and a key element in their armies. Charles V's eminently practical approach to the defence of France and the gradual erosion of English power were perhaps another reason why Froissart chooses to emphasize great deeds of knighthood. Such deeds, he implies, are no longer as frequent as they should be: his task is to encourage such feats of arms by describing those of the past. There is a lull in knightly festivals after 1360, and they do not reappear until the last decade of the century. When they do, after the truce of Leulinghem in 1389, they are international gatherings of a kind that had not been seen for a century. The famous jousts at St Inglevert in 1390 are the first occasion when numbers of English and French knights had appeared in the lists together for as long as men could remember, and Froissart dwells on them in loving detail. The challenges of men like Jean Werchin led to the *pas d'armes* of the fifteenth century, where single knights offered to appear at a specified place and defend it against all comers, and the roster of combatants was again international. The heroes of these international events sought, as their predecessors had done in Prussia, honour and fame for their knightly achievements. Honour as an individual replaced the allegiance to the monarch which was at the heart of the Company of the Garter; and membership of the sovereign's personal order of knighthood likewise depended on individual honour rather than companionship in arms.

In the 1360s, Giovanni Boccaccio wrote his great poem on the lives and deaths of great princes, translated seventy years later by John Lydgate, a monk at Bury St Edmunds. One of the princes included was King Arthur, and Boccaccio tells us that the knights of the Round Table had 'laws and ordinances' which they had to obey. These prove to be the general principles of knighthood found in earlier writers, transformed into a formal code; but the idea that there was 'an especial law' for the companions of the Round Table, and that they should 'relate all that they had done, whether to their honour or shame, to those who were charged with keeping the history of the Round Table', is very much a concept of Boccaccio's own day, close to the rules of the Order of the Ship in Naples. Lydgate calls these 'laws and ordinances' 'statutes' and talks of the order's 'register', both of which echo the arrangements of the Garter in the 1430s. By this time, the translation of the religious confraternity of the Company of the Garter into the Order of the Garter is complete, and it has itself become the model for the Arthurian Round

Table from which it was once supposed to have been derived. With its own officer, an established heraldic history and a properly kept register, it has become an institution of honour under the crown; and so it has remained to this day.

One last transformation remained: that of St George's chapel itself. Edward IV was very mindful of his namesake and ancestor, and sought to model himself on the heroic figure of Edward III. He appointed Richard Beauchamp, bishop of Salisbury, to supervise the work in 1473, and by 1478 the work was involving so many stonecutters that, as in the building campaign for the house of the Round Table in 1344, other projects were seriously disrupted by a shortage of workmen: the university authorities in Oxford complained of the effect on their work on the new divinity schools. It transformed the relatively modest original chapel of the College of St George into one of the great monuments of fifteenth-century England, a rival to Henry VI's plans for Eton and King's College Cambridge. St George's was to be the Yorkist riposte to these Lancastrian foundations, and was designated by Edward IV as his last resting place. Fittingly, all three chapels were completed by the Tudors, whose dynasty brought the rivalry of the two branches of Edward III's descendants to an end.

Epilogue: The Legends

The Company of the Garter was a religious confraternity, but its membership was restricted to knights; which is why, during Edward III's reign, ladies played almost no visible role in it. We know that the queen had a stall in the chapel and can assume that some of her attendant ladies would have been present at the services, but that is all. The 'ladies of the Garter', as we have seen, are likely to have been an innovation of Joan of Kent as Richard II's mother. And the great romantic myth about the involvement of ladies in the foundation of the company is a fifteenth-century invention. With the creation of purely honorific orders in the years following the institution of the Garter, the object of Edward III's fraternity was obscured by the fame of its members, and their image, as projected in the pages of Froissart, overlaid the founder's original intentions. Because of their great deeds, so foreign writers thought, it must have been knightly and therefore designed to honour ladies.

This new image of the Garter first appears in a fifteenth-century Catalan romance by Joan Martorell, *Tirant the White*, whose hero visits King Arthur's court, just as Martorell had visited England in 1439–40. This is the account given by one of the knights of the origin of the order, 'similar to King Arthur's Knights of the Round Table in olden days':

> the king asked his guests to wait a few days longer, for he wished to announce the founding of a new order comprised of irreproachable knights. This order's inspiration, as I and all these knights heard it from the king's own lips, came from an incident one day when we were dancing ... Many knights were dancing with ladies, and by chance one damsel named Madresilva drew near the king. As she whirled, her left garter, which was trimmed with silk, fell off ... do not imagine, my lord,

that she was fairer or more genteel than others. She has a rather flirtatious way of dancing and talking, though she sings reasonably well, yet one might have found three hundred comelier and more gracious damsels present. All the same, there is no accounting for men's tastes and whims. One of the knights near the king said: 'Madresilva, you have lost your leg armour. You must have a bad page who failed to fasten it well.'

She blushed slightly and stooped to pick it up, but another knight rushed over and grabbed it. The king then summoned the knight and said: 'Fasten it to my left stocking below the knee.'[1]

The knight goes on to tell how the king wore the garter openly for more than four months; the queen never said anything, and it was only a favourite servant who eventually reproached him for his behaviour, saying that all the foreigners, the queen, her ladies and his subjects were amazed that he could honour 'such an insignificant damsel' in this way. 'The king replied: "So the queen is disgruntled and my guests are displeased!", and he said in French: "*Puni soit qui mal y pense*. [Let him be punished who thinks ill of it.] Now I swear before God that I shall found a new knightly order upon this incident: a fraternity that shall be remembered as long as the world endures."[2] The narrator goes on to describe, reasonably accurately, the way in which the knights are seated in St George's chapel, with their swords and helmets displayed and their escutcheon fixed to the back of the stall, as well as the robes of the knights and the penalties for failing to wear the garter in public. The name 'Madresilva' is intriguing, since it is the Spanish for honeysuckle, called in English woodbine; and one of the mottoes embroidered on Edward's court garments was 'Sure as the woodbine'.[3] There must be a connection, but there is no evidence that will help us to explain the link.

The account is a mixture of reality and romance in the style of Froissart – whom Martorell may well have read. But its tone is also faintly disparaging: Madresilva is depicted as sexually attractive rather than as an ideal object of courtly love, and the whole episode turns on the king's whimsical and irrational fancy of wearing the dropped garter. The motto is distorted, and the image we are left with is of an arrogant ruler untroubled by any kind of ideals. Either Martorell invented the tale, and it passed into popular myth, or he himself heard a scurrilous tale of a kind which could be found in connection with other knightly orders. Elias Ashmole, the great seventeenth-century historian of the

Garter, writes of the Burgundian Order of the Golden Fleece, which has considerable parallels with the Garter:

> even that also hath met with the same fate; and the Institution reported to have risen from an effeminate ground: for it is said, that its Founder entering one morning into the chamber of a most beautiful lady of Bruges (generally esteemed his mistress) found upon her toilette, a fleece of Low Country wool; whence some of his followers taking occasion of sport, as at a thing unusually seen in a lady's chamber, he . . . vowed that such as made it the subject of their derision should never be honoured with a collar of the order thereof, which he intended to establish to express the love he bore that lady.[4]

Likewise, the Order of the Collar in Savoy, which incorporated love-knots in its device, was rumoured to be based on a bracelet sent to the count of Savoy by his mistress. Neither of these stories is true – the Golden Fleece has its roots in classical mythology, and the Order of the Collar is unequivocally dedicated to the Virgin Mary.

A story of this kind was certainly current in England by 1463, when an Italian cleric, Mondonus Belvaleti, wrote a learned Latin treatise on the symbolism of the Order of the Garter for Edward IV. He reports the popular version discreetly, saying only that 'many assert that this order took its beginning from the feminine sex, from a lewd and forbidden affection'.[5] Another Catalan author, Roís de Corella, had probably heard of Martorell's story by 1480 when he spoke of 'the disorderly rule of the Garter'.[6] It is possible that the real context of Martorell's romance is not that of 1439–40, but that of the court of Edward IV in the 1460s. The character of the king in *Tirant the White* would fit Edward IV, impulsive and noted for his love affairs, much better than his great-grandfather. By the early sixteenth century, another Italian writing in England, Polydore Vergil, had picked up Martorell's story, and included a close paraphrase of it in his *English History* in 1534.

> But the reason for the founding of the order is utterly uncertain; popular tradition nowadays declares that Edward at some time picked up from the ground a garter from the stocking of his queen or mistress, which had become unloosed by some chance, and had fallen. As some of the knights began to laugh and jeer at this, he is reputed to have said that in a very little while the same garter would be held by them in the highest honour.

And not long after, he is said to have founded this order and given it the title by which he showed those knights who had laughed at him how to judge his actions. Such is popular tradition. English writers have been modestly superstitious, perhaps fearing to commit lèse-majesté, if they made known such unworthy things; and they have preferred to remain silent about them, whereas matters should really be seen otherwise: something that rises from a petty or sordid origin increases all the more in dignity.[7]

It is William Camden in 1607 who first names the lady of Martorell's and Vergil's romantic tradition as the countess of Salisbury. However, this is given only as a secondary possibility for the origin of the order: his first suggestion is quite different:

> In this place [Windsor], king *Edward* the third, for to adorne martiall prowesse, with honors, the guerdon of vertue, ordained that most noble order and society of knights, whom (as some report) for his owne garter given forth as signall of a battaile that sped fortunately, hee called knights of the Garter: who weare on their left legge somewhat under the knee, a blew garter: carying this Empresse [motto] wrought with golden letters in French HONY SOIT QUI MAL Y PENSE, and fasten the same with a buckle of gold as with the bond of a most inward society, in token of concord and unity, that there might bee among them a certaine consociation and communion of vertues. But others there be, that doe attribute it unto the garter of the Queene or rather of *Joan* Countesse of Salisburie, a Lady of incomparable beauty, which fell from her as shee daunced, and the King tooke up from the floore: for, when a number of Nobles and Gentle men standing by laughed thereat, he made answere againe, that shortly it would come to passe that garter should bee in high honour and estimation. This is the common and most received report: Neither need this seeme to be a base originall thereof, considering how, as one saith
>
> *Nobilitas sub amore jacet*
> Nobility lies under love.[8]

Camden's preferred origin of the Garter as 'signal of a battle' is an interesting one, suggesting that it might have been an identifying badge of some sort; it is just possible that the Garter was such a badge at Crécy before its adoption for the company, but there is no firm evidence for the idea, nor are there any parallels for the use of a badge in this way. In his second story, which he has lifted from Polydore Vergil, he is quite clearly embellishing it by making a link with Joan of Kent, who was nominally countess of Salisbury after her then husband became earl in 1344 until the marriage was declared void in 1349.

It is Jean le Bel who recounts the story of Edward's rape of the countess of Salisbury. The countess is said to have been defending Wark Castle, a great fortress on the Scottish border which did indeed belong to the earl, and which was attacked in June 1340. At the time, William Montagu, her husband, was imprisoned in France after his capture at Lille in April 1340. He was released in September of that year, so the episode is firmly placed in the summer of 1340. Edward was in Flanders for most of 1340, but was in England from late February to late June, but did not go further north than Hertford. Edward is said to have gone to the countess's aid with his troops, and to have fallen in love with her, but was firmly put in his place by the countess. Two years later, he holds a great feast and jousts in London in August, and invites the countess, who comes reluctantly. Again, the king was indeed in London in August 1342, and held a feast at the time specified. The following year, while the earl and Robert d'Artois were in Brittany, according to the story, Edward went to Wark to see the countess again. Once more, the movements of the earl are accurately represented, but Edward himself returned from Brittany in March, and spent the rest of the year in the south of England. The rape is therefore supposed to have taken place in the summer of 1343, before the earl's return from Brittany. Le Bel does not pull his punches in describing the king's violence:

> that night, as he lay in the splendid bed provided for him, a bed befitting his station, and knew that the noble lady was in her chamber and the whole household and all his retainers except his privy chamberlains were asleep, he rose and ordered his chamberlains not to get in his way, no matter what he did, or they'd find themselves at the end of a noose. And he entered the lady's chamber, locked the door of the adjoining room so that her maids couldn't help her, and seized her and stopped her mouth – so hard that she uttered only two or three cries – and then forced himself upon her, so painfully, so punishingly, that no woman ever was so brutally abused. And he left her lying there, unconscious, bleeding from her nose and mouth and elsewhere: it was a distressing and a grievous wrong. Then he left next morning without saying a word, and returned to

London, deeply disturbed about what he'd done. From that day forth the good lady was never happy again; her heart was so troubled that she never again shared in festivities or mixed with worthy people.[9]

When the countess tells her husband what has happened, he goes abroad, and dies there: he did in fact leave for Algeciras in the autumn of 1343, but returned safely. He, and probably the countess, attended the Windsor feast of 1344 at which he played a prominent part, but he had been taken ill a few days earlier, performed poorly in the tournament, and died – 'of natural causes', says Murimuth – shortly afterwards.

Whoever concocted the story must have done so after the earl's departure for Algeciras, as all the historical details are correct up to that point. Overlaid on this historically accurate account is a tale which is obviously derived from Livy's account of the rape of Lucretia, well known throughout the middle ages, and used by writers from St Augustine onwards. There are a number of late fourteenth-century versions, including those by Chaucer, Christine de Pisan, Boccaccio and Gower. The central themes are the same in both: the infatuation of a king, Sextus Tarquinius/Edward, for the wife of one of his commanders; the heroine's beauty and chastity; the first encounter and return when the husband is absent; the invasion of her bedchamber; and the heroine's confession to her husband.[10] Jean le Bel, our only detailed authority for the episode, was convinced of its truth by the historical context in which it was set; it is unlikely, given his initial scepticism, that he was responsible for weaving in these details. The most probable source is someone in the French court well informed about the earl's movements, which were generally known to anyone with an interest in English affairs, who also had a literary background. It is reminiscent of the propaganda against the Knights Templar produced when Philip the Fair engineered their downfall in 1307. As such, it is no real reflection on Edward's character or the morals of his court, but is a rare historical survival of a piece of expert propaganda.[11] Its nearest parallel is the story of Joan of Kent artfully luring the prince of Wales into marriage, a much more innocent tale but one which also discredits the English royal family.[12]

Le Bel names the countess only casually, in a linking paragraph taking up the story after Edward's first visit to Wark; he calls her 'Alice', which is either a slip of the pen or an amendment by a copyist, thereby confusing generations of later historians into trying to unravel this puzzle.[13] Froissart himself has grave problems with the story, emasculating it and turning it into a love story in one version of his chronicles: he actually denies it directly, both on the grounds that the king would never commit such a crime, and also because he has tried to find supporting evidence: 'Now I declare that I know England well, where I have lived for long periods at the royal court and also with the great lords of the country. And I have never heard tell of this rape although I have asked people about it who must have known if it had ever happened.'[14] The story was in circulation in France in the late fourteenth century, since four French chronicles mention it, in almost identical wording which summarizes very briefly the events described by Le Bel. They are almost certainly copying each other, and one of them is from the abbey of St Denis, the centre where the official French royal chronicles were written. The story of the rape is a brief paragraph which attempts to explain the execution of Olivier Clisson and the exile of Godefroy d'Harcourt:

> After the king had returned home, the countess of Salisbury lamented to her husband that she had been raped by the king of England; the earl was very despondent and sad, and summoned his friends. He went with them to the court of the king of England where in the presence of the king and the peers of the kingdom, he surrendered all his lands and left them to his daughter, since he had no son, in such a way that his wife would be endowed with them during her lifetime.
>
> Then, leaving the court, he sent his defiance to King Edward and crossed to France to King Philip, and gave him letters about the alliance of Olivier Clisson and Godefroy d'Harcourt with the king of England. And soon afterwards he left France, and after that no one ever saw him.[15]

This is all sheer nonsense: William Montagu, first earl of Salisbury, had a son, remained in England and was loyal to Edward until his death. If we place the composition of the story in 1343, while Salisbury was still alive, it looks like an attempt to discredit both Edward and his closest friend, and also to implicate the latter in the summary execution of Clisson which had produced such a hostile reaction among the French nobility. Le Bel seems, unusually, to have fallen for this carefully composed piece of propaganda. It is almost certainly a deliberate fabrication commissioned by the French authorities to show that Edward was unprincipled and treacherous; its effect was not what they had hoped for.[16] It had little impact on contemporaries, yet it became embedded in later versions of Edward's history, and Froissart's sanitized version led Polydore Vergil to associate it with the founding of the Order of the Garter. What began as a denigration of Edward's character ended by casting him in the role of romantic lover.

Within a few years of Edward's death, an unknown writer penned a eulogy of the late king, which was later translated into English.[17] It is an idealized portrait of a king who was said to have outshone all his predecessors, and most of it is conventional – his devoutness, generosity, moderation and good governance of his realm – or rhetorical: 'there sprang and shone so much grace in him that anyone who had seen his face or had dreamed of him, was sure that anything that happened to him that day would be joyful and to his liking'. His fortunes in war are emphasized, for 'he was a man very bold of heart, who did not dread any mischance, harm or misfortune which might befall a noble warrior, and he was fortunate both by land and sea. And in all battles and encounters he always had the victory, and great glory and worship.'

Medieval writers did not like innovation; tradition was more important than 'newfangled things' and it is only with the distance of the centuries that we can perhaps see Edward's achievements more clearly. By positioning himself, like Arthur at the Round Table, as first among equals, a knight among knights, he gained the trust of the great lords who had brought down his father and troubled his grandfather's reign, and earned their respect by his willingness to fight alongside them. If caution prevented him from leading from the front, there were moments when he was prepared to throw himself into the fray, at Sluys, at Calais and at Winchelsea, or to strike boldly and unexpectedly, as in his dramatic crossing back to England in 1340. Swift action when the time was ripe was perhaps something he had learnt from William Montagu when he seized Mortimer in 1330; it was a lesson that he remembered throughout his military career. Likewise, he might play the part of the traditional knight on occasions, but he was also an innovator and an improviser. If the reading of the tactics at Crécy is correct, he used a combination of new technology – the longbow had only recently come to the fore, and cannons were entirely novel in battle – with a brilliant inventiveness, creating a strong position with the available resources in unfavourable terrain. And because of the strong mutual trust he had built between himself and his commanders, they both contributed to his tactical decisions and respected his judgement. It is this cohesion between Edward and his leading knights that is commemorated in the Company of the Garter.

Appendix 1
The English Battle Formation at Crécy:
A Hypothetical Reconstruction

In chapter 7, it was argued that the account by Giovanni Villani of the English battle formation is the most reliable that has come down to us. This is a hypothetical reconstruction of that formation, which according to Villani was centred on a formation of carts. In the open chalk country of Crécy, such an artificial defensive structure would be very valuable. The only natural defences mentioned by the chroniclers are a wood on the left flank (anonymous Roman chronicle) and hedges (*Norman Chronicle*),[1] very different from the terrain of battles such as Halidon Hill, Morlaix and Poitiers, where the battle formation was determined by the substantial presence of woods and hedges. The contours of the landscape do present some features which were potentially useful. It is reasonably probable that Edward's position was above the modern village of Crécy, on the ridge which overlooks the valley of the river Maye; and he may well have placed his men so that the one obstacle on this hillside, the steep sixteen-foot-high bank of the Vallée des Clercs, forced the French to attack from a particular direction. No attacking army could cross this obstacle at speed.

In such circumstances, Villani's declaration that 'they enclosed the army with carts, of which they had plenty, both of their own and from the country' and his description of the creation of an artificial fortress of carts rings true, as we have argued. Diagram B shows a possible and highly tentative reconstruction of how this might have worked. The formation would probably have faced more or less due south, at the head of one of the valleys which run up to the ridge from the river. The carts

---

[1] *Istoire et croniques de Flandres*, 42, specifies that it was behind the army. Hedges: p. 227 above.

were probably drawn up in a roughly circular formation, and may have been two or more deep, chained wheel to wheel, judging from the evidence from Mons-en-Pévèle in 1304 and from the Hussite wars in the fifteenth century. Use of carts to provide a fortified encampment to protect the baggage is widely attested in the thirteenth and fourteenth centuries, and Philip Preston has suggested that the practice of surrounding the army with carts might also have been used when encamping for the night. Certainly there were men with the army who were practised in manoeuvring the four-wheeled carts into an array of some kind, and Edward had arrived at the battlefield two days before, according to the records of both the 'Kitchen Journal' and the itinerary in the Cottonian manuscript.[2] He had more than enough time to ride over the ground, select a suitable position and organize the creation of the array of carts. Furthermore, the evidence points to the availability of enough carts to create such a circle, though the anonymous Roman chronicler's assertion that he brought 3,000 carts with him on the expedition is definitely too high. As a working figure, let us take the recent estimate of a ratio of carts to men of 1:20,[3] giving 700 carts for an army of 14,000 men.

Let us assume a length for each cart of six feet when drawn up in formation, positioned lengthways around the perimeter with the shafts raised to close the gaps which would otherwise be left between the carts. If the carts were arranged in a double row, this would give a ring 700 yards in circumference, to which we have to add the gap of 100 yards at the entrance. This gives an enclosed area of about 20,000 square yards. Andrew Ayton estimates the total army at around 2,800 men at arms, 3,000 mounted archers and 8,000 infantry, about 14,000 men in all.[4] The suggested deployment is as follows: within the ring were about 3,000 men at arms and 8,000 infantry; the archers were deployed on the carts, or outside on the wings. Also within the ring were the horses for the men at arms, giving a total of about 11,000 men and 3,000 horses. The only available calculation for the space occupied by a medieval army drawn up in battle formation is for the Swiss army at the battle of Morat in 1476, where 10,000 men are thought to have occupied an area of 3,600 square yards (60 yards × 60 yards). If we allow an

---

[2] TNA E 101/390/11; BL MS Cotton Cleopatra D.VII. See Baker, *Chronicon*, 252, 254. For the 'Kitchen Journal', see p. 26.
[3] Harari, 'Strategy and Supply in Fourteenth-Century Campaigns', 318.
[4] Ayton and Preston, *Crécy*, 189.

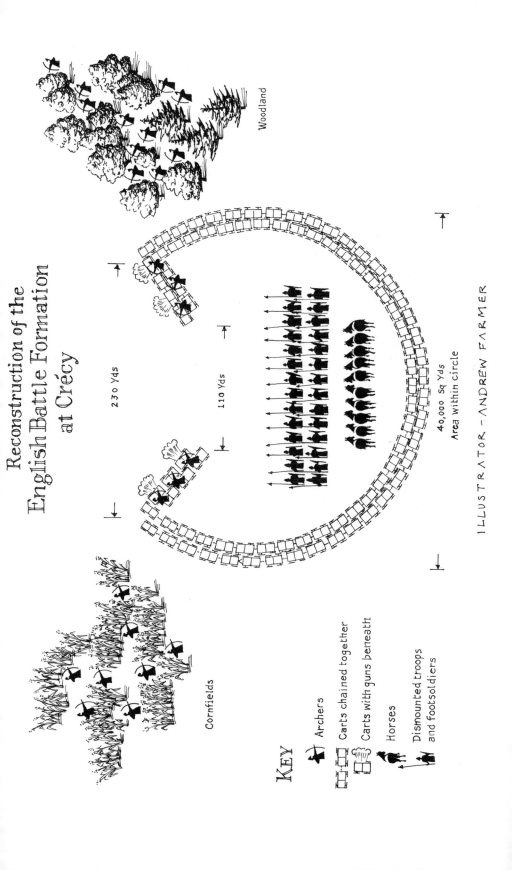

Reconstruction of the English Battle Formation at Crécy

230 Yds

110 Yds

Woodland

Cornfields

40,000 Sq Yds
Area within circle

ILLUSTRATOR ~ ANDREW FARMER

KEY

Archers

Carts chained together

Carts with guns beneath

Horses

Dismounted troops and footsoldiers

increased space of 0.5 square yards for each man, and an estimated 2 square yards for each horse, this gives a total of 11,500 square yards, leaving adequate room for formation and manoeuvre. These are of necessity purely theoretical calculations, but they indicate that there is nothing impossible about the idea of the cart fortification with the bulk of the English army inside it. The entrance of 100 yards or less, while open enough to invite the enemy to attempt an attack, would be a death trap given the covering fire from the archers on the carts. The carts were probably not in an exact square, but in a diamond or circle, to provide a better forward line of fire for the archers. Diagram B is a very tentative suggestion as to how this would have worked.

Villani makes it clear that there was a substantial opening in the array, sufficient to allow the passage of numbers of men at arms; equally, this opening created 'a narrow place'. This imitated artificially a feature found at Halidon Hill, and to a lesser extent at Morlaix and Poitiers, a valley which acted as a narrowing funnel, compressing the attacking force into a front which meant that they could not maintain their formation. Nor were superior numbers a striking advantage under such conditions, as only a relatively small number of men would be engaged at any one time.

Edward added to this defensive formation which restricted the area of action a skilful deployment of his most effective long-range weapon, the archers. If we are to believe the evidence of Villani and the anonymous Roman chronicler, which is supported in general terms by other chronicles, there were two wings of archers outside the circle. These were concealed, one in an unidentified wood, and the other in tall standing corn. The distance between these wings, according to Robert Hardy, should have been no greater than 500 yards to give proper covering fire, and the suggested size of the array of carts fits well with this calculation. Furthermore, Edward placed archers on the carts. Villani's evidence on this is detailed, and controversial. It would seem that they were concealed and protected by the canvas of the carts, which would have been supported on wooden hoops (as in the famous illustration from the Luttrell Psalter of an admittedly luxurious royal travelling wagon[5]). These carts were perhaps placed at an angle to the entrance to the array of carts, so that the crossfire would cover the gap to deadly effect; and

[5] Plate 24.

their supplies of arrows were in barrels on the carts, within easy reach. Furthermore – and this is admittedly a speculation – if the front row of carts were empty, it would be extremely difficult to reach the archers with a lance if a knight did penetrate to the carts themselves. Men on foot would have to clamber up the wheels to get at them; later Bohemian battle wagons carried ladders for the occupants to get up and down.

The guns were, according to Villani, positioned beneath the carts. They would have been relatively small, probably 'ribalds',[6] and such a placing would be perfectly possible. They would probably have been better at causing panic among the horses than actually inflicting serious injury, except at a relatively short range; it is unlikely that all 100 were in use.

Once the archers were in position, and the men at arms were drawn up in battle order within the array, the archers would conceal themselves. From the foot of the hill, the approaching French would have seen a small army standing in an array of carts which looked not unlike the traditional method of guarding the rear of a defensive position. The carts would have served to conceal the true numbers within the ring, and would have made the English army seem a tempting target.

As soon as the first French forces came within range, the archers on the wings would have stood up and begun their deadly volleys. This was what the Genoese crossbowmen encountered, and a commander with some control over his troops would have halted the attack to consider how to deal with the archers. Instead, the uncontrolled French cavalry rode over the crossbowmen, wasting their energy on attacking their own men, into the second trap, the archers concealed at the entrance under the canvas of the carts.

Even so, the sheer mass of the French cavalry enabled them to force their way into the 'narrow place', where the prince of Wales's men awaited them. It was in this 'small area' that, according to Edward himself, the real slaughter took place. The defensive array and the ambush had done their work, and the superior numbers of the French army were no longer an advantage. The battle was not won, however; but, in the struggle that ensued, the discipline and battle experience of the English were the decisive factors. It is possible that the manoeuvre used

[6] See p. 182 above.

at Poitiers, an encircling movement from the rear of the English army to attack the enemy from an unexpected quarter, may have been employed, and that this later became the story of the rescue of the prince of Wales. There would have been time to disengage a couple of dozen carts once it was clear that the main action was at the front of the array, so the existence of the circle would not have prevented such a manoeuvre.

If we are to accept this reconstruction as a possibility, it would mean that the emphasis of Edward's military thinking went beyond the creation of an army which was well organized and formed of men who had fought together, in some cases for two decades, to the deployment of the latest technology, and – as important as either of these factors – a genuine understanding of tactics and of the need for a specific type of site in order to make the most effective use of his archers. If he could not find the terrain that he needed, he was prepared to create by artificial means the necessary obstacles and constraints that would hinder the enemy.

Appendix 2
Eustace (Sauchet) d'Auberchicourt

The Auberchicourt family appear early in Edward III's life. Nicholas d'Auberchicourt[1] was lord of Buignicourt, on the borders of Hainault, where the young Edward stayed with his mother before their return to England in 1326. Among others at the castle at the time was the lord of Aisne and three of the Mauny brothers, among them Walter Mauny. The queen's escort from Buignicourt included Nicholas d'Auberchicourt, also called Nicholas but known as Colart. He sailed with her to England and was present at her landing at the Orwell estuary.[2] Five years later, Nicholas was knighted by Edward; he was given lands to maintain the estate of knighthood on 8 October 1331, and the grant specifies that this was as a reward for assistance at a crucial moment of the king's life: 'for good service while we were in foreign parts, and also when we came with Isabella queen of England, our dearest mother, to our kingdom'.[3]

Nicholas d'Auberchicourt returned to Hainault, and went on crusade to Prussia with William I of Hainault in 1336–7, after which we hear nothing more of him.[4] The castle of Auberchicourt was apparently burnt by the French garrisons of Douai and Lille in 1337.[5] It is his eldest son Nicholas (Colart) who appears in 1352 and 1355 as provost of Valenciennes,[6] and this gives added force to Froissart's account of the

---

[1] There are at least fifteen different spellings of the name in medieval records. I have standardized to the modern spelling of the place name, which is now in Ponthieu. For the genealogy of the family, see Feuchère, *Auberchicourt*, 53 ff.

[2] Froissart, *Chroniques*, Amiens version, 58, 62, 72.

[3] *Foedera*, ii.ii.824. He also fought in the 1327 campaign in Scotland: Froissart, *Chroniques*, Amiens version, 114.

[4] Paravicini, *Die Preussenreisen*, i.94.

[5] Lapierre, *La Guerre de cent ans dans l'Argonne*, 10; the author explains the brutality of Eustace's activities in 1358–9 as an act of revenge for this episode.

[6] Feuchère, *Auberchicourt*, 58.

Auberchicourts' involvement with Edward, as they would almost certainly have known each other. There were two or three younger brothers: we have clear records of Eustace and Gilles, the latter being bailiff of two estates near Cambrai in 1350.[7] It is possible that Eustace was employed by the count of Hainault, William II, as a squire in his household; Staes or Staesken, the Dutch for Eustace, appears in this role while the count went on pilgrimage to Jerusalem and then on crusade to Prussia. Given that this was a rare name in Dutch at this time, and that his father had accompanied William I on crusade, this seems a plausible identification; no other person named Staes occurs in these accounts. His activities during this period are very similar to those of Heinken Oem, who subsequently appears in the service of the prince of Wales as Henry Eam: indeed, in one instance, Staes and Heinken Oem appear in adjoining entries. The business which he is recorded as performing is very similar to that carried out by Heinken Oem, and he is called the count's 'kammerling' or member of his chamber.

If this identification is correct, his career and that of Oem run parallel: he moves to England on the death of William II at Staveren in September 1345, in which case his next appearance is an entry in the English patent rolls for 1345. On 20 October, Sausetus Daubrichecourt is given all the chattels of John Wardedieu, indicted for the death of Robert Poteman.[8] These lands were in Sussex, and included the future site of Bodiam Castle. But Wardedieu was then cleared of felony, and the grant to Sausetus never took effect. His daughter married Edward Dalyngrigge, who built Bodiam in 1385. In 1347, Froissart tells us that the six burghers of Calais pardoned at the request of Walter Mauny and Queen Philippa were escorted through the English lines by Sanse d'Aubrecicourt and Paon de Roet. The wife of Nicholas lord of Buignicourt was from the Roeux family and Paon de Roet or Roeux may have been his cousin (and later Chaucer's father-in-law).[9] This entry would place him firmly in the group of Hainaulters around the queen. A Dabrichcourt is next recorded in the accounts of the prince of Wales: Stacy Dabrichcourt brings him money to gamble with the queen on 18 September 1348, and appears again as Tassyn Dabrigcourt, recipient of a

---

[7] Ibid., 68.
[8] *CPR 1343–1345*, 557.
[9] Feuchère, *Auberchicourt*, 57; Froissart, *Chroniques*, Amiens version, 849.

gift of £6 13s. 4d. from the prince on 6 November, probably in 1353.[10] These are all Eustace, but both his Christian name or nickname and his surname are subject to the vagaries of fourteenth-century spelling: I have found at least fifteen variant versions of his surname.

Meanwhile, in the accounts of Margaret countess of Hainault, the prince's aunt, we find Nicholas d'Auberchicourt paid the substantial sum of £200 on 1 August 1353, which he is owed for wages to his brother Sausset d'Auberchicourt, who has served the duchess in the wars in Zeeland and on the Maas.[11] In 1355, we find an entry which connects Eustace d'Auberchicourt with both the prince of Wales and the countess of Hainault: on 4 May 1355, the prince arranges for his aunt's clerk, Stephen de Maulyons, to pay 100 crowns to Eustace out of a debt which Stephen owed to the prince, implying that Eustace was in Hainault at the time.

So we have Sausset, Sanse, Stacy and Tassin d'Auberchicourt in the English records for 1345 to 1355, and no records for Eustace during the period when these names appear. The only subsequent record relating to a man with a similar name to Sausset or Sanse is the early copies of the statutes of the Company of the Garter, which call him Sanchet. Now of these names, Sanchet is not found elsewhere. Stacy and Tassin are probably variations of Eustace (or Ustasse, as the name is frequently spelled in the chronicles). Could Sausset and Eustace be the same man?[12]

Sausset is a very rare name, apparently confined to a few families on the borders of Ponthieu and Hainault. There is a Sausset in the d'Aisne family: the lord of Aisne is mentioned as present at Buignicourt in 1326. This man's son is named Gerard, and Sausset is clearly a nickname. He first appears in the records under his real name. In 1339 he is Gerardo dicto Sausseto d'Enne,[13] but in 1342 he becomes simply Sausset d'Aisne, and as bailiff of Hainaut he is also referred to as Sausset without his real name.[14] Furthermore, Sanse de Biaureau and Sauses de Bousoit appear

[10] *RBP*, iv.76, 158.

[11] *Cartulaire de Hainaut*, 770: 'Par lettres medame, données à Caisnoit le mercredi nuit Saint Pière entrant aoust l'an dessusdit, payetà monsigneur Nicole d'Auberchicourt, lesquels medame le contesse pooit devoir à lui pour monsigneur Sausset d'Auberchicourt, sen frère, liquel servi ma dite dame en ses wières de Zélande et sur le Maize, si qu'il appert par chesle lettre ij^c l.'

[12] This suggestion has been made by a number of historians, notably Kervyn de Lettenhove in his edition of Froissart, xx.197, but usually without any supporting arguments.

[13] *Cartulaire de Hainaut*, 100.

[14] Ibid., 103, 211, 217, 241, 286.

in Isabella's entourage on her way to England in 1326 and among the Hainault knights who fought in the Scottish campaign in 1327.[15] Both of them are also known in the Hainault records as Sausse or Sausset.[16] Because of the difficulty of distinguishing 'n' and 'u' in Gothic script, the likely reading for 'Sanse' is 'Sause', a variation on Sausset and the mysterious Sanchet would become 'Sauchet', similarly a version of Sausset. It is noteworthy that the representation of Auberchicourt in the book compiled by William Bruges, the first Garter king at arms, one of the images for the windows he had made for St George's, Stamford, clearly reads Sausetus, as does Hollar's engraving of the images from the window.[17]

The meaning of this nickname has unfortunately been lost. The only modern writer to discuss the adoption of nicknames in Hainault at this period implies that it is in some way pejorative, but fails to give any justification for this idea: he suggests that it might mean red-faced or blotchy.[18] Subsequent dictionaries of names assume that it is related to 'sausse', sauce, and hence derives from the cook's red face. But this begs the question as to why there should be a group of men from the same small circle of families with the same disfigurement (though it could conceivably have been hereditary). It seems much more likely that it is some kind of private language whose meaning was soon forgotten.[19]

If Sausset is a nickname, and there are no documents that imply the existence of both Sausset and Eustace at the same time, it is strong evidence that the two are identical. All that is missing to complete the proof is an entry in the records like that for 'Gerard dit Sausset d'Aisne', which would read 'Eustace dit Sausset d'Auberchicourt'. I would argue that we should substitute Eustace's name for that of the mysterious 'Sanchet' in the list of Garter knights, particularly in view of the late date of the statutes and the problems involved in identifying the original members of the company. The next test of this hypothesis is to look at the career of Eustace d'Auberchicourt and to see how far it corresponds with the patterns we can detect in the careers of other Garter knights.

[15] Froissart, *Chroniques*, Rome version, 71, 114.
[16] For example, *Cartulaire de Hainaut*, 755: Sausse de Biauriu; 243: Sausset, sire de Boussoit.
[17] Hollar's engraving is in Ashmole, *Order of the Garter*, 643.
[18] Edouard Poncelet; see Hemricourt, *Œuvres*, ccxxvii–ccxxviii.
[19] Ibid., ccxxix, for examples from the later fourteenth and fifteenth centuries.

From 1355 onwards it is easy to trace Eustace d'Auberchicourt. The payment to him in May 1355 may have been a retainer, for in the autumn of 1355 he was in Aquitaine with the prince of Wales, and appears in the accounts kept by John Henxteworth from 20 September 1355 onwards. He probably travelled from England with the prince, and was with John Ghistels, possibly the son of Wulfart Ghistels.[20] Payments to them both appear on 1 October, on 10 December on the return from the raid to Narbonne that autumn, on 8 January 1356, and finally a gift of 40s. 6d. to each of them on 5 February.[21] After this Ghistels disappears from the accounts, and Auberchicourt's name appears alone: there are entries in February, March and April for his wages, and a final damaged entry on the last page apparently for wages to 30 June.[22] However, the partnership with John Ghistels continued, as in 1358 they owed one of the prince's officers £46 for money advanced to them, which the prince paid on their behalf.[23] Froissart also mentions them together in his lists of knights who fought in this campaign, and it is possible that they had entered into a partnership agreement whereby they shared the profits and expenses of the war.[24]

It is from the beginning of this raid by the prince of Wales that Auberchicourt appears regularly in Froissart's chronicle. As with the other Hainault knights, most of his exploits must have been told to Froissart by eyewitnesses or by Auberchicourt himself. Froissart says that, 'as I was afterwards told', the inhabitants of Carcassonne had tried to defend themselves by fixing chains across the streets, but Auberchicourt jumped over two or three of these and laid into the defenders with his sword, while elsewhere the English archers drove them back.[25] In the 1356 campaign he is mentioned as taking part in a skirmish at Romorantin.[26] The capture of the counts of Joigny and Auxerre is related in considerable detail by Froissart, and is again evidently based on an oral account, with

[20] Froissart, *Chroniques*, Rome version, 114, 440; Wulfart also served William II of Hainault in 1344: Hamaker, *De rekeningen der grafelijkheid van Holland*, xxvi.381, 395.
[21] Henxteworth, m. 1d, m. 4d, m. 9d, m. 13; a damaged entry on m. 5d for Auberchicourt might have included Ghistels' name.
[22] Ibid., m. 14, m. 15, m. 16, m. 17, m. 28.
[23] *RBP*, iv.264.
[24] Froissart, *Chroniques*, SHF, iv.136 (1355 raid); v.32 (battle of Poitiers); Froissart, *Chroniques*, ed. Lettenhove, v.378 (Poitiers campaign).
[25] Froissart, *Chroniques*, SHF, iv.166.
[26] Ibid., v.5.

some apparently authentic detail.[27] Auberchicourt was among a group
of soldiers, including the captal de Buch, Bartholomew Burghersh the
younger and Aimery de Pommiers, sent to reconnoitre the enemy positions; they encountered a French squadron which outnumbered them,
and turned back, leading the enemy towards the prince and his army,
who counter-attacked. In the ensuing encounter, the two counts were
captured. The same fate befell Auberchicourt himself an hour or two
later, when he was taken prisoner by a German knight; however, John
Ghistels was able to rescue him.[28]

So far, Auberchicourt's activities – at least seen through Froissart's
possibly rose-tinted lenses – had been entirely orthodox. But, like many
other knights, he found the truce signed in Bordeaux in 1357 had
brought his military career and hence his income to a temporary end. As
a younger son, he had little in the way of lands, although he was well
connected. Along with men of more humble birth who owed their
knightly status entirely to their activities in the field, Eustace became a
freebooter, one of the leaders of the dreaded companies, operating in
Champagne on his own account in collaboration with a group of
like-minded soldiers. He established himself in southern Champagne, a
rich area with several royal castles, in the autumn of 1358, and spent
the following year as one of the leaders of an army under the joint command of himself, Peter Audley (perhaps James Audley's younger brother)
and Albrecht, a German mercenary with a brutal reputation who may
be the same as Albert Sterz, a German captain executed in Italy eight
years later. Eustace seized Nogent-sur-Seine, among a number of other
towns and castles, and made it his headquarters.[29]

Froissart paints an idealized picture of Auberchicourt's behaviour
during this period, emphasizing his success and his chivalric encounters,
and dwelling particularly on his lady, Elizabeth of Juliers, niece of
Queen Philippa. He represents Elizabeth as sending him letters, greet-
ings and other signs, and Auberchicourt as inspired by the love of this

[27] Ibid., 14. The 'bushes and heather' leading up to the edge of the wood correspond closely
to the terrain of the battlefield at Poitiers; but see Ainsworth, *Jean Froissart and the Fabric
of History*, 219–53, for the literary element in Froissart's landscape descriptions.
[28] Froissart, *Chroniques*, SHF, v.16–17, 35, 41. This reinforces the idea that they were in
partnership, as Ghistels would have been liable for Auberchicourt's ransom if he had
remained in captivity.
[29] Le Bel, *Chronique*, ii.276–9 [243–5].

'young, fresh and pretty' beauty 'of the greatest blood in the kingdom'.[30] The reality of this campaign was very different. His men were responsible for a reign of terror which included an episode at Rosnay when they entered the church during mass, seized the chalice from the priest's hands and led him off as a prisoner. Elsewhere in France, the chaos after the capture of John II at Poitiers meant that such marauding went unpunished; but Eustace was unlucky in that the royal lieutenants in Champagne were well organized and prepared to act. They could raise troops from the towns, which, if not well trained, were plentiful, and could call on the local knights to serve in defence of their county. The freebooters would be outnumbered in any battle, and were not in a position to provision their strongholds to withstand a long siege. Eustace's response was to assemble his troops outside the town, and to fight a defensive battle, a tactic which had a reasonable chance of success, as at Crécy.[31] He succeeded, if we are to believe Froissart, in driving off the first two divisions of the French force, and in holding the third; but the arrival of the fresh troops in the French fourth division was too much for the small force at his command, and he himself was seriously wounded and captured. The French returned to Troyes, but the knight who had taken Auberchicourt prisoner knew that Eustace would be in danger of lynching because he was so hated for his behaviour, and took him elsewhere to recover.

Auberchicourt was able to raise his ransom of 22,000 *moutons* in a few months; on his release Elizabeth is said to have sent him a fine white courser.[32] He resumed his activities as a freebooter, and seized the town of Attigny on the Aisne as his base. His men found fifteen large tuns of wine there, and became very drunk: a house was burnt, and with it twenty of the English and forty horses.[33] Shortly afterwards, Edward III's army reached Reims, to begin their siege of that city, and Auberchicourt made contact with them: he is said to have sent them supplies from the stores he found at Attigny.[34] Early in 1360 he went on a foraging raid with Henry of Grosmont, but despite doing serious damage to towns and villages, they failed to return with enough supplies to prevent

[30] Froissart, *Chroniques*, SHF, v.159–60.
[31] Ibid., 165–73; *Chronique normande du XIVe siècle*, 140.
[32] Froissart, *Chroniques*, SHF, v.160.
[33] Ibid., 183.
[34] Ibid., 213.

Edward's lifting of the siege on 11 January.[35] After Edward's departure, he continued his ravages unabated; Jean le Bel believed that he was acting under Edward's orders, and bemoaned the fact that the French authorities in Champagne had failed 'up to the day when this was written' to do anything about Auberchicourt. In the end the local population seem to have bought him out: in May and June 1360 the count of Flanders ordered them to pay the 25,000 *deniers d'or* which they had promised on his surrender of Attigny and another castle.[36] The duke of Bar bought the fortress of Authey in June 1360 for 1,200 gold florins.[37]

Auberchicourt was certainly in Edward's service later in the year, as one of the commissioners who confirmed the treaty of Brétigny at Calais on 4 October 1360.[38] Five days earlier, he had made a prestigious marriage to the lady of Froissart's stories, Elizabeth of Juliers.[39] Her father, William of Juliers, was at one point very close to the king, who appointed him his 'private and very special sovereign secretary' in 1339, and created him earl of Cambridge in 1340.[40] On the death of her husband John earl of Kent in 1352, Elizabeth had become a nun at Waverley abbey, and the correspondence which Froissart depicts seems improbable. For Elizabeth it was a way out of the convent, for Auberchicourt it was a splendid opportunity for social and financial advancement. Both parties had to do penance for this illicit marriage, but they do not seem to have incurred any disfavour at court. Auberchicourt, as a second son, had relatively little in the way of lands, and his wife brought him a modest group of manors, her widow's portion from the estate of John of Kent. More important, however, he was now closely connected to the royal family: Elizabeth was sister-in-law to Joan of Kent, who was to become princess of Wales in 1361. Soon after the marriage, they sold the manors of Woking and Sutton to the prince of Wales.[41]

Auberchicourt continued in the king's service: he was supposed to go

[35] Sumption, *The Hundred Years War*, iii. 432.
[36] Orders printed from Archive du nord, B1596, fo. 174ᵛ, in Lapierre, *La Guerre de cent ans dans l'Argonne*, 118.
[37] Froissart, *Chroniques*, ed. Lettenhove, xx.198.
[38] *Foedera*, iii.i.518.
[39] The Alice Dabrechicourt who appears as a damsel of Queen Philippa in 1358 (*CPR 1358–1361*, 131) could have been his first wife, or his sister; we have no further evidence.
[40] Ormrod, *Edward III*, 127.
[41] *RBP*, iv.500, 503, 524.

to Brittany in the spring of 1363. Instead he took a substantial force – 350 mounted soldiers – to Ireland in 1363; he had twenty horses for himself and his retinue. However, the treaty of Brétigny meant that there was little official military activity by the English, and the following year he entered the service of Charles of Navarre, whom he was to serve for the remainder of his life. He took part in the battle of Auray in 1364 alongside John Chandos, but then returned to his earlier existence as a freebooter, for which he was severely reprimanded by Edward III.

When du Guesclin was captured at Auray, it seems that he held the castle of Carentan, of which Auberchicourt was nominally guardian. In July 1365 Auberchicourt was party to a deal by which du Guesclin sold it back to Charles of Navarre for 14,000 francs.[42] However, instead of returning to Normandy, he spent the next eighteen months involved in the French and English invasions of Castile, in the course of which he played a very ambiguous role as a kind of English agent nominally in the pay of Charles of Navarre.[43]

He did not remain to witness the disastrous outcome of the expedition after the victory, with Pedro unable to meet his debts to the prince of Wales and his army. Auberchicourt was by then in Tudela, where he received 3,000 francs from Charles of Navarre, a gift which probably marks his return to service with Navarre.[44] By the spring of the following year, he was back in Normandy, trying to eject Breton freebooters from Charles of Navarre's castles in the region.[45] John Chandos evidently collaborated with him, as there is a writ for payments to both Eustace and John for getting rid of the companies at this period.[46] He was once again captain of Carentan, as in 1364; it is possible that he had never surrendered this office.

Charles of Navarre came to Normandy in 1369, but the prince of Wales summoned Auberchicourt to help to suppress the growing revolt in Aquitaine. Charles was reluctant to let him go, but eventually relented. Auberchicourt took ship to St Malo, and then rode to Nantes and through Poitou to Angoulême.[47]

---

[42] Guesclin, *Letters*, 57, no. 152.
[43] See p. 454 above.
[44] *Archivo General de Navarra, Comptos*, vi.397, document 952.
[45] *Compte des recettes et dépenses du roi de Navarre*, 31, 33, 35–6, 42, 45.
[46] Ibid., 449.
[47] Froissart, *Chroniques*, SHF, vii.132–3.

John Chandos had preceded him to the prince's court, and Auber-chicourt joined his expedition that summer, fighting along the valley of the Garonne and at the siege of Domme. He seems to have stayed in Aquitaine for almost three years.[48] He and Walter Huet (an old col-league from the Spanish wars) were sent with 400 men to take over the castle of Rochechouart, but were driven off by Bertrand du Guesclin.[49] Late in 1370 he was at Belleperche when the mother of the duke of Bourbon was captured, and helped to arrange her exchange for Simon Burley, one of the prince's household knights.[50] He was also at the siege of Limoges in September 1370.[51] It was probably in the following year that, according to Froissart, he was captured at Pierre-Buffière near Limoges when he entered a castle which he believed to be in the hands of a lord friendly to the English and was taken prisoner by the Breton captain who was in fact holding it. His ransom was 12,000 francs; he could raise only part of it, but the duke of Bourbon, grateful for Auber-chicourt's help in releasing his mother, loaned him the rest. His son, whom Froissart calls François, remained with the duke as hostage for the repayment of the loan.[52] He returned to Normandy before the end of 1372, and died at Carentan, of which he had been captain since 1368, in December. His Navarrese squire Ferrant Martin de Merlo was with him.[53]

Auberchicourt was probably quite young when he died: if the Crécy–Calais campaign was his first experience of warfare, he would have been around forty-five in 1372. He seems to have had a remarkably varied and action-packed career.

He may have had two sons, François and William.[54] The eldest must

---

[48] Letters of protection for a year were issued for him, staying in Aquitaine with Edward prince of Wales. TNA C 61/83, m. 2 and m. 9; in October 1371 letters were issued for a year for Edmund de Munden, staying in his company in Aquitaine. These were repeated in November 1372 (TNA C 61/84, m. 2; C 61/85, m. 2).

[49] Froissart, Chroniques, ed. Lettenhove, xx.198.

[50] Froissart, Chroniques, SHF, vii.219, 224.

[51] Ibid., 244.

[52] Froissart, Chroniques, SHF, viii.ii.6.

[53] Froissart, Chroniques, ed. Lettenhove, xi.390.

[54] William's tomb was at St Mary's, Bridport in Dorset until the nineteenth century. John Leland notes the inscription in his Itinerary, i.245: 'Hic jacet Gulielmus, filius Elizabeth de Julers, Comitissae Cantiae, consanguinae Philippae quondam Reginae Angl.'

have been born before 1366, when his father swore liege homage to the king of Navarre on behalf of himself and his first-born son.

Auberchicourt's career corresponds for the most part to the pattern of similar Garter knights. He belongs to the entourage of the prince of Wales, but has also personal links to Edward III and Philippa, and is one of the Hainaulters in England associated with the queen. His service at Calais – we do not know whether he was at Crécy, but there is no reason why he should not have been – and at Poitiers is a common feature of the careers of the members of the company. Like Walter Mauny, he retained some interests in Hainault, but was less involved since he was a younger son, while Mauny had inherited the family estates there. His marriage makes him one of the knights with links by marriage to the royal house.

More problematic, and more interesting, is his time in the service of the king of Navarre. Charles the Bad's extraordinary political manoeuvrings must have baffled and infuriated both the French and English kings in equal measure, but in general we find Auberchicourt in Navarrese employ when Charles was either neutral or allied to the English. And his liege homage to Charles makes it clear that his prime loyalty is to Edward and the prince of Wales. It seems that he may have been acting with Edward's tacit approval, as a way of undermining the French, particularly during the period 1358–9 and again in 1365–6. This is similar to the tacit encouragement given to the English lords who had lost their Scottish lands in 1332. If Froissart is right about Elizabeth of Juliers's correspondence with him, he was clearly in touch with England in 1358–9, but it is equally plain that he failed to respect the normal conventions of warfare. Again, the career of Hugh Wrottesley offers a parallel for this lawlessness among the Garter knights.[55]

As to the convoluted politics of the Great Company's activities in Spain in 1366, Auberchicourt was clearly disobeying Edward's instructions to return in December 1365, along with Hugh Calveley. It is just possible that he was in effect keeping an eye on Charles of Navarre for Edward, and that he spent his time in Navarrese service rather than as an active member of the Great Company, though, like Calveley, he only returned to Bordeaux when it was clear there was nothing more to be gained in Castile. Even after his participation in the battle of Nájera, his

[55] See pp. 319–22 above.

service was still divided between the prince of Wales and the king of Navarre. There were perhaps personal loyalties at work as well: in 1364, 1367 and 1368–9 we find him fighting under the leadership of John Chandos. The reality behind Froissart's portrait of 'a very valiant knight'[56] points to a man whose lifestyle was much more ruthless, devious and precarious.

---

[56] Froissart, *Chroniques*, SHF, viii.ii.6.

Appendix 3
Sources for Biographical Material on the Companions of the Garter Elected before 1361

The following knights are not in *ODNB*; references are given to published material, and brief biographies are supplied for those knights for whom there is no printed biography apart from those in Beltz, *Memorials of the Garter*. Dates of admission to the Company of the Garter are approximate.

Eustace (Sanchet) d'Auberchicourt (KG 1349) See Appendix 2.

John Beauchamp (KG 1349) John Beauchamp was the younger brother of Thomas Beauchamp, earl of Warwick, and spent his life as a professional soldier. He first appears in the records at the Dunstable tournament of 1334, listed next to his brother.[1] He was part of his brother's retinue in 1337 in Scotland, and was in William Montagu's retinue in the following year in Flanders.[2] He appears as a household knight for the first time in this year.[3] He fought at Sluys in 1340,[4] and in Brittany in 1342, with his own retinue of three esquires.[5]

He was on the Crécy campaign of 1346 in the king's retinue, and served until Edward returned to England after the siege of Calais.[6] It was only after the campaign that he became a banneret; he appears at the tournament

---

[1] Long, 'Roll of the Arms of the Knights at the Tournament at Dunstable', 394.
[2] Ayton, *Knights and Warhorses*, 249–50.
[3] Shenton, 'The English Court', 255.
[4] *Complete Peerage*, ii.50.
[5] Ayton, *Knights and Warhorses*, 263.
[6] Wrottesley, *Crécy and Calais*, 176.

at Canterbury in 1348.[7] Shortly afterwards he was appointed captain of Calais, with responsibility for the ships stationed there.[8] In 1351 he was defeated in a battle at Ardres by a larger French force, and captured.[9] He may have been imprisoned for a year or two, as he was reappointed captain in January 1355, and a new indenture was drawn up for the same appointment in February 1356 for a year.[10] In June 1358 he was sent on an unsuccessful mission to negotiate an alliance with Brabant.[11] He served on the Reims campaign of 1359–60,[12] and in 1360 he was appointed constable of the Tower of London and of Dover Castle. He held these posts briefly, as he died unmarried on 2 December 1360. His tomb in St Paul's cathedral was later mistaken for that of Humphrey duke of Gloucester.[13]

Hugh Courtenay (KG 1349) Hugh Courtenay was born in 1326, and was therefore four years older than the prince of Wales. He was heir to the earl of Devon; his father, also called Hugh, was incapacitated in some way, since he never appears in the records as a soldier after he became earl in 1340. In 1347 Hugh the younger and the earl's brother-in-law the earl of Northampton petitioned that he should be excused any military service overseas. Hugh fought in the king's division on the Crécy campaign with a small retinue.[14] He was at the Eltham tournament of 1348, where he was given a hood embroidered with dancing men; the other recipients were Henry of Grosmont, John Lisle and John Grey.[15] Hugh was the first of the Garter knights to die, almost certainly of the plague: Queen Philippa laid cloth of gold on his tomb at Forde abbey in Dorset on 2 September 1349.[16]

Henry Eam *see* **Henry Oem**

[7] Nicolas, 'Observations on the Garter', 43.
[8] *Complete Peerage*, ii.50; *Foedera*, iii.i.75.
[9] Baker, *Chronicon*, 116; *Chronique normande du XIVᵉ siècle*, 101.
[10] *Complete Peerage*, ii.50; *Foedera*, iii.i.324.
[11] Trautz, *Die Könige von England*, 379.
[12] Ayton, *Knights and Warhorses*, 205.
[13] Stow, *Survey of the cities of London and Westminster*, i.335.
[14] Wrottesley, *Crécy and Calais*, 199: two knights, eight esquires and eight archers.
[15] Nicolas, 'Observations on the Garter', 41.
[16] TNA E 36/205, fo. 6.

Richard Fitzsimon (KG 1349)   Richard Fitzsimon first appears at the Dunstable tournament of 1334,[17] and then in Flanders in the service of Reginald Cobham.[18] He served with Henry of Grosmont in 1344 on his diplomatic mission to Castile, during which he attended the siege of the Moorish fortress at Algeciras, and again in 1345–6 in Aquitaine; he evidently returned home early in 1346.[19] He served on the Crécy campaign in the retinue of Robert Ufford, but is also named as being in the retinue of the king and of the prince.[20] He was the standard-bearer of Edward prince of Wales at the battle of Crécy, and was rewarded accordingly.[21] He appears to have died in 1358–9.[22]

William Fitzwarin (KG 1349)   Sir William Fitzwarin was the second son of Fulk, second Baron Fitzwarin, and his wife Alianore de Beauchamp, daughter of John, Lord Beauchamp, of Somerset. Fulk had a distinguished career under Edward II, and was constable of the army during the civil wars of 1322. William's elder brother, Fulk the younger, was similarly an important figure in Edward III's campaigns, and was assumed to have been the founding member of the Order of the Garter when the stall plates at Windsor were first put up in the 1420s.

However, it was William who had a close connection with the royal household. We do not know when he was born, but it seems to have been in the period 1305–10. We find him in attendance on Queen Philippa at Windsor on 22 October 1330, in her chamber,[23] and it is in her service that he most frequently appears. He was appointed governor of Montgomery Castle in 1330, after the execution of Roger Mortimer, earl of March, the previous castellan; he held this position until 1355, when Roger's son was able to reclaim the family lands which had been forfeited because of his father's treason. By 1332 he had also been given the castellany of Knaresborough, which was held by Queen Philippa, and was the queen's chamberlain.[24] He was in the king's household in

---

[17] Long, 'Roll of the Arms of the Knights at the Tournament at Dunstable', 393.
[18] Beltz, *Memorials of the Garter*, 60.
[19] *Foedera*, iii.i.11, 40; Fowler, 'Henry of Grosmont', iv.250.
[20] Wrottesley, *Crécy and Calais*, 96, 118, 119, 160, 185.
[21] See p. 234 above.
[22] Wrottesley, *Crécy and Calais*, 189.
[23] Manchester, John Rylands, MS 235, fo. 10ᵛ.
[24] BL MS Cotton Galba E.III, fo. 184ʳ.

1333–4 as knight of the Marshalsea of the king's hall, and continued as a household knight until at least 1337. He was evidently a highly valued and trusted servant of both king and queen, as in 1335 he was granted the marriage of Elizabeth, widow of William Latimer, 'for long and gratuitous service to the king and queen Philippa', 'if she will marry him'; if not, he was to have the fee payable to the king on her remarriage. She chose not to marry him; he married Amicia, the daughter of a neighbour in Dorset, at some time before 1341. In 1336 he was promised an income of £30 per year 'for service to the king and queen Philippa', and received as part of this lands in Dorset.[25]

William first appears on a diplomatic mission in October 1330, when he is sent with two clerics to make an alliance with John duke of Brabant.[26] Over the next sixteen years he was regularly employed on diplomatic business, particularly where alliances were concerned. He was chosen to approach Alfonso XI of Castile in 1335 to explore the possibility of a match between his eldest son and Edward III's elder daughter Isabella, then aged three, though the alliance did not materialize. In August 1336 he went to Austria with a similar proposal, for the marriage of the eldest son of Duke Otto with Princess Joan, who was a year younger than Isabella. Again, the alliance did not materialize. He went to the count of Guelders in January 1338 for a conference of the local princes, returning via Hainault by 14 March. At the end of the year, five of his servants were accused of the murder at Antwerp of Oliver, son of Oliver Ingham, then seneschal of Aquitaine, and a very important figure in Edward's entourage. Once the war against France began, he was employed on military tasks such as gathering a force of Welsh footsoldiers in July 1338. When Edward III mounted his raid on France, and an encounter with the French army was expected at La Flamengrie, Fitzwarin appears as one of the nineteen named knights listed as being in the king's battalion. He had a modest retinue, and was paid £128 18s. 8d. in June 1340 and £140 in March 1341. In 1342 he served as a banneret in Brittany with one knight and eight esquires.

In the Crécy campaign, he fought, as would be expected, in the king's division, with a similar retinue to that in Brittany.[27] His retinue included men

[25] Marriage grant, CPR 1334–1338, 179; income grant, CPR 1334–1338, 320.
[26] CCR, Lists and Indexes II, 1900, 189.
[27] Ayton and Preston, Crécy, 246. The Acta Bellicosa (Acts of War) omits him from the list of bannerets in the king's division, but the St Omer chronicle names him, and he is on the

from Hereford and Somerset, as well as his brother John.[28] He was with the king throughout the siege of Calais, and accompanied him on his return to England. He then seems to have rejoined the queen's household, as he is paid as a knight of the queen's bodyguard in 1349–50. He was paid the substantial sum of £266 13s. 4d. in 1350 for services in Flanders and Germany, but this may be a question of wages in respect of his missions abroad over the previous twelve years or more; such belated settlements were far from uncommon. In the same year, he led a pilgrimage to Rome.[29]

He was back in England in 1351, when he was again paid as a member of the queen's household. But thereafter he disappears from the records of active knights, whether on campaign or as administrator at home. Apart from his surrender of Montgomery Castle in 1355, there is only a commission of inquiry in 1357. About the time of his return from Rome, in June 1351, he obtained a licence to give lands and rent to support three chaplains at Wantage to celebrate masses 'for the good estate of the king, queen Philippa and him, and for their souls when they are dead'.[30] Seven years later, because he had not yet made the grants, he asked for the licence to be applied to a grant he wished to make to the friars of Hounslow instead. Yet it was at Wantage that he was buried; his tomb is one of the two surviving memorials to the first Garter knights. The effigies of Sir William and his wife are much defaced by the ravages of iconoclasts and visitors scratching their names in the soft alabaster. The Garter is still visible over his armour, but any decoration or inscription has long since gone, and it is no more than a plain band.

Frank van Hale (KG 1359) A Flemish knight, probably born in the 1320s, and brother of Simon Hale, a member of the king's household in 1328–30 who had come over with Philippa of Hainault and who lent Edward £400 in January 1339; he was said to have been better known as Simon de Mirabel.[31] Frank van Hale first appears in the English records in Flanders in 1341, receiving the substantial sum of £90 per annum as his retaining fee.[32] He served as a banneret in Henry of Grosmont's army

payrolls.
[28] Wrottesley, *Crécy and Calais*, 150, 173, 176.
[29] See pp. 330–33 above.
[30] *CPR 1350–1354*, 108.
[31] Note by Kervyn de Lettenhove in Froissart, *Chroniques*, ed. Lettenhove, ii.513.
[32] TNA E 101/389/8, m. 9.

in Gascony in 1345; Froissart says that he was at the siege of Bergerac, and he was certainly made keeper of the castle of Rochefort, guarding the mouth of the river Charente, in 1346. In 1349 he was appointed seneschal of the duchy, and accompanied Grosmont on his raid to Toulouse in November and December that year. He was in Grosmont's service in 1351, when he prepared the way, with Stephen de Cosington,[33] for talks between the duke and the count of Flanders. He served on the Reims expedition, probably in Grosmont's retinue, and was among the knights of the Garter named to negotiate the treaty of Brétigny, and was also a guarantor of it.[34] His connection with the house of Lancaster evidently continued after Grosmont's death, as he was paid an annuity in the 1370s through his attorney.[35] However, from 1363 onwards he appears in attendance on the count of Flanders as holding a fief from him as a witness to various acts, the last being in 1373. He was engaged again in peace negotiations in 1375,[36] and probably died shortly after that.

Otho Holland (KG 1349)   Otho, brother of Thomas Holland, is a shadowy figure. In 1342 he fought in Brittany with two esquires,[37] and was a household knight in 1343.[38] In 1350 he was given custody of Raoul count of Eu when Edward purchased him from Thomas, but guarded him so negligently that the count was seen armed and without an escort on the streets of Calais, for which Otho was imprisoned by the marshal of the king's court.[39] He may have fought alongside his brother for much of his career, and was with him in Brittany in 1355. The following year it was Otho who captured Castle Cornet on Jersey in his brother's name. He died in Normandy, presumably in the company of his brother, in September 1359. His lands were in Derbyshire[40] and in Staffordshire.

John, Lord Lisle (of Rougemont) (KG 1349)   See *Complete Peerage*, viii.73–6.

---

[33] Fowler, *The King's Lieutenant*, 101.
[34] *Foedera*, iii.i.531, 535.
[35] Beltz, *Memorials of the Garter*, 126.
[36] *Foedera*, iii.ii.1024–5.
[37] Ayton, *Knights and Warhorses*, 264.
[38] TNA E 36/204, fo. 86.
[39] Beltz, *Memorials of the Garter*, 85.
[40] BL Wolley Charter I.16, with his seal.

Henry Oem (KG 1349) For his career in service of William II, see pp. 324–5; for his service to the prince of Wales, see pp. 188–9, 325–6. Nothing else is known about him.

John Sully (KG 1353) For the career of John Sully, who very probably succeeded Henry Oem, we depend largely on his testimony in the Scrope–Grosvenor case in the Court of Chivalry.[41] He gave evidence in 1388, and stated his age as 102. If he was really born in 1276, he was 32 when he first fought in Scotland in 1315, and 84 when he fought at the battle of Najéra. A more realistic assessment would be that he was born about 1296. He said that he was at the first of Edward III's great victories, at Halidon Hill in 1333, and he is recorded at the Dunstable tournament in 1334.[42] He fought in Flanders in 1338 in William Montagu's retinue.[43] On the Crécy campaign, he transferred to the retinue of Richard Fitzalan, earl of Arundel.[44] He also claimed, probably correctly, to have fought at Winchelsea. He was certainly retained by the prince from 1353 onwards, and that year was given a handsome new year's gift by the prince of Wales of a silver cup and ewer.[45] He became one of his close associates: when the prince ordered five green hats in 1355, they were for himself, Roger Mortimer, Bartholomew Burghersh, Nigel Loring and Sully.[46] Sully went to Gascony in 1355, fought on that year's campaign and at Poitiers, and returned to Gascony with the prince in 1365.[47] After the battle of Najéra, he remained in Aquitaine, and the last mention of him is in 1370, until commissioners were sent to interview him for the Scrope–Grosvenor case in his retirement at Iddesleigh, where he was attended by his squire Richard Baker.

Thomas Ufford (KG 1360) Thomas Ufford was born sometime before 1334, the second son of Robert Ufford, first earl of Suffolk. He appears as a party to a transaction between his father and Edward Montagu in

---

[41] See p. 379 above.
[42] Long, 'Roll of the Arms of the Knights at the Tournament at Dunstable', 393.
[43] Ayton, *Knights and Warhorses*, 249.
[44] Wrottesley, *Crécy and Calais*, 97.
[45] *RBP*, iv.70, 80.
[46] *RBP*, iv.230.
[47] Henxteworth, m. 4; Nicolas, *Scrope–Grosvenor Controversy*, ii.240–43.

August 1352, possibly to do with a marriage.[48] He was listed as one of the knights going on Henry of Grosmont's abortive expedition to Normandy in 1355,[49] and three years later he was retained by Grosmont,[50] which implies that he fought in the Reims campaign of 1359–60. He was probably elected to the company in 1360 on the death of Roger Mortimer: at the time he was heir to the earldom of Suffolk. He was issued with Garter robes in 1362 and 1363,[51] and went abroad, probably with the prince of Wales, in 1364.[52] He fought on the Spanish campaign of 1366–7,[53] and presumably died there, as he predeceased his father, who died in 1368.

Richard de la Vache (KG 1355) Richard de la Vache served with Henry of Grosmont in Brittany in 1342–3,[54] and was a knight of the chamber by 1348: he fought in the tournament at Lichfield in that year.[55] His family were relatively modest knights from Buckinghamshire, and it is possible that his marriage to Amy de la Vache, who was connected in some way with Philippa's household, was his way into the royal circle.[56] He was one of the knights summoned back from England in May 1347 in anticipation of Philip of Valois's arrival before Calais with an army, and his presence in that list makes it likely that he was already a knight of the household, and therefore fought in the king's division at Crécy. He had been appointed to supervise the array of men at arms from Buckinghamshire and Bedfordshire in March 1346, and, as several of his fellow-arrayers for other counties were household knights, this would confirm that he too was one of them.[57] He does not seem to have served in any subsequent campaign, and was appointed constable of the Tower of London in 1361, a largely administrative post. He was issued

---

[48] Mutual recognizances for 2,500 marks, 26 August 1352: *CCR 1349–1354*, 503.
[49] Fowler, 'Henry of Grosmont', iv.261.
[50] *CPR 1358–1361*, 16.
[51] TNA E 361/4, rot. 7 and rot. 8d.
[52] *CPR 1361–1364*, 472.
[53] Chandos Herald, *La Vie du Prince Noir*, ll. 2247, 2461, 3231.
[54] Fowler, 'Henry of Grosmont', iv.262.
[55] Nicolas, 'Observations on the Garter', 26–9.
[56] Beltz, *Memorials of the Garter*, 106–7.
[57] Wrottesley, *A History of the Family of Wrottesley of Wrottesley*, 78–9.

with Garter robes in 1361–3.[58] He succeeded John Chandos as under-chamberlain in 1363 and died in 1366.

Thomas Wale (KG 1349) Thomas Wale is another obscure figure, lord of a modest manor in Northamptonshire, born in 1303.[59] His first military record is a summons for the Scottish campaign in 1333.[60] He fought in Flanders in the retinue of William Montagu in 1338,[61] and under William Bohun, earl of Northampton, in Brittany in 1342. He went to Brittany with Richard Fitzalan in 1344.[62] There is a gift of a silver-gilt cup to him in the prince of Wales's register in the list drawn up in 1353, and he is described as 'the prince's bachelor'.[63] He died in Gascony on 26 October 1352, leaving no heir.[64]

Hugh Wrottesley (KG 1349) See pp. 320–23. For a full account of his career, see George Wrottesley, *A History of the Family of Wrottesley of Wrottesley.*

[58] TNA E 361/4, rot. 4, rot. 7 and rot. 8d.
[59] Beltz, *Memorials of the Garter*, 63.
[60] *Foedera*, ii.ii.856.
[61] *Foedera*, ii.ii.1048.
[62] *Foedera*, iii.i.10.
[63] *RBP*, iv.73.
[64] Beltz, *Memorials of the Garter*, 63.

Appendix 4
Chronological List of Royal Tournaments of Edward III

Most tournaments are discussed in the text, and references can be found in the relevant notes. References given below are only for those tournaments not referenced in the main text. Only the ninety-five tournaments where Edward himself is known or believed to have attended are included in the list; records of other tournaments held by individuals at which the king was not present are very sparse, and were probably infrequent. Likewise, records of attendance at the tournaments are erratic, and the names of knights known to have been present are not included here; where there is such information, the tournament is asterisked and the names can be traced in the sources referred to in the footnotes.

Dating has been done by cross-reference to the itinerary printed in Ormrod, *Edward III*, 610–31, and is inevitably tentative in many cases.

Year	Date	Place
1327	February	London[1]
1327	April[2]	
1327	23–7 December	Worcester
1328	9–14 January	Clipstone
1328	15 January	Blyth[3]
1328	17–18 January	Rothwell

[1] To celebrate coronation; TNA E 361/3, rot. 9 m. 2d, rot. 10 m. 1.
[2] Held by John Bohun, earl of Hereford; TNA DL 10/250.
[3] TNA DL 41/335; Smyth, *Lives of the Berkeleys*, i.235.

Year	Date	Place
1328	25–8 January	York
1328	24 May–23 June	Northampton[4]
1328	31 May	Hereford
1328	25 September	Thetford[5]
1328	31 October–31 December	Wigmore
1329	2 January	Coventry
1329	6–9 March	Guildford
1329	June	Amiens
1329	13–19 June	Canterbury
1329	25 June	Dartford
1329	2–3 July	Reigate
1329	12 August–4 September	Gloucester
1329	8–13 September	Hereford
1329	8–13 September	Wigmore
1329	28 September–7 October	Worcester
1329	8–12 October	Dunstable*
1330	?18 February	Westminster*
1330	c. 25 March	Winchester[6]
1330	22–7 July	Woodstock
1330	28 July	Northampton[7]
1330	16 September	Nottingham[8]
1330	13 November	Clarendon
1330	28 November	Westminster
1330	20 December	Guildford
1331	20 January	Westminster
1331	1–7 February	King's Langley[9]
1331	26 April	Dartford*
1331	1–21 May	Havering-atte-Bower*
1331	25 May–4 June	Newmarket*
1331	16–19 June	Stepney*
1331	during summer?	Lichfield*[10]

[4] Ibid., 235.
[5] TNA C 47/6/1, m. 5.
[6] Possibly Mortimer's celebration of the execution of Edmund earl of Kent; E 101/361/3, rot. 16d m. 1.
[7] London, Society of Antiquaries, MS 541, note sewn to m. 3, fair copy m. 3.
[8] Ibid.
[9] TNA E 361/3, rot. 19 m. 1d.
[10] TNA E 101/385/7, m. 1; E 361/3, rot. 19 m. 1d.

Year	Date	Place
1331	20 August	Bedford[11]
1331	22–5 September	Cheapside*
1332	16 June	Woodstock*
1334	16–26 January	Dunstable*
1334	?1–6 February	Woodstock[12]
1334	?9 February	Newmarket
1334	16–18 May	Burstwick[13]
1334	12–17 July	Nottingham
1334	?11–12 September	Guildford[14]
1334	13–30 September	Smithfield[15]
1337	?10 April	?[16]
1338	?	Windsor[17]
1339	1–31 January	Antwerp[18]
1339	1–6 November	Brussels[19]
1340	12–18 April	Windsor[20]
1340	1 October–27 November	Ghent[21]
1340	Between 9 and 15 December 1340	Le Bure[22]
1340	c. 25 December	Reading
1341	2 February	King's Langley
1341	20 February	Norwich
1341	1–10 June	King's Langley*
1341	4 October	Westminster[23]

[11] TNA E 361/3, rot. 19 m. 1d.
[12] For tournaments at Woodstock and Newmarket, see Ormrod, *Edward III*, 143 and note; and BL Add. MS 46350, rot. 7.
[13] TNA E 101/386/15; BL Add MS. 46350, rot. 7.
[14] TNA E 101/386/15.
[15] *Annales Paulini*, i.361; possibly celebration of military successes in Scotland.
[16] BL Add. MS 60584, fo. 38ᵛ.
[17] TNA E 361/3, m. 40a.
[18] TNA E 101/388/11; churching of Philippa, baptism of Lionel.
[19] TNA E 101/388/11; *Chronographia Regum Francorum*, ii.85.
[20] TNA E 101/388/11; E 361/3, m. 40a.
[21] TNA E 101/388/11.
[22] TNA DL /25/983; king may not have been present, jousts organized by Henry of Grosmont.
[23] TNA E 101/389/12.

APPENDIX 4

Year	Date	Place
1342	?23–5 January	York
1342	January?	Hull
1342	11–12 February	Dunstable*
1342	10–14 April	Northampton*
1342	1–13 July	Eltham*
1343	24–7 June	Smithfield*[24]
1343	10 March onwards	Canterbury, Hereford[25]
1344	15–24 January	Windsor*
1344	15 November–30 December	Bungay*[26]
1344	30 November	Leicester*[27]
1344	21–7 December	Norwich[28]
1345	?	Winchester*[29]
1348	mid-February	Reading[30]
1348	February?	Bury St Edmunds*[31]
1348	20 April	Lincoln[32]
1348	4–12 May	Lichfield*
1348	14–19 May	Windsor*
1348	20 May	Eltham
1348	14 July	Canterbury*
1349	23 April	Windsor
1349	24 June	Windsor[33]
1350	25 November–8 December	Reading[34]
1350	6 December	Norwich[35]
1351	?	Bristol[36]

[24] TNA C 47/6/1, m. 16; *Murimuth*, 146, 230–31; *Annales Paulini*, ii.361.
[25] *Murimuth*, 146.
[26] TNA C 47/6/1, m. 4.
[27] Knighton, *Chronicle*, 50–51.
[28] Blomefield, *Norfolk*, iii.86.
[29] BL MS Harleian 4304, fo. 19ᵛ.
[30] Nicolas, 'Observations on the Garter', 38–9; TNA E 101/391/15, m. 10; E 372/207, m. 50; E 403/340.
[31] TNA E 372/207, m. 50; C 47/6/1, m. 4; *RBP*, iv.67.
[32] Baker, *Chronicon*, 97.
[33] Ibid., 101; TNA E 372/207, m. 50.
[34] TNA E 361/3, m. 49a.
[35] Blomefield, *Norfolk*, iii.94; Norfolk Record Office, Norwich bailiffs' account for 1349.
[36] TNA E 372/207, m. 50.

Year	Date	Place
1353	19–27 March	Smithfield[37]
1353	31 December	Eltham[38]
1355	22 February	Woodstock[39]
1357	?24 May	Smithfield*[40]
1358	1 January	Bristol
1358	23 April	Windsor
1359	27–9 May	Smithfield*[41]
1361	27 May	Smithfield[42]
1362	19 April	Smithfield[43]
1363	1 November	Smithfield[44]
1377	February	Smithfield[45]
1377	4 June	Smithfield[46]

[37] *Avesbury*, 419; in honour of Breton visitors.
[38] Ibid.
[39] Ibid., 422; *RBP*, iv.165; churching of Philippa, baptism of Thomas.
[40] John of Reading, *Chronica*, 129; Walsingham, *Historia Anglicana*, i.285, 296.
[41] John of Reading *Chronica*, 131; *RBP*, iv.323; *Brut*, ii.309; marriage of John of Gaunt and Blanche of Lancaster.
[42] TNA E 101/393/15 for date; *RBP*, iv.324; marriage of earl of Richmond.
[43] John of Reading, *Chronica*, 152–3; *RBP*, iv.475.
[44] TNA E 101/571/16, E 101/393/15, m. 13, E 101/394/16, mm. 5, 14, 17; Venette, *Chronicle*, 114. Four kings were present on this occasion: Edward, David II of Scotland, John II of France and Peter I of Cyprus.
[45] TNA E 101/397/20, mm. 18, 19, 21.
[46] TNA E 101/392/20, m. 6; planned but cancelled.

Appendix 5
The Statutes of the Garter

A translation into English by Lisa Barber from the Latin version of the earliest known text of the Statutes of the Order of the Garter, with footnote annotations for any significant difference between this Latin text and the earliest, very slightly later, text in French.[1]

1. In honour of Almighty God, of St Mary the glorious Virgin, and of St George the martyr, our supreme lord, Edward III, king of England, in the twenty-third year of his reign ordained, established and founded a certain company or knightly order within his castle of Windsor, in this manner: Firstly, he decreed himself to be the sovereign of the said company or order, his eldest son the prince of Wales, the duke of Lancaster, the earl of Warwick, the captal de Buch, the earl of Stafford, the earl of Salisbury, Lord Mortimer, Sir John Lisle, Sir Bartholomew Burghersh the younger, Sir John Beauchamp, Lord Mohun, Sir Hugh Courtenay, Sir Thomas Holland, Sir John Grey, Sir Richard Fitzsimon, Sir Miles Stapleton, Sir Thomas Wale, Sir Hugh Wrottesley, Sir Nigel Loring, Sir John Chandos, Sir James Audley, Sir Otho Holland, Sir Henry Eam, Sir 'Sanchet d'Abridgecourt', Sir Walter Pavely.

2. It was agreed that the king of England, whoever it shall be at the time,[2] shall in perpetuity be the Sovereign of this Order of St George or Company of the Garter.

3. Item, it is agreed that none shall be elected as a member of the said order unless he be of noble birth and a knight without reproach, since

---

[1] The original of the earliest known Latin text is found in Oxford, Bodleian Library, MS Ashmole 1128, and is printed in Ashmole, *Order of the Garter*, appendix I. The earliest French text is found in a number of manuscripts, and is edited by Lisa Jefferson [Barber], 'MS Arundel 48 and the Earliest Statutes of the Order of the Garter'.

[2] The French text says 'the king and his heirs, kings of England', which is slightly different.

the institution of the order does not admit those of low birth nor the reprobate.[3]

4. And the aforesaid twenty-six fellow-knights and companions of this order[4] shall wear the mantle and garter as ordained at the said castle as often as they shall be present there, that is to say each time that they enter the chapel of St George or the chapter house in order to hold a chapter or to regulate any matter pertaining to the order. And in the same manner[5] they shall proceed on St George's Eve, moving as a procession with the sovereign of the order or his deputy from the king's great chamber as far as the chapel or the chapter house, and they shall return in the same manner. They shall then sit wearing their mantles and garters on the said eve at the time of supper, both those who wish to take supper and those who do not eat, until the usual time for departure from the said great chamber.[6] And thus robed also they shall proceed the next day towards the said chapel and return from there, as also at the time of dinner and thereafter, until the sovereign or his deputy shall remove his own insignia of the order. Thus also when proceeding to the second vespers and returning therefrom, as also at the time of supper and thereafter, they shall be dressed as on the eve, until such time as the sovereign of the order shall decree it to be time for departure.[7]

5. And thirteen secular canons are ordained, who must be priests at the time of their induction or who must be preferred to the priesthood within the following year, and also thirteen vicars who shall be priests at the time of their admission or at the latest by the time of the next following ordinations, who shall celebrate continually for the souls of all the faithful deceased. These aforenamed canons shall be presented by the aforenamed founders of the order,[8] that is to say that each of the

---

[3] The French text lacks the last phrase, has nothing more in this article after 'reproach'.
[4] The order is not specifically limited to twenty-six members in the statutes, but this number is implied throughout.
[5] The French text says that 'they shall likewise wear their mantles'.
[6] The French text says until 'la voydie' = 'the void, or voidee': the parting dish of wine with spiced delicacies, brought round to mark the end of a feast or ceremonial evening.
[7] Here again the French text says 'until the voidee'.
[8] There is a contradiction here, if the present founders and the aforenamed founders are different – 'that is to say that each of the present founders' implies that they are the same as the 'aforenamed founders' who are to do the presentation. This passage must be corrupt and words are missing. The reservation of later presentations to the sovereign confirms the identity of 'present founders' and 'aforenamed founders'.

present founders shall present his canon to the warden of the college.[9] However, if one of the canons shall die, neither he who last presented him nor any other of the companions of the order shall afterwards present, but only the sovereign of the order shall present to that canonry from that time forward in perpetuity. And thus it is unanimously agreed for the presentations of all other canons to be reserved to the sovereign alone.

6. Item, it is agreed that the aforesaid canons shall each have a mantle of cloth of purple colour[10] with a roundel of the arms of St George.

7. Item, it is ordained that twenty-six veteran knights,[11] who have no means of sustenance, shall have there in the honour of God and of the blessed George a sufficient maintenance, that they may continually serve God in prayers. And for the election of those veteran knights it is ordained in the same manner as for the presentation of the aforesaid canons, thus that both the elections of the veterans as also the presentations of the canons are reserved to the sovereign alone.

8. Item, it is agreed that the said veteran knights shall each have a mantle of red with an escutcheon of the arms of St George but without the garter.

9. Item, it is agreed that if the sovereign of this order or company shall perchance be unable to attend the celebration of the feast of St George, [he shall nominate a deputy to hold][12] the chapter meeting at the hour of terce and the celebration of the feast on the next day, at the expense of the sovereign of the order. But such a deputy shall not make new observances or ordinances. However, it shall be permitted to him to correct and redress those who transgress the statutes of the order which follow.

[9] This ruling has provoked a fair amount of discussion among modern scholars; it is clear that it does not date from the first institution of the order, since it refers to 'quilibet fundatorum modernorum', or in French 'chacun des fondeurs qui sont a present', the Latin of 'modernorum' making it clear that these are not the original twenty-six first founders. At what date this ordinance was issued has not been determined, but Peter Begent tentatively suggested that one should consider the period between 1352 and 1368 (Begent and Chesshyre, *The Most Noble Order of the Garter*, 27).

[10] The French text says 'murrey' = mulberry colour.

[11] The French text throughout calls them 'povres chevaliers' = poor knights, the title by which they came to be known in English until a much later date.

[12] There is clearly an omission of several words in the manuscript here, but the sense is clear and can also be supplied from the French version of the text, which in addition says that the nomination of a deputy should be 'par ses lettres' = by letter.

10. Item, each year on St George's Eve shall be held a meeting of all the companions of the Order of St George, at the said castle of Windsor, whether they be within the kingdom of England or outside it but that they may conveniently be able to come thither,[13] and there they must attend the church service and shall wear their mantle at the time of the celebration of divine service, being each in their stalls in their respective places. And each of them shall have in the chapel above his stall his helmet and his sword which, in memory[14] of him and for the protection of the church, shall stay there for the period of his lifetime, in the manner that the noble and chivalrous order requires. But in the eventuality that the feast of St George shall fall within the fifteen days following Easter Day, the said feast of St George shall be postponed until the second Sunday after Easter Day, so that each of the companions of the order may in due manner be able to come to that feast without having to ride on horseback on any of the three days that follow Easter Day.[15]

11. Item, that they shall gather together in the said place on St George's Eve, at the hour of terce, and if any do not come thus at the appointed time and have no excuse acceptable to the sovereign of the order or his deputy, they must be punished by the sovereign of the order and the chapter,[16] in this manner that, because of this negligence, they shall not enter the chapter on this occasion, but shall wait outside at the door, and they shall have no voice in any matter that may be dealt with in the said chapter on that occasion. And if any do not come before the beginning of vespers, they shall not enter their stalls then, but shall stand down below in front of their stalls in the customary place for the candlebearers,[17] for the duration of the said vespers at which they did not arrive on time. And a like penalty is ordained for those who do not

[13] Is the meaning in effect 'as long as they are conveniently able to come thither', i.e. if they are too far away or occupied in something which they cannot break off, then they are excused?

[14] The French text says 'en signifiance', not in memory. The French is a better reading, because 'memory' implies that the knight is dead.

[15] The Church maintained a ban on riding (the basis for which is Exodus 20: 10) after vespers each Saturday and on Sundays and during feast days. The last sentence may be a later addition.

[16] The French text here refers to a preceding agreement as to the punishment, made in a chapter meeting: 'auront leur penance selon l'accord du chapistre. Et l'accord est que ...'.

[17] Or candelabra or candlesticks. The French version says 'in the choristers' place'. Thirty-eight candelabra were bought for the chapel; they were probably on the choristers' stalls, as in present Oxbridge college chapels.

arrive before the beginning of Solemn Mass[18] or of vespers on the following day. And whoever does not come to the celebration of the feast, having no excuse acceptable to the sovereign of the order, he shall be ordered in the name of penance that he shall not enter his stall at the next following feast but shall stand outside and in front of his stall in the aforementioned place during the time of first vespers, and at the time of the procession on the next day he shall walk in front of the three processional crosses, and coming into the choir again he shall stand in the aforementioned low place until the offertory, when he shall be the last to offer. And when he has performed these penances thus, he shall come straight away before the sovereign's stall or that of his deputy to ask for pardon. And then the said sovereign or his deputy shall restore him to his stall and to his former status. If he once more absent himself for a second time from the feast of St George held the next following year, without an excuse acceptable to the sovereign or his deputy, and being within the kingdom of England, then he shall not from that time forward enter his stall until he has, within that said chapel upon the altar of St George, offered a jewel to the value of twenty English marks. And he shall double the fine each year from then onwards until he be reconciled.

12. Item, that all companions of the order, wherever they may be, shall wear their mantle of bluet each year, inclusively from the hour of first vespers on St George's Eve until second vespers on the day following, in the same manner as they would if they were present in person with the sovereign of the order or his deputy, for the whole time that this feast is to be celebrated, provided yet that they be in a place wherein they enjoy their liberty.[19]

13. Item, it is agreed that if any one of the said company should appear publicly[20] without his garter, as soon as this shall be brought to attention or noted,[21] he shall pay to the warden and college half a mark, in the same manner as others previously have paid who have been established to be guilty of the same fault.

14. Item, it is agreed that at the time of the offertory at High Mass,

---

[18] Or High Mass.

[19] The French version has additionally at the end of this article: 'Notwithstanding the prorogation of the feast'.

[20] The French text says 'should be found in public'.

[21] The French text says 'tentost aprés la chalenge' = straight after this is challenged.

the two companions who are opposite each other in their stalls shall always come forward together to make their offering. And if it happen that one of these be absent, then his companion who should be opposite to him shall come forward alone and shall make his offering on his own. And it is to be noted that the sovereign of the order at the time of a procession in the said chapel shall move forward behind the whole body of the companions.

15. Item, it is recorded that on each morrow of St George's Day, before the companions take leave of each other or depart, a requiem mass is to be celebrated for the souls of all the faithful departed,[22] and that the whole company should be there in its entirety, unless there be some reasonable hindrance for anyone, or unless he have the permission of the sovereign of the order or his deputy before he departs from there.

16. Item, it is agreed that each of the companions shall leave his mantle there, [ready] for unexpected visits and in order to observe the precepts and salutary admonitions of the aforesaid sovereign.

17. Item, it is deemed appropriate that if it should happen that anyone of the said company or order shall travel through the said castle of Windsor, he shall enter [there] in honour of the place, if he is conveniently able and is not hindered by any just and reasonable cause. And that before he enter the chapel he shall put on his mantle, for he should not enter except clothed in his mantle. And the canons present there at that time shall come to meet him, and shall lead him devoutly into the chapel. And if he shall happen to arrive at the time of mass, he shall wait there in the honour of God and St George and shall hear that same mass. But if he arrive after midday, he shall enter in the manner and form stated and shall then wait until the canons have once recited the psalm De Profundis for the souls of all the faithful departed,[23] and he shall make an offering once the psalm has been said. But if anyone of the said company shall ride through the midst of the town and not enter the chapel and make an offering according to this agreement, for each time that he has not done this, he shall for the virtue of obedience walk a mile[24] on foot towards the said chapel and shall offer one penny in the honour of St George.

---

[22] The French text says the requiem mass is to be sung 'for the souls of companions who have died and for all Christians'.
[23] The French text says 'for the souls of all Christians'.
[24] The French text lays down 'une lieue' = a league.

18. Item, it is agreed that the sovereign of the order, immediately after the death of one of the companions has been made known to him, shall see to it that 1,000 masses are celebrated for the soul of him who has died, and each foreign king shall have 800 masses celebrated for the soul of him who has died, the prince of Wales 700, each duke 600, each earl 300, each baron[25] 200 and each knight bachelor 100 masses.[26] And if the sovereign of the order or any other shall not have had this done within the quarter of the year after he has been notified of the death, he shall be obliged to double the number of masses in total of those to which his status or rank obliged him from the beginning, and if he be in arrears by half a year, then he must double them again in the same manner, and thus from time to time until the end of the year, and then he shall redouble the years in the same manner.

19. Item, it is agreed that as often as one of the companions of the order shall depart this life, the sovereign of the order or his deputy, having assured himself that the report be trustworthy, shall have all the companions who are within his kingdom of England and who are able to get there summoned by letter that they should meet together to elect a new companion, within six weeks after the notification of the death, in a convenient place which the sovereign shall designate for this purpose. When all are thus met together, or six of them at least besides the sovereign or his deputy, each one who shall be present at the election shall nominate nine qualified persons, whom he shall believe to be free from all ignominy or shame, who shall be subjects of the sovereign of the order or others, foreigners not subject to him but who yet shall not favour or uphold any party opposed to the said sovereign, that is to say three earls or those of higher rank, three barons and three knights bachelor, and these nominations shall be written down by the chief prelate of the order, that is to say the bishop of Winchester whoever he be at the time, and in his absence the dean of the college, or the registrar, and in their absence the oldest resident of the aforesaid college, and these nominations having been made by all the companions or at least six of them as said above, they shall be shown by him who has written them down to the sovereign of the order or his deputy, who shall choose from those

---

[25] The French gives a number of 200 for bannerets rather than barons.
[26] The text Ashmole was having copied had two interpolated additions, one for a marquess (450 masses) and one for a viscount (250 masses). These additions date from 1446.

nominated in this manner and shall admit the one who has obtained the greatest number of votes and who shall seem to him most fit to the honour of the order and the usefulness of the kingdom and of the king.[27] And in the event that any of the companions shall not come to the election in the following manner, he shall be punished only if he was not prevented by just cause. But if he adduce just and demonstrable cause for his absence, this must be approved by the sovereign or his deputy. But if the cause of his absence shall perchance be found insufficiently justified, and having been summoned he does not come to the election as is stated above, it is agreed that he shall pay one mark as a penalty to the warden and college, and, when he is next in a chapter meeting, he shall sit in front of the sovereign or his deputy and of the whole company, in the middle of the chapter house and on the ground, until he be reinstated by the sovereign or his deputy.

20. Item, it is agreed that in the event that one of the knights of the said Company of the Garter shall die, and another be elected in his place, as soon after the election as he is elected he shall have the garter as a sign that he is one of the companions of the Garter, and he shall have the mantle as his livery of the order at the time of his induction into his stall and not before. And in the event that he die before he has been installed, he shall not be named as one of the founders since he has not had full possession of his status, but he shall have half the number of the aforesaid masses since he had the livery of the Garter and withal nothing more. And if one thus elected shall not come to the said place with all proper speed after he has received the garter, so that he may be installed, and certainly within the year after his election if he be living within the kingdom of England, and have no excuse acceptable to the sovereign or his deputy and the Company of the Garter, then his election shall be straightway declared invalid and void, and then the sovereign of the order or his deputy shall together with the company proceed to a new election. And neither the sword nor the helmet of any elected companion shall be affixed above his stall until he come to the castle, but shall be placed outside and in front of his stall, this being so that if such an elected companion do not come to the castle, as it is said above, his sword and his helmet shall not be taken down from above in unseemly fashion but shall be removed in a manner befitting unim-

---

[27] The French text says 'the most profitable (or useful) to the crown and the kingdom'.

paired knightly honour, and shall be taken out of the choir in courtly
and honest fashion and shall remain from henceforward at the communal service and use of the aforesaid college.

21. Item, it is agreed that all foreigners who shall be elected to the
company of the said Order of the Garter shall be notified of their election by the sovereign of the order, and the garter and mantle and the
statutes of the order under the common seal shall be sent to them with
all proper speed but at the expense of the sovereign of the order. And all
foreigners shall be notified within four months following the time of
their election, in order that they may be able to consider from the contents of the statutes whether they wish to accept such an election. And
also that all foreigners elected thus, of whatever rank or dignity they
may be, within the space of eight months after they have been notified
of their election by the sovereign or his deputy, and after reception of
the garter, shall send a procurator who shall adequately be seen to be
sufficient in status to the elected man. With the proviso, however, that
such a procurator who is to be installed in his place shall be a knight
free from all opprobrium, who at the time of his arrival for this purpose
shall bring with him from him who has sent him a mantle of the order
of blue silk, and also a sword and his helmet[28] which are to remain in the
College itself.[29] That this mantle shall be laid over the right arm of such
a procurator by the sovereign of the order or his deputy at the time of
his aforesaid installation, and he shall keep it there over his said right
arm during the canonical hours next following the installation which he
shall take in the name of his aforesaid lord or master. But the said procurator once installed shall not wear such a mantle afterwards, nor shall
he enter the chapter meeting nor have any voice there by virtue of any
powers that may have been attributed to him. And it is to be known that
this favour of installation by proxy shall only be accorded to foreigners
who for this reason are unable to come in person, so that they may participate in the masses and devout prayers of the order, of half of which
they would be deprived if they were not installed before they died.

[28] The French text of Arundel 48 adds here the crest as well: 'son heaulme, son tymbre et
son espee', which is interesting as the Latin text gives only the helmet and sword here, and
both texts give only these for English-born companions, whereas here the crest is added for
foreigners (stranger knights).
[29] The French text says they are to remain there 'pour tousjours' = for ever.

22. Item, it is agreed that if any earl, baron[30] or knight bachelor of the said order shall die, he who shall succeed in his place, whether he be an earl, a baron or a knight bachelor, shall hold the same stall as his predecessor, whatever his rank may be. Nor shall any to be elected change this succession except the prince of Wales, who shall always hold the stall opposite to that of the sovereign after he has been elected. Thus it may happen that an earl can occupy the stall of a knight, and vice versa. And this is ordained so that it shall be known who were the first founders of the order.

23. Item, it is agreed that each companion of the order at the time of his first entry, shall give a fixed sum of money according to the eminence of his rank, for the support of the canons and the poor veteran knights living there and also for the increase of alms perpetually ordained there: that is to say the sovereign of the order 40 marks, a foreign king 20 pounds, the prince of Wales 20 marks, each duke 10 pounds, each earl 10 marks, each baron[31] 100 shillings and each knight bachelor 5 marks. And these pious gifts are thus established in order that each who enters this knightly order shall more worthily obtain the name, title and privilege of being one of the founders.[32] For it is judged worthy and suitable that he who is added to the number of the founders shall give generously for the sake of this benefit or name.[33] And until such sums have been paid in this manner in correct proportion as devised here at the time of his first entry, neither the sword nor the helmet of such an entrant shall be affixed above his stall. And it is to be known that the sovereign of the order shall be liable to pay the expenses of the entry of any foreigners who shall be elected, at the time of the installation of their procurators.

24. Item, it is agreed that whenever one of the first founders of this company or order shall die, an escutcheon of metal of his arms, and his helmet, shall be affixed to the back of his stall. And the other founders who succeed later shall have their escutcheons and helmets placed in similar fashion but somewhat below those of the first founders. And

[30] Here and below the French text refers to a banneret, rather than a baron.
[31] Here again the French text gives 'banneret'.
[32] The French text adds here 'of this same order'.
[33] This sentence: 'For it is judged ... or name', does not appear at all in the French version.

their escutcheons and helmets shall not be of such great value[34] as those of the first founders.

25. Item, that each upon entering shall promise and swear either in person or through a suitable and sufficient procurator to be installed in his name, that he will well and faithfully observe the statutes of the order to the utmost of his ability. And it is to be observed that no one shall receive installation by procurator except only foreigners who for that reason are not conveniently able to attend in person.

26. Item, it is agreed that in the event that the sovereign of the order shall be outside his kingdom of England at the time of the installation of one of the companions of the Garter, or if perchance he is not able to perform in person those duties which pertain to him by virtue of his office, he may entrust his powers and full capacities in this matter to one of the companions of the same order to carry out those appropriate duties which should pertain to his own office were he present.[35]

27. Item, it is agreed that a common seal shall be made, which shall be in the custody of him whom the sovereign of the order shall wish to appoint to this duty.

28. Item, that each of the companions of the aforesaid order shall from henceforth have a copy of the statutes of the order under the aforesaid common seal, and the original copy of the statutes shall be sealed by the same seal and shall remain in perpetuity within the treasury of the said college,[36] and that after the death of each companion of the aforesaid order, his executors shall be obliged to return those same statutes to the college, and to hand them over to the warden of the college.

29. Item, it is agreed that none of the knights of the Order of St George and of the Company of the Garter shall leave the kingdom of England without the knowledge and permission of the said sovereign. And it is therefore agreed that if some knightly expedition arise, or anything else which may be perceived to result in knightly honour, the sovereign of the order shall be obliged to prefer by his grace the companions of the order to all others in such knightly actions.

---

[34] The French text says that they shall not be as big as those of the first founders. Neither injunction has been followed in practice.
[35] The French text says that this shall be done 'in his [the sovereign's] name'.
[36] What follows here: 'and that after ... college', is, in the French text, allocated to a separate article.

30. Item, that no companion of the order shall lift arms against another companion unless it be in the war of his liege lord or in his own just cause. And if it should happen that one of the companions of the order be retained by a certain lord, or shall uphold the party and cause of a certain lord, and that later an adverse party should wish to retain any other companion of the order to defend its opposing cause, then no such companion secondarily requested shall consent to this, but shall be obliged to excuse himself on the grounds that his companion has been previously retained or armed by the opposing party. And on this account each companion of the order, when he is retained by anyone, shall be obliged to make an exception and to stipulate that he shall be entirely and with full quittance excused from all service in advancing or waging a war if it shall be that one of his companions of the Company of the Garter has been previously retained by the opposing side and armed in that cause. And if he who is secondarily retained has not known that one of his companions of the Garter had been previously retained by or had taken up arms for the opposing party, then as soon as this shall come to his notice he shall be obliged to relinquish completely all such service and totally to excuse himself.

31. Item, all licences to fellow-knights of the said company granting leave to travel around to those who wish to gain honour through the exercise of knightly arts, and also all other written documents whether they be letters of certification or letters of instruction which shall be seen to concern the order, must be issued[37] through the sovereign of the order under the common seal, which shall remain in the custody of one of the companions of the order according to the wishes of the aforesaid sovereign. And if he who has custody of the seal shall for reasonable cause move out of the sovereign's presence, he shall hand over that same seal into the custody of another companion of the same order who is present with the sovereign and whom that same sovereign shall designate to have custody of that same seal; thus that the common seal shall never be removed from the presence of the sovereign while that same sovereign be within his kingdom of England. And in similar fashion, in the absence of the sovereign of the order, his deputy shall see to it that this be done with the aforesaid seal.

---

[37] The French text states that this is 'doresenavant' = from henceforth.

32. Item, it is agreed that if any (other)[38] knight of the said company or order, moved by a spirit of devotion, shall desire to make his residence permanently in the said castle of Windsor, he shall be required to provide for the necessities of his life and of his dwelling from his own private means.

[33. Item,[39] that if any other knight who is not one of the said company shall, by devotion, wish to live there, then his living arrangements shall be made acccording to the agreement of the sovereign and the company.]

34. Item, it is agreed that in the event that any knight who is not one of the said Company of the Garter, or any other person,[40] shall wish to donate in any year ten pounds[41] or more to the said college, in order to participate in the support of the prayers to be said there, then the name of such a donor shall be recorded in the Calendar of Benefactors, so that the canons and veteran knights shall be able to pray for him in perpetuity.

35. Item, it is agreed that if any of the canons shall die, and the sovereign of the order shall be outside his kingdom of England, then the warden or dean of the college, whoever he shall be at the time, shall send letters accordingly to the sovereign of the order, so that the sovereign shall be able to present whom he wishes to enter that canonry.

36. Item, a registrar[42] shall be appointed by the sovereign and the company of the order, who shall be more learned than the others of the college, and he must be present at each chapter meeting that is held of the order, for the registration and enactment of each and every election and the names of those elected, and the punishments imposed and the reasons for punishments that pertain to the said order,[43] and this from chapter to chapter annually. And the said registrar shall be sworn upon

---

[38] The word 'alius' = 'other' is a scribal error in this text, caused by the similarity in wording of the next statute, which the scribe has omitted, again no doubt by eyeslip caused by the similarities of wording.

[39] Ashmole has annotated the text here to say 'The 33. Art. of E3 & H5 statts is here omitted.' I give the text above as translated from the French of Arundel 48.

[40] The French text gives 'Item, it is agreed that if any knight or any other person shall wish . . .'.

[41] The French text gives no monetary value, just 'any lands or rents'.

[42] By tradition in the order he has always been called 'Register'.

[43] The French text has additionally here that he must record the reconciliations of those punished, and all other acts and the reasons for them that appertain to the said order.

his receiving office that he shall faithfully keep the register, and that at the beginning of each chapter meeting held on St George's Eve each year, all matters registered the previous year shall there be publicly read out in the presence of the sovereign and the company of the order, so that if anything be badly described and worthy of correction, it may be amended in due form.

Abbreviations

Age of Edward III	*The Age of Edward III*, ed. J. S. Bothwell (Woodbridge, 2001)
Avesbury	*Chronicon Roberti de Avesbury*, in *Chronica Adae Murimuth et Roberti de Avesbury*, ed. E. M. Thompson, RS 93 (London, 1889)
Baker, *Chronicon*	*Chronicon Geoffrey le Baker de Swynebroke*, ed. Edward Maunde Thompson (Oxford, 1889)
BL	British Library
BN	Bibliothèque Nationale
CCR	*Calendar of Close Rolls* (London, 1900–63)
CPR	*Calendar of Patent Rolls* (London, 1891–1916)
EETS	Early English Text Society
EHR	*English Historical Review*
Froissart, *Chroniques*, Amiens version	Jean Froissart, *Chroniques Livre I: Le Manuscrit d'Amiens*, ed. George T. Diller, 5 vols. (Geneva, 1991–8)
Froissart, *Chroniques*, Besançon version	Jean Froissart, *Chroniques Livre III: Le Manuscrit Saint-Vincent de Besançon*, ed. Peter F. Ainsworth, 1 vol. to date (Geneva, 2007–)
Froissart, *Chroniques*, Rome version	Jean Froissart, *Chroniques: début du premier livre. Édition du manuscrit de Rome Reg. lat. 869*, ed. George T. Diller (Geneva, 1972)
Froissart, *Chroniques*, SHF	Jean Froissart, *Chroniques*, ed. Simeon Luce *et al.*, 13 vols. (in progress), SHF (Paris, 1869–)
Froissart, *Chroniques*, ed. Lettenhove	*Œuvres de Froissart: Chroniques*, ed. Kervyn de Lettenhove, 26 vols. (Paris, 1867–77)
Henxteworth	London, Duchy of Cornwall Office, Daybook of John Henxteworth
Historia Roffensis	(*Rochester History*) BL MS Cotton Faustina B.V
History of the King's Works	R. A. Brown, H. M. Colvin and A. J. Taylor, *The History of the King's Works: The Middle Ages*, 2 vols. (London, 1963)

Livre Charny	Michael Taylor (ed.), 'A Critical Edition of Geoffroy de Charny's *Livre Charny* and the *Demandes pour la Joute, les Tournois et la Guerre*', Ph.D. thesis, University of North Carolina at Chapel Hill, 1977
MED	*Middle English Dictionary*: http://quod.lib.umich.edu/m/med/lookup.html
Murimuth	*Chronicon Adae Murimuth*, in *Chronica Adae Murimuth et Roberti de Avesbury*, ed. E. M. Thompson, RS 93 (London, 1889)
ODNB	*Oxford Dictionary of National Biography*: www.oxforddnb.com
PROME	*The Parliament Rolls of Medieval England 1275–1504*, general editor Chris Given-Wilson (Woodbridge, 2005)
RBP	*Register of Edward the Black Prince*, 4 vols. (London, 1930–33)
RS	Rolls Series, London
SHF	Société de l'Histoire de France
TNA	The National Archives
TRHS	*Transactions of the Royal Historical Society*

Bibliography

PRIMARY SOURCES

A. Manuscripts

Cambridge, Corpus Christi College, MS 170
Eton College, MS 213
Heidelberg, Universitätsbibliothek, MS Cod. Pal. Germ. 848
London, British Library:

Add. MS 38823	MS Cotton Galba E.III
Add. MS 42130	MS Cotton Galba E.XIV
Add. MS 46350	MS Cotton Nero C.VIII
Add. MS 60584	MS Cotton Nero D.VII
MS Cotton Caligula D.III, item 76	MS Harleian 4304
MS Cotton Cleopatra D.VII	MS Harleian 5001
MS Cotton Faustina B.V	Wolley Charter I.16

London, Duchy of Cornwall Office, Daybook of John Henxteworth
London, The National Archives:

C 47/6/1	E 101/361/3
C 61/83	E 101/382/9
C 61/84	E 101/382/17
C 61/85	E 101/383/8
C 76/45	E 101/384/6
C 241/147	E 101/384/14
DL 10/250	E 101/385/4
DL 25/983	E 101/385/7
DL 40/1/11	E 101/386/2
DL 41/335	E 101/386/9
E 36/144	E 101/386/15
E 36/204	E 101/386/16
E 36/205	E 101/386/18
E 36/278	E 101/387/14
E 43/20	E 101/387/25

E 101/388/8
E 101/388/11
E 101/389/8
E 101/389/12
E 101/389/14
E 101/390/2
E 101/390/11
E 101/391/1
E 101/391/5
E 101/391/15
E 101/392/4
E 101/392/20
E 101/393/4
E 101/393/11
E 101/393/15

E 101/394/16
E 101/397/20
E 101/398/22
E 101/571/16
E 361/2
E 361/3
E 361/4
E 372/207
E 379/198
E 403/246
E 403/340
E 403/388
E 404/7/43
E 404/17/357–9
SC8/63/3125

London, Society of Antiquaries:
MS 208
MS 541
MS 545
Manchester, John Rylands Library, MSS 234 and 235
Oxford, Bodleian Library:
MS Ashmole 1128
MS Douce 231
MS Lat. Hist. a.2
Oxford, Corpus Christi College, MS 78
Pamplona, Archivio General de Navarra, Register 120, counter-roll for January 1365
Paris, Bibliothèque Nationale:
MS français 693 (St Omer chronicle)
MS français 5001
Windsor, St George's Chapel, Precentor's Rolls, XV.56.16, 22 and 23

B. Printed Sources

Accounts of the English Crown with Italian Merchant Societies, 1272–1345, ed. Adrian R. Bell, Chris Brooks and Tony K. Moore, List and Index Society 331 (London, 2009).

Actes et documents anciens intéressant la Belgique, ed. Henri Laurent (Brussels, 1933).

The Acts of War of Edward III (Acta Bellicosa), tr. in *Life and Campaigns of the Black Prince*, 26–40; the original is edited, with some omissions, in J. Moisant, *Le Prince Noir en Aquitaine, 1355–1356 – 1362–1370* (Paris, 1894), 157–74.

Alfonso X 'El Sabio', *Las siete partidas*, tr. S. Parsons Scott, ed. R. I. Burns, SJ, 5 vols. (Philadelphia, 2001).

[*Amadis de Gaule*] Nicolas de Herberay seigneur des Essars, *Le quatriesme livre de Amadis de Gaule* (Paris, 1555).

[Ambroise] *The History of the Holy War: Ambroise's Estoire de la Guerre Sainte*, ed. Marianne Ailes and Malcolm Barber, 2 vols. (Woodbridge, 2003).

Anglo-Scottish Relations 1174–1328, ed. and tr. E. L. G. Stones, Oxford Medieval Texts (Oxford, 1965).

Annales Gandenses, ed. and tr. Hilda Johnstone (Oxford, 1985).

Annales Paulini, in *Chronicles of the Reigns of Edward I and Edward II*, ed. William Stubbs, 2 vols., RS 76 (London, 1882).

The Anonimalle Chronicle 1333–1381, ed. V. H. Galbraith (Manchester, 1927).

Anonimo romano, *Cronica*, ed. Giuseppe Porta (Milan, 1979; abbreviated edn., Milan, 1981).

[Anonymus Cantuariensis] *Chronicon Anonymi Cantuariensis = The Chronicle of Anonymous of Canterbury, 1346–1365*, ed. and tr. Charity Scott-Stokes and Chris Given-Wilson, Oxford Medieval Texts (Oxford, 2008).

The Antient Kalendars and Inventories of the Treasury of His Majesty's Exchequer, ed. Sir Francis Palgrave, 3 vols. (London, 1836).

Archivo General de Navarra, Catálogo de la seccion de Comptos: Documentos, ed. José Rámon Castro (Pamplona, 1952–74).

Arnould, E. J. F., *Étude sur le Livre des saintes médécines du duc Henri de Lancastre* (Paris, 1948).

[Avesbury] *Chronicon Roberti de Avesbury*, in *Chronica Adae Murimuth et Roberti de Avesbury*, ed. E. M. Thompson, RS 93 (London, 1889).

[Baker, Geoffrey] *The chronicle of Geoffrey Le Baker*, tr. David Preest, intro. and notes by Richard Barber (Woodbridge, 2012).

Barbour, John, *The Bruce*, ed. and tr. A. A. M. Duncan (Edinburgh, 1997).

'Benedict of Peterborough', *Gesta Regis Henrici Secundi Benedicti Abbas*, ed. W. Stubbs, 2 vols., RS 49 (London, 1867).

Beneš z Weitmile, *Chronicon*, in *Fontes Rerum Bohemicarum*, vol. iv, ed. Josef Emler (Prague, 1884).

Boehmer, J. F., *Acta imperii selecta* (Innsbruck, 1870).

[Boucicaut] *Le Livre de fais du bon messire Jehan le Maingre, dit Bouciquaut*, ed. Denis Lalande (Geneva, 1985).

The Brut or The Chronicles of England, ed. Friedrich W. D. Brie, 2 vols., EETS OS 131, 136 (London, 1906–8).

Calendar of Charter Rolls, 1341–1417 (London, 1916).

Calendar of Inquisitions Miscellaneous (London, 1916).

Calendar of Liberate Rolls, 1240–1245 (London, 1931).

Calendar of Wills proved and enrolled in the court of Husting, London A.D. 1258–A.D.1688, ed. Reginald R. Sharpe, 3 vols. (London, 1890).

Cambridge Gild Records, ed. Mary Bateson, Cambridge Antiquarian Society, octavo series XXXIX (Cambridge, 1903).

Cartulaire des Comtes de Hainaut de l'avènement de Guillaume II à la mort de Jacqueline de Bavière, ed. Léopold Devillers, vol. i (Brussels, 1881).

Chandos Herald, *La Vie du Prince Noir*, ed. D. Tyson, Beihefte zur Zeitschrift für Romanische Philologie 147 (Tübingen, 1975).

Charny, Geoffroy de, *The* Book of Chivalry *of Geoffroi de Charny: Text, Context, and Translation*, ed. Richard W. Kaeuper and Elspeth Kennedy (Philadelphia, 1996).

Chevalier, Ulysse, *Choix de documents inédits sur le Dauphiné* (Lyons, 1874).

Chronica Monasterii de Melsa, ed. E. A. Bond, 3 vols., RS (London, 1868).

The Chronicle of Glastonbury: An Edition, Translation and Study of John of Glastonbury's Cronica sive Antiquitates Glastoniensis Ecclesie, ed. James Carley, tr. David Townsend (Woodbridge, 1985).

[*Chronicle of Lanercost*] *Chronicon de Lanercost: 1201–1346. E codice Cottoniano nunc primum typis mandate*, ed. Joseph Stevenson, Maitland Club (Edinburgh, 1839).

Chronicles of London, ed. C. L. Kingsford (Oxford, 1905).

Chronicon Adae Murimuth, in *Chronica Adae Murimuth et Roberti de Avesbury*, ed. E. M. Thompson, RS 93 (London, 1889).

Chronique artésienne (1295–1304) et chronique tournaisienne, ed. F. Funck-Brentano (Paris, 1899).

Chronique des quatre premiers Valois, ed. Simeon Luce, SHF (Paris, 1862).

Chronique des règnes de Jean II et Charles V, ed. R. Delachenal, 4 vols., SHF (Paris, 1910–20).

Chronique du religieux de Saint-Denis, ed. L. Bellaguet, 6 vols. (Paris, 1839–52).

Chronique latine de Guillaume de Nangis de 1113 à 1300, avec les continuations de 1300 à 1368, ed. H. Géraud, 2 vols., SHF (Paris, 1843).

Chronique normande du XIVᵉ siècle, ed. Auguste et Émile Molinier, SHF (Paris, 1882).

Chronique parisienne anonyme de 1316 à 1339, ed. A. Hellot, Mémoires de la Société de l'Histoire de Paris et de l'Île-de-France XI (1884).

Chroniques de Saint-Martial de Limoges, ed. H. Duplès-Agier, SHF (Paris, 1874).

Chronographia Regum Francorum, ed. H. Moranvillé, 3 vols., SHF (Paris, 1891–7).

Clement VI, *Lettres closes, patentes et curiales*, ed. Eugène Déprez, 2 vols., Bibliothèque des Écoles Françaises d'Athènes et Rome, 3rd ser. III (Paris, 1901).

Cochon, Pierre, *Chronique normande*, ed. Ch. de Robillard de Beaurepaire, Société de l'Histoire de Normandie (Rouen, 1870).

Le compte des recettes et dépenses du roi de Navarre en France et en Normandie de 1367 à 1370, ed. E. Izarn (Paris, 1885).

Crónicas de los reyes de Castilla, ed. Cayetano Rosell, 3 vols., Biblioteca de autores españoles 66, 68, 70 (Madrid, 1875–8).

Croniques de London depuis l'an 44 Hen. III jusqu'à l'an 17 Edw. III, ed. George J. Aungier, Camden Society XXVIII (London, 1844).

Delpit, Jules, *Collection générale des documents français qui se trouvent en Angleterre* (Paris, 1874).

Documents des archives de la chambre des comptes de Navarre (1196–1384), ed. Jean-Auguste Brutails, Bibliothèque de l'École des Hautes Études 84 (Paris, 1890).

Dugdale, William, *Monasticon anglicanum*, ed. John Caley, Henry Ellis and the Revd Bulkeley Bandinel, 6 vols. in 8 pts. (London, 1846).

Eulogium historiarum sive temporis, ed. F. S. Haydon, 3 vols., RS 9 (London, 1863).

Foedera, Conventiones, Literare et Cujuscunque Genera Acta Publica, ed. T. Rymer, 4 vols. in 7 parts (London, 1816–30).

Froissart, Jean, *Chroniques Livre I: Le Manuscrit d'Amiens*, ed. George T. Diller, 5 vols. (Geneva, 1991–8).

—— *Chroniques Livre III: Le Manuscrit Saint-Vincent de Besançon*, ed. Peter F. Ainsworth (Geneva, 2007–).

—— *Chroniques: début du premier livre. Édition du manuscrit de Rome Reg. lat. 869*, ed. George T. Diller (Geneva, 1972).

—— *Chroniques*, ed. Simeon Luce *et al.*, 13 vols. (in progress), SHF (Paris, 1869–).

—— *Œuvres de Froissart: Chroniques*, ed. Kervyn de Lettenhove, 26 vols. (Paris, 1867–77).

—— *Chronicles of England, France, Spain, and the adjoining countries*, tr. Thomas Johnes, 2 vols. (London, 1848).

'La Geste des Nobles François', ed. in [Denis-François Secousse,] *Recueil de pieces servant de preuves aux Mémoires sur les Troubles excites en France par Charles II, dit le mauvais, roi de Navarre et comte d'Evreux* (Paris, 1775), ii. 631–55.

Les Grandes chroniques de France, ed. J. Viard, 10 vols., SHF (Paris, 1920–53).

Les Grandes chroniques de France: Chronique des règnes de Jean II et de Charles V, ed. R. Delachenal, 10 vols., SHF (Paris, 1919).

Gray, Sir Thomas, *Scalacronica 1272–1363*, ed. and tr. Andy King, Publications of the Surtees Society ccix (Woodbridge, 2005).

[Guesclin] *Letters, Orders and Musters of Bertrand du Guesclin, 1357–1380*, ed. Michael Jones (Woodbridge, 2004).

Guiart, Guillaume, 'Branche des royaus lignages', in Natalis (Noël) de Wailly and Léopold Delisle (eds.), *Recueil des historiens des Gaules et de la France XXII* (Paris, 1865).

Hamaker, H. G. (ed.), *De rekeningen der grafelijkheid van Holland onder het Henegouwsche Huis*, Werken uitgegeven door het Historisch Genootschap gevestigd te Utrecht, new series xxi, xxiv, xxvi (1875, 1876, 1878).

Hemingburgh, Walter of, *De Gestis Regum Angliae*, ed. Hans Claude Hamilton, 2 vols., English Historical Society (London, 1848).

Hemricourt, Jacques d', *Le Miroir des Nobles de Hesbaye* (Brussels, 1673).

[Hemricourt] *Œuvres de Jacques de Hemricourt*, ed. C. de Borman, Alphonse Bayot and Edouard Poncelet (Brussels, 1931).

Histoire de Guillaume le Maréchal, ed. A. J. Holden and D. Crouch, tr. S. Gregory, Anglo-Norman Text Society Occasional Publications 4–6 (London, 2006–7).

Historiae Anglicanae Scriptores Decem, ed. Roger Twysden (London, 1652).

Hoccleve, Thomas, *The Minor Poems*, ed. Frederick J. Furnivall and I. Gollancz, rev. Jerome Mitchell and A. I. Doyle, EETS Extra Series 61 (London, 1970).

Hodenc, Raoul de, *Le roman des eles*, with the anonymous *Ordene de chevalerie*, ed. and tr. Keith Busby (Amsterdam, 1983).

Istoire et croniques de Flandre, d'après les textes de divers manuscrits, ed. Kervyn de Lettenhove, 2 vols. (Brussels, 1879–80).

John of Arderne, *Treatises of Fistula in Ano*, ed. D'Arcy Power, EETS OS 139 (London, 1910).

John of Gaunt's Register, ed. Sydney Armitage-Smith, Camden Society 3rd series 20, 21 (London, 1911).

The Kirkstall Abbey Chronicles, ed. John Taylor, Publications of the Thoresby Society XLII (Leeds, 1952).

[Knighton, Henry] *Chronicon Henrici Knighton vel Cnitthon, Monachi Leycestrensis*, ed. J. R. Lumby, 2 vols., RS (London, 1889–95).

—— *Knighton's Chronicle*, ed. and tr. G. H. Martin, Oxford Medieval Texts (Oxford, 1995).

Laborde, Leon de, *Notice des émaux, bijoux et objets divers, exposés dans les galleries du Musée du Louvre*, vol. ii (Paris, 1853).

Lancelot-Grail: The Old French Arthurian Vulgate and post-Vulgate in translation, general editor Norris J. Lacy, 10 vols. (Woodbridge and Rochester, NY, 2010); originally 5 vols. (New York, 1993–6). References are by part, chapter and section, and are identical in both editions.

The Lay of Mantel, ed. and tr. Glyn Burgess, and Leslie C. Brook, Arthurian Archives: French Arthurian Literature V (Woodbridge, 2013).

Le Bel, Jean, *Chronique de Jean le Bel*, ed. J. Viard and E. Déprez, 2 vols., SHF (Paris, 1904–5, repr. Geneva, 1977); numbers in square brackets refer to the English version, *Jean le Bel's True Chronicle*, tr. Nigel Bryant (Woodbridge, 2011).

The Life and Campaigns of the Black Prince, ed. and tr. Richard Barber (Woodbridge, 1986).

Le Livre de seyntz medicines: The Unpublished Devotional Treatise of Henry of Lancaster. Text, ed. E. T. Arnould, Anglo-Norman Texts 2 (Oxford, 1940).

[Li Muisit] *Chronique et annales de Gilles Le Muisis, Abbé de Saint-Martin de Tournai (1272–1352)*, ed. H. Lemaître, SHF (Paris, 1906).

Llull, Ramon, *Llibre de L'Orde de Cavalleria*, ed. Marina Gusta (Barcelona, 1980).

L[ong], C. E., 'Roll of the Arms of the Knights at the Tournament at Dunstable in 7 Edw. III', *Collectanea Topographica et Genealogica*, 4 (1837), 389–95.

López de Ayala, Pero, *Corónica del rey don Pedro*, ed. Constance L. and Heanon M. Wilkins (Madison, 1985).

[Malory, Sir Thomas] *The Works of Sir Thomas Malory*, ed. P. J. C. Field (Woodbridge, 2013).

Martin, Kurt (ed.), *Minnesänger: vierundzwanzig farbige Wiedergaben aus der Manessischen Liederhandschrift*, vol. 1 (Baden-Baden, 1966).

Martorell, Joanot, and Joan de Galba, Martí, *Tirant lo Blanc*, tr. David H. Rosenthal (London, 1984).

[Mathias von Nuewenburg] *Die Chronik des Mathias von Neuenburg*, ed. A. Hofmeister, Monumenta Germaniae Historica, Scriptores Rerum Germanicum, n.s. 4 (Leipzig, 1924–37).

Milemete, Walter de, *De nobilitatibus, sapientiis, et prudentiis regum*, ed. M. R. James, Roxburghe Club (London, 1913).

[*Morte Arthure*] *The Death of Arthur*, tr. Simon Armitage (London, 2012).

[Murimuth] *Adami Murimuthensis Chronica Sui Temporis*, ed. Thomas Hog, English Historical Society 20 (London, 1846).

Paris, Jean de, *Memoriale historiarum*, in Natalis (Noël) and Daniel Guigniaut (eds.), *Recueil des historiens des Gaules et de la France* XXI (Paris, 1855).

The Parliament Rolls of Medieval England 1275–1504, general editor Chris Given-Wilson (Woodbridge, 2005).

Perceforest, parts I–V, ed. Gilles Roussineau, Textes littéraires français (Geneva, 1987–2012; the original vol. 1 by Jane Taylor is replaced by Roussineau's edition of 2007).

Perceforest: The Prehistory of King Arthur's Britain, tr. Nigel Bryant, Arthurian Studies LXXVII (Woodbridge, 2011).

Political Thought in Early Fourteenth Century England: Treatises by Walter of Milemete, William of Pagula, and William of Ockham, ed. and tr. Cary J. Nederman, Medieval and Renaissance Texts and Studies 250 (Tempe, Ariz., 2002).

Prince, A. E., 'A Letter of Edward the Black Prince describing the Battle of Najéra in 1367', *EHR* 41 (1926), 416–18.

Reading, John of, *Chronica Johannis de Reading et Anonymi Cantuariensis 1346–1367*, ed. James Tait (Manchester, 1914).

Récits d'un bourgeois de Valenciennes, ed. Kervyn de Lettenhove (Louvain, 1877).

Registrum Simonis de Sudbiria, Diocesis Londoniensis, ed. R. C. Fowler, 2 vols., Canterbury and York Society xxxiv, xxxviii (Oxford, 1927–38).

Report from the Lords Committee for All Matters Touching the Dignity of a Peer, 5 vols. (London, 1820–29).

Riley, H. T., *Memorials of London and London Life in the XIIIth, XIVth, and XVth Centuries* (London, 1868).

Le Roman en prose de Tristan, ed. E. Löseth, Bibliothèque de l'École Pratique des Hautes Études 82 (Paris, 1890, repr. Geneva, 1974).

The Romance of Alexander: A Collotype Facsimile of MS. Bodley 264, ed. M. R. James (Oxford, 1933).

The Rule of the Templars, ed. and tr. Julie Upton-Ward (Woodbridge, 1992).

Secretum Secretorum: Nine English Versions, ed. M. A. Manzalaoui, EETS OS 276 (Oxford, 1977).

Sir Gawain and the Green Knight, tr. Brian Stone (Harmondsworth, 1974).

Smit, H. J. (ed.), *De rekeningen der graven en gravinnen uit het Henegouwsche Huis*, Werken uitgegeven door het Historisch Genootschap gevestigd te Utrecht, 3rd series, xlvi, liv, lxix (1924–39).

Storie pistoresi, ed. Silvio Ardastro Barbi, in L. A. Muratori (ed.), *Rerum Italicarum Scriptores*, XI, pt. v (Castello, 1927).

Taylor, Michael (ed.), 'A Critical Edition of Geoffroy de Charny's *Livre Charny* and the *Demandes pour la Joute, les Tournois et la Guerre*', Ph.D. thesis, University of North Carolina at Chapel Hill, 1977.

Vegetius, *Epitoma rei militaris*, ed. M. D. Reeve (Oxford, 2004).

[Venette] *The Chronicle of Jean de Venette*, tr. Jean Birdsall, ed. Richard A. Newhall, Records of Civilization, Sources and Studies L (New York, 1953).

Villani, Giovanni, *Nuova cronica*, ed. Giuseppe Porta, 3 vols. (Parma, 1990–91).

Villani, Matteo, *Cronica*, ed. Giuseppe Porta, 2 vols. (Parma, 1995).

Vita Edwardi Secundi, in *Chronicles of the Reigns of Edward I and Edward II*, ed. William Stubbs, 2 vols., RS 76 (London, 1882).

Voragine, Jacopo de, *Legenda Aurea*, ed. T. Graesse (Dresden and Leipzig, 1846).

The Vows of the Heron: A Middle French Vowing Poem, ed. J. L. Grigsby and Norris J. Lacy (New York, 1992).

[Walsingham, Thomas] *Chronicon Angliae ad anno domini 1328 usque ad annum 1388, auctore monacho quodam Sancti Albani*, ed. Edward Maunde Thompson, RS (London, 1874).

—— *Historia Anglicana*, ed. H. T. Riley, 2 vols., RS 28.i (London, 1863–4).

Walter of Peterborough, 'Prince Edward's Expedition into Spain, and the battle of Najara', in T. Wright (ed.), *Political Poems and Songs*, 2 vols., RS 14 (London, 1859–61), i.97–122.

Wynnere and Wastoure, ed. Stephanie Trigg, EETS OS 297 (Oxford, 1990).

SECONDARY SOURCES

Ainsworth, Peter, *Jean Froissart and the Fabric of History: Truth, Myth, and Fiction in the* Chroniques (Oxford, 1990).

Alexander, Jonathan, and Binski, Paul, *Age of Chivalry: Art in Plantagenet England 1200–1400* (London, 1987).

Anstis, John, *The Register of the most noble Order of the Garter*, 2 vols. (London, 1724).

Antiquarian Repertory, ed. F. Grose, 4 vols. (London, 1807).

Archer, R., 'The Estates and Finances of Margaret of Brotherton', *Historical Research*, 60 (1987), 267–78.

Ashmole, Elias, *The Institution, Laws & Ceremonies of the most noble Order of the Garter* (London, 1672).

Ayton, Andrew, 'Edward III and the English Aristocracy at the Beginning of the Hundred Years' War', in Matthew Strickland (ed.), *Armies, Chivalry and Warfare in Medieval Britain and France*, Harlaxton Medieval Studies VII (Stamford, 1998).

—— 'The English Army and the Normandy Campaign of 1346', in D. Bates and Anne Curry (eds.), *England and Normandy in the Middle Ages* (London, 1994).

—— *Knights and Warhorses: Military Service and the English Aristocracy under Edward III* (Woodbridge, 1994).

—— 'Knights, Esquires and Military Service: The Evidence of the Court of Chivalry', in Andrew Ayton and J. L. Price (eds.), *The Medieval Military Revolution* (London, 1995), 81–4.

—— 'Sir Thomas Ughtred and the Edwardian Military Revolution', in *Age of Edward III*, 107–33.

—— and Preston, Sir Philip, *The Battle of Crécy, 1346*, Warfare in History (Woodbridge, 2005).

Barber, Richard, 'Edward III's Arthurian Enthusiasms Revisited: Perceforest in the Context of Philippa of Hainault and the Round Table Feast of 1344', *Arthurian Literature*, 30, forthcoming.

—— *Edward, Prince of Wales and Aquitaine* (London and New York, 1978).

—— and Barker, Juliet, *Tournaments: Jousts, Chivalry and Pageants in the Middle Ages* (Woodbridge, 1989).

Barker, Juliet, *The Tournament in England, 1100–1400* (Woodbridge, 1986).

Barnes, Joshua, *The History of that Most Victorious Monarch Edward III* (London, 1688).

Barnie, John, *War in Medieval Society: Social Values and the Hundred Years War, 1337–99* (London, 1974).

Bautier, R.-H., Sornay, J., and Muret, F. (eds.), *Les Sources de l'histoire économique . . . des états de la maison de Bourgogne, i. Archives des principautés territoriale, ii. Les Principautés du nord* (Paris, 1984).

Begent, Peter J., and Chesshyre, Hubert, *The Most Noble Order of the Garter: 650 Years* (London, 1999).

Bell, Adrian R., 'Medieval Chroniclers as War Correspondents during the Hundred Years' War: The Earl of Arundel's Campaign of 1387', in Chris Given-Wilson (ed.), *Fourteenth Century England VI* (Woodbridge, 2010), 171–84.

—— *War and the Soldier in the Fourteenth Century* (Woodbridge, 2004).

Bellamy, J. G., 'The Coterel Gang: An Anatomy of a Band of Fourteenth-Century Criminals', *EHR* 79 (1964), 698–717.

Beltz, George Frederick, *Memorials of the Order of the Garter, from its foundation to the present time with Biographical Notices of the Knights in the reigns of Edward III. and Richard II.* (London, 1841).

Belvaletus, Mondonus, *Catechismus ordinis Equitum Perisc'lidis Anglicanae . . .* (Cologne, 1631).

Benedictow, Ole, *The Black Death, 1346–1353: The Complete History* (Woodbridge, 2004).

Bennett, Michael J., *Community, Class and Careerism: Cheshire and Lancashire Society in the Age of* Sir Gawain and the Green Knight (Cambridge, 1983).

Berard, Christopher, 'Edward III's Abandoned Order of the Round Table', *Arthurian Literature*, 29 (2012), 1–40.

Biddle, Martin, *King Arthur's Round Table: An Archaeological Investigation* (Woodbridge, 2000).

Billot, Claudine, *Les Saintes Chapelles royales et princières* (Paris, 1998).

—— 'Les Saintes Chapelles (XIIIᵉ siècle-XVIᵉ siècle): Approche comparée de fondations dynastiques', *Revue de l'histoire de l'église en France*, 73 (1987), 229–48.

Binski, Paul, *Westminster Abbey and the Plantagenets: Kingship and the Representation of Power* (London, 1995).

Birch, Debra J., *Pilgrimage to Rome in the Middle Ages* (Woodbridge, 1998).

Blatchly, John, and MacCulloch, Diarmaid, *Miracles in Lady Lane: The Ipswich Shrine at the Westgate* (Ipswich, 2013).

Bliese, John R. E., 'Rhetoric and Morale: A Study of Battle Orations from the Central Middle Ages', *Journal of Medieval History*, 15 (1989), 201–20.

Blomefield, Francis, *An Essay towards a Topographical History of the County of Norfolk*, 6 vols. (London, 1808).

Bock, Friedrich, *Das deutsch–englische Bündnis von 1335–42* (Munich, 1956).

—— 'Some New Documents Illustrating the Early Years of the Hundred Years War (1353–1356)', *Bulletin of the John Rylands Library*, 15 (1931), 60–83.

Bock, Nicolas, 'L'Ordre du Saint-Esprit au Droit Désir. Enluminure, cérémonial et idéologie monarchique au XIVᵉ siècle', in Nicolas Bock, Peter Kurmann, Serena Romano and Jean-Michel Spieser (eds.), *Art, cérémonial et liturgie au moyen-âge* (Rome, 2002).

Bond, Maurice, *The Inventories of St George's Chapel, Windsor Castle 1384–1667* (Windsor, 1947).

Booth, P. H. W., 'Taxation and Public Order: Cheshire in 1353', *Northern History*, 12 (1967), 16–31.

Bothwell, J. S. (ed.). *The Age of Edward III* (Woodbridge, 2001).

—— *Edward III and the English Peerage, Royal Patronage, Social Mobility and Political Control in 14th-Century England* (Woodbridge, 2004).

—— 'Edward III, the English Peerage and the 1337 Earls', in *Age of Edward III*, 35–52.

Boulton, D'Arcy Jonathan Dacre, *The Knights of the Crown: The Monarchical Orders of Knighthood in Later Medieval Europe 1325–1520*, 2nd edn. (Woodbridge, 2000).

—— 'The Middle French Statutes of the Monarchical Order of the Ship (Naples, 1381); A Critical Edition, with Introduction and Notes', *Mediaeval Studies*, 47 (1985), 176–271.

Bowers, Roger, 'The Music and Musical Establishment of St George's Chapel', in Colin Richmond and Eileen Scarff (eds.), *St George's Chapel, Windsor, in the Later Middle Ages* (Windsor, 2001), 171–90.

Brindle, Steven, 'The First St George's Chapel', in Nigel Saul and Tim Tatton-Brown (eds.), *St George's Chapel Windsor: History and Heritage* (Wimborne Minster, 2010), 36–44.

Brooke, Christopher, 'Chaucer's Parson and Edmund Gonville: Contrasting Roles of Fourteenth Century Incumbents', in David M. Smith (ed.), *Studies in Clergy and Ministry in Medieval England*, Borthwick Studies in History 1 (York, 1991), 1–16.

—— *A History of Gonville and Caius College* (Woodbridge, 1985).

Broome, Dorothy M., 'The Ransom of John II King of France 1360–70', Camden 3rd series XXXVII, *Camden Miscellany*, 14 (1926).

Brown, Elizabeth A. R., 'Diplomacy, Adultery and Domestic Politics at the Court of Philip the Fair: Queen Isabelle's Mission to France in 1314', in J. S. Hamilton and Patricia J. Bradley (eds.), *Documenting the Past* (Woodbridge, 1989), 53–84.

—— 'The King's Conundrum: Endowing Queens and Loyal Servants, Ensuring Salvation, and Protecting the Patrimony in Fourteenth Century France', in J. A. Burrow and Ian P. Wei (eds.), *Medieval Futures* (Woodbridge, 2000), 115–66.

Brown, Michelle, *The Luttrell Psalter Commentary* (London, 2006; issued with facsimile of the manuscript).

Brown, R. A., Colvin, H. M., and Taylor, A. J., *The History of the King's Works: The Middle Ages*, 2 vols. (London, 1963).

Bryant, Nigel (tr. and ed.), *Chrétien de Troyes: Perceval: The Story of the Grail* (Woodbridge, 1982).

Bullock-Davies, Constance, *Register of Royal and Baronial Domestic Minstrels 1272–1327* (Woodbridge, 1986).

Burne, A. H., 'The Battle of Poitiers', *EHR* 53 (1938), 21–52.

—— 'Cannons at Crécy', *Royal Artillery Journal*, 77 (1939), 335–44.

—— *The Crecy War: A Military History of the Hundred Years War from 1337 to the Peace of Bretigny, 1360* (London, 1955).

Burrow, J. A., *Thomas Hoccleve*, Authors of the Middle Ages 4 (Aldershot, 1994).

Burtscher, Michael, *The Fitzalans: Earls of Arundel and Surrey, Lords of the Welsh Marches (1267–1415)* (Little Logaston, 2008).

—— 'The Missing Earl: Richard Fitzalan, Earl of Arundel and the Order of the Garter', *Coat of Arms*, 3rd series, 3/1 (2007), 93–101.

Butterfield, Ardis, *The Familiar Enemy: Chaucer, Language, and Nation in the Hundred Years War* (Oxford, 2009).

Camden, William, *Britannia*, tr. Philemon Holland (London, 1610).

Campanelli, Maurizio, 'A New Account of the Battle of Crécy from Fourteenth-Century Rome', forthcoming.

Capra, Pierre, 'Les Bases sociales du pouvoir anglo-gascon au milieu du xive siècle', *Le Moyen Âge*, 81 (1975), 273–99, 447–73.

—— 'Le Séjour du Prince Noir, Lieutenant du Roi, à l'archevêché de Bordeaux', *Revue historique de Bordeaux*, 7 (1958), 241–52.

Carey, Richard J. (ed.), *Jean de le Mote, Le Parfait du Paon*, University of North Carolina Studies in the Romance Languages and Literatures 118 (Chapel Hill, NC, 1972).

Carolus Barré, M. L., 'Benoit XII et la mission charitable de Bernard Carit', *Mélanges d'archéologie et d'histoire, École française de Rome*, 62 (1950), 165–232.

Carpentier, Élisabeth, 'L'Historiographie de la bataille de Poitiers au quatorzième siècle', *Revue historique*, 263 (1980), 21–58.

Carruthers, Leo, 'The Duke of Clarence and the Earls of March: Garter Knights and *Sir Gawain and the Green Knight*', *Medium Aevum*, 70 (2001), 66–79.

Cavanaugh, Susan, 'A Study of Books Privately Owned in England: 1300–1450', Ph.D. thesis, University of Pennsylvania, 1980.

Cazelles, R., *La Société politique et la crise de la royauté sous Philippe de Valois* (Paris, 1958).

—— *Société politique, noblesse et couronne sous Jean le Bon et Charles V* (Paris, 1982).

Channel Pilot, vol. 2, 11th edn. [Hydrographic Department, Admiralty] (London, 1952).

Chaplais, Pierre, 'Règlement des conflits internationaux franco-anglais au XIVe siècle (1293–1377)', *Le Moyen Âge*, 57 (1951), 269–302.

Chareyron, Nicole, *Jean le Bel: Le Maître de Froissart, grand imagier de la guerre de cent ans*, Bibliothèque du Moyen Âge 7 (Brussels, 1996).

Cheetham, Francis, *Alabaster Images of Medieval England* (Woodbridge, 2003).

—— *English Medieval Alabasters* (Oxford, 1984).

Chettle, H. F., 'The *Boni Homines* of Ashridge and Edington', *Downside Review*, 62 (1944), 40–55.

Christensen, Eric, *The Northern Crusades: The Baltic and the Catholic Frontier 1100–1525* (London, 1980).

Collins, Hugh E. L., *The Order of the Garter 1348–1461: Chivalry and Politics in Late Medieval England* (Oxford, 2000).

Colón, Germán, 'Premiers échos de l'Ordre de la Jarretière', *Zeitschrift für Romanische Philologie*, 81 (1965), 441–53.

The Complete Peerage, by G. E. C[okayne], ed. Vicary Gibbs, 12 vols. in 13 parts (London, 1910–59).

Conrad, Klaus, 'Der dritte Litauerzug König Johanns von Böhmen und der Rücktritt des Hochmeisters Ludolf König', in *Festschrift für Hermann Heimpel*, Veröffentlichungen des Max-Planck-Instituts für Geschichte 36 (Göttingen, 1971), ii.382–401.

Contamine, Philippe, 'Geoffroy de Charny (début du XIVᵉ siècle-1356)', in *Histoire et société: mélanges offerts à Georges Duby* (Aix-en-Provence, 1992), 107–21.

—— Giry-Deloison, Charles, and Keen, Maurice H. (eds.), *Guerre et société en France, en Angleterre et en Bourgogne XIVᵉ-XVᵉ siècle* (Villeneuve d'Ascq, 1991).

Cook, G. H., *English Collegiate Churches* (London, 1959).

Cooke, W. G. and Boulton, D'A. J. D., 'Sir Gawain and the Green Knight: A Poem for Henry of Grosmont?', *Medium Aevum*, 68 (1999), 42–54.

Coote, Lesley A., *Prophecy and Public Affairs in Later Medieval England* (Woodbridge, 2000).

Coss, Peter, and Keen, Maurice (eds.), *Heraldry, Pageantry and Social Display in Medieval England* (Woodbridge, 2002).

Crouch, David, 'The Court of Henry II of England in the 1180s, and the Office of King of Arms', *Coat of Arms*, 3rd series, 6 (2010), 47–56.

—— *Tournament* (London, 2005).

—— Carpenter, D. A., and Coss, P. R., 'Bastard Feudalism Revisited', *Past and Present*, 131 (1991), 165–203.

Crow, M. M., and Olson, C. C. (eds.), *Chaucer Life-Records* (Oxford, 1966).

Crowfoot, Elisabeth, Pritchard, Frances, and Staniland, Kay, *Textiles and Clothing*, Medieval Finds from Excavations in London 4, 2nd edn. (Woodbridge, 2001).

Cruse, Mark, *Illuminating the* Roman d'Alexandre: *Oxford, Bodleian Library, MS Bodley 264* (Woodbridge, 2011).

Cunliffe, Tom, *The Shell Channel Pilot* (St Ives, 2010).

Curry, Anne, and Hughes, Michael (eds.), *Arms, Armies and Fortifications in the Hundred Years War* (Woodbridge, 1994).

Cushway, Graham, *Edward III and the War at Sea: The English Navy, 1327–1377* (Woodbridge, 2011).

Cuttino, G. P., 'Historical Revision: The Causes of the Hundred Years' War', *Speculum*, 31 (1956), 463–77.

Daly, L. J., 'The Conclusion of Walter Burley's Commentary on the *Politics*: Books I to IV', *Manuscripta*, 12 (1968), 163, 213.

Daumet, Georges, 'L'Ordre castillan de l'écharpe (Banda)', *Bulletin hispanique*, 25 (1923), 1–32.

de Graaf, Roland, *Oorlog om Holland 1000–1375* (Hilversum, 1996).

Delachenal, Roland, *Histoire de Charles V*, 5 vols. (Paris, 1909–31).

Delcorno Branco, Daniela, *Boccaccio e le storie di re Artù* (Bologna, 1991).

Delisle, Léopold, *Histoire du château et des sires de Saint-Sauveur-Le-Vicomte* (Valognes, 1867).

Denholm Young, N., 'Edward III and Bermondsey Priory', in his *Collected Papers* (Cardiff, 1969).

—— *History and Heraldry* (Oxford, 1965).

—— 'The Tournament in the Thirteenth Century', in R. W. Hunt *et al.* (eds.), *Studies Presented to F. M. Powicke* (Oxford, 1948).

Déprez, Eugène, 'La Bataille de Najéra: Le communiqué du Prince Noir', *Revue historique*, 136 (1921), 37–59.

De Santi, G., 'L'Expédition du prince noir en 1355 d'après le journal d'un de ses compagnons', *Mémoires de l'Académie des Sciences de Toulouse*, 10/5 (1904), 181–223.

Devon, Frederick, *Issues of the Exchequer* (London, 1837).

DeVries, Kelly, *Infantry Warfare in the Early Fourteenth Century* (Woodbridge, 1996).

—— 'The Use of the Pavise in the Hundred Years War', *Arms and Armour*, 4 (2007), 93–100.

Dictionary of British Arms, ed. Thomas Woodcock, Janet Grant and Ian Graham, 3 vols. in progress (London, 1996–).

Dictionary of Medieval Latin from British Sources, ed. D. R. Howlett (Oxford, 1975–).

Diller, G. T., 'Robert d'Artois et l'historicité des Chroniques de Froissart', *Le Moyen Âge*, 86 (1980), 217–31.

Doherty, P. C., 'Isabella, Queen of England 1308–1330', Oxford D.Phil. thesis, 1977.

Douch, R., 'The Career, Lands and Family of William Montagu, Earl of Salisbury', *Bulletin of the Institute of Historical Research*, 24 (1951), 85–8.

Du Cange, Charles Dufresne, sieur, *Dissertations sur l'histoire de Saint Louys*, Du Cry d'Armes, dissertation XI, in *Glossarium Mediae et Infimae Latinitatis*, VII (Paris, 1850), 28–35.

Durdík, Jan, *Hussitisches Heerwesen* (Berlin, 1961) (translated from the Czech).

Dygo, Marian, 'The Political Role of the Cult of the Virgin Mary in Teutonic Prussia in the Fourteenth and Fifteenth Centuries', *Journal of Medieval History*, 15 (1989), 63–80.

Ellmers, Detlev, 'The Cog as Cargo Carrier', in Robert Gardiner (ed.), *Cogs, Caravels and Galleons* (London, 1994), 29–46.

Engel, Pál, *The Realm of St Stephen: A History of Medieval Hungary, 895–1526*, ed. Andrew Ayton (London, 2001).

Feuchère, Pierre, *Les Vieilles Familles chevaleresques du nord de France*, 1.i: *Auberchicourt* (Fontenay-le-Comte, 1945).

Fleckenstein, Josef (ed.), *Das ritterliche Turnier im Mittelalter*, Veröffentlichungen des Max-Planck-Instituts für Geschichte 80 (Göttingen, 1985).

Foucard, C., *Lo statuto della Compagnia della Giarretiera istituta da Edoardo III, Re d'Inghilterra MCCCL* (Modena, 1878).

Fowler, Kenneth, 'Henry of Grosmont, First Duke of Lancaster, 1310–1361', Ph.D. thesis, University of Leeds, 1961 (contains documentary appendix not in printed version).

—— (ed.), *The Hundred Years War* (London, 1971).

—— *The King's Lieutenant: Henry of Grosmont, First Duke of Lancaster 1310–1361* (London, 1969).

—— *Medieval Mercenaries*, 1: *The Great Companies* (Oxford, 2001).

—— 'News from the Front: Letters and Dispatches of the Fourteenth Century', in Philippe Contamine, Maurice Keen *et al.* (eds.), *Guerre et Société en France, en Angleterre et en Bourgogne XIVᵉ –XVᵉ siècle* (Lille, 1991), 63–92.

Fügedi, Erik, 'Turniere im mittelalterlichen Ungarn', in Josef Fleckenstein (ed.), *Das ritterliche Turnier im Mittelalter*, Veröffentlichungen des Max-Planck-Instituts für Geschichte 80 (Göttingen, 1985), 390–400.

Galbraith, V. H., 'Extracts from the Historia Aurea and a French "Brut" (1317–1347)', *EHR* 43 (1928), 203–17.

Galway, Margaret, 'The Foundation of the Order of the Garter', *University of Birmingham Historical Journal*, 7 (1959), 18–35.

Gardiner, Robert (ed.), *Cogs, Caravels and Galleons* (London, 1994).

Geddes, Jane, 'Medieval Decorative Ironwork in St George's Chapel', in Nigel Saul and Tim Tatton-Brown (eds.), *St George's Chapel Windsor: History and Heritage* (Wimborne Minster, 2010), 63–8.

Gillespie, James L., 'Ladies of the Fraternity of Saint George and of the Society of the Garter', *Albion*, 17 (1985), 259–78.

Given-Wilson, Chris, *Chronicles: The Writing of History in Medieval England* (London, 2004).

—— 'The Exequies of Edward III and the Royal Funeral Ceremony in Late Medieval England', *EHR* 124 (2009), 257–82.

—— (ed.), *Fourteenth Century England II* (Woodbridge, 2002).

—— (ed.), *Fourteenth Century England VI* (Woodbridge, 2010).

—— 'Royal Charter Witness Lists 1327–1399', *Medieval Prosopography*, 12/2 (1991), 35–93.

—— *The Royal Household and the King's Affinity: Service, Politics and Finance in England 1360–1413* (New Haven and London, 1986).

—— 'Wealth and Credit, Public and Private: The Earls of Arundel, 1306–1397', *EHR* 106 (1991), 1–26.

—— and Bériac, Françoise, 'Edward III's Prisoners of War: The Battle of Poitiers and its Context', *EHR* 116 (2001), 802–33.

Good, Jonathan, *The Cult of Saint George in Medieval England* (Woodbridge, 2009).

Goodall, John A. A., 'The Aerary Porch and its Influence on Late Medieval English Vaulting', in Nigel Saul (ed.), *St George's Chapel Windsor in the Fourteenth Century* (Woodbridge, 2005), 165–202.

—— *The English Castle 1066–1650* (New Haven and London, 2011).

Goodman, Anthony, *John of Gaunt: The Exercise of Princely Power in Fourteenth-Century Europe* (Harlow, 1992).

Gransden, Antonia, 'The Alleged Rape by Edward III of the Countess of Salisbury', *EHR* 87 (1972), 333–44.

—— *Historical Writing in England II: c.1307 to the Early Sixteenth Century* (London, 1982).

Green, David, *The Black Prince* (Stroud, 2001).

Green, Richard Firth, 'King Richard II's Books Revisited', *The Library*, 5th series, 31 (1976), 235–9.

Greene, C., and Whittingham, A. B., 'Excavations at Walsingham Priory, Norfolk, 1961', *Archaeological Journal*, 125 (1968), 255–90.

Greene, R. L. (ed.), *A Selection of English Carols* (Oxford, 1962).

Greenstreet, James, 'Powell's Roll', *The Reliquary*, new series 3 (1889), 144–52.

—— '[Sixth] Nobility Roll', *Notes and Queries*, 6th series, 1 (1880), 351–2, 370–71.

—— 'Thomas Jenyns' Book', *The Antiquary*, 1 (1880), 205–9; 2 (1885–7), 97–101, 238–44; *Walfords Magazine and Bibliographer*, 8–12 [BL Add. MS 40851].

Grimsley, M., and Rogers, C. J., *Civilians in the Path of War* (Lincoln, Nebr., 2002).

Guenée, Bernard, *Between Church and State: The Lives of Four French Prelates in the Late Middle Ages*, tr. Arthur Goldhammer (Chicago, 1991).

Guesnon, A., 'Documents inédits sur l'invasion anglaise et les états au temps de Philippe VI et Jean le Bon', *Bulletin philologique et historique du Comité des Travaux historiques et scientifiques* (1897), 208–59.

Gumus, T. Tolga, 'A Tale of Two Codices: The Medieval Registers of the Order of the Garter', *Comitatus*, 37 (2006), 86–110.

Hanna, Ralph, *London Literature 1300–1380* (Cambridge, 2005).

Harari, Yuval Noah, 'Strategy and Supply in Fourteenth-Century Western European Invasion Campaigns', *Journal of Military History*, 64 (2000), 297–333.

Harriss, G. L., *King, Parliament and Public Finance in Medieval England to 1369* (Oxford, 1975).

Hay, Denis, 'The Division of the Spoils of War in Fourteenth Century England', *TRHS*, 5th series, 4 (1954), 91–109.

Hayez, M., 'Un exemple de culture historique au xve siècle: *La geste des nobles françois*', *École française de Rome: Mélanges d'archéologie et d'histoire*, 75 (1963), 127–78.

Hewitt, H. J., *The Black Prince's Expedition of 1355–1357* (Manchester, 1958).

—— *The Organization of War under Edward III, 1338–62* (Manchester, 1966).

Holmes, G. A., *The Estates of the Higher Nobility in Fourteenth-Century England* (Cambridge, 1957).

Hóman, Balínt, *Gli angioini di Napoli in Ungheria, 1290–1403* (Rome, 1938).

Hoskins, Peter, *In the Steps of the Black Prince: The Road to Poitiers, 1355–1356* (Woodbridge, 2011).

Howe, Emily, 'Divine Kingship and Dynastic Display: The Altar Wall Murals of St Stephen's Chapel, Westminster', *Antiquaries Journal*, 81 (2001), 259–303.

Huet, G., 'Les Traditions arthuriennes chez le chroniqueur Louis de Velthem', *Le Moyen Âge*, 36 (1913), 173, 197.

Huot, Sylvia, *Postcolonial Fictions in the 'Roman de Perceforest': Cultural Identities and Hybridities* (Cambridge, 2007).

Ingledew, Francis, *Sir Gawain and the Green Knight and the Order of the Garter* (Notre Dame, Ind., 2006).

Jaeger, C. Stephen, *Ennobling Love: In Search of a Lost Sensibility* (Philadelphia, 1999).

Janse, Antheun, *Ridderschap in Holland: portret van een Adellijke Elite in de late Middeleeuwen* (Hilversum, 2001).

—— 'Tourneyers and Spectators', in Steven Gunn and Antheun Janse (eds.), *The Court as Stage* (Woodbridge, 2006), 39–52.

Jeayes, I. H., *Catalogue of the Charters and Muniments at Berkeley Castle* (Bristol, 1892).

Jefferson, Lisa, 'MS Arundel 48 and the Earliest Statutes of the Order of the Garter', *EHR* 109 (1994), 356–84.

—— 'Two Fifteenth-Century Manuscripts of the Statutes of the Order of the Garter', *English Manuscript Studies*, 5 (1995), 18–35.

Johnstone, H., *Edward of Caernarvon* (Manchester, 1946).

Jones, Michael, *Ducal Brittany 1364–1399: Relations with England and France during the Reign of Duke John IV* (Oxford, 1970).

—— 'Edward III's Captains in Brittany', in W. M. Ormrod (ed.), *England in the Fourteenth Century: Proceedings of the 1985 Harlaxton Symposium* (Woodbridge, 1986), 99–118.

—— 'Sir John de Hardreshull, King's Lieutenant in Brittany', *Nottingham Medieval Studies*, 31 (1987), 76–95.

—— and Walker, Simon, 'Private Indentures for Life Service in Peace and War 1278–1476', *Camden Miscellany*, 32 (1994), 1–190.

Jones, Robert W., *Bloodied Banners: Martial Display on the Medieval Battlefield* (Woodbridge, 2010).

Kaeuper, Richard W., *Chivalry and Violence in Medieval Europe* (Oxford, 2001).
—— *Holy Warriors: The Religious Ideology of Chivalry* (Philadelphia, 2009).
—— *War, Justice and Public Order: England and France in the Later Middle Ages* (Oxford, 1988).
Keegan, John, *The Face of Battle* (London, 1977).
Keen, Lawrence, and Scarff, Eileen, *Windsor: Medieval Art, Archeology and Architecture in the Thames Valley*, BAA Transactions 25 (Leeds, 2002).
Keen, Maurice, 'Chivalry and the Aristocracy', in Michael Jones (ed.), *The New Cambridge Medieval History*, vol. 6: *c.1300–c.1415* (Cambridge, 2000), 209–21.
—— 'Chivalry, Heralds and History', in R. H. C. Davis and J. M. Wallace-Hadrill (eds.), *The Writing of History in the Middle Ages: Essays Presented to Richard William Southern* (Oxford, 1981), 393–414.
—— *The Laws of War in the Late Middle Ages* (London, 1968).
—— *Origins of the English Gentleman: Heraldry, Chivalry and Gentility in Medieval England, c.1300–c.1500* (Stroud, 2002).
Keeney, B. C., 'Military Service and the Development of Nationalism in England', *Speculum*, 22 (1947), 541–5.
Kerr, Jill, 'The East Window of Gloucester Cathedral', in *Medieval Art and Architecture at Gloucester and Tewkesbury*, British Archaeological Association Conference Transactions, VII (1985), 116–29.
Knowles, David, and Grimes, W. F., *Charterhouse: The Medieval Foundation in the Light of Recent Discoveries* (London, 1954).
—— and Hadcock, R. Neville, *Medieval Religious Houses: England and Wales* (London, 1971).
Krochalis, Jeanne, '*Magna tabula*: The Glastonbury Tablets', in James Carley (ed.), *Glastonbury and the Arthurian Tradition* (Woodbridge, 2001), 435–568.
Kruse, Holger, Paravicini, Werner, and Ranft, Andreas (eds.), *Ritterorden und Adelsgesellschaften in spätmittelalterlichen Deutschland* (Frankfurt, 1991).
Lachaud, Frédérique, 'Les Tentes et l'activité militaire: les guerres d'Édouard Ier Plantagenet (1272–1307)', *Mélanges de l'École française de Rome: Moyen-Âge*, 111/1 (1999), 443–61.
Lambert, Craig L., *Shipping the Medieval Military: English Military Logistics in the Fourteenth Century* (Woodbridge, 2011).
Lapierre, A., *La Guerre de cent ans dans l'Argonne et le Rethelois* (Sedan, 1900).
Le Patourel, J., 'Edward III and the Kingdom of France', *History*, 43 (1958).
—— 'The Treaty of Brétigny 1360', *TRHS*, 5th series, 10 (1960), 19–39.
Leland, John, *Itinerary through England and Wales*, ed. Lucy Toulmin Smith (London, 1964).
Leroux, Alfred, 'Le Sac de la cité de Limoges et son relèvement, 1370–1464', *Bulletin de la société archéologique et historique du Limousin*, 56 (1908), 175–9.

Lester, G. A., *Sir John Paston's Grete Boke* (Cambridge, 1984).

Lewis, N. B., 'The Organisation of Indentured Retinues in Fourteenth-Century England', *TRHS*, 4th series, 27 (1945), 29–39.

Liebnitz, Karl, 'Die Manuskripte des Walter de Milemete', *Waffen und Kostumkunde*, 34 (1992), 117–31.

Lindenbaum, Sheila, 'The Smithfield Tournament of 1390', *Journal of Medieval and Renaissance Studies*, 20 (1990), 1–20.

Livingstone, Marilyn, and Witzel, Morgen, *The Road to Crécy: The English Invasion of France 1346* (Harlow, 2005).

London, H. S., *The Life of William Bruges, the First Garter King of Arms*, Harleian Society, CXI/CXII (London, 1970).

Loomis, Laura Hibbard, 'Secular Dramatics in the Royal Palace, Paris, 1378, 1389, and Chaucer's "Tregetoures"', *Speculum*, 33 (1958), 242–55.

Loomis, R. S., 'Edward I, Arthurian Enthusiast', *Speculum*, 28 (1953), 114–27.

Lucas, H. S., 'Edward III and the Poet Chronicler John Boendale', *Speculum*, 12 (1937), 367–9.

—— *The Low Countries and the Hundred Years War, 1326–1347*, University of Michigan Publications, History and Political Science, VIII (Ann Arbor, 1929).

Luce, Simeon, 'Du Guesclin au siège de Rennes', *Bibliothèque de l'École des Chartes*, 53 (1891), 615–18.

Luxford, Julian, 'King Arthur's Tomb at Glastonbury: The Relocation of 1368 in Context', *Arthurian Literature*, 29 (2012), 41–52.

Luzzati, M., *Giovanni Villani e la compagnia dei Buonaccorsi* (Rome, 1971).

McDonald, Nicola, and Ormrod, W. M. (eds.), *Rites of Passage: Cultures of Transition in the Fourteenth Century* (Woodbridge, 2004).

McFarlane, K. B., 'Bastard Feudalism', *Bulletin of the Institute of Historical Research*, 20 (1943–5), 161–80.

—— *The Nobility of Later Medieval England* (Oxford, 1973).

McHardy, A. K., 'Some Reflections on Edward III's Use of Propaganda', in *Age of Edward III*, 171–83.

Mackinnon, James, *The History of Edward III (1327–1377)* (London, 1900).

Majláth, Béla, 'A Kolos Család Czímeres Levele', *Turul*, 5 (1887), 156–9.

Malderghem, Jean van, *La Bataille de Staveren* (Brussels, 1870).

Marks, Richard, 'Some Early Representations of the Garter in Stained Glass', *Report of the Society of Friends of St George's*, 5/4 (1972–3), 154–6.

May, Theresa, 'The Cobhams in Royal Administration 1200–1400', *Archaeologia Cantiana*, 82 (1967), 1–31.

Melchiori, G. (ed.), *King Edward III* (Cambridge, 1998).

Melville, Gert, 'Pourquoi des hérauts d'armes? Les raisons d'une institution', *Revue du Nord*, 88 (2006), 491–502.

Michael, M. A., 'A Manuscript Wedding Gift from Philippa of Hainault to Edward III', *Burlington Magazine*, 127 (1985), 582–98.

Michaud, Claude, 'The Kingdoms of Central Europe in the Fourteenth Century', in Michael Jones (ed.), *The New Cambridge Medieval History*, vol. 6: *c.1300–c.1415* (Cambridge, 2000), 735–63.

Moisant, J., *Le Prince Noir en Aquitaine, 1355–1356 – 1362–1370* (Paris, 1894).

Molinier, Émile, 'Étude sur la vie d'Arnoul d'Audrehem', *Mémoires présentés . . . à l'Académie des inscriptions et belles-lettres de l'Institut de France. Deuxième série: Antiquités de la France* VI (Paris, 1883).

Mooney, Linne R., 'Some New Light on Thomas Hoccleve', *Studies in the Age of Chaucer*, 29 (2007), 293–340.

Morgan, D. A. L., 'The Banner-Bearer of Christ: How God Became an English-man Revisited', in Nigel Saul (ed.), *St George's Chapel Windsor in the Fourteenth Century* (Woodbridge, 2005), 51–62.

Morgan, Nigel, *Early Gothic Manuscripts [II] 1250–1285*, A Survey of Manu-scripts Illuminated in the British Isles IV (London, 1988).

Morris, Marc, 'Edward I and the Knights of the Round Table', in Paul Brand and Sean Cunningham (eds.), *Foundations of Medieval Scholarship: Records Edited in Honour of David Crook* (York, 2008), 57–76.

Mortimer, Ian, *The Perfect King: The Life of Edward III, Father of the English Nation* (London, 2006).

Munby, Julian, Barber, Richard, and Brown, Richard, *Edward III's Round Table at Windsor: The House of the Round Table and the Windsor Festival of 1344* (Woodbridge, 2007).

Newton, Stella Mary, *Fashion in the Age of the Black Prince: A Study of the Years 1340–1345* (Woodbridge, 1980).

—— 'Queen Philippa's Squirrel Suit', in M. Flury-Lemberg and K. Stolleis (eds.), *Documenta Textilia: Festschrift für Sigrid Müller-Christensen* (Munich, 1981), 342–8.

Nicholson, Ranald, *Edward III and the Scots: The Formative Years of a Military Career* (Oxford, 1965).

Nicolas, Sir Nicolas Harris, *The controversy between Sir R. Scrope and Sir R. Grosvenor in the Court of Chivalry, A.D. MCCCLXXXV–MCCCXC*, 2 vols. (London, 1832).

—— *History of the Orders of Knighthood*, 3 vols. (London, 1841).

—— 'Observations on the Institution of the Most Noble Order of the Garter', *Archaeologia*, 31 (1846), 1–163.

—— *A Roll of Arms compiled in the Reign of Edward III* (London, 1829).

Oberman, Heiko A., and Weishepl, James A., 'The Sermo epinicius Ascribed to Thomas Bradwardine', *Archives d'histoire doctrinale et littéraire du moyen âge*, 25 (1958), 295–329.

Offler, H. S., 'Thomas Bradwardine's "Victory Sermon" in 1346', repr. in H. S. Offler, *Church and Crown in the Fourteenth Century* (Aldershot, 2000), item XIII.

Ormrod, W. Mark, *Edward III* (London, 2011).

—— 'Edward III and his Family', *Journal of British Studies*, 26 (1987), 398–442.

—— 'Edward III and the Recovery of Royal Authority in England 1340–1360', *History*, 72 (1987), 4–19.

—— (ed.), *England in the Fourteenth Century: Proceedings of the 1985 Harlaxton Symposium* (Woodbridge, 1986).

—— 'For Arthur and St George: Edward III, Windsor Castle and the Order of the Garter', in Nigel Saul (ed.), *St George's Chapel Windsor in the Fourteenth Century* (Woodbridge, 2005), 13–34.

—— (ed.), *Fourteenth Century England VII* (Woodbridge, 2012).

—— 'The Personal Religion of Edward III', *Speculum*, 64 (1989), 849–77.

—— *The Reign of Edward III* (Stroud, 2000).

Owen, A., *Le Traité de Walter de Bibbesworth sur la langue française* (Paris, 1929).

Owst, G. R., *Preaching in Medieval England*, Cambridge Studies in Medieval Life and Thought (Cambridge, 1926).

Palmer, John (ed.), *Froissart: Historian* (Woodbridge, 1981).

Pannier, Léopold, *La Noble-maison de Saint-Ouen: La villa Clippiacum et l'ordre de l'Étoile d'après les documents originaux* (Paris, 1872).

Pantin, W. A., 'A Medieval Treatise on Letter-Writing, with Examples, from the Rylands Latin MS. 394', *Bulletin of the John Rylands Library*, 13 (1929), 326–82.

Paravicini, Werner, 'Armoriaux et histoire culturelle: Le Rôle d'Armes des "Meilleurs Trois"', in Werner Paravicini, *Noblesse: Studien zum adeligen Leben im spätmittelalterlichen Europa* (Sigmaringen, 2012), 471–88.

—— 'L'Office d'armes: historiographie, sources, problématique', *Revue du Nord*, 88 (2006), 467–90 (special issue on *Le Héraut, figure européenne (XIVᵉ–XVIᵉ siècle)*).

—— *Die Preussenreisen des Europäischen Adels*, 2 vols. (in progress), Beihefte der Francia 17 (Sigmaringen, 1989–).

Parisse, Michel, 'Le Tournoi en France, des origines à la fin du XIIIᵉ siècle', in Josef Fleckenstein (ed.), *Das ritterliche Turnier im Mittelalter*, Veröffentlichungen des Max-Planck-Instituts für Geschichte 80 (Göttingen, 1985), 174–211.

Pastoureau, Michel, *L'Armorial Bellenville* (Lathuile, 1974).

Pauli, Sebastiano, *Codice diplomatico del sacro militare ordine gerosolimitano oggi di Malta*, 2 vols. (Lucca, 1738).

Pépin, Guilhem, 'Towards a Rehabilitation of Froissart's Credibility: The Non Fictitious Bascot de Mauléon', in Adrian R. Bell, Anne Curry *et al.* (eds.), *The Soldier Experience in the Fourteenth Century* (Woodbridge, 2011), 175–90.

Perroy, E., 'France, England, and Navarre from 1359 to 1364', *Bulletin of the Institute of Historical Research*, 13 (1935–6), 152–3.

Phillips, Seymour, *Edward II* (New Haven and London, 2010).

Pór, Antal, 'Az Anjou ház és örökösei, 1301–1439', in S. Szilágyi (ed.), *A Magyar nemzet története*, Köt 3 (Budapest, 1895), 133–9.

Powicke, M. R., 'Edward II and Military Obligation', *Speculum*, 31 (1956), 92–119.

—— *Military Obligation in Medieval England: A Study in Liberty and Duty* (Oxford, 1962).

Prentout, Henri, 'La Prise de Caen par Édouard III – 1346', *Mémoires de l'académie nationale des sciences, arts et belles-lettres de Caen* (1904), 225–95.

Preston, Sir Philip, 'The Traditional Battlefield of Crécy', in Andrew Ayton and Preston, *The Battle of Crécy, 1346*, Warfare in History (Woodbridge, 2005), 109–37.

Prestwich, Michael, *Edward I* (London, 1988).

—— 'English Armies in the Early Stages of the Hundred Years War: A Scheme in 1341', *Bulletin of the Institute of Historical Research*, 56 (1983), 102–13.

—— 'The English at the Battle of Neville's Cross', in David Rollason and Michael Prestwich (eds.), *The Battle of Neville's Cross 1346*, Studies in North-Eastern History 2 (Stamford, 1998), 1–14.

—— *Plantagenet England, 1225–1360* (Oxford, 2005).

—— *The Three Edwards: War and State in England 1272–1377* (London, 1980).

Prince, A. E., 'The Indenture System under Edward III', in J. G. Edwards, V. H. Galbraith and E. F. Jacob (eds.), *Historical Essays in Honour of James Tait* (Manchester, 1933), 283–97.

—— 'A Letter of Edward the Black Prince Describing the Battle of Najéra in 1367', *EHR* 41 (1926), 415–18.

—— 'The Payment of Army Wages in Edward III's Reign', *Speculum*, 19 (1944), 137–60.

—— 'The Strength of English Armies in the Reign of Edward III', *EHR* 46 (1931), 353–71.

Pryor, J. H., 'Transportation of Horses by Sea during the Crusades', *Mariner's Mirror*, 68 (1982), 9–30, 103–25.

Ragone, Franca, *Giovanni Villani e i suoi continuatori: La scrittura delle cronache a Firenze nel trecento*, Istituto Storico Italiano per il medio evo, Nuovi studi storici 43 (Rome, 1998).

Rastall, Richard, 'Minstrels of the English Royal Households, 25 Edward I – 1 Henry VIII: An Inventory', *Royal Musical Association Research Chronicle*, 4 (1964), 7–20.

Renouard, Yves, 'L'Ordre de la jarretière et l'ordre de l'étoile', *Le Moyen Âge*, 55 (1949), 281–300.

Revard, Carter, 'Courtly Romances in the Privy Wardrobe', in Evelyn Mullally and John Thompson (eds.), *The Court and Cultural Diversity* (Woodbridge, 1997), 297–308.

Riches, Samantha, *St George: Hero, Martyr and Myth* (Stroud, 2000).

Richmond, Colin, and Scarff, Eileen, *St George's Chapel Windsor in the Late Middle Ages*, Windsor Historical Monographs 17 (Windsor, 2001).

Rigg, A. G., 'Propaganda of the Hundred Years War: Poems on the Battles of Crecy and Durham (1346). A Critical Edition', *Traditio*, 54 (1999), 169–211.

Riquer, Martí de, *L'Arnes del Cavaller* (Barcelona, 1968).

Robbins, R. H., *Historical Poems of the XIVth and XVth Centuries* (New York, 1959).

Roberts, A. K. B., *St George's Chapel, Windsor Castle, 1348–1416: a Study in Early Collegiate Administration* (Windsor, 1951).

Rogers, Clifford J., 'By Fire and Sword: *Bellum hostile* and "Civilians" in the Hundred Years' War', in M. Grimsley and C. J. Rogers, *Civilians in the Path of War* (Lincoln, Nebr., 2002), 33–78.

—— 'Edward III and the Dialectics of Strategy 1327–1360', *TRHS*, 6th series, 4 (1994), 83–101.

—— 'The Military Revolutions of the Hundred Years' War', *Journal of Military History*, 57 (1993), 241–78.

—— *War Cruel and Sharp: English Strategy under Edward III* (Woodbridge, 2000).

—— *The Wars of Edward III: Sources and Interpretations* (Woodbridge, 1999).

Rogers, Nicholas, *England in the Fourteenth Century: Proceedings of the 1991 Harlaxton Symposium*, Harlaxton Medieval Studies III (Stamford, 1993).

Rollason, David, and Prestwich, Michael (eds.), *The Battle of Neville's Cross 1346*, Studies in North-Eastern History 2 (Stamford, 1998).

Roy, É., *Études sur le théâtre français du XIVᵉ et du XVᵉ siècle: La comédie sans titre . . . et les Miracles de Notre-Dame* (Dijon, 1901).

Rubin, Miri, *The Hollow Crown: A History of Britain in the Later Middle Ages* (London, 2005).

Runyan, T. J., 'The Cog as Warship', in Robert Gardiner (ed.), *Cogs, Caravels and Galleons* (London, 1994), 47–58.

—— 'Ships and Mariners in Later Medieval England', *Journal of British Studies*, 16 (1977), 1–17.

Russell, P. E., *The English Intervention in Spain and Portugal in the Time of Edward III and Richard II* (Oxford, 1955).

Safford, E. W., 'An Account of the Expenses of Eleanor, Sister of Edward III, on the Occasion of her Marriage to Reynald, Count of Guelders', *Archaeologia*, 77 (1928), 111–40.

St John, Graham, 'Dying beyond the Seas: Testamentary Preparation for Campaigning during the Hundred Years War', in W. M. Ormrod (ed.), *Fourteenth Century England VII* (Woodbridge, 2012), 177–96.

—— 'War, the Church and English Men-at-Arms', in Chris Given-Wilson (ed.), *Fourteenth Century England VI* (Woodbridge, 2010), 73–93.

St John Hope, W. H., *The History of the London Charterhouse* (London, 1925).

—— *The Stall Plates of the Knights of the Order of the Garter, 1348–1485* (Westminster, 1901).

—— *Windsor Castle: An Architectural History*, 2 vols. (London, 1913).

Salter, Elizabeth, 'The Timeliness of *Wynnere and Wastoure*', *Medium Aevum*, 47 (1980), 40–65.

Sandberger, Dietrich, *Studien ueber das Rittertum in England, vornehmlich waehrend des 14 Jahrhunderts*, Historische Studien 310 (Berlin, 1937).

Sandler, Lucy Freeman, *Gothic Manuscripts 1285–1385*, 2 vols., A Survey of Manuscripts Illuminated in the British Isles V (London, 1985).

Saul, Nigel, *English Church Monuments in the Middle Ages* (Oxford, 2009).

—— 'The Growth of a Mausoleum: The Pre-1600 Tombs and Brasses of St George's Chapel, Windsor', *Antiquaries Journal*, 87 (2007), 220–58.

—— *For Honour and Fame: Chivalry in England 1066–1500* (London, 2011).

—— *Knights and Esquires: The Gloucestershire Gentry in the Fourteenth Century* (Oxford, 1981).

—— *Richard II* (New Haven and London, 1997).

—— 'Servants of God and Crown', in Saul (ed.), *St George's Chapel Windsor in the Fourteenth Century* (Woodbridge, 2005), 97–115.

—— and Tatton-Brown, Tim (eds.), *St George's Chapel Windsor: History and Heritage* (Wimborne Minster, 2010).

Saunders, Corinne, *Rape and Ravishment in the Literature of Medieval England* (Woodbridge, 2001).

Schmolke-Hasselmann, Beate, 'The Round Table: Ideal, Fiction, Reality', *Arthurian Literature*, 2 (1982), 41–75.

Schneider, Diethard, *Der englische Hosenbandorden: Beiträge zur Entstehung und Entwicklung des 'The Most Noble Order of the Garter' (1348–1702) mit einem Ausblick bis 1983*, 2 vols. (Bonn, 1988).

Selden, John, *Titles of Honor* (London, 1672).

Shenton, Caroline, 'The English Court and the Restoration of Royal Prestige', Oxford D.Phil., 1995.

—— 'Royal Interest in Glastonbury and Cadbury: Two Arthurian Itineraries, 1278 and 1331', *EHR* 114 (1999), 1249–55.

Sherborne, J. W., 'Indentured Retinues and English Expeditions to France', *EHR* 79 (1964), 718–46.

Shrewsbury, J. F. D., *The History of Bubonic Plague* (Cambridge, 1970).

Siddons, Michael, *Heraldic Badges in England and Wales*, 4 vols. (London, 2009).

Simpkin, David, *The English Aristocracy at War: From the Welsh Wars of Edward I to the Battle of Bannockburn* (Woodbridge, 2008).

Smith, J. T., *Antiquities of Westminster: The Old Palace; St Stephen's Chapel (now the House of Commons)* (London, 1807).

Smith, Kathryn A., *The Taymouth Hours: Stories and the Construction of Self in Late Medieval England* (London, 2012).

Smyth, John, *The Lives of the Berkeleys* . . ., ed. Sir John Maclean, 2 vols., Bristol and Gloucester Archaeological Society (Bristol, 1883–5).

Snead, G., 'The Careers of Four Fourteenth Century Military Commanders', MA thesis, UKC history, record id 440276, University of Kent, 1968.

Spencer, Brian, *Pilgrim Souvenirs and Secular Badges*, Medieval Finds from Excavations in London 7 (Woodbridge, 2010).

Spufford, Peter, *Money and its Use in Medieval Europe* (Cambridge, 1988).

—— *Power and Profit: The Merchant in Medieval Europe* (London, 2002).

Squibb, G. C., *The High Court of Chivalry* (Oxford, 1959).

Staniland, Kay, 'Clothing and Textiles at the Court of Edward III, 1342–1352', in Joanna Bird *et al.* (eds.), *Collectanea Londiniensa*, 223–34, Special Paper 2, London and Middlesex Archaeological Society (London, 1978).

—— 'Court Style, Painters, and the Great Wardrobe', in W. M. Ormrod (ed.), *England in the Fourteenth Century: Proceedings of the 1985 Harlaxton Symposium* (Woodbridge, 1986), 236–46.

—— 'The Great Wardrobe Accounts as a Source for Historians of Fourteenth-Century Clothing and Textiles', *Textile History*, 20 (1989), 275–81.

—— 'Medieval Courtly Splendour', *Costume*, 14 (1980), 7–23.

Stanley, Arthur P., *Historical Memorials of Canterbury* (London, 1912).

Stones, E. L. G., *Anglo-Scottish Relations 1174–1328* (Oxford, 1965).

—— 'The Folvilles of Ashby-Folville, Leicestershire, and their Associates in Crime, 1326–1347', *TRHS*, 5th series, 7 (1957), 117–36.

Stow, John, *A Survey of the cities of London and Westminster*, ed. John Strype, 6 vols. (London, 1720).

Stratford, Jenny, *Richard II and the English Royal Treasure* (Woodbridge, 2012).

Strickland, Matthew (ed.), *Armies, Chivalry and Warfare in Medieval Britain and France*, Harlaxton Medieval Studies VII (Stamford, 1998).

—— and Hardy, Robert, *The Great Warbow* (Stroud, 2005).

Strong, Roy, *Art and Power: Renaissance Festivals 1450–1650* (Woodbridge, 1984).

Sumption, Jonathan, *The Hundred Years War*, vol. i: *Trial by Battle* (London, 1990).

—— *The Hundred Years War*, vol. ii: *Trial by Fire* (London, 1999).

—— *The Hundred Years War*, vol. iii: *Divided Houses* (London, 2009).

Tatton-Brown, Tim, 'The Deanery, Windsor Castle', *Antiquaries Journal*, 78 (1998), 345–90.

Taylor, Craig, 'Edward III and the Plantagenet Claim to the French Throne', in *Age of Edward III*, 155–69.

—— 'English Writings on Chivalry and Warfare during the Hundred Years War', in Peter Coss and Christopher Tyerman (eds.), *Soldiers, Nobles and Gentlemen: Essays in Honour of Maurice Keen* (Woodbridge, 2009).

—— 'The Salic Law, French Queenship, and the Defense of Women in the Late Middle Ages', *French Historical Studies*, 29 (2006), 543–64.

Taylor, John, *English Historical Literature in the Fourteenth Century* (Oxford, 1987).

—— *The Universal Chronicle of Ranulf Higden* (Oxford, 1966).

Tobler, Adolf, *Altfranzösisches Wörterbuch*, ed. Erhard Lommatzsch (Stuttgart, 1915–).

Toman, H., *Husitské válečnictví za doby Žižkovy a Prokopovy* (Prague, 1898).

Topham, John, *Some Account of the Collegiate Chapel of St Stephen, Westminster* (London, 1795).

Tourneur-Aumont, J. M., *La Bataille de Poitiers (1356) et la construction de la France* (Paris, 1940).

Tout, T. F., *Chapters in the Administrative History of Mediaeval England*, 6 vols. (Manchester, 1920–33).

—— 'Firearms in England in the Fourteenth Century', *EHR* 26 (1911), 666–702.

—— 'The Household of the Chancery and its Disintegration', in H. W. C. Davis (ed.), *Essays in History Presented to Reginald Lane Poole* (Oxford, 1927).

—— *The Place of the Reign of Edward II in English History* (Manchester, 1914).

—— 'Some Neglected Fights between Crecy and Poitiers', *EHR* 20 (1905), 726–30.

—— 'The Tactics of the Battles of Boroughbridge and Morlaix', *EHR* 19 (1904), 711–15.

Tracy, Charles, *English Gothic Choirstalls 1200–1400* (Woodbridge, 1987).

Trautz, Fritz, *Die Könige von England und des Reich 1272–1377* (Heidelberg, 1961).

—— 'Die Reise eines Englischen Gesandten nach Ungarn im Jahre 1346', *Mitteilungen des Instituts für Österreichischen Geschichte*, 60 (1952), 359–68.

Trigg , Stephanie, 'The Vulgar History of the Order of the Garter', in G. McMullan and D. Matthews (eds.), *Reading the Medieval in Early Modern England* (Cambridge, 2007), 91–105.

Trowell, Brian, 'A Fourteenth Century Ceremonial Motet and its Composer', *Acta Musicologica*, 29 (1957), 65–75.

Tucoo-Chala, Pierre, 'Froissart dans le Midi pyrénéen', in J. J. N. Palmer (ed.), *Froissart: Historian* (Woodbridge, 1981).

Tudor-Craig, Pamela, 'The Fonts of St George's Chapel', in Nigel Saul (ed.), *St George's Chapel Windsor in the Fourteenth Century* (Woodbridge, 2005), 151–64.

Tyson, Diana B., 'Jean le Bel, Annalist or Artist? A Literary Appraisal', in Sally Burch North (ed.), *Studies in Medieval French Language and Literature Presented to Brian Woledge* (Geneva, 1988), 217–26.

—— 'Jean le Bel, Portrait of a Chronicler', *Journal of Medieval History*, 12 (1986), 315–32.

Vale, Juliet, 'Arthur in English Society', in W. R. J. Barron (ed.), *The Arthur of the English: The Arthurian Legend in Medieval English Life and Literature* (Cardiff, 2001), 185–96.

—— *Edward III and Chivalry: Chivalric Society and its Context 1270–1350* (Woodbridge, 1982).

—— 'Image and Identity in the Order of the Garter', in Nigel Saul (ed.), *St George's Chapel Windsor in the Fourteenth Century* (Woodbridge, 2005), 35–50.

Vale, Malcolm, *The Princely Court: Medieval Courts and Culture in North-West Europe 1270–1380* (Oxford, 2001).

van Buren, Anne H., *Illuminating Fashion: Dress in the Art of Medieval France and the Netherlands 1325–1515* (New York, 2011).

van Oostrom, Frits Pieter, *Court and Culture: Dutch Literature 1350–1450* (Berkeley, 1992).

Vattier, A., 'Fondation de l'Ordre de l'Étoile', *Comité archéologique de Senlis, Comptes-rendus et Mémoires*, 2nd series, 10 (1885), 32–47.

Verbruggen, J., *The Art of Warfare in Western Europe during the Middle Ages*, 2nd edn. (Woodbridge, 1997).

[Vergil, Polydore] *Polydori Vergili Historiae Anglicanae* . . . (Basle, 1555, repr. Menston, 1972).

Viard, Jules, 'La Campagne de juillet-août 1346 et la bataille de Crécy', *Le Moyen Âge*, 2nd series, 27 (1926), 1–84.

—— 'Le Siège de Calais', *Le Moyen Âge*, 2nd series, 30 (1929), 129–89.

Villanueva, Lorenzo Tadeo de, 'Memoria sobre la Orden de Caballería de la Banda de Castilla', *Boletín de la Real Academia de Historia*, 72 (1918), 436–65, 552–75.

Wagner, Anthony R., *A Catalogue of English Mediaeval Rolls of Arms*, Aspilogia i (London, 1950), and corrections in *Rolls of Arms: Henry III*, Aspilogia ii (London, 1967).

—— *Heralds and Heraldry in the Middle Ages: An Inquiry into the Growth of the Armorial Function of Heralds*, 2nd edn. (Oxford, 1956).

—— and Mann, J. G., 'A Fifteenth-Century Description of the Brass of Sir Hugh Hastings at Elsing, Norfolk', *Antiquaries Journal*, 19 (1939), 421–8.

Walker, Simon, *The Lancastrian Affinity 1361–1399* (Oxford, 1990).

Walthey, Andrew, 'The Marriage of Edward III and the Transmission of French Motets to England', *Journal of the American Musicological Society*, 45 (1992), 1–29.

—— 'The Peace of 1360–1369 and Anglo-French Musical Relations', *Early Music History*, 9 (1990), 129–74.

Warner, Sir George, *Queen Mary's Psalter* (London, 1912).

Wentersdorf, Karl P., 'The Clandestine Marriages of the Fair Maid of Kent', *Journal of Medieval History*, 5 (1979), 203–31.

Wheatley, Abigail, *The Idea of the Castle* (Woodbridge, 2004).

Whiting, B. J., 'The Vows of the Heron', *Speculum*, 20 (1945), 261–78.

Willard, James F., Morris, William A., and Dunham, William H., Jr, *The English Government at Work, 1327–1336* (Cambridge, Mass., 1940–50).

Willement, T., *Willement's Roll: A Roll of Arms of the Reign of Richard II* (London, 1834).

[Wotton, Sir Henry] *The Life and Letters of Sir Henry Wotton*, ed. Logan Pearsall Smith, 2 vols. (Oxford, 1907).

Wright, Nicholas, *Knights and Peasants: The Hundred Years War in the French Countryside* (Woodbridge, 1998).

Wrottesley, George, *Crécy and Calais, from the Original Records in the Public Record Office* (London, 1898).

—— *A History of the Family of Wrottesley of Wrottesley*, William Salt Archaeological Society, Collections, new series vi.ii (London, 1903).

Notes

DIFFERENT VOICES: READING THE EVIDENCE

1. *Channel Pilot*, 358; Cunliffe, *Shell Channel Pilot*, 258–9, 283–5.
2. Sumption, *The Hundred Years War*, i.x.
3. Le Bel, *Chronique*, i.viii, quoting Jean d'Outremeuse.
4. Hemricourt, *Le Miroir des Nobles*, 157–8.
5. Tyson, 'Jean le Bel, Annalist or Artist? A Literary Appraisal', 218.
6. Tyson, 'Jean le Bel, Portrait of a Chronicler', 316. Sir Thomas Gray and Chandos Herald (see pp. 15–17 below) are the only other examples, and neither describes warfare in any detail.
7. Le Bel, *Chronique*, i.xvi.
8. Le Bel, *Chronique*, i.1–4 [21–2].
9. See pp. 489–90 below.
10. Le Bel, *Chronique*, ii.105 [181].
11. Froissart, *Chroniques*, Rome version, 217.
12. Le Bel, *Chronique*, i.212.
13. Chareyron, *Jean le Bel*, 60–65.
14. *Récits d'un bourgeois de Valenciennes*, 54–8.
15. Froissart, *Chroniques*, Amiens version, i.1.
16. Bell, 'Medieval Chroniclers as War Correspondents during the Hundred Years' War', 179–80, 183 (for his general conclusions on the value of chronicles as evidence).
17. Tucoo-Chala, 'Froissart dans le Midi pyrénéen', 130.
18. Ibid., 118–31.
19. Froissart, *Chroniques*, Besançon version, i.210–34; Pépin, 'Towards a Rehabilitation of Froissart's Credibility', 175–90.
20. Froissart, *Chroniques*, SHF, i.6.
21. Ainsworth, *Jean Froissart and the Fabric of History*, 254–302.
22. Ibid., 300.
23. Diller, 'Robert d'Artois et l'historicité', 229–31.
24. *Amadis de Gaule*, fo. a.iiij.
25. Li Muisit, *Chroniques et annales*, xiv.

26. Guenée, *Between Church and State*, 74.
27. Li Muisit, *Chroniques et annales*, 131.
28. Ibid., xv.
29. They are said to have cut off children's feet, hands or ears, saying 'This is to show that the king of England has been here': Li Muisit, *Chroniques et annales*, 118. The papal commissioners who visited the area in 1341 confirmed the destruction wrought in the area, as much by Tournai's neighbours from Hainault and Brabant as by the English, and record the inhabitants' complaints, but do not note such atrocities. See Carolus Barré, 'Benoit XII et la mission charitable de Bernard Carit', 165–232.
30. Venette, *Chronicle*.
31. Gray, *Scalacronica*, xxxi ff.
32. BL MS Harleian 4304, fo. 17ᵛ; if this is the case, the Thomas Gray who repulsed a Scottish raid in 1341 would have been his father.
33. See p. 21 below.
34. It survives in a summary made by John Leland in the mid-sixteenth century, printed in Gray, *Scalacronica*, 134–41.
35. We do not know his name, but it could well be Faucon herald at arms, who 'came with letters to the prince [of Wales] from Sir John de Chaundos, then beyond the seas' on 1 October 1354. *RBP*, iv.163.
36. Chandos Herald, *La Vie du Prince Noir*, 14–18.
37. *Life and Campaigns of the Black Prince*, 100.
38. Ibid., 85. For another poem on the campaign, this time with a view to praising John of Gaunt and in Latin, see Walter of Peterborough, 'Prince Edward's Expedition'. Walter's Latin verse does not help the author's rather confused account, though his details are sometimes accurate.
39. *Life and Campaigns of the Black Prince*, 89.
40. Ibid., 114–15.
41. Henry of Grosmont wrote a not dissimilar confessional, *Le Livre des seyntz medicines*; see p. 326 below.
42. López de Ayala, *Coronica del rey don Pedro*, 157. I am grateful to Elspeth Ferguson for the translation.
43. *Chronique des règnes de Jean II et Charles V*; Ainsworth, *Jean Froissart and the Fabric of History*, 64–9.
44. For the annals of St Paul's, Adam Murimuth, Robert of Avesbury and the French chronicle of London, see Gransden, *Historical Writing in England II: c.1307 to the Early Sixteenth Century*, 61–72.
45. For these three chronicles, see *Annales Paulini*, *Murimuth* and *Avesbury*.
46. See p. 24 below.
47. Munby *et al.*, *Edward III's Round Table at Windsor*, 182–7.
48. *Avesbury*, 279.
49. Ibid., 285.

50. Ibid., 408–10.
51. *Croniques de London*, 76.
52. Gransden, *Historical Writing in England II*, 73–6.
53. This is particularly true of the unpublished text in Corpus Christi College Oxford MS 78, on Edward prince of Wales in Aquitaine.
54. See introduction to English translation of Baker, *Chronicon*.
55. *Chronique des quatre premiers Valois*, ed. Simeon Luce, 230–31.
56. Ibid., 123–5. The marriage was said to be the reason why the prince went to Aquitaine in 1362.
57. *Chronique normande du XIVᵉ siècle*.
58. Kenneth Fowler, 'News from the Front', 67–76; for Rodez, see ibid., p. 68.
59. See *Foedera*, iii.i.1209; other examples are in *Foedera* iii.i.858, 910, 1025, 1089 and iii.ii.45, 70, 81, 87, 341, 442. For a similar letter sent by Edward I, see *Foedera*, i.ii.872. See also McHardy, 'Some Reflections on Edward III's Use of Propaganda'.
60. Fowler, 'News from the Front', 83–4. This was presumably the *cedula* enclosed with a letter to the towns and sheriffs of England on 3 August 1346 (*Foedera*, iii.ii.88).
61. *Foedera*, iii.i.1129.
62. For *The Acts of War of Edward III*, see *Life and Campaigns of the Black Prince*, 26–40.
63. Translated in Riley, *Memorials of London and London Life*, 285–8.
64. Prince, 'A Letter of Edward the Black Prince', trans. in *Life and Campaigns of the Black Prince*, 83.
65. *Murimuth*, 212–14, in Latin; *Avesbury*, 358–62 and 367–9, both in French.
66. *Avesbury*, 445–7; *Life and Campaigns of the Black Prince*, 55–6.
67. For what follows, see Spufford, *Power and Profit*, 25–7.
68. Giovanni Villani, *Nuova cronica*, ed. Giuseppe Porta.
69. Christa Hammerl, 'The Earthquake of January 25th, 1348, Discussion of Sources', 6–7, http://emidius.mi.ingv.it/RHISE/ii_2oham/ii_2oham.html, accessed 01/09/2010.
70. Some further details are recorded in a chronicle from Pistoia, but these could simply be elaborations of what Villani says, rather than independent evidence. *Storie pistoresi*, 223.
71. Matteo Villani, *Cronica*, ed. Giuseppe Porta.
72. Letter from Johann von Schönfeld to Gottfried bishop of Passau, in Boehmer, *Acta imperii*, 750.
73. Carpentier, 'L'Historiographie de la bataille de Poitiers au quatorzième siècle'.
74. Anonimo romano, *Cronica*, ed. Giuseppe Porta (Milan, 1979) is the first full edition of the text. For a full study of the section on Crécy, see Maurizio Campanelli, 'A New Account of the Battle of Crécy from Fourteenth-Century

Rome', forthcoming. I am most grateful to Dr Campanelli for allowing me to see his text in advance of publication.

75. The phrase is from Robert Macfarlane, *The Old Ways* (London, 2012), 311.
76. *Foedera*, iii.i.88-90.

PROLOGUE: THE POLITICAL BACKGROUND

1. Prestwich, *Edward I*, 406-10.
2. Phillips, *Edward II*, 441 and n.
3. Seymour Phillips, Edward's most recent biographer, is 'inclined to take the letter at face value', but points out that it could be an elaborate cover-up of a relationship with Mortimer. See *Historiae Anglicanae Scriptores Decem*, where it is quoted by the bishop of Hereford in 1334, defending himself against charges that he was behind Isabella's defection (cols. 2767-8).
4. It was part of Isabella's dowry in 1303.
5. Phillips, *Edward II*, 543.

CHAPTER 1. EDWARD, PHILIPPA AND
THEIR COMRADES 1327-1330

1. Ormrod, *Edward III*, 19-24, for what follows.
2. Ibid., 20.
3. Denholm Young, 'Edward III and Bermondsey Priory', 213-20.
4. Shenton, 'The English Court', 115.
5. Ormrod, *Edward III*, 56. Some sources name Jean de Hainault; Le Bel, who may have been present, does not mention the knighting ceremony (*Chronique*, i.33 [33]).
6. *CPR 1327-1330*, 39; Chandos was granted £40 p.a. in revenue, less than Edward Bohun as son of the earl of Hereford, but much more than the other two knights named in the writ, who got 40s. each. This would support the idea that he was already a man of mature years. *CPR 1330-1334*, 173.
7. TNA E 101/383/8, m. 2.
8. Mortimer, *The Perfect King*, 60.
9. Ibid., 61-2, portrays Edward as eager to attack, and being restrained by Mortimer. The role played by Mortimer is ignored by Le Bel, but the English *Brut* chronicle portrays him as engaging in double-dealing with the Scots, preventing Thomas of Brotherton from ordering an attack and even disrupting the night-watch so that the Scots could withdraw unseen (ii.250-51).
10. Le Bel, *Chronique*, i.65 [45].
11. The dating of these in Mortimer, *The Perfect King*, 449, seems wrong: there are no dates in the accounts, the king was not at Worcester from 25 to 30

November, and the Clipstone and Rothwell dates make more sense after Christmas rather than before Edward II's funeral. For the entries for Worcester, Clipstone and Rothwell in the wardrobe accounts, see TNA E 101/382/9, mm. 15–16; E 101/383, mm. 2, 3; the York tournament is mentioned in Smyth, *Lives of the Berkeleys*, i.325.

12. Barker, *Tournament in England*, 56–8, 191–2.

13. Ibid., 50.

14. *Annales Paulini*, ii.264.

15. *RBP*, iii.59.

16. Munby *et al.*, *Edward III's Round Table at Windsor*, 135–6.

17. *Eulogium historiarum*, iii.227.

18. Denholm Young, 'The Tournament in the Thirteenth Century', 245.

19. *Murimuth*, 57; Baker, *Chronicon*, 42; Knighton, *Chronicon*, RS edn., i.449 (placed at Bedford in error).

20. Hemingburgh, *De Gestis*, ii.300.

21. *Avesbury*, 284; Dugdale, *Monasticon anglicanum*, vi, pt. 1, 352; TNA E 101/382/17; E 101/384, fo. 16ᵛ; E 101/398/22, m. 4.

22. Bryant, *Chrétien de Troyes: Perceval: The Story of the Grail*, 121.

23. Le Bel, *Chronique*, i.102 [59].

24. For a full account of the 'Craddok' material, see Barber, 'Edward III's Arthurian Enthusiasms Revisited', forthcoming.

25. Le Bel, *Chronique*, i.80 [51].

26. Edmund died in 1331, and Geoffrey inherited a lordship in France, so played no part in English affairs after the 1330s.

27. Walsingham, *Historia Anglicana*, i.304.

28. Baker, *Chronicon*, 48.

29. For example, in 1333 (*CPR 1330–1334*, 425) and in 1345 (*CPR 1343–1345*, 549); in both cases the offence was theft, and the convict was pregnant.

30. The counts of Hainault were also counts of Holland: William I of Hainault was also William III of Holland, and is often cited as William III as a result. Philippa's brother later became William II of Hainault and William IV of Holland.

31. *Accounts of the English Crown with Italian Merchant Societies*, ed. Bell *et al.*, 189.

32. Manchester, John Rylands, MS 235, fo. 11ᵛ.

33. See pp. 83, 156, 173 below on round table re-enactments.

34. Janse, *Ridderschap in Holland*, 339.

35. Smit, *De rekeningen der graven en gravinnen uit het Henegouwsche Huis*, xlvi.654.

36. Paravicini, *Die Preussenreisen*, i.57 for William II's Prussian journeys. His journey to Prussia explains his absence from Edward's Round Table feast in January 1344: see pp. 54–5 above.

37. Hamaker, *De rekeningen der grafelijkheid van Holland*, xxvi.85–88, 207, 333, 335, 338.
38. The Dutch pound was 20 shillings of silver, weighing 30 grams in all; Smit, *De rekeningen der graven en gravinnen uit het Henegouwsche Huis*, lxix.208.
39. Ibid., 129 for his armourer's journeys with horses for tournaments; several tournaments did not take place, and the count failed to appear on other occasions. Janse, 'Tourneyers and Spectators', 44, says that the count 'participated in at least ten tournaments in 1344 and 1345'.
40. For a survey of Philippa's possible commissioning of manuscripts, see Smith, *The Taymouth Hours*, 18.
41. See p. 181 below.
42. On this manuscript, see Sandler, *Gothic Manuscripts*, ii.103–5; Michael, 'A Manuscript Wedding Gift from Philippa of Hainaut to Edward III'; and Wathey, 'The Marriage of Edward III and the Transmission of French Motets to England'.
43. Coote, *Prophecy and Public Affairs*, 126.
44. Mortimer, *The Perfect King*, 182–5.
45. Ormrod, *Edward III*, 464–5, 534–7.
46. Coventry: Smyth, *Lives of the Berkeleys*, i.325; Guildford: ibid.; Nicolas, *Scrope–Grosvenor Controversy*, i.133; TNA E 361/3, m. 13a; E 101/384/6, rot. 2 m. 1; E 101/389/14, m. 2.
47. *Chronographia Regum Francorum*, ii.12; *Récits d'un bourgeois de Valenciennes*, 153.
48. *Croniques de London*, 62; TNA E 101/384/6, rot. 2 m. 1. There was a further tournament at Reigate, probably on 2–3 July: TNA E 101/384/6, rot. 2 m. 2.
49. TNA E 101/384/6, rot. 2 m. 4.
50. For all four tournaments, see TNA E 101/384/6, rot. 2 m. 1.
51. TNA C 47/6/1, mm. 2, 4; Nicolas, *Scrope–Grosvenor Controversy*, i.133; TNA E 101/384/6, rot. 2 m. 1; E 101/384/14; E 403/246.
52. All the details in this paragraph are from TNA E 101/384/6, rot. 2.
53. Vale, 'Image and Identity', 36; BL Add. MS 60584, m. 8ᵛ; Stanley, *Historical Memorials*, 168.
54. Le Bel, *Chronique*, 51.
55. London, Society of Antiquaries, MS 541, m. 4.
56. *Brut*, i.267.
57. London, Society of Antiquaries, MS 541, m. 3, records armour issued in 1330 to the king for a tournament at Woodstock. He was there from 22 to 27 July, which covers the period forty days after the prince's birth, and this is the most likely explanation for the tournament there.
58. See Newton, 'Queen Philippa's Squirrel Suit'.

59. *CPR 1327–1330*, 516, 517, 520, 530.
60. *PROME*, iv.103.
61. Baker, *Chronicon*, 45.
62. See Shenton, 'The English Court', 25. The only contemporary evidence is slight: see Doherty, 'Isabella, Queen of England', 287, for documents where she names Mortimer her heir in 1329–30.
63. *Brut*, ii.269–71; Gray, *Scalacronica*, 104–7.
64. Shenton, 'The English Court', 18, 20, says that he was not present at the coup because he is not included in the pardons, and that the same applies to Humphrey Bohun and Ralph Stafford; but see *ODNB*, s.v. William Bohun, where W. M. Ormrod accepts the evidence of the *Brut*. They may not have been directly involved in the action, or their pardons may not have survived, but their subsequent careers would point to their being members of this fairly select group.
65. Gray, *Scalacronica*, 107.
66. *Brut*, ii.271.
67. Baker, *Chronicon*, 47f.
68. Thornham is obscure: all that we know is that he joined the Knights Hospitaller in 1331, and had to be pardoned for the murder at Nottingham in order to do so.
69. *Brut*, ii.271.
70. Baker, *Chronicon*, 46.
71. Ormrod, *Edward III*, 134–5.
72. Powicke, 'Edward II and Military Obligation', 103. This is earlier than any citation in *MED*.
73. *Murimuth*, 60.
74. Shenton, 'The English Court', 194–5.

CHAPTER 2. 'A JOLLY YOUNG LIFE': TOURNAMENTS, FESTIVALS, DISPLAY

1. Gray, *Scalacronica*, 106–7.
2. London, Society of Antiquaries, MS 541, note sewn to m. 3, fair copy m. 3.
3. Parisse, 'Le Tournoi en France', 182, explores the possible derivations. It had a generalized meaning of a battle on horseback by the late twelfth century, and it is often found as a synonym for *hastiludia*.
4. *Annales Paulini*, 352–3; *Murimuth*, 63. There is a problem with the dating of this tournament, which has been associated with Edward's homage of 1329. However, *Annales Paulini* places it after the coup of 1330, and gives a date of 2 May, while *Murimuth* dates it to the end of April 1331. This seems to me to indicate that it is the same event, and a deliberate public appearance by the king, as if he had not been abroad. Furthermore, he was

only at Dartford in 1329 at late as 25 June. Walsingham, *Historia Anglicana*, i.193, says it was within a fortnight of his return from France in 1331.

5. *History of the King's Works*, ii.956–7.

6. TNA E 101/385/7, m. 2; E 361/3, rot. 10 m. 1d.

7. The entries in the accounts appear to be in chronological order, but this cannot be relied on. TNA E 101/385/7, m. 1; E361/3, rot. 19 m. 1d.

8. *Annales Paulini*, 353–4; TNA E 101/385/7, m. 1; Walsingham, *Historia Anglicana*, i.193.

9. *Annales Paulini*, 354–5.

10. Ibid.; TNA E101/385/7, m. 1; *Murimuth*, 63; Walsingham, *Historia Anglicana*, i.193; *Avesbury*, 286; *Croniques de London*, 62.

11. TNA E 361/3, rot. 19 m. 1d. The entries in his account appear to be in chronological order, and largely correspond in this respect with TNA E 101/385/7. Apart from Lichfield, they can be dated with the help of the king's itinerary: Ormrod, *Edward III*, 613–14.

12. See Appendix 4, 'Chronological List of Royal Tournaments of Edward III' for details. The London tournaments are: 1331, Stepney, Cheapside; 1334, Smithfield; 1343, Smithfield; 1344, Windsor (citizens invited); 1353, Smithfield; 1357, Smithfield; 1359, Smithfield; 1361, Smithfield; 1362, Cheapside (planned), Smithfield; 1363, Smithfield.

13. Strong, *Art and Power*, 21–2.

14. Barber and Barker, *Tournaments*, 107.

15. Vale, *Edward III and Chivalry*, 35.

16. *Lancelot-Grail*, Lancelot 5, 155:387.

17. *Foedera*, iii.i.5; *CPR 1343–1345*, 196. Grosmont left England at the end of March 1344 for Spain, and was still away at midsummer; in the following years he was in Aquitaine in 1345–6 and at Calais in 1347. It was only in 1348 that the fraternity did indeed hold jousts, and even then we hear nothing further of it (Baker, *Chronicon*, 97).

18. See Appendix 4.

19. See Long, 'Roll of the Arms of the Knights at the Tournament at Dunstable'.

20. *Chronicle of Lanercost*, quoted in Gransden, *Historical Writing in England II*, 13.

21. Villanueva, 'Memoria sobre la Orden de Caballería de la Banda de Castilla', 570–73, chs. 22 and 23; Daumet, 'L'Ordre castillan de l'écharpe', 28–9.

22. See p. 310 below for the circumstances.

23. TNA E 101/384/6, rot. 2 mm. 1–2.

24. *Murimuth*, 173–5.

25. John of Reading, *Chronica*, 151; Anonymus Cantuariensis, *Chronicon*, 118–19.

26. Barber and Barker, *Tournaments*, 98.

27. TNA E 101/391/5.

28. TNA E372/207, m. 50. Vale, *Edward III and Chivalry*, 175, misreads the entry: there are no merchants involved.
29. BL Add. MS 60584, m. 57.
30. TNA E 101/388/8, m. 5; E 101/385/4, m. 79.
31. Newton, *Fashion in the Age of the Black Prince*, 77–8.
32. Knighton, *Chronicle*, 76–7.
33. Vale, *The Princely Court*, 25.
34. *Chronique du religieux de Saint-Denis*, ii.64–71; Froissart, *Chroniques*, ed. Lettenhove, xv.84–92.
35. TNA E 101/394/16, m. 6.
36. See p. 484 below for the transformation of this into the story of the damsel Madresilva (Honeysuckle) in a fifteenth-century Catalan romance.
37. TNA E101/390/1, m. 2; E101/389/14, m. 2; Vale, *Edward III and Chivalry*, 64.
38. Siddons, *Heraldic Badges*, ii.i.239–45.
39. Wotton, *Life and Letters*, ii.17.
40. See Loomis, 'Secular Dramatics in the Royal Palace ... and Chaucer's "Tregetoures"'.
41. *Sir Gawain and the Green Knight*, 22.
42. Ibid., 24.
43. Ibid., 31.
44. Heidelberg, Universitätsbibliothek, MS Cod. Pal. Germ. 848, fos. 42^v, 197^v, 237, 52^r and 229^v.
45. Martin, *Minnesänger*, 7.
46. There may be a connection with his nickname, 'the Black Prince', from his supposed habit of wearing black armour. *RBP*, iv.245–6. Plates covered with cloth of gold and with blue velvet are mentioned in another list: *RBP*, iv.323–4.
47. Newton, *Fashion in the Age of the Black Prince*, 62–3.
48. Tout, *Chapters*, vi.105.
49. Staniland, 'The Great Wardrobe Accounts', 276.
50. Crowfoot *et al.*, *Textiles and Clothing*, 88. See also, for what follows, Staniland, 'Medieval Courtly Splendour' and 'Clothing and Textiles at the Court of Edward III'.
51. London, Society of Antiquaries, MS 208, fo. 9.
52. Nicolas, 'Observations on the Garter', 52.
53. Tout, *Chapters*, iv.390.
54. See p. 164 below.
55. For what follows, see Lachaud, 'Les Tentes et l'activité militaire'.
56. See Staniland, 'Court Style, Painters, and the Great Wardrobe'.
57. BL Add. MS 42130, fos. 181^v–182^r.

58. Safford, 'Expenses of Eleanor on her Marriage to Reynald, Count of Guelders', 114–15.
59. *Brut*, ii.297; John of Reading, *Chronica*, 88. Stella Newton points out (*Fashion in the Age of the Black Prince*, 9) that the *Brut* author misunderstands several terms in the Latin version. I have combined the two versions.
60. Newton, *Fashion in the Age of the Black Prince*, 8–11, 53–6.
61. Van Buren, *Illuminating Fashion*, 44–6.
62. Venette, *Chronicle*, 34.
63. Newton, *Fashion in the Age of the Black Prince*, 35, 36.
64. Cruse, *Illuminating the* Roman d'Alexandre, 183–94.
65. See Vale, *The Princely Court*, 212–13, on *The Vows of the Peacock* in court culture of the period.
66. *Récits d'un bourgeois de Valenciennes*, 48–9.
67. Quoted in Huot, *Postcolonial Fictions*, 2.
68. See *The Romance of Alexander: A Collotype Facsimile of MS. Bodley 264*; this is largely monochrome, but the five colour plates give some idea of its splendour.
69. Knighton, *Chronicle*, 93–5.
70. See Bothwell, 'Edward III, the English Peerage and the 1337 Earls'.
71. Although they were rarely together before the coup of 1330, Henry may have met Edward at the tournaments at Blyth and Hereford in 1328, and again at Northampton in July 1330; he was certainly at the Cheapside tournament in 1331, and at the queen's churching at Woodstock in 1332. See Fowler, *The King's Lieutenant*, 27–8.
72. *Antient Kalendars*, iii.164–5.

CHAPTER 3. APPRENTICESHIP IN WAR: SCOTLAND AND FLANDERS 1332–1340

1. Gray, *Scalacronica*, 106–7.
2. Strictly speaking, the Dunbars were earls of March, but I have used the alternative name to avoid confusion with the Mortimer earls of March in England.
3. Nicholson, *Edward III and the Scots*, 133.
4. *Chronicle of Lanercost*, 268.
5. The best account of the battle is in Rogers, *War Cruel and Sharp*, 39–46.
6. TNA E 361/3, rot. 19 m. 1d; DL 40/1/11, fo. 52ᵛ; BL Add. MS 46350, rot. 7; BL MS Cotton Galba E.III, fo. 183ᵛ.
7. TNA E 101/386/2, m. 7.
8. It is not clear if he actually served during the campaign; the writ for payment of his wages was cancelled. He did serve in 1334–5, but died during 1335. *CCR 1337–1339*, 7–8.

9. Rogers, *War Cruel and Sharp*, 69 n. 139. Documentation for this campaign is slight.

10. The date of Joan's birth is uncertain; if the normal forty days for Philippa's churching was observed, the feast for her churching on 8–10 March 1334 would give a date of 26–9 January 1334. See TNA E 101/386/16, m. 7, and Mortimer, *The Perfect King*, 433, 501.

11. TNA E 361/2, rot. 4 m. 13; TNA E 101/386/18, m. 23.

12. TNA E 101/389/14, m. 2.

13. *Lancelot-Grail*, Lancelot 1, 11:108; Lancelot 3, 86:215.

14. *Lancelot* is framed by King Claudas's dispossession of Lancelot, Lionel and Bors as children at the beginning of the story, and by the defeat of Claudas and restoration of their lands at the end. See index of proper names in *Lancelot-Grail* for full references.

15. Ormrod, *Edward III*, 99.

16. TNA E 361/3, rot. 24 m. 1d. See Tobler–Lommatzsch, *Altfranzösisches Wörterbuch*, 5.i, col. 501: the phrase 'escu lionel' occurs in the twelfth-century *chanson de geste Raoul de Cambrai* and elsewhere.

17. I am grateful to Thomas Woodcock, Garter King of Arms, for pointing out the identification of the shield. See *Dictionary of British Arms*, ii.223.

18. BL MS Cotton Nero C.VIII, fos. 233 ff.

19. *Historia Roffensis*, quoted in Rogers, *The Wars of Edward III*, 44.

20. Rogers, *War Cruel and Sharp*, 101.

21. *Historia Roffensis*, fo. 78.

22. Rogers, *War Cruel and Sharp*, 116 n. 181; Ayton, *Knights and Warhorses*, 257.

23. Gray, *Scalacronica*, 124–5.

24. Cazelles, *La Société politique*, 80–81.

25. *CPR 1330–1334*, 565. He was, however, sent again in 1337.

26. Baker, *Chronicon*, 56.

27. *Report on the Dignity of a Peer*, v.28–32.

28. Gray, *Scalacronica*, 123.

29. Edward of Woodstock, the king's eldest son, aged seven, succeeded John as earl of Cornwall; the earl of Norfolk had no heir.

30. *CPR 1338–1340*, 91, 95.

31. Ayton, 'Edward III and the English Aristocracy', 193.

32. Sumption, *The Hundred Years War*, i.51, estimates the magnate families at '150 to 200'.

33. McFarlane, *The Nobility of Later Medieval England*, 120.

34. Ayton, 'Edward III and the English Aristocracy', 184.

35. TNA E 101/388/8, m. 6.

36. Ibid.

37. TNA E 101/388/8, m. 1.

38. Not all of those who sealed were present in Flanders; for instance, Henry Percy was in the north of England in command of military activity on the Scottish border.
39. BL MS Cotton Caligula D.III, printed in Froissart, *Chroniques*, ed. Lettenhove, xviii.85–94.
40. Le Bel, *Chronique*, i.163 [81].
41. Rogers, *War Cruel and Sharp*, 173; TNA E 101/388/11.
42. See Rogers, *The Wars of Edward III*, 81–2.
43. TNA E 101/388/11; E 361/3, m. 40a.
44. *Avesbury*, 311.
45. I have followed the most recent account of the battle in Cushway, *Edward III and the War at Sea*, 92–100.
46. Philip's letter setting out the terms is in Fowler, 'Henry of Grosmont', appendix, 41.
47. *Croniques de London*, 84.
48. *Foedera*, ii.ii.1141.

CHAPTER 4. THE KINGDOM OF FRANCE

1. See Owen, *Le Traité de Walter de Bibbesworth*.
2. *Chronica Monasterii de Melsa*, iii.57. The abbey held lands at Nafferton.
3. Ponthieu had only been English since Edward's step-grandmother, Margaret of France, brought it as her dowry in 1299.
4. Baker, *Chronicon*, reflects this attitude in a more extreme form, calling Philip VI and John II 'the crowned one of France' rather than king of France, to emphasize that they were not the rightful occupants of the throne.
5. Taylor, 'The Salic Law', 550–52. The Roman *lex voconia*, in St Augustine's view, conflicted with the biblical tradition, which allowed women to inherit property. The crown, however, was not private property, but a public office, and a form of priestly office as well, from which women should be barred.
6. Cazelles, *La Société politique*, 53–7; see also Taylor, 'Edward III and the Plantagenet Claim to the French Throne'.
7. Cazelles, *La Société politique*, 72.
8. Ibid., 42–3.
9. *Chronique latine de Guillaume de Nangis*, ii.96–7.
10. John XXII mentions this in a letter congratulating him on his victory, quoted in DeVries, *Infantry Warfare*, 107.
11. The best account of the historical background is Whiting, 'The Vows of the Heron'. See also Butterfield, *The Familiar Enemy*, 115–16, and Vale, *The Princely Court*, 213–18. The most recent edition of *Vows of the Heron* is that of J. L. Grigsby and Norris J. Lacy.
12. Le Bel, *Chronique*, i.163 [81].

13. Sumption, *The Hundred Years War*, ii.412.
14. Eustace d'Auberchicourt until his death in 1368 (see Appendix 2), and then John Chandos.
15. *Grandes chroniques*, ed. Viard, ix.248.
16. *Historia Roffensis*, fo. 92.
17. See p. 234 below.
18. Anonimo romano, *Cronica*, abbreviated edn., 93.
19. Sumption, *The Hundred Years War*, i.562.
20. In fact he was beheaded in the courtyard of the Hôtel de Nesle on the morning of the 18th.
21. Le Bel, *Chronique*, i.198–200 [214–15].
22. Chareyron, *Jean le Bel*, 90–104, examines all the accounts in detail, and concludes that none can be said to solve the problem. Villani's version seems the most plausible.
23. *PROME*, v.35–6.
24. Cazelles, *Société politique, noblesse et couronne*, 40–43.
25. Delachenal, *Histoire de Charles V*, iii.553; although the writer requests that the letter be burnt immediately, a copy survives in a collection of documents relating to negotiations with France in BL MS Cotton Caligula D.III (item 76, not 170 as in Delachenal).
26. Cazelles, *Société politique, noblesse et couronne*, 309.
27. Luce, 'Du Guesclin au siège de Rennes'.
28. i.e. du Guesclin; Froissart, *Chroniques*, SHF, vi.117–19.
29. Sumption, *The Hundred Years War*, ii.215. For *regard* see p. 396 below.
30. *Récits d'un bourgeois de Valenciennes*, 220.

CHAPTER 5. 'AS IT WAS IN THE DAYS OF KING ARTHUR'

1. *History of the King's Works*, ii.950–54.
2. TNA E 101/388/11 (Norwich); *Foedera*, iii.ii.1145 (Ingham), 1146 (Norwich). *Murimuth*, 117 n. for series of tournaments, followed by Baker, *Chronicon*, 73.
3. TNA C 47/6/1, m. 18 ('the parson of Osmundeston', now Scole, near Diss).
4. TNA E 101/390/2, m. 4.
5. Ibid. m. 1.
6. There were jousts of war with the Scots at the end of December (*Murimuth*, 123) and tournaments on the return southwards at York and Hull (*Chronica Monasterii de Melsa*, iii.49).
7. *Murimuth*, 123–4, 223; Baker, *Chronicon*, 75; TNA C 47/6/1, mm. 2, 4; E 36/204, fo. 21ᵛ; E 101/389/14; *Chronica Monasterii de Melsa*, iii.49; *Brut*, ii.296.

8. *Murimuth*, 124, 223; *Chronica Monasterii de Melsa*, iii.49; TNA E 101/389/14. Froissart, *Chroniques*, Rome version, 563–4, has a garbled account confusing this tournament with that at Northampton, and incorporating a largely fictitious passage from Jean le Bel, *Chronique*, ii.2–4 [146–7], which is perhaps a distant echo of the Eltham occasion.

9. *Murimuth*, 121.

10. Jones, 'Edward III's Captains in Brittany', 107 n.

11. Cushway, *Edward III and the War at Sea*, 112.

12. Baker, *Chronicon*, 76.

13. *Murimuth*, 128.

14. *PROME*, iv.368.

15. Loomis, 'Edward I, Arthurian Enthusiast'.

16. Morris, 'Edward I and the Knights of the Round Table', 62.

17. *Chronicle of Glastonbury*, 245.

18. *Vita Edwardi Secundi*, in *Chronicles of the Reigns of Edward I and Edward II*, i.91.

19. Stones, *Anglo-Scottish Relations*, 197.

20. Shenton, 'Royal Interest in Glastonbury and Cadbury', 1254.

21. Luxford, 'King Arthur's Tomb at Glastonbury', 50.

22. Le Bel, *Chronique*, i.118–19 [65].

23. For an outline of Isabella's activities as a bibliophile, and a list of manuscripts possibly associated with her, see Smith, *The Taymouth Hours*, 16–17.

24. BL Add. MS 60584, m. 27ᵛ. See Revard, 'Courtly Romances in the Privy Wardrobe', 304–6, for details of all Isabella's borrowings.

25. TNA E 101/393/4, fo. 8; BL MS Cotton Galba E.XIV.

26. Cavanaugh, 'Books Privately Owned in England', 844–61.

27. The nature of John Flete's 'final account' is discussed in Revard, 'Courtly Romances in the Privy Wardrobe', 299, 303, 306–7.

28. *Dictionary of Medieval Latin*, s.v. 'romancia'.

29. BL Add. MS 60584, m. 26ᵛ.

30. Green, 'King Richard II's Books Revisited', 237; the list is printed in Cavanaugh, 'Books Privately Owned in England', 279.

31. This would identify it as a version of Chrétien de Troyes's *Perceval*, in which the two heroes figure with almost equal prominence.

32. *Antient Kalendars*, iii.265; Vale, *Edward III and Chivalry*, 45, 125.

33. Alfonso X, *Las siete partidas*, ii.428–9.

34. See p. 78 above.

35. 'Benedict of Peterborough', ii.159.

36. *Le Roman en prose de Tristan*, 424.

37. Johnstone, *Edward of Caernarvon*, 18.

38. Murimuth's chronicle exists in three versions: for full texts and translations, see Munby *et al.*, *Edward III's Round Table*, appendix C.

39. BN MS français 693, fo. 254.

40. The section of Gray's *Scalacronica* which described the event survives only in a sixteenth-century summary (135), which confuses the Round Table feast with the foundation of the Order of the Garter. Froissart's account (*Chroniques*, Rome version, 595–6), which makes the same mistake, was written many years later, after the early records of the Order of the Garter had been lost.

41. Newton, *Fashion in the Age of the Black Prince*, 18–20. The pawning seems to have been symbolic rather than related to the value of the crown. A list of crowns and circlets in BL Add. MS 60584, fo. 58^v, shows the maximum value of any one of the crowns in Edward's possession in 1336 to have been £75.

42. Nicolas, 'Observations on the Garter', 6.

43. Walsingham, *Historia Anglicana*, i.263.

44. *Brut*, i.262.

45. Quoted in Schmolke-Hasselmann, 'The Round Table: Ideal, Fiction, Reality', 48.

46. The only exception is in the Merlin section of the *Lancelot-Grail*, where Merlin chooses fifty knights for Uther Pendragon when he establishes the table (Merlin 3:54); it is not at this point called the 'Round Table'. This passage is based on Robert de Boron's *Merlin*.

47. *Lancelot-Grail*, Merlin Continuation 60:16.

48. Ibid., Post-Vulgate Quest 107:359.

49. Ibid., 120:67.

50. Munby *et al.*, *Edward III's Round Table*, 238–39; *Chronicle of Lanercost*, 341, notes that 'excessive provisions' were used, 'as befitted the royal majesty'.

51. The expenditure listed by St John Hope, *Windsor Castle*, i.178–219, totals £6,868 8s. 4d. for sixty months, giving an average of £114 14s. 8d. per month.

52. *Morte Arthure*, ll. 16–22.

53. St John Hope, *Windsor Castle*, i.111.

54. *Antiquarian Repertory*, ed. F. Grose, i.324.

55. *CPR 1247–1258*, 157.

56. Munby *et al.*, *Edward III's Round Table*, 86; for the following discussion, see ibid., 84–99, 149–52.

57. *Perceforest*, ed. Roussineau, *Première partie*, ii.294; tr. Bryant, 258.

58. Barber, 'Edward III's Arthurian Enthusiasms Revisited'.

59. Wheatley, *The Idea of the Castle*, ch. 4, 'The Imperial Castle'.

60. Strong, *Art and Power*, 19.

61. Ormrod, *Edward III*, 261–2.

62. de Graaf, *Oorlog om Holland*, 285–97.

63. Giovanni Villani, *Nuova cronica*, iii.409: 'more than five thousand pounds sterling'.

CHAPTER 6. THE CRÉCY CAMPAIGN

1. For what follows, see Lambert, *Shipping the Medieval Military*, esp. ch. 3.
2. See below (p. 193) for the number of ships needed to transport 10,000 horses (500). This leaves 500 or more larger ships to transport 13,600 troops and a number of non-military personnel, as well as the provisions. The chroniclers, who all overestimate the strength of the army, are closer to the mark on the number of ships (Baker and Avesbury both give about 1,000; Murimuth gives 750 at the end of June, with further vessels still arriving before the departure a week later).
3. Cushway, *Edward III and the War at Sea*, appendix 2.
4. Livingstone and Witzel, *Road to Crécy*, 95.
5. Lambert, *Shipping the Medieval Military*, 136.
6. It is possible that the undated list of ships available to the king at the end of seventeenth-century copies of the army retinues (e.g. BL Add. MS 38823) may be related to the Crécy campaign.
7. Ayton and Preston, *Crécy*, 236.
8. Hewitt, *The Organization of War under Edward III*, 152.
9. Tout, 'Firearms in England', 689; further guns were supplied for the siege of Calais, but it is the use of guns in battle which is novel, as guns had not been employed at Berwick in 1333.
10. *Life and Campaigns of the Black Prince*, 30.
11. For numbers of carts, see Chapter 7.
12. TNA E 101/393/11, rot. 62.
13. e.g. TNA E 101/393/11, rot. 63.
14. Livingstone and Witzel, *Road to Crécy*, 89.
15. See p. 198 below on the policy of intimidation as against acceptance into the king's peace, i.e. changing sides.
16. Hewitt, *Organization of War under Edward III*, 53-6.
17. Wrottesley, *Crécy and Calais*, 193-4. The lower figure is for retinues with more than 300 men, the higher for retinues of more than 100 men; we do not know enough about the arrangements for feeding the army at large to do more than estimate.
18. TNA E 101/393/11, rot. 60.
19. It is described as 'salted' in the accounts; ibid., rot. 62.
20. Ibid., rot. 58d.
21. Ayton and Preston, *Crécy*, 181.
22. Ibid., 189.
23. The surviving lists are for the whole campaign up to 23 November 1347, when the bulk of the troops had returned from the siege of Calais: Wrottesley, *Crécy and Calais*, 193, 201. There are no accurate numbers for the actual battle.
24. *RBP*, i.14.

25. Ayton and Preston, *Crécy*, 207.
26. *RBP*, i.163.
27. *RBP*, ii.46.
28. Jones and Walker, 'Private Indentures for Life Service in Peace and War 1278–1476'.
29. Full text in Fowler, *The King's Lieutenant*, 234.
30. Prince, 'Indenture System', 293.
31. *Life and Campaigns of the Black Prince*, 29.
32. Nicholson, *Edward III and the Scots*, 17, 174.
33. Hay, 'The Division of the Spoils of War', 108–9.
34. Ibid., 101.
35. Ayton, *Knights and Warhorses*, 130–37.
36. *Life and Campaigns of the Black Prince*, 29.
37. Pryor, 'Transportation of Horses by Sea during the Crusades'. In the Sicilian ships, there is an item for the purchase of rings, evidently for securing their bridles as in a stable. Pryor interprets the rings as supports for slings which lifted the horses off their feet for the duration of the voyage; this is still found in modern veterinary practice, where a horse will be put in slings if it has a foot injury, so that it can stand comfortably for long periods on three legs.
38. Manchester, John Rylands, MS 234, fo. 50; fifteen grooms are listed as keepers of one destrier.
39. Henxteworth, m. 1, payment for windage at the start of the expedition to Gascony in 1355.
40. Ambroise, *History of the Holy War*, ii.53.
41. Printed in Le Bel, *Chronique*, ii.338.
42. *Life and Campaigns of the Black Prince*, 14. There is no supporting evidence that he had made arrangements for his arrival in Gascony, whereas he does seem to have made arrangements for a possible rendezvous with the Flemish army in Picardy before setting out.
43. Tidal information from Admiralty Easy Tide website, http://easytide.ukho.gov.uk.
44. Sumption, *The Hundred Years War*, i.494.
45. Ibid., 499.
46. *Life and Campaigns of the Black Prince*, 15.
47. The *Acts of War* lists many of the commanders, and others are named in the St Omer chronicle. I have excluded four clerks and the bishop of Durham.
48. For Hastings's campaign, which ended around 25 August, see Sumption, *The Hundred Years War*, i.498–9, 503, 512, 519, 524.
49. Viard, 'La Campagne de juillet-août 1346', 15. The French sources say that the castle was 'sold', but it seems more likely that the French commanders recognized Edward as king of France and were put on his payroll.
50. *Life and Campaigns of the Black Prince*, 30.
51. Viard, 'La Campagne de juillet-août 1346', 18.

52. *Chronique normande du XIVe siècle*, 76.

53. See pp. 308–9 below for the far-reaching consequences on Thomas Holland's career, and indeed on the succession to the English throne: without this money, Holland would not have regained Joan of Kent, and she would not have been free to marry the prince of Wales on Holland's death.

54. *Life and Campaigns of the Black Prince*, 34.

55. Papirius Masso and Thomas Warton, cited in Prentout, 'La Prise de Caen', 261.

56. Delpit, *Collection générale*, 72.

57. Avesbury, 364.

58. *Chronique normande du XIVe siècle*, 77 n. 1.

59. *Eulogium historiarum*, iii.206.

60. Edward III to his council, in Fowler, 'News from the Front', 84.

61. *Eulogium historiarum*, in *Life and Campaigns of the Black Prince*, 35.

62. *Eulogium historiarum* calls him 'du Bois'.

63. There is some confusion over the sequence of events at Gaillon and La Roche-Guyon: see Viard, 'La Campagne de juillet-août 1346', 41–3. However, Viard is mistaken in saying that La Roche-Guyon was not taken, as the *Acts of War* (Cambridge, Corpus Christi College, MS 170, fo. 102^r) specifically quotes a rhyme which says that 'the fleur-de-lis will lose its name when Rocheguyon is wounded', because the castle was reputedly impregnable. The same rhyme is quoted in *Chronica Monasterii de Melsa*, iii.56.

64. *Récits d'un bourgeois de Valenciennes*, 223.

65. *Grandes chroniques*, ed. Viard, ix.278.

66. *Life and Campaigns of the Black Prince*, 39.

67. Le Bel, *Chronique*, ii.92 [176–7].

68. *Life and Campaigns of the Black Prince*, 19.

69. Ibid., 22.

70. *Récits d'un bourgeois de Valenciennes*, 227.

71. BN MS français 693, fo. 260^v.

72. Le Bel, *Chronique*, ii.96 [178].

73. Knighton, *Chronicle*, 60–61.

74. Information from local noticeboards at St Valéry, September 2012.

75. *Chronica Monasterii de Melsa*, iii.57.

76. Data from http://easytide.ukho.gov.uk, adjusted back to the Julian calendar.

77. *Life and Campaigns of the Black Prince*, 22.

78. See the discussion in Preston, 'The Traditional Battlefield of Crécy': although he believes that the traditional battlefield is the most likely candidate, the problems and uncertainties are fully explored.

CHAPTER 7. THE BATTLE AT CRÉCY

1. See Keegan, 'The Personal Angle of Vision', in *The Face of Battle*, 128–33.
2. Li Muisit, *Chroniques et annales*, 161.
3. *Life and Campaigns of the Black Prince*, 22.
4. Ibid., 19–20.
5. *Acts of War*, 27.
6. *PROME*, iii.389–92.
7. Matteo Villani, *Cronica*, i.46, says that Edward 'arranged all his carts at the front *a modo d'una schiera*', in ranks or in a group, and that he put armed knights on top of the carts. The knights would not have been much use in that position, and his account seems to be entirely a garbled version of that of his brother.
8. Villani writes 'bombarde', but these were described as ribalds in the royal accounts, and were therefore smaller than the guns usually described as bombards. They would have been similar to that illustrated in Milemete's treatise of 1326.
9. 'pallottole di ferro', 'pellets of iron'. This is confirmed by a writ of 4 March 1346, referring to 'pellotis et pulvere' for the 100 'ribalds' shipped for the Crécy campaign: Tout, 'Firearms in England', 688.
10. 'dentro al carrino': I have translated 'carrino' as 'array of carts' below, as it does not specify the actual formation in which the carts were drawn up.
11. This corresponds to the 'small area' mentioned in Edward III's letter on the battle.
12. It was not unusual to give the prince of Wales his anticipated title, even during his father's lifetime.
13. Giovanni Villani, *Nuova cronica*, i.450–59.
14. Anonimo romano, *Cronica*, abbreviated edn., 5. In his introduction, the chronicler says that he has used oral sources, but this applies mainly to the section on Rome.
15. See Campanelli, 'A New Account of the Battle of Crécy from Fourteenth-Century Rome', forthcoming.
16. As at Waterloo, where the English identified the advancing Imperial Guard in the same way.
17. This would be 22 August by the modern Julian calendar, but still a late harvest.
18. The text reads 'crossbowmen' (*valestrieri*), but the English did not use crossbows.
19. 'soprastare', literally 'stand above'.
20. *Istoire et croniques de Flandre*, ii.42–3.
21. BN MS français 693, fo. 261ᵛ. Names are distorted throughout this text: I have normalized as follows:

Berinc = Warwick, Suatere = Fitzwalter, Werdon = Verdon, Stryvelyn = Stirling, Poinghe = Poynings, Frarin = Fitzwarin, Causmale = Carswell. I have not been able to identify the lords of 'Tringas' and 'Baruf'. Seventeen of the thirty-four names occur in the *Acts of War*. For a slightly different interpretation, and comments on St Omer's errors, see Ayton in Ayton and Preston, *Crécy*, 165–6, 242–4. The 'lord of Man' is Sir William Montagu, who became earl of Salisbury in 1349.

22. *Historia Roffensis*, fo. 92.

23. i.e. the *Grandes chroniques*, *Chronique des quatre premiers Valois*, and *Chronographia Regum Francorum*.

24. *Chronique normande du XIVe siècle*, 81.

25. *Istoire et croniques de Flandre*, 42.

26. Mathias von Nuewenburg, *Chronik*, 398.

27. Le Bel and *Chronica Monasterii de Melsa* treat the carts as the usual wagon park to the rear of the army, found in most medieval battles (Froissart takes his account from Le Bel).

28. Baker, *Chronicon*, 67.

29. Vegetius, *Epitoma rei militaris*, 3.10.16–18.

30. Toman, *Husitské válečnictví za doby Žižkovy a Prokopovy*, 403–4.

31. Durdík, *Hussitisches Heerwesen*, 151–63.

32. The fullest account is in DeVries, *Infantry Warfare*, 32–48.

33. *Annales Gandenses*, 66; Paris, *Memoriale*, 643; *Chronique artésienne*, 84; Guiart, 'Branche des royaus lignages', 291.

34. Guiart, 'Branche des royaus lignages', ll. 20085–20110.

35. Harari, 'Strategy and Supply in Fourteenth-Century Campaigns', 318.

36. Anonimo romano, *Cronica*, abbreviated edn., 87.

37. Le Bel, *Chronique*, ii.299 [251].

38. See Ch. 6, n. 38 above.

39. Baker, *Chronicon*, 84.

40. Strickland and Hardy, *The Great Warbow*, 295–7.

41. Baker, *Chronicon*, 84.

42. Ayton, in Ayton and Preston, *Crécy*, 328, and *Dictionary of Medieval Latin*, s.v. 'ericius'. It is also used of siege machines, one of the group of such engines which even in classical times were named after animals, the best-known being the *testudo* or tortoise. It may seem a small point, but a great deal of ink has been spilt over the crucial question of the formation of the archers in this battle.

43. Mathias von Nuewenburg, *Chronik*, 398.

44. Baker, *Chronicon*, 84.

45. *lo conte Valentino*: Aymar VI de Poitiers, count of Diois and Valentinois.

46. The *catenelle* or small chains; not immediately identifiable as part of a suit of armour.

47. *Adoardetto*, literally 'little Edward', an insulting way of referring to the prince.

48. Anonimo romano, *Cronica*, abbreviated edn., 92–3.
49. *Chronique normande du XIVe siècle*, 81; the *Chronographia Regum Francorum*, ii.233, is the only other source to mention it: 'And in that battle the prince of Wales was captured by the count of Flanders, but later rescued.'
50. Thomas Daniel was specifically rewarded for raising the banner, but Fitzsimon may have taken charge of it again once the enemy had retreated.
51. Baker, *Chronicon*, 85.
52. Froissart, *Chronicles*, tr. Thomas Johnes, i.167; original in Froissart, *Chroniques*, SHF, i.281. Sir Thomas Norwich is not found in the official British records.
53. 'et fut honteux', literally 'and was ashamed'. *Récits d'un bourgeois de Valenciennes*, 234.
54. His name is given as 'Sir Haun di Tornello'; I have not been able to identify him.
55. Anonimo romano, *Cronica*, abbreviated edn., 95–7.
56. Beneš z Weitmile, *Chronicon*, iv.514.
57. BN MS français 693, fo. 262^v.
58. John of Arderne, *Treatises*, xxvii n.
59. Le Bel, *Chronique*, i.102 [180].
60. Technically, according to the Church, a day of truce; but the rule was rarely observed in the field.
61. *Récits d'un bourgeois de Valenciennes*, 230.
62. There is a modern viewing point where the mill is thought to have stood, though its precise position is not known.
63. Cochon, *Chronique normande*, 69.
64. *Murimuth*, 216; *Storie pistoresi*, 222; *Eulogium historiarum*, iii.210–11.
65. *Chronique des quatre premiers Valois*, 16.
66. BN MS français 693, fos. 262^v–263.
67. Le Bel, *Chroniques*, ii.108 [183].
68. A cloth attached to the helmet covering the neck which was usually blazoned with the owner's arms.
69. *Récits d'un bourgeois de Valenciennes*, 235.
70. Delisle, *Histoire de Saint-Sauveur*, 67–8, 88–9, 95–9.
71. BN MS français 693, fo. 263; this is confirmed by *Istoire et croniques de Flandre*, 44, but this information may have come from St Omer.
72. Anonimo romano, *Cronica*, abbreviated edn., 96.
73. Giovanni Villani, *Nuova cronica*, 458.
74. Baker, *Chronicon*, 85–6.
75. Facetiously named 'good day' (*goedendag*) from the warm welcome they gave to the enemy.
76. *Life and Campaigns of the Black Prince*, 23.
77. Ibid., 25.
78. *RBP*, i.14.

79. Prestwich, 'The English at the Battle of Neville's Cross', 1–14.
80. 2 Corinthians 2: 14.
81. Offler, 'Thomas Bradwardine's "Victory Sermon"', 4–6.
82. *Chronica Monasterii de Melsa*, iii.63–4.
83. Viard, 'Le Siège de Calais', 163.
84. BN MS français 693, fos. 272–3; Viard, 'Le Siège de Calais', 157.
85. *Avesbury*, 386.
86. Le Bel, *Chronique*, ii.113 [184]; Knighton, *Chronicle*, 78–80.
87. Le Bel, *Chronique*, ii. 157 [199].
88. Baker, *Chronicon*, 91.
89. 'runcino' – Chaucer's 'rouncy'.
90. Le Bel, *Chronique*, ii.161–7 [200–203].
91. 'Hay the Whit Swan', according to TNA E 372/207, m. 50.
92. See p. 79 above for full details.
93. See in particular the full-page images in Martin, *Minnesänger*, where peacock feathers are used.
94. Edward was at Lichfield only once in 1348, from 4 to 12 May; he was at Windsor in May, June and July, and at Eltham in May and July, so the dating is not certain. The dating of 9 April in the accounts for the Lichfield tournament (Nicolas, 'Observations on the Garter', 26) is clearly an error. Baker (*Chronicon*, 101) dates the Windsor tournament as being at midsummer 1349, but he gives the names of the French captives present, two of whom are known from the accounts to have been at Windsor in 1348. Baker's chronology is particularly difficult at this point: he still appears to be following Murimuth's curious habit of starting the year at Michaelmas, which suggests Murimuth's chronicle (or a continuation) may have covered these years. He goes on to say that the captives hunted at Clarendon: Edward was at Odiham, known for its hunting (*History of the King's Works*, ii.766), Woodstock and Clarendon in August and September. See Ormrod, 'For Arthur and St George', 19 n. 30. For other details of these tournaments, see Nicolas, 'Observations on the Garter', 26–30, 39, 40–42; TNA E 101/391/15, mm. 7, 9, 10; E 372/207, m. 50; *RBP*, iv.72–3.
95. Baker, *Chronicon*, 101.
96. Ormrod, *Edward III*, 306 n. 28. A date of 9 July seems unlikely, since the Canterbury jousts would almost certainly have been cancelled if this was the case.

CHAPTER 8. THE ROYAL CHAPELS AND THE COLLEGE OF ST GEORGE AT WINDSOR

1. *Foedera*, iii.i.167.
2. *Foedera*, iv.50.
3. See Cook, *English Collegiate Churches*, 12–17, and Knowles and Hadcock, *Medieval Religious Houses*, 420–44.

4. The canons of the great cathedrals also technically belonged to secular colleges, but these colleges had been set up after the foundation of the church to which they belonged.
5. Stow, *A Survey of the cities of London and Westminster*, vi.54.
6. Ormrod, 'The Personal Religion of Edward III', 857.
7. *Victoria County Histories, London*, i.461.
8. *Chronica Monasterii de Melsa*, iii.51-2.
9. *Eulogium historiarum*, iii.213.
10. See Howe, 'Divine Kingship and Dynastic Display'.
11. *Calendar of Charter Rolls 1341-1417*, p. 134.
12. *Wynnere and Wastoure*, l. 503.
13. Stratford, *Richard II and the English Royal Treasure*, 209, item R 706.
14. Howe, 'Divine Kingship and Dynastic Display', 262.
15. Tracy, *English Gothic Choirstalls*, 50.
16. Howe, 'Divine Kingship and Dynastic Display', 264.
17. Topham, *Some Account of the Collegiate Chapel of St Stephen*, 8 (note to plate VIII).
18. See Billot, *Les Saintes Chapelles*.
19. Edward I had begun to rebuild the chapel in 1297 in the style of the Sainte-Chapelle, but at that point there was no re-foundation of the chapel, and no claim to the kingdom of France, but simply a princely rivalry. See Alexander and Binski, *Age of Chivalry*, cat. no. 324.
20. Bowers, 'The Music and Musical Establishment of St George's Chapel', 174-5.
21. Ormrod, 'Edward III and his Family', 408, 413.
22. *Calendar of Liberate Rolls 1240-1245*, 205.
23. *History of the King's Works*, ii.1016.
24. Ibid., 862-3.
25. Biddle, *King Arthur's Round Table*, 78-80 (dating of woodwork), 398-402 (Windsor connection). Given Edward IV's known Arthurian enthusiasm and use of the rose en soleil, as well as Harding's mention of the Round Table as hanging there, a dating in the 1460s on cultural grounds seems much more probable.
26. See list in Good, *The Cult of Saint George in Medieval England*, 155-9; unfortunately, few dates can be given. However, only a handful are for monastic institutions, or for pre-Conquest churches: see Morgan, 'The Banner-Bearer of Christ', 56.
27. Good, *The Cult of Saint George in Medieval England*, 52-9.
28. *History of the King's Works*, i.481. The cost also included a similar figure of a pilgrim.
29. Oxford, Bodleian Library, MS Douce 231, fo. 1^r. See Sandler, *Gothic Manuscripts*, ii.95-6.

30. Milemete, *De nobilitatibus*, xxi. See also *Secretum Secretorum*, ed. Manzalaoui.
31. *Political Thought in Early Fourteenth Century England*, 21.
32. Voragine, *Legenda Aurea*, s.v. Julian, 145; Lambeth Apocalypse: illustrated in Good, *The Cult of Saint George in Medieval England*, pl. 2. For descriptions of the manuscripts, see Morgan, *Early Gothic Manuscripts*, ii.104; Warner, *Queen Mary's Psalter*, 45–6, pls. 223–4; Sandler, *Gothic Manuscripts*, ii.108.
33. Modernized from Greene, *Selection of English Carols*, 227.
34. BL MS Harleian 5001, fos. 24–24ᵛ; this is a seventeenth-century copy of the prince's wardrobe book for 1306–7. The garters and shoes are recorded as being 'for the Scottish wars', but this is probably an error and the comment should apply to the previous item, banners of St George and St Edward.
35. *Calendar of Inquisitions Miscellaneous*, ii.130, C87/25, goods of prisoners taken after the battle of Boroughbridge.
36. e.g. in Boulton, *Knights of the Crown*, 157–8.
37. TNA E 101/386/9, m. 12, and E 101/386/18, m. 58.
38. TNA E 101/387/25, m. 7.
39. *Calendar of Inquisitions Miscellaneous*, ii.434, C145/5, goods of the dean of Wolverhampton.
40. Arnould, *Étude sur le Livre des saintes médécines*, 72.
41. *Eulogium historiarum*, iii.231.
42. BL Add. MS 42130, fo. 158ᵛ; Brown, *The Luttrell Psalter Commentary*, 150.
43. *MED*, s.v. garter (2a), (1).
44. See p. 311 below.
45. TNA E 101/391/5; Rolleston's account roll is E 101/391/15; and the pipe roll is E 372/207, m. 50.
46. St Gregory is reputed to have said 'Non angli sed angeli' when he first encountered pale-skinned English boys at a slave market. See Bede, *Historia ecclesiastica*, ii.i.
47. TNA E 43/20 (1329–30); C 241/147/100 and C 241/147/130 (1367, 1368).
48. *RBP*, iv.66–77; Tout, *Chapters*, iv.434.
49. The first entries in the account go back to the time of Northwell's predecessor.
50. TNA E 101/388/8, m. 3.
51. Vale, *Edward III and Chivalry*, 149 n. 36, dates the streamers to 1346–7; Ormrod, *Edward III*, 303, suggests the dating of 1348–9. For other examples of streamers, see TNA E 101/387/14, m. 2, m. 23; E 101/388/8, m. 2; E 101/390/2, mm. 4–5; E 101/392/4, m. 2, m. 7; E 361/3, rot. 40d.
52. *Dictionary of Medieval Latin*, s.v. 'chlamys'.
53. TNA E 372/207, m. 50, m. 1/2.

54. See p. 255 above. Newton, *Fashion in the Age of the Black Prince*, 44, claims that *blu/bluettus*, the term used, is rare elsewhere, but see for example BL Add. MS 60584, fos. 9 ff.

55. TNA E 36/278, fo. 45.

56. *RBP*, iv.72–3.

57. TNA E 101/391/1, fo. 7.

58. Camden, *Britannia*, 278.

59. Vale, *Edward III and Chivalry*, 83–4.

60. *PROME*, iv.413, 447, 453–4; see also Harriss, *King, Parliament*, 372–3.

61. See p. 488 below.

62. Prince of Wales's accounts, TNA E 36/144, fo. 45^r (*de societate garter*); E 101/394/16, mm. 6, 7, 15, 18 (*societas* in all cases); accounts for 1383 and 1387 cited by Anstis, *Register*, i.10 n., 11 n. *Societas* is defined by the *Dictionary of Medieval Latin* as a 'company' in this context, with a secondary meaning of 'fellowship'; as *compaignie* is used by the French sources I have used 'company' throughout.

63. Accounts for 1399 and 1416, cited by Anstis, *Register*, i.13 n., 15 n. Baker is writing in the context of the foundation of the College of St George, and calls them both *fraternitas* and *comitiva*, a company.

64. Anstis, *Register*, ii.50 n.

65. See Jefferson, 'MS Arundel 48 and the Earliest Statutes of the Order of the Garter'.

66. See p. 528 below for the later clauses providing for a different feast day if St George's Day was too close to Easter.

67. St John, 'Dying beyond the Seas', 196. The calculation is taken from Boulton, *Knights of the Crown*, 140.

68. *John of Gaunt's Register*, ii.51.

69. Jefferson, 'MS Arundel 48 and the Earliest Statutes of the Order of the Garter', 379; see below, Appendix 5, notes 22 and 23.

70. Roberts, *St George's Chapel, Windsor Castle*, 8.

71. Saul, 'Servants of God and Crown', 98.

72. Roberts, *St George's Chapel, Windsor Castle*, 65.

73. St John Hope, *Windsor Castle*, i.152, 223.

74. *CPR 1361–1364*, 498.

75. *CCR 1343–1346*, 30 September 1343; *CPR 1361–1364*, 587; *CCR 1360–1364*, 30 September 1360; *CPR 1364–1367*, 342.

76. Tout, *Chapters*, iv.331.

77. *RBP*, iv.162, 456, 556.

78. *CPR 1361–1364*, 23; Roberts, *St George's Chapel, Windsor Castle*, 13.

79. TNA E 404/17/357–9.

80. Gray, *Scalacronica*, 150–51; on the event as a whole see Berard, 'Edward III's Abandoned Order of the Round Table', 35–8.

81. TNA E 403/388, 9 March and 12 March 1358.
82. Knighton, *Chronicle*, 158–9; *CCR 1354–1360*, 489; *RBP*, iv.252.
83. Anonymus Cantuariensis, *Chronicon*, 45.
84. Delachenal, *Histoire de Charles V*, ii.65–7.
85. Matteo Villani, *Cronica*, ii.182, 196–7; *Eulogium historiarum*, iii.227; John of Reading, *Chronica*, 130. See Ragone, *Giovanni Villani e i suoi continuatori*, 230–32, for Matteo Villani's connection to the court of Naples and to Niccolò Acciaioli, and hence to the chivalric world of the Company of the Knot.
86. John of Reading, *Chronica*, 131; *RBP*, iv.323; *Brut*, ii.309.
87. Vale, *Edward III and Chivalry*, 86.
88. Ibid., 88.
89. Mortimer, *The Perfect King*, 427–9.
90. TNA E 372/207, m. 50 (2).
91. See p. 346 below.
92. Antal Pór, 'Az Anjou ház és örökösei', including facsimile and edition of text of charter.
93. Statute X, in Daumet, 'L'Ordre castillan de l'écharpe', 25; not in second redaction of statutes.
94. Statute XXI, ibid., 27; statute XVI in Villanueva, 'Memoria sobre la Orden de Caballería de la Banda de Castilla', 567.
95. Clement VI, *Lettres closes*, ii.33.
96. For what follows, see Ormrod, *Edward III*, 320–21.
97. Ormrod's claim that 'The Black Prince took an extensive entourage ... in 1352' is a misreading of an account for 1348 entered belatedly in the records for 1352. *RBP*, iv.72–3.
98. *CPR 1354–1358*, 527; the entry for 21 April is entered as at Windsor.
99. 'Under Arthur's reign, the sheltered people ...'
100. Bowers, 'The Music and Musical Establishment of St George's Chapel', 178–9. *Sub Arcturo* is recorded on Herald HAVPCD 236 (1999).
101. See Brindle, 'The First St George's Chapel'.
102. Jane Geddes, 'Medieval Decorative Ironwork in St George's Chapel', 63–5.
103. St John Hope, *Windsor Castle*, i.143.
104. Kerr, 'The East Window of Gloucester Cathedral', 125–7.
105. Eton College MS 213; the figure for the height of the sills is from Brindle, 'The First St George's Chapel', 44.
106. Tracy, *English Gothic Choirstalls*, 53 and pl. 166.
107. Begent and Chesshyre, *The Most Noble Order of the Garter*, 25–6, 32; ordinances in 1431–2 imply that the canons only occupied the high stalls if the knights were absent, because if a knight was attending the service, the canon was to move to the lower stalls; but the 1522 statutes say specifically that, in the absence of any knights, the canons may sit 'in the high seats next unto the stalls of the said knights'.

108. St John Hope, *Windsor Castle*, ii.374.
109. Jefferson, 'MS Arundel 48 and the Earliest Statutes of the Order of the Garter', 378.
110. St John Hope, *Windsor Castle*, i.138, 139. Thirty-eight iron candlesticks were bought for the chapel, which were probably for the stalls, but this does not really help in working out the layout (forty-eight would be the expected number). They may have been positioned in front of the lower stalls.
111. Ibid., ii.374.
112. Bond, *The Inventories of St George's Chapel*, 59, 268–9.
113. St John Hope, *Windsor Castle*, i.133.
114. Ibid., 139.
115. Ibid., 162.
116. Tudor-Craig, 'The Fonts of St George's Chapel', 154.
117. St John Hope, *Windsor Castle*, i.131.
118. Cheetham, *English Medieval Alabasters*, 13.
119. Cheetham, *Alabaster Images of Medieval England*, 177.
120. Bond, *The Inventories of St George's Chapel*, 50–61.
121. Ibid., 4.
122. Ibid., 74–5.
123. Ibid., 41–7.
124. Given-Wilson, 'The Exequies of Edward III', 277–80.
125. I owe this observation to Karen Watts of the Royal Armouries, in response to an enquiry about pre-1350 examples of display of arms over tombs.
126. Goodall, 'The Aerary Porch', 169.
127. St John Hope, *Windsor Castle*, ii.506. The only entry which definitely implies a separate chapter house for the canons is that for glazing in 1430–31, so it is possible that in the fourteenth century it was shared with the canons. See also Tatton-Brown, 'The Deanery, Windsor Castle', 350, for the correct interpretation of the layout of the chapter house.
128. See p. 295 below for a discussion of the fate of the early records of the order.
129. Tatton-Brown, 'The Deanery, Windsor Castle', 350.

CHAPTER 9. 'THE COMPANY OF THE KNIGHTS OF SAINT GEORGE *DE LA GARTIERE*'

1. Jefferson, 'MS Arundel 48 and the Earliest Statutes of the Order of the Garter', 373–5.
2. As translated by Lisa Barber; see Appendix 5, 'The Statutes of the Garter'.
3. The data for 1351 is: Mortlake, 28 April, [ceremony (according to clause 10) 30 April], Westminster, 1–2 May; and for 1362: Windsor, 27–8 April, [ceremony (according to clause 10) 30 April], Westminster, 1–5 May.

4. Jefferson, 'MS Arundel 48 and the Earliest Statutes of the Order of the Garter', 374.
5. *Foedera*, iv.50.
6. Oxford, Bodleian Library, MS Lat. Hist. a.2; see Krochalis, '*Magna tabula*: The Glastonbury Tablets'.
7. Ibid., 519–21.
8. Windsor, St George's Chapel Precentor's Rolls, XV.56.16.
9. Ibid., 22 and 23. The latter roll ends on 29 September 1417; the feast of the Exaltation was on 14 September.
10. René d'Anjou, in the statutes of his Order of the Crescent, founded in 1448, imitated the Windsor tables, ordering that tables should be put up in Angers cathedral 'four feet high or thereabouts, on which were the arms, together with the helm and war cry, of each of the knights and squires of the order'. Du Cange, *Dissertations*, 46.
11. Ashmole, *Order of the Garter*, 191.
12. See St John Hope, *The Stall Plates of the Knights of the Order of the Garter.*
13. Baker, *Chronicon*, 109. He uses *fraternitas* and *comitiva*. The latter description only recurs in an entry on the issue rolls in 1401 to the 'officium virgarii comitive de Garteri', the office of verger of the Company of the Garter (TNA E 404/17/357).
14. He uses the word 'blueto', bluet, for blue, which corresponds to the entries in the wardrobe accounts (p. 273 and note above).
15. Nicolas, *History of the Orders of Knighthood*, ii.54. For example, Richard Fitzsimon, traditionally said to have died in 1348–9, seems to have died a decade later; see p. 513 and note.
16. See Appendix 2.
17. See p. 325 below.
18. See clause 19 of the statutes, p. 531 below.
19. Some of these deaths may have been due to causes other than the plague, but there is some doubt about both the nature and duration of the outbreak. Shrewsbury, *The History of Bubonic Plague*, 128, believes it may have started in the autumn of 1360, and may have been influenza.
20. TNA E 101/393/15, m. 14.
21. I owe this suggestion to Lisa Jefferson.
22. The king and the prince of Wales are excluded from the analysis which follows. John Sully is included, as he is likely to have been elected in 1353, not 1361; see p. 300 above.
23. Fowler, 'News from the Front', 85.
24. Devon, Warwick, Arundel, Lancaster, Hereford, Oxford. Kent and Pembroke were under age.
25. See *ODNB*, s.v. John de Vere, seventh earl of Oxford.

26. See above for the question of the date of the first meeting of the knights: he may have been chosen and not installed.
27. The fullest account of his career is in Burtscher, *The Fitzalans*, 33–68.
28. See p. 96 above for jewels as currency rather than display alone.
29. See p. 314 below.
30. The medieval text which uses this nickname has proved elusive: the earliest reference I can find is in *Complete Peerage*, i.242 in 1912, which does not quote a source.
31. Newton, *Fashion in the Age of the Black Prince*, 93–4.
32. Boulton, *Knights of the Crown*, 300.
33. Burtscher, *The Fitzalans*, 48, also thinks that the marriage was at the root of his exclusion.
34. *Life and Campaigns of the Black Prince*, 33–4.
35. Edward's four younger sons, and Sir Thomas Holland's younger brother Otho.
36. There were grants of revenue to William Montagu in December 1347 (*CPR 1345–1348*, 443–4) and a royal licence for him to raise money a year later by mortgaging estates he would inherit (*CPR 1348–1350*, 213).
37. Quoted in Wentersdorf, 'The Clandestine Marriages of the Fair Maid of Kent', 220.
38. Matteo Villani, *Cronica*, ii.544. He says that Joan was quite old, had already been married to two 'minor barons' and had several children.
39. *Chronique des quatre premiers Valois*, 123–5.
40. Possibly Sir Bernard Brocas, who had fought with him at Poitiers and was a leading Gascon lord, is intended.
41. One was probably a chantry chapel in the crypt at Canterbury cathedral. See Wentersdorf, 'The Clandestine Marriages of the Fair Maid of Kent', 217–19 and appendices C–G.
42. *RBP*, iv.428.
43. Chandos Herald, *La Vie du Prince Noir*, ll. 3771–2.
44. Two apparent instances in Edward's reign do not relate to Garter robes: in 1358 Philippa was given £500 for her clothes for the very lavish St George's Day feast of that year; the same applies to the issue of robes to Isabella, the king's eldest daughter, in 1361 (TNA E 101/393/15, m. 3, where the garment is a 'corset'). However, in 1376, when she was married to Enguerrand de Coucy, who was a companion of the Garter, she was issued with robes 'de secta militum de Garterio' (TNA E 101/397/20). For the entries in Richard II's reign, see Anstis, *Register*, i.10–15 nn.
45. Gillespie, 'Ladies of the Fraternity of Saint George and the Garter', exaggerates the formal element of these gifts, but has a useful coverage of the entries relating to them. Collins, *The Order of the Garter*, 79–83, rightly points out the fact that many ladies were part of the royal family or closely related to it.
46. Thomas of Woodstock, Edward's youngest son, became a knight in 1380.

47. Richard II and Henry of Derby, the future Henry IV, became knights in 1376-7.
48. *Complete Peerage*, i.344 n.
49. Jeanne was the wife of Philip V. See the accounts by Elizabeth A. R. Brown of this affair in 'The King's Conundrum' and 'Diplomacy, Adultery and Domestic Politics at the Court of Philip the Fair', especially pp. 74-7. A promised extended study by the same author never appeared.
50. Gray, *Scalacronica*, 66-7.
51. Archer, 'The Estates and Finances of Margaret of Brotherton', 269-70.
52. TNA SC8/63/3125.
53. Wrottesley, *Crécy and Calais*, 196 nn.
54. Goodall, *The English Castle 1066-1650*, 265.
55. *Croniques de London*, 90.
56. It was demolished during the Civil War; the modern castle is a nineteenth- and twentieth-century replica.
57. *Foedera*, iii.507.
58. See Wrottesley, *A History of the Family of Wrottesley of Wrottesley.*
59. Ibid., 147.
60. Booth, 'Taxation and Public Order', 25.
61. Bellamy, 'The Coterel Gang'; Stones, 'The Folvilles of Ashby-Folville'.
62. The case of Eustace d'Auberchicourt is even more complex than that of Henry Eam, and is explored in Appendix 2.
63. Hamaker, *De rekeningen der grafelijkheid van Holland*, xxi.246.
64. Janse, *Ridderschap in Holland*, 320.
65. Hamaker, *De rekeningen der grafelijkheid van Holland*, xxvi.81.
66. Ibid., 83.
67. Ibid., 103.
68. Conrad, 'Der dritte Litauerzug König Johanns von Böhmen', 383-4.
69. *Le Livre de seyntz medicines.*
70. Arnould, *Étude sur le Livre des saintes médécines*, 76.
71. TNA C 47/6/1, m. 1.
72. St John, 'War, the Church and English Men-at-Arms', 76.
73. Spencer, *Pilgrim Souvenirs and Secular Badges*, 272-6.
74. *RBP*, iv.73, 163.
75. TNA E 36/204, fo. 72^r. See also Blatchly and MacCulloch, *Miracles in Lady Lane*, 10-11.
76. See p. 262.
77. John of Reading, *Chronica*, 132-3. *Wynnere and Wastoure*, ll. 496-503, merely points to Edward's interest in Cologne, before the poem breaks off abruptly.
78. Including their attendants, the group was at least 361 people. *Foedera*, iii.ii.203.
79. Birch, *Pilgrimage to Rome in the Middle Ages*, 197-9.

80. Indulgences promised remission of punishment for sins in advance, which became one of the major abuses of the medieval Church.
81. Birch, *Pilgrimage to Rome in the Middle Ages*, 47. It may have been open earlier, but is not recorded until the thirteenth century.
82. Spufford, *Power and Profit*, 200.
83. See Chettle, 'The *Boni Homines*'.
84. Knowles and Grimes, *Charterhouse*, 49, 87–92.
85. Ibid., 6.
86. Brooke, 'Chaucer's Parson and Edmund Gonville', 6–8.
87. *Cambridge Gild Records*, 49–50. Tamworth can be identified as John Clement of Tamworth since his wife Alice is named in both the records of the guild and in his will (*Calendar of Wills in the court of Husting*, ii.167). He was the head of the royal chancery and seems to have run a small training school for chancery clerks: see Tout, 'The Household of the Chancery', 72.
88. BL MS Cotton Nero D.VII, fo. 105ᵛ.
89. Stanley, *Historical Memorials of Canterbury*, 164–71.
90. St John Hope, *The London Charterhouse*, 94–5, from the cartulary of the Charterhouse. The copy of the will in Archbishop Sudbury's register does not mention the effigy: *Registrum Simonis de Sudbiria*, i.1–3.
91. Froissart, *Chroniques*, SHF, viii.ii.287.
92. Ibid., vii.163.
93. Knowles and Grimes, *Charterhouse*, appendix C, 87–92. The report states that 'the cranial capacity is exceptionally large ...'
94. Greene and Whittingham, 'Excavations at Walsingham Priory', 269.

CHAPTER 10. KNIGHTLY ASSOCIATIONS: ORDERS, COMPANIES, FRATERNITIES

1. Pauli, *Codice diplomatico del ordine di Malta*, ii.80.
2. Antal Pór, 'Az Anjou ház és örökösei', pp. 138–9; the Latin is 'societas fraternalis militie tytulo sancti Georgii insigniti'. Compare 'fratres militie Templi', in the Templars' own records.
3. The exact date is uncertain, as we only have a charter issued in April 1326 with amendments to the original statutes: Boulton, *Knights of the Crown*, 30.
4. Engel, *The Realm of St Stephen*, 130–34.
5. Ibid., 146.
6. Ibid., 183–4.
7. Tout, *Chapters*, ii.148.
8. Boulton, *Knights of the Crown*, 42.
9. Minorite chronicle, s.a.1342, translated from Latin and quoted in Fügedi, 'Turniere im mittelalterlichen Ungarn', 395.

10. Majláth, 'A Kolos Czalád Czímeres Levele'; Fügedi, 'Turniere im mittelalterlichen Ungarn', 394.
11. Trautz, 'Die Reise eines Englischen Gesandten', 367.
12. They survive only in an eighteenth-century copy, printed in Chevalier, *Choix de documents inédits sur le Dauphiné*, ii.35–9.
13. Billot, *Les Saintes Chapelles*, 232.
14. Clement VI, *Lettres closes*, 32.
15. Billot, *Les Saintes Chapelles*, 232.
16. Clement VI, *Lettres closes*, 33.
17. French version of the Latin original in Vattier, 'Fondation de l'Ordre de l'Étoile', 42.
18. French original ibid., 37. Le Bel's figure of 300 is wrong; John's letter (Vattier, 'fondation de l'Ordre de L'Étoile', 39) clearly states 'cinq cens'.
19. Le Bel, *Chronique*, ii.204–7 [216–17].
20. 'four arpents' in the original. The *arpent* was a unit of length roughly equivalent, in medieval France, to 75 yards.
21. Modernized from *The Works of Sir Thomas Malory*, ed. Field, 786.
22. Alfonso X, *Las siete partidas*, ii.428.
23. Pannier, *La Noble-maison de Saint-Ouen*, 90.
24. The date of Epiphany is given in *Chroniques des quatres premiers Valois*, 23. For what follows, see Pannier, *La Noble-maison de Saint-Ouen*, 63 ff.
25. Ibid., 73–4.
26. The accounts (Pannier, 74) wrongly call him 'patriarch of Jerusalem'.
27. At Mauron, on 14 August 1352. Le Bel's phrase here is 'ilz firent sy soubtillement par une embusche qu'ilz firent', but there is no suggestion elsewhere that the French were exactly 'ambushed' at Mauron, and 'embusche' should probably be understood as a deft tactical ploy.
28. Le Bel, *Chronique*, ii.206 [217]. There is an account of the order in the long chronicle of Kirkstall, which says that the knights were 'moved rather by untamed courage than judgement', and claims that 140 were killed. *Kirkstall Chronicles*, 95.
29. Also called the Company of the Knot, from its device.
30. Matteo Villani, *Cronica*, ii.579.
31. Quoted in Boulton, *Knights of the Crown*, 236; for the full details of this order, see ibid., 211–40, and Bock, 'L'Ordre du Saint-Esprit au Droit Désir'.
32. The order is often referred to as the Order of the Band. Its Spanish name is *banda*, whose first meaning is 'sash', and all visual representations quite clearly show a sash worn diagonally over armour. See Riquer, *L'Arnes del Cavaller*, plate opposite p. 77, showing Henry of Trastamara and his son wearing the sash.
33. *Crónica de rey don Alfonso el Onceno*, in *Crónicas de los reyes de Castilla*, i.231–2.

34. Villanueva, 'Memoria sobre la Orden de Caballería de la Banda de Castilla', 436–65, 552–75.
35. Boulton, *Knights of the Crown*, 77–80.
36. This law code of the kingdom of Castile is at the foundation of modern Spanish law, and, through the former Spanish colonies of the southern United States, is a strong influence on the laws of Texas, California and Louisiana. The first translation was made by a lawyer in Chicago in the 1930s, and issued in looseleaf form for legal use.
37. This later became three times a year: see statute 15 in the version edited by Villanueva, 'Memoria sobre la Orden de Caballería de la Banda de Castilla', 566.
38. This was also a function of the Order of Santiago (St James); the first *casa de merced* for exchange of prisoners was established as early as 1170. The Trinitarians, founded in France in 1198, and the Order of Our Lady of Mercy, started in Barcelona in 1218, were orders wholly dedicated to ransoming Christian prisoners.
39. López de Ayala, *Corónica del rey don Pedro*, 164.

CHAPTER 11. KNIGHTS IN THEIR OWN WORDS

1. Llull, *Llibre de l'Orde de Cavalleria*, 35.
2. Ibid., 60.
3. Ibid., 50.
4. Kaeuper, *Chivalry and Violence in Medieval Europe*, 278.
5. See Charny, *The* Book of Chivalry, 3–17; Contamine, 'Geoffroy de Charny'.
6. *Murimuth*, 129.
7. The writ for the attorneys is dated October 1343: *CPR 1343–1345*, 130.
8. See pp. 415–16 below.
9. Baker, *Chronicon*, 103.
10. Wagner, *Heralds and Heraldry in the Middle Ages*, 21–3; Keen, *Origins of the English Gentleman*, ch. 2.
11. Charny, *The* Book of Chivalry, 85.
12. Ibid., 111.
13. Ibid., 115.
14. *Livre Charny*, ll. 548–600.
15. See Lester, *Sir John Paston's Grete Boke*, 34–57, on knightly miscellanies.
16. Taylor, 'English Writings on Chivalry and Warfare during the Hundred Years War', 74 ff.
17. See Squibb, *The High Court of Chivalry*, 2–3.
18. *PROME*, vii.148.
19. Reproduced in Keen, *Origins of the English Gentleman*, 40.

20. TNA C 47/6/1, m. 4.
21. For the Robert Laton case, see p. 478 below.
22. Keen, *Laws of War*, 55–6, 260–63.
23. See p. 381 below for chaucer's evidence on this.
24. Nicolas, *Scrope–Grosvenor Controversy*, i.124.
25. Ayton, 'Knights, Esquires and Military Service', 88.
26. Ibid., 95.
27. Nicolas, *Scrope–Grosvenor Controversy*, i.155–6.
28. Ibid., 178–9.
29. Ibid., 124–5.
30. Ayton, 'Knights, Esquires and Military Service', 87.
31. Keen, *Origins of the English Gentleman*, 51–2.
32. Paravicini, *Die Preussenreisen*, i.59, 94.
33. Quoted ibid., i.272, from *Scriptores rerum prussicarum* (Leipzig, 1861–), iii.599.
34. Paravicini, *Die Preussenreisen*, i.259, 263.
35. See p. 355 above
36. For what follows, see Paravicini, *Preussenreisen*, i.316–34, which quotes the original texts and gives a full discussion.
37. Ibid., 316–17. The account was written down some fifty years later.
38. Pannier, *La Noble-maison de Saint-Ouen*, 90.
39. Paravicini, *Preussenreisen*, i.337.
40. Ibid., ii.13 and tables 48–9.
41. Ibid., i.123. The document to which Paravicini refers is unfortunately in the unpublished third volume of his work, but appears to be the *Armorial Belleville*, ed. Pastoureau and Popoff, fos. 55ᵛ–57ᵛ. See also Paravicini, 'Armoriaux et histoire culturelle'.
42. Paravicini, *Preussenreisen*, i.123.
43. Gray, *Scalacronica*, 139 (John Leland's summary of lost text), confirmed by Baker, *Chronicon*, 119–20.
44. Paravicini, *Preussenreisen*, i.124.
45. Ibid., ii.28–9.
46. Boucicaut, *Le Livre de fais du bon messire Jehan le Maingre, dit Bouciquaut*, 42.
47. Paravicini, *Preussenreisen*, ii.24–5.

CHAPTER 12. LAWS OF WAR AND THE REALITY OF WARFARE

1. Le Bel, *Chronique*, i.69–70 [47].
2. Baker, *Chronicon*, 85.
3. *Récits d'un bourgeois de Valenciennes*, 234.

4. Ayton, *Knights and Warhorses*, 225, for average prices; pp. 59–60 for details on spare horses.

5. Henxteworth, m. 1, m. 1d, m. 3, m. 5d, m. 9, m. 10, m. 12, m. 13, m. 14, m. 14d.

6. Ayton, *Knights and Warhorses*, 239–41.

7. Prince, 'Indenture System', 291.

8. Keen, *Laws of War*, ch. IX, 139–55.

9. Ayton, *Knights and Warhorses*, 127–31.

10. 'Demandes pour la Joute', in *Livre Charny*, demande 52, 117.

11. Henxteworth, m. 24, 22 June 1356.

12. For what follows, see Keen, *Laws of War*, ch. X, 151–85.

13. *RBP*, iv.339.

14. i.e. with the shield point upwards.

15. See Broome, 'The Ransom of John II King of France 1360–70'.

16. 'Demandes pour la Joute', in *Livre Charny*, demande 74, 128.

17. Walthey, 'The Peace of 1360–1369', 142–3.

18. Laborde, *Notice des émaux du Musée du Louvre*, ii.112. I am grateful to Ronald Lightbown for pointing out this entry.

19. Baker, *Chronicon*, 152.

20. López de Ayala, *Corónica del rey don Pedro*, 165–6.

21. Keen, *Laws of War*, 53.

22. The highest ransom at Najéra was half as much again, for the count of Denia, and took twenty-three years to collect; the rights were sold on by the prince to the king, who resold them to the heirs of the captors. The sureties spent the intervening years in captivity in England.

23. Hayez, 'Un exemple de culture historique', 162.

24. 'La Geste des Nobles François', ii.634. The text and manuscript (BN MS français 5001, fo. 15ᵛ) read 'pour l'introduction des nobles': I have emended to 'instruction'.

25. Froissart, *Chroniques*, SHF, vi.119.

26. Keen, *Laws of War*, 197–206.

27. Le Bel, *Chronique*, ii.118–19 [186].

28. Ibid., ii.164–7 [202–3].

29. Froissart, *Chroniques*, SHF, iv.56–7.

30. Leroux, 'Le Sac de la cité de Limoges et son relèvement'; Walsingham, *Chronicon Angliae*, 67; *Chroniques de Saint-Martial*, 154.

31. Keen, *Laws of War*, 129–33.

CHAPTER 13. THE GARTER COMPANIONS AT WAR

1. Jean le Bel's figure: it is blank in Baker's account. Le Bel, *Chronique*, ii.177 [206]; Baker, *Chronicon*, 103.

2. *Avesbury* says that it was 'subtiliter elevatus', cunningly built, 409.

3. *Chronique normande du XIVe siècle*, 104.
4. Baker, *Chronicon*, 109.
5. Froissart, *Chroniques*, SHF, iv.90, though his list is unreliable and adds some unlikely names; Sir John Lisle: *CPR 1350–1354*, 43.
6. TNA E 379/198, rot. 36 m. 1, and TNA E 372/207, rot. 51. I owe this reference to Dr Thom Richardson of the Royal Armouries, who discusses it in his forthcoming thesis on the armourers' accounts of Edward III's reign. For the use of pavises in England, see DeVries, 'The Use of the Pavise', 93–5.
7. *Wynnere and Wastoure*, ll. 295–8; the Garter motto is at l. 68.
8. Li Muisit, *Chroniques et annales*, 278.
9. Froissart, *Chronicles*, tr. Johnes, i.198. See also Froissart, *Chroniques*, SHF, iv.93–4.
10. *RBP*, ii.77.
11. *RBP*, iv.143–5.
12. Henxteworth, m. 23.
13. Ibid., m. 9, m. 10, m. 12; Baker, *Chronicon*, 128.
14. *Life and Campaigns of the Black Prince*, 50.
15. Baker, *Chronicon*, 131; echoed by Matteo Villani, *Cronica*, i.709: 'this country, where there was no memory among those living there at the time of war having disturbed it'.
16. *Life and Campaigns of the Black Prince*, 54.
17. Baker, *Chronicon*, 136.
18. The river Save, a tributary of the Garonne.
19. *Life and Campaigns of the Black Prince*, 54–5.
20. The quarrel is reported by Baker, *Chronicon*, 137–8, and in more detail by Matteo Villani, *Cronica*, i.709–10.
21. *Life and Campaigns of the Black Prince*, 52.
22. Matteo Villani, *Cronica*, i.709.
23. The main accounts of the campaign are those of Geoffrey le Baker and *Eulogium historiarum*. Matteo Villani, writing within a few years of the battle, gives an extensive account, but is better informed about the negotiations with the cardinals and about the French situation than he is about the English manoeuvres (*Cronica*, ii.21–41). See Carpentier, 'L'Historiographie de la bataille de Poitiers'.
24. Sumption, *The Hundred Years War*, ii.246.
25. Tourneur-Aumont, *La Bataille de Poitiers*.
26. Hewitt, *The Black Prince's Expedition*, 115.
27. Quoted in *ODNB*, s.v. 'Thomas Beauchamp, eleventh earl of Warwick (1313/14–1369)'.
28. Crécy (*Brut*, ii.298–9): 'And for al this, the same unglorious Philip withdrowe him ... wherfore it was seyd in commune among his owne peple "Nostre beall Retret", that is for to sey, "Our faire withdraweth hym".'

Poitiers (Baker, *Chronicon*, 149, my translation): 'what the invincible French would call "a fair retreat".'

29. Delachenal, *Histoire de Charles V*, i.237.
30. Matteo Villani, *Cronica*, ii.36.
31. Ibid., 38.
32. Baker, *Chronicon*, 142–5; Sallust, *Catiline Conspiracy*, 58. Catiline's speech to his troops before the battle in which he is killed was famous as a piece of rhetoric.
33. Le Bel, *Chronique*, ii.237 [228].
34. Froissart, *Chroniques*, SHF, v.153–4.
35. Ibid., 162.
36. Delachenal, *Histoire de Charles V*, ii.25–6.
37. Matteo Villani, *Cronica*, ii.295–6.
38. Le Bel, *Chronique*, ii.287 [247].
39. Ibid., 299 [251–2].
40. Ibid., 291–2 [249].
41. Froissart, *Chroniques*, SHF, v.202.
42. Knighton, *Chronicle*, 168–71.
43. Matteo Villani, *Cronica*, ii.383.
44. *Chronique des quatre premiers Valois*, 105–6, describes an assault on the city by the men of the prince of Wales, but the description of the attack, on the Paris gate, is very generalized, and unsupported by any other evidence. Delachenal, *Histoire de Charles V*, ii.159, dismisses it as fiction and is probably correct, even though Sumption, *The Hundred Years War*, ii.431, believes that it did take place. It seems out of line with the whole ethos of the campaign, unless it was a rather half-hearted attempt to test the strength of the defences. *Les Grandes chroniques*, ed. Viard, vi.167, say categorically that he left without ever attacking the city.
45. Venette, *Chronicle*, 98–9.
46. *Les Grandes chroniques de France*, ed. Delachenal, i.257.
47. Venette, *Chronicle*, 102.
48. *Anonimalle Chronicle*, 46. Black Monday was the traditional name for Easter Monday, which was in fact a week earlier.
49. *Chronicles of London*, 13.
50. Knighton, *Chronicle*, 179.
51. Venette, *Chronicle*, 103.
52. Knighton, *Chronicle*, 179.
53. *Foedera*, iii.ii.630.
54. Brittany: TNA C 76/45, m. 3 (I owe this reference to Professor Michael Jones). Ireland: CCR 1360–1364, 450; Ayton, *Knights and Warhorses*, 77, 198 n. 10, 202, 203 n. 33.
55. *Archivo General de Navarra, Comptos*, v, document 202, 84.
56. Froissart, *Chroniques*, ed. Lettenhove, vii.497.

57. He seems to have fought alongside Chandos in 1362 or earlier: there is a payment to him for John Chandos's expenses on 13 April 1362. See TNA E 404/7/43.
58. There are several contemporary accounts of the battle, summarized in Sumption, *The Hundred Years War*, ii.518–20.
59. *Foedera*, iii.ii.754–5.
60. *Foedera*, iii.ii.779.
61. *Archivio General de Navarra*, register 120, counter-roll for January 1365–January 1366 (I owe this reference to Professor Michael Jones).
62. *Archivo General de Navarra, Comptos*, vi.28, documents 56 and 57.
63. However, Froissart says that in late March Henry of Trastamara kept Eustace d'Auberchicourt and Hugh Calveley with him, and said that he wanted them for a proposed crusade against Granada. Froissart, *Chroniques*, ed. Lettenhove, vii.95.
64. *Documents des archives de la chambre des comptes de Navarre*, 142; Fowler, *Medieval Mercenaries*, 175; Crow and Olson, *Chaucer Life-Records*, 65. Chaucer's wife Philippa was the daughter of Pain de Roet, a Hainault neighbour and possible companion in arms of Auberchicourt.
65. Fowler, *Medieval Mercenaries*, 173.
66. Guesclin, *Letters*, 57, no. 152.
67. *Archivo General de Navarra, Comptos*, vi.66–7, documents 151 and 153.
68. Gray, *Scalacronica*, 191.
69. Chandos Herald, *La Vie du Prince Noir*, ll. 1965–2000. Chandos had refused point-blank to join the Great Company: Froissart, *Chroniques*, ed. Lettenhove, vii.88.
70. Russell, *English Intervention in Spain and Portugal*, 78.
71. Sons of his old comrades Ralph Stafford and Robert Ufford; both became companions of the Garter.
72. See p. 402 above.
73. This would now be termed a spinel; it weighs thirty-four grams, is the size of a small egg and is the largest uncut example in the world.

CHAPTER 14. THE MOST NOBLE ORDER OF THE GARTER

1. Beltz, *Memorials of the Garter*, 152, quotes Coucy as writing that it had been 'his honour and pride' to wear it; but this is not in the printed text. *Foedera*, iv.18.
2. See Appendix 2.
3. Boulton, *Knights of the Crown*, 294–7; see also Boulton, 'The Middle French Statutes of the Monarchical Order of the Ship'.

4. Saul, *Richard II*, 337, affirms that 'it was invariably his habit to return to Windsor for the annual Garter ceremonies', but the itinerary which he prints does not entirely bear this out, partly because we cannot be as sure of his whereabouts as in the case of Edward III. Anstis, *Register*, ii.55, can find records for only fourteen of the twenty-two years of his reign.

5. See pp. 296-7 above.

6. See Lindenbaum, 'The Smithfield Tournament of 1390'.

7. Crow and Olson, *Chaucer Life-Records*, 472.

8. *Brut*, ii.343. If Richard made the two foreigners knights of the order, there can have been only twenty-two Garter knights in the tournament, and the *Brut* evidence does seem to be unreliable.

9. Original in Beltz, *Memorials of the Garter*, appendix XV, 405-6.

10. *Femina* (Trinity College, Cambridge, MS B 14.40), ed. William Rothwell, The Anglo-Norman On-Line Hub 2005, http://www.anglo-norman.net/texts/.

11. Crow and Olson, *Chaucer Life-Records*, 412, 458-62.

12. See for example Cooke and Boulton, '*Sir Gawain and the Green Knight*: A Poem for Henry of Grosmont?' and Carruthers, 'The Duke of Clarence and the Earls of March'.

13. Hoccleve, *Minor Poems*, 41-3; Burrow, *Thomas Hoccleve*, 21-2.

14. Mooney, 'Some New Light on Thomas Hoccleve', 297-307.

15. 'unus militum de illo inclito et excellente ordine militaris de la gartour': *PROME*, ix.124, where the translation uses 'military order', instead of the more accurate 'knightly order'.

16. Pantin, 'Medieval Treatise on Letter-Writing', 382. The king's deputy was probably Humphrey duke of Gloucester, who presided on St George's Day of that year: Anstis, *Register*, ii.70.

17. Minstrels themselves were very ill-defined: the word has a wide range of meanings, and its origin seems to have been related to 'ministering' to someone, whether as a servant or a craftsman. Only later did it acquire the modern meaning of a musician or singer.

18. See Paravicini, 'L'Office d'armes'.

19. See Crouch, 'The Court of Henry II and the Office of King of Arms'.

20. Bullock-Davies, *Register of Royal and Baronial Domestic Minstrels*, 21-2.

21. Ibid., 24-5.

22. Ibid., 110.

23. Little (Parvus): ibid., 139-44; Morel: ibid., 123-5; Norris: ibid., 137.

24. The best general account is still Wagner, *Heralds and Heraldry in the Middle Ages*, 25-40. Henry le Norrois: *Histoire de Guillaume le Maréchal*, 266-7.

25. Bullock-Davies, *Register of Royal and Baronial Domestic Minstrels*, 123-5, 137. The last record for Nicholas Morel is in 1297; Robert Parvus appears until 1320.

26. 'No king of arms or minstrels may carry concealed weapons on them other than their blunted swords. The kings of arms should wear only their tabards'; translation in Crouch, *Tournament*, 202.

27. See Wagner, *A Catalogue of English Mediaeval Rolls of Arms*; the early rolls are discussed in Wagner, *Heralds and Heraldry in the Middle Ages*, 48–55; Denholm Young, *History and Heraldry*, 41–63; and most recently in Simpkin, *English Aristocracy at War*, 20–25.

28. Hemingburgh, *De Gestis*, i.323.

29. Wagner, *Heralds and Heraldry in the Middle Ages*, 35.

30. Ibid., 159.

31. *RBP*, iv.108, where he is listed next to the king's messenger; and iv.163, 168, twice given the substantial sum of 100s. in 1355; given 66s. 8d. in 1358. Other heralds appear in his accounts as early as 1348 (William Stafford, given a plate 'of the companionship of the Garter' on 18 December).

32. See his testimony in TNA C 47/6/1, m. 4. He had served with Ufford at Sluys and Calais, and on the Reims campaign.

33. van Oostrom, *Court and Culture*, 129.

34. *Avesbury*, 464.

35. Ormrod, *Edward III*, 320.

36. 'qu'il prist ung heroult congnoissant armes', Le Bel, *Chronique*, ii.108. Froissart describes the French and English heralds working together to identify the dead, but does not name individual heralds; the operation is directed by five English knights and recorded by four clerks. Froissart, *Chroniques*, Rome version, 737.

37. Nicolas, *Scrope–Grosvenor Controversy*, i.111, ii.300.

38. Froissart, *Chroniques*, Amiens version, i.1. Revising the text for the Rome version of his chronicle, he ends the sentence at '. . . reporters of such affairs'. Froissart, *Chroniques*, Rome version, 35.

39. Froissart, *Chroniques*, Rome version, i.197–8. For the likely date of composition see ibid., xxii.

40. Wagner, *Heralds and Heraldry in the Middle Ages*, 39–40.

41. See van Oostrom, *Court and Culture*, ch. iv.

42. See Melville, 'Pourquoi des hérauts d'armes?'.

EPILOGUE: THE LEGENDS

1. Martorell, *Tirant lo Blanc*, 121.

2. Ibid., 122.

3. See p. 81 above.

4. Ashmole, *Order of the Garter*, 181.

5. Belvaletus, *Catechismus*, 7.

6. Colón, 'Premiers échos', 448–53.

7. Vergil, *Polydori Vergili Historiae Anglicanae*, 379.
8. Camden, *Britannia*, 278.
9. Le Bel, *Chronique*, ii.31 [155].
10. Saunders, *Rape and Ravishment*, 174.
11. There are a number of modern discussions of the episode. The most authoritative is that of Gransden, 'The Alleged Rape by Edward III of the Countess of Salisbury'. See also Chareyron, *Jean le Bel*, 308–23, who suggests that Uther's rape of Ygerne in Arthurian legend may have been a model; but Uther is disguised as her husband, and the violence represented by Le Bel is absent. Ingeldew, *Sir Gawain and the Green Knight and the Order of the Garter*, 46–57, unconvincingly attempts to link this episode, as representative of the morals of the court, to the great alliterative poem.
12. See p. 310 above.
13. The beginning of ch. LXI reads: 'You have earlier heard how King Edward had had to conduct a series of mighty wars in many lands and marches, at vast cost and expense: in Picardy, Normandy, Gascony, Saintonge, Poitou, Brittany and Scotland. And you've also heard of his passionate love for the valiant lady of Salisbury, named Alice; he couldn't help himself, even though the Earl of Salisbury was one of his closest counsellors and most loyal servants. And so it was that, for love of that lady and in his longing to see her . . .' (Le Bel, *Chronique*, ii.1 [146]).
14. Froissart, *Chroniques*, Amiens version, ii.332.
15. *Chronographia Regum Francorum*, ii.204–5; see also *Chronique normande du XIVe siècle*, 54 and *Istoire et croniques de Flandre*, ii.9, which give even briefer accounts of the affair.
16. See Ormrod, 'For Arthur and St George', 29.
17. The origin of this piece is unknown, and it seems to have been added originally to a copy of Ralph Higden's encyclopaedic *Polychronicon*, possibly at St Albans. It is printed in Murimuth, *Adami Murimuthensis Chronica Sui Temporis*, 224–7; an addition critical of his taxations and exactions is printed from BL Add. MS 12118, fo. 157, in John of Reading, *Chronica*, 91. See Taylor, *The Universal Chronicle of Ranulf Higden*, 117–19, 122–3.

Index

Abbeville 208
Acciaioli family, Italian bankers 26
Acciaioli, Niccolò 360
accidents, in tournaments 72, 150
Acre, fall of (1291) 382
The Acts of War of Edward III 23,
    25–6
    on battle of Crécy 215–16, 232
    Crécy campaign 192, 196,
      200, 204
admiralty 179–80
adultery 315–16
Agen, Aquitaine 38
Agincourt, battle of (1415),
    prisoners 404
Aiguillon, siege 196, 197
aketons (jackets) 65–6
alabaster, from Tutbury 288
Alamans, Guillaume 350
'Albamala', count of, and son, death
    at Crécy 220
Albrecht (Albert Sterz) 504
Albret, Arnaud Amanieu, lord of
    456, 460
Alençon, Charles, count of
    at Crécy 147, 219, 220,
      233, 235
    death at Crécy 134, 243
Alexander the Great
    connection with Arthurian
      legend 173–4

influence of story 91–3
Aleyn, John, composer of motet 284
Alfonso IX, king of Castile 376
Alfonso X (the Wise), king of Castile
    357, 362–3
    Las siete partidas (law code) 363,
      601*n*
    and Order of Santiago 345, 601*n*
Alfonso XI, king of Castile 74, 78
    and Templars 345, 360
altars, portable 328
Amadeus of Savoy, Order of the
    Collar 466
Amadis de Gaula 13
Amiens 57, 108, 147
    Philip VI at 206, 220
Angevin empire 34
Angoulême 138
    tournament (1365) 311
Anjou, Louis, count (later duke) of
    350, 431
    as prisoner 401
Anjou, René d', duke of
    Order of the Crescent 596*n*
    on tournaments 173
anniversaries, importance of 278–9
Antwerp 114
Aquitaine 33–4, 35, 108, 125
    formal confiscation 38, 108, 109
Arabs, conversion of (in Spain) 366
Aragon, Order of Montesa 345

archers
  at Crécy 230–32, 496–7
  longbowmen 101
  at Poitiers 436–7
  see also crossbowmen
Arderne, Isabel 317
Arderne, John 240
aristocracy 125
  new French peerages 141
  twelve peerages of France 140–41
  see also earls; knights
Armagnac, Jean d', count of 421, 423,
  424, 426, 428, 430
  at Najéra 460
  on Poitiers 438
armies
  feudal summons to 145–6
  organization 377, 433, 434–5
  recruitment 145–6
  see also English army; French
  army; Scottish army
armour
  in accounts 50
  ailettes 58
  changing styles 85, 90
  at Crécy 223
  decorated with garters 272–3, 274
  Edward III's suits of 101, 102
  Hainault style 58
  plate 85, 90
arms see coats of arms; heraldry
arrière-ban, summons to army 145–6
Artevelde, Jacob van 176
Arthur, King, and Arthurian legend
  265, 356–7
  Company of the Garter as model
  for Round Table 481–2
  erroneous links with Garter
  470, 483–4
  influence of 51–2, 82–4
  Lionel in 101–2
  and nature of war 160

ownership and readership of
  romances 158–9, 160
Prose Lancelot 101
Quest of the Holy Grail 102
and Round Table 156–7,
  165, 167–9
Sir Gawain and the Green
  Knight 83–4
Artois, Jeanne d', countess of 131
Artois, Robert d', count of 13,
  108, 487
  in England 151
  expedition to Brittany 153, 154
  and Philip VI 131, 132
Ashmole, Elias 484–5
  account of the Company of the
  Garter 296–7
Ashridge, Hertfordshire, house of
  canons 333
Athelstan, king, of all Britain 35
Athens, duke of 252
Atholl, Catherine, countess of 106
Atholl, John Campbell, earl of 105
Attewood, Edward 204
Attigny, near Reims 447, 505
Auberchicourt, Eustace d' (Sauchet)
  (KG 1349) 55, 299, 300, 312,
  499–510
  career 503–10
  and Charles of Navarre 442, 452–3,
  454–5, 465, 507–8, 509–10
  as freebooter and mercenary 407,
  452, 504, 505–6
  as Garter knight 302, 324
  in Gascony (1355) 422
  and Great Company 457, 509
  identification 500–502
  in Ireland 507
  marriage to Elizabeth of Juliers
  312, 504–5, 506, 509
  at Najéra 509
  at Poitiers 393, 403, 436, 505

in Prussia 389
ransoms 404, 505, 508
Reims campaign 447
variants of name 500–502
Auberchicourt, François d' 508–9
Auberchicourt, Gilles d' 500
Auberchicourt, Nicholas (Colart) d',
   of Buignicourt 499–500, 501
Auberchicourt, Nicholas d', of
   Buignicourt 499
Auberchicourt, William d' 508–9
Auberoche, battle of (1345) 176, 191
Aubrey, Andrew, mayor of London
   121, 126
Audley of Heighley, James 322–3
Audley, Hugh, earl of Gloucester 109,
   154–5, 303
   at battle of Winchelsea (1350) 416
Audley, Margaret 313, 316, 318
Audley, Peter 442, 504
Audley, Sir James (KG 1349) 25,
   313, 396
   funeral 338
   as Garter knight 302, 323
   in Gascony (1355) 422
   at Poitiers 405, 431, 435, 437,
     439, 441
   in Prussia 388
   Reims campaign 447–8
   'unlawful' operations 407
Audrehem, Arnoul d', French marshal
   143–4, 401–2
   and Castile 454, 458
   at Najéra 460, 461
   at Poitiers 435, 436, 440
Auray, battle of (1364) 143, 507
Auxerre 448
Auxerre, John, count of 407, 503
Avesbury, Robert of, chronicle
   20, 25
   on battle of Crécy 215–16
   and Sluys 119

Avignon, peace conference (1343–4)
   155, 175
Ayton, Andrew 494

baboons 79
Bacon, John 159
Badlesmere, Elizabeth 317
Baie de la Seine 3
Baker, Geoffrey le see le Baker
Baker, Richard 517
Baldwin II, emperor of
   Byzantium 264
Balliol, Edward 98, 99
   and 1336 campaign 105
   Halidon Hill 100
   as king of Scotland 98, 103, 104–5
banditry, after Poitiers 393
bankers, Italian 26–7
bannerets (knights banneret) 52,
   103, 111
   Crécy campaign 188
banners 87–8, 406–7
   in battle 234, 377
   to identify leaders 407
   used to indicate war to the
     death 407
Bannockburn, battle of (1314) 328
Bar, county of, ransom 448, 506
Barcelona 455
Bardi family, Italian bankers 26, 27
Barroso, Cardinal Gómez 18
'Baruf', lord of, at battle of Crécy 227
Bascot de Mauleon, knight 11–12
Basset, Lord, at battle of Winchelsea
   (1350) 416
Bassett, Ralph 297
Bateman, William, bishop of
   Norwich 335
battle, descriptions of 392–3
Bayeux, surrender of 202
beards, long 91
Beauchamp, Guy 451

Beauchamp, Sir John (KG 1349) 113,
298, 328, 396, 511–12
death 338, 405
ransom 404
Beauchamp, Philippa 313
Beauchamp, Richard, bishop of
Salisbury 482
Beauchamp, Thomas, 11th earl of
Warwick (KG 1349) 72, 103,
113, 154, 312, 328, 336, 389
Brittany 197
at Calais 249
capture of archbishop of Sens 403
Crécy campaign 187, 192, 206,
208, 210
at Crécy 220, 226, 236
as Garter knight 286, 302
in Gascony (1355) 421, 422, 423
monument 338
at Paris 449
at Poitiers 435, 436, 437, 439
and Reims campaign 446
in Scotland 106
Warwick Castle 318
at Winchelsea (1350) 416
Beauchamp, Thomas, the younger 467
Beaufort, Henry, chancellor 471
as bishop of Winchester 284
Beaujeu, lord of, French marshal 252
Beaumont, Henry of 99, 106
capture at Dundarg 104
claim to earldom of Buchan
97–8, 107
as guardian of Edward as prince
45, 57
at Halidon Hill 100
Beaumont, (John of Artois) count of,
at Crécy 233
Beaumont, John, Lord 150
death in tournament at
Northampton 72
beaver hats 91
Bedford 57, 69

Belvaleti, Mondonus 485
Benedictine order 343
Bereford, Simon 61
Bergerac 176
Berkeley Castle, death
of Edward II at 43
Berkeley, Maurice, 4th baron Berkeley
58, 61, 66, 99, 104, 317
at Buironfosse 117
at Crécy 226
at Guildford Christmas feast 113
shield in Gloucester cathedral
window 286
Berkeley, Thomas, 3rd baron Berkeley
43, 57, 61, 68, 99, 317
shield in Gloucester cathedral
window 286
Bernard, Arnaud 424
Bernier, Jean, provost of Hainault,
chronicler 9, 93
on crossing of Somme 208, 209
Bertrand, Robert, French commander
133, 143, 147, 197, 199, 202
Berwick, siege of (1333) 99–100, 410
Bibbesworth, Walter of, glossary 125,
269, 470–71
Bigod, Roger, earl of Norfolk 36, 38
Black Death 256, 300, 332
Blanche of Bourbon, wedding 91
Blanche, queen of Navarre 51
Blanchetaque, Somme crossing 208,
211, 218
Blankmouster, John de 399
Blois, Charles de 94, 132, 143,
256, 359
claim to Brittany 151–3, 452, 453
defeat (1346) 196
Blois, John, count of 387
Blois, Louis, count of 147
at Crécy 219, 220, 233
Blome, John, licence to search
Glastonbury for Joseph of
Arimathea 157

Blount, Sir John 162
blue, colour 272–3
boar, as emblem 401
Boccaccio, Giovanni 360, 481
Bohun family 21, 22, 82
Bohun, Edward (twin of William) 46, 52, 61, 66, 99, 303
Bohun, Humphrey, 3rd earl of Hereford 36
Bohun, Humphrey, 6th earl of Hereford 63, 110
  death (1361) 405
Bohun, Humphrey, 7th earl of Hereford and earl of Northampton 312, 388–9
Bohun, William, earl of Northampton (KG 1349) 312, 328, 395–6
  and 1345 campaign 176
  in Brittany 152–3, 155
  at Buironfosse 117
  at Calais 249, 252, 253
  in Crécy campaign 187, 188, 192, 205
  at Crécy 220, 226
  death of plague 300
  and Edward III 66, 103, 109, 110
  in France (1339) 116
  as Garter knight 298, 302, 303
  marriage 317
  and Mortimer 63
  at Paris 449
  Reims campaign 446
  in Scotland 99, 106, 379
  shield in Gloucester cathedral window 286
  and Walden priory 337
  at Winchelsea 416
Bois, Piers du, of Ghent 11
Boniface VIII, Pope 331
Bonington, Gilbert, goldsmith 286

The Book of Arms of Bavaria 480
The Book of Arms of Guelders 480
Book of Chivalry (Charny) 370–73
The Book of Holy Medicines (Grosmont) 269, 326–7
Book of the Order of Knighthood (Llull) 126, 366–8
The Book of the Sash 363
The Book of Treasures 56
books
  Arthurian romances 158–9, 160
  illustrated 55–6
  reading of 159–60
books of hours 326
booty 396–8
  acquisition of 375
  Gascony campaign 428
  taken at Caen 200, 202, 306
Bordeaux, St Seurin reredos 288
Bordeaux, truce of (1357) 442
Born, Bertran de 474
Botetourt, Baldwin 437
Boucicaut, Marshal (Jean de Meingre), French marshal 25, 143, 144
  in Prussia 390
  at Romorantin 431
Bouillon, Godfrey of 83
Bourbon, Jacques de, count of La Marche 451
  constable of France 142, 251, 424, 427
  as prisoner after Poitiers 403
Bourbon, Louis II, duke of 508
Bourbon, Pierre, duke of, at Calais 252
Bourchier, Sir Robert, at Crécy 226
Bourges 430
  'sainte-chapelle' at 352
Bourne, Henry, scribe 296
Bozzuto, Giacomo 358
Brabant, John, duke of 116, 120–21

Bradeston, Thomas 66, 99, 104, 317
  at Buironfosse 117
  at Crécy 226
  at Guildford Christmas feast 113
  shield in Gloucester cathedral 286
  at tournaments 57, 73, 77, 255
Bradninch (Bradnynch, Bradenynche),
  manor of 325, 394
Bradwardine, Thomas, chancellor of
  St Paul's 248
Brandenburg, Frederick von 229
Braose, Sir Thomas de, at Crécy 226
Brest, Brittany 153
Brétigny, treaty of (1361) 319, 401,
  450–51, 506
Brian, Guy, at Winchelsea (1350) 416
bridges, timber for 182
Brienne, Walter de 91, 142
Brignais, battle of (1362) 451
Briquet, Robert 457
Brisebarre, Jean, *The Restoration of
  the Peacock* 92, 93
Bristol, tournament 50
Brittany
  campaigns (1342–3) 110–11,
    151–5
  civil war 452–3
  dispute over 132–3
  Grosmont in 428
  truce (1343) 155
Brittany, dukes of *see* Montfort, Jean
  (III, IV and V)
Brocas, Bernard, sieur de 310, 597*n*
Brotherton, Margaret of 312, 316
Brotherton, Thomas of, earl of
  Norfolk 41–2, 47, 60, 70, 316
Bruce, Robert 97
Bruges, Peter of, lance-maker 59
Bruges, Richard, Lancaster herald 473
Bruges, William, Garter king of arms
  473, 480
  and arms of d'Auberchicourt 502
Bruiant, herald 475, 479

Brussels
  cloth weaving 86
  tournament 54
Brut chronicle 16, 21, 60
  on fall of Mortimer 63, 64
  on fashion 89
  on Round Table festival 163
  and Smithfield jousts (1390) 469
Buch, captal de *see* Grailly
Buironfosse, confrontation at (1339)
  117–18, 130–31, 132
Bungay, Hugh of, armourer 269
Buonaccorsi company, Italian
  bankers 26–7
Burchester, John of, mason 318
burdeicium (*bohort*, *burdis*), practice
  tournament 68
Burghersh family 312, 313
Burghersh, Bartholomew 58, 125,
  155, 313
  and *Acts of War of Edward III* 24
  admiral of the west 179, 194
  at Calais 216, 252
  at Crécy 211, 226
Burghersh, Bartholomew, the younger
  (KG 1349) 396, 504
  Crécy campaign 198
  at Crécy 226
  Ewyas Harold castle 319
  as Garter knight 302, 313
  in Gascony (1355) 422
  and pilgrimage 330
  at Poitiers 431, 435, 437
  Reims campaign 448
  tomb at Walsingham
    330, 339
Burghersh, Henry, bishop of Lincoln
  95–6, 313
  at Buironfosse 117
  diplomatic missions 113
  and French campaign (1340)
    120–21
  report on battle of Crécy 216

Burghersh, Joan 312
Burgos 455, 457
Burgundy, (Eudes IV) duke of 135
Burgundy, Philip the Good of 470
Burley, Simon 508
Burnell, Nicholas, claim to
   arms 371
Burstwick, tournament 102
Burwell, Robert, wood carver 287
Bury, Richard of, bishop
   of Durham 62
   at Crécy 236, 392
   Crécy campaign 192
   funeral of John of Bohemia 244
Bury St Edmunds 296
   tournament (1348) 255
buttons 90
Buxhull, Alan 467

Cadsand, island of 113
Caen 23
   booty 200, 202, 306, 396
   capture of 214, 393, 409
   defence of 199–200, 202
Caerlaverock, siege of (1300)
   266, 476
Caerphilly 42
Calais 3, 245–7
   capture of (1349) 415–17
   Philip VI at 130–31
   Philippa at 53, 246, 410
   siege of 135, 246–53, 377;
   connection with Company of
   the Garter 277, 302, 306;
   mortality rate 405; unconditional surrender 252–4, 409–10
   surprise attack by French
   (1350) 20
Calveley, Hugh 453, 454, 455, 457,
   458, 509
   at Najéra 460
Cambrai 116
Cambrai, bishop of 116

Cambridge, colleges 259, 334–5
   Corpus Christi 334–5
   Gonville and Caius 334–5
   Trinity Hall 335
Camden, William
   on knights of the Garter 275
   and story of countess of Salisbury
   486–7
Cange, Charles Dufresne du 232
Canterbury 35
   joust (1348) 255
   tournament 58
Canterbury cathedral 261
   shrine of Thomas Becket 266,
   329, 330
Cantilupe, Sir William, at
   Crécy 226
captain, role in tournaments 73
Carcassonne 426, 503
Carentan 198–9
   castle of 452, 507
carpenters, for Crécy campaign 182
carriages, royal 88, 496
Carswell, Sir William, at Crécy 226
carts
   for Crécy campaign 182
   as defensive array 219, 220, 223–4,
   227–30, 493–4, 496–7
   knights and 228
   numbers of 230
   for Reims campaign 444
Cassel, French attack on 250
Cassel, battle of (1328) 245
Castile
   campaign against 454–62, 507
   Order of Santiago 344–5, 361
   Order of the Sash 277, 282–3,
   361–4
   proposed alliance with 176
Castilian ships
   as threat to English shipping
   462–3
   at Winchelsea 417–18

castles
building of 174
of Garter knights 318–23
Causton, Sir Robert, at Crécy 226
Cernay, near Reims 447–8
Chalgrave, church 336
Chalon, Jean de 453
Chandos, Edward 46
Chandos, John (KG 1349) 17, 25, 46,
313, 328, 396
booty 397
and Brittany 155, 452
capture of du Guesclin 403
castle in Normandy 319
constable of Aquitaine 454
and d'Auberchicourt 507, 508, 510
death at Lussac 404–5
as Garter knight 302, 323
gifts to 273, 274
and Great Company 407, 457
at Loire 431
masses for 278
at Najéra 460
at Paris 449
at Poitiers 435, 437, 439
at Winchelsea (1350) 416, 420
Chandos Herald, chronicler
16–17, 329
on Gascony (1355) 421
The Life of the Black Prince 16
chapels, royal 259–64
see also St Edward's, Windsor; St
Stephen's, Westminster
charity 333
Charlemagne, emperor 34–5
Charles IV, king of France 129, 131
and Edward II 38–40
and Queen Isabella 41
Charles V, king of France 19, 83, 451
as dauphin 139–40; and civil war
in France 441–2, 443; at
Poitiers 435, 438; and Reims
campaign 445; at Tours 431

and defence of France 480–81
Charles VI, king of France 81
Charles, king of Navarre ('the Bad')
137–8, 144
and Auberchicourt 442, 452–3,
454–5
and civil war in France 441–2
Charles of Bohemia 147, 219, 220
at Crécy 219, 233
and death of father 221,
238–9, 244
Charny, Geoffroy de 153, 252, 358,
368–75
on acquisition of booty 397
and Aimeric di Pavia 415–17
Book of Charny 370, 373–4
Book of Chivalry 370–73, 374
capture of (1349) 416
on costs of warfare 395
death at Poitiers 440
descriptions of warfare 373–4
and knightly honour 464
member of Company of the
Star 370
Questions on Jousts, Tournaments
and War 370, 374–5, 397
as standard-bearer of oriflamme
369, 370
Chartres 449
Châtellerault 432
Châtillon, Gaucher de 447
Châtres 449
Chaucer, Geoffrey 606n
capture 448
and Company of the Garter 471
evidence in Scrope v Grosvenor 380
safe conduct for 455
and Smithfield jousts (1390) 469
'The Franklin's Tale' 83
Chauvigny 432
Cheapside
joust (1331) 70–71
tournament (1361) 78

Cherbourg 3
Chester 247
Chevereston, Sir John, at Crécy 226
Cheyne, Alan, at Poitiers 437
Chrétien de Troyes 168
    Perceval 52, 158
Christianity *see* religion
Christmas, festivals 77
Chronicle of Alfonso XI 361
*Chronicle of the First Four Valois
    Kings* (1380s) 22, 231
    on battle of Crécy 241–2
    on marriage of prince of Wales to
        Joan of Kent 310
chronicles 5–23
    Flemish 217
    French 19, 22–3
    outside London 21–2
    see also Brut; Froissart; Gray,
        Thomas; Le Baker; Le Bel, Jean;
        Li Muisit; Murimuth, Adam;
        Roman chronicle
Chronicles of Flanders, on battle of
    Crécy 225–6, 227, 241
churches
    armorial displays 381
    rebuilding and enlargement
        335–7
City of London, and court 71
Clarence, duke of *see* Lionel (of
    Antwerp)
Clarenceaux, Andrew, king of arms
    476–7
Clarendon, tournament 67
Clement V, Pope 352
Clement VI, Pope 141, 283, 307,
    331–2
Clement, John, of Tamworth
    335, 599*n*
clergy
    and loyalty to papacy 127
    resistance to taxation 36, 38
    at St Stephen's 263–4

Clermont, Jean de, marshal of France
    143, 144, 424, 431
    at Poitiers 435, 436–7, 440
Clinton, William (later earl of
    Huntingdon) 52, 99, 103,
        150, 303
    admiral of the west 119, 179
    at Calais 251
    creation of earldom 109
    in Crécy campaign 187, 202, 203
    diplomatic missions 108, 112–13
    and French campaign (1340)
        120–21
    as judge in Court of Chivalry 378
    and Mortimer 63, 66, 95
    regency council 114
    said to be at Crécy 226
    at tournaments 69, 73
    at Winchelsea (1350) 416
Clipstone, tournament at 48, 50
Clisson, Olivier 132–3, 151, 489
    execution 156, 176
clock, at Windsor 182
coats of arms
    and dishonour 378, 399, 400
    display on battlefields 418–19
    displayed upside down 378
    reversed 378, 399
    rolls of 476
    of St George 58
    visual collections 475–6
Cobham, Reginald, 1st baron
    Cobham (KG 1349) 99,
        104, 193
    at Buironfosse 117
    at Calais 252, 253
    capture of count of Longueville 403
    and count of Dammartin 398
    Crécy campaign 198
    at Crécy 226, 236, 477; and
        aftermath of battle 242–3
    death of plague 300
    as Garter knight 300, 302

Cobham – *cont.*
in Gascony (1355) 421, 422, 423
as judge in Court of Chivalry 378
marriage 317
monument in Lingfield church
336, 338
at Poitiers 435
and Sluys 119
with Teutonic Knights 388
at Winchelsea (1350) 416
Cocherel, battle of (1364) 143, 407
coinage, new gold (1344) 175
Cold Norton, priory 336
College of Arms, foundation
(1420) 474
College of St George *see* Windsor:
College of St George
colleges, secular 259
Cambridge 334–5
Oxford 259
Cologne 35
shrine of Three Kings at 262, 330
Cologne, John of, armourer 71,
78–9, 87
accounts 270–72
Garter robes 274
supply of garters 269, 270
Cologne, William of 271
commissions of array, to recruit
foot-soldiers 186–7
Company of the Garter 4, 5, 464–82
administrative changes 468
'Black Book' 468
Bruges's Garter Book 473
expulsions 468
first mention in accounts 273
founding of 244, 274–7
heraldry 85
ladies' robes 311, 597*n*
legends 483–91
officials 279–80
poor knights 298–9
record-keeping 468, 473

as religious confraternity 244,
277–9, 465
Richard II and 467–70
St George's Day assembly
274, 278
statutes 275, 277, 525–38; earliest
surviving version (1415) 293–5
symbolism of 485
and tournaments 468–70
see also College of St George;
Company of the Garter,
companions
Company of the Garter, companions
bachelors 323–6
challenged to tournament (1408)
469–70
choice of 275, 365
companions to 1360 (first group)
301–6
and conflict of loyalties 464
and court culture 73
deaths among 300
deaths in battle 404–5
descendants of original members
464
elections of foreigners 469
family networks of great lords
312–13
funerals 337–8
honorific appointments 470
list of names in 1415 copy of
statutes 293
lists of 293, 295–300
masses for 278
monuments 338–9
omissions from early membership
303–6
at Poitiers 434, 435–7
religious interests of 326–37
resignations 465
royal family network 307–12, 464
succession, problems of 295
tables of members 295–6, 468

with Teutonic Knights 384,
388–9
use of term Order 465
at war 415–63
women and 483–4
women of Garter families
313–17
Company of the Holy Spirit (Naples)
352, 359–60
Company of Knights of Our Lady of
the Noble House of St Ouen
(Company of the Star) 352,
353–60, 370, 374
badge 355
first assembly and feast 357
inspiration of Round Table for
356–7
membership 355, 357–8
rules and obligations 355–6
Company of the Knot 365
Congregation (Company) of the
Virgin and St George 283, 351,
352–3
Constanza of Castile 462
Copham, Thomas, armourer 59
Corder, Gawan, at Crécy 211
Corfe Castle 60
Cormicy 448
Cornwall, John 469–70
Cosington, Stephen 77, 378, 455
costumes
buckram armour 255
for festivals and revels 78–9, 93,
113–14
gifts of robes 112, 164, 282
at King's Langley 150
livery 80
opulence 85
peacock 255
team uniforms 65–6, 79–81
for tournaments 58–9, 85,
160, 164
see also fabrics; fashion; uniforms

Cotentin peninsula 197, 198
Coterel gang 323
Coucy, Enguerrand de 314, 597n
as earl of Bedford, resignation
from Garter 465
court
and city of London 71
costumes and fashions 94
role of jousts and tournaments 73
social culture of 65–6
splendour and extravagance 95
Court of Chivalry 305, 376–81
cases 377–9
evidence 477–8
judges 378
and test of 'public fame' 381, 479
and use of arms 371
witnesses 379–81
Courtenay, Hugh, 9th earl of Devon
110, 304
Courtenay, Sir Hugh (KG 1349)
298, 299, 300, 304,
312, 512
courtly love 371, 373
Courtrai, battle of (1302) 244–5
Couvin, Watriquet de 93
Coventry, tournament 57
Crabbe, John, admiral 119, 403
'Craddok', society of 51–2, 65,
80, 160
Craon, Jean de, archbishop of Reims
446–7
Craon, lord of 431
Crécy
approach to 211–12, 218
castle 208
Crécy, battle of (1346) 17, 27,
213–56, 369
aftermath 237–8, 242–4
analysis 213–14
archers at 230–32
battlefield 28, 211–12, 223–4
casualties 215, 220–21

Crécy, battle – *cont.*
chroniclers of 15, 213, 215–22, 225–8
  and Company of the Garter
    277, 278
  defensive array of carts 219, 220,
    223–4, 227–30
  descriptions of battle 219–20,
    223–5, 236–7
  and disloyalty to Philip VI 134
  English battle formation 218,
    230–32, 493–8
  eyewitness accounts 214–15
  French attack in disorder 233–4
  French deployment 146–7,
    218–19, 233
  French militias at 145, 233
  German troops 233, 238, 239
  legends 222
  loss of *oriflamme* 234
  no quarter given 241, 404
  numbers 221–2
  participants 226–7
  records of fallen 477
  reports of in Europe 213, 244–5
  Rome chronicle account 222–5
  Villani on 217–22
Crécy campaign 20, 178–212, 392
  connection with Company of the
    Garter 277, 278, 302, 306
  disputes over rights to arms 377–8
  Edward's intentions 197–8, 205–6
  fleet at Portsmouth 178–80
  food for 182–3
  French reaction to landing 196–7
  landing at La Hogue 143, 192,
    194, 196
  provisions for 184–5
  troops for 180, 185–92
  weapons 180–82
Cresswell, John 457
Crombek, John 64
crossbowmen 28

Genoese 146, 197, 217, 218–19,
  225, 233
crowns, pawned 163–4, 169, 170,
  583*n*
crusades 381–7
  and family honour 381
  and orders of knighthood 343–4
  Palestine 382
  in Prussia 382–90
Csák, Matthew 346
Culbean, battle of (1335) 105
Cupar Castle, siege 106
Cusance, William of, keeper of
  household 44

Dagworth, Thomas, and Brittany
  155, 196
Dalyngrigge, Edward 500
Dammartin, count of 229
  as prisoner 398–9
Damory, Richard 44
dancing, at festivals 77
Daniel, Thomas 200
  at Crécy 234, 589*n*
Daniers, John 50
Darcy, Sir John, at Crécy 226
Darcy, Sir John (son), at Crécy 226
Dartford
  nunnery 333
  tournament 58, 69, 575–6*n*
Dashwood, Sir Thomas, at Crécy 226
Datini company, Italian bankers 26
David II, king of Scotland 16, 80, 85,
  97, 256
  and Balliol 105
  captured at Neville's Cross 248
  in France 104
  debts, to finance campaigns 394–6
Denia, count of 460, 603*n*
Despenser family 316
Despenser, Edward, 3rd Lord
  Despenser (KG 1361) 422

Despenser, Eleanor 44
Despenser, Hugh (son), 2nd Lord
  Despenser
  in Brittany 152
  Crécy campaign 198
  at Crécy 226
Despenser, Hugh, the younger, 1st
  Lord Despenser 39, 157
  and Edward II 42
  and Queen Isabella 40–41
Despenser, Isabella, marriage to
  Richard Fitzalan 304–5, 314
Despenser, Sir Philip 162
Dinis, king of Portugal 345
diplomatic missions, to Flanders 108,
  112–13
disasters
  attributed to extravagant fashions
    90, 91
  attributed to tournament
    costumes 78
Domme, siege of 508
domus, house for Round Table 172,
  173, 174
Doria, Anton 219
  death at Crécy 221
Doria, Sir Otto, at battle of Crécy
  223, 224
Douce Book of Hours 266
Douglas, Archibald, and Berwick 99
Douglas, James, Scots commander 48
Douglas, William, Scottish knight 105,
  145, 435
dragon, on English standard 242, 407
Dunbar, earl of 98, 578n
Dunstable 41–2
  tournament (1334) 58, 73, 76, 101
  tournament/festival (1342) 82,
    102, 150
Dunstable priory 336
Dupplin Moor, battle of (1332)
  15, 101

Durazzo, Charles of, Order of the
  Ship 466
Durham 248
dyes, scarlet 86

Eam, Sir Henry see Oem, Henry
earls
  as military leaders 110, 187–8
  new, as Garter knights 303–4
  new creations (1337) 109, 110
  'Earls' rebellion' (1400) 468
Edington, William, treasurer 194
  as bishop of Winchester 284
Edward I, King 35, 260
  and Arthurian legend 161
  attempts to raise armies against
    France 36, 38
  code for tournaments 49
  and St Stephen's, Westminster 259
  Statuta armorum (1292) 475
  and Wales 174, 289
Edward II, King 33, 36, 39, 266
  and Arthurian legend 161
  bans on tournaments 49
  death 43, 60
  deposition 42–3
  favourites 39
  and Gascon expedition 38, 39
  and homage to Charles IV
    38–9, 40
  purchase of garters 269
  rumours of escape 29, 60
  and Windsor 260
Edward III, King 4, 175, 490
  accession 33, 42–3, 46
  advance on Paris 448–9
  affair with Alice Perrers 56–7
  and alleged rape of countess of
    Salisbury 7, 486, 487–90
  appointed imperial vicar-general at
    Koblenz (1338) 114
  and Aquitaine 40, 62

Edward III – *cont.*
  as army commander 100–101,
    463, 490
  and Arthur: comparison with
    157–8, 490; interest in 159–61
  and Audrehem 144
  and Charles of Navarre 442
  claim to French throne 33, 123,
    125, 151
  and concept of Company of the
    Garter 277; purchase of garters
    269; and story of lady's garter
    485–6
  at Crécy 213, 241, 244
  crisis (1340–41) 121–2, 149
  early life 44–6
  and execution of earl of Kent
    60–61
  expedition to Brittany 153–4
  family: marriage to Philippa 56–7;
    relations with father 44–5;
    relations with Isabella 45, 51;
    sons 57
  household 44, 45
  as innovator 182, 232–3, 490–91
  invasion of Normandy 3–4
  love of falconry 418
  and mercenaries in France 451–2
  and Mortimer 61–4
  and opposition to war in France
    121–2
  and preparations for 1343
    campaign 156, 176–7
  and Reims campaign (1359)
    443–8
  relations with Philip VI 57–8, 69,
    128, 130
  religious foundations 333
  and Round Table project 167–9
  royal council (advisers) 23,
    140, 490
  and Scotland 46–8, 97–108; ride to
    Perth (1336) 106

  and supporters 95–6, 103–4,
    109–10, 111–12, 490–91
  and taking of Calais (1349)
    415–17
  and tournaments: armour 85;
    enthusiasm for 50–52, 67–8,
    69–71; as 'Lionel' 101–2, 174;
    participation as simple knight
    73, 76–7, 151
  and Virgin Mary 260–61
Edward IV, King 376
  appointments to Company of the
    Garter 470
  and St George's chapel 482
  and symbolism of Order of the
    Garter 485–6
Edward, Prince of Wales (the Black
    Prince) 23, 61, 398, 463
  accounts 271, 273
  adoption of black ostrich
    feather 240
  Crécy campaign 187, 192,
    199, 200
  at Crécy 213, 224,
    226, 392–3; banner 234, 235–7;
    reputed capture 134, 234–6
  and cult of Trinity 328–9
  funeral instructions 337–8
  in Gascony (1355) 421–3, 424,
    426–8
  marriage to Joan of Kent 24–5, 76,
    290, 314
  at Nájera 460–62
  and papal envoys 431–2
  and Pedro I of Castile 454, 456
  at Poitiers 435–7, 438–41
  religious foundations 333
  shield in Gloucester cathedral 286
  siege of Limoges 410
  in Spain 457, 459
  at Winchelsea 416, 419–20
Eland, William 64
Elbeuf 204

Eleanor of Aquitaine 474
  marriage to Henry II of
    England 34
  marriage to Louis VII 33
Eleanor (of Woodstock), sister of
    Edward III 44
  marriage to Reginald, count of
    Guelders 89
Elsing, Norfolk, Hugh Hastings
    monument 338
Eltham Palace
  tournament (1342) 150–51
  tournament (1348) 255, 272
embroidery 86, 87
  opus anglicanum 87
encampment, on campaign 183
England
  knightly culture 351
  royal councils 140
English army
  for 1334 invasion of Scotland
    103, 185
  after Crécy 245–6
  after Najéra 464, 480–81
  assembled at Portsmouth for Crécy
    campaign 180
  and battle formation at Crécy
    493–8
  battlefield experience 148
  casualties in Hundred Years War
    404–5
  contracts of service 146,
    188–90
  earls as leaders 110
  esprit de corps 392, 434, 440
  and knightly honour 464
  organization of 145, 190,
    192–4
  pay 146, 190–91, 394, 396
  at Poitiers 432–3, 435–7, 438–40
  and profits of war 191–2, 396–8
  recruitment 146, 156, 185–92
  reputation 463

  see also Crécy, battle of (1346);
    Crécy campaign
English Channel, wind and tides 178,
    194, 196
English language 125, 127–8
Erpingham, Thomas 468
Esplechin, truce of (1340) 74, 121,
    151, 384
esquires, role of 380
Essarts, Herberay des 13
Eu, Raoul III, count of 256, 368
  as constable of France 135, 136,
    142, 147
  and Crécy campaign 196,
    199, 200
Eu, Raoul IV, count of 142
  at Caen 389, 403
Ewyas Harold castle 319
exchequer, royal, tally system 281

fabrics
  damask 86
  linen 86
  silk 86
  velvet 85, 86
  woollen cloth 86
  see also fashion
Falkirk, battle of (1298) 476
fashion 85–7, 89–95
  blue cloth 272–3
  buttons 90
  embroidery 86, 87
  fastenings 90
  furs 86–7
  Hainault 58, 59
  hats 91, 305
  jagged edges 89, 90
  liripipes 94
  parti-coloured garments 90–91, 94
  pictorial designs 86
  sleeves 90
  tailoring 90–91
  see also costumes; fabrics

Faversham, tournament 49
Fay, Godemar du, and crossing of
    Somme 208, 211
Felton, Thomas 458, 459
Felton, William 458–9
Ferne, John, *The Blazon of
    Gentrie* 172
Ferrers, Henry, at Guildford
    Christmas feast 113
Ferrers, Sir John, at Najéra 25
Ferrers, Ralph 380
Ferrers, Sir Robert, at battle of
    Crécy 226
festivals 77–89
    in 1342: 150
    after Crécy 254–6
    with Arthurian themes 82–4
    French 81
    'round tables' 173
    scenery 79, 88
    see also costumes; tournaments
feudalism, in France 35
finances *see* treasury, royal
Fitzalan, Sir Edmund 314
Fitzalan, Richard, 8th earl of
    Arundel 468
Fitzalan, Richard, 9th earl of Arundel
    111, 150, 517
    admiralty 179
    banking activities 304, 395–6
    at Crécy (called 'son of the earl of
        Warenne') 220, 226
    and Crécy campaign 187
    at Guildford Christmas feast 113
    marriages 304–5, 314, 316
    not Garter knight 304–6
    shield in Gloucester cathedral 286
    at Winchelsea (1350) 416
Fitzalan of Bedale, Katharine 317
Fitzsimon, Sir Richard (KG 1349)
    298, 299–300, 302, 513
    at Crécy 234, 235–6, 589n, 596n

Fitzwalter, Lord, at battle of
    Crécy 226
Fitzwarin, Fulk, the younger 513
Fitzwarin, John 515
Fitzwarin, Sir William (KG 1349) 86,
    99, 103, 298, 300, 302, 396,
    513–15
    at Buironfosse 117
    at Crécy 226
    death, of plague 300
    monument at Wantage 338, 515
    and parish of Wantage 336
    pilgrimage to Rome 330–32
    with Teutonic Knights 388
Flanders 245
    and 1345 campaign 176
    alliance against France
        112–13, 114
    relations with France 250–51
    war in (1339–40) 74
    war with France (1304) 229–30
Flanders, Guy of, prisoner after
    Cadzand 403
Flanders, Louis de Nevers, count of
    112, 147, 506
    at Crécy 219, 220, 223,
        224, 233
Flanders, Margaret of 310
Flete, John, privy wardrobe 158
Florence, trading companies 26–7
Flote, Guillaume, French
    chancellor 252
Foix-Béarn, Gaston III, lord of
    (Phoebus) 11, 139
Folville gang 323
food
    for Crécy campaign 182–3,
        184–5
    fish 185
    meat 184
    poultry 183, 185
    for St George's Day festival 283

France 123–48, 351
  1339 campaign in 116–18
  and battle of Sluys 119–20
  campaigns against 108, 110–11,
    112–21
  civil war after Poitiers 441–2
  claimants to throne 123, 124
  Company of the Virgin and St
    George 283, 351, 352–3
  debts to Italian bankers 250
  'free companies' of mercenaries
    451–2, 454
  heralds 474
  hostility to aristocracy 250
  kingship in 34–5
  knightly ideals 131, 376
  naval war with (1293–4) 35
  relations with 33–4, 35–6
  royal council 139, 140–41
  'sainte-chapelles' 263–4, 352–3
  tenure of English lands in 36, 38,
    126–7
  treachery in 131–6, 235
Fraternal Society of St George,
    Hungary 282, 346–50, 360
  political purpose 348–9
  rules and obligations 348–9
  uniform 349
Frederick II, Emperor 174
French army 142–5
  battle cry 143
  constable 143
  at Crécy 146–7, 218–19, 497–8
  and hostility to nobility 250
  lack of cohesion 146–7, 440
  marshals 143–4
  mercenaries 146
  morale 148
  oriflamme (standard) 215
  at Poitiers 145, 148, 435,
    437–9, 440
  recruitment 144–5

French court
  extravagant fashion 91
  masks and disguises 81
French language 125
  Arthurian histories in 158
Froissart, Jean, chronicler 5, 6, 9–13,
    16, 54
  on Audrehem 143–4
  on battle of Crécy 222, 228, 232,
    236–7
  on battle of Winchelsea (1350)
    419–20
  on Charny 370
  connection of Garter with
    Arthurian Round Table
    470, 483
  on d'Auberchicourt 499–500, 503,
    504–5
  on death of John of Bohemia 240
  on death of John Chandos
    404–5
  on funeral of James Audley 338
  on heralds 478
  and knighthood 174
  and knightly honour 464, 481
  and legend of rape of countess of
    Salisbury by Edward III 489
  Meliador romance 10
  on peace of Brétigny 450
  on Poitiers 438
  on Reims campaign 446
  Rome manuscript 12, 13
  on royal revels 81
  on surrender of Calais 253, 410
funerals, of companions 337–8
furs 86–7
  ermine 87
  miniver 87
Fyfield, Richard 379

Gaillon, castle 204
gambling 372

Garter badge 268–74, 401
  on College carpets 290–91
  at Crécy 486–7
  use of colour blue 272–3, 276–7
Garter Company see Company
  of the Garter
Garter king of arms, office of 473
Garter motto 81, 84, 272, 275–6, 486
  on manuscript of Sir Gawain and
    the Green Knight 471
garter(s)
  on costumes 272–3
  as emblem 275
  as items of clothing 268–70
  jewelled 269, 272
  legend of lady's loss of 483–4
  women's 270
Gascony 3, 35, 148
  1355 campaign 394, 421–4, 426–8
  border dispute (1323) 38
Gaunt, John of, son of Edward III,
  duke of Lancaster (KG) 57,
  76, 255–6
  and Castile 456–7, 458, 462
  marriage 313, 462
  at Najéra 460
  Reims campaign 444, 446,
    447–8
Gaveston, Piers 39, 266
  tournament at Wallingford
    (1307) 49
Geldern, duke of 387
Gelre herald see Heynenzoon
Genoese crossbowmen 146
  at Crécy 217, 218–19, 225, 233
  in Normandy 197
Genoese galleys 154
  at battle of Sluys 120
  at Brest 153
Germany
  crusades in Prussia 382–90
  Manesse manuscript 85
  see also Cologne; Teutonic Knights

Ghent, jousts at 118
Ghistels, John 503, 504
Ghistels, Wulfart 206, 208, 503
  in France (1339) 117
Glastonbury
  and Arthurian legend 157, 161
  tables of history of monastery
    295, 296
Gloucester, tournament 58
Gloucester, Thomas (of Woodstock),
  1st duke of 82, 92, 158, 172,
  597n
Glover's Roll 476
gold, in textiles 86
The Golden Legend 268
Gonville, Edmund 334–5
Grailly, Jean de, captal de Buch (KG
  1349) 143, 297, 388, 504
  capture of duke of Bourbon 403
  as Garter knight 302
  in Gascony (1355) 421, 423
  at Najéra 460
  at Poitiers 439
  ransom 404
Grandes chroniques 19, 133, 205
Grandisson, John, Bishop of
  Exeter 329
graves, mass 243
Gray, Thomas, chronicler 15–16
  on adultery 315
  on Edward III's pleasures 67
  on fall of Mortimer 63, 64
  on Henry Beaumont and
    Scotland 97
  on Montagu 107
  on new earldoms 109
  on Pedro I 455–6
  Scalacronica 63, 280, 370,
    375, 583n
  on tournaments 280, 283
'Great Company' 454, 457
Grey, Sir John, 1st baron Grey de
  Rotherfield (KG 1349) 103, 317

at Crécy 226
as Garter knight 298, 302
Grimaldi, Carlo 219, 223, 224
death at Crécy 220
Grosmont, Eleanor of, marriage to
Richard Fitzalan 304–5, 314
Grosmont, Henry of, earl of Derby
(later earl of Leicester and duke
of Lancaster) (KG 1349) 68, 95,
109, 312, 328
and 1345 campaign 176, 420–21
at Auberoche 191
Book of Holy Medicines 269,
326–7
book on laws of war 406
and Brittany 155, 196, 428, 431
at Buironfosse 117
at Calais 251, 252, 253
Crécy campaign 187–8
death of plague (1361) 300, 405
endowments 333, 335
in France (1339) 116
as Garter knight 302
and Henry IV (grandfather of) 467
as judge in Court of Chivalry
378, 478
negotiates peace of Brétigny 450
at Paris 449
and Reims campaign 445, 446,
447–8, 449, 450
at Rennes 143
at Round Table festival (1344) 162
Scottish campaigns 99, 103, 105–6
shield in Gloucester cathedral 286
with Teutonic Knights 388
and tournaments 72–3, 113–14,
255
use of heralds 477
at Winchelsea 416, 419
Grosmont, Maud 313
Grosvenor, Robert 378–9
Guelders, Reginald, count (later duke)
of 89, 163, 469

herald of 480
Guernsey, invasion (1339) 22
guerre mortelle, banners to indicate 407
Guesclin, Bertrand du, French
constable 142–3, 407, 508
in Brittany 453
and Castile 454, 455, 457, 458
at Najéra 460, 461, 462
as prisoner after Auray 403, 507
ransom 402–3
Guildford
Christmas feast (1337) 79, 113–14
Christmas feast (1340) 149
Christmas feast (1347) 78–9,
80, 254–5
entertainments 270–71
tournaments 57, 67, 102
guilds, costumes 80
Guines, castle 136, 253, 416
raid on 249
guns
at battle of Crécy 497
bombards 181
cannons 182
for Crécy campaign 181–2
multi-barrelled 182
ribalds 587n
Gurney, Thomas 43
Gynewell, John, Grosmont's
steward 335

Hainault
entourage at English court 53, 54,
111, 312
fashions 58, 59
Garter knights from 323–6
military contingents in England
46–7, 55
Hainault, counts of 573n
and Alexander the Great 92–3
see also Philippa
Hainault, Jean de 6, 7, 8, 9, 41, 54
at Buironfosse 117

Hainault, Jean de – *cont.*
  at Crécy 54, 134, 217, 219, 233
  in France (1339) 116
  and Philip VI at Crécy 240–41
  and Scottish campaigns 46–7
  at tournaments 59
Hainault, Jeanne of, dowager
  countess 120
Hainault, Margaret, countess of 501
Hainault, William I of 9, 41, 53–4, 55,
  93, 499
Hainault, William II of 53–4,
  324, 500
  and 1339 campaign in France 116
  alliance with France 176
  knightly career 54–5
  with Teutonic Knights 384–5, 389,
  390
  at tournaments 150–51
Hale, Sir Frank van (KG 1359) 302,
  515–16
Hale, Simon (Simon de Mirabel) 515
Halidon Hill, battle of (1333) 21, 74,
  100–101
Hammes, castle of 249
Hanseatic League 87, 126
Harcourt, count of
  at Crécy 219
  death at Crécy 220, 243
Harcourt, Godefroy d' 133, 151, 176
  at Crécy 235, 243
  and Crécy campaign 196, 197,
  199, 202, 203, 206, 210
  exile of 489
Hardreshull, John, and Brittany 155
Hardy, Robert 496
  The Great Warbow 231
Harfleur, port of 196–7
hastiludium (joust) 68
Hastings, Sir Hugh 203
  Crécy campaign 198
  monument 338

Hastings, Hugh III 381
Hastings, John, 2nd earl of
  Pembroke 381
  at La Rochelle (1372) 462
Hastings, Laurence, 1st earl of
  Pembroke 155, 286
  and 1339 campaign in France 116
  and 1345 campaign 176, 187
  at Buironfosse 117
Hastings, Ralph 189
hats 91, 305
Havering, tournament 69
Hemricourt, Jacques d' 6, 7, 8
Hennebont, Brittany 152
Henry II, King
  and Arthurian legend 161, 167
  marriage to Eleanor of Aquitaine 34
Henry III, King
  and 'round table' festivals 173
  and St Edward's, Windsor 260
  and St Stephen's, Westminster 259
Henry IV, King 384, 467
  and 1408 challenge to Garter
  knights 469–70
  and Company of the Garter 280,
  295–6, 466–7, 472
Henry V, King 400
  and Company of the Garter as
  knightly order 470, 471–3
  and statutes of the Garter 295,
  472–3
Henry of Trastamara, king of Castile
  144, 606n
  alliance with Charles of
  Navarre 457
  crowned king at Burgos 455
  at Najéra 459–62
  war against Pedro I 454, 455–6,
  457–9
Henxteworth, John 394, 424, 503
heraldry
  banners 87–8

crests 85
 development of 75, 126
 'lion shield' 102
 public displays of 381
 records 479
 on royal carriage 89
 and use of arms 371
heralds
 equated with minstrels 474–5
 formal appointments of 473, 479–80
 formal authority 478–9
 French 474
 heraldic titles 475
 and identification of knights in
  battle 242–3, 476, 477
 and kings of arms 474–6
 as messengers 477, 478
 regulation of 473, 474–81
 at tournaments 72, 474
Hereford, tournaments 51, 58
Herland, William, wood carver 288
Hesdin, Philip VI at 251
Hewitt, H.J. 434–5
Heynenzoon, Claes, king of heralds
  of the Rhine (Gelre herald)
  388, 480
 Lobdichten 480
Hoccleve, Thomas, poet 471–2
Holland, John, earl of
  Huntingdon 312
Holland, Sir Otho (KG 1349) 516
Holland, Thomas, 1st earl of Kent
  (KG 1349) 135, 516, 586n
 at battle of Winchelsea
  (1350) 416
 and Brittany 155
 at Buironfosse 117
 at Caen 200
 at Calais 253
 capture of Raoul of Eu 403
 Crécy campaign 204
 death of plague (1360) 300

marriage to Joan of Kent 308–9
 with Teutonic Knights 388, 389
Holy Cross, feast of 296
honour
 and dishonour 378, 400
 family 381
 of knights 372–3, 464, 473–4, 481
Hope, William St John 297
horses
 for Crécy campaign 180
 shipping of 193–4, 585n
 in tournaments 75
Howard, John, admiral 250
Huet, Walter 508
Humbert II, ruler of Vienne 348, 350,
  351, 358, 369
Hungary, Fraternal Society of St
  George 282, 346–50, 360
Hungerford, Walter 472
Hurley, William, master carpenter 287
Hus, John 229

Ibelin, John of 173
indentures, 'for peace or war' 189
Ingham church, Norfolk 336
Ingham, Joan 317
Ingham, Oliver 149, 152, 317, 336
Ingham, Oliver (son) 514
Isabella, daughter of Edward III 87,
  99, 265, 514
 marriage to Enguerrand de Coucy
  314, 465, 597n
Isabella, Queen 33, 58, 128, 314–15
 books of Arthurian romances 158
 and deposition of Edward II 42–3
 and execution of earl of Kent 60
 and fall of Mortimer 63–4
 in France (1325) 39–40
 marriage to Edward II 36
 and Mortimer 40–41, 51,
  52, 62
Isle of Man 45

Italy
    textiles 86
    trading companies and bankers
        26–7, 126

Jacquerie uprising 15
Jaime III, king of Majorca 50, 220,
        223, 224, 233
Jaime IV, king of Majorca 460
James, M.R. 267
jaques (jackets) 94
Jeanne, queen of France 129, 315
Jerusalem
    conquest (1099) 83
    defence and fall of 343–4
    pilgrimage to 330
jewellery, confiscated 96
Joan, daughter of Edward III 87, 101,
        314, 514
Joan of Kent *see* Kent, Joan,
    countess of
Joan of the Tower, sister of Edward
    III, wife of David II of Scotland
    44, 97, 159, 313–14
John of Bohemia, king 147
    at Crécy 219, 223, 224, 233,
        240–41
    death at Crécy 220, 234,
        237–40, 243–4
    funeral 221, 243–4
    and knightly pursuits 347–8
    and Teutonic Knights 383
John of Eltham, brother of Edward III
    44, 104
John of Gaunt *see* Gaunt
John II, king of France 135–7,
        305, 388
    and 1355 Gascony campaign
        428, 430
    and battle of Poitiers 431, 432,
        435–6, 438–9, 440; capture 15,
        27, 139, 440, 441
    in Brittany 430

and Charles of Navarre 137–8
Company of Knights of Our Lady
    352, 353–60
Company of the Virgin and St
    George 283, 351, 352–3
death (1364) 451
as duke of Normandy 141, 154,
    202, 352, 353
hat 91
military tactics 145
as prisoner 175, 280, 281,
    400–401, 443
ransom 400–401, 450
John, king of England 35
Joigny, count of 503
Joseph of Arimathea 157
jousting 73, 371
    as court event 73
    hastiludium 68
    lists 172
    merchants as spectators 126
    at night 50
    themes 77–8
    see also tournaments
Juan I, king of Castile 462
Juan II, king of Castile 364
Juliers, Elizabeth of 312, 452, 504–5,
    506, 509
Juliers, William, margrave of (d. 1302)
    229, 245
Juliers, William, margrave and duke of
    252, 506
'just war' 397

Károly I, king of Hungary 346–8, 351,
    360–61
Keegan, John 214
Keith, William, warden of Berwick 99
Kenilworth 42
    tournament 51
Kennington, tournament 49
Kent, Edmund of Woodstock, 1st earl
    of 38, 39, 41, 43, 47, 60

arrest and execution 60–61
Kent, Joan, countess of 308–12
  in Aquitaine 311
  as 'lady of the Garter' 483
  marriage to Edward, Prince of
    Wales 24–5, 290, 309–11, 488
  marriage to Thomas Holland 308–9
  marriage to William Montagu
    308–9, 487–9
Kent, John, 3rd earl of 506
Kent, 4th earl of see Holland, Thomas
Kerdeston, Sir William, at battle of
  Crécy 226
kings and kingship 34–5
  coronation 35
  election 34
  in France 129–30
King's Langley, tournament (1341)
  149
Kirkby, John 189–90
'Kitchen Journal', Walter Wetewang
  26, 494
knighthood 46, 343
  and Arthurian legend 168, 174
  as competitive 371
  and honour 372–3
  and individual 371
  as international 125–6
  knightly deeds 8, 371
  manuals of 366–75
  and reputation 372, 381
  see also knights
knighthood, orders of 465–6
  focus on honour 473–4
  secular 29, 360
knightly societies 282–3
  Fraternal Society of St George 282,
    346–50
  and monarch as leader 364–5
  and tournaments 282
Knighton, Henry 68, 80, 450
  on crossing of Somme 209
  on fashion 94

  on siege of Calais 252
knights
  cost of equipment 394–5
  Crécy campaign 188
  education and literacy of 374,
    375–6
  longevity 379–80
  'public fame' 372, 381
  regional loyalties 379
  retinues in war 393–5
  role as aggressor 406
  role in society and state 367–8
  see also knighthood; knights of the
    household; tournaments
Knights Hospitallers, Order of
  343–4
  prior of 233
knights of the household 103–4,
  111–12, 142
  robes 112
  and Round Table project 172
Knights Templar, Order of 29,
  343–4
  Philip the Fair and 315, 345, 360
Kniprode, Winrich von, grand master
  of Teutonic Knights 384,
  385, 389–90
Knolles, Robert, mercenary 457
Königsberg 389
  table of honour of Teutonic
    Knights 385–7
Kyeser, Conrad, Bellifortis 229
Kynebell, Robert, wood carver 287

la Beche, Sir Nicholas de 121
la Cerda, Charles de 138, 141, 142,
  250
La Hogue see St Vaast-la-Hogue
la More, Thomas de 22
la Mote, Jean de 93
  Perfection of the Peacock 92
la Pole, William de 126
La Réole, near Bordeaux 38

La Roche-Guyon, castle 204, 586*n*
La Rochelle, battle of (1372) 462–3
la Vache, Sir Richard de (KG 1355)
    518–19
la Warre, Roger de 196
Lambeth Apocalypse 268
Lancaster, earls of (later dukes of) 21
    see also Gaunt, John of; Grosmont,
        Henry of
Lancaster, Edmund, 1st earl of 51
Lancaster, Henry, 3rd earl of (and
    Leicester) 42, 46
    blindness 95, 110, 303
    and Mortimer 57
    at Stanhope Park 47
Lancaster, Thomas, 2nd earl 266, 301
lands, grants of 95, 109
Langley, Edmund of, earl of Cambridge
    (KG) 53, 76, 150, 256
    and Reims campaign 446
Languedoc 430
Lannoy, Gilbert de 385
Laon 135
Latimer, William, 4th baron 64,
    155, 467
    as chamberlain 464
    as Garter knight 64, 303
Laton, Robert 478
law of arms 405
'law of the nations' 405–6
Lawrence (ship) 272
laws of war 405–7
Lay of mantel 51
le Baker, Geoffrey, chronicler 21–2,
    26, 28, 64
    on battle of Crécy 222, 231, 234,
        236, 242
    on battle of Morlaix 153
    on battle of Poitiers 434, 438,
        439, 441
    on battle of Winchelsea (1350)
        416, 419
    on Charny 370, 415–16

on Garter foundation 275
on Gascony campaign (1355) 424
list of original Garter members
    297–9
on Miles Stapleton 328
on St George's Day tournament
    (1349) 281–2
on surrender of Calais 253
le Bel, Jean, canon of Liège, chronicler
    6–9, 12, 47, 54, 375
    on 1342 campaign 152
    on battle of Crécy 228, 230,
        240, 242–3
    on battle of Mauron 358–9
    on Buironfosse 132
    on capture of John II 441
    comparison of Edward III with
        Arthur 157
    on Crécy campaign 206, 209
    on d'Auberchicourt 506
    and legend of rape of countess of
        Salisbury by Edward III 487–90
    on Lille expedition 118
    on Reims campaign 444, 445
    on siege of Calais 252
    on surrender of Calais 253–4,
        409–10
    on truce of Bordeaux 442
Le Crotoy 203, 206, 208
Le Hem, tournament 82
Le Mans, 'sainte-chapelle' 352
Le Moine de Basle (Heinrich Münch)
    239–40
Le Morte Darthur (Malory) 370, 375
le Ros, William 196
Leicester, earl of see Grosmont, Henry
Leo VI, Emperor 228–9
Léon, Hervé, lord of 152
Leopartie 202
Lesparre, lord of 421
letters, as sources 20, 23–6
Li Muisit, Gilles, chronicler 13–15
    on battle of Crécy 214, 232

on battle of Winchelsea (1350) 419
on Philip VI 130
Libourne 456
Lichfield
joust (1331) 69
joust (1348) 73, 255, 590n
Lille, expedition to 118
Limoges
monastery of St Martial 410
siege of 410, 508
Limousin 35
Lincoln, company of knights 72
Lion, Espan du, squire 11
Lionel (of Antwerp), duke of
Clarence (KG) 76, 82, 255–6,
312, 314
betrothal 150
birth 116
in Gascony (1355) 421
and Reims campaign 446
Lisieux 202–3
Lisle, John, Lord, of Rougemont (KG
1349) 293, 298, 302, 319, 516
at Crécy 226
death (1355) 404
in Gascony (1355) 421, 422, 423
at Winchelsea (1350) 416, 417
literature
Anglo-French shared 125–6
Anglo-Saxon tradition 128
Lithuania, crusades in 384
Little, Robert, herald 475, 476
livery 80, 87
Llull, Ramon, Book of the Order of
Knighthood 126, 366–8
Llywelyn, defeat of (1285) 157, 158
loans, to finance campaigns 395–6
Lochindorb Castle 106
Logroño, Castile 458, 459
Loire, bridges 431
Lollard heresy 471–2
London
as centre for histories 19

Charterhouse 333–4
chronicle (in French 1330s)
20–21
longbows, and arrows, for Crécy
campaign 181
Longueville, count of, as prisoner after
Poitiers 403
Longuyon, Jacques de, The Vows of
the Peacock 92, 93
López de Ayala, Pero, poet and
chronicler 17–18, 402
Chronicle of King Pedro 460
at Nájera 364, 460, 461
Rhyme of the Palace 17–18
Loring, Nigel, chamberlain to Edward
Prince of Wales (KG 1349) 23,
323, 328, 396
as Garter knight 302, 313
in Gascony (1355) 422
at Poitiers 437
religious benefactions 336
with Teutonic Knights 388
Lorraine, Raoul, duke of 233, 385
Louis IV, German emperor
114, 330
Louis VII, king of France 33, 34
Louis IX, king and saint, of France
263–4
Louis X, king of France 128–9, 140
Louis of Taranto, king of Naples 352,
359–60
Lovel, William, as judge in Court of
Chivalry 378
Lovell versus Morley 328,
378, 380
Lucy, Thomas 46
ludi (king's games) 77
Lundy Island 42
Luttrell, Andrew 331
Luttrell, Beatrice 331
Luttrell, Geoffrey 331
Luttrell Psalter 89, 269–70, 496
Lydgate, John 172, 481

McFarlane, K.B. 111
Madresilva, fictional damsel 483–4
magnates
  communication with, during
    campaigns 74, 114
  Edward III's relations with 111,
    112, 149
  in France 142
Maignelay, Sir Tristan de, standard-
  bearer 386, 438
Maldon, Geoffrey of, monk 199, 202
Malory, Thomas 16
  Le Morte Darthur 370, 375, 470
Maltravers, John, steward 61
Man, lord of see Montagu, William,
  2nd earl of Salisbury
Manesse manuscript 85
Mar, earl of 98
Marcel, Étienne 139
March, earls of
  tournaments 68
  see also Mortimer, Roger
March, Edmund, 3rd earl of 467
Marck, raid on 249
Margaret (of Windsor), daughter of
  Edward III 76
Marie de France 81, 168
Marienburg, headquarters of Teutonic
  Knights 383, 384
Marlborough, Maundy money
  (1344) 175
Marmion, Avice 317
marriage
  and adultery 315–16
  choice of husband 314–15
  function of priests 307
  and regional alliances 317
  spousals 307–8
  within prohibited degrees 307
Marshal, William 474
Martin de Merlo, Ferrant 508
Martorell, Joan, Tirant the White
  483–4, 485, 486

Mary (of Waltham), daughter of
  Edward III, marriage to earl of
  Richmond (heir to duke of
  Brittany) 76, 313
masks 57
  at festivals 77–8, 254–5
  for tournaments 59, 70, 78–9, 160
Maunsell, John 64
Mauny, Anne 381
Mauny, Olivier 462
Mauny, Walter, knight (KG 1349) 13,
  52, 59–60, 98
  and 1345 campaign 176
  and Brittany 8, 152
  at Buironfosse 117
  at Calais 252, 253–4, 410
  and costs of campaigning 395
  in France (1339) 116, 117
  funeral 278, 337–9
  as Garter knight 298, 302, 464
  as judge in Court of Chivalry 378
  at Paris 449
  prisoners of 403
  and Reims campaign 445
  religious foundations 333–5
  at Sluys 113, 119
  at tournaments and festivals 54,
    69, 113
  wife 312, 316
  at Winchelsea (1350) 416
Mauron, battle of (1352) 358–9
Maxstoke castle 303
Meaux abbey
  abbot of 127
  chronicle 210
Meingre, Jean de see Boucicaut
Meissen, Frederick, margrave of 445
mêlée (mock warfare) 68, 173
  to open tournaments 71–2
Melton, William, Archbishop of
  York 60
mercenaries, 'free companies' in
  France 451–2, 454

merchants, links with France 126
Merton
  Christmas games 79
  Epiphony games 82
Meulan, bridge at 204
Midsummer Day, tournaments 76
Mildenhale, Robert, armourer 418
Milemete, Walter 56, 181, 267, 497
military religious orders 360
miniver, squirrel fur 87
Minot, Laurence 29
minstrels 607n
  commentary at tournaments 72
  heralds as 474–5
Miranda, Castile 458
Mohun, Elizabeth 312
Mohun, Sir John de, Lord Mohun
  (KG 1349) 298, 302, 312, 313
  cost of warfare 394, 396
Molyns, John 64, 113
monasteries, chroniclers in 18–19
Monclar, Gascony 423
Monington, Walter de, Abbot of
  Glastonbury 157
Monmouth, Geoffrey of
  and image of Arthur 160, 167
  and Round Table 165
Mons-en-Pévèle, battle of (1304)
  229–30, 244–5, 494
Montagu family 312
Montagu, Edward, in France
  (1339) 116
Montagu, Philippa 312
Montagu, William, 1st earl of
  Salisbury, lord of Man 15–16,
  20, 109, 328
  and 1335–6 Scottish campaign
  105, 106
  at Buironfosse 117
  captured in France (1339/40) 16,
  116, 121, 228
  death (1344) 302–3
  diplomatic missions 112–13

  and Edward III 65, 66, 95, 103,
  107–8
  expedition to Lille 118
  at Guildford Christmas feast
  113–14
  and Mortimer 63, 64–5, 95
  and Philip VI 108
  ransom 404
  at Round Table festival (1344) 162
  in Scotland 99, 106, 107
  at tournaments 52, 58, 67–8,
  70–71, 73, 150
Montagu, William, 2nd earl of
  Salisbury, lord of Man (KG
  1349) 314, 388, 399
  at battle of Winchelsea (1350) 416
  Crécy campaign 196
  at Crécy 226
  as Garter knight 302, 303
  in Gascony (1355) 421, 422, 423
  marriage to Elizabeth Mohun 312
  marriage to Joan of Kent 308–9,
  312, 487–9
Montacute priory at Bisham 337
  at Poitiers 435, 436–7
  and Reims campaign 446
Montfort, Jean III de, duke of
  Brittany 151
Montfort, Jean IV de, duke of
  Brittany, earl of Richmond 41,
  132, 321, 469
  death 176
  escape from Paris 176
Montfort, Jean V de, duke of Brittany
  as heir to Brittany 151–2, 446, 452
  release 155, 175
Montfort, Jeanne de, countess of
  Brittany 8, 152
Montfort, Ralph 321
Montfort, Simon de 476
Montgomery, Sir John de,
  admiral 250
  at Crécy 226

Montiel, battle of (1369) 462
'Montjoie St Denis', war cry 407
Montmorency, Charles de 147
monuments 338–9
  brasses 338, 339
Morat, battle of (1476) 494
Moray, Thomas, 1st earl of 97
More, Walter atte 349, 476
Moreau de Fiennes, Robert,
  constable 142
Morel, Nicholas, herald 475
Morlaix, siege of 153
Morley, Robert, Lord 58,
  328, 381
  admiral of the north 119, 179
  as captain at tournaments 70,
  73, 150
  claim to arms 371
  at Crécy 226–7
  death 451
Morley, Thomas, Lord 378
Morley, William, Lord 381, 479
Morte Arthure 160
  and Round Table 171
Mortimer family 312
Mortimer, Edmund 96
Mortimer, Geoffrey 58, 61
Mortimer, Ian 281
Mortimer, Roger, 1st earl of March
  21, 60–62
  downfall 61–4, 95–6
  as earl of March 51, 57, 297
  and Edward III 46
  and Isabella 33, 40–41, 51, 52, 62
  and opposition to Edward II
  39, 42, 43
  sons of 46, 52
  at Stanhope Park 47
  tournaments 50–51, 58, 67
Mortimer, Roger, 2nd earl of March
  (KG 1349) 280, 337
  Crécy campaign 196, 198
  at Crécy 226

  death (1360) 405, 450
  marriage to Philippa Montagu 312
  and Reims campaign 405, 444,
  445, 446
Mortimer, Roger, grandson 96
mottoes 81–2
  swan 82
Mowbray, Thomas 467–8, 470
Murimuth, Adam, chronicler 19–20,
  21, 25, 275
  on 1344 Windsor festival 161–2,
  169, 178
  on battle of Crécy 215–17
  on Charny 369
  on Edward's claim to France 151
  on William Montagu 488
  on Wyville 66
Murkirk, Francolin of, painter 59
Murray, Andrew 106, 152
music
  at festivals 77
  polyphonic 284
Musshon, John, herald 477, 608n
Mussidan, lord of 421
mystery plays 77

Najéra, battle of (1367) 17, 143, 245,
  402, 459–62
  captives 461
  Order of the Sash at 364
Namur, Guy, count of 106, 245
Namur, Robert of, at Winchelsea
  (1350) 416, 419–20
Nantes, raid on 154
Naples
  Order of the Holy Spirit 352,
  359–60
  Order of the Ship 305
Narbonne 426
Navarre 454–5
Navarre, Louis de 453
Nefyn, Wales, tournament 157
Neith Cross, relic 289, 296

Nesle, Guy de 147
Neville, Ida, Lady 331
Neville, John 58, 63, 66, 99
Neville, John, of Raby (KG 1369) 103
Neville, Ralph 66, 467
Neville's Cross, battle of (1346)
    16, 248
Nevsky, Alexander 383
Newark, house of canons 333
Newmarket
    tournament (1331) 69
    tournament (1334) 102
Newstead Abbey 263
Nicolas, Sir Nicolas Harris 299
nobility, Anglo-Norman 127
Norman Chronicle (1369–72) 23
    on battle of Crécy 227, 231–2,
        235, 241, 493
Normandy 110, 125
    duchy of 33–4
    loss of 34, 35
Norrois, name 479
Norrois, Andrew, herald 475
Norrois, Henry le 475
Norroy herald 475
Northampton
    great council (1336) 106
    tournaments 49, 150, 475
Northampton, earl of *see* Bohun,
    William
Northampton, treaty of (1328) 97
Northburgh, Michael 25
    on battle of Crécy 215
    as bishop of London 334
    Crécy campaign 197
Northwell, William, keeper of Prince
    of Wales's wardrobe 271, 273–4
Norwich, tournament (1341) 68,
    149–50
Norwich, bishop of (William
    Ayermin) 41
Norwich, Thomas, at Crécy 236–7
Norwich, William 317

'Notre Dame, Guesclin', war cry 407
Nottingham
    great council (1330) 62–3
    great council (1337) 110
    tournament (1334) 102
Nouaillé
    abbey of 432
    bridge at 436
Noyers, Mile de 141, 234
Nuewenburg, Mathias von, on battle
    of Crécy 227–8, 233

Ockley, William 43
Oem (Eam), Henry (Heinken) (KG
    1349) 55, 300, 330, 500, 517
    in Prussia 389
    retinue 393–4
    service with prince of Wales 188–9,
        302, 324–6
Offord, John, chancellor 194
Oldcastle, Sir John 471
Order of the Collar (Savoy)
    466, 485
Order of the Garter *see* Company of
    the Garter
Order of the Golden Fleece
    466, 485
Order of Our Lady of Mercy
    (Barcelona) 601*n*
Order of St Catherine 350–51
Order of Santiago 345, 601*n*
Order of the Sash 74, 277, 282–3
    361–4
    emblem of sash 364
    Jews among 455–6
    as military corps 363–4
    and oath of loyalty 465–6
    rules for admission 362
    statutes 361–2
    tournaments 363
    uniform 361
Order of the Ship (Naples) 466, 481
Order of the Sword (Cyprus) 466

oriflamme (French standard) 19,
141, 215
loss at Crécy 215, 234, 243
at siege of Calais 250
to indicate war to the death 407
Origo, Iris, *The Merchant of Prato* 26
Orléans, Charles, duke of 376, 400
Orléans, Philip, duke of 137, 148,
435, 438
captured at Poitiers 440
Orleton, Adam, bishop of Hereford 42
Ostrevant, count of 469
Otford, Christmas feast (1348)
79, 255
Otto, duke of Brunswick 388
Oxford, colleges 259
Oxford, earls of *see* Vere, John de;
Vere, Robert de
Oxford, Robert of, bookseller 55

Page, John, scribe/painter 296, 468
Painter-Stainers guild 88
painters, at St Stephen's 262
Pamplona 457–8
Pancio, Master, king's physician 66
papacy
and crusades 382
Edward III's letters to 62
envoys 431–2
settlement of 1293–4 war 35
taxes 78
Paris 19, 252
advance on (1360) 448–9
royal feast (1378) 83
St Louis's palace 263
Sainte-Chapelle 263–4
Paris, Matthew, chronicle 475–6
parliament 74
role in selection of officials
122, 149
support for campaign after
Crécy 246

parliaments
(1341) 122
(May 1343) 155
Paston, John 375–6
Paveley, Sir Walter (KG 1349) 328,
330
as Garter knight 298
with Teutonic Knights 388
Pavia, Aimeric di 369, 370
and Charny 415–17
pavises (shields), for archers on ships
418–19
peacock, romances of 92–3
Pedro, king of Castile 143, 364,
454–8, 462
Peipus, lake, battle of (1242) 383
Pembridge, Richard 467
Pembroke, earl of *see* Hastings,
Laurence
Penbrugge, William 58
Perceforest, romance of 93
and Round Table building 173
Perceval see Chrétien de Troyes
Percy, Henry (KG 1365) 103, 379
Pere IV, king of Aragon 455, 457
Perrers, Alice, mistress of Edward III
56–7
Perth 106
Perton family 320
Perton, John 320, 321
Peruzzi family, Italian bankers 26
Peshall, Adam 322
Peter I, king of Cyprus 85
Order of the Sword 466
Peterborough, Walter of 459, 570n
Petrarch 448
on John II of France 136–7
Philip II Augustus, king of France
34, 35
Philip IV the Fair, king of France 29,
35–6, 229, 245
adultery of daughters-in-law 315

and Knights Templar 315, 345, 360

Philip V, king of France 123, 129, 137

Philip VI of Valois, king of France 33, 128–31
  and 1339 invasion 116–18
  at Buironfosse 117–18
  capture of Montagu and Ufford 118–19
  claim to throne 123, 128–30
  at Crécy 131, 233, 240–41
  and crusade 221
  Edward III's homage to 57–8, 108
  and English crossing of Somme 208–9
  pageants 71
  purchase of Viennois from Humbert 351
  relations with magnates 155–6
  and Round Table occasion 162–3
  royal council 141
  and Scotland 104, 105–6, 108
  and siege of Calais 246–7, 249–52, 410
  as soldier 130–31
  strategy in Crécy campaign 197–8, 203, 204, 205–6
  treachery against 131–6

Philippa of Hainault, Queen 52–4, 55–7, 76, 396
  at Calais 246, 254, 410
  'churching' 61, 76, 99, 116, 150
  entourage 52–4, 499
  fashions 58, 270
  marriage to Edward III 41, 48, 56–7, 106–7
  mottoes 81–2
  ownership of books 92, 159
  patronage of arts 9, 55–6
  pet squirrels 89
  and Romance of Alexander 92

Pieres, Jean 465
Pierre-Buffière, castle 508
pilgrimage, Garter companions and 330–32
play-acting
  at festivals 77, 81
  and role-playing 82–3
Poissy, repair of bridge 182, 204–5
Poitiers 33–4
Poitiers, battle of (1356) 27, 148, 245, 432–41
  English army 435–7, 438–40
  French battle plan 435, 437–9, 440
  lawlessness after 393
  prisoners taken 404
Poitiers, (John) count of 430–31
Poitou 35
Pomfret, Henry 378
Pommiers, Aimery de 504
Pont-Hébert 199
Ponthieu 41, 208, 580n
Poor Knights of Windsor 298–9
Portsmouth, Crécy fleet at 178–80
Portugal, Order of Christ 345
Poteman, Robert 500
Potenhale, John 369–70
Pountney, John, merchant 126
pourpoints or jaques (jackets) 94
Poynings, Michael, Lord, at battle of Crécy 226
Poynings, Thomas
  in France (1339) 116
  at Guildford Christmas feast 113
preachers, and knightly ideals 376
Preston, Philip 494
prisoners
  capture, as contract 398
  and dishonour 400
  and ransom 400
  terms of captivity 400

private war 407
provisions
　for Crécy campaign 184–5
　Reims campaign 444–6,
　　447–8, 450
Prussia, crusades in 382–90
purveyancers, royal, and food on
　campaign 184

Queen Mary's Psalter 268

ransoms 191, 398–405, 603n
　and breaches of faith 401–2
　Charny on 375
　of Garter knights 404
　as matter of contract 406
　part payment 400, 603n
　as safeguard against death in battle
　　404–5
　Teutonic Knights and 389–90
Reading
　tournament (1340) 149
　tournament (1348) 255
Reading, John of, chronicler 89,
　90, 445
real tennis 372
Reims 35
　siege 446–7, 605n
Reims campaign (1359) 148, 443–8
　provisions 444–6, 447–8
relics
　in St George's chapel 289
　at St Stephen's 264
religion 326–37
　allegory 326–7
　charity 333
　and Christian moral justification
　　for war 405
　personal devotion 326–7
　and pilgrimage 330–32
religious foundations 333–5
religious orders
　of knighthood 465

military 360
Rennes, siege of 143
'Renno', duke of 220
The Restoration of the Peacock 92, 93
retinues, in Crécy campaign
　187–9, 584n
reysen (journeys) (winter campaigns in
　Prussia) 383, 384, 385, 387–90
　weather 387–8
Rhodes, island of 344
Rhys ap Gruffudd 43
Ribemont, Eustace de 416
Richard I, King 'the Lionheart'
　35, 59
　and Excalibur 161
Richard II, King 17, 311, 480
　and Company of the Garter 467–8
　courtiers 467–8
　deposition 466, 467
Richeldis of Walsingham 339
Richmond, (John of Brittany),
　earl of 41
Rienzo, Cola di 91
Robert, king of Aragon 345
Robert, Master, illuminator 55
Robessart, Lewis 472
Rochester chronicler 54, 104, 134
　on battle of Crécy 227
Rodez, France 23
Roet (Roeux), Paon de 500, 606n
Roger, Pierre (later Pope Clement
　VI) 141
Roís de Corella 485
Rolleston, Thomas, clerk of privy
　wardrobe 270, 282
Roman chronicle 28, 134
　on battle of Crécy 222–5, 230,
　　231, 233, 493
　on death of John of Bohemia
　　237–9, 244
Romance of Alexander 80, 92, 93
Romance of Brut 165
Romance of Fauveyn (Fauvel) 56, 80

romances 375–6
Rome, pilgrimage to 330–32
Romorantin 431, 503
Roncesvalles pass 457
Rothwell, Yorkshire, tournament 48
Rouen 147, 198, 203
Rougemont castle 319
Round Table
    in Arthurian legend 165,
        167–9, 470
    building of house for (Windsor)
        164–5, 170–71, 172–4
    Company of the Garter as model
        for 481–2
    Edward I's (at Winchester) 156–7
    festivities at Windsor (January
        1344) 20, 77, 83, 87, 156–7,
        161–4, 280, 351; founding
        ceremony 162, 169–71, 175
    membership of 168–9, 170
    solemn oath 170
royal commission, for recruitment 186
Rufus, Vivelin, Jew from Strasbourg
    163–4
Russell, Theobald, claim to arms 371
Russia, crusades in 384

Sabraham, Nicholas 379–80
safe conducts 408
St Albans abbey 18, 336
St Albans chronicler 312
St Albans, Hugh of, painter 88–9
St Amant, Sir Aymery de, at Crécy 226
St Andrew, Edmund of, Master, wood
    carver 263
St Catherine, Order of 350–51
St Cloud 205
St Denis monastery, Paris 19, 81
St Edmund, cult of 330
St Edward the Confessor 330
St Edward's chapel, Windsor 260
    rededication 260–61
St George

dedications to 265–7
legend of 267–8
as patron of Edward III 262
as patron saint of England 354
'St George', war cry 407
St George, cross of 58
    as nationalist symbol 267
    used by Edward I 266
    used by Edward III 47
St George's Chapel see Windsor: St
    George's Chapel
St George's Day
    Garter assembly 274, 278, 294
    jousts 280
    as major court festival 283–4
    tournament (1349) 281–2
    Windsor pageant (1358) 77,
        280–81
St Germain-des-Près 205
St Germain-en-Laye 205
St Inglevert, jousts of 469, 481
St Isidore, Etymologies 222
St Katharine's by the Tower, hospital
    of 287
St Lô 199
St Mary Graces monastery, near
    Tower of London 261, 330
St Mercurius, legend of 267–8
St Omer 249
St Omer chronicle 163, 209
    on battle of Crécy 226–7
    on death of John of Bohemia
        239–40, 244
    on siege of Calais 249
St Ouen, royal manor of 354
St Paul's chronicle 19, 69, 70–71
St Sauveur-le-Vicomte, castle 133,
    196, 319
St Stephen's chapel, Westminster
    261–4, 291–2
    as dynastic chapel 264
    murals 263
    origins 259–60

St Stephen's chapel – *cont.*
  rededication 260
  refurbishment 261–3
  seating 262–3
St Vaast-la-Hogue 197, 380
  English landing at 143, 192, 194
St Valéry 210
St Venant, lord of 137, 250–51, 252
Salisbury 57
Salisbury, countess of, alleged rape by
  Edward III 7, 486, 487–90
Salisbury, earls of *see* Montagu,
  William
Salm, count of, at Crécy 220, 233
Samogitians, crusades against 384
Sancerre, count of, death at Crécy 220
Sangatte, French army at 252
Santiago de Compostela 387
Say, Lord, at Crécy 226
Scales, Robert, 3rd baron 378
  at Crécy 226
scenery, at feasts and festivals 79,
  88, 113
Scole, parson of 150
Scot, Robert 453
Scotland 46, 97–108, 150
  1327 expedition 391–2
  1334 invasion 103–4
  1336 campaign 105–7
  Beaumont's campaign 98
  castles 107
  claims of English lords in 97, 99
  draft treaty with (1336) 105
  Edward III and 46–8, 60
  Edward II's campaign (1322) 45
  Philip VI of France and 104,
    105–6, 108
Scottish army 100
Scrope, Geoffrey 57, 108
  and French campaign (1340)
    120–21
Scrope, Henry, baron Scrope of
  Masham 472

Scrope, Richard, baron Scrope of
  Bolton 378
Scrope, Stephen 380
Scrope *v.* Grosvenor (1386) 11, 378, 380
Seaford, Sussex, table (of
  information) 296
The Secret of Secrets 56, 266–7
Seine, river 204
  crossing of 205–6
Sens, archbishop of, as prisoner after
  Poitiers 403
Seton, Alexander, warden of Berwick
  99, 411
Shareshull, William 320
ships
  for Crécy expedition 178–9, 584n
  for horses 193–4, 585n
  payrolls 179–80
  and profits of war 192
  provisioning 180
  and siege of Calais 249–50
  supplies after Crécy 245–6
Shrovetide, tournaments 76, 149
sieges
  bombards for use in 181
  Charny's description of 373–4
  ending by agreement 409, 410–11
  and hostages 411
  taking by storm 408, 409
  unconditional surrender 408, 409–10
Sigismund, emperor of Germany 470
silk 86
  cloth of gold 86
single combat 75
Sir Gawain and the Green Knight 375
  Garter motto on manuscript 471
Sluys
  attack on (1337) 113
  battle of (1340) 22, 119–20
Smithfield
  tournaments and jousts 72, 78,
    103; (1390) 469
Smithfield Decretals 268

Somme, river 203
  crossing of 208–11, 218
Song of Roland 140
Spain
  campaign in (1367) 17
  reconquista 344–5, 364, 366
  see also Aragon; Castile
squires, practice tournaments 68
squirrels
  fur 87
  pet 89
Stafford Augustinian priory 336
Stafford family 82, 313
Stafford, Hugh 313, 458
Stafford, Ralph, 1st earl of
    (KG 1349) 46, 52, 98,
    312, 328
  and 1345 campaign 176
  in Brittany 153, 321
  castle at Stafford 318
  at Crécy 236
  as Garter knight 303
  in Gascony (1355) 421
  marriage to Margaret Audley 313,
    316
  and Mortimer 63
  Stafford Augustinian priory 336
Stafford, Ralph, grandson, murder
    of 312
Stafford, Richard 25
  Reims campaign 446
Stafford, William, herald 273, 608n
stained-glass
  at St George's Chapel, Windsor 286
  at Gloucester cathedral 286
  makers, at St Stephen's 262
  at Stamford, showing Garter
    knights 473
standard-bearers, status of 375
Standerwyk, William 80
Stanhope Park 47–8
Stapledon, Walter, bishop of Exeter 40
  as guardian of Edward as prince 45

Stapleton, Sir Miles (KG 1349) 162,
    317, 327–8
  death 405
  Ingham church 336
  with Teutonic Knights 388
Statute of Treasons (1352) 136
Staveren, (1344) 55, 176, 323
Steelyard, London 87, 126
Stephen, King 259
Stepney 49
  joust (1331) 69–70, 71
Stirling, Sir John, at Crécy
    198, 226
Stratford, John, Archbishop of
    Canterbury 22, 56, 74, 318
  opposition to war in France
    121–2
  and Philip VI 108
  relations with Edward III 140
  at St Paul's 20
  and Sluys 119
Stratford, Ralph, bishop of London
    333–4
streamers (flags) 88, 272
Suffolk, John, herald to Robert Ufford
    378, 477
Sully, Sir John (KG 1353) 300, 325,
    379, 517, 596n
  in retinue of prince of Wales 189
Sumption, Jonathan 6, 135
  on Poitiers 433
swan badge and motto 82
Sy, Thomas, verger of Company 280

table of honour 386
tailoring 90–91
  king's tailor 87
Taktika (Byzantine treatise) 228–9
Talbot, Gilbert 46, 99
Talbot, Richard 369
  Crécy campaign 204
  at Crécy 226
  shield in Gloucester cathedral 286

Tancarville, Jean de, army commander
378, 451
prisoner after Caen 200, 256
Tancred of Sicily 161
Tannenberg, battle of (1410) 383
taxation 36, 38
papal 78
to fund campaigns in France 118,
120, 121, 156
Taymouth Hours 55, 268
teams
at festivals 79–80
at tournaments 65–6
Tello, Don 458, 460
tents and pavilions 88, 418–19
for Crécy campaign 183
Teutonic Knights 54, 344
choice of knights 385
crusades in Prussia 382–7
English knights with 384
reysen 383, 385, 387–90
table of honour (Ehrentisch)
385–7
textiles see fabrics; fashion
Thornham, Thomas, knight 64
Thurie, castle of 12
tides
English channel 178, 194, 196
Somme estuary 210
Tirant the White (Catalan romance)
483–4, 485, 486
Topham, John, on murals in St
Stephen's 263
torneamentum, use of word 68
Toulouse 50, 424
Tournai 14
siege of 74, 120
tournaments 48, 67–95, 371
1341 series 149–51
accidents 72, 150
after Crécy 254–6
after Halidon Hill 102–3

bans 49, 68
chronological list 520–24
and Company of the Garter
468–70
connected with Company of the
Garter 280–82, 283
costumes for 58–9
Edward III's 57–9, 520–24
Fraternal Society of St George 349
groups of knights 52, 469–70
judges 75
for knights of the Sash 363
mêlée to open 71–2
prizes 75
regulations and rules 48–50, 74–5
role of captain 73
single combat 75
as social occasions 75–6
for special occasions 59, 74,
76–7, 99
treatise on 173
William II of Hainault's 54–5
see also festivals
Tours 431
Tower of London, armourers 87, 182
trading companies, Italian 26–7
Trailly, John, squire 398–9
treason, defined 136
treasury, royal 60
accounts for clothing and entertainments 270–74
audit of royal finances 122
exchequer tally system 281
and expenditure on tournaments
and festivals 84–5
expense of Round Table festival
163–4, 170
'great wardrobe' expenses 85–6
Treves, archbishop of 163
'Tringas', lord of, at Crécy 227
Trinitarians 336, 601n
Trinity, cult of 328

Troarn, abbey of 202
Trussell, William, at Poitiers 437
Turplington, Hugh 63

Ufford, Edmund 189
Ufford, Ralph, at Guildford Christmas
    feast 113
Ufford, Sir Robert, 1st earl of
    Suffolk (KG 1349) 66,
    95, 109
  admiral of the north 179
  at Buironfosse 117
  capture and ransom 228, 404
  and Crécy campaign 187
  at Crécy 226
  expedition to Lille 118
  as Garter knight (1349) 298,
    302, 303
  in Gascony (1355) 421, 422
  at Guildford Christmas
    feast 113
  herald 477
  marriage 313, 317
  and Mortimer 63, 95
  at Poitiers 435
  and Reims campaign 446
  in Scotland 103, 106
  at tournaments 66, 150
Ufford, Sir Thomas (KG 1359) 458,
    517–18
Ufford, William 117, 467
Ughtred, Thomas, 1st baron (KG
    1349) 98, 99, 103, 404
  at Crécy 226
  as Garter knight 300, 301
  in Scotland 106
uniforms
  guilds 80
  livery 80, 87
  and team costumes 79–81
  for Welsh infantry 187
  see also costumes

Vale, Juliet 276, 281
Vale Royal Abbey, Cheshire 78
Valenciennes 9
Valenciennes chronicle
  on aftermath of Crécy 237
  on battle of Crécy 217, 233,
    235–6, 240–41
  on crossing of Somme
    208, 209
Valentinois, count of 235
Vannes, Brittany 154, 155
Vaquier, Nicolas, armourer to John II
    of France 357
Vegetius, treatise on warfare 228
velvets 85, 86
Venette, Jean de 15
  on advance on Paris 448–50
  on fashion 91
  on peace of Brétigny
    450, 451
Verdon, Sir Robert, at Crécy 226
Vere, John de, 7th earl of Oxford
    303–4, 421, 422
  Crécy campaign 187
  at Crécy 226
  in Gascony (1355) 423
  at Poitiers 435, 436–7
  and Reims campaign 446
Vere, Richard de 196
Vere, Robert de, 9th earl of Oxford
    and duke of Ireland 467–8, 470
  expulsion from Company of the
    Garter 468
Vergil, Polydore 487, 490
  English History (1534) 485–6
Vermelles, Sir Hutin de 386
Vernon, on Seine 204
Vienne, Jean de, commander of Calais
    251, 253–4
Viennois (Dauphiné), Order of St
    Catherine 350–51
Vikings, in Normandy 33

Villani, Giovanni
  account of battle of Crécy 217–22,
    237, 241, 493, 496, 497
  on fashion 91
  New Chronicle 26–7, 28
Villani, Matteo 27, 28
  on 1358 joust at Windsor 281
  on Gascony campaign 428
  on marriage of prince of Wales to
    Joan of Kent 310
  on Poitiers 438
  on truce of Bordeaux 442
Villeneuve le Hardi, English camp at
    248–9, 251, 252
Vincennes 40
Virgin Mary
  dedications to 260–61, 266
  devotion of Edward III to 329
Visconti, Violante 314
visitations, of College of St George
    (1378) 295
Vizcaya, Basque province 456, 462
Vladislav II of Poland 383
Volaunt, William, king of heralds 476
The Vows of the Heron 132, 267
The Vows of the Peacock 92, 93

Wace, Robert 165, 167, 168
wages, for troops 187
Wake, Blanche, widow of Thomas,
    Lord 330–31
Walden priory, Essex 337
Wale, Sir Thomas (KG 1349)
    298, 518
Wales
  Edward I's castles in 174
  Neith Cross from 289
Walkefare, Robert 64
Wallingford, tournament (1307) 49
Walsingham, shrine of Virgin Mary at
    260, 329, 330
Walsingham, Thomas 53

on house of the Round Table
    164–5, 170–71
  on siege of Limoges 410
Wantage 336
war
  booty 396–8
  Charny's description of
    373–4, 391
  finances of 393–405
  income from 396
  in king's name ('just war') 397
  laws of 405–7
  Le Bel's descriptions 391–2
  long campaigns 392
  private 407
  profits of 191–2, 242, 306, 396
  and ransoms 398–405
  rules of engagement 406
  see also English army; French army
war cries
  national 407
  personal (family) 407
Warbleton, John, claim to
    arms 371
Wardedieu, John 500
Warenne, John de, 7th earl of Surrey
    39, 319
Wark castle 487–8
Warrington, tournament 50
Warwick Castle 318
Warwick, earl of *see* Beauchamp,
    Thomas
Warwick, St Mary's church 336
  Thomas Beauchamp's monument
    338
Wauncy, Edmund 437
Waurin, Robert de 147
weapons
  bows and arrows 181
  for Crécy campaign 180–82
  guns 181–2
  swords and lances 181

Weitmile, Beneš z, Bohemian
  chronicler 239
Welsh troops
  archers at Crécy 219
  and Brittany campaign 155
  infantry in Crécy campaign 187
Werchin, John de, seneschal of
  Hainault 469–70, 481
West, Thomas, knight 64
Westminster
  parliament (1330) 65
  tournament 67, 69, 102
Westminster, Brother William of,
  paintings by 286
Wetewang, Walter
  'Kitchen Journal' 26, 494
  treasurer 187
Weymouth, arrival of Black Death
  256
Wharton, Thomas 202
Whitehorse, William, usher of
  Company 279–80
Wigmore
  tournament (1328) 51, 68
  tournament (1329) 58,
    59, 102
Wigmore castle 96
Wigmore priory 51, 68, 337
William I, the Conqueror, Duke of
  Normandy 33
William (of Windsor), son of Edward
  III 256, 271, 274
William of York, St 295
Winchelsea, battle of (1350) 138,
  417–18, 419–20
Winchelsey, Robert, archbishop of
  Canterbury 38
Winchester 57
  Castle 265
  Edward I's Round Table at
    156–7, 265
  parliament (1330) 60

Winchester, bishop(s) of, as prelate(s) of
  Company of the Garter 283–4
Windsor
  1358 pageant (St George's Day) 77,
    280–81
  building of house of the Round
    Table 164–5, 170–71, 172–4,
    274, 482
  College of St George 264–8, 465;
    canons 279; founding of 274;
    precentor's rolls 296
  Edward IV's chapel 284, 287
  festival (1344) 20, 83, 156–7,
    161–4, 169–71, 477
  Henry III's chapel 284, 285
  Henry VII's Lady Chapel 284, 285
  joust (1348) 255
  as pre-eminent castle 265
  revels (1352) 79
  St George's chapel 264–8, 274,
    284–91, 594nn, 595n; altars
    287, 289; architecture 284–91;
    carpets 290–91; choir screen
    288; choirstalls 287–8; exterior
    290–91; font 288; furnishings
    289–90; glass 286; music 284;
    rebuilt by Edward IV 284,
    287, 482; reredos 288–9;
    stall plates 297; statues 288;
    vestments 289
  St George's Day jousts 280
Windsor tables 468
wine, for Crécy campaign 185
Wingfield, John 25, 404
  on Gascony campaign 424, 427–8
Winner and Waster (poem) 262,
  418–19
Woodland, Walter,
  standard-bearer 437
Woodstock 61, 99, 265
  tournament (1334) 102
Worcester, tournament 58

Worcester, bishop of 396
Wotton, Sir Henry 82
Wrottesley, Sir Hugh (KG 1349) 298,
    313, 519
  career and estate 319–23, 395
  marriage 317
  and ransom money 403, 404
Wyard, John 61–2
Wykeham, William of
  as bishop of Winchester 284
  remodelling of Windsor Castle 171
Wynkeley, Richard 209

on battle of Crécy 215, 241
Wyville, Robert, bishop of
    Salisbury 66

York
  government at 99
  royal feast (1322) 44, 45
  St Mary's abbey, chronicle 445–6
York Minster, tables (of information)
    at 295

Zouche, William 248

Exam 70-640: *TS: Windows Server® 2008 Active Directory®, Configuring*

Objective	Chapter	Lesson
Configuring Domain Name System (DNS) for Active Directory (16 percent)		
Configure zones.	9	1
Configure DNS server settings.	9	2
Configure zone transfers and replication.	9	2
Configuring the Active Directory Infrastructure (25 percent)		
Configure a forest or a domain.	1, 10, 12	Chapter 1, Lessons 1, 2 Chapter 10, Lessons 1, 2 Chapter 12, Lessons 1, 2
Configure trusts.	12	2
Configure sites.	11	1, 2
Configure Active Directory replication.	8, 10, 11	Chapter 8, Lesson 3 Chapter 10, Lesson 3 Chapter 11, Lesson 3
Configure the global catalog.	11	2
Configure operations masters.	10	2
Configuring Additional Active Directory Server Roles (9 percent)		
Configure Active Directory Lightweight Directory Service (AD LDS).	14	1, 2
Configure Active Directory Rights Management Service (AD RMS).	16	1, 2
Configure the read-only domain controller (RODC).	8	3
Configure Active Directory Federation Services (AD FS).	17	1, 2
Creating and Maintaining Active Directory Objects (24 percent)		
Automate creation of Active Directory accounts.	3, 4, 5	Chapter 3, Lessons 1, 2 Chapter 4, Lessons 1, 2 Chapter 5, Lessons 1, 2
Maintain Active Directory accounts.	2, 3, 4, 5	Chapter 2, Lessons 2, 3 Chapter 3, Lessons 1, 2, 3 Chapter 4, Lessons 1, 2, 3 Chapter 5, Lessons 1, 2, 3
Create and apply Group Policy objects (GPOs).	6	1, 2, 3
Configure GPO templates.	6, 7	Chapter 6, Lessons 1, 2, 3 Chapter 7, Lessons 1, 2, 3
Configure software deployment GPOs.	7	3
Configure account policies.	8	1
Configure audit policy by using GPOs.	7, 8	Chapter 7, Lesson 4 Chapter 8, Lesson 2
Maintaining the Active Directory Environment (13 percent)		
Configure backup and recovery.	13	2
Perform offline maintenance.	13	1
Monitor Active Directory.	6, 11, 13	Chapter 6, Lesson 3 Chapter 11, Lesson 3 Chapter 13, Lesson 1

Objective	Chapter	Lesson
Configuring Active Directory Certificate Services (13 percent)		
Install Active Directory Certificate Services.	15	1
Configure CA server settings.	15	2
Manage certificate templates.	15	2
Manage enrollments.	15	2
Manage certificate revocations.	15	2

MCTS Self-Paced Training Kit (Exam 70-640): Configuring Windows Server® 2008 Active Directory®

Dan Holme,
Nelson Ruest, and
Danielle Ruest

PUBLISHED BY
Microsoft Press
A Division of Microsoft Corporation
One Microsoft Way
Redmond, Washington 98052-6399

Copyright © 2008 by Dan Holme

Library of Congress Control Number: 2008923653

Printed and bound in the United States of America.

1 2 3 4 5 6 7 8 9   QWT   3 2 1 0 9 8

Distributed in Canada by H.B. Fenn and Company Ltd.

A CIP catalogue record for this book is available from the British Library.

Microsoft Press books are available through booksellers and distributors worldwide. For further information about international editions, contact your local Microsoft Corporation office or contact Microsoft Press International directly at fax (425) 936-7329. Visit our Web site at www.microsoft.com/mspress. Send comments to tkinput@microsoft.com.

Microsoft, Microsoft Press, Access, Active Directory, ActiveX, BitLocker, Excel, Hyper-V, Internet Explorer, JScript, MSDN, Outlook, PowerPoint, SharePoint, SQL Server, Visio, Visual Basic, Windows, Windows Live, Windows NT, Windows PowerShell, Windows Server, and Windows Vista are either registered trademarks or trademarks of Microsoft Corporation in the United States and/or other countries. Other product and company names mentioned herein may be the trademarks of their respective owners.

The example companies, organizations, products, domain names, e-mail addresses, logos, people, places, and events depicted herein are fictitious. No association with any real company, organization, product, domain name, e-mail address, logo, person, place, or event is intended or should be inferred.

This book expresses the author's views and opinions. The information contained in this book is provided without any express, statutory, or implied warranties. Neither the authors, Microsoft Corporation, nor its resellers, or distributors will be held liable for any damages caused or alleged to be caused either directly or indirectly by this book.

Acquisitions Editor: Ken Jones
Developmental Editor: Laura Sackerman
Project Editor: Maureen Zimmerman
Editorial Production: nSight, Inc.
Technical Reviewers: Bob Hogan, Bob Dean; Technical Review services provided by Content Master, a member of CM Group, Ltd.
Cover: Tom Draper Design

Body Part No. X14-33191

About the Authors

Dan Holme

Dan Holme, a graduate of Yale University and Thunderbird, has spent more than a decade as a consultant and trainer, delivering solutions to tens of thousands of IT professionals from the most prestigious organizations and corporations around the world. Dan's company, Intelliem, specializes in boosting the productivity of IT professionals and end users by creating advanced, customized solutions that integrate clients' specific design and configuration into productivity-focused tools, training, and knowledge management services. Dan is also a contributing editor for *Windows IT Pro* magazine, an MVP (Office SharePoint Server), and the community lead of *officesharepointpro.com*. From his base in beautiful Maui, Dan travels around the globe supporting customers and delivering Windows technologies training. Immediately following the release of this Training Kit, he will be preparing for the Beijing Olympic Games as the Windows Technologies Consultant for NBC television, a role he also played in Torino in 2006.

Danielle Ruest

Danielle Ruest is passionate about helping people make the most of computer technology. She is a senior enterprise workflow architect and consultant with over 20 years of experience in project implementations. Her customers include governments and private enterprises of all sizes. Throughout her career, she has led change-management processes, developed and delivered training, provided technical writing services, and managed communications programs during complex technology implementation projects. More recently, Danielle has been involved in the design and support of test, development, and production infrastructures based on virtualization technologies. She is an MVP for the Virtual Machine product line.

Nelson Ruest

Nelson Ruest is passionate about doing things *right* with Microsoft technologies. He is a senior enterprise IT architect with over 25 years of experience. He was one of Canada's first Microsoft Certified Systems Engineers (MCSEs) and Microsoft Certified Trainers. In his IT career, he has been a computer operator, systems administrator, trainer, Help desk operator, support engineer, IT manager, project manager, and now, IT architect. He has also taken part in numerous migration projects, where he was responsible for everything from project management to systems design in both the private and public sectors. He is an MVP for the Windows Server product line.

Nelson and Danielle work for Resolutions Enterprises, a consulting firm focused on IT infrastructure design. Resolutions Enterprises can be found at *http://www.reso-net.com*. Both are authors of multiple books, notably the free *The Definitive Guide to Vista Migration* (*http://www.realtime-nexus.com/dgvm.htm*) and *Microsoft Windows Server 2008: The Complete Reference* (McGraw-Hill Osborne, 2008) (*http://www.mhprofessional.com/product.php?cat=112&isbn=0072263652*).

Tony Northrup

Tony Northrup, MVP, MCSE, MCTS, and CISSP, is a Windows consultant and author living in Phillipston, Massachusetts. Tony started programming before Windows 1.0 was released but has focused on Windows administration and development for the past 15 years. He has written more than a dozen books covering Windows networking, security, and development. Among other titles, Tony is coauthor of *Microsoft Windows Server 2003 Resource Kit* (Microsoft Press, 2005) and *Windows Vista Resource Kit* (Microsoft Press, 2007).

When he's not consulting or writing, Tony enjoys photography, remote-controlled flight, and golf. Tony lives with his cat, Sam, and his dog, Sandi. You can learn more about Tony by visiting his technical blog at *http://www.vistaclues.com* or his personal Web site at *http://www.northrup.org*.

Contents at a Glance

1	Installation	1
2	Administration	33
3	Users	85
4	Groups	139
5	Computers	187
6	Group Policy Infrastructure	229
7	Group Policy Settings	289
8	Authentication	355
9	Integrating Domain Name System with AD DS	393
10	Domain Controllers	459
11	Sites and Replication	507
12	Domains and Forests	555
13	Directory Business Continuity	607
14	Active Directory Lightweight Directory Services	685
15	Active Directory Certificate Services and Public Key Infrastructures	723
16	Active Directory Rights Management Services	781
17	Active Directory Federation Services	825
	Answers	875
	Index	921

Table of Contents

Introduction xxix

    Making the Most of the Training Kit xxx

    Setup and Hardware Requirements xxx

    Software Requirements and Setup xxxi

    Using the CD xxxi

        How to Install the Practice Tests xxxii

        How to Use the Practice Tests xxxii

    How to Uninstall the Practice Tests xxxiii

    Microsoft Certified Professional Program xxxiv

    Technical Support xxxiv

1   Installation 1

    Before You Begin 2

    Lesson 1: Installing Active Directory Domain Services 3

        Active Directory, Identity and Access 3

        Beyond Identity and Access 8

        Components of an Active Directory Infrastructure 8

        Preparing to Create a New Windows Server 2008 Forest 11

        Adding the AD DS Role Using the Windows Interface 12

        Creating a Domain Controller 13

        Creating a Windows Server 2008 Forest 14

        Lesson Summary 21

        Lesson Review 21

What do you think of this book? We want to hear from you!

Microsoft is interested in hearing your feedback so we can continually improve our books and learning resources for you. To participate in a brief online survey, please visit:

www.microsoft.com/learning/booksurvey/

Lesson 2: Active Directory Domain Services on Server Core 23

    Understanding Server Core. 23

    Installing Server Core 24

    Performing Initial Configuration Tasks 25

    Adding AD DS to a Server Core Installation. 26

    Removing Domain Controllers 26

    Installing a Server Core Domain Controller 27

    Lesson Summary. 29

    Lesson Review 30

Chapter Review. 31

Key Terms. 31

Case Scenario 32

    Case Scenario: Creating an Active Directory Forest 32

Take a Practice Test. 32

2   Administration. 33

Before You Begin 33

Lesson 1: Working with Active Directory Snap-ins. 35

    Understanding the Microsoft Management Console 35

    Active Directory Administration Tools. 36

    Finding the Active Directory Administrative Tools 37

    Adding the Administrative Tools to Your Start Menu 37

    Running Administrative Tools with Alternate Credentials 37

    Creating a Custom Console with Active Directory Snap-ins 38

    Saving and Distributing a Custom Console 39

    Creating and Managing a Custom MMC 40

    Lesson Summary. 44

    Lesson Review 45

Lesson 2: Creating Objects in Active Directory. 46

    Creating an Organizational Unit. 46

    Creating a User Object. 48

    Creating a Group Object 50

    Creating a Computer Object. 52

    Finding Objects in Active Directory 54

Finding Objects by Using *Dsquery* 59

Understanding DNs, RDNs, and CNs. 60

Creating and Locating Objects in Active Directory. 61

Lesson Summary. 67

Lesson Review 67

Lesson 3: Delegation and Security of Active Directory Objects. 69

Understanding Delegation 69

Viewing the ACL of an Active Directory Object. 70

Object, Property, and Control Access Rights 72

Assigning a Permission Using the Advanced Security Settings Dialog Box. . . .72

Understanding and Managing Permissions with Inheritance 73

Delegating Administrative Tasks with the Delegation Of Control Wizard 74

Reporting and Viewing Permissions 75

Removing or Resetting Permissions on an Object 75

Understanding Effective Permissions 76

Designing an OU Structure to Support Delegation 77

Delegating Administrative Tasks 78

Lesson Summary. 79

Lesson Review 80

Chapter Review. 81

Key Terms 81

Case Scenario 82

Case Scenario: Organizational Units and Delegation 82

Suggested Practices. 82

Maintain Active Directory Accounts 82

Take a Practice Test 84

3   Users. 85

Before You Begin 86

Lesson 1: Automating the Creation of User Accounts. 87

Creating Users with Templates. 87

Using Active Directory Command-Line Tools 88

Creating Users with *Dsadd* 89

Importing Users with *CSVDE* 90

Importing Users with *LDIFDE* 90

Automating the Creation of User Accounts 93

Lesson Summary 96

Lesson Review 96

Lesson 2: Creating Users with Windows PowerShell and VBScript 98

Introducing Windows PowerShell 98

Understanding Windows PowerShell Syntax, Cmdlets, and Objects 99

Getting Help 101

Using Variables 102

Using Aliases 102

Namespaces, Providers, and PSDrives 103

Creating a User with Windows PowerShell 103

Importing Users from a Database with Windows PowerShell 106

Executing a Windows PowerShell Script 108

Introducing VBScript 108

Creating a User with VBScript 109

VBScript vs. Windows PowerShell 109

Creating Users with Windows PowerShell and VBScript 110

Lesson Summary 112

Lesson Review 112

Lesson 3: Supporting User Objects and Accounts 114

Managing User Attributes with Active Directory Users and Computers 114

Understanding Name and Account Attributes 118

Managing User Attributes with *Dsmod* and *Dsget* 121

Managing User Attributes with Windows PowerShell and VBScript 123

Administering User Accounts 124

Supporting User Objects and Accounts 130

Lesson Summary 133

Lesson Review 133

Chapter Review 135

Key Terms 135

Case Scenario 136

Case Scenario: Import User Accounts 136

Suggested Practices 136

Automate the Creation of User Accounts 136

Maintain Active Directory Accounts 137

Take a Practice Test 137

4   Groups **139**

Before You Begin 139

Lesson 1: Creating and Managing Groups 141

Managing an Enterprise with Groups 141

Defining Group Naming Conventions 143

Understanding Group Types 145

Understanding Group Scope 145

Converting Group Scope and Type 149

Managing Group Membership 151

Developing a Group Management Strategy 153

Creating and Managing Groups 155

Lesson Summary 156

Lesson Review 157

Lesson 2: Automating the Creation and Management of Groups 159

Creating Groups with *Dsadd* 159

Importing Groups with *CSVDE* 160

Managing Groups with *LDIFDE* 161

Retrieving Group Membership with *Dsget* 162

Changing Group Membership with *Dsmod* 162

Moving and Renaming Groups with *Dsmove* 163

Deleting Groups with *Dsrm* 163

Managing Group Membership with Windows PowerShell and VBScript . . . 164

Automating the Creation and Management of Groups 165

Lesson Summary 167

Lesson Review 167

Lesson 3: Administering Groups in an Enterprise 169

Best Practices for Group Attributes 169

Protecting Groups from Accidental Deletion 171

Delegating the Management of Group Membership 172

Understanding Shadow Groups 176

Default Groups 177

Special Identities 179

Administering Groups in an Enterprise 180

Lesson Summary 181

Lesson Review 182

Chapter Review 184

Key Terms 184

Case Scenario 185

Case Scenario: Implementing a Group Strategy 185

Suggested Practices 185

Automating Group Membership and Shadow Groups 186

Take a Practice Test 186

5   Computers 187

Before You Begin 188

Lesson 1: Creating Computers and Joining the Domain 189

Understanding Workgroups, Domains, and Trusts 189

Identifying Requirements for Joining a Computer to the Domain 190

Computers Container 190

Creating OUs for Computers 190

Delegating Permission to Create Computers 192

Prestaging a Computer Account 192

Joining a Computer to the Domain 193

Importance of Prestaging Computer Objects 195

Creating Computers and Joining the Domain 198

Lesson Summary 201

Lesson Review 202

Lesson 2: Automating the Creation of Computer Objects 203

Importing Computers with *CSVDE* 203

Importing Computers with *LDIFDE* 204

Creating Computers with *Dsadd* 205

Creating Computers with *Netdom* 205

Creating Computers with Windows PowerShell 206

Creating Computers with VBScript 208

Create and Manage a Custom MMC. 209

Lesson Summary. 211

Lesson Review. 212

Lesson 3: Supporting Computer Objects and Accounts 213

Configuring Computer Properties. 213

Moving a Computer. 214

Managing a Computer from the Active Directory Users and
Computers Snap-In 215

Understanding the Computer's Logon and Secure Channel. 216

Recognizing Computer Account Problems 216

Resetting a Computer Account 217

Renaming a Computer 218

Disabling and Enabling Computer Accounts. 219

Deleting Computer Accounts. 220

Recycling Computers. 220

Supporting Computer Objects and Accounts 221

Lesson Summary. 222

Lesson Review. 223

Chapter Review. 224

Key Terms 224

Case Scenarios 224

Case Scenario 1: Creating Computer Objects and Joining the Domain 225

Case Scenario 2: Automating the Creation of Computer Objects 225

Suggested Practices. 225

Create and Maintain Computer Accounts 225

Take a Practice Test 227

6   Group Policy Infrastructure **229**

Before You Begin 230

Lesson 1: Implementing Group Policy 231

An Overview and Review of Group Policy 231

Group Policy Objects 237

Policy Settings. 241

Administrative Templates Node 244

Implementing Group Policy 248

Lesson Summary. 252

Lesson Review 253

Lesson 2: Managing Group Policy Scope. 255

GPO Links. 255

GPO Inheritance and Precedence 257

Using Security Filtering to Modify GPO Scope 262

WMI Filters. 264

Enabling or Disabling GPOs and GPO Nodes 266

Targeting Preferences. 267

Group Policy Processing. 268

Loopback Policy Processing 270

Configuring Group Policy Scope 272

Lesson Summary. 275

Lesson Review 276

Lesson 3: Supporting Group Policy. 277

Resultant Set of Policy 277

Examining Policy Event Logs. 281

Configuring Group Policy Scope 281

Lesson Summary. 284

Lesson Review 285

Chapter Review 286

Key Terms. 286

Case Scenario 287

Case Scenario: Implementing Group Policy. 287

Suggested Practices 287

Create and Apply Group Policy Objects (GPOs). 287

Take a Practice Test. 288

7   Group Policy Settings. 289

Before You Begin 289

Lesson 1: Delegating the Support of Computers 291

Understanding Restricted Groups Policies 291

Delegating Administration Using Restricted Groups Policies
with the Member Of Setting. 294

Delegating Membership Using Group Policy 295

Lesson Summary. 298

Lesson Review. 298

Lesson 2: Managing Security Settings 300

Configuring the Local Security Policy 300

Managing Security Configuration with Security Templates. 302

The Security Configuration Wizard 309

Settings, Templates, Policies, and GPOs 314

Managing Security Settings 315

Lesson Summary. 320

Lesson Review. 321

Lesson 3: Managing Software with Group Policy Software Installation 322

Understanding Group Policy Software Installation. 322

Preparing an SDP 325

Creating a Software Deployment GPO 325

Managing the Scope of a Software Deployment GPO. 327

Maintaining Applications Deployed with Group Policy 327

GPSI and Slow Links. 329

Managing Software with Group Policy Software Installation 329

Lesson Summary. 332

Lesson Review. 332

Lesson 4: Auditing. 335

Audit Policy. 335

Auditing Access to Files and Folders. 337

Auditing Directory Service Changes 341

Auditing. 342

Lesson Summary. 346

Lesson Review. 346

Chapter Review. 348

Key Terms 349

Case Scenarios 350

Case Scenario 1: Software Installation with Group Policy
Software Installation 350
Case Scenario 2: Security Configuration 350
Suggested Practices 351
Restricted Groups 351
Security Configuration 352
Take a Practice Test 354

8   Authentication 355
Before You Begin 356
Lesson 1: Configuring Password and Lockout Policies 357
Understanding Password Policies 357
Understanding Account Lockout Policies 359
Configuring the Domain Password and Lockout Policy 360
Fine-Grained Password and Lockout Policy 360
Understanding Password Settings Objects 361
PSO Precedence and Resultant PSO 362
PSOs and OUs 362
Configuring Password and Lockout Policies 363
Lesson Summary 366
Lesson Review 367
Lesson 2: Auditing Authentication 368
Account Logon and Logon Events 368
Configuring Authentication-Related Audit Policies 369
Scoping Audit Policies 370
Viewing Logon Events 371
Auditing Authentication 371
Lesson Summary 372
Lesson Review 373
Lesson 3: Configuring Read-Only Domain Controllers 374
Authentication and Domain Controller Placement in a Branch Office 374
Read-Only Domain Controllers 375
Deploying an RODC 377
Password Replication Policy 380

Administer RODC Credentials Caching. 381

Administrative Role Separation 383

Configuring Read-Only Domain Controllers 383

Lesson Summary. 386

Lesson Review 387

Chapter Review. 389

Key Terms 389

Case Scenarios 390

Case Scenario 1: Increasing the Security of Administrative Accounts. 390

Case Scenario 2: Increasing the Security and Reliability of
Branch Office Authentication. 391

Suggested Practices. 391

Configure Multiple Password Settings Objects 391

Recover from a Stolen Read-Only Domain Controller 392

Take a Practice Test 392

9   Integrating Domain Name System with AD DS. 393

DNS and IPv6 395

The Peer Name Resolution Protocol 397

DNS Structures 398

The Split-Brain Syndrome 400

Before You Begin 403

Lesson 1: Understanding and Installing Domain Name System 406

Understanding DNS. 406

Windows Server DNS Features 414

Integration with AD DS 417

Installing the DNS Service 419

Lesson Summary. 429

Lesson Review. 429

Lesson 2: Configuring and Using Domain Name System 431

Configuring DNS 431

Forwarders vs. Root Hints 439

Single-Label Name Management 441

DNS and DHCP Considerations 443

Working with Application Directory Partitions 445

Administering DNS Servers. 448

Finalizing a DNS Server Configuration in a Forest. 450

Lesson Summary. 452

Lesson Review 452

Chapter Review. 455

Key Terms. 456

Case Scenario 456

Case Scenario: Block Specific DNS Names. 456

Suggested Practices 456

Working with DNS 456

Take a Practice Test. 457

10   Domain Controllers 459

Before You Begin 459

Lesson 1: Installing Domain Controllers. 461

Installing a Domain Controller with the Windows Interface 461

Unattended Installation Options and Answer Files. 462

Installing a New Windows Server 2008 Forest. 464

Installing Additional Domain Controllers in a Domain. 465

Installing a New Windows Server 2008 Child Domain 467

Installing a New Domain Tree. 468

Staging the Installation of an RODC 469

Installing AD DS from Media 472

Removing a Domain Controller 473

Installing Domain Controllers. 474

Lesson Summary. 476

Lesson Review 477

Lesson 2: Configuring Operations Masters 478

Understanding Single Master Operations. 478

Forest-Wide Operations Master Roles. 480

Domain-Wide Operations Master Roles 480

Placing Operations Masters. 483

Identifying Operations Masters 484

Transferring Operations Master Roles. 485

Recognizing Operations Master Failures 486

Seizing Operations Master Roles. 487

Returning a Role to Its Original Holder. 488

Transferring Operations Master Roles. 489

Lesson Summary. 491

Lesson Review 492

Lesson 3: Configuring DFS Replication of SYSVOL. 494

Raising the Domain Functional Level 494

Understanding Migration Stages. 495

Migrating SYSVOL Replication to DFS-R 496

Configuring DFS Replication of SYSVOL. 497

Lesson Summary. 502

Lesson Review 502

Chapter Review. 504

Key Terms 504

Case Scenario 504

Case Scenario: Upgrading a Domain 505

Suggested Practices. 505

Upgrade a Windows Server 2003 Domain. 505

Take a Practice Test 506

11   Sites and Replication 507

Before You Begin 508

Lesson 1: Configuring Sites and Subnets. 509

Understanding Sites. 509

Planning Sites 510

Defining Sites 512

Managing Domain Controllers in Sites. 515

Understanding Domain Controller Location 516

Configuring Sites and Subnets. 519

Lesson Summary. 520

Lesson Review. 521

Lesson 2: Configuring the Global Catalog and Application Directory Partitions . 522
  Reviewing Active Directory Partitions 522
  Understanding the Global Catalog 523
  Placing GC Servers 523
  Configuring a Global Catalog Server. 524
  Universal Group Membership Caching 524
  Understanding Application Directory Partitions 525
  Replication and Directory Partitions 527
  Lesson Summary. 529
  Lesson Review 529
Lesson 3: Configuring Replication. 531
  Understanding Active Directory Replication 531
  Connection Objects 532
  The Knowledge Consistency Checker 533
  Intrasite Replication 534
  Site Links. 535
  Bridgehead Servers. 538
  Configuring Intersite Replication 539
  Monitoring Replication 543
  Configuring Replication. 545
  Lesson Summary. 547
  Lesson Review 547
Chapter Review. 550
Key Terms. 551
Case Scenario 551
  Case Scenario: Configuring Sites and Subnets 551
Suggested Practices 553
  Monitor and Manage Replication 553
Take a Practice Test. 554

12 Domains and Forests 555
Before You Begin 555
Lesson 1: Understanding Domain and Forest Functional Levels 557
  Understanding Functional Levels. 557

Domain Functional Levels. 557

Forest Functional Levels 560

Raising the Domain and Forest Functional Levels. 563

Lesson Summary. 565

Lesson Review 565

Lesson 2: Managing Multiple Domains and Trust Relationships 567

Defining Your Forest and Domain Structure 567

Moving Objects Between Domains and Forests 572

Understanding Trust Relationships 576

Authentication Protocols and Trust Relationships. 579

Manual Trusts 583

Administering Trusts 590

Securing Trust Relationships. 591

Administering a Trust Relationship 595

Lesson Summary. 601

Lesson Review 602

Chapter Review. 604

Chapter Summary 604

Case Scenario 605

Case Scenario: Managing Multiple Domains and Forests. 605

Suggested Practices. 605

Configure a Forest or Domain 605

Take a Practice Test 606

13   Directory Business Continuity 607

Before You Begin 608

Lesson 1: Proactive Directory Maintenance and Data Store Protection. 610

Twelve Categories of AD DS Administration 612

Performing Online Maintenance. 622

Performing Offline Maintenance. 623

Relying on Built-in Directory Protection Measures. 624

Relying on Windows Server Backup to Protect the Directory. 629

Performing Proactive Restores. 638

Protecting DCs as Virtual Machines 648

Working with the AD DS Database 650

Lesson Summary 657

Lesson Review 658

Lesson 2: Proactive Directory Performance Management 660

Managing System Resources 660

Working with Windows System Resource Manager 672

AD DS Performance Analysis 675

Lesson Summary 680

Lesson Review 680

Chapter Review 682

Key Terms 683

Case Scenario 683

Case Scenario: Working with Lost and Found Data 683

Suggested Practices 684

Proactive Directory Maintenance 684

Take a Practice Test 684

14   Active Directory Lightweight Directory Services 685

Before You Begin 687

Lesson 1: Understanding and Installing AD LDS 690

Understanding AD LDS 690

AD LDS Scenarios 692

Installing AD LDS 694

Installing AD LDS 696

Lesson Summary 699

Lesson Review 699

Lesson 2: Configuring and Using AD LDS 701

Working with AD LDS Tools 701

Creating AD LDS Instances 703

Working with AD LDS Instances 709

Working with AD LDS Instances 714

Lesson Summary 718

Lesson Review 719

Chapter Review 720

Chapter Summary 720

Key Terms 721

Case Scenario 721

    Case Scenario: Determine AD LDS Instance Prerequisites 721

Suggested Practices. 721

    Work with AD LDS Instances 722

Take a Practice Test 722

15   Active Directory Certificate Services and Public Key Infrastructures. . 723

Before You Begin 727

Lesson 1: Understanding and Installing Active Directory Certificate Services. . . . 730

    Understanding AD CS 731

    Installing AD CS 740

    Installing a CA Hierarchy. 742

    Lesson Summary. 750

    Lesson Review 751

Lesson 2: Configuring and Using Active Directory Certificate Services 753

    Finalizing the Configuration of an Issuing CA. 753

    Finalizing the Configuration of an Online Responder 759

    Considerations for the Use and Management of AD CS 763

    Working with Enterprise PKI. 765

    Protecting Your AD CS Configuration. 766

    Configuring and Using AD CS 767

    Lesson Summary. 773

    Lesson Review 774

Chapter Review. 776

Key Terms 777

Case Scenario 777

    Case Scenario: Manage Certificate Revocation. 777

Suggested Practices. 778

    Working with AD CS 778

Take a Practice Test 779

16   Active Directory Rights Management Services **781**

Before You Begin 784

Lesson 1: Understanding and Installing Active Directory Rights
Management Services 786

    Understanding AD RMS. 786

    Installing Active Directory Rights Management Services. 794

    Installing AD RMS 802

    Lesson Summary. 807

    Lesson Review 808

Lesson 2: Configuring and Using Active Directory Rights Management Services. 809

    Configuring AD RMS 810

    Creating a Rights Policy Template 819

    Lesson Summary. 820

    Lesson Review 821

Chapter Review. 822

Key Terms. 823

Case Scenario 823

    Case Scenario: Prepare to Work with an External AD RMS Cluster 823

Suggested Practices 823

    Work with AD RMS 824

Take a Practice Test. 824

17   Active Directory Federation Services. **825**

The Purpose of a Firewall 826

Active Directory Federation Services. 827

Before You Begin 829

Lesson 1: Understanding Active Directory Federation Services. 832

    The AD FS Authentication Process. 833

    Working with AD FS Designs. 836

    Understanding AD FS Components. 838

    Installing Active Directory Federation Services 845

    Prepare an AD FS Deployment. 849

Lesson Summary. 852

Lesson Review 853

Lesson 2: Configuring and Using Active Directory Federation Services. 854

Finalize the Configuration of AD FS 854

Using and Managing AD FS 855

Finalizing the AD FS Configuration 857

Lesson Summary. 869

Lesson Review 870

Chapter Review. 871

Key Terms 872

Case Scenario 872

Case Scenario: Choose the Right AD Technology 872

Suggested Practices. 873

Prepare for AD FS. 873

Take a Practice Test 873

Answers. 875

Index 921

What do you think of this book? We want to hear from you!

Microsoft is interested in hearing your feedback so we can continually improve our books and learning resources for you. To participate in a brief online survey, please visit:

www.microsoft.com/learning/booksurvey/

Heartfelt Thanks

Nelson, Danielle, Tony, and I would like to pay tribute to the incredible folks at Microsoft Press for giving us the opportunity to contribute to the Windows Server 2008 training and certification effort. Starting with Laura Sackerman and Ken Jones: you pulled us together in 2007 and created a framework that was both comfortable and effective, bringing out the best in us as authors and resulting in what we believe is a tremendous resource for the Windows IT professional community. Thanks for giving us the chance to write about a technology we love! Maureen Zimmerman, your tireless attention to detail and nurturing of the process brought us, and this training kit, across a finish line that at times seemed elusive. I know I owe you special thanks for your faith in me and your support and "props" along the way. Bob Hogan, you kept us honest and contributed great ideas to the cause. Kerin Forsyth, you make us sound better than we really are. Bob Dean, we all are grateful that with your efforts, the practice test questions for this training kit are first class. And Chris Norton, without you, there wouldn't be a page to look at, let alone hundreds of pages of valuable training and reference. Thanks to all of you, from all of us!

Finally, my own deepest gratitude goes to my Einstein, and we all thank our families, our friends, and our muses who make it possible and worthwhile.

Introduction

This training kit is designed for IT professionals who support or plan to support Microsoft Windows Server 2008 Active Directory Domain Services (AD DS) and who also plan to take the Microsoft Certified Technology Specialist (MCTS) 70-640 examination. It is assumed that, before you begin using this kit, you have a solid foundation-level understanding of Microsoft Windows client and server operating systems and common Internet technologies. The MCTS exam, and this book, assume that you have at least one year of experience administering AD DS.

The material covered in this training kit and on the 70-640 exam builds on your understanding and experience to help you implement AD DS in distributed environments that can include complex network services and multiple locations and domain controllers. By using this training kit, you will learn how to do the following:

- Deploy Active Directory Domain Services, Active Directory Lightweight Directory Services, Active Directory Certificate Services, Active Directory Federation Services, and Active Directory Rights Management Services in a forest or domain.
- Upgrade existing domain controllers, domains, and forests to Windows Server 2008.
- Efficiently administer and automate the administration of users, groups, and computers.
- Manage the configuration and security of a domain by using Group Policy, fine-grained password policies, directory services auditing, and the Security Configuration Wizard.
- Implement effective name resolution with Domain Name System (DNS) on Windows Server 2008.
- Plan, configure, and support the replication of Active Directory data within and between sites.
- Add, remove, maintain, and back up domain controllers.
- Enable authentication between domains and forests.
- Implement new capabilities and functionality offered by Windows Server 2008.

Find additional content online   As new or updated material that complements your book becomes available, it will be posted on the Microsoft Press Online Windows Server and Client Web site. Based on the final build of Windows Server 2008, the type of material you might find includes updates to book content, articles, links to companion content, errata, sample chapters, and more. This Web site will be available soon at *http://www.microsoft.com/learning/books/online/serverclient* and will be updated periodically.

Making the Most of the Training Kit

This training kit will prepare you for the 70-640 MCTS exam, which covers a large number of concepts and skills related to the implementation and administration of AD DS on Windows Server 2008. To provide you with the best possible learning experience, each lesson in the training kit includes content, practices, and review questions, and each chapter adds case scenario exercises and suggested practices. The companion CD provides links to external resources and dozens of sample questions.

We recommend that you take advantage of each of these components in the training kit. Some concepts or skills are easiest to learn within the context of a practice or sample questions, so these concepts and skills might be introduced in the practices or sample questions and not in the main body of the lesson. Don't make the mistake of reading the lessons and not performing the practices or of performing practices and taking sample exams without reading the lessons. Even if you do not have an environment with which to perform practices, at least read and think through the steps so that you gain the benefit of the new ideas they introduce.

Setup and Hardware Requirements

Practice exercises are a valuable component of this training kit. They enable you to experience important skills directly, reinforce material discussed in lessons, and even introduce new concepts. Each lesson and practice describes the requirements for exercises. Although many lessons require only one computer, configured as a domain controller for a sample domain named *contoso.com*, some lessons require additional computers acting as a second domain controller in the domain, as a domain controller in another domain in the same forest, as a domain controller in another forest, or as a server performing other roles.

The chapters that cover AD DS (chapters 1–13) require, at most, three machines running simultaneously. Chapters covering other Active Directory roles require up to seven machines running simultaneously to provide a comprehensive experience with the technology.

It is highly recommended that you use virtual machines rather than physical computers to work through the lessons and practices. Doing so will reduce the time and expense of configuring physical computers. You can use Virtual PC 2007 or later or Virtual Server 2005 R2 or later, which you can download for free at *http://www.microsoft.com/downloads*. You can use other virtualization software instead, such as VMware Workstation or VMware Server, which can be downloaded at *http://www.vmware.com*. Refer to the documentation of your selected virtualization software for guidance regarding the creation of virtual machines for Windows Server 2008.

Windows Server 2008 can run comfortably with 512 megabytes (MB) of memory in small environments such as the sample *contoso.com* domain. As you provision virtual machines, be sure to give each machine at least 512 MB of RAM. It is recommended that the physical host running the virtual machines have sufficient physical RAM for the host operating system and each of the concurrently running virtual machines. If you encounter performance bottlenecks while running multiple virtual machines on a single physical host, consider running virtual machines on different physical hosts. Ensure that all virtual machines can network with each other. It is highly recommended that the environment be totally disconnected from your production environment.

The authors recommend that you preserve each of the virtual machines you create until you have completed the training kit. After each chapter, create a backup or snapshot of the virtual machines used in that chapter so that you can reuse them as required in later exercises.

Software Requirements and Setup

You must have a copy of Windows Server 2008 to perform the exercises in this training kit. Several exercises require Windows Server 2003, and some optional exercises require Windows Vista.

Evaluation versions of Windows Server 2008 can be downloaded from *http://www.microsoft.com /downloads*. To perform the exercises in this training kit, you can install either the Standard or Enterprise editions, and you can use either 32-bit or 64-bit versions, according to the hardware or virtualization platform you have selected. Chapter 1, "Installation," includes setup instructions for the first domain controller in the *contoso.com* domain, which is used throughout this training kit. Lessons that require an additional computer provide guidance regarding the configuration of that computer.

Using the CD

A companion CD, included with this training kit, contains the following:

- **Practice tests**   You can reinforce your understanding of how to configure Windows Server 2008 by using electronic practice tests you customize to meet your needs from the pool of Lesson Review questions in this book. Alternatively, you can practice for the 70-640 certification exam by using tests created from a pool of 200 realistic exam questions, which give you many practice scenarios to ensure that you are prepared.
- **An eBook**   An electronic version (eBook) of this book is included for when you do not want to carry the printed book with you. The eBook is in Portable Document Format (PDF), and you can view it by using Adobe Acrobat or Adobe Reader.
- **Sample chapters**   Sample chapters from other Microsoft Press titles on Windows Server 2008 are offered on the CD. These chapters are in PDF.

> **Digital Content for Digital Book Readers:** If you bought a digital-only edition of this book, you can enjoy select content from the print edition's companion CD. Visit **http://go.microsoft.com/fwlink /?LinkId=114977** to get your downloadable content. This content is always up-to-date and available to all readers.

How to Install the Practice Tests

To install the practice test software from the companion CD to your hard disk, do the following:

1. Insert the companion CD into your CD drive and accept the license agreement. A CD menu appears.

   NOTE If the CD menu does not appear

   If the CD menu or the license agreement does not appear, AutoRun might be disabled on your computer. Refer to the Readme.txt file on the CD-ROM for alternate installation instructions.

2. Click Practice Tests and follow the instructions on the screen.

How to Use the Practice Tests

To start the practice test software, follow these steps.

1. Click Start\All Programs\Microsoft Press Training Kit Exam Prep.

   A window appears that shows all the Microsoft Press training kit exam prep suites installed on your computer.

2. Double-click the lesson review or practice test you want to use.

   NOTE Lesson reviews vs. practice tests

   Select the (70-640) TS: Configuring Windows Server 2008 Active Directory *lesson review* to use the questions from the "Lesson Review" sections of this book. Select the (70-640) TS: Configuring Windows Server 2008 Active Directory *practice test* to use a pool of 200 questions similar to those that appear on the 70-640 certification exam.

Lesson Review Options

When you start a lesson review, the Custom Mode dialog box appears so that you can configure your test. You can click OK to accept the defaults, or you can customize the number of questions you want, how the practice test software works, which exam objectives you want the questions to relate to, and whether you want your lesson review to be timed. If you are retaking a test, you can select whether you want to see all the questions again or only the questions you missed or did not answer.

After you click OK, your lesson review starts.

- To take the test, answer the questions and use the Next and Previous buttons to move from question to question.
- After you answer an individual question, if you want to see which answers are correct—along with an explanation of each correct answer—click Explanation.
- If you prefer to wait until the end of the test to see how you did, answer all the questions and then click Score Test. You will see a summary of the exam objectives you chose and the percentage of questions you got right overall and per objective. You can print a copy of your test, review your answers, or retake the test.

Practice Test Options

When you start a practice test, you choose whether to take the test in Certification Mode, Study Mode, or Custom Mode.

- **Certification Mode**   Closely resembles the experience of taking a certification exam. The test has a set number of questions. It is timed, and you cannot pause and restart the timer.
- **Study Mode**   Creates an untimed test in which you can review the correct answers and the explanations after you answer each question.
- **Custom Mode**   Gives you full control over the test options so that you can customize them as you like.

In all modes, the user interface when you are taking the test is basically the same but with different options enabled or disabled, depending on the mode. The main options are discussed in the previous section, "Lesson Review Options."

When you review your answer to an individual practice test question, a "References" section is provided that lists where in the training kit you can find the information that relates to that question and provides links to other sources of information. After you click Test Results to score your entire practice test, you can click the Learning Plan tab to see a list of references for every objective.

How to Uninstall the Practice Tests

To uninstall the practice test software for a training kit, use the Add Or Remove Programs option (Windows XP) or the Programs And Features option (Windows Vista) in Windows Control Panel.

Microsoft Certified Professional Program

The Microsoft certifications provide the best method to prove your command of current Microsoft products and technologies. The exams and corresponding certifications are developed to validate your mastery of critical competencies as you design and develop or implement and support solutions with Microsoft products and technologies. Computer professionals who become Microsoft certified are recognized as experts and are sought after industry-wide. Certification brings a variety of benefits to the individual and to employers and organizations.

MORE INFO   All the Microsoft certifications

For a full list of Microsoft certifications, go to *http://www.microsoft.com/learning/mcp/default.asp*.

Technical Support

Every effort has been made to ensure the accuracy of this book and the contents of the companion CD. If you have comments, questions, or ideas regarding this book or the companion CD, please send them to Microsoft Press by using either of the following methods:

- E-mail: tkinput@microsoft.com
- Postal mail at:

  Microsoft Press
  Attn: *MCTS Self-Paced Training Kit (Exam 70-640): Configuring Windows Server 2008 Active Directory*, Editor
  One Microsoft Way
  Redmond, WA 98052-6399

For additional support information regarding this book and the CD-ROM (including answers to commonly asked questions about installation and use), visit the Microsoft Press Book and CD Support Web site at *http://www.microsoft.com/learning/support/books*. To connect directly to Microsoft Knowledge Base and enter a query, visit *http://support.microsoft.com/search*. For support information regarding Microsoft software, connect to *http://support.microsoft.com*.

Chapter 1

Installation

Active Directory Domain Services (AD DS) and its related services form the foundation for enterprise networks running Microsoft Windows as, together, they act as tools to store information about the identities of users, computers, and services; to authenticate a user or computer; and to provide a mechanism with which the user or computer can access resources in the enterprise. In this chapter, you will begin your exploration of Windows Server 2008 Active Directory by installing the Active Directory Domain Services role and creating a domain controller in a new Active Directory forest. You will find that Windows Server 2008 continues the evolution of Active Directory by enhancing many of the concepts and features with which you are familiar from your experience with Active Directory.

This chapter focuses on the creation of a new Active Directory forest with a single domain in a single domain controller. The practice exercises in this chapter will guide you through the creation of a domain named *contoso.com* that you will use for all other practices in this training kit. Later, in Chapter 8, "Authentication," Chapter 10, "Domain Controllers," and Chapter 12, "Domains and Forests," you will learn to implement other scenarios, including multidomain forests, upgrades of existing forests to Windows Server 2008, and advanced installation options. In Chapter 14, "Active Directory Lightweight Directory Services," Chapter 15, "Active Directory Certificate Services and Public Key Infrastructures," Chapter 16, "Active Directory Rights Management Services," and Chapter 17, "Active Directory Federation Services," you will learn the details of other Active Directory services such as Active Directory Lightweight Directory Services, Active Directory Certificate Services and public key infrastructure, Active Directory Rights Management Service, and Active Directory Federated Services.

Exam objectives in this chapter:
- Configuring the Active Directory Infrastructure
  - Configure a forest or a domain.

Lessons in this chapter:

- Lesson 1: Installing Active Directory Domain Services 3
- Lesson 2: Active Directory Domain Services on Server Core 23

Before You Begin

To complete the lessons in this chapter, you must have done the following:

■ Obtained two computers on which you will install Windows Server 2008. The computers can be physical systems that meet the minimum hardware requirements for Windows Server 2008 found at *http://technet.microsoft.com/en-us/windowsserver/2008/bb414778.aspx.* You will need at least 512 MB of RAM, 10 GB of free hard disk space, and an x86 processor with a minimum clock speed of 1GHz or an x64 processor with a minimum clock speed of 1.4 GHz. Alternatively, you can use virtual machines that meet the same requirements.

■ Obtained an evaluation version of Windows Server 2008. At the time of writing, links to evaluation versions are available on the Windows Server 2008 Home Page at *http://www.microsoft.com/windowsserver2008.*

Real World

Dan Holme

Domain controllers perform identity and access management functions that are critical to the integrity and security of a Windows enterprise. Therefore, most organizations choose to dedicate the role of domain controller, meaning that a domain controller does not provide other functions such as file and print servers. In previous versions of Windows, however, when you promote a server to a domain controller, other services continue to be available whether or not they are in use. These additional unnecessary services increase the need to apply patches and security updates and expose the domain controller to additional susceptibility to attack. Windows Server 2008 addresses these concerns through its role-based architecture, so that a server begins its life as a fairly lean installation of Windows to which roles and their associated services and features are added. Additionally, the new Server Core installation of Windows Server 2008 provides a minimal installation of Windows that even forgoes a graphical user interface (GUI) in favor of a command prompt. In this chapter, you will gain firsthand experience with these important characteristics of Windows Server 2008 domain controllers. These changes to the architecture and feature set of Windows Server 2008 domain controllers will help you and other enterprises further improve the security, stability, and manageability of your identity and access management infrastructure.

Lesson 1: Installing Active Directory Domain Services

Active Directory Domain Services (AD DS) provides the functionality of an identity and access (IDA) solution for enterprise networks. In this lesson, you will learn about AD DS and other Active Directory roles supported by Windows Server 2008. You will also explore Server Manager, the tool with which you can configure server roles, and the improved Active Directory Domain Services Installation Wizard. This lesson also reviews key concepts of IDA and Active Directory.

After this lesson, you will be able to:
- Explain the role of identity and access in an enterprise network.
- Understand the relationship between Active Directory services.
- Configure a domain controller with the Active Directory Domain Services (AD DS) role, using the Windows interface.

Estimated lesson time: 60 minutes

Active Directory, Identity and Access

As mentioned in the introductions to the chapter and this lesson, Active Directory provides the IDA solution for enterprise networks running Windows. IDA is necessary to maintain the security of enterprise resources such as files, e-mail, applications, and databases. An IDA infrastructure should do the following:

- **Store information about users, groups, computers, and other identities** An identity is, in the broadest sense, a representation of an entity that will perform actions on the enterprise network. For example, a user will open documents from a shared folder on a server. The document will be secured with permissions on an access control list (ACL). Access to the document is managed by the security subsystem of the server, which compares the identity of the user to the identities on the ACL to determine whether the user's request for access will be granted or denied. Computers, groups, services, and other objects also perform actions on the network, and they must be represented by identities. Among the information stored about an identity are properties that uniquely identify the object, such as a user name or a security identifier (SID), and the password for the identity. The *identity store* is, therefore, one component of an IDA infrastructure. The Active Directory data store, also known as the directory, is an identity store. The directory itself is hosted on and managed by a domain controller—a server performing the AD DS role.

- **Authenticate an identity**   The server will not grant the user access to the document unless the server can verify the identity presented in the access request as valid. To validate the identity, the user provides secrets known only to the user and the IDA infrastructure. Those secrets are compared to the information in the identity store in a process called *authentication.*

Kerberos Authentication in an Active Directory Domain

In an Active Directory domain, a protocol called Kerberos is used to authenticate identities. When a user or computer logs on to the domain, Kerberos authenticates its credentials and issues a package of information called a ticket granting ticket (TGT). Before the user connects to the server to request the document, a Kerberos request is sent to a domain controller along with the TGT that identifies the authenticated user. The domain controller issues the user another package of information called a service ticket that identifies the authenticated user to the server. The user presents the service ticket to the server, which accepts the service ticket as proof that the user has been authenticated.

These Kerberos transactions result in a single network logon. After the user or computer has initially logged on and has been granted a TGT, the user is authenticated within the entire domain and can be granted service tickets that identify the user to any service. All of this ticket activity is managed by the Kerberos clients and services built into Windows and is transparent to the user.

- **Control access**   The IDA infrastructure is responsible for protecting confidential information such as the information stored in the document. Access to confidential information must be managed according to the policies of the enterprise. The ACL on the document reflects a security policy composed of permissions that specify access levels for particular identities. The security subsystem of the server in this example is performing the access control functionality in the IDA infrastructure.
- **Provide an audit trail**   An enterprise might want to monitor changes to and activities within the IDA infrastructure, so it must provide a mechanism by which to manage auditing.

AD DS is not the only component of IDA that is supported by Windows Server 2008. With the release of Windows Server 2008, Microsoft has consolidated a number of previously separate components into an integrated IDA platform. Active Directory itself now includes five technologies, each of which can be identified with a keyword that identifies the purpose of the technology, as shown in Figure 1-1.

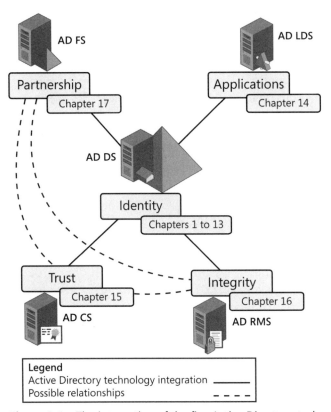

Figure 1-1   The integration of the five Active Directory technologies

These five technologies comprise a complete IDA solution:

■ **Active Directory Domain Services (Identity)**   AD DS, as described earlier, is designed to provide a central repository for identity management within an organization. AD DS provides authentication and authorization services in a network and supports object management through Group Policy. AD DS also provides information management and sharing services, enabling users to find any component—file servers, printers, groups, and other users—by searching the directory. Because of this, AD DS is often referred to as a network operating system directory service. AD DS is the primary Active Directory technology and should be deployed in every network that runs Windows Server 2008 operating systems. AD DS is covered in chapters 1 through 13.

For a guide outlining best practices for the design of Active Directory, download the free "Chapter 3: Designing the Active Directory" from *Windows Server 2003, Best Practices for Enterprise Deployments* at *http://www.reso-net.com/Documents/007222343X_Ch03.pdf*.

MORE INFO   AD DS design

For updated information on creating an Active Directory Domain Services design, look up *Windows Server 2008: The Complete Reference,* by Ruest and Ruest (McGraw-Hill Osborne, in press).

■   **Active Directory Lightweight Directory Services (Applications)**   Essentially a standalone version of Active Directory, the Active Directory Lightweight Directory Services (AD LDS) role, formerly known as Active Directory Application Mode (ADAM), provides support for directory-enabled applications. AD LDS is really a subset of AD DS because both are based on the same core code. The AD LDS directory stores and replicates only application-related information. It is commonly used by applications that require a directory store but do not require the information to be replicated as widely as to all domain controllers. AD LDS also enables you to deploy a custom schema to support an application without modifying the schema of AD DS. The AD LDS role is truly lightweight and supports multiple data stores on a single system, so each application can be deployed with its own directory, schema, assigned Lightweight Directory Access Protocol (LDAP) and SSL ports, and application event log. AD LDS does not rely on AD DS, so it can be used in a standalone or workgroup environment. However, in domain environments, AD LDS can use AD DS for the authentication of Windows security principals (users, groups, and computers). AD LDS can also be used to provide authentication services in exposed networks such as extranets. Once again, using AD LDS in this situation provides less risk than using AD DS. AD LDS is covered in Chapter 14.

■   **Active Directory Certificate Services (Trust)**   Organizations can use Active Directory Certificate Services (AD CS) to set up a certificate authority for issuing digital certificates as part of a public key infrastructure (PKI) that binds the identity of a person, device, or service to a corresponding private key. Certificates can be used to authenticate users and computers, provide Web-based authentication, support smart card authentication, and support applications, including secure wireless networks, virtual private networks (VPNs), Internet Protocol security (IPSec), Encrypting File System (EFS), digital signatures, and more. AD CS provides an efficient and secure way to issue and manage certificates. You can use AD CS to provide these services to external communities. If you do so, AD CS should be linked with an external, renowned CA that will prove to others you are who you say you are. AD CS is designed to create trust in an untrustworthy world; as such, it must rely on proven processes that certify that each person or computer that obtains a certificate has been thoroughly verified and approved. In internal networks, AD CS can integrate with AD DS to provision users and computers automatically with certificates. AD CS is covered in Chapter 15.

For more information on PKI infrastructures and how to apply them in your organization, visit *http://www.reso-net.com/articles.asp?m=8* and look for the "Advanced Public Key Infrastructures" section.

- **Active Directory Rights Management Services (Integrity)** Although a server running Windows can prevent or allow access to a document based on the document's ACL, there have been few ways to control what happens to the document and its content after a user has opened it. Active Directory Rights Management Services (AD RMS) is an information-protection technology that enables you to implement persistent usage policy templates that define allowed and unauthorized use whether online, offline, inside, or outside the firewall. For example, you could configure a template that allows users to read a document but not to print or copy its contents. By doing so, you can ensure the integrity of the data you generate, protect intellectual property, and control who can do what with the documents your organization produces. AD RMS requires an Active Directory domain with domain controllers running Windows 2000 Server with Service Pack 3 (SP3) or later; IIS; a database server such as Microsoft SQL Server 2008; the AD RMS client that can be downloaded from the Microsoft Download Center and is included by default in Windows Vista and Windows Server 2008; and an RMS-enabled browser or application such as Microsoft Internet Explorer, Microsoft Office, Microsoft Word, Microsoft Outlook, or Microsoft PowerPoint. AD RMS can rely on AD CS to embed certificates within documents as well as in AD DS to manage access rights. AD RMS is covered in Chapter 16.
- **Active Directory Federation Services (Partnership)** Active Directory Federation Services (AD FS) enables an organization to extend IDA across multiple platforms, including both Windows and non-Windows environments, and to project identity and access rights across security boundaries to trusted partners. In a federated environment, each organization maintains and manages its own identities, but each organization can also securely project and accept identities from other organizations. Users are authenticated in one network but can access resources in another—a process known as single sign-on (SSO). AD FS supports partnerships because it allows different organizations to share access to extranet applications while relying on their own internal AD DS structures to provide the actual authentication process. To do so, AD FS extends your internal AD DS structure to the external world through common Transmission Control Protocol/Internet Protocol (TCP/IP) ports such as 80 (HTTP) and 443 (Secure HTTP, or HTTPS). It normally resides in the perimeter network. AD FS can rely on AD CS to create trusted servers and on AD RMS to provide external protection for intellectual property. AD FS is covered in Chapter 17.

Together, the Active Directory roles provide an integrated IDA solution. AD DS or AD LDS provides foundational directory services in both domain and standalone implementations. AD CS provides trusted credentials in the form of PKI digital certificates. AD RMS protects the integrity of information contained in documents. And AD FS supports partnerships by eliminating the need for federated environments to create multiple, separate identities for a single security principal.

Beyond Identity and Access

Active Directory delivers more than just an IDA solution, however. It also provides the mechanisms to support, manage, and configure resources in distributed network environments.

A set of rules, the *schema*, defines the classes of objects and attributes that can be contained in the directory. The fact that Active Directory has user objects that include a user name and password, for example, is because the schema defines the *user* object class, the two attributes, and the association between the object class and attributes.

Policy-based administration eases the management burden of even the largest, most complex networks by providing a single point at which to configure settings that are then deployed to multiple systems. You will learn about such policies, including Group Policy, audit policies, and fine-grained password policies in Chapter 6, "Group Policy Infrastructure," Chapter 7, "Group Policy Settings," and Chapter 8.

Replication services distribute directory data across a network. This includes both the data store itself as well as data required to implement policies and configuration, including logon scripts. In Chapter 8, Chapter 11, "Sites and Replication," and Chapter 10, you will learn about Active Directory replication. There is even a separate partition of the data store named *configuration* that maintains information about network configuration, topology, and services.

Several components and technologies enable you to query Active Directory and locate objects in the data store. A partition of the data store called the *global catalog* (also known as the *partial attribute set*) contains information about every object in the directory. It is a type of index that can be used to locate objects in the directory. Programmatic interfaces such as Active Directory Services Interface (ADSI) and protocols such as LDAP can be used to read and manipulate the data store.

The Active Directory data store can also be used to support applications and services not directly related to AD DS. Within the database, application partitions can store data to support applications that require replicated data. The domain name system (DNS) service on a server running Windows Server 2008 can store its information in a database called an Active Directory integrated zone, which is maintained as an application partition in AD DS and replicated using Active Directory replication services.

Components of an Active Directory Infrastructure

The first 13 chapters of this training kit will focus on the installation, configuration, and management of AD DS. AD DS provides the foundation for IDA in and management of an enterprise network. It is worthwhile to spend a few moments reviewing the components of an Active Directory infrastructure.

For more details about Active Directory, refer to the product help installed with Windows Server 2008 and to the TechCenter for Windows Server 2008 located at *http://technet.microsoft.com/en-us /windowsserver/2008/default.aspx.*

- **Active Directory data store** As mentioned in the previous section, AD DS stores its identities in the directory—a data store hosted on domain controllers. The directory is a single file named Ntds.dit and is located by default in the %SystemRoot%\Ntds folder on a domain controller. The database is divided into several partitions, including the schema, configuration, global catalog, and the domain naming context that contains the data about objects within a domain—the users, groups, and computers, for example.
- **Domain controllers** Domain controllers, also referred to as DCs, are servers that perform the AD DS role. As part of that role, they also run the Kerberos Key Distribution Center (KDC) service, which performs authentication, and other Active Directory services. Chapter 10 details the roles performed by DCs.
- **Domain** One or more domain controllers are required to create an Active Directory *domain*. A domain is an administrative unit within which certain capabilities and characteristics are shared. First, all domain controllers replicate the domain's partition of the data store, which contains among other things the identity data for the domain's users, groups, and computers. Because all DCs maintain the same identity store, any DC can authenticate any identity in a domain. Additionally, a domain is a scope of administrative policies such as password complexity and account lockout policies. Such policies configured in one domain affect all accounts in the domain and do not affect accounts in other domains. Changes can be made to objects in the Active Directory database by any domain controller and will replicate to all other domain controllers. Therefore, in networks where replication of all data between domain controllers cannot be supported, it might be necessary to implement more than one domain to manage the replication of subsets of identities. You will learn more about domains in Chapter 12.
- **Forest** A *forest* is a collection of one or more Active Directory domains. The first domain installed in a forest is called the *forest root domain*. A forest contains a single definition of network configuration and a single instance of the directory schema. A forest is a single instance of the directory—no data is replicated by Active Directory outside the boundaries of the forest. Therefore, the forest defines a security boundary. Chapter 12 will explore the concept of the forest further.
- **Tree** The DNS namespace of domains in a forest creates trees within the forest. If a domain is a subdomain of another domain, the two domains are considered a tree. For example, if the *treyresearch.net* forest contains two domains, *treyresearch.net* and *antarctica.treyresearch.net,* those domains constitute a contiguous portion of the DNS namespace, so they are a single tree. If, conversely, the two domains are *treyresearch.net*

and *proseware.com*, which are not contiguous in the DNS namespace, the domain is considered to have two trees. Trees are the direct result of the DNS names chosen for domains in the forest.

Figure 1-2 illustrates an Active Directory forest for Trey Research, which maintains a small operation at a field station in Antarctica. Because the link from Antarctica to the headquarters is expensive, slow, and unreliable, Antarctica is configured as a separate domain. The DNS name of the forest is *treyresearch.net*. The Antarctica domain is a child domain in the DNS namespace, *antarctica.treyresearch.net*, so it is considered a child domain in the domain tree.

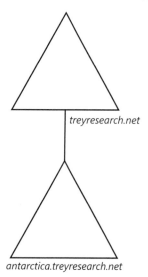

treyresearch.net

antarctica.treyresearch.net

Figure 1-2   An Active Directory forest with two domains

- **Functional level**   The functionality available in an Active Directory domain or forest depends on its *functional level*. The functional level is an AD DS setting that enables advanced domain-wide or forest-wide AD DS features. There are three domain functional levels, Windows 2000 native, Windows Server 2003, and Windows Server 2008 and two forest functional levels, Microsoft Windows Server 2003 and Windows Server 2008. As you raise the functional level of a domain or forest, features provided by that version of Windows become available to AD DS. For example, when the domain functional level is raised to Windows Server 2008, a new attribute becomes available that reveals the last time a user successfully logged on to a computer, the computer to which the user last logged on, and the number of failed logon attempts since the last logon. The important thing to know about functional levels is that they determine the versions of Windows permitted on domain controllers. Before you raise the domain functional level to Windows Server 2008, all domain controllers must be running Windows Server 2008. Chapter 12, details domain and forest functional levels.

- **Organizational units**   Active Directory is a hierarchical database. Objects in the data store can be collected in containers. One type of container is the object class called *container*. You have seen the default containers, including Users, Computers, and Builtin, when you open the Active Directory Users and Computers snap-in. Another type of container is the organizational unit (OU). OUs provide not only a container for objects but also a scope with which to manage the objects. That is because OUs can have objects called Group Policy objects (GPOs) linked to them. GPOs can contain configuration settings that will then be applied automatically by users or computers in an OU. In Chapter 2, "Administration," you will learn more about OUs, and in Chapter 6, you will explore GPOs.
- **Sites**   When you consider the network topology of a distributed enterprise, you will certainly discuss the network's sites. Sites in Active Directory, however, have a very specific meaning because there is a specific object class called *site*. An Active Directory site is an object that represents a portion of the enterprise within which network connectivity is good. A site creates a boundary of replication and service usage. Domain controllers within a site replicate changes within seconds. Changes are replicated between sites on a controlled basis with the assumption that intersite connections are slow, expensive, or unreliable compared to the connections within a site. Additionally, clients will prefer to use distributed services provided by servers in their site or in the closest site. For example, when a user logs on to the domain, the Windows client first attempts to authenticate with a domain controller in its site. Only if no domain controller is available in the site will the client attempt to authenticate with a DC in another site. Chapter 11 details the configuration and functionality of Active Directory sites.

Each of these components is discussed in detail later in this training kit. At this point, if you are less familiar with Active Directory, it is important only that you have a basic understanding of the terminology, the components, and their relationships.

Preparing to Create a New Windows Server 2008 Forest

Before you install the AD DS role on a server and promote it to act as a domain controller, plan your Active Directory infrastructure. Some of the information you will need to create a domain controller includes the following:

- The domain's name and DNS name. A domain must have a unique DNS name, for example, *contoso.com*, as well as a short name, for example, CONTOSO, called a NetBIOS name. NetBIOS is a network protocol that has been used since the first versions of Microsoft Windows NT and is still used by some applications.
- Whether the domain will need to support domain controllers running previous versions of Windows. When you create a new Active Directory forest, you will configure the functional level. If the domain will include only Windows Server 2008 domain controllers,

you can set the functional level accordingly to benefit from the enhanced features introduced by this version of Windows.

■ Details for how DNS will be implemented to support Active Directory. It is a best practice to implement DNS for your Windows domain zones by using Windows DNS Service, as you will learn in Chapter 9, "Integrating Domain Name System with AD DS"; however, it is possible to support a Windows domain on a third-party DNS service.

■ IP configuration for the domain controller. Domain controllers require static IP addresses and subnet mask values. Additionally, the domain controller must be configured with a DNS server address to perform name resolution. If you are creating a new forest and will run Windows DNS Service on the domain controller, you can configure the DNS address to point to the server's own IP address. After DNS is installed, the server can look to itself to resolve DNS names.

■ The user name and password of an account in the server's Administrators group. The account must have a password—the password cannot be blank.

■ The location in which the data store (including *Ntds.dit*) and system volume (SYSVOL) should be installed. By default, these stores are created in %SystemRoot%, for example, C:\Windows, in the NTDS and SYSVOL folders, respectively. When creating a domain controller, you can redirect these stores to other drives.

MORE INFO   Deployment of AD DS

This list comprises the settings that you will be prompted to configure when creating a domain controller. There are a number of additional considerations regarding the deployment of AD DS in an enterprise setting. See the Windows Server 2008 Technical Library at *http:// technet2.microsoft.com/windowsserver2008/en/library/bab0f1a1-54aa-4cef-9164- 139e8bcc44751033.mspx* for more information.

Adding the AD DS Role Using the Windows Interface

After you have collected the prerequisite information listed earlier, you are ready to add the AD DS role. There are several ways to do so. In this lesson, you will learn how to create a domain controller by using the Windows interface. In the next lesson, you will learn to do so using the command line.

Windows Server 2008 provides role-based configuration, installing only the components and services required for the roles a server plays. This role-based server management is reflected in the new administrative console, Server Manager, shown in Figure 1-3. Server Manager consolidates the information, tools, and resources needed to support a server's roles.

You can add roles to a server by using the Add Roles link on the home page of Server Manager or by right-clicking the Roles node in the console tree and choosing Add Roles. The Add Roles Wizard presents a list of roles available for installation and steps you through the installation of selected roles.

Figure 1-3   Server Manager

Practice It   Exercise 3, "Install a New Windows Server 2008 Forest with the Windows Interface," at the end of this lesson guides you through adding the AD DS role, using the Windows interface.

Creating a Domain Controller

After you add the AD DS role, the files required to perform the role are installed on the server; however, the server is not yet acting as a domain controller. You must subsequently run the Active Directory Domain Services Installation Wizard, which can be launched using the *Dcpromo.exe* command, to configure, initialize, and start Active Directory.

Practice It   Exercise 4, "Install a New Windows Server 2008 Forest," at the end of this lesson guides you through configuration of AD DS, using the Active Directory Domain Services Installation Wizard.

Quick Check

- You want to use a new server running Windows Server 2008 as a domain controller in your Active Directory domain. Which command do you use to launch configuration of the domain controller?

Quick Check Answer

- *Dcpromo.exe*

PRACTICE Creating a Windows Server 2008 Forest

In this practice, you will create the AD DS forest for Contoso, Ltd. This forest will be used for exercises throughout this training kit. You will begin by installing Windows Server 2008 and performing post-installation configuration tasks. You will then add the AD DS role and promote the server to a domain controller in the *contoso.com* forest, using the Active Directory Domain Services Installation Wizard.

▶ **Exercise 1   Install Windows Server 2008**

In this exercise, you will install Windows Server 2008 on a computer or virtual machine.

1. Insert the Windows Server 2008 installation DVD.

    If you are using a virtual machine (VM), you might have the option to mount an ISO image of the installation DVD. Consult the VM Help documentation for guidance.

2. Power on the system.

    If the system's hard disk is empty, the system should boot to the DVD. If there is data on the disk, you might be prompted to press a key to boot to the DVD.

    If the system does not boot to the DVD or offer you a boot menu, go to the BIOS settings of the computer and configure the boot order to ensure that the system boots to the DVD.

    The Install Windows Wizard appears, shown in Figure 1-4.

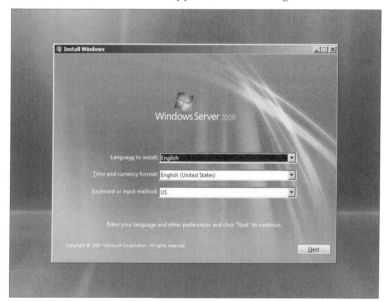

Figure 1-4   The Install Windows Wizard

3. Select the language, regional setting, and keyboard layout that are correct for your system and click Next.

4. Click Install Now.

   You are presented with a list of versions to install, as shown in Figure 1-5. If you are using an x64 computer, you will be presented with x64 versions rather than with x86 versions.

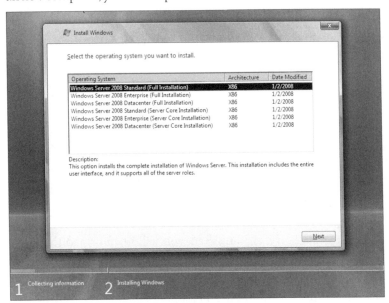

Figure 1-5   The Select The Operating System You Want To Install page

5. Select Windows Server 2008 Standard (Full Installation) and click Next.

6. Select the I Accept The License Terms check box and click Next.

7. Click Custom (Advanced).

8. On the Where Do You Want to Install Windows page, select the disk on which you want to install Windows Server 2008.

   If you need to create, delete, extend, or format partitions or if you need to load a custom mass storage driver to access the disk subsystem, click Driver Options (Advanced).

9. Click Next.

   The Installing Windows dialog box appears, shown in Figure 1-6. The window keeps you apprised of the progress of Windows installation.

   Installation of Windows Server 2008, like that of Windows Vista, is image-based. Therefore, installation is significantly faster than previous versions of Windows even though the operating systems themselves are much larger than earlier versions. The computer will reboot one or more times during installation.

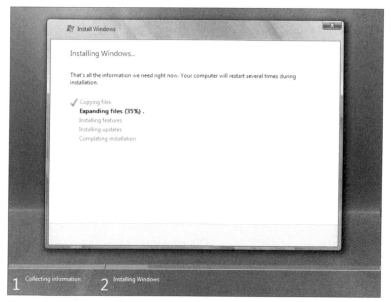

Figure 1-6   The Installing Windows page

When the installation has completed, you will be informed that the user's password must be changed before logging on the first time.

10. Click OK.

11. Type a password for the Administrator account in both the New Password and Confirm Password boxes and press Enter.

    The password must be at least seven characters long and must have at least three of four character types:

    ❏ Uppercase: A–Z

    ❏ Lowercase: a–z

    ❏ Numeric: 0–9

    ❏ Nonalphanumeric: symbols such as $, #, @, and !

NOTE   Do not forget this password

Without it, you will not be able to log on to the server to perform other exercises in this training kit.

---

12. Click OK.

    The desktop for the Administrator account appears.

▶ Exercise 2   **Perform Post-Installation Configuration**

In this exercise, you will perform post-installation configuration of the server to prepare the server with the name and TCP/IP settings required for exercises in this training kit.

1. Wait for the desktop for the Administrator account to appear.

    The Initial Configuration Tasks window appears, as shown in Figure 1-7. This tool is designed to make it easy for you to perform best practice, post-installation configuration tasks.

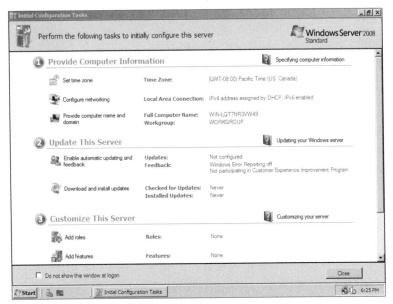

Figure 1-7   The Initial Configuration Tasks window

2. Use the Initial Configuration Tasks window to configure the following settings:
    ❑   Time zone: as appropriate for your environment.
    ❑   Computer name: SERVER01. Do not restart until instructed to do so later in this exercise.

3. Click the Configure Networking link in the Initial Configuration Tasks window and make sure the server's IP configuration is appropriate for your environment.

4. If the server has connection to the Internet, it is highly recommended to click the Download And Install Updates link so that you can update the server with the latest security updates from Microsoft.

5. After the server is updated, restart the server.

    The remaining exercises in this training kit will create a domain using IP addresses in the 10.0.0.11–10.0.0.20 range, with a subnet mask of 255.255.255.0. If these addresses are used in your production environment, and if the server is connected to your production environment, you must change the IP addresses in this book accordingly so that the *contoso.com* domain you create in these practices does not conflict with your production network.

6. In the Initial Configuration Tasks window, click the Configure Networking link.

   The Network Connections dialog box appears.

7. Select Local Area Connection.

8. On the toolbar, click Change Settings Of This Connection.

9. Select Internet Protocol Version 4 (TCP/IPv4) and click Properties.

   Windows Server 2008 also provides native support for Internet Protocol Version 6 (TCP/IPv6).

10. Click Use The Following IP Address. Enter the following configuration:
    - ❑ IP address: **10.0.0.11**
    - ❑ Subnet mask: **255.255.255.0**
    - ❑ Default gateway: **10.0.0.1**
    - ❑ Preferred DNS server: **10.0.0.11**

11. Click OK, and then click Close.

12. Note the Add Roles and Add Features links in the Initial Configuration Tasks window.

    In the next exercise, you will use Server Manager to add roles and features to SERVER01. These links are another way to perform the same tasks.

    The Initial Configuration Tasks window will appear each time you log on to the server.

13. Select the Do Not Show This Window At Logon check box to prevent the window from appearing.

    If you need to open the Initial Configuration Tasks window in the future, you do so by running the *Oobe.exe* command.

14. Click the Close button at the bottom of the Initial Configuration Tasks window.

    Server Manager appears. Server Manager enables you to configure and administer the roles and features of a server running Windows Server 2008. You will use Server Manager in the next exercise.

NOTE   Create a snapshot of your virtual machine

If you are using a virtual machine to perform this exercise, and if the virtual machine enables you to create point-in-time snapshots of the machine's state, create a snapshot at this time. This baseline installation of Windows Server 2008 can be used to perform the exercises in this chapter, which enable you to experiment with the variety of methods of adding the AD DS role.

▶ **Exercise 3 Install a New Windows Server 2008 Forest with the Windows Interface**

In this exercise, you will add the AD DS role to the server you installed and configured in Exercise 1, "Install Windows Server 2008," and Exercise 2, "Perform Post-Installation Configuration."

1. If Server Manager is not open, open it from the Administrative Tools program group.
2. In the Roles Summary section of the home page, click Add Roles.

   The Add Roles Wizard appears.
3. Click Next.
4. On the Select Server Roles page, select the check box next to Active Directory Domain Services. Click Next.
5. On the Active Directory Domain Services page, click Next.
6. On the Confirm Installation Selections page, click Install.

   The Installation Progress page reports the status of installation tasks.
7. On the Installation Results page, confirm that the installation succeeded and click Close.

   In the Roles Summary section of the Server Manager home page, you'll notice an error message indicated by a red circle with a white x. You'll also notice a message in the Active Directory Domain Services section of the page. Both of these links will take you to the Active Directory Domain Services role page of Server Manager, shown in Figure 1-8. The message shown reminds you that it is necessary to run *Dcpromo.exe*, which you will do in the next exercise.

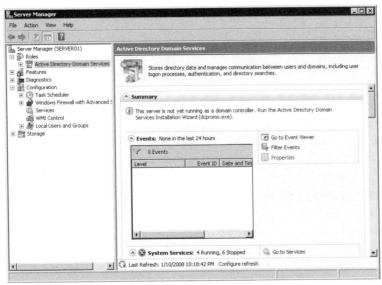

Figure 1-8 The Active Directory Domain Services roles page in Server Manager

▶ **Exercise 4   Install a New Windows Server 2008 Forest**

In this exercise, you will use the Active Directory Domain Services Installation Wizard (*Dcpromo.exe*) to create a new Windows Server 2008 forest.

1. Click Start, click Run, type **Dcpromo.exe**, and then click OK.

NOTE   *Dcpromo* **will add the AD DS role if necessary**

In the previous exercise, you added the AD DS role by using Server Manager. However, if you run *Dcpromo.exe* on a server that does not yet have the AD DS role installed, *Dcpromo.exe* will install the role automatically.

The Active Directory Domain Services Installation Wizard appears. In Chapter 10, you will learn about advanced modes of the wizard.

2. Click Next.

3. On the Operating System Compatibility page, review the warning about the default security settings for Windows Server 2008 domain controllers, and then click Next.

4. On the Choose a Deployment Configuration page, select Create A New Domain In A New Forest, and click Next.

5. On the Name The Forest Root Domain page, type **contoso.com**, and then click Next.

   The system performs a check to ensure that the DNS and NetBIOS names are not already in use on the network.

6. On the Set Forest Functional Level page, choose Windows Server 2008, and then click Next.

   Each of the functional levels is described in the Details box on the page. Choosing Windows Server 2008 forest functional level ensures that all domains in the forest operate at the Windows Server 2008 domain functional level, which enables several new features provided by Windows Server 2008. You will learn about functional levels in Chapter 12.

   The Additional Domain Controller Options page appears. DNS Server is selected by default. The Active Directory Domain Services Installation Wizard will create a DNS infrastructure during AD DS installation. The first domain controller in a forest must be a global catalog (GC) server and cannot be a read-only domain controller (RODC).

7. Click Next.

   A Static IP assignment warning appears. Because discussion of IPv6 is beyond the scope of this training kit, you did not assign a static IPv6 address to the server in Exercise 2. You did assign a static IPv4 address in Exercise 2, and later exercises will use IPv4. You can, therefore, ignore this warning in the context of the exercise.

8. Click Yes, The Computer Will Use A Dynamically Assigned IP Address (Not Recommended).

A warning appears that informs you that a delegation for the DNS server cannot be created. In the context of this exercise, you can ignore this error. Delegations of DNS domains will be discussed in Chapter 9.

9. Click Yes to close the Active Directory Domain Services Installation Wizard warning message.

10. On the Location For Database, Log Files, And SYSVOL page, accept the default locations for the database file, the directory service log files, and the SYSVOL files and click Next.

    The best practice in a production environment is to store these files on three separate volumes that do not contain applications or other files not related to AD DS. This best practices design improves performance and increases the efficiency of backup and restore.

11. On the Directory Services Restore Mode Administrator Password page, type a strong password in both the Password and Confirmed Password boxes. Click Next.

    Do not forget the password you assigned to the Directory Services Restore Mode Administrator.

12. On the Summary page, review your selections.

    If any settings are incorrect, click Back to make modifications.

13. Click Next.

    Configuration of AD DS begins. The server will require a reboot when the process is completed. Optionally, select the Reboot On Completion check box.

Lesson Summary

- Active Directory services comprise an integrated solution for identity and access in enterprise networks.
- Active Directory Domain Services (AD DS) provide the directory service and authentication components of IDA. Additionally, AD DS facilitates management of even large, complex, distributed networks.
- Windows Server 2008 systems are configured based on the roles they play. You can add the AD DS role by using Server Manager.
- Use *Dcpromo.exe* to configure AD DS and create a domain controller.

Lesson Review

You can use the following questions to test your knowledge of the information in Lesson 1, "Installing Active Directory Domain Services." The questions are also available on the companion CD if you prefer to review them in electronic form.

NOTE Answers

Answers to these questions and explanations of why each answer choice is right or wrong are located in the "Answers" section at the end of the book.

1. Which of the following are required to create a domain controller successfully? (Choose all that apply.)

   A. A valid DNS domain name

   B. A valid NetBIOS name

   C. A DHCP server to assign an IP address to the domain controller

   D. A DNS server

2. Trey Research has recently acquired Litware, Inc. Because of regulatory issues related to data replication, it is decided to configure a child domain in the forest for Litware users and computers. The Trey Research forest currently contains only Windows Server 2008 domain controllers. The new domain will be created by promoting a Windows Server 2008 domain controller, but you might need to use existing Windows Server 2003 systems as domain controllers in the Litware domain. Which functional levels will be appropriate to configure?

   A. Windows Server 2008 forest functional level and Windows Server 2008 domain functional level for the Litware domain

   B. Windows Server 2008 forest functional level and Windows Server 2003 domain functional level for the Litware domain

   C. Windows Server 2003 forest functional level and Windows Server 2008 domain functional level for the Litware domain

   D. Windows Server 2003 forest functional level and Windows Server 2003 domain functional level for the Litware domain

Lesson 2: Active Directory Domain Services on Server Core

Many organizations want to implement the maximum available security for servers acting as domain controllers because of the sensitive nature of information stored in the directory—particularly user passwords. Although the role-based configuration of Windows Server 2008 reduces the security surface of a server by installing only the components and services required by its roles, it is possible to reduce its servers and security surface further by installing Server Core. A Server Core installation is a minimal installation of Windows that forgoes even the Windows Explorer GUI and the Microsoft .NET Framework. You can administer a Server Core installation remotely, using GUI tools; however, to configure and manage a server locally, you must use command-line tools. In this lesson, you will learn to create a domain controller from the command line within a Server Core installation. You will also learn how to remove domain controllers from a domain.

After this lesson, you will be able to:
- Identify the benefits and functionality of installing Server Core.
- Install and configure Server Core.
- Add and remove Active Directory Domain Services (AD DS), using command-line tools.

Estimated lesson time: 60 minutes

Understanding Server Core

Windows Server 2008 (Server Core Installation), better known as Server Core, is a minimal installation of Windows that consumes about 3 GB of disk space and less than 256 MB of memory. Server Core installation limits the server roles and features that can be added but can improve the security and manageability of the server by reducing its attack surface. The number of services and components running at any one time are limited, so there are fewer opportunities for an intruder to compromise the server. Server Core also reduces the management burden of the server, which requires fewer updates and less maintenance.

Server Core supports nine server roles:

- Active Directory Domain Services
- Active Directory Lightweight Directory Services (AD LDS)
- Dynamic Host Configuration Protocol (DHCP) Server
- DNS Server
- File Services
- Print Server

- Streaming Media Services
- Web Server (IIS) (as a static Web server—ASP.NET cannot be installed)
- Hyper-V (Windows Server Virtualization)

Server core also supports these 11 optional features:

- Microsoft Failover Cluster
- Network Load Balancing
- Subsystem for UNIX-based applications
- Windows Backup
- Multipath I/O
- Removable Storage Management
- Windows Bitlocker Drive Encryption
- Simple Network Management Protocol (SNMP)
- Windows Internet Naming Service (WINS)
- Telnet client
- Quality of Service (QoS)

Installing Server Core

You can install Server Core by using the same steps presented in Exercise 1 of Lesson 1. The differences between a full installation and a Server Core installation are, first, that you select Server Core Installation in the Installing Windows Wizard shown in Figure 1-9, and that when the installation is complete and you log on, a command prompt appears rather than the Windows Explorer interface.

NOTE The blank initial Administrator password

When you install Windows Server 2008 from the installation DVD, the initial password for the Administrator account is blank. When you log on to the server for the first time, use a blank password. You will be prompted to change the password on first log on.

Practice It   Exercise 1, "Install Server Core," in the practice at the end of this lesson, steps you through the installation of Server Core.

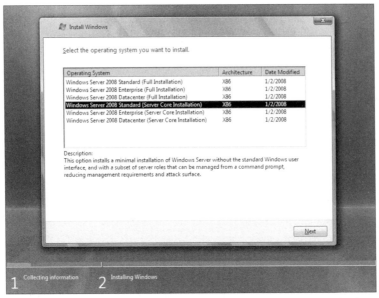

Figure 1-9   The Operating Systems selection page of the Install Windows Wizard

Performing Initial Configuration Tasks

On a full installation of Windows Server 2008, the Initial Configuration Tasks window appears to guide you through post-installation configuration of the server. Server Core provides no GUI, so you must complete the tasks by using command-line tools. Table 1-1 lists common configuration tasks and the commands you can use. To learn more about any command, open a command prompt and type the name of the command followed by /?.

Table 1-1   Server Core Configuration Commands

Task	Command
Change the Administrator password	When you log on with Ctrl + Alt + Del, you will be prompted to change the password. You can also type the following command: *Net user administrator **
Set a static IPv4 configuration	*Netsh interface ipv4*
Activate Windows Server	*Cscript c:\windows\system32\slmgr.vbs −ato*
Join a domain	*Netdom*
Add Server Core roles, components, or features	*Ocsetup.exe* package or feature Note that the package or feature names are case sensitive.

Table 1-1   Server Core Configuration Commands

Task	Command
Display installed roles, components, and features	*Oclist.exe*
Enable Remote Desktop	*Cscript c:\windows\system32\scregedit.wsf /AR 0*
Promote a domain controller	*Dcpromo.exe*
Configure DNS	*Dnscmd.exe*
Configure DFS	*Dfscmd.exe*

Practice It   Exercise 2, "Perform Post-Installation Configuration on Server Core," in the practice at the end of this lesson, steps you through the initial configuration of a Server Core installation of Windows Server 2008.

The *Ocsetup.exe* command is used to add supported Server Core roles and features to the server. The exception to this rule is AD DS. Do not use *Ocsetup.exe* to add or remove AD DS. Use *Dcpromo.exe* instead.

Adding AD DS to a Server Core Installation

Because there is no Active Directory Domain Services Installation Wizard in Server Core, you must use the command line to run *Dcpromo.exe* with parameters that configure AD DS. To learn about the parameters of *Dcpromo.exe*, open a command line and type **dcpromo.exe /?**. Each configuration scenario has additional usage information. For example, type **dcpromo.exe /?:Promotion** for detailed usage instructions for promoting a domain controller.

MORE INFO   Unattended installation parameters
You can find a listing of unattended installation parameters at *http://technet2.microsoft.com /windowsserver2008/en/library/bcd89659-402d-46fb-8535-8da1feb8d4111033.mspx*.

Practice It   You will add AD DS to a Server Core installation during Exercise 3, "Create a Domain Controller with Server Core," in the practice at the end of this lesson.

Removing Domain Controllers

Occasionally, you might have a reason to take a domain controller offline for extended maintenance or to remove it permanently. It is important that you remove a domain controller correctly so that the information about the domain controller is cleaned up in Active Directory.

To remove a domain controller, use the *Dcpromo.exe* command. If you run the command on a domain controller by using the Windows interface, the Active Directory Domain Services Installation Wizard will step you through the process. If you want to use the command line or are removing AD DS from a Server Core installation, type **dcpromo.exe /?:Demotion** for usage information regarding parameters for the demotion operation.

Practice It   In Exercise 4, "Remove a Domain Controller," in the practice at the end of the lesson, you will remove a domain controller by using the *Dcpromo.exe* command.

When you demote a domain controller, you must provide a password that will be assigned to the local Administrator account of the server after demotion.

PRACTICE Installing a Server Core Domain Controller

In this exercise, you will add a domain controller to the *contoso.com* forest you created in the Lesson 1 practice. To increase the security and reduce the management overhead of the new DC, you will promote a server running Server Core to a domain controller. Before performing the exercises in this practice, you must have completed the practice in Lesson 1.

▶ Exercise 1   Install Server Core

In this exercise, you will install Server Core on a computer or virtual machine.

1. Insert the Windows Server 2008 installation DVD.

    If you are using a VM, you might have the option to mount an ISO image of the installation DVD. Consult the VM Help documentation for guidance.

2. Power on the system.

    If the system's hard disk is empty, the system should boot to the DVD. If there is data on the disk, you might be prompted to press a key to boot to the DVD.

    If the system does not boot to the DVD or offer you a boot menu, go to the BIOS settings of the computer and configure the boot order to ensure that the system boots to the DVD.

3. Select the language, regional setting, and keyboard layout that are correct for your system and click Next.

4. Click Install Now.

5. Select Windows Server 2008 Standard (Server Core Installation) and click Next.

6. Select the I Accept The License Terms check box and click Next.

7. Click Custom (Advanced).

8. On the Where Do You Want To Install Windows page, select the disk on which you want to install Windows Server 2008.

    If you need to create, delete, extend, or format partitions, or if you need to load a custom mass storage driver to access the disk subsystem, click Driver Options (Advanced).

9. Click Next.

10. When installation has completed, log on to the system.

   The initial password for the Administrator account is blank

11. You will be prompted to change the password. Enter a password for the Administrator account in both the New Password and Confirm Password boxes and press Enter.

   The password must be at least seven characters long and must have at least three of four character types:

   ❑ Upper case: A–Z

   ❑ Lower case: a–z

   ❑ Numeric: 0–9

   ❑ Nonalphanumeric: symbols such as $, #, @, and !

NOTE   Do not forget this password

Without it, you will not be able to log on to the server to perform other exercises in this training kit.

---

12. Click OK.

   The command prompt for the Administrator account appears.

▶ **Exercise 2   Perform Post-Installation Configuration on Server Core**

In this exercise, you will perform post-installation configuration of the server to prepare it with the name and TCP/IP settings required for the remaining exercises in this lesson.

1. Rename the server by typing **netdom renamecomputer %computername% /newname: SERVER02**. You will be prompted to press **Y** to confirm the operation.

2. Set the IPv4 address of the server by typing each of the following commands:

```
netsh interface ipv4 set address name="Local Area Connection"
source=static address=10.0.0.12 mask=255.255.255.0
gateway=10.0.0.1 1

netsh interface ipv4 set dns name="Local Area Connection"
source=static address=10.0.0.11 primary
```

3. Confirm the IP configuration you entered previously with the command **ipconfig /all**.

4. Restart by typing **shutdown –r –t 0**.

5. Log on as Administrator.

6. Join the domain with the command **netdom join %computername% /domain: contoso.com**.

7. Restart by typing **shutdown –r –t 0**, and then log on again as Administrator.

8. Display installed server roles by typing oclist.

   Note the package identifier for the DNS server role: DNS-Server-Core-Role.

9. Type **ocsetup** and press Enter.

Surprise! There is a minor amount of GUI in Server Core.

10. Click OK to close the window.

11. Type **ocsetup DNS-Server-Core-Role**.

Package identifiers are case sensitive.

12. Type **oclist** and confirm that the DNS server role is installed.

▶ **Exercise 3 Create a Domain Controller with Server Core**

In this exercise, you will add the AD DS role to the Server Core installation, using the *Dcpromo.exe* command.

1. Type **dcpromo.exe /?** and press Enter.

Review the usage information.

2. Type **dcpromo.exe /?:Promotion** and press Enter.

Review the usage information.

3. Type the following command to add and configure the AD DS role:

```
dcpromo /unattend /replicaOrNewDomain:replica
/replicaDomainDNSName:contoso.com /ConfirmGC:Yes
/UserName:CONTOSO\Adminsitrator /Password:* /safeModeAdminPassword:P@ssword
```

4. When prompted to enter network credentials, type the password for the Administrator account in the *contoso.com* domain and click OK.

The AD DS role will be installed and configured, and then the server will reboot.

▶ **Exercise 4 Remove a Domain Controller**

In this exercise, you will remove AD DS from the Server Core installation.

1. Log on to the Server Core installation as Administrator.

2. Type **dcpromo /unattend /AdministratorPassword:***password* where *password* is a strong password that will become the local Administrator password of the server after AD DS has been removed. Press Enter.

Lesson Summary

- Windows Server 2008 Server Core Installation, better known simply as Server Core, is a minimal installation of Windows that supports a subset of server roles and features.

- Server Core can improve the security and manageability of Windows servers.

- The *Ocsetup.exe* command is used to add and remove Server Core roles except for AD DS, which is added by using *Dcpromo.exe*.

- You can fully configure an automated promotion or demotion operation by using the *Dcpromo.exe /unattend* command with parameters appropriate for the operation.

Lesson Review

You can use the following questions to test your knowledge of the information in Lesson 2, "Active Directory Domain Services on Server Core." The questions are also available on the companion CD if you prefer to review them in electronic form.

NOTE   Answers

Answers to these questions and explanations of why each answer choice is right or wrong are located in the "Answers" section at the end of the book.

---

1. You are logged on as Administrator to SERVER02, one of four domain controllers in the *contoso.com* domain that run Server Core. You want to demote the domain controller. Which of the following is required?

    A. The local Administrator password

    B. The credentials for a user in the Domain Admins group

    C. The credentials for a user in the Domain Controllers group

    D. The address of a DNS server

2. SERVER02 is running Server Core. It is already configured with the AD DS role. You want to add Active Directory Certificate Services (AD CS) to the server. What must you do?

    A. Install the Active Directory Certificate Services role.

    B. Install the Active Directory Federated Services role.

    C. Install the AD RMS role.

    D. Reinstall the server as Windows Server 2008 (Full Installation).

Chapter Review

To further practice and reinforce the skills you learned in this chapter, you can perform the following tasks:

- Review the chapter summary.
- Review the list of key terms introduced in this chapter.
- Complete the case scenario. This scenario sets up a real-world situation involving the topics of this chapter and asks you to create a solution.
- Take a practice test.

Chapter Summary

- Active Directory services perform identity access and management functions to support an organization's network.
- A domain controller hosts the Active Directory data store and related services. Domain controllers are created by adding the AD DS role and then configuring AD DS by using *Dcpromo.exe*.
- Server Core enables you to reduce the management costs and increase the security of your domain controllers.

Key Terms

Use these key terms to understand better the concepts covered in this chapter.

- **authentication**   The mechanism by which an identity is validated by comparing secrets such as passwords provided by the user or computer compared to secrets maintained in the identity store.
- **domain**   An administrative unit of Active Directory. Within a domain, all domain controllers replicate information about objects such as users, groups, and computers in the domain.
- **forest**   The boundary of an instance of Active Directory. A forest contains one or more domains. All domains in the forest replicate the schema and configuration partitions of the directory.
- **forest root domain**   The first domain created in a forest.
- **functional level**   A setting that determines which features of Active Directory are enabled within a domain or forest. The functional level limits the versions of Windows that can be used by domain controllers in a domain or forest.
- **global catalog (or partial attribute set)**   A partition of the Active Directory data store that contains a subset of attributes for every object in the Active Directory forest. The global catalog is used for efficient object queries and location.

- **identity store** A database of information regarding users, groups, computers, and other security principals. Attributes stored in an identity store include user names and passwords.
- **Kerberos** A standard protocol used by Active Directory for authentication.
- **schema** A definition of the attributes and object classes supported by Active Directory.
- **site** An Active Directory object that represents a portion of the network with reliable connectivity. Within a site, domain controllers replicate updates within seconds, and clients attempt to use the services within their site before obtaining the services from other sites.

Case Scenario

In the following case scenario, you will apply what you've learned about Server Core installation and related Active Directory Domain Services. You can find answers to these questions in the "Answers" section at the end of this book.

Case Scenario: Creating an Active Directory Forest

You have been asked to create a new Active Directory forest for a new research project at Trey Research. Because of the sensitive nature of the project, you must ensure that the directory is as secure as possible. You are considering the option of using a Server Core installation on the two servers that will act as domain controllers.

1. Can you create an Active Directory forest by using only Server Core servers?
2. Which command will you use to configure static IP addresses on the servers?
3. Which command will you use to add the DNS server role?
4. Which command will you use to add Active Directory Domain Services?

Take a Practice Test

The practice tests on this book's companion CD offer many options. For example, you can test yourself on just one exam objective, or you can test yourself on all the 70-640 certification exam content. You can set up the test so that it closely simulates the experience of taking a certification exam, or you can set it up in study mode so that you can look at the correct answers and explanations after you answer each question.

MORE INFO Practice tests

For details about all the practice test options available, see the "How to Use the Practice Tests" section in this book's introduction.

Chapter 2
Administration

Most administrators first experience Active Directory Domain Services (AD DS) by opening Active Directory Users And Computers and creating user, computer, or group objects within the organizational units (OUs) of a domain. Such tasks are fundamental to the job requirements of an IT professional in an Active Directory environment, so now that you have created a domain in Chapter 1, "Installation," you can address the tools, tips, and best practices regarding the creation of these objects. Later chapters will explore each of these object classes in detail.

In this chapter, you will also look at two important, higher-level concerns within an enterprise: how to locate objects in the directory and how to ensure that Active Directory is secure while enabling support personnel to perform the tasks required of their roles.

Exam objectives in this chapter:
- Creating and Maintaining Active Directory Objects
  - Maintain Active Directory accounts

Lessons in this chapter:
- Lesson 1: Working with Active Directory Snap-ins 35
- Lesson 2: Creating Objects in Active Directory 46
- Lesson 3: Delegation and Security of Active Directory Objects 69

Before You Begin

To complete the lessons in this chapter, you must have installed Windows Server 2008 on a physical computer or virtual machine. The machine should be named SERVER01 and should be a domain controller in the *contoso.com* domain. The details for this setup are presented in Chapter 1.

Real World

Dan Holme

You are certainly familiar with administrative tools, such as the Active Directory Users and Computers snap-in, and the basic skills required to create organizational units, users, computers, and groups. This chapter reviews those tools and skills so that you can fill in any gaps in your knowledge. More important, however, this chapter introduces ways you can elevate your productivity and effectiveness as an administrator. I find that many administrators continue to use the default consoles and, therefore, have to open multiple tools to do their jobs, instead of creating a single, customized Microsoft Management Console (MMC) that contains all the snap-ins they need. I also see administrators diving deep into their OU structure to locate and manage objects rather than taking advantage of the power of Saved Queries to virtualize the view of their domains. Although this chapter covers only one exam objective, "Maintain Active Directory accounts," the tips and guidance I provide here is some of the most valuable in the book because it will enable you to work more efficiently and more securely every day in the real world of your enterprise.

Lesson 1: Working with Active Directory Snap-ins

The Active Directory administrative tools, or snap-ins, expose the functionality you require to support the directory service. In this lesson, you will identify and locate the most important Active Directory snap-ins. You will also learn how to work effectively with them, using alternate credentials, and how to build custom consoles that can be distributed to administrators in your organization.

> **After this lesson, you will be able to:**
> - Work with Microsoft Management Console.
> - Identify the most important Active Directory administrative snap-ins.
> - Install the Remote Server Administration Tools (RSAT) on Windows Server 2008 and Windows Vista.
> - Launch administrative tools with alternate credentials, using Run As Administrator.
> - Create, manage, and distribute a custom MMC.
>
> **Estimated lesson time: 35 minutes**

Understanding the Microsoft Management Console

Windows administrative tools share a common framework called the Microsoft Management Console (MMC). The MMC displays tools in a customizable window with a left pane that displays the console tree (similar to the Windows Explorer tree) and a center pane that displays details. An Actions pane on the right exposes commands, called actions by MMC. Figure 2-1 shows an example.

To control the visibility of the left and right panes, use the Show/Hide Console Tree and Show/Hide Action Pane buttons or the *Customize* command on the View menu.

Administrative tools, called *snap-ins*, use the console tree and details pane of the console to provide administrative functionality. You can think of an MMC as a tool belt to which you can attach one or more tools (snap-ins). Snap-ins cannot be launched directly; they can function within the context of an MMC only. Most of the tools in the Administrative Tools folder constitute a single console with a single snap-in. These tools include Event Viewer, Services, and Task Scheduler. Other tools, such as Computer Management, are consoles that contain multiple snap-ins, including some that exist as standalone consoles. For example, the Computer Management console contains Event Viewer, Services, and Task Scheduler.

As you are administering Windows with snap-ins, you will be performing commands, called *actions* by the MMC, that you can find in the console's Action menu, on the context menu that appears when you right-click, and in the Actions pane on the right side of the console. Most experienced administrators find the context menu to be the most productive way to perform actions in an MMC snap-in. If you use the context menu exclusively, you can turn off the Actions pane so that you have a larger area to display information in the details pane.

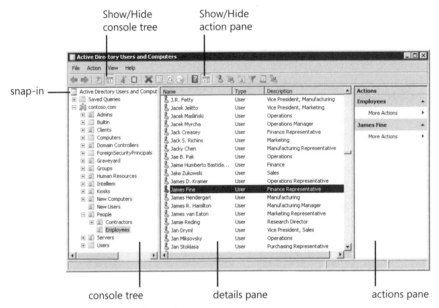

Figure 2-1 An MMC and snap-in

There are two types of MMC: preconfigured and custom. Preconfigured consoles are installed automatically when you add a role or feature, to support administration of that role or feature. They function in user mode, so you cannot modify them or save them. The user, however, can create custom consoles to provide exactly the tools and functionality required. In the following sections, you will look at both preconfigured and custom consoles.

Active Directory Administration Tools

Most Active Directory administration is performed with the following snap-ins and consoles:

- **Active Directory Users and Computers** Manage most common day-to-day resources, including users, groups, computers, printers, and shared folders. This is likely to be the most heavily used snap-in for an Active Directory administrator.
- **Active Directory Sites and Services** Manage replication, network topology, and related services. You will use this snap-in heavily in Chapter 11, "Sites and Replication."
- **Active Directory Domains and Trusts** Configure and maintain trust relationships and the domain and forest functional levels. This tool will be discussed in Chapter 13, "Domains and Forests."

■ **Active Directory Schema**   Examine and modify the definition of Active Directory attributes and object classes. This schema is the "blueprint" for Active Directory. It is rarely viewed and even more rarely changed. Therefore, the Active Directory Schema snap-in is not installed by default.

Active Directory snap-ins and consoles are installed when you add the AD DS role to a server. Two commonly used Active Directory administrative tools are added to Server Manager when you install the AD DS role: the Active Directory Users and Computers snap-in and the Active Directory Sites and Services snap-in. However, to administer Active Directory from a system that is not a domain controller, you must install the RSAT, a feature that can be installed from the Features node of Server Manager on Windows Server 2008. It can be downloaded from Microsoft and installed on clients running Windows Vista Service Pack 1.

Finding the Active Directory Administrative Tools

You can find two Active Directory snap-ins in Server Manager by expanding Roles and Active Directory Domain Services. All tools, however, can be found in the Administrative Tools folder, which itself is found in Control Panel. In the classic view of Control Panel, you will see the Administrative Tools folder displayed. Using the Control Panel Home view, you can find administrative tools in System And Maintenance.

Adding the Administrative Tools to Your Start Menu

By default, administrative tools are not added to the Start menu on Windows Vista clients. You can make the administrative tools easier to access by adding them to your Start menu.

1. Right-click the Start button and choose Properties.
2. Click Customize.
3. If you are using the default Start menu, scroll to System Administrative Tools and select Display On The All Programs Menu And The Start Menu or Display On The All Programs Menu. If you are using the Classic Start menu, select Display Administrative Tools.
4. Click OK twice.

Running Administrative Tools with Alternate Credentials

Many administrators log on to their computers by using their administrative accounts. This practice is dangerous because an administrative account has more privileges and access to more of the network than a standard user account. Therefore, malware that is launched with administrative credentials can cause significant damage. To avoid this problem, do not log on as an administrator. Instead, log on as a standard user and use the Run As Administrator feature to launch administrative tools in the security context of an administrative account:

1. Right-click the shortcut for an executable, Control Panel applet, or MMC that you want to launch, and then choose Run As Administrator. If you do not see the command, try holding down the Shift key and right-clicking.

   The User Account Control dialog box appears, as shown in Figure 2-2.

Figure 2-2   The User Account Control dialog box prompting for administrative credentials

2. Enter the user name and password of your administrative account.

3. Click OK.

If you will be running an application regularly as an administrator, create a new shortcut that preconfigures Run As Administrator. Create a shortcut and open the Properties dialog box for the shortcut. Click the Advanced button and select Run As Administrator. When you launch the shortcut, the User Account Control dialog box will appear.

Creating a Custom Console with Active Directory Snap-ins

It's easier to administer Windows when the tools you need are in one place and can be customized to meet your needs. You can achieve this by creating a custom administrative MMC which, continuing our tool belt metaphor, is a tool belt made just for you. When you create a custom MMC, you can:

- Add multiple snap-ins so that you do not have to switch between consoles to perform your job tasks and so that you have to launch only one console with Run As Administrator.
- Save the console to be used regularly.
- Distribute the console to other administrators.
- Centralize consoles in a shared location for unified, customized administration.

To create a custom MMC, open an empty MMC by clicking the Start button. Then, in the Start Search box, type **mmc.exe** and press Enter. The *Add/Remove Snap-in* command in the File menu enables you to add, remove, reorder, and manage the console's snap-ins.

Practice It Exercise 1, "Create a Custom MMC," Exercise 2, "Add a Snap-in to an MMC," and Exercise 3, "Manage the Snap-ins of an MMC," in the practice at the end of this lesson step you through the skills related to creating a custom MMC with multiple snap-ins.

Saving and Distributing a Custom Console

If you plan to distribute a console, it is recommended to save the console in user mode. To change a console's mode, choose Options from the File menu. By default, new consoles are saved in author mode, which enables adding and removing snap-ins, viewing all portions of the console tree, and saving customizations. User mode, by contrast, restricts the functionality of the console so that it cannot be changed. There are three types of user modes, described in Table 2-1. User Mode – Full Access is commonly selected for a console provided to skilled administrators with diverse job tasks requiring broad use of the console snap-ins. User Mode – Limited Access (multiple window and single window) is a locked-down mode and is, therefore, selected for a console provided to administrators with a more narrow set of job tasks.

Table 2-1 MMC Console Modes

Mode	Use when
Author	You want to continue customizing the console.
User Mode – Full Access	You want users of the console to be able to navigate between and use all snap-ins. Users will not be able to add or remove snap-ins or change the properties of snap-ins or the console.
User Mode – Limited Access, multiple window	You want users to navigate to and use only the snap-ins that you have made visible in the console tree, and you want to preconfigure multiple windows that focus on specific snap-ins. Users will not be able to open new windows.
User Mode – Limited Access, single window	You want users to navigate to and use only the snap-ins that you have made visible in the console tree within a single window.

After a console is no longer saved in author mode, you—the original author—can make changes to the console by right-clicking the saved console and choosing Author.

Practice It Exercise 4, "Prepare a Console for Distribution to Users," in the practice at the end of the lesson, guides you through saving a console in user mode so that it can be locked down for deployment to other administrators.

Consoles are saved with the .msc file extension. The default location to which consoles are saved is the Administrative Tools folder, but not the folder in Control Panel. Rather, they are saved in the Start menu folder of your user profile: *%userprofile%*\AppData\Roaming \Microsoft\Windows\StartMenu.

This location is problematic because it is secured with permissions so that only your user account has access to the console. The best practice is to log on to your computer with an account that is not privileged and then run administrative tools such as your custom console with alternate credentials that have sufficient privilege to perform administrative tasks. Because two accounts will be involved, saving the console to the Start menu subfolder of one account's user profile will mean additional navigation, at a minimum, and access-denied errors in a worst-case scenario.

Save your consoles to a location that can be accessed by both your user and your administrative credentials. It is recommended to save consoles to a shared folder on the network so that you can access your tools when you are logged on to other computers. Optionally, the folder can be made accessible by other administrators to create a centralized store of customized consoles. You can also save consoles to a portable device such as a USB drive, or you can even send a console as an e-mail attachment.

It is important to remember that consoles are basically a set of instructions that are interpreted by *mmc.exe*—instructions that specify which snap-ins to add and which computers to manage with those snap-ins. Consoles do not contain the snap-ins themselves. Therefore, a console will not function properly if the snap-ins it contains have not been installed, so be sure you have installed appropriate snap-ins from RSAT on systems on which you will use the console.

Quick Check

- Describe the difference between a console saved in user mode and in author mode.

Quick Check Answer

- Author mode enables a user to add and remove snap-ins and thoroughly customize the console. User mode prevents users from making changes to the console.

PRACTICE Creating and Managing a Custom MMC

In this practice, you will create a custom MMC. You will add, remove, and reorder snap-ins. You will then prepare the console for distribution to other administrators.

▶ Exercise 1   Create a Custom MMC

In this exercise, you will create a custom MMC with the Active Directory Users and Computers, Active Directory Schema, and Computer Management snap-ins. These tools are useful for administering Active Directory and domain controllers.

1. Log on to SERVER01 as Administrator.
2. Click the Start button and, in the Start Search box, type **mmc.exe** and press Enter.

    An empty MMC appears. By default, the new console window is not maximized within the MMC. Maximize it to take advantage of the application's full size.

3. Choose Add/Remove Snap-in from the File menu.

    The Add Or Remove Snap-ins dialog box, shown in Figure 2-3, appears.

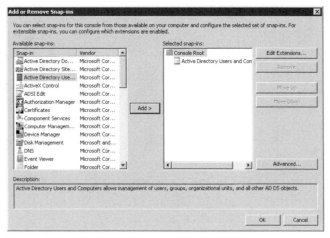

Figure 2-3   The Add Or Remove Snap-ins dialog box

    If you do not see the snap-ins listed that you want, be sure you've installed the RSAT.

4. In the Add Or Remove Snap-ins dialog box, select Active Directory Users And Computers from the Available Snap-ins list.
5. Click the Add button to add it to the Selected Snap-ins list.

    Notice that the Active Directory Schema snap-in is not available to add. The Active Directory Schema snap-in is installed with the Active Directory Domain Services role with the RSAT, but it is not registered, so it does not appear.

6. Click OK to close the Add Or Remove Snap-ins dialog box.
7. Click the Start button. In the Start Search box, type **cmd.exe**.
8. At the command prompt, type the **regsvr32.exe schmmgmt.dll** command.

    This command registers the dynamic link library (DLL) for the Active Directory Schema snap-in. This is necessary to do one time on a system before you can add the snap-in to a console.

9. A prompt will appear that indicates the registration was successful. Click OK.

10. Return to your custom MMC and repeat steps 2–6 to add the Active Directory Schema snap-in.

11. Choose Add/Remove Snap-in from the File menu.

12. In the Add Or Remove Snap-ins dialog box, select Computer Management from the Available Snap-ins list.

13. Click the Add button to add it to the Selected Snap-ins list.

    When a snap-in supports remote administration, you are prompted to select the computer you wish to manage, as shown in Figure 2-4.

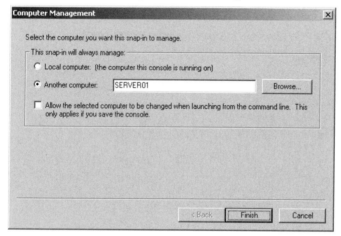

Figure 2-4   Selecting the computer to be managed by a snap-in

   ❑ To manage the computer on which the console is running, select Local Computer. This does not refer solely to the computer on which you are creating the console. If you launch the console from another computer, the console will manage that computer.

   ❑ To specify a single computer that the snap-in should manage, select Another Computer. Then, enter the computer's name or click Browse to select the computer.

14. Choose Another Computer and type **SERVER01** as the computer name.

15. Click Finish.

16. Click OK to close the Add Or Remove Snap-ins dialog box.

17. Choose Save from the File menu and save the console to your desktop with the name **MyConsole.msc**.

18. Close the console.

▶ **Exercise 2   Add a Snap-in to an MMC**

In this exercise, you will add Event Viewer to the console you created in Exercise 1. Event Viewer is useful to monitor activity on domain controllers.

1. Open MyConsole.msc.

   If you did not save the console to your desktop in Exercise 1, and instead saved the console to the default location, you will find it in the Start\All Programs\Administrative Tools folder.

2. Choose Add/Remove Snap-in from the File menu.

3. In the Add Or Remove Snap-ins dialog box, select Event Viewer from the Available Snap-ins list.

4. Click the Add button to add it to the Selected Snap-ins list.

   You will be prompted to select a computer to manage.

5. Choose Another Computer and type **SERVER01** as the computer name.

6. Click OK.

7. Click OK to close the Add Or Remove Snap-ins dialog box.

8. Save and close the console.

▶ **Exercise 3   Manage the Snap-ins of an MMC**

In this exercise, you will change the order of snap-ins and delete a snap-in. You will also learn about extension snap-ins.

1. Open MyConsole.msc.

2. Choose Add/Remove Snap-in from the File menu.

3. In the list of Selected snap-ins, select Event Viewer.

4. Click the Move Up button.

5. Select Active Directory Schema.

6. Click the Remove button.

7. In the list of Selected snap-ins, select Computer Management.

8. Click Edit Extensions.

   Extensions are snap-ins that exist within another snap-in to provide additional functionality. The Computer Management snap-in has many familiar snap-ins as extensions, each of which you can enable or disable.

9. Select Enable Only Selected Extensions.

10. Deselect Event Viewer. You have already added Event Viewer as a standalone snap-in for the console.

11. Click OK to close the Extensions For Computer Management dialog box.

12. Click OK to close the Add Or Remove Snap-in dialog box.

13. Save and close the console.

▶ **Exercise 4   Prepare a Console for Distribution to Users**

In this exercise, you will save your console in user mode so that users cannot add, remove, or modify snap-ins. Keep in mind that MMC users are typically administrators themselves.

1. Open MyConsole.msc.

2. Choose Options from the File menu.

3. In the Console Mode drop-down list, choose User Mode – Full Access.

4. Click OK.

5. Save and close the console.

6. Open the console by double-clicking it.

7. Click the File menu. Note that there is no *Add/Remove Snap-in* command.

8. Close the console.

9. Right-click the console and choose Author.

10. Click the File menu. In author mode, the *Add/Remove Snap-in* command appears.

11. Close the console.

Lesson Summary

- Windows administrative tools are snap-ins that can be added to an MMC. Active Directory Users And Computers and other Active Directory management snap-ins are also added to Server Manager and are contained in preconfigured consoles in the Administrative Tools folder.

- Administrators should not log on to their computers with administrative credentials. Instead, they should use a standard user account for logon and launch administrative tools by using the *Run As Administrator* command.

- Create a custom MMC that contains all the snap-ins you require to perform your job tasks. Such a console can be saved to a location where you, and possibly other administrators, can access it and launch it with administrative credentials. Ideally, this should be the only tool you need to run as administrator if it is fully customized to your needs.

- It is recommended that you save a console in user mode so that changes cannot be made to the console or its snap-ins.

- Consoles require that the appropriate administrative tools have been installed. Otherwise, console snap-ins will not function properly.

Lesson Review

You can use the following questions to test your knowledge of the information in Lesson 1, "Working with Active Directory Snap-ins." The questions are also available on the companion CD if you prefer to review them in electronic form.

NOTE Answers

Answers to these questions and explanations of why each answer choice is right or wrong are located in the "Answers" section at the end of the book.

---

1. You are a support professional for Contoso, Ltd. The domain's administrators have distributed a custom console with the Active Directory Users and Computers snap-in. When you open the console and attempt to reset a user's password, you receive Access Denied errors. You are certain that you have been delegated permission to reset passwords for users. What is the best solution?

    A. Close the custom console and open Server Manager. Use the Active Directory Users and Computers snap-in in Server Manager.

    B. Close the custom console and open a command prompt. Type **dsa.msc**.

    C. Close the custom console, and then right-click the console and choose Run As Administrator. Type the credentials for your secondary administrative account.

    D. Close the custom console, and then right-click the console and open a command prompt. Use the *DSMOD USER* command with the *-p* switch to change the user's password.

Lesson 2: Creating Objects in Active Directory

Active Directory is a directory service, and it is the role of a directory service to maintain information about enterprise resources, including users, groups, and computers. Resources are divided into OUs to facilitate manageability and visibility—that is, they can make it easier to find objects. In this lesson, you will learn how to create OUs, users, groups, and computers. You will also learn important skills to help you locate and find objects when you need them.

If you are experienced with Active Directory, you will be able to review the first few sections in this lesson quickly, but you might want to pay particular attention to the later sections, beginning with "Find Objects in Active Directory," because they will help you make better use of Active Directory tools.

The practice exercises at the end of this lesson will be important for you to complete because they create some of the objects that will be used in future practices.

After this lesson, you will be able to:
- Create users, groups, computers, and organizational units.
- Disable protection to delete an organizational unit.
- Customize and take advantage of views and features of the Active Directory Users and Computers snap-in to work effectively with objects in the directory.
- Create saved queries to provide rule-based views of objects in the directory.

Estimated lesson time: 45 minutes

Creating an Organizational Unit

Organizational units (OUs) are administrative containers within Active Directory that are used to collect objects that share common requirements for administration, configuration, or visibility. What this means will become clearer as you learn more about OU design and management. For now, just understand that OUs provide an administrative hierarchy similar to the folder hierarchy of a disk drive: OUs create *collections* of objects that belong together for *administration*. The term *administration* is emphasized here because OUs are not used to assign permissions to resources—that is what groups are for. Users are placed into groups that are given permission to resources. OUs are administrative containers within which those users and groups can be managed by administrators.

To create an organizational unit:

1. Open the Active Directory Users And Computers snap-in.
2. Right-click the Domain node or the OU node in which you want to add the new OU, choose New, and then select Organizational Unit.

3. Type the name of the organizational unit.

   Be sure to follow the naming conventions of your organization.

4. Select Protect Container From Accidental Deletion.

   You'll learn more about this option later in this section.

5. Click OK.

   OUs have other properties that can be useful to configure. These properties can be set after the object has been created.

6. Right-click the OU and choose Properties.

   Follow the naming conventions and other standards and processes of your organization. You can use the *Description* field to explain the purpose of an OU.

   If an OU represents a physical location, such as an office, the OU's address properties can be useful.

   The Managed By tab can be used to link to the user or group that is responsible for the OU. Click the Change button underneath the Name box. By default, the Select User, Contact, Or Group dialog box that appears does not, despite its name, search for groups; to search for groups, you must first click the Object Types button and select Groups. You'll learn about the Select Users, Contacts, Or Groups dialog box later in this lesson. The remaining contact information on the Managed By tab is populated from the account specified in the Name box. The Managed By tab is used solely for contact infor-mation—the specified user or group does not gain any permissions or access to the OU.

7. Click OK.

The Windows Server 2008 administrative tools add a new option: the Protect Container From Accidental Deletion. This option adds a safety switch to the OU so that it cannot be accidentally deleted. Two permissions are added to the OU: Everyone::Deny::Delete and Every-one::Deny::Delete Subtree. No user, not even an administrator, will be able to delete the OU and its contents accidentally. It is highly recommended that you enable this protection for all new OUs.

If you want to delete the OU, you must first turn off the safety switch. To delete a protected OU, follow these steps:

1. In the Active Directory Users And Computers snap-in, click the View menu and select Advanced Features.

2. Right-click the OU and choose Properties.

3. Click the Object tab.

   If you do not see the Object tab, you did not enable Advanced Features in step 1.

4. Clear the check box labeled Protect Object From Accidental Deletion.

5. Click OK.

6. Right-click the OU and choose Delete.

7. You will be prompted to confirm that you want to delete the OU. Click Yes.

8. If the OU contains any other objects, you will be prompted by the Confirm Subtree Deletion dialog box to confirm that you want to delete the OU and all the objects it contains. Click Yes.

Quick Check

■ You attempt to delete an OU and receive an insufficient privileges error. You are logged on as a member of Domain Admins, so you are certain you should have permission to delete an OU. What is happening and what must you change to delete the OU?

Quick Check Answer

■ The OU is protected from accidental deletion. You must deselect the option to protect the object from accidental deletion. The option is located on the Object tab of the OU's Properties dialog box, which is accessible only when Advanced Features is enabled.

Creating a User Object

To create a new user in Active Directory, perform the following steps. Be certain to follow the naming conventions and processes specified by your organization.

1. Open the Active Directory Users And Computers snap-in.

2. In the console tree, expand the node that represents your domain (for instance, *contoso.com*) and navigate to the OU or container (for example, Users) in which you want to create the user account.

3. Right-click the OU or container, choose New, and then select User.

   The New Object – User dialog box appears, as shown in Figure 2-5.

4. In First Name, type the user's first name.

5. In Initials, type the user's middle initial(s).

   Note that this property is, in fact, meant for the initials of a user's middle name, not the initials of the user's first and last name.

6. In Last Name, type the user's last name.

7. The *Full Name* field is populated automatically. Make modifications to it if necessary.

   The *Full Name* field is used to create several attributes of a user object, most notably the common name (CN), and to display name properties. The CN of a user is the name displayed in the details pane of the snap-in. It must be unique within the container or OU. Therefore, if you are creating a user object for a person with the same name as an existing user in the same OU or container, you will need to enter a unique name in the *Full Name* field.

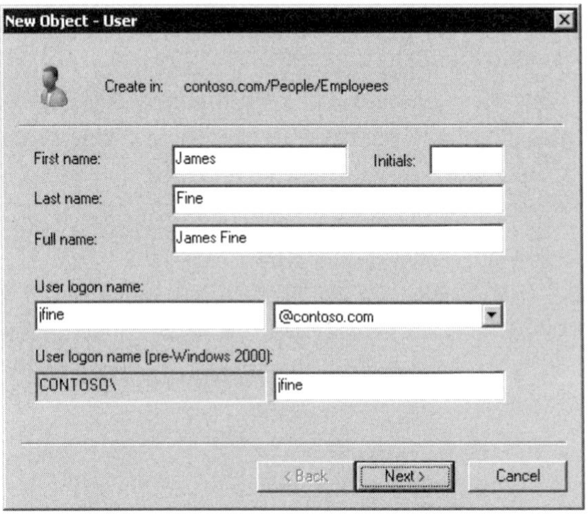

Figure 2-5   New Object – User dialog box

8. In User Logon Name, type the name that the user will log on with and, from the drop-down list, select the user principle name (UPN) suffix that will be appended to the user logon name following the @ symbol.

   User names in Active Directory can contain some special characters (including periods, hyphens, and apostrophes), which enable you to generate accurate user names such as O'Hara and Smith-Bates. However, certain applications can have other restrictions, so it is recommended to use only standard letters and numerals until you have fully tested the applications in your enterprise for compatibility with special characters in logon names.

   The list of available UPN suffixes can be managed using the Active Directory Domains And Trusts snap-in. Right-click the root of the snap-in, Active Directory Domains And Trusts, choose Properties, and then use the UPN Suffixes tab to add or remove suffixes. The DNS name of your Active Directory domain will always be available as a suffix and cannot be removed.

9. In the User logon name (Pre-Windows 2000) box of the Active Directory Users And Computers snap-in, enter the pre-Windows 2000 logon name, often called the down-level logon name.

   In Chapter 3, "Users," you will learn about the two different logon names.

10. Click Next.

11. Enter an initial password for the user in the Password and Confirm Password boxes.

12. Select User Must Change Password At Next Logon.

    It is recommended that you always select this option so that the user can create a new password unknown to the IT staff. Appropriate support staff members can always reset the user's password at a future date if they need to log on as the user or access the user's resources. However, only users should know their passwords on a day-to-day basis.

13. Click Next.

14. Review the summary and click Finish.

The New Object – User interface enables you to configure a limited number of account-related properties such as name and password settings. However, a user object in Active Directory supports dozens of additional properties. These can be configured after the object has been created.

15. Right-click the user object you created and choose Properties.

16. Configure user properties.

Be certain to follow the naming conventions and other standards of your organization.

You will learn more about many of the user properties in Chapter 3 and Chapter 8, "Authentication."

17. Click OK.

Creating a Group Object

Groups are an important class of object because they are used to collect users, computers, and other groups to create a single point of management. The most straightforward and common use of a group is to grant permissions to a shared folder. If a group has been given read access to a folder, for example, then any of the group's members will be able to read the folder. You do not have to grant read access directly to each individual member; you can manage access to the folder simply by adding and removing members of the group.

To create a group:

1. Open the Active Directory Users And Computers snap-in.

2. In the console tree, expand the node that represents your domain (for instance, *contoso.com*) and navigate to the OU or container (such as Users) in which you want to create the group.

3. Right-click the OU or container, choose New, and then select Group.

The New Object – Group dialog box appears, as shown in Figure 2-6.

4. Type the name of the new group in the Group Name box.

Most organizations have naming conventions that specify how group names should be created. Be sure to follow the guidelines of your organization.

By default, the name you type is also entered as the pre-Windows 2000 name of the new group. It is very highly recommended that you keep the two names the same.

5. Do not change the name in the Group Name (Pre-Windows 2000) box.

6. Choose the Group type.

❑ A Security group can be given permissions to resources. It can also be configured as an e-mail distribution list.

❏ A Distribution group is an e-mail–enabled group that cannot be given permissions to resources and is, therefore, used only when a group is an e-mail distribution list that has no possible requirement for access to resources.

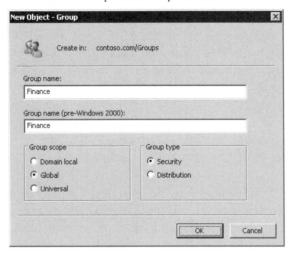

Figure 2-6   The New Object – Group dialog box

7. Select the Group Scope.

   ❏ A Global group is used to identify users based on criteria such as job function, location, and so on.

   ❏ A Domain local group is used to collect users and groups who share similar resource access needs, such as all users who need to be able to modify a project report.

   ❏ A Universal group is used to collect users and groups from multiple domains.

   Group scope will be discussed in more detail in Chapter 4, "Groups."

   Note that if the domain in which you are creating the group object is at a mixed or interim domain functional level, you can select only Domain Local or Global scopes for security groups. Domain functional levels will be discussed in Chapter 13, "Domains and Forests."

8. Click OK.

   Group objects have a number of properties that are useful to configure. These can be specified after the object has been created.

9. Right-click the group and choose Properties.

10. Enter the properties for the group.

    Be sure to follow the naming conventions and other standards of your organization.

    The group's Members and Member Of tabs specify who belongs to the group and what groups the group itself belongs to. Group membership will be discussed in Chapter 4.

The group's *Description* field, because it is easily visible in the details pane of the Active Directory Users And Computers snap-in, is a good place to summarize the purpose of the group and the contact information for the individual(s) responsible for deciding who is and is not a member of the group.

The group's *Notes* field can be used to provide more detail about the group.

The Managed By tab can be used to link to the user or group that is responsible for the group. Click the Change button underneath the Name box. To search for a group, you must first click the Object Types button and select Groups. The Select User, Contact, Or Group dialog box will be discussed later in this lesson.

The remaining contact information on the Managed By tab is populated from the account specified in the Name box. The Managed By tab is typically used for contact information so that if a user wants to join the group, you can decide who in the business should be contacted to authorize the new member. However, if you select the Manager Can Update Membership List option, the account specified in the Name box will be given permission to add and remove members of the group. This is one method to delegate administrative control over the group. Other delegation options are discussed in Lesson 3.

11. Click OK.

Creating a Computer Object

Computers are represented as accounts and objects in Active Directory, just as users are. In fact, behind the scenes, a computer logs on to the domain just as a user does. The computer has a user name—the computer's name with a dollar sign appended, for instance, DESKTOP101$—and a password that is established when you join the computer to the domain, and it's changed automatically every thirty days or so thereafter. To create a computer object in Active Directory:

1. Open the Active Directory Users And Computers snap-in.
2. In the console tree, expand the node that represents your domain (such as *contoso.com*) and navigate to the OU or container (for instance, Users) in which you want to create the computer.
3. Right-click the OU or container, choose New, and then select Computer.

   The New Object – Computer dialog box appears, as seen in Figure 2-7.
4. In the Computer Name box, type the computer's name.

   Your entry will automatically populate the Computer Name (Pre-Windows 2000) box.
5. Do not change the name in the Computer Name (Pre-Windows 2000) box.
6. The account specified in the *User Or Group* field will be able to join the computer to the domain. The default value is Domain Admins. Click Change to select another group or user.

Generally, you will select a group that represents your deployment, desktop support, or help desk team. You can also select the user to whom the computer is assigned. You will explore the issues related to joining the computer to the domain in Chapter 5, "Computers."

7. Do not select the check box labeled Assign This Computer Account As A Pre-Windows 2000 Computer unless the account is for a computer running Microsoft Windows NT 4.0.

Figure 2-7   The New Object – Computer dialog box

8. Click OK.

   Computer objects have a number of properties that are useful to configure. These can be specified after the object has been created.

9. Right-click the computer and choose Properties.

10. Enter the properties for the computer.

   Be sure to follow the naming conventions and other standards of your organization.

   The computer's *Description* field can be used to indicate who the computer is assigned to, its role (for instance, a training-room computer), or other descriptive information. Because Description is visible in the details pane of the Active Directory Users And Computers snap-in, it is a good place to store the information you find most useful to know about a computer.

   There are several properties that describe the computer, including DNS Name, DC Type, Site, Operating System Name, Version, and Service Pack. These properties will be populated automatically when the computer joins the domain.

   The Managed By tab can be used to link to the user or group responsible for the computer. Click the Change button underneath the Name box. To search for groups, you must first click the Object Types button and select Groups. The Select Users, Contacts,

Or Groups dialog box is discussed later in this lesson. The remaining contact information on the Managed By tab is populated from the account specified in the Name box.
The Managed By tab is typically used for contact information. Some organizations use
the tab to indicate the support team (group) responsible for the computer. Others use
the information to track the user to whom the computer is assigned.

11. Click OK.

Finding Objects in Active Directory

You have learned how to create objects in Active Directory, but what good is information in a
directory service if you can't get it out of the directory as well? You will need to locate objects
in Active Directory on many occasions:

- **Granting permissions**   When you configure permissions for a file or folder, you must
  select the group (or user) to which permissions should be assigned.
- **Adding members to groups**   A group's membership can consist of users, computers,
  groups, or any combination of the three. When you add an object as a member of a
  group, you must select the object.
- **Creating links**   Linked properties are properties of one object that refer to another
  object. Group membership is, in fact, a linked property. Other linked properties, such as
  the *Managed By* attribute discussed earlier, are also links. When you specify the *Managed
  By* name, you must select the appropriate user or group.
- **Looking up an object**   You can search for any object in your Active Directory domain.

There are many other situations that will entail searching Active Directory, and you will
encounter several user interfaces. In this section, you'll learn some techniques for working
with each.

Controlling the View of Objects in the Active Directory Users and Computers Snap-in

The details pane of the Active Directory Users and Computers snap-in can be customized to
help you work effectively with the objects in your directory. Use the *Add/Remove Columns*
command on the View menu to add columns to the details pane. Not every attribute is available to be displayed as a column, but you are certain to find columns that will be useful to display such as User Logon Name. You might also find columns that are unnecessary. If your
OUs have only one type of object (user or computer, for example), the Type column might not
be helpful.

When a column is visible, you can change the order of columns by dragging the column headings to the left or right. You can also sort the view in the details pane by clicking the column:
the first click will sort in ascending order, the second in descending order, just like Windows
Explorer. A common customization is to add the Last Name column to a view of users so they

can be sorted by last name. It is generally easier to find users by last name than by the Name column, which is the CN and generally first name/last name.

Using Saved Queries

Windows Server 2003 introduced the Saved Queries node of the Active Directory Users and Computers snap-in. This powerful function enables you to create rule-driven views of your domain, displaying objects across one or more OUs. To create a saved query:

1. Open the Active Directory Users And Computers snap-in.

    Saved Queries is not available in the Active Directory Users And Computers snap-in that is part of Server Manager. You must use the Active Directory Users And Computers console or a custom console with the snap-in.

2. Right-click Saved Queries, choose New, and then select Query.

3. Type a name for the query.

4. Optionally, enter a description.

5. Click Browse to locate the root for the query.

    The search will be limited to the domain or OU you select. It is recommended to narrow your search as much as possible to improve search performance.

6. Click Define Query to define your query.

7. In the Find Common Queries dialog box, select the type of object you want to query.

    The tabs in the dialog box and the input controls on each tab change to provide options that are appropriate for the selected query.

8. Click OK.

After your query is created, it is saved within the instance of the Active Directory Users And Computers snap-in, so if you open the Active Directory Users And Computers console (*dsa.msc*), your query will be available the next time you open the console. If you created the saved query in a custom console, it will be available in that custom console. To transfer saved queries to other consoles or users, you can export the saved query as an XML file and then import it to the target snap-in.

The view in the details pane of the saved query can be customized as described earlier, with specific columns and sorting. A very important benefit of saved queries is that the customized view is specific to each saved query. When you add the Last Name column to the "normal" view of an OU, the Last Name column is actually added to the view of *every* OU, so you will see an empty Last Name column even for an OU of computers or groups. With saved queries, you can add the Last Name column to a query for user objects and other columns for other saved queries.

Saved queries are a powerful way to virtualize the view of your directory and monitor for issues such as disabled or locked accounts. Learning to create and manage saved queries is a worthwhile use of your time.

MORE INFO   Saved queries

The following site is highly recommended for details and examples of saved queries: *http://www.petri.co.il/saved_queries_in_windows_2003_dsa.htm.*

Using the Select Users, Contacts, Computers, Or Groups Dialog Box

When you add a member to a group, assign a permission, or create a linked property, you are presented with the Select Users, Contacts, Computers, Or Groups dialog box shown in Figure 2-8. This dialog box is referred to as the *Select dialog box* throughout this training kit. If you'd like to see an example, open the properties of a group object, click the Members tab, and then click the Add button.

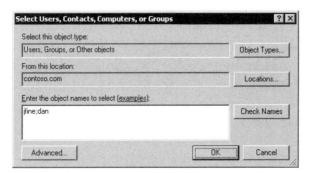

Figure 2-8   Select Users, Contacts, Computers, Or Groups dialog box

If you know the names of the objects you need, you can type them directly into the Enter The Object Names To Select text box. Multiple names can be entered, separated by semicolons, as shown in Figure 2-8. When you click OK, Windows looks up each item in the list and converts it into a link to the object, then closes the dialog box. The Check Names button also converts each name to a link but leaves the dialog box open, as shown in Figure 2-9.

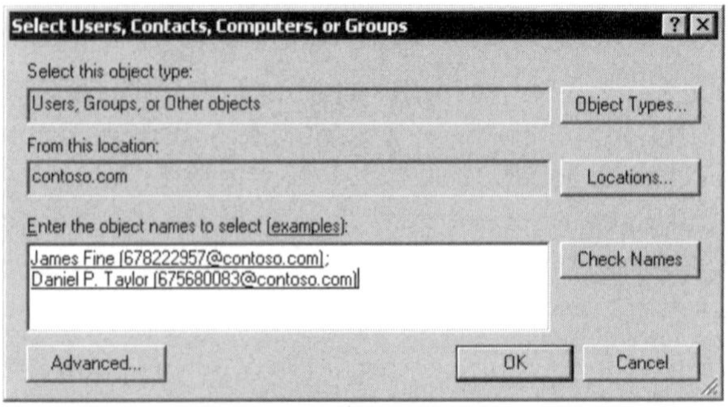

Figure 2-9   Names resolved to links using the Check Names button

You do not need to enter the full name; you can enter partial names instead. For example, Figure 2-8 shows the names jfine and dan. When you click OK or Check Names, Windows will attempt to convert your partial name to the correct object. If there is only one matching object, such as the logon name jfine, the name will be resolved as shown in Figure 2-9. If there are multiple matches, such as the name Dan, the Multiple Names Found box, shown in Figure 2-10, appears. Select the correct name(s) and click OK. The selected name appears as shown in Figure 2-9.

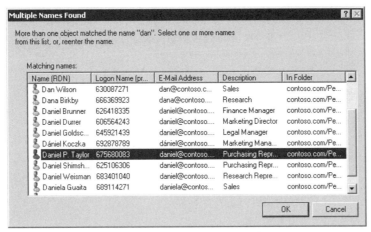

Figure 2-10   The Multiple Names Found dialog box

By default, the Select dialog box searches the entire domain. If you are getting too many results and wish to narrow the scope of your search, or if you need to search another domain or the local users and groups on a domain member, click Locations.

Additionally, the Select dialog box, despite its full name—Select Users, Contacts, Computers, Or Groups—rarely searches all four object types. When you add members to a group, for example, computers are not searched by default. If you enter a computer name, it will not be resolved correctly. When you specify Name on the Managed By tab, groups are not searched by default. You must make sure that the Select dialog box is scoped to resolve the types of objects you want to select. Click the Object Types button, use the Object Types dialog box shown in Figure 2-11 to select the correct types, and then click OK.

If you are having trouble locating the objects you want, click the Advanced button on the Select dialog box. The advanced view, shown in Figure 2-12, enables you to search both name and description fields as well as disabled accounts, nonexpiring passwords, and stale accounts that have not logged on for a specific period of time. Some of the fields on the Common Queries tab might be disabled, depending on the object type you are searching. Click the Object Types button to specify exactly the type of object you want.

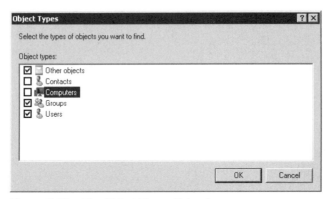

Figure 2-11   The Object Types dialog box

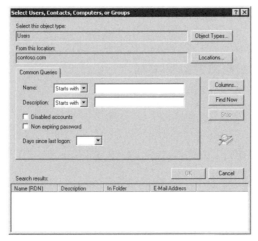

Figure 2-12   The advanced view of the Select dialog box

Using the *Find* Commands

Windows systems also provide the Active Directory query tool, called the Find box by many administrators. One way to launch the Find box is to click the Find Objects In Active Directory Domain Services button on the toolbar in the Active Directory Users And Computers snap-in. The button and the resulting Find box are shown in Figure 2-13.

Use the Find drop-down list to specify the type(s) of objects you want to query or select Common Queries or Custom Search. The In drop-down list specifies the scope of the search. It is recommended that, whenever possible, you narrow the scope of the search to avoid the performance impact of a large, domain-wide search. Together, the Find and the In lists define the scope of the search.

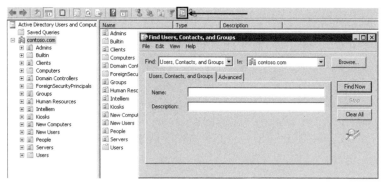

Figure 2-13   The Find box

Next, configure the search criteria. Commonly used fields are available as criteria based on the type of query you are performing. For the most complete, advanced control over the query, choose Custom Search in the Find drop-down list. If you choose Custom Search and then click the Advanced tab, you can build powerful LDAP queries. For example, the query **OU=*main*** searches for any OU with a name that contains *main* and would return the Domain Controllers OU. Without the custom search, you can search based on the text at the *beginning* of the name only; the custom search with wildcards enables you to build a "contains" search.

When you have specified your search scope and criteria, click Find Now. The results will appear. You can then right-click any item in the results list and perform commands such as *Move*, *Delete*, and *Properties*.

The Find box also appears in other Windows locations, including the Add Printer Wizard when locating a network printer. The Network folder also has a Search Active Directory button. You can add a custom shortcut, perhaps to your Start menu or desktop, to make searches even more accessible. The target of the shortcut should be *rundll32 dsquery,OpenQueryWindow*.

Finding Objects by Using *Dsquery*

Windows provides command-line utilities that perform functionality similar to that of user interface tools, such as the Active Directory Users and Computers snap-in. Many of those commands begin with the letters DS, so they are often referred to as *the DS commands*. *Dsquery* can locate objects in Active Directory.

Dsquery, like other DS commands, is well documented. Type **dsquery.exe /?** to learn its syntax and usage. Most DS commands are used by specifying the object class you want the command to work against. For example, you would type **dsquery user** to look for a user, whereas *Dsquery computer*, *Dsquery group*, and *Dsquery ou* would query for their respective object types. Following the object type specifier, you can use switches to indicate the criteria for the query. Each object can be located by its name, for example, with the *-name* switch. Most objects can be queried based on the description (*-desc*). Security principals can be located based on their pre-Windows 2000 logon name (*-samid*). To learn which properties may be queried, type **dsquery objecttype /?**.

For example, if you want to locate all users whose names begin with "Jam," you would type **dsquery user -name jam***. After the property switch, *name* in this case, you can enter the criteria, which are not case sensitive and can include wildcards such as the asterisk, which represents any zero or more characters. The *Dsquery* command returns matching objects with their distinguished names (DNs) by default, as you can see in Figure 2-14.

```
c:\>dsquery user -name jam*
"CN=James D. Kramer,OU=Employees,OU=People,DC=contoso,DC=com"
"CN=James Fine,OU=People,DC=contoso,DC=com"
"CN=James Hendergart,OU=Employees,OU=People,DC=contoso,DC=com"
"CN=James R. Hamilton,OU=Employees,OU=People,DC=contoso,DC=com"
"CN=James van Eaton,OU=Employees,OU=People,DC=contoso,DC=com"
"CN=Jamie Reding,OU=Employees,OU=People,DC=contoso,DC=com"
```

Figure 2-14   The *Dsquery* command

If DNs are not the way you'd like to see the results, add the *-o* switch to the *Dsquery* command. You can add *-o samid*, for example, to return the results with pre-Windows 2000 logon names, or *-o upn* to return the list as user logon names, called UPNs.

Understanding DNs, RDNs, and CNs

DNs are a kind of path to an object in Active Directory. Each object in Active Directory has a completely unique DN. Our user, James Fine, has the DN CN=James Fine,OU=People,DC=contoso,DC=com.

You can see what is happening: the DN is a path starting at the object and working up to the top-level domain in the *contoso.com* DNS namespace. As mentioned earlier, CN stands for common name, and when you create a user, the Full Name box is used to create the CN of the user object. OU means organizational unit, not surprisingly. And DC means domain component.

The portion of the DN prior to the first OU or container is called the *relative distinguished name*, or RDN. In the case of James Fine, the RDN of the object is CN=James Fine. Not every RDN is a CN. The DN of the People OU is OU=People,DC=contoso,DC=com. The RDN of the People OU is, therefore, OU=People.

Because the DN of an object must be unique within the directory service, the RDN of an object must be unique within its container. That's why if you hire a second James Fine, and if both user objects should be in the same OU, you will have to give that user a different CN. The same logic applies as files in a folder: you cannot have two files with identical names in a single folder.

You will encounter DNs regularly as you work with Active Directory, just as you encounter file paths regularly if you work with files and folders. It's very important to be able to read them and interpret them.

PRACTICE Creating and Locating Objects in Active Directory

In this practice, you will create and then locate objects in Active Directory. You will create OUs, users, groups, and computers. You will then create a saved query and customize the view of that saved query. The objects you create in this practice will be used in other practices in this training kit.

▶ **Exercise 1   Create Organizational Units**

The default Users and Computers containers are provided to facilitate the setup of and migration to an Active Directory domain. It is recommended that you create OUs that reflect your administrative model and that you use these OUs to create and manage objects in your directory service. In this exercise, you will create OUs for the example domain, *contoso.com*. These OUs will be used in practices and exercises later in this training kit.

1. Log on to SERVER01 as Administrator.
2. Open the Active Directory Users And Computers snap-in.
3. Expand the Domain node.
4. Right-click the Domain node, choose New, and then select Organizational Unit.
5. Type the name of the organizational unit: **People**.
6. Select Protect Container From Accidental Deletion.
7. Click OK.
8. Right-click the OU and choose Properties.
9. In the *Description* field, type **Non-administrative user identities**.
10. Click OK.
11. Repeat steps 2–10 to create the following OUs.

OU Name	OU Description
Clients	Client computers
Groups	Non-administrative groups
Admins	Administrative identities and groups
Servers	Servers

▶ **Exercise 2   Create Users**

Now that you have created OUs in the *contoso.com* domain, you are ready to populate the directory service with objects. In this exercise, you will create several users in two of the OUs you created in Exercise 1, "Create Organizational Units." These user objects will be used in practices and exercises later in this training kit.

1. Log on to SERVER01 as Administrator and open the Active Directory Users And Computers snap-in.

2. Follow the procedure in the "Creating a User Object" section earlier in the chapter and create the following users in the People OU. For each user, create a complex, secure password. Remember the passwords you assign—you will be logging on as these user accounts in other exercises and practices in this training kit.

3. In the console tree, expand the Domain node, *contoso.com*, and select the People OU.

4. Right-click the People OU, choose New, and then select User.

 The New Object – User dialog box appears.

5. In First Name, type the user's first name: **Dan**.

6. In Last Name, type the user's last name: **Holme**.

7. In User Logon Name, type the user's logon name: **dholme**.

8. In the User Logon Name (Pre-Windows 2000) text box, enter the pre-Windows 2000 logon name: **dholme**.

9. Click Next.

10. Enter an initial password for the user in the Password and Confirm Password boxes.

 The default password policy for an Active Directory domain requires a password of seven or more characters. Additionally, the password must contain three of four character types: upper case (A–Z), lower case (a–z), numeric (0–9), and nonalphanumeric (for example, ! @ # $ %). The password cannot contain any of the user's name or logon name attributes.

 Remember the password you assign to this user; you will be logging on as this user account in other exercises and practices in this training kit.

 Many training resources suggest using a generic password such as P@ssword. You may use a generic password for the practices in this training kit; however, it is recommended that you create unique passwords, even in a practice, so that you are using best practices even in a lab environment.

11. Select User Must Change Password At Next Logon.

12. Click Next.

13. Review the summary and click Finish.

14. Right-click the user object you created and choose Properties.

15. Examine the attributes that can be configured in the Properties dialog box. Do not change any of the user's properties at this time.

16. Click OK.

17. Repeat steps 3–12 and create the following users in the People OU.
 - ❏ James Fine
   - First name: James
   - Last name: Fine

- Full name: James Fine
- User logon name: jfine
  ❑ Barbara Mayer
    - First name: Barbara
    - Last name: Mayer
    - Full name: Barbara Mayer
    - User logon name: bmayer
    - Pre-Windows 2000 logon name: bmayer
  ❑ Barbara Moreland
    - First name: Barbara
    - Last name: Moreland
    - Full name: Barbara Moreland
    - User logon name: bmoreland
    - Pre-Windows 2000 logon name: bmoreland

18. Repeat steps 3–12 and create a user account for yourself in the People OU. For the user logon name, use your first initial and last name, for example, dholme for Dan Holme. Create a complex, secure password and remember it because you will be logging on as this account in other exercises and practices in this training kit.

19. Repeat steps 3–12 and create an administrative account for yourself in the Admins OU. This account will be given administrative privileges. Create the user object in the Admins OU rather than in the People OU. For the user logon name, use your first initial and last name, followed by _admin, for instance, dholme_admin for Dan Holme's administrative account. Create a complex, secure password and remember it because you will be logging on as this account in other exercises and practices in this training kit.

▶ **Exercise 3   Create Computers**

Computer accounts should be created before joining machines to the domain. In this exercise, you will create several computers in two of the OUs you created in Exercise 1. These computer objects will be used in practices and exercises later in this training kit.

1. Log on to SERVER01 as Administrator and open the Active Directory Users And Computers snap-in.

2. In the console tree, expand the Domain node, *contoso.com*, and select the Servers OU.

3. Right-click the Servers OU, choose New, and then select Computer.
   The New Object – Computer dialog box appears.

4. In the Computer Name box, type the computer's name: **FILESERVER01**.
   Your entry will automatically populate the Computer Name (Pre-Windows 2000) box.

5. Do not change the name in the Computer Name (Pre-Windows 2000) box.

6. Take note of the account specified in the User Or Group Field text box. Do not change the value at this time.

7. Do not select the check box labeled Assign This Computer Account As A Pre-Windows 2000 Computer.

8. Click OK.

9. Right-click the computer and choose Properties.

10. Examine the properties that are available for a computer. Do not change any attributes at this time.

11. Click OK.

12. Repeat steps 3–8 to create computer objects for the following computers:
    - ❑ SHAREPOINT02
    - ❑ EXCHANGE03

13. Repeat steps 3–8 and create the following computers in the Clients OU rather than in the Servers OU.
    - ❑ DESKTOP101
    - ❑ DESKTOP102
    - ❑ LAPTOP103

▶ **Exercise 4   Create Groups**

It is a best practice to manage objects in groups rather than to manage each object individually. In this exercise, you will create several groups in two of the OUs you created in Exercise 1. These groups will be used in practices and exercises later in this training kit.

1. Log on to SERVER01 as Administrator and open the Active Directory Users And Computers snap-in.

2. In the console tree, expand the Domain node, *contoso.com*, and select the Groups OU.

3. Right-click the Groups OU, choose New, and then select Group.

   The New Object – Group dialog box appears.

4. Type the name of the new group in the Group Name text box: **Finance**.

5. Do not change the name in the Group Name (Pre-Windows 2000) box.

6. Select the Group Type: Security.

7. Select the Group Scope: Global.

8. Click OK.

   Group objects have a number of properties that are useful to configure. These can be specified after the object has been created.

9. Right-click the group and choose Properties.
10. Examine the properties available for the group. Do not change any attributes at this time.
11. Click OK.
12. Repeat steps 3–8 to create the following global security groups in the Groups OU:
    - ❑ Finance Managers
    - ❑ Sales
    - ❑ APP_Office 2007
13. Repeat steps 3–8 to create the following global security groups in the Admins OU rather than in the Groups OU.
    - ❑ Help Desk
    - ❑ Windows Administrators

▶ **Exercise 5   Add Users and Computers to Groups**

Now that you have created groups, you can add objects as members of the groups. In this exercise, you will add users and computers to groups. Along the way, you will gain experience with the Select dialog box that is used in some procedures to locate objects in Active Directory.

1. Log on to SERVER01 as Administrator and open the Active Directory Users And Computers snap-in.
2. Open the properties of your administrative account in the Admins OU.
3. Click the Member Of tab.
4. Click the Add button.
5. In the Select Groups dialog box, type the name **Domain Admins**.
6. Click OK.
7. Click OK again to close the account properties.
8. Open the properties of the Help Desk group in the Admins OU.
9. Click the Members tab.
10. Click the Add button.
11. In the Select dialog box, type **Barb**.
12. Click Check Names.
    The Multiple Names Found box appears.
13. Select Barbara Mayer and click OK.
14. Click OK to close the Select dialog box.
15. Click OK again to close the group properties.
16. Open the properties of the APP_Office 2007 group in the Groups OU.
17. Click the Members tab.

18. Click the Add button.
19. In the Select dialog box, type **DESKTOP101**.
20. Click Check Names.

    A Name Not Found dialog box appears, indicating that the object you specified could not be resolved.

21. Click Cancel to close the Name Not Found box.
22. In the Select box, click Object Types.
23. Select Computers as an object type and click OK.
24. Click Check Names. The name will resolve now that the Select box is including computers in its resolution.
25. Click OK.

▶ **Exercise 6   Find Objects in Active Directory**

When you need to find an object in your domain's directory service, it is sometimes more efficient to use search functionality than to click through your OU structure to browse for the object. In this exercise, you will use three interfaces for locating objects in Active Directory.

1. Log on to SERVER01 and open the Active Directory Users And Computers snap-in.
2. Click the Find Objects In Active Directory Domain Services button.
3. Make sure the In drop-down list is set to *contoso.com* (the domain name).
4. In the Name box, type **Barb**.
5. Click Find Now.
6. The two users named Barbara should appear in the Search results.
7. Close the Find box.
8. Open Network from the Start menu.
9. Click Search Active Directory.
10. Repeat steps 3–7.
11. In the Active Directory Users And Computers snap-in, right-click the Saved Queries node, choose New, and then choose Query.

    If Saved Queries is not visible, close the console and open the Active Directory Users And Computers console from the Administrative Tools folder of Control Panel.

12. In the Name box, type **All Users**.
13. In the Description box, type **Users for the entire domain**.
14. Click Define Query.
15. On the Users tab, in the Name box, choose Has A Value.

16. Click OK twice to close the dialog boxes.

     The results of the saved query appear. Note that it shows the users from both the People OU and the Admins OU.

17. Choose View, and then click Add/Remove Columns.

18. In the Available columns list, select Last Name and click the Add button.

19. In the Displayed columns list, select Type and click the Remove button.

20. Click OK.

21. Drag the Last Name column heading so that it is between Name and Description.

22. Click the Last Name column heading so that users are sorted alphabetically by last name.

Lesson Summary

- Organizational units (OUs) are administrative containers that collect objects sharing similar requirements for administration, configuration, or visibility. They provide a way to access and manage a collection of users, groups, computers, or other objects easily. An OU cannot be given permission to a resource such as a shared folder.

- When you create an object such as a user, computer, or group, you are able to configure only a limited number of its properties while creating it. After creating the object, you can open its properties and configure the attributes that were not visible during creation.

- Object properties such as Description, Managed By, and Notes can be used to document important information about an object.

- By default, OUs are created with protection, which prevents the accidental deletion of the OU. To disable protection, you must turn on Advanced Features from the View menu. Then, in the properties of the OU, click the Object tab to deselect protection.

Lesson Review

You can use the following questions to test your knowledge of the information in Lesson 2, "Creating Objects in Active Directory." The questions are also available on the companion CD if you prefer to review them in electronic form.

NOTE Answers

Answers to these questions and explanations of why each answer choice is right or wrong are located in the "Answers" section at the end of the book.

---

1. You have opened a command prompt, using Run As Administrator, with credentials in the Domain Admins group. You use the *Dsrm* command to remove an OU that had been created accidentally by James, a member of the Administrators group of the domain. You receive the response: Dsrm Failed: Access Is Denied. What is the cause of the error?

    A. You must launch the command prompt as a member of Administrators to perform Active Directory tasks.

    B. Only Administrators can delete OUs.

    C. Only the owner of the OU can delete an OU.

    D. The OU is protected from deletion.

Lesson 3: Delegation and Security of Active Directory Objects

In previous lessons of this chapter, you've learned how to create users, groups, computers, and OUs and how to access the properties of those objects. Your ability to perform those actions was dependent on your membership in the Administrators group of the domain. You would not want every user on your help desk team to be a member of the domain's Administrators group just to reset user passwords and unlock user accounts. Instead, you should enable the help desk and each role in your organization to perform the tasks that are required of the role and no more. In this lesson, you'll learn how to delegate specific administrative tasks within Active Directory, which is achieved by changing the access control lists (ACLs) on Active Directory objects.

> **After this lesson, you will be able to:**
> - Describe the business purpose of delegation.
> - Assign permissions to Active Directory objects by using the security editor user interfaces and the Delegation of Control Wizard.
> - View and report permissions on Active Directory objects by using user interface and command-line tools.
> - Evaluate effective permissions for a user or group.
> - Reset the permissions on an object to its default.
> - Describe the relationship between delegation and OU design.
>
> **Estimated lesson time: 35 minutes**

Understanding Delegation

In most organizations, there is more than one administrator, and as organizations grow, administrative tasks are often distributed to various administrators or support organizations. For example, in many organizations, the help desk is able to reset user passwords and unlock the accounts of users who are locked out. This capability of the help desk is a delegated administrative task. The help desk cannot, usually, create new user accounts, but it can make specific changes to existing user accounts.

All Active Directory objects, such as the users, computers, and groups you created in the previous lesson, can be secured using a list of permissions, so you could give your help desk permission to reset passwords on user objects. The permissions on an object are called *access control entries* (ACEs), and they are assigned to users, groups, or computers (called *security principals*). ACEs are saved in the object's discretionary access control list (DACL). The DACL is a part of the object's ACL, which also contains the system access control list (SACL) that includes auditing settings. This might sound familiar to you if you have studied the permissions on files and folders—the terms and concepts are identical.

The delegation of administrative control, also called the delegation of control or just delegation, simply means assigning permissions that manage access to objects and properties in Active Directory. Just as you can give a group the ability to change files in a folder, you can give a group the ability to reset passwords on user objects.

Viewing the ACL of an Active Directory Object

At the lowest level is the ACL on an individual user object in Active Directory. To view the ACL on an object:

1. Open the Active Directory Users And Computers snap-in.
2. Click the View menu and select Advanced Features.
3. Right-click an object and choose Properties.
4. Click the Security tab.

   If Advanced Features is not enabled, you will not see the Security tab in an object's Properties dialog box.

   The Security tab of the object's Properties dialog box is shown in Figure 2-15.

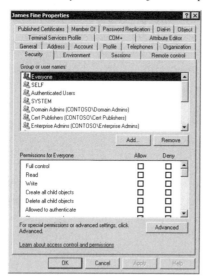

Figure 2-15   The Security tab of an Active Directory object's Properties dialog box

5. Click the Advanced button.

   The Security tab shows a very high-level overview of the security principals that have been given permissions to the object, but in the case of Active Directory ACLs, the Security tab is rarely detailed enough to provide the information you need to interpret or manage the ACL. You should always click Advanced to open the Advanced Security Settings dialog box.

The dialog box showing Advanced Security Settings for an object appears, shown in Figure 2-16.

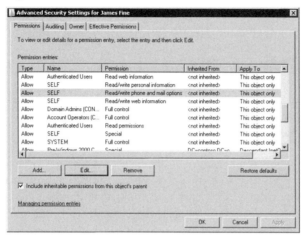

Figure 2-16   The Advanced Security Settings dialog box for an Active Directory object

The Permissions tab of the Advanced Security Settings dialog box shows the DACL of the object. You can see in Figure 2-16 that ACEs are summarized on a line of the Permission entries list. In this dialog box, you are not seeing the granular ACEs of the DACL. For example, the permission entry that is selected in Figure 2-16 is actually composed of two ACEs.

6. To see the granular ACEs of a permission entry, select the entry and click Edit.

   The Permission Entry dialog box appears, detailing the specific ACEs that make up the entry, as in Figure 2-17.

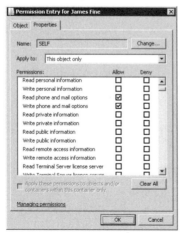

Figure 2-17   The Permission Entry dialog box

> ### Quick Check
> - You want to view the permissions assigned to an OU. You open the OU's Properties dialog box and there is no Security tab visible. What must you do?
>
> ### Quick Check Answer
> - In the Active Directory Users And Computers snap-in, click the View menu and select Advanced Features.

Object, Property, and Control Access Rights

The DACL of an object enables you to assign permissions to specific properties of an object. As you saw in Figure 2-17, you can allow (or deny) permission to change phone and e-mail options. This is in fact not just one property; it is a property set that includes multiple specific properties. Property sets make it easier to manage permissions to commonly used collections of properties. But you could get even more granular and allow or deny permission to change just the mobile telephone number or just the home street address.

Permissions can also be assigned to manage control access rights, which are actions such as changing or resetting a password. The difference between those two control access rights is important to understand. If you have the right to *change* a password, you must know and enter the current password before making the change. If you have the right to *reset* a password, you are not required to know the previous password.

Finally, permissions can be assigned to objects. For example, the ability to change permissions on an object is controlled by the Allow::Modify Permissions ACE. Object permissions also control whether you are able to create child objects. For example, you might give your desktop support team permissions to create computer objects in the OU for your desktops and laptops. The Allow::Create Computer Objects ACE would be assigned to the desktop support team at the OU.

The type and scope of permissions are managed using the two tabs, Object and Properties, and the Apply To drop-down lists on each tab.

Assigning a Permission Using the Advanced Security Settings Dialog Box

Imagine a scenario in which you want to allow the help desk to change the password on James Fine's account. In this section, you will learn to do it the most complicated way first: by assigning the ACE on the DACL of the user object. Later, you'll learn how to perform the delegation by using the Delegation Of Control Wizard for the entire OU of users, and you'll see why this latter practice is recommended.

1. Open the Active Directory Users And Computers snap-in.
2. Click the View menu and select Advanced Features.
3. Right-click an object and choose Properties.
4. Click the Security tab.
5. Click the Advanced button.
6. Click the Add button.

   If you have User Account Control enabled, you might need to click Edit and, perhaps, enter administrative credentials before the Add button will appear.

7. In the Select dialog box, select the security principal to which permissions will be assigned.

   It is an important best practice to assign permissions to groups, not to individual users.

   In your example, you would select your Help Desk group.

8. Click OK.

   The Permission Entry dialog box appears.

9. Configure the permissions you want to assign.

   For our example, on the Object tab, scroll down the list of Permissions and select Allow::Reset Password.

10. Click OK to close each dialog box.

Understanding and Managing Permissions with Inheritance

You can imagine that assigning the help desk permission to reset passwords for each individual user object would be quite time-consuming. Luckily, you don't have to and, in fact, it's a terrible practice to assign permissions to individual objects in Active Directory. Instead, you will assign permissions to organizational units. The permissions you assign to an OU will be inherited by all objects in the OU. Thus, if you give the help desk permission to reset passwords for user objects, and you attach that permission to the OU that contains your users, all user objects within that OU will inherit that permission. With one step, you'll have delegated that administrative task.

Inheritance is an easy concept to understand. Child objects inherit the permissions of the parent container or OU. That container or OU in turn inherits its permissions from its parent container, OU, or, if it is a first-level container or OU, from the domain itself. The reason child objects inherit permissions from their parents is that, by default, each new object is created with the Include Inheritable Permissions From This Object's Parent option enabled. You can see the option in Figure 2-16.

Note, however, that as the option indicates, only *inheritable* permissions will be inherited by the child object. Not every permission, however, is inheritable. For example, the permission to reset passwords assigned to an OU would not be inherited by group objects because group objects do not have a password attribute. So inheritance can be scoped to specific object classes: passwords are applicable to user objects, not to groups. Additionally, you can use the Apply To box of the Permission Entry dialog box to scope the inheritance of a permission. The conversation can start to get very complicated. What you should know is that, by default, new objects inherit inheritable permissions from their parent object—usually an OU or container.

What if the permission being inherited is not appropriate? Two things can be done to modify the permissions that a child object is inheriting. First, you can disable inheritance by deselecting the Include Inheritable Permissions From This Object's Parent option in the Advanced Security Settings dialog box. When you do, the object will no longer inherit any permissions from its parent—all permissions will be explicitly defined for the child object. This is generally not a good practice because it creates an exception to the rule that is being created by the permissions of the parent containers.

The second option is to allow inheritance but override the inherited permission with a permission assigned specifically to the child object—an explicit permission. Explicit permissions always override permissions that are inherited from parent objects. This has an important implication: an explicit permission that *allows* access will actually override an inherited permission that *denies* the same access. If that sounds counterintuitive to you, it is not: the rule is being defined by a parent (deny), but the child object has been configured to be an exception (allow).

Exam Tip   Look out for scenarios in which access or delegation are not performing as expected either because inheritance has been broken—the child is no longer inheriting permissions from its parent—or because the child object has an explicit permission that overrides the permissions of the parent.

Delegating Administrative Tasks with the Delegation Of Control Wizard

You've seen the complexity of the DACL, and you've probably gleaned that managing permissions by using the Permission Entry dialog box is not a simple task. Luckily, the best practice is not to manage permissions by using the security interfaces but, rather, to use the Delegation of Control Wizard. The following procedure details the use of the wizard.

1. Open the Active Directory Users And Computers snap-in.
2. Right-click the node (Domain or OU) for which you want to delegate administrative tasks or control and choose Delegate Control.

    In this example, you would select the OU that contains your users.

    The Delegation of Control Wizard is displayed to guide you through the required steps.

3. Click Next.

    You will first select the administrative group to which you are granting privileges.

4. On the Users or Groups page, click the Add button.

5. Use the Select dialog box to select the group and click OK.

6. Click Next.

    Next, you will specify the specific task you wish to assign that group.

7. On the Tasks To Delegate page, select the task.

    In this example, you would select Reset User Passwords and Force Password Change at Next Logon.

8. Click Next.

9. Review the summary of the actions that have been performed and click Finish.

    The Delegation of Control Wizard applies the ACEs that are required to enable the selected group to perform the specified task.

Reporting and Viewing Permissions

There are several other ways to view and report permissions when you need to know who can do what. You've already seen that you can view permissions on the DACL by using the Advanced Security Settings and Permission Entry dialog boxes.

Dsacls.exe is also available as a command-line tool that reports on directory service objects. If you type the command, followed by the distinguished name of an object, you will see a report of the object's permissions. For example, this command will produce a report of the permissions associated with the People OU:

```
dsacls.exe "ou=People,dc=contoso,dc=com"
```

Dsacls can also be used to set permissions—to delegate. Type **dsacls.exe /?** for help regarding the syntax and usage of *Dsacls*.

Removing or Resetting Permissions on an Object

How do you remove or reset permissions that have been delegated? Unfortunately, there is no undelegate command. You must use the Advanced Security Settings and Permission Entry dialog boxes to remove permissions. If you want to reset the permissions on the object back to the defaults, open the Advanced Security Settings dialog box and click Restore Defaults. The default permissions are defined by the Active Directory schema for the class of object. After you've restored the defaults, you can reconfigure the explicit permissions you want to add to the DACL. *Dsacls* also provides the */s* switch to reset permissions to the schema-defined defaults, and the */t* switch makes the change for the entire tree—the object and all its child objects. For example, to reset permissions on the People OU and all its child OUs and objects, you would type:

```
dsacls "ou=People,dc=contoso,dc=com" /resetDefaultDACL
```

Understanding Effective Permissions

Effective permissions are the resulting permissions for a security principal, such as a user or group, based on the cumulative effect of each inherited and explicit ACE. Your ability to reset a user's password, for example, can be due to your membership in a group that was allowed Reset Password permission on an OU several levels above the user object. The inherited permission assigned to a group to which you belong resulted in an effective permission of Allow::Reset Password. Your effective permissions can be complicated when you consider allow and deny permissions, explicit and inherited ACEs, and the fact that you might belong to multiple groups, each of which might be assigned different permissions.

Permissions, whether assigned to your user account or to a group to which you belong, are equivalent. In the end, an ACE applies to you, the user. The best practice is to manage permissions by assigning them to groups, but it is also possible to assign ACEs to individual users or computers. Just because a permission has been assigned directly to you, the user, doesn't mean that permission is either more important or less important than a permission assigned to a group to which you belong.

Permissions that allow access (allow permissions) are cumulative. When you belong to several groups, and those groups have been granted permissions that allow a variety of tasks, you will be able to perform all the tasks assigned to all those groups as well as tasks assigned directly to your user account.

Permissions that deny access (deny permissions) override an equivalent allow permission. If you are in one group that has been allowed the permission to reset passwords, and another group that has been denied permission to reset passwords, the deny permission will prevent you from resetting passwords.

NOTE   Use Deny permissions sparingly

It is generally unnecessary to assign deny permissions. If you simply do not assign an allow permission, users cannot perform the task. Before assigning a deny permission, check to see whether you could achieve your goal by removing an allow permission instead. Use deny permissions rarely and thoughtfully.

Each permission is granular. Even though you've been denied the ability to reset passwords, you might still have the ability, through other allow permissions, to change the user's logon name or e-mail address.

Finally, you learned earlier in this lesson that child objects inherit the inheritable permissions of parent objects by default and that explicit permissions can override inheritable permissions. This means that an explicit allow permission will actually override an inherited deny permission.

Unfortunately, the complex interaction of user, group, explicit, inherited, allow, and deny permissions can make evaluating effective permissions a bit of a chore. There is an Effective Permissions tab in the Advanced Security Settings dialog box of an Active Directory object, but the tab is practically useless; it does not expose enough permissions to provide the kind of detailed information you will require. You can use the permissions reported by the *Dsacls* command or on the Permissions tab of the Advanced Security Settings dialog box to begin evaluating effective permissions, but it will be a manual task.

MORE INFO Role-based access control

The best way to manage delegation in Active Directory is through role-based access control. Although this approach will not be covered on the certification exam, it is well worth understanding for real-world implementation of delegation. See *Windows Administration Resource Kit: Productivity Solutions for IT Professionals,* by Dan Holme (Microsoft Press, 2008) for more information.

Designing an OU Structure to Support Delegation

OUs are, as you now know, administrative containers. They contain objects that share similar requirements for administration, configuration, and visibility. You now understand the first of those requirements: administration. Objects that will be administered the same way, by the same administrators, should be contained within a single OU. By placing your users in a single OU called "People," you can delegate the help desk permission to change all users' passwords by assigning one permission to one OU. Any other permissions that affect what an administrator can do to a user object will be assigned at the People OU. For example, you might allow your HR managers to disable user accounts in the event of an employee's termination. You would delegate that permission, again, to the People OU.

Remember that administrators should be logging on to their systems with user credentials and launching administrative tools with the credentials of a secondary account that has appropriate permissions to perform administrative tasks. Those secondary accounts are the administrative accounts of the enterprise. It is not appropriate for the frontline help desk to be able to reset passwords on such privileged accounts, and you probably would not want HR managers to disable administrative accounts. Therefore, administrative accounts are being administered differently than nonadminstrative user accounts. That's why you have a separate OU, Admins, for administrative user objects. That OU will be delegated quite differently than the People OU.

Similarly, you might delegate the desktop support team the ability to add computer objects to the Clients OU, which contains your desktops and laptops, but not to the Servers OU, where only your Server Administration group has permissions to create and manage computer objects.

The primary role of OUs is to scope delegation efficiently, to apply permissions to objects and sub-OUs. When you design an Active Directory environment, you always begin by designing an OU structure that will make delegation efficient—a structure that reflects the administrative model of your organization. Rarely does object administration in Active Directory look like your organizational chart. Typically, all normal user accounts are supported the same way, by the same team, so user objects are often found in a single OU or in a single OU branch. Quite often, an organization that has a centralized help desk function to support users will also have a centralized desktop support function, in which case, all client computer objects would be within a single OU or single OU branch. However, if desktop support is decentralized, you would be likely to find that the Clients OU is divided into sub-OUs representing geographic locations so that each location is delegated to allow the local support team to add computer objects to the domain in that location.

Design OUs, first, to enable the efficient delegation of objects in the directory. Once you have achieved that design, you will refine the design to facilitate the configuration of computers and users through Group Policy, which will be discussed in Chapter 6, "Group Policy Infrastructure." Active Directory design is an art and a science.

PRACTICE Delegating Administrative Tasks

In this practice, you will manage the delegation of administrative tasks within the *contoso.com* domain and view the resulting changes to ACLs on Active Directory objects. Before performing the exercises in this practice, you must perform the practice in Lesson 2, "Practice: Creating and Locating Objects in Active Directory." The OUs created in that practice are required for these exercises.

▶ **Exercise 1   Delegate Control for Support of User Accounts**

In this exercise, you will enable the Help Desk to support users by resetting passwords and unlocking user accounts in the People OU.

1. Log on to SERVER01 as Administrator and open the Active Directory Users And Computers snap-in.
2. Expand the Domain node, *contoso.com*, right-click the People OU, and choose Delegate Control to launch the Delegation Of Control Wizard.
3. Click Next.
4. On the Users Or Groups page, click the Add button.
5. Using the Select dialog box, type **Help Desk**, and then click OK.
6. Click Next.

7. On the Tasks To Delegate page, select the Reset User Passwords And Force Password Change At Next Logon task.

8. Click Next.

9. Review the summary of the actions that have been performed and click Finish.

▶ **Exercise 2   View Delegated Permissions**

In this exercise, you will view the permissions you assigned to the Help Desk.

1. Log on to SERVER01 as Administrator and open the Active Directory Users And Computers snap-in.

2. Right-click the People OU and choose Properties.

   Note that the Security tab is not visible. If Advanced Features is not enabled, you will not see the Security tab in an object's Properties dialog box.

3. Click OK to close the Properties dialog box.

4. Click the View menu and select Advanced Features.

5. Right-click the People OU and choose Properties.

6. Click the Security tab.

7. Click the Advanced button.

8. In the Permission Entries list, select the first permission assigned to the Help Desk.

9. Click the Edit button.

10. In the Permission Entry dialog box, locate the permission that is assigned, and then click OK to close the dialog box.

11. Repeat steps 8–10 for the second permission entry assigned to the Help Desk.

12. Repeat steps 2–11 to view the ACL of a user in the People OU and to examine the inherited permissions assigned to the Help Desk.

13. Open the command prompt, type **dsacls "ou=people,dc=contoso,dc=com"**, and press Enter.

14. Locate the permissions assigned to the Help Desk.

Lesson Summary

- Delegation of control in Active Directory enables an organization to assign specific administrative tasks to appropriate teams and individuals.

- Delegation is the result of permissions, or ACEs, on the DACL of Active Directory objects.

- The DACL can be viewed and modified using the Advanced Security Settings of the object's Properties dialog box.

- The Delegation of Control Wizard simplifies the underlying complexity of object ACLs by enabling you to assign tasks to groups.

- Permissions on an object can be reset to their defaults by using the Advanced Security Settings dialog box or *Dsacls* with the */resetDefaultDACL* switch.
- It is a best practice to delegate control by using organizational units. Objects within the OUs will inherit the permissions of their parent OUs.
- Inheritance can be modified by disabling inheritance on a child object or by applying an explicit permission to the child object that overrides the inherited permission.
- Effective permissions are the result of user, group, allow, deny, inherited, and explicit permissions. Deny permissions override allow permissions, but explicit permissions override inherited permissions. Therefore, an explicit allow permission will override an inherited deny permission.

Lesson Review

You can use the following questions to test your knowledge of the information in Lesson 3, "Delegation and Security of Active Directory Objects." The questions are also available on the companion CD if you prefer to review them in electronic form.

NOTE   Answers

Answers to these questions and explanations of why each answer choice is right or wrong are located in the "Answers" section at the end of the book.

---

1. You want to enable your help desk to reset user passwords and unlock user accounts. Which of the following tools can be used? (Choose all that apply.)
   - A. The Delegation of Control Wizard
   - B. DSACLS
   - C. DSUTIL
   - D. The Advanced Security Settings dialog box

Chapter Review

To further practice and reinforce the skills you learned in this chapter, you can perform the following tasks:

- Review the chapter summary.
- Review the list of key terms introduced in this chapter.
- Complete the case scenario. This scenario sets up a real-world situation involving the topics of this chapter and asks you to create a solution.
- Complete the suggested practices.
- Take a practice test.

Chapter Summary

- The Active Directory Users and Computers snap-in, which is part of Server Manager and of the Active Directory Users and Computers console, can be also be added to custom consoles and distributed to administrators.
- As you create objects with the Active Directory Users and Computers snap-in, you are able to configure a limited number of initial properties. After an object is created, you can populate a much larger set of properties. These properties can be used in saved queries to provide customizable views of your enterprise objects.
- Organizational units should be used to delegate administrative control so that teams in your enterprise can perform the tasks required of their role. With inheritance enabled, objects will inherit the permissions of their parent OUs.

Key Terms

Use these key terms to understand better the concepts covered in this chapter.

- **delegation** Assignment of an administrative task. Delegation within Active Directory is achieved by modifying the DACL of an object. A common example is delegation of the ability to reset user passwords to a help desk role. By assigning the help desk the Allow::Reset Passwords control access right on an OU, members of the help desk role will be able to reset passwords for all user objects within the OU.
- **saved query** A view of Active Directory objects based on search criteria. Saved Queries, a node within the Active Directory Users and Computers snap-in, allow enables you to specify the type and properties of objects that you want to look for. Results are returned in the details pane of the snap-in.

Case Scenario

In the following case scenario, you will apply what you've learned about Active Directory snap-ins and object creation, delegation, and security. You can find answers to these questions in the "Answers" section at the end of this book.

Case Scenario: Organizational Units and Delegation

You are an administrator at Contoso, Ltd. Contoso's Active Directory was created when the organization was very small. One OU was created for users and one for computers. Now, the organization spans five geographic sites around the world, with over 1,000 employees. At each site, one or two members of desktop support personnel provide help to users with desktop applications and are responsible for installing systems and joining them to the domain. In addition, a small team at headquarters occasionally installs systems, joins them to the domain, and ships them to the site. If a user has forgotten his or her password, a centralized help desk telephone number is directed to one of the support personnel members on call, regardless of which site the user is in. Answer the following questions for your manager, who is concerned about manageability and least privilege, and explain how delegation would be managed:

1. Should computer objects remain in a single OU, or should the objects be divided by site? If divided, should the site OUs be under a single parent OU?

2. Should the ability to manage computer objects in sites be delegated directly to the user accounts of the desktop support personnel, or should groups be created, even though those groups might have only one or two members?

3. Should users be divided by site or remain within a single OU?

Suggested Practices

To help you successfully master the exam objectives presented in this chapter, complete the following tasks.

Maintain Active Directory Accounts

In this practice, you will validate that delegation has been successful, and you will experience what happens when an administrator attempts to perform a task that has not been delegated. You will also experience the results of inheritance and of OU protection.

To perform this practice, you must have performed the practices in Lesson 2 and Lesson 3. Specifically, ensure that:

- There is a user account in the Admins OU.
- There is a Help Desk group in the Admins OU.
- There is a user account for Barbara Mayer and at least one other user account in the People OU.
- The user Barbara Mayer is a member of the Help Desk group.
- The Help Desk group has been delegated the Reset User Passwords and Force Password Change at Next Logon permissions for the People OU.

In addition, make sure that the Domain Users group is a member of the Print Operators group, which can be found in the Builtin container. This will enable all sample users in the practice domain to log on to the SERVER01 domain controller. This is important for the practices in this training kit, but you should not allow users to log on to domain controllers in your production environment, so do not make Domain Users members of the Print Operators group in your production environment.

- **Practice 1**   Log on to SERVER01 as Barbara Mayer. She is a member of the Help Desk group. Validate that she can reset the password of users other than her own in the People OU. Then attempt to change the password of a user account in the Admins OU. Investigate the results.

- **Practice 2**   Log on to SERVER01 as Administrator. Create a new OU within the People OU, called Branch. When you create the Branch OU, ensure that the Protect Container From Accidental Deletion option is selected because you will delete this OU after this practice. Create a user account in the OU. Open the DACL of the user object in the Advanced Security Settings dialog box. Note the permissions assigned to the Help Desk. Are they explicit or inherited? If inherited, where are they inherited from? Open the DACL of the Branch OU in the Advanced Security Settings dialog box. Deselect the Include Inheritable Permissions From This Object's Parent option.

Log off and log on as Barbara Mayer. Validate that she can reset the password of a user in the People OU. Now attempt to reset the password of the user in the Branch OU. Access is denied.

Log off and log on as Administrator. Troubleshoot Barbara's lack of access by restoring inheritance to the Branch OU. Log off and log on as Barbara to validate the results. Can she successfully reset the password of a user in the Branch OU?

- **Practice 3** Log on to SERVER01 as Barbara Mayer. Attempt to delete the Branch OU. Access is denied. Log off and log on as Administrator. Attempt to delete the Branch OU. Access is denied. Open the properties of the Branch OU. Look for the Object tab. If it is not visible, turn on the Advanced Features view of the Active Directory Users And Computers snap-in. On the Object tab, unprotect the Branch OU. Finally, delete the Branch OU and the user account within it.

Take a Practice Test

The practice tests on this book's companion CD offer many options. For example, you can test yourself on just one exam objective, or you can test yourself on all the 70-640 certification exam content. You can set up the test so that it closely simulates the experience of taking a certification exam, or you can set it up in study mode so that you can look at the correct answers and explanations after you answer each question.

MORE INFO   Practice tests

For details about all the practice test options available, see the "How to Use the Practice Tests" section in this book's introduction.

Chapter 3

Users

Chapter 1, "Installation," introduced Active Directory Domain Services (AD DS) as an identity and access solution. User accounts stored in the directory are the fundamental component of identity. Because of their importance, knowledge of user accounts and the tasks related to support them is critical to the success of an administrator in a Microsoft Windows enterprise.

Your ability to work effectively with user accounts can make a big difference in your overall productivity. Skills that are effective to create or modify a single user account, such as the procedures described in Chapter 2, "Administration," can become clumsy and inefficient when you are working with large numbers of accounts, such as when creating the accounts of newly hired employees.

In this chapter, you will learn how to apply tools and techniques to automate the creation and management of users and to locate and manipulate user objects and their attributes. Along the way, you will be introduced to Microsoft Windows PowerShell, which represents the future of command line–based and automated administration for Windows technologies. You will learn a variety of options for performing each of the most common administrative tasks.

The certification exam will expect you to have a very basic understanding of the purpose and syntax of command-line utilities, Windows PowerShell, and Microsoft Visual Basic Script (VBScript). However, this chapter goes beyond the expectations of the exam to provide a solid introduction to scripting and automation. Practice what you learn in this chapter, not because you'll need to be a scripting guru to pass the exam but because the more you can automate those tedious administrative tasks, the more you can elevate your productivity and your success.

Exam objectives in this chapter:
- Creating and Maintaining Active Directory Objects
  - ❏ Automate creation of Active Directory accounts.
  - ❏ Maintain Active Directory accounts.

Lessons in this chapter:
- Lesson 1: Automating the Creation of User Accounts. 87
- Lesson 2: Creating Users with Windows PowerShell and VBScript 98
- Lesson 3: Supporting User Objects and Accounts. 114

Before You Begin

To complete the practices in this chapter, you must have created a domain controller named SERVER01 in a domain named *contoso.com*. See Chapter 1 for detailed steps for this task.

Real World

Dan Holme

It's really amazing to stop and consider how much of our time as Windows administrators is spent performing basic tasks related to user objects. Each day in an enterprise network brings with it a unique set of challenges related to user management. Employees are hired, moved, married, and divorced, and most eventually leave the organization. As human beings, they make mistakes like forgetting passwords or locking out their accounts by logging on incorrectly.

Administrators must respond to all these changes, and user accounts are so complicated, with so many properties, that even the most well-intentioned administrators often stray from the procedures and conventions they've established. I believe that the key to efficient, effective, consistent, and secure user environments begins with raising the skill set of administrators.

Lesson 1: Automating the Creation of User Accounts

In Chapter 2, you learned how to create a user account in the Active Directory Users and Computers snap-in. Although the procedures discussed in Chapter 2 can be applied to create a small number of users, you will need more advanced techniques to automate the creation of user accounts when a large number of users must be added to the domain. In this lesson, you will learn several of these techniques.

After this lesson, you will be able to:
- Create users from user account templates.
- Import users with *CSVDE*.
- Import users with *LDIFDE*.

Estimated lesson time: 30 minutes

Creating Users with Templates

Users in a domain often share many similar properties. For example, all sales representatives can belong to the same security groups, log on to the network during similar hours, and have home folders and roaming profiles stored on the same server. When you create a new user, you can simply copy an existing user account rather than create a blank account and populate each property.

Since the days of Microsoft Windows NT 4.0, Windows has supported the concept of user account templates. A user account template is a generic user account prepopulated with common properties. For example, you can create a template account for sales representatives that is preconfigured with group memberships, logon hours, a home folder, and roaming profile path.

NOTE Disable template user accounts

The template account should not be used to log on to the network, so be sure to disable the account.

To create a user based on the template, select Copy from the shortcut menu. The Copy Object – User Wizard appears. You are prompted for the name, logon name, and password settings of the new user. A number of properties of the template are copied to the new user account. After a user account is created, you can view its properties, grouped by tab, in the Properties dialog box. Some of the tabs and properties that appear are the following:

- **General** No properties are copied from the General tab
- **Address** P.O. box, city, state or province, zip or postal code, and country or region. Note that the street address itself is not copied
- **Account** Logon hours, logon workstations, account options, and account expiration
- **Profile** Profile path, logon script, home drive, and home folder path

- **Organization**   Department, company, and manager
- **Member Of**   Group membership and primary group

NOTE   What you see isn't all you get

User accounts have additional properties that are not visible on the standard tabs in the Active Directory Users and Computers snap-in. These hidden attributes include useful properties such as assistant, division, employee type, and employee ID. To view these properties, click the View menu in the Active Directory Users and Computers snap-in and select the Advanced Features option. Then open the properties of a user account and click the Attribute Editor tab. Several of these attributes, including assistant, division, and employee type, are also copied from a template to a new account.

> ## What Is Copied Is Not Enough
>
> Many administrators consider the list of copied attributes to be somewhat limited. For example, you might want the job title and street address attributes to be copied. You can actually modify the Active Directory schema to include additional attributes when duplicating a user. See Knowledge Base article 827832 at *http://support.microsoft .com/kb/827832* for instructions.
>
> However, you will be well served to use more advanced methods for automating the creation of user accounts. Later in this chapter, you will learn to use directory service (DS) commands, Comma-Separated Values Data Exchange (CSVDE), LDAP Data Interchange Format Data Exchange (LDIFDE), and Windows PowerShell to automate administrative tasks. With these tools, you will have full control over the process used to provision a new account.

Using Active Directory Command-Line Tools

In Chapter 2, you were introduced to *Dsquery.exe*, one of a suite of Active Directory command-line tools collectively called *DS commands*. The following DS commands are supported in Windows Server 2008:

- *Dsadd*   Creates an object in the directory.
- *Dsget*   Returns specified attributes of an object.
- *Dsmod*   Modifies specified attributes of an object.
- *Dsmove*   Moves an object to a new container or OU.
- *Dsrm*   Removes an object, all objects in the subtree beneath a container object, or both.
- *Dsquery*   Performs a query based on parameters provided at the command line and returns a list of matching objects. By default, the result set is presented as the distinguished

names (DNs) of each object, but you can use the *–o* parameter with modifiers such as *dn*, *rdn*, *upn*, or *samid* to receive the results as DNs, relative DNs, user principal names (UPNs), or pre-Windows 2000 logon names (security accounts manager [SAM] IDs).

Most of the DS commands take two modifiers after the command itself: the object type and the object's DN. For example, the following command adds a user account for Mike Fitzmaurice:

```
dsadd user "cn=Mike Fitzmaurice,ou=People,dc=contoso,dc=com"
```

The object type, *user*, immediately follows the command. After the object type is the object's DN. When the object's DN includes a space, surround the DN with quotes. The following command removes the same user:

```
dsrm user "cn=Mike Fitzmaurice,ou=People,dc=contoso,dc=com"
```

DS commands that read or manipulate attributes of objects include *Dsquery.exe*, *Dsget.exe*, and *Dsmod.exe*. To specify an attribute, include it as a parameter after the object's DN. For example, the following command retrieves the home folder path for Mike Fitzmaurice:

```
dsget user "cn=Mike Fitzmaurice,ou=People,dc=contoso,dc=com" –hmdir
```

The parameter of a DS command that represents an attribute, for example, *hmdir*, is not always the same as the name of the attribute in the Active Directory Users and Computers snap-in or in the schema.

Creating Users with *Dsadd*

Use the *Dsadd* command to create objects in Active Directory. The *DSADD USER UserDN* command creates a user object and accepts parameters that specify properties of the user. The following command shows the basic parameters required to create a user account:

```
dsadd user "User DN" –samid pre-Windows 2000 logon name
-pwd {Password | *} –mustchpwd yes
```

The *pwd* parameter specifies the password. If it is set to an asterisk (*), you are prompted for a user password. The *mustchpwd* parameter specifies that the user must change the password at next logon.

DSADD USER accepts a number of parameters that specify properties of the user object. Most parameter names are self-explanatory: *-email*, *-profile*, and *-company*, for example. Type **DSADD USER /?** or search the Windows Server 2008 Help And Support Center for thorough documentation of the *DSADD USER* parameters.

The special token *$username$* represents the SAM ID in the value of the *-email*, *-hmdir*, *-profile*, and *-webpg* parameters. For example, to configure a home folder for a user when creating the user with the *DSADD USER* command shown earlier, add the following parameter:

```
-hmdir \\server01\users\$username$\documents
```

Importing Users with *CSVDE*

CSVDE is a command-line tool that imports or exports Active Directory objects from or to a comma-delimited text file (also known as a comma-separated value text file, or .csv file). Comma-delimited files can be created, modified, and opened with tools as familiar as Notepad and Microsoft Office Excel. If you have user information in existing Excel or Microsoft Office Access databases, you will find that *CSVDE* is a powerful way to take advantage of that information to automate user account creation.

The basic syntax of the *CSVDE* command is:

```
csvde [-i] [-f Filename] [-k]
```

The *i* parameter specifies import mode; without it, the default mode of *CSVDE* is export. The *-f* parameter identifies the file name to import from or export to. The *-k* parameter is useful during import operations because it instructs *CSVDE* to ignore errors including Object Already Exists, Constraint Violation, and Attribute Or Value Already Exists.

The import file itself is a comma-delimited text file (.csv or .txt) in which the first line defines the imported attributes by their Lightweight Directory Access Protocol (LDAP) attribute names. Each object follows, one per line, and must contain exactly the attributes listed on the first line. Here's a sample file:

```
DN,objectClass,sAMAccountName,sn,givenName,userPrincipalName
"cn=Lisa Andrews,ou=People,dc=contoso,dc=com",user,lisa.andrews,
Lisa,Andrews,lisa.andrews@contoso.com
```

This file, when imported by the *CSVDE* command, will create a user object for Lisa Andrews in the People OU. The user logon names, last name and first name, are configured by the file. You cannot use the *CSVDE* to import passwords, and without a password, the user account will be disabled initially. After you have reset the password, you can enable the object.

In Chapter 4, "Groups," and Chapter 5, "Computers," you will use *CSVDE* to import computers and groups. For more information about *CSVDE*, including details regarding its parameters and usage to export directory objects, type **csvde /?** or search the Windows Server 2008 Help and Support Center.

Importing Users with *LDIFDE*

You can also use *Ldifde.exe* to import or export Active Directory objects, including users. The Lightweight Directory Access Protocol Data Interchange Format (LDIF) is a draft Internet standard for file format that can be used to perform batch operations against directories that conform to the LDAP standards. LDIF supports both import and export operations as well as batch operations that modify objects in the directory. The *LDIFDE* command implements these batch operations by using LDIF files.

The LDIF file format consists of a block of lines that, together, constitute a single operation. Multiple operations in a single file are separated by a blank line. Each line comprising an operation consists of an attribute name followed by a colon and the value of the attribute. For example, suppose you wanted to import user objects for two sales representatives, named April Stewart and Tony Krijnen. The contents of the LDIF file would look similar to the following example:

```
DN: CN=April Stewart,OU=People,DC=contoso,DC=com
changeType: add
CN: April Stewart
objectClass: user
sAMAccountName: april.stewart
userPrincipalName: april.stewart@contoso.com
givenName: April
sn: Stewart
displayName: Stewart, April
mail: april.stewart@contoso.com
description: Sales Representative in the USA
title: Sales Representative
department: Sales
company: Contoso, Ltd.

DN: CN=Tony Krijnen,OU=People,DC=contoso,DC=com
changeType: add
CN: Tony Krijnen
objectClass: user
sAMAccountName: tony.krijnen
userPrincipalName: tony.krijnen@contoso.com
givenName: Tony
sn: Krijnen
displayName: Krijnen, Tony
mail: tony.krijnen@contoso.com
description: Sales Representative in The Netherlands
title: Sales Representative
department: Sales
company: Contoso, Ltd.
```

Each operation begins with the *DN* attribute of the object that is the target of the operation. The next line, *changeType*, specifies the type of operation: *add*, *modify*, or *delete*.

As you can see, the LDIF file format is not as intuitive or familiar as the comma-separated text format. However, because the LDIF format is also a standard, many directory services and databases can export LDIF files.

After creating or obtaining an LDIF file, you can perform the operations specified by the file by using the *LDIFDE* command. From a command prompt, type **ldifde /?** for usage information. The two most important switches for the *LDIFDE* command are:

- *-i* Turn on Import mode. Without this parameter, *LDIFDE* exports information.
- *-f Filename* The file from which to import, or to which to export.

For example, the following command will import objects from the file named Newusers.ldf:

```
ldifde -i -f newusers.ldf
```

The command accepts a variety of modifications using parameters. The most useful parameters are summarized in Table 3-1.

Table 3-1   *LDIFDE* Parameters

Command	Usage
General parameters	
-i	Import mode. (The default is Export mode.)
-f filename	Import or export file name.
-s servername	The domain controller to bind to for the query.
-c FromDN ToDN	Convert occurrences of *FromDN* to *ToDN*. This is useful when importing objects from another domain, for example.
-v	Turn on Verbose mode.
-j path	Log file location.
-?	Help.
Export-specific parameters	
-d RootDN	The root of the LDAP search. The default is the root of the domain.
-r Filter	LDAP search filter. The default is (objectClass=*), meaning all objects.
-p SearchScope	The scope, or depth, of the search. Can be *subtree* (the container and all child containers), *base* (the immediate child objects of the container only), or *onelevel* (the container and its immediate child containers).
-l list	Comma-separated list of attributes to include in export for resulting objects. Useful if you want to export a limited number of attributes.
-o list	List of attributes (comma-separated) to omit from export for resulting objects. Useful if you want to export all but a few attributes.
Import-specific parameters	
-k	Ignore errors and continue processing if Constraint Violation or Object Already Exists errors appear.

Exam Tip   For the 70-640 certification exam, you should understand that both *CSVDE* and *LDIFDE* are able to import and export objects by using their respective file formats. Both commands are in the export mode by default and require the *-i* parameter to specify import mode. Only *LDIFDE* is capable of modifying existing objects or removing objects. Neither command enables you to import a user's password. Only *Dsadd* supports specifying the password. If you import users with *CSVDE* or *LDIFDE*, the accounts will be disabled until you reset their passwords and enable the accounts.

PRACTICE Automating the Creation of User Accounts

In this practice, you will create a number of user accounts with automated methods discussed in this lesson. To perform the exercises in this practice, you will need the following objects in the *contoso.com* domain:

- A first-level OU named People
- A first-level OU named Groups
- A global security group in the Groups OU named Sales

▶ **Exercise 1   Create Users with a User Account Template**

In this exercise, you will create a user account template that is prepopulated with properties for sales representatives. You will then create a user account for a new sales representative by copying the user account template.

1. Log on to SERVER01 as Administrator.
2. Open the Active Directory Users And Computers snap-in and expand the domain.
3. Right-click the People OU, choose New, and then select User.
4. In the First Name box, type **_Sales**, including the underscore character.
5. In the Last Name box, type **Template**.
6. In the User Logon Name box, type **_salestemplate**, including the underscore character. Click Next.
7. Type a complex password in the Password and Confirm Password boxes.
8. Select the Account Is Disabled check box. Click Next. Click Finish.

    Notice that the underscore character at the beginning of the account's name ensures that the template appears at the top of the list of users in the People OU. Notice also that the icon of the user object includes a down arrow, indicating that the account is disabled.

9. Double-click the template account to open its Properties dialog box.
10. Click the Organization tab.
11. In the Department box, type **Sales**.
12. In the Company box, type **Contoso, Ltd.**
13. Click the Member Of tab.
14. Click the Add button.
15. Type **Sales**, and then click OK.
16. Click the Profile tab.
17. In the Profile Path box, type **\\server01\profiles\%username%**.
18. Click OK.

    You have now created a template account that can be copied to generate new user accounts for sales representatives. Next, you will create an account based on the user account template.

19. Right-click _Sales Template and choose Copy.

The Copy Object – User dialog box appears.

20. In the First Name box, type **Jeff**.

21. In the Last Name box, type **Ford**.

22. In the User Logon Name box, type **jeff.ford**. Click Next.

23. Type a complex password in the Password and Confirm Password boxes.

24. Clear the Account Is Disabled check box.

25. Click Next, and then click Finish.

26. Open the properties of the Jeff Ford account and confirm that the attributes you configured in the template were copied to the new account.

▶ **Exercise 2   Create a User with the *Dsadd* Command**

In this exercise, you will use the *Dsadd* command to create a user account for Mike Fitzmaurice in the People OU.

1. Open a command prompt.

2. Type the following command on one line, and then press Enter:

```
dsadd user "cn=Mike Fitzmaurice,ou=People,dc=contoso,dc=com"
-samid mike.fitz -pwd * -mustchpwd yes -hmdir
\\server01\users\%username%\documents -hmdrv U:
```

3. You will be prompted to enter a password for the user twice. Type a password that is complex and at least seven characters long.

4. Open the Active Directory Users And Computers snap-in and open the properties of Mike's user account. Confirm that the properties you entered on the command line appear in the account.

▶ **Exercise 3   Import Users with *CSVDE***

In the previous two exercises, you created users one at a time. In this exercise, you will use a comma-delimited text file to import two users.

1. Open Notepad and enter the following three lines. Each of the following bullets represents one line of text. Do not include the bullets in the Notepad document.

  ❑ DN,objectClass,sAMAccountName,sn,givenName,userPrincipalName

  ❑ "cn=Lisa Andrews,ou=People,dc=contoso,dc=com",user,lisa.andrews,
  Lisa,Andrews,lisa.andrews@contoso.com

  ❑ "cn=David Jones,ou=People,dc=contoso,dc=com",user,david.jones,
  David,Jones,david.jones@contoso.com

2. Save the file to your Documents folder with the name **Newusers.txt**.

3. Open a command prompt.

4. Type **cd %userprofile%\Documents** and press Enter.

5. Type **csvde -i -f newusers.txt -k** and press Enter.

   The three users are imported. If you encounter any errors, examine the text file for typographical problems.

6. Open the Active Directory Users And Computers snap-in and confirm that the users were created successfully.

   If you have had the Active Directory Users And Computers snap-in open during this exercise, you might have to refresh your view to see the newly created accounts.

7. Examine the accounts to confirm that first name, last name, user principal name, and pre-Windows 2000 logon name are populated according to the instructions in NewUsers.txt.

▶ **Exercise 4   Import Users with *LDIFDE***

Like *CSVDE*, *LDIFDE* can be used to import users. The LDIF file format, however, is not a typical delimited text file. In this exercise, you will use *LDIFDE* to import two users.

1. Open Notepad and type the following lines. Be sure to include the blank line between the two operations.

   ```
   DN: CN=April Stewart,OU=People,DC=contoso,DC=com
   changeType: add
   CN: April Stewart
   objectClass: user
   sAMAccountName: april.stewart
   userPrincipalName: april.stewart@contoso.com
   givenName: April
   sn: Stewart
   displayName: Stewart, April
   mail: april.stewart@contoso.com
   description: Sales Representative in the USA
   title: Sales Representative
   department: Sales
   company: Contoso, Ltd.

   DN: CN=Tony Krijnen,OU=People,DC=contoso,DC=com
   changeType: add
   CN: Tony Krijnen
   objectClass: user
   sAMAccountName: tony.krijnen
   userPrincipalName: tony.krijnen@contoso.com
   givenName: Tony
   sn: Krijnen
   displayName: Krijnen, Tony
   mail: tony.krijnen@contoso.com
   description: Sales Representative in The Netherlands
   title: Sales Representative
   department: Sales
   company: Contoso, Ltd.
   ```

2. Save the file to your Documents folder with the name **Newusers.ldf**. Surround the file name with quotes; otherwise, Notepad will add a .txt extension.

Although you can import LDIF files with any extension, it is convention to use the .ldf extension.

3. Open a command prompt.

4. Type **cd %userprofile%\Documents** and press Enter.

5. Type **ldifde -i -f newusers.ldf -k** and press Enter.

   The two users are imported. If you encounter any errors, examine the text file for typographical problems.

6. Open the Active Directory Users And Computers snap-in and confirm that the users were created successfully.

   If you have had the Active Directory Users And Computers snap-in open during this exercise, you might have to refresh your view to see the newly created accounts.

7. Examine the accounts to confirm that user properties are populated according to the instructions in Newusers.ldf.

Lesson Summary

- You can copy a user account in Active Directory to create a new account. A small subset of account properties are copied. To create a user account template, create a user and pre-populate the appropriate attributes. Then, disable the template account so that it cannot be used for authentication. Copy the template as a basis for new user accounts.

- The *Dsadd* command enables you to create user objects from the command line, with parameters that specify properties of the user.

- You can import a comma-delimited text file of users and their properties with the *CSVDE* command.

- Use *LDIFDE* to perform operations in Active Directory, including adding, changing, and removing users. The LDIF file that specifies such operations is a standard format that enables the interchange of data between directories.

Lesson Review

You can use the following questions to test your knowledge of the information in Lesson 1, "Automating the Creation of User Accounts." The questions are also available on the companion CD if you prefer to review them in electronic form.

NOTE Answers

Answers to these questions and explanations of why each answer choice is right or wrong are located in the "Answers" section at the end of the book.

1. You are an administrator at a large university, and you have just been sent an Excel file containing information about 2,000 students who will enter the school in two weeks. You want to create user accounts for the new students with as little effort as possible. Which of the following tasks should you perform?

    A. Create a user account template and copy it for each student.

    B. Run *LDIFDE -i.*

    C. Use *CSVDE -i.*

    D. Run the *DSADD USER* command.

2. You are an administrator at a large university. Which command can be used to delete user accounts for students who graduated?

    A. *LDIFDE*

    B. *Dsmod*

    C. *DEL*

    D. *CSVDE*

Lesson 2: Creating Users with Windows PowerShell and VBScript

In Lesson 1, you learned how to use command-line tools to add or import user accounts. In this lesson, you will discover two of the most powerful tools for performing and automating administrative tasks: Windows PowerShell and VBScript. Both of these tools enable you to create scripts that can automate the creation of user accounts. Windows PowerShell also enables you to create users from a twenty-first century command shell that lives up to its middle name, *Power*.

After this lesson, you will be able to:
- Install the Windows PowerShell feature on Windows Server 2008.
- Identify key elements of the Windows PowerShell syntax, including cmdlets, variables, aliases, namespaces, and providers.
- Create a user in Windows PowerShell.
- Create a user in VBScript.

Estimated lesson time: 75 minutes

Introducing Windows PowerShell

Windows PowerShell is a powerful tool for performing and automating administrative tasks in Windows Server 2008.

Exam Tip   This section introduces you to Windows PowerShell so that you can become familiar with this important administrative tool. You are not expected to create Windows PowerShell scripts on the 70-640 exam; however, you should be able to recognize cmdlets used for basic Active Directory tasks such as those described in this training kit. If you want to learn to administer using Windows PowerShell, refer to *Windows PowerShell Scripting Guide* by Ed Wilson (Microsoft Press, 2008).

Windows PowerShell is both a command-line shell and a scripting language including more than 130 command-line tools called *cmdlets* (pronounced, "command-lets") that follow extremely consistent syntax and naming conventions and can be extended with custom cmdlets. Unlike traditional command shells such as *Cmd.exe* in Windows or BASH in Unix that operate by sending a text command a separate process or utility and then returning the results of that command as text, Windows PowerShell performs direct manipulation of Microsoft .NET Framework objects at the command line.

Windows PowerShell is installed as a feature of Windows Server 2008. Open Server Manager and click the Add Features link to install Windows PowerShell. After you have installed Windows PowerShell, you can open it from the Start menu. It is likely that you will use Windows

PowerShell often enough to warrant creating a shortcut in a more accessible location. Right-click Windows PowerShell in the Windows PowerShell program group and choose Pin To Start Menu. The Windows PowerShell command shell looks very similar to the command prompt of *Cmd.exe* except that the default background color is dark blue, and the prompt includes *PS*. Figure 3-1 shows the Windows PowerShell.

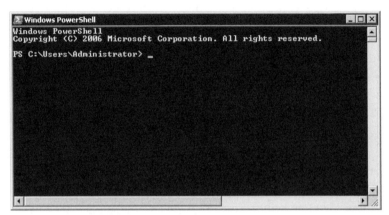

Figure 3-1   The Windows PowerShell console

NOTE   One Windows, one shell

Windows PowerShell enables you to use launch programs and execute commands that are identical to those in the command shell. Therefore, Windows PowerShell is backward compatible for administrators. If you use Windows PowerShell, you can perform administrative tasks either with familiar *Cmd.exe* commands or with Windows PowerShell directives.

Understanding Windows PowerShell Syntax, Cmdlets, and Objects

In traditional shells such as *Cmd.exe*, you issue commands such as *dir* or *copy* that access utilities built into the shell, or you call executable programs such as *attrib.exe* or *xcopy.exe*, many of which accept parameters from the command line and return feedback in the form of output, errors, and error codes.

In Windows PowerShell, you issue directives by using cmdlets. A cmdlet is a single-feature command that manipulates an object. Cmdlets use a Verb-Noun syntax—a verb and a noun separated by a hyphen. Examples include Get-Service and Start-Service.

NOTE   Cmdlets support direct entry and scripting

Cmdlets can be typed into the Windows PowerShell interactively or saved in script files (*.PS1) that are then executed by Windows PowerShell.

What Is an Object?

An object is a programming construct. From a technical perspective, a .NET object is an instance of a .NET class that consists of data and the operations associated with that data. Think of an object as a virtual representation of a resource of some kind. For example, when you use the Get-Service *cmdlet* in Windows PowerShell, the cmdlet returns one or more objects representing services. Objects can have *properties* that represent data, or attributes, maintained by the resource. An object representing a service, for example, has properties for the service name and its startup state. When you get a property, you are retrieving the data of the resource. When you set a property, you are writing that data to the resource.

Objects also have *methods*, which are actions that you can perform on the object. The service object has *start* and *stop* methods, for example. When you perform a method on the object that represents the resource, you perform the action on the resource itself.

These cmdlets do not pass commands or parameters to other utilities or programs but, rather, operate on .NET objects directly. If you type the cmdlet Get-Service, Windows PowerShell returns a *collection* of objects for all services. It presents the results of the cmdlet as a table showing the service, its name, and its display name, as shown in Figure 3-2.

Figure 3-2   The Get-Service cmdlet

These simple commands can be used together by combining or *pipelining* to create more complex directives. For example, pipelining the Get-Service cmdlet to the Format-List cmdlet produces a different result, as Figure 3-3 shows.

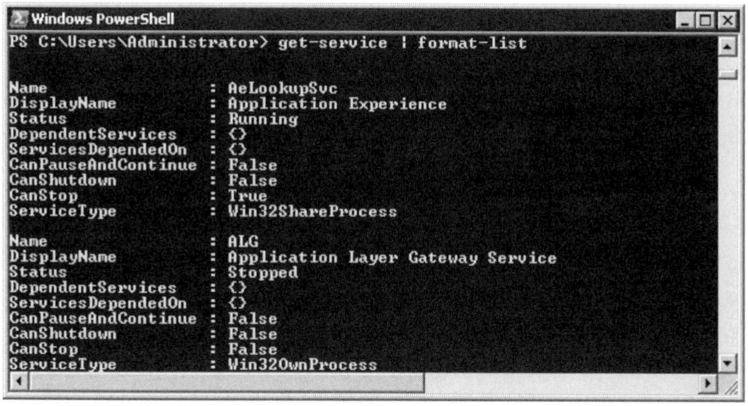

Figure 3-3   The Format-List cmdlet operating on the collection generated by Get-Service

Notice that the Format-List cmdlet produces far more detail than the default output of the Get-Service cmdlet. This reveals an important point. The Get-Service cmdlet is not just returning a static list of three attributes of services; it is returning objects representing the services. When those objects are pipelined, or passed, to the Format-List cmdlet, Format-List is able to work directly with those objects and display all the attributes of the services.

NOTE   **Subtle but important difference**

This is quite different from the standard Windows command shell, in which the output of one command piped to another command can be only text. If this were *Cmd.exe*, a *"format list"* command could reformat only the three pieces of information provided by a *"get-service"* command.

The Format-List cmdlet makes decisions about which attributes to display. You can direct it to show all properties by adding a parameter, *property*, with a value of all represented by an asterisk (*). The following command will list all available properties of all services:

```
get-service | format-list –property *
```

Getting Help

The Windows PowerShell Get-Help cmdlet is the best place to start looking for information, especially when you are just getting started with Windows PowerShell. The simplest form of help is provided by typing the Get-Help cmdlet followed by the cmdlet name you want help with, for example:

```
get-help get-service
```

You can get more detailed help by adding the *detailed* or *full* parameters, for example, *get-help get-command -detailed* or *get-help get-command -full*.

Using Variables

If you are repeatedly issuing a path or object definition, you can assign it to a variable to reduce your level of effort. Variables in Windows PowerShell always begin with a dollar sign ($). For example, you can assign the variable *$DNS* to represent the object retrieved by the Get-Service DNS cmdlet:

```
$DNS=get-service DNS
```

When you assign an object to a variable, you create an *object reference.* You can retrieve properties of the object by using dot (.) properties. For example, to return the status of the DNS service, type the following:

```
$DNS.status
```

A special *pipeline variable* can be used as a placeholder for the current object within the current pipeline. The pipeline variable is $_. For example, to get a list of all running services, type the following:

```
get-service | where-object { $_.status -eq "Running" }
```

This directive retrieves all services and pipes the objects to the Where-Object cmdlet, which evaluates each object in the pipeline to determine whether the object represented by the pipeline variable $_ has a status property equal to *Running.*

Using Aliases

An *alias* is an alternative way to refer to a cmdlet. For example, the Where-Object *cmdlet* previously shown has an alias of, simply, Where, so the code shown previously could be shortened to the following:

```
get-service | where { $_.status -eq "Running" }
```

Many of the Windows PowerShell cmdlets have already been assigned aliases. For example, the cmdlet that displays the contents of a folder on a disk is Get-ChildItem. This cmdlet has been given the alias Dir, equivalent to the Windows command shell command, and the alias Ls, for users more accustomed to a UNIX shell.

How do you determine which cmdlet is behind an alias? Type **alias**, as in the following example:

```
alias dir
```

The output will reveal that Dir is an alias for Get-ChildItem.

Whereas Windows PowerShell provides aliases for command-shell commands, Windows PowerShell cmdlets do not take the same parameters as *Cmd.exe* commands. For example, to retrieve a directory of folders and all subfolders at the command prompt, type **dir /s**. In Windows PowerShell, type **dir -recurse**.

Namespaces, Providers, and PSDrives

Cmdlets operate against objects in a namespace. A folder on a disk is an example of a namespace—a hierarchy that can be navigated. Namespaces are created by providers, which you can think of as drivers. For example, the file system has a Windows PowerShell provider, as does the registry, so Windows PowerShell can directly access and manipulate objects in the namespaces of those providers.

You are certainly familiar with the concept of representing the namespace of a disk volume with a letter or representing a shared network folder's namespace as a mapped drive letter. In Windows PowerShell, namespaces from any provider can be represented as *PSDrives*. Windows PowerShell automatically creates a PSDrive for each drive letter already defined by Windows.

Windows PowerShell takes this concept to the next level by creating additional PSDrives for commonly required resources. For example, it creates two drives, *HKCU* and *HKLM*, for the HKEY_CURRENT_USER and HKEY_LOCAL_MACHINE registry hives. Now you can navigate and manipulate the registry as easily as you can a file system. Type the following in the Windows PowerShell:

```
cd hklm:\software
dir
```

Drives are also created for aliases, environment, certificates, functions, and variables. To list the PSDrives that have been created, type **get-psdrive**.

Creating a User with Windows PowerShell

You are now ready to learn how to apply Windows PowerShell to create a user in Active Directory. The most basic Windows PowerShell script to create a user will look similar to the following:

```
$objOU=[ADSI]"LDAP://OU=People,DC=contoso,DC=com"
$objUser=$objOU.Create("user","CN=Mary North")
$objUser.Put("sAMAccountName","mary.north")
$objUser.SetInfo()
```

This code exemplifies the four basic steps to creating an object in Active Directory with Windows PowerShell:

1. Connect to the container—for example, the OU—in which the object will be created.
2. Invoke the *Create* method of the container with the object class and relative distinguished name (RDN) of the new object.
3. Populate attributes of the object with its *Put* method.
4. Commit changes to Active Directory with the object's *SetInfo* method.

Each of these steps is examined in detail in the following sections.

Connecting to an Active Directory Container

To create an object such as a user, you ask the object's container to create the object. So you begin by performing an action—a method—on the container. The first step, then, is to connect to the container. Windows PowerShell uses the Active Directory Services Interface (ADSI) type adapter to tap into Active Directory objects. A *type adapter* is a translator between the complex and sometimes quirky nature of a .NET Framework object and the simplified and consistent structure of Windows PowerShell. To connect to an Active Directory object, you submit an LDAP query string, which is simply the LDAP:// protocol moniker followed by the DN of the object. So the first line of code is as follows:

```
$objOU=[ADSI]"LDAP://OU=People,DC=contoso,DC=com"
```

Windows PowerShell uses the ADSI type adapter to create an object reference to the People OU and assigns it to a variable. The variable name *objOU* reflects programming standards that suggest a three-letter prefix to identify the type of variable, but variable names can be anything you'd like as long as they start with a dollar sign.

Invoking the *Create* Method

At this point, the variable *$objOU* is a reference to the People OU. You can now ask the container to create the object, using the container's *Create* method. The *Create* method requires two parameters, passed as arguments: the object class and the RDN of the object. An object's RDN is the portion of its name beneath its parent container. Most object classes use the format CN=*object name* as their RDNs. The RDN of an OU, however, is OU=*organizational unit name*, and the RDN of a domain is DC=*domain name*. The following line, then, creates a user object with the RDN specified as CN=*Mary North*.

```
$objUser=$objOU.Create("user","CN=Mary North")
```

The resulting object is assigned to the variable *$objUser*, which will represent the object and enable you to manipulate it.

Populating User Attributes

It's important to remember that the new object and the changes you make are not saved until you commit the changes, and you cannot commit the changes successfully until all required attributes are populated. The required attribute for user objects is the pre-Windows 2000 logon name. The LDAP name for this attribute is *sAMAccountName*. Therefore, the next line of code assigns the *sAMAccountName* to the object, using the *Put* method. *Put* is a standard method for writing a property of an object. *Get* is a standard method for retrieving a property. The resulting code is:

```
$objUser.Put("sAMAccountName","mary.north")
```

There are other mandatory attributes for a user object, including its security identifier (SID), but those attributes are created automatically by Active Directory when you commit a new user to the directory.

Committing Changes with the *SetInfo* Method

To commit the changes, use the Active Directory object's *SetInfo* method, as in the following line of code:

```
$objUser.SetInfo()
```

Populating Additional User Attributes

The preceding commands create a user with only the mandatory *sAMAccountName* attribute configured. You should populate other user attributes when creating a user object. You just learned to use the *Put* method of a user object to write a property. All you have to do is use the same method repeatedly, specifying each attribute you want to add. Examine the following code:

```
$objUser.put("sAMAccountName",$samAccountName)
$objUser.put("userPrincipalName",$userPrincipalName)
$objUser.put("displayName",$displayName)
$objUser.put("givenName",$givenName)
$objUser.put("sn",$sn)
$objUser.put("description",$description)
$objUser.put("company",$company)
$objUser.put("department",$department)
$objUser.put("title",$title)
$objUser.put("mail",$mail)
$objUser.SetInfo()
```

Each of these commands populates an attribute of a user with the value stored in a variable. Don't forget to use the *SetInfo()* method of the user object to commit the changes to Active Directory! Until you use *SetInfo()*, the changes you make are occurring only in your local copy of the object. The *SetInfo()* method evaluates your object's properties for validity. If you configured an invalid value for an attribute, you will receive an error on the *SetInfo()* line. Using the *GetInfo()* method of the user object reloads the original object, effectively undoing all your changes.

If you're not sure what the LDAP name for an attribute is, click the Attribute Editor tab of a user account in the Active Directory Users And Computers snap-in. The tab is visible when you select Advanced Features from the View menu. The Attribute Editor shows all attributes of an object, including their LDAP names and values. You can also use either of these commands to show properties that are populated for a user object:

```
$objUser.psbase.properties
$objUser | get-member
```

NOTE **Multivalued attributes are different**

Although most user attributes are single valued, some are multivalued. If an attribute takes multiple values, use the *PutEx()* method of the user object. Perform a search on the Internet with the following keywords: *PowerShell user array PutEx*, and you will find numerous community resources that will help you learn the nuances of working with multivalued attributes.

And what about the user's password? You do not use *Put* to set a user's password. Instead, you use the *SetPassword* method, as in the following command:

```
$objUser.SetPassword("COmp!exP@ssw0rd")
```

Unfortunately, *SetPassword* can be used only *after* you've created the user and invoked the *Set-Info()* method. That means, in fact, you are creating the account before assigning it a password. That's not a bug or a limitation of Windows PowerShell—it's a reality of Kerberos and LDAP. However, it's secure because the account is created in the disabled state.

You must then enable the account. The status of an account is a flag that is also not manipulated with the *Put* command. Instead, you use the following command:

```
$objUser.psbase.InvokeSet("AccountDisabled",$false)
$objUser.SetInfo()
```

Importing Users from a Database with Windows PowerShell

Although you will not be expected to understand database imports with Windows PowerShell for the 70-640 examination, learning how to do so can be a tremendous benefit to your efforts to automate the creation of users. As you'll see, it takes only a few lines of additional code with the powerful cmdlets of Windows PowerShell.

Assume that you receive an Excel worksheet from the human resources department with information about newly hired employees. Excel can save the file as a comma-delimited text file (.csv), which can be imported by Windows PowerShell. The first line of the .csv file must have field names followed by the information about each user. As a simple example, consider the following .csv file saved as Newusers.csv:

Newusers.csv
```
cn,sAMAccountName,FirstName,LastName
John Woods,john.woods,Johnathan,Woods
Kim Akers,kim.akers,Kimberly,Akers
```

Notice that the field names do not have to match the LDAP attribute names. They will be mapped to attribute names by the script.

Windows PowerShell can import this data source with one command:

```
$dataSource=import-csv "newusers.csv"
```

After you import the data source, you must loop through each record in the data source. This is performed with a *foreach* block, which takes the following format:

```
foreach($dataRecord in $datasource)
{
    # do whatever you want to do
}
```

The ForEach cmdlet loops through each object or record in the data source and assigns the current object to the *$dataRecord* variable, so the *$dataRecord* variable represents the current record. You can now look at the actual fields in each record, which become properties of the *$dataRecord* variable. For example, the first name of the first user is:

```
$dataRecord.FirstName
```

You can assign it to a variable:

```
$givenName = $dataRecord.FirstName
```

Again, it is not necessary for the variable or the field name to match the LDAP attribute name. The mapping is performed when you write the variable containing the value to the attribute itself:

```
$objUser.Put("givenName",$givenName)
```

The LDAP attribute, *givenName*, is in quotes. Only when you refer to the actual attribute of an object must you use the correct name. It certainly makes it easier to follow the code, however, if data source field names and variable names reflect the attribute names.

Putting it together, you can create a user import script:

Userimport.ps1
```
$objOU=[ADSI]"LDAP://OU=People,DC=contoso,DC=com"
$dataSource=import-csv "NewUsers.csv"
foreach($dataRecord in $datasource) {
    #map variables to data source
    $cn=$dataRecord.cn
    $sAMAccountName=$dataRecord.sAMAccountName
    $givenName=$dataRecord.FirstName
    $sn=$dataRecord.LastName
    $displayName=$sn + ", " + $givenName
    $userPrincipalName=$givenName + "." + $sn + "@contoso.com"

    #create the user object
    $objUser=$objOU.Create("user","CN="+$cn)
    $objUser.Put("sAMAccountName",$sAMAccountName)
    $objUser.Put("userPrincipalName",$userPrincipalName)
    $objUser.Put("displayName",$displayName)
    $objUser.Put("givenName",$givenName)
    $objUser.Put("sn",$sn)
    $objUser.SetInfo()
```

```
$objUser.SetPassword("COmp!exP@ssw0rd")
$objUser.psbase.InvokeSet("AccountDisabled",$false)
$objUser.SetInfo()
}
```

The first line of the script connects to the container, the OU in which all new users will be created. The next two lines connect to the data source and loop through each record, assigning each record to a variable, *$dataRecord*. The *foreach* block does two things. First, it maps fields in the data source to variables. Then it creates a user.

Notice that some variables are constructed by concatenating (appending) two fields. The *$displayName* variable takes the *LastName, FirstName* format, and the *$userPrincipalName* variable takes the *FirstName.LastName@contoso.com* format.

The user is created by invoking the *Create* method of the OU. Attributes of the user are populated and committed, and then the password is set and the account is enabled. Voilà!

Executing a Windows PowerShell Script

By default, Windows PowerShell prevents the execution of scripts as a security measure. To run a script that you have created, you must change the execution policy of Windows PowerShell with the following command:

```
set-executionpolicy remotesigned
```

The execution policy specifies which scripts can be run. The command just shown configures Windows PowerShell so that it will run local scripts but will require scripts from remote sources to be signed. Changing the execution policy has security implications, so you should read the information about running Windows PowerShell scripts at *http://www.microsoft.com/technet/scriptcenter/topics/winpsh/manual/run.mspx#EXC*.

After you've set the execution policy, you can run your script. but do not run it by name alone—you will receive an error. You must specify the path to the script! A shortcut is to use the *.\scriptname* notation, which indicates the current directory, so the following command will execute the user import script:

```
.\UserImport.ps1
```

Introducing VBScript

VBScript is a scripting language that supports the automation of administrative tasks on all current versions of Windows. VBScript files are text files typically edited with Notepad or a script editor and saved with a .vbs extension. To execute a script, you can double-click it, which opens the script, using *Wscript.exe*. Alternatively, from the command line, you can run the script with *Cscript.exe*, using the following syntax:

```
cscript.exe scriptname
```

Both *Wscript.exe* and *Cscript.exe* are components of the Windows Scripting Host (WSH), which is the automation framework installed on all current versions of Windows that supports several scripting languages, including VBScript.

Creating a User with VBScript

Because VBScript also uses the ADSI interface to manipulate Active Directory, the process for creating a user in VBScript is identical to the process in Windows PowerShell. A simple script for creating a user follows:

```
Set objOU=GetObject("LDAP://OU=People,DC=contoso,DC=com")
Set objUser=objOU.Create("user","CN=Mary North")
objUser.Put "sAMAccountName","mary.north"
objUser.SetInfo()
```

The script first connects to the container, the OU in which the user will be created. VBScript uses the GetObject statement to connect to an ADSI object by its distinguished name. When you assign an object to a variable in VBScript, you use the Set statement to create the object reference.

The second line of code invokes the *Create* method of the OU to create an object of a specific class and with a specific relative distinguished name, just as in the Windows PowerShell example. Because the result of the method is an object, you again have to use the Set statement to assign the object reference to a variable.

The third line uses the *Put* method of the user object, but VBScript does not use parentheses to pass the parameters to the argument. The fourth line is identical to Windows PowerShell; it commits the changes. Save the script as Newuser.vbs and execute it from the command shell, or from Windows PowerShell, with this command:

```
cscript.exe newusers.vbs
```

VBScript vs. Windows PowerShell

VBScript has two major advantages over Windows PowerShell. The first is the fact that VBScript scripts can be run on all current versions of Windows using the WSH, whereas Windows PowerShell must be downloaded and installed on versions of Windows prior to Windows Server 2008 and requires .NET Framework 2.0 or greater. The second advantage of VBScript is that it has been around for many years, so there is an extraordinary amount of experience, knowledge, and community-posted information on the Internet.

However, WSH does not provide a shell for directly executing commands. Additionally, VBScript as a language is not a particularly rich scripting language and does not fully use the .NET Framework. Although the WSH exists on Windows Server 2008 and VBScript is still supported, the way of the future is Windows PowerShell. That is why it was presented first in this lesson.

The disadvantages of Windows PowerShell are the inverse of the VBScript advantages. The very fact that Windows PowerShell is new means that it is a product still in development. In the previous sections, you learned to create user accounts with Windows PowerShell. The techniques and code you learned are fairly complex in the bigger picture of Windows PowerShell. In fact, they are almost identical to VBScript.

That's because in the current version of Windows PowerShell, there is very limited support for Active Directory administration. Unlike Windows Management Interface (WMI) and Microsoft Exchange Server, which have very rich Windows PowerShell providers, Active Directory support is limited to the ADSI type adapter, which is quirky and awkward and, ultimately, relies on ADSI just as VBScript does. In future versions of Windows PowerShell, an Active Directory provider will be introduced that will make working with Active Directory objects as easy as working with files in a file system.

Remember that on the 70-640 exam, you are not expected to create scripts in either Windows PowerShell or VBScript. Be able to recognize a script that follows the correct process to create a user: Connect to the OU, create the object, populate its properties, and then commit the changes.

PRACTICE Creating Users with Windows PowerShell and VBScript

In this practice, you will create a number of user accounts with automated methods discussed in this lesson. To perform the exercises in this practice, you will need the first-level OU object, named People, in the *contoso.com* domain.

▶ **Exercise 1   Install Windows PowerShell**

In preparation for exercises that use Windows PowerShell for administrative tasks, you will install the Windows PowerShell feature in this exercise.

1. Open Server Manager.
2. Click the Features node in the console tree.
3. Click the Add Features link.
4. Select Windows PowerShell from the Features list. Click Next.
5. Click Install.
6. When the installation is complete, click Close.
7. Right-click Windows PowerShell in the Windows PowerShell program group and choose Pin To Start Menu.

▶ **Exercise 2   Create a User with Windows PowerShell**

Now that Windows PowerShell is installed, you will use it to create a user in Active Directory.

1. Open Windows PowerShell.
2. Connect to the People OU by typing the following command:

```
$objOU=[ADSI]"LDAP://OU=People,DC=contoso,DC=com"
```

3. Create a user object in the OU by typing the following command:

```
$objUser=$objOU.Create("user","CN=Mary North")
```

4. Assign the mandatory attribute, the user's pre-Windows 2000 logon name, by typing the following command:

```
$objUser.Put("sAMAccountName","mary.north")
```

5. Commit the changes to Active Directory by typing the following command:

```
$objUser.SetInfo()
```

6. Confirm that the object was created by typing the following command:

```
$objUser.distinguishedName
```

   The user's distinguished name should be returned.

7. Examine the user attributes that Active Directory configured automatically by typing the following command:

```
$objUser | get-member
```

   This command pipes the object representing the user to the Get-Member cmdlet, which enumerates, or lists, the populated attributes.

▶ **Exercise 3   Create a New User with a Windows PowerShell Script**

In Exercise 2, "Create a User with Windows PowerShell," you created a user by entering commands directly into Windows PowerShell. In this exercise, you will create a Windows PowerShell script that automates the creation of a user.

1. Open Notepad.

   Type the following lines of code:

```
$objOU=[ADSI]"LDAP://OU=People,DC=contoso,DC=com"
$objUser=$objOU.Create("user","CN=Scott Mitchell")
$objUser.Put("sAMAccountName","scott.mitchell")
$objUser.SetInfo()
```

2. Save the script in your Documents folder as "Newuser.ps1", including the quotes so that Notepad does not add a .txt extension.

3. Open Windows PowerShell.

4. Type **get-childitem** and press Enter.

   The Get-ChildItem cmdlet enumerates all child objects of the object currently in the pipe. At the Windows PowerShell prompt, the current directory is in the pipe.

5. Type **dir** and press Enter.

   The *dir* alias refers to the Get-ChildItem cmdlet.

6. Type **cd documents** and press Enter.

   You should now be in your Documents folder.

7. Enable script execution by typing the following command:

```
set-exceutionpolicy remotesigned
```

8. Execute the script by typing .**newuser.ps1** and pressing Enter.

   The .\ notation provides the current path as the path to the script. Without .\, an error is thrown.

9. Confirm that the user was created successfully in Active Directory.

▶ **Exercise 4   Create a New User with a VBScript Script**

In this exercise, you will create a VBScript script that automates the creation of a user.

1. Open Notepad.
2. Type the following lines of code:

```
Set objOU=GetObject("LDAP://OU=People,DC=contoso,DC=com")
Set objUser=objOU.Create("user","CN=Linda Mitchell")
objUser.Put "sAMAccountName","linda.mitchell"
objUser.SetInfo()
```

3. Save the script in your Documents folder as "Newuser.vbs", including the quotes so that Notepad does not add a .txt extension.
4. Open the command prompt.
5. Type **cd %userprofile%\\documents** and press Enter.
6. Execute the script by typing **cscript.exe newuser.vbs**.
7. Confirm that the user was created successfully in Active Directory.

Lesson Summary

- Windows PowerShell provides support for performing administrative tasks from a command line and from scripts. Windows PowerShell is a feature of Windows Server 2008 and can be downloaded for Windows Server 2003, Windows Vista, and Windows XP.

- VBScript is a scripting language that can be processed by the Windows Scripting Host, a component that exists in all current versions of Windows.

- To create an Active Directory object by using Windows PowerShell or VBScript, you connect to the container—the OU, for example—and then create the object, populate its properties, and commit changes to Active Directory with the *SetInfo* method.

Lesson Review

You can use the following questions to test your knowledge of the information in Lesson 2, "Creating Users with Windows PowerShell and VBScript." The questions are also available on the companion CD if you prefer to review them in electronic form.

NOTE **Answers**

Answers to these questions and explanations of why each answer choice is right or wrong are located in the "Answers" section at the end of the book.

1. You want to create a user object with Windows PowerShell. Which of the following must you do?

    A. Use the Create-User cmdlet.

    B. Use the *NewUser* method of ADSI.

    C. Invoke the *Create* method of an OU.

    D. Use the *set objUser=CreateObject* statement.

2. You want to create a user object with a single command. Which of the following should you do?

    A. Use the Create-Item cmdlet.

    B. Use the *SetInfo* method.

    C. Use the *Create* method of an OU.

    D. Use the *Dsadd* command.

3. Which of the following lines of Windows PowerShell code are necessary to create a user object in the People OU? (Choose all that apply. Each correct answer is a part of the solution.)

    A. `$objUser=$objOU.Create("user","CN=Jeff Ford")`

    B. `$objUser.SetInfo()`

    C. `$objUser=CreateObject("LDAP://CN=Jeff Ford,OU=People,DC=contoso,DC=com")`

    D. `$objOU=[ADSI]"LDAP://OU=People,DC=contoso,DC=com"`

Lesson 3: Supporting User Objects and Accounts

The first two lessons of this chapter detailed the methods with which to create user accounts. That is only the first step in the life cycle of a user in a domain. After creating the user, you must configure attributes that define both the properties of the security principal (the account) and properties that manage the user. You must also know how and when to administer the account—to perform password resets and to unlock the account. Finally, you must be able to move the user between OUs and, eventually, deprovision the account by disabling or deleting it. This lesson will cover the procedures used to support a user object through its life cycle—procedures you can perform using both the Windows interface and the command line or automation tools.

> **After this lesson, you will be able to:**
> - Identify the purpose and requirements of user account attributes and user name properties.
> - View and modify hidden attributes of user objects.
> - Modify attributes of multiple users simultaneously.
> - Manage users with the Active Directory Users And Computers snap-in, DS commands, Windows PowerShell, and VBScript.
> - Perform common administrative tasks to support user accounts.
>
> **Estimated lesson time: 90 minutes**

Managing User Attributes with Active Directory Users and Computers

When you create a user with the Active Directory Users and Computers snapin New Object–User Wizard, you are prompted for some common properties, including logon names, password, and user first and last names. A user object in Active Directory, however, supports dozens of additional properties that you can configure at any time with the Active Directory Users and Computers snap-in.

To read and modify the attributes of a user object, right-click the user and choose Properties. The user's Properties dialog box appears, as shown in Figure 3-4. Attributes of a user object fall into several broad categories that appear on tabs of the dialog box:

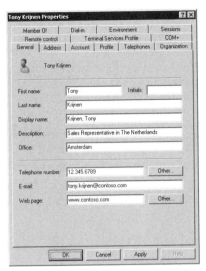

Figure 3-4 The Properties dialog box for a user

- **Account attributes: the Account tab** These properties include logon names, password, and account flags. Many of these attributes can be configured when you create a new user with the Active Directory Users and Computers snap-in. The "Account Properties" section details account attributes.

- **Personal information: the General, Address, Telephones, and Organization tabs** The General tab exposes the name properties that are configured when you create a user object, as well as basic description and contact information. The Address and Telephones tabs provide detailed contact information. The Telephones tab is also where Microsoft chose to put the *Notes* field, which maps to the *info* attribute and is a very useful general-purpose text field that is underused by many enterprises. The Organization tab shows job title, department, company, and organizational relationships.

- **User configuration management: the Profile tab** Here you can configure the user's profile path, logon script, and home folder.

- **Group membership: the Member Of tab** You can add the user to and remove the user from groups and change the user's primary group. Group memberships and the primary group will be discussed in Chapter 5, "Computers."

- **Terminal services: the Terminal Services Profile, Environment, Remote Control, and Sessions tabs** These four tabs enable you to configure and manage the user's experience when the user is connected to a Terminal Services session.

MORE INFO Terminal Services settings

For more information about configuring Terminal Services settings, see *MCTS: Configuring Windows Server 2008 Applications Infrastructure*, by J.C. Mackin and Anil Desai (Microsoft Press, 2008).

- **Remote access: the Dial-in tab**   You can enable and configure remote access permission for a user on the Dial-in tab.
- **Applications: the COM+ tab**   This tab enables you to assign the users to an Active Directory COM+ partition set. This feature facilitates the management of distributed applications and is beyond the scope of the 70-640 exam.

Viewing All Attributes

A user object has even more properties than are visible in its Properties dialog box. Some of the so-called hidden properties can be quite useful to your enterprise. To uncover hidden user attributes, you must turn on the Attribute Editor, a new feature in Windows Server 2008. Click the View menu and select the Advanced Features option. Then open the Properties dialog box of the user, and the Attribute Editor tab will be visible, as shown in Figure 3-5.

Figure 3-5   The Attribute Editor tab

The Attribute Editor displays all the system attributes of the selected object. The Filter button enables you to choose to see even more attributes, including backlinks and constructed attributes. Backlinks are attributes that result from references to the object from other objects. The easiest way to understand backlinks is to look at an example: the *memberOf* attribute. When a user is added to a group, it is the group's *member* attribute that is changed—the distinguished name of the user is added to this multivalued attribute. Therefore, the *member* attribute of a group is called a *forward link* attribute. A user's *memberOf* attribute is updated automatically by Active Directory when the user is referred to by a group's *member* attribute. You do not ever write directly to the user's *memberOf* attribute; it is dynamically maintained by Active Directory.

A *constructed* attribute is one of the results from a calculation performed by Active Directory. An example is the *tokenGroups* attribute. This attribute is a list of the security identifiers (SIDs) of all the groups to which the user belongs, including nested groups. To determine the value of *tokenGroups*, Active Directory must calculate the effective membership of the user, which takes a few processor cycles. Therefore, the attribute is not stored as part of the user object or dynamically maintained. Instead, it is calculated when needed. Because of the processing required to produce constructed attributes, the Attribute Editor does not display them by default. They also cannot be used in LDAP queries.

As you can see in Figure 3-5, some attributes of a user object could be quite useful, including *division*, *employeeID*, *employeeNumber*, and *employeeType*. Although the attributes are not shown on the standard tabs of a user object, they are now available through the Attribute Editor, and they can be accessed programmatically with Windows PowerShell or VBScript.

MORE INFO **Hidden attributes of objects**

For more information on using hidden attributes of objects and extending the schema with custom attributes, see *Windows Administration Resource Kit: Productivity Solutions for IT Professionals* by Dan Holme (Microsoft Press, 2008).

Managing Attributes of Multiple Users

The Active Directory Users and Computers snap-in enables you to modify the properties of multiple user objects simultaneously. Select several user objects by holding the Ctrl key as you click each user or using any other multiselection technique. Be certain that you select only objects of one class, such as users. After you have multiselected the objects, right-click any one of them and choose Properties.

When you have multiselected the user objects, a subset of properties is available for modification.

- **General** Description, Office, Telephone Number, Fax, Web Page, E-mail
- **Account** UPN Suffix, Logon Hours, Computer Restrictions (logon workstations), all Account Options, Account Expires
- **Address** Street, P.O. Box, City, State/Province, ZIP/Postal Code, Country/Region
- **Profile** Profile Path, Logon Script, and Home Folder
- **Organization** Title, Department, Company, Manager

Exam Tip Be sure to know which properties can be modified for multiple users simultaneously. Exam scenarios and simulations that suggest a need to change many user object properties as quickly as possible are often testing your understanding of multiselecting. In the real world, remember that you can and should use automation tools such as Dsmod, Windows PowerShell, and VBScript.

Understanding Name and Account Attributes

Two sets of attributes tend to appear on the certification exams and to present challenges to Windows administrators: name attributes and account attributes.

User Object Names

Several attributes are related to the name of a user object and an account. It is important to understand the distinctions between them.

- A user's *sAMAccountName* attribute (the pre-Windows 2000 logon name) must be unique for the entire domain. Many organizations use initials or some combination of first and last name to generate the *sAMAccountName*. That approach can be problematic because an organization of any size is likely to have users with names similar enough that the rules for generating the *sAMAccountName* would generate a duplicate name, so exceptions have to be built into the system and, eventually, the rules are riddled with exceptions. This problem is solved if the employee number or some other unique attribute of the users is used for the *sAMAccountName*. If you have the ability to direct the naming conventions at your organization, a unique, name-independent logon name is recommended.

- The *userPrincipalName* (UPN) attribute consists of a logon name and a UPN suffix which is, by default, the DNS name of the domain in which you create the object. The UPN must be unique for the entire forest. E-mail addresses, which must be unique for the whole world, certainly meet that requirement. Consider using e-mail addresses as UPNs. If your Active Directory domain name is not the same as your e-mail domain name, you must add the e-mail domain name as an available UPN suffix. To do this, open the Active Directory Domains And Trusts snap-in, right-click the root of the snap-in, and choose Properties.

- The RDN must be unique within an OU. For users, this means the *cn* attribute must be unique within the OU. This can be a tricky one. If you have a single, flat OU for users that already contains a user named Scott Miller, and you hire a second Scott Miller, his user object cannot have the same common name as the first. Unfortunately, there's no perfect answer to this problem for all organizations. Design a naming standard that applies a single rule for all CNs. Perhaps the CN should include an employee's number— for example, *Scott Miller (645928)*. If your OU structure for user accounts is flat, be prepared to address this challenge.

  Additionally, many organizations choose to configure the *cn* attribute as *LastName, FirstName* because by doing so, you can sort users by last name in the Active Directory Users and Computers snap-in. This is not a recommended method to achieve the goal. Instead of using a last-name-first format for *cn*, add the Last Name column to your view in the Active Directory Users And Computers snap-in by clicking the View menu and choosing Add/Remove Columns. Then click the Last Name column header to sort by last name.

■ The *displayName* attribute appears in the Exchange global address list (GAL). It can be easier to locate users in the GAL if they are sorted by last name, so you can create a naming convention for your organization that specifies that the *displayName* attribute takes the *LastName, FirstName* syntax.

Account Properties

On the Account tab of a user's Properties dialog box, shown in Figure 3-6, are the attributes directly related to the fact that a user is a security principal, meaning that it is an identity to which permissions and rights can be assigned. Other security principals include computers, groups, and the *inetOrgPerson* object class.

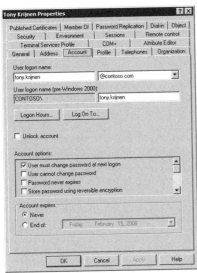

Figure 3-6   Account properties of a user object

Several of the account properties are worth highlighting because they are potentially quite useful and are not self-explanatory. Table 3-2 describes these properties.

Table 3-2   User Account Properties

Property	Description
Logon Hours	Click Logon Hours to configure the hours during which a user is allowed to log on to the network.
Log On To	Click Log On To if you want to limit the workstations to which the user can log on. This is called Computer Restrictions in other parts of the user interface and maps to the *userWorkstations* attribute. You must have NetBIOS over TCP/IP enabled for this feature to restrict users, because it uses the computer name rather than the Media Access Control (MAC) address of its network card to restrict logon.

Table 3-2   User Account Properties

Property	Description
User Must Change Password At Next Logon	Select this check box if you want the user to change the password you have entered the first time he or she logs on. You cannot select this option if you have selected Password Never Expires. Selecting this option will automatically clear the mutually exclusive option User Cannot Change Password.
User Cannot Change Password	Select this check box if you have more than one person using the same domain user account (such as Guest) or to maintain control over user account passwords. This option is commonly used to manage service account passwords. You cannot select this option if you have selected User Must Change Password At Next Logon.
Password Never Expires	Select this check box if you never want the password to expire. This option will automatically clear the User Must Change Password At Next Logon setting because they are mutually exclusive. This option is commonly used to manage service account passwords.
Account Is Disabled	Select this check box to disable the user account, for example, when creating an object for a newly hired employee who does not yet need access to the network.
Store Password Using Reversible Encryption	This option, which stores the password in Active Directory without using Active Directory's powerful, nonreversible encryption hashing algorithm, exists to support applications that require knowledge of the user password. If it is not absolutely required, do not enable this option because it weakens password security significantly. Passwords stored using reversible encryption are similar to those stored as plaintext. Macintosh clients using the AppleTalk protocol require knowledge of the user password. If a user logs on using a Macintosh client, you will need to select this option.
Smart Card Is Required For Interactive Logon	Smart cards are portable, tamper-resistant hardware devices that store unique identification information for a user. They are attached to, or inserted into, a system and provide an additional, physical identification component to the authentication process.
Account Is Trusted For Delegation	This option enables a service account to impersonate a user to access network resources on behalf of a user. This option is not typically selected, certainly not for a user object representing a human being. It is used more often for service accounts in three-tier (or multitier) application infrastructures.
Account Expires	Use the Account Expires controls to specify when an account expires.

NOTE Configure highly complex passwords for service accounts

Services require credentials with which to access system resources. Many services require a domain user account with which to authenticate, and it is common to specify that the account password never expires. In such situations, be sure you use a long, complex password. If the service account is used by services on a limited number of systems, you can increase the security of the account by configuring the Log On To property with the list of systems using the service account.

Managing User Attributes with *Dsmod* and *Dsget*

The *Dsmod* and *Dsget* commands are two Active Directory command-line tools, called DS commands. You encountered *Dsquery* in Chapter 2 and *Dsadd* in Lesson 1 of this chapter.

Dsmod

Dsmod modifies the attributes of one or more existing objects. DS commands were introduced in Lesson 1. Like other DS commands, the *Dsmod* basic syntax is:

```
dsmod user UserDN ... parameters
```

The *UserDN* parameter specifies the distinguished name of the user to modify. The remaining parameters indicate the attribute to change and the new value. For example, the following command changes the *Office* attribute of Tony Krijnen:

```
dsmod "cn=Tony Krijnen,ou=People,dc=contoso,dc=com" –office "Amsterdam"
```

The attribute parameters do not map directly to the names of LDAP attributes of a user object. For example, the *dept* parameter of the *DSMOD USER* command modifies the *department* attribute of a user object. Additionally, *DSMOD USER* can modify only a subset of user attributes. Type **DSMOD USER /?** for usage information and a list of supported parameters.

Piping Multiple DNs to *Dsmod*

The *UserDN* parameter of the *Dsmod* command does not have to be entered directly into the command line. There are two other ways to pipe DNs to it. The first is to enter the DNs into the console. Let's assume you need to change the *office* attribute of two users, Linda Mitchell and Scott Mitchell, to reflect their relocation to the Sydney office. At the command prompt, type the following command:

```
dsmod user –office "Sydney"
```

The *UserDN* parameter is missing. The console (the command prompt) waits for you to enter DNs of users. Enter one per line, surrounded with quotes, pressing Enter at the end of each DN. After entering the last DN and pressing Enter, press Ctrl+Z at the beginning of the next line and press Enter to indicate that you are finished. The command will then execute against each of the DNs you have entered.

A more sophisticated way to send DNs to the *Dsmod* command is by piping the results of a *Dsquery* command. *Dsquery* was covered in Chapter 2; it searches Active Directory for specified criteria and returns the DNs of matching objects. For example, to change the *office* attribute of Linda and Scott Mitchell's accounts to Sydney, use the following command:

```
dsquery user -name "* Mitchell" | dsmod user -office "Sydney"
```

The *DSMOD USER* command searches Active Directory for users whose names end with *Mitchell*. The resulting objects' DNs are then piped to *DSMOD USER*, which changes the *office* attribute to *Sydney*.

As another example, assume you want to assign all users a home folder on SERVER01. The following command changes the *homeDirectory* and *homeDrive* attributes of user objects in the People OU:

```
dsquery user "ou=People,dc=contoso,dc=com" | dsmod user
-hmdir "\\server01\users\%username%\documents" -hmdrv "U:"
```

As mentioned in Lesson 1, the special *%username%* token can be used to represent the *sAMAccountName* of user objects when using DS commands to configure the value of the *-email*, *-hmdir*, *-profile*, and *-webpg* parameters.

Dsget

The *Dsget* command gets and outputs selected attributes of one or more objects. Its syntax, like that of *Dsmod*, is:

```
dsget user UserDN... parameters
```

You can supply the DNs of one or more user objects by specifying them on the command line, separated by spaces; by entering them in the console; or by piping the results of a *DSQUERY USER* command. Unlike *Dsadd* and *Dsmod*, *Dsget* takes only a parameter and not an associated value. For example, *Dsget* takes the *samid* parameter like *Dsadd* does, but it does not take a value. Instead, it reports the current value of the attribute. For example, to display the pre-Windows 2000 logon name of Jeff Ford in the People OU, use the following command:

```
dsget user "cn=Jeff Ford,ou=People,dc=contoso,dc=com" -samid
```

To display the pre-Windows 2000 logon names of all users in the Sydney office, use this command:

```
dsquery user -office "Sydney" | dsget user -samid
```

Managing User Attributes with Windows PowerShell and VBScript

To read an attribute of a user object with Windows PowerShell or VBScript, you use the ADSI to connect to the user object, a process called *binding*. In Lesson 2, you connected to an OU to create an object. After the object exists, you connect directly to the object. One way to do so is with the Active Directory services path (*aDSPath*) of the object, which is the "LDAP://" protocol moniker followed by the distinguished name of the object.

The Windows PowerShell command for connecting to the user account of Jeff Ford in the People OU is:

```
$objUser=[ADSI]"LDAP://cn=Jeff Ford,ou=People,dc=contoso,dc=com"
```

The VBScript equivalent is:

```
Set objUser=GetObject("LDAP://cn=Jeff Ford,ou=People,dc=contoso,dc=com"
```

Remember that Windows PowerShell specifies the ADSI type adapter, and VBScript uses *GetObject*. VBScript uses the Set statement to assign an object reference to a variable. Windows PowerShell does not use the Set statement and prefixes all variables with a dollar sign.

After you have a variable that references the object, you can get its properties. For example, in Windows PowerShell, type the following to report the user's *sAMAccountName* attribute:

```
$objUser.Get("sAMAccountName")
```

In VBScript, you must indicate that you want to output the attribute. A common way to do that is with the WScript.Echo statement, as follows:

```
WScript.Echo objUser.Get("sAMAccountName")
```

You will often see a shorthand form called the *.property* (pronounced "dot-property") format, such as *$objUser.sAMAccountName* in Windows PowerShell and *objUser.sAMAccountName* in VBScript. Although this method works most of the time, it is recommended to specify the *Get* method, particularly when working with Active Directory objects in Windows PowerShell.

If you want to modify an attribute, you need to perform three steps:

1. Connect to the user object.
2. Modify an attribute.
3. Commit the change.

You've already seen how to connect to the object. The second step is to change the attribute. Most attributes are simple, single-valued attributes and can be changed with the *Put* method of the object. For example, in Windows PowerShell:

```
$objUser.put("company","Contoso, Ltd.")
```

and in VBScript:

```
objUser.put "company","Contoso, Ltd."
```

The only difference here is that VBScript does not use parentheses to pass the parameters to the *Put* method.

You can set multiple attributes during the second step. After all attributes have been specified, you must commit the changes to the directory with *SetInfo*. The Windows PowerShell version is:

```
$objUser.SetInfo()
```

The VBScript version is identical, except for the variable name:

```
objUser.SetInfo()
```

Putting the three steps together, you have a Windows PowerShell script:

```
$objUser=[ADSI]"LDAP://cn=Jeff Ford,ou=People,dc=contoso,dc=com"
$objUser.put("company","Contoso, Ltd.")
$objUser.SetInfo()
```

In VBScript, the code is as follows:

```
Set objUser=GetObject("LDAP://cn=Jeff Ford,ou=People,dc=contoso,dc=com"
objUser.put "company","Contoso, Ltd."
objUser.SetInfo()
```

What if you want to delete an attribute entirely? You must first connect to the object. Then you can set an attribute to a blank string, "" if it is a string attribute or to 0 if it is a numeric attribute and 0 if 0 is an appropriate representation of "empty." However, you can also delete the attribute entirely, assuming it is not a mandatory attribute. To do so, you must use the *PutEx* method of the user object. To delete the *office* attribute, for example, you would use the following code in Windows PowerShell:

```
$objUser.PutEx(1, "office", 0)
$objUser.SetInfo()
```

In VBScript, you would use the following lines to delete an attribute:

```
objUser.PutEx 1, "office", 0
objUser.SetInfo()
```

Administering User Accounts

The primary purpose of user objects in Active Directory is to support authentication of a human being or of a service. Accounts are provisioned, administered, and, eventually, deprovisioned. The most common administrative tasks related to user accounts are resetting a password, unlocking an account, disabling, enabling, deleting, moving, and renaming user objects.

The following sections will examine each of these tasks and how they can be performed using the Windows interface, Windows PowerShell, VBScript, or the command prompt. Each of these tasks requires you to have appropriate permissions to the user objects. Delegating administrative permissions was discussed in Chapter 2.

Resetting a User's Password

If the user forgets his or her password and attempts to log on, he or she will receive a logon message, as shown in Figure 3-7.

Before the user can log on successfully, you will have to reset that password. You do not need to know the user's old password to do so. Simply right-click the user's object in Active Directory and choose Reset Password. The Reset Password dialog box, shown in Figure 3-8, appears. Enter the new password in both the New Password and Confirm Password boxes. It is a best practice to select the User Must Change Password At Next Logon option so that the user's password is known only to the user.

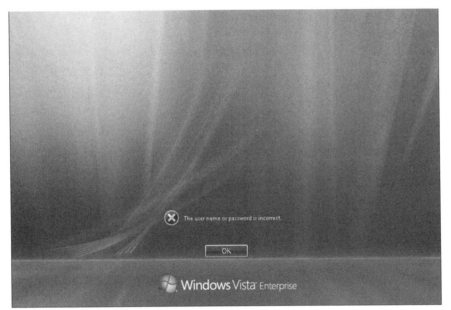

The user name or password is incorrect.

OK

Windows Vista Enterprise

Figure 3-7   A logon message notifying a user that the user name or password is invalid

Reset Password	? X

New password:

Confirm password:

☑ User must change password at next logon

The user must logoff and then logon again for the change to take effect.

Account Lockout Status on this Domain Controller: Unlocked

☐ Unlock the user's account

OK   Cancel

Figure 3-8   The Reset Password dialog box

You can also use a DS command to reset a user's password and, optionally, to force the user to change that password at the next logon. Type the following command:

```
dsmod user UserDN -pwd NewPassword -mustchpwd yes
```

Using Windows PowerShell, type the following commands:

```
$objUser=[ADSI]"LDAP://UserDN'
$objUser.SetPassword("NewPassword")
```

Note that, unlike other attributes, you do not use *SetInfo* after using *SetPassword* to configure the user's password. However, if you want to force the user to change passwords at the next logon, you do as follows:

```
$objUser.Put ("pwdLastSet",0)
$objUser.SetInfo()
```

In VBScript, the code is very similar:

```
Set objUser=GetObject("LDAP://UserDN")
objUser.SetPassword "NewPassword"
objUser.Put "pwdLastSet",0
objUser.SetInfo
```

It is even possible to import passwords, using *LDIFDE*, a command introduced in Lesson 1. See Knowledge Base article 263991 at *http://support.microsoft.com/default.aspx?scid=kb;en-us;263991* for information.

Unlocking a User Account

In Chapter 8, "Authentication," you will learn to configure password and account lockout policies. A lockout policy is designed to prevent an intruder from attempting to penetrate the enterprise network by logging on repeatedly with various passwords until he or she finds a correct password. When a user attempts to log on with an incorrect password, a logon failure is generated. When too many logon failures occur within a specified period of time defined by the lockout policy, the account is locked out. The next time the user attempts to log on, a notification clearly states the account lockout.

NOTE Watch for drives mapped with alternate credentials

A common cause of account lockout is a drive mapped with alternate credentials. If the alternate credentials' password is changed, and the Windows client attempts repeatedly to connect to the drive, that account will be locked out.

Your lockout policy can define a period of time after which a lockout account is automatically unlocked. But when a user is trying to log on and discovers he or she is locked out, it is likely he or she will contact the help desk for support. You can unlock a user account by right-clicking the account, choosing Properties, clicking the Account tab, and selecting the Unlock Account check box.

Windows Server 2008 also adds the option to unlock a user's account when you choose the *Reset Password* command. Select the Unlock The User's Account check box, shown in Figure 3-8. This method is particularly handy when a user's account has become locked out because the user did, in fact, forget the password. You can now assign a new password, specify that the user must change the password at next logon, and unlock the user's account in one dialog box.

Unfortunately, neither the command line nor Windows PowerShell provides a native tool for unlocking accounts. To unlock a user with VBScript, use the following code:

```
Set objUser = GetObject("LDAP://UserDN")
objUser.IsAccountLocked = False
objUser.SetInfo
```

Disabling and Enabling a User Account

User accounts are security principals—identities that can be given access to network resources. Because each user is a member of Domain Users and of the Authenticated Users special identity, each user account has at least read access to a vast amount of information in Active Directory and on your file systems unless you have been severe and unusually successful at locking down access control lists (ACLs).

Therefore, it is important not to leave user accounts open. That means you should configure password policies and auditing—both discussed in Chapter 8—and procedures to ensure that accounts are being used appropriately. If a user account is provisioned before it is needed, or if an employee will be absent for an extended period of time, disable the account.

To disable an account in the Active Directory Users And Computers snap-in, right-click a user and choose Disable. From the command line, you can use *Dsmod.exe*, as in the following example:

```
dsmod user UserDN -disabled yes
```

With Windows PowerShell, as you learned in Lesson 2, you must use a roundabout method to set the flag:

```
$objUser=[ADSI]"LDAP://UserDN"
$objUser.psbase.InvokeSet('Account Disabled',$true)
$objUser.SetInfo()
```

VBScript is more straightforward:

```
Set objUser = GetObject("LDAP://UserDN")
objUser.AccountDisabled=TRUE
```

Enabling an account is just a matter of *yes* to *no* for the *Dsmod.exe* command:

```
dsmod user UserDN -disabled no
```

In the Windows PowerShell commands shown earlier, change *$true* to *$false* and, in VBScript, change *TRUE* to *FALSE*.

Deleting a User Account

When an account is no longer necessary, you can delete it from your directory. However, it is critical to consider that after the account has been deleted, it is eventually purged entirely from the directory. You cannot simply re-create a new account with the same name as a deleted account and hope it has the same group memberships and access to resources; it will not. The loss of the user's SID and of its group memberships can cause significant problems if, later, you realize you need the account.

Therefore, many organizations choose to deprovision a user account in stages. First, the account is disabled. After a period of time, it is deleted. Active Directory actually maintains a subset of the account's properties—most notably its SID—for a period of time called the *tombstone lifetime*, 60 days by default. After that time, the account's record is removed from the directory.

You can also consider recycling a user account. If a user leaves your organization, it's possible you will eventually hire a replacement who will need very similar resource access, group memberships, and user rights as the previous user. You can disable the account until a replacement is found and then rename the account to match the new user's name. The previous user's SID, group memberships, and resource access are thereby transferred to the replacement.

To delete a user account in Active Directory, select the user and press Delete or right-click the user and choose Delete. You will be prompted to confirm your choice because of the significant implications of deleting a security principal.

You can delete objects from Active Directory by using the *Dsrm* command, another of the DS commands. *Dsrm* uses a simple syntax:

```
dsrm UserDN
```

Notice that *Dsrm* is not followed by the *user* object class as are the other DS commands.

To delete a user from Active Directory, using Windows PowerShell, you connect to the parent container—the OU—and use the container's *Delete* method. This might seem slightly strange, but it parallels the fact that you use the container's *Create* method to create a user. The following two Windows PowerShell commands will delete a user:

```
$objOU = [ADSI]"LDAP://organizational unit's DN"
$objOU.Delete("user","CN=UserCN")
```

VBScript uses the same approach, with its unique syntax:

```
Set objOU = GetObject(LDAP://organizational unit's DN")
objOU.Delete "user","CN=UserCN"
```

Moving a User Account

If you need to move a user object in Active Directory, you can drag and drop it in the Active Directory Users and Computers snap-in. However, it is more accurate to right-click the user and choose the *Move* command. Keep in mind that when you move a user, you might change the Group Policy objects (GPOs) that apply to that user. GPOs are discussed in Chapter 6, "Group Policy Infrastructure."

To move a user with a command-line tool, use *Dsmove*. *Dsmove* uses the following syntax:

```
dsmove UserDN -newparent TargetOUDN
```

Dsmove does not specify a *user* object class. Instead, it simply indicates the DN of the user to move and, in the *TargetOUDN* placeholder, the distinguished name of the OU to which the user will be moved.

To move a user in Windows PowerShell, you must use the *psbase.MoveTo* method. The following two lines of code will move a user:

```
$objUser=[ADSI]"LDAP://UserDN"
$objUser.psbase.MoveTo("LDAP://TargetOUDN")
```

This is another example of a workaround required because this version of Windows PowerShell does not deliver an Active Directory provider. Some day in the future, you will be able to use the Move-Item cmdlet as you can with the file system and registry providers, but not yet.

In VBScript, you use an approach that seems a bit backward. You connect to the target container and then you grab the user object and move it to the container. The following two lines of code do the trick:

```
Set objOU = GetObject("LDAP://TargetOUDN")
objOU.MoveHere "LDAP://UserDN", vbNullString
```

The intrinsic constant *vbNullString* passes *Null* to the *MoveHere* method, instructing it that you want the object to keep its current CN.

Renaming a User Account

In the "User Object Names" section, you learned about many of the names associated with a user account. When a user account needs to be renamed, there can be one or more attributes you must change. To rename a user in Active Directory, right-click the user and choose Rename. Type the new common name (CN) for the user and press Enter. The Rename User dialog box appears and prompts you to enter the Full Name (which maps to the *cn* and *name* attributes), First Name, Last Name, Display Name, User Logon Name, and User Logon Name (Pre-Windows 2000).

From a command prompt, you can use *Dsmod.exe* with the following syntax:

```
dsmod user UserDN [-upn UPN][-fn FirstName][-mi Initial][-ln LastName]
[-dn DisplayName][-email EmailAddress]
```

You cannot change the *samAccountName* attribute by using *Dsmod.exe*, and you cannot change the CN of the object by using *Dsmod.exe*.

To change the CN of an object from a command shell, you must use Windows PowerShell or VBScript. In Windows PowerShell, two lines of code work:

```
$objUser=[ADSI]"LDAP://UserDN"
$objUser.psbase.rename("CN=New CN")
```

You can also change other name attributes, using the *Put* method of the user object.

To rename a user with VBScript, use a variation of the *MoveHere* method shown in the previous section:

```
Set objOU = GetObject("LDAP://CurrentOUDN")
objOU.MoveHere "LDAP://UserDN", "CN=New CN"
```

In these two lines, you connect to the user's current OU and use the *MoveHere* method of the OU to apply a new CN to the user.

PRACTICE Supporting User Objects and Accounts

In this practice, you will perform procedures that reflect common tasks required to support users in an enterprise environment. To perform the exercises in this practice, you should have performed the practices in Lesson 1 and Lesson 2 so that the following user objects exist in the People OU:

- Tony Krijnen
- Linda Mitchell
- Scott Mitchell
- April Stewart

▶ **Exercise 1   View All Attributes of a User**

In this exercise, you will discover the Attribute Editor and use it to reveal and modify user attributes that are not visible in the Active Directory Users and Computers snap-in.

1. Log on to SERVER01 as Administrator and open the Active Directory Users And Computers snap-in.
2. In the People OU, right-click Tony Krijnen and choose Properties.
3. Examine the tabs of the Properties dialog box.

   What attributes are visible? Do you see any that you have not seen before? Do you see any attributes that, if configured, can provide useful information to your enterprise?
4. Click the Telephones tab and enter information into the *Notes* field. Click OK.
5. Click the View menu and select Advanced Features.
6. Open the properties of Tony Krijnen again and click the Attribute Editor tab.

7. Scroll to locate the *info* attribute.

   What do you see there?

8. Locate the *division* attribute, double-click it, type **Subsidiary**, and then click OK.

9. Locate the *employeeID* attribute, double-click it, type **104839**, and then click OK.

10. Examine other attributes that are visible in the Attribute Editor.

    What attributes do you see that are not visible in the Active Directory Users and Computers snap-in? Can any of the hidden attributes, if configured, provide useful information to your enterprise?

11. Click OK to close the Properties dialog box.

▶ **Exercise 2   Manage Attributes of Multiple Objects**

In this exercise, you will select multiple objects and configure properties of the objects.

1. In the People OU, select Scott Mitchell.

2. Hold the Ctrl key and select Linda Mitchell and April Stewart.

   You should have three users selected now.

3. Right-click any of the selected users and choose Properties.

   A Properties dialog box appears with a subset of user properties that can be applied to multiple users simultaneously.

4. On the General tab, select the Office check box and type **Miami** in the Office text box.

5. Click the Account tab.

   In this scenario, these three users work on weekdays. They are not allowed to log on during the weekend.

6. Select the Logon Hours check box, and then click the Logon Hours button.

7. Click Sunday and click the Logon Denied button.

8. Click Saturday and click the Logon Denied button. Then click OK.

   Additionally, the three users are allowed to log on to only specific computers in the enterprise.

9. Select the Computer Restrictions check box, and then click the Log On To button.

10. Select The Following Computers option.

11. In the Computer Name box, type **DESKTOP101** and click Add.

12. Repeat the process to add **DESKTOP102** and **DESKTOP103**. Then click OK.

13. On the Address tab, select the Street, City, State/Province, and ZIP/Postal Code check boxes. Enter fictitious address information in these boxes.

14. Click the Profile tab and configure the **\\server01\%username%\documents** home folder.

15. Click the Organizational tab and configure the company name, **Contoso, Ltd**.

16. Click OK.

17. Open the user objects to confirm that the changes were applied.

▶ **Exercise 3   Manage User Attributes with DS Commands**

In this scenario, Linda and Scott Mitchell are relocating from Miami to Sydney. They will be taking three weeks to perform the relocation. You will manage their accounts through the process.

1. Open Windows PowerShell.

   Windows PowerShell can launch executables just like the command prompt.

2. Spend some time considering how you could, with a single command, change the *office* attribute of the two users to *Sydney* and disable the accounts so that the accounts cannot be used while the employees are away. What command would you issue?

3. Type the following command and press Enter:

   ```
   dsquery user -name "* Mitchell" | dsmod user -office "Sydney" -disabled yes
   ```

4. In the Active Directory Users And Computers snap-in, open the user accounts to confirm the changes were made.

5. You need to make a record of the users' pre-Windows 2000 logon names and user principal names. What single command could you enter to show you that information?

6. Type the following command and press Enter:

   ```
   dsquery user -name "* Mitchell" | dsget user -samid -upn
   ```

   The Mitchells have arrived in Sydney. It is now time to enable their accounts.

7. In Windows PowerShell, type the following lines:

   ```
   $objUser = [ADSI]"LDAP://CN=Linda Mitchell,OU=People,DC=contoso,DC=com"
   $objUser.psbase.InvokeSet('AccountDisabled',$false)
   $objUser.SetInfo()
   ```

8. In the Active Directory Users And Computers snap-in, confirm that Linda Mitchell's account is once again enabled.

9. Right-click Scott Mitchell's account and choose Enable Account.

▶ **Exercise 4   Reset a Password and Unlock a User Account**

While he was relocating from Miami to Sydney, Scott Mitchell forgot his password. After you enabled his account, he attempted to log on several times with an incorrect password, and then his account was locked. In this exercise, you will reset Scott's password and unlock his account.

1. In the Active Directory Users And Computers snap-in, select the People OU.

2. In the details pane, right-click Scott Mitchell's account and choose Reset Password.

3. Enter a new password for Scott in the New Password and Confirm Password boxes.

4. Ensure that the User Must Change Password At Next Logon check box is selected.

5. Select the Unlock The User's Account check box.

6. Click OK.

Lesson Summary

- Use the Attribute Editor to view and modify all attributes of a user object.
- User account properties can restrict the workstations to which a user logs on, the hours during which logon is allowed, and the date that the account will expire on.
- You can modify the attributes of multiple objects simultaneously by using *Dsmod.exe* or by multiselecting objects in the Active Directory Users And Computers snap-in. However, the properties you can change with each method are limited. You can use a script, for example, a VBScript or Windows PowerShell script, to modify attributes of objects as well.
- When you delete a user account, you cannot create an account with the same name; the new account will not belong to the same groups or have the same resource access. You will have to rebuild those memberships and permissions for the new account.

Lesson Review

You can use the following questions to test your knowledge of the information in Lesson 3, "Supporting User Objects and Accounts." The questions are also available on the companion CD if you prefer to review them in electronic form.

NOTE Answers

Answers to these questions and explanations of why each answer choice is right or wrong are located in the "Answers" section at the end of the book.

---

1. You want to set the Office property of ten users in two different OUs. The users currently have the Office property configured as *Miammi*. You recently discovered the typographic error and want to change it to *Miami*. What can you do to make the change? (Choose all that apply.)
    - A. Select all ten users by holding the Ctrl key and opening the Properties dialog box.
    - B. Use *Dsget* and *Dsmod*.
    - C. Use *Dsquery* and *Dsmod*.
    - D. Use Get-Item and Move-Item.
2. You want to move a user from the Paris OU to the Moscow OU. Which tools can you use? (Choose all that apply.)
    - A. Move-Item
    - B. The *MoveHere* method of the Moscow OU
    - C. *Dsmove*
    - D. *Redirusr.exe*
    - E. Active Directory Migration Tool

3. A user reports that she is receiving a logon message that states, "Your account is configured to prevent you from using the computer. Please try another computer." What should you do to enable her to log on to the computer?

   A. Click the Log On To button on the Account tab of her user account.

   B. Click the Allowed To Join Domain button in the New Computer dialog box.

   C. Use the *Dsmove* command.

   D. Give her the right to log on locally, using the local security policy of the computer.

Chapter Review

To further practice and reinforce the skills you learned in this chapter, you can perform the following tasks:

- Review the chapter summary.
- Review the list of key terms introduced in this chapter.
- Complete the case scenario. This scenario sets up a real-world situation involving the topics of this chapter and asks you to create a solution.
- Complete the suggested practices.
- Take a practice test.

Chapter Summary

- A variety of tools are at your disposal for managing user objects through the life cycle of the account.
- VBScript and Windows PowerShell are powerful ways to automate administrative tasks. Although neither tool is the solution for all problems, there are more samples and resources for administering Active Directory with VBScript than with Windows PowerShell. However, the future of command-based administration and automation is clearly in Windows PowerShell.
- Because users are security principals, it is particularly important to manage accounts carefully and to be comfortable with the tasks, including resetting passwords; unlocking, enabling, and disabling accounts; moving and renaming accounts; and, eventually, deleting accounts.
- If you have a data source of user information, it is likely that you will be able to import it into Active Directory with *CSVDE*, Windows PowerShell, or VBScript.

Key Terms

Use these key terms to understand better the concepts covered in this chapter.

- **method**   In the context of programming or scripting, an action performed on an object. For example, you can use the *SetPassword* method of a user object to perform a secure password reset. You can use the *Create* method of a container object in Active Directory to create a new user, group, or computer.
- **object**   In the context of programming or scripting, a data structure that represents a system resource. For example, an object might represent a user account in Active Directory. Objects expose properties or attributes, methods or actions.

Case Scenario

In the following case scenario, you will apply what you've learned about creating and maintaining user accounts. You can find answers to these questions in the "Answers" section at the end of this book.

Case Scenario: Import User Accounts

You are an administrator at a large university. Each term, you receive a file containing information about incoming students. Your job is to create a user account for each of the new students. The file you receive is created in Excel, and it contains name and contact information for each student. The user accounts you create must have logon names, display names, and e-mail addresses that follow the naming conventions established for the university. For example, logon names are constructed using the student's last name followed by the first letter of his or her first name. E-mail addresses are constructed to follow the first.last@domain.edu format. Your manager has asked you to have all accounts created four weeks before the beginning of the new term. In the past, you have created the accounts manually. This year, you want to automate the creation of the user accounts.

1. Which tool discussed in this chapter should you use to import the user accounts from the database? Why do you believe that tool is better than the other available user import tools?

2. What can you do to increase the security of the accounts you are creating, considering that they will be created four weeks before they are used for the first time?

3. After creating the accounts, you realize that you forgot to populate the *company* attribute with the name of your university. All the new student accounts are in a single year. What can you do quickly to populate that attribute, using the Active Directory Users and Computers snap-in or the command prompt?

Suggested Practices

To help you successfully master the exam objectives presented in this chapter, complete the following tasks.

Automate the Creation of User Accounts

In the first practice, you will use one method to create a large number of user accounts. In the second practice, which is optional and advanced, you will use a different method.

- **Practice 1** Create an Excel worksheet that will serve as a database of user accounts. In the first row of the worksheet, type the following LDAP attribute names, one attribute per column: *distinguishedName*, *objectClass*, *givenName*, *sn*, *sAMAccountName*. Populate the file with sample data. Remember that *givenName* is the user's first name, and *sn* is the user's last name. Use the sample in Exercise 3, "Import Users with *CSVDE*," of Lesson 1 if you need assistance. Save the file as a comma-separated text file. Use the *CSVDE* command to import the file.

■ **Practice 2**   In Chapter 2, you examined a script that can use a .csv file to create users. Modify the script to import users from your .csv file. Construct attributes such as *userPrincipalName* and *displayName* in the script, as the sample in Chapter 2 illustrated.

Maintain Active Directory Accounts

In this practice, you will apply the methods presented in Chapter 3, "Users," for managing user accounts.

■ **Practice**   Chapter 3 illustrated a number of options for performing administrative tasks to support user accounts. It will be an extremely valuable learning experience to step through the examples provided in the chapter and apply them, hands on. Treat each of the commands and scripts illustrated in this chapter as a practice.

Take a Practice Test

The practice tests on this book's companion CD offer many options. For example, you can test yourself on just one exam objective, or you can test yourself on all the 70-640 certification exam content. You can set up the test so that it closely simulates the experience of taking a certification exam, or you can set it up in study mode so that you can look at the correct answers and explanations after you answer each question.

MORE INFO   Practice tests

For details about all the practice test options available, see the "How to Use the Practice Tests" section in this book's introduction.

Chapter 4

Groups

Although users and computers, and even services, change over time, business roles and rules tend to remain more stable. Your business probably has a finance role, which requires certain capabilities in the enterprise. The user or users who perform that role will change, but the role will remain. For that reason, it is not practical to manage an enterprise by assigning rights and permissions to individual user, computer, or service identities. Management tasks should be associated with groups. In this training kit, you will use groups to identify administrative and user roles, to filter Group Policy, to assign unique password policies, to assign rights and permissions, and more. To prepare for those tasks, in this lesson you will learn how to create, modify, delete, and support group objects in an Active Directory Domain Services (AD DS) domain.

Exam objectives in this chapter:

- Creating and Maintaining Active Directory Objects
    - ❏ Automate creation of Active Directory accounts.
    - ❏ Maintain Active Directory accounts.

Lessons in this chapter:

- Lesson 1: Creating and Managing Groups 141
- Lesson 2: Automating the Creation and Management of Groups 159
- Lesson 3: Administering Groups in an Enterprise 169

Before You Begin

This chapter applies Microsoft Windows PowerShell, Microsoft VBScript, Comma-Separated Values Data Exchange (*CSVDE*), and LDAP Data Interchange Format Data Exchange (*LDIFDE*) to the task of automating computer account creation. Read Lesson 1, "Automating the Creation of User Accounts," and Lesson 2, "Creating Users with Windows PowerShell and VBScript," of Chapter 3, "Users," prior to reading this chapter.

In addition, to perform exercises in this chapter, you must have created a domain controller named SERVER01 in a domain named *contoso.com*. See Chapter 1, "Installation," for detailed steps for this task.

Real World

Dan Holme

Efficient and effective group management is a tremendous enabler for security, consistency, and productivity in an IT environment. As a consultant, I spend a lot of time with clients, aligning technology with their business needs. In the case of Microsoft Windows technologies, that entails defining and implementing business roles and rules so that administration can be defined, documented, and automated. And that process often requires improving clients' group management knowledge, technologies, and processes. Many IT professionals have come into Windows Server 2008 Active Directory with former practices that do not take advantage of groups as fully as possible. In fact, I've seen so much wasted productivity and decreased security due to poor group management that I dedicated two chapters of my book, *Windows Administration Resource Kit: Productivity Solutions for IT Professionals* (Microsoft Press, 2008), to improving and automating group management. In this lesson, you will learn what you need to know for the certification exam, and I share with you a few of the tips and best practices you'll need to make the most of groups in a production environment. I highly recommend reading the resource kit for more information, guidance, and fantastic tools related to group management.

Lesson 1: Creating and Managing Groups

You are certainly familiar with the purpose of groups: to collect items and manage them as a single entity. The implementation of group management in Active Directory is not intuitive because Active Directory is designed to support large, distributed environments, so it includes seven types of groups: two types of domain groups with three scopes each and local security groups. In this lesson, you will learn the purpose each of these groups serves, and you'll learn to align your business requirements with the potentially complex options that Active Directory provides.

After this lesson, you will be able to:
- Create groups by using the Active Directory Users and Computers snap-in.
- Manage and convert group type and scope.
- Identify the types of objects that can be members of groups of various scopes.
- Manage group membership.
- Develop a group management strategy.

Estimated lesson time: 45 minutes

Managing an Enterprise with Groups

Groups are security principals with a security identifier (SID) that, through their *member* attribute, collect other security principals (users, computers, contacts, and other groups) to facilitate management.

Imagine that all 100 users in the sales department require read-level access to a shared folder on a server: It is not manageable to assign permissions to each user individually. When new salespeople are hired, you will have to add the new accounts to the access control list (ACL) of the folder. When accounts are deleted, you will have to remove the permissions from the ACL, or else you will be left with the missing account entry on the ACL, shown in 4-1, which results from a SID on the ACL that refers to an account that cannot be resolved. Imagine now that all 100 users in the sales department require access to 10 shared folders on three servers. The management challenges just increased significantly.

You have, no doubt, learned that although assigning permissions to a resource to an individual identity—user or computer—is possible, the best practice is to assign a single permission to a group and then to manage access to the resource simply by changing membership of the group.

Figure 4-1 An ACL with a SID that refers to an account that can no longer be resolved

So, to continue the example, you could create a group called Sales and assign the group the Allow Read permission on the 10 shared folders on the three servers. Now, you have a *single point of management*. The Sales group effectively manages access to the shared folder. You can add new sales users to the group, and they will gain access to the 10 shared folders. When you delete an account, it is automatically deleted from the group, so you will not have irresolvable SIDs on your ACLs. There's an extra benefit also: because your ACL will remain stable with the Sales group having Allow Read permission, your backups will be easier. When you change the ACL of a folder, the ACL propagates to all child files and folders, setting the Archive flag and thereby requiring a backup of all files, even if the contents of the files have not changed.

Imagine, now, that it is not only salespeople who require read access to the folders. Marketing department employees and the sales consultants hired by your organization also require Read permission to the same folders. You could add those groups to the ACL of the folders, but soon you will end up with an ACL with multiple permissions, this time assigning the Allow Read permission to multiple groups instead of multiple users. To give the three groups permission to the 10 folders on the three servers, you will have to add 30 permissions! The next group that requires access will require 10 more changes to grant permissions to the ACLs of the 10 shared folders. What if eight users, who are not salespeople, marketing employees, or consultants, have business need for Read access to the 10 folders? Do you add their individual user accounts to the ACLs?

You can see quickly that using only one type of group—a group that defines the business roles of users—is not enabling effective management of access to the 10 folders. The solution is to recognize that two types of management must exist to manage this scenario effectively. You must manage the users as collections, based upon their business roles, and you must manage access to the 10 folders. The 10 folders are also a collection of items: They are a single resource that just happens to be distributed across 10 folders on three servers. You are trying to manage Read access to that resource collection. You need a single point of management with which to manage access to the resource collection.

This requires another group—a group that represents read access to the 10 folders on the three servers. Imagine that a group is created called ACL_Sales Folders_Read. This group will be assigned the Allow Read permission on the 10 folders. The sales, marketing, and consultants groups, along with the eight individual users, will all be members of the ACL_Sales Folders_Read group. As additional groups or users require access to the folders, they will be added to that group. It also becomes much easier to report who has access to the folders. Instead of having to examine the ACLs on each of the 10 folders, you simply examine the membership of the ACL_Sales Folders Read group.

This approach to managing the enterprise with groups is called *role-based management*. You define roles of users based on business characteristics—for example, department or division affiliation such as sales, marketing, and consultants—and you reflect your business rules such as which roles and individuals can access the 10 folders.

You can achieve both management tasks, using groups in a directory. Roles are represented by groups that contain users, computers, and other roles. That's right—roles can include other roles. For example, a Managers role might include the Sales Managers, Finance Managers, and Production Managers roles. Rules, such as the rule that defines Read access to the 10 folders, are represented by groups as well. Rule groups contain role groups and, occasionally, individual users or computers such as the eight users in the example.

To achieve manageability of an enterprise of any size or complexity, you will need to manage groups effectively and have an infrastructure of groups that provide single points of management for roles and rules. That means, technically, that you will need groups that can include as members users, computers, other groups, and, possibly, security principals from other domains.

For more information about role-based management, see *Windows Administration Resource Kit: Productivity Solutions for IT Professionals*.

Defining Group Naming Conventions

To create a group by using the Active Directory Users And Computers snap-in, simply right-click the OU in which you want to create a group, choose New, and select Group. The New Object – Group dialog box, shown in Figure 4-2, enables you to specify fundamental properties of the new group.

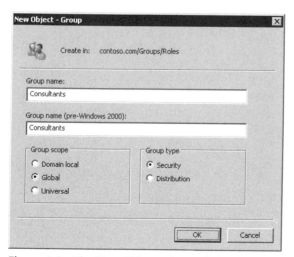

Figure 4-2   The New Object – Group dialog box

The first properties you must configure are the group's names. A group, like a user or computer, has several names. The first, shown in the Group Name box in Figure 4-2, is used by Windows 2000 and later systems to identify the object—it becomes the *cn* and *name* attributes of the object. The second, the pre-Windows 2000 name, is the *sAMAccountName* attribute, used to identify the group to computers running Microsoft Windows NT 4.0 and to some devices such as network attached storage (NAS) devices running non-Microsoft operating systems. The *cn* and *name* attributes must be unique only within the container—the OU—in which the group exists. The *sAMAccountName* must be unique in the entire domain. Technically, the *sAMAccountName* could be a different value than the *cn* and *name*, but it is highly discouraged to do so. Pick a name that is unique in the domain and use it in both name fields in the New Object – Group dialog box.

The name you choose should help you manage the group and manage your enterprise on a day-to-day basis. It is recommended to follow a naming convention that identifies the type of group and the purpose of the group. The example in the previous section used a group name, ACL_Sales Folder_Read. The prefix indicates that the group is used to assign permissions to a folder: It is used on access control lists. The main part of the name describes the resource that is being managed with the group: the sales folder. The suffix further defines what is being managed by the group: read access. A delimiter—in this case, an underscore—is used to separate parts of the name. Note that the delimiter is not used between the words *Sales* and *Folder*. Spaces are acceptable in group names—you will just need to enclose group names in quotes when you refer to them on command lines. You can create scripts that use the delimiter to deconstruct group names to facilitate auditing and reporting. Keep in mind that role groups that define user roles will often be used by nontechnical users. For example, you might e-mail enable the Sales group so that it can be used as an e-mail distribution list. Therefore, it is recommended that you do not use prefixes on role group names—keep the names user-friendly and descriptive.

For more information about managing groups effectively, see *Windows Administration Resource Kit: Productivity Solutions for IT Professionals.*

Understanding Group Types

There are two types of groups: security and distribution. When you create a group, you make the selection of the group type in the New Object – Group dialog box.

Distribution groups are used primarily by e-mail applications. These groups are not security enabled; they do not have SIDs, so they cannot be given permissions to resources. Sending a message to a distribution group sends the message to all members of the group.

Security groups are security principals with SIDs. These groups can, therefore, be used as permission entries in ACLs to control security for resource access. Security groups can also be used as distribution groups by e-mail applications. If a group will be used to manage security, it must be a security group.

Because security groups can be used for both resource access and e-mail distribution, many organizations use only security groups. However, it is recommended that if a group will be used only for e-mail distribution, you should create the group as a distribution group. Otherwise, the group is assigned a SID, and the SID is added to the user's security access token, which can lead to unnecessary token bloat.

Understanding Group Scope

Groups have members: users, computers, and other groups. Groups can be members of other groups, and groups can be referred to by ACLs, Group Policy object (GPO) filters, and other management components. *Group scope* affects each of these characteristics of a group: what it can contain, what it can belong to, and where it can be used. There are four group scopes: global, domain local, local, and universal.

The characteristics that define each scope fall into these categories:

- **Replication**   Where is the group defined and to what systems is the group replicated?
- **Membership**   What types of security principals can the group contain as members? Can the group include security principals from trusted domains?

  In Chapter 12, "Domains and Forests," you will learn about trust relationships, or *trusts*. A trust enables a domain to refer to another domain for user authentication, to include security principals from the other domain as group members, and to assign permissions to security principals in the other domain. The terminology used can be confusing. If Domain A trusts Domain B, then Domain A is the *trusting* domain and Domain B is the *trusted* domain. Domain A accepts the credentials of users in Domain B. It forwards requests by Domain B users to authenticate to a domain controller in Domain B because it *trusts* the identity store and authentication service of Domain B. Domain A can add

Domain B's security principals to groups and ACLs in Domain A. See Chapter 12 for more detail.

Exam Tip   In the context of group membership, remember that if Domain A trusts Domain B, Domain B is *trusted*, and its users and global groups can be members of domain local groups in Domain A. Additionally, Domain B's users and global groups can be assigned permissions to resources in Domain A.

- **Availability**   Where can the group be used? Is the group available to add to another group? Is the group available to add to an ACL?

Keep these broad characteristics in mind as you explore the details of each group scope.

Local Groups

Local groups are truly local—defined on and available to a single computer. Local groups are created in the security accounts manager (SAM) database of a domain member computer. Both workstations and servers have local groups. In a workgroup, you use local groups to manage security of resources on a system. In a domain, however, managing the local groups of individual computers becomes unwieldy and is, for the most part, unnecessary. It is not recommended to create custom local groups on domain members. In fact, the Users and Administrators local groups are the only local groups that you should be concerned with managing in a domain environment. To summarize:

- **Replication**   A local group is defined only in the local SAM database of a domain member server. The group and its membership are not replicated to any other system.
- **Membership**   A local group can include as members:
    - Any security principals from the domain: users, computers, global groups, or domain local groups.
    - Users, computers, and global groups from any domain in the forest.
    - Users, computers, and global groups from any trusted domain.
    - Universal groups defined in any domain in the forest.
- **Availability**   A local group has only computer-wide scope. It can be used in ACLs on the local computer only. A local group cannot be a member of any other group.

Domain Local Groups

Domain local groups are used primarily to manage permissions to resources. For example, the ACL_Sales Folder_Read group discussed earlier in the lesson would be created as a domain local group. Domain local groups have the following characteristics:

- **Replication** A domain local group is defined in the domain naming context. The group object and its membership (the *member* attribute) are replicated to every domain controller in the domain.
- **Membership** A domain local group can include as members:
  - Any security principals from the domain: users, computers, global groups, or other domain local groups.
  - Users, computers, and global groups from any domain in the forest.
  - Users, computers, and global groups from any trusted domain.
  - Universal groups defined in any domain in the forest.
- **Availability** A domain local group can be added to ACLs on any resource on any domain member. Additionally, a domain local group can be a member of other domain local groups or even computer local groups.

The membership capabilities of a domain local group are identical to those of local groups, but the replication and availability of the domain local group makes it useful across the entire domain. The domain local group is, therefore, well suited for defining business management rules, such as access rules, because the group can be applied anywhere in the domain, and it can include members of any type within the domain and members from trusted domains as well.

Global Groups

Global groups are used primarily to define collections of domain objects based on business roles. Role groups, such as the Sales and Marketing groups mentioned earlier, as well as roles of computers such as a Sales Laptops group, will be created as global groups. Global groups have the following characteristics:

- **Replication** A global group is defined in the domain naming context. The group object, including the *member* attribute, is replicated to all domain controllers in the domain.
- **Membership** A global group can include as members users, computers, and other global groups in the same domain only.
- **Availability** A global group is available for use by all domain members as well as by all other domains in the forest and all trusting external domains. A global group can be a member of any domain local or universal group in the domain or in the forest. It can also be a member of any domain local group in a trusting domain. Finally, a global group can be added to ACLs in the domain, in the forest, or in trusting domains.

As you can see, global groups have the most limited membership (only users, computers, and global groups from the same domain) but the broadest availability across the domain, the forest, and trusting domains. That is why they are well suited to defining roles, because roles are generally collections of objects from the same directory.

Universal Groups

Universal groups are useful in multidomain forests. They enable you to define roles, or to manage resources, that span more than one domain. The best way to understand universal groups is through an example. Trey Research has a forest with three domains: Americas, Asia, and Europe. Each domain has user accounts and a global group called Regional Managers that includes the managers of that region. Remember that global groups can contain only users from the same domain. A universal group called Trey Research Regional Managers is created, and the three Regional Managers groups are added as members. The Trey Research Regional Managers group, therefore, defines a role for the entire forest. As users are added to any one of the Regional Managers groups, they will, through group nesting, be a member of the Trey Research Regional Managers.

Trey Research is planning to release a new product that requires collaboration across its regions. Resources related to the project are stored on file servers in each domain. To define who can modify files related to the new product, a universal group is created called *ACL_New Product_Modify*. That group is assigned the Allow Modify permission to the shared folders on each of the file servers in each of the domains. The Trey Research Regional Managers group is made a member of the ACL_New Product_Modify group, as are various global groups and a handful of users from each of the regions.

As you can see from this example, universal groups can help you represent and consolidate groups that span domains in a forest and help you define rules that can be applied across the forest. Universal groups have the following characteristics:

- **Replication**   A universal group is defined in a single domain in the forest but is replicated to the global catalog. You will learn more about the global catalog in Chapter 10, "Domain Controllers." Objects in the global catalog will be readily accessible across the forest.
- **Membership**   A universal group can include as members users, global groups, and other universal groups from any domain in the forest.
- **Availability**   A universal group can be a member of a universal group or domain local group anywhere in the forest. Additionally, a universal group can be used to manage resources, for example, to assign permissions anywhere in the forest.

Summarizing Group Membership Possibilities

Both on the 70-640 examination and in day-to-day administration, it is important for you to be completely familiar with the membership characteristics of each group scope.

Table 4-1 summarizes the objects that can be members of each group scope.

Table 4-1 **Group Scope and Members**

Group Scope	Members from the same domain	Members from another domain in the same forest	Members from a trusted external domain
Local	Users Computers Global groups Universal groups Domain local groups Local users defined on the same computer as the local group	Users Computers Global groups Universal groups	Users Computers Global groups
Domain Local	Users Computers Global groups Domain local groups Universal groups	Users Computers Global groups Universal groups	Users Computers Global groups
Universal	Users Computers Global groups Universal groups	Users Computers Global groups Universal groups.	N/A
Global	Users Computers Global groups	N/A	N/A

Quick Check

- Which types of objects can be members of a global group in a domain?

Quick Check Answer

- Global groups can contain only users, computers, and other global groups from the same domain.

Converting Group Scope and Type

If, after creating a group, you determine that you need to modify the group's scope or type, you can do so. Open the Properties dialog box of an existing group and, on the General tab, shown in Figure 4-3, you will see the existing scope and type. At least one more scope and type are available to be selected.

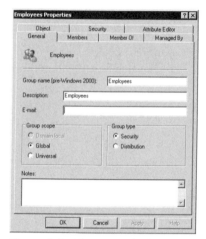

Figure 4-3   The General tab of a group's Properties dialog box

You can convert the group type at any time by changing the selection in the Group Type section of the General tab. Be cautious, however. When you convert a group from security to distribution, any resources to which the group had been assigned permission will no longer be accessible in the same way. After the group becomes a distribution group, users who log on to the domain will no longer include the group's SID in their security access tokens.

You can change the group scope in one of the following ways:

- Global to universal
- Domain local to universal
- Universal to global
- Universal to domain local

The only scope changes that you cannot make directly are from global to domain local or domain local to global. However, you can make these changes indirectly by first converting to universal scope and then converting to the desired scope, so all scope changes are possible.

Remember, however, that a group's scope determines the types of objects that can be members of the group. If a group already contains members or is a member of another group, you will be prevented from changing scope. For example, if a global group is a member of another global group, you cannot change the first group to universal scope, because a universal group cannot be a member of a global group. An explanatory error message will display such as that shown in Figure 4-4. You must correct the membership conflicts before you can change the group's scope.

Figure 4-4 The error produced when a group's membership will not allow a change of scope

The *Dsmod* command, introduced in Chapter 3, can be used to change group type and scope by using the following syntax:

```
dsmod group GroupDN -secgrp { yes | no } -scope { 1 | g | u }
```

The *GroupDN* is the distinguished name of the group to modify. The following two parameters affect group scope and type:

- **-secgrp { yes | no }** specifies group type: security (*yes*) or distribution (*no*).
- **-scope { l | g | u }** determines the group scope: domain local (*l*), global (*g*), or universal (*u*).

Managing Group Membership

When you need to add or remove members of a group, you have several methods by which to do so. First, you can open the group's Properties dialog box and click the Members tab. To remove a member, simply select the member and click Remove. To add a member, click the Add button. The Select Users, Computers, Or Groups dialog box appears, as shown in Figure 4-5.

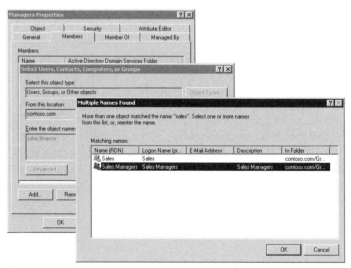

Figure 4-5 Adding a member to a group

Several tips are worth mentioning about this process:

- In the Select dialog box, in the Enter The Object Names box, you can type multiple accounts separated by semicolons. For example, in Figure 4-5, both *sales* and *finance* were entered. They are separated by a semicolon.

- You can type partial names of accounts—you do not need to type the full name. Windows searches Active Directory for accounts that begin with the name you entered. If there is only one match, Windows selects it automatically. If there are multiple accounts that match, the Multiple Names Found dialog box appears, enabling you to select the specific object you want. This shortcut—typing partial names—can save time adding members to groups and can help when you don't remember the exact name of a member.

- By default, Windows searches only for users and groups that match the names you enter in the Select dialog box. If you want to add computers to a group, you must click the Options button and select Computers.

- By default, Windows searches only domain groups. If you want to add local accounts, click the Locations button in the Select dialog box.

- If you cannot find the member you want to add, click the Advanced button in the Select dialog box. A more powerful query window will appear, giving you more options for searching Active Directory.

You can also add an object to a group in the Active Directory Users And Computers snap-in by opening the properties of the object and clicking its Member Of tab. Click the Add button and select the group. Similarly, you can right-click one or more selected objects and use the *Add To Group* command.

The *Member* and *MemberOf* Attributes

When you add a member to a group, you change the group's *member* attribute. The *member* attribute is a multivalued attribute. Each member is a value represented by the distinguished name (DN) of the member. If the member is moved or renamed, Active Directory automatically updates the *member* attributes of groups that include the member.

When you add a member to a group, the member's *memberOf* attribute is also updated, indirectly. The *memberOf* attribute is a special type of attribute called a *backlink*. It is updated by Active Directory when a forward link attribute, such as *member*, refers to the object. When you add a member to a group, you are always changing the *member* attribute. Therefore, when you use the Member Of tab of an object to add to a group, you are actually changing the group's *member* attribute. Active Directory updates the *memberOf* attribute automatically.

Helping Membership Changes Take Effect Quickly

When you add a user to a group, the membership does not take effect immediately. Group membership is evaluated at logon for a user (at startup for a computer). Therefore, a user will have to log off and log on before the membership change becomes a part of the user's token.

Additionally, there can be a delay while the group membership change replicates. Replication will be discussed in Chapter 11, "Sites and Replication." This is particularly true if your enterprise has more than one Active Directory site. You can facilitate the speed with which a change affects a user by making the change on a domain controller in the user's site. Right-click the domain in the Active Directory Users And Computers snap-in and choose Change Domain Controller.

Developing a Group Management Strategy

Adding groups to other groups—a process called *nesting*—can create a hierarchy of groups that support your business roles and rules. Now that you have learned the business purposes and technical characteristics of groups, it is time to align the two in a strategy for group management.

Earlier in this lesson, you learned which types of objects *can* be members of each group scope. Now it is time to identify which types of objects *should* be members of each group scope. This leads to the best practice for group nesting, known as AGDLA:

- **A**ccounts (user and computer identities) are members of
- **G**lobal groups that represent business roles. Those role groups (global groups) are members of
- **D**omain **L**ocal groups that represent management rules—which have Read permission to a specific collection of folders, for example. These rule groups (domain local groups) are added to
- **A**ccess control lists (ACLs), which provide the level of access required by the rule.

In a multidomain forest, there are universal groups, as well, that fit in between global and domain local. Global groups from multiple domains are members of a single universal group. That universal group is a member of domain local groups in multiple domains. You can remember the nesting as AGUDLA.

This best practice for implementing group nesting translates well even in multidomain scenarios. Consider Figure 4-6, which represents a group implementation that reflects not only the technical view of group management best practices (AGDLA) but also the business view of role-based, rule-based management.

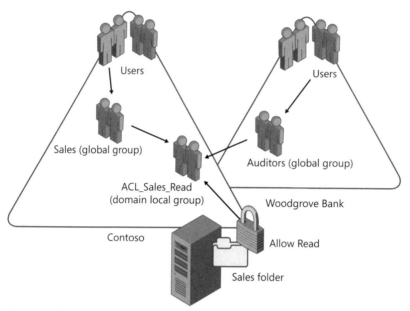

Figure 4-6 A group management implementation

Consider the following scenario. The sales force at Contoso, Ltd., has just completed their fiscal year. Sales files from the previous year are in a folder called Sales. The sales force needs read access to the Sales folder. Additionally, a team of auditors from Woodgrove Bank, a potential investor, require Read access to the Sales folder to perform the audit. The steps to implement the security required by this scenario are as follows:

1. Assign users with common job responsibilities or other business characteristics to role groups implemented as global security groups.

   This happens separately in each domain. Sales people at Contoso are added to a Sales role group. Auditors at Woodgrove Bank are added to an Auditors role group.

2. Create a group to represent the business rule regarding who can access the Sales folder with Read permission.

   This is implemented in the domain containing the resource to which the rule applies. In this case, it is the Contoso domain in which the Sales folder resides. The rule group is created as a domain local group.

3. Add the role groups to whom the business rule applies to the rule group.

   These groups can come from any domain in the forest or from a trusted domain such as Woodgrove Bank. Global groups from trusted external domains, or from any domain in the same forest, can be a member of a domain local group.

4. Assign the permission that implements the required level of access.

   In this case, grant the Allow Read permission to the domain local group.

This strategy results in single points of management, reducing the management burden. There is one point of management that defines who is in Sales or who is an Auditor. Those roles, of course, are likely to have a variety of permissions to resources beyond simply the Sales folder. There is another single point of management to determine who has Read access to the Sales folder. The Sales folder might not just be a single folder on a single server; it could be a collection of folders across multiple servers, each of which assigns Allow Read permission to the single domain local group.

PRACTICE Creating and Managing Groups

In this practice, you will create groups, experiment with group membership, and convert group type and scope. Before performing the exercises in this practice, you need to create the following objects in the *contoso.com* domain:

- A first-level OU named Groups
- A first-level OU named People
- User objects in the People OU for Linda Mitchell, Scott Mitchell, Jeff Ford, Mike Fitzmaurice, Mike Danseglio, and Tony Krijnen

▶ **Exercise 1   Create Groups**

In this exercise, you will create groups of different scopes and types.

1. Log on to SERVER01 as Administrator and open the Active Directory Users And Computers snap-in. Select Groups OU in the console tree.
2. Right-click Groups OU, choose New, and then select Group.
3. In the Group Name box, type **Sales**.
4. Select the Global group scope and Security group type. Click OK.
5. Right-click the Sales group and choose Properties.
6. Click the Members tab.
7. Click the Add button.
8. Type **Jeff; Tony** and click OK.
9. Click OK to close the Properties dialog box.
10. Repeat steps 2–4 to create two global security groups named **Marketing** and **Consultants**.
11. Repeat steps 2–4 to create a domain local security group named **ACL_Sales Folder_Read**.
12. Open the properties of the ACL_Sales Folder_Read group.
13. Click the Member tab.
14. Click Add.
15. Type **Sales;Marketing;Consultants** and click OK.
16. Click Add.

17. Type **Linda** and click OK.
18. Click OK to close the Properties dialog box.
19. Open the Properties dialog box of the Marketing group.
20. Click the Member tab and click Add.
21. Type **ACL_Sales Folder_Read** and click OK.

    You are unable to add a domain local group to a global group.
22. Cancel out of all open dialog boxes.
23. Create a folder named **Sales** on the C drive.
24. Right-click the Sales folder, choose Properties, and click the Security tab.
25. Click Edit, and then click Add.
26. Click Advanced, and then click Find Now.

    Notice that by using a prefix for group names, such as the *ACL_* prefix for resource access groups, you can find them quickly, grouped together at the top of the list.
27. Cancel out of all open dialog boxes.
28. Right-click Groups, choose New, and then select Group.
29. In the Group Name box, type **Employees**.
30. Select the Domain Local group scope and the Distribution group type. Click OK.

▶ Exercise 2   Convert Group Type and Scope

In this exercise, you will learn how to convert group type and scope.

1. Right-click the Employees group and choose Properties.
2. Change the group type to Distribution.
3. Click Apply.

   Consider: Can you change the group scope from Domain Local to Global? How?
4. Change the group scope to Universal. Click Apply.
5. Change the group scope to Global. Click Apply.
6. Click OK to close the Properties dialog box.

Lesson Summary

■ There are two types of groups: security and distribution. Security groups can be assigned permissions although distribution groups are used primarily as e-mail distribution lists.

■ In addition to local groups, which are maintained only in the local SAM database of a domain member server, there are three domain group scopes: global, domain local, and universal.

- The group scope affects the group's replication, the types of objects that can be members of the group, and the group's availability to be a member of another group or to be used for management tasks such as assigning permissions.
- You can convert group type and scope after creating the group.

Lesson Review

You can use the following questions to test your knowledge of the information in Lesson 1, "Creating and Managing Groups." The questions are also available on the companion CD if you prefer to review them in electronic form.

NOTE Answers

Answers to these questions and explanations of why each answer choice is right or wrong are located in the "Answers" section at the end of the book.

---

1. A new project requires that users in your domain and in the domain of a partner organization have access to a shared folder on your file server. Which type of group should you create to manage the access to the shared folder?

    A. Universal security group

    B. Domain local security group

    C. Global security group

    D. Domain local distribution group

2. Your domain includes a global distribution group named Company Update. It has been used to send company news by e-mail to its members. You have decided to allow all members to contribute to the newsletter by creating a shared folder on a file server. What must you do to allow group members access to the shared folder?

    A. Change the group scope to domain local.

    B. Change the group scope to universal.

    C. Add the group to the Domain Users group.

    D. Use *Dsmod* with the *−secgrp yes* switch.

3. You have created a global security group in the *contoso.com* domain named Corporate Managers. Which members can be added to the group? (Choose all that apply.)

    A. Sales Managers, a global group in the *fabrikam.com* domain, a trusted domain of a partner company

    B. Sales Managers, a global group in the *tailspintoys.com* domain, a domain in the *contoso.com* forest

C. Linda Mitchell, a user in the *tailspintoys.com* domain, a domain in the *contoso.com* forest

D. Jeff Ford, a user in the *fabrikam.com* domain, a trusted domain of a partner company

E. Mike Danseglio, a user in the *contoso.com* domain

F. Sales Executives, a global group in the *contoso.com* domain

G. Sales Directors, a domain local group in the *contoso.com* domain

H. European Sales Managers, a universal group in the *contoso.com* forest

Lesson 2: Automating the Creation and Management of Groups

In Lesson 1, you learned the steps for creating groups, choosing group scope and type, and configuring group membership, using the Active Directory Users and Computers snap-in. When you need to create more than one group at a time, or when you want to automate group creation, you must turn to other tools. Chapter 3 introduced you to command-line and automation tools, including *CSVDE*, *LDIFDE*, *Dsadd*, Windows PowerShell, and VBScript. These tools can also be used to automate the creation and management of group objects. In this lesson, you'll learn how to manage the life cycle of group objects, from birth to death, using command-line and automation tools.

After this lesson, you will be able to:
- Create groups with *Dsadd*, *CSVDE*, and *LDIFDE*.
- Modify groups' membership with *Dsmod*, *LDIFDE*, Windows PowerShell, and VBScript.
- Enumerate group membership with *Dsget*.
- Move and delete groups with *Dsmove* and *Dsrm*.

Estimated lesson time: 45 minutes

Creating Groups with *Dsadd*

The *Dsadd* command, introduced in Chapter 3, enables you to add objects to Active Directory. To add a group, type the command **dsadd group *GroupDN***, where *GroupDN* is the DN of the group, such as "CN=Finance Managers,OU=Groups,DC=contoso,DC=com." Be certain to surround the DN with quotes if the DN includes spaces. For example, to create a new global security group named Marketing in the Groups OU of the *contoso.com* domain, the command would be:

```
dsadd group "CN=Marketing,OU=Groups,DC=contoso,DC=com"
   -samid Marketing -secgrp yes -scope g
```

You can also provide the *GroupDN* parameter by one of the following ways:

- By piping a list of DNs from another command such as *Dsquery*.
- By typing each DN on the command line, separated by spaces.
- By leaving the DN parameter empty, at which point you can type the DNs one at a time at the keyboard console of the command prompt. Press Enter after each DN. Press Ctrl + Z and Enter after the last DN.

Because you can include more than one DN on the command line, separated by a space, you can generate multiple groups at once with *Dsadd*. The *Dsadd* command can also configure group attributes of the groups you create with the following optional parameters:

- **−secgrp { yes | no }** specifies group type: security (*yes*) or distribution (*no*).
- **−scope { l | g | u }** determines the group scope: domain local (*l*), global (*g*), or universal (*u*).
- **−samid** *Name* specifies the *sAMAccountName* of the group. If not specified, the name of the group from its DN is used. It is recommended that the *sAMAccountName* and the group name be the same, so you do not need to include this parameter when using *Dsadd*.
- **−desc** *Description* configures the group's description.
- **−members** *MemberDN* adds members to the group. Members are specified by their DNs in a space-separated list.
- **−memberof** *GroupDN* ... makes the new group a member of one or more existing groups. The groups are specified by their DNs in a space-separated list.

Importing Groups with *CSVDE*

Chapter 3 also introduced you to *CSVDE*, which imports data from comma-separated values (.csv) files. It is also able to export data to a .csv file. The following example shows a .csv file that will create a group, Marketing, and populate the group with two initial members, Linda Mitchell and Scott Mitchell.

```
objectClass,sAMAccountName,DN,member
group,Marketing,"CN=Marketing,OU=Groups,DC=contoso,DC=com",
    "CN=Linda Mitchell,OU=People,DC=contoso,DC=com;CN=Scott Mitchell,
    OU=People,DC=contoso,DC=com"
```

The objects listed in the *member* attribute must already exist in the directory service. Their DNs are separated by semicolons within the *member* column.

You can import this file into Active Directory by using the command:

```
csvde -i -f "Filename" [-k]
```

The *−i* parameter specifies import mode. Without it, *CSVDE* uses export mode. The *−f* parameter precedes the filename, and the *−k* parameter ensures that processing continues even if errors are encountered.

Exam Tip   *CSVDE* can be used to create objects, not to modify existing objects. You cannot use *CSVDE* to import members to existing groups.

Managing Groups with *LDIFDE*

LDIFDE, as you learned in Chapter 3, is a tool that imports and exports files in the Lightweight Directory Access Protocol Data Interchange Format (LDIF) format. LDIF files are text files within which operations are specified by a block of lines separated by a blank line. Each operation begins with the DN attribute of the object that is the target of the operation. The next line, *changeType*, specifies the type of operation: *add*, *modify*, or *delete*.

The following LDIF file creates two groups, Finance and Research, in the Groups OU of the *contoso.com* domain:

```
DN: CN=Finance,OU=Groups,DC=contoso,DC=com
changeType: add
CN: Finance
description: Finance Users
objectClass: group
sAMAccountName: Finance

DN: CN=Research,OU=Groups,DC=contoso,DC=com
changeType: add
CN: Research
description: Research Users
objectClass: group
sAMAccountName: Research
```

Convention would suggest saving the file with an .ldf extension, for example Groups.ldf. To import the groups into the directory, issue the *Ldifde.exe* command as shown here:

```
ldifde -i -f groups.ldf
```

Modifying Group Membership with *LDIFDE*

LDIFDE can also be used to modify existing objects in Active Directory, using LDIF operations with a *changeType* of *modify*. To add two members to the Finance group, the LDIF file would be:

```
dn: CN=Finance,OU=Groups,DC=contoso,DC=com
changetype: modify
add: member
member: CN=April Stewart,OU=People,dc=contoso,dc=com
member: CN=Mike Fitzmaurice,OU=People,dc=contoso,dc=com
-
```

The *changeType* is set to *modify*, and then the change operation is specified: *add* objects to the *member* attribute. Each new member is then listed on a separate line that begins with the *member* attribute name. The change operation is terminated with a line containing a single dash. Changing the third line to the following would remove the two specified members from the group:

```
delete: member
```

Retrieving Group Membership with *Dsget*

The *Dsmod* and *Dsget* commands discussed in Chapter 3 are particularly helpful for managing the membership of groups. There is no option in the Active Directory Users and Computers snap-in to list all the members of a group, including nested members. You can see only direct members of a group on the group's Members tab. Similarly, there is no way to list all the groups to which a user or computer belongs, including nested groups. You can see only direct membership on the user's or computer's Member Of tab.

The *Dsget* command enables you to retrieve a complete list of a group's membership, including nested members, with the following syntax:

```
dsget group "GroupDN" -members [-expand]
```

The *expand* option performs the magic of expanding nested groups' members.

Similarly, the *Dsget* command can be used to retrieve a complete list of groups to which a user or computer belongs, again by using the *expand* option in the following commands:

```
dsget user "UserDN" -memberof [-expand]
dsget computer "ComputerDN" -memberof [-expand]
```

The *memberof* option returns the value of the user's or computer's *memberOf* attribute, showing the groups to which the object directly belongs. By adding the *expand* option, those groups are searched recursively, producing an exhaustive list of all groups to which object the user belongs in the domain.

Changing Group Membership with *Dsmod*

The *Dsmod* command was applied in Lesson 1 to modify the scope and type of a group. The command's basic syntax is:

```
dsmod group "GroupDN" [options]
```

You can use options such as *samid* and *desc* to modify the *sAMAccountName* and *description* attributes of the group. Most useful, however, are the options that enable you to modify a group's membership:

- **–addmbr "*Member DN*"**   Adds members to the group
- **–rmmbr "*Member DN*"**   Removes members from the group

As with all DS commands, *Member DN* is the distinguished name of another Active Directory object, surrounded by quotes if the DN includes spaces. Multiple *Member DN* entries can be included, separated by spaces. For example, to add Mike Danseglio to the Research group, the *Dsmod* command would be:

```
dsmod group "CN=Research,OU=Groups,DC=contoso,DC=com"
   -addmbr "CN=Mike Danseglio,OU=People,DC=contoso,DC=com"
```

You can use *Dsget* in combination with *Dsmod* to copy group membership. In the following example, the *Dsget* command is used to get information about all the members of the Sales group and then, by piping that list to *Dsmod*, to add those users to the Marketing group:

```
dsget group "CN=Sales,OU=Groups,DC=contoso,DC=com" -members |
    dsmod group "CN=Marketing,OU=Groups,DC=contoso,DC=com" -addmbr
```

Moving and Renaming Groups with *Dsmove*

The *Dsmove* command, also discussed in Chapter 3, enables you to move or rename an object within a domain. You cannot use it to move objects between domains. Its basic syntax is:

```
dsmove ObjectDN [-newname NewName] [-newparent TargetOUDN]
```

The object is specified by using its distinguished name in the *ObjectDN* parameter. To rename the object, specify its new common name as the value of the *newname* parameter. To move an object to a new location, specify the distinguished name of the target container as the value of the *newparent* parameter.

For example, to change the name of the Marketing group to Public Relations, type:

```
dsmove "CN=Marketing,OU=Groups,DC=contoso,DC=com"
    -newname "Public Relations"
```

To then move that group to the Marketing OU, type:

```
dsmove "CN=Public Relations,OU=Groups,DC=contoso,DC=com"
    -newparent "OU=Marketing,DC=contoso,DC=com"
```

NOTE You're not limited to the command line

You can also move or rename a group in the Active Directory Users And Computers snap-in by right-clicking the group and choosing Move or Rename from the context menu.

Deleting Groups with *Dsrm*

Dsrm can be used to delete a group or any other Active Directory object. The basic syntax of *Dsrm* is:

```
dsrm ObjectDN ... [-subtree [-exclude]] [-noprompt] [-c]
```

The object is specified by its distinguished name in the *ObjectDN* parameter. You will be prompted to confirm the deletion of each object unless you specify the *noprompt* option. The −c switch puts *Dsrm* into continuous operation mode, in which errors are reported, but the command keeps processing additional objects. Without the −c switch, processing halts on the first error.

To delete the Public Relations group, type:

```
dsrm "CN=Public Relations,OU=Marketing,DC=contoso,DC=com"
```

You can also delete a group in the Active Directory Users And Computers snap-in by right-clicking the group and choosing the *Delete* command.

NOTE   Know the impact before deleting a group

When you delete a group, you are removing a point of management in your organization. Be certain you have evaluated the environment to verify that there are no permissions or other resources that rely on the group. Deleting a group is a serious action with potentially significant consequences. It is recommended that, before you delete a group, you record its membership and remove all members for a period of time to determine whether the members lose access to any resources. If anything goes wrong, simply re-add the members. If the test succeeds, then delete the group.

Managing Group Membership with Windows PowerShell and VBScript

It is unlikely that you will need to understand the intricacies of managing group membership for the 70-640 examination, and an exhaustive discussion of scripting groups is beyond the scope of this book. See *Windows Administration Resource Kit: Productivity Solutions for IT Professionals* for detailed discussions about automating group management with VBScript.

However, it doesn't hurt to know the basics. In both VBScript and Windows PowerShell, there are several ways to manipulate group membership—a group's *member* attribute—but the most common and effective involve these steps:

1. Determine the *aDSPath* of the member. The *aDSPath* takes the form, *LDAP://<DN of member>*.
2. Connect to the group.
3. Use the *Add* or *Remove* method of the group object, specifying the *aDSPath* of the member.

A Windows PowerShell script that adds Mike Danseglio to the Research group would, therefore, be:

```
$MemberADSPath = "LDAP://CN=Mike Danseglio,OU=People,DC=contoso,DC=com"
$objGroup = [ADSI]"LDAP://CN=Research,OU=Groups,DC=contoso,DC=com"
$objGroup.Add ($MemberADSPath)
```

In VBScript, the script would be:

```
MemberADSPath = "LDAP://CN=Mike Danseglio,OU=People,DC=contoso,DC=com"
Set objGroup = GetObject("LDAP://CN=Research,OU=Groups,DC=contoso,DC=com")
objGroup.Add MemberADSPath
```

To remove members, use the *Remove* method instead of the *Add* method. The remainder of each script remains the same.

PRACTICE Automating the Creation and Management of Groups

In this practice, you will use DS commands, *CSVDE*, and *LDIFDE* to perform group management tasks. Before performing the exercises in this practice, you need to create the following objects in the *contoso.com* domain:

- A first-level OU named Groups
- A first-level OU named People
- User objects in the People OU for Linda Mitchell, Scott Mitchell, Jeff Ford, Mike Fitzmaurice, Mike Danseglio, April Stewart, and Tony Krijnen.

In addition, *delete* any groups with the following names: Finance, Accounting.

▶ **Exercise 1   Create a Group with *Dsadd***

In this exercise, you will use *Dsadd* to create a group. *Dsadd* can create a group, and even populate its membership, with a single command.

1. Log on to SERVER01 as Administrator.
2. Open a command prompt and type the following command on one line. Then press Enter:

```
dsadd group "CN=Finance,OU=Groups,DC=contoso,DC=com"
    -samid Finance -secgrp yes -scope g
```

3. Open the Active Directory Users And Computers snap-in and confirm that the group was created successfully. If the Active Directory Users And Computers snap-in was open prior to performing step 2, refresh the view.

▶ **Exercise 2   Import Groups with *CSVDE***

1. Log on to SERVER01 as Administrator.
2. Open Notepad and type the following lines. Each bullet is one line of text in Notepad but do not include the bullets:
   - objectClass,sAMAccountName,DN,member
   - group,Accounting,"CN=Accounting,OU=Groups,DC=contoso,DC=com",
     "CN=Linda Mitchell,OU=People,DC=contoso,DC=com;
     CN=Scott Mitchell,OU=People,DC=contoso,DC=com"
3. Save the file to your Documents folder with the name "**Importgroups.csv**" including the quotes so that Notepad doesn't add a .txt extension.
4. Open a command prompt and type the following command:

```
csvde -i -f "%userprofile%\importgroups.csv"
```

5. Open the Active Directory Users And Computers snap-in and check to confirm that the groups were created successfully. You might need to refresh the view if the Active Directory Users And Computers snap-in was open prior to performing the step.

▶ Exercise 3   Modify Group Membership with *LDIFDE*

CSVDE cannot modify the membership of existing groups, but *LDIFDE* can. In this exercise, you will use *LDIFDE* to modify the group membership of the Accounting group you imported in Exercise 2, "Import Groups with *CSVDE*."

1. Open Notepad and type the following lines:

    ```
    dn: CN=Accounting,OU=Groups,DC=contoso,DC=com
    changetype: modify
    add: member
    member: CN=April
    Stewart,OU=People,dc=contoso,dc=com
    member: CN=Mike Fitzmaurice,OU=People,dc=contoso,dc=com
    -

    dn: CN= Accounting,OU=Groups,DC=contoso,DC=com
    changetype: modify
    delete: member
    member: CN=Linda Mitchell,OU=People,dc=contoso,dc=com
    -
    ```

    Be sure to include the dashes after each block and the blank line between the two blocks.

2. Save the file to your Documents folder as "**Membershipchange.ldf**" including the quotes, so that Notepad does not add a .txt extension.

3. Open a command prompt.

4. Type the following command and press Enter:

    ```
    ldifde -i -f "%userprofile%\documents\membershipchange.ldf"
    ```

5. Using the Active Directory Users And Computers snap-in, confirm that the membership of the Accounting group changed according to the instructions of the LDIF file. It should now include April Stewart, Mike Fitzmaurice, and Scott Mitchell.

▶ Exercise 4   Modify Group Membership with *Dsmod*

In this exercise, you will add a user and a group to the Finance group, using the *Dsmod* command.

1. Open a command prompt.

2. Type the following command to change the membership of the Finance group:

    ```
    dsmod group "CN=Finance,OU=Groups,DC=contoso,DC=com" -addmbr "CN=Tony
    Krijnen,OU=People,DC=contoso,DC=com"
    "CN=Accounting,OU=Groups,DC=contoso,DC=com"
    ```

3. In the Active Directory Users And Computers snap-in, confirm that the membership of the Finance group consists of Tony Krijnen and the Accounting group.

▶ Exercise 5   Confirm Group Membership with *Dsget*

Evaluating effective group membership is difficult with the Active Directory Users and Computers snap-in but is easy with the *Dsget* command. In this exercise, you will look at both the full membership of a group and the group memberships of a user.

1. Open a command prompt.

2. List the direct members of the Accounting group by typing the following command and then pressing Enter:

    ```
    dsget group "CN=Accounting,OU=Groups,DC=contoso,DC=com" -members
    ```

3. List the direct members of the Finance group by typing the following command and then pressing Enter:

    ```
    dsget group "CN=Finance,OU=Groups,DC=contoso,DC=com" -members
    ```

4. List the full list of members of the Finance group by typing the following command and then pressing Enter:

    ```
    dsget group "CN=Finance,OU=Groups,DC=contoso,DC=com" -members -expand
    ```

5. List the direct group membership of Scott Mitchell by typing the following command and then pressing Enter:

    ```
    dsget user "CN=Scott Mitchell,OU=People,DC=contoso,DC=com" -memberof
    ```

6. List the full group membership of Scott Mitchell by typing the following command on one line and then pressing Enter:

    ```
    dsget user "CN=Scott Mitchell,OU=People,DC=contoso,DC=com"
        -memberof -expand
    ```

Lesson Summary

- You can create groups with *Dsadd*, *CSVDE*, and *LDIFDE*.
- *LDIFDE* and *Dsmod* can modify the membership of existing groups.
- The *Dsget* command can list the full membership of a group or the full list of groups to which a user belongs, including nested groups.

Lesson Review

You can use the following questions to test your knowledge of the information in Lesson 2, "Automating the Creation and Management of Groups." The questions are also available on the companion CD if you prefer to review them in electronic form.

NOTE Answers

Answers to these questions and explanations of why each answer choice is right or wrong are located in the "Answers" section at the end of the book.

1. Which of the following can be used to remove members from a group? (Choose all that apply.)

    A. Remove-Item

    B. *Dsrm*

    C. *Dsmod*

    D. *LDIFDE*

    E. *CSVDE*

2. You are using *Dsmod* to add a domain local group named GroupA to a global group named GroupB. You are receiving errors. Which command will solve the problem so that you can then add GroupA to GroupB? (Choose all that apply.)

    A. *Dsrm.exe*

    B. *Dsmod.exe*

    C. *Dsquery.exe*

    D. *Dsget.exe*

3. Your management has asked you to produce a list of all users who belong to the Special Project group, including those users belonging to groups nested into Special Project. Which of the following can you use?

    A. Get-Members

    B. *Dsquery.exe*

    C. *LDIFDE*

    D. *Dsget.exe*

Lesson 3: Administering Groups in an Enterprise

Lesson 1 and Lesson 2 prepared you to perform daily administrative tasks related to groups in Active Directory. You learned to create, modify, and delete groups, using a variety of tools and procedures. This lesson rounds out your exploration of groups by preparing you to take advantage of useful group attributes for documenting groups, to delegate the management of group membership to specific administrative teams or individuals, and to break away from reliance on some of the Active Directory and Windows default groups.

After this lesson, you will be able to:
- Document the purpose of a group by using the group's attributes.
- Prevent a group from being accidentally deleted.
- Delegate management of a group's membership.
- Create a shadow group.
- Recognize and manage default domain groups.
- Assign permissions to special identities.

Estimated lesson time: 45 minutes

Best Practices for Group Attributes

Creating a group in Active Directory is easy. It is not so easy to make sure that the group is used correctly over time. You can facilitate the correct management and use of a group by documenting its purpose to help administrators understand how and when to use the group. There are several best practices, which, although they are unlikely to be addressed by the certification exam, will prove immensely useful to your enterprise group administration:

- **Establish and adhere to a strict naming convention**   Lesson 1 addressed a suggested naming convention. In the context of ongoing group administration, establishing and following group naming standards increases administrative productivity. Using prefixes to indicate the purpose of a group, and a consistent delimiter between the prefix and the descriptive part of the group names, can help locate the correct group for a particular purpose. For example, the prefix APP can be used to designate groups that are used to manage applications, and the prefix ACL can be used for groups that are assigned permissions on ACLs. With such prefixes, it becomes easier to locate and interpret the purpose of groups named APP_Accounting versus ACL_Accounting_Read. The former is used to manage the deployment of the accounting software, and the latter provides read access to the accounting folder. Prefixes also help group the names of groups in the user interface. Figure 4-7 shows an example. When attempting to locate a group to use in assigning permissions to a folder, you can type the prefix *ACL_* in the Select dialog box and click OK. A Multiple Names Found dialog box appears showing only the *ACL_* groups in the directory, thereby ensuring that permissions will be assigned to a group that is designed to manage resource access.

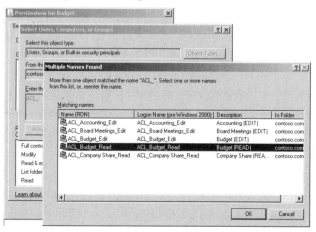

Figure 4-7   Selecting a group by using a group prefix to narrow down to the correct type of group

■ **Summarize a group's purpose with its *description* attribute**   Use the *description* attribute of a group to summarize the group's purpose. Because the Description column is enabled by default in the details pane of the Active Directory Users and Computers snap-in, the group's purpose can be highly visible to administrators.

■ **Detail a group's purpose in its Notes**   When you open a group's Properties dialog box, the *Notes* field, at the bottom of the General tab, can be used to document the group's purpose. For example, you can list the folders to which a group has been given permission, as shown in Figure 4-8.

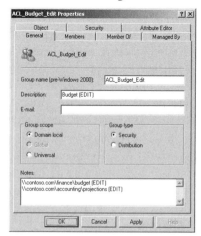

Figure 4-8   A group's Properties dialog box, showing the *Notes* field used to detail the group's purpose

Protecting Groups from Accidental Deletion

Deleting a group has a high impact on administrators and, potentially, on security. Consider a group that has been used to manage access to resources. If the group is deleted, access to that resource is changed. Either users who should be able to access the resource are suddenly prevented from access, creating a denial-of-service scenario, or if you had used the group to deny access to a resource with a Deny permission, inappropriate access to the resource becomes possible.

Additionally, if you re-create the group, the new group object will have a new SID, which will not match the SIDs on ACLs of resources. Instead, you must perform object recovery to reanimate the deleted group before the tombstone interval is reached. When a group has been deleted for the tombstone interval—60 days by default—the group and its SID are permanently deleted from Active Directory. When you reanimate a tombstoned object, you must re-create most of its attributes, including, significantly, the *member* attribute of group objects. That means you must rebuild the group membership after restoring the deleted object. Alternatively, you can perform an authoritative restore or, in Windows Server 2008, turn to your Active Directory snapshots to recover both the group and its membership. Authoritative restore and snapshots are discussed in Chapter 13, "Maintenance, Backup, and Recovery."

MORE INFO   Recovering deleted groups

You can learn more about recovering deleted groups and their memberships in Knowledge Base article 840001, which you can find at *http://support.microsoft.com/kb/840001/en-us*.

In any event, it is safe to say that recovering a deleted group is a skill you should hope to use only in disaster recovery fire drills, not in a production environment. Protect yourself from the potentially devastating results of group object deletion by protecting each group you create from deletion. Windows Server 2008 makes it easy to protect any object from accidental deletion. To protect an object, follow these steps:

1. In the Active Directory Users And Computers snap-in, click the View menu and make sure that Advanced Features is selected.
2. Open the Properties dialog box for a group.
3. On the Object tab, select the Protect Object From Accidental Deletion check box.
4. Click OK.
    This is one of the few places in Windows where you actually have to click OK. Clicking Apply does not modify the ACL based on your selection.

The Protect Object From Accidental Deletion option applies an access control entry (ACE) to the ACL of the object that explicitly denies the Everyone group both the Delete permission and the Delete Subtree permission. If you really do want to delete the group, you can return to the Object tab of the Properties dialog box and clear the Protect Object From Accidental Deletion check box.

Delegating the Management of Group Membership

After a group has been created, you might want to delegate the management of the group's membership to a team or an individual who has the business responsibility for the resource that the group manages. For example, assume that your finance manager is responsible for creating next year's budget. You create a shared folder for the budget and assign Write permission to a group named *ACL_Budget_Edit*. If someone needs access to the budget folder, he or she contacts the help desk to enter a request, the help desk contacts the finance manager for business approval, and then the help desk adds the user to the ACL_Budget_Edit group. You can improve the responsiveness and accountability of the process by allowing the finance manager to change the group's membership. Then, users needing access can request access directly from the finance manager, who can make the change, removing the intermediate step of the help desk. To delegate the management of a group's membership, you must assign to the finance manager the Allow Write Member permission for the group. The *member* attribute is the multivalued attribute that is the group's membership. There are several ways to delegate the Write Member permission. Two of them are covered in the following sections.

Delegating Membership Management with the Managed By Tab

The easiest way to delegate membership management of a single group is to use the Managed By tab. The Managed By tab of a group object's Properties dialog box, shown in Figure 4-9, serves two purposes. First it provides contact information related to the manager of a group. You can use this information to contact the business owner of a group to obtain approval prior to adding a user to the group.

The second purpose served by the Managed By tab is to manage the delegation of the *member* attribute. Note the check box shown in Figure 4-9. It is labeled Manager Can Update Membership List. When selected, the user or group shown in the Name box is given the WriteMember permission. If you change or clear the manager, the appropriate change is made to the group's ACL.

NOTE   Click OK

This is another of the strange and rare places where you must actually click OK to implement the change. Clicking Apply does not change the ACL on the group.

Figure 4-9   The Managed By tab of a group's Properties dialog box

It is not quite so easy to insert a group into the Managed By tab of another group. When you click the Change button, the Select User, Contact, Or Group dialog box appears, shown in Figure 4-10. If you enter the name of a group and click OK, an error occurs. That's because this dialog box is not configured to accept groups as valid object types, even though *Group* is in the name of the dialog box itself. To work around this odd limitation, click the Object Types button, and then select the check box next to Groups. Click OK to close both the Object Types and Select dialog boxes. Be sure to select the Manager Can Update Membership List check box if you want to assign the WriteMember permission to the group. When a group is used on the Managed By tab, no contact information is visible because groups do not maintain contact-related attributes.

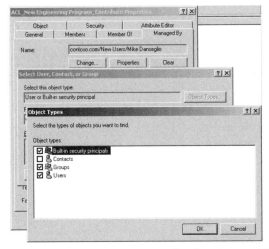

Figure 4-10   Selecting a group for the Managed By tab

Delegating Membership Management Using Advanced Security Settings

You can use the Advanced Security Settings dialog box to assign the Allow Write Member permission directly. You can assign the permission for an individual group or for all the groups in an OU.

Delegate the management of membership for an individual group

1. In the Active Directory Users And Computers snap-in, click the View menu and make sure Advanced Features is selected.
2. Right-click the groups' OU and choose Properties.
3. Click the Security tab.
4. Click the Advanced button.
5. In the Advanced Security Settings dialog box, click the Add button.

    If the Add button is not visible, click the Edit button, and then click the Add button.
6. In the Select dialog box, enter the name for the group to whom you want to grant permission or click Browse to search for the group. When you are finished, click OK.

    The Permission Entry dialog box appears.
7. Click the Properties tab.
8. In the Apply To drop-down list, choose This Object And All Descendant Objects.
9. In the Permissions list, select the Allow check boxes for the Read Members and Write Members permissions.

    By default, all users have the Read Members permission, so that permission is not required. However, role-based access control is best implemented by assigning all the permissions required to achieve the desired capability rather than relying on permissions assigned indirectly.

    Figure 4-11 shows the resulting Permission Entry dialog box.

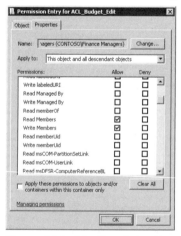

Figure 4-11   The Permission Entry dialog box showing the delegation of group membership management for a group

10. Click OK to close each of the security dialog boxes.

Delegate the ability to manage membership for all groups in an OU

1. In the Active Directory Users And Computers snap-in, click the View menu and make sure Advanced Features is selected.
2. Right-click the groups' OU and choose Properties.
3. Click the Security tab.
4. Click the Advanced button.
5. In the Advanced Security Settings dialog box, click the Add button.

    If the Add button is not visible, click the Edit button, and then click the Add button.
6. In the Select dialog box, enter the name for the group to whom you want to grant permission or click Browse to search for the group. When you are finished, click OK.

    The Permission Entry dialog box appears.
7. Click the Properties tab.
8. In the Apply To drop-down list, choose Descendant Group Objects. If you are using earlier versions of the Active Directory Users And Computers snap-in, choose Group Objects.
9. In the Permissions list, select the Allow check boxes for the Read Members and Write Members permissions.

    By default, all users have the Read Members permission, so that permission is not required. However, role-based access control is best implemented by assigning all the permissions required to achieve the desired capability rather than relying on permissions assigned indirectly.

    Figure 4-12 shows the resulting Permission Entry dialog box.

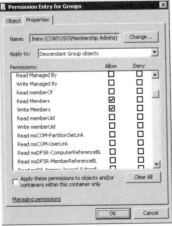

Figure 4-12 The Permission Entry dialog box showing the delegation of group membership management for all groups in the Groups OU

10. Click OK to close each of the security dialog boxes.

Understanding Shadow Groups

Most management of an enterprise is implemented with groups. Groups are assigned permission to resources. Groups can be used to filter the scope of Group Policy objects. Groups are assigned fine-grained password policies. Groups can be used as collections for configuration management tools such as Microsoft System Center Configuration Manager. The list goes on. OUs, however, are not used as frequently to manage the enterprise, and in some cases, they cannot be used. For instance, OUs cannot be assigned permissions to resources, nor can they be assigned fine-grained password policies (discussed in Chapter 8, "Authentication"). Instead, the primary purpose of an OU is to provide a scope of management for the delegation of administrative permissions for the objects in that OU. In other words, an OU of users enables you to delegate to your help desk the ability to reset passwords for all users in the OU. OUs are administrative containers.

The reason for this separation of purpose between OUs and groups is that OUs do not provide the same flexibility as groups. A user or computer (or other object) can only exist within the context of a single OU whereas a security principal can belong to many groups. Therefore, groups are used for aligning identities with the capabilities required by those identities.

Sometimes, you might want to manage using an OU when it is not possible. For example, you might want to give all users in an OU access to a folder. Or you might want to assign a unique password policy to users in an OU. You cannot do so directly, but you can achieve your goal by creating what is called a *shadow group*. A shadow group is a group that contains the same users as an OU. More accurately, a shadow group contains users that meet a certain criterion.

The easiest way to create a shadow group is to create the group; then, in the OU containing the users, press Ctrl + A to select all users. Right-click any selected user and choose Add To Group. Type the name of the group and click OK.

Exam Tip   On the 70-640 exam, be prepared to see the term *shadow group* in use. Know that it means a group that contains, as members, the users in an OU.

Unfortunately, Windows does not yet provide a way to maintain the membership of a shadow group dynamically. When you add or remove a user to or from the OU, you must also add or remove the user to or from the shadow group.

MORE INFO   Maintaining shadow groups dynamically

See *Windows Administration Resource Kit: Productivity Solutions for IT Professionals* for scripts that will help maintain shadow groups dynamically.

Default Groups

A number of groups are created automatically on a server running Windows Server 2008. These are called *default local groups*, and they include well-known groups such as Administrators, Backup Operators, and Remote Desktop Users. Additional groups are created in a domain, in both the Builtin and Users containers, including Domain Admins, Enterprise Admins, and Schema Admins. The following list provides a summary of capabilities of the subset of default groups that have significant permissions and user rights related to the management of Active Directory:

- **Enterprise Admins (Users container of the forest root domain)** This group is a member of the Administrators group in every domain in the forest, giving it complete access to the configuration of all domain controllers. It also owns the Configuration partition of the directory and has full control of the domain naming context in all forest domains.

- **Schema Admins (Users container of the forest root domain)** This group owns and has full control of the Active Directory schema.

- **Administrators (Builtin container of each domain)** This group has complete control over all domain controllers and data in the domain naming context. It can change the membership of all other administrative groups in the domain, and the Administrators group in the forest root domain can change the membership of Enterprise Admins, Schema Admins, and Domain Admins. The Administrators group in the forest root domain is arguably the most powerful service administration group in the forest.

- **Domain Admins (Users container of each domain)** This group is added to the Administrators group of its domain. Therefore, it inherits all the capabilities of the Administrators group. It is also, by default, added to the local Administrators group of each domain member computer, giving Domain Admins ownership of all domain computers.

- **Server Operators (Builtin container of each domain)** This group can perform maintenance tasks on domain controllers. It has the right to log on locally, start and stop services, perform backup and restore operations, format disks, create or delete shares, and shut down domain controllers. By default, this group has no members.

- **Account Operators (Builtin container of each domain)** This group can create, modify, and delete accounts for users, groups, and computers located in any organizational unit in the domain (except the Domain Controllers OU) as well as in the Users and Computers container. Account Operators cannot modify accounts that are members of the Administrators or Domain Admins groups, nor can they modify those groups. Account Operators can also log on locally to domain controllers. By default, this group has no members.

- **Backup Operators (Builtin container of each domain)** This group can perform backup and restore operations on domain controllers as well as log on locally and shut down domain controllers. By default, this group has no members.
- **Print Operators (Builtin container of each domain)** This group can maintain print queues on domain controllers. It can also log on locally and shut down domain controllers.

The default groups that provide administrative privileges should be managed carefully because they typically have broader privileges than are necessary for most delegated environments and because they often apply protection to their members.

The Account Operators group is a perfect example. If you examine its capabilities in the preceding list, you will see that its rights are very broad, indeed. It can even log on locally to a domain controller. In very small enterprises, such rights will probably be appropriate for one or two individuals who might be domain administrators anyway. In enterprises of any size, the rights and permissions granted to Account Operators are usually far too broad.

Additionally, Account Operators is, like the other administrative groups listed previously, a *protected group*. Protected groups are defined by the operating system and cannot be unprotected. Members of a protected group become protected. The result of protection is that the permissions (ACLs) of members are modified so that they no longer inherit permissions from their OU but, rather, receive a copy of an ACL that is quite restrictive. For example, if Jeff Ford is added to the Account Operators group, his account becomes protected and the help desk, which can reset all other user passwords in the People OU, cannot reset Jeff Ford's password.

MORE INFO Protected accounts

For more information about protected accounts, see Knowledge Base article 817433 at *http://support.microsoft.com/?kbid=817433*. If you want to search the Internet for resources, use the keyword *adminSDHolder*.

For these reasons—overdelegation and protection—strive to avoid adding users to the groups listed previously that do not have members by default: Account Operators, Backup Operators, Server Operators, and Print Operators. Instead, create custom groups to which you assign permissions and user rights that achieve your business and administrative requirements. For example, if Scott Mitchell should be able to perform backup operations on a domain controller but should not be able to perform restore operations that could lead to database rollback or corruption and should not be able to shut down a domain controller, don't put Scott in the Backup Operators group. Instead, create a group and assign it only the Backup Files And Directories user right; then add Scott as a member.

MORE INFO   Default group capabilities information

There is an exhaustive reference to the default groups in a domain and to the default local groups on Microsoft TechNet. If you are not familiar with the default groups and their capabilities, you should prepare for the examination by reading them. The default domain groups reference is at *http:// technet2.microsoft.com/WindowsServer/en/library/1631acad-ef34-4f77-9c2e-94a62f8846cf1033.mspx*, and the default local groups reference is at *http://technet2.microsoft.com/WindowsServer/en/library/ f6e01e51-14ea-48f4-97fc-5288a9a4a9b11033.mspx*.

Special Identities

Windows and Active Directory also support *special identities*, groups for which membership is controlled by the operating system. You cannot view the groups in any list in the Active Directory Users and Computers snap-in, for example. You cannot view or modify the membership of these special identities, and you cannot add them to other groups. You can, however, use these groups to assign rights and permissions. The most important special identities, often referred to as groups for convenience, are described in the following list:

- **Anonymous Logon**   Represents connections to a computer and its resources that are made without supplying a user name and password. Prior to Microsoft Windows Server 2003, this group was a member of the Everyone group. Beginning in Windows Server 2003, this group is no longer a default member of the Everyone group.
- **Authenticated Users**   Represents identities that have been authenticated. This group does not include Guest, even if the Guest account has a password.
- **Everyone**   Includes Authenticated Users and Guest. On computers running versions of Windows earlier than Windows Server 2003, this group includes Anonymous Logon.
- **Interactive**   Represents users accessing a resource while logged on locally to the computer hosting the resource, as opposed to accessing the resource over the network. When a user accesses any given resource on a computer to which the user is logged on locally, the user is automatically added to the Interactive group for that resource. Interactive also includes users logged on through a remote desktop connection.
- **Network**   Represents users accessing a resource over the network, as opposed to users who are logged on locally at the computer hosting the resource. When a user accesses any given resource over the network, the user is automatically added to the Network group for that resource.

The importance of these special identities is that they enable you to provide access to resources based on the type of authentication or connection rather than on the user account. For example, you could create a folder on a system that allows users to view its contents when logged on locally to the system but does not allow the same users to view the contents from a mapped drive over the network. This would be achieved by assigning permissions to the Interactive special identity.

PRACTICE **Administering Groups in an Enterprise**

In this practice, you will perform best-practices group management tasks to improve the administration of groups in the *contoso.com* domain. To perform the exercises in this practice, you will need the following objects in the *contoso.com* domain:

- A first-level OU named Groups.
- A global security group named Finance in the Groups OU.
- A first-level OU named People.
- A user account named Mike Danseglio in the People OU. Populate the user account with sample contact information: address, phone, and e-mail. Make sure the account is *not* required to change the password at the next logon.

In addition, ensure that the Domain Users group is a member of the Print Operators group, which can be found in the Builtin container. This will enable all sample users in the practice domain to log on to the domain controller, SERVER01. This is important for the practices in this training kit, but you should not allow users to log on to domain controllers in your production environment, so do not make Domain Users members of the Print Operators group in your production environment.

▶ **Exercise 1   Create a Well-Documented Group**

In this exercise, you will create a group to manage access to the Budget folder, and you will follow the best-practices guidelines presented in this lesson.

1. Log on to SERVER01 as Administrator and open the Active Directory Users And Computers snap-in.
2. Select the Groups OU in the console tree.
3. Right-click the Groups OU, choose New, and then select Group.
   The New Object – Group dialog box appears.
4. In the Group Name box, type **ACL_Budget_Edit**.
5. Select Domain Local in the Group Scope section and Security in the Group Type section, and then click OK.
6. Click the View menu and ensure that Advanced Features is selected.
7. Right-click the ACL_Budget_Edit group and choose Properties.
8. Click the Object tab.
9. Select the Protect Object From Accidental Deletion check box and click OK.
10. Open the group's Properties again.
11. In the Description box, type **BUDGET (EDIT)**.

12. In the *Notes* field, type the following paths to represent the folders that have permissions assigned to this group:

    \\server23\data$\finance\budget
    \\server32\data$\finance\revenue projections

13. Click OK.

▶ **Exercise 2   Delegate Management of Group Membership**

In this exercise, you will give Mike Danseglio the ability to manage the membership of the ACL_Budget_Edit group.

1. Open the Properties dialog box of the ACL_Budget_Edit group.
2. Click the Managed By tab.
3. Click the Change button.
4. Type the user name for Mike Danseglio and click OK.
5. Select the Manager Can Update Membership List check box. Click OK.

▶ **Exercise 3   Validate the Delegation of Membership Management**

In this exercise, you will test the delegation you performed in Exercise 2, "Delegate Management of Group Membership," by modifying the membership of the group as Mike Danseglio.

1. Open a command prompt.
2. Type the following command: **runas /user:Username cmd.exe**, where *Username* is the user name for Mike Danseglio.
3. When prompted, enter the password for Mike Danseglio.

    A new command prompt window appears, running as Mike Danseglio.
4. Type the following command and press Enter:

    ```
    dsmod group "CN=ACL_Budget_Edit,OU=Groups,DC=contoso,DC=com" -addmbr
    "CN=Finance,OU=Groups,DC=contoso,DC=com"
    ```
5. Close the command prompt.
6. In the Active Directory Users And Computers snap-in, examine the membership of the ACL_Budget_Edit group and confirm that the Finance group was added successfully.

Lesson Summary

- Use the *Description* and *Notes* fields in a group's Properties dialog box to document the purpose of the group.
- The Managed By tab enables you to specify a user or group that is responsible for a group. You can also select the Manager Can Update Membership List check box to delegate membership management to the user or group indicated on the Managed By tab.
- To delegate the management of group membership, you grant the Allow Write Members permission.

- Use the Protect Object From Accidental Deletion check box to prevent the potential security and management problems created when a group is accidentally deleted.

- Windows Server 2008 and Active Directory contain default groups with significant permissions and user rights. You should not add users to the default domain groups that do not already have members (Account Operators, Backup Operators, Print Operators, and Server Operators), and you should seriously restrict membership in other service administration groups (Enterprise Admins, Domain Admins, Schema Admins, and Administrators).

- Special identities such as Authenticated Users, Everyone, Interactive, and Network can be used to assign rights and permissions. Their membership is determined by the operating system and cannot be viewed or modified.

Lesson Review

You can use the following questions to test your knowledge of the information in Lesson 3, "Administering Groups in an Enterprise." The questions are also available on the companion CD if you prefer to review them in electronic form.

NOTE Answers

Answers to these questions and explanations of why each answer choice is right or wrong are located in the "Answers" section at the end of the book.

1. Your company is conducting a meeting for a special project. The data is particularly confidential. The team is meeting in a conference room, and you have configured a folder on the conference room computer that grants permission to the team members. You want to ensure that team members access the data only while logged on to the computer in the conference room, not from other computers in the enterprise. What must you do?

   A. Assign the Allow Read permission to the Interactive group.

   B. Assign the Allow Read permission to the team group.

   C. Assign the Deny Traverse Folders permission to the team group.

   D. Assign the Deny Full Control permission to the Network group.

2. You want to allow a user named Mike Danseglio to add and remove users from a group called Special Project. Where can you configure this permission?

    A. The Members tab of the group

    B. The Security tab of Mike Danseglio's user object

    C. The Member Of tab of Mike Danseglio's user object

    D. The Managed By tab of the group

3. Which of the following groups can shut down a domain controller? (Choose all that apply.)

    A. Account Operators

    B. Print Operators

    C. Backup Operators

    D. Server Operators

    E. Interactive

Chapter Review

To further practice and reinforce the skills you learned in this chapter, you can perform the following tasks:

- Review the chapter summary.
- Review the list of key terms introduced in this chapter.
- Complete the case scenario. This scenario sets up a real-world situation involving the topics of this chapter and asks you to create a solution.
- Complete the suggested practices.
- Take a practice test.

Chapter Summary

- Group scopes (global, universal, domain local, and universal) define group characteristics related to membership, replication, and availability of the group.
- In an enterprise, role-based management suggests that groups should be viewed as either defining a role or defining a business rule. Role groups are generally implemented as global groups, and rules are defined using domain local groups.
- A group's *member* attribute is a multivalued attribute containing the DNs of the group's members. Each member's *memberOf* attribute is automatically updated to reflect changes in membership. When you add a user to a group, you are always changing the group's *member* attribute. The *memberOf* attribute, which is read-only, is called a backlink.
- You can delegate the management of group membership by assigning the Allow Write Members permission, which grants write permission to the *member* attribute.
- Directory Services tools such as *Dsquery*, *Dsget*, and *Dsmod* can be used to list, create, and modify groups and their membership.
- *CSVDE* and *LDIFDE* can import and export groups. Additionally, *LDIFDE* can modify the membership of existing groups.
- The *Dsadd*, *Dsmove*, and *Dsrm* commands can add, move, and delete groups, respectively.

Key Terms

Use these key terms to understand better the concepts covered in this chapter.

- **backlink**   A type of read-only attribute that is automatically updated when its corresponding forward link attribute changes. For example, a group's *member* attribute is a forward link attribute, paired with the *memberOf* attribute. When a group's *member* attribute is changed to reflect an update in the group's membership, the *memberOf* attribute of affected objects is automatically updated by Active Directory.

- **shadow group**   A group that contains all users in an OU, or all users that meet a specific criteriona. A shadow group is a concept, not a type of group; you must create a shadow group manually, add all users to it, and update its membership according to changes in your environment.
- **special identities**   Users and groups that are dynamically maintained by the operating system, such as Authenticated Users, Everyone, and Anonymous Logon. You can assign rights and permissions to special identities, but you cannot view or manage their membership.

Case Scenario

In the following case scenario, you will apply what you've learned about administering groups in an enterprise. You can find answers to these questions in the "Answers" section at the end of this book.

Case Scenario: Implementing a Group Strategy

You are an administrator at Trey Research. A new product development initiative called Sliced Bread is underway, and there is confidential information about the project in shared folders on three servers in three different sites. Users in Research, Marketing, and Finance need access to the project data. Additionally, the CEO and her assistant need access. Of these, only Marketing and Research require Write access. Several interns are currently working in the Marketing department, and you want to prevent them from gaining access. Finally, a team of auditors from Woodgrove Bank, an investor in Trey Research, need Read access as well. You have a trust relationship configured so that the Trey Research domain trusts the Woodgrove Bank domain.

1. What types and scopes of groups do you create to represent the user roles in Trey Research? What type and scope of group do you ask administrators at Woodgrove Bank to create to represent the auditors' role?
2. What types and scopes of groups do you create to manage Read and Write access to the Sliced Bread folders?
3. Describe the nesting of users and groups you implement to achieve the security required by this project.

Suggested Practices

To help you successfully master the exam objectives presented in this chapter, complete the following tasks.

Automating Group Membership and Shadow Groups

In this practice, you will create a shadow group to reflect the user accounts in the People OU. You will apply the *Dsquery* and *Dsmod* commands to keep the membership up to date.

To perform this practice, you must have the following objects in the *contoso.com* domain:

- A first-level OU named Groups
- An OU named People
- Several sample user accounts in the People OU
- **Practice 1** In the Groups OU, create a global security group named People. Then click the People OU in the tree pane of the Active Directory Users And Computers snap-in. Click any user in the details pane and press Ctrl + A to select all. Right-click any selected user and choose Add To Group. Add the users to the People group. Examine the Members tab of the People group to confirm that all users were added successfully.
- **Practice 2** Open a command prompt. Delete the People group you created in Practice 1. Type the following two commands to create the People shadow group:

```
dsadd group "CN=People,OU=Groups,DC=contoso,DC=com" -secgrp yes -scope g
dsquery user "OU=People,DC=contoso,DC=com" |
    dsmod group "CN=People,OU=Groups,DC=contoso,DC=com" -addmbr
```

- **Practice 3** In a command prompt, type the following two commands to remove all members of the group and repopulate it with the current users in the People OU:

```
dsget group "CN=People,OU=Groups,DC=contoso,DC=com" -members |
    dsmod group "CN=People,OU=Groups,DC=contoso,DC=com" -rmmbr
dsquery user "OU=People,DC=contoso,DC=com" |
    dsmod group "CN=People,OU=Groups,DC=contoso,DC=com" -addmbr
```

Take a Practice Test

The practice tests on this book's companion CD offer many options. For example, you can test yourself on just one exam objective, or you can test yourself on all the 70-640 certification exam content. You can set up the test so that it closely simulates the experience of taking a certification exam, or you can set it up in study mode so that you can look at the correct answers and explanations after you answer each question.

MORE INFO   Practice tests

For details about all the practice test options available, see the "How to Use the Practice Tests" section in this book's introduction.

Chapter 5

Computers

Computers in a domain are security principals, like users are. They have an account with a logon name and password that Microsoft Windows changes automatically every 30 days or so. They authenticate with the domain. They can belong to groups, have access to resources, and be configured by Group Policy. And, like users, computers sometimes lose track of their passwords, requiring a reset, or have accounts that need to be disabled or enabled.

Managing computers—both the objects in Active Directory Domain Services (AD DS) and the physical devices—is part of the day-to-day work of most IT professionals. New systems are added to the organization, computers are taken offline for repairs, computers are exchanged between users or roles, and older equipment is retired or upgraded, leading to the acquisition of replacement systems. Each of these activities requires managing the identity of the computer represented by its object, or account, and Active Directory.

Unfortunately, most enterprises do not invest the same kind of care and process in the creation and management of computer accounts as they do for user accounts, even though both are security principals. In this chapter, you will learn how to create computer objects, which include attributes required for the object to be an account. You will learn how to support computer accounts through their life cycle, including configuration, troubleshooting, repairing, and deprovisioning computer objects. You will also deepen your understanding of the process through which a computer joins a domain, so that you can identify and avoid potential points of failure.

Exam objectives in this chapter:
- Creating and Maintaining Active Directory Objects
  - ❑ Automate creation of Active Directory accounts.
  - ❑ Maintain Active Directory accounts.

Lessons in this chapter:
- Lesson 1: Creating Computers and Joining the Domain 189
- Lesson 2: Automating the Creation of Computer Objects 203
- Lesson 3: Supporting Computer Objects and Accounts........................ 213

Before You Begin

This chapter applies Microsoft Windows PowerShell, Microsoft VBScript, *CSVDE*, and *LDIFDE* to the task of automating computer account creation. Please read Lesson 1, "Automating the Creation of User Accounts," and Lesson 2, "Creating Users with Windows PowerShell and VBScript," of Chapter 3, "Users," prior to reading this chapter.

Real World

Dan Holme

"Computers are people, too," or at least in Active Directory they are. In fact, computers have the *objectClass* attribute of *user*. They have accounts, just as users do. They can even forget their passwords, like users do. Because computers are security principals and can be used to scope Group Policy (as you'll learn in the next chapter), it is important to treat computer accounts with the same care as you'd treat user accounts.

I'm sure you've run into a situation when you had to remove a computer from a domain and then had it rejoin the domain. As you will see in Lesson 3, "Supporting Computer Objects and Accounts," that's a bad practice, equivalent to deleting and re-creating a user's account just because the user forgot his or her password. That's just one example of scenarios I see regularly, in which administrators are a bit less careful with computer accounts than they probably should be.

In this lesson, you'll learn the best practices for supporting computer accounts with the same level of respect as other security principals (including users and groups) in the domain. You'll also learn how to use command-line tools, VBScript, and Windows PowerShell scripts to automate the creation and management of computer objects. You'll see a lot of similarities to the procedures discussed in Chapter 3. Why? Because computers are people, too!

Lesson 1: Creating Computers and Joining the Domain

The default configuration of Windows Server 2008—as well as of Microsoft Windows Server 2003, Windows Vista, Windows XP, and Windows 2000—is that the computer belongs to a workgroup. Before you can log on to a computer with a domain account, that computer must belong to the domain. To join the domain, the computer must have an account in the domain which, like a user account, includes a logon name (*sAMAccountName*), a password, and a security identifier (SID) that uniquely represent the computer as a security principal in the domain. Those credentials enable the computer to authenticate against the domain and to create a secure relationship that then enables users to log on to the system with domain accounts. In this lesson, you will learn the steps to prepare the domain for a new computer account, and you will explore the process through which a computer joins the domain.

After this lesson, you will be able to:
- Design an OU structure for computers.
- Create computer objects in the domain.
- Delegate the creation of computer objects.
- Join computers to the domain.
- Redirect the default computer container.
- Prevent nonadministrative users from creating computers and joining the domain.

Estimated lesson time: 45 minutes

Understanding Workgroups, Domains, and Trusts

In a workgroup, each system maintains an identity store of user and group accounts against which users can be authenticated and access can begin. The local identity store on each computer is called the Security Accounts Manager (SAM) database. If a user logs on to a workgroup computer, the system authenticates the user against its local SAM database. If a user connects to another system, to access a file for example, the user is re-authenticated against the identity store of the remote system. From a security perspective, a workgroup computer is, for all intents and purposes, a standalone system.

When a computer joins a domain, it delegates the task of authenticating users to the domain. Although the computer continues to maintain its SAM database to support local user and group accounts, user accounts will typically be created in the central domain directory. When a user logs on to the computer with a domain account, the user is now authenticated by a domain controller rather than by the SAM. Said another way, the computer now *trusts* another authority to validate a user's identity. Trust relationships are generally discussed in the context of two domains, as you will learn in Chapter 12, "Domains and Forests," but there is also a trust between each domain member computer and its domain that is established when the computer joins the domain.

Identifying Requirements for Joining a Computer to the Domain

Three things are required for you to join a computer to an Active Directory domain:

- A computer object must be created in the directory service.
- You must have appropriate permissions to the computer object. The permissions allow you to join a computer with the same name as the object to the domain.
- You must be a member of the local Administrators group on the computer to change its domain or workgroup membership.

The next sections examine each of these requirements.

Computers Container

Before you create a computer object in the directory service—the first of the three requirements for joining a computer to the domain—you must have a place to put it. When you create a domain, the Computers container is created by default (CN=Computers, . . .). This container is not an organizational unit (OU); it is an object of class *container*. There are subtle but important differences between a container and an OU. You cannot create an OU within a container, so you cannot subdivide the Computers OU, and you cannot link a Group Policy object to a container. Therefore, it is highly recommended to create custom OUs to host computer objects instead of using the Computers container.

Creating OUs for Computers

Most organizations create at least two OUs for computer objects: one to host computer accounts for clients—desktops, laptops, and other user systems—and another for servers. These two OUs are in addition to the Domain Controllers OU created by default during the installation of Active Directory. In each of these OUs, computer objects are created. There is no technical difference between a computer object in a clients OU and a computer object in a servers or domain controllers OU; computer objects are computer objects. But separate OUs are typically created to provide unique scopes of management so that you can delegate management of client objects to one team and server objects to another.

Your administrative model might necessitate further dividing your client and server OUs. Many organizations create sub-OUs beneath a server OU to collect and manage specific types of servers, for example, an OU for file and print servers and an OU for database servers. By doing so, the team of administrators for each type of server can be delegated permissions to manage computer objects in the appropriate OU. Similarly, geographically distributed organizations with local desktop support teams often divide a parent OU for clients into sub-OUs for each site. This approach enables each site's support team to create computer objects in the site for client computers and join computers to the domain by using those computer objects. This is an example only; what is most important is that your OU structure reflects your administrative model so that your OUs provide single points of management for the delegation of administration.

Figure 5-1 illustrates a typical OU design for an organization whose server administration teams are focused on specific types of servers and whose desktop support teams are focused on clients in specific geographical areas.

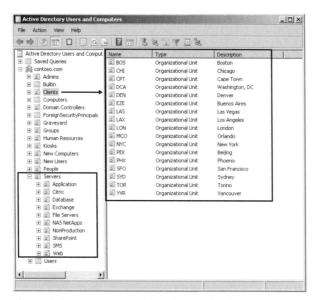

Figure 5-1   A common OU design illustrating site-based administration of clients and role-based administration of servers

Additionally, separate OUs enable you to create different baseline configurations, using different Group Policy objects (GPOs) linked to the client and the server OUs. Group Policy, discussed in detail in Chapter 6, "Group Policy Infrastructure," enables you to specify configuration for collections of computers by linking GPOs that contain configuration instructions to OUs. It is common for organizations to separate clients into desktop and laptop OUs. GPOs specifying desktop or laptop configuration can then be linked to appropriate OUs.

If your organization has decentralized, site-based administration and wants to manage unique configurations for desktops and laptops, you face a design dilemma. Should you divide your clients OU based on administration and then subdivide desktops and laptops, or should you divide your clients OU into desktop and laptop OUs and then subdivide based on administration? The options are illustrated in Figure 5-2. Because the primary design driver for Active Directory OUs is the efficient delegation of administration through the inheritance of access control lists (ACLs) on OUs, the design on the left would be recommended.

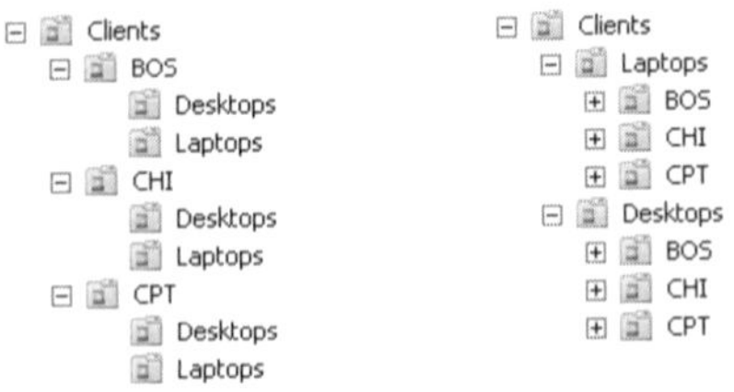

Figure 5-2   OU design options

Delegating Permission to Create Computers

By default, the Enterprise Admins, Domain Admins, Administrators, and Account Operators groups have permission to create computer objects in any new OU. However, as discussed in Chapter 4, "Groups," it is recommended that you tightly restrict membership in the first three groups and that you do not add administrators to the Account Operators group.

Instead, delegate the permission to create computer objects to appropriate administrators or support personnel. The permission required to create a computer object is Create Computer Objects. This permission, assigned to a group for an OU, allows members of the group to create computer objects in that OU. For example, you might allow your desktop support team to create computer objects in the clients OU and allow your file server administrators to create computer objects in the file servers OU.

Practice It   Exercise 3, "Delegate the Ability to Create Computer Objects," at the end of this lesson, steps you through the procedure required to delegate the creation of computer objects.

Prestaging a Computer Account

After you have been given permission to create computer objects, you can do so by right-clicking the OU and choosing Computer from the New menu. The New Object – Computer dialog box, shown in Figure 5-3, appears.

Enter the computer name, following the naming convention of your enterprise, and select the user or group that will be allowed to join the computer to the domain with this account. The two computer names—Computer Name and Computer Name (Pre-Windows 2000)—should be the same; there is rarely, if ever, a justification for configuring them separately.

NOTE   The New Object – Computer Wizard over-delegates

The permissions that are applied to the user or group you select in the New Object – Computer Wizard are more than are necessary simply to join a computer to the domain. The selected user or group is also given the ability to modify the computer object in other ways. For guidance regarding a least-privilege approach to delegating permission to join a computer to the domain, see *Windows Administration Resource Kit: Productivity Solutions for IT Professionals* by Dan Holme (Microsoft Press, 2008).

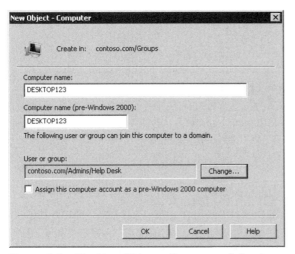

Figure 5-3   The New Object – Computer dialog box

The process you have completed to create a computer account before joining the computer to the domain is called *prestaging* the account. The advantage of performing this procedure is that the account is in the correct OU and is, therefore, delegated according to the security policy defined by the ACL of the OU and is within the scope of GPOs linked to the OU before the computer joins the domain. Prestaging is highly recommended for reasons discussed in the "Importance of Prestaging Computer Objects" section.

Joining a Computer to the Domain

By prestaging the computer object, you fulfill the first two requirements for joining a computer to a domain: the computer object exists, and you have specified who has permissions to join a computer with the same name to the domain. Now, a local administrator of the computer can change the computer's domain membership and enter the specified domain credentials to complete the process successfully. To join a computer to the domain, follow these steps:

1. Log on to the computer with credentials that belong to the local Administrators group on the computer.

   Only local administrators can alter the domain or workgroup membership of a computer.

2. Open the System properties, using one of the following methods:

   ❏ Windows XP, Windows Server 2003: Right-click My Computer and choose Properties.

   ❏ Windows Vista, Windows Server 2008: Right-click Computer; choose Properties; and then, in the Computer Name, Domain, And Workgroup Settings section, click Change Settings. Click if prompted.

3. Click the Computer Name tab.

4. Click Change.

5. Under Member Of, select Domain.

6. Type the name of the domain you want to join.

NOTE   Use the full DNS name of the domain

Use the full DNS name of the Active Directory domain. Not only is this more accurate and more likely to succeed, but if it does not succeed, it indicates a possible problem with DNS name resolution that should be rectified before joining the computer to the domain.

---

7. Click OK.

8. Windows prompts for the credentials of your user account in the domain.

   The domain checks to see whether a computer object already exists with the name of the computer. One of the following three things happens:

   ❑ If the object exists and a computer with that name has already joined the domain, an error message is returned, and you cannot join the computer to the domain.

   ❑ If the object exists and it is prestaged—a computer with the same name has not joined the domain—the domain confirms that the domain credentials you entered have permission to join the domain using that account. These permissions are discussed in the "Prestaging a Computer Account" section.

   ❑ If the computer account is not prestaged, Windows checks to see whether you have permissions to create a new computer object in the default computer container. If you do have permissions to create a new computer object in the default computer container, the object is created with the name of the computer. This method of joining a domain is supported for backward compatibility, but is not recommended. It is recommended to prestage the account as indicated earlier and as detailed in the next section, "The Importance of Prestaging Computer Objects."

   The computer then joins the domain by assuming the identity of its Active Directory object. It configures its SID to match the domain computer account's SID and sets an initial password with the domain. The computer then performs other tasks related to joining the domain. It adds the Domain Admins group to the local Administrators group and the Domain Users group to the local Users group.

9. You are prompted to restart the computer. Click OK to close this message box.

10. Click Close (in Windows Vista) or OK (in Windows XP) to close the System Properties dialog box.

11. You are prompted, again, to restart the computer, after which the system is fully a member of the domain, and you can log on using domain credentials.

The *Netdom.exe* command enables you to join a computer to the domain from the command line. The basic syntax of the command is:

```
netdom join MachineName /Domain:DomainName [/OU:"DN of OU"]
    [/UserO:LocalUsername] [/PasswordO:{LocalPassword|*} ]
    [/UserD:DomainUsername] [/PasswordD:{DomainPassword|*} ]
    [/SecurePasswordPrompt] [/REBoot[:TimeInSeconds]]
```

It can be useful to join a computer to a domain from the command line, first, because it can be included in a script that performs other actions. Second, *Netdom.exe* can be used to join a computer *remotely* to the domain. Third, *Netdom.exe* enables you to specify the OU for the computer object. The command's parameters are, for the most part, self-explanatory. *UserO* and *PasswordO* are credentials that are members of the workgroup computer's local Administrators group. Specifying * for the password causes *Netdom.exe* to prompt for the password on the command line. *UserD* and *PasswordD* are domain credentials with permission to create a computer object, if the account is not prestaged, or to join a computer to a prestaged account. The *REBoot* parameter causes the system to reboot after joining the domain. The default timeout is 30 seconds. The *SecurePasswordPrompt* parameter displays a pop-up for credentials when * is specified for either *PasswordO* or *PasswordD*.

Importance of Prestaging Computer Objects

The best practice is to prestage a computer account prior to joining the computer to the domain. Unfortunately, Windows enables you to join a computer to a domain without following best practices. You can log on to a workgroup computer as a local administrator and change the computer's membership to the domain. Then, on demand, Windows creates a computer object in the default computer container, gives you permission to join a computer to that object, and joins the system to the domain.

There are three problems with this behavior of Windows. First, the computer account created automatically by Windows is placed in the default computer container, which is not where the computer object belongs in most enterprises. Second, you must move the computer from the default computer container into the correct OU, which is an extra step that is often forgotten. Third, any user can join a computer to the domain—no domain-level administrative permissions are required. Because a computer object is a security principal, and because the creator of a computer object owns the object and can change its attributes, this exposes a potential security vulnerability. The next sections detail these disadvantages.

Configuring the Default Computer Container

When you join a computer to the domain and the computer object does not already exist in Active Directory, Windows automatically creates a computer account in the default computer container, which is called Computers (CN=Computers,DC=*domain*, by default). The problem with this relates to the discussion of OU design earlier in the lesson. If you have implemented the best practices described there, you have delegated permissions to administer computer objects in specific OUs for clients and servers. Additionally, you might have linked GPOs to those OUs to manage the configuration of these computer objects. If a new computer object is created outside of those OUs, in the default computer container, the permissions and configuration it inherits from its parent container will be different than what it should have received. You will then need to remember to move the computer from the default container to the correct OU after joining the domain.

Two steps are recommended to reduce the likelihood of this problem. First, always try to prestage computer accounts. If an account is prestaged for a computer in the correct OU, then when the computer joins the domain, it will use the existing account and will be subject to the correct delegation and configuration.

Second, to reduce the impact of systems being joined to the domain without a prestaged account, change the default computer container so that it is not the Computers container itself but, instead, is an OU that is subject to appropriate delegation and configuration. For example, if you have an OU called Clients, you can instruct Windows to use that OU as the default computer container, so that if computers are joined to the domain without prestaged accounts, the objects are created in the Clients OU.

The *Redircmp.exe* command, available on domain controllers, redirects the default computer container with the following syntax:

```
redircmp "DN of OU for new computer objects"
```

Now, if a computer joins the domain without a prestaged computer account, Windows creates the computer object in the specified organizational unit.

Redirecting the Default User Container

The same concepts apply to the creation of user accounts. By default, if a user account is created using an earlier practice that does not specify the OU for the account, the object is created in the default user container (CN=Users,DC=*domain*, by default). The *Redirusr.exe* command, available on domain controllers, can redirect the default container to an actual OU that is delegated and configured appropriately. *Redirusr*, like *Redircmp*, takes a single parameter: the distinguished name of the OU that will become the default user container.

Exam Tip   The *Redircmp.exe* command redirects the default computer container to a specified OU. *Redirusr.exe* does the same for the default user container. You might see these two commands used as *distracters*—presented as potential (but incorrect) answers to questions that have nothing to do with the default computer or user containers. As you look at any exam question, evaluate the possible answers to determine whether the answers are proposing to use real commands but in the wrong application of those commands.

Restricting the Ability of Users to Create Computers

When a computer account is prestaged, the permissions on the account determine who is allowed to join that computer to the domain. When an account is not prestaged, Windows will, by default, allow any authenticated user to create a computer object in the default computer container. In fact, Windows will allow any authenticated user to create up to ten computer objects in the default computer container. The creator of a computer object, by default, has permission to join that computer to the domain. It is through this mechanism that any authenticated user can join ten computers to the domain without any explicit permissions to do so.

The ten-computer quota is configured by the *ms-DS-MachineAccountQuota* attribute of the domain. It allows any authenticated user to join a computer to the domain, no questions asked. This is problematic from a security perspective because computers are security principals, and the creator of a security principal has permission to manage that computer's properties. In a way, the quota is like allowing any domain user to create ten user accounts, without any controls.

It is highly recommended that you close this loophole so that nonadministrative users cannot join computers to the domain. To change the *ms-DS-MachineAccountQuota* attribute, follow these steps:

1. Open ADSI Edit from the Administrative Tools folder.
2. Right-click ADSI Edit and choose Connect To.
3. In the Connection Point section, choose Select A Well Known Naming Context and, from the drop-down list, choose Default Naming Context.
4. Click OK.
5. Expand Default Naming Context.
6. Right-click the dc=contoso,dc=com domain folder, for example, and choose Properties.
7. Select ms-DS-MachineAccountQuota and click Edit.
8. Type **0**.
9. Click OK.

The Authenticated Users group also is assigned the user right to add workstations to the domain, but you do not have to modify this right if you have changed the default value of the *ms-DS-MachineAccountQuota* attribute.

After you have changed the *ms-DS-MachineAccountQuota* attribute to zero, you can be assured that the only users who can join computers to the domain are those who have been specifically delegated permission to join prestaged computer objects or to create new computer objects.

> **Quick Check**
>
> ■ What two things determine whether you can join a computer account to the domain?
>
> **Quick Check Answer**
>
> ■ To join a computer to a prestaged account, you must be given permission on the account to join it to the domain. If the account is not prestaged, the *ms-DS-MachineAccountQuota* attribute will determine the number of computers you can join to the domain in the default computer container without explicit permission.

After you've eliminated this loophole, you must make sure you have given appropriate administrators explicit permission to create computer objects in the correct OUs, as described in the "Delegating Permission to Create Computers" section; otherwise, the error message shown in Figure 5-4 will appear.

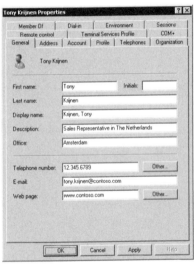

Figure 5-4   An error message appearing when a user has exceeded the default computer account quota specified by the *ms-DS-MachineAccountQuota* attribute

PRACTICE Creating Computers and Joining the Domain

In this practice, you will implement best practices for creating computers and joining systems to the domain. You will begin by creating an OU structure to host new computer objects. You will then create prestaged computer objects and delegate permission to join the computers to the domain. You will delegate permission to create computer objects, using the *Dsacls.exe* command, and you will redirect the default computer container.

Before performing the exercises, you must create the following objects in the *contoso.com* domain:

- A first-level OU named Admins with a sub-OU named Groups.
- A global security group in the Admins\Groups OU named Server Admins.
- A global security group in the Admins\Groups OU named Help Desk.
- A first-level OU named People.
- A user in the People OU named Jeff Ford. The user is a member of Domain Users and Server Admins.
- A user in the People OU named Linda Mitchell. The user is a member of Domain Users and Help Desk.

In addition, make sure that the Domain Users group is a member of the Print Operators group, which can be found in the Builtin container. This will enable all sample users in the practice domain to log on to the SERVER01 domain controller. This is important for the practices in this training kit, but you should not allow users to log on to domain controllers in your production environment, so do not make Domain Users members of the Print Operators group in your production environment.

▶ **Exercise 1   Create OUs for Client and Server Computer Objects**

Before you can create computer accounts, you must create OUs for the objects. In this exercise, you will create OUs for server and computer objects.

1. Log on to SERVER01 as Administrator.
2. Open the Active Directory Users And Computers snap-in and expand the domain.
3. Right-click the *contoso.com* domain, choose New, and then select Organizational Unit.
4. Type **Clients** and click OK.
5. Right-click the *contoso.com* domain, choose New, and then select Organizational Unit.
6. Type **Servers** and click OK.

▶ **Exercise 2   Create Computer Objects**

After an OU has been created for computer objects, you can prestage accounts for computers that will join the domain. In this exercise, you will prestage an account for a client and an account for a server and delegate the ability to join the computer to the domain.

1. Right-click the Clients OU, choose New, and then select Computer.
2. The New Object – Computer dialog box appears, as shown in Figure 5-3.
3. Type the computer's name in the Computer Name box: **DESKTOP101**.
4. Click the Change button next to the User Or Group box.
5. In the Select User Or Group dialog box that appears, type the name of the user or group that will be allowed to join the computer to the domain: **Help Desk**. Click OK.

6. Click OK to close the New Object – Computer dialog box.

7. Right-click the Servers OU, choose New, and then select Computer.

8. The New Object – Computer dialog box appears, as shown in Figure 5-3.

9. Type the computer's name in the Computer Name box: **SERVER02**.

10. Click the Change button next to the User Or Group box.

11. In the Select User Or Group dialog box that appears, enter the name of the user or group that will be allowed to join the computer to the domain: **Server Admins**. Click OK.

12. Click OK to close the New Object – Computer dialog box.

▶ **Exercise 3   Delegate the Ability to Create Computer Objects**

You must have permission to create computer objects to create accounts as you did in Exercise 2, "Create Computer Objects." The Administrator account has such permissions, but you might want to delegate the ability to create computer accounts to other groups. In this exercise, you will delegate least-privilege permissions to create computer objects.

1. On SERVER01, open the Active Directory Users And Computers snap-in.

2. Click the View menu and ensure that Advanced Features is selected.

3. Right-click Clients and choose Properties.

4. Click the Security tab.

5. Click Advanced.

6. Click Add.

7. Type **Help Desk** and click OK.

8. Click the Object tab.

9. In the Apply To drop-down list, choose This Object And All Descendant Objects.

10. In the Permissions list, select the check box for Allow next to the Create Computer Objects.

11. Click OK three times to close all dialog boxes.

12. You can test your delegation by launching a command prompt as Linda Mitchell and performing Exercise 1, "Create a Computer with *Dsadd*," in Lesson 2, "Automating the Creation of Computer Objects."

▶ **Exercise 4   Redirect the Default Computer Container**

It is recommended to redirect the default computer container so that any new computer objects generated by joining a computer to the domain without a prestaged account will be created in a managed OU rather than in the Computers container. In this exercise, you will use *Redircmp.exe* to redirect the default computer container.

1. On SERVER01, open a command prompt.

2. Type the following command and press Enter:

```
redircmp "OU=Clients,DC=contoso,DC=com"
```

▶ **Optional Exercise 5   Join a Computer to the Domain**

In this exercise, you will join a computer to the domain. This requires a second system, which would be either a server named SERVER02 running Windows Server 2008 or a client named DESKTOP101 running Windows Vista. If the computer has another name, you must either rename it or create a computer object for it in the correct OU, using the steps in Exercise 2 as a reference.

1. Log on to the workgroup computer with credentials that belong to the local Administrators group on the computer.
2. Open the System properties, using one of the following methods:
    ❏ Open System from Control Panel.
    ❏ Right-click Computer in the Start menu.
    ❏ Press the Windows key and the Pause key.
3. In the Computer Name, Domain, And Workgroup Settings section, click Change Settings. Click Continue if prompted.
4. Click the Computer Name tab.
5. Click Change.
6. Under Member Of, select Domain.
7. Type the name of the domain you want to join: **contoso.com**.
8. Click OK.

    The computer attempts to contact the domain. Windows prompts for the credentials of your user account in the domain.
9. Enter domain credentials and click OK.
    ❏ If you are joining SERVER02 to the domain, enter the credentials of Jeff Ford, who belongs to the Server Admins group.
    ❏ If you are joining DESKTOP101 to the domain, enter the credentials of Linda Mitchell, who belongs to the Help Desk group.
10. You are prompted to restart the computer. Click OK to close this message box.
11. Click Close to close the System Properties dialog box.
12. You are prompted, again, to restart the computer.

Lesson Summary

- The Computers container does not support linking Group Policy objects or creating child OUs. Create an OU structure to reflect the administrative model of your organization.
- Always prestage computer accounts, which means that you create a computer object in Active Directory prior to joining the system to the domain.

- To join the domain successfully, you must be a local Administrator of the computer, a computer account must be created, and you must provide domain credentials that have permission on the computer object to join the domain.

- You use *Redircmp.exe* to redirect the default computer container to an OU that has been delegated and configured to meet your business requirements.

- The *ms-DS-MachineAccountQuota* allows all authenticated users to join up to ten systems to the domain. Windows will create computer objects for the systems in the default computer container. Reduce this quota to zero to prevent nonadministrative users from creating security principals.

Lesson Review

You can use the following questions to test your knowledge of the information in Lesson 1, "Creating Computers and Joining the Domain." The questions are also available on the companion CD if you prefer to review them in electronic form.

NOTE   Answers

Answers to these questions and explanations of why each answer choice is right or wrong are located in the "Answers" section at the end of the book.

---

1. You want to require all new computer accounts created when computers join the domain to be placed in the Clients OU. Which command should you use?

    A. *Dsmove*

    B. Move-Item

    C. *Netdom*

    D. *Redircmp*

2. You want to prevent nonadministrative users from joining computers to the domain. What should you do?

    A. Set *ms-DS-MachineAccountQuota* to zero.

    B. Set *ms-DS-DefaultQuota* to zero.

    C. Remove the Add Workstations To Domain user right from Authenticated Users.

    D. On the domain, deny the Authenticated Users group the Create Computer Objects permission.

3. You want to join a remote computer to the domain. Which command should you use?

    A. *Dsadd.exe*

    B. *Netdom.exe*

    C. *Dctest.exe*

    D. *System.cpl*

Lesson 2: Automating the Creation of Computer Objects

The steps you learned in Lesson 1 for creating a computer account become burdensome if you must create dozens or even hundreds of computer accounts at the same time. Commands such as *CSVDE*, *LDIFDE*, and *Dsadd*, as well as VBScript and Windows PowerShell scripts, can import and automate the creation of computer objects. Scripts can also enable you to *provision* computer objects, that is, to perform business logic such as the enforcement of computer naming conventions. In this lesson, you will learn to import, automate, and provision computer objects. You will build upon the knowledge of these commands that you gained from reading Lesson 1 and Lesson 2 of Chapter 3, which are a prerequisite for this lesson.

After this lesson, you will be able to:
- Use *CSVDE* and *LDIFDE* to import computers.
- Create computers with *Dsadd*.
- Create computers with *Netdom*.
- Create computers with Windows PowerShell.
- Create computers with VBScript.

Estimated lesson time: 30 minutes

Importing Computers with *CSVDE*

You were introduced to the *Comma-Separated Values Data Exchange* (*CSVDE*) command in Lesson 1 of Chapter 3. *CSVDE* is a command-line tool that imports or exports Active Directory objects from or to a comma-delimited text file (also known as a comma-separated value text file, or .csv file). The basic syntax of the *CSVDE* command is:

```
csvde [-i] [-f "Filename"] [-k]
```

The *–i* parameter specifies import mode; without it, the default mode of *CSVDE* is export. The *–f* parameter identifies the file name to import from or export to. The *–k* parameter is useful during import operations because it instructs *CSVDE* to ignore errors including Object Already Exists, Constraint Violation, and Attribute Or Value Already Exists.

Comma-delimited files can be created, modified, and opened with tools as familiar as Notepad and Microsoft Office Excel. The first line of the file defines the attributes by their Lightweight Directory Access Protocol (LDAP) attribute names. Each object follows, one per line, and must contain exactly the attributes listed on the first line. A sample file is shown in Excel in Figure 5-5.

When importing computers, be sure to include the *userAccountControl* attribute and set it to 4096. This attribute ensures that the computer will be able to join the account. Also include the pre-Windows 2000 logon name of the computer, the *sAMAccountName* attribute, which is the name of the computer followed by a dollar sign ($) as shown in Figure 5-5.

	A	B	C	D	E
1	DN	objectClass	name	userAccountControl	sAMAccountName
2	CN=DESKTOP103,OU=Clients,DC=contoso,DC=con	computer	DESKTOP103	4096	DESKTOP103$
3	CN=DESKTOP104,OU=Clients,DC=contoso,DC=con	computer	DESKTOP104	4096	DESKTOP104$
4	CN=SERVER02,OU=Servers,DC=contoso,DC=com	computer	SERVER02	4096	SERVER02$

Figure 5-5   A .csv file, opened in Excel, that will create three computer accounts

---

MORE INFO   In Chapter 3 and Chapter 4, you used the *CSVDE* command to import users and groups. For more information about *CSVDE*, including details regarding its parameters and usage to export directory objects, type csvde /? or search the Windows Server 2008 Help and Support Center.

Importing Computers with *LDIFDE*

Chapter 3 also introduced you to *Ldifde.exe*, which imports data from files in the Lightweight Directory Access Protocol Data Interchange Format (LDIF) format. LDIF files are text files within which operations are specified by a block of lines separated by a blank line. Each operation begins with the *DN* attribute of the object that is the target of the operation. The next line, *changeType*, specifies the type of operation: *add*, *modify*, or *delete*.

The following listing is an LDIF file that will create two server accounts:

```
dn: CN=SERVER10,OU=Servers,DC=contoso,DC=com
changetype: add
objectClass: top
objectClass: person
objectClass: organizationalPerson
objectClass: user
objectClass: computer
cn: SERVER10
userAccountControl: 4096
sAMAccountName: SERVER10$

dn: CN= SERVER11,OU= Servers,DC=contoso,DC=com
changetype: add
objectClass: top
objectClass: person
objectClass: organizationalPerson
objectClass: user
objectClass: computer
cn: SERVER11
userAccountControl: 4096
sAMAccountName: SERVER11$
```

The basic syntax of the *LDIFDE* command is similar to that of the *CSVDE* command:

```
ldifde [-i] [-f "Filename"] [-k]
```

By default, *LDIFDE* is in export mode. The −i parameter specifies import mode. You must specify the −f mode to identify the file you are using for import or export. *LDIFDE* will stop when it encounters errors unless you specify the −k parameter, in which case, *LDIFDE* continues processing.

Exam Tip   Remember that the default mode of *CSVDE* and *LDIFDE* is export. You must use the −i parameter to import objects.

Creating Computers with *Dsadd*

The *Dsadd* command has been used in previous chapters to create objects in Active Directory. To create computer objects, simply type **dsadd computer *ComputerDN*** where ComputerDN is the distinguished name (DN) of the computer, such as CN=Desktop123,OU=Desktops,DC =contoso,DC=com.

If the computer's DN includes a space, surround the entire DN with quotation marks. The *ComputerDN* parameter can include more than one distinguished name for new computer objects, making *Dsadd Computer* a handy way to generate multiple objects at once. The parameter can be entered in one of the following ways:

- By piping a list of DNs from another command such as *Dsquery*.
- By typing each DN on the command line, separated by spaces.
- By leaving the *DN* parameter empty, at which point, you can type the DNs, one at a time, at the keyboard console of the command prompt. Press Enter after each DN. Press Ctrl+Z and Enter after the last DN.

The *Dsadd Computer* command can take the following optional parameters after the DN parameter:

- -samid *SAMName*
- -desc *Description*
- -loc *Location*

Creating Computers with *Netdom*

The *Netdom* command is also able to perform a variety of domain account and security tasks from the command line. In Lesson 1, you learned to use *Netdom* to join a computer to the domain. You can also use it to create a computer account by typing the following command:

```
netdom add ComputerName /domain:DomainName [/ou:OUDN]
[/userd:User /PasswordD:Password]
```

This command creates the computer account for *ComputerName* in the domain indicated by the *domain* parameter, using the credentials specified by *UserD* and *PasswordD*. The *ou* parameter causes the object to be created in the OU specified by the *OUDN* distinguished name following the parameter. If no *OUDN* is supplied, the computer account is created in the default computer container. The user credentials must have permissions to create computer objects.

Creating Computers with Windows PowerShell

Chapter 3 introduced you to Windows PowerShell, the new administrative and automation shell for Windows platforms. You learned how to create users in that chapter. As with user objects, you can create computer objects by following these high-level steps:

1. Connect to the container (the OU) in which you want to create a computer.
2. Use the *Create* method of the container to create the computer.
3. Populate mandatory attributes.
4. Commit your changes.

To connect to an OU in Windows PowerShell, type the following at a PowerShell prompt:

```
$objOU = [ADSI]"LDAP://DN of OU'
```

The command creates an object reference stored in the *$objOU* variable that represents the OU. You can now invoke the methods of the OU, using the *$objOU* variable. To create a computer, use the *Create* method by typing the following:

```
$objComputer = $objOU.Create("computer","CN=Computer CN")
```

Next, you must configure two attributes. The first is the computer's pre-Windows 2000 logon name, the *sAMAccountName* attribute, which is the computer's name appended with a dollar sign ($). The second is the computer's *userAccountControl* attribute, which must be set to 4096 (0x1000 in hexadecimal). The *userAccountControl* attribute is a series of flags, 1 bit each. This bit indicates that the account is for a domain member. Without it, a computer will not be able to join the domain by using the account. To set these two attributes, type the following:

```
$objComputer.Put("sAMAccountName", "ComputerName$")
$objComputer.Put("userAccountControl", 4096)
```

You can set other attributes at this time as well. For example, you can set *description* or *info*. When you have finished configuring attributes, you must commit your changes with the following code.

```
$objComputer.SetInfo()
```

Importing Computers from a Database with Windows PowerShell

On the 70-640 examination, it is highly unlikely that you will need to know how to connect to a database and create computers with Windows PowerShell. However, such knowledge can be a tremendous benefit in your production environment. Assume you receive a list of computers that are being shipped from your vendor. You want to prestage computer accounts for those systems.

You can easily do so with a Windows PowerShell script. With scripts, you can also perform business logic such as enforcing naming standards. In this section, you will learn how to do so.

Windows PowerShell can connect to and expose a data source such as a .csv file, which you can create in Excel. So, for example, you could paste the asset tags from the list of computers you received from your vendor into an Excel worksheet, as shown in Figure 5-6, and save the worksheet as a .csv file with a name such as Assets.csv.

	A	B
1	**AssetTag**	**Type**
2	A849XD	Desktop
3	D82KE8	Desktop
4	ELW938	Laptop
5	XKD8G0	Laptop
6	93JX9D	Laptop
7	SJ0GJ3	Laptop

Figure 5-6   A simple Excel data source of computer asset tags

Assume that you want to import these computers into your domain, and you want them to follow two rules. First, laptops and desktops are in separate OUs, specifically the Laptops OU and the Desktops OU, under your Clients OU. Second, your computer naming convention is to prefix the asset tag with an L or a D, for laptop or desktop, respectively. For example, the computer name for the first computer listed in Figure 5-6 would be DA849XD. These two simple rules are examples of what would be called *logic* in the context of programming.

A script that would import computers from the file would look similar to the following code. Line numbers have been added to facilitate discussing the code.

```
1.  $dataSource=import-csv "Assets.csv"
2.  foreach($dataRecord in $datasource) {
3.      #map variables to data source
4.      $AssetTag = $dataRecord.AssetTag
5.      $Type = $dataRecord.Type

6.      #determine name
7.      $ComputerName = $Type.substring(0,1) + $AssetTag
8.      $sAMAccountName=$ComputerName + "$"
9.      #determine OU
10.     $strOUADsPath = "LDAP://OU=" + $Type + "s" + `
11.          ",OU=Clients,DC=contoso,DC=com"

12.     #create the computer object
13.     $objOU=[ADSI]$strOUADsPath
14.     $objComputer=$objOU.Create("computer","CN="+$ComputerName)
15.     $objComputer.Put("sAMAccountName",$sAMAccountName)
16.     $objComputer.Put("userAccountControl",4096)
17.     $objComputer.SetInfo()
18. }
```

Lines 13–17 are identical to the commands shown in the previous section, except that in line 13, a variable is used rather than a hard-coded path to the OU. These lines are part of a block of code, bounded by lines 2 and 18, that are repeated for each record in the data source. The data source is defined in line 1, using the same Import-Csv cmdlet you learned about in Chapter 3. Line 2 uses a *foreach* collection (*foreach* is an alias for ForEach-Object) to loop through each record in the data source.

Lines 4 and 5 assign the two fields in each record to variables. Lines 6–11 perform the business logic. Line 7 creates the computer name, using the first character of the *Type* field (a *D* or an *L*) and appending *AssetTag*. Line 8 creates the *sAMAccountName* attribute by adding a dollar sign to the computer name. Line 10 creates the path to the OU for the object. The back tick mark at the end of line 10 is a line continuation character; it means that the code continues on line 11. Therefore, lines 10 and 11 are actually a single line of code. The logic indicated that a Desktop asset *Type* goes into the Desktops OU, so the type has an *s* added to it.

As you can see from this script, it is possible and not terribly difficult to create a data-driven provisioning system for new computer objects. Define your data sources and define your business logic, and Windows PowerShell scripts can do the rest.

Creating Computers with VBScript

VBScript uses the same Active Directory Services Interface (ADSI) as does Windows PowerShell to manipulate Active Directory objects, so the steps to create a computer are identical: connect to the container, create the object, populate its attributes, and commit the changes. The following code will create a computer in the domain:

```
Set objOU = GetObject("LDAP://DN of OU")
Set objComputer = objOU.Create("computer","CN=Computer CN")
objComputer.Put "sAMAccountName", "ComputerName$"
objComputer.Put "userAccountControl", 4096
objComputer.SetInfo
```

The code is very similar to the Windows PowerShell commands in lines 13–17 of the script presented in the previous section.

NOTE **VBScript does databases**

In the previous section, you learned how to use a .csv file as a data source for a Windows PowerShell script. VBScript can also load and use data from .csv files, but it is not as elegant as the Windows PowerShell Import-Csv cmdlet.

PRACTICE   Create and Manage a Custom MMC

In this practice, you will implement automation to import and create computers in the *contoso.com* domain. Before performing the exercises in this practice, be sure that you have the following objects in the *contoso.com* domain.

- A first-level OU called Clients
- A first-level OU called Servers

You must also have installed the Windows PowerShell feature. The practice in Chapter 3, Lesson 2 has instructions.

▶ **Exercise 1   Create a Computer with *Dsadd***

The *Dsadd* command enables you to add a computer from the command line. An advantage of the *Dsadd* command is that it requires only the computer's DN. It creates the *sAMAccountName* and *userAccountControl* attributes automatically. In this exercise, you will create a computer with *Dsadd.exe*.

1. Log on to SERVER01 as Administrator.
2. Open a command prompt.
3. Type the following command and press Enter:

   ```
   dsadd computer "CN=DESKTOP152,OU=Clients,DC=contoso,DC=com"
   ```

4. Using the Active Directory Users And Computers snap-in, verify that the computer was created successfully.

▶ **Exercise 2   Import Computers by Using *CSVDE***

When you want to create more than a few computers, you might find it easier to import the computer objects from a data source such as a .csv file. In this exercise, you will use *CSVDE* to import computer accounts from a .csv file.

1. Open Notepad.
2. Type the following lines into Notepad. Each bullet is one line. Do not include the bullets in the Notepad file.
   - DN,objectClass,name,userAccountControl,sAMAccountName
   - "CN=DESKTOP103,OU=Clients,DC=contoso,DC=com",computer, DESKTOP103,4096,DESKTOP103$
   - "CN=DESKTOP104,OU=Clients,DC=contoso,DC=com",computer, DESKTOP104,4096,DESKTOP104$
   - "CN=SERVER02,OU=Servers,DC=contoso,DC=com",computer, SERVER02,4096,SERVER02$
3. Save the file to your Documents folder with the name "**Computers.csv**" including the quotes so that Notepad does not add a .txt extension.

4. Open a command prompt.

5. Type the following command, and then press Enter:

```
csvde -i -f "%userprofile%\documents\computers.csv"
```

6. Open the Active Directory Users And Computers snap-in and verify that the computer objects were created successfully.

▶ Exercise 3   Import Computers from an LDIF File

LDIF files are not as familiar to most administrators as .csv files, but they are powerful and relatively easy to master. In this exercise, you will create an LDIF file and import it by using *Ldifde.exe*.

1. Open Notepad.

2. Enter the following into Notepad, making certain to include a blank line between the two operations (before the *dn* line for *SERVER11*):

```
dn: CN=SERVER10,OU=Servers,DC=contoso,DC=com
changetype: add
objectClass: top
objectClass: person
objectClass: organizationalPerson
objectClass: user
objectClass: computer
cn: SERVER10
userAccountControl: 4096
sAMAccountName: SERVER10$

dn: CN= SERVER11,OU=Servers,DC=contoso,DC=com
changetype: add
objectClass: top
objectClass: person
objectClass: organizationalPerson
objectClass: user
objectClass: computer
cn: SERVER11 userAccountControl: 4096
sAMAccountName: SERVER11$
```

3. Save the file to your Documents folder with the name "Computers.ldf" including the quotation marks so Notepad doesn't add a .txt extension.

4. Open a command prompt.

5. Type the following command, and then press Enter:

```
ldifde -i -f "%userprofile%\documents\computers.ldf"
```

6. Open the Active Directory Users And Computers snap-in and verify that the computers were created successfully.

▶ **Exercise 4   Create a Computer with Windows PowerShell**

Windows PowerShell enables you to use ADSI to create and manipulate Active Directory objects. In this exercise, you will create a computer with Windows PowerShell.

1. Open Windows PowerShell.
2. Type the following commands, pressing Enter after each:

```
$objOU = [ADSI]"LDAP://OU=Clients,DC=contoso,DC=com"
$objComputer = $objOU.Create("computer","CN=DESKTOP154")
$objComputer.Put("sAMAccountName", "DESKTOP154$")
$objComputer.Put("userAccountControl", 4096)
$objComputer.SetInfo()
```

3. Open the Active Directory Users And Computers snap-in and confirm that DESKTOP154 was created in the Clients OU.

▶ **Exercise 5   Create a Computer with VBScript**

You can also use VBScript to create a computer. In this exercise, you will create a computer by writing a VBScript and executing it.

1. Open Notepad.
2. Type the following code into Notepad:

```
Set objOU = GetObject("LDAP://OU=Clients,DC=contoso,DC=com ")
Set objComputer = objOU.Create("computer","CN= DESKTOP155")
objComputer.Put "sAMAccountName", " DESKTOP155$"
objComputer.Put "userAccountControl", 4096
objComputer.SetInfo
```

3. Save the file to your Documents folder with the name "**CreateComputer.vbs**" including the quotes so that Notepad doesn't add a .txt extension.
4. Open a command prompt and type the following command:

```
cscript "%userprofile%\documents\createcomputer.vbs"
```

5. Open the Active Directory Users And Computers snap-in and verify that the computer was created successfully.

Lesson Summary

■ Use *CSVDE* to import computers from comma-delimited text files, which can be edited using tools as simple as Notepad or Excel.

■ Use *LDIFDE* to import LDIF files containing computer add operations.

■ *Dsadd* can add a computer to the domain with a single command.

■ VBScript and Windows PowerShell can add computers, using ADSI.

Lesson Review

You can use the following questions to test your knowledge of the information in Lesson 2, "Automating the Creation of Computer Objects." The questions are also available on the companion CD if you prefer to review them in electronic form.

NOTE Answers

Answers to these questions and explanations of why each answer choice is right or wrong are located in the "Answers" section at the end of the book.

---

1. Your manager has just asked you to create an account for DESKTOP234. Which of the following enables you to do that in one step?

    A. *CSVDE*

    B. *LDIFDE*

    C. *Dsadd*

    D. Windows PowerShell

    E. VBScript

2. Your hardware vendor has just given you an Excel worksheet containing the asset tags of computers that will be delivered next week. You want to create computer objects for the computers in advance. Your naming convention specifies that computers' names are their asset tags. Which of the following tools can you use to import the computers? (Choose all that apply.)

    A. *CSVDE*

    B. *LDIFDE*

    C. *Dsadd*

    D. Windows PowerShell

    E. VBScript

Lesson 3: Supporting Computer Objects and Accounts

A computer account begins its life cycle when it is created and when the computer joins the domain. Day-to-day administrative tasks include configuring computer properties; moving the computer between OUs; managing the computer itself; renaming, resetting, disabling, enabling, and, eventually, deleting the computer object. This lesson looks closely at the computer properties and procedures involved with these tasks and will equip you to administer computers in a domain.

After this lesson, you will be able to:
- Configure the properties of a computer running Active Directory.
- Move a computer between OUs.
- Rename a computer.
- Disable and enable computer accounts.
- Reset the secure channel of a domain member computer.
- Perform administrative tasks with the Active Directory Users and Computers snap-in, command-line commands, VBScript, and Windows PowerShell.

Estimated lesson time: 45 minutes

Configuring Computer Properties

When you create a computer object, you are prompted to configure only the most fundamental attributes, including the computer name and the delegation to join the computer to the domain. Computers have several properties that are not visible when creating the computer object, and you should configure these properties as part of the process of staging the computer account.

Open a computer object's Properties dialog box to set its location and description, configure its group memberships and dial-in permissions, and link it to the user object of the user to whom the computer is assigned. The Operating System tab is read-only. The information will be blank until a computer has joined the domain, using that account, at which time, the client publishes the information to its account.

Several object classes in Active Directory support the *managedBy* attribute that is shown on the Managed By tab. This linked attribute creates a cross-reference to a user object. All other properties—the addresses and telephone numbers—are displayed directly from the user object. They are not stored as part of the computer object itself.

On the Member Of tab of a computer's Properties dialog box, you can add the computer to groups. The ability to manage computers in groups is an important and often underused feature of Active Directory. A group to which computers belong can be used to assign resource access permissions to the computer or to filter the application of a GPO.

As with users and groups, it is possible to multiselect more than one computer object and subsequently manage or modify properties of all selected computers simultaneously.

Configuring Computer Attributes with *Dsmod*

The *Dsmod* command, which you learned about in Chapter 3 and Chapter 4, is able to modify only the *description* and the *location* attributes. It uses the following syntax:

```
dsmod computer "DN of Computer" [-desc Description] [-loc Location]
```

Configuring Computer Attributes with Windows PowerShell or VBScript

In Windows PowerShell and VBScript, you can change attributes of a computer with three steps:

1. Connect to the computer using ADSI and the *aDSPath* attribute of the computer in the form "LDAP://*Distinguished Name of Computer.*"
2. Use the *Put* method of the computer object to set single-valued attributes.
3. Use the *SetInfo* method to commit changes to the object.

The Windows PowerShell commands are as follows:

```
$objComputer = [ADSI]"LDAP://DN of Computer"
$objComputer.Put ("property", value)
$objComputer.SetInfo()
```

The VBScript code follows this format:

```
Set objComputer = GetObject("LDAP://DN of Computer")
objComputer.Put "property",
value objComputer.SetInfo
```

In both cases, if the value is a text value, it must be surrounded by quotes.

Moving a Computer

Many organizations have multiple OUs for computer objects. Some domains, for example, have computer OUs based on geographic sites, as shown in Figure 5-2. If you have more than one OU for computers, it is likely that someday you will need to move a computer between OUs.

You can move a computer in the Active Directory Users and Computers snap-in using either drag and drop or the *Move* command, available when you right-click a computer.

You must have appropriate permissions to move an object in Active Directory. Default permissions allow Account Operators to move computer objects between containers, including the Computers container and any OUs *except* into or out of the Domain Controllers OU. Administrators, which include Domain Admins and Enterprise Admins, can move computer objects between any containers, including the Computers container, the Domain Controllers OU, and any other OUs. There is no way to delegate the specific task of moving an object in Active Directory. Instead, your ability to move a computer is derived from your ability to delete an object in the source container and create an object in the destination container. When you move the object, you are not actually deleting and re-creating it; those are just the permissions that are evaluated to allow you to perform a move.

The *Dsmove* command allows you to move a computer object or any other object. The syntax of *Dsmove* is:

```
dsmove ObjectDN [-newname NewName] [-newparent ParentDN]
```

The *newname* parameter enables you to rename an object. The *newparent* parameter enables you to move an object. To move a computer named DESKTOP153 from the Computers container to the Clients OU, you would type the following:

```
dsmove "CN=DESKTOP153,CN=Computers,DC=contoso,DC=com" -newparent
"OU=Clients,DC=contoso,DC=com"
```

To move a computer in Windows PowerShell, you must use the *psbase.MoveTo* method. The following two lines of code will move a computer:

```
$objUser=[ADSI]"LDAP://ComputerDN "
$objUser.psbase.MoveTo("LDAP://TargetOUDN")
```

With VBScript, you connect to the source container and use the container's *MoveHere* method:

```
Set objOU = GetObject("LDAP://TargetOUDN")
objOU.MoveHere "LDAP://ComputerDN", vbNullString
```

Before you move a computer, consider the implications to delegation and configuration. The target OU might have different permissions than the originating OU, in which case, the object will inherit new permissions affecting who is able to manage the object further. The target OU might also be within the scope of different GPOs, which would change the configuration of settings on the system itself.

Managing a Computer from the Active Directory Users and Computers Snap-In

One of the beneficial but lesser used features of the Active Directory Users and Computers snap-in is the *Manage* command. Select a computer in the Active Directory Users and Computers snap-in, right-click it, and choose Manage. The Computer Management console opens, focused on the selected computer, giving you instant access to the computer's event logs, local users and groups, shared folder configuration, and other management extensions. The tool is launched with the credentials used to run the Active Directory Users and Computers snap-in, so you must be running the Active Directory Users and Computers snap-in as a member of the remote computer's Administrators group to gain the maximum functionality from the Computer Management console.

Understanding the Computer's Logon and Secure Channel

Every member computer in an Active Directory domain maintains a computer account with a user name (*sAMAccountName*) and password, just like a user account does. The computer stores its password in the form of a local security authority (LSA) secret and changes its password with the domain every 30 days or so. The Netlogon service uses the credentials to log on to the domain, which establishes the secure channel with a domain controller.

Recognizing Computer Account Problems

Computer accounts and the secure relationships between computers and their domain are robust. However, certain scenarios might arise in which a computer is no longer able to authenticate with the domain. Examples of such scenarios include:

- After reinstalling the operating system on a workstation, the workstation is unable to authenticate even though the technician used the same computer name. Because the new installation generated a new SID and because the new computer does not know the computer account password in the domain, it does not belong to the domain and cannot authenticate to the domain.

- A computer is completely restored from backup and is unable to authenticate. It is likely that the computer changed its password with the domain after the backup operation. Computers change their passwords every 30 days, and Active Directory remembers the current and previous password. If the restore operation restored the computer with a significantly outdated password, the computer will not be able to authenticate.

- A computer's LSA secret gets out of synch with the password known by the domain. You can think of this as the computer forgetting its password, although it did not forget its password; it just disagrees with the domain over what the password really is. When this happens, the computer cannot authenticate and the secure channel cannot be created.

The most common signs of computer account problems are:

- Messages at logon indicate that a domain controller cannot be contacted, that the computer account might be missing, that the password on the computer account is incorrect, or that the trust (another way of saying "the secure relationship") between the computer and the domain has been lost. An example is shown in Figure 5-7.

Figure 5-7   An error message indicating a failed secure channel

■ Error messages or events in the event log indicating similar problems or suggesting that passwords, trusts, secure channels, or relationships with the domain or a domain controller have failed. One such error is NETLOGON Event ID 3210: Failed To Authenticate, which appears in the computer's event log.

■ A computer account is missing in Active Directory.

Resetting a Computer Account

When the secure channel fails, you must reset it. Many administrators do so by removing the computer from the domain, putting it in a workgroup, and then rejoining the domain. This is not a good practice because it has the potential to delete the computer account altogether, which loses the computer's SID and, more important, its group memberships. When you rejoin the domain, even though the computer has the same name, the account has a new SID, and all the group memberships of the previous computer object must be re-created.

NOTE   Do not remove a computer from the domain and rejoin it

If the trust with the domain has been lost, do not remove a computer from the domain and rejoin it. Instead, reset the secure channel.

To reset the secure channel between a domain member and the domain, use the Active Directory Users and Computers snap-in, *Dsmod.exe*, *Netdom.exe*, or *Nltest.exe*. By resetting the account, the computer's SID remains the same and it maintains its group memberships.

■ **The Active Directory Users and Computers snap-in**   Right-click a computer and choose Reset Account. Click Yes to confirm your choice. The computer will then need to be rejoined to the domain, requiring a reboot.

■ *Dsmod*   Type the command, **dsmod computer "*Computer DN*" −reset**. You will have to rejoin the computer to the domain and reboot the computer.

■ *Netdom*   Type the command **netdom reset MachineName /domain DomainName / UserO UserName /PasswordO** {*Password* | ***} where the credentials belong to the local Administrators group of the computer. This command resets the secure channel by attempting to reset the password on both the computer and the domain, so it does not require rejoining or rebooting.

- **Nltest**   On the computer that has lost its trust, type the command **nltest /server:*Server Name* /sc_reset:*DOMAIN**DomainController***, for example, *nltest /server:SERVER02 / sc_reset:CONTOSO\\SERVER01*. This command, like *Netdom.exe*, attempts to reset the secure channel by resetting the password both on the computer and in the domain, so it does not require rejoining or rebooting.

Because *Nltest.exe* and *Netdom.exe* reset the secure channel without requiring a reboot, try those commands first. Only if not successful should you use the *Reset Account* command or *Dsmod* to reset the computer account.

Quick Check

- A user complains that when she attempts to log on, she receives an error message indicating the trust with the domain has been lost. You want to attempt to reset the secure channel without rebooting her system. Which two commands can you use?

Quick Check Answer

- The *Netdom.exe* and *Nltest.exe* commands reset the secure channel without requiring you to rejoin the computer to the domain and, therefore, they require no reboot.

Renaming a Computer

When you rename a computer, you must be careful to do it correctly. Remember that the computer uses its name to authenticate with the domain, so if you rename only the domain object, or only the computer itself, they will be out of synch. You must rename the computer in such a way that both the computer and the domain object are changed.

You can rename a computer correctly by logging on to the computer itself, either locally or with a remote desktop session. Open the System properties from Control Panel and, in the Computer Name, Domain, And Workgroup Settings section, click Change Settings. Click Continue if prompted, and then click the Change button on the Computer Name tab.

From the command prompt, you can use the *Netdom* command with the following syntax:

```
netdom renamecomputer MachineName /NewName:NewName
    [/User0:LocalUsername] [/Password0:{LocalPassword|*} ]
    [/UserD:DomainUsername] [/PasswordD:{DomainPassword|*} ]
    [/SecurePasswordPrompt] [/REBoot[:TimeInSeconds]]
```

In addition to specifying the computer to rename (*MachineName*) and the desired new name (*NewName*), you must have credentials that are a member of the local Administrators group on the computer and credentials that have permission to rename the domain computer object. By default, *Netdom.exe* will use the credentials with which the command is executed. You can specify credentials, using *UserO* and *PasswordO* for the credentials in the computer's local Administrators group, and *UserD* and *PasswordD* for the domain credentials with permission to rename the computer object. Specifying * for the password causes *Netdom.exe* to prompt for the password on the command line. The *SecurePasswordPrompt* parameter displays a pop-up for credentials when * is specified for either *PasswordO* or *PasswordD*. After you rename a computer, you must reboot it. The *REBoot* parameter causes the system to reboot after 30 seconds unless otherwise specified by *TimeInSeconds*.

When you rename a computer, you can adversely affect services running on it. For example, Active Directory Certificate Services (AD CS) relies on the server's name. Be certain to consider the impact of renaming a computer before doing so. Do not use these methods to rename a domain controller.

Disabling and Enabling Computer Accounts

If a computer is taken offline or is not to be used for an extended period of time, consider disabling the account. This recommendation reflects the security principle that an identity store allows authentication only of the minimum number of accounts required to achieve the goals of an organization. Disabling the account does not modify the computer's SID or group membership, so when the computer is brought back online, the account can be enabled.

You can disable a computer by right-clicking it and choosing Disable Account. A disabled account appears with a down-arrow icon in the Active Directory Users and Computers snap-in, as shown in Figure 5-8.

DESKTOP153

Figure 5-8 A disabled computer account

While an account is disabled, the computer cannot create a secure channel with the domain. The result is that users who have not previously logged on to the computer, and who, therefore, do not have cached credentials on the computer, will be unable to log on until the secure channel is reestablished by enabling the account.

To enable a computer account, simply select the computer and choose the *Enable Account* command from the context menu.

To disable or enable a computer from the command prompt, use the *Dsmod* command. The syntax used to disable or enable computers is:

```
DSMOD COMPUTER ComputerDN –DISABLED YES
DSMOD COMPUTER ComputerDN –DISABLED NO
```

Deleting Computer Accounts

You have learned that computer accounts, like user accounts, maintain a unique SID, which enables an administrator to grant permissions to computers. Also like user accounts, computers can belong to groups. Therefore, like user accounts, it is important to understand the effect of deleting a computer account. When a computer account is deleted, its group memberships and SID are lost. If the deletion is accidental, and another computer account is created with the same name, it is nonetheless a new account with a new SID. Group memberships must be reestablished, and any permissions assigned to the deleted computer must be reassigned to the new account. Delete computer objects only when you are certain that you no longer require those security-related attributes of the object.

To delete a computer account using Active Directory Users and Computers, right-click the computer object and, from the context menu, choose the *Delete* command. You will be prompted to confirm the deletion and, because deletion is not reversible, the default response to the prompt is No. Select Yes, and the object is deleted.

The *Dsrm* command introduced in Chapter 3 enables you to delete a computer object from the command prompt. To delete a computer with *Dsrm*, type:

DSRM *ObjectDN*

where *ObjectDN* is the distinguished name of the computer, such as "CN=Desktop154, OU=Clients,DC=contoso,DC=com." Again, you will be prompted to confirm the deletion.

Recycling Computers

If a computer account's group memberships and SID, and the permissions assigned to that SID, are important to the operations of a domain, you do not want to delete that account. So what would you do if a computer was replaced with a new system with upgraded hardware? Such is another scenario in which you would reset a computer account.

Resetting a computer account resets its password but maintains all the computer object's properties. With a reset password, the account becomes, in effect, available for use. Any computer can then join the domain using that account, including the upgraded system. In effect, you've recycled the computer account, assigning it to a new piece of hardware. You can even rename the account. The SID and group memberships remain.

As you learned earlier in this lesson, the *Reset Account* command is available in the context menu when you right-click a computer object. The *Dsmod* command can also be used to reset a computer account by typing **dsmod computer "*ComputerDN*" -reset.**

PRACTICE **Supporting Computer Objects and Accounts**

In this practice, you will support and troubleshoot computer accounts with the skills you learned in this chapter. To perform the exercises in this practice, you must have the following objects in the *contoso.com* domain.

- A first-level OU named Clients.
- Two computer objects, DESKTOP154 and DESKTOP155, in the Clients OU.
- An OU named Desktops and an OU named Laptops in the Clients OU.
- A first-level OU named People.
- User accounts in the People OU for Linda Mitchell and Scott Mitchell. Populate sample contact information for the accounts: address, telephone, and e-mail.
- A first-level OU named Groups.
- A group in the Groups OU named Sales Desktops.

▶ **Exercise 1   Manage Computer Objects**

In this exercise, you will perform several common administrative tasks related to computers as you support the computers assigned to Linda Mitchell and Scott Mitchell, two salespeople at Contoso, Ltd.

1. Log on to SERVER01 as Administrator.
2. Open the Active Directory Users And Computers snap-in.
3. Select the Clients OU.
4. In the details pane, right-click DESKTOP154 and choose Properties.
5. Click the Managed By tab.
6. Click the Change button.
7. Type the user name for Scott Mitchell and click OK.

    The Managed By tab reflects the contact information you populated in Scott Mitchell's user object.
8. Click the Properties button.

    The Properties button on the Managed By tab takes you to the object referred to by the *managedBy* attribute.
9. Click OK to close each dialog box.
10. Repeat steps 4–9 to associate DESKTOP155 with Linda Mitchell.
11. In the console details pane of the Clients OU, select both DESKTOP154 and DESKTOP155.
12. Drag both objects into the Desktops OU. Click Yes to confirm your action.
13. In the console tree, select the Desktops OU.
14. In the details pane, select both DESKTOP154 and DESKTOP155.

15.   Right-click one of the two selected computers and choose Properties.

    The Properties For Multiple Items dialog box appears.

16.   Select the Change The Description Text For All Selected Objects check box and type **Sales Desktop**. Click OK.

17.   With both computers selected, right-click one of the selected computers and choose Add To A Group.

18.   Type **Sales Desktops** and click OK.

    A success message appears.

19.   Click OK.

20.   In the console tree, select the Domain Controllers OU.

21.   In the details pane, right-click SERVER01 and choose Manage.

22.   The Computer Management console appears, focused on SERVER01.

▶ **Exercise 2   Troubleshoot Computer Accounts**

In this exercise, you will simulate resetting the secure channel on a domain member. If you have a second computer joined to the *contoso.com* domain, you can use its name in step 4 of this exercise to actually perform a secure channel reset.

1.   Open a command prompt.

2.   The *Nltest* command can test the secure channel and perform a number of useful domain-related tests. Type **nltest /?** and review the options supported by *Nltest.exe*.

3.   The *Netdom* command performs a number of tasks related to computers and to the domain. Type **netdom /?** and review the options supported by *Netdom.exe*.

4.   Simulate resetting a computer's secure channel by typing **netdom reset desktop154**. You will receive an error, The RPC Server Is Not Available, because the system is not online.

Lesson Summary

- You can configure computer properties by using the Active Directory Users and Computers snap-in, *Dsmod*, Windows PowerShell, or VBScript.

- Computers maintain accounts that, like users, include a SID and group memberships. Be careful about deleting computer objects. Disabling computer objects allows you to enable the objects again when the computer needs to participate in the domain.

- When a computer's secure channel is broken, you can use the *Reset Account* command in the Active Directory Users and Computers snap-in, the *Dsmod* command, *Netdom.exe*, or *nltest.exe* to reset the secure channel.

Lesson Review

You can use the following questions to test your knowledge of the information in Lesson 3, "Supporting Computer Objects and Accounts." The questions are also available on the companion CD if you prefer to review them in electronic form.

NOTE Answers

Answers to these questions and explanations of why each answer choice is right or wrong are located in the "Answers" section at the end of the book.

1. A server administrator reports Failed To Authenticate events in the event log of a file server. What should you do?

   A. Reset the server account.

   B. Reset the password of the server administrator.

   C. Disable and enable the server account.

   D. Delete the account of the server administrator.

2. A computer has permissions assigned to its account to support a system service. It also belongs to 15 groups. The computer is being replaced with new hardware. The new hardware has a new asset tag, and your naming convention uses the asset tag as the computer name. What should you do? (Choose all that apply. Each correct answer is a part of the solution.)

   A. Delete the computer account for the existing system.

   B. Create a computer account for the new system.

   C. Reset the computer account for the existing system.

   D. Rename the computer account for the existing system.

   E. Join the new system to the domain.

3. Your enterprise recently created a child domain to support a research project in a remote location. Computer accounts for researchers were moved to the new domain. When you open Active Directory Users And Computers, the objects for those computers are displayed with a down-arrow icon. What is the most appropriate course of action?

   A. Reset the accounts.

   B. Disable the accounts.

   C. Enable the accounts.

   D. Delete the accounts.

Chapter Review

To further practice and reinforce the skills you learned in this chapter, you can perform the following tasks:

- Review the chapter summary.
- Review the key term introduced in this chapter.
- Complete the case scenarios. These scenarios set up real-world situations involving the topics of this chapter and ask you to create a solution.
- Complete the suggested practices.
- Take a practice test.

Chapter Summary

- Computers maintain accounts which, like users, include a logon name, security identifier (SID), and password. Computer accounts must, therefore, be created, managed, and supported with the same level of care as user accounts.
- You can create computer accounts, using the Active Directory Users and Computers snap-in, *Dsadd*, *Netdom.exe*, Windows PowerShell, and VBScript.
- You should prestage computer accounts before joining computers to the domain.
- You must have permissions on the Active Directory OU to create a computer object, and you must have permissions on the computer object to join a computer to the domain.
- If a computer's secure channel is broken and it loses its trust with the domain, you should reset the account, using *Netdom.exe*, *Nltest.exe*, *Dsmod*, or the Active Directory Users and Computers snap-in.

Key Terms

Use this key term to understand better the concepts covered in this chapter.

- **secure channel**   The encrypted communications stream between a computer and the domain. The secure channel is established by the Netlogon service, which authenticates to the domain, using the computer's user name and password.

Case Scenarios

In the following case scenarios, you will apply what you've learned about creating and supporting computer objects, automating their creation, and joining domains. You can find answers to these questions in the "Answers" section at the end of this book.

Case Scenario 1: Creating Computer Objects and Joining the Domain

During your security audit, you discover a number of computers in the Computers container. This is against your procedures, which dictate that a computer account should be pre-staged in the Clients OU. You are concerned about this fact because the Computers container is not within the scope of Group Policy objects that apply your corporate security baseline settings. You want to restrict administrators and users from adding computers to the Computers container.

1. Under what circumstances are computers added to the Computers container?
2. How can you ensure that computers are added to the Clients OU by default?
3. What can you do to prevent nonadministrative users from joining computers to the domain?

Case Scenario 2: Automating the Creation of Computer Objects

You recently ordered 100 laptops to support expansion of your remote sales force. The vendor sent you a list of asset tags as an Excel file. You want to create computer accounts for the systems, using the asset tags as the computer names.

1. Which tool will you use to import the computers?
2. You import the computers into a single, new OU. You want to disable all the accounts with a single command line. What command can you use?
3. You open one of the imported objects in the Active Directory Users and Computers snap-in and realize you forgot to configure the *Description* attribute to be *Sales Laptop*. How can you configure the description for all 100 systems within the Active Directory Users and Computers snap-in?

Suggested Practices

To help you successfully master the exam objectives presented in this chapter, complete the following tasks.

Create and Maintain Computer Accounts

In this practice, you will perform key administrative tasks that support the life cycle of a computer in a domain.

To perform this practice, you must have the following objects in the *contoso.com* domain:

- A first-level OU named Clients
- A first-level OU named Servers
- A first-level OU named Admins with a child OU named Groups

- A group named Help Desk in the Admins OU
- A first-level OU named People
- A user account for Linda Mitchell and April Stewart in the People OU
- Linda Mitchell as a member of the Help Desk group

Finally, you will need a second computer that can be used to join the domain. The computer can be a system running either Windows Server 2008 or Windows Vista, and it must be in a workgroup. Name the computer **DESKTOP555**.

- **Practice 1**   Log on to SERVER01 as Administrator and, in the Clients OU, create a computer account for DESKTOP555. In the User Or Group section, click Change and select the Help Desk group so that the Help Desk group can join the computer to the domain.

- **Practice 2**   Log on to DESKTOP555 as Administrator. Join the domain. When prompted for domain credentials, enter the user name and password for Linda Mitchell. Restart the system and log on as the domain user April Stewart.

- **Practice 3**   Open the Active Directory Users And Computers snap-in, right-click DESKTOP555, and choose Reset Account. This completely breaks the secure channel between DESKTOP555 and the domain. Attempt to log on to DESKTOP555 as Linda Mitchell. You will receive an error message explaining that the trust with the domain has been broken. Because you used the *Reset Account* command to break the secure channel, you will not be successful using *Netdom.exe* or *Nltest.exe* to repair the secure channel. Under normal troubleshooting scenarios, you should try those tools first. In this case, rejoin the computer to the domain.

- **Practice 4**   Remove DESKTOP555 from the domain, putting it back in a workgroup. Be certain its account has been deleted from Active Directory. Use the *Redircmp.exe* command to redirect the default computer container to the Clients OU. Log on to DESKTOP555 as Administrator and join the domain. When prompted for credentials, enter those of April Stewart as standard user. The computer will join the domain with a new object in the Clients OU. Remove the computer from the domain again. Follow the procedures in Lesson 1 in the "Restricting the Ability of Users to Create Computers" section to reduce *ms-DS-MachineAccountQuota* to zero. Then try to join DESKTOP555 to the domain again with April Stewart's standard user credentials. Your attempt should be prevented with the warning message shown in Figure 5-4.

Take a Practice Test

The practice tests on this book's companion CD offer many options. For example, you can test yourself on just one exam objective, or you can test yourself on all the 70-640 certification exam content. You can set up the test so that it closely simulates the experience of taking a certification exam, or you can set it up in study mode so that you can look at the correct answers and explanations after you answer each question.

MORE INFO   Practice tests

For details about all the practice test options available, see the "How to Use the Practice Tests" section in this book's introduction.

Chapter 6
Group Policy Infrastructure

In Chapter 1, "Installation," you learned that Active Directory Domain Services (AD DS) provides the foundational services of an identity and access solution for enterprise networks running Microsoft Windows and that AD DS goes further to support the management and configuration of even the largest, most complex networks. Chapter 2, "Administration," Chapter 3, "Users," Chapter 4, "Groups," and Chapter 5, "Computers," focused on the administration of Active Directory directory service security principals: users, groups, and computers. Now you will begin an examination of the management and configuration of users and computers by using Group Policy. Group Policy provides an infrastructure within which settings can be defined centrally and deployed to users and computers in the enterprise.

In an environment managed by a well-implemented Group Policy infrastructure, little or no configuration needs to be made by directly touching a desktop. All configuration is defined, enforced, and updated using settings in Group Policy objects (GPOs) that affect a portion of the enterprise as broad as an entire site or domain or as narrow as a single organizational unit (OU) or group. In this chapter, you will learn what Group Policy is, how it works, and how best to implement Group Policy in your organization. The remaining chapters in this training kit will apply Group Policy to specific management tasks such as security configuration, software deployment, password policy, and auditing.

Exam objectives in this chapter:
- Creating and Maintaining Active Directory Objects
    - ❏ Create and apply Group Policy objects (GPOs).
    - ❏ Configure GPO templates.
- Maintaining the Active Directory Environment
    - ❏ Monitor Active Directory.

Lessons in this chapter:
- Lesson 1: Implementing Group Policy. 231
- Lesson 2: Managing Group Policy Scope. 255
- Lesson 3: Supporting Group Policy 277

Before You Begin

To complete the practices in this chapter, you must have created a domain controller named SERVER01 in a domain named *contoso.com*. See Chapter 1 for detailed steps for this task.

Real World

Dan Holme

Many of my clients are attempting to do more with less: to increase security, decrease costs, and increase user productivity. All these goals are easier to achieve when you are able to manage change and configuration in your organization. When a new security concern arises, you want to be able to respond quickly to plug any holes. When help desk logs indicate a high number of calls from users requiring help to configure something on their systems, you want to be able to deploy a change centrally that proactively helps users work more effectively. If a new piece of software is required to win new business, you want to deploy it quickly. These are just a few examples of the types of change and configuration management I see tackled every day in enterprises large and small. Group Policy is a phenomenal technology that can deliver a great amount of value to an organization. Too often, I see Group Policy underused or poorly designed. In this chapter, you will learn the workings of Group Policy. Not only will your knowledge help you answer a number of Group Policy questions on the certification exam, but your expertise in Group Policy will be a great asset to your IT organization.

Lesson 1: Implementing Group Policy

A Group Policy infrastructure has a lot of moving parts. It is important that you understand not only what each part does but also how the parts work together and why you might want to assemble them in various configurations. In this lesson, you will get a comprehensive overview of Group Policy: its components, its functions, and its inner workings.

After this lesson, you will be able to:
- Identify the components of Group Policy.
- Explain the fundamentals of Group Policy processing.
- Create, edit, and link Group Policy objects.
- Create the central store for administrative templates.
- Search for specific policy settings in a GPO.
- Create a GPO from a Starter GPO.

Estimated lesson time: 90 minutes

An Overview and Review of Group Policy

Group Policy is a feature of Windows that enables you to manage change and configuration for users and computers from a central point of administration. If you are less familiar with the concepts of Group Policy, it is helpful to keep in mind at all times that Group Policy is all about configuring a setting for one or more users or one or more computers. There are thousands of configuration settings that can be managed with Group Policy, using one infrastructure that is administered with one set of tools.

Policy Settings

The most granular component of the Group Policy is an individual *policy setting*, also known simply as a *policy*, that defines a specific configuration change to apply. For example, a policy setting exists that prevents a user from accessing registry editing tools. If you define that policy setting and apply it to the user, the user will be unable to run tools such as *Regedit.exe*. Another policy setting is available that allows you to disable the local Administrator account. You can use this policy setting to disable the Administrator account on all user desktops and laptops, for example.

These two examples illustrate an important point: that some policy settings affect a user, regardless of the computer to which the user logs on, and other policy settings affect a computer, regardless of which user logs on to that computer. Policy settings such as the setting that prevents access to registry editing tools are often referred to as *user configuration settings* or *user settings*. The policy setting that disables the Administrator account and similar settings are often referred to as *computer configuration settings* or *computer settings*.

Group Policy Objects (GPOs)

Policy settings are defined and exist within a *Group Policy object (GPO)*. A GPO is an object that contains one or more policy settings and thereby applies one or more configuration settings for a user or computer.

Creating and Managing GPOs

GPOs can be managed in Active Directory by using the Group Policy Management console (GPMC), shown in Figure 6-1. They are displayed in a container named Group Policy Objects. Right-click the Group Policy Objects container and choose New to create a GPO.

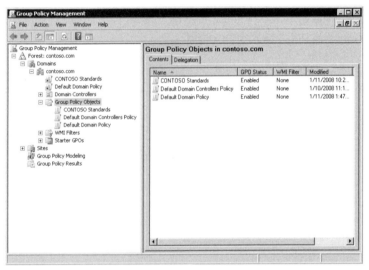

Figure 6-1   The Group Policy Management console

Editing a GPO

To modify the settings of a GPO, right-click the GPO and choose Edit. The GPO opens in the Group Policy Management Editor (GPME) snap-in, formerly known as the Group Policy Object Editor (GPO Editor), shown in Figure 6-2.

The GPME displays the thousands of policy settings available in a GPO in an organized hierarchy that begins with the division between computer settings and user settings: the Computer Configuration node and the User Configuration node. The next levels of the hierarchy are two nodes called Policies and Preferences. You will learn about the difference between these two nodes as this lesson progresses. Drilling deeper into the hierarchy, the GPME displays folders, also called nodes or policy setting groups. Within the folders are the policy settings themselves. Prevent Access To Registry Editing Tools is selected in Figure 6-2. To define a policy setting, double-click the policy setting. The policy setting's Properties dialog box appears, as shown in Figure 6-3.

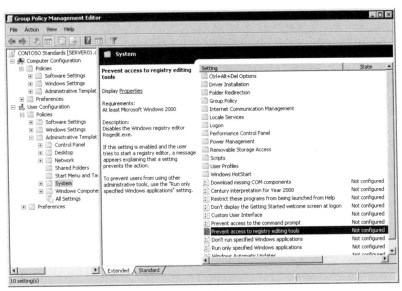

Figure 6-2   Group Policy Management Editor

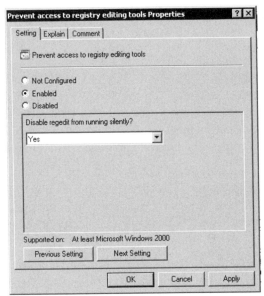

Figure 6-3   The Properties dialog box of a policy setting

Configuring a Policy Setting

A policy setting can have three states: Not Configured, Enabled, and Disabled. As you can see in Figure 6-2, in a new GPO every policy setting is Not Configured. This means that the GPO will not modify the existing configuration of that particular setting for a user or computer. If you enable or disable a policy setting, a change will be made to the configuration of users and computers to which the GPO is applied. The effect of the change depends on the policy setting itself. For example, if you enable the Prevent Access To Registry Editing Tools policy setting, users will be unable to launch the *Regedit.exe* Registry Editor. If you disable the policy setting, you ensure that users can launch the Registry Editor. Notice the double negative in this policy setting: You disable a policy that prevents an action, so you allow the action.

NOTE   Understand and test all policy settings

Many policy settings are complex, and the effect of enabling or disabling them might not be immediately clear. Also, some policy settings affect only certain versions of Windows. Be sure to review a
policy setting's explanatory text in the GPME detail pane, shown in Figure 6-2, or on the Explain tab
of the policy setting's Properties dialog box seen in Figure 6-3. Additionally, always test the effects
of a policy setting, and its interactions with other policy settings, before deploying a change in the
production environment.

Some policy settings bundle several configurations into one policy and might require additional parameters. In Figure 6-3, you can see that by enabling the policy to restrict registry editing tools, you can also define whether registry files can be merged into the system silently,
using *regedit /s*.

Scope

Configuration is defined by policy settings in Group Policy objects. However, the configuration changes in a GPO do not affect computers or users in your enterprise until you have specified the computers or users to which the GPO applies. This is called *scoping* a GPO. The *scope*
of a GPO is the collection of users and computers that will apply the settings in the GPO.

You can use several methods to manage the scope of GPOs. The first is the *GPO link*. GPOs can
be linked to sites, domains, and OUs in Active Directory. The site, domain, or OU then
becomes the maximum scope of the GPO. All computers and users within the site, domain, or
OU, including those in child OUs, will be affected by the configurations specified by policy settings in the GPO. A single GPO can be linked to more than one site or OU.

You can further narrow the scope of the GPO with one of two types of filters: *security filters* that
specify global security groups to which the GPO should or should not apply, and *Windows
Management Instrumentation (WMI) filters* that specify a scope, using characteristics of a system
such as operating system version or free disk space. Use Security filters and WMI filters to narrow or specify the scope within the initial scope created by the GPO link.

Scoping GPOs is detailed in Lesson 2, "Managing Group Policy Scope."

Resultant Set of Policy

Computers and users within the scope of a GPO will apply the policy settings specified in the GPO. An individual user or computer is likely to be within the scope of multiple GPOs linked to the sites, domain, or OUs in which the user or computer exists. This leads to the possibility that policy settings might be configured differently in multiple GPOs. You must be able to understand and evaluate the *Resultant Set of Policy (RSoP)*, which determines the settings that are applied by a client when the settings are configured divergently in more than one GPO. RSoP will be examined in Lesson 3, "Supporting Group Policy."

Group Policy Refresh

When are policies applied? Policy settings in the Computer Configuration node are applied at system startup and every 90–120 minutes thereafter. User Configuration policy settings are applied at logon and every 90–120 minutes thereafter. The application of policies is called *Group Policy refresh*.

Manually Refreshing Group Policy with GPUpdate

When you are experimenting with Group Policy or trying to troubleshoot Group Policy processing, you might need to initiate a Group Policy refresh manually so that you do not have to wait for the next background refresh. The *Gpupdate.exe* command can be used to initiate a Group Policy refresh. Used on its own, *Gpupdate.exe* triggers processing identical to a background Group Policy refresh. Both computer policy and user policy is refreshed. Use the */target:computer* or */target:user* parameter to limit the refresh to computer or user settings, respectively. During background refresh, by default, settings are applied only if the GPO has been updated. The */force* switch causes the system to reapply all settings in all GPOs scoped to the user or computer. Some policy settings require a logoff or reboot before they actually take effect. The */logoff* and */boot* switches of *Gpupdate.exe* cause a logoff or reboot, respectively, if settings are applied that require one. In Windows 2000, the *Secedit.exe* command was used to refresh policy, so you might encounter a mention of the *Secedit.exe* command on the exam.

Group Policy Client and Client-Side Extensions

And how, exactly, are the policy settings applied? When Group Policy refresh begins, a service running on all Windows systems (called the Group Policy client in Windows Vista and Windows Server 2008) determines which GPOs apply to the computer or user. It downloads any GPOs that it does not already have cached. Then a series of processes called *client-side extensions* (CSEs) do the work of interpreting the settings in a GPO and making appropriate changes to the local computer or to the currently logged-on user. There are CSEs for each major category of policy setting. For example, a CSE applies security changes, a CSE executes startup and logon scripts, a CSE installs software, and a CSE makes changes to registry keys and values. Each version of Windows has added CSEs to extend the functional reach of Group Policy. Several dozen CSEs are now in Windows Server 2008. One of the more important concepts to remember about Group Policy is that it is really client driven. The Group Policy client pulls the GPOs from the domain, triggering the CSEs to apply settings locally. Group Policy is not a "push" technology.

The behavior of CSEs can be configured using Group Policy, in fact. Most CSEs will apply settings in a GPO only if that GPO has changed. This behavior improves overall policy processing by eliminating redundant applications of the same settings. Most policies are applied in such a way that standard users cannot change the setting on their system—they will always be subject to the configuration enforced by Group Policy. However, some settings can be changed by standard users, and many can be changed if a user is an Administrator on that system. If users in your environment are administrators on their computers, consider configuring CSEs to reapply policy settings even if the GPO has not changed. That way, if an administrative user changes a configuration so that it is no longer compliant with policy, the configuration will be reset to its compliant state at the next Group Policy refresh.

NOTE **Configure CSEs to reapply policy settings even if the GPO has not changed**

You can configure CSEs to reapply policy settings, even if the GPO has not changed, at background refresh. To do so, configure a GPO scoped to computers and define the settings in the Computer Configuration\Policies\Administrative Templates\System\ Group Policy node. For each CSE you want to configure, open its policy processing policy setting, for example, Registry Policy Processing for the Registry CSE. Click Enabled and select the check box labeled Process Even If The Group Policy Objects Have Not Changed.

An important exception to the default policy processing settings is settings managed by the Security CSE. Security settings are reapplied every 16 hours even if a GPO has not changed.

NOTE **The Always Wait For Network At Startup And Logon policy setting**

It is highly recommended that you enable the Always Wait For Network At Startup And Logon policy setting for all Windows XP and Windows Vista clients. Without this setting, by default, Windows XP and Windows Vista clients perform only background refreshes, meaning that a client might start up and a user might log on without receiving the latest policies from the domain. The setting is located in Computer Configuration\Policies\Administrative Templates\System\Logon. Be sure to read the policy setting's explanatory text.

Slow Links and Disconnected Systems

One of the tasks that can be automated and managed with Group Policy is software installation. Group Policy Software Installation (GPSI) is supported by the software installation CSE. You can configure a GPO to install one or more software packages. Imagine, however, if a user were to connect to your network over a slow connection. You would not want large software packages to be transferred over the slow link because performance would be problematic.

The Group Policy client addresses this concern by detecting the speed of the connection to the domain and determining whether the connection should be considered a slow link. That determination is then used by each CSE to decide whether to apply settings. The software extension, for example, is configured to forgo policy processing so that software is not installed if a slow link is detected. By default, a link is considered to be slow if it is less than 500 kilobits per second (kbps).

If a user is working disconnected from the network, the settings previously applied by Group Policy will continue to take effect, so a user's experience is identical whether on the network or working away from the network. There are exceptions to this rule, most notably that startup, logon, logoff, and shutdown scripts will not run if the user is disconnected.

If a remote user connects to the network on a Windows Vista or Windows Server 2008 system, the Group Policy client wakes up and determines whether a Group Policy refresh window has been missed. If so, it performs a Group Policy refresh to obtain the latest GPOs from the domain. Again, the CSEs determine, based on their policy processing settings, whether settings in those GPOs are applied.

Group Policy Objects

Now that you have a broad-stroke understanding of Group Policy and its components, you can look more closely at each component. In this section, you will examine GPOs in detail. To manage configuration for users and computers, you create GPOs that contain the policy settings you require. Each computer has several GPOs stored locally on the system—the *local GPOs*—and can be within the scope of any number of domain-based GPOs.

Local GPOs

Computers running Windows 2000, Windows XP, and Microsoft Windows Server 2003 each have one local GPO, which can manage configuration of that system. The local GPO exists whether or not the computer is part of domain, workgroup, or a non-networked environment. It is stored in %SystemRoot%\System32\GroupPolicy. The policies in the local GPO affect only the computer on which the GPO is stored. By default, only the Security Settings policies are configured on a system's local GPO. All other policies are set at Not Configured.

When a computer does not belong to an Active Directory domain, the local policy is useful to configure and enforce configuration on that computer. However, in an Active Directory domain, settings in GPOs that are linked to the site, domain, or OUs will override local GPO settings and are easier to manage than GPOs on individual computers.

Windows Vista and Windows Server 2008 systems have multiple local GPOs. The Local Computer GPO is the same as the GPO in previous versions of Windows. In the Computer

Configuration node, configure all computer-related settings. In the User Configuration node, configure settings you want to apply to all users on the computer. The user settings in the Local Computer GPO can be modified by the user settings in two new local GPOs: Administrators and Non-Administrators. These two GPOs apply user settings to a logged-on user who is a member of the local Administrators group or is not, respectively. You can further refine user settings with a local GPO that applies to a specific user account. User-specific local GPOs are associated with local, not domain, user accounts.

RSoP is easy for computer settings: the Local Computer GPO is the only local GPO that can apply computer settings. User settings in a user-specific GPO will override conflicting settings in the Administrators and Non-Administrators GPOs, which themselves override settings in the Local Computer GPO. The concept is simple: the more specific the local GPO, the higher the precedence of its settings.

To create and edit local GPOs, click the Start button and, in the Start Search box, type **mmc.exe**. An empty Microsoft Management console (MMC) opens. Click File and choose Add/Remove Snap-in. Select the Group Policy Object Editor and click Add. A dialog box will appear, prompting you to select the GPO to edit. The Local Computer GPO is selected by default. If you want to edit another local GPO, click the Browse button. On the Users tab, you will find the Non-Administrators and Administrators GPOs and one GPO for each local user. Select the GPO and click OK. Click Finish and then OK to close each of the dialog boxes, and the Group Policy Object editor will be added, focused on the selected GPO.

Keep in mind that local GPOs are designed for nondomain environments. Configure them for your computer at home, for example, to manage the settings for your spouse or children. In a domain environment, settings in domain-based GPOs override conflicting settings in local GPOs, and it is a best practice to manage configuration by using domain-based GPOs.

Domain-Based GPOs

Domain-based GPOs are created in Active Directory and stored on domain controllers. They are used to manage configuration centrally for users and computers in the domain. The remainder of this training kit refers to domain-based GPOs rather than to local GPOs, unless otherwise specified.

When AD DS is installed, two default GPOs are created:

- **Default Domain Policy** This GPO is linked to the domain and has no security group or WMI filters. Therefore, it affects all users and computers in the domain (including computers that are domain controllers). This GPO contains policy settings that specify password, account lockout, and Kerberos policies. As discussed in Chapter 8, "Authentication," modify the existing settings to align with your enterprise password and account lockout policies but do not add unrelated policy settings to this GPO. If you need to configure other settings to apply broadly in your domain, create additional GPOs linked to the domain.

- **Default Domain Controllers Policy**   This GPO is linked to the Domain Controllers OU. Because computer accounts for domain controllers are kept exclusively in the Domain Controllers OU, and other computer accounts should be kept in other OUs, this GPO affects only domain controllers. The Default Domain Controllers GPO should be modified to implement your auditing policies, as discussed in Chapter 7, "Group Policy Settings," and in Chapter 8. It should also be modified to assign user rights required on domain controllers.

Creating, Linking, and Editing GPOs

To create a GPO, right-click the Group Policy Objects container and choose New. You must have permission to the Group Policy Objects container to create a GPO.

By default, the Domain Admins group and the Group Policy Creator Owners group are delegated the ability to create GPOs. To delegate permission to other groups, select the Group Policy Objects container in the GPME console tree and then click the Delegation tab in the console details pane.

After you have created a GPO, you can create the initial scope of the GPO by linking it to a site, domain, or OU. To link a GPO, right-click the container and choose Link An Existing GPO. Note that you will not see your sites in the Sites node of the GPMC until you right-click Sites, choose Show Sites, and select the Sites you want to manage. You can also create and link a GPO with a single step by right-clicking a site, domain, or OU and choosing Create A GPO In This Domain And Link It Here.

You must have permission to link GPOs to a site, domain, or OU. In the GPMC, select the container in the console tree and then click the Delegation tab in the console details pane. From the Permission drop-down list, select Link GPOs. The users and groups displayed hold the permission for the selected OU. Click the Add or Remove buttons to modify the delegation.

To edit a GPO, right-click the GPO in the Group Policy Objects container and choose Edit. The GPO is opened in the GPME. You must have at least Read permission to open the GPO in this way. To make changes to a GPO, you must have Write permission to the GPO. Permissions for the GPO can be set by selecting the GPO in the Group Policy Objects container and then clicking the Delegation tab in the details pane.

The GPME will display the name of the GPO as the root node. The GPME also displays the domain in which the GPO is defined and the server from which the GPO was opened and to which changes will be saved. The root node is in the *GPOName [ServerName]* format. In Figure 6-2, the root node is CONTOSO Standards [SERVER01.contoso.com] Policy. The GPO name is CONTOSO Standards, and it was opened from SERVER01.contoso.com, meaning that the GPO is defined in the *contoso.com* domain.

GPO Storage

Group Policy settings are presented as GPOs in Active Directory user interface tools, but a GPO is actually two components: a Group Policy Container (GPC) and Group Policy Template (GPT). The GPC is an Active Directory object stored in the Group Policy Objects container within the domain naming context of the directory. Like all Active Directory objects, each GPC includes a globally unique identifier (GUID) attribute that uniquely identifies the object within Active Directory. The GPC defines basic attributes of the GPO, but it does not contain any of the settings. The settings are contained in the GPT, a collection of files stored in the SYSVOL of each domain controller in the %SystemRoot%\SYSVOL\Domain\Policies*GPO GUID* path, where *GPO GUID* is the GUID of the GPC. When you make changes to the settings of a GPO, the changes are saved to the GPT of the server from which the GPO was opened.

By default, when Group Policy refresh occurs, the CSEs apply settings in a GPO only if the GPO has been updated. The Group Policy client can identify an updated GPO by its version number. Each GPO has a version number that is incremented each time a change is made. The version number is stored as an attribute of the GPC and in a text file, GPT.ini, in the GPT folder. The Group Policy client knows the version number of each GPO it has previously applied. If, during Group Policy refresh, it discovers that the version number of the GPC has been changed, the CSEs will be informed that the GPO is updated.

Quick Check

- Describe the default Group Policy processing behavior, including refresh intervals and CSE application of policy settings.

Quick Check Answer

- Every 90–120 minutes, the Group Policy Client service determines which GPOs are scoped to the user or computer and downloads any GPOs that have been updated, based on the GPOs' version numbers. CSEs process the policies in the GPOs according to their policy processing configuration. By default, most CSEs apply policy settings only if a GPO has been updated. Some CSEs also do not apply settings if a slow link is detected.

GPO Replication

The two parts of a GPO are replicated between domain controllers by using distinct mechanisms. The GPC in Active Directory is replicated by the Directory Replication Agent (DRA), using a topology generated by the Knowledge Consistency Checker (KCC). You will learn more about these services in Chapter 11, "Sites and Replication." The result is that the GPC is replicated within seconds to all domain controllers in a site and is replicated between sites based on your intersite replication configuration, which will also be discussed in Chapter 11.

The GPT in the SYSVOL is replicated using one of two technologies. The File Replication Service (FRS) is used to replicate SYSVOL in domains running Windows Server 2008, Windows Server 2003, and Windows 2000. If all domain controllers are running Windows Server 2008, you can configure SYSVOL replication, using Distributed File System Replication (DFS-R), a much more efficient and robust mechanism.

Because the GPC and GPT are replicated separately, it is possible for them to become out of synch for a short time. Typically, when this happens, the GPC will replicate to a domain controller first. Systems that obtained their ordered list of GPOs from that domain controller will identify the new GPC, will attempt to download the GPT, and will notice the version numbers are not the same. A policy processing error will be recorded in the event logs. If the reverse happens, and the GPO replicates to a domain controller before the GPC, clients obtaining their ordered list of GPOs from that domain controller will not be notified of the new GPO until the GPC has replicated.

You can download from the Microsoft Download Center the Group Policy Verification Tool, *Gpotool.exe*, which is part of Windows Resource Kits. This tool reports the status of GPOs in the domain and can identify instances in which, on a domain controller, the GPC and the GPT do not have the same version. For more information about *Gpotool.exe*, type **gpotool** /? at the command line.

Exam Tip   *Gpotool.exe* is used to troubleshoot GPO status, including problems caused by the replication of GPOs, leading to inconsistent versions of a GPC and GPT.

Policy Settings

Group Policy settings, also known simply as policies, are contained in a GPO and are viewed and modified using the GPME. In this section, you will look more closely at the categories of settings available in a GPO.

Computer Configuration and User Configuration

There are two major divisions of policy settings: computer settings, contained in the Computer Configuration node, and user settings, contained in the User Configuration node. The Computer Configuration node contains the settings that are applied to computers, regardless of who logs on to them. Computer settings are applied when the operating system starts up and during background refresh every 90–120 minutes thereafter. The User Configuration node contains settings that are applied when a user logs on to the computer and during background refresh every 90–120 minutes thereafter.

Within the Computer Configuration and User Configuration nodes are the Policies and Preferences nodes. Policies are settings that are configured and behave similarly to the policy settings in earlier versions of Windows. Preferences are introduced in Windows Server 2008. The following sections examine these nodes.

Software Settings Node

Within the Policies nodes within Computer Configuration and User Configuration are a hierarchy of folders containing policy settings. Because there are thousands of settings, it is beyond the scope of the exam and of this training kit to examine individual settings. It is worthwhile, however, to define the broad categories of settings in the folders. The first of these nodes is the Software Settings node, which contains only the Software Installation extension. The Software Installation extension helps you specify how applications are installed and maintained within your organization. It also provides a place for independent software vendors to add settings. Software deployment with Group Policy is discussed in Chapter 7.

Windows Settings Node

In both the Computer Configuration and User Configuration nodes, the Policies node contains a Windows Settings node that includes the Scripts, Security Settings, and Policy-Based QoS nodes.

The *Scripts* extension enables you to specify two types of scripts: startup/shutdown (in the Computer Configuration node) and logon/logoff (in the User Configuration node). Startup/shutdown scripts run at computer startup or shutdown. Logon/logoff scripts run when a user logs on or off the computer. When you assign multiple logon/logoff or startup/shutdown scripts to a user or computer, the scripts CSE executes the scripts from top to bottom. You can determine the order of execution for multiple scripts in the Properties dialog box. When a computer is shut down, the CSE first processes logoff scripts, followed by shutdown scripts. By default, the timeout value for processing scripts is 10 minutes. If the logoff and shutdown scripts require more than 10 minutes to process, you must adjust the timeout value with a policy setting. You can use any ActiveX scripting language to write scripts. Some possibilities include Microsoft Visual Basic, Scripting Edition (VBScript), Microsoft JScript, Perl, and Microsoft MS DOS style batch files (.bat and .cmd). Logon scripts on a shared network directory in another forest are supported for network logon across forests.

The Security Settings node allows a security administrator to configure security, using GPOs. This can be done after, or instead of, using a security template to set system security. For a detailed discussion of system security and the Security Settings node, refer to Chapter 7.

The Policy-Based QoS node defines policies that manage network traffic. For example, you might want to ensure that users in the Finance department have priority for running a critical network application during the end-of-year financial reporting period. Policy-Based QoS enables you to do that.

In the User Configuration node only, the Windows Settings folder contains the additional Remote Installation Services, Folder Redirection, and Internet Explorer Maintenance nodes.

Remote Installation Services (RIS) policies control the behavior of a remote operating system installation, using RIS. Folder Redirection enables you to redirect user data and settings folders (AppData, Desktop, Documents, Pictures, Music, and Favorites, for example) from their default user profile location to an alternate location on the network, where they can be centrally managed. *Internet Explorer Maintenance* enables you to administer and customize Microsoft Internet Explorer.

Administrative Templates Node

In both the Computer Configuration and User Configuration nodes, the Administrative Templates node contains registry-based Group Policy settings. There are thousands of such settings available for configuring the user and computer environment. As an administrator, you might spend a significant amount of time manipulating these settings. To assist you with the settings, a description of each policy setting is available in two locations:

- On the Explain tab in the Properties dialog box for the setting. In addition, the Settings tab in the Properties dialog box for the setting lists the required operating system or software for the setting.
- On the Extended tab of the GPME. The Extended tab appears on the bottom of the right details pane and provides a description of each selected setting in a column between the console tree and the settings pane. The required operating system or software for each setting is also listed.

The Administrative Templates node is discussed in detail in the "Administrative Templates" section.

Preferences Node

Underneath both Computer Configuration and User Configuration is a Preferences node. New to Windows Server 2008, preferences provide more than 20 CSEs to help you manage an incredible number of additional settings, including:

- Applications such as Microsoft Office 2003 and Office 2007
- Mapped drives
- Registry settings
- Power options
- Folder options
- Regional options
- Starch menu options

Preferences also enables you to deploy the following:

- Files and folders
- Printers

- Scheduled tasks
- Network connections

Many enterprises will also benefit from Preferences because the options can be used to enable or disable hardware devices or classes of devices. For example, you can use Preferences to prevent USB hard drives, including personal media players, from being connected to computers.

The new version of the GPME that supports configuring Preferences is available for download for Windows Vista SP1 from the Microsoft Download Center at *http://www.microsoft.com /downloads*. To apply preferences, systems require the preferences CSEs, which Windows Server 2008 includes. CSEs for Windows XP, Windows Server 2003, and Windows Vista can be downloaded from the Microsoft Download Center.

The interface you use to configure many preferences looks identical to the Windows user interface in which you would make the change manually. Figure 6-4 shows a Folder Options (Windows XP) preference *item*—a collection of settings that are processed by the preferences CSE. You will recognize the similarity to the Folder Options application in Control Panel.

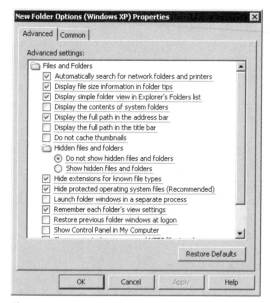

Figure 6-4   A Folder Options preference item

Administrative Templates Node

Policies in the Administrative Templates node in the Computer Configuration node modify registry values in the HKEY_LOCAL_MACHINE (HKLM) key. Policies in the Administrative Templates node in the User Configuration node modify registry values in the

HKEY_CURRENT_USER (HKCU) key. Most of the registry values that are modified by the default policies are located in one of the following four reserved trees:

- HKLM\Software\Policies (computer settings)
- HKCU\Software\Policies (user settings)
- HKLM\Software\Microsoft\Windows\CurrentVersion\Policies (computer settings)
- HKCU\Software\Microsoft\Windows\CurrentVersion\Policies (user settings)

An *administrative template* is a text file that specifies the registry change to be made and that generates the user interface to configure the Administrative Templates policy settings in the GPME. Figure 6-3 shows the properties dialog box for the Prevent Access To Registry Editing Tools. The fact that the setting exists, and that it provides a drop-down list with which to disable *Regedit.exe* from running silently, is determined in an administrative template. The registry setting that is made based on how you configure the policy is also defined in the administrative template.

You can add new administrative templates to the GPME by right-clicking the Administrative Templates node and choosing Add/Remove Templates. Some software vendors provide administrative templates as a mechanism to manage the configuration of their application centrally. For example, you can obtain administrative templates for all recent versions of Microsoft Office from the Microsoft Downloads Center. You can also create your own custom administrative templates. A tutorial on creating custom administrative templates is beyond the scope of this training kit.

In versions of Windows prior to Windows Vista, an administrative template had an .adm extension. ADM files have several drawbacks. First, all localization must be performed within the ADM file. That is, if you want to create an ADM file to help deploy configuration in a multilingual organization, you would need separate ADM files for each language to provide a user interface for administrators who speak that language. If you were to decide later to make a modification related to the registry settings managed by the templates, you would need to make the change to each ADM file.

The second problem with ADM files is the way they are stored. An ADM file is stored as part of the GPT in the SYSVOL. If an ADM file is used in multiple GPOs, it is stored multiple times, contributing to SYSVOL bloat. There were also challenges maintaining version control over ADM files.

In Windows Vista and Windows Server 2008, an administrative template is a pair of XML files, one with an .admx extension that specifies changes to be made to the registry and the other with an .adml extension that provides a language-specific user interface in the GPME. When changes need to be made to settings managed by the administrative template, they can be made to the single ADMX file. Any administrator who modifies a GPO that uses the template accesses the same ADMX file and calls the appropriate ADML file to populate the user interface.

NOTE   No need to take sides

ADM and ADMX/ADML administrative templates can coexist.

Central Store

As was previously stated, ADM files are stored as part of the GPO itself. When you edit a GPO that uses administrative templates in the ADM format, the GPME loads the ADM from the GPC to produce the user interface. When ADMX/ADML files are used as administrative templates, the GPO contains only the data that the client needs for processing Group Policy, and when you edit the GPO, the GPME pulls the ADMX and ADML files from the local workstation.

This works well for smaller organizations, but for complex environments that include custom administrative templates or that require more centralized control, Windows Server 2008 introduces the central store. The central store is a single folder in SYSVOL that holds all the ADMX and ADML files that are required. After you have set up the central store, the GPME recognizes it and loads all administrative templates from the central store instead of from the local computer.

To create a central store, create a folder called PolicyDefinitions in the *FQDN*\SYSVOL *FQDN*\Policies path. For example, the central store for the *contoso.com* domain would be \\contoso.com\SYSVOL\contoso.com\Policies\PolicyDefinitions. Then, copy all files from the %SystemRoot%\PolicyDefinitions folder of a Windows Server 2008 system to the new SYSVOL PolicyDefinitions folder. These will include the .admx files and the .adml files in a language-specific subfolder of %SystemRoot%\PolicyDefinitions. For example, English (United States) ADML files are located in %SystemRoot%\PolicyDefinitions\en-us. Copy them into *FQDN* \SYSVOL*FQDN*\Policies\PolicyDefinitions\en-us. If additional languages are required, copy the folder that contains the ADML files to the central store. When you have copied all ADMX and ADML files, the PolicyDefinitions folder on the domain controller should contain the ADMX files and one or more folders containing language-specific ADML files.

Exam Tip   If logging on to a domain controller, locally or by using Remote Desktop, the local path to the PolicyDefinitions folder is %SystemRoot%\SYSVOL\domain\Policies\PolicyDefinitions.

Filtering Administrative Template Policy Settings

A weakness of the Group Policy editing tools in previous versions of Windows is the inability to search for a specific policy setting. With thousands of policies to choose from, it can be difficult to locate exactly the setting you want to configure. The new GPME in Windows Server 2008 solves this problem for Administrative Template settings: you can now create filters to locate specific policy settings.

To create a filter, right-click Administrative Templates and choose Filter Options. To locate a specific policy, select Enable Keyword Filters, enter the words with which to filter, and select the fields within which to search. Figure 6-5 shows an example of a search for policy settings related to the screen saver.

In the top section of the Filter Options dialog box shown in Figure 6-5, you can filter the view to show only policy settings that are configured. This can help you locate and modify settings that are already specified in the GPO.

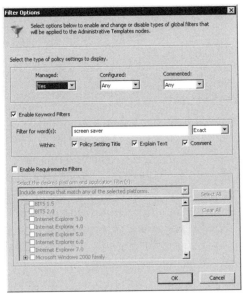

Figure 6-5   Filtering the Administrative Templates policy settings

Commenting

You can also search and filter based on policy-setting comments. Windows Server 2008 enables you to add comments to policy settings in the Administrative Templates node. Double-click a policy setting and click the Comment tab. It is a best practice to add comments to configured policy settings as a way to document the justification for a setting and its intended effect. You should also add comments to the GPO itself. Windows Server 2008 enables you to attach comments to a GPO. In the GPME, right-click the root node in the console tree and choose Properties; then click the Comment tab.

Starter GPOs

Another new Group Policy feature in Windows Server 2008 is starter GPOs. A starter GPO contains Administrative Template settings. You can create a new GPO from a starter GPO, in which case, the new GPO is prepopulated with a copy of the settings in Starter GPO. A starter

GPO is, in effect, a template. Unfortunately, Microsoft had already been using the term *template* in the context of administrative templates, so another name had to be found. When you create a new GPO, you can still choose to begin with a blank GPO, or you can select one of the preexisting starter GPOs or a custom starter GPO.

NOTE   **When you need more than administrative template settings**

Starter GPOs can contain only Administrative Templates policy settings. You can also copy and paste entire GPOs in the Group Policy Objects container of the Group Policy Management console so that you have a new GPO with all the settings of the source GPO. To transfer settings between GPOs in different domains or forests, right-click a GPO and choose Back Up. In the target domain, create a new GPO, right-click it, and choose Import Settings. You will be able to import the settings of the backed-up GPO.

Managed and Unmanaged Policy Settings

There is a nuance to the registry policy settings configured by the Administrative Templates node that is important to understand: the difference between managed and unmanaged policy settings. The registry policy settings that have been discussed so far and that are encountered in the practices of this chapter are examples of managed policy settings. A managed policy setting effects a configuration change of some kind when the setting is applied by a GPO. When the user or computer is no longer within the scope of the GPO, the configuration reverts to its original state automatically. For example, if a GPO prevents access to registry editing tools and then the GPO is deleted, disabled, or scoped so that it no longer applies to users, those users will regain access to registry editing tools at the next policy refresh.

In contrast, an unmanaged policy setting makes a change that is persistent in the registry. If the GPO no longer applies, the setting remains. This is often called *tattooing* the registry. To reverse the effect of the policy setting, you must deploy a change that reverts the configuration to the desired state.

By default, the GPME hides unmanaged policy settings to discourage you from implementing a configuration that is difficult to revert. However, you can make many useful changes with unmanaged policy settings, particularly for custom administrative templates to manage configuration for applications. To control which policy settings are visible, right-click Administrative Templates and choose Filter Options. Make a selection from the Managed drop-down list.

PRACTICE Implementing Group Policy

In this practice, you will implement configuration in the *contoso.com* domain by using Group Policy. You will create, configure, and scope GPOs. You will also gain hands-on experience with the new features of Group Policy in Windows Server 2008.

▶ **Exercise 1   Create, Edit, and Scope a Group Policy Object**

In this exercise, you will create a GPO that implements a setting mandated by the corporate security policy of Contoso, Ltd., and scope the setting to all users and computers in the domain.

1. Log on to SERVER01 as Administrator.
2. Open the Group Policy Management console from the Administrative Tools folder.
3. Expand Forest, Domains, the *contoso.com* domain, and the Group Policy Objects container.
4. Right-click the Group Policy Objects Container in the console tree and choose New.
5. In the Name box, type **CONTOSO Standards**. Click OK.
6. Right-click the CONTOSO Standards GPO and choose Edit.

   Group Policy Management Editor appears.
7. Right-click the root node of the console, CONTOSO Standard, and choose Properties.
8. Click the Comment tab and type **Contoso corporate standard policies. Settings are scoped to all users and computers in the domain. Person responsible for this GPO:** *your name*. Then click OK.

   In this scenario, the Contoso corporate IT security policy specifies that computers cannot be left unattended and logged on for more than 10 minutes. To meet this requirement, you will configure the screen saver timeout and password-protected screen saver policy settings. You will use the new search capability of Windows Server 2008 Group Policy to locate the policy settings.
9. Expand User Configuration\Policies\Administrative Templates.
10. Spend a few moments browsing the settings beneath this node. Review the explanatory text of policy settings that sound interesting to you. Do not make any configuration changes.
11. Right-click Administrative Templates in the User Configuration node and choose Filter Options.
12. Select the Enable Keyword Filters check box.
13. In the Filter for Word(s) text box, type **screen saver**.
14. In the drop-down list next to the text box, choose Exact.
15. Click OK.

    Administrative Templates policy settings are filtered to show only those that contain the words *screen saver*.
16. Browse to examine the screen saver policies that you have found.
17. In the Control Panel\Display node, click the policy setting Screen Saver Timeout. Note the explanatory text in the left margin of the console's details pane.
18. Double-click the policy setting Screen Saver Timeout.

19. Review the explanatory text on the Explain tab.

20. Click the Setting tab and select Enabled.

21. In the Seconds box, type **600**.

22. On the Comment tab, type **Corporate IT Security Policy implemented with this policy in combination with Password Protect the Screen Saver.**

23. Click OK.

24. Double-click the Password Protect The Screen Saver policy setting.

25. Select Enabled.

26. On the Comment tab, type **Corporate IT Security Policy implemented with this policy in combination with Screen Saver Timeout.**

27. Click OK.

28. Close the GPME.

    Changes you make in the GPME are saved in real time. There is no Save command.

29. In the Group Policy Management console, right-click the *contoso.com* domain and choose Link An Existing GPO.

30. Select the CONTOSO Standards GPO and click OK.

▶ **Exercise 2   View the Effects of Group Policy Application**

In this exercise, you will experience the effect of the Group Policy setting you configured in Exercise 1, "Create, Edit, and Scope a Group Policy Object," and you will practice triggering a manual policy refresh, using *Gpupdate.exe*.

1. On SERVER01, right-click the desktop and choose Personalize.

2. Click Screen Saver.

3. Note that you can change the screen saver timeout and the option to display the logon screen on resume. Close the Screen Saver Settings dialog box.

4. Open a command prompt and type **gpupdate.exe /force /boot /logoff**.

    These options of the *Gpupdate.exe* command invoke the most complete Group Policy refresh. Wait until both user and computer policies have been updated.

5. Return to the Screen Saver Settings dialog box. Note that you can no longer change the screen saver timeout or resume option.

▶ **Exercise 3   Explore a GPO**

Now that you've seen a GPO in action, you will explore the GPO itself to learn about the inner workings of Group Policy.

1. In the Group Policy Management console, select the CONTOSO Standards GPO in the Group Policy Objects container.

2. On the Scope tab, notice that the GPO reports its links in the Links section.

3. Click the Settings tab to see a report of the policy settings in the GPO.

If you have Internet Explorer Enhanced Security Configuration (ESC) enabled, you will be prompted to confirm that you want to add *about:security_mmc.exe* to your Trusted Sites zone.

4. Click the Show All link at the top of this settings report to expand all sections of the report. Notice that the policy setting comments you added are part of the settings report.

5. Point at the text for the policy Screen Saver Timeout. Notice that the policy title is actually a hyperlink. Click the link to reveal the explanatory text for the policy setting.

6. Click the Details tab. Notice that your GPO comments appear on this tab along with GPO version information.

7. Write down the Unique ID shown on the Details tab.

8. Open the following folder: \\contoso.com\SYSVOL\contoso.com\Policies.

9. Double-click the folder with the same name as the GPO's Unique ID.

   This is the GPT of the GPO.

▶ **Exercise 4   Explore Administrative Templates**

Administrative templates provide the instructions with which the GPME creates a user interface to configure Administrative Templates policy settings and specify the registry changes that must be made based on those policy settings. In this exercise, you will examine an administrative template.

1. Open the %SystemRoot%\PolicyDefinitions folder.

2. Open the en-us folder or the folder for your region and language.

3. Double-click ControlPanelDisplay.adml. Choose the Select A Program From A List Of Installed Programs option and click OK. Choose to open the file with Notepad and click OK.

4. Turn on Word Wrap from the Format menu.

5. Search for the ScreenSaverIsSecure text.

6. Note the label for the setting and, on the next line, the explanatory text.

7. Close the file and navigate up to the PolicyDefinitions folder.

8. Double-click ControlPanelDisplay.admx. Choose the Select A Program From A List Of Installed Programs option and click OK. Choose to open the file with Notepad and click OK.

9. Search for the text shown here:

```
<policy name="ScreenSaverIsSecure" class="User"
displayName="$(string.ScreenSaverIsSecure)"
explainText="$(string.ScreenSaverIsSecure_Help)"
key="Software\Policies\Microsoft\Windows\Control Panel\Desktop"
valueName="ScreenSaverIsSecure">
     <parentCategory ref="Display" />
     <supportedOn ref="windows:SUPPORTED_Win2kSP1" />
     <enabledValue>
```

```
        <string>1</string>
      </enabledValue>
      <disabledValue>
        <string>0</string>
      </disabledValue>
    </policy>
```

10. Identify the parts of the template that define the following:
    - ❏ The name of the policy setting that appears in the GPME
    - ❏ The explanatory text for the policy setting
    - ❏ The registry key and value affected by the policy setting
    - ❏ The data put into the registry if the policy is enabled
    - ❏ The data put into the registry if the policy is disabled

▶ **Exercise 5   Creating a Central Store**

In this exercise, you will create a central store of administrative templates to centralize the management of templates.

1. In the Group Policy Management console, right-click CONTOSO Standards and choose Edit.
2. Expand User Configuration\Policies\Administrative Template.
3. Note that the node reports Policy Definitions (ADMX Files) Retrieved From The Local Machine.
4. Close the GPME.
5. Open the following folder: \\contoso.com\SYSVOL\contoso.com\Policies.
6. Create a folder named **PolicyDefinitions**.
7. Copy the contents of %SystemRoot%\PolicyDefinitions to the folder you created in the previous step.
8. In the Group Policy Management console, right-click CONTOSO Standards and choose Edit.
9. Expand User Configuration\Policies\Administrative Template.
10. Note that the node reports Policy Definitions (ADMX Files) Retrieved From The Central Store.

Lesson Summary

- GPOs contain policy settings that define configuration. When GPOs are scoped to a site, domain, or OU, users and computers within the scope of the GPO apply its policy settings.
- Processes on Windows clients determine the GPOs that must be downloaded and applied. Group Policy processing occurs at startup and every 90–120 minutes thereafter for computer settings and at logon and every 90–120 minutes thereafter for user settings.

- By default, CSEs apply settings only if the GPO has changed, except for Security settings, which are applied every 16 hours, whether or not the GPO is changed. CSEs can be configured to reapply settings at each policy refresh and to apply or skip policy application if a slow link is detected.
- Windows Server 2008 introduces Group Policy Preferences, which add more than 20 CSEs to manage a wide variety of user and computer settings.
- Administrative templates (.adm or .admx/.adml files) define the user interface and registry changes for policy settings in the Administrative Templates node of the GPO.
- You can centralize the management of administrative templates by creating a central store.
- Windows Server 2008 also adds the ability to attach comments to GPOs and policy settings and to create new GPOs based on starter GPOs that contain a baseline of Administrative Templates policy settings.

Lesson Review

You can use the following questions to test your knowledge of the information in Lesson 1, "Implementing Group Policy." The questions are also available on the companion CD if you prefer to review them in electronic form.

NOTE   Answers

Answers to these questions and explanations of why each answer choice is right or wrong are located in the "Answers" section at the end of the book.

1. Litware, Inc., has three business units, each represented by an OU in the *litwareinc.com* domain. The business unit administrators want the ability to manage Group Policy for the users and computers in their OUs. Which actions do you perform to give the administrators the ability to manage Group Policy fully for their business units? (Choose all that apply. Each correct answer is a part of the solution.)

   A. Copy administrative templates from the central store to the PolicyDefinitions folder on the administrators' Windows Vista workstations.

   B. Add business unit administrators to the Group Policy Creator Owners group.

   C. Delegate Link GPOs permission to the administrators in the *litwareinc.com* domain.

   D. Delegate Link GPOs permission to the each business unit's administrators in the business unit's OU.

2. You are an administrator at Contoso, Ltd. The *contoso.com* domain has a child domain, *es.contoso.com*, for the branch in Spain. Administrators of that domain have asked you to provide a Spanish-language interface for Group Policy Management Editor. How can you provide Spanish-language versions of administrative templates?

   A. Log on to a domain controller in the *es.contoso.com* domain, open %SystemRoot% \SYSVOL\domain\Policies\PolicyDefinitions, and copy the ADM files to the ES folder.

   B. Copy ADML files to the \\es.contoso.com\SYSVOL\es.contoso.com\policies\ PolicyDefinitions\es folder.

   C. Log on to a domain controller in the *es.contoso.com* domain, open %System-Root%\SYSVOL\domain\Policies\PolicyDefinitions, and copy the ADMX files to the ES folder.

   D. Install the Boot.wim file from the Windows Server 2008 CD on a domain controller in the child domain.

3. You are an administrator at Contoso, Ltd. At a recent conference, you had a conversation with administrators at Fabrikam, Inc. You discussed a particularly successful set of configurations you have deployed using a GPO. The Fabrikam administrators have asked you to copy the GPO to their domain. Which steps can you and the Fabrikam administrators perform?

   A. Right-click the Contoso GPO and choose Save Report. Create a GPO in the Fabrikam domain, right-click it, and choose Import.

   B. Right-click the Contoso GPO and choose Back Up. Right-click the Group Policy Objects container in the Fabrikam domain and choose Restore From Backup.

   C. Right-click the Contoso GPO and choose Back Up. Create a GPO in the Fabrikam domain, right-click it, and choose Paste.

   D. Right-click the Contoso GPO and choose Back Up. Create a GPO in the Fabrikam domain, right-click it, and choose Import Settings.

Lesson 2: Managing Group Policy Scope

A GPO is, by itself, just a collection of configuration instructions that will be processed by the CSEs of computers. Until the GPO is scoped, it does not apply to any users or computers. The GPO's scope determines which computers' CSEs will receive and process the GPO, and only the computers or users within the scope of a GPO will apply the settings in that GPO. Several mechanisms are used to scope a GPO:

- The GPO link to a site, domain, or OU and whether that link is enabled
- The Enforce option of a GPO
- The Block Inheritance option on an OU
- Security group filtering
- WMI filtering
- Policy node enabling or disabling
- Preferences targeting
- Loopback policy processing

You must be able to define the users or computers to which configuration is deployed, and therefore, you must master the art of scoping GPOs. In this lesson, you will learn each of the mechanisms with which you can scope a GPO and, in the process, the concepts of Group Policy application, inheritance, and precedence.

After this lesson, you will be able to:
- Manage GPO links.
- Evaluate GPO inheritance and precedence.
- Understand the Block Inheritance and Enforced link options.
- Use security filtering to narrow the scope of a GPO.
- Apply a WMI filter to a GPO.
- Implement loopback policy preferences.

Estimated lesson time: 90 minutes

GPO Links

A GPO can be linked to one or more Active Directory sites, domains, or OUs. After a policy is linked to a site, domain, or OU, the users or computers and users in that container are within the scope of the GPO, including computers and users in child OUs.

As you learned in Lesson 1, you can link a GPO to the domain or to an OU by right-clicking it and choosing Link An Existing GPO. If you have not yet created a GPO, you can choose Create A GPO In This Domain, And Link It Here. You can choose the same commands to link a GPO to a site, but by default, your Active Directory sites are not visible in the GPME; you must first right-click Sites and choose Show Sites.

> ## Site-Linked GPOs and Domain Controller Placement
>
> A GPO linked to a site affects all computers in the site without regard to the domain to which the computers belong (as long as all computers belong to the same Active Directory forest). Therefore, by linking a GPO to a site, that GPO can be applied to multiple domains within a forest. Site-linked GPOs are stored on domain controllers in the domain in which the GPO was created. Therefore, domain controllers for that domain must be accessible for site-linked GPOs to be applied correctly. If you implement site-linked policies, you must consider policy application when planning your network infrastructure. Either place a domain controller from the GPO's domain in the site to which the policy is linked or ensure that WAN connectivity provides accessibility to a domain controller in the GPO's domain.

When you link a GPO to a site, domain, or OU, you define the initial scope of the GPO. Select a GPO and click the Scope tab to identify the containers to which the GPO is linked. In the details pane of the GPMC, the GPO links are displayed in the first section of the Scope tab, as seen in Figure 6-6.

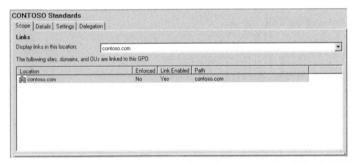

Figure 6-6   A GPO's links displayed on the Scope tab of the GPMC

The impact of the GPO's links is that the Group Policy client will download the GPO if either the computer or the user objects fall within the scope of the link. The GPO will be downloaded only if it is new or updated. The Group Policy client caches the GPO to make policy refresh more efficient.

Linking a GPO to Multiple OUs

You can link a GPO to more than one site, domain, or OU. It is common, for example, to apply configuration to computers in several OUs. You can define the configuration in a single GPO and link that GPO to each OU. If you later change settings in the GPO, your changes will apply to all OUs to which the GPO is linked.

Deleting or Disabling a GPO Link

After you have linked a GPO, the GPO link appears in the GPMC underneath this site, domain, or OU. The icon for the GPO link has a small shortcut arrow. When you right-click the GPO link, a context menu appears, as shown in Figure 6-7.

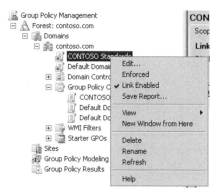

Figure 6-7 The context menu of a GPO link

You can delete a GPO link by choosing Delete from the context menu. Deleting a GPO link does not delete the GPO itself, which remains in that Group Policy Objects container. Deleting the link does change the scope of the GPO so that it no longer applies to computers and users within a site, domain, or OU to which it was previously linked.

You can also modify a GPO link by disabling it. Right-click the GPO link and deselect the Link Enabled option. Disabling the link also changes the scope of the GPO so that it no longer applies to computers and users within that container. However, the link remains so that it can be easily re-enabled.

GPO Inheritance and Precedence

A policy setting can be configured in more than one GPO, and GPOs can be in conflict with one another. For example, a policy setting can be enabled in one GPO, disabled in another GPO, and not configured in a third GPO. In this case, the *precedence* of the GPOs determines which policy setting the client applies. A GPO with higher precedence will prevail over a GPO with lower precedence. Precedence is shown as a number in the GPMC. The smaller the number—that is, the closer to 1—the higher the precedence, so a GPO with a precedence of 1 will prevail over other GPOs. Select the domain or OU and then click the Group Policy Inheritance tab to view the precedence of each GPO.

When a policy setting is enabled or disabled in a GPO with higher precedence, the configured setting takes effect. However, remember that policy settings are set to Not Configured by default. If a policy setting is not configured in a GPO with higher precedence, the policy setting (either enabled or disabled) in a GPO with lower precedence will take effect.

A site, domain, or OU can have more than one GPO linked to it. The link order of GPOs determines the precedence of GPOs in such a scenario. GPOs with higher-link order take precedence over GPOs with lower-link order. When you select an OU in the GPMC, the Linked Group Policy Objects tab shows the link order of GPOs linked to that OU.

The default behavior of Group Policy is that GPOs linked to a higher-level container are inherited by lower-level containers. When a computer starts up or a user logs on, the Group Policy client examines the location of the computer or user object in Active Directory and evaluates the GPOs with scopes that include the computer or user. Then the client-side extensions apply policy settings from these GPOs. Policies are applied sequentially, beginning with the policies linked to the site, followed by those linked to the domain, followed by those linked to OUs— from the top-level OU down to the OU in which the user or computer object exists. It is a layered application of settings, so a GPO that is applied later in the process, because it has higher precedence, will override settings applied earlier in the process. This default order of applying GPOs is illustrated in Figure 6-8.

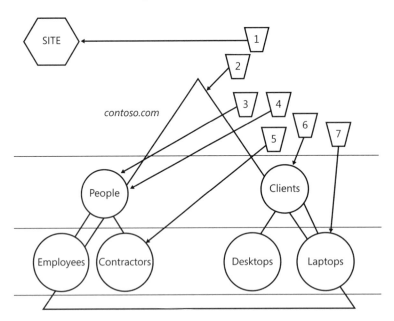

GPO processing order for the Contractors OU = 1, 2, 3, 4, 5
GPO processing order for the Laptops OU = 1, 2, 6, 7

Figure 6-8   Default processing of site, domain, and OU GPOs

Exam Tip   Be certain to memorize the default domain policy processing order: site, domain, OU; remember that domain policy settings are applied after and, therefore, take precedence over settings in local GPOs.

This sequential application of GPOs creates an effect called *policy inheritance*. Policies are inherited, so the resultant set of group policies for a user or computer will be the cumulative effect of site, domain, and OU policies.

By default, inherited GPOs have lower precedence than GPOs linked directly to the container. In a practical example, you might configure a policy setting to disable the use of registry-editing tools for all users in the domain by configuring the policy setting in a GPO linked to the domain. That GPO, and its policy setting, will be inherited by all users within the domain. However, you probably want administrators to be able to use registry-editing tools, so you will link a GPO to the OU that contains administrators' accounts and configure the policy setting to allow the use of registry-editing tools. Because the GPO linked to the administrators' OU takes higher precedence than the inherited GPO, administrators will be able to use registry-editing tools.

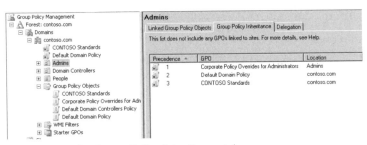

Figure 6-9   The Group Policy inheritance tab

Figure 6-9 shows this example. A policy setting that restricts registry-editing tools is defined in the CONTOSO Standards GPO, linked to the *contoso.com* domain. In the Corporate Policy Overrides For Administrators GPO, a policy setting specifically allows the use of registry-editing tools. The administrator's GPO is linked to the Admins OU. When you select an OU such as the Admins OU, the details pane of the GPMC displays a Group Policy Inheritance tab that reveals GPO precedence for that OU. You can see that the Corporate Policy Overrides For Administrators GPO has precedence. Any setting in that GPO that is in conflict with a setting in CONTOSO Standards will be applied from the administrators GPO. Therefore, users in the Admins OU will be able to use registry editing tools, although users elsewhere in the domain will not be able to. As you can see from this simple example, the default order of precedence ensures that the policy that is closest to the user or computer prevails.

Precedence of Multiple Linked Group Policy Objects

An OU, domain, or site can have more than one GPO linked to it. In the event of multiple Group Policy objects, the objects' *link order* determines their precedence. In Figure 6-10, two GPOs are linked to the People OU. The object higher on the list, with a link order of 1, has the highest precedence. Therefore, settings that are enabled or disabled in the Power User Configuration GPO will have precedence over these same settings in the Standard User Configuration GPO.

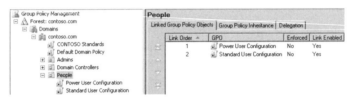

Figure 6-10   GPO link order

Blocking Inheritance

A domain or OU can be configured to prevent the inheritance of policy settings. To block inheritance, right-click the domain or OU in the GPME and choose Block Inheritance.

The Block Inheritance option is a property of a domain or OU, so it blocks *all* Group Policy settings from GPOs linked to parents in the Group Policy hierarchy. When you block inheritance on an OU, for example, GPO application begins with any GPOs linked directly to that OU–GPOs linked to higher-level OUs, the domain, or the site will not apply.

The Block Inheritance option should be used sparingly, if ever. Blocking inheritance makes it more difficult to evaluate Group Policy precedence and inheritance. In the section, "Using Security Filtering to Modify GPO Scope," you will learn how to scope a GPO so that it applies to only a subset of objects or so that it is prevented from applying to a subset of objects. With security group filtering, you can carefully scope a GPO so that it applies to only the correct users and computers in the first place, making it unnecessary to use the Block Inheritance option.

Enforcing a GPO Link

In addition, a GPO link can be set to Enforced. To do this, right-click a GPO link and choose Enforced from the context menu shown in Figure 6-7. When a GPO link is set to Enforced, the GPO takes the highest level of precedence; policy settings in that GPO will prevail over any conflicting policy settings in other GPOs. In addition, a link that is enforced will apply to child containers even when those containers are set to Block Inheritance. The Enforced option causes the policy to apply to all objects within its scope. Enforced will cause policies to override any conflicting policies and will apply regardless of whether a Block Inheritance option is set.

In Figure 6-11, Block Policy Inheritance has been applied to the Clients OU. As a result, GPO 1, which is applied to the site, is blocked and does not apply to the Clients OU. However, GPO 2, linked to the domain with the Enforced option, does apply. In fact, it is applied last in the processing order, meaning that its settings will override those of GPOs 6 and 7.

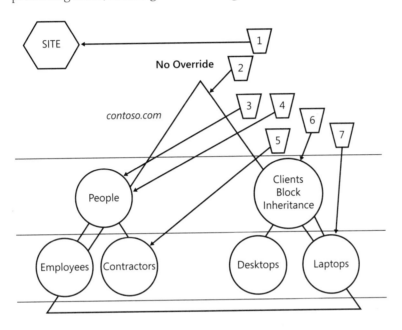

GPO processing order for the Contractors OU = 1, 3, 4, 5, 2
GPO processing order for the Laptops OU = 6, 7, 2

Figure 6-11   Policy processing with Block Inheritance and Enforced options

When you configure a GPO that defines configuration mandated by your corporate IT security and usage policies, you want to ensure that those settings are not overridden by other GPOs. You can do this by enforcing the link of the GPO. Figure 6-12 shows just this scenario. Configuration mandated by corporate policies is deployed in the CONTOSO Corporate IT Security & Usage GPO, which is linked with an enforced link to the *contoso.com* domain. The icon for the GPO link has a padlock on it—the visual indicator of an enforced link. On the People OU, the Group Policy Inheritance tab shows that the GPO takes precedence even over the GPOs linked to the People OU itself.

To facilitate evaluation of GPO precedence, you can simply select an OU (or domain) and click the Group Policy Inheritance tab. This tab will display the resulting precedence of GPOs, accounting for GPO link, link order, inheritance blocking, and link enforcement. This tab does not account for policies that are linked to a site, nor does it account for GPO security or WMI filtering.

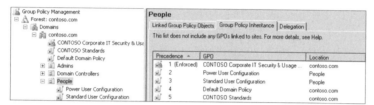

Figure 6-12   The precedence of the GPO with an enforced link

---

Exam Tip   Although it is recommended to use the Block Inheritance and Enforced options sparingly in your Group Policy infrastructure, the 70-640 exam will expect you to understand the effect of both options.

Using Security Filtering to Modify GPO Scope

By now, you've learned that you can link a GPO to a site, domain, or OU. However, you might need to apply GPOs only to certain groups of users or computers rather than to all users or computers within the scope of the GPO. Although you cannot directly link a GPO to a security group, there is a way to apply GPOs to specific security groups. The policies in a GPO apply only to users who have Allow Read and Allow Apply Group Policy permissions to the GPO.

Each GPO has an access control list (ACL) that defines permissions to the GPO. Two permissions, Allow Read and Allow Apply Group Policy are required for a GPO to apply to a user or computer. If a GPO is scoped to a computer, for example, by its link to the computer's OU, but the computer does not have Read and Apply Group Policy permissions, it will not download and apply the GPO. Therefore, by setting the appropriate permissions for security groups, you can filter a GPO so that its settings apply only to the computers and users you specify.

By default, Authenticated Users are given the Allow Apply Group Policy permission on each new GPO. This means that by default, *all* users and computers are affected by the GPOs set for their domain, site, or OU regardless of the other groups in which they might be members. Therefore, there are two ways of filtering GPO scope:

- Remove the Apply Group Policy permission (currently set to Allow) for the Authenticated Users group but do not set this permission to Deny. Then determine the groups to which the GPO should be applied and set the Read and Apply Group Policy permissions for these groups to Allow.

- Determine the groups to which the GPO should not be applied and set the Apply Group Policy permission for these groups to Deny. If you deny the Apply Group Policy permission to a GPO, the user or computer will not apply settings in the GPO, even if the user or computer is a member of another group that is allowed the Apply Group Policy Permission.

Filtering a GPO to Apply to Specific Groups

To apply a GPO to a specific security group, select the GPO in the Group Policy Objects container in the GPMC. In the Security Filtering section, select the Authenticated Users group and click Remove. Click OK to confirm the change and then click Add. Select the group to which you want the policy to apply and click OK. The result will look similar to Figure 6-13–the Authenticated Users group is not listed, and the specific group to which the policy should apply is listed.

NOTE **Use global security groups to filter GPOs**

GPOs can be filtered only with global security groups—not with domain local security groups.

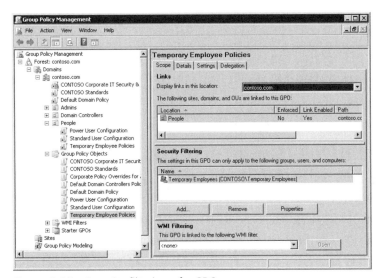

Figure 6-13 Security filtering of a GPO

Filtering a GPO to Exclude Specific Groups

Unfortunately, the Scope tab of a GPO does not allow you to exclude specific groups. To exclude a group–that is, to deny the Apply Group Policy permission–you must click the Delegation tab. Click the Advanced button, and the Security Settings dialog box appears. Click the Add button in the Security Settings dialog box, select the group you want to exclude from the GPO, and click OK. The group you selected is given the Allow Read permission by default. Deselect that permission check box and select the Deny Apply Group Policy. Figure 6-14 shows an example that denies the Help Desk group the Apply Group Policy permission and, therefore, excludes the group from the scope of the GPO.

When you click the OK button in the Security Settings dialog box, you will be warned that Deny permissions override other permissions. Because of this, it is recommended that you use

Deny permissions sparingly. Microsoft Windows reminds you of this best practice with the warning message and by the far more laborious process to exclude groups with the Deny Apply Group Policy permission than to include groups in the Security Filtering section of the Scope tab.

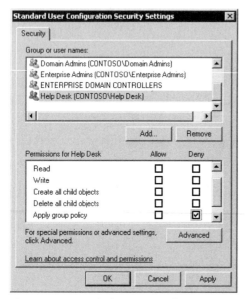

Figure 6-14   Excluding a group from the scope of a GPO with the Deny Apply Group Policy permission

---

NOTE   Deny permissions are not exposed on the Scope tab

Unfortunately, when you exclude a group, the exclusion is not shown in the Security Filtering section of the Scope tab. This is yet one more reason to use Deny permissions sparingly.

WMI Filters

Windows Management Instrumentation (WMI) is a management infrastructure technology that enables administrators to monitor and control managed objects in the network. A WMI query is capable of filtering systems based on characteristics, including RAM, processor speed, disk capacity, IP address, operating system version and service pack level, installed applications, and printer properties. Because WMI exposes almost every property of every object within a computer, the list of attributes that can be used in a WMI query is virtually unlimited. WMI queries are written using WMI query language (WQL).

You can use a WMI query to create a WMI filter, with which a GPO can be filtered. A good way to understand the purpose of a WMI filter, both for the certification exams and for real-world implementation, is through examples. Group Policy can be used to deploy software applications and service packs—a capability that is discussed in Chapter 7. You might create a GPO to deploy an application and then use a WMI filter to specify that the policy should apply only to computers with a certain operating system and service pack, Windows XP SP3, for example. The WMI query to identify such systems is:

```
Select * FROM Win32_OperatingSystem WHERE Caption="Microsoft
Windows XP Professional" AND CSDVersion="Service Pack 3"
```

When the Group Policy client evaluates GPOs it has downloaded to determine which should be handed off to the CSEs for processing, it performs the query against the local system. If the system meets the criteria of the query, the query result is a logical *True*, and the CSEs will process the GPO.

WMI exposes *namespaces*, within which are classes that can be queried. Many useful classes, including *Win32_Operating System*, are found in a class called *root\CIMv2*.

To create a WMI filter, right-click the WMI Filters node in the GPME and choose New. Type a name and description for the filter, and then click the Add button. In the Namespace box, type the namespace for your query. In the Query box, enter the query. Then click OK.

To filter a GPO with a WMI filter, click the Scope tab of a GPO, click the WMI drop-down list, and select the WMI filter. A GPO can be filtered by only one WMI filter, but that WMI filter can be a complex query, using multiple criteria. A single WMI filter can be linked to, and thereby used to filter, one or more GPOs. The General tab of a WMI filter, shown in Figure 6-15, displays the GPOs that use the WMI filter.

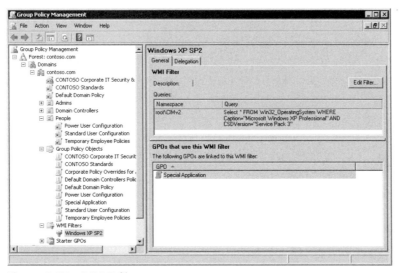

Figure 6-15   A WMI filter

There are three significant caveats regarding WMI filters. First, the WQL syntax of WMI queries can be challenging to master. You can often find examples on the Internet when you search using the keywords *WMI filter* and *WMI query* along with a description of the query you want to create.

MORE INFO   WMI filter examples

You can find examples of WMI filters at *http://technet2.microsoft.com/windowsserver/en/library /a16cffa4-83b3-430b-b826-9bf81c0d39a71033.mspx?mfr=true*. You can also refer to the Windows Management Instrumentation (WMI) software development kit (SDK), located at *http:// msdn2.microsoft.com/en-us/library/aa394582.aspx*.

Second, WMI filters are expensive in terms of Group Policy processing performance. Because the Group Policy client must perform the WMI query at each policy processing interval, there is a slight impact on system performance every 90–120 minutes. With the performance of today's computers, the impact might not be noticeable, but you should certainly test the effects of a WMI filter prior to deploying it widely in your production environment.

Third, WMI filters are not processed by computers running Windows 2000. If a GPO is filtered with a WMI filter, a Windows 2000 system ignores the filter and processes the GPO as if the results of the filter were *True*.

Exam Tip   Although it is unlikely that you will be asked to recognize WQL queries on the 70-640 exam, you should be familiar with the basic functionality of WMI queries as discussed in this section. Be certain to remember that Windows 2000 systems will apply settings in GPOs with WMI filters because Windows 2000 ignores WMI filters during policy processing.

Enabling or Disabling GPOs and GPO Nodes

You can prevent the settings in the Computer Configuration or User Configuration nodes from being processed during policy refresh by changing GPO Status. On the Details tab of a GPO, shown in Figure 6-16, click the GPO Status drop-down list and choose one of the following:

- **Enabled**   Both computer configuration settings and user configuration settings will be processed by CSEs during policy refresh.
- **All Settings Disabled**   CSEs will not process the GPO to policy refresh.
- **Computer Configuration Settings Disabled**   During computer policy refresh, computer configuration settings in the GPO will be applied. The GPO will not be processed during user policy refresh.
- **User Configuration Settings Disabled**   During user policy refresh, user configuration settings in the GPO will be applied. The GPO will not be processed during computer policy refresh.

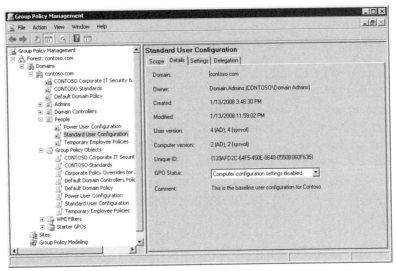

Figure 6-16   The Details tab of a GPO

You can configure GPO Status to optimize policy processing. If a GPO contains only user settings, for example, setting GPO Status to disable computer settings will prevent the Group Policy client from attempting to process the GPO during computer policy refresh. Because the
GPO contains no computer settings, there is no need to process the GPO, and you can save a
few cycles of the processor.

NOTE   Use disabled GPOs for disaster recovery

You can define a configuration that should take effect in case of an emergency, security incident, or
other disasters in a GPO and link the GPO so that it is scoped to appropriate users and computers.
Then, disable the GPO. In the event that you require the configuration to be deployed, simply
enable the GPO.

Targeting Preferences

Preferences, which are new to Windows Server 2008, have a built-in scoping mechanism
called *item-level targeting*. You can have multiple preference items in a single GPO, and each
preference item can be targeted or filtered. So, for example, you could have a single GPO with
a preference that specifies folder options for engineers and another item that specifies folder
options for sales people. You can target the items by using a security group or OU. There are
over a dozen other criteria that can be used, including hardware and network characteristics,
date and time, LDAP queries, and more.

NOTE   **Preferences can target within a GPO**

What's new about preferences is that you can target multiple preferences items within a single GPO instead of requiring multiple GPOs. With traditional policies, you often need multiple GPOs filtered to individual groups to apply variations of settings.

Like WMI filters, item-level targeting of preferences requires the CSE to perform a query to determine whether to apply the settings in a preferences item. You must be aware of the potential performance impact of item-level targeting, particularly if you use options such as LDAP queries, which require processing time and a response from a domain controller to process. As you design your Group Policy infrastructure, balance the configuration management benefits of item-level targeting against the performance impact you discover during testing in a lab.

Group Policy Processing

Now that you have learned more about the concepts, components, and scoping of Group Policy, you are ready to examine Group Policy processing closely. As you read this section, keep in mind that Group Policy is all about applying configurations defined by GPOs, that GPOs are applied in an order (site, domain, and OU), and that GPOs applied later in the order have higher precedence; their settings, when applied, will override settings applied earlier. The following sequence details the process through which settings in a domain-based GPO are applied to affect a computer or user:

1. The computer starts, and the network starts. Remote Procedure Call System Service (RPCSS) and Multiple Universal Naming Convention Provider (MUP) are started. The Group Policy client is started.

2. The Group Policy client obtains an ordered list of GPOs scoped to the computer.

   The order of the list determines the order of GPO processing, which is, by default, local, site, domain, and OU:

   a. Local GPOs. Each computer running Windows Server 2003, Windows XP, and Windows 2000 has exactly one GPO stored locally. Windows Vista and Windows Server 2008 have multiple local GPOs. The precedence of local GPOs is discussed in the "Local GPOs" section in Lesson 1.

   b. Site GPOs. Any GPOs that have been linked to the site are added to the ordered list next. When multiple GPOs are linked to a site (or domain or OU), the *link order*, configured on the Scope tab, determines the order in which they are added to the list. The GPO that is highest on the list, with the number closest to 1, has the highest precedence, and is added to the list last. It will, therefore, be applied last, and its settings will override those of GPOs applied earlier.

   c. Domain GPOs. Multiple domain-linked GPOs are added as specified by the link order.

NOTE   Domain-linked policies are not inherited by child domains

Policies from a parent domain are not inherited by a child domain. Each domain maintains distinct policy links. However, computers in several domains might be within the scope of a GPO linked to a site.

---

   d.   OU GPOs. GPOs linked to the OU highest in the Active Directory hierarchy are added to the ordered list, followed by GPOs linked to its child OU, and so on. Finally, the GPOs linked to the OU that contains the computer are added. If several group policies are linked to an OU, they are added in the order specified by the link order.

   e.   Enforced GPOs. These are added at the end of the ordered list, so their settings will be applied at the end of the process and will, therefore, override settings of GPOs earlier in the list and in the process. As a point of trivia, enforced GPOs are added to the list in reverse order: OU, domain, and then site. This is relevant when you apply corporate security policies in a domain-linked, enforced GPO. That GPO will be at the end of the ordered list and will be applied last, so its settings will take precedence.

3.   The GPOs are processed synchronously in the order specified by the ordered list. This means that settings in the local GPOs are processed first, followed by GPOs linked to the site, the domain, and the OUs containing the user or computer. GPOs linked to the OU of which the computer or user is a direct member are processed last, followed by enforced GPOs.

   As each GPO is processed, the system determines whether its settings should be applied based on the GPO status for the computer node (enabled or disabled) and whether the computer has the Allow Group Policy permission. If a WMI filter is applied to the GPO, and if the computer is running Windows XP or later, it performs the WQL query specified in the filter.

4.   If the GPO should be applied to the system, CSEs trigger to process the GPO settings. Policy settings in GPOs will overwrite policies of previously applied GPOs in the following ways:

   ❑   If a policy setting is configured (set to Enabled or Disabled) in a GPO linked to a parent container (OU, domain, or site), and the same policy setting is Not Configured in GPOs linked to its child container, the resultant set of policies for users and computers in the child container will include the parent's policy setting. If the child container is configured with the Block Inheritance option, the parent setting is not inherited unless the GPO link is configured with the Enforced option.

   ❑   If a policy setting is configured (set to Enabled or Disabled) for a parent container, and the same policy setting *is* configured for a child, the child container's setting

overrides the setting inherited from the parent. If the parent GPO link is configured with the Enforced option, the parent setting has precedence.

❑ If a policy setting of GPOs linked to parent containers is Not Configured, and the
child OU setting is also Not Configured, the resultant policy setting is the setting
that results from the processing of local GPOs. If the resultant setting of local
GPOs is also Not Configured, the resultant configuration is the Windows default
setting.

5. When the user logs on, steps 2, 3, and 4 are repeated for user settings. The client obtains
an ordered list of GPOs scoped to the user, examines each GPO synchronously, and
hands over GPOs that should be applied to the appropriate CSEs for processing. This
step is modified if User Loopback Group Policy Processing is enabled. Loopback policy
processing is discussed in the next section.

**NOTE   Policy settings in both the Computer Configuration and User Configuration
nodes**

Most policy settings are specific to either the User Configuration or Computer Configuration
node. A small handful of settings appear in both nodes. Although in most situations the setting in the Computer Configuration node will override the setting in the User Configuration
node, it is important to read the explanatory text accompanying the policy setting to understand the setting's effect and its application.

---

6. Every 90–120 minutes after computer startup, computer policy refresh occurs, and steps
2, 3, and 4 are repeated for computer settings.

7. Every 90–120 minutes after user logon, user policy refresh occurs, and steps 2, 3, and 4
are repeated for user settings.

NOTE   Settings might not take effect immediately

Although most settings are applied during a background policy refresh, some CSEs do not
apply the setting until the next startup or logon event. Newly added startup and logon script
policies, for example, will not run until the next computer startup or logon. Software installation, discussed in Chapter 7, will occur at the next startup if the software is assigned in computer settings. Changes to folder redirection policies will not take effect until the next logon.

Loopback Policy Processing

By default, a user's settings come from GPOs scoped to the user object in Active Directory.
Regardless of which computer the user logs on to, the resultant set of policies that determine
the user's environment will be the same. There are situations, however, when you might want
to configure a user differently, depending on the computer in use. For example, you might
want to lock down and standardize user desktops when users log on to computers in closely
managed environments such as conference rooms, reception areas, laboratories, classrooms,

and kiosks. Imagine a scenario in which you want to enforce a standard corporate appearance for the Windows desktop on all computers in conference rooms and other public areas of your office. How could you centrally manage this configuration, using Group Policy? Policy settings that configure desktop appearance are located in the User Configuration node of a GPO. Therefore, by default, the settings apply to users, regardless of which computer they log on to. The default policy processing does not give you a way to scope user settings to apply to computers, regardless of which user logs on. That's where loopback policy processing comes in.

Loopback policy processing alters the default algorithm used by the Group Policy client to obtain the ordered list of GPOs that should be applied to a user's configuration. Instead of user configuration being determined by the User Configuration node of GPOs that are scoped to the user object, user configuration can be determined by the User Configuration node policies of GPOs that are scoped to the *computer* object.

The User Group Policy Loopback Processing Mode policy, located in the Computer Configuration\Policies\Administrative Templates\System\Group Policy folder in Group Policy Management Editor, can be, like all policy settings, set to Not Configured, Enabled, or Disabled. When enabled, the policy can specify Replace or Merge mode.

- **Replace** In this case, the GPO list for the user (obtained in step 5 in the "Group Policy Processing" section) is replaced in its entirety by the GPO list already obtained for the computer at computer startup (during step 2). The settings in the User Configuration policies of the computer's GPOs are applied to the user. Replace mode is useful in a situation such as a classroom, where users should receive a *standard configuration* rather than the configuration applied to those users in a less managed environment.

- **Merge** In this case, the GPO list obtained for the computer at computer startup (step 2 in the "Group Policy Processing" section) is appended to the GPO list obtained for the user when logging on (step 5). Because the GPO list obtained for the computer is applied later, settings in GPOs on the computer's list have precedence if they conflict with settings in the user's list. This mode would be useful to apply *additional settings* to users' typical configurations. For example, you might allow a user to receive his or her typical configuration when logging on to a computer in a conference room or reception area but replace the wallpaper with a standard bitmap and disable the use of certain applications or devices.

Exam Tip The 70-640 exam is likely to include several questions that test your knowledge of Group Policy scope. Sometimes, questions that seem to be addressing the technical details of a policy setting are, in fact, testing your ability to scope the setting to appropriate systems. When you encounter Group Policy questions, ask yourself, "Is this really about a specific policy setting, or is it about the scope of that setting?"

PRACTICE Configuring Group Policy Scope

In this practice, you will follow a scenario that builds upon the GPO you created and configured in Lesson 1. In each vignette, you will refine your application of Group Policy scoping.
Before performing these exercises, complete the exercises in Lesson 1.

▶ **Exercise 1   Create a GPO with a Policy Setting That Takes Precedence over a Conflicting
Setting**

Imagine you are an administrator of the *contoso.com* domain. The CONTOSO Standards GPO,
linked to the domain, configures a policy setting that requires a ten-minute screen saver timeout. An engineer reports that a critical application that performs lengthy calculations crashes
when the screens saver starts, and the engineer has asked you to prevent the setting from
applying to the team of engineers that use the application every day.

1. Log on to SERVER01 as Administrator.
2. Open the Active Directory Users And Computers snap-in and create a first-level OU
   called People and a child OU called Engineers.
3. Open the GPMC.
4. Right-click the Engineers OU and choose Create A GPO In This Domain, And Link It Here.
5. Enter the name **Engineering Application Override** and click OK.
6. Expand the Engineers OU, right-click the GPO, and choose Edit.
7. Expand User Configuration\Policies\Administrative Templates\Control Panel\Display.
8. Double-click the Screen Saver Timeout policy setting.
9. Click Disabled, and then click OK.
10. Close the GPME.
11. In the GPMC, select the Engineers OU, and then click the Group Policy Inheritance tab.
12. Notice that the Engineering Application Override GPO has precedence over the CON-
    TOSO Standards GPO.

    The setting you configured, which explicitly disables the screen saver, will override the
    setting in the CONTOSO Standards GPO.

▶ **Exercise 2   Configure the Enforced Option**

You want to ensure that all systems receive changes to Group Policy as quickly as possible. To
do this, you want to enable the Always Wait For The Network Group Policy setting described
in Lesson 1. You do not want any administrators to override the policy; it must be enforced for
all systems.

1. In the GPMC, right-click the *contoso.com* domain and choose Create A GPO In This
   Domain, And Link It Here.
2. Enter the name **Enforced Domain Policies** and click OK.
3. Right-click the GPO and choose Edit.

4. Expand Computer Configuration\Policies\Administrative Templates\System\Logon.

5. Double-click the Always Wait For The Network At Computer Startup And Logon policy setting.

6. Select Enabled and click OK.

7. Close the GPME.

8. Right-click the Enforced Domain Policies GPO and choose Enforced.

9. Select the Engineers OU, and then click the Group Policy Inheritance tab.

    Note that your enforced domain GPO has precedence even over GPOs linked to the Engineers OU. Settings in a GPO such as Engineering Application Override cannot successfully override settings in an enforced GPO.

▶ **Exercise 3   Configure Security Filtering**

As time passes, you discover that a small number of users must be exempted from the screen saver timeout policy configured by the CONTOSO Standards GPO. You decide that it is no longer practical to use overriding settings. Instead, you will use security filtering to manage the scope of the GPO.

1. Open the Active Directory Users And Computers snap-in and create an OU called Groups. Within it, create a global security group named **GPO_CONTOSO Standards_Exceptions**.

2. In the GPMC, select the Group Policy Objects container.

3. Right-click the Engineering Application Override GPO and choose Delete. Click Yes to confirm your choice.

4. Select the CONTOSO Standards GPO in the Group Policy Objects container.

5. Click the Delegation tab.

6. Click the Advanced button.

7. In the Security Settings dialog box, click the Add button.

8. Type the name of the group and click OK.

9. In the permissions list, scroll down and select the Deny permission for Apply Group Policy. Then click OK.

10. Click Yes to confirm your choice.

11. Note the entry shown on the Delegation tab in the Allowed Permissions column for the GPO_CONTOSO Standards_Exceptions group.

12. Click the Scope tab and examine the Security Filtering section.

    The default security filtering of the new GPO is that the Authenticated Users group has the Allow Apply Group Policy permission, so all users and computers within the scope of the GPO link will apply the settings in the GPO. Now, you have configured a group with the Deny Apply Group Policy permission, which overrides the Allow permission. If any user requires exemption from the policies in the CONTOSO Standards GPO, you can simply add the computer to the group.

▶ **Exercise 4   Loopback Policy Processing**

Recently, a salesperson at Contoso, Ltd., turned on his computer to give a presentation to an important customer, and the desktop wallpaper was a picture that exhibited questionable taste on the part of the salesperson. The management of Contoso, Ltd., has asked you to ensure that the laptops used by salespeople will have no wallpaper. It is not necessary to manage the wallpaper of salespeople when they are logged on to desktop computers at the office. Because policy settings that manage wallpaper are user configuration settings, but you need to apply the settings to sales laptops, you must use loopback policy processing. In addition, the computer objects for sales laptops are scattered across several OUs, so you will use security filtering to apply the GPO to a group rather than to an OU of sales laptops.

1. Open the Active Directory Users And Computers snap-in and create a global security group called **Sales Laptops** in the Groups OU. Also create an OU called Clients for client computer objects.

2. In the GPMC, right-click the Group Policy Objects container and choose New.

3. In the Name box, type **Sales Laptop Configuration** and click OK.

4. Right-click the GPO and choose Edit.

5. Expand User Configuration\Policies\Administrative Templates\Desktop\Desktop.

6. Double-click the Desktop Wallpaper policy setting.

7. Click the Explain tab and review the explanatory text.

8. Click the Comment tab and type **Corporate standard wallpaper for sales laptops**.

9. Click the Settings tab.

10. Select Enabled.

11. In the Wallpaper Name box, type **c:\windows\web\Wallpaper\server.jpg**.

12. Click OK.

13. Expand Computer Configuration\Policies\Administrative Templates\System\Group Policy.

14. Double-click the User Group Policy Loopback Processing Mode policy setting.

15. Click Enabled and, in the Mode drop-down list, select Merge.

16. Click OK and close the GPME.

17. In the GPMC, select the Sales Laptop Configuration GPO in the Group Policy Objects container.

18. On the Scope tab, in the Security Filtering section, select the Authenticated Users group and click the Remove button. Click OK to confirm your choice.

19. Click the Add button in the Security Filtering section.

20. Type the group name, **Sales Laptops**, and click OK.

21. Right-click the Clients OU and choose Link An Existing GPO.
22. Select Sales Laptop Configuration and click OK.

    You have now filtered a GPO so that it applies only to objects in the Sales Laptops group. You can add computer objects for sales laptops as members of the group, and those laptops will be within the scope of the GPO. The GPO configures the laptops to perform loopback policy processing in Merge mode. When a user logs on to one of the laptops, user configuration settings scoped to the user are applied and then user configuration settings in GPOs scoped to the computer are applied, including the Sales Laptop Configuration GPO.

Lesson Summary

- The initial scope of the GPO is established by GPO links. A GPO can be linked to one or more sites, domains, or OUs. The scope of the GPO can be further refined using security filtering or WMI filters.

- CSEs apply GPOs in the following order: local GPOs, GPOs linked to the site in which a user or computer logs on, GPOs linked to the user or computer domain, and then GPOs linked to OUs. The layered application of policy settings creates the effect of policy inheritance.

- Policy inheritance can be blocked by configuring the Block Inheritance option on a domain or OU.

- A GPO link can be set to Enforced. The settings in an enforced GPO are applied to computers and users within the scope of the GPO, even if the Block Inheritance option is set. Additionally, settings in an enforced GPO take precedence, so they will override conflicting settings.

- You can use security filtering to specify the groups to which a GPO will apply or the groups that will be exempted from the GPO. Only global security groups can be used to filter GPOs.

- Under normal policy processing, during user policy refresh (at logon and every 90–120 minutes thereafter), the system applies user configuration policy settings from GPOs scoped to the logged-on user.

- Loopback policy processing causes the system to change the way it applies GPOs during user policy refresh. In Merge mode, after applying settings from GPOs scoped to the logged on user, the system applies policy settings from GPOs scoped to the computer. These settings take precedence over conflicting settings from user GPOs. In loopback processing Replace mode, user configuration settings from GPOs scoped to the logged-on user are not applied. Instead, only user configuration settings from GPOs scoped to the computer are applied.

Lesson Review

You can use the following questions to test your knowledge of the information in Lesson 2, "Managing Group Policy Scope." The questions are also available on the companion CD if you prefer to review them in electronic form.

NOTE   Answers

Answers to these questions and explanations of why each answer choice is right or wrong are located in the "Answers" section at the end of the book.

---

1. You want to deploy a GPO named Northwind Lockdown that applies configuration to all users at Northwind Traders. However, you want to ensure that the settings do not apply to members of the Domain Admins group. How can you achieve this goal? (Choose all that apply.)

    A. Link the Northwind Lockdown GPO to the domain, and then right-click the domain and choose Block Inheritance.

    B. Link the Northwind Lockdown GPO to the domain, right-click the OU that contains the user accounts of all users in the Domain Admins group, and choose Block Inheritance.

    C. Link the Northwind Lockdown GPO to the domain, and then assign the Domain Admins group the Deny Apply Group Policy permission.

    D. Link the Northwind Lockdown GPO to the domain, and then configure security filtering so that the GPO applies to Domain Users.

2. You want to create a standard lockdown desktop experience for users when they log on to computers in your company's conference and training rooms. You have created a GPO called Public Computers Configuration with desktop restrictions defined in the User Configuration node. What additional steps must you take? (Choose all that apply. Each correct answer is a part of the solution.)

    A. Enable the User Group Policy Loopback Processing Mode policy setting.

    B. Link the GPO to the OU containing user accounts.

    C. Select the Block Inheritance option on the OU containing conference and training room computers.

    D. Link the GPO to the OU containing conference and training room computers.

Lesson 3: Supporting Group Policy

Group Policy application can be complex to analyze and understand, with the interaction of multiple settings in multiple GPOs scoped using a variety of methods. You must be equipped to effectively evaluate and troubleshoot your Group Policy implementation, to identify potential problems before they arise, and to solve unforeseen challenges. Microsoft Windows provides two tools that are indispensible for supporting Group Policy: Resultant Set of Policy (RSOP) and the Group Policy Operational Logs. In this lesson, you will explore the use of these tools in both proactive and reactive troubleshooting and support scenarios.

After this lesson, you will be able to:
- Analyze the set of GPOs and policy settings that have been applied to a user or computer
- Proactively model the impact of Group Policy or Active Directory changes on resultant set of policy
- Locate the event logs containing Group-Policy related events

Estimated lesson time: 30 minutes

Resultant Set of Policy

In Lesson 2, you learned that a user or computer can be within the scope of multiple GPOs. Group Policy inheritance, filters, and exceptions are complex, and it's often difficult to determine just which policy settings will apply. *Resultant Set of Policy (RSoP)* is the net effect of GPOs applied to a user or computer, taking into account GPO links, exceptions such as Enforced and Block Inheritance, and the application of security and WMI filters. RSoP is also a collection of tools that help you evaluate, model, and troubleshoot the application Group Policy settings. RSoP can query a local or remote computer and report back the exact settings that were applied to the computer and to any user who has logged on to the computer. RSoP can also model the policy settings that are anticipated to be applied to a user or computer under a variety of scenarios, including moving the object between OUs or sites or changing the object's group membership. With these capabilities, RSoP can help you manage and troubleshoot conflicting policies.

Windows Server 2008 provides the following tools for performing RSoP analysis:

- The Group Policy Results Wizard
- The Group Policy Modeling Wizard
- *Gpresult.exe*

Generating RSoP Reports with the Group Policy Results Wizard

To help you analyze the cumulative effect of GPOs and policy settings on a user or computer in your organization, the Group Policy Management console includes the Group Policy Results Wizard. If you want to understand exactly which policy settings have applied to a user or computer and why, the Group Policy Results Wizard is the tool to use.

The Group Policy Results Wizard is able to reach into the WMI provider on a local or remote computer running Window Vista, Windows XP, Windows Server 2003, and Windows Server 2008. The WMI provider can report everything there is to know about the way Group Policy was applied to the system. It knows when processing occurred, which GPOs were applied, which GPOs were not applied and why, errors that were encountered, the exact policy settings that took precedence, and their source GPO.

There are several requirements for running the Group Policy Results Wizard:

- You must have administrative credentials on the target computer.
- The target computer must be running Windows XP or later. The Group Policy Results Wizard cannot access Windows 2000 systems.
- You must be able to access WMI on the target computer. That means that it must be powered on, connected to the network, and accessible through ports 135 and 445.

> **NOTE   Enable remote administration of client computers**
>
> Performing RSoP analysis by using Group Policy Results Wizard is just one example of remote administration. Windows XP SP2, Windows Vista, and Windows Server 2008 include a firewall that prevents unsolicited inbound connections even from members of the Administrators group. Group Policy provides a simple way to enable remote administration. In the Computer Configuration\Policies\Administrative Templates\Network\Network Connections\Windows Firewall\Domain Profile folder, you will find a policy setting named Windows Firewall: Allow Inbound Remote Administration Exception. When you enable this policy setting, you can specify the IP addresses or subnets from which inbound remote administration packets will be accepted. As with all policy settings, review the explanatory text on the Explain tab and test the effect of the policy in a lab environment before deploying it in production.

- The WMI service must be started on the target computer.
- If you want to analyze RSoP for a user, that user must have logged on at least once to the computer. It is not necessary for the user to be currently logged on.

After you have ensured that the requirements are met, you are ready to run an RSoP analysis. Right-click Group Policy Results in the GPMC and choose Group Policy Results Wizard. The wizard prompts you to select a computer. It then connects to the WMI provider on that computer and provides a list of users that have logged on to it. You can then select one of the users or opt to skip RSoP analysis for user configuration policies.

The wizard produces a detailed RSoP report in a dynamic HTML format. If Internet Explorer ESC is enabled, you will be prompted to allow the console to display the dynamic content. Each section of the report can be expanded or collapsed by clicking the Show or Hide link or by double-clicking the heading of the section. The report is displayed on three tabs:

- **Summary**   The Summary tab displays the status of Group Policy processing at the last refresh. You can identify information that was collected about the system, the GPOs that were applied and denied, security group membership that might have affected GPOs filtered with security groups, WMI filters that were analyzed, and the status of CSEs.
- **Settings**   The Settings tab displays the resultant set of policy settings applied to the computer or user. This tab shows you exactly what has happened to the user through the effects of your Group Policy implementation. A tremendous amount of information can be gleaned from the Settings tab, but some data isn't reported, such as IPSec, wireless, and disk quota policy settings.
- **Policy Events**   The Policy Events tab displays Group Policy events from the event logs of the target computer.

After you have generated an RSoP report with the Group Policy Results Wizard, you can right-click the report to rerun the query, print the report, or save the report as either an XML file or an HTML file that maintains the dynamic expanding and collapsing sections. Either file type can be opened with Internet Explorer, so the RSoP report is portable outside the GPMC. If you right-click the node of the report itself, underneath the Group Policy Results folder in the console tree, you can switch to Advanced View. In Advanced View, RSoP is displayed using the RSoP snap-in, which exposes all applied settings, including IPSec, wireless, and disk quota policies.

Generating RSoP Reports with *Gpresult.exe*

The *Gpresult.exe* command is the command-line version of the Group Policy Results Wizard. *Gpresult* taps into the same WMI provider as the wizard, produces the same information, and, in fact, enables you to create the same graphical reports. *Gpresult* runs on Windows Vista, Windows XP, Windows Server 2003, and Windows Server 2008. Windows 2000 includes a *Gpresult.exe* command, which produces a limited report of Group Policy processing but is not as sophisticated as the command included in later versions of Windows.

When you run the *Gpresult* command, you are likely to use the following options:

- **/s *computername***   Specifies the name or IP address of a remote system. If you use a dot (.) as the computer name, or do not include the /s option, the RSoP analysis is performed on the local computer.
- **/scope [user | computer]**   Displays RSoP analysis for user or computer settings. If you omit the */scope* option, RSoP analysis includes both user and computer settings.
- **/user *username***   Specifies the name of the user for which RSoP data is to be displayed.
- **/r**   Displays a summary of RSoP data.

- **/v**   Displays verbose RSoP data that presents the most meaningful information.
- **/z**   Displays super verbose data, including the details of all policy settings applied to the system. Often, this is more information than you will require for typical Group Policy troubleshooting.
- **/u** *domain\user* **/p** *password*   Provides credentials that are in the Administrators group of a remote system. Without these credentials, *Gpresult* runs using the credentials with which you are logged on.
- **[/x | /h]** *filename*   Saves the reports in XML or HTML format, respectively. These options are available in Windows Vista SP1 and Windows Server 2008.

Quick Check

- You want to perform RSoP analysis on a remote system. Which two tools can you use?

Quick Check Answer

- The Group Policy Results Wizard and *Gpupdate.exe* can be used to perform your top analysis on a remote system.

Troubleshooting Group Policy with the Group Policy Results Wizard and *Gpresult.exe*

As an administrator, you will likely encounter scenarios that require Group Policy troubleshooting. You might need to diagnose and solve problems, including:

- GPOs are not applied at all.
- The resultant set of policies for a computer or user are not those that were expected.

The Group Policy Results Wizard and *Gpresult.exe* will often provide the most valuable insight into Group Policy processing and application problems. Remember that these tools examine the WMI RSoP provider to report exactly what happened on a system. Examining the RSoP report will often point you to GPOs that are scoped incorrectly or policy processing errors that prevented the application of GPOs settings.

Performing What-If Analyses with the Group Policy Modeling Wizard

If you move a computer or user between sites, domains, or OUs, or change its security group membership, the GPOs scoped to that user or computer will change and, therefore, the RSoP for the computer or user will be different. RSoP will also change if slow link or loopback processing occurs or if there is a change to a system characteristic that is targeted by a WMI filter.

Before you make any of these changes, you should evaluate the potential impact to the RSoP of the user or computer. The Group Policy Results Wizard can perform RSoP analysis only on what has actually happened. To predict the future and to perform what-if analyses, you can use the Group Policy Modeling Wizard.

Right-click the Group Policy Modeling node in the GPMC. Choose Group Policy Modeling Wizard and perform the steps in the wizard. Modeling is performed by conducting a simulation on a domain controller, so you are first asked to select a domain controller that is running Windows Server 2003 or later. You do not need to be logged on locally to the domain controller, but the modeling request will be performed on the domain controller. You are then asked to specify the settings for the simulation:

- Select a user or computer object to evaluate or specify the OU, site, or domain to evaluate.
- Choose whether slow link processing should be simulated.
- Specify to simulate loopback processing and, if so, choose Replace or Merge mode.
- Select a site to simulate.
- Select security groups for the user and for the computer.
- Choose which WMI filters to apply in the simulation of user and computer policy processing.

When you have specified the settings for the simulation, a report is produced that is very similar to the Group Policy Results report discussed earlier. The Summary tab shows an overview of which GPOs will be processed, and the Settings tab details the policy settings that will be applied to the user or computer. This report, too, can be saved by right-clicking it and choosing Save Report.

Examining Policy Event Logs

Windows Vista and Windows Server 2008 improve your ability to troubleshoot Group Policy not only with RSoP tools but also with improved logging of Group Policy events. In the System log, you will find high-level information about Group Policy, including errors created by the Group Policy client when it cannot connect to a domain controller or locate GPOs. The Application log captures events recorded by CSEs. A new log, called the Group Policy Operational Log, provides detailed information about Group Policy processing. To find these logs, open the Event Viewer snap-in or console. The System and Application logs are in the Windows Logs node. The Group Policy Operational Log is found in Applications And Services Logs\Microsoft\Windows\GroupPolicy\Operational. This log will not be available until after you use the Group Policy Modeling Wizard initially.

PRACTICE Configuring Group Policy Scope

In this practice, you will follow a scenario that builds upon the GPOs you created and configured in Lesson 1 and Lesson 2. You will perform RSoP results and modeling analysis and examine policy-related events in the event logs. To perform these exercises, you must have completed the practices in Lesson 1 and Lesson 2.

▶ **Exercise 1   Use the Group Policy Results Wizard**

In this exercise, you will use the Group Policy Results Wizard to examine RSoP on SERVER01. You will confirm that the policies you created in Lesson 1 and Lesson 2 have applied.

1. Log on to SERVER01 as Administrator.
2. Open a command prompt and type **gpupdate.exe /force /boot** to initiate a Group Policy refresh. Wait for the process host to reboot. Make a note of the current system time; you will need to know the time of the refresh in Exercise 3, "View Policy Events."
3. Log on to SERVER01 as Administrator and open the Group Policy Management console.
4. Expand Forest.
5. Right-click Group Policy Results and choose Group Policy Results Wizard.
6. Click Next.
7. On the Computer Selection page, select This Computer and click Next.
8. On the User Selection page, select Display Policy Settings For, select Select A Specific User, and select CONTOSO\Administrator. Then click Next.
9. On the Summary Of Selections page, review your settings and click Next.
10. Click Finish.

    The RSoP report appears in the details pane of the console.

11. On the Summary tab, click the Show All link at the top of the report.
12. Review the Group Policy Summary results. For both user and computer configuration, identify the time of the last policy refresh and the list of allowed and denied GPOs. Identify the components that were used to process policy settings.
13. Click the Settings tab and click the Show All link at the top of the page. Review the settings that were applied during user and computer policy application and identify the GPO from which the settings were obtained.
14. Click the Policy Events tab and locate the event that logs the policy refresh you triggered with the *Gpupdate.exe* command in step 2.
15. Click the Summary tab, right-click the page, and choose Save Report. Save the report as an HTML file to your Documents folder with a name of your choice.
16. Open the saved RSoP report from your Documents folder.

▶ **Exercise 2   Use the *Gpresult.exe* Command**

In this exercise, you will perform RSoP analysis from the command line, using *Gpresult.exe*.

1. Open a command prompt.
2. Type **gpresult /r** and press Enter.

    RSoP summary results are displayed. The information is very similar to the Summary tab of the RSoP report produced by the Group Policy Results Wizard.

3. Type **gpresult /v** and press Enter.

    A more detailed RSoP report is produced. Notice many of the Group Policy settings applied by the client are listed in this report.

4. Type **gpresult /z** and press Enter.

    The most detailed RSoP report is produced.

5. Type **gpresult /h:"%userprofile%\Documents\RSOP.html"** and press Enter.

    An RSoP report is saved as an HTML file to your Documents folder.

6. Open the saved RSoP report from your documents folder. Compare the report, its information, and its formatting to the RSoP report you saved in the previous exercise.

▶ **Exercise 3   View Policy Events**

As a client performs a policy refresh, Group Policy components log entries to the Windows event logs. In this exercise, you will locate and examine Group Policy–related events.

1. Open the Event Viewer console from the Administrative Tools folder.

2. Expand Windows Logs\System.

3. Locate events with GroupPolicy as the Source. You can even click the Filter Current Log link in the Actions pane and then select GroupPolicy in the Event Sources drop-down list.

4. Review the information associated with GroupPolicy events.

5. Click the Application node in the console tree underneath Windows Logs.

6. Sort the Application log by the Source column.

7. Review the logs by Source and identify the Group Policy events that have been entered in this log.

    Which events are related to Group Policy application, and which are related to the activities you have been performing to manage Group Policy?

8. In the console tree, expand Applications And Services Logs\Microsoft\Windows \GroupPolicy\Operational.

9. Locate the first event related in the Group Policy refresh you initiated in Exercise 1, "Use the Group Policy Results Wizard," with the *Gpupdate.exe* command. Review that event and the events that followed it.

▶ **Exercise 4   Perform Group Policy Modeling**

In this exercise, you will use Group Policy modeling to evaluate the potential effect of your policy settings on users who log on to sales laptops.

1. Open the Active Directory Users And Computers snap-in.

2. Create a user account for Mike Danseglio in the People OU.

3. Create an OU in the domain called **Clients**.

4. Create a computer account in the Clients OU called **LAPTOP101**.

5. Add LAPTOP101 and Domain Users to the Sales Laptops group.

   It is an underdocumented fact that when you combine the loopback processing with security group filtering, the application of user settings during policy refresh uses the credentials of the computer to determine which GPOs to apply as part of the loopback processing, but the logged-on user must also have the Apply Group Policy permission for the GPO to be successfully applied.

6. In the Group Policy Management console, expand Forest.

7. Right-click Group Policy Modeling and choose Group Policy Modeling Wizard.

8. Click Next.

9. On the Domain Controller Selection page, click Next.

10. On the User And Computer Selection page, in the User Information section, click the User button, click Browse, and then select Mike Danseglio.

11. In the Computer Information section, click the Computer button, click Browse, and select LAPTOP101 as the computer.

12. Click Next.

13. On the Advanced Simulation Options page, select the Loopback Processing check box and select Merge.

    Even though the Sales Laptop Configuration GPO specifies the loopback processing, you must instruct the Group Policy Modeling Wizard to consider loopback processing in its simulation.

14. Click Next.

15. On the Alternate Active Directory Paths page, click Next.

16. On the User Security Groups page, click Next.

17. On the Computer Security Groups page, click Next.

18. On the WMI Filters For Users page, click Next.

19. On the WMI Filters For Computers page, click. Next.

20. Review your settings on the Summary Of Selections page. Click Next, and then click Finish.

Lesson Summary

- RSoP reports can be generated in the Windows interface by using the Group Policy Results Wizard, a component of the GPMC. RSoP reports reveal the actual results of policy processing at the last policy refresh.

- RSoP reports can be generated from the command line, using *Gpresult.exe*. The */scope* option can be used to generate a report containing only user or computer settings. The */s* switch can be used to run *Gpresult.exe* against a remote system.

- The Group Policy Modeling Wizard enables you to simulate the application of Group Policy to evaluate the possible effect of changes to your Group Policy infrastructure or of moving users and computers between OUs and groups.
- Group Policy components create entries in the Windows event logs.

Lesson Review

You can use the following questions to test your knowledge of the information in Lesson 3, "Supporting Group Policy." The questions are also available on the companion CD if you prefer to review them in electronic form.

NOTE Answers

Answers to these questions and explanations of why each answer choice is right or wrong are located in the "Answers" section at the end of the book.

---

1. A user calls the help desk at your organization and reports problems that you suspect might be related to changes that were recently made to Group Policy. You want to examine information regarding Group Policy processing on her system. Which tools can you use to gather this information remotely? (Choose all that apply.)

   A. Group Policy Modeling Wizard

   B. Group Policy Results Wizard

   C. *Gpupdate.exe*

   D. *Gpresult.exe*

   E. *Msconfig.exe*

2. You are the administrator at Contoso, Ltd. The *contoso.com* domain has five GPOs linked to the domain, one of which configures the password-protected screen saver and screen saver timeout required by corporate policy. Some users report that the screen saver is not launching after 10 minutes as expected. How do you know when the GPO was applied?

   A. Run *Gpresult.exe* for the users.

   B. Run *Gpresult.exe* –*computer*.

   C. Run *Gpresult* –*scope computer*.

   D. Run *Gpupdate.exe* /*Target:User*.

Chapter Review

To further practice and reinforce the skills you learned in this chapter, you can perform the following tasks:

- Review the chapter summary.
- Review the list of key terms introduced in this chapter.
- Complete the case scenario. This scenario sets up a real-world situation involving the topics of this chapter and asks you to create a solution.
- Complete the suggested practices.
- Take a practice test.

Chapter Summary

- Group Policy enables you to manage and change configuration centrally in an enterprise environment.
- There are thousands of policy settings that can be configured within a GPO. By default, these policy settings are set to Not Configured. When a setting is enabled or disabled, it effects a change.
- GPOs can be scoped to apply to users and computers with a variety of mechanisms, including links to sites, domains, and OUs. You can also filter GPOs with security groups and WMI filters.
- You can support and troubleshoot Group Policy with tools, including RSoP tools and event logs.

Key Terms

Use these key terms to understand better the concepts covered in this chapter.

- **Group Policy object (GPO)**   A collection of policy settings that determine configuration.
- **policy setting or policy**   A configuration or change within a Group Policy object.
- **Resultant Set of Policies (RSoP)**   The net effect of policy settings applied by Group Policy, accounting for GPO scope links, security filters, WMI filters, and options such as Block Inheritance and Enforced.
- **scope**   In the context of Group Policy, the users or computers to which a GPO applies.

Case Scenario

In the following case scenario, you will apply what you've learned about implementing GPOs, managing Group Policy scope, and supporting Group Policy. You can find answers to these questions in the "Answers" section at the end of this book.

Case Scenario: Implementing Group Policy

You are an administrator at Northwind Traders. Your company is converting to a new enterprise resource planning (ERP) application and, in the process, will be conducting a large number of training sessions. You are responsible for configuring the computers in the training rooms, and you want to provide a single, consistent user experience for any student who logs on to the systems. For example, you want to implement a specific desktop wallpaper, prevent users from accessing registry editing tools, and disable the password-protected screen saver policy that is implemented by a GPO linked to the domain.

1. Are the policy settings that will configure the desired desktop environment found in the Computer Configuration or the User Configuration node of a GPO?
2. After you configure the settings, should you link the GPO to the OU containing user accounts or to the OU containing the training computers?
3. What must you do to ensure that the settings are applied when users log on to computers in the training rooms and not when they log on to their normal computers?
4. What setting must be configured to prevent policy settings that normally apply to users from being applied when the users log on to training computers?
5. What must you do to prevent the domain's screen saver policies from applying to training room computers?

Suggested Practices

To help you successfully master the exam objectives presented in this chapter, complete the following tasks.

Create and Apply Group Policy Objects (GPOs)

In this practice, you will configure the environment proposed in the case scenario. You will create an OU for training room computers and configure a standard user desktop experience for those computers, using loopback Group Policy processing. You will also prevent a domain policy from applying to training room computers. You will confirm your work by performing RSoP analysis.

- **Practice 1**   Create an OU called **Training Room**. Create several sample computer objects within the OU. Then, create a global security group called **Training Room Computers** and add the computer objects as members of the group.
- **Practice 2**   Create a GPO called **Training Room Configuration**. In the GPO, enable a policy that prevents access to registry editing tools and configure a standard desktop wallpaper. Both of these settings are user configuration settings in the Administrative Templates node. If you need assistance finding them, filter the settings with keywords. In the Computer Configuration node, locate the administrative templates setting that enables loopback policy processing. Enable this setting and choose to implement loopback processing in Replace mode.
- **Practice 3**   Link the Training Room Configuration GPO to the Training Room OU.
- **Practice 4**   In Lesson 1, you created the CONTOSO Standards GPO and configured it to implement screen saver policy settings. If you no longer have this GPO, perform Exercise 1 of Lesson 1. Using the Delegation tab of the GPO, add a permission that denies the Training Room Computers group the Apply Group Policy permission.
- **Practice 5**   Use the Group Policy Modeling Wizard to evaluate RSoP for a user logging on to one of the sample computers. Be sure in the wizard to select the option to simulate loopback processing and Replace mode.

Take a Practice Test

The practice tests on this book's companion CD offer many options. For example, you can test yourself on just one exam objective, or you can test yourself on all the 70-640 certification exam content. You can set up the test so that it closely simulates the experience of taking a certification exam, or you can set it up in study mode so that you can look at the correct answers and explanations after you answer each question.

MORE INFO   Practice tests

For details about all the practice test options available, see the "How to Use the Practice Tests" section in this book's introduction.

Chapter 7

Group Policy Settings

Group Policy can be used to manage the configuration of an enormous variety of components and features of Microsoft Windows. In the previous chapter, you learned how to configure a Group Policy infrastructure. In this chapter, you will learn to apply that infrastructure to manage several types of configuration related to security and software installation. You will also discover tools, such as the Security Configuration Wizard, that make it easier to determine which settings should be configured based on a server's roles. Finally, you will learn how to configure auditing of files and folders and of Active Directory Domain Services (AD DS) changes.

Exam objectives in this chapter:
- Creating and Maintaining Active Directory Objects
  - ❑ Create and apply Group Policy objects (GPOs).
  - ❑ Configure GPO templates.
  - ❑ Configure audit policy by using GPOs.

Lessons in this chapter:
- Lesson 1: Delegating the Support of Computers 291
- Lesson 2: Managing Security Settings 300
- Lesson 3: Managing Software with Group Policy Software Installation 322
- Lesson 4: Auditing 335

Before You Begin

To complete the practices in this chapter, you must have created a domain controller named SERVER01 in a domain named *contoso.com*. See Chapter 1, "Installation," for detailed steps to perform this task.

Real World

Dan Holme

I am often brought in by clients to perform "sanity checks" on their Active Directory implementations. These sanity checks involve an examination of Group Policy settings and a discussion of how to take better advantage of Group Policy to manage change and configuration. It amazes me that a full eight years after the introduction of Group Policy, many organizations do not yet use its full capability, particularly in the area of security. Three of the four lessons in this chapter focus on the interaction between security configuration and Group Policy. Configuration such as the membership of the Administrators group and assignment of user rights, service startup modes, and audit policies can be effectively managed with Group Policy. What you will learn in this chapter will not only help you pass the 70-640 exam; it will also help you increase the manageability and security of your entire enterprise. This includes Active Directory itself. For the past eight years, I've constantly been asked, "How can I know what changes have been made by administrators in Active Directory?" Now, thanks to the new Directory Service Changes auditing in Windows Server 2008, you can simply check your security log. Even if you are already using policy to manage your security configuration, this new feature, along with the vastly improved Security Configuration Wizard, will surely take your security management capabilities to a higher level.

Lesson 1: Delegating the Support of Computers

Many enterprises have one or more members of personnel dedicated to supporting end users, a role often referred to as the *help desk*, *desktop support*, or just *support*. Help desk personnel are often asked to perform troubleshooting, configuration, or other support tasks on client computers, and these tasks often require administrative privileges. Therefore, the credentials used by support personnel must be at the level of a member of the local Administrators group on client computers, but desktop support personnel do not need the high level of privilege given to the Domain Admins group, so it is not recommended to place them in that group. Instead, configure client systems so that a group representing support personnel is added to the local Administrators group. Restricted groups policies enable you to do just that, and in this lesson, you will learn how to use restricted groups policies to add the help desk personnel to the local Administrators group of clients and, thereby, to delegate support of those computers to the help desk. The same approach can be used to delegate the administration of any scope of computers to the team responsible for those systems.

After this lesson, you will be able to:

■ Delegate the administration of computers.

■ Use Group Policy to modify or enforce the membership of groups.

Estimated lesson time: 30 minutes

Understanding Restricted Groups Policies

When you edit a Group Policy object (GPO) and expand the Computer Configuration node, the Policies node, the Windows Settings node, and the Security Settings node, you will find the Restricted Groups policy node, shown in Figure 7-1.

Figure 7-1   The Restricted Groups policy node of a Group Policy object

Restricted groups policy settings enable you to manage the membership of groups. There are two types of settings: This Group Is A Member Of (the Member Of setting) and Members Of This Group (the Members setting). Figure 7-2 shows examples.

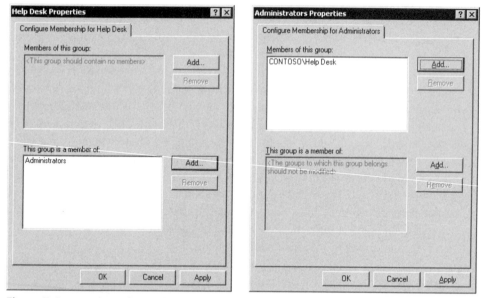

Figure 7-2   Member Of and Members restricted groups policies

It's very important to understand the difference between these two settings. A Member Of setting specifies that the group specified by the policy is a member of another group. On the left side of Figure 7-2, you can see a typical example: The CONTOSO\Help Desk group is a member of the Administrators group. When a computer applies this policy setting, it ensures that the Help Desk group from the domain becomes a member of its local Administrators group. If there is more than one GPO with restricted groups policies, each Member Of policy is applied. For example, if a GPO linked to the Clients organizational unit (OU) specifies CONTOSO\Help Desk as a member of Administrators, and a second GPO linked to the NYC OU (a sub-OU of the Clients OU) specifies CONTOSO\NYC Support as a member of Administrators, a computer in the NYC OU will add both the Help Desk and NYC Support groups to its Administrators group in addition to any existing members of the group such as Domain Admins. This example is illustrated in Figure 7-3. As you can see, restricted groups policies that use the Member Of setting are cumulative.

Figure 7-3   Results of restricted groups policies using the Member Of setting

The second type of restricted groups policy setting is the Members setting, which specifies the entire membership of the group specified by the policy. The right side of Figure 7-2 shows a typical example: the Administrators group's Members list is specified as CONTOSO\Help Desk. When a computer applies this policy setting, it ensures that the local Administrators group's membership consists *only* of CONTOSO\Help Desk. Any members not specified in the policy are removed, including Domain Admins. The Members setting is the authoritative policy—it defines the final list of members. If there is more than one GPO with restricted group policies, the GPO with the highest priority will prevail. For example, if a GPO linked to the Clients OU specifies the Administrators group membership as CONTOSO\Help Desk, and another GPO linked to the NYC OU specifies the Administrators group membership as CONTOSO\NYC Support, computers in the NYC OU will have only the NYC Support group in their Administrators group. This example is illustrated in Figure 7-4.

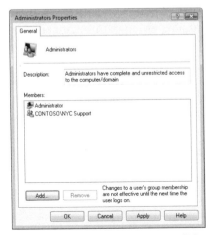

Figure 7-4   Restricted groups policies using the Members setting

In your enterprise, be careful to design and test your restricted groups policies to ensure that they achieve the desired result. Do not mix GPOs that use the Member Of and the Members settings—use one approach or the other.

Exam Tip   On the 70-640 exam, be able to identify the differences between restricted groups policies that use the Member Of setting and those that use the Members setting. Remember that Member Of settings are cumulative and that if GPOs use the Members setting, only the Members setting with the highest GPO processing priority will be applied, and its list of members will prevail.

Delegating Administration Using Restricted Groups Policies with the Member Of Setting

You can use restricted groups policies with the Member Of setting to manage the delegation of administrative privileges for computers by following these steps:

1. In Group Policy Management Editor, navigate to Computer Configuration\Policies\Windows Settings\Security Settings\Restricted Groups.
2. Right-click Restricted Groups and choose Add Group.
3. Click the Browse button and, in the Select Groups dialog box, type the name of the group you want to add to the Administrators group, for example, **CONTOSO\Help Desk**, and click OK.
4. Click OK to close the Add Group dialog box.
   A Properties dialog box appears.
5. Click the Add button next to the This Group Is A Member Of section.
6. Type **Administrators** and click OK.
   The Properties group policy setting should look something like the left side of Figure 7-2.
7. Click OK again to close the Properties dialog box.

Delegating the membership of the local Administrators group in this manner adds the group specified in step 3 to that group. It does not remove any existing members of the Administrators group. The group policy simply tells the client, "Make sure this group is a member of the local Administrators group." This allows for the possibility that individual systems could have other users or groups in their local Administrators group. This group policy setting is also cumulative. If multiple GPOs configure different security principals as members of the local Administrators group, all will be added to the group.

To take complete control of the local Administrators group, follow these steps:

1. In Group Policy Management Editor, navigate to Computer Configuration\Windows Settings\Security Settings\Restricted Groups.
2. Right-click Restricted Groups and choose Add Group.

3. Type **Administrators** and click OK.

   A Properties dialog box appears.

4. Click the Add button next to the Members Of This Group section.

5. Click the Browse button and type the name of the group you want to make the sole member of the Administrators group—for example, **CONTOSO\Help Desk**—and click OK.

6. Click OK again to close the Add Member dialog box.

   The group policy setting Properties should look something like the right side of Figure 7-2.

7. Click OK again to close the Properties dialog box.

When you use the Members setting of a restricted groups policy, the Members list defines the final membership of the specified group. The steps just listed result in a GPO that authoritatively manages the Administrators group. When a computer applies this GPO, it will add all members specified by the GPO and will remove all members not specified by the GPO, including Domain Admins. Only the local Administrator account will not be removed from the Administrators group because Administrator is a permanent and nonremovable member of Administrators.

Quick Check

- You want to add a group to the local Administrators group on computers without removing accounts that already exist in the group. Describe the restricted groups policy you should create.

Quick Check Answer

- Create a restricted groups policy for the group you wish to add. Use the Member Of policy setting (This Group Is A Member Of) and specify Administrators.

PRACTICE Delegating Membership Using Group Policy

In this practice, you will use Group Policy to delegate the membership of the Administrators group. You will first create a GPO with a restricted groups policy setting that ensures that the Help Desk group is a member of the Administrators group on all client systems. You will then create a GPO that adds the NYC Support group to Administrators on clients in the NYC OU. Finally, you will confirm that in the NYC OU, both the Help Desk and NYC Support groups are administrators.

To perform this practice, you will need the following objects in the *contoso.com* domain:

- A first-level OU named Admins with a sub-OU named Admin Groups.
- A global security group named Help Desk in the Admins\Admin Groups OU.
- A global security group named NYC Support in the Admins\Admin Groups OU.

- A first-level OU named Clients.
- An OU named NYC in the Clients OU.
- A computer object named DESKTOP101 in the NYC OU.

▶ **Exercise 1   Delegate the Administration of All Clients in the Domain**

In this exercise, you will create a GPO with a restricted groups policy setting that ensures that the Help Desk group is a member of the Administrators group on all client systems.

1. In the Group Policy Management console, expand Forest\Domains\contoso.com. Select the Group Policy Objects container.
2. Right-click the Group Policy Objects container and choose New.
3. In the Name box, type **Corporate Help Desk** and click OK.
4. Right-click the GPO and choose Edit.
5. In Group Policy Management Editor, navigate to Computer Configuration\Policies \Windows Settings\Security Settings\Restricted Groups.
6. Right-click Restricted Groups and choose Add Group.
7. Click the Browse button and, in the Select Groups dialog box, type **CONTOSO\Help Desk** and click OK.
8. Click OK to close the Add Group dialog box.
9. Click the Add button next to the This Group Is A Member Of section.
10. Type **Administrators** and click OK.
    The group policy setting Properties should look like the left side of Figure 7-2.
11. Click OK again to close the Properties dialog box.
12. Close Group Policy Management Editor.
13. In the Group Policy Management console, right-click the Clients OU and choose Link An Existing GPO.
14. Select the Corporate Help Desk GPO and click OK.

▶ **Exercise 2   Delegate the Administration of a Subset of Clients in the Domain**

In this exercise, you will create a GPO with a restricted groups policy setting that adds the NYC Support group to the Administrators group on all client systems in the NYC OU.

1. In the Group Policy Management console, expand Forest\Domains\Contoso.com. Select the Group Policy Objects container.
2. Right-click the Group Policy Objects container and choose New.
3. In the Name box, type **New York Support** and click OK.
4. Right-click the GPO and choose Edit.
5. Repeat steps 5–12 of Exercise 1, "Delegate the Administration of All Clients in the Domain," except type **CONTOSO\NYC Support** as the group name in step 7.

6. In the Group Policy Management console, right-click the Clients\NYC OU and choose Link An Existing GPO.

7. Select the New York Support GPO and click OK.

▶ Exercise 3   Confirm the Cumulative Application of Member Of Policies

You can use Group Policy Modeling to produce a report of the effective policies applied to a computer or user. In this exercise, you will use Group Policy Modeling to confirm that a computer in the NYC OU will include both the Help Desk and NYC Support groups in its Administrators group.

1. In the Group Policy Management console, expand Forest and select the Group Policy Modeling node.

2. Right-click the Group Policy Modeling node and choose Group Policy Modeling Wizard.

3. Click Next.

4. On the Domain Controller Selection page, click Next.

5. On the User And Computer Selection page, in the Computer Information section, click the Browse button.

6. Expand the domain and the Clients OU, and then select the NYC OU.

7. Click OK.

8. Select the Skip To The Final Page Of This Wizard Without Collecting Additional Data check box.

9. Click Next.

10. On the Summary Of Selections page, click Next.

11. Click Finish.

    The Group Policy Modeling report appears.

12. Click the Settings tab.

13. Double-click Security Settings.

14. Double-click Restricted Groups.

    You should see both the Help Desk and NYC Support groups listed. Restricted groups policies using the This Group Is A Member Of setting are cumulative. Notice the report does not specify that the listed groups belong to Administrators. This is a limitation of the report.

▶ Optional Exercise 4   Confirm the Membership of the Administrators Group

If your test environment includes a computer named DESKTOP101 that is a member of the *contoso.com* domain, you can start the computer, log on as the domain's Administrator, and open the Computer Management console from the Administrative Tools folder in Control Panel. In Computer Management, expand the Local Users And Groups node and, in the Groups folder, open the Administrators group. You should see the following members listed:

- CONTOSO\Help Desk, applied by the Corporate Help Desk GPO
- CONTOSO\NYC Support, applied by the New York Support GPO
- Domain Admins, made a member of Administrators when the computer joined the domain
- The local Administrator account, a default member that cannot be removed

Lesson Summary

- To delegate support of computers in your domain, you must manage the membership of the Administrators groups on those systems.
- GPOs using the Member Of setting of restricted groups policies can add domain groups to the Administrators group. Member Of settings are cumulative, so multiple GPOs can add groups to Administrators.
- A GPO using the Members setting of restricted groups policies can define the membership of the Administrators group. The Members setting is final and authoritative. If more than one GPO applies to a computer, only the GPO with the highest precedence will determine the membership of the Administrators group.

Lesson Review

You can use the following questions to test your knowledge of the information in Lesson 1, "Delegating the Support of Computers." The questions are also available on the companion CD if you prefer to review them in electronic form.

NOTE   Answers

Answers to these questions and explanations of why each answer choice is right or wrong are located in the "Answers" section at the end of the book.

---

1. The *contoso.com* domain contains a GPO named Corporate Help Desk, linked to the Clients OU, and a GPO named Sydney Support linked to the Sydney OU within the Clients OU. The Corporate Help Desk GPO includes a restricted groups policy for the CONTOSO\Help Desk group that specifies This Group Is A Member Of Administrators. The Sydney Support GPO includes a restricted groups policy for the CONTOSO\Sydney Support group that specifies This Group Is A Member Of Administrators. A computer named DESKTOP234 joins the domain in the Sydney OU. Which of the following accounts will be a member of the Administrators group on DESKTOP234? (Choose all that apply.)

    A. Administrator

    B. Domain Admins

    C. Sydney Support

    D. Help Desk

    E. Remote Desktop Users

2. The *contoso.com* domain contains a GPO named Corporate Help Desk, linked to the Clients OU, and a GPO named Sydney Support linked to the Sydney OU within the Clients OU. The Corporate Help Desk GPO includes a restricted groups policy for the Administrators group that specifies the Members Of This Group setting to be CONTOSO\Help Desk. The Sydney Support GPO includes a restricted groups policy for the Administrators group that specifies the Members Of This Group setting to be CONTOSO\Sydney Support. A computer named DESKTOP234 joins the domain in the Sydney OU. Which of the following accounts will be a member of the Administrators group on DESKTOP234? (Choose all that apply.)

    A. Administrator

    B. Domain Admins

    C. Sydney Support

    D. Help Desk

    E. Remote Desktop Users

3. The *contoso.com* domain contains a GPO named Corporate Help Desk, linked to the Clients OU, and a GPO named Sydney Support linked to the Sydney OU within the Clients OU. The Corporate Help Desk GPO includes a restricted groups policy for the Administrators group that specifies the Members Of This Group setting to be CONTOSO\Help Desk. The Sydney Support GPO includes a restricted groups policy for the CONTOSO\Sydney Support group that specifies This Group Is A Member Of Administrators. A computer named DESKTOP234 joins the domain in the Sydney OU. Which of the following accounts will be a member of the Administrators group on DESKTOP234? (Choose all that apply.)

    A. Administrator

    B. Domain Admins

    C. Sydney Support

    D. Help Desk

    E. Remote Desktop Users

Lesson 2: Managing Security Settings

Security is a primary concern for all Windows administrators. Windows Server 2008 includes numerous settings that affect the services that are running, the ports that are open, the network packets that are allowed into or out of the system, the rights and permissions of users, and the activities that are audited. There is an enormous number of settings that can be managed, and unfortunately, there is no magic formula that applies the perfect security configuration to a server. The appropriate security configuration for a server depends on the roles that server plays, the mix of operating systems in the environment, and the security policies of the organization, which themselves depend on compliance regulations enforced from outside the organization.

Therefore, you must work to determine and configure the security settings that are required for servers in your organization, and you must be prepared to manage those settings in a way that centralizes and optimizes security configuration. Windows Server 2008 provides several mechanisms with which to configure security settings on one or more systems. In this lesson, you will discover these mechanisms and their interactions.

After this lesson, you will be able to:
- ■ Configure security settings on a computer using the Local Security Policy.
- ■ Create and apply security templates to manage security configuration.
- ■ Analyze security configuration based on security templates.
- ■ Create, edit, and apply security policies using the Security Configuration Wizard.
- ■ Deploy security configuration with Group Policy.

Estimated lesson time: 60 minutes

Configuring the Local Security Policy

Each server running Windows Server 2008 maintains a collection of security settings that can be managed using the local GPO. You can configure the local GPO by using the Group Policy Object Editor snap-in or the Local Security Policy console. The available policy setting categories are shown in Figure 7-5.

This lesson focuses on the mechanisms with which to configure and manage security settings rather than on the details of the settings themselves. Many of the settings—including account policies, audit policy, and user rights assignment—are discussed elsewhere in this training kit.

Figure 7-5 The security settings available in the local GPO

Because domain controllers (DCs) do not have local user accounts—only domain accounts—the policies in the Account Policies container of the local GPO on DCs cannot be configured. Instead, account policies for the domain should be configured as part of a domain-linked GPO such as the Default Domain Policy GPO. Account policies are discussed in the first lesson of Chapter 8, "Authentication."

The settings found in the local Security Settings policies are a subset of the policies that can be configured using domain-based Group Policy, shown in Figure 7-6. As you learned in Chapter 6, "Group Policy Infrastructure," it is a best practice to manage configuration by using domain-based Group Policy rather than on a machine-by-machine basis using local Group Policy. This is particularly true for domain controllers. The Default Domain Controllers Policy GPO is created when the first domain controller is promoted for a new domain. It is linked to the Domain Controllers OU and should be used to manage baseline security settings for all DCs in the domain so that DCs are consistently configured.

Figure 7-6   Security settings in a domain-based GPO

Managing Security Configuration with Security Templates

The second mechanism for managing security configuration is the security template. A security template is a collection of configuration settings stored as a text file with the .inf extension. As you can see in Figure 7-7, a security template contains settings that are a subset of the settings available in a domain-based GPO but a somewhat different subset than those managed by the local GPO. The tools used to manage security templates present settings in an interface that enables you to save your security configurations as files and deploy them when and where they are needed. You can also use a security template to analyze the compliance of a computer's current configuration against the desired configuration.

Figure 7-7   Security settings in a security template

There are several advantages to storing security configuration in security templates. For example, because the templates are plaintext files, you can work with them manually as with any text file, cutting and pasting sections as needed. Further, templates make it easy to store security configurations of various types so that you can easily apply different levels of security to computers performing different roles.

Security templates enable you to configure any of the following types of policies and settings:

- **Account Policies**   Enables you to specify password restrictions, account lockout policies, and Kerberos policies
- **Local Policies**   Enables you to configure audit policies, user rights assignments, and security options policies
- **Event Log Policies**   Enables you to configure maximum event log sizes and rollover policies
- **Restricted Groups**   Enables you to specify the users who are permitted to be members of specific groups
- **System Services**   Enables you to specify the startup types and permissions for system services
- **Registry Permissions**   Enables you to set access control permissions for specific registry keys
- **File System Permissions**   Enables you to specify access control permissions for NTFS files and folders

You can deploy security templates in a variety of ways, using Active Directory Group Policy Objects, the Security Configuration And Analysis snap-in, or *Secedit.exe*. When you associate a security template with an Active Directory object, the settings in the template become part of the GPO associated with the object. You can also apply a security template directly to a computer, in which case, the settings in the template become part of the computer's local policies. You will learn about each of these options in this section.

Using the Security Templates Snap-in

To work with security templates, you use the Security Templates snap-in. Windows Server 2008 does not include a console with the Security Templates snap-in, so you have to create one yourself using the MMC *Add/Remove Snap-in* command. The snap-in creates a folder called Security and a subfolder called Templates in your Documents folder, and the Documents \Security\Templates folder becomes the template search path, where you can store one or more security templates.

You can create a new security template by right-clicking the node that represents your template search path–C:\Users\Documents\Administrator\Security\Templates, for example–and choosing New Template. You can also create a template that reflects the current configuration of a server; you'll learn how to do that in the "Creating a Security Template" section.

Settings are configured in the template in the same way that settings are configured in a GPO. The Security Templates snap-in is used to configure settings in a security template. It is just an editor—it does not play any role in actually applying those settings to a system. Configure security settings in a template by using the Security Templates snap-in. Although the template itself is a text file, the syntax can be confusing. Using the snap-in ensures that settings are changed using the proper syntax. The exception to this rule is adding Registry settings that are not already listed in the Local Policies\Security Option portion of the template. As new security settings become known, if they can be configured using a Registry key, you can add them to a security template. To do so, you add them to the Registry Values section of the template.

MORE INFO   Adding custom registry settings

The article "How to Add Custom Registry Settings to Security Configuration Editor" helps you understand how to perform this task. You can find it at *http://support.microsoft.com/?kbid=214752*.

NOTE   Save your settings

Be sure to save your changes to a security template by right-clicking the template and choosing Save.

When you install a server or promote it to a domain controller, a default security template is applied by Windows. You can find that template in the %SystemRoot%\Security\Templates folder. On a domain controller, the template is called DC security.inf. You should not modify this template directly, but you can copy it to your template search path and modify the copy.

NOTE   Security templates in Windows Server 2008 and in earlier versions of Windows

In previous versions of Windows, a number of security templates were available to modify and apply to a computer. The new role-based configuration of Windows Server 2008 and the improved Security Configuration Manager have made these templates unnecessary.

Deploying Security Templates by Using Group Policy Objects

Creating and modifying security templates does not improve security unless you apply those templates. To configure a number of computers in a single operation, you can import a security template into the Group Policy Object for a domain, site, or organizational unit object in Active Directory. To import a security template into a GPO, right-click the Security Settings node and choose Import Policy. In the Import Policy From dialog box, if you select the Clear This Database Before Importing check box, all security settings in the GPO will be erased prior to importing the template settings, so the GPO's security settings will match the template's settings. If you leave the Clear This Database Before Importing check box deselected, the GPO's security policy settings will remain and the templates settings will be imported. Any settings defined in the GPO that are also defined in the template will be replaced with the template's setting.

Security Configuration and Analysis Tool

You can use the Security Configuration and Analysis snap-in to apply a security template to a computer interactively. The snap-in also provides the ability to analyze the current system security configuration and compare it to a baseline saved as a security template. This enables you to determine quickly whether someone has changed a computer's security settings and whether the system conforms to your organization's security policies.

As with the Security Templates snap-in, Windows Server 2008 does not include a console with the Security Configuration and Analysis snap-in, so you must add the snap-in to a console yourself.

To use the Security Configuration and Analysis snap-in, you must first create a database that will contain a collection of security settings. The database is the interface between the actual security settings on the computer and the settings stored in your security templates. Create a database (or open an existing one) by right-clicking the Security Configuration And Analysis node in the console tree.

You can then import one or more security templates. If you import more than one template, you must decide whether to clear the database. If the database is cleared, only the settings in the new template will be part of the database. If the database is not cleared, additional template settings that are defined will override settings from previously imported templates. If settings in newly imported templates are not defined, the settings in the database from previously imported templates will remain. To summarize, the Security Configuration and Analysis snap-in creates a database of security settings composed of imported security template settings. The settings in the database can be applied to the computer or used to analyze the computer's compliance and discrepancies with the desired state.

IMPORTANT   Database settings vs. the computer's settings

Remember that settings in a database do not modify the computer's settings or the settings in a template until that database is either used to configure the computer or exported to a template.

Applying Security Templates to a Computer

After you have imported one or more templates to create the database, you can apply the database settings to the computer. Right-click Security Configuration And Analysis and choose Configure Computer Now. You will be prompted for a path to an error log that will be generated during the application of settings. After applying the settings, examine the error log for any problems.

> **Quick Check**
>
> - Describe the procedure used to apply a security template to a computer.
>
> **Quick Check Answer**
>
> - Use the Security Configuration and Analysis snap-in to create a database. Import the template into the database. Configure the computer by using the database.

Analyzing the Security Configuration of a Computer

Before applying the database settings to a computer, you might want to analyze the computer's current configuration to identify discrepancies. Right-click Security Configuration And Analysis and choose Analyze Computer Now. The system prompts you for the location of its error log file and then proceeds to compare the computer's current settings to the settings in the database. After the analysis is complete, the console produces a report such as the one shown in Figure 7-8.

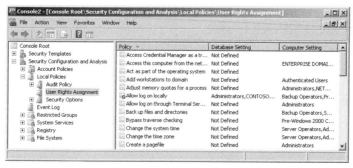

Figure 7-8   The Security Configuration and Analysis snap-in displays an analysis of the computer's configuration.

Unlike the display of policy settings in the Group Policy Management Editor, Group Policy Object Editor, Local Security Policy, or Security Templates snap-ins, the report shows for each policy the setting defined in the database (which was derived from the templates you imported) and the computer's current setting. The two settings are compared, and the comparison result is displayed as a flag on the policy name. For example, in Figure 7-8, the Allow Log On Locally policy setting is showing a discrepancy between the database setting and the computer setting. The meanings of the flags are as follows:

- **X in a red circle**   Indicates that the policy is defined both in the database and on the computer but that the configured values do not match
- **Green check mark in a white circle**   Indicates that the policy is defined both in the database and on the computer and that the configured values do match

- **Question mark in a white circle**   Indicates that the policy is not defined in the database and, therefore, was not analyzed or that the user running the analysis did not have the permissions needed to access the policy on the computer
- **Exclamation point in a white circle**   Indicates that the policy is defined in the database but does not exist on the computer
- **No flag**   Indicates that the policy is not defined in the database or on the computer

Correcting Security Setting Discrepancies

As you examine the elements of the database and compare its settings with those of the computer, you might find discrepancies and want to make changes to the computer's configuration or to the database to bring the two settings into alignment. You can double-click any policy setting to display its Properties dialog box and modify its value in the database. After you've made changes to the database, you can apply the database settings to the computer by performing the steps described earlier, in the section, "Applying Security Templates to a Computer."

CAUTION   **Applying or exporting database changes**

Modifying a policy value in the Security Configuration and Analysis snap-in changes the database value only, not the actual computer setting. For the changes you make to take effect on the computer, you must either apply the database settings to the computer using the *Configure Computer Now* command or export the database to a new template and apply it to the computer, using a GPO or the *Secedit.exe* command (discussed in the "*Secedit.exe*" section).

Alternatively, you can modify the computer's security settings directly by using the Local Security Policy console, by modifying the appropriate Group Policy Object, or by manually manipulating file system or registry permissions. After making such changes, return to the Security Configuration And Analysis snap-in and choose the *Analyze Computer Now* command to refresh the analysis of the computer's settings compared to the database.

Creating a Security Template

You can create a new security template from the database by right-clicking Security Configuration And Analysis and selecting Export Template. The template will contain the settings in the database, which have been imported from one or more security templates and which you have modified to reflect the current settings of the analyzed computer.

IMPORTANT   **Exporting the database to a template**

The Export Template feature creates a new template from the current database settings at the time you execute the command, not from the computer's current settings.

Secedit.exe

Secedit.exe is a command-line utility that can perform the same functions as the Security Configuration and Analysis snap-in. The advantage of *Secedit.exe* is that you can call it from scripts and batch files, enabling you to automate your security template deployments. Another big advantage of *Secedit.exe* is that you can use it to apply only part of a security template to a computer, something you cannot do with the Security Configuration and Analysis snap-in or with Group Policy Objects. For example, if you want to apply the file system's permissions from a template but leave all the other settings alone, *Secedit.exe* is the only way to do it.

To use *Secedit.exe*, you run the program from the command prompt with one of the following six main parameters, plus additional parameters for each function:

- **Configure**   Applies all or part of a security database to the local computer. You can also configure the program to import a security template into the specified database before applying the database settings to the computer.
- **Analyze**   Compares the computer's current security settings with those in a security database. You can configure the program to import a security template into the database before performing the analysis. The program stores the results of the analysis in the database itself, which you can view later, using the Security Configuration and Analysis snap-in.
- **Import**   Imports all or part of a security template into a specific security database.
- **Export**   Exports all or part of the settings from a security database to a new security template.
- **Validate**   Verifies that a security template is using the correct internal syntax.
- **Generaterollback**   Creates a security template you can use to restore a system to its original configuration after applying another template.

For example, to configure the machine by using a template called BaselineSecurity, use the following command:

```
secedit /configure /db BaselineSecurity.sdb
/cfg BaselineSecurity.inf /log BaselineSecurity.log
```

To create a rollback template for the BaselineSecurity template, use the following command:

```
secedit /generaterollback /cfg BaselineSecurity.inf
/rbk BaselineSecurityRollback.inf
/log BaselineSecurityRollback.log
```

MORE INFO   *Secedit.exe*

For full details regarding *Secedit.exe* and its switches, see *http://technet2.microsoft.com/windowsserver/en/library/b1007de8-a11a-4d88-9370-25e2445605871033.mspx?mfr=true.*

The Security Configuration Wizard

The Security Configuration Wizard can be used to enhance the security of a server by closing ports and disabling services not required for the server's roles. The Security Configuration Wizard can be launched from the home page of Server Manager, in the Security Information section, or from the Administrative Tools folder. There is also a command-line version of the tool, *scwcmd.exe*. Type **scwcmd.exe /?** at the command prompt for help on the command or see *http://technet2.microsoft.com/windowsserver2008/en/library/a222cb38-db08-4bf1-b9cf-6ec566c239e91033.mspx?mfr=true*.

The Security Configuration Wizard is a next-generation security management tool. It is more advanced than the Security Configuration and Analysis snap-in and role-based in accordance with the new role-based configuration of Windows Server 2008. The Security Configuration Wizard creates a security policy—an .xml file—that configures services, network security including firewall rules, registry values, audit policy, and other settings based on the roles of a server. That security policy can then be modified, applied to another server, or transformed into a GPO for deployment to multiple systems.

Creating a Security Policy

To create a security policy, you launch the Security Configuration Wizard from the Administrative Tools folder or the Security Information section on the home page of Server Manager. You can open the Security Configuration Wizard Help file by clicking the Security Configuration Wizard link on the first page of the wizard. Click Next and choose Create A New Security Policy. Click Next and enter the name of the server to scan and analyze. The security policy will be based on the roles being performed by the specified server. You must be an administrator on the server for the analysis of its roles to proceed. Ensure also that all applications using inbound IP ports are running prior to running the Security Configuration Wizard.

When you click Next, the Security Configuration Wizard begins the analysis of the selected server's roles. It uses a security configuration database that defines services and ports required for each server role supported by the Security Configuration Wizard. The security configuration database is a set of .xml files installed in %SystemRoot%\Security\Msscw\Kbs.

NOTE **Centralizing the security configuration database**

In an enterprise environment, centralize the security configuration database so that administrators use the same database when running the Security Configuration Wizard. Copy the files in the %SystemRoot%\Security\Msscw\Kbs folder to a network folder; then launch the Security Configuration Wizard with the *Scw.exe* command, using the syntax **scw.exe /kb *DatabaseLocation***. For example, the command *scw.exe /kb \\server01\scwkb* launches the Security Configuration Wizard, using the security configuration database in the shared folder scwkb on SERVER01.

The Security Configuration Wizard uses the security configuration database to scan the selected server and identifies the following:

- Roles that are installed on the server
- Roles likely being performed by the server
- Services installed on the server but not defined in the security configuration database
- IP addresses and subnets configured for the server

The information discovered about the server is saved in a file named Main.xml. This server-specific file is called the *configuration database*, not to be confused with the security configuration database used by the Security Configuration Wizard to perform the analysis. You can display this file by clicking the View Configuration Database button on the Processing Security Configuration page. The initial settings in the configuration database are called the *baseline settings*.

After the server has been scanned and the configuration database has been created, you have the opportunity to modify the database, which will then be used to generate the security policy to configure services, firewall rules, registry settings, and audit policies. The security policy can then be applied to the server or to other servers playing similar roles. The Security Configuration Wizard presents each of these four categories of the security policy in a section—a series of wizard pages.

- **Role-Based Service Configuration**   The outcome of this section is a set of policies that configure the startup state of services on the server. You want to ensure that only the services required by the server's roles start and that other services do not start. To achieve this outcome, the Security Configuration Wizard presents pages that display the server roles, client features, and administration and other options detected on the scanned server. You can add or remove roles, features, and options to reflect the desired role configuration. The last page of the section, titled "Confirm Service Changes" and shown in Figure 7-9, shows the changes that will be made to services based on the roles you specify.

  The server shown in Figure 7-9 is a domain controller, and you can see that the AD DS service is currently configured to start automatically; the policy will also set the service to start automatically to support the AD DS role. However, audio is not required for a DC, so the service named Audiosrv used by the Windows Audio option will be configured by the policy as disabled.

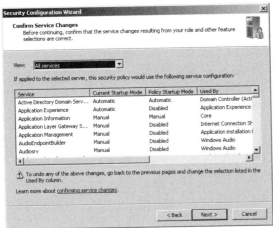

Figure 7-9 The Confirm Service Changes page of the Security Configuration Wizard

You cannot change the startup states on the Confirm Service Changes page of the Security Configuration Wizard. Instead, you must click the Back button to locate the role, service, or option indicated in the Used By column and either select or deselect that item. The service startup policies on the Confirm Service Changes page are determined by the selected roles, services, and options. Those not selected will result in service startup policy settings of disabled.

It is conceivable that the server on which you run the Security Configuration Wizard has services that are not defined by the Security Configuration Wizard security configuration database. The Select Additional Services page of the wizard enables you to include those services in the security policy so that, if the services exist on a system to which you apply the policy, those services will be started according to the startup setting in the baseline configuration database.

It is also conceivable that a server to which you apply the security policy might have services not found on the server from which you created the security policy. The Handling Unspecified Services page enables you to specify whether such services should be disabled or allowed to remain in their current startup mode.

- **Network Security** The Network Security section produces the firewall settings of the security policy. Those settings will be applied by Windows Firewall with Advanced Security. Like the Role-Based Service Configuration section, the Network Security section displays a page of settings derived from the baseline settings in the configuration database. The settings in the Network Security section, however, are firewall rules rather than service startup modes. Figure 7-10 shows the rule that allows incoming ping requests to a domain controller. You can edit existing rules or add and remove custom rules.

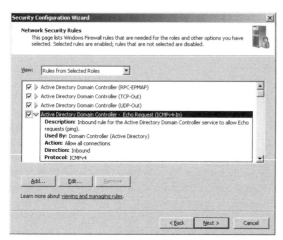

Figure 7-10   The Network Security Rules page of the Security Configuration Wizard

Windows Firewall with Advanced Security combines Internet Protocol security (IPSec) and a stateful firewall that inspects and filters all IP version 4 (IPv4) and IP version 6 (IPv6) packets, discarding unsolicited packets unless a firewall rule has been created to allow traffic explicitly to a port number, application name, or service name. The security policy generated by the Security Configuration Wizard manages firewall rules, but IPSec configuration is not provided by the Security Configuration Wizard.

- **Registry Settings**   The Registry Settings section configures protocols used to communicate with other computers. These wizard pages determine server message block (SMB) packet signing, Lightweight Directory Access Protocol (LDAP) signing, LAN Manager (LM) authentication levels, and storage of password LM hash values. Each of these settings is described on the appropriate page, and a link on each page takes you to a Security Configuration Wizard Help page that details the setting.

- **Audit Policy**   The Audit Policy section generates settings that manage the auditing of success and failure events and the file system objects that are audited. Additionally, the section enables you to incorporate a security template called SCWAudit.inf into the security policy. Use the Security Templates snap-in, described earlier in this lesson, to examine the settings in the template, which is located in %SystemRoot%\Security\Msscw\Kbs.

You can skip any of the last three sections you do not want to include in your security policy. When all the configuration sections have been completed or skipped, the Security Configuration Wizard presents the Security Policy section. The Security Policy File Name page, shown in Figure 7-11, enables you to specify a path, a name, and a description for the security policy.

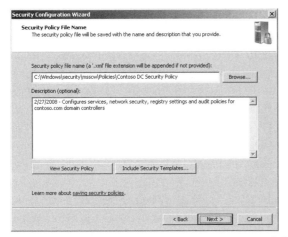

Figure 7-11   The Security Policy File Name page of the Security Configuration Wizard

Click the View Security Policy button to examine the settings of the security policy, which are very well documented by the Security Configuration Wizard. You can also import a security template into the security policy. Security templates, discussed earlier in this lesson in the "Managing Security Configuration with Security Templates" section, contain settings that are not provided by Managing Security Configuration with Security Templates, including restricted groups, event log policies, and file system and registry security policies. By including a security template, you can incorporate a richer collection of configuration settings in the security policy. If any settings in the security template conflict with the Security Configuration Wizard, the settings in the Security Configuration Wizard will take precedence. When you click the Next button, you are given the option to apply the security template to the server immediately or to apply the policy later.

Editing a Security Policy

You can edit a saved security policy by launching the Security Configuration Wizard and choosing Edit An Existing Security Policy on the Configuration Action page. Click the Browse button to locate the policy .xml file. When prompted to select a server, select the server that was used to create the security policy.

Applying a Security Policy

To apply a security policy to a server, open the Security Configuration Wizard and, on the Configuration Action page, choose Apply An Existing Security Policy. Click the Browse button to locate the policy .xml file. The server you specify on the Select Server page is the server to which the policy will be applied. Many of the changes specified in a security policy, including the addition of firewall rules for applications already running and the disabling of services, require that you restart the server. Therefore, as a best practice, it is recommended to restart a server any time you apply a security policy.

Rolling Back an Applied Security Policy

If a security policy is applied and causes undesirable results, you can roll back the changes by launching the Security Configuration Wizard and choosing Rollback The Last Applied Security Policy as the configuration action. When a security policy is applied by the Security Configuration Wizard, a rollback file is generated that stores the original settings of the system. The rollback process applies the rollback file.

Modifying Settings of an Applied Security Policy

Alternatively, if an applied security template does not produce an ideal configuration, you can manually change settings by using the Local Security Policy console discussed at the beginning of this lesson in the "Configuring the Local Security Policy" section. Thus, you can see the whole picture of security configuration, from manual settings to the generation of security templates to the creation of security policies with the Security Configuration Wizard, which can incorporate security templates, to the application of security policies and back to the manual configuration of settings.

Deploying a Security Policy Using Group Policy

You can apply a security policy created by the Security Configuration Wizard to a server by using the Security Configuration Wizard itself, by using the *Scwcmd.exe* command, or by transforming the security policy into a GPO. To transform a security policy into a GPO, log on as a domain administrator and run *Scwcmd.exe* with the *transform* command. For example, the *scwcmd transform /p:"Contoso DC Security.xml" /g:"Contoso DC Security GPO"* command will create a GPO called *Contoso DC Security GPO* with settings imported from the *Contoso DC Security.xml* security policy file. The resulting GPO can then be linked to an appropriate scope—site, domain, or OU—by using the Group Policy Management console. Be sure to type **scwcmd.exe transform /?** for help and guidance about this process.

Settings, Templates, Policies, and GPOs

As suggested in the introduction to this lesson, there are a number of mechanisms with which to manage security settings. You can use tools such as the Local Security Policy console to modify settings on an individual system. You can use security templates, which have existed since Windows 2000, to manage settings on one or more systems and to compare the current state of a system's configuration against the desired configuration defined by the template. Security policies generated by the Security Configuration Wizard are the most recent addition to the security configuration management toolset. They are role-based .xml files that define service startup modes, firewall rules, audit policies, and some registry settings. Security policies can incorporate security templates. Both security templates and security policies can be deployed using Group Policy.

The plethora of tools available can make it difficult to identify the best practice for managing security on one or more systems. Plan to use Group Policy whenever possible to deploy security configuration. You can generate a GPO from a role-based security policy produced by the Security Configuration Wizard, which itself incorporates additional settings from a security template. After the GPO has been generated, you can make additional changes to the GPO by using the Group Policy Management Editor snap-in. Settings not managed by Group Policy can be configured on a server-by-server basis, using the local GPO security settings.

PRACTICE **Managing Security Settings**

In this practice, you will manage security settings, using each of the tools discussed in this lesson. To perform the exercises in this practice, you must have the following objects in the directory service for the *contoso.com* domain:

- A first-level OU named Admins.
- An OU named Admin Groups in the Admins OU.
- A global security group named SYS_DC Remote Desktop in the Admins\ Admin Groups OU. The group must be a member of the Remote Desktop Users group. This membership gives the SYS_DC Remote Desktop group the permissions required to connect to the RDP-Tcp connection.

Alternatively, you can add the SYS_DC Remote Desktop group to the access control list (ACL) of the RDP-Tcp connection, using the Terminal Services Configuration console. Right-click RDP-Tcp and choose Properties; then click the Security tab, click the Add button, and type **SYS_DC Remote Desktop**. Click OK twice to close the dialog boxes.

▶ **Exercise 1   Configure the Local Security Policy**

In this exercise, you will use the local security policy to enable a group to log on using Remote Desktop to the domain controller named SERVER01. The local security policy of a domain controller affects only that individual DC—it is not replicated between DCs.

1. Log on to SERVER01 as Administrator.
2. Open the Local Security Policy console from the Administrative Tools folder.
3. Expand Security Settings\Local Policies\User Rights Assignment.
4. In the details pane, double-click Allow Log On Through Terminal Services.
5. Click Add User Or Group.
6. Type **CONTOSO\SYS_DC Remote Desktop** and click OK.
7. Click OK again.

   If you want to test the results of this exercise by logging on to the DC, using Remote Desktop as a member of the SYS_DC Remote Desktop group, create a user account and add it to the group. Be sure that the group is a member of Remote Desktop Users or has been given permission to connect to the RDP-Tcp connection as described earlier.

You will now remove the setting because you will manage the setting by using other tools in later exercises.

8. Double-click Allow Log On Through Terminal Services.
9. Select CONTOSO\SYS_DC Remote Desktop.
10. Click Remove.
11. Click OK.

▶ **Exercise 2 Create a Security Template**

In this exercise, you will create a security template that gives the SYS_DC Remote Desktop group the right to log on using Remote Desktop.

1. Log on to SERVER01 as Administrator.
2. Click Run from the Start menu.
3. Type **mmc** and press Enter.
4. Choose Add/Remove Snap-in from the File menu.
5. Select Security Templates from the Available Snap-ins list and click the Add button. Click OK.
6. Choose Save from the File menu and save the console to your desktop with the name **Security Management**.
7. Right-click C:\Users\Administrator\Documents\Security\Templates and choose New Template.
8. Type **DC Remote Desktop** and click OK.
9. Expand DC Remote Desktop\Local Policies\User Rights Assignment.
10. In the details pane, double-click Allow Log On Through Terminal Services.
11. Select Define These Policy Settings In The Template.
12. Click Add User Or Group.
13. Type **CONTOSO\SYS_DC Remote Desktop** and click OK.
14. Click OK.
15. Right-click DC Remote Desktop and choose Save.

▶ **Exercise 3 Use the Security Configuration and Analysis Snap-in**

In this exercise, you will analyze the configuration of SERVER01, using the DC Remote Desktop security template to identify discrepancies between the server's current configuration and the desired configuration defined in the template. You will then create a new security template.

1. Log on to SERVER01 as Administrator. Open the Security Management console you created and saved in Exercise 2, "Create a Security Template."
2. Choose Add/Remove Snap-in from the File menu.
3. Select Security Configuration And Analysis from the Available Snap-ins list and click the Add button. Click OK.

4. Choose Save from the File menu to save the modified console.

5. Select the Security Configuration And Analysis console tree node.

6. Right-click the same node and choose Open Database.

    The *Open Database* command enables you to create a new security database.

7. Type **SERVER01Test** and click Open.

    The Import Template dialog box appears.

8. Select the DC Remote Desktop template you created in Exercise 2 and click Open.

9. Right-click Security Configuration And Analysis and choose Analyze Computer Now.

10. Click OK to confirm the default path for the error log.

11. Expand Local Policies and select User Rights Assignment.

12. Notice that the Allow Log On Through Terminal Services policy is flagged with a red circle and an X. This indicates a discrepancy between the database setting and the computer setting.

13. Double-click Allow Log On Through Terminal Services.

14. Notice the discrepancies. The computer is not configured to allow the SYS_DC Remote Desktop Users group to log on through Terminal Services

15. Notice also that the Computer Setting currently allows Administrators to log on through Terminal Services. This is an important setting that should be incorporated into the database.

16. Click the check box next to Administrators under Database Setting, and then click OK. This will add the right for Administrators to log on through Terminal Services to the database. It does not change the template, and it does not affect the current configuration of the computer.

17. Right-click Security Configuration And Analysis and choose Save.

    This saves the security database, which includes the settings imported from the template plus the change you made to allow Administrators to log on through Terminal Services. The hint displayed in the status bar when you choose the *Save* command suggests that you are saving the template. That is incorrect. You are saving the database.

18. Right-click Security Configuration And Analysis and choose Export Template.

19. Select DC Remote Desktop and click Save.

    You have now replaced the template created in Exercise 2 with the settings defined in the database of the Security Configuration and Analysis snap-in.

20. Close and reopen your Security Management console.

    This is necessary to refresh fully the settings shown in the Security Templates snap-in.

21. Expand C:\Users\Administrator\Documents\Security\Templates\DC Remote Desktop \Local Policies\User Rights Assignment.

22. In the details pane, double-click Allow Log On Through Terminal Services.

23. Notice that both the Administrators and SYS_DC Remote Desktop groups are allowed to log on through Terminal Services in the security template.

24. Right-click Security Configuration And Analysis and choose Configure Computer Now.

25. Click OK to confirm the error log path.

    The settings in the database are applied to the server. You will now confirm that the change to the user right was applied.

26. Open the Local Security Policy console from the Administrative Tools folder.

    If the console was already open during this exercise, right-click Security Settings and choose Reload.

27. Expand Security Settings\Local Policies\User Rights Assignment. Double-click Allow Log On Through Terminal Services.

28. Confirm that both Administrators and SYS_DC Remote Desktop are listed.

    The Local Security Policy console displays the actual, current settings of the server.

▶ **Exercise 4   Use the Security Configuration Wizard**

In this exercise, you will use the Security Configuration Wizard to create a security policy for domain controllers in the *contoso.com* domain based on the configuration of SERVER01.

1. Log on to SERVER01 as Administrator.

2. Open the Security Configuration Wizard from the Administrative Tools folder.

3. Click Next.

4. Select Create A New Security Policy and click Next.

5. Accept the default server name, SERVER01, and click Next.

6. On the Processing Security Configuration Database page, you can optionally click View Configuration Database and explore the configuration that was discovered on SERVER01.

7. Click Next and, on the Role Based Service Configuration section introduction page, click Next.

8. On the Select Server Roles, Select Client Features, Select Administration And Other Options, Select Additional Services, and Handling Unspecified Services pages, you can optionally explore the settings that were discovered on SERVER01, but do not change any settings. Click Next on each page.

9. On the Confirm Service Changes page, click the View drop-down list and choose All Services. Examine the settings in the Current Startup Mode column, which reflect service startup modes on SERVER01, and compare them to the settings in the Policy Startup Mode column. Click the View drop-down list and choose Changed Services. Click Next.

10. On the Network Security section introduction page, click Next.

11. On the Network Security Rules page, you can optionally examine the firewall rules derived from the configuration of SERVER01. Do not change any settings. Click Next.

12. On the Registry Settings section introduction page, click Next.

13. Click through each page of the Registry Settings section. Examine the settings, but do not change any of them. When the Registry Settings Summary page appears, examine the settings and click Next.

14. On the Audit Policy section introduction page, click Next.

15. On the System Audit Policy page, examine but do not change the settings. Click Next.

16. On the Audit Policy Summary page, examine the settings in the Current Setting and Policy Setting columns. Click Next.

17. On the Save Security Policy section introduction page, click Next.

18. In the Security Policy File Name text box, type **DC Security Policy**.

19. Click Include Security Templates.

20. Click Add.

21. Browse to locate the DC Remote Desktop template created in Exercise 3, "Use the Security Configuration And Analysis Snap-In," located in your Documents\Security\Templates folder. When you have located and selected the template, click Open.

22. Click OK to close the Include Security Templates dialog box.

23. Click View Security Policy to examine the settings in the security policy. You will be prompted to confirm the use of the ActiveX control; click Yes. Close the window after you have examined the policy, and then click Next in the Security Configuration Wizard window.

24. Accept the Apply Later default setting and click Next.

25. Click Finish.

▶ **Exercise 5   Transform a Security Configuration Wizard Security Policy to a Group Policy**

In this exercise, you will convert the security policy generated in Exercise 4, "Use the Security Configuration Wizard," to a GPO, which could then be deployed to computers by using Group Policy.

1. Log on to SERVER01 as Administrator.

2. Open the command prompt.

3. Type **cd c:\windows\security\msscw\policies** and press Enter.

4. Type **scwcmd transform /?** and press Enter.

5. Type **scwcmd transform /p:"DC Security Policy.xml" /g:"DC Security Policy"** and press Enter.

6. Open the Group Policy Management console from the Administrative Tools folder.

7. Expand the console tree nodes Forest, Domains, *contoso.com*, and Group Policy Objects.

8. Select DC Security Policy.

   This is the GPO created by the *Scwcmd.exe* command.

9. Click the Settings tab to examine the settings of the GPO.

10. Click the Show link next to Security Settings.

11. Click the Show link next to Local Policies / User Rights Assignment.

12. Confirm that the BUILTIN\Administrators and CONTOSO\SYS_DC Remote Desktop groups are given the Allow Log On Through Terminal Services user right.

    The GPO is not applied to DCs because it is not linked to the Domain Controllers OU. In this practice, do not link the GPO to the domain, site, or any OU. In a production environment, you would spend more time examining, configuring, and testing security settings in the security policy before deploying it as a GPO to production domain controllers.

Lesson Summary

- Security settings can be configured using the local GPO on an individual computer. The local GPO can be edited using the Group Policy Object Editor snap-in or the Local Security Policy console.

- Security settings can be defined in a security template with the Security Templates snap-in. Security templates can define a large number of security-related settings.

- Security templates can be used by the Security Configuration and Analysis snap-in to create a database. The snap-in can then analyze the configuration of a system for discrepancies between the computer's current settings and those specified in the database. The snap-in can also apply the database settings to the computer or export the database settings to a security template.

- *Secedit.exe* is the command-line tool that performs and extends the functionality of the Security Configuration and Analysis snap-in.

- Security policies are collections of settings created by the Security Configuration Wizard that define service startup modes, firewall rules, certain registry settings, and audit policies. The Security Configuration Wizard creates security policies based on the roles of a server.

- A security policy can incorporate the settings in a security template. In the event of conflicting settings, the settings in the security policy take precedence.

- *Scwcmd.exe* is the command-line tool that performs and extends the functionality of the Security Configuration Wizard.

- You can import a security template into a GPO.

- You can use *Scwcmd.exe transform* to convert a security policy into a GPO.

Lesson Review

You can use the following questions to test your knowledge of the information in Lesson 2, "Managing Security Settings." The questions are also available on the companion CD if you prefer to review them in electronic form.

NOTE Answers

Answers to these questions and explanations of why each answer choice is right or wrong are located in the "Answers" section at the end of the book.

---

1. You want to deploy security settings to multiple servers by using Group Policy. The settings need to apply the user rights that you have configured and validated on a server in your test environment. Which tool should you use?

    A. Local Security Policy

    B. Security Configuration And Analysis

    C. Security Configuration Wizard

    D. Security Templates

2. You want to deploy security settings to multiple servers by using Group Policy. The settings need to configure services, firewall rules, and audit policies appropriate for servers in your enterprise that act as file and print servers. Which tool would be the best choice for you to use?

    A. Local Security Policy

    B. Security Configuration And Analysis

    C. Security Configuration Wizard

    D. Security Templates

3. You created a security policy by using the Security Configuration Wizard. Now you want to deploy the settings in that security policy to the servers in your Servers OU. Which of the following steps are required? (Choose two. Each correct answer is a part of the solution.)

    A. Use *Scwcmd.exe /transform*.

    B. Create a Group Policy Object in the Group Policy Objects container.

    C. Right-click the Security Settings node of a GPO and choose Import.

    D. Link the GPO to the Servers OU.

Lesson 3: Managing Software with Group Policy Software Installation

You might be aware of several tools that can be used to deploy software within an organization, including Microsoft System Center Configuration Manager (Configuration Manager) and its predecessor, Microsoft Systems Management Server (SMS). Although these tools provide great benefits, including features to meter software use and inventory systems, you can effectively deploy most software without these tools, using only Group Policy software installation (GPSI).

After this lesson, you will be able to:
- Deploy software using GPSI to computers and users.
- Remove software installed originally with GPSI.

Estimated lesson time: 45 minutes

Understanding Group Policy Software Installation

Group Policy software installation (GPSI) is used to create a managed software environment that has the following characteristics:

- Users have access to the applications they need to do their jobs, no matter which computer they log on to.
- Computers have the required applications, without intervention from a technical support representative.
- Applications can be updated, maintained, or removed to meet the needs of the organization.

The software installation extension is one of the many client-side extensions (CSEs) that support change and configuration management using Group Policy. CSEs were discussed in Chapter 6. The extension enables you to manage the initial deployment, the upgrades, and the removal of software centrally. All configuration of the software deployment is managed within a GPO, using procedures detailed later in this lesson.

Windows Installer Packages

GPSI uses the Windows Installer service to install, maintain, and remove software. The Windows Installer service manages software, using information contained in the application's Windows Installer package. The Windows Installer package is in a file with an .msi extension that describes the installed state of the application. The package contains explicit instructions regarding the installation and removal of an application. You can customize Windows Installer packages by using one of the following types of files:

- **Transform (.mst) files**   These files provide a means for customizing the installation of an application. Some applications provide wizards or templates that permit a user to create transforms. For example, Adobe provides an enterprise deployment tool for Adobe Acrobat Reader that generates a transform. Many enterprises use the transform to configure agreement with the end user license agreement and to disable certain features of the application such as automatic updates that involve access to the Internet.

- **Patch (.msp) files**   These files are used to update an existing .msi file for security updates, bug fixes, and service packs. An .msp file provides instructions about applying the updated files and registry keys in the software patch, service pack, or software update. For example, updates to Microsoft Office 2003 and later are provided as .msp files.

NOTE   Installation of .msp and .mst files

You cannot deploy .mst or .msp files alone. They must be applied to an existing Windows Installer package.

GPSI can make limited use of non-MSI application files (.zap file), also known as down-level application packages, that specify the location of the software distribution point (SDP) and the setup command. See knowledge base article 231747 at *http://support.microsoft.com/?kbid= 231747* for details. Most organizations do not use .zap files, however, because the installation of the application requires the user to have administrative privileges on the system. When GPSI installs an application by using a Windows Installer package, the user does not require administrative privileges, allowing for a more secure enterprise.

NOTE   GPSI and Windows Installer packages

GPSI can fully manage applications only if the applications are deployed using Windows Installer packages. Other tools, including Configuration Manager and SMS, can manage applications that use other deployment mechanisms.

The .msi file, transforms, and other files required to install an application are stored in a shared SDP.

Software Deployment Options

You can deploy software by assigning applications to users or computers or by publishing applications for users. You *assign* required or mandatory software to users or to computers. You *publish* software that users might find useful in performing their jobs.

Exam Tip   Know the difference between assigning applications and publishing applications.

Assigning Applications   When you assign an application to a user, the application's local registry settings, including filename extensions, are updated and its shortcuts are created on the Start menu or desktop, thus advertising the availability of the application. The application advertisement follows the user regardless of which physical computer he or she logs on to. This application is installed the first time the user activates the application on the computer, either by selecting the application on the Start menu or by opening a document associated with the application. When you assign an application to the computer, the application is installed during the computer's startup process.

Publishing Applications   When you publish an application to users, the application does not appear as if it is installed on the users' computers. No shortcuts are visible on the desktop or Start menu. Instead, the application appears as an available application for the user to install using Add Or Remove Programs in Control Panel on a Windows XP system or in Programs And Features on a Windows Server 2008 and Windows Vista system. Additionally, the application can be installed when a user opens a file type associated with the application. For example, if Acrobat Reader is advertised to users, it will be installed if a user opens a file with a .pdf extension.

Given that applications can be either assigned or published and targeted to users or computers, you can establish a workable combination to meet your software management goals. Table 7-1 details the different software deployment options.

Table 7-1   Software Deployment Options

	Publish (User Only)	**Assign (User)**	**Assign (Computer)**
After deployment of the GPO, the software is available for installation:	The next time a user logs on.	The next time a user logs on.	The next time the computer starts.
Typically, the user installs the software from:	The Control Panel Add Or Remove Programs (Windows XP) or Programs And Features (Windows Server 2008 and Windows Vista) applications.	Start menu or desktop shortcut. An application can also be configured to install automatically at logon.	The software is installed automatically when the computer starts up.
If the software is not installed and the user opens a file associated with the software, does the software install?	Yes (if auto-install is enabled).	Yes.	Does not apply; the software is already installed.

Table 7-1 **Software Deployment Options**

	Publish (User Only)	**Assign (User)**	**Assign (Computer)**
Can the user remove the software by using Control Panel?	Yes, and the user can choose to install it again from Control Panel.	Yes, and the software is available for installation again from the Start menu shortcuts or file associations.	No. Only a local administrator can remove the software; a user can run a repair on the software.
Supported installation files:	Windows Installer packages (.msi files), .zap files.	Windows Installer packages (.msi files).	Windows Installer packages (.msi files).

Quick Check

- You want to use GPSI to deploy an administrative tool so that it is available for administrators on any system to which they log on. You do not want the tool to install automatically because administrators do not need the tool on each computer, but you want the tool to be easily installed. Should you publish or assign the application? Describe how an administrator will install the tool.

Quick Check Answer

- Publish the application. An administrator will use the Programs And Features Control Panel application on a Windows Server 2008 and Windows Vista system or Add/Remove Programs on a Windows XP system to install the application.

Preparing an SDP

Now that you understand GPSI at a high level, you are ready to prepare the SDP. The SDP is simply a shared folder from which users and computers can install applications. Create a shared folder and create a separate folder for each application. Then copy the software package, modifications, and all other necessary files to the application folders. Set appropriate permissions on the folders that allow users or computers Read And Execute permission—the minimum permission required to install an application successfully from the SDP. The administrators of the SDP must be able to change and delete files to maintain the SDP over time.

Creating a Software Deployment GPO

To create a software deployment GPO, use the Group Policy Management console to create a new GPO or select an existing GPO. Edit the GPO, using Group Policy Management Editor. Expand the console nodes User Configuration\Policies\Software Settings\Software Installation. Alternatively, select the Software Installation node in the Computer Configuration branch. Right-click Software Installation, choose New, and then select Package. Browse to locate the .msi file for the application. Click Open. The Deploy Software dialog box appears, shown in Figure 7-12. Select Published, Assigned, or Advanced. You cannot publish an application to computers, so the option will not be available if you are creating the package in the Software Installation node in Computer Configuration.

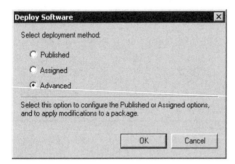

Figure 7-12   The Deploy Software dialog box

The Advanced option enables you to specify whether the application is published or assigned and gives you the opportunity to configure advanced properties of the software package. Therefore, it is recommended that you choose Advanced. The package properties dialog box then appears. Among the more important properties that you can configure are the following choices:

- **Deployment Type**   On the Deployment tab, configure Published or Assigned.
- **Deployment Options**   Based on the selected deployment type, different choices will appear in the Deployment Options section. These options, along with other settings on the Deployment tab, manage the behavior of the application installation.
- **Uninstall This Application When It Falls Out Of The Scope Of Management**   If this option is selected, the application will be automatically removed when the GPO no longer applies to the user or computer.
- **Upgrades**   On the Upgrades tab, you can specify the software that this package will upgrade. Upgrades are discussed in the "Maintaining Applications Deployed with Group Policy" section later in this lesson.
- **Categories**   The Categories tab enables you to associate the package with one or more categories. Categories are used when an application is published to a user. When the user goes to Control Panel to install a program, applications published using GPSI are presented in groups based on these categories.

    To create categories that are available to associate with packages, right-click Software Installation and choose Properties; then click the Categories tab.

- **Modifications**   If you have a transform (.mst file) that customizes the package, click the Add button to associate the transform with the package. Most tabs in the package Properties dialog box are available for you to change settings at any time. However, the Modifications tab is available only when you create the new package and choose the Advanced option shown in Figure 7-12.

Managing the Scope of a Software Deployment GPO

After you have created a software deployment GPO, you can scope the GPO to distribute the software to appropriate computers or users. In many software management scenarios, applications should be assigned to computers rather than to users. This is because most software licenses allow an application to be installed on one computer, and if the application is assigned to a user, the application will be installed on each computer to which the user logs on.

As you learned in Chapter 6, you can scope a GPO by linking the GPO to an OU or by filtering the GPO so that it applies only to a selected global security group. Many organizations have found that it is easiest to manage software by linking an application's GPO to the domain and filtering the GPO with a global security group that contains the users and computers to which the application should be deployed. For example, a GPO that deploys the XML Notepad tool (available from the Microsoft downloads site at *http://www.microsoft.com/downloads*) would be linked to the domain and filtered with a group containing developers that require the tool. The group would have a descriptive name that indicates its purpose to manage the deployment of XML Notepad—*APP_XML Notepad*, for example.

Exam Tip   On the 70-640 exam, you are likely to encounter questions that present software installation scenarios but are in fact testing your knowledge of how to scope a GPO effectively. As you read questions on the exam, try to identify what knowledge the question is really targeting.

Maintaining Applications Deployed with Group Policy

After a computer has installed an application by using the Windows Installer package specified by a GPO, the computer will not attempt to reinstall the application at each Group Policy refresh. There might be scenarios in which you want to force systems to reinstall the application. For example, small changes might have been made to the original Windows Installer package. To redeploy an application deployed with Group Policy, right-click the package in the GPO, choose All Tasks, and then select Redeploy Application.

You can also upgrade an application that has been deployed with GPSI. Create a package for the new version of the application in the Software Installation node of the GPO. The package can be in the same GPO as the package for the previous version or in any different GPO. Right-click the package and choose Properties. Click the Upgrades tab, and then click the Add button. The Add Upgrade Package dialog box appears, shown in Figure 7-13.

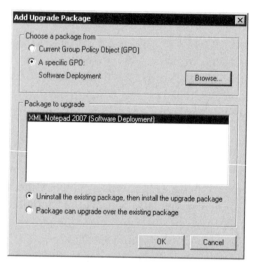

Figure 7-13   The Add Upgrade Package dialog box

Select whether the package for the previous version of the application is in the current GPO or in another GPO. If the previous package is in another GPO, click the Browse button to select that GPO. Then select the package from the Package To Upgrade list. Based on your knowledge of the application's upgrade behavior, choose one of the upgrade options shown at the bottom of Figure 7-13. Then click OK.

You can also remove an application that was deployed with GPSI. To do so, right-click the package, choose All Tasks, and then select Remove. In the Remove Software dialog box, choose one of the following two options:

- **Immediately Uninstall The Software From Users And Computers**   This option, known as *forced removal*, causes computers to remove the application. The software installation extension will remove an application when the computer restarts if the application was deployed with a package in the Computer Configuration portion of the GPO. If the package is in the User Configuration portion, the application will be uninstalled the next time the user logs on.

- **Allows Users To Continue To Use The Software, But Prevents New Installations**   This setting, known as *optional removal*, causes the software installation extension to avoid adding the package to systems that do not yet have the package installed. Computers that had previously installed the application do not forcibly uninstall the application, so users can continue using it.

If you use one of these two options to remove software using GPSI, it is important that you allow the settings in the GPO to propagate to all computers within the scope of the GPO before you delete, disable, or unlink the GPO. Clients need to receive this setting that specifies forced or optional removal. If the GPO is deleted or no longer applied before all clients have received this setting, the software is not removed according to your instructions. This is particularly important in environments with mobile users on laptop computers that might not connect to the network on a regular basis.

If, when creating the software package, you chose the Uninstall This Application When It Falls Out Of The Scope Of Management option, you can simply delete, disable, or unlink the GPO, and the application will be forcibly removed by all clients that have the installed package with that setting.

GPSI and Slow Links

When a client performs a Group Policy refresh, it tests the performance of the network to determine whether it is connected using a slow link defined by default as 500 kilobits per second (kbps). Each client-side extension is configured to process Group Policy or to skip the application of settings on a slow link. By default, GPSI does not process Group Policy settings over a slow link because the installation of software over a slow link could cause significant delays.

You can change the slow link policy processing behavior of each client-side extension, using policy settings located in Computer Configuration\Policies\Administrative Templates\System\Group Policy. For example, you could modify the behavior of the software installation extension so that it does process policies over a slow link.

You can also change the connection speed threshold that constitutes a slow link. By configuring a low threshold for the connection speed, you can convince the client-side extensions that a connection is not a slow link, even if it actually is. There are separate Group Policy Slow Link Detection policy settings for computer policy processing and user policy processing. The policies are in the Administrative Templates\System\Group Policy folders in Computer Configuration and User Configuration.

PRACTICE Managing Software with Group Policy Software Installation

In this practice, you will install, upgrade, and remove software, using GPSI. You will practice software management by using XML Notepad, a simple XML editor available from the Microsoft downloads site. To perform this practice, you must complete the following preparatory steps:

- Create a first-level OU named **Groups** and, within that OU, create an OU called **Applications**.
- In the Applications OU, create a global security group named **APP_XML Notepad** to represent the users and computer to which XML Notepad is deployed.
- Create a folder named **Software** on the C drive of SERVER01. Within that folder, create a folder named **XML Notepad**. In the XML Notepad folder, give the APP_XML Notepad

group Read And Execute permission. Share the Software folder with the share name Software and grant the Everyone group the Allow Full Control share permission.

■ Download XML Notepad from the Microsoft downloads site at *http://www.microsoft.com /downloads*. Save it to the Software\XML Notepad folder. Make a note of the version you have downloaded. At the time of writing this chapter, the current version is XML Notepad 2007.

▶ **Exercise 1   Create a Software Deployment GPO**

In this exercise, you will create a GPO that deploys XML Notepad to developers who require the application.

1. Log on to SERVER01 as Administrator.
2. Open the Group Policy Management console.
3. Right-click the Group Policy Objects container and choose New.
4. In the Name box, type the name of the application, for example **XML Notepad**, and then click OK.
5. Right-click the XML Notepad GPO and choose Edit.
6. Expand User Configuration\Policies\Software Settings.
7. Right-click Software Installation, choose New, and then select Package.
8. In the File Name text box, type the network path to the software distribution folder, for example, **\\server01\software**; select the Windows Installer package, for example, XmlNotepad.msi; and then click Open.
9. In the Deploy Software dialog box, select Advanced and click OK.
10. On the General tab, note that the name of the package includes the version, for example, XML Notepad 2007.
11. Click the Deployment tab.
12. Select Assigned.
13. Select the Install This Application At Logon check box.
14. Select Uninstall This Application When It Falls Out Of The Scope Of Management.
15. Click OK.
16. Close Group Policy Management Editor.
17. In the Group Policy Management console, select the XML Notepad GPO in the Group Policy Objects container.
18. Click the Scope tab.
19. In the Security Filtering section, select Authenticated Users and click Remove. Click OK to confirm your action.
20. Click the Add button.

21. Type the name of the group that represents users and computers to which the application should be deployed, for example **APP_XML Notepad**.

22. Click OK.

    The GPO is now filtered to apply only to the APP_XML Notepad group. However, the GPO settings will not apply until it is linked to an OU, to a site, or to the domain.

23. Right-click the domain, *contoso.com*, and choose Link An Existing GPO.

24. Select XML Notepad from the Group Policy Objects list and click OK.

    You can optionally test the GPO by adding the Administrator account to the APP_XML Notepad group. Log off and then log on. XML Notepad will be installed when you log on.

▶ **Exercise 2   Upgrade an Application**

In this exercise, you will simulate deploying an upgraded version of XML Notepad.

1. Log on to SERVER01 as Administrator.

2. Open the Group Policy Management console.

3. Right-click the XML Notepad GPO in the Group Policy Objects container and choose Edit.

4. Expand User Configuration\Policies\Software Settings.

5. Right-click Software Installation, choose New, and then select Package.

6. In the File Name text box, enter the network path to the software distribution folder, for example, **\\server01\software**; select the .msi file name; and click Open.

    This exercise will use the existing XmlNotepad.msi file as if it is an updated version of XML Notepad.

7. Click Open.

8. In the Deploy Software dialog box, select Advanced and click OK.

9. On the General tab, change the name of the package to suggest that it is the next version of the application, for example, **XML Notepad 2008**.

10. Click the Deployment tab.

11. Select Assigned.

12. Select the Install This Application At Logon check box.

13. Click the Upgrades tab.

14. Click the Add button.

15. Select the Current Group Policy Object (GPO) option.

16. In the Package To Upgrade list, select the package for the simulated earlier version, XML Notepad 2007, for example.

17. Select Uninstall The Existing Package, and then select Then Install The Upgrade Package.

18. Click OK.

19. Click OK again.

If this were an actual upgrade, the new package would upgrade the previous version of the application as clients applied the XML Notepad GPO. Because this is only a simulation of an upgrade, you can remove the simulated upgrade package.

20. Right-click the package that you just created to simulate an upgrade, choose All Tasks, and then select Remove.

21. In the Remove Software dialog box, select the Immediately Uninstall The Software From Users And Computers option.

22. Click OK.

Lesson Summary

- Group Policy Software Installation (GPSI) can be used to deploy, maintain, upgrade, and remove software.

- You can assign a software package in the Computer Configuration portion of a GPO. Client computers within the scope of the GPO will install the application at startup.

- You can assign a software package in the User Configuration portion of a GPO. The application will be installed when a user launches the application by using a shortcut in the Start menu or opens a file type associated with the application. You can optionally configure a user assigned application to install at logon.

- You can publish a software package in the User Configuration portion of a GPO. The application will be advertised in the Programs And Features Control Panel application on Windows Server 2008 and Windows Vista clients and in the Add/Remove Programs Control Panel application on Windows XP clients.

- Transforms (.mst files) can be used to modify the behavior of a Windows Installer package deployed using GPSI.

- Applications managed using GPSI can be redeployed or removed by the software installation extension.

- A software package can be configured to upgrade other applications deployed using GPSI.

- GPSI settings are not applied when a slow link is detected.

Lesson Review

You can use the following questions to test your knowledge of the information in Lesson 3, "Managing Software with Group Policy Software Installation." The questions are also available on the companion CD if you prefer to review them in electronic form.

NOTE   Answers

Answers to these questions and explanations of why each answer choice is right or wrong are located in the "Answers" section at the end of the book.

1. You want to deploy an application by using Group Policy to client computers in the headquarters and in a branch office. The branch office is connected to the headquarters with a wide area network connection that is 364 kbps. What steps must you take to deploy the software? (Choose two. Each correct answer is part of the solution.)

    A. Create a GPO that applies to all client computers in the headquarters and branch office. In the GPO, create a software package in the User Configuration node that assigns the application.

    B. Create a GPO that applies to all client computers in the headquarters and branch office. In the GPO, create a software package in the Computer Configuration node that assigns the application.

    C. In a GPO that applies to all computers, configure the slow link detection policy connection speed in the User Configuration node to 256 kbps.

    D. In a GPO that applies to computers in the branch office, configure the slow link detection policy connection speed in the Computer Configuration node to 256 kbps.

    E. In a GPO that applies to computers in the branch office, configure the slow link detection policy connection speed in the Computer Configuration node to 1,000 kbps.

2. In your domain, the Employees OU contains all user accounts. Each site has an OU within which a Sales OU contains accounts for the computers in the Sales department at that site. You want to deploy an application so that it is available to all users in the organization's Sales departments. Which methods can you use? (Choose all that apply.)

    A. Create a GPO linked to the domain. Create a group containing all Sales users. Filter the GPO so that it applies only to the group. In the GPO's User Configuration policies, create a software package that assigns the application.

    B. Create a GPO linked to each site's Sales OU. In the GPO's User Configuration policies, create a software package that assigns the application.

    C. Create a GPO linked to the domain. Create a group containing all Sales users. Filter the GPO so that it applies only to the group. In the GPO's Computer Configuration policies, create a software package that assigns the application.

    D. Create a GPO linked to each site's Sales OU. In the GPO User Configuration policies, create a software package that assigns the application. In the GPO's Computer Configuration, enable loopback policy processing in merge mode.

3. Your organization consists of ten branch offices. Within your Active Directory, an Employees OU is divided into ten child OUs containing user accounts at each branch office. You want to deploy an application to users at four branches. The application should be fully installed before the user opens the application for the first time. Which steps should you take? (Choose four. Each correct answer is a part of the solution.)

   A. Create a software deployment GPO linked to the Employees OU.

   B. Create a package in the User Configuration polices that publishes the application.

   C. Select the Install This Application At Logon deployment option.

   D. Create a shadow group that includes the users in the four branches. Filter the software deployment GPO so that it applies only to the shadow group.

   E. Create a package in the User Configuration policies that assigns the application.

   F. Select the Required Upgrade For Existing Packages option.

Lesson 4: Auditing

Auditing is an important component of security. Auditing logs specified activities in your enterprise to the Windows Security log, which you can then monitor to understand those activities and to identify issues that warrant further investigation. Auditing can log successful activities to provide documentation of changes. It can also log failed and potentially malicious attempts to access enterprise resources. Auditing involves up to three management tools: audit policy, auditing settings on objects, and the Security log. In this lesson, you will learn how to configure auditing to address several common scenarios.

After this lesson, you will be able to:
- Configure audit policy.
- Configure auditing settings on file system and directory service objects.
- Implement Windows Server 2008 new Directory Service Changes auditing.
- View the Security log, using the Event Viewer snap-in.

Estimated lesson time: 45 minutes

Audit Policy

Audit Policy configures a system to audit categories of activities. If Audit Policy is not enabled, a server will not audit those activities. Figure 7-14 shows the Audit Policy node of a GPO expanded.

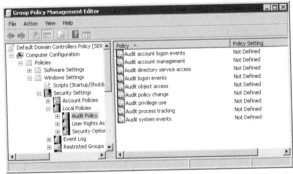

Figure 7-14   The Audit Policy node of a GPO

To configure auditing, you must define the policy setting. Double-click any policy setting and select the Define These Policy Settings check box. Then select whether to enable auditing of Success events, Failure events, or both. Table 7-2 defines each audit policy and its default settings on a Windows Server 2008 domain controller.

Table 7-2 **Audit Policies**

Audit Policy Setting	Explanation	Default Setting for Windows Server 2008 Domain Controllers
Audit Account Logon Events	Creates an event when a user or computer attempts to authenticate using an Active Directory account. For example, when a user logs on to any computer in the domain, an account logon event is generated.	Successful and failed account logons are audited.
Audit Logon Events	Creates an event when a user logs on interactively (locally) to a computer or over the network (remotely). For example, if a workstation and a server are configured to audit logon events, the workstation audits a user logging on directly to that workstation. When the user connects to a shared folder on the server, the server logs that remote logon. When a user logs on, the domain controller records a logon event because logon scripts and policies are retrieved from the DC.	Successful and failed logons are audited.
Audit Account Management	Audits events, including the creation, deletion, or modification of user, group, or computer accounts and the resetting of user passwords.	Successful account management activities are audited.
Audit Directory Service Access	Audits events that are specified in the system SACL, which is seen in an Active Directory object's Properties Advanced Security Settings dialog box. In addition to defining the audit policy with this setting, you must also configure auditing for the specific object or objects using the SACL of the object or objects. This policy is similar to the Audit Object Access policy used to audit files and folders, but this policy applies to Active Directory objects.	Successful directory service access events are audited, but few objects' SACLs specify audit settings. See the discussion in the "Auditing Directory Services Changes" section for more information.
Audit Policy Change	Audits changes to user rights assignment policies, audit policies, or trust policies.	Successful policy changes are audited.
Audit Privilege Use	Audits the use of a privilege or user right. See the explanatory text for this policy in Group Policy Management Editor (GPME).	No auditing is performed, by default.
Audit System Events	Audits system restart, shutdown, or changes that affect the system or security log.	Successful and failed system events are audited.

Table 7-2 **Audit Policies**

Audit Policy Setting	Explanation	Default Setting for Windows Server 2008 Domain Controllers
Audit Process Tracking	Audits events such as program activation and process exit. See the explanatory text for this policy in GPME.	Successful process tracking events are audited.
Audit Object Access	Audits access to objects such as files, folders, registry keys, and printers that have their own SACLs. In addition to enabling this audit policy, you must configure the auditing entries in objects' SACLs.	Successful object access events are audited.

Exam Tip   Microsoft certification exams often test your knowledge of audit policies at a high level. Commit the information in Table 7-2 to memory and you are likely to be able to answer one or more exam items correctly.

As you can see, most major Active Directory events are already audited by domain controllers, assuming that the events are successful. Therefore, the creation of a user, the resetting of a user's password, the logon to the domain, and the retrieval of a user's logon scripts are all logged.

However, not all failure events are audited by default. You might need to implement additional failure auditing based on your organization's IT security policies and requirements. Auditing failed account logon events, for example, will expose malicious attempts to access the domain by repeatedly trying to log on as a domain user account without yet knowing the account's password. Auditing failed account management events can reveal someone attempting to manipulate the membership of a security-sensitive group.

One of the most important tasks you must fulfill is to balance and align Audit Policy with your corporate policies and reality. Your corporate policy might state that all failed logons and successful changes to Active Directory users and groups must be audited. That's easy to achieve in Active Directory. But how, exactly, are you going to use that information? Verbose auditing logs are useless if you don't know how or don't have the tools to manage those logs effectively. To implement auditing, you must have the business requirement to audit, a well-configured audit policy, and the tools with which to manage audited events.

Auditing Access to Files and Folders

Many organizations elect to audit file system access to provide insight into resource usage and potential security issues. Windows Server 2008 supports granular auditing based on user or group accounts and the specific actions performed by those accounts. To configure auditing, you must complete three steps: specify auditing settings, enable audit policy, and evaluate events in the security log.

Specifying Auditing Settings on a File or Folder

You can audit access to a file or folder by adding auditing entries to its SACL. To access the SACL and its audit entries, open the Properties dialog box and click the Security tab. Then click the Advanced button and click the Auditing tab. The Advanced Security Settings dialog box of a folder named Confidential Data is shown in Figure 7-15.

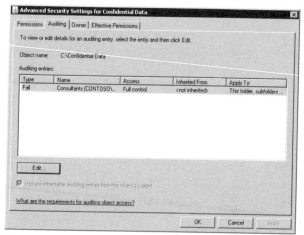

Figure 7-15   The Advanced Security Settings dialog box of a folder named Confidential Data

To add an entry, click the Edit button to open the Auditing tab in Edit mode. Click the Add button to select the user, group, or computer to audit. Then, in the Auditing Entry dialog box shown in Figure 7-16, indicate the type of access to audit.

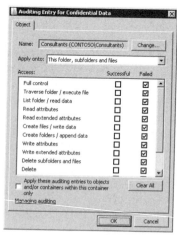

Figure 7-16   The Auditing Entry dialog box

You are able to audit for successes, failures, or both as the specified user, group, or computer attempts to access the resource by using one or more of the granular access levels.

You can audit successes for the following purposes:

- To log resource access for reporting and billing
- To monitor access that would suggest users are performing actions greater than what you had planned, indicating that permissions are too generous
- To identify access that is out of character for a particular account, which might be a sign that a user account has been breached by a hacker

Auditing failed events enables you:

- To monitor for malicious attempts to access a resource to which access has been denied.
- To identify failed attempts to access a file or folder to which a user does require access. This would indicate that the permissions are not sufficient to achieve a business requirement.

Auditing entries direct Windows to audit the successful or failed activities of a security principal (user, group, or computer) to use a specific permission. The example in Figure 7-15 audits for unsuccessful attempts by users in the Consultants group to access data in the Confidential Data folder at any level. It does that by configuring an auditing entry for Full Control access. Full Control includes all the individual access levels, so this entry covers any type of access. If a Consultant group member attempts access of any kind and fails, the activity will be logged.

Typically, auditing entries reflect the permission entries for the object. In other words, you would configure the Confidential Data folder with permissions that prevent members of the Consultants group from accessing its contents. You would then use auditing to monitor members of the Consultants group who nonetheless attempt to access the folder. Keep in mind, of course, that a member of the Consultants group can also belong to another group that does have permission to access the folder. Because that access will be successful, the activity is not logged. Therefore, if you really are concerned about keeping users out of a folder and making sure they do not access it in any way, monitor failed access attempts; however, also audit successful access to identify situations in which a user is accessing the folder through another group membership that is potentially incorrect.

NOTE Don't over-audit

Audit logs have the tendency to get quite large quite rapidly, so a golden rule for auditing is to configure the bare minimum required to achieve the business task. Specifying to audit the successes and failures on an active data folder for the Everyone group using Full Control (all permissions) would generate enormous audit logs that could affect the performance of the server and make locating a specific audited event all but impossible.

Enabling Audit Policy

Configuring auditing entries in the security descriptor of a file or folder does not, in itself, enable auditing. Auditing must be enabled by defining the Audit Object Access setting shown in Figure 7-17. After auditing is enabled, the security subsystem begins to pay attention to the audit settings and to log access as directed by those settings.

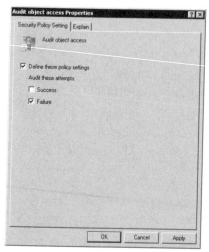

Figure 7-17   The Audit Object Access policy

The policy setting must be applied to the server that contains the object being audited. You can configure the policy setting in the server's local GPO or use a GPO scoped to the server.

You can define the policy then to audit Success events, Failure events, or both. The policy setting (shown in Figure 7-17) must specify auditing of Success or Failure attempts that match the type of auditing entry in the object's SACL (shown in Figure 7-16). For example, to log a failed attempt by a member of the Consultants group to access the Confidential Data folder, you must configure the Audit Object Access policy to audit failures, and you must configure the SACL of the Confidential Data folder to audit failures. If Audit Policy audits successes only, the failure entries in the folder's SACL will not trigger logging.

NOTE   Making sure Audit Policy matches auditing entries

Remember that access that is audited and logged is the combination of the audit entries on specific files and folders and the settings in Audit Policy. If you've configured audit entries to log failures, but the policy enables only logging for successes, your audit logs will remain empty.

Evaluating Events in the Security Log

After you have enabled the Audit Object Access policy setting and specified the access you want to audit, using object SACLs, the system will begin to log access according to the audit entries. You can view the resulting events in the Security log of the server. Open the Event Viewer console from Administrative Tools. Expand Windows Logs\Security.

Exam Tip   Auditing access to objects such as files and folders requires three components. First, the Audit Object Access policy must be enabled and configured to audit Success or Failure events as appropriate for the scenario. Second, the SACL of the object must be configured to audit successful or failed access. Third, you must examine the Security log. Audit Policy is often managed using a GPO, so the GPO must be scoped to apply to the server with the file or folder, which is usually a file server rather than a domain controller. Some exam questions that appear to be testing your knowledge of auditing are actually testing your ability to scope a GPO with Audit Policy to the correct servers.

Auditing Directory Service Changes

Just as the Audit Object Access policy enables you to log attempts to access objects such as files and folders, the Audit Directory Service Access policy enables you to log attempts to access objects in Active Directory. The same basic principles apply. You configure the policy to audit success or failure. You then configure the SACL of the Active Directory object to specify the types of access you want to audit.

As an example, if you want to monitor changes to the membership of a security-sensitive group such as Domain Admins, you can enable the Audit Directory Service Access policy to audit Success events. You can then open the SACL of the Domain Admins group and configure an auditing entry for successful modifications of the group's *member* attribute. You will do this in an exercise in this lesson's practice.

In Microsoft Windows Server 2003 and Windows 2000 Server, you could audit directory service access and you would be notified that an object, or the property of an object, had been changed, but you could not identify the previous and new values of the attribute that had changed. For example, an event could be logged indicating that a particular user changed the *member* attribute of Domain Admins, but you could not determine exactly what change was made.

Windows Server 2008 adds an auditing category called Directory Service Changes. The important distinction between Directory Service Changes and Directory Service Access is that with Directory Service Changes auditing, you can identify the previous and current values of a changed attribute.

Directory Service Changes is not enabled in Windows Server 2008 by default. Instead, Directory Service Access is enabled to mimic the auditing functionality of previous versions of Windows.

To enable auditing of successful Directory Service Changes, open a command prompt on a domain controller and type this command:

```
auditpol /set /subcategory:"directory service changes" /success:enable
```

Exam Tip   The *auditpol* command is used to enable auditing of directory service changes.

You must still modify the SACL of objects to specify which attributes should be audited. Although you can use the preceding command to enable Directory Service Changes auditing in a lab and explore the events that are generated, don't implement this in a domain until you've read the documentation on TechNet, starting with the step-by-step guide found at *http://technet2.microsoft.com/windowsserver2008/en/library/a9c25483-89e2-4202-881c-ea8e02b4b2a51033.mspx*.

When Directory Service Changes auditing is enabled, and auditing entries are configured in the SACL of directory service objects, events are logged to the Security log that clearly indicate the attribute that was changed and when the change was made. In most cases, event log entries will show the previous and current value of the changed attribute.

Quick Check

- You want to audit changes to properties of user accounts provided for temporary employees. When a change is made, you want to see the previous and new value of the changed attribute. What type of auditing do you perform?

Quick Check Answer

- Directory Services Changes auditing

PRACTICE Auditing

In this practice, you will configure auditing settings, enable audit policies for object access, and filter for specific events in the Security log. The business objective is to monitor a folder containing confidential data that should not be accessed by users in the Consultants group. You will also configure auditing to monitor changes to the membership of the Domain Admins group. To perform this practice, you must complete the following preparatory tasks:

- Create a folder called Confidential Data on the C drive.
- Create a global security group called Consultants.
- Add the Consultants group to the Print Operators group.
  This is a shortcut that will allow a user in the Consultants group to log on locally to SERVER01, which is a domain controller in this exercise.
- Create a user named James Fine and add the user to the Consultants group.

▶ **Exercise 1   Configure Permissions and Audit Settings**

In this exercise, you will configure permissions on the Confidential Data folder to deny access to consultants. You will then enable auditing of attempts by consultants to access the folder.

1. Log on to SERVER01 as Administrator.
2. Open the properties of the C:\Confidential Data folder and click the Security tab.
3. Click Edit.
4. Click Add.
5. Type **Consultants** and click OK.
6. Click the Deny check box for the Full Control permission.
7. Click Apply. Click Yes to confirm the use of a Deny permission.
8. Click OK to close the Permissions dialog box.
9. Click Advanced.
10. Click the Auditing tab.
11. Click Edit.
12. Click Add.
13. Type **Consultants** and click OK.
14. In the Auditing Entry dialog box, select the check box under Failed next to Full Control.
15. Click OK to close all dialog boxes.

▶ **Exercise 2   Enable Audit Policy**

Because SERVER01 is a domain controller, you will use the existing Domain Controller Security Policy GPO to enable auditing. On a standalone server, you would enable auditing by using Local Security Policy or a GPO scoped to the server.

1. Open the Group Policy Management console and select the Group Policy Objects container.
2. Right-click the Domain Controller Security Policy and choose Edit.
3. Expand Computer Configuration\Policies\Windows Settings\Security Settings\Local Policies\Audit Policy.
4. Double-click Audit Object Access.
5. Select Define These Policy Settings.
6. Select the Failure check box.
7. Click OK, and then close the console.
8. To refresh the policy and ensure that all settings have been applied, open a command prompt and type the command **gpupdate**.

▶ **Exercise 3   Generate Audit Events**

You will now attempt to access the Confidential Data folder as a member of the Consultants group.

1. Log on to SERVER01 as James Fine.
2. Open My Computer and browse to C:\Confidential Data. Attempt to open the folder.
3. Create a text file on your desktop and attempt to cut and paste the file into the Confidential Data folder.

▶ **Exercise 4   Examine the Security Log**

You can now view the attempts by a consultant to access the Confidential Data folder.

1. Log on to SERVER01 as Administrator.
2. Open Event Viewer from the Administrative Tools folder.
3. Expand Windows Logs\Security.
4. Which types of events do you see in the Security log? Remember that policies can enable auditing for numerous security-related actions, including directory service access, account management, logon, and more. Notice that the source of events indicated in the Source column is Microsoft Windows security auditing.
5. To filter the log and narrow the scope of your search, click the Filter Current Log link in the Actions pane.
6. Configure the filter to be as narrow as possible.

   What do you know about the event you are trying to locate? You know it occurred within the last hour, that the source is Microsoft Windows security auditing, and that it is a File System event.
7. Check your work by referring to Figure 7-18.

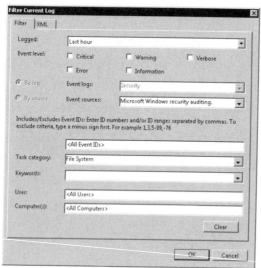

Figure 7-18   Filtering the Security Log for recent File System events

8. Click OK.

Can you more easily locate the events generated when James Fine attempted to access the Confidential Data folder?

You could not filter for the C:\Confidential Data folder name in the Filter dialog box shown in Figure 7-18. But you can locate events for that folder by exporting the file to a log analysis tool or even to a text file.

9. Click the Save Filter Log File As link in the Actions pane.

10. In the Save As dialog box, click the Desktop link in the Favorite Links pane.

11. Click the Save As Type drop-down list and choose Text.

12. In the File Name text box, type **Audit Log Export**.

13. Click Save.

14. Open the resulting text file in Notepad and search for instances of C:\Confidential Data.

▶ **Exercise 5   Use Directory Services Changes Auditing**

In this exercise, you will see the Directory Service Access auditing that is enabled by default in Windows Server 2008 and Windows Server 2003. You will then implement the new Directory Services Changes auditing of Windows Server 2008 to monitor changes to the Domain Admins group.

1. Open the Active Directory Users And Computers snap-in.

2. Click the View menu and ensure that Advanced Features is selected.

3. Select the Users container.

4. Right-click Domain Admins and choose Properties.

5. Click the Security tab, and then click Advanced.

6. Click the Auditing tab, and then click Add.

7. Type **Everyone**, and then click OK.

8. In the Auditing Entry dialog box, click the Properties tab.

9. Select the check box below Successful and next to Write Members.

10. Click OK.

11. Click OK to close the Advanced Security Settings dialog box.

   You have specified to audit any changes to the *member* attribute of the Domain Admins group. You will now make two changes to the group's membership.

12. Click the Members tab.

13. Add the user James Fine and click Apply.

14. Select James Fine, click Remove, and then click Apply.

15. Click OK to close the Domain Admins Properties dialog box.

16. Open the Security log and locate the events that were generated when you added and removed James Fine. The Event ID is 4662. Examine the information provided on the General tab.

You will be able to identify that a user (Administrator) accessed an object (Domain Admins) and used a Write Property access. The property itself is displayed as a globally unique identifier (GUID)—you cannot readily identify that the *member* attribute was changed. The event also does not detail the change that was made to the property.

You will now enable Directory Service Changes auditing, a new feature of Windows Server 2008.

17.   Open a command prompt and type the following command:

```
auditpol /set /subcategory:"directory service changes" /success:enable
```

18.   Open the properties of Domain Admins and add James Fine to the group.

19.   Return to the Event Viewer snap-in and refresh the view of the Security log. You should see both a Directory Service Access event (Event ID 5136) and a Directory Service Changes event (Event ID 5136). If you do not see the Directory Service Changes event, wait a few moments, and then refresh the view again. It can take a few seconds for the Directory Service Changes event to be logged.

20.   Examine the information in the Directory Service Changes event.

The information on the General tab clearly indicates that a user (Administrator) made a change to an object in the directory (Domain Admins) and that the specific change made was adding James Fine.

Lesson Summary

- Audit Policy defines whether success or failure events are audited. There are a number of audit policies related to specific types of activities such as account logon, object access, and directory service changes.

- To audit file system access, you must add auditing entries to the SACL of a file or folder, define the Audit Object Access policy setting, and evaluate resulting audit entries in the Security log.

- Windows Server 2008 enables a more detailed auditing of changes to objects in Active Directory. You can use the *Auditpol.exe* command to enable this new category of auditing. Events display the attribute that was changed and clearly indicate the type of change that was made or the previous and current value of the attribute.

Lesson Review

You can use the following questions to test your knowledge of the information in Lesson 4, "Auditing." The questions are also available on the companion CD if you prefer to review them in electronic form.

NOTE Answers

Answers to these questions and explanations of why each answer choice is right or wrong are located in the "Answers" section at the end of the book.

1. You are concerned that an individual is trying to gain access to computers by logging on with valid domain user names and a variety of attempted passwords. Which audit policy should you configure and monitor for such activities?

   A. Logon Event failures

   B. Directory Service Access failures

   C. Privilege Use successes

   D. Account Logon Event failures

   E. Account Management failures

2. You want to audit changes to attributes of user accounts used by administrators in your organization. When a change is made, you want to see both the previous and changed values of the attribute. What must you do to achieve your goal?

   A. Define Account Management audit policy.

   B. Use the *Auditpol.exe* command.

   C. Enable Privilege Use auditing.

   D. Define Directory Service Access audit policy.

3. Your organization includes 10 file servers, which have computer accounts in the Servers OU of your domain. A GPO named Server Configuration is linked to the Servers OU. On five of the servers, a folder called Confidential Data exists. You have hired a team of consultants to assist on a project, and you want to ensure that those consultants cannot access the Confidential Data folder. You configure permissions on the folder to prevent access by consultants, and you want to audit any attempt by consultants to open or manipulate the folder. Which steps must you take? (Choose three. Each correct answer is part of the solution.)

   A. Add audit entries to the Confidential Data folder to audit successful Full Control access.

   B. Evaluate entries in the Security logs on the domain controllers.

   C. Define the Audit Directory Service Access policy in the Server Configuration GPO.

   D. Define the Audit Object Access policy in the Default Domain Controllers GPO.

   E. Define the Audit Object Access policy in the Server Configuration GPO.

   F. Evaluate entries in the Security logs on each file server.

   G. Add audit entries to the Confidential Data folder to audit failed Full Control access.

Chapter Review

To further practice and reinforce the skills you learned in this chapter, you can perform the following tasks:

- Review the chapter summary.
- Review the list of key terms introduced in this chapter.
- Complete the case scenarios. These scenarios set up real-world situations involving the topics of this chapter and ask you to create a solution.
- Complete the suggested practices.
- Take a practice test.

Chapter Summary

- Group Policy can be used to configure the membership of groups, security settings, software management, and auditing.
- In addition to the Group Policy Management console and a Group Policy Management Editor, numerous tools affect Group Policy, including security templates, the Security Configuration Wizard, *Scwcmd.exe*, and *Auditpol.exe*.
- It is critical that you know how to scope GPOs effectively, both for the 70-640 exam and for the success of Group Policy in your enterprise.
- Restricted groups policies can add members to a group in a cumulative manner or can define the single, authoritative membership of a group.
- The new Security Configuration Wizard creates role-based security policies that can incorporate security templates managed by snap-ins that have existed in previous versions of Windows. The *Scwcmd.exe* command can transform a security policy into a GPO.
- Software can be assigned to users or computers or can be published to users for installation using Control Panel. Group Policy Software Installation can also manage the redeployment, upgrade, or removal of an application.
- Auditing file system access, directory service access, or directory service changes requires defining Audit Policy and auditing entries in the SACL of objects.

Key Terms

Use these key terms to understand better the concepts covered in this chapter.

- **audit policy**   A setting that configures the logging of security-related activities.

- **delegation**   An assignment of administrative responsibility. A grant of permission to perform an administrative task.

- **Extensible Markup Language (XML)**   An abbreviated version of the Standard Generalized Markup Language (SGML). XML enables the flexible development of user-defined document types and provides a nonproprietary, persistent, and verifiable file format for the storage and transmission of text and data both on and off the Internet.

- **firewall**   A hardware or software product designed to isolate a system or network from another network. Traditionally used to protect a private network from intrusion from the Internet, firewall technology is now included in Windows through Windows Firewall With Advanced Security. A firewall inspects inbound or outbound packets or both and determines, based on rules, which packets to allow to the other side of the firewall.

- **Lightweight Directory Access Protocol (LDAP)**   The primary access protocol for Active Directory. LDAP version 3 is defined by a set of Proposed Standard documents in Internet Engineering Task Force (IETF) RFC 2251.

- **local Group Policy object**   A Group Policy object (GPO) stored on each computer running Windows. Settings in a local GPO are overwritten by conflicting settings in Active Directory–based GPOs.

- **security template**   A collection of security-related configuration settings stored as a text file with a .inf extension. You can use the Security Configuration and Analysis snap-in to create a database based on the security template to analyze the compliance of a computer with the settings in the template or to apply the settings in the template to a computer.

- **service**   A process that performs a specific system function to support applications or other services. Some examples of services are Active Directory Domain Services, DFS Replication, Netlogon, Server, Task Scheduler, and Windows Event Log.

- **Windows Installer package (.msi file)**   A database that contains instructions about the installation and removal of one or more applications.

- **Windows Installer transform (.mst file)**   A file that customizes a Windows Installer package. Some applications support the use of transforms to automate or customize application installation. See Windows Installer package.

Case Scenarios

In the following case scenarios, you will apply what you've learned about managing security settings, Group Policy with software installation, and auditing. You can find answers to these questions in the "Answers" section at the end of this book.

Case Scenario 1: Software Installation with Group Policy Software Installation

You are an administrator at Contoso, Ltd. You will be deploying a new application to the users in your mobile sales force, and you would like to do so using Group Policy software installation (GPSI). In your Active Directory, all users are in the Employees OU, and all client computer accounts are in the Clients OU. The application is licensed per machine. When sales personnel are at the office, they log on to other systems such as computers in conference rooms. You want to ensure that the application is installed only on the sales force's desktops and laptops—not on other computers. You have created a transform that automates installation of the application's Windows Installer package.

1. Should the package for the application be created in the Computer Configuration node or User Configuration node of a GPO? Why?
2. When you create the package, should you choose Publish, Assign, or Advanced? Why?
3. How should you scope the GPO so that it applies only to the mobile sales force users?

Case Scenario 2: Security Configuration

You are an administrator at Contoso, Ltd. You maintain twenty servers for the Human Resources department—servers that are distributed across seven global sites. The Salaries folder is replicated to a server in each site. Because the folder contains highly sensitive information about employee compensation, you have been asked to secure it thoroughly and audit inappropriate attempts to access it. You have applied NTFS permissions that allow only appropriate HR personnel access to the Salaries folders—even the Administrators groups on the servers do not have access. Of course, members of a server's Administrators group can always take ownership of a resource and give themselves permissions, but that can be audited as well. To improve the security of these servers and their sensitive data further, you want to ensure that only your user account and that of the vice president of HR are administrators of the server—the vice president's account is to be used as a backup when you are not available. You want to deploy this configuration to all seven servers without having to reproduce each step manually. You are not delegated permissions to create or modify Group Policy objects in your organization.

1. You must audit inappropriate attempts to access the Salaries folder. You are also to audit any access to the folder by members of the Administrators group on the server, including attempts to take ownership of the folder. What auditing entries should you configure on the Salaries folder?

2. What policy setting should you configure to enforce the limited membership of the Administrators group? Can you remove the Administrator account with this policy?

3. Which audit policies should you configure?

4. How can you deploy this configuration to the seven servers without Group Policy?

5. Can policy settings in Active Directory–based GPOs override your settings? If so, how can you monitor the servers occasionally to ensure that your configuration is not being changed?

Suggested Practices

To help you successfully master the exam objectives presented in this chapter, complete the following tasks.

Restricted Groups

In this practice, you will create a best practices framework for the delegation of support for client computers. You will configure the Administrators group on client computers so that it includes the corporate Help Desk and a support group specific to a geographical site. Administrators will not include Domain Admins.

To perform this practice, you must have the following objects in the Active Directory domain:

- A first-level OU named Admins.
- Two child OUs in the Admins OU: Identities and Groups.
- A global security group named Help Desk in the Admins\ Admin Groups OU.
- A global security group named NYC Support in the Admins\ Admin Groups OU.
- One or more user accounts representing corporate help desk personnel in the Admins\Identities OU. These users are members of the Help Desk group.
- One or more users representing members of the New York desktop support team in the Admins\Identities OU. These users are members of the NYC Support group.
- A first-level OU named Clients.
- An OU named NYC in the Clients OU.
- A computer object named DESKTOP101 in the Clients\NYC OU.
- **Practice 1**   In this practice, you will create intermediate groups to manage the delegation of administration. Create two domain local security groups in the Admins\Groups OU: SYS_Clients_Admins and SYS_NYC_Admins. Add the Help Desk group as a member of SYS_Clients_Admins and add the NYC Support group as a member of SYS_NYC_Admins.
- **Practice 2**   Create a GPO that defines the membership of Administrators as *only* the SYS_Clients_Admins group. Refer to the steps in Exercise 2, "Delegate the Administration of a Subset of Clients in the Domain," of Lesson 1 if you need help. In this practice,

however, you must create a restricted groups policy for Administrators that uses the Members Of This Group setting and specifies SYS_Clients_Admins. Scope the GPO to apply to all computers in the Clients OU.

- **Practice 3**   This practice is identical to Exercise 3, "Confirm the Cumulative Application of Member Of Policies," of Lesson 1. Create a GPO that ensures that the SYS_NYC_Admins group is a member of Administrators. Create a restricted group policy for SYS_NYC_Admins that uses the This Group Is A Member Of setting and specifies Administrators. Scope the GPO to apply to all computers in the NYC OU.

- **Practice 4**   Use Resultant Set of Policy (RSoP) Modeling and verify that the Administrators group contains SYS_Clients_Admins and SYS_NYC_Admins. Refer to Exercise 3 in Lesson 1 for the required steps if you need assistance. If you have a test computer named DESKTOP101 joined to the domain, refer to Optional Exercise 4, "Confirm the Membership of the Administrators Group," in Lesson 1 for the required steps to log on and validate the membership of the Administrators group. On DESKTOP101, you will see that the Administrators group no longer includes Domain Admins.

This practice appears similar to the practice in Lesson 1, but it varies in two significant ways. First, Practice 2 uses the Members setting of a restricted groups policy, which has the effect of removing the Domain Admins group from the local Administrators group. This is a best practice because the Domain Admins group should be used only for directory service and domain controller–related administration, not for universal system support. Second, in Lesson 1, you used Group Policy to add the Help Desk and NYC Support groups directly to the Administrators group of clients. In this practice, you added the intermediate groups—SYS_Clients_Admins and SYS_NYC_Admins—to the Administrators group on client systems, so the help desk and NYC support teams are still members, but indirectly. The advantage of the indirect structure is that if other groups need to be members of the Administrators group, you do not need to change your policies and configuration—you simply add them to the domain local group. If, for example, you deploy an application that requires local administrative credentials on all clients, you do not need to touch each system, and you do not need to change your GPOs. You simply add the application's account to the SYS_Clients_Admins group. Similarly, if a team of auditors is assigned to examine all computers in New York, you add the team to the SYS_NYC_Admins group. No change to security configuration or GPOs is required.

Security Configuration

In this practice, you will implement a security configuration similar to that proposed in Case Scenario 2, "Security Configuration." Review Case Scenario 2 before proceeding. You will need the following objects in Active Directory to perform these practices:

- A first-level OU named Admins with a sub-OU named Admin Groups
- A group in the Admin Groups OU named HR Server Admins

- A first-level OU named Groups
- A group in the Groups OU named Human Resources

In addition, you will need a folder named Salaries on the C drive of SERVER01.

- **Practice 1**   In the Security Templates snap-in, create a new security template called **HR Server**. In the Local Policies\Audit Policy node, configure Audit Object Access to audit success and failure events and configure Audit Privilege Use to audit successes. In the Restricted Groups node, add a new restricted group policy for Administrators that defines Members Of This Group as HR Server Admins. In Active Directory Users And Computers, make a note of the current membership of the Administrators group (in the BUILTIN OU) so that you can restore the membership to this state after the practice. Save the template by right-clicking HR Server and choosing Save.

- **Practice 2**   Case Scenario 2 suggested that you would manually configure permissions and auditing entries on the Salaries folder. Windows provides file system policies that enable you to configure permissions and auditing entries through policies so that you do not have to do so manually and so that security can be reapplied and enforced through policy. In the HR Server security template, right-click the File System node and choose Add File. In the dialog box that appears, type **C:\Salaries** in the Folder text box and click OK. In the Database Security dialog box, remove all entries and add a permission for Human Resources that gives the group Full Control permission. That should be the only permission applied. Click the Advanced button and click the Auditing tab. Add an auditing entry for Everyone that audits failed full-control access. Add a second auditing entry for Administrators that audits successful full-control access. Click OK to close all dialog boxes, accepting all defaults that are presented. Save the template by right-clicking HR Server and choosing Save.

- **Practice 3**   In the Security Configuration And Analysis snap-in, open a new database named **HR Server Configuration**. Import the HR Server template you created in Practices 1 and 2. Right-click Security Configuration And Analysis and choose Analyze Computer Now. Click OK. Examine the three nodes of security settings that you modified: Audit Policy, Restricted Groups, and File System. Locate the discrepancies between the computer's current settings and the settings in the template.

- **Practice 4**   Right-click Security Configuration And Analysis and choose Configure Computer Now. Click OK. Confirm the changes that were made by examining the membership of the Administrators group in the BUILTIN OU and by examining the security and auditing settings on the C:\Salaries folder.

Be sure to reset the membership of the Administrators group to the original members you recorded in Practice 1. If you did not record the original membership of the group, make sure that Enterprise Admins and Domain Admins are members.

Take a Practice Test

The practice tests on this book's companion CD offer many options. For example, you can test yourself on just one exam objective, or you can test yourself on all the 70-640 certification exam content. You can set up the test so that it closely simulates the experience of taking a certification exam, or you can set it up in study mode so that you can look at the correct answers and explanations after you answer each question.

MORE INFO   **Practice tests**

For details about all the practice test options available, see the "How to Use the Practice Tests" section in this book's introduction.

Chapter 8
Authentication

When a user logs on to an Active Directory Domain Services (AD DS) domain, she enters her user name and password, and the client uses those credentials to *authenticate* the user—to validate the user's identity against her Active Directory account. In Chapter 3, "Users," you learned how to create and manage user accounts and their properties, including their passwords. In this chapter, you will explore the domain-side components of authentication, including the policies that specify password requirements and the auditing of authentication-related activities. You will also discover two new options, password settings objects (PSOs) and read-only domain controllers (RODCs).

Exam objectives in this chapter:
- Creating and Maintaining Active Directory Objects
  - Configure account policies.
  - Configure audit policy by using GPOs.
- Configuring the Active Directory Infrastructure
  - Configure Active Directory replication.
- Configuring Additional Active Directory Server Roles
  - Configure the read-only domain controller (RODC).

Lessons in this chapter:

- Lesson 1: Configuring Password and Lockout Policies 357
- Lesson 2: Auditing Authentication 368
- Lesson 3: Configuring Read-Only Domain Controllers 374

Before You Begin

To complete the lessons in this chapter, you must have installed a domain controller named SERVER01 in the *contoso.com* domain.

Real World

Dan Holme

As I work with clients to implement AD DS, I must constantly balance the need to maintain high levels of security with the need to continue conducting the client's business. With versions of Microsoft Windows prior to Windows Server 2008, I constantly ran into two scenarios in which this balance was particularly difficult to reach. The first relates to the security of user accounts with high levels of privilege within the enterprise. Such accounts are particularly attractive to hackers, so they should be locked down with particularly lengthy and complex passwords. In earlier versions of Windows, only one password policy could be applied to all accounts in the domain. Therefore, I either had to apply the highly restrictive password policy to all users in the domain, which was never a palatable solution, or ask administrators to follow the more restrictive policy but with no way to require compliance. Windows Server 2008 introduces fine-grained password policies that can be used to apply more or less restrictive passwords after requirements to groups or users in a domain.

Branch offices were also highly problematic because I had to balance the user's need to be authenticated quickly and reliably against the branch office's desire to centralize control over the physical security of domain controllers. Placing a domain controller in a branch office would clearly improve performance for users in the office but would also typically expose the domain controller to lower levels of security than those maintained at the data center. Coming to the rescue once again, Windows Server 2008 can act as a read-only domain controller, authenticating users and the branch office without storing all domain user credentials, thus reducing the risk to the enterprise in the event of a stolen branch office domain controller.

If you have worked with Active Directory for any period of time, you already appreciate the value of fine-grained password policies and read-only domain controllers. If you are new to Active Directory, you are lucky to be able to work with these much-anticipated new features.

Lesson 1: Configuring Password and Lockout Policies

In a Windows Server 2008 domain, users are required to change their password every 42 days, and a password must be at least seven characters long and meet complexity requirements including the use of three of four character types: uppercase, lowercase, numeric, and nonalphanumeric. Three password policies—maximum password age, password length, and password complexity—are among the first policies encountered by administrators and users alike in an Active Directory domain. Rarely do these default settings align precisely with the password security requirements of an organization. Your organization might require passwords to be changed more or less frequently or to be longer. In this lesson, you'll learn how to implement your enterprise's password and lockout policies by modifying the Default Domain Policy Group Policy object (GPO).

There are exceptions to every rule, and you likely have exceptions to your password policies. To enhance the security of your domain, you can set more restrictive password requirements for accounts assigned to administrators, for accounts used by services such as Microsoft SQL Server, or for a backup utility. In earlier versions of Windows, this was not possible; a single password policy applied to all accounts in the domain. In this lesson, you will learn to configure fine-grained password policies, a new feature in Windows Server 2008 that enables you to assign different password policies to users and groups in your domain.

> **After this lesson, you will be able to:**
> - Implement your domain password policy.
> - Configure and assign fine-grained password policies.
>
> **Estimated lesson time: 45 minutes**

Understanding Password Policies

Your domain's password policy is configured by a GPO scoped to the domain. Within the GPO, in the Computer Configuration\Policies\Windows Settings\ Security Settings\ Account Policies \Password Policy node, you can configure the policy settings that determine password requirements. The Password Policy node is shown in Figure 8-1.

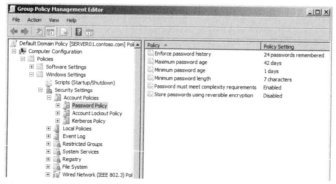

Figure 8-1   The Password Policy node of a GPO

You can understand the effects of the policies by considering the life cycle of a user password. A user will be required to change his or her password within the number of days specified by the Maximum Password Age policy setting. When the user enters a new password, the length of the new password will be compared to the number of characters in the Minimum Password Length policy. If the Password Must Meet Complexity Requirements policy is enabled, the password must contain at least three of four character types:

- Uppercase—for example, A–Z
- Lowercase—for example, a–z
- Numeric—0–9
- Nonalphanumeric—symbols such as !, #, %, or &

If the new password meets requirements, Active Directory puts the password through a mathematical algorithm that produces a representation of the password called the *hash code*. The hash code is unique; no two passwords can create the same hash code. The algorithm used to create the hash code is called a one-way function. You cannot put the hash code through a reverse function to derive the password. The fact that a hash code, and not the password itself, is stored in Active Directory helps increase the security of the user account.

Occasionally, applications require the ability to read a user's password. This is not possible because, by default, only the hash code is stored in Active Directory. To support such applications, you can enable the Store Passwords Using Reversible Encryption policy. This policy is not enabled by default, but if you enable the policy, user passwords are stored in an encrypted form that can be decrypted by the application. Reversible encryption significantly reduces the security of your domain, so it is disabled by default, and you should strive to eliminate applications that require direct access to passwords.

Additionally, Active Directory can check a cache of the user's previous hash codes to make sure that the new password is not the same as the user's previous passwords. The number of previous passwords against which a new password is evaluated is determined by the Enforce Password History policy. By default, Windows maintains the previous 24 hash codes.

If a user is determined to reuse a password when the password expiration period occurs, he or she could simply change the password 25 times to work around the password history. To prevent that from happening, the Minimum Password Age policy specifies an amount of time that must pass between password changes. By default, it is one day. Therefore, the determined user would have to change his or her password once a day for 25 days to reuse a password. This type of deterrent is generally successful at discouraging such behavior.

Each of these policy settings affects a user who changes his or her password. The settings do not affect an administrator using the Reset Password command to change another user's password.

Understanding Account Lockout Policies

An intruder can gain access to the resources in your domain by determining a valid user name and password. User names are relatively easy to identify because most organizations create user names from an employee's e-mail address, initials, combinations of first and last names, or employee IDs. When a user name is known, the intruder must determine the correct password by guessing or by repeatedly logging on with combinations of characters or words until the logon is successful.

This type of attack can be thwarted by limiting the number of incorrect logons that are allowed. That is exactly what account lockout policies achieve. Account lockout policies are located in the node of the GPO directly below Password Policy. The Account Lockout Policy node is shown in Figure 8-2.

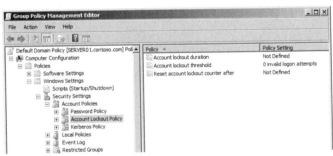

Figure 8-2   The Account Lockout Policy node of a GPO

Three settings are related to account lockout. The first, Account Lockout Threshold, determines the number of invalid logon attempts permitted within a time specified by the Account Lockout Duration policy. If an attack results in more unsuccessful logons within that timeframe, the user account is locked out. When an account is locked out, Active Directory will deny logon to that account, even if the correct password is specified.

An administrator can unlock a locked user account by following the procedure you learned in Chapter 3. You can also configure Active Directory to unlock the account automatically after a delay specified by the Reset Account Lockout Counter After policy setting.

Configuring the Domain Password and Lockout Policy

Active Directory supports one set of password and lockout policies for a domain. These policies are configured in a GPO that is scoped to the domain. A new domain contains a GPO called the Default Domain Policy that is linked to the domain and that includes the default policy settings shown in Figure 8-1 and Figure 8-2. You can change the settings by editing the Default Domain Policy.

Practice It You can practice configuring a domain's password and lockout policies in Exercise 1, "Configure the Domain's Password and Lockout Policies," in the practice for this lesson.

The password settings configured in the Default Domain Policy affect all user accounts in the domain. The settings can be overridden, however, by the password-related properties of the individual user accounts. On the Account tab of a user's Properties dialog box, you can specify settings such as Password Never Expires or Store Passwords Using Reversible Encryption. For example, if five users have an application that requires direct access to their passwords, you can configure the accounts for those users to store their passwords, using reversible encryption.

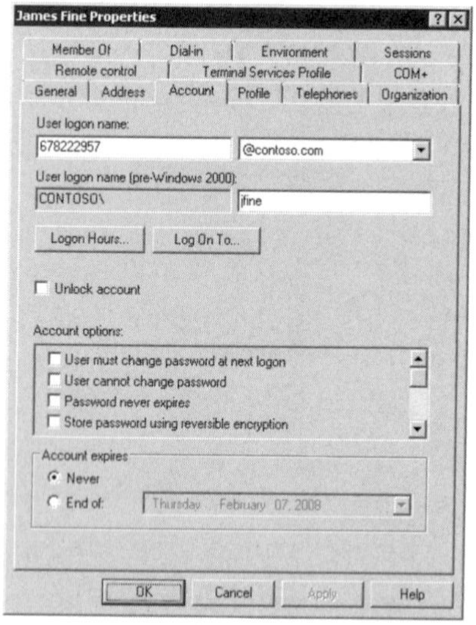

Figure 8-3 Password-related properties of a user account

Fine-Grained Password and Lockout Policy

You can also override the domain password and lockout policy by using a new feature of Windows Server 2008 called *fine-grained password and lockout policy*, often shortened to simply *fine-grained password policy*. Fine-grained password policy enables you to configure a policy that applies to one or more groups or users in your domain. To use fine-grained password policy, your domain must be at the Windows Server 2008 domain functional level described in Chapter 12, "Domains and Forests."

This feature is a highly anticipated addition to Active Directory. There are several scenarios for which fine-grained password policy can be used to increase the security of your domain. Accounts used by administrators are delegated privileges to modify objects in Active Directory; therefore, if an intruder compromises an administrator's account, more damage can be done to the domain than could be done through the account of a standard user. For that reason, consider implementing stricter password requirements for administrative accounts. For example, you might require greater password length and more frequent password changes.

Accounts used by services such as SQL Server also require special treatment in a domain. A service performs its tasks with credentials that must be authenticated with a user name and password just like those of a human user. However, most services are not capable of changing their own password, so administrators configure service accounts with the Password Never Expires option enabled. When an account's password will not be changed, make sure the password is difficult to compromise. You can use fine-grained password policies to specify an extremely long minimum password length and no password expiration.

Understanding Password Settings Objects

The settings managed by fine-grained password policy are identical to those in the Password Policy and Accounts Policy nodes of a GPO. However, fine-grained password policies are not implemented as part of Group Policy, nor are they applied as part of a GPO. Instead, there is a separate class of object in Active Directory that maintains the settings for fine-grained password policy: the *password settings object* (PSO).

Exam Tip There can be one, and only one, authoritative set of password and lockout policy settings that applies to all users in a domain. Those settings are configured in the Default Domain Policy GPO. Fine-grained password policies, which apply to individual groups or users in the domain, are implemented using PSOs.

Most Active Directory objects can be managed with user-friendly graphical user interface (GUI) tools such as the Active Directory Users and Computers snap-in. You manage PSOs, however, with low-level tools, including ADSI Edit.

MORE INFO Password Policy Basic

Although it will not be addressed on the 70-640 exam, it is highly recommended that you use Password Policy Basic by Special Operations Software to manage fine-grained password policy. The GUI tool can be downloaded free from *http://www.specopssoft.com*.

You can create one or more PSOs in your domain. Each PSO contains a complete set of password and lockout policy settings. A PSO is applied by linking the PSO to one or more global security groups or users. For example, to configure a strict password policy for administrative accounts, create a global security group, add the service user accounts as members, and link a PSO to the group. Applying fine-grained password policies to a group in this manner is more manageable than applying the policies to each individual user account. If you create a new service account, you simply add it to the group, and the account becomes managed by the PSO.

PSO Precedence and Resultant PSO

A PSO can be linked to more than one group or user, an individual group or user can have more than one PSO linked to it, and a user can belong to multiple groups. So which fine-grained password and lockout policy settings apply to a user? One and only one PSO determines the password and lockout settings for a user; this PSO is called the *resultant PSO*. Each PSO has an attribute that determines the precedence of the PSO. The precedence value is any number greater than 0, where the number 1 indicates highest precedence. If multiple PSOs apply to a user, the PSO with the highest precedence (closest to 1) takes effect. The rules that determine precedence are as follows:

- If multiple PSOs apply to groups to which the user belongs, the PSO with the highest precedence prevails.
- If one or more PSOs are linked directly to the user, PSOs linked to groups are ignored, regardless of their precedence. The user-linked PSO with highest precedence prevails.
- If one or more PSOs have the same precedence value, Active Directory must make a choice. It picks the PSO with the lowest globally unique identifier (GUID). GUIDs are like serial numbers for Active Directory objects—no two objects have the same GUID. GUIDs have no particular meaning—they are just identifiers—so choosing the PSO with the lowest GUID is, in effect, an arbitrary decision. Configure PSOs with unique, specific precedence values so that you avoid this scenario.

These rules determine the resultant PSO. Active Directory exposes the resultant PSO in a user object attribute, so you can readily identify the PSO that will affect a user. You will examine that attribute in the practice at the end of this lesson. PSOs contain all password and lockout settings, so there is no inheritance or merging of settings. The resultant PSO is the authoritative PSO.

PSOs and OUs

PSOs can be linked to global security groups or users. PSOs cannot be linked to organizational units (OUs). If you want to apply password and lockout policies to users in an OU, you must create a global security group that includes all the users in the OU. This type of group is called a *shadow group*—its membership shadows, or mimics, the membership of an OU.

> ## Quick Check
> - You want to require that administrators maintain a password of at least 15 characters and change the password every 45 days. The administrators' user accounts are in an OU called Admins. You do not want to apply the restrictive password policy to all domain users. What do you do?
> ## Quick Check Answer
> - Create a global security group that contains all users in the Admins OU. Create a PSO that configures the password policies and link the PSO to the group.

Shadow groups are conceptual, not technical objects. You simply create a group and add the users that belong to the OU. If you change the membership of the OU, you must also change the membership of the group.

MORE INFO Shadow groups

Additional information about PSOs and shadow groups is available at *http://technet2.microsoft.com /windowsserver2008/en/library/2199dcf7-68fd-4315-87cc-ade35f8978ea1033.mspx?mfr=true.*

MORE INFO Maintaining shadow group membership with scripts

You can use scripts to maintain the membership of shadow groups dynamically so that they always reflect the users in OUs. You can find example scripts in *Windows Administration Resource Kit: Productivity Solutions for IT Professionals* by Dan Holme (Microsoft Press, 2008).

PRACTICE Configuring Password and Lockout Policies

In this practice, you will use Group Policy to configure the domain-wide password and lockout policies for *contoso.com*. You will then secure administrative accounts by configuring more restrictive, fine-grained password and lockout policies.

▶ **Exercise 1   Configure the Domain's Password and Lockout Policies**

In this exercise, you will modify the Default Domain Policy GPO to implement a password and lockout policy for users in the *contoso.com* domain.

1. Log on to SERVER01 as Administrator.
2. Open the Group Policy Management console from the Administrative Tools folder.
3. Expand Forest, Domains, and *contoso.com*.
4. Right-click Default Domain Policy underneath the *contoso.com* domain and choose Edit. You might be prompted with a reminder that you are changing the settings of a GPO.

5. Click OK.

   The Group Policy Management Editor appears.

6. Expand Computer Configuration\Policies\Security Settings\Account Policies, and then select Password Policy.

7. Double-click the following policy settings in the console details pane and configure the settings indicated:

   ❑ Maximum Password Age: 90 Days

   ❑ Minimum Password Length: 10 characters

8. Select Account Lockout Policy in the console tree.

9. Double-click the Account Lockout Threshold policy setting and configure it for 5 Invalid Logon Attempts. Then click OK.

10. A Suggested Value Changes window appears. Click OK.

    The values for Account Lockout Duration and Reset Account Lockout Counter After are automatically set to 30 minutes.

11. Close the Group Policy Management Editor window.

▶ **Exercise 2   Create a Password Settings Object**

In this exercise, you will create a PSO that applies a restrictive, fine-grained password policy to users in the Domain Admins group. Before you proceed with this exercise, confirm that the Domain Admins group is in the Users container. If it is not, move it to the Users container.

1. Open ADSI Edit from the Administrative Tools folder.

2. Right-click ADSI Edit and choose Connect To.

3. In the Name box, type **contoso.com**. Click OK.

4. Expand *contoso.com* and select DC=contoso,DC=com.

5. Expand DC=contoso,DC=com and select CN=System.

6. Expand CN=System and select CN= Password Settings Container.

   All PSOs are created and stored in the Password Settings Container (PSC).

7. Right-click the PSC, choose New, and then select Object.

   The Create Object dialog box appears. It prompts you to select the type of object to create. There is only one choice: msDS-PasswordSettings—the technical name for the object class referred to as a PSO.

8. Click Next.

   You are then prompted for the value for each attribute of a PSO. The attributes are similar to those found in the GPO you examined in Exercise 1.

9. Configure each attribute as indicated in the following list. Click Next after each attribute.

   ❑ Common Name: **My Domain Admins PSO**. This is the friendly name of the PSO.

   ❑ msDS-PasswordSettingsPrecedence: **1**. This PSO has the highest possible precedence because its value is the closest to 1.

❑ msDS-PasswordReversibleEncryptionEnabled: **False**. The password is not stored using reversible encryption.

❑ msDS-PasswordHistoryLength: **30**. The user cannot reuse any of the last 30 passwords.

❑ msDS-PasswordComplexityEnabled: **True**. Password complexity rules are enforced.

❑ msDS-MinimumPasswordLength: **15**. Passwords must be at least 15 characters long.

❑ msDS-MinimumPasswordAge: **1:00:00:00**. A user cannot change his or her password within one day of a previous change. The format is d:hh:mm:ss (days, hours, minutes, seconds).

❑ MaximumPasswordAge: **45:00:00:00**. The password must be changed every 45 days.

❑ msDS-LockoutThreshold: **5**. Five invalid logons within the time frame specified by XXX (the next attribute) will result in account lockout.

❑ msDS-LockoutObservationWindow: **0:01:00:00**. Five invalid logons (specified by the previous attribute) within one hour will result in account lockout.

❑ msDS-LockoutDuration: **1:00:00:00**. An account, if locked out, will remain locked for one day or until it is unlocked manually. A value of zero will result in the account remaining locked out until an administrator unlocks it.

The attributes listed are required. After clicking Next on the *msDS-LockoutDuration* attribute page, you will be able to configure the optional attribute.

10. Click the More Attributes button.

11. In the Edit Attributes box, type **CN=DomainAdmins,CN=Users,DC=contoso,DC=com** and click OK.

Click Finish.

▶ **Exercise 3   Identify the Resultant PSO for a User**

In this exercise, you will identify the PSO that controls the password and lockout policies for an individual user.

1. Open the Active Directory Users And Computers snap-in.

2. Click the View menu and make sure that Advanced Features is selected.

3. Expand the *contoso.com* domain and click the Users container in the console tree.

4. Right-click the Administrator account and choose Properties.

5. Click the Attribute Editor tab.

6. Click the Filter button and make sure that Constructed is selected.

The attribute you will locate in the next step is a *constructed* attribute, meaning that the resultant PSO is not a hard-coded attribute of a user; rather, it is calculated by examining the PSOs linked to a user in real time.

7. In the Attributes list, locate *msDS-ResultantPSO*.

8. Identify the PSO that affects the user.

The My Domain Admins PSO that you created in Exercise 2, "Create a Password Settings Object," is the resultant PSO for the Administrator account.

▶ **Exercise 4   Delete a PSO**

In this exercise, you will delete the PSO you created in Exercise 2 so that its settings do not affect you in later exercises.

1. Repeat steps 1–6 of Exercise 2 to select the Password Settings container in ADSI Edit.

2. In the console details pane, select CN=My Domain Admins PSO.

3. Press Delete.

4. Click Yes.

Lesson Summary

- Password policy settings determine when a password can or must be changed and what the requirements of the new password are.

- Account lockout settings cause Active Directory to lock out a user account if a specified number of invalid logons occurs within a specified period of time. Lockout helps prevent intruders from repeatedly attempting to log on to a user account in an effort to guess the user's password.

- A domain can have only one set of password and lockout policies that affect all users in the domain. These policies are defined using Group Policy. You can modify the default settings in the Default Domain Policy GPO to configure the policies for your organization.

- Windows Server 2008 gives you the option to specify different password and lockout policies for global security groups and users in your domain. Fine-grained password policies are deployed not with Group Policy but with password settings objects.

- If more than one PSO applies to a user or to groups to which a user belongs, a single PSO, called the resultant PSO, determines the effective password and lockout policies for the user. The PSO with the highest precedence (precedence value closest to 1) will prevail. If one or more PSOs are linked directly to the user rather than indirectly to groups, group-linked PSOs are not evaluated to determine the resultant PSO, and the user-linked PSO with the highest precedence will prevail.

Lesson Review

You can use the following questions to test your knowledge of the information in Lesson 1, "Configuring Password and Lockout Policies." The questions are also available on the companion CD if you prefer to review them in electronic form.

NOTE   Answers

Answers to these questions and explanations of why each answer choice is right or wrong are located in the "Answers" section at the end of the book.

1. You are an administrator at Tailspin Toys. Your Active Directory domain includes an OU called Service Accounts that contains all user accounts. Because you have configured service accounts with passwords that never expire, you want to apply a password policy that requires passwords of at least 40 characters. Which of the following steps should you perform? (Choose all that apply. Each correct answer is part of the solution.)

    A. Set the Minimum Password Length policy in the Default Domain Policy GPO.

    B. Link a PSO to the Service Accounts OU.

    C. Create a group called Service Accounts.

    D. Link a PSO to the Service Accounts group.

    E. Add all service accounts as members of the Service Accounts group.

2. You want to configure account lockout policy so that a locked account will not be unlocked automatically. Rather, you want to require an administrator to unlock the account. Which configuration change should you make?

    A. Configure the Account Lockout Duration policy setting to 100.

    B. Configure the Account Lockout Duration policy setting to 1.

    C. Configure the Account Lockout Threshold to 0.

    D. Configure the Account Lockout Duration policy setting to 0.

3. As you evaluate the password settings objects in your domain, you discover a PSO named PSO1 with a precedence value of 1 that is linked to a group named Help Desk. Another PSO, named PSO2, with a precedence value of 99, is linked to a group named Support. Mike Danseglio is a member of both the Help Desk and Support groups. You discover that two PSOs are linked directly to Mike. PSO3 has a precedence value of 50, and PSO4 has a precedence value of 200. Which PSO is the resultant PSO for Mike?

    A. PSO1

    B. PSO2

    C. PSO3

    D. PSO4

Lesson 2: Auditing Authentication

In Chapter 7, "Group Policy Settings," you learned to configure auditing for several types of activities, including access to folders and changes to directory service objects. Windows Server 2008 also enables you to audit the logon activity of users in a domain. By auditing successful logons, you can look for instances in which an account is being used at unusual times or in unexpected locations, which might indicate that an intruder is logging on to the account. Auditing failed logons can reveal attempts by intruders to compromise an account. In this lesson, you will learn to configure logon auditing.

> **After this lesson, you will be able to:**
> - Configure auditing of authentication-related activity.
> - Distinguish between account logon and logon events.
> - Identify authentication-related events in the Security log.
>
> **Estimated lesson time: 30 minutes**

Account Logon and Logon Events

This lesson examines two specific policy settings: Audit Account Logon Events and Audit Logon Events. It is important to understand the difference between these two similarly named policy settings.

When a user logs on to any computer in the domain using his or her domain user account, a domain controller authenticates the attempt to log on to the domain account. This generates an account logon event on the domain controller.

The computer to which the user logs on—for example, the user's laptop—generates a logon event. The computer did not authenticate the user against his or her account; it passed the account to a domain controller for validation. The computer did, however, allow the user to log on interactively to the computer. Therefore, the event is a logon event.

When the user connects to a folder on a server in the domain, that server authorizes the user for a type of logon called a network logon. Again, the server does not authenticate the user; it relies on the ticket given to the user by the domain controller. But the connection by the user generates a logon event on the server.

Exam Tip   Be certain that you can distinguish between *account logon events* and *logon events*. The simplest way to remember the difference is that an account logon event occurs where the account lives: on the domain controller that authenticates the user. A logon event occurs on the computer to which the user logs on interactively. It also occurs on the file server to which the user connects using a network logon.

Configuring Authentication-Related Audit Policies

Account logon and logon events can be audited by Windows Server 2008. The settings that manage auditing are located in a GPO in the Computer Configuration\Policies\Windows Settings \Security Settings\Local Policies\Audit Policy node. The Audit Policy node and the two settings are shown in Figure 8-4.

Figure 8-4   Authentication-related policy settings

To configure an audit policy, double-click the policy, and its properties dialog box appears. The Audit Account Logon Events Properties dialog box is shown in Figure 8-5.

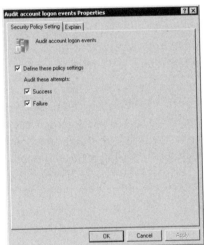

Figure 8-5   The Audit Account Logon Events Properties dialog box

The policy setting can be configured to one of the following four states:

- **Not defined**   If the Define These Policy Settings check box is cleared, the policy setting is not defined. In this case, the server will audit the event based on its default settings or on the settings specified in another GPO.

- **Defined for no auditing**   If the Define These Policy Settings check box is selected, but the Success and Failure check boxes are cleared, the server will not audit the event.

- **Audit successful events**   If the Define These Policy Settings check box is selected, and the Success checkbox is selected, the server will log successful events in its Security log.

■ **Audit failed to events**   If the Define These Policy Settings check box is selected, and the Failure check box is selected, the server will log unsuccessful events in its Security log.

A server's audit behavior is determined by the setting that wins based on the rules of policy application discussed in Chapter 6, "Group Policy Infrastructure."

Scoping Audit Policies

As with all policy settings, be careful to scope settings so that they affect the correct systems. For example, if you want to audit attempts by users to connect to file servers in your enterprise, you can configure logon event auditing in a GPO linked to the OU that contains your file servers. Alternatively, if you want to audit logons by users to desktops in your human resources department, you can configure logon event auditing in a GPO linked to the OU containing human resources computer objects. Remember that domain users logging on to a client computer or connecting to a server will generate a logon event—not an account logon event—on that system.

Only domain controllers generate account logon events for domain users. Remember that an account logon event occurs on the domain controller that authenticates a domain user, regardless of where that user logs on. If you want to audit logons to domain accounts, scope account logon event auditing to affect only domain controllers. In fact, the Default Domain Controllers GPO that is created when you install your first domain controller is an ideal GPO in which to configure account logon audit policies.

In the previous section, you learned that if an event auditing policy is not defined, the system will audit based on the settings in other GPOs or on its default setting. In Windows Server 2008, the default setting is to audit successful account logon events and successful logon events, so both types of events are, if successful, entered in the server's Security log. If you want to audit failures or turn off auditing, you will need to define the appropriate setting in the audit policy.

Quick Check

■ You are concerned that an intruder is attempting to gain access to your network by guessing a user's password. You want to identify the times at which the intruder is trying to log on. What type of event should you audit? Should you configure the policy setting in the Default Domain Policy or in the Default Domain Controllers Policy?

Quick Check Answer

■ Enable auditing of failed account logon events (not logon events) in the Default Domain Controllers GPO. Only domain controllers generate account logon events related to the authentication of domain users. The Default Domain Controllers GPO is scoped correctly to apply only to domain controllers.

Viewing Logon Events

Account logon and logon events, if audited, appear in the Security log of the system that generated the event. Figure 8-6 shows an example. Thus, if you are auditing logons to computers in the human resources department, the events are entered in each computer's Security log. Similarly, if you are auditing unsuccessful account logons to identify potential intrusion attempts, the events are entered in each domain controller's Security log. This means, by default, you will need to examine the Security logs of all domain controllers to get a complete picture of account logon events in your domain.

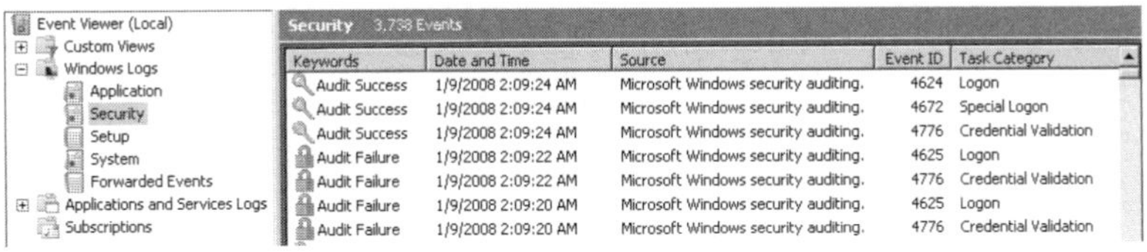

Figure 8-6 Authentication events in the Security log

As you can imagine, in a complex environment with multiple domain controllers and many users, auditing account logons or logons can generate a tremendous number of events. If there are too many events, it can be difficult to identify problematic events worthy of closer investigation. Balance the amount of logging you perform with the security requirements of your business and the resources you have available to analyze logged events.

PRACTICE Auditing Authentication

In this practice, you will use Group Policy to enable auditing of logon activity by users in the *contoso.com* domain. You will then generate logon events and view the resulting entries in the event logs.

▶ **Exercise 1   Configure Auditing of Account Logon Events**

In this exercise, you will modify the Default Domain Controllers Policy GPO to implement auditing of both successful and failed logons by users in the domain.

1. Open the Group Policy Management console.
2. Expand Forest\Domains\Contoso.com\Domain Controllers.
3. Right-click Default Domain Controllers Policy and select Edit.
   Group Policy Management Editor appears.
4. Expand Computer Configuration\Policies\Windows at Settings\Security Settings\Local Policies, and then select Audit Policy.
5. Double-click Audit Account Logon Events.
6. Select the Define These Policy Settings check box.
7. Select both the Success and Failure check boxes. Click OK.

8. Double-click Audit Logon Events.
9. Select the Define These Policy Settings check box.
10. Select both the Success and Failure check boxes. Click OK.
11. Close Group Policy Management Editor.
12. Click Start and click Command Prompt.
13. Type **gpupdate.exe /force**.

    This command causes SERVER01 to update its policies, at which time the new auditing settings take effect.

▶ **Exercise 2   Generate Account Logon Events**

In this exercise, you will generate account logon events by logging on with both incorrect and correct passwords.

1. Log off of SERVER01.
2. Attempt to log on as Administrator with an incorrect password. Repeat this step once or twice.
3. Log on to SERVER01 with the correct password.

▶ **Exercise 3   Examine Account Logon Events**

In this exercise, you will view the events generated by the logon activities in Exercise 2.

1. Open Event Viewer from the Administrative Tools folder.
2. Expand Windows Logs, and then select Security.
3. Identify the failed and successful events.

Lesson Summary

- Account logon events occur on a domain controller as it authenticates users logging on anywhere in the domain.
- Logon events occur on systems to which users log on, for example, to their individual desktops and laptops. Logon events are also generated in response to a network logon, for example, when a user connects to a file server.
- By default, Windows Server 2008 systems audit successful account logon and logon events.
- To examine account logon events in your domain, you must look at the individual event logs from each domain controller.

Lesson Review

You can use the following questions to test your knowledge of the information in Lesson 2, "Auditing Authentication." The questions are also available on the companion CD if you prefer to review them in electronic form.

NOTE Answers

Answers to these questions and explanations of why each answer choice is right or wrong are located in the "Answers" section at the end of the book.

---

1. You want to obtain a log that will help you isolate the times of day that failed logons are causing a user's account to be locked out. Which policy should you configure?

   A. Define the Audit Account Logon Events policy setting for Success events in the Default Domain Policy GPO.

   B. Define the Audit Account Logon Events policy setting for Failure events in the Default Domain Policy GPO.

   C. Define the Audit Logon Events policy setting for Success events in the Default Domain Policy GPO.

   D. Define the Audit Logon Events policy setting for Failure events in the Default Domain Policy GPO.

2. You want to keep track of when users log on to computers in the human resources department of Adventure Works. Which of the following methods will enable you to obtain this information?

   A. Configure the policy setting to audit successful account logon events in the Default Domain Controllers GPO. Examine the event log of the first domain controller you installed in the domain.

   B. Configure the policy setting to audit successful logon events in a GPO linked to the OU containing user accounts for employees in the human resources department. Examine the event logs of each computer in the human resources department.

   C. Configure the policy setting to audit successful logon events in a GPO linked to the OU containing computer accounts in the human resources department. Examine the event logs of each computer in the human resources department.

   D. Configure the policy setting to audit successful account logon events in a GPO linked to the OU containing computer accounts in the human resources department. Examine the event logs of each domain controller.

Lesson 3: Configuring Read-Only Domain Controllers

Branch offices present a unique challenge to an enterprise's IT staff: if a branch office is separated from the hub site by a wide area network (WAN) link, should you place a domain controller (DC) in the branch office? In previous versions of Windows, the answer to this question was not a simple one. Windows Server 2008, however, introduces a new type of DC—the read-only domain controller (RODC)—that makes the question easier to answer. In this lesson, you will explore the issues related to branch office authentication and DC placement, and you will learn how to implement and support a branch-office RODC.

After this lesson, you will be able to:
- Identify the business requirements for RODCs.
- Install an RODC.
- Configure password replication policy.
- Monitor the caching of credentials on an RODC.

Estimated lesson time: 60 minutes

Authentication and Domain Controller Placement in a Branch Office

Consider a scenario in which an enterprise is characterized by a hub site and several branch offices. The branch offices connect to the hub site over WAN links that might be congested, expensive, slow, or unreliable. Users in the branch office must be authenticated by Active Directory to access resources in the domain. Should a DC be placed in the branch office?

In branch office scenarios, many IT services are centralized in a hub site. The hub site is carefully maintained by the IT staff and includes secure facilities for services. The branch offices, however, offer inadequate security for servers and might have insufficient IT staff to support the servers.

If a DC is not placed in the branch office, authentication and service ticket activities will be directed to the hub site over the WAN link. Authentication occurs when a user first logs on to his or her computer in the morning. *Service tickets* are a component of the Kerberos authentication mechanism used by Windows Server 2008 domains. You can think of a service ticket as a key issued by the domain controller to a user. The key allows the user to connect to a service such as the File and Print services on a file server. When a user first tries to access a specific service, the user's client requests a service ticket from the domain controller. Because users typically connect to multiple services during a workday, service ticket activity happens regularly. Authentication and service ticket activity over the WAN link between a branch office and a hub site can result in slow or unreliable performance.

If a DC is placed in the branch office, authentication is much more efficient, but there are several potentially significant risks. A DC maintains a copy of all attributes of all objects in its domain, including secrets such as information related to user passwords. If a DC is accessed or stolen, it becomes possible for a determined expert to identify valid user names and passwords, at which point the entire domain is compromised. At a minimum, you must reset the passwords of every user account in the domain. Because the security of servers at branch offices is often less than ideal, a branch office DC poses a considerable security risk.

A second concern is that the changes to the Active Directory database on a branch office DC replicate to the hub site and to all other DCs in the environment. Therefore, corruption to the branch office DC poses a risk to the integrity of the enterprise directory service. For example, if a branch office administrator performs a restore of the DC from an outdated backup, there can be significant repercussions for the entire domain.

The third concern relates to administration. A branch office domain controller might require maintenance, for example, a new device driver. To perform maintenance on a standard domain controller, you must log on as a member of the Administrators group on the domain controller, which means you are effectively an administrator of the domain. It might not be appropriate to grant that level of capability to a support team at a branch office.

Read-Only Domain Controllers

These concerns—security, directory service integrity, and administration—left many enterprises with a difficult choice to make, and there was no best practices answer. The RODC is designed specifically to address the branch office scenario. An RODC is a domain controller, typically placed in the branch office, that maintains a copy of all objects in the domain and all attributes except secrets such as password-related properties. When a user in the branch office logs on, the RODC receives the request and forwards it to a domain controller in the hub site for authentication.

You are able to configure a password replication policy (PRP) for the RODC that specifies user accounts the RODC is allowed to cache. If the user logging on is included in the PRP, the RODC caches that user's credentials, so the next time authentication is requested, the RODC can perform the task locally. As users who are included in the PRP log on, the RODC builds its cache of credentials so that it can perform authentication locally for those users. These concepts are illustrated in Figure 8-7.

Because the RODC maintains only a subset of user credentials, if the RODC is compromised or stolen, the effect of the security exposure is limited; only the user accounts that had been cached on the RODC must have their passwords changed. Writable domain controllers maintain a list of all cached credentials on individual RODCs. When you delete the account of the stolen or compromised RODC from Active Directory, you are given the option to reset the passwords of all user accounts that were cached on the RODC. The RODC replicates changes to Active Directory from DCs in the hub site. Replication is one way (from a writable domain controller to a RODC); no changes to the RODC are replicated to any other domain controller. This eliminates the exposure of the directory service to corruption resulting from changes made to a compromised branch office DC. Finally, RODCs, unlike writable DCs, have a local Administrators group. You can give one or more local support personnel the ability to maintain an RODC fully, without granting them the equivalence of domain administrators.

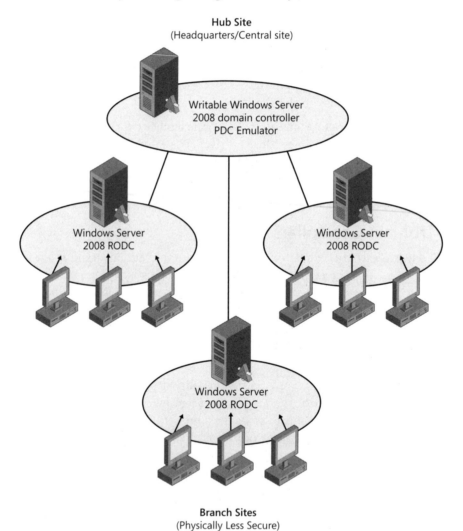

Figure 8-7   A branch office scenario supported by RODCs

Deploying an RODC

The high-level steps to install an RODC are as follows:

1. Ensure that the forest functional level is Windows Server 2003 or higher.
2. If the forest has any DCs running Microsoft Windows Server 2003, run *Adprep /rodcprep*.
3. Ensure that at least one writable DC is running Windows Server 2008.
4. Install the RODC.

Each of these steps is detailed in the following sections.

Verifying and Configuring Forest Functional Level of Windows Server 2003 or Higher

Functional levels enable features unique to specific versions of Windows and are, therefore, dependent on the versions of Windows running on domain controllers. If all domain controllers are Windows Server 2003 or later, the domain functional level can be set to Windows Server 2003. If all domains are at Windows Server 2003 domain functional level, the forest functional level can be set to Windows Server 2003. Domain and forest functional levels are discussed in detail in Chapter 12.

RODCs require that the forest functional level is Windows Server 2003 or higher. That means that all domain controllers in the entire forest are running Windows Server 2003 or later. To determine the functional level of your forest, open Active Directory Domains And Trusts from the Administrative Tools folder, right-click the name of the forest, choose Properties, and verify the forest functional level, as shown in Figure 8-8. Any user can verify the forest functional level in this way.

If the forest functional level is not at least Windows Server 2003, examine the properties of each domain to identify any domains for which the domain functional level is not at least Windows Server 2003. If you find such a domain, you must ensure that all domain controllers in the domain are running Windows Server 2003. Then, in Active Directory Domains And Trusts, right-click the domain and choose Raise Domain Functional Level. After you have raised each domain functional level to at least Windows Server 2003, right-click the root node of the Active Directory Domains And Trusts snap-in and choose Raise Forest Functional Level. In the Select An Available Forest Functional Level drop-down list, choose Windows Server 2003 and click Raise. You must be an administrator of a domain to raise the domain's functional level. To raise the forest functional level, you must be either a member of the Domain Admins group in the forest root domain or a member of the Enterprise Admins group.

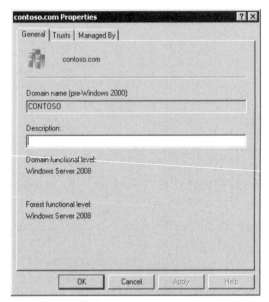

Figure 8-8   The forest Properties dialog box

Running *Adprep /rodcprep*

If you are upgrading an existing forest to include domain controllers running Windows Server 2008, you must run *Adprep /rodcprep*. This command configures permissions so that RODCs are able to replicate DNS application directory partitions. DNS application directory partitions are discussed in Chapter 9, "Integrating Domain Name System with AD DS." If you are creating a new Active Directory forest and it will have only domain controllers running Windows Server 2008, you do not need to run *Adprep /rodcprep*.

You can find this command in the *cdrom*\Sources\Adprep folder of the Windows Server 2008 installation DVD. Copy the folder to the domain controller acting as the schema master. The schema master role is discussed in Chapter 10, "Domain Controllers." Log on to the schema master as a member of the Enterprise Admins group, open a command prompt, change directories to the Adprep folder, and type **adprep /rodcprep**.

Placing a Writable Windows Server 2008 Domain Controller

An RODC must replicate domain updates from a writable domain controller running Windows Server 2008. It is critical that an RODC is able to establish a replication connection with a writable Windows Server 2008 domain controller. Ideally, the writable Windows Server 2008 domain controller should be in the closest site—the hub site. In Chapter 11, "Sites and Replication," you'll learn about Active Directory replication, sites, and site links. If you want the RODC to act as a DNS server, the writable Windows Server 2008 domain controller must also host the DNS domain zone.

Quick Check

■ Your domain consists of a central site and four branch offices. A central site has two domain controllers. Each branch office site has one domain controller. All domain controllers run Windows Server 2003. Your company decides to open a fifth branch office, and you want to configure it with a new Windows Server 2008 RODC. What must you do before introducing the first RODC into your domain?

Quick Check Answer

■ You must first ensure that the forest functional level is Windows Server 2003. Then, you must upgrade one of the existing domain controllers to Windows Server 2008 so that there is one writable Windows Server 2008 domain controller. You must also run *Adprep /rodcprep* from the Windows Server 2008 installation DVD.

Installing an RODC

After completing the preparatory steps, you can install an RODC. An RODC can be either a full or Server Core installation of Windows Server 2008. With a full installation of Windows Server 2008, you can use the Active Directory Domain Services Installation Wizard to create an RODC. Simply select Read-Only Domain Controller (RODC) on the Additional Domain Controller Options page of the wizard, as shown in Figure 8-9.

Figure 8-9   Creating an RODC with the Active Directory Domain Services Installation Wizard

---

Practice It   Exercise 1, "Install an RODC," in the practice at the end of this lesson walks you through the use of the Active Directory Domain Services Installation Wizard to create an RODC.

Alternatively, you can use the *Dcpromo.exe* command with the */unattend* switch to create the RODC. On a Server Core installation of Windows Server 2008, you must use the *Dcpromo.exe /unattend* command.

It is also possible to delegate the installation of the RODC, which enables a user who is not a domain administrator to create the RODC, by adding a new server in the branch office and running *Dcpromo.exe*. To delegate the installation of an RODC, pre-create the computer account for the RODC in the Domain Controllers OU and specify the credentials that will be used to add the RODC to the domain. That user can then attach a server running Windows Server 2008 to the RODC account. The server must be a member of a workgroup—not of the domain—when creating an RODC by using delegated installation.

MORE INFO   Options for installing an RODC

For details regarding other options for installing an RODC, including delegated installation, see "Step-by-Step Guide for Read-only Domain Controllers" at *http://technet2.microsoft.com /windowsserver2008/en/library/ea8d253e-0646-490c-93d3-b78c5e1d9db71033.mspx?mfr=true*.

Password Replication Policy

Password Replication Policy (PRP) determines which users' credentials can be cached on a specific RODC. If PRP allows an RODC to cache a user's credentials, then authentication and service ticket activities of that user can be processed by the RODC. If a user's credentials cannot be cached on an RODC, authentication and service ticket activities are referred by the RODC to a writable domain controller.

A PRP of an RODC is determined by two multivalued attributes of the RODC computer account. These attributes are commonly known as the Allowed List and the Denied List. If a user's account is on the Allowed List, the user's credentials are cached. You can include groups on the Allowed List, in which case all users who belong to the group can have their credentials cached on the RODC. If the user is on both the Allowed List and the Denied List, the user's credentials will not be cached—the Denied List takes precedence.

Configure Domain-Wide Password Replication Policy

To facilitate the management of PRP, Windows Server 2008 creates two domain local security groups in the Users container of Active Directory. The first, named Allowed RODC Password Replication Group, is added to the Allowed List of each new RODC. By default, the group has no members. Therefore, by default, a new RODC will not cache any user's credentials. If there are users whose credentials you want to be cached by all domain RODCs, add those users to the Allowed RODC Password Replication Group.

The second group is named Denied RODC Password Replication Group. It is added to the Denied List of each new RODC. If there are users whose credentials you want to ensure are never cached by domain RODCs, add those users to the Denied RODC Password Replication Group. By default, this group contains security-sensitive accounts that are members of groups including Domain Admins, Enterprise Admins, and Group Policy Creator Owners.

NOTE   Computers are people, too

Remember that it is not only users who generate authentication and service ticket activity. Computers in a branch office also require such activity. To improve performance of systems in a branch office, allow the branch RODC to cache computer credentials as well.

Configure RODC-Specific Password Replication Policy

The two groups described in the previous section provide a method to manage PRP on all RODCs. However, to support a branch office scenario most efficiently, you need to allow the RODC in each branch office to cache user and computer credentials in that specific location. Therefore, you need to configure the Allowed List and the Denied List of each RODC.

To configure an RODC PRP, open the properties of the RODC computer account in the Domain Controllers OU. On the Password Replication Policy tab, shown in Figure 8-10, you can view the current PRP settings and add or remove users or groups from the PRP.

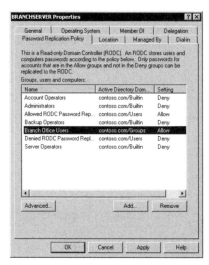

Figure 8-10   The Password Replication Policy tab of an RODC

Administer RODC Credentials Caching

When you click the Advanced button on the Password Replication Policy tab shown in Figure 8-10, an Advanced Password Replication Policy dialog box appears. An example is shown in Figure 8-11.

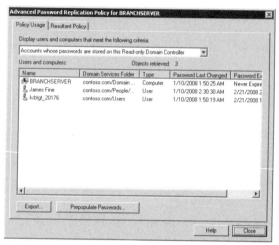

Figure 8-11   The Advanced Password Replication Policy dialog box

The drop-down list at the top of the Policy Usage tab enables you to select one of two reports for the RODC:

- **Accounts Whose Passwords Are Stored On This Read-Only Domain Controller**   Displays the list of user and computer credentials that are currently cached on the RODC. Use this list to determine whether credentials are being cached that you do not want to be cached on the RODC; modify the PRP accordingly.

- **Accounts That Have Been Authenticated To This Read-Only Domain Controller**   Displays the list of user and computer credentials that have been referred to a writable domain controller for authentication or service ticket processing. Use this list to identify users or computers that are attempting to authenticate with the RODC. If any of these accounts are not being cached, consider adding them to the PRP.

In the same dialog box, the Resultant Policy tab enables you to evaluate the effective caching policy for an individual user or computer. Click the Add button to select a user or computer account for evaluation.

You can also use the Advanced Password Replication Policy dialog box to prepopulate credentials in the RODC cache. If a user or computer is on the allow list of an RODC, the account credentials can be cached on the RODC but will not be cached until the authentication or service ticket events cause the RODC to replicate the credentials from a writable domain controller. By prepopulating credentials in the RODC cache for users and computers in the branch office, for example, you can ensure that authentication and service ticket activity will be processed locally by the RODC even when the user or computer is authenticating for the first time. To prepopulate credentials, click the Prepopulate Passwords button and select the appropriate users and computers.

Administrative Role Separation

RODCs in branch offices can require maintenance such as an updated device driver. Additionally, small branch offices might combine the RODC with the file server role on a single system, in which case it will be important to be able to back up the system. RODCs support local administration through a feature called *administrative role separation*. Each RODC maintains a local database of groups for specific administrative purposes. You can add domain user accounts to these local roles to enable support of a specific RODC.

You can configure administrative role separation by using the *Ddsmgmt.exe* command. To add a user to the Administrators role on an RODC, follow these steps:

1. Open a command prompt on the RODC.
2. Type **dsmgmt** and press Enter.
3. Type **local roles** and press Enter.

    At the *local roles* prompt, you can type **?** and press Enter for a list of commands. You can also type **list roles** and press Enter for a list of local roles.

4. Type **add** *username* **administrators**, where *username* is the pre-Windows 2000 logon name of a domain user, and press Enter.

You can repeat this process to add other users to the various local roles on an RODC.

MORE INFO Improving authentication and security

RODCs are a valuable new feature for improving authentication and security in branch offices. Be sure to read the detailed documentation on the Microsoft Web site at *http://technet2.microsoft.com /windowsserver2008/en/library/ea8d253e-0646-490c-93d3-b78c5e1d9db71033.mspx*.

PRACTICE Configuring Read-Only Domain Controllers

In this practice, you will implement read-only domain controllers in a simulation of a branch office scenario. You will install an RODC, configure password replication policy, monitor credential caching, and prepopulate credentials on the RODC. To perform this practice, you must complete the following preparatory tasks:

- Install a second server running Windows Server 2008. Name the server **BRANCH-SERVER**. Set the server's IP configuration as follows:
  - IP Address: 10.0.0.12
  - Subnet Mask: 255.255.255.0
  - Default Gateway: 10.0.0.1
  - DNS Server: 10.0.0.11 (the address of SERVER01)

■ Create the following Active Directory objects:

    ❑ A global security group named Branch Office Users

    ❑ A user named James Fine, who is a member of Branch Office Users

    ❑ A user named Adam Carter, who is a member of Branch Office Users

    ❑ A user named Mike Danseglio, who is not a member of Branch Office Users

■ Add the Domain Users group as a member of the Print Operators group.

IMPORTANT   A word about permission levels

This is a shortcut that allows standard user accounts to log on to the domain controllers that you will use in these exercises. In a production environment, it is not recommended to allow standard users to log on to domain controllers.

▶ **Exercise 1   Install an RODC**

In this exercise, you will configure the BRANCHSERVER server as an RODC in the *contoso.com* domain.

1. Log on to BRANCHSERVER as Administrator.

2. Click Start and click Run.

3. Type **dcpromo** and click OK.

    A window appears that informs you the Active Directory Domain Services binaries are being installed. When installation is completed, the Active Directory Domain Services Installation Wizard appears.

4. Click Next.

5. On the Operating System Compatibility page, click Next.

6. On the Choose A Deployment Configuration page, select the Existing Forest option, and then select Add A Domain Controller To An Existing Domain. Click Next.

7. On the Network Credentials page, type **contoso.com**.

8. Click the Set button.

9. In the User Name box, type **Administrator**.

10. In the Password box, type the password for the domain's Administrator account. Click OK.

11. Click Next.

12. On the Select A Domain page, select *contoso.com* and click Next.

13. On the Select A Site page, select Default-First-Site-Name and click Next.

    In a production environment, you would select the site for the branch office in which the RODC is being installed. Sites are discussed in Chapter 11.

14. On the Additional Domain Controller Options page, select Read-Only Domain Controller (RODC). Also ensure that DNS Server and Global Catalog are selected. Then click Next.

15. On the Delegation Of RODC Installation And Administration page, click Next.

16. On the Location For Database, Log Files, And SYSVOL page, click Next.

17. On the Directory Services Restore Mode Administrator Password page, type a password in the Password and Confirm Password boxes, and then click Next.

18. On the Summary page, click Next.

19. In the progress window, select the Reboot On Completion check box.

▶ **Exercise 2   Configure Password Replication Policy**

In this exercise, you will configure PRP at the domain level and for an individual RODC. PRP determines whether the credentials of a user or computer are cached on an RODC.

1. Log on to SERVER01 as Administrator.

2. Open the Active Directory Users And Computers snap-in.

3. Expand the domain and select the Users container.

4. Examine the default membership of the Allowed RODC Password Replication Group.

5. Open the properties of the Denied RODC Password Replication Group.

6. Add the DNS Admins group as a member of the Denied RODC Password Replication Group.

7. Select the Domain Controllers OU.

8. Open the properties of BRANCHSERVER.

9. Click the Password Replication Policy tab.

10. Identify the PRP settings for the two groups, Allowed RODC Password Replication Group and Denied RODC Password Replication Group.

11. Click the Add button.

12. Select Allow Passwords For The Account To Replicate To This RODC and click OK.

13. In the Select Users, Computers, Or Groups dialog box, type **Branch Office Users** and click OK.

14. Click OK.

▶ **Exercise 3   Monitor Credential Caching**

In this exercise, you will simulate the logon of several users to the branch office server. You will then evaluate the credentials caching of the server.

1. Log on to BRANCHSERVER as James Fine, and then log off.

2. Log on to BRANCHSERVER as Mike Danseglio, and then log off.

3. Log on to SERVER01 as Administrator and open the Active Directory Users And Computers snap-in.

4. Open the properties of BRANCHSERVER in the Domain Controllers OU.

5. Click the Password Replication Policy tab.

6. Click the Advanced button.

7. On the Policy Usage tab, in the Display Users And Computers That Meet The Following Criteria drop-down list, select Accounts Whose Passwords Are Stored On This Read-Only Domain Controller.

8. Locate the entry for James Fine.

   Because you had configured the PRP to allow caching of credentials for users in the Branch Office Users group, James Fine's credentials were cached when he logged on in step 1. Mike Danseglio's credentials are not cached.

9. In the drop-down list, select Accounts That Have Been Authenticated To This Read-Only Domain Controller.

10. Locate the entries for James Fine and Mike Danseglio.

11. Click Close, and then click OK.

▶ **Exercise 4   Prepopulate Credentials Caching**

In this exercise, you will prepopulate the cache of the RODC with the credentials of a user.

1. Log on to SERVER01 as Administrator and open the Active Directory Users And Computers snap-in.

2. Open the properties of BRANCHSERVER in the Domain Controllers OU.

3. Click the Password Replication Policy tab.

4. Click the Advanced button.

5. Click the Prepopulate Passwords button.

6. Type **Adam Carter** and click OK.

7. Click Yes to confirm that you want to send the credentials to the RODC.

8. On the Policy Usage tab, select Accounts Whose Passwords Are Stored On This Read-Only Domain Controller.

9. Locate the entry for Adam Carter.

   Adam's credentials are now cached on the RODC.

10. Click OK.

Lesson Summary

- RODCs contain a read-only copy of the Active Directory database.

- An RODC replicates updates to the domain from a writable domain controller using inbound-only replication.

- Password replication policy defines whether the credentials of the user or computer are cached on an RODC. The Allowed RODC Password Replication Group and Denied RODC Password Replication Group are in the Allowed List and Denied List, respectively, or in each new RODC. You can, therefore, use the two groups to manage a domain-wide password replication policy. You can further configure the individual PRP of each domain controller.

- An RODC can be supported by configuring administrator role separation to enable one or more users to perform administrative tasks without granting those users permissions to other domain controllers or to the domain. The *Dsmgmt.exe* command implements administrator role separation.

- An RODC requires a Windows Server 2008 writable domain controller in the same domain. Additionally, the forest functional level must be at least Windows Server 2003, and the *Adprep /rodcprep* command must be run prior to installing the first RODC.

Lesson Review

You can use the following questions to test your knowledge of the information in Lesson 3, "Configuring Read-Only Domain Controllers." The questions are also available on the companion CD if you prefer to review them in electronic form.

NOTE Answers

Answers to these questions and explanations of why each answer choice is right or wrong are located in the "Answers" section at the end of the book.

---

1. Your domain consists of five domain controllers, one of which is running Windows Server 2008. All other DCs are running Windows Server 2003. What must you do before installing a read-only domain controller?

    A. Upgrade all domain controllers to Windows Server 2008.

    B. Run *Adprep /rodcprep*.

    C. Run *Dsmgmt*.

    D. Run *Dcpromo /unattend*.

2. During a recent burglary at a branch office of Tailspin Toys, the branch office RODC was stolen. Where can you find out which users' credentials were stored on the RODC?

    A. The Policy Usage tab

    B. The membership of the Allowed RODC Password Replication Group

    C. The membership of the Denied RODC Password Replication Group

    D. The Resultant Policy tab

3. Next week, five users are relocating to one of the ten overseas branch offices of Litware, Inc. Each branch office contains an RODC. You want to ensure that when the users log on for the first time in the branch office, they do not experience problems authenticating over the WAN link to the data center. Which steps should you perform? (Choose all that apply.)

    A. Add the five users to the Allowed RODC Password Replication Group.

    B. Add the five users to the Password Replication Policy tab of the branch office RODC.

    C. Add the five users to the Log On Locally security policy of the Default Domain Controllers Policy GPO.

    D. Click Prepopulate Passwords.

Chapter Review

To further practice and reinforce the skills you learned in this chapter, you can perform the following tasks:

- Review the chapter summary.
- Review the list of key terms introduced in this chapter.
- Complete the case scenarios. These scenarios set up real-world situations involving the topics of this chapter and ask you to create a solution.
- Complete the suggested practices.
- Take a practice test.

Chapter Summary

- Windows Server 2008 enables you to specify password and account lockout settings for the entire domain by modifying the Default Domain Policy GPO. You can then use fine-grained password and lockout policies contained in password settings objects (PSOs) to configure specific policies for groups or individual users.
- When a domain user logs on to a computer in a domain, the computer generates a logon event, and the domain generates an account logon event. These events can be audited to monitor authentication activity. By default, Windows Server 2008 audits successful account logon and logon events.
- Read-only domain controllers (RODCs) provide valuable support for branch office scenarios by authenticating users in the branch office. RODCs reduce the security risk associated with placing a domain controller in a less secure site. You can configure which credentials an RODC will cache. You can also delegate administration of the RODC without granting permissions to other domain controllers or to the domain.

Key Terms

Use these key terms to understand better the concepts covered in this chapter.

- **password replication policy (PRP)**   A policy that determines which user credentials can be cached on a read-only domain controller. An RODC PRP includes an Allowed List and a Denied List. Credentials of users on the Allowed List can be cached by the RODC. If a user is on both the Allowed List and the Denied List, the user's credentials are not cached.
- **password settings object (PSO)**   A collection of settings that define password requirements and account lockout policies for a subset of users in a domain. PSOs can be

applied to groups and individual users in a domain to configure policies that are different from the domain-wide password and lockout policies defined by Group Policy.

- **read-only domain controller (RODC)**   A domain controller that maintains a copy of Active Directory with all objects and attributes except for user credentials. An RODC obtains domain updates from a writable domain controller using inbound-only replication. RODCs are particularly well suited for branch office scenarios.
- **resultant PSO**   The password settings object that applies to a user. The resultant PSO is calculated by examining the precedence value of all PSOs linked to a user's groups and directly to the user.

Case Scenarios

In the following case scenarios, you will apply what you've learned about fine-grained password policies and RODCs. You can find answers to these questions in the "Answers" section at the end of this book.

Case Scenario 1: Increasing the Security of Administrative Accounts

You are an administrator at Contoso, Ltd., which recently won a contract to deliver an important and secret new product. The contract requires that you increase the security of your Active Directory domain. You must ensure that accounts used by domain administrators are at least 25 characters long and are changed every 30 days. You believe it would not be reasonable to enforce such strict requirements on all users, so you wish to limit the scope of the new password requirements to only domain administrators. Additionally, you are required by the contract to monitor attempts by potential intruders to gain access to the network by using an administrative account.

1. Your domain currently contains four Windows Server 2003 domain controllers and eight Windows Server 2008 domain controllers. What must you do before you are able to implement fine-grained password policies that meet the requirements of the new contract?

2. Which tool do you use to configure fine-grained password and lockout policies?

3. You return from a vacation and discover that other administrators have created several new password settings objects (PSOs) with precedence values ranging from 10–50. You want to ensure that the PSO you created for domain administrators has the highest precedence so that it always takes effect for those users. What value should you assign to the precedence of your PSO?

4. How will you configure the domain to monitor attempts by potential intruders to gain access to the network by using an administrative account? Which GPO will you modify? Which settings will you define?

Case Scenario 2: Increasing the Security and Reliability of Branch Office Authentication

You are an administrator at Contoso, Ltd. You maintain the domain's directory service on four domain controllers at a data center in your main site. The domain controllers run Windows Server 2003. Contoso has decided to open a new office overseas. Initially, the office will have ten salespeople. You are concerned about the speed, expense, and reliability of the connection from the branch office to the data center, so you decide to place a read-only domain controller in the branch office.

1. What must you do to your existing domain controllers and to functional levels before you can install an RODC?

2. Due to customs regulations, you decide to ask one of the employees in the branch office to purchase a server locally. Can you allow the employee to create an RODC without giving the user domain administrative credentials?

3. You want the same user to be able to log on to the RODC to perform regular maintenance. Which command should you use to configure administrator role separation?

Suggested Practices

To help you successfully master the exam objectives presented in this chapter, complete the following tasks.

Configure Multiple Password Settings Objects

In this practice, you will experience the effects of PSO precedence by creating several PSOs that apply to a single user and evaluating the resultant PSO for that user.

To perform this practice, create the following objects in the *contoso.com* domain:

- A global security group named **Human Resources**
- A global security group named **Secure Users**
- A user account named **James Fine** that is a member of both the Human Resources and Secure Users groups
- **Practice 1** Create a PSO named *PSO1* that is linked to the Human Resources group. Give *PSO1* a precedence value of *10*. You can use any valid settings for the other attributes of the PSO. Create a second PSO named *PSO2* and give it a precedence value of *5*. You can use any valid settings for the other attributes of the PSO. Use the steps in Exercise 2, "Create a Password Settings Object," of Lesson 1 as a reference if you require any reminders for creating a PSO.

- **Practice 2** Identify the PSO that affects James Fine. Use the steps in Exercise 3, "Identify the Resultant PSO for a User," of Lesson 1 as a guide to evaluating resultant PSOs. Which PSO applies to James Fine?
- **Practice 3** Create a PSO named **PSO3** that is linked to James Fine's user account. Give *PSO3* a precedence value of *20*. You can use any valid settings for the other attributes of the PSO. Use the steps in Exercise 2 of Lesson 1 as a reference if you require any reminders for creating a PSO. Use the steps in Exercise 3 of Lesson 1 as a guide to evaluating resultant PSO. Identify the PSO that affects James Fine.

Recover from a Stolen Read-Only Domain Controller

In this practice, you will learn how to recover if an RODC is stolen or compromised, by simulating the loss of the server named BRANCHSERVER. To perform this practice, you must have completed the practice in Lesson 3, "Configuring Read-Only Domain Controllers."

When an RODC is stolen or compromised, any user credentials that had been cached on the RODC should be considered suspect and should be reset. Therefore, you must identify the credentials that had been cached on the RODC and reset the passwords of each account.

- **Practice 1** Determine the user and computer accounts that had been cached on BRANCHSERVER by examining the Policy Usage tab of the BRANCHSERVER Advanced Password Replication Policy dialog box. Use the steps in Exercise 3, "Monitor Credential Caching," of Lesson 3 if you require reminders for how to identify accounts whose passwords were stored on the RODC. Export the list to a file on your desktop.
- **Practice 2** Open the Active Directory Users And Computers snap-in and, in the Domain Controllers OU, select BRANCHSERVER. Press the Delete key and click Yes. Examine the options you have for automatically resetting user and computer passwords.

Take a Practice Test

The practice tests on this book's companion CD offer many options. For example, you can test yourself on just one exam objective, or you can test yourself on all the 70-640 certification exam content. You can set up the test so that it closely simulates the experience of taking a certification exam, or you can set it up in study mode so that you can look at the correct answers and explanations after you answer each question.

MORE INFO   Practice tests

For details about all the practice test options available, see the "How to Use the Practice Tests" section in this book's introduction.

Chapter 9

Integrating Domain Name System with AD DS

Without the Domain Name System (DNS), using the Internet would not be easy. Oh, you could still use the Internet because the underlying technology for the Internet is really TCP/IP, but going to *http://207.46.198.248* isn't quite like going to *http://Technet.microsoft.com*, especially when you have to type the address in your browser. When you look up a new technology such as Windows Server 2008 in Windows Live Search and receive a collection of IP addresses hosting information as the result of your query, it doesn't inspire confidence that these sites are safe to navigate to. IP addresses do not mean much to humans whereas domain names do.

This is why users rely so much on DNS: it translates IP addresses into common terms or domain names that humans can relate to more easily. In fact, DNS is at the very core of the TCP/IP protocol, whether it is IPv4—the traditional, 32-bit addressing scheme—or IPv6, the new, 128-bit addressing scheme that is built into Windows Server 2008. Each time you set up a system in a network, it will be identified by its IP address or addresses. In a Windows Server 2008 network running Active Directory Domain Services (AD DS), each of the devices linked to the directory will also be linked to the DNS name resolution system and will rely on it to identify each of the services it interacts with.

For example, when you boot a computer that is part of a domain, a standard process takes place. This process begins by the identification of service location records (SRV) from a DNS server to identify the closest domain controller (DC). Then, after DNS has done its work, the authentication process between the computer and the DC can begin. However, without the name resolution for the SRV by DNS, it would be difficult for AD DS to authenticate a member computer.

Because it provides the translation of IP addresses to names, DNS enables programming standards through common names in applications. When programmers know they need a process that will support the discovery of a specific service, they use a common name for that service; then, when the customer implements the DNS service along with the new application, DNS will render the common name to the actual IP address assigned to the computer hosting the service.

In addition, because it is a technology designed to manage naming on the Internet, DNS is one of the technologies contained within Windows Server 2008 that enables you to extend the authority of your network to the outside world. Like Active Directory Certificate Services

(AD CS), Active Directory Rights Management Services (AD RMS), Active Directory Lightweight Directory Services (AD LDS), and Active Directory Federation Services (AD FS), DNS is integrated with AD DS, but it can also run independently in a perimeter network and beyond. (See Figure 9-1.) When it does so, it enables other organizations and individuals to locate you from anywhere in the world. When they find you, they can interact with you or the applications you might share with customers, partners, mobile users, and anyone else through some form of electronic communication.

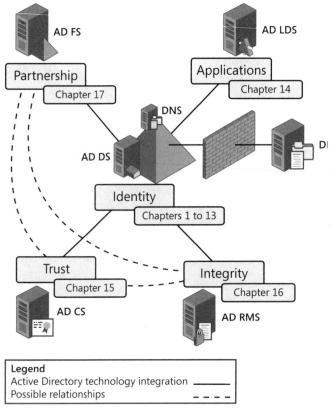

Figure 9-1 DNS extends your organization's authority beyond the borders of your internal network

Whether it communicates on the Internet or in your internal network, DNS always relies on TCP/IP port 53. All clients and servers are tuned to this port to locate and identify information about the computer names they need to interact with.

The naming structure supported by DNS is hierarchical. Names begin with a root and extend from the root when additional tiers are added to the hierarchy. The actual root of the DNS hierarchy is the dot (.) itself. However, this dot is not used in Internet naming. Commonly, standard root names are registered on the Internet and include names such as .com, .biz., .net,

.info, .name, .ms, .edu, .gov, .org, and so on. Organizations can link to the Internet through the binding of a common name with the root name. For example, *Microsoft.com* is two levels down from the root name but three levels down from the actual DNS root, as shown in Figure 9-2. *Technet.microsoft.com* is three levels down from the name but four from the DNS root and so on. AD DS relies on this hierarchy to create the domain structure of a forest.

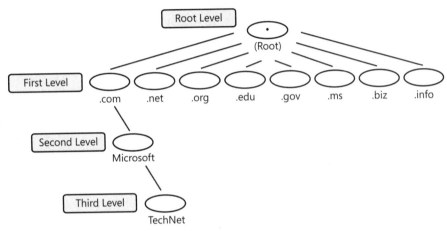

Figure 9-2   The DNS hierarchy of the Internet

DNS and IPv6

In Windows Server 2008, DNS has been updated to integrate with IPv6. Unlike IPv4, which is composed of four octets of binary digits to form the 32-bit IP address, IPv6 uses eight 16-bit pieces to form the 128-bit IP that is usually displayed in hexadecimal format. For example, FE80:: refers to the autogenerated link-local IPv6 address Windows Vista or Windows Server 2008 will assign to your computer if you rely on the Dynamic Host Configuration Protocol (DHCP) and there is no available DHCP server to respond with an actual address. The FE80:: address is the same as the Automatic Private IP Addressing (APIPA) address your system will generate if the same thing happens with an IPv4 address allocation.

In IPv6, each time a 16-bit address piece is composed of all zeros, you can concatenate the address and represent it with two colons (::). The two colons will represent any number of 16-bit sections that are composed of all zeros as long as they are contiguous. This facilitates writing out IPv6 addresses; otherwise, IPv6 notation could become quite complex.

Like IPv4, IPv6 provides several types of addresses:

- **Link-local**   Addresses that enable direct neighbors to communicate with each other. Any computer on the same network segment will be able to communicate with any other by using this address type. This is the address type assigned by default when IPv6 is turned on but does not use a static address and cannot communicate with a dynamic address provider such as a DHCPv6 server. These addresses are similar to the 169.254.0.0/16 addresses used by the APIPA process.

■ **Site-local**   Addresses that support private address spaces and you can use internally without having your own IPv6 address allocation. Site-local addresses can be routed, but should never have a routed connection to the Internet. They are similar to the 10.0.0.0/8, 172.16.0.0/12, and 192.168.0.0/16 addresses organizations use internally with IPv4.

■ **Global unicast**   Addresses that are entirely unique and can be used on the Internet to identify an interface. These addresses are routable on the Internet and enable direct communication to any device. These are comparable to the public IPv4 addresses organizations use on the Internet today.

The boon of IPv6 is the sheer number of addresses it provides. With the world population booming, the number of services and devices requiring IP addresses increasing, and the number of IPv4 addresses dwindling, it is time for the IP infrastructure of the Internet to evolve to the next level. By providing 340 billion billion billion billion—or 2^{128} addresses—IPv6 should support the next stage of the Internet for a long time. All you have to do is compare it to the 4 billion IPv4 addresses to see the difference.

Table 9-1 outlines the most common IPv6 address types.

Table 9-1   Common IPv6 Address Types

Address Type	Format	Description
Unspecified	::	Indicates the absence of an address. Comparable to 0.0.0.0 in IPv4.
Loopback	::1	Indicates the loopback interface and enables a node to send packets to itself. Comparable to 127.0.0.1 in IPv4.
Link-local	FE80::	Local network browsing address only. Comparable to APIPA or addresses in the 169.254.0.0/16 range in IPv4. Unroutable by IPv6 routers.
Site-local	FEC0::	Site-level internal address space. Routable but not to the Internet. Comparable to addresses in the 10.0.0.0/8, 172.16.0.0/12, and 192.168.0.0/16 ranges in IPv4.
Global unicast	All others	Unique addresses assigned to specific interfaces.

To comply with Internet standards and support the move to IPv6, DNS in Windows Server 2008 has been updated to support the longer address form of the IPv6 specification. IPv6 is installed and enabled by default in both Windows Vista and Windows Server 2008. This means that you can use this technology, at least internally, with little risk. It will be some time before all the elements that require an IPv6 connection to the Internet—intrusion detection systems, firewalls, anti-spam filtering, and so on—have been upgraded to support secure IPv6 transmissions.

MORE INFO   IPv6

For more information on IPv6, go to *http://www.microsoft.com/technet/network/ipv6/ipv6rfc.mspx*.

The Peer Name Resolution Protocol

Because they fully support IPv6, Windows Server 2008 and Windows Vista also include a secondary name resolution system called Peer Name Resolution Protocol (PNRP). Unlike DNS, which relies on a hierarchical naming structure, PNRP relies on peer systems to resolve the location of a computer system. Basically, PNRP is a referral system that performs lookups based on known data. For example, if you need to look up Computer A and you are near Computers B and C, your system will ask Computer B if it knows Computer A. If Computer B says yes, it will provide you with a link to Computer A. If not, your system will ask Computer C if it knows Computer A and then use the same process as with Computer B. If neither Computer B nor Computer C knows Computer A, your system will send a request to other computers near it until it finds one that knows of Computer A.

PNRP includes several features that are different from the DNS service:

- It is a distributed naming system that does not rely on a central server to locate objects. It is almost entirely serverless, but in some instances, servers are required to develop the name resolution process by themselves. Windows Server 2008 includes PNRP server components as an add-on feature.

- PNRP can scale to billions of names, unlike the DNS service, which will host only a small number of names and will then rely on another DNS server to locate the names over which it is not authoritative.

- Because it is distributed and relies on clients as much as servers, PNRP is fault tolerant. Several computers can host the same name, providing multiple paths to that name.

- Name publication is instantaneous, free, and does not require administrative intervention in the way DNS does.

- Names are updated in real time, unlike DNS, which relies heavily on caching to improve performance. Because of this, PNRP does not return stale addresses the way a DNS server, especially an earlier, nondynamic DNS server, can.

- PNRP also supports the naming of services as well as of computers because the PNRP name includes an address, a port, and a potential payload such as a service's function.

■ PNRP names can be protected through digital signatures. Protecting the names in this way ensures that they cannot be spoofed or replaced with counterfeit names by malicious users.

To provide resolution services, PNRP relies on the concept of a cloud. Two different clouds can exist. The first is the global cloud and includes the entire IPv6 global address scope, which encompasses the entire Internet. The second is a link-local cloud and is based on the link-local IPv6 address scope. Local links usually represent a single subnet. There can be several link-local clouds but only a single global cloud.

Just as the world has not fully moved to IPv6 yet, it also hasn't moved to PNRP and continues to rely on DNS to provide name resolution services. However, PNRP is an important new technology that will have a greater and greater impact on Internet operation as organizations move to IPv6.

MORE INFO   PNRP

For more information on PNRP, go to *http://technet.microsoft.com/en-us/library/bb726971.aspx*.

DNS Structures

DNS has been around since the Internet was first developed and has evolved with it. Because of this, the DNS service in Windows Server 2008 can provide a number of roles. There are three possible types of DNS servers:

■ **Dynamic DNS servers**   Servers that are designed to accept name registrations from a wide variety of devices through dynamic updates are deemed to be dynamic DNS (DDNS) servers. DDNS is designed to enable devices—clients and servers—to self-register to the DNS server so that other devices can locate them. When the DNS service runs on a DC and is integrated with the directory service, it runs in DDNS mode, enabling computers that use DHCP to register their own names within it automatically. This enables AD DS to locate the client when it needs to send it management data such as Group Policy objects (GPOs). DDNS servers are read-write servers, but they accept registrations from known entities only.

Exam Tip   Note that the exam does not include direct references to dynamic DNS. It will, however, refer to dynamic updates as well as to Active Directory–integrated DNS zones. Any time a DNS server is updated automatically through authorized clients, it is a DDNS. Keep this in mind when taking the exam.

■ **Read-write DNS servers**   Earlier DNS servers that are not running in dynamic mode but that will accept writes from known sources such as authorized operators are deemed read-write DNS servers. The most common type of read-write DNS server is the primary

DNS server. Primary DNS servers are usually deployed in perimeter networks and are not integrated with AD DS.

■ **Read-only DNS servers**   DNS servers that hold a read-only copy of DNS data that originates from another location are deemed read-only DNS servers. In Windows Server 2008, there are two types of read-only DNS servers. The first is the secondary DNS server. Secondary DNS servers are linked to primary DNS servers and will accept and host DNS data provided by the primary parent server. They make data available locally but cannot be modified because they support only one-way replication from the primary. A second type of read-only DNS server in Windows Server 2008 is the DNS server that runs on a read-only DC (RODC). These servers run primary read-only zones when integrated with RODCs.

Using these three types of DNS servers, you can construct a name resolution strategy that meets all your naming requirements. (See Figure 9-3.) For example, you could pair DDNS servers with every domain controller in your network because the DNS data is usually integrated with the directory store. Because it is contained in the directory store, the DNS data is replicated to every DC in a domain and sometimes in a forest through the same mechanism that replicates directory traffic. This means each DC has a local copy of DNS data. Installing the DNS service on the DC automatically gives it access to this data and can provide local rather than remote name resolution services, avoiding wide area network (WAN) traffic. In addition, you can use the RODC DNS service in read-only mode in unsecured locations within your network, locations that warrant local services but do not have local administrative staff. You can also use the standalone primary DNS service in perimeter networks. These servers contain few records but support access to any application or service you host in your perimeter. Last, you could use read-only secondary DNS servers in unsecured locations facing the Internet.

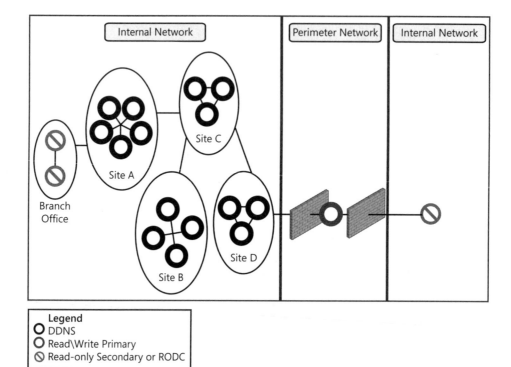

Figure 9-3 DNS server placement in a Windows Server 2008 network: DDNS follows DCs, primaries are protected, and RODCs are internal, whereas secondaries are external

---

MORE INFO Domain Name System

For more information on DNS, go to *http://technet2.microsoft.com/windowsserver2008/en/servermanager/dnsserver.mspx*.

The Split-Brain Syndrome

One of the most basic tenets of internetworking is the segregation of the internal network from the Internet. Small and large organizations alike will endeavor to protect their internal network through a variety of systems and technology. The most common protection mechanism is the firewall, which protects your network by blocking entry of undesirable traffic through the control of TCP/IP ports. Accepted ports are open and all unacceptable ports are closed. It's as simple as that.

Similarly, when you work with Windows Server 2008 and especially with AD DS, you will need to work with two namespaces. Because AD DS directories are based on the DNS hierarchical naming system, you must use a properly formed DNS name, often called a fully qualified domain name (FQDN), to name your directory forests and the domains they contain. Frequently, organizations use the same name they use to represent themselves on the Internet.

For example, this book suggests names such as *contoso.com* or *woodgrovebank.com* as potential names for your internal networks. This is by no means a best practice. This book uses these names because they are legally acceptable names that Microsoft Press is allowed to use to represent fictitious organizations. However, using the same name internally for your AD DS directory structure as you use for your external exposure to the Internet means you must implement a split-brain DNS service.

That's because you need to maintain two namespaces for two purposes all across a firewall. Nothing could be more complex. Your users must be able to locate both internal and external resources that rely on the same name. If Contoso, Ltd., used *contoso.com* for both its internal and its external namespaces in real life, its DNS administrators would need to manage the separation manually between internal and external name resolution mechanisms.

However, if Contoso used *contoso.com* exclusively for its external presence and used a corresponding name with a different extension, for example, .net, for its internal AD DS namespace, the DNS administrators would have to do nothing to segregate the two namespaces. The very fact that they use different roots automatically segregates the names and the two DNS services that would be used to support them. The only thing that needs to transit through the firewall is standard name references you would normally use for any name that is not located within your network.

In addition, it is very easy for Contoso to buy and maintain all the possible combinations of its Internet name, including common roots such as .com, .net, .info, .ms, .ws, and more. This way, Contoso knows it can use any of the names it owns for any forest implementation, production, testing, development, or staging or for whichever purpose it needs it and never conflict with anyone else even if it faces a merger or an acquisition.

Issues that commonly arise around this topic are often based on the ownership of the DNS service. Traditionally, network operators own previous DNS services and, very often, these DNS services are maintained in environments that are not Microsoft Windows–based. However, Windows and, especially, AD DS are designed to rely very tightly on the Windows DNS service. Although it is possible to use Windows with non-Windows DNS servers, it is not recommended because it requires so much more work. When you use the Windows DNS service and integrate it with your AD DS service, everything becomes automatic. When you don't, everything remains manual and, very often, you'll find that specific components don't work because the manual configuration was not completed or was misconfigured by non-Windows system administrators.

If you are in this situation and you must run two DNS technologies, the best and ideal network configuration is to use a whole-brain approach and rely on two different namespaces, integrate the internal namespace with Windows DNS servers running on DCs, and simply link the two namespaces through standard DNS resolution mechanisms. This will provide you with the implementation that will require the least amount of administrative effort and ensure that all services work at all times. (See Figure 9-4.)

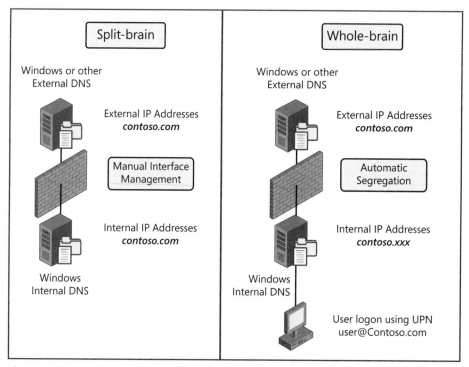

Figure 9-4   Split-brain vs. whole-brain DNS structures

Further, you needn't worry about users. If you are using a different namespace internally, but you want them to log on with the external network name, for example, *contoso.com*, just add it as the preferred user principal name (UPN) suffix in your directory. DNS will be simpler to manage, your internal network will be protected from external access, and your users won't know the difference!

MORE INFO   **Split-brain DNS**

For more information on split-brain DNS setups, go to *http://www.microsoft.com/serviceproviders/resources/techresarticlesdnssplit.mspx.*

Exam objectives in this chapter:

- Configuring Domain Name System (DNS) for Active Directory
    - ❏ Configure zones.
    - ❏ Configure DNS server settings.
    - ❏ Configure zone transfers and replication.

Lessons in this chapter:

- Lesson 1: Understanding and Installing Domain Name System................ 406
- Lesson 2: Configuring and Using Domain Name System...................... 431

Before You Begin

To complete the lessons in this chapter, you must have done the following:

- Installed Windows Server 2008 on a physical or virtual computer that should be named SERVER10 and should be a standalone server. This computer will host the DNS server and DC service you will install and create through the exercises in this chapter. Assign an IPv4 address from one of the private ranges, for example, 192.168.x.x, and map its DNS server address to its own address.

- Installed Windows Server 2008 on a physical or virtual computer that should be named SERVER20 and should be a standalone server. This computer will host the DNS server and DC service you will install and create through the exercises in this chapter. Assign an IPv4 address from one of the private ranges, for example, 192.168.x.x, and map its DNS server address to the address you assigned to SERVER10.

- Installed Windows Server 2008 on a physical or virtual computer that should be named SERVER30 and should be a standalone server. This computer will host the DNS server and DC service you will install and create through the exercises in this chapter. Assign an IPv4 address from one of the private ranges, for example, 192.168.x.x, and map its DNS server address to the address you assigned to SERVER10.

We strongly recommend using virtual machines (VMs) in support of the exercises. The DC and DNS server roles are ideal for virtualization through either Microsoft Virtual Server 2005 R2 or Windows Server 2008 Hyper-V.

Real World

Danielle Ruest and Nelson Ruest

In late 2002, we were putting finishing touches to our second book: *Windows Server 2003, Best Practices for Enterprise Deployments* for McGraw-Hill Osborne. This book was based on our experiences with customers in designing and deploying Windows 2000–based Active Directory (AD) structures. One feature that intrigued us the most was the new application directory partition feature in Microsoft Windows Server 2003. According to the documentation provided with the beta versions, application directory partitions would be used to store DNS data within the directory and control their replication scope.

As our customers would create best-practices forests, using a forest root domain and a single, global child production domain, we discovered that when you created the forest root domain, DNS data was properly located within the forest root domain partition, but when you created a child domain, the data would not be stored automatically within the child domain partition. This caused a serious problem with DNS data. All our customers would use a two-DC forest root to keep it as secure as possible and to control access to forest root administration tightly. Because of this, the forest root DCs would always be located within central headquarter sites. The child production domain, however, would be highly distributed and include domain controllers within each remote site that had more than a certain number of users.

Because DNS data for the child domain was actually included in the forest root domain partition and not in the child partition, each client had to perform DNS lookups over the WAN to contact the forest root DCs. However, if DNS data was to be stored in the directory and made available to DCs, it should be in the local DC, not in a remote DC.

We discovered that we could change the replication scope of the child domain DNS data after the directory service was deployed, but we have always been proponents of doing things right in the first place, not correcting them afterward. This meant we needed to find a way to make sure the DNS data would be stored in the proper location during installation rather than later.

We contacted the Microsoft Active Directory development team and reported this DNS behavior as a bug, and they agreed that this should be corrected at installation, not afterward. Further research demonstrated that because a child domain namespace is an extension of the root domain's namespace, the child domain name would resolve properly during the verification checks the Active Directory Installation Wizard performed. Because of this, the wizard would store the data within the forest root domain. In fact, the wizard was behaving properly; we just didn't give it enough information.

Further investigation revealed that if you created a manual DNS delegation before creating the child domain, the wizard would locate the data properly within the child domain partition—the manual delegation would point to a server that did not exist yet because the child domain was not created. For example, if you had a root domain named *treyresearch.net* and a child domain that would be named *intranet.treyresearch.net*, you would point the delegation to a server named *servername*.intranet.treyresearch.net. Because no server of that name existed until the child domain was actually created, the delegation would contain dummy data and would be called a dummy DNS delegation. When the wizard would run, it would find this server in DNS and try to use it to resolve the child domain's DNS name. The resolution would fail and force the wizard to install DNS during the creation of the domain and create the appropriate DNS data partition.

The Active Directory Domain Services Installation Wizard now properly creates delegations for child domains. Many AD implementations based on Windows Server 2003 did not locate DNS data in the proper partition during installation, and only IT administrators who knew how to use the dummy delegation before creating a child domain were aware of the issue. Windows Server 2008 has resolved this problem.

Lesson 1: Understanding and Installing Domain Name System

Domain name resolution is a complex process that relies on a naming hierarchy to match IP addresses, both IPv4 and IPv6, to system names. DNS name resolution also supports the identification of service locations. This is how the AD DS logon process works. In fact, DNS plays an essential role in this process and, because of this, services such as those provided by AD DS would simply not be possible without the DNS service.

To do this, the DNS service relies on name records. Records can be inscribed manually, such as in a primary DNS server that provides read-write services. However, writes are supported only from administrators, or they can be inscribed automatically such as with dynamic DNS servers that accept name records from devices. Smart devices such as computers running editions of Windows 2000, Windows XP, Windows 2003, Windows Vista, or Windows Server 2008 can register their own names within a DDNS, but devices running earlier operating systems such as Microsoft Windows NT cannot. Former devices will rely on the DHCP to perform the inscription for them; however, this is a less secure implementation of a DDNS infrastructure.

DNS contains a host of record types that can be used to provide name resolution for specific service types or specific computer types. In addition, these records are stored within DNS zones—special placeholders that provide a given name resolution functionality for a specific namespace.

Understanding the various components of the Windows Server 2008 DNS service is critical to understanding how it works and how it should be used.

MORE INFO   DNS in Windows Server 2008

For more information on DNS in Windows Server 2008, go to *http://technet2.microsoft.com/ windowsserver2008/en/servermanager/dnsserver.mspx*.

> **After this lesson, you will be able to:**
> - Understand when to use DNS.
> - Install DNS.
> - Locate and view the DNS installation.
>
> **Estimated lesson time: 70 minutes**

Understanding DNS

The first thing to understand when working with DNS is how it works to resolve a name. You already know that DNS relies on a hierarchy of servers because a DNS server cannot hold all possible name records within itself. Because of this, the DNS service relies on name referrals to perform name resolution. (See Figure 9-5.)

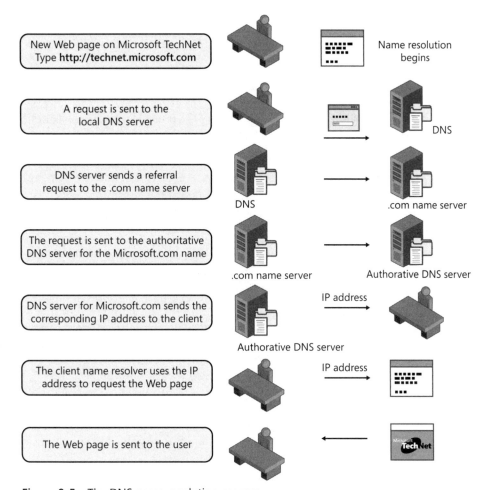

Figure 9-5 The DNS name resolution process

Here's how name resolution works:

1. You try to look up a Web page on the Microsoft TechNet Web site. To do so, you type *http://technet.microsoft.com* in the address bar of your browser and press Enter. That's when name resolution begins.

2. Your computer sends out a request to its local DNS server or at least to one of the servers listed in its IP configuration settings for the name.

3. If this server does not include the name in its own database or cache, it sends a referral request to the name server. Because the Microsoft site name ends in .com, the DNS server sends the referral to the .com name server.

4. The .com name server is the authority for all names that end in the .com suffix. This server knows the location of all DNS servers that are the final authorities for a particular name ending with .com. In this case, it sends the request to the authoritative DNS server for the *microsoft.com* name.

5. The DNS server for *microsoft.com* sends the corresponding IP address for the requested page to the client computer.

6. The name resolver on the client uses the IP address to request the actual page from its Internet provider.

7. If the page is not already in the local cache of the Internet provider, it requests the actual page and sends it to the client.

This name resolution procedure occurs within seconds, and the Web page appears almost as fast as you type it, depending on the speed of your connection and the current load of the requested server. That's what happens when you look at the green progress bar at the bottom of your browser. The actual progress also includes downloading content such as text and graphics to your own computer.

DNS is a system that does not and cannot work alone. It must rely on other servers to operate. In addition, the DNS service includes a terminology of its own. Table 9-2 outlines the most common terms you will encounter when working with DNS.

Table 9-2   DNS Terms and Concepts

Term	Description
Active Directory Integrated (ADI) zone	When a DNS zone is integrated with Active Directory, it is hosted in the AD DS database, *NTDS.dit*, and is replicated throughout the directory with other directory data.
Aging	DNS records are associated with an age or a Time to Live (TTL). When the record lasts beyond its age, it is no longer valid and can result in false positives, giving users the impression they are going to a specific location when the location is no longer valid.
Application directory partitions	When DNS data is stored within AD DS directory databases, it is replicated by default with the directory data it is associated with. However, you can define a custom replication scope for DNS data. For example, DNS data that belongs to a root domain for a forest must be made available to the entire forest whereas DNS data for a specific domain is really required only for that domain. You control DNS data replication scopes through application directory partitions.

Table 9-2   **DNS Terms and Concepts**

Term	Description
DDNS	This is a DNS service that can be automatically updated by the clients that rely on it. In Windows Server 2008, you install DDNS whenever you choose to install the DNS service with AD DS. Because all the clients in a DDNS implementation have AD DS accounts, they are deemed secure clients and are authorized to update the DNS server with their record information.
DNS Notify	Traditional or former DNS servers manage data in local files. These files are located on the primary server. They are then transferred through a polling and zone transfer mechanism to read only secondary servers. However, large zones will often require frequent record updating. This could lead to incorrect records located within the secondary server. To correct this situation, DNS uses a special notification process that notifies slave servers that an update is available, which then prompts a zone transfer to the read-only servers.
Domain DNS zone	This is the zone that contains the records for a particular domain, either a root or a child domain, within an AD DS forest structure.
Forest DNS zone	This is the zone that contains the records that pertain to an entire forest within an AD DS forest structure.
Forward lookup	DNS supports two types of lookups: forward or reverse. A forward lookup relies on a client providing an FQDN to the server. The server then matches this FQDN to the corresponding IP address.
Forward lookup zone	This comprises DNS containers—databases or text files—that include name resolutions for forward lookups.
Forwarders	DNS servers have two mechanisms for name resolution: forwarders or root hints. DNS servers that provide name resolution services to the internal network will often rely on forwarders to forward any request they cannot resolve on their own to a trusted external DNS server. Windows Server 2008 also includes the ability to rely on conditional forwarders or forwarders that are used only when specific conditions are met in a request. For example, if the name is for an internal domain, but not one managed by this server, it can automatically forward the request to the internal name server for that domain.
GlobalNames Zone (GNZ)	NetBIOS names are single-label names that do not use the FQDN format. For example, down-level computer names are single-label names. Traditionally, these names are managed by Windows Internet Name Service (WINS). In an effort to remove this prior service from a Windows-based network, Microsoft has implemented the GlobalNames Zone in DNS in Windows Server 2008. GNZs can contain single-label names and replace WINS in a Windows-based network.

Table 9-2 **DNS Terms and Concepts**

Term	Description
Legacy DNS	Nondynamic DNS servers that rely on manual updating of zone records are deemed legacy DNS servers. Because it complies with the set of request for comments (RFC) that define and standardize the DNS protocol on the Internet, Windows Server 2008 can support former DNS services as well as the dynamic DNS service required by AD DS. Legacy DNS servers host either primary or secondary zones.
Name recursion	Name resolutions can be either iterative or recursive. In an iterative request, each DNS server holds only part of the answer for a query and must rely on other DNS servers to complete the query. In a recursive query, the DNS server will hold the complete answer and provide it to the requester. Because of record aging, it is possible for a recursive query to respond with an erroneous IP address.
Primary zones	These are zones that contain read-write information for a particular domain. Primary zones are stored on nondynamic or dynamic DNS servers. When stored on nondynamic DNS servers, primary zones are contained within text files and are edited manually by an administrator. When stored on DDNS servers, primary zones are contained within Active Directory and are updated either automatically by each record holder or manually by an administrator.
Resource records	These are the name records contained within DNS databases. Resource records usually link an IP address with an FQDN.
Reverse lookup	DNS supports two types of lookups: forward or reverse. A reverse lookup relies on a client providing an IP address and requesting the FQDN that corresponds to the address.
Reverse lookup zone	This zone comprises DNS containers—databases or text files—that include name resolutions for reverse lookups for a particular domain.
Root hints	DNS servers have two mechanisms for name resolution: forwarders or root hints. DNS servers that provide name resolution services to the internal network but also have a direct connection to the Internet can rely on root hints to locate authoritative servers for root names such as .com, .org, .net, and so on in the Internet and provide resolution services to internal clients. By default, Windows Server 2008 DNS servers rely on root hints for external name resolution. These hints are regularly updated through Microsoft Windows Update. Root hints are contained within a special file named Cache.dns, which can also be used to reset root hints in the event of issues with the external name resolution process.

Table 9-2 DNS Terms and Concepts

Term	Description
Round robin	DNS services can be used to provide some form of high availability. This is done by creating multiple records for the same resource, each with a different IP address. When queried, the DNS server will provide the first address, then the second address, then the third, and so on, balancing the load between multiple servers that host the same service. For example, Microsoft Exchange Server 2007 Edge Transport Server—servers that face the Internet to accept and send internal e-mail—rely on the round robin process to provide e-mail load balancing.
Secondary zone	A secondary zone is a read-only zone obtained from a primary DNS server. Secondary zones provide local DNS resolution in highly distributed networks.
Server scavenging	A feature that was introduced with the dynamic DNS service released with Windows 2000 Server. Because records have an age or time to live, they can become stale when they extend beyond their expected duration. Server scavenging will scour the DNS database to locate records that have aged beyond their usefulness and automatically remove them.
Single-label names	NetBIOS names that do not use the FQDN format. For example, down-level computer names are single-label names. These names include 16 characters and do not support special characters such as dots. Only the first 15 characters of a single-label name can be used because the sixteenth character is reserved by the system to complete the name. Traditionally, these names are managed by WINS. In Windows Server 2008, you can rely on the GNZ in DNS to replace WINS.
Start of Authority (SOA) record	This is a special DNS record that outlines domain information such as the update schedule for the records it contains, the intervals other DNS servers should use to verify updates, and the date and time of the last update as well as other information such as contacts for the domain and so on. Only one SOA record can be contained within a specific zone file. Each zone file should contain a particular SOA record.
Stub zone	This is a special zone type that contains only the records of other DNS servers that maintain the actual zone itself. This can speed name resolution and reduce the likelihood of errors because stub zones are used as referrals to other, authoritative DNS servers for a zone.
TTL	Each DNS record is given a TTL value. This value determines the valid duration of the record. When it expires, the record can be deleted through scavenging. However, if the record is still valid before its TTL value expires, you can renew the record and, therefore, renew its TTL value.

Table 9-2   **DNS Terms and Concepts**

Term	Description
Zone delegations	Delegations are used to help you manage different namespace sections better. For example, Microsoft might want to delegate different sections of its namespace, notably the MSDN or TechNet sections of *Microsoft.com*, to have them administered by other divisions in the company. When managing DNS namespaces in AD DS, you must delegate new domain-based zones when you create the domain; otherwise, the zone will be managed at the forest level and not at the domain level as it should be. In Windows Server 2003, this delegation had to be created manually before creating the domain. In Windows Server 2008, the Active Directory Domain Services Installation Wizard will perform the delegation automatically when you create a child domain.
Zone scavenging	Scavenging scours the DNS server to remove stale or outdated records whose age has gone beyond their TTL value. Zone scavenging applies when scavenging is applied to a single zone as opposed to the entire server.
Zone transfers	These are the transactions DNS servers use to replicate information from one server to another. Full zone transfers transfer the entire content of a zone to one or more other DNS servers. Incremental transfers send only a subset of the data. Traditionally, full transfers are referred to as Asynchronous Full Transfer (AXFR) whereas incremental transfers are dubbed Incremental Zone Transfer (IXFR). Windows Server 2008 also supports secure zone transfers, which are performed through AD DS multimaster replication.

The Windows Server 2008 DNS service supports three zone types, as shown in Figure 9-6:

- **Primary Zone** Zones that can be integrated with AD DS or that can be of the former, standard type. These zones are authoritative for the namespace they contain. Primary zones are read-write zones except when located on RODCs.

- **Secondary Zone** Zones that are of the former, standard type and are only a replica of the data maintained by a primary or authoritative server for a namespace. When you create a secondary zone, you must tell DNS the address of the primary zone or source of the zone data.

- **Stub Zone** Zones that are nothing but pointers to other, authoritative servers for the namespace they maintain. Once again, when you create a stub zone, you must specify a list of server(s) that are authoritative for the namespace.

Each zone type can be stored either in a text file or within an Active Directory directory store partition.

Exam Tip   Keep these zone types in mind for the exam. You can change from one zone type to another in DNS, but remember that the most useful zone type is the primary zone. This is the type used by AD DS when you integrate the DNS service with it.

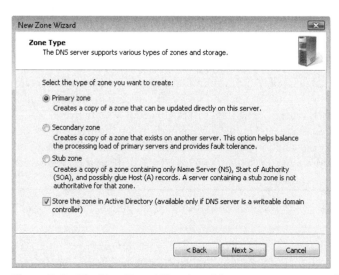

Figure 9-6   The New Zone Wizard enables you to create any of the three supported zones

Zones are containers that include information about the objects they manage. This information is in the form of records. DNS can contain several types of records. Table 9-3 outlines the most common record types used in DNS in Windows Server 2008.

Table 9-3   DNS Record Types in Windows Server 2008

Record Type	Usage
Alias (CNAME)	Used to create an alternate record or alias DNS name for a name that is already specified as another record type in a specific zone. This is also known as a canonical name (CNAME). For example, if you want to create a record such as *intranet.contoso.com* to point to a server or server farm hosting Microsoft Office SharePoint Server, you would create it as an alias record. This facilitates usage by providing a more functional name than the server name.
Host (A or AAAA) records	The most common record type in DNS. They represent computer objects in the namespace and are used to resolve a specific IP address to a device.

Table 9-3   DNS Record Types in Windows Server 2008

Record Type	Usage
Mail exchanger (MX)	Routes e-mail messages to a specific namespace. For example, the MX record for *contoso.com* would indicate that all e-mail directed to *contoso.com* should pass through the host or hosts identified by this record.
Pointer (PTR)	Points to a specific location within the namespace. PTR records are usually used to provide reverse lookup capabilities within the namespace.
Service location (SRV)	Indicates the location of a specific TCP/IP service. For example, if you want to use Microsoft Office Communications Server, you must create a session initiation protocol (SIP) service location record to indicate to all the devices that rely on this service where it is situated in your network. Similarly, AD DS creates several service location records in support of the logon or the Group Policy distribution processes. Service location records usually consist of the IP address for the server as well as the TCP/IP port on which the service is available.

The records in Table 9-3 provide the main functionality of DNS in a Windows Server 2008 implementation.

Exam Tip   Table 9-3 lists the most common record types. However, review all the record types the Windows Server 2008 DNS server supports in preparation for the exam.

Windows Server DNS Features

The Windows Server 2008 DNS server complies fully with the RFC generated by the Internet Engineering Task Force (IETF, found at *http://www.ietf.org*) for Internet technology standards, but, in addition, it also includes a series of features that are designed to support the network operating system (NOS) features of AD DS. The DNS server in Windows Server 2008 can also operate with non-Windows-based DNS servers because it complies with all the RFCs related to the DNS service.

When the DNS service is integrated with AD DS, you can store DNS data in different locations within the directory database. DNS data can be stored within the domain partition of the directory. You choose this option for data that references the domain itself. For example, a child domain within a forest would normally have its data stored within its own domain partition to make the data available to all DNS servers in the domain. You can also store data within application directory partitions. Unlike domain partitions, application directory partitions have a controllable replication scope. For example, forest DNS data is stored in an application directory partition that spans the entire forest, making this data available to any DNS server within the forest. By default, Windows Server DNS creates two application directory partitions to host DNS data in each forest. These partitions are respectively named

ForestDnsZones and DomainDnsZones. In addition, DomainDnsZones is created in each child domain within a forest to host data for that domain.

Exam Tip DNS replication scopes are a key section of the exam. Examine them in your DNS server implementations and understand the contents of each scope type.

In addition, the DNS service in Windows Server 2008 has been improved to support background zone loading. When a DNS server hosts a large number of zones and records hosted in AD DS, it might take time for the server to boot because, traditionally, it needs to load all zone data before servicing requests. By using background loading, the DNS service can begin to respond to requests more quickly as it continues to load zone data in the background after the computer is started and logon is initiated.

To support the new read-only domain controller role, DNS has been updated to provide read-only DNS data for primary zones hosted on the RODC. This further secures the role and ensures that no one can create records from potentially unprotected servers to spoof the network.

Exam Tip Remember that DNS zones in RODCs are read-only *primary* DNS zones. Traditionally, read-only zones are secondary zones.

In an effort to support the removal of the WINS service from networks while still providing support for single-label names or names that do not include the parent name in their own (for example, SERVER10 instead of SERVER10.Contoso.com), DNS has been updated to include a GNZ. This zone can be used to host a small number of names with static IP addresses.

Exam Tip Keep in mind that you use GNZs to replace WINS implementations but only when you have a small number of single-label names to manage. Single-label or NetBIOS names are often required for previous applications that cannot work with the more complex FQDN structure. In fact, single-label names stem from older Windows NT–based networks or applications. In most cases, organizations should have been able to deprecate these applications and remove them from their networks, but some exceptions might remain. GNZs are designed to support these few remaining applications. However, if an organization needs to run a multitude of single-label names, you will need to implement the WINS service along with DNS.

Finally, in an effort to provide further protection against spoofing, DNS now supports the addition of global query block lists. When clients use protocols such as the Web Proxy Automatic Discovery Protocol (WPAD) or the Intra-site Automatic Tunnel Addressing Protocol (ISATAP) and rely on DNS to resolve host names, they can be vulnerable to malicious users who take advantage of dynamic updates to register computers that are not legitimate hosts.

WPAD is normally the protocol Web browsers rely on to discover network proxy server settings. Spoofing this address could lead users to malicious servers that impersonate legitimate proxy servers and potentially compromise a network. ISATAP is a transition protocol that enables IPV4 and IPv6 networks to work together. It does this by encapsulating IPv6 packets in IPv4 format to transmit them through routers. It does not support dynamic router discovery. Instead, it relies on a potential routers list to identify potential ISATAP routers. If this list is compromised, IPv6 packets could be routed to malicious routers and compromised in turn.

You can reduce the potential for these vulnerabilities by using global query block lists that contain specific blocked address ranges. Only the leftmost portion of an FQDN is included in global query block lists. When the DNS server receives a query that includes this name, it returns an answer as if no record existed. By default, the DNS server will generate this list at installation or during an upgrade of an existing DNS service. If either of the two protocols exists, the one that exists will not be blocked. If they do not exist, they will both be blocked. In addition, you can add your own names to this list to block names you do not want to be operational in your network.

MORE INFO Global query block lists

For more information on global query block lists, search for DNS global query block lists on the Microsoft Web site. You can download a document on the subject.

In short, the DNS service in Windows Server 2008 provides full support for all the standard features you would expect in a DNS server but also includes custom features that are available in Windows only.

Quick Check

1. What are the most common address types in IPv6 and which type is used by default on Windows Server 2008 and Windows Vista systems?
2. What is a major difference between the PNRP and DNS?
3. Which are the two types of read-only DNS servers supported by Windows Server 2008?
4. What is the first step in an AD DS logon process?
5. Which type of delegations can the Active Directory Domain Services Installation Wizard automatically remove?

Quick Check Answers

1. The most common IPv6 address types are link-local, site-local, and global unicast. By default, Windows Server 2008 and Windows Vista are designed to use dynamic IPv6 addresses. However, when no DHCPv6 servers are present in a network, IPv6 automatically assigns a link-local address to the interface.

2. One major difference between PNRP and DNS is the number of records each can contain. PNRP can scale to contain millions of name records; DNS is much more modest and relies on a hierarchy of servers to validate names.

3. The DNS server supports two read-only modes in Windows Server 2008. The first is the traditional, or legacy, secondary DNS. Secondary DNS servers are subordinate to one or more primary servers and contain only a copy of the information provided to them by a read-write source. The second type of read-only server is the one included in an RODC. This DNS server, however, includes *primary* read-only zones.

4. The first step in an AD DS logon process is a DNS request sent to locate the SRV for the closest domain controller. When this record is resolved, the logon process can begin through exchanges with the domain controller.

5. The Active Directory Domain Services Installation Wizard supports the removal of any delegation you have control over. This means it will properly remove child domain delegations, but it cannot remove top-level delegations because the root servers are on the Internet, and you do not have access to these servers.

Integration with AD DS

Because of its special Windows features, always deploy the Windows DNS server when you deploy AD DS. You can rely on a third-party DNS server to provide name resolution support for AD DS also, but it is significantly more work to set up and prepare this DNS server than to use the one built into Windows. When you use the Windows DNS server with AD DS, all DNS content is configured by default. This is why DNS installation is integrated with the domain controller promotion wizard. Installing DNS with AD DS performs several tasks that are usually completely transparent to the administrator running the wizard. These operations occur only during the creation of a forest, a domain tree within an existing forest, or a new domain within an existing forest.

If the AD DS deployment is for a forest root domain, DNS will create placeholders for the forward lookup zones (FLZ), the reverse lookup zones (RLZ) and conditional forwarders (CF). Then, it will generate two new zones within the FLZ. The first will be a container for the entire forest for the namespace you created during the installation of AD DS. This zone is usually named _msdcs.*domainname*. For example, for the *contoso.com* domain, this zone is called *_msdcs.contoso.com.* In addition, it creates a zone within the FLZ for the root domain itself, as shown in Figure 9-7.

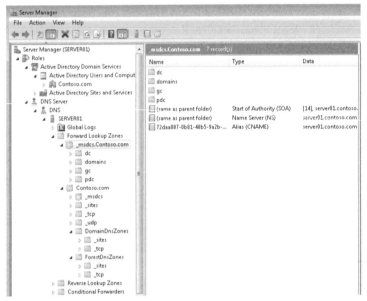

Figure 9-7   Forward lookup zones for the *contoso.com* forest

When the AD DS process creates a domain tree in an existing forest, it requires a manual delegation before the domain tree is created. Because the name of the domain tree is different from the root domain name—it must be different because that is the definition of a tree within a forest—the wizard cannot create the delegation on its own. When two DNS namespaces are different, neither has the authority to delegate information for the other, hence the need for a manual delegation. Then, after the delegation has been created, the AD DS Installation Wizard will create the DNS namespace and store it appropriately within the domain tree's new domain partition.

When the AD DS process creates a child domain in an existing forest, it automatically creates a delegation within the top-level root domain and then properly stores the DNS data for the child domain in the child domain's partition.

To remove a domain, you must run the Active Directory Domain Services Installation Wizard once again to remove the domain controller role, and then you can remove the AD DS role. However, because there is no interface to access the wizard anywhere, you must type **Dcpromo.exe** in the Search box of the Start menu to launch the wizard. When you remove the DC role, it will also remove DNS data created for a domain if this DC is the last DC in a domain. Also, if the DC is a global catalog (GC) server, it will give you a warning during the demotion because GCs support the search function in AD DS. During the removal of the DC role, you will be prompted to remove DNS delegations, as shown in Figure 9-8. If this is a top-level domain such as a forest or tree root domain, make sure you clear this option; otherwise, you will receive an error because the wizard will ask you for credentials to delete the delegation. Because you do not have root-level credentials (for names such as .com, .net, .org, and so on), you cannot provide them and, therefore, cannot delete (or create, for that matter) root-level delegations. However, if it is a child domain, select to delete the DNS delegation and it will work properly.

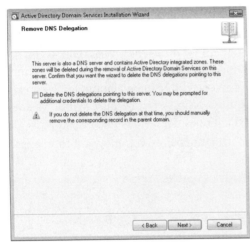

Figure 9-8   Removing DNS delegations with the AD DS Installation Wizard

PRACTICE Installing the DNS Service

In this practice, you will install the DNS service. In the first exercise, you will install the DNS service in standalone mode to explore how you would create a legacy primary server. Then, you will install AD DS and create a root domain in a new forest. This will create forest DNS zones in the DNS server. In the third exercise, you will create a manual zone delegation to prepare for the integration of a new domain tree into your new forest. Then, you will install AD DS and create a new domain tree within the same forest as the first server. This creates tree-based zones in DNS by relying on the delegation you created. Finally, you will install AD DS and create a child domain to view child domain zones in DNS. Note that in this case, the wizard will properly create the appropriate delegations for the child domain. This exercise requires that SERVER10, SERVER20, and SERVER30 be running.

▶ **Exercise 1   Install a Primary DNS Server**

In this exercise, you will use a standalone computer to install the DNS service and view how it operates in nondynamic mode. This exercise is performed on SERVER10.

1. Log on to Server10 with the local administrator account.
2. In Server Manager, right-click the Roles node and select Add Roles.

3. Review the Before You Begin page and click Next.

4. On the Select Server Roles page of the Add Roles Wizard, select DNS Server and click Next.

5. Review the information in the DNS Server page and click Next.

6. Review your choices and click Install.

7. Examine the installation results and click Close.

   Your installation is complete.

8. Move to the DNS Server node in Server Manager and expand all its sections. You might need to close and reopen Server Manager to refresh the nodes.

   As you can see, the DNS installation creates all the containers required to run the DNS service in Windows Server 2008, but because this is the process you would normally use to install a legacy DNS server, no information is created within the DNS container structure. (See Figure 9-9.) Legacy DNS servers require manual input for the creation of zone information. You can automate the input process, but because Windows does not know why you want to use this DNS server, it does not create data for you.

9. Explore the DNS Server container structure before you move on to Exercise 2, "Install AD DS and Create a New Forest."

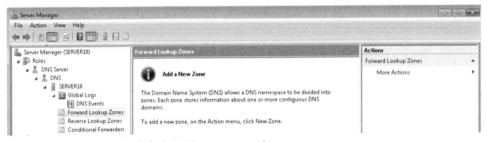

Figure 9-9 Viewing the default DNS server containers

▶ **Exercise 2   Install AD DS and Create a New Forest**

In this exercise, you will use a standalone computer to install the AD DS role and then create a new forest. After AD DS is installed, you will use the Active Directory Domain Services Installation Wizard to create a root domain in a new forest.

1. Log on to Server10 with the local administrator account.

2. In Server Manager, right-click the Roles node and select Add Roles.

3. Review the Before You Begin screen and click Next.

4. On the Select Server Roles page of the Add Roles Wizard, select Active Directory Domain Services and click Next.

5. Review the information on the Active Directory Domain Services page and click Next.

6. Confirm your choices and click Install.

7. Examine the installation results and click Close.

   Your installation is complete.

8. Next, click the Active Directory Domain Services node in Server Manager.

9. Click Run The Active Directory Domain Services Installation Wizard in the details pane. This launches the Active Directory Domain Services Installation Wizard.

10. Click Next.

11. Review the information on the Operating System Compatibility page and click Next.

12. On the Choose A Deployment Configuration page, choose Create A New Domain In A New Forest and click Next.

13. On the Name The Forest Root Domain page, type **treyresearch.net** and click Next.

    You use a name with the .net extension because you do not want to use a split-brain DNS model. Trey Research uses a public name with the .com extension on the Internet but a name with the .net extension internally. Trey Research has purchased both domain names and knows that because it owns them, no one can use the names for AD DS structures. If Trey Research ever faces a merger or acquisition, it will be much easier for the company to integrate its own forest with another to streamline IT operations for the new organization.

14. On the Set Forest Functional Level page, select Windows Server 2008 from the drop-down list and click Next.

15. On the Additional Domain Controller Options page, verify that DNS Server and Global Catalog are both selected and click Next. Note that the DNS Server service is already installed on this server.

16. If you did not assign a static IP address, the Active Directory Domain Services Installation Wizard will give you a warning because you are using a dynamic IP address. Click the Yes, The Computer Will Use A Dynamically Assigned IP Address (Not Recommended) option.

17. The Active Directory Domain Services Installation Wizard will warn you that it cannot create a delegation for this server. Click Yes.

    You get this error message for two reasons. First, because you assigned this server's own IP address as the DNS server in its network configuration, you cannot reach a proper DNS server to create the delegation. Second, even if you could reach a proper DNS server, you are using a name based on a top-level root name (.net), and you would not have the authorization to create the delegation in the server hosting root addresses for the that extension.

18. On the Location For Database, Log Files And SYSVOL page, accept the default locations and click Next.

19. On the Directory Services Restore Mode Administrator Password page, type a strong password, confirm it, and click Next.

20. Confirm your settings on the Summary page and click Next.

21. Select the Reboot On Completion check box and wait for the operation to complete.

22.   After the computer has been rebooted, log on with the newly created domain credentials (TreyResearch\Administrator) and move to the DNS Server node in Server Manager.

Review the changes the AD DS setup created within the forward lookup zones of this new forest. Note that DNS data is divided into two sections, one that affects the entire forest and another that affects only the root domain, as shown in Figure 9-10.

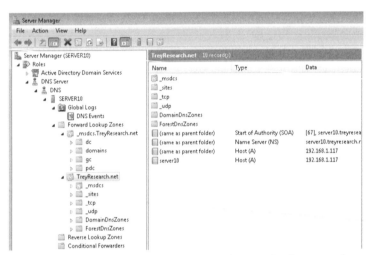

Figure 9-10   Active Directory Domain Services entries for a new forest

▶ **Exercise 3   Create a Manual Zone Delegation**

In this exercise, performed on SERVER10, you will use the newly created domain controller for the *treyresearch.net* domain to create a manual DNS zone delegation. This delegation will be used in Exercise 4, "Install AD DS and Create a New Domain Tree," to load DNS data for a domain tree. It will not contain any data when you create it and will point to a nonexistent server—a server that is not yet created; this is called a dummy DNS delegation. Also, because a domain tree uses a different DNS name than the forest, you will need to create a new FLZ for the tree; otherwise, you would not be able to use the new name in the delegation.

1.   Log on to Server10 with the domain administrator account.

2.   In Server Manager, expand the DNS Server node and click the Forward Lookup Zones node.

3.   Right-click Forward Lookup Zones and select New Zone.
This launches the New Zone Wizard.

4.   Click Next.

5. On the Zone Type page, select Primary Zone and make sure the Store The Zone In Active Directory check box is selected. Click Next.

   You must create a new zone to host the delegation because if you tried to store the delegation in an existing zone, it would automatically add the name suffix for this zone. Because a domain tree is distinguished from the forest namespace by its name suffix, you must create a new zone to host it.

6. On the Active Directory Zone Replication Scope page, select To All DNS Servers In This Domain: *treyresearch.net* and click Next. This will place the DNS data in the DomainDnsZones application directory partition for the *treyresearch.net* domain.

7. On the Zone Name page, type **northwindtraders.com** and click Next.

   Trey Research has decided to expand its operations and create a new division that will be focused on new sportswear related to Trey's latest discoveries and inventions. Because of this, they need to create a new domain tree in their existing forest.

IMPORTANT Using name extensions other than .com

You would normally use a name extension other than .com to protect your internal network from possible name conflicts and to avoid the split-brain syndrome, but using a .com extension is valid for the purposes of this exercise.

8. On the Dynamic Update page, select Allow Only Secure Dynamic Updates (Recommended For Active Directory) and click Next.

   Dynamic updates are not really required for this zone because it will host a delegation only, but using this setting will allow for eventual growth if the Trey Research strategy for this domain changes in the future.

9. Click Finish to create the zone.

10. Move to the *northwindtraders.com* zone and select it.

    The DNS server is peculiar in that it does not provide you with context menu options until you have selected the item first. You need to select the item with the left mouse button, and then you can use the right mouse button to view the context menu.

11. Right-click the *northwindtraders.com* zone and select New Delegation.

    This launches the New Delegation Wizard.

12. Click Next.

13. On the Delegated Domain Name page, type **SERVER20**, which should list SERVER20 .northwindtraders.com as the FQDN, and click Next.

14. On the Name Servers page, click Add and type the FQDN of the server you will create for this zone.

    The value should be SERVER20.northwindtraders.com.

15. Move to the IP Addresses Of This NS Record section of the dialog box, click <Click Here To Add An IP Address>, and then type the IP address you assigned to SERVER20. Click OK.

16. Click Next and then Finish to create the delegation.

    The dialog box will give you an error because the *northwindtraders.com* domain is not yet created, and a server with an FQDN of SERVER20.northwindtraders.com does not yet exist, hence the dummy delegation name for this type of delegation.

IMPORTANT   **Add name servers to a delegation**

In a production environment, you should have at least two or more name servers for this delegation. In this exercise, one is enough, but when you create any AD DS domain, always create at least two DCs. You should, therefore, return to this delegation after the second server is created and add it to the delegation to provide fault tolerance for it.

▶ **Exercise 4   Install AD DS and Create a New Domain Tree**

In this exercise, you will use a standalone computer to install the AD DS role and then create a new domain tree in an existing forest. This exercise is performed on SERVER20, but SERVER10 must also be running. After AD DS is installed, you will use the Active Directory Domain Services Installation Wizard to create a new domain tree in an existing forest.

1. Log on to SERVER20 with the local administrator account.

2. In Server Manager, right-click the Roles node and select Add Roles.

3. Review the Before You Begin screen and click Next.

4. On the Select Server Roles page of the Add Roles Wizard, select Active Directory Domain Services and click Next.

5. Review the information on the Active Directory Domain Services page and click Next.

6. Confirm your choices and click Install.

7. Examine the installation results and click Close. Your installation is complete.

8. Next, click the Active Directory Domain Services node in Server Manager.

9. Click Run The Active Directory Domain Services Installation Wizard in the details pane.

10. This launches the Active Directory Domain Services Installation Wizard. Select the Use Advanced Mode Installation check box, and then click Next.

    This option enables you to create a new domain tree.

11. Review the information on the Operating System Compatibility page and click Next.

12. On the Choose A Deployment Configuration page, select Existing Forest, select Create A New Domain In An Existing Forest, select the Create A New Domain Tree Root Instead Of A New Child Domain check box, and click Next.

13. On the Network Credentials page, type **treyresearch.net**, and then click Set to enter alternate credentials. Type **treyresearch.net\administrator** or the equivalent account name and the password. Click OK, and then click Next.

14. On the Name The New Domain Tree Root page, type **northwindtraders.com** and click Next.

15. On the Domain NetBIOS Name page, accept the proposed name and click Next.

    This page appears because you are running the wizard in advanced mode. Note that the name does not include the final *s* because it is limited to fifteen characters. The sixteenth is always reserved by the system.

16. On the Select A Site page, accept the default and click Next. This page also appears because you are running the wizard in advanced mode.

17. On the Additional Domain Controller Options page, verify that the DNS Server check box is selected. Select the Global Catalog check box, and then click Next.

    Note that one authoritative DNS server has been found for this domain. This is the server in your delegation and is the server you are now creating.

18. If you did not assign a static IP address, the Active Directory Domain Services Installation Wizard will give you a warning because you are using a dynamic IP address. Click the Yes, The Computer Will Use A Dynamically Assigned IP Address (Not Recommended) option.

    The AD DS Installation Wizard will warn you that it has detected an existing DNS infrastructure for this domain and, because of this, you now have two choices: to attempt to create a DNS delegation or to omit it. See Figure 9-11.

19. Select No, Do Not Create The DNS Delegation and click Next.

    You select No because you already created the delegation manually. The wizard cannot create this delegation because it would attempt to create it in a .com root name DNS server, and you do not have access rights to this server.

20. On the Source Domain Controller page, verify that Let The Wizard Choose An Appropriate Domain Controller is selected and click Next.

21. On the Location For Database, Log Files And SYSVOL page, accept the default locations and click Next.

22. On the Directory Services Restore Mode Administrator Password page, type a strong password, confirm it, and click Next.

23. Confirm your settings on the Summary page and click Next. Select the Reboot On Completion check box and wait for the operation to complete.

24. When the computer has been rebooted, log on with the new domain credentials (NorthwindTraders\Administrator or equivalent) and move to the DNS Server node in Server Manager. Review the changes the AD DS setup created within the FLZs of this new domain tree. Note that DNS data includes a container for this tree only and not for the domain. (See Figure 9-12.)

Any child domains created under this tree root would also create delegations of their own and would be listed in this zone.

Figure 9-11   The Create DNS Delegation page

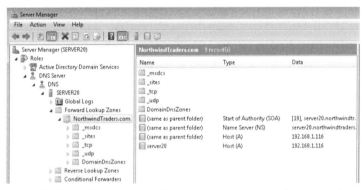

Figure 9-12   Active Directory Domain Services entries for a new domain tree in an existing forest

▶ **Exercise 5   Install AD DS and Create a Child Domain**

In this exercise, you will use a standalone computer to install the AD DS role and then create a new child domain. This exercise is performed on SERVER30. After AD DS is installed, you will use the Active Directory Domain Services Installation Wizard to create a child domain in the Trey Research forest.

1. Log on to SERVER30 with the local administrator account.
2. In Server Manager, right-click the Roles node and select Add Roles.
3. Review the Before You Begin screen and click Next.
4. On the Select Server Roles page of the Add Roles Wizard, select Active Directory Domain Services and click Next.
5. Review the information in the AD DS page and click Next.
6. Confirm your choices and click Install.
7. Examine the installation results and click Close.
    Your installation is complete.
8. Next, click the Active Directory Domain Services node in Server Manager.
9. Click Run The Active Directory Domain Services Installation Wizard in the details pane.
    This launches the Active Directory Domain Services Installation Wizard.
10. Click Next.
11. Review the information on the Operating System Compatibility page and click Next.
12. On the Choose a Deployment Configuration page, choose Existing Forest and Create A New Domain In An Existing Forest and click Next.
13. On the Network Credentials page, type **treyresearch.net** and click Set to add proper credentials.
14. In the Network Credentials dialog box, type **treyresearch\administrator** or equivalent, type the password, click OK, and click Next.
15. On the Name The New Domain page, type **treyresearch.net** as the FQDN of the parent domain, type **intranet** in the single label of the child domain field, and click Next.
    The complete FQDN should be *intranet.treyresearch.net*.
    When you create a global child production domain, you name it with an appropriate name such as Intranet. This provides a clear demarcation for users and clearly shows that they are in an internal, protected network.
16. On the Select a Site page, use the default settings and click Next.

17. On the Additional Domain Controller Options page, verify that the DNS Server check box is selected and select the Global Catalog check box. Click Next.

    Note that there are no authoritative DNS servers for this domain name.

    If you did not assign a static IP address, the Active Directory Domain Services Installation Wizard will give you a warning because you are using a dynamic IP address.

18. Click the Yes, The Computer Will Use A Dynamically Assigned IP Address (Not Recommended) option.

19. On the Location For Database, Log Files And SYSVOL page, accept the default locations and click Next.

20. On the Directory Services Restore Mode Administrator Password page, type a strong password, confirm it, and click Next.

21. Confirm your settings on the Summary page and click Next.

    Note that in this case, the wizard will create a DNS delegation for this domain. (See Figure 9-13.) This is because the parent domain is authoritative for the *treyresearch.net* zone and can, therefore, create a proper delegation for the child domain.

22. Select the Reboot On Completion check box and wait for the operation to complete.

23. When the computer has been rebooted, log on with the newly created domain credentials (Intranet\Administrator or equivalent) and move to the DNS Server node in Server Manager.

24. Review the changes the AD DS setup created within the FLZs of this new domain. Note that DNS data is in only one section that affects this particular domain, as shown in Figure 9-14. Also, if you return to SERVER10, you will see that a new DNS delegation (a gray icon instead of yellow) has been created for this child domain in the *treyresearch.net* FLZ.

Figure 9-13   The Active Directory Domain Services Installation Summary page

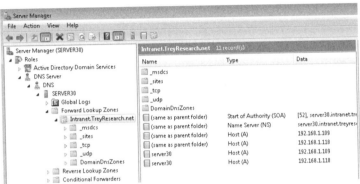

Figure 9-14 Active Directory Domain Services entries for a new child domain in an existing forest

Lesson Summary

- DNS is a name resolution system that relies on a hierarchical naming structure to map IP addresses to FQDNs, which are in the *object.namespace.rootname* format.

- AD DS also relies on a hierarchical structure. In fact, the AD DS forest structure is based entirely on the hierarchical structure found in DNS.

- Because Windows Server 2008 has been updated to support IPv6, and IPv6 is installed by default with link-local addresses, the DNS server in Windows Server 2008 provides support for the longer 128-bit address format used by IPv6.

- DNS Server can host three types of zones. Primary zones are read-write zones that contain data in support of name resolution for a given namespace. Secondary zones are read-only zones that contain a copy of a primary zone. Stub zones are pointers to other DNS servers and contain only the authoritative servers for the namespace they point to. Each zone type can be integrated with AD DS to be stored in the directory database.

Lesson Review

You can use the following questions to test your knowledge of the information in Lesson 1, "Understanding and Installing Domain Name System." The questions are also available on the companion CD if you prefer to review them in electronic form.

NOTE Answers

Answers to these questions and explanations of why each answer choice is right or wrong are located in the "Answers" section at the end of the book.

1. You are an administrator for Contoso, Ltd. Your organization has decided to move to Windows Server 2008 and, because of your past experience, you have decided to create a new server implementation instead of upgrading your existing infrastructure. After the new infrastructure has been created, you will move all data—accounts, directory settings, and more—to the new forest you will implement with Windows Server 2008. You have been asked to create the initial forest structure. This forest includes a root domain, a global child production domain, and a domain tree. The forest is named with a .net extension, and the domain tree uses a .ms extension to differentiate it from the production forest. You successfully create the forest root domain and the child domain, but when you come to the domain tree, you find that you cannot locate the domain tree option. What could be the problem?

    A. You cannot create a domain tree with the Active Directory Domain Services Installation Wizard. You must use the command-line *Dcpromo.exe* command to do so.

    B. You are not logged on with the appropriate credentials.

    C. You must return to the Welcome page of the wizard to select the Advanced mode of the wizard.

    D. The server you are using is not a member of the forest root domain.

2. You are an administrator for Contoso, Ltd. Your organization has decided to move to Windows Server 2008 and, because of your past experience, you have decided to create a new server implementation instead of upgrading your existing infrastructure. After the new infrastructure has been created, you will move all data—accounts, directory settings, and more—to the new forest you will implement with Windows Server 2008. You have been asked to create the initial forest structure. This forest includes a root domain, a global child production domain, and a domain tree. The forest is named with a .net extension, and the domain tree uses a .ms extension to differentiate it from the production forest. You successfully create the forest root domain and the child domain, but when you come to the domain tree, you find that you cannot create the delegation, no matter which options you try or which credentials you provide. What could be the problem? (Choose all that apply.)

    A. You must select the advanced mode of the wizard to create the delegation.

    B. You must create a manual delegation before creating the domain tree.

    C. You must tell the wizard to create the delegation during the creation of the domain tree and provide appropriate credentials.

    D. You must tell the wizard to omit the creation of the delegation during the creation of the domain tree.

    E. You must create the delegation manually after the domain tree has been created.

Lesson 2: Configuring and Using Domain Name System

When you install the DNS Server role with AD DS, there is little configuration to be done. FLZs are created automatically; replication is configured automatically because it rides on the AD DS multimaster replication system, and you don't even need to add records because all computer systems running Windows 2000 or later can register and update their own records in the dynamic DNS AD DS requires.

However, some operations are not performed automatically. For example, the DNS server configuration does not, by default, include RLZs. It is a good idea to add them to support reverse lookups. In addition, the DNS server needs configuration finalization. For example, you must set it to support record scavenging, automatically deleting outdated records.

It is also a very good idea to review all the DNS server content to become familiar with it and ensure that all data and values correspond to your actual requirements.

After this lesson, you will be able to:
- Finalize the configuration of your DNS servers.
- Administer DNS servers and DNS replication.

Estimated lesson time: 40 minutes

Configuring DNS

The DNS configuration involves several activities. These include:

- Considering the security of your DNS servers to reduce their attack surface.
- Configuring scavenging settings for the server as a whole.
- Finalizing the configuration of your FLZs.
- Creating RLZs.
- Adding custom records to FLZs for specific services and resources.

It is also a good idea to make sure your DNS replication is working properly and that all DNS data is being replicated properly.

Security Considerations for the DNS Server Role

DNS servers that are exposed to the Internet are notorious targets for malicious users. The most common attack is a denial-of-service (DoS) attack that floods the DNS service with so many requests that the service cannot respond to valid requests. Another common attack form occurs when an attacker tries to obtain all the data contained within a DNS server, intending to use it to identify the object a network contains. This is called *footprinting the network*. Two more attack types attempt to modify data within the DNS server or redirect user queries from a valid DNS server to another DNS server that would be under the control of the attacker. The latter usually occurs through the modification of DNS data contained within the DNS cache. Remember that DNS uses in-memory caching to increase the speed of responses to queries. When this data is corrupted, users can receive invalid responses to their queries.

This is why it is important to apply common security measures to your DNS installations. When you use a whole-brain approach to DNS configuration and you rely on DNS integration with AD DS in your internal network, your internal DNS servers are much less prone to attack because they do not share a namespace with the outside world and are, therefore, protected from external access by firewalls, which do not allow external users to access your internal DNS servers. This does not mean that internal servers do not need protection. Any time an untrusted user can connect to your network either through the wired connections or through wireless access, your infrastructure is at risk. This is why extensive screening is a good practice whenever you allow someone you are not familiar with to connect to your network. It is not because you are inside the firewall that everything is protected by default.

Consider a different security approach with internal vs. external DNS servers. When servers are in an external or perimeter network, they should be highly secured. One good protection method is to use a secondary or subordinate server only whenever the server is exposed to the outside world. Then, you configure the zone updates to occur only from known sources that are included within DNS itself.

In internal networks, tie the DNS Server role to the DC role and ensure that they support secure dynamic updates only. This will help protect them from obtaining or transmitting erroneous data. Verify DNS data on a regular basis to validate it and monitor your DNS event logs to identify potential security issues quickly if they arise.

Exam Tip   The exam focuses on DNS usage with AD DS. Because of this, it does not cover external or standalone DNS servers. If you find you need to configure an external DNS server, you can look up more information on DNS security at *http://technet2.microsoft.com/windowsserver/en/library /fea46d0d-2de7-4da0-9c6f-2bb0ae9ca7e91033.mspx?mfr=true.*

Working with DNS Server Settings

DNS stores name records for a specific period of time. Each name record is assigned a TTL value. When this value expires, the record should be removed to avoid providing false positive results to users performing lookups on the name. Fortunately, the DNS server in Windows Server 2008 can perform this task automatically through server or zone scavenging. When applied to the server, scavenging cleans all active zones on the server. When applied to a particular zone, only the records for the zone are scavenged.

Configuring Scavenging for All Zones   To set scavenging for an entire server, you must assign the setting through the server's action menu.

1. Right-click the server name in the DNS node of Server Manager and choose Set Aging/ Scavenging For All Zones.

2. Select the Scavenge Stale Resource Records check box to enable the feature.

   No-Refresh Interval refers to the time between the most recent refresh of a record stamp and the moment when the system allows the timestamp to be refreshed again. Refresh Interval refers to the earliest moment when a record may be updated or when it may be scavenged if no updates have been applied. The default value of seven days is sufficient for most networks.

3. Leave the default values as is and click OK.

4. Because you set the values for existing zones, DNS also enables you to set it for any future zone you create, including Active Directory–integrated zones. Select the Apply These Settings To The Existing Active Directory-Integrated Zones check box and click OK.

Your DNS zones are set to remove stale records. Make sure you apply these settings to every DNS server in your network. Make this part of your default configuration for DNS servers. If you need to modify the setting for a single zone, you must use the Properties dialog box for that zone. Zone scavenging is performed by using the General tab and clicking the Aging button.

You'll note that in the server's context menu, you can also manually initiate scavenging by clicking Scavenge Stale Resource Records. You use this operation when you discover that your servers are sending out stale data.

If you do discover that records are stale, you can also use the *Clear Cache* command from the same context menu. Because the DNS server relies heavily on the in-memory cache to improve performance, you might have scavenged records from the database but find they are still in the cache, which might still be providing false positives.

Finalizing FLZ Configuration   When you examine the Properties dialog box for a FLZ, you'll find that there are several options you can set for each zone. Make a point of examining these options and configure the following settings for each production DNS zone as a best practice:

- On the General tab, make sure each internal DNS zone is Active Directory-Integrated, uses the proper replication scope, and supports Secure Only dynamic updates.
  - ❏ Domain-based DNS zones should replicate to all DNS servers in the domain. Each DC that also hosts the DNS role will include the zone.
  - ❏ Forest DNS zones should replicate to all DNS servers in the forest.
  - ❏ If you maintain Windows 2000 Server DCs in your network, you must use the To All Domain Controllers In This Domain (For Windows 2000 Compatibility) option because Windows 2000 Server does not support application directory partitions.
  - ❏ You can also set replication to custom application directory partitions, but you must create the partition first.

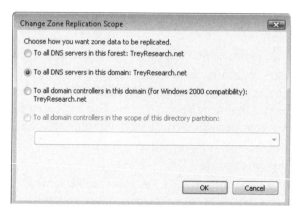

- On the Name Servers tab, ensure that each DNS zone includes at least two name severs. Just as you would create at least two DCs for each domain, create two DNS servers for each zone as a best practice.

- On the WINS tab, assign WINS lookups only if you cannot use GNZs and you must deploy WINS. This lesson will discuss single-label name management further in a later section.

- On the Zone Transfers tab, set the name servers to which you allow this zone to be transferred upon request. If this zone is integrated with Active Directory, zone transfers are not required. This tab is mostly used for previous DNS server installations.

- On the Security tab, review the default security settings. These settings use the appropriate configuration for most networks, but in highly secure implementations, they might need to be revised and modified.

- The final tab is the SOA. SOA records identify the zone and its related information such as owner, operator, update schedules, and so on. These records include the following information:

  - ❏ Serial Number, which is assigned when your zone is created. You can increment the serial number if you need to change its value.

  - ❏ Primary Server is the master server for this zone. This is usually the server where the zone was first created.

  - ❏ Responsible Person should list the operator name for this server. Normally, this is a standard term such as Hostmaster or Operations. By default, Windows Server 2008 assigns hostmaster.*dnszonename* where dnszonename is the FQDN of the zone. Responsible Person entries are based on Responsible Person records. These records are not created by default. Create a proper Responsible Person record for each zone or, at the very least, for each master DNS server and assign it to this value.

  - ❏ The SOA lists the various intervals and time-based settings for the record. These include the Refresh Interval, the Retry Interval, the Expires After setting, and the

Minimum (Default) TTL for the record. Default values are acceptable for most record types.

❑ The last value of the SOA is the TTL For This Record. Note that it is assigned to the same value as the Minimum (Default) TTL value listed above it in the dialog box.

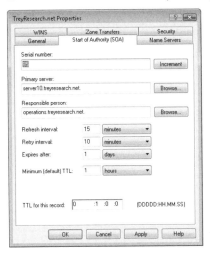

Finalize these settings for each zone you manage on your DNS servers.

Creating a Responsible Person Record   As mentioned earlier, each zone should be assigned a Responsible Person (RP) as a best practice. This means you need at least one RP record in your DNS configuration. Use the context menu for the zone you want to host this record in to create the record. Keep in mind that you will require different items for the creation of this record. These include:

■ **A common group name**   This name will be displayed in the record.

■ **A group mailbox in the directory**   It is best to use a group mailbox to make sure the messages sent to this address are treated in a timely fashion.

■ **A text record to include with the Responsible Person record**   The text record can indicate information about your organization and its DNS management policies.

Use the following procedure to create the RP record. Begin with the Text Record.

1. Right-click the zone name and choose Other New Records.

2. In the Select A Resource Record Type list, scroll down to select Text (TXT) and click Create Record.

3. In the New Resource Record dialog box, type the name of the record, for example, **Disclaimer**, and move to the Text entry box.

4. Type your message. Click OK to create the record. This returns you to the Resource Record Type dialog box.

This should include information about who you are and what your DNS management practices are. You might consider preparing the message in a word processor and then pasting it in this dialog box because the text box does not include any proofing capabilities.

5. In the Select A Resource Record Type list, scroll up to select Responsible Person (RP) and click Create Record.

6. In the New Resource Record dialog box, type the name of the record in the Host Or Domain text box, for example, **Operations**, and click Browse to locate the mailbox of the responsible person. You can also type the address if you know it.

7. Click Browse to locate your newly created text record. Navigate to the zone you are working with to locate the text record, select it, and click OK.

8. Click OK to create the record. Click Done to close the Resource Record Type dialog box.

9. Return to the zone Properties dialog box or double-click the Start Of Authority record to assign the RP record to the SOA record.

Perform these operations for each zone you manage. It is always better to configure the zone completely than to have to figure out what to do if issues arise and nothing is configured.

Creating Reverse Lookup Zones

Small networks with few computers, for example, fewer than 500, might not require RLZs. These zones are used to provide resolution from an IP address to a name instead of a name to an IP address. These are most often used by applications. For example, a secure Web application will use a reverse lookup to verify that the computer it is communicating with is actually the right computer and not another computer impersonating it. If you do not have any such application in your network, then you can safely do without RLZs.

However, clients that have the ability to update their own DNS records dynamically will also create a PTR record—a reverse record that maps the IP address to the name—and try to store it within the RLZ that corresponds to the FLZ their name record is located in. If there is no RLZ, these records will never be generated.

MORE INFO   **How dynamic updates work**

For more information on dynamic updates and how they work, go to *http://technet2.microsoft.com/ windowsserver/en/library/e760737e-9e55-458d-b5ed-a1ae9e04819e1033.mspx?mfr=true.*

If you need RLZs, create them for the corresponding FLZs. Create a zone for each named FLZ. In an Active Directory–integrated DNS implementation, you would create a RLZ for each domain DNS zone. In a multidomain forest, this would include the root domain, any child domain, and any domain trees. Use the following procedure:

1. Move to the Reverse Lookup Zone section of the DNS node in Server Manager.

2. Right-click Reverse Lookup Zone and select New Zone.

3. Review the information on the Welcome page and click Next.

4. Select Primary Zone, make sure the Store The Zone In Active Directory check box is selected, and click Next.

5. Because RLZs are tied to a specific domain name, apply To All DNS Servers In This Domain and click Next.

6. On the Reverse Lookup Zone Name page, select either IPv4 or IPv6 and click Next.

   Remember that reverse lookups map an IP address to a name. You need to create an RLZ for the type of IP addressing you are using in the network. If you are using both IPv6 and IPv4, you must create two zones.

   You generate the zone name on the next page. This page will differ, depending on the IP version you are using.

7. If you are using IPv4, type the network ID for the zone. Note that as you type the network address, the name is automatically generated in the lower part of the page under Reverse Lookup Zone Name.

8. Click Next.

   If you are using IPv6, you can add up to eight zones at once. Remember that IPv6 addresses use hexadecimal format. For example, if you are using site-local addresses in your network, you might type **fe80::/64** as the address scope. This will automatically generate the zone name in the Reverse Lookup Zones section of the page. If one zone is all you need, you can move on from this page.

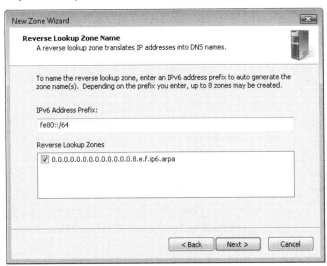

9. On the next page, select which type of dynamic update you want to allow. In most cases, select Allow Only Secure Dynamic Updates and click Next. Click Finish to create the zone.

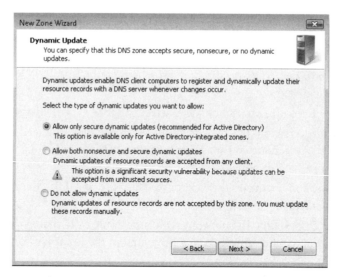

As soon as the zones are created, they will begin supporting record hosting when the next dynamic update refresh occurs on your client systems.

Exam Tip Practice working with zones and zone properties because they are an important part of the exam topics.

Quick Check

1. Why should you configure scavenging and aging on a DNS server?
2. When should you create reverse lookup zones?

Quick Check Answers

1. Every DNS name record is assigned a TTL value when created. This value determines when the information in the record is no longer valid. If the record is not renewed, then it becomes a stale record. Aging and scavenging on the DNS server will automatically remove stale records to limit the possibility of false positives when users request data from the DNS server.

2. Reverse lookup zones are mostly useful for secure Web applications, which must validate the IP address provided by the systems they communicate with. If a network does not include any such application, then reverse lookup zones are not required.

Creating Custom Records

The last step in a DNS server configuration is the creation of custom records for the FLZs. Custom records are created manually and will provide a variety of services in your network. For example, you might need to create the following:

- An MX record to point to your e-mail servers.
- An alias record such as intranet.*domainname* to point to an Office SharePoint Server server farm to support collaboration in your network.
- SRV records for various services in your network. For example, you must create SIP records for Microsoft Office Communication Server deployments.

Time will tell which custom records you need. In an internal network, manually created records should be infrequent because of the dynamic update process initiated by client systems.

Exam Tip   Practice record creation because it is also an important topic on the exam.

Forwarders vs. Root Hints

Name resolution is performed by two main methods. DNS servers will either contain root hints that enable them to identify and locate authoritative DNS servers for root names or rely on forwarders to link them to another server that will perform the lookup for them.

By default, Windows DNS Server relies on root hints to perform lookups. This means that if your users need to perform a lookup on the Internet, your DNS servers will communicate with the name servers. In smaller organizations, this is quite acceptable because even if your DNS servers expose themselves by communicating directly with the Internet, they are the ones who initiate the communication. External systems reply to the initiated communication only and cannot initiate the communication themselves.

However, in highly secure networks, you might prefer to rely on forwarders instead of root hints. For example, you might place two standalone DNS servers in your perimeter network and link the internal DNS servers to these servers through forwarders. Each time the internal servers need to resolve an Internet name, they link to one of the servers in the perimeter and ask it to perform the lookup for them. This way, the only servers to communicate outside the network are the more secure standalone servers in the perimeter.

Forwarders are configured as part of the properties of the DNS server and are accessed from the Forwarders tab in the DNS server Properties dialog box. (See Figure 9-15.) If you are configuring forwarders for security purposes, make sure you uncheck the Use Root Hints option if no forwarders are available; otherwise, your internal DNS servers will communicate directly with the Internet if your servers in the perimeter do not respond.

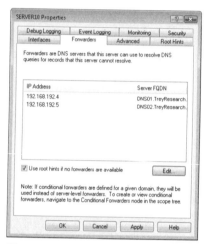

Figure 9-15   Configuring forwarders in DNS

You can also use conditional forwarders in your DNS configuration. Conditional forwarders are used to forward DN requests when specific conditions are met. For example, if you want to link two namespaces but only when users request a particular name, you would use conditional forwarders.

For example, consider the following scenario. Your network includes two forests. The first is the production forest, the one that contains all the accounts users use to work together in your organization. The second is a special forest that was created to test the AD DS integration of third-party applications with the AD DS forest schema before they are deployed in your production forest. Because of the schema changes, you do not want to link your forests together through a forest trust. Therefore, you create conditional forwarders in each forest so that users in the production domain, mostly developers and IT professionals, can link from the production to the staging domain.

Conditional forwarders include their own container in DNS Server.

1. To create a new conditional forwarder, right-click the Conditional Forwarders node and select New Conditional Forwarder.
2. Type the name of the DNS domain you want to forward to.
3. Click <Click Here To Add An IP Address Or DNS Name> and type the server's IP address.
4. Add at least two servers to the list.
5. As a best practice, store the conditional forwarder in Active Directory and determine which replication scope to apply to the forwarder. Click OK.

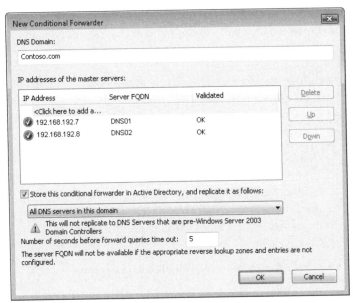

In the preceding example, you would replicate the data only to the production domain because you do not need to replicate it to the entire forest. In other cases, you might need to replicate it to the entire forest.

Note that when you create a conditional forwarder, it creates a new container for the domain you will forward to under the Conditional Forwarders node. From now on, each time your users request a name resolution that contains this domain name, your DNS servers will automatically forward it to the DNS servers you provided in the list.

Single-Label Name Management

When you want to manage single-label names, you will need to create a GNZ manually. A single GNZ is required for each forest. The basic process of creating a GNZ requires five steps, but it involves an operation on each DNS server in the forest. If you are using AD DS–integrated DNS servers and each of your DCs is also running the DNS service, you must perform this operation on each DC. This means using domain administrator credentials to complete the operation.

- Create the GlobalNames FLZ.
- Set its replication scope to all DNS servers in the forest.
- Do not enable dynamic updates for this zone.
- Enable GNZ support on each DNS server in the forest.
- Add single-label names to the DNS zone.

Configuration is performed through the command line because there is no graphical interface to access this feature. However, you can create the GNZ through Server Manager, but enabling

GNZ support in a DNS server requires a modification of the Windows Registry. This modification is performed with the *Dnscmd.exe* command and uses the following format:

```
dnscmd /config /enableglobalnamessupport 1
```

This command needs to be run on each DNS server in the forest. If you need to support single-label names and you do not want to use WINS, you might want to make this command part of your standard DNS server installation and configuration process. You need to restart the DNS service when the command has been run.

After you have enabled GNZ support, you can begin to add records. GNZ names are aliases because each object in your network already has a host name in DNS. You create an alias and point it to the corresponding FQDN for the object. GNZ aliases, like WINS names, cannot have more than 15 characters—they actually use 16 characters, but the system reserves the last character. If you want to create the names through a command file, use the following command format for each name:

```
dnscmd dnsservername /recordadd globalnames singlelabelname cname
correspondingdnsname
```

Where *dnsservername* is the name of the DNS server that you are adding the name to, the *singlelabelname* is the 15-character name you want to add, and *correspondingdnsname* is the FQDN of the object whose GNZ name you are adding.

MORE INFO   GlobalNames zones

For more information on GNZs, view the DNS GlobalNames Zone Deployment document at *http://www.microsoft.com/downloads/details.aspx?FamilyID=1c6b31cd-3dd9-4c3f-8acd-3201 a57194f1&displaylang=en*.

DNS and WINS

If you are in a network that requires a multitude of single-label names and you cannot provide support for them through a GNZ because there are simply too many names to manage, install the WINS service on at least two servers in your network. WINS will then automatically generate and manage names for each object in the network. Remember that WINS services are a feature of Windows Server 2008, not a role, and that it is an outdated technology that has not been updated since the original release of Windows Server 2003.

If you do deploy WINS, remember that:

- WINS does not appear in Server Manager. To administer WINS, you must use the WINS console in the Administrative Tools program group.
- WINS supports IPv4 addresses only and will not be updated to support IPv6.

- You need at least two WINS servers to provide fault tolerance for single-label names in your network. These two servers should be configured to use push/pull synchronization to make sure both name databases are synchronized at all times.

- You need to ensure that the values for WINS are specified in the DHCP settings you send to computers requiring dynamic IPv4 addresses. Two settings are required. The first lists the name servers and the second identifies which type of node each client will work with.

  - ❑ 044 WINS/NBNS Servers identifies which servers host the WINS service.

  - ❑ 046 WINS/NBT Node Type identifies how nodes interact with WINS. The most commonly used node type is 0x8 or the Hybrid node type. This minimizes the amount of broadcasting required in single-label name networks.

- You can also integrate WINS and DNS by modifying the properties of an FLZ. This property sheet includes a WINS tab that is unused unless you have WINS servers in your network. (See Figure 9-16.) This feature is useful in networks in which many clients rely on WINS and it is possible that some of the client device names will not be present in DNS. However, all Windows operating systems since Windows 2000 can participate in a dynamic DNS infrastructure. Networks that run earlier clients than Windows 2000 are becoming very rare.

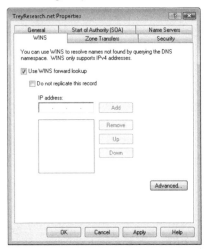

Figure 9-16 Linking DNS with WINS to provide both FQDN and single-label name resolution

DNS and DHCP Considerations

When you work with dynamic DNS and you integrate the DNS service with the AD DS directory store, you must change the traditional approach network administrators use to configure DHCP settings that are provided to each client device that relies on dynamic IP addresses, whether they are IPv4 or IPv6.

Traditionally, network administrators provide as few as two central DNS servers in the server options of the DHCP settings. This provides all client devices with the DNS addresses they need to resolve both internal and external FQDNs, but because the servers were centrally located, any client that was in a remote site would need to perform a DNS lookup over the WAN.

However, with the integration of DNS and especially DNS data with the directory store, DNS data is now available wherever there is a DC and, to provide authentication services wherever clients are located, DCs are distributed throughout a network. In fact, some organizations have DCs available wherever there are at least 20 clients. With the advent of server virtualization through Hyper-V as well as DC hardening through the RODC, DCs can be even more prevalent in networks. This means that DNS data, even read-only DNS data, will be available in each remote site or branch office. Clients can use servers in their local site to perform FQDN lookups.

However, for clients to perform the lookup locally, they must know about the presence of local DNS servers. Imagine the following scenario:

- A client in a remote site uses a dynamic IP address allocated through DHCP.
- There are two DCs in the remote site.
- DNS is integrated with the directory and is replicated with the domain partition.
- DHCP sends out values for only two DNS servers in a central site.
- When the client boots in the morning, it performs a DNS lookup to locate its closest DC to log on.
- The DNS lookup occurs over the WAN to request the name resolution from one of the two central DCs.
- The central DNS servers look up the client's site and find that there are two local DCs to support logon.
- The DNS server returns the location of the closest DC to the client, once again over the WAN.
- The client contacts its local DC to log on.

In this scenario, the client cannot log on if there is no WAN connectivity even though the DNS data is stored locally within the two DCs!

Because of this, DHCP options must be modified as follows:

- The server scope should continue to provide at least two addresses for centrally located DNS servers for redundancy purposes. If the local DCs is down, clients will still be able to log on, albeit over the WAN.
- Each individual address scope should include options for name resolution servers, and these records should point to the DCs that are local to the site the scope is assigned to. This means adding the *006 DNS Servers* value to each individual scope in DHCP.

■ All DCs should also be running the DNS Server role. That's all you have to do. If a DNS zone is stored in the AD DS directory store, it will be made available to the DNS service as soon as you install the DNS Server role on the DC. There is nothing more to configure except global DNS server settings.

Keep this in mind when planning to integrate DNS with DHCP.

Working with Application Directory Partitions

In certain circumstances, you will want to create custom application directory partitions in support of DNS data replication. Remember that application directory partitions control the replication scope of the data they contain. The DNS server creates two application directory partitions when it is installed with AD DS in a forest, one for forest data and one for domain data in each domain, but under certain conditions, these two scopes might not be appropriate, especially in complex forests.

Consider this scenario. Your forest includes three domains: the forest root, a global child production domain, and a development domain. You created the development domain because your developers have special access right requirements and you do not want to grant them these access rights in the production domain. All production domain users except for system administrators have standard user access rights. In the development domain, however, you can grant developers higher access rights–rights to create, modify, or delete objects–because this domain does not affect production operations.

In addition, you created only a single account for each developer. This account is located in the global child production domain and has standard user rights, but through the transitive trusts inherent in each forest, developers can use their accounts from the production domain to access objects in the development domain where their production domain accounts have higher access rights.

By default, name resolution between the two child domains passes through the forest root domain. Developers access this domain on a constant basis every day, so to provide them with faster name resolution, you create a custom application directory partition to share the DNS records between the development and the production domains. This means that because the data is available in the partition, production DNS servers will not need to pass through the forest root domain to resolve development domain names. (See Figure 9-17.)

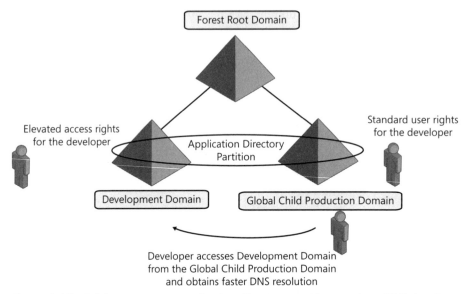

Figure 9-17 Relying on custom application directory partitions to share DNS data between two child domains

Creating and Assigning Custom Application Directory Partitions

Custom application directory partitions are created through the command line with the *Dnscmd.exe* command. There is no interface for creating these partitions. However, after they are created, the partitions can be assigned through the graphical interface. You can perform each operation through the command line if you prefer. You must perform three tasks:

■ Create the partition.
■ Enlist DNS servers into the partition.
■ Assign the zones whose replication scope you want to change to the newly created partition.

To create an application directory partition, you must be a member of the Enterprise Admins groups because you must have full access to the forest.

1. Log on to a DNS server with an account that is a member of the Enterprise Admins group for the forest.
2. Launch an elevated command prompt through the context menu and the *Run as* administrator command.
3. Type the following command:

   dnscmd *dnsservername* /createdirectorypartition *partitionfqdn*

   where the *dnsservername* is the FQDN of your DNS server or its IP address, and *partition-fqdn* is the FQDN of the partition you want to create.

For example, if you want to create a new partition on SERVER10 and name it partition01.treyresearch.net, you would use the following command:

```
dnscmd server10.treyresearch.net /createdirectorypartition
partition01.treyresearch.net
```

4. Enlist the server into the partition. Once again, you use the *Dnscmd.exe* command. Type the following command:

   dnscmd *dnsservername* /enlistdirectorypartition *partitionfqdn*

   You need to repeat this command for each DNS server you want to enlist into the partition. Note that the server you use to create the partition is enlisted by default. In the preceding scenario, you would need to enlist all the DNS servers for the production domain as well as all the DNS servers for the development domain into the partition. For example, if you want to enlist SERVER30—a server of the child domain—as an additional server into the new partition named partition01.treyresearch.net, you would use the following command:

   ```
   dnscmd server30.intranet.treyresearch.net /enlistdirectorypartition
   partition01.treyresearch.net
   ```

   Now you can change the replication scope of the zones you want to make available to the members of the new application directory partition.

5. Return to the DNS node in Server Manager, right-click the name of the zone you want to change, and select Properties.

6. On the General tab, click the Change button to change the replication scope.

7. In the Change Zone Replication Scope dialog box, select To All Domain Controllers In The Scope Of This Directory Partition and click the drop-down list to select your new partition. Click OK twice.

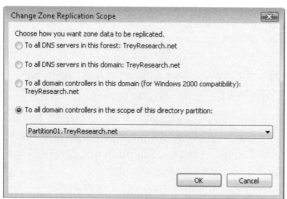

Be careful when you work with application directory partitions because many of the commands are manually entered. If you make a mistake, you could damage the replication scope of your servers and, therefore, disable name resolution.

MORE INFO Application directory partitions

For more information on application directory partitions, go to *http://technet2.microsoft.com/ windowsserver2008/en/library/2e2e0678-1775-4cdd-8779-32d5c281540f1033.mspx?mfr=true.*

Exam Tip Replication scopes and application directory partitions are an important part of the exam. Be sure you understand them fully.

Administering DNS Servers

You've already seen several tools in operation through practices and detailed step-by-step lists. However, you might need to work with other tools when working with your DNS servers. Table 9-4 outlines the different tools you can use to support DNS operations and management.

Table 9-4 Common DNS Administration Tools

Tool	Task	Location
DNS Manager	Perform initial configuration of a new server. Connect to and manage a local DNS server. Add and remove forward and reverse lookup zones. Add, remove, and update resource records in zones. Modify how zones are stored and replicated between servers. Modify how server processes queries and handles dynamic update. Modify security for specific zones or resource records. Perform maintenance. Monitor contents of the server cache. Tune advanced server options. Configure and perform aging and scavenging of stale resource records.	Administrative Tools program group or Server Manager
Dnscmd	Manage all aspects of DNS servers. This is the most powerful command-line tool for DNS administration. Common switches include: ■ */info* to obtain server information. ■ */config* to modify server configuration parameters. ■ */statistics* to obtain operational statistics from a server. ■ */clearcache* to clear and reset the cache. ■ */startscavenging* to initiate a scavenging operation. ■ */directorypartitioninfo* for information about partitions. ■ */exportsettings* to create a backup file of your server's settings.	Command line

Table 9-4 **Common DNS Administration Tools**

Tool	Task	Location
Dnslint	Diagnose common DNS name resolution issues. Common switches include: ■ */d* to request domain name resolution tests. ■ */ql* to verify DNS query tests from a list. ■ */ad* to verify records specifically related to Active Directory.	
Event Viewer	There are two options for monitoring DNS servers: ■ Default logging of DNS server event messages to the DNS server log. ■ Debug options for trace logging to a text file on the DNS server. This option is enabled through the DNS server's Properties dialog box and is disabled by default. Use it only for debugging purposes.	Server Manager
Ipconfig	Display and modify IP configuration details. Common switches include: ■ */all* to display all network configuration settings on a system. ■ */renew* to request a dynamic IPv4 address renewal from DHCP. ■ */renew6* to request a dynamic IPv6 address renewal from DHCP. ■ */release* to release a dynamic IPv4 address. ■ */release6* to release a dynamic IPv6 address. ■ */flushdns* to clear the DNS resolver cache on a system. ■ */registerdns* to renew a dynamic DNS registration for a system.	Command line
Nslookup	Perform query testing of the DNS domain namespace. *Nslookup* is also a command interpreter that is entered by simply typing **nslookup** at the command line. Type **exit** to return to the command line. However, it can also be used directly. To do so, type **nslookup** followed by the hostname or the IP address of the computer you are looking for.	Command line
System Monitor	Create charts and graphs of server performance trends. Determine performance benchmarks.	Server Manager, Diagnostics, Reliability, and Performance

Exam Tip   Run through each of these tools. DNS operation is an important part of the exam.

Little will go wrong with your internal DNS implementations if you follow the guidelines outlined here. However, there is always the possibility of uncontrolled issues. This is why you should become familiar with the tools listed in Table 9-4. Examine DNS events and understand them.

MORE INFO   **DNS troubleshooting and potential resolutions**

For more information on DNS troubleshooting and potential resolutions to DNS issues, go to *http://technet2.microsoft.com/windowsserver2008/en/library/8e3f7e44-91dd-44c4-81cf-158cea7089021033.mspx?mfr=true*. To obtain *Dnslint.exe*, go to *http://support.microsoft.com/kb/321045*.

PRACTICE **Finalizing a DNS Server Configuration in a Forest**

In this practice, you will work with the DNS service to finalize its configuration. First, you will enable single-label name management in the Trey Research forest. Then you will create single-label names to populate your GNZ. Finally, you will modify a global query block list to protect your servers from dynamic entry spoofing.

▶ **Exercise 1   Single-Label Name Management**

In this exercise, you will create and configure a GNZ for the *treyresearch.net* forest. This operation is manual and will require domain administrator credentials because your DNS servers are running on DCs. This exercise will require SERVER10, SERVER20, and SERVER30.

1. Log on to SERVER10 with treyresearch\administrator.
2. In Server Manager, select the Forward Lookup Zones node in the DNS role.
3. Right-click Forward Lookup Zone to select New Zone from the context menu.
4. Review the welcome information and click Next.
5. Select Primary Zone and make sure you select the Store The Zone In Active Directory check box. Click Next.
6. On the next page, select To All DNS Servers In This Forest:TreyResearch.net and click Next.
7. On the Zone Name page, type **GlobalNames** and click Next.
8. On the Dynamic Update page, select Do Not Allow Dynamic Updates and click Next.
   You do not allow dynamic updates in this zone because all single-label names are created manually in DNS.
9. Click Finish to create the zone.
   Now, enable GNZ support on this DNS server. You need to do this through an elevated command line.
10. From the Start menu, right-click Command Prompt to select Run As Administrator.
11. Type the following command:
    ```
    dnscmd /config /enableglobalnamessupport 1
    ```

12. Close the command prompt and return to Server Manager. Right-click SERVER10 under the DNS node, select All Tasks, and choose Restart to recycle the DNS service on this server.

13. Repeat steps 10–12 on SERVER20 and SERVER30.

14. Return to SERVER10 to add single-label names.

▶ **Exercise 2   Create Single-Label Names**

In this exercise, you will create single-label names within the GNZ on SERVER10. This operation is manual and will require domain administrator credentials because your DNS servers are running on DCs. You will add a single-label record for each of your three servers.

1. Log on to SERVER10 with treyresearch\administrator.

2. In Server Manager, select the GlobalNames FLZ node in the DNS role.

3. Right-click GlobalNames to select New Alias (CNAME) from the context menu.

4. In the *Alias Name* field, type **SERVER10**, move to *Fully Qualified Domain Name (FQDN) For Target Host* field, and type **SERVER10.treyresearch.net**.

   Remember that like WINS names, single-label DNS names cannot have more than 15 characters—they actually use 16 characters, but the system reserves the last character. Also, single-label or NetBIOS names tend always to be in uppercase. Use uppercase to create your single-label names as a best practice.

5. Do not select the Allow Any Authenticated User To Update All DNS Records With The Same Name. This Setting Applies Only To DNS Records For A New Name check box.

6. Click OK to create the single-label name.

7. Use the command line to create the other two single-label names you need. From the Start menu, right-click Command Prompt to select Run As Administrator.

8. Type the following commands:

```
dnscmd server10.treyresearch.net /recordadd globalnames server20 cname
server20.northwindtraders.com

dnscmd server10.treyresearch.net /recordadd globalnames server30 cname
server30.intranet.treyresearch.net
```

9. Close the command prompt and return to the GNZ in Server Manager to view the new records. Use the Refresh button to update the details view.

   If you have many names to add, you might want to script this operation to simplify it.

▶ **Exercise 3   Modify a Global Query Block List**

In this exercise, you will modify an existing global query block list on SERVER10. This operation is manual and will require domain administrator credentials because your DNS server is running on a DC. You will add a special DNS name, **manufacturing**, to the list to block name resolution for any object that uses this name.

1. Log on to SERVER10 with treyresearch\administrator.
2. Use the command line to modify the block list. From the Start menu, right-click Command Prompt to select Run As Administrator.
3. Type the following commands:

```
dnscmd /config /globalqueryblocklist wpad isatap manufacturing
```

You must add the existing names in the block list, WPAD and ISATAP, to the command to ensure that they continue to be blocked. Make a note of the new name to ensure that you continue to block it if you need to add another name at a later date.
4. Close the command prompt.

Your block list is configured.

Lesson Summary

■ After the DNS server is installed, its configuration must be completed. DNS configuration settings include a review of the security parameters, scavenging and aging settings, zone configuration, and possible RLZ creations.

■ Each forward lookup or stub zone includes a SOA record. This record should be properly configured to include the e-mail address of the responsible parties for DNS operation as well as information about your DNS operating standards.

■ If you require single-label name management in your network, you will need to determine whether you will be using GNZs or the WINS service. GNZs are used when only a select list of names is required. If a multitude of names is required, you must deploy WINS.

■ By default, DNS servers rely on root hints for name resolution. You can also use forwarders, which direct the DNS server to another DNS server under special circumstances.

■ By default, replication scopes for DNS data integrated with Active Directory will automatically span the proper number of DNS servers. However, under special circumstances, you can create manual application directory partitions to control the replication scope more precisely.

Lesson Review

You can use the following questions to test your knowledge of the information in Lesson 2, "Configuring and Using Domain Name System." The questions are also available on the companion CD if you prefer to review them in electronic form.

NOTE Answers

Answers to these questions and explanations of why each answer choice is right or wrong are located in the "Answers" section at the end of the book.

1. You are the DNS administrator for the *contoso.com* internal forward lookup zone. You have been asked to complete the configuration of this zone now that it has been created. What should you do? (Choose all that apply).

    A. Configure scavenging for the zone.

    B. Validate the replication scope for the zone.

    C. Create custom records for the zone.

    D. Create a text (TXT) record for the zone.

    E. Assign an e-mail address to the zone.

    F. Delete unused records in the zone.

    G. Create a reverse lookup zone for the zone.

2. You are a system administrator for the *treyresearch.net* domain. Your organization has decided to create a new development domain to segregate development from the production domain. Because of compliance issues, all users of the production domain except operational staff must be granted only standard user rights. This means that for developers to be able to work, they must be granted rights other than in the production domain. However, because developers will be using the new domain on a regular basis, it has been determined that a new application directory partition must be created to support faster DNS name resolution between the two domains. All forward lookup zones are Active Directory–integrated zones. You must assign this new partition to a forward lookup zone. However, when you go to assign it, it is not available. What could be the problem? (Choose all that apply.)

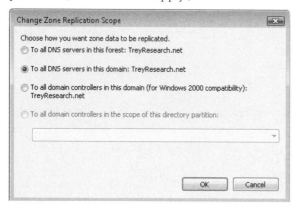

A. You must log on with domain administrator credentials.

B. You must enlist the server you are using in the partition.

C. You must log on with enterprise administrator credentials.

D. You must use the command line to assign the zone to the partition.

E. You cannot change the replication scope of a forward lookup zone after it is created.

Chapter Review

To further practice and reinforce the skills you learned in this chapter, you can perform the following tasks:

- Review the chapter summary.
- Review the list of key terms introduced in this chapter.
- Complete the case scenario. This scenario sets up a real-world situation involving the topics of this chapter and asks you to create a solution.
- Complete the suggested practices.
- Take a practice test.

Chapter Summary

- The most common types of DNS structures are the dynamic DNS server, the primary DNS server, and the secondary DNS server. Dynamic DNS servers will accept automatic name registration from authorized entities within their network. Primary DNS servers are read-write servers that are usually maintained by authorized administrators. Names can be entered manually or through automated processes but are not entered dynamically. Secondary DNS servers are usually subordinate servers that include read-only data that has originated from another DNS server, usually a primary DNS server. DNS in Windows Server 2008 also includes another type of read-only DNS server, the read-only DC DNS server, which hosts read-only *primary* DNS zones.

- A typical Windows Server 2008 DNS scenario can include up to four DNS server deployments. The first and most prolific is the dynamic DNS server, which is integrated with every DC in the network. Read-write DCs will also contain read-write DNS servers. In remote sites that do not have local administrative staff but require a DC for availability purposes, read-only DCs will also include read-only DNS servers. External networks will include at least one primary standalone DNS, which will be maintained manually. If more DNS servers are required, they should be secondary, read-only DNS servers. Read-only DNS servers are more secure than read-write servers and should be deployed in areas that demand the highest security levels.

- To support further the move to IPv6, Windows Server 2008 also supports the Peer Name Resolution Protocol and includes a PRNP server that can help promote name resolution. PNRP and DNS do not work the same way and do not include the same features. However, most organizations will continue to rely on DNS to support name resolution for the time being. For example, AD DS hierarchies are not supported in PNRP. This is a good reason to continue using DNS for the time being.

Key Terms

Use these key terms to understand better the concepts covered in this chapter.

- **record** A valid entry in a DNS zone that provides a correspondence between an IPv4 or IPv6 address and a fully qualified domain name.
- **zone** A special container in DNS that includes records that will resolve to valid IP addresses. Zones address a specific namespace and only one namespace.

Case Scenario

In the following case scenario, you will apply what you've learned about Domain Name System services. You can find answers to the questions in this scenario in the "Answers" section at the end of this book.

Case Scenario: Block Specific DNS Names

In the past, Trey Research has had problems with the Biometrics and the Biology departments when unauthorized users in these departments set up their own non-Windows servers to run their research programs. These servers were set up with little or no care for security and were quickly taken over by malicious users. After they were compromised, the servers started sending out dynamic updates for the Biometrics department, spoofing valid addresses. Now, Trey Research wants to ensure that this can never occur again. They have taken administrative measures to ensure that if other non-Windows operating systems are needed, they are installed according to proper IT guidelines.

Which other technical measure could Trey Research take to ensure that these two departments do not cause issues with DNS name resolution in the internal network?

Suggested Practices

To help you successfully master the exam objectives presented in this chapter, complete the following tasks.

Working with DNS

DNS in Windows Server 2008 is tightly integrated with Active Directory Domain Services. Therefore, you should practice working with dynamic DNS systems that support AD DS. Use the following practices to do so.

- **Practice 1** Practice installing and uninstalling DNS both on its own and through the Active Directory Domain Services Installation Wizard in as many scenarios as possible. In addition, create manual delegations and compare their interaction with the installation process to the automatically created delegations the wizard generates. This will familiarize you with the various pages presented by the wizards.

■ **Practice 2**   Work with zones, creating each of the three supported zone types one after the other. Try as many configuration options as possible. Then, create as many different record types as possible. This will familiarize you with the different dialog boxes and wizards used to configure zones and records.

■ **Practice 3**   Work with the command-line tools and try as many different switches as possible for each tool. The *Dnscmd.exe* command, especially, will be present on the exam. Familiarity with this command will help you understand its function better.

■ **Practice 4**   Work with the DNS event log and tracing log and examine their content. Familiarity with DNS logging is essential for any DNS operator.

Take a Practice Test

The practice tests on this book's companion CD offer many options. For example, you can test yourself on just one exam objective, or you can test yourself on all the 70-640 certification exam content. You can set up the test so that it closely simulates the experience of taking a certification exam, or you can set it up in study mode so that you can look at the correct answers and explanations after you answer each question.

MORE INFO   **Practice tests**

For details about all the practice test options available, see the "How to Use the Practice Tests" section in this book's introduction.

Chapter 10
Domain Controllers

Domain controllers (DCs) host the directory service and perform the services that support identity and access management in a Microsoft Windows enterprise. To this point in the training kit, you have learned to support the logical and management components of an Active Directory Domain Services (AD DS) infrastructure: users, groups, computers, and Group Policy. Each of these components is contained in the directory database and in SYSVOL on domain controllers. In this chapter, you will begin your exploration of the service-level components of Active Directory, starting with the domain controllers themselves. You will learn how to add Windows Server 2008 domain controllers to a forest or domain, how to prepare a Microsoft Windows Server 2003 forest or domain for its first Windows Server 2008 DC, how to manage the roles performed by DCs, and how to migrate the replication of SYSVOL from the File Replication Service (FRS) used in previous versions of Windows to the Distributed File System Replication (DFS-R) mechanism that provides more robust and manageable replication.

Exam objectives in this chapter:
- Configure a forest or a domain.
- Configure Active Directory replication.
- Configure operations masters.

Lessons in this chapter:
- Lesson 1: Installing Domain Controllers. 461
- Lesson 2: Configuring Operations Masters. 478
- Lesson 3: Configuring DFS Replication of SYSVOL 494

Before You Begin

To complete the practices in this chapter, you must have created a domain controller named SERVER01 in a domain named *contoso.com* and a member server, with a full installation, joined to the domain named SERVER02. See Chapter 1, "Installation," for detailed steps for this task.

Real World

Dan Holme

Active Directory enables you to configure a domain and a forest with a single domain controller. But that's not enough. Domain controllers provide functionality critical to the identity and access management requirements of an enterprise, and if a domain controller fails, you must have a way to provide continuity of service. That's why it's very important to have at least two DCs in a domain. As soon as you start adding DCs to a domain, you start needing to consider replication, and in this chapter, you'll learn about one of the exciting new features of Windows Server 2008: DFS-R of SYSVOL. FRS, used by previous versions of Windows and supported by Windows Server 2008 for backward compatibility, has been a notorious weak spot prone to problems and difficult to troubleshoot. To take advantage of this feature, all domain controllers must be running Windows Server 2008, so you'll need to know how to prepare an existing forest for its first Windows Server 2008 DC—another objective of this chapter. Finally, as you add domain controllers to an enterprise, you need to consider the placement of single master operations, which are special roles assigned to one DC in a forest or domain. By the time you're through with this chapter, you'll have the skills to improve the redundancy, performance, and manageability of multiple domain controllers in your enterprise.

Lesson 1: Installing Domain Controllers

In Chapter 1, you used the Add Roles Wizard in Server Manager to install Active Directory Domain Services (AD DS). Then you used the Active Directory Domain Services Installation Wizard to create the first DC in the *contoso.com* forest. Because DCs are critical to authentication, it is highly recommended to maintain at least two domain controllers in each domain in your forest to provide a level of fault tolerance in the event that one DC fails. You might also need to add domain controllers to remote sites or create new domains or trees in your Active Directory forest. In this lesson, you will learn user-interface, command-line, and unattended methods for installing domain controllers in a variety of scenarios.

> **After this lesson, you will be able to:**
> - Install a DC, using the Windows interface, *Dcpromo.exe* command-line parameters, or an answer file for unattended installation.
> - Add Windows Server 2008 DCs to a domain or forest with Windows Server 2003 and Windows 2000 Server DCs.
> - Create new domains and trees.
> - Perform a staged installation of a read-only domain controller.
> - Install a DC from installation media to reduce network replication.
> - Remove a domain controller.
>
> **Estimated lesson time: 60 minutes**

Installing a Domain Controller with the Windows Interface

If you want to use the Windows interface to install a domain controller, there are two major steps. First, you must install the AD DS role, which, as you learned in Chapter 1, can be accomplished using the Add Roles Wizard in Server Manager. After the AD DS role installation has copied the binaries required for the role to the server, you must install and configure AD DS by launching the Active Directory Domain Services Installation Wizard, using one of these methods:

- Click Start and, in the Start Search box, type **dcpromo** and click OK.
- When you complete the Add Roles Wizard, click the link to launch the Active Directory Domain Services Installation Wizard.
- After adding the AD DS role, links will appear in Server Manager that remind you to run the Active Directory Domain Services Installation Wizard. Click any of those links.

The Active Directory Domain Services Installation Wizard is shown in Figure 10-1.

Figure 10-1 The Active Directory Domain Services Installation Wizard

---

NOTE All-in-one wizard

Microsoft documentation for Windows Server 2008 emphasizes the role-based model, so it recommends you add the AD DS role and then run *Dcpromo.exe* (the Active Directory Domain Services Installation Wizard). However, you can simply run *Dcpromo.exe* and, as a first step, the wizard detects that the AD DS binaries are not installed and adds the AD DS role automatically.

Unattended Installation Options and Answer Files

You can also add or remove a domain controller at the command line, using unattended installation supported by the Windows Server 2008 version of *Dcpromo.exe*. Unattended installation options provide values to the Active Directory Domain Services Installation Wizard. For example, the NewDomainDNSName option specifies a fully qualified domain name (FQDN) for a new domain.

These options can be provided at the command line by typing **dcpromo /*unattendOption:value*,** for example, **dcpromo /newdomaindnsname:contoso.com**. Alternatively, you can provide the options in an unattended installation answer file. The answer file is a text file that contains a section heading, [DCINSTALL], followed by options and their values in the *option=value* form. For example, the following file provides the NewDomainDNSName option:

```
[DCINSTALL]
NewDomainDNSName=contoso.com
```

The answer file is called by adding its path to the *unattend* parameter, for example:

```
dcpromo /unattend:"path to answer file"
```

The options in the answer file can be overridden by parameters on the command line. For example, if the NewDomainDNSName option is specified in the answer file and the /New-DomainDNSName parameter is used on the command line, the value on the command line takes precedence. If any required values are neither in the answer file nor on the command line, the Active Directory Domain Services Installation Wizard will prompt for the answers, so you can use the answer file to partially automate an installation, providing a subset of configuration values to be used during an interactive installation.

The wizard is not available when running *Dcpromo.exe* from the command line in Server Core. In that case, the *Dcpromo.exe* command will return with an error code.

For a complete list of parameters that you can specify as part of an unattended installation of AD DS, open an elevated command prompt and type the following command:

```
dcpromo /?[:operation]
```

where *operation* is one of the following:

- **Promotion** returns all parameters you can use when creating a domain controller.
- **CreateDCAccount** returns all parameters you can use when creating a prestaged account for a read-only domain controller (RODC).
- **UseExistingAccount** returns all parameters you can use to attach a new DC to a prestaged RODC account.
- **Demotion** returns all parameters you can use when removing a domain controller.

MORE INFO *Dcpromo* **parameters and unattended installation**

For a complete reference of *Dcpromo* parameters and unattended installation options, see *http://go.microsoft.com/fwlink/?LinkID=101181*.

NOTE **Generate an answer file**

When you use the Windows interface to create a domain controller, the Active Directory Domain Services Installation Wizard gives you the option, on the Summary page, to export your settings to an answer file. If you need to create an answer file for use from the command line, for example, on a Server Core installation, you can use this shortcut to create an answer file with the correct options and values.

Installing a New Windows Server 2008 Forest

Chapter 1 discussed the installation of the first Windows Server 2008 DC in a new forest, using the Windows interface. Exercise 3, "Install a New Windows Server 2008 Forest with the Windows Interface," and Exercise 4, "Install a New Windows Server 2008 Forest," of Lesson 1, "Installing Active Directory Domain Services," in that chapter detailed the steps to add the AD DS role to a server by using Server Manager and then to run *Dcpromo.exe* to promote the server to a domain controller. When creating a new forest root domain, you must specify the forest root Domain Name System (DNS) name, its NetBIOS name, and the forest and domain functional levels. The first domain controller cannot be a read-only domain controller and must be a global catalog (GC) server. If the Active Directory Domain Services Installation Wizard detects that it is necessary to install or configure DNS, it does it automatically.

You can also use an answer file by typing **dcpromo /unattend:**"*path to answer file*", where the answer file contains unattended installation options and values. The following example contains the minimum parameters for an unattended installation of a new Windows Server 2008 domain controller in a new forest:

```
[DCINSTALL]
ReplicaOrNewDomain=domain
NewDomain=forest
NewDomainDNSName=fully qualified DNS name
DomainNetBiosName=domain NetBIOS name
ForestLevel={0=Windows 2000 Server Native;
             2=Windows Server 2003 Native;
             3=Windows Server 2008}
DomainLevel={0=Windows Server 2000 Native;
             2=Windows Server 2003 Native;
             3=Windows Server 2008}
InstallDNS=yes
DatabasePath="path to folder on a local volume"
LogPath="path to folder on a local volume"
SYSVOLPath="path to folder on a local volume"
SafeModeAdminPassword=password
RebootOnCompletion=yes
```

You can also specify one or more unattended installation parameters and values at the command line. For example, if you don't want the Directory Services Restore Mode password in the answer file, leave the entry blank and specify the */SafeModeAdminPassword:password* parameter when you run *Dcpromo.exe*.

You can also include all options on the command line itself. The following example creates the first domain controller in a new forest in which you don't expect to install any Windows Server 2003 domain controllers:

```
dcpromo /unattend /installDNS:yes /dnsOnNetwork:yes
   /replicaOrNewDomain:domain /newDomain:forest
   /newDomainDnsName:contoso.com /DomainNetbiosName:contoso
```

```
/databasePath:"e:\ntds" /logPath:"f:\ntdslogs" /sysvolpath:"g:\sysvol"
/safeModeAdminPassword:password /forestLevel:3 /domainLevel:3
/rebootOnCompletion:yes
```

Installing Additional Domain Controllers in a Domain

If you have a domain with at least one domain controller running Windows 2000 Server, Windows Server 2003, or Windows Server 2008, you can create additional domain controllers to distribute authentication, create a level of fault tolerance in the event any one DC fails, or provide authentication in remote sites.

Installing the First Windows Server 2008 Domain Controller in an Existing Forest or Domain

If you have an existing forest with domain controllers running Windows Server 2003 or Windows 2000 Server, you must prepare them prior to creating your first Windows Server 2008 domain controller. That's because there are objects and attributes that Windows Server 2008 adds to the directory that previous versions of Windows don't understand. Therefore, the schema must be updated. The schema is the definition of the attributes and object classes that can exist within a domain. It is like the catalog for what can be created in other directory partitions. To prepare the forest schema for Windows Server 2008, follow these steps:

1. Log on to the schema master as a member of the Enterprise Admins, Schema Admins, and Domain Admins groups.

    Lesson 2, "Configuring Operations Masters," discusses operations masters and provides steps for identifying which domain controller is the schema master.

2. Copy the contents of the \Sources\Adprep folder from the Windows Server 2008 DVD to a folder on the schema master.

3. Open a command prompt and change directories to the Adprep folder.

4. Type **adprep /forestprep** and press Enter.

5. If you plan to install an RODC in any domain in the forest, type **adprep /rodcprep** and press Enter.

NOTE RODCPREP, anytime

You can also run *Adprep /rodcprep* at any time in a Windows 2000 Server or Windows Server 2003 forest. It does not have to be run in conjunction with */forestprep*; however, you must run it and allow its changes to replicate throughout the forest prior to installing the first RODC. You can run *Adprep /rodcprep* from any DC as long as you are logged on as a member of the Enterprise Admins group.

Exam Tip The *Adprep /rodcprep* command is required before installing an RODC into any domain in an existing forest with Windows Server 2003 or Windows 2000 Server domain controllers. It is not necessary if the forest is a new forest consisting only of Windows Server 2008 domain controllers.

You must allow time for the operation to complete. After the changes have replicated throughout the forest, you can continue to prepare the domains for Windows Server 2008. To prepare a Windows 2000 Server or Windows Server 2003 domain for Windows Server 2008, perform these steps:

1. Log on to the domain infrastructure operations master as a member of Domain Admins.
   Lesson 2 provides steps for identifying which domain controller is the infrastructure operations master.

2. Copy the contents of the \Sources\Adprep folder from the Windows Server 2008 DVD to a folder on the infrastructure master.

3. Open a command prompt and change directories to the Adprep folder.

4. Type **adprep /domainprep /gpprep** and press Enter.
   On Windows Server 2003, you might receive an error message stating that updates were unnecessary. You can ignore this message.

Allow the change to replicate throughout the forest before you install a domain controller that runs Windows Server 2008.

Installing an Additional Domain Controller

Additional domain controllers can be added by installing AD DS and launching the Active Directory Domain Services Installation Wizard. You are prompted to choose the deployment configuration; to enter network credentials; to select a domain and site for the new DC; and to configure the DC with additional options such as DNS Server, Global Catalog, or Read-Only Domain Controller. The remaining steps are the same as for the first domain controller: configuring file locations and the Directory Services Restore Mode Administrator password.

If you have one domain controller in a domain, and if you select the Use Advanced Mode Installation check box on the Welcome To The Active Directory Domain Services Installation Wizard page, you are able to configure advanced options, which are:

- **Install From Media** By default, a new domain controller replicates all data for all directory partitions it will host from other domain controllers during the Active Directory Domain Services Installation Wizard. To improve the performance of installation, particularly over slow links, you can use installation media created by existing domain controllers. Installation media is a form of backup. The new DC is able to read data from the installation media directly and then replicate only updates from other domain controllers. Install From Media (IFM) is discussed in the "Installing AD DS from Media" section.

■ **Source Domain Controller**   If you want to specify the domain controller from which the new DC replicates its data, you can click Use This Specific Domain Controller.

NOTE *Dcpromo /adv* **is still supported**

In Windows Server 2003, *Dcpromo /adv* was used to specify advanced installation options. The *adv* parameter is still supported; it simply pre-selects the Use Advanced Mode Installation check box on the Welcome page.

To use *Dcpromo.exe* with command-line parameters to specify unattended installation options, you can use the minimal parameters shown in the following example:

```
dcpromo /unattend /replicaOrNewDomain:replica
    /replicaDomainDNSName:contoso.com /installDNS:yes /confirmGC:yes
    /databasePath:"e:\ntds" /logPath:"f:\ntdslogs" /sysvolpath:"g:\sysvol"
    /safeModeAdminPassword:password /rebootOnCompletion:yes
```

If you are not logged on to the server with domain credentials, specify the *userdomain* and *username* parameters as well. A minimal answer file for an additional domain controller in an existing domain is as follows:

```
[DCINSTALL]
ReplicaOrNewDomain=replica
ReplicaDomainDNSName=FQDN of domain to join
UserDomain=FQDN of domain of user account
UserName=DOMAIN\username (in Administrators group of the domain)
Password=password for user specified by UserName (* to prompt)
InstallDNS=yes
ConfirmGC=yes
DatabasePath="path to folder on a local volume"
LogPath="path to folder on a local volume"
SYSVOLPath="path to folder on a local volume"
SafeModeAdminPassword=password
RebootOnCompletion=yes
```

Installing a New Windows Server 2008 Child Domain

If you have an existing domain, you can create a new child domain by creating a Windows Server 2008 domain controller. Before you do, however, you must run *Adprep /forestprep,* as described in the "Installing the First Windows Server 2008 Domain Controller in an Existing Forest or Domain" section.

Then install AD DS and launch the Active Directory Domain Services Installation Wizard and, on the Choose A Deployment Configuration page, click Existing Forest and Create A New Domain In An Existing Forest. You are prompted to select the domain functional level.

Because it is the first DC in the domain, it cannot be an RODC, and it cannot be installed from media. If you select the Use Advanced Mode Installation check box on the Welcome page, the wizard presents you with a Source Domain Controller page on which you specify a domain controller from which to replicate the configuration and schema partitions.

Using *Dcpromo.exe*, you can create a child domain with the minimal options shown in the following command:

```
dcpromo /unattend /installDNS:yes
    /replicaOrNewDomain:domain /newDomain:child
    /ParentDomainDNSName:contoso.com
    /newDomainDnsName:subsidiary.contoso.com /childName:subsidiary
    /DomainNetbiosName:subsidiary
    /databasePath:"e:\ntds" /logPath:"f:\ntdslogs" /sysvolpath:"g:\sysvol"
    /safeModeAdminPassword:password /forestLevel:3 /domainLevel:3
    /rebootOnCompletion:yes
```

The following answer file reflects the same minimal parameters:

```
[DCINSTALL]
ReplicaOrNewDomain=domain
NewDomain=child
ParentDomainDNSName=FQDN of parent domain
UserDomain=FQDN of user specified by UserName
UserName= DOMAIN\username (in Administrators group of ParentDomainDNSName)
Password=password for user specified by UserName or * for prompt
ChildName=single-label prefix for domain
            (Child domain FQDN will be ChildName.ParentDomainDNSName)
DomainNetBiosName=Domain NetBIOS name
DomainLevel=domain functional level (not lower than current forest level)
InstallDNS=yes
CreateDNSDelegation=yes
DNSDelegationUserName=DOMAIN\username with permissions to create
                       DNS delegation, if different than UserName, above
DNSDelegationPassword=password for DNSDelegationUserName or * for prompt
DatabasePath="path to folder on a local volume"
LogPath="path to folder on a local volume"
SYSVOLPath="path to folder on a local volume"
SafeModeAdminPassword=password
RebootOnCompletion=yes
```

Installing a New Domain Tree

You learned in Chapter 1 that in an Active Directory forest, a tree is composed of one or more domains that share contiguous DNS namespace. So, for example, the *contoso.com* and *subsidiary. contoso.com* domains would be in a single tree. Additional trees are simply additional domains that are not in the same namespace. For example, if Contoso, Ltd., bought Tailspin Toys, the *tailspintoys.com* domain would be in a separate tree in the domain. There is very little functional difference between a child domain and a domain in another tree, and the process for creating a new tree is, therefore, very similar to creating a child domain.

First, you must run *Adprep /forestprep*, as described in the "Installing the First Windows Server 2008 Domain Controller in an Existing Forest or Domain" section. Then you can install AD DS and run the Active Directory Domain Services Installation Wizard. You must select Use Advanced Mode Installation on the Welcome page of the wizard. On the Choose A Deployment Configuration page, click Existing Forest, select Create A New Domain In An Existing Forest, and select Create A New Domain Tree Root Instead Of A New Child Domain. The rest of the process is identical to creating a new child domain.

The following options provided as parameters to *Dcpromo.exe* create a new tree for the *tailspintoys.com* domain within the *contoso.com* forest:

```
dcpromo /unattend /installDNS:yes
    /replicaOrNewDomain:domain /newDomain:tree
    /newDomainDnsName:tailspintoys.com /DomainNetbiosName:tailspintoys
    /databasePath:"e:\ntds" /logPath:"f:\ntdslogs" /sysvolpath:"g:\sysvol"
    /safeModeAdminPassword:password /domainLevel:2
    /rebootOnCompletion:yes
```

The domain functional level is configured at 2—Windows Server 2003 Native—so the domain could include Windows Server 2003 domain controllers. An unattended installation answer file that creates the same new tree would look similar to the following:

```
[DCINSTALL]
ReplicaOrNewDomain=domain
NewDomain=tree
NewDomainDNSName=FQDN of new domain
DomainNetBiosName=NetBIOS name of new domain
UserDomain=FQDN of user specified by UserName
UserName= DOMAIN\username (in Administrators group of ParentDomainDNSName)
Password=password for user specified by UserName or * for prompt
DomainLevel=domain functional level (not lower than current forest level)
InstallDNS=yes
ConfirmGC=yes
CreateDNSDNSDelegation=yes
DNSDelegationUserName=account with permissions to create DNS delegation
                     required only if different than UserName, above
DNSDelegationPassword=password for DNSDelegationUserName or * for prompt
DatabasePath="path to folder on a local volume"
LogPath="path to folder on a local volume"
SYSVOLPath="path to folder on a local volume"
SafeModeAdminPassword=password
RebootOnCompletion=yes
```

Staging the Installation of an RODC

As you remember from Chapter 8, "Authentication," RODCs are designed to support branch office scenarios by providing authentication local to the site while mitigating the security and data integrity risks associated with placing a DC in a less well-controlled environment. Many times, there are few or no IT support personnel in a branch office. How, then, should a domain controller be created in a branch office?

To answer this question, Windows Server 2008 enables you to create a staged, or delegated, installation of an RODC. The process includes two stages:

- **Create the account for the RODC**   A member of Domain Admins creates an account for the RODC in Active Directory. The parameters related to the RODC are specified at this time: the name, the Active Directory site in which the RODC will be created, and, optionally, the user or group that can complete the next stage of the installation.

- **Attach the server to the RODC account**   After the account has been created, AD DS is installed, and the RODC is attached to the domain. These steps can be the users or groups specified when the RODC account was prestaged; these users do not require any privileged group membership. A server can also be attached by a member of Domain Admins or Enterprise Admins, but the ability to delegate this stage to a nonprivileged user makes it much easier to deploy RODCs in branches without IT support. The domain controller will replicate its data from another writable DC in the domain, or you can use the IFM method discussed in the "Installing AD DS from Media" section.

NOTE   Promote from a workgroup

When you create an RODC by using the staged approach—when you attach an RODC to a pre-staged account—the server must be a member of a workgroup, not of the domain, when you launch *Dcpromo.exe* or the Active Directory Domain Services Installation Wizard. The wizard will look in the domain for the existing account with its name and will attach to that account.

Creating the Prestaged Account for the RODC

To create the account for the RODC, using the Active Directory Users and Computers snap-in, right-click the Domain Controllers OU and choose Pre-Create Read-Only Domain Controller Account. A wizard appears that is very similar to the Active Directory Domain Services Installation Wizard. You are asked to specify the RODC name and site. You are also able to configure the password replication policy, as detailed in Chapter 8.

On the Delegation Of RODC Installation And Administration page, you can specify one security principal—user or group—that can attach the server to the RODC account you create. The user or group will also have local administrative rights on the RODC after the installation. It is recommended that you delegate to a group rather than to a user. If you do not specify a user or group, only members of the Domain Admins or Enterprise Admins groups can attach the server to the account.

MORE INFO   Creating prestaged RODC accounts

You can create prestaged RODC accounts by using *Dcpromo.exe* with numerous parameters or by creating an answer file for *Dcpromo.exe*. The steps for doing so are detailed at *http://technet2.microsoft.com/windowsserver2008/en/library/f349e1e7-c3ce-4850-9e50-d8886c866b521033.mspx?mfr=true*.

Attaching a Server to the RODC Account

After you have prestaged the account, the server can be attached to it. You cannot simply launch the Active Directory Domain Services Installation Wizard. You must do so by typing **dcpromo /useexistingaccount:attach**. The wizard prompts for network credentials and then finds the RODC account in the domain indicated by the credentials. Remaining steps are similar to other domain controller promotion operations.

To use an answer file, provide the following options and values:

```
[DCINSTALL]
ReplicaDomainDNSName=FQDN of domain to join
UserDomain=FQDN of user specified by UserName
UserName=DOMAIN\username (in Administrators group of the domain)
Password=password for user specified by UserName
InstallDNS=yes
ConfirmGC=yes
DatabasePath="path to folder on a local volume"
LogPath="path to folder on a local volume"
SYSVOLPath="path to folder on a local volume"
SafeModeAdminPassword=password
RebootOnCompletion=yes
```

Run *Dcpromo* with the unattend:"answer file path" and the UseExistingAccount:Attach options, as in the following example:

```
dcpromo /useexistingaccount:attache /unattend:"c:\rodcanswer.txt"
```

All the options just shown in the answer file can also be specified or overridden directly on the command line. Just type a command similar to the following:

```
dcpromo /unattend /UseExistingAccount:Attach /ReplicaDomainDNSName:contoso.com
    /UserDomain:contoso.com /UserName:contoso\dan /password:*
    /databasePath:"e:\ntds" /logPath:"f:\ntdslogs" /sysvolpath:"g:\sysvol"
    /safeModeAdminPassword:password /rebootOnCompletion:yes
```

> ### Quick Check
>
> ■ You administer a domain containing Windows Server 2003 domain controllers. You want to allow a manager at a remote site to promote a member server at a remote site to an RODC. You do not want to give the manager administrative credentials in the domain. What steps must you and the manager take?
>
> ### Quick Check Answer
>
> ■ You must run *Adprep /rodcprep* to prepare the domain for the RODC. You must then prestage the RODC account, delegating to the manager the ability to attach the domain controller to the account. The manager will run *Dcpromo.exe* with the UseExistingAccount option to attach the server, but first, the server must be removed from the domain and placed in a workgroup.

Installing AD DS from Media

When you add domain controllers to a forest, data from existing directory partitions are replicated to the new DC. In an environment with a large directory or where bandwidth is constrained between a new DC and a writable DC from which to replicate, you can install AD DS more efficiently by using the IFM option. Installing from media involves creating *installation media*—a specialized backup of Active Directory that can be used by the Active Directory Domain Services Installation Wizard as a data source for populating the directory on a new DC. Then the new DC will replicate only updates from another writable DC, so if the installation media is recent, you can minimize the impact of replication to a new DC.

Remember that it is not only the directory that must be replicated to a new DC but SYSVOL as well. When you create your installation media, you can specify whether to include SYSVOL on the installation media.

Using IFM also enables you to control the timing of impact to your network bandwidth. You can, for example, create installation media and transfer it to a remote site during off hours, then create the domain controller during normal business hours. Because the installation media is from the local site, impact to the network is reduced, and only updates will be replicated over the link to the remote site.

To create installation media, open a command prompt on a writable domain controller, running Windows Server 2008. The installation media is compatible across platforms. Run *Ntdsutil.exe* and then, at the ntdsutil prompt, type the **activate instance ntds** command and then the **ifm** command. At the *ifm:* prompt, type one of the following commands, based on the type of installation media you want to create:

■ **create sysvol full** *path*   Creates installation media with SYSVOL for a writable domain controller in the folder specified by *Path*

- **create full** *path*   Creates installation media without SYSVOL for a writable domain controller or an Active Directory Lightweight Directory Services (AD LDS) instance in the folder specified by *Path*
- **create sysvol rodc** *path*   Creates installation media with SYSVOL for a read-only domain controller in the folder specified by *Path*
- **create rodc** *path*   Creates installation media without SYSVOL for a read-only domain controller in the folder specified by *Path*

When you run the Active Directory Domain Services Installation Wizard, select the Use Advanced Mode Installation check box, and you will be presented the Install From Media page later in the wizard. Choose Replicate Data From Media At The Following Location. You can use the ReplicationSourcePath installation option in an answer file or on the *Dcpromo.exe* command line.

Practice It   Exercise 3, "Create Installation Media," in the practice at the end of this lesson, steps you through the process of creating installation media with *Ntdsutil.exe*.

Removing a Domain Controller

You can remove a domain controller by using *Dcpromo.exe*, either to launch the Active Directory Domain Services Installation Wizard or from a command prompt, specifying options at the command line or in an answer file. When a domain controller is removed while it has connectivity to the domain, it updates the forest metadata about the domain controller so that the directory knows the DC has been removed.

MORE INFO   Removing a domain controller

For detailed steps for removing a domain controller, see *http://technet2.microsoft.com /windowsserver2008/en/library/9260bb40-a808-422f-b33b-c3d2330f5eb81033.mspx*.

If a domain controller must be demoted while it cannot contact the domain, you must use the forceremoval option of *Dcpromo.exe*. Type **dcpromo /forceremoval**, and the Active Directory Domain Services Installation Wizard steps you through the process. You are presented warnings related to any roles the domain controller hosts. Read each warning and, after you have mitigated or accepted the impact of the warning, click Yes. You can suppress warnings, using the demotefsmo:yes option of *Dcpromo.exe*. After the DC has been removed, you must manually clean up the forest metadata.

MORE INFO   Performing metadata cleanup

See article 216498 in the Microsoft Knowledge Base for information about performing metadata cleanup. The article is located at *http://go.microsoft.com/fwlink/?LinkId=80481*.

PRACTICE **Installing Domain Controllers**

In this practice, you will perform the steps required to install an additional domain controller in the *contoso.com* domain. You will install AD DS and configure an additional DC, using the Active Directory Domain Services Installation Wizard. *You will not complete the installation.* Instead, you will save the settings as an answer file. You will then use the settings to perform an unattended installation, using the *Dcpromo.exe* command with installation options.

To perform this exercise, you will need a second server running Windows Server 2008 full installation. The server must be named SERVER02, and it should be joined to the *contoso.com* domain. Its configuration should be as follows:

- Computer Name: SERVER02
- Domain Membership: *contoso.com*
- IPv4 address: 10.0.0.12
- Subnet Mask: 255.255.255.0
- Default Gateway: 10.0.0.1
- DNS Server: 10.0.0.11

▶ **Exercise 1   Create an Additional DC with the Active Directory Domain Services Installation Wizard**

In this exercise, you will use the Active Directory Domain Services Installation Wizard (*Dcpromo.exe*) to create an additional domain controller in the *contoso.com* domain. You will not complete the installation, however. Instead, you will save the settings as an answer file, which will be used in the next exercise.

1. Log on to SERVER02 as CONTOSO\Administrator.
2. Click Start, click Run, type **Dcpromo.exe**, and press Enter.
3. Click Next.
4. On the Operating System Compatibility page, review the warning about the default security settings for Windows Server 2008 domain controllers, and then click Next.
5. On the Choose A Deployment Configuration page, select Existing Forest, select Add A Domain Controller To An Existing Domain, and then click Next.
6. On the Network Credentials page, type **contoso.com** in the text box, select My Current Logged On Credentials, and then click Next.
7. On the Select A Domain page, select *contoso.com* and click Next.
8. On the Select A Site page, select Default-First-Site-Name and click Next.
   The Additional Domain Controller Options page appears. DNS Server and Global Catalog are selected by default.
9. Clear the Global Catalog and DNS Server check boxes, and then click Next.
   An Infrastructure Master Configuration Conflict warning appears. You will learn about the infrastructure master in Lesson 2, so you will ignore this error.

10. Click Do Not Transfer The Infrastructure Master Role To This Domain Controller. I Will Correct The Configuration Later.
11. On the Location For Database, Log Files, And SYSVOL page, accept the default locations for the database file, the directory service log files, and the SYSVOL files and click Next.

    The best practice in a production environment is to store these files on three separate volumes that do not contain applications or other files not related to AD DS. This best practices design improves performance and increases the efficiency of backup and restore.
12. On the Directory Services Restore Mode Administrator Password page, type a strong password in both the Password and Confirmed Password boxes. Click Next.

    Do not forget the password you assigned to the Directory Services Restore Mode Administrator.
13. On the Summary page, review your selections.

    If any settings are incorrect, click Back to make modifications.
14. Click Export Settings.
15. Click Browse Folders.
16. Select Desktop.
17. In the File Name box, type **AdditionalDC** and click Save.

    A message appears indicating that settings were saved successfully.
18. Click OK.
19. On the Active Directory Domain Services Installation Wizard Summary page, click Cancel.
20. Click Yes to confirm that you are cancelling the installation of the DC.

▶ **Exercise 2   Add a Domain Controller from the Command Line**

In this exercise, you will examine the answer file you created in Exercise 1, "Create an Additional DC with the Active Directory Domain Services Installation Wizard." You will use the installation options in the answer file to create a *Dcpromo.exe* command line to install the additional domain controller.

1. Open the AdditionalDC.txt file you created in Exercise 1.
2. Examine the answers in the file. Can you identify what some of the options mean?

   Tip: Lines beginning with a semicolon are comments or inactive lines that have been commented out.
3. Open a command prompt.

   You will be building a command line, using the options in the answer file. Position the windows so you can see both Notepad and the command prompt or print the answer file for reference.
4. Determine the command line to install the domain controller with the configuration contained in the answer file.

   Parameters on the command line take the form /*option:value* whereas, in the answer file, they take the form *option=value*.

5. Type the following command and press Enter:

```
dcpromo /unattend /replicaornewdomain:replica
/replicadomaindnsname:contoso.com /sitename:Default-First-Site-Name
/installDNS:No /confirmGC:No /CreateDNSDelegation:No
/databasepath:"C:\Windows\NTDS" /logpath:"C:\Windows\NTDS"
/sysvolpath:"C:\Windows\SYSVOL" /safemodeadminpassword:password
/transferimroleifnecessary:no
```

where *password* is a complex password.

6. Installation will complete, and the server will reboot.

▶ **Exercise 3   Create Installation Media**

You can reduce the amount of replication required to create a domain controller by promoting the domain controller, using the IFM option. IFM requires that you provide installation media, which is, in effect, a backup of Active Directory. In this exercise, you will create the installation media.

1. Log on to SERVER01 as Administrator.
2. Open a command prompt.
3. Type **ntdsutil** and press Enter.
4. Type **activate instance ntds** and press Enter.
5. Type **ifm** and press Enter.
6. Type **?** and press Enter to list the commands available in IFM mode.
7. Type **create sysvol full c:\IFM** and press Enter.

    The installation media files are copied to C:\Ifm.

Lesson Summary

■ AD DS can be installed by running *Dcpromo.exe*, which launches the Active Directory Domain Services Installation Wizard or, with the unattend option, can obtain installation options from the command line or an answer file.

■ When you introduce the first Windows Server 2008 domain controller into an existing forest, you must run *Adprep /forestprep*. Before you introduce the first Windows Server 2008 DC into an existing domain, you must run *Adprep /domainprep /gpprep*.

■ Before you install the first RODC in a domain containing Windows 2000 Server or Windows Server 2003 DCs, you must run *Adprep /rodcprep*.

■ To perform a staged installation of an RODC, you create the account for the RODC and specify the user or group that will be able to attach the RODC to the account.

■ To reduce replication requirements, you can create installation media and use the media as a source when performing a domain controller promotion.

Lesson Review

You can use the following questions to test your knowledge of the information in Lesson 1, "Installing Domain Controllers." The questions are also available on the companion CD if you prefer to review them in electronic form.

NOTE Answers

Answers to these questions and explanations of why each answer choice is right or wrong are located in the "Answers" section at the end of the book.

---

1. You are an administrator at Trey Research. The Trey Research forest consists of three domains, each of which includes two domain controllers running Windows Server 2003. You want to upgrade one of the domain controllers to Windows Server 2008. What must you do first?

   A. Upgrade the domain controller's operating system to Windows Server 2008.
   B. Run the *Adprep.exe /domainprep /gpprep* command.
   C. Run the Active Directory Domain Services Installation Wizard.
   D. Run the *Adprep.exe /forestprep* command.
   E. Run the *Adprep.exe /rodcprep* command.

2. You are an administrator at Contoso, Ltd. The domain was built using Windows Server 2008 domain controllers. You want to improve authentication at a remote site by promoting a member server at the site to a read-only domain controller. There is no IT support at the site, so you want the site's manager to perform the promotion. You do not want to give her administrative credentials in the domain. Which steps must you or the manager take? (Choose all that apply. Each correct answer is part of the solution.)

   A. Run *Adprep /rodcprep*.
   B. Create the RODC account in the Domain Controllers OU.
   C. Run *Dcpromo.exe* with the UseExistingAccount option.
   D. Remove the server from the domain.

3. You want to promote a server to act as a domain controller, but you are concerned about the replication traffic that will occur during the promotion and its impact on the slow link between the server's site and the data center where all other domain controllers are located, so you choose to promote the server, using a backup of the directory from another domain controller. What must you do to create the installation media?

   A. Run *Ntbackup.exe* and select System State.
   B. Install the Windows Server Backup Features.
   C. Run *Ntdsutil.exe* in the IFM mode and use the *Create Sysvol Full* command.
   D. Copy *ntds.dit* and SYSVOL from a domain controller to a location in the remote site.

Lesson 2: Configuring Operations Masters

In an Active Directory domain, all domain controllers are equivalent. They are all capable of writing to the database and replicating changes to other domain controllers. However, in any multimaster replication topology, certain operations must be performed by one and only one system. In an Active Directory domain, *operations masters* are domain controllers that play a specific role. Other domain controllers are capable of playing the role but do not. This lesson will introduce you to the five operations masters found in Active Directory forests and domains. You will learn their purposes, how to identify the operations masters in your enterprise, and the nuances of administering and transferring roles.

After this lesson, you will be able to:
- Define the purpose of the five single master operations in Active Directory forests.
- Identify the domain controllers performing operations master roles.
- Plan the placement of operations master roles.
- Transfer and seize operations master roles.

Estimated lesson time: 45 minutes

Understanding Single Master Operations

In any replicated database, some changes must be performed by one and only one replica because they are impractical to perform in a multimaster fashion. Active Directory is no exception. A limited number of operations are not permitted to occur at different places at the same time and must be the responsibility of only one domain controller in a domain or forest. These operations, and the domain controllers that perform them, are referred to by a variety of terms:

- *Operations masters*
- *Operations master roles*
- *Single master roles*
- *Operations tokens*
- *Flexible single master operations (FSMOs)*

Regardless of the term used, the idea is the same. One domain controller performs a function, and while it does, no other domain controller performs that function.

Not Déjà Vu

If you were an administrator in the days of Microsoft Windows NT 4.0, the concept of operations masters might sound similar to Windows NT primary domain controllers (PDCs). However, single master operations are characteristic of any replicated database, and Active Directory single master operations bear striking differences to Windows NT 4.0 PDCs:

- All Active Directory domain controllers are capable of performing single master operations. The domain controller that actually does perform an operation is the domain controller that currently holds the operation's token.
- An operation token, and thus the role, can be transferred easily to another domain controller without a reboot.
- To reduce the risk of single points of failure, the operations tokens can be distributed among multiple DCs.

AD DS contains five operations master roles. Two roles are performed for the entire forest:

- Domain naming
- Schema

Three roles are performed in each domain:

- Relative identifier (RID)
- Infrastructure
- PDC Emulator

Each of these roles is detailed in the following sections. In a forest with a single domain, there are, therefore, five operations masters. In a forest with two domains, there are eight operations masters because the three domain master roles are implemented separately in each of the two domains.

Exam Tip   Commit to memory the list of forest-wide and domain single master operations. You are likely to encounter questions that test your knowledge of which roles apply to the entire forest and which are domain specific. Exam questions are cast in scenarios and, often, the scenarios provide so much detail that you can lose sight of what is really being asked. When you read items on the certification exam, always ask yourself, "What is really being tested?" Sometimes what is being tested is different from, and simpler than, what the scenario in the question would lead you to believe.

Forest-Wide Operations Master Roles

The schema master and the domain naming master must be unique in the forest. Each role is performed by only one domain controller in the entire forest.

Domain Naming Master Role

The domain naming role is used when adding or removing domains in the forest. When you add or remove a domain, the domain naming master must be accessible, or the operation will fail.

Schema Master Role

The domain controller holding the schema master role is responsible for making any changes to the forest's schema. All other DCs hold read-only replicas of the schema. If you want to modify the schema or install an application that modifies the schema, it is recommended you do so on the domain controller holding the schema master role. Otherwise, changes you request must be sent to the schema master to be written into the schema.

Domain-Wide Operations Master Roles

Each domain maintains three single master operations: RID, Infrastructure, and PDC Emulator. Each role is performed by only one domain controller in the domain.

RID Master Role

The RID master plays an integral part in the generation of security identifiers (SIDs) for security principals such as users, groups, and computers. The SID of a security principal must be unique. Because any domain controller can create accounts and, therefore, SIDs, a mechanism is necessary to ensure that the SIDs generated by a DC are unique. Active Directory domain controllers generate SIDs by assigning a unique RID to the domain SID. The RID master for the domain allocates pools of unique RIDs to each domain controller in the domain. Thus, each domain controller can be confident that the SIDs it generates are unique.

NOTE The RID master role is like DHCP for SIDs

If you are familiar with the concept that you allocate a scope of IP addresses for the Dynamic Host Configuration Protocol (DHCP) server to assign to clients, you can draw a parallel to the RID master, which allocates pools of RIDs to domain controllers for the creation of SIDs.

Infrastructure Master Role

In a multidomain environment, it is common for an object to reference objects in other domains. For example, a group can include members from another domain. Its multivalued *member* attribute contains the distinguished names of each member. If the member in the other domain is moved or renamed, the infrastructure master of the group's domain updates the group's *member* attribute accordingly.

NOTE   The infrastructure master

You can think of the infrastructure master as a tracking device for group members from other domains. When those members are renamed or moved in the other domain, the infrastructure master identifies the change and makes appropriate changes to group memberships so that the memberships are kept up to date.

Phantoms of the Directory

Although you are not expected to understand the internals of the infrastructure master role for the certification exam, such understanding can be helpful in the production environment. When you add a member from another domain into a group in your domain, the group's *member* attribute is appended with the distinguished name of the new member. However, your domain might not always have access to a domain controller from the member's domain, so Active Directory creates a phantom object to represent the member. The phantom object includes only the member's SID, distinguished name (DN), and globally unique identifier (GUID). If the member is moved or renamed in its domain, its GUID does not change, but its DN changes. If the object is moved between domains, its SID also changes. The infrastructure master periodically—every two days by default—contacts a GC or a DC in the member domain. At that time, the infrastructure master looks for each phantom object, using the GUID of the phantom object. It updates the DN of the phantom objects with the current DN of the object. Any change is then propagated to the *member* attribute of groups.

After a member is moved or renamed in another domain, and until the infrastructure master has updated DNs, you might look at the membership of a group using the Active Directory Users and Computers snap-in, for example, and the group might appear not to include that member. However, the member continues to belong to the group. The member's *memberOf* attribute still refers to the group, so the *memberOf* attribute and the *tokenGroups* constructed attribute are unchanged. There is no compromise to security; it is only an administrator looking at that particular group membership that would notice the temporary inconsistency.

PDC Emulator Role

The PDC Emulator role performs multiple, crucial functions for a domain:

- **Emulates a Primary Domain Controller (PDC) for backward compatibility** In the days of Windows NT 4.0 domains, only the PDC could make changes to the directory. Previous tools, utilities, and clients written to support Windows NT 4.0 are unaware that all Active Directory domain controllers can write to the directory, so such tools request a connection to the PDC. The domain controller with the PDC Emulator role registers itself as a PDC so that down-level applications can locate a writable domain controller. Such applications are less common now that Active Directory is nearly 10 years old, and if your enterprise includes such applications, work to upgrade them for full Active Directory compatibility.

- **Participates in special password update handling for the domain** When a user's password is reset or changed, the domain controller that makes the change replicates the change immediately to the PDC emulator. This special replication ensures that the domain controllers know about the new password as quickly as possible. If a user attempts to log on immediately after changing passwords, the domain controller responding to the user's logon request might not know about the new password. Before it rejects the logon attempt, that domain controller forwards the authentication request to a PDC emulator, which verifies that the new password is correct and instructs the domain controller to accept the logon request. This function means that any time a user enters an incorrect password, the authentication is forwarded to the PDC emulator for a second opinion. The PDC emulator, therefore, should be highly accessible to all clients in the domain. It should be a well-connected, high-performance DC.

- **Manages Group Policy updates within a domain** If a Group Policy object (GPO) is modified on two DCs at approximately the same time, there could be conflicts between the two versions that could not be reconciled as the GPO replicates. To avoid this situation, the PDC emulator acts as the focal point for all Group Policy changes. When you open a GPO in Group Policy Management Editor (GPME), the GPME binds to the domain controller performing the PDC emulator role. Therefore, all changes to GPOs are made on the PDC emulator by default.

- **Provides a master time source for the domain** Active Directory, Kerberos, File Replication Service (FRS), and DFS-R each rely on timestamps, so synchronizing the time across all systems in a domain is crucial. The PDC emulator in the forest root domain is the time master for the entire forest, by default. The PDC emulator in each domain synchronizes its time with the forest root PDC emulator. Other domain controllers in the domain synchronize their clocks against that domain's PDC emulator. All other domain members synchronize their time with their preferred domain controller. This hierarchical structure of time synchronization, all implemented through the Win32Time service, ensures consistency of time. Universal Time Coordinate (UTC) is synchronized, and the time displayed to users is adjusted based on the time zone setting of the computer.

MORE INFO   **Change the time service only one way**

It is highly recommended to allow Windows to maintain its native, default time synchronization mechanisms. The only change you should make is to configure the PDC emulator of the forest root domain to synchronize with an extra time source. If you do not specify a time source for the PDC emulator, the System event log will contain errors reminding you to do so. See *http://go.microsoft.com/fwlink/?LinkId=91969*, and the articles it refers to, for more information.

■ **Acts as the domain master browser**   When you open Network in Windows, you see a list of workgroups and domains, and when you open a workgroup or domain, you see a list of computers. These two lists, called *browse lists*, are created by the Browser service. In each network segment, a master browser creates the browse list: the lists of workgroups, domains, and servers in that segment. The domain master browser serves to merge the lists of each master browser so that browse clients can retrieve a comprehensive browse list.

Placing Operations Masters

When you create the forest root domain with its first domain controller, all five operations master roles are performed by the domain controller. As you add domain controllers to the domain, you can transfer the operations master role assignments to other domain controllers to balance the load among domain controllers or to optimize placement of a single master operation. The best practices for the placement of operations master roles are as follows:

■ **Co-locate the schema master and domain naming master**   The schema master and domain naming master roles should be placed on a single domain controller that is a GC server. These roles are rarely used, and the domain controller hosting them should be tightly secured. The domain naming master must be hosted on a GC server because when a new domain is added, the master must ensure that there is no object of any type with the same name as the new domain. The GC's partial replica contains the name of every object in the forest. The load of these operations master roles is very light unless schema modifications are being made.

■ **Co-locate the RID master and PDC Emulator roles**   Place the RID and PDC Emulator roles on a single domain controller. If the load mandates that the roles be placed on two separate domain controllers, those two systems should be physically well connected and have explicit connection objects created in Active Directory so that they are direct replication partners. They should also be direct replication partners with domain controllers that you have selected as standby operations masters.

■ **Place the infrastructure master on a DC that is not a GC**   The infrastructure master should be placed on a domain controller that is not a GC server but is physically well connected to a GC server. The infrastructure master should have explicit connection objects in Active Directory to that GC server so that they are direct replication partners.

The infrastructure master can be placed on the same domain controller that acts as the RID master and PDC emulator.

NOTE It doesn't matter if they're all GCs

If all DCs in a domain are GC servers—which indeed is a best practices recommendation that will be discussed in Chapter 11, "Sites and Replication"—you do not need to worry about which DC is the infrastructure master. When all DCs are GCs, all DCs have up-to-date information about every object in the forest, which eliminates the need for the infrastructure master role.

- **Have a failover plan** In following sections, you will learn to transfer single operations master roles between domain controllers, which is necessary if there is lengthy planned or unplanned downtime of an operations master. Determine, in advance, a plan for transferring operations roles to other DCs in the event that one operations master is offline.

Identifying Operations Masters

To implement your role placement plan, you must know which DCs are currently performing single master operations roles. Each role is exposed in an Active Directory administrative tool as well as in other user interface and command-line tools. To identify the current master for each role, use the following tools:

- **PDC Emulator: The Active Directory Users And Computers snap-in** Right-click the domain and choose Operations Masters. Click the PDC tab. An example is shown in Figure 10-2, which indicates that SERVER01.contoso.com is currently the PDC operations master.

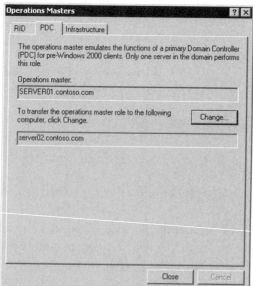

Figure 10-2 PDC Operations Master

- **RID Master: The Active Directory Users And Computers snap-in**   Right-click the domain and choose Operations Masters. Click the RID tab.
- **Infrastructure Master: The Active Directory Users And Computers snap-in**   Right-click the domain and choose Operations Masters. Click the Infrastructure tab.
- **Domain Naming: The Active Directory Domains And Trusts snap-in**   Right-click the root node of the snap-in (Active Directory Domains And Trusts) and choose Operations Master.
- **Schema Master: The Active Directory Schema snap-in**   Right-click the root node of the snap-in (Active Directory Schema) and choose Operations Master.

NOTE   **Registering the Active Directory Schema snap-in**

You must register the Active Directory Schema snap-in before you can create a custom Microsoft Management Console (MMC) with the snap-in. At a command prompt, type **regsvr32 schmmgmt.dll**.

You can also use several other tools to identify operations masters, including the following commands:

```
ntdsutil
roles
connections
connect to server DomainControllerFQDN:portnumber
quit
select operation target
list roles for connected server"
quit
quit
quit

dcdiag /test:knowsofroleholders /v

netdom query fsmo
```

Practice It   Exercise 1, "Identify Operations Masters," in the practice at the end of this lesson, steps you through the identification of operations masters.

Transferring Operations Master Roles

You can transfer a single operations master role easily. You will transfer roles in the following scenarios:

- When you establish your forest, all five roles are performed by the first domain controller you install. When you add a domain to the forest, all three domain roles are performed by the first domain controller in that domain. As you add domain controllers, you can distribute the roles to reduce single-point-of-failure instances and improve performance.

- If you plan to take a domain controller offline that is currently holding an operations master role, transfer that role to another domain controller prior to taking it offline.

- If you are decommissioning a domain controller that currently holds an operations master role, transfer that role to another domain controller prior to decommissioning. The Active Directory Domain Services Installation Wizard will attempt to do so automatically, but you should prepare for demoting a domain controller by transferring its roles.

To transfer an operations master role, follow these steps:

1. Open the administrative tool that exposes the current master.

   For example, open the Active Directory Users And Computers snap-in to transfer any of the three domain master roles.

2. Connect to the domain controller to which you are transferring the role.

   This is accomplished by right-clicking the root node of the snap-in and choosing Change Domain Controller or Change Active Directory Domain Controller. (The command differs between snap-ins.)

3. Open the Operations Master dialog box, which will show you the domain controller currently holding the role token for the operation. Click the Change button to transfer the role to the domain controller to which you are connected.

Practice It   Exercise 2, "Transfer an Operations Master Role," in the practice at the end of this lesson, steps you through the transfer of an operations master role.

When you transfer an operations master role, both the current master and the new master are online. The token is transferred, the new master immediately begins to perform the role, and the former master immediately ceases to perform the role. This is the preferred method of moving operations master roles.

It is recommended to make sure that the new role holder is up to date with replication from the former role holder before transferring the role. You can use skills introduced in Chapter 11 to force replication between the two systems.

Recognizing Operations Master Failures

Several operations master roles can be unavailable for quite some time before their absence becomes a problem. Other master roles play a crucial role in the day-to-day operation of your enterprise. You can identify problems with operations masters by examining the Directory Service event log.

However, you will often discover that an operations master has failed when you attempt to perform a function managed by the master, and the function fails. For example, if the RID master fails, eventually you will be prevented from creating new security principals.

Seizing Operations Master Roles

If a domain controller performing a single master operation fails, and you cannot bring the system back to service, you have the option of seizing the operations token. When you seize a role, you designate a new master without gracefully removing the role from the failed master.

Seizing a role is a drastic action, so before seizing a role, think carefully about whether it is necessary. Determine the cause and expected duration of the offline operations master. If the operations master can be brought online in sufficient time, wait. What is sufficient time? It depends on the impact of the role that has failed:

- **PDC emulator failure**   The PDC emulator is the operations master that will have the most immediate impact on normal operations and on users if it becomes unavailable. Fortunately, the PDC Emulator role can be seized to another domain controller and then transferred back to the original role holder when the system comes back online.

- **Infrastructure master failure**   A failure of the infrastructure master will be noticeable to administrators but not to users. Because the master is responsible for updating the names of group members from other domains, it can appear as if group membership is incorrect although, as mentioned earlier in this lesson, membership is not actually affected. You can seize the infrastructure master role to another domain controller and then transfer it back to the previous role holder when that system comes online.

- **RID master failure**   A failed RID master will eventually prevent domain controllers from creating new SIDs and, therefore, will prevent you from creating new accounts for users, groups, or computers. However, domain controllers receive a sizable pool of RIDs from the RID master, so unless you are generating numerous new accounts, you can often go for some time without the RID master online while it is being repaired. Seizing this role to another domain controller is a significant action. After the RID master role has been seized, the domain controller that had been performing the role cannot be brought back online.

- **Schema master failure**   The schema master role is necessary only when schema modifications are being made, either directly by an administrator or by installing an Active Directory integrated application that changes the schema. At other times, the role is not necessary. It can remain offline indefinitely until schema changes are necessary. Seizing this role to another domain controller is a significant action. After the schema master role has been seized, the domain controller that had been performing the role cannot be brought back online.

- **Domain naming master failure**   The domain naming master role is necessary only when you add a domain to the forest or remove a domain from a forest. Until such changes are required to your domain infrastructure, the domain naming master role can remain offline for an indefinite period of time. Seizing this role to another domain controller is a significant action. After the domain naming master role has been seized, the domain controller that had been performing the role cannot be brought back online.

Although you can transfer roles by using the administrative tools, you must use *Ntdsutil.exe* to seize a role. To seize an operations master role, perform the following steps:

1. From the command prompt, type **ntdsutil** and press Enter.
2. At the ntdsutil prompt, type **roles** and press Enter.

   The next steps establish a connection to the domain controller you want to perform the single master operation role.
3. At the fsmo maintenance prompt, type **connections** and press Enter.
4. At the server connections prompt, type **connect to server** *DomainControllerFQDN* and press Enter.

   DomainControllerFQDN is the FQDN of the domain controller you want to perform the role.

   Ntdsutil responds that it has connected to the server.
5. At the server connections prompt, type **quit** and press Enter.
6. At the fsmo maintenance prompt, type **seize** *role* and press Enter.

   Role is one of the following:

   a. schema master
   b. domain naming master
   c. RID master
   d. PDC
   e. infrastructure master
7. At the fsmo maintenance prompt, type **quit** and press Enter.
8. At the ntdsutil prompt, type **quit** and press Enter.

Returning a Role to Its Original Holder

To provide for planned downtime of a domain controller if a role has been transferred, not seized, the role can be transferred back to the original domain controller.

If, however, a role has been seized and the former master is able to be brought back online, you must be very careful. The PDC emulator and infrastructure master are the only operations master roles that can be transferred back to the original master after having been seized.

NOTE   Do not return a seized schema, domain naming, or RID master to service

After seizing the schema, domain naming, or RID roles, you must completely decommission the original domain controller.

If you have seized the schema, domain naming, or RID roles to another domain controller, you must not bring the original domain controller back online without first completely decommissioning it. That means you must keep the original role holder physically discon-nected from the network, and you must remove AD DS by using the *Dcpromo /forceremoval* command. You must also clean the metadata for that domain controller as described in *http://go.microsoft.com/fwlink/?LinkId=80481*.

After the domain controller has been completely removed from Active Directory, if you want the server to rejoin the domain, you can connect it to the network and join the domain. If you want it to be a domain controller, you can promote it. If you want it to resume performing the operations master role, you can transfer the role back to the DC.

NOTE   Better to rebuild

Because of the critical nature of domain controllers, it is recommended that you completely reinstall the former domain controller in this scenario.

Quick Check

- You need to upgrade the power supply and motherboard of SERVER01, the domain controller performing the PDC Emulator operations master role. You want to ensure continuity of services provided by the PDC emulator. Describe the pro-cess of transferring the role to SERVER02, another domain controller, and trans-ferring it back after SERVER01 has been upgraded. Which tools will you use, and which steps will you perform?

Quick Check Answer

- Prior to performing the upgrade, make sure the standby operations master is up to date with replication from the PDC emulator. Then open the Active Directory Users And Computers snap-in, right-click the domain, and choose Change Domain Controller. Select SERVER02. Right-click the domain and choose Opera-tions Masters. Click the PDC tab and click Change. The role is transferred. When SERVER01 comes back online, right-click the domain, choose Change Domain Controller, and select SERVER01. Right-click the domain, choose Operations Mas-ters, click the PDC tab, and click Change.

PRACTICE **Transferring Operations Master Roles**

In this practice, you will identify the operations masters in the *contoso.com* domain, and you will transfer an operations master to another domain controller to take the current master offline for maintenance. To perform Exercise 2 in this practice, you must have completed "Practice: Installing Domain Controllers" in Lesson 1 so that you have a second domain con-troller, SERVER02, in the domain.

▶ **Exercise 1   Identify Operations Masters**

In this exercise, you will use both user interface and command-line tools to identify operations masters in the *contoso.com* domain.

1. Log on to SERVER01 as Administrator.
2. Open the Active Directory Users And Computers snap-in.
3. Right-click the *contoso.com* domain and choose Operations Masters.
4. Click the tab for each operations master.

   The tabs identify the domain controllers currently performing the single master operations roles for the domain: PDC emulator, RID master, and Infrastructure master.
5. Click Close.
6. Open the Active Directory Domains And Trusts snap-in.
7. Right-click the root node of the snap-in, Active Directory Domains And Trusts, and choose Operations Master.

   The dialog box identifies the domain controller performing the domain naming master role.
8. Click Close.

   The Active Directory Schema snap-in does not have a console of its own and cannot be added to a custom console until you have registered the snap-in.
9. Open a command prompt, type **regsvr32 schmmgmt.dll**, and press Enter.
10. Click OK to close the message box that appears.
11. Click Start and, in the Start Search box, type **mmc.exe**, and press Enter.
12. Choose Add/Remove Snap-In from the File menu.
13. From the Available snap-ins list, choose Active Directory Schema, click Add, and then click OK.
14. Right-click the root node of the snap-in, Active Directory Schema, and choose Operations Master.

    The dialog box that appears identifies the domain controller currently performing the schema master role.
15. Click Close.
16. Open a command prompt, type the command **netdom query fsmo**, and press Enter.

    All operations masters are listed.

▶ **Exercise 2   Transfer an Operations Master Role**

In this exercise, you will prepare to take the operations master offline by transferring its role to another domain controller. You will then simulate taking it offline, bringing it back online, and returning the operations master role.

1. Open the Active Directory Users And Computers snap-in.

2. Right-click the *contoso.com* domain and choose Change Domain Controller.

3. In the list of directory servers, select server02.contoso.com and click OK.

   Before transferring an operations master, you must connect to the domain controller to which the role will be transferred.

   The root node of the snap-in indicates the domain controller to which you are connected: Active Directory Users And Computers [server02.contoso.com].

4. Right-click the *contoso.com* domain and choose Operations Masters.

5. Click the PDC tab.

   The tab indicates that SERVER01.contoso.com currently holds the role token. SERVER02.contoso.com is listed in the second dialog box. It should appear similar to Figure 10-2.

6. Click the Change button.

   An Active Directory Domain Services dialog box prompts you to confirm the transfer of the operations master role.

7. Click Yes.

   An Active Directory Domain Services dialog box confirms the role was successfully transferred.

8. Click OK, and then click Close.

9. Simulate taking SERVER01 offline for maintenance by shutting down the server.

10. Simulate bringing the server back online by starting the server.

    Remember you cannot bring a domain controller back online if the RID, schema, or domain naming roles have been seized. But you can bring it back online if a role was transferred.

11. Repeat steps 1–8, this time connecting to SERVER01 and transferring the operations master role back to SERVER01.

Lesson Summary

- Operations master roles are assigned to domain controllers to perform single master operations.
- There are five operations master roles. Two are unique to the entire forest: schema and domain naming. Three are unique to each domain: PDC Emulator, RID, and infrastructure.
- The infrastructure master must be placed on a domain controller that is not a GC unless all DCs in the domain are GC servers.
- You can transfer a role by using Windows tools or *Ntdsutil.exe*. Transferring a role is the preferred method for managing operations masters.
- You can seize a role, using *Ntdsutil.exe*. This should be done only when the former role holder cannot be brought back online in sufficient time. Only the PDC Emulator and

infrastructure roles can be transferred back to the original holder when it comes back online. DCs that held schema, RID, or domain naming roles must be completely decommissioned if those roles are seized.

Lesson Review

You can use the following questions to test your knowledge of the information in Lesson 2, "Configuring Operations Masters." The questions are also available on the companion CD if you prefer to review them in electronic form.

NOTE   Answers

Answers to these questions and explanations of why each answer choice is right or wrong are located in the "Answers" section at the end of the book.

---

1. You are an administrator at Contoso, Ltd. The *contoso.com* domain consists of two sites. At the headquarters, one domain controller, named SERVER01, is a GC server and performs all five operations master roles. The second domain controller at the headquarters is named SERVER02. SERVER02 is not a GC and performs no operations master roles. At the branch office, the domain controller is named SERVER03, and it is a GC server. Which change to the operations master role placement must you make?

    A.   Transfer the infrastructure master to SERVER03.

    B.   Transfer the RID master to SERVER02.

    C.   Transfer the schema master to SERVER02.

    D.   Transfer the domain naming master to SERVER03.

    E.   Transfer the infrastructure master to SERVER02.

2. You are an administrator at Contoso, Ltd. The forest consists of two domains, *contoso.com* and *windows.contoso.com*. Currently, SERVER02.windows.contoso.com performs all five operations master roles. You are going to decommission the *windows.contoso.com* domain and move all accounts into *contoso.com*. You want to transfer all operations masters to SERVER01.contoso.com. Which operations masters do you transfer? (Choose all that apply.)

    A.   Infrastructure master

    B.   PDC emulator

    C.   RID master

    D.   Schema master

    E.   Domain naming master

3. You are an administrator at Contoso, Ltd. The *contoso.com* domain has five domain controllers. You want to move all domain operations masters to SERVER02.contoso.com. Which masters do you move? (Choose all that apply.)

    A. Infrastructure master

    B. PDC emulator

    C. RID master

    D. Schema master

    E. Domain naming master

Lesson 3: Configuring DFS Replication of SYSVOL

SYSVOL, a folder located at %SystemRoot%\SYSVOL by default, contains logon scripts, group policy templates (GPTs), and other resources critical to the health and management of an Active Directory domain. Ideally, SYSVOL should be consistent on each domain controller. However, changes to Group Policy objects and to logon scripts are made from time to time, so you must ensure that those changes are replicated effectively and efficiently to all domain controllers. In previous versions of Windows, the FRS was used to replicate the contents of SYSVOL between domain controllers. FRS has limitations in both capacity and performance that cause it to break occasionally. Unfortunately, troubleshooting and configuring FRS is quite difficult. In Windows Server 2008 domains, you have the option to use DFS-R to replicate the contents of SYSVOL. In this lesson, you will learn how to migrate SYSVOL from FRS to DFS-R.

After this lesson, you will be able to:
- Raise the domain functional level.
- Migrate SYSVOL replication from FRS to DFS-R.

Estimated lesson time: 60 minutes

Raising the Domain Functional Level

In Chapter 12, "Domains and Forests," you will learn about forest and domain functional levels. A domain's functional level is a setting that both restricts the operating systems that are supported as domain controllers in a domain and enables additional functionality in Active Directory. A domain with a Windows Server 2008 domain controller can be at one of three functional levels: Windows 2000 Native, Windows Server 2003 Native, and Windows Server 2008. At Windows 2000 Native domain functional level, domain controllers can be running Windows 2000 Server or Windows Server 2003. At Windows Server 2003 Native domain functional level, domain controllers can be running Windows Server 2003. At Windows Server 2008 domain functional level, all domain controllers must be running Windows Server 2008.

As you raise functional levels, new capabilities of Active Directory are enabled. At Windows Server 2008 domain functional level, for example, you can use DFS-R to replicate SYSVOL. Simply upgrading all domain controllers to Windows Server 2008 is not enough: You must specifically raise the domain functional level. You do this by using Active Directory Domains and Trusts. Right-click the domain and choose Raise Domain Functional Level. Then select Windows Server 2008 as the desired functional level and click Raise. After you've set the domain functional level to Windows Server 2008, you cannot add domain controllers running Windows Server 2003 or Windows 2000 Server. The functional level is associated only with domain controller operating systems; member servers and workstations can be running Windows Server 2003, Windows 2000 Server, Windows Vista, Windows XP, or Windows 2000 Workstation.

Quick Check

■ You are the administrator of Northwind Traders. The domain consists of three domain controllers. You have upgraded two of them to Windows Server 2008. The third is still running Windows Server 2003. You want to establish DFS-R as the replication mechanism for SYSVOL. What must you do?

Quick Check Answer

■ You must upgrade the third domain controller to Windows Server 2008 and then raise the domain functional level to Windows Server 2008.

Understanding Migration Stages

Because SYSVOL is critical to the health and functionality of your domain, Windows does not provide a mechanism with which to convert replication of SYSVOL from FRS to DFS-R instantly. In fact, migration to DFS-R involves creating a parallel SYSVOL structure. When the parallel structure is successfully in place, clients are redirected to the new structure as the domain's system volume. When the operation has proven successful, you can eliminate FRS.

Migration to DFS-R thus consists of four stages or *states*:

■ **0 (start)**   The default state of a domain controller. Only FRS is used to replicate SYSVOL.

■ **1 (prepared)**   A copy of SYSVOL is created in a folder called SYSVOL_DFSR and is added to a replication set. DFS-R begins to replicate the contents of the SYSVOL_DFSR folders on all domain controllers. However, FRS continues to replicate the original SYSVOL folders and clients continue to use SYSVOL.

■ **2 (redirected)**   The SYSVOL share, which originally refers to SYSVOL\sysvol, is changed to refer to SYSVOL_DFSR\sysvol. Clients now use the SYSVOL_DFSR folder to obtain logon scripts and Group Policy templates.

■ **3 (eliminated)**   Replication of the old SYSVOL folder by FRS is stopped. The original SYSVOL folder is not deleted, however, so if you want to remove it entirely, you must do so manually.

You move your domain controllers through these stages, using the *Dfsrmig.exe* command. You will use three options with *Dfsrmig.exe*:

■ **setglobalstate** *state*   The setglobalstate option configures the current global DFSR migration state, which applies to all domain controllers. The state is specified by the *state* parameter, which is 0–3. Each domain controller will be notified of the new DFSR migration state and will migrate to that state automatically.

- **getglobalstate**   The getglobalstate option reports the current global DFSR migration state.

- **getmigrationstate**   The getmigrationstate option reports the current migration state of each domain controller. Because it might take time for domain controllers to be notified of the new global DFSR migration state, and because it might take even more time for a DC to make the changes required by that state, DCs will not be synchronized with the global state instantly. The getmigrationstate option enables you to monitor the progress of DCs toward the current global DFSR migration state.

If there is a problem moving from one state to the next higher state, you can revert to previous states by using the setglobalstate option. However, after you have used the setglobalstate option to specify state 3 (eliminated), you cannot revert to earlier states.

Migrating SYSVOL Replication to DFS-R

To migrate SYSVOL replication from FRS to DFS-R, perform the following steps:

1. Open the Active Directory Domains And Trusts snap-in.
2. Right-click the domain and choose Raise Domain Functional Level.
3. If the Current Domain Functional Level box does not indicate Windows Server 2008, choose Windows Server 2008 from the Select An Available Domain Functional Level list.
4. Click Raise. Click OK twice in response to the dialog boxes that appear.
5. Log on to a domain controller and open a command prompt.
6. Type **dfsrmig /setglobalstate 1**.
7. Type **dfsrmig /getmigrationstate** to query the progress of DCs toward the Prepared global state. Repeat this step until the state has been attained by all DCs.

    This can take 15 minutes to an hour or longer.
8. Type **dfsrmig /setglobalstate 2**.
9. Type **dfsrmig /getmigrationstate** to query the progress of DCs toward the Redirected global state. Repeat this step until the state has been attained by all DCs.

    This can take 15 minutes to an hour or longer.
10. Type **dfsrmig /setglobalstate 3**.

    After you begin migration from state 2 (prepared) to state 3 (replicated), any changes made to the SYSVOL folder will have to be replicated manually to the SYSVOL_DFSR folder.
11. Type **dfsrmig /getmigrationstate** to query the progress of DCs toward the Eliminated global state. Repeat this step until the state has been attained by all DCs. This can take 15 minutes to an hour or longer.

    For more information about the *Dfsrmig.exe* command, type **dfsrmig.exe /?**.

PRACTICE Configuring DFS Replication of SYSVOL

In this practice, you will experience SYSVOL replication and migrate the replication mechanism from FRS to DFS-R. You will then verify that SYSVOL is being replicated by DFS-R.

Other practices in the training kit have required Windows Server 2008 forest functional level. To perform the exercises in this practice, you will need a domain running at Windows Server 2003 domain functional level, so you must create a new forest running at Windows Server 2003 forest functional level consisting of one domain at Windows Server 2003 domain functional level and two domain controllers. To prepare for this practice, perform the following tasks:

- Install a server running Windows Server 2008 full installation. The server must be named SERVER01. Its configuration should be as follows:
    - ❏ Computer Name: SERVER01
    - ❏ Workgroup membership: WORKGROUP
    - ❏ IPv4 address: 10.0.0.11
    - ❏ Subnet Mask: 255.255.255.0
    - ❏ Default Gateway: 10.0.0.1
    - ❏ DNS Server: 10.0.0.11

    Use the procedures described in Lesson 1, "Installing Active Directory Domain Services," of Chapter 1 if you need assistance installing Windows Server 2008.

- Promote SERVER01 as a domain controller in a new forest named *contoso.com*. Select Windows Server 2003 forest and domain functional levels. Allow the Active Directory Domain Services Installation Wizard to install DNS on the domain controller.

    Use the steps in Exercise 1, "Install Windows Server 2008," of Lesson 1 of Chapter 1 if you need assistance promoting the domain controller. Be certain, however, to select Windows Server 2003 forest and domain functional levels.

- Install a second server running Windows Server 2008 full installation. The server must be named SERVER02. Its configuration should be as follows:
    - ❏ Computer Name: SERVER02
    - ❏ Workgroup membership: WORKGROUP
    - ❏ IPv4 address: 10.0.0.12
    - ❏ Subnet Mask: 255.255.255.0
    - ❏ Default Gateway: 10.0.0.1
    - ❏ DNS Server: 10.0.0.11

    Use the procedures described in Lesson 1 of Chapter 1 if you need assistance installing Windows Server 2008.

■ Promote SERVER02 as an additional domain controller in the *contoso.com* domain. Do not make it a GC or DNS server.

Use the steps in Exercise 1 of Lesson 1 of this chapter if you need assistance promoting SERVER02.

▶ **Exercise 1   Experience SYSVOL Replication**

In this exercise, you will experience SYSVOL replication by adding a logon script to the NET-LOGON share and observing its replication to another domain controller.

1. Log on to SERVER01 as Administrator.
2. Open %SystemRoot%\Sysvol\Domain\Scripts.
3. Create a new text file called **Sample Logon Script**.
4. Log on to SERVER02 as Administrator.
5. Open %SystemRoot%\Sysvol\Domain\Scripts.
6. Confirm that the text file has replicated to the SERVER02 Scripts folder.

▶ **Exercise 2   Prepare to Migrate to DFS-R**

Before you can migrate replication of SYSVOL to DFS-R, the domain must contain only Windows Server 2008 domain controllers, and the domain functional level must be raised to Windows Server 2008. In this exercise, you will confirm the fact that DFS-R migration is not supported in other domain functional levels. You will also install the DFS administrative tools.

1. On SERVER01, open the Active Directory Domains And Trusts snap-in.
2. Right-click the *contoso.com* domain and choose Raise Domain Functional Level.
3. Confirm that the Current Domain Functional Level is Windows Server 2003.
4. Cancel out of the dialog box without raising the functional level.
5. Open a command prompt.
6. Type **dfsrmig /getglobalstate** and press Enter.

   A message appears informing you that *Dfsrmig* is supported only on domains at the Windows Server 2008 functional level.
7. Open the Active Directory Domains And Trusts snap-in.
8. Right-click the *contoso.com* domain and choose Raise Domain Functional Level.
9. Confirm that the Select An Available Domain Functional Level list indicates Windows Server 2008.
10. Click Raise. Click OK to confirm your change.

    A message appears informing you that the functional level was raised successfully.
11. Click OK.
12. At the command prompt, type **dfsrmig /getglobalstate** and press Enter.

    A message appears informing you that DFSR migration has not yet initialized.

▶ Exercise 3   Migrate Replication of SYSVOL to DFS-R

In this exercise, you will migrate SYSVOL replication from FRS to DFS-R.

1. On SERVER01, open a command prompt.

2. Type **dfsrmig /setglobalstate 0** and press Enter.

   The following message appears:

   ```
   Current DFSR global state: 'Start'
   New DFSR global state: 'Start'
   Invalid state change requested.
   ```

   The default global state is already 0, 'Start,' so your command is not valid. However, this does serve to initialize DFSR migration.

3. Type **dfsrmig /getglobalstate** and press Enter.

   The following message appears:

   ```
   Current DFSR global state: 'Start'
   Succeeded.
   ```

4. Type **dfsrmig /getmigrationstate** and press Enter.

   The following message appears:

   ```
   All Domain Controllers have migrated successfully to Global state
   ('Start').
   Migration has reached a consistent state on all Domain Controllers.
   Succeeded.
   ```

5. Type **dfsrmig /setglobalstate 1** and press Enter.

   The following message appears:

   ```
   Current DFSR global state: 'Start'
   New DFSR global state: 'Prepared'

   Migration will proceed to 'Prepared' state. DFSR service will
   copy the contents of SYSVOL to SYSVOL_DFSR
   folder.

   If any DC is unable to start migration then try manual polling.
   OR Run with option /CreateGlobalObjects.
   Migration can start anytime between 15 min to 1 hour.
   Succeeded.
   ```

6. Type **dfsrmig /getmigrationstate** and press Enter.

   A message appears that reflects the migration state of each domain controller. Migration can take up to 15 minutes. Repeat this step until you receive the following message that indicates migration has progressed to the 'Prepared' state and is successful:

   ```
   All Domain Controllers have migrated successfully to Global state
   ('Prepared').
   Migration has reached a consistent state on all Domain Controllers.
   Succeeded.
   ```

When you receive the message just shown, continue to step 7.

During migration to the 'Prepared' state, you might see one of these messages:

```
The following Domain Controllers are not in sync with Global state
('Prepared'):


Domain Controller (Local Migration State) - DC Type
===================================================

SERVER01 ('Start') - Primary DC
SERVER02 ('Start') - Writable DC

Migration has not yet reached a consistent state on all Domain Controllers.
State information might be stale due to AD latency.
```

or

```
The following Domain Controllers are not in sync with Global state
('Prepared'):


Domain Controller (Local Migration State) - DC Type
===================================================

SERVER01 ('Start') - Primary DC
SERVER02 ('Waiting For Initial Sync') - Writable DC

Migration has not yet reached a consistent state on all Domain Controllers.
State information might be stale due to AD latency.
```

or

```
The following Domain Controllers are not in sync with Global state
('Prepared'):


Domain Controller (Local Migration State) - DC Type
===================================================

SERVER02 ('Waiting For Initial Sync') - Writable DC

Migration has not yet reached a consistent state on all Domain Controllers.
State information might be stale due to AD latency.
```

7. Open the Event Viewer console from the Administrative Tools program group.

8. Expand Applications And Services Logs and select DFS Replication.

9. Locate the event with event ID 8014 and open its properties.

   You should see the details shown in Figure 10-3.

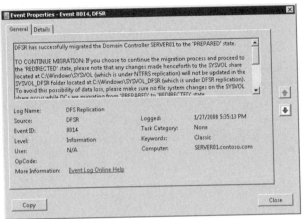

Figure 10-3 DFS-R event indicating successful migration to the 'Prepared' state

Type **dfsrmig /setglobalstate 2** and press Enter.

The following message appears:

```
Current DFSR global state: 'Prepared'
New DFSR global state: 'Redirected'

Migration will proceed to 'Redirected' state. The SYSVOL share will be
changed to SYSVOL_DFSR folder.

If any changes have been made to the SYSVOL share during the state
transition from 'Prepared' to 'Redirected', please robocopy the changes
from SYSVOL to SYSVOL_DFSR on any replicated RWDC.
Succeeded.
```

10. Type **dfsrmig /getmigrationstate** and press Enter.

A message appears that reflects the migration state of each domain controller. Migration can take up to 15 minutes. Repeat this step until you receive the following message that indicates migration has progressed to the 'Prepared' state and is successful:

```
All Domain Controllers have migrated successfully to Global state
('Redirected').
Migration has reached a consistent state on all Domain Controllers.
Succeeded.
```

When you receive the message just shown, continue to step 12.

During migration, you might receive messages like the following:

```
The following Domain Controllers are not in sync with Global state
('Redirected'):

Domain Controller (Local Migration State) - DC Type
========================================================

SERVER02 ('Prepared') - Writable DC

Migration has not yet reached a consistent state on all Domain Controllers.
State information might be stale due to AD latency.
```

11. Type **net share** and press Enter.
12. Confirm that the NETLOGON share refers to the %SystemRoot%\SYSVOL_DFSR\Sysvol\contoso.com\Scripts folder.
13. Confirm that the SYSVOL share refers to the %SystemRoot%\SYSVOL_DFSR\Sysvol folder.
14. In Windows Explorer, open the %SystemRoot%\SYSVOL_DFSR\Sysvol\contoso.com\Scripts folder.
15. Confirm that the Sample Logon Script file was migrated to the new Scripts folder.
16. Create a new text file named **Sample Logon Script DFSR**.
17. On SERVER02, confirm that the file replicated to the %SystemRoot%\SYSVOL_DFSR\Sysvol\contoso.com\Scripts folder.

Lesson Summary

- You cannot use DFS-R to replicate SYSVOL until the domain is at Windows Server 2008 functional level.
- The *Dfsrmig.exe* command manages the migration from the FRS-replicated SYSVOL folder to the DFS-R replicated SYSVOL_DFSR folder.
- There are four migration states: Start, Prepared, Redirected, and Eliminated. You can revert to previous states until you have configured the state as Eliminated.

Lesson Review

You can use the following questions to test your knowledge of the information in Lesson 3, "Configuring DFS Replication of SYSVOL." The questions are also available on the companion CD if you prefer to review them in electronic form.

NOTE Answers

Answers to these questions and explanations of why each answer choice is right or wrong are located in the "Answers" section at the end of the book.

1. You are an administrator at Trey Research. Your domain consists of three domain controllers, two running Windows Server 2008 and one running Windows Server 2003. The forest root domain has two domain controllers, both running Windows Server 2003. You want to replicate SYSVOL in your domain, using DFS-R. What steps must you take? (Choose all that apply. Each correct answer is part of the solution.)

    A. Upgrade the forest root domain controllers to Windows Server 2008.

    B. Configure the forest functional level to Windows Server 2008.

    C. Upgrade your Windows Server 2003 domain controller to Windows Server 2008.

    D. Configure the domain functional level of your domain to Windows Server 2008.

    E. Configure the domain functional level of the forest root domain to Windows Server 2008.

2. You want to configure Active Directory so that replication of logon scripts is managed using DFS-R. Which command do you use?

    A. *Dfsrmig.exe*

    B. *Repadmin.exe*

    C. *Dfsutil.exe*

    D. *Dfscmd.exe*

Chapter Review

To further practice and reinforce the skills you learned in this chapter, you can perform the following tasks:

- Review the chapter summary.
- Review the key term introduced in this chapter.
- Complete the case scenario. This scenario sets up a real-world situation involving the topics of this chapter and asks you to create a solution.
- Complete the suggested practices.
- Take a practice test.

Chapter Summary

- Domain controllers in an Active Directory domain replicate changes in a multimaster fashion; however, certain roles are performed by a single domain controller.
- When you add new domain controllers to a domain, you can transfer operations master roles to decrease single-point-of-failure instances, to increase performance, or to accommodate planned downtime.
- Before you add the first Windows Server 2008 domain controller to a forest, you must run *Adprep /forestprep* and *Adprep /domainprep /gpprep*.
- After all domain controllers are running Windows Server 2008, you can raise the domain functional level to Windows Server 2008, which enables you to begin migrating replication of SYSVOL to the more robust DFS-R technology.

Key Terms

Use this key term to understand better the concepts covered in this chapter.

- **operations master** A domain controller that performs a single-master operation. There are five single-master operations: schema, domain naming, infrastructure, RID, and PDC emulator.

Case Scenario

In the following case scenario, you will apply what you've learned about installing domain controllers and configuring operations masters. You can find answers to these questions in the "Answers" section at the end of this book.

Case Scenario: Upgrading a Domain

You are a consultant who has been hired by Contoso, Ltd., to provide guidance during the upgrade of the *contoso.com* forest to Windows Server 2008 domain controllers. The forest consists of two domains, *contoso.com* and *subsidiary.contoso.com*. Both domains contain three domain controllers running Windows Server 2003.

1. What must you do before installing any Windows Server 2008 domain controllers in the *contoso.com* forest?

2. The *subsidiary.contoso.com* domain consists of three small branch offices, each with a domain controller. The management of Contoso wants all three branch office DCs to be read-only. Is this possible and, if so, how?

3. You are planning to upgrade SERVER01 in the forest root domain, which performs all forest and domain single master operations. What should you do prior to upgrading the server?

Suggested Practices

To help you successfully master the exam objectives presented in this chapter, complete the following tasks.

Upgrade a Windows Server 2003 Domain

In this practice, you will upgrade a Windows Server 2003 domain to Windows Server 2008. To perform these practices, you must have two servers available.

- **Practice 1**   Install a server running Windows Server 2003. Promote it to a domain controller in a new forest. Configure its domain and forest functional levels to Windows Server 2003.

- **Practice 2**   Run *Adprep /forestprep* and *Adprep /domainprep /gpprep* from the Windows Server 2008 installation DVD \Sources\Adprep folder.

- **Practice 3**   Install a server running Windows Server 2008 and join the domain. Promote the server to a domain controller, including DNS and global catalog.

- **Practice 4**   Transfer all operations master roles to the new domain controller.

- **Practice 5 (Option 1)**   Upgrade the first domain controller to Windows Server 2008.

- **Practice 5 (Option 2)**   Demote the Windows Server 2003 domain controller and remove it from the domain to a workgroup. Format the disk. Install Windows Server 2008 and join the domain. Promote the server to a domain controller. Transfer all operations master roles back to the system.

Take a Practice Test

The practice tests on this book's companion CD offer many options. For example, you can test yourself on just one exam objective, or you can test yourself on all the 70-640 certification exam content. You can set up the test so that it closely simulates the experience of taking a certification exam, or you can set it up in study mode so that you can look at the correct answers and explanations after you answer each question.

MORE INFO **Practice tests**

For details about all the practice test options available, see the "How to Use the Practice Tests" section in this book's introduction.

Chapter 11
Sites and Replication

You've learned in previous chapters that domain controllers (DCs) in a Windows Server 2008 domain are peers. Each maintains a copy of the directory, each performs similar services to support authentication of security principals, and changes made on any one domain controller will be replicated to all other domain controllers. As an administrator of a Microsoft Windows enterprise, one of your tasks is to ensure that authentication is provided as efficiently as possible, and that replication between domain controllers is optimized. Active Directory Domain Services (AD DS) sites are the core component of the directory service that supports the goals of service localization and replication. In this chapter, you will learn how to create a distributed directory service that supports domain controllers in portions of your network that are separated by expensive, slow, or unreliable links. You'll learn where domain controllers should be placed and how to manage replication and service usage. You'll also learn how to control which data is replicated to each domain controller by configuring global catalogs (GCs) and application partitions.

Exam objectives in this chapter:
- Configuring the Active Directory Infrastructure
    - ❏ Configure the global catalog.
    - ❏ Configure sites.
    - ❏ Configure Active Directory replication.
- Maintaining the Active Directory Environment
    - ❏ Monitor Active Directory.

Lessons in this chapter:
- Lesson 1: Configuring Sites and Subnets 509
- Lesson 2: Configuring the Global Catalog and Application Directory Partitions . . . 522
- Lesson 3: Configuring Replication 531

Before You Begin

To complete the practices in this chapter, you must have created two domain controllers named SERVER01 and SERVER02 in a domain named *contoso.com*. See Chapter 1, "Installation," and Chapter 10, "Domain Controllers," for detailed steps for this task.

Real World

Dan Holme

As you learned in the previous chapter, it is important to have more than one domain controller in a domain to provide continuity of service in the event that one domain controller fails. That rule of thumb—at least two DCs per domain—assumes that all servers and clients in your environment are well connected to the DCs. But what happens if you have several network locations separated by links that are not LAN speed? And what must you do if those intersite links are unreliable? Well, then, you must make a determination whether to place domain controllers in remote locations and how to manage replication of the directory to those domain controllers. On the 70-640 exam, the focus on Active Directory sites is their relationship to replication, and you will certainly learn how to manage replication in this chapter. But sites are also important in highly connected environments because they enable you to manage *service localization*—that is, ensure that when a service is available from multiple servers, a client uses the most efficient server. Throughout this chapter, keep your eye on the relationship between sites and service localization as well, because although it might not be as important on the exam, it is certainly important in your production environment.

Lesson 1: Configuring Sites and Subnets

Active Directory represents human beings by user objects in the directory service. It represents machines by computer objects. It represents network topology with objects called *sites* and *subnets*. Active Directory site objects are used to manage replication and service localization and, fortunately, in many environments, the configuration of sites and subnets can be quite straightforward. In this lesson, you will learn the fundamental concepts and techniques required to configure and manage sites and subnets.

After this lesson, you will be able to:

- Identify the roles of sites and subnets.
- Describe the process with which a client locates a domain controller.
- Configure sites and subnets.
- Manage domain controller server objects in sites.

Estimated lesson time: 45 minutes

Understanding Sites

When administrators describe their network infrastructure, they often mention how many sites comprise their enterprise. To most administrators, a site is a physical location, an office or city, for example. Sites are connected by links—network links that might be as basic as dial-up connections or as sophisticated as fiber links. Together, the physical locations and links make up the network infrastructure.

Active Directory represents the network infrastructure with objects called *sites* and *site links*, and although the words are similar, these objects are not identical to the sites and links described by administrators. This lesson focuses on sites, and Lesson 3, "Configuring Replication," discusses site links.

It's important to understand the properties and roles of sites in Active Directory to understand the subtle distinction between Active Directory sites and network sites. Active Directory sites are objects in the directory, specifically in the Configuration container (CN=Configuration,DC=*forest root domain*). These objects are used to achieve two service management tasks:

- To manage replication traffic
- To facilitate service localization

Replication Traffic

Replication is the transfer of changes between domain controllers. When you add a user or change a user's password, for example, the change you make is committed to the directory by one domain controller. That change must be communicated to all other domain controllers in the domain.

Active Directory assumes there are two types of networks within your enterprise: highly connected and less highly connected. Conceptually, a change made to Active Directory should replicate immediately to other domain controllers within the highly connected network in which the change was made. However, you might not want the change to replicate immediately over a slower, more expensive, or less reliable link to another site. Instead, you might want to manage replication over less highly connected segments of your enterprise to optimize performance, reduce costs, or manage bandwidth.

An Active Directory site represents a highly connected portion of your enterprise. When you define a site, the domain controllers within the site replicate changes almost instantly. Replication between sites can be scheduled and managed.

Service Localization

Active Directory is a distributed service. That is, assuming you have at least two domain controllers, there are multiple servers (domain controllers) providing the same services of authentication and directory access. If you have more than one network site, and if you place a domain controller in each, you want to encourage clients to authenticate against the domain controller in their site. This is an example of service localization.

Active Directory sites help you localize services, including those provided by domain controllers. During logon, Windows clients are automatically directed to a domain controller in their site. If a domain controller is not available in their site, they are directed to a DC in another site that will be able to authenticate the client efficiently.

Other services can be localized as well. Distributed File System Namespaces (DFS Namespaces), for example, is a localized service. DFS clients will obtain replicated resources from the most efficient server, based on their Active Directory site. In fact, because clients know what site they are in, any distributed service could be written to take advantage of the Active Directory site structure to provide intelligent localization of service usage.

Planning Sites

Because sites are used to optimize replication and to enable service localization, you must spend time designing your Active Directory site structure. Active Directory sites might not map one to one with your network's sites. Consider two scenarios:

- You have offices in two distinct locations. You place one domain controller in each location. The locations are highly connected, and to improve performance, you decide to configure a single Active Directory site that includes both locations.

- You have an enterprise on a large, highly connected campus. From a replication perspective, the enterprise could be considered a single site. However, you want to encourage clients to use distributed services in their location, so you configure multiple sites to support service localization.

Therefore, an Active Directory site can include more than one network site or be a subset of a single network site. The key is to remember that sites serve both replication management and service localization roles. Several characteristics of your enterprise can be used to help you determine which sites are necessary:

Connection Speed

An Active Directory site represents a unit of the network that is characterized by fast, reliable, inexpensive connectivity. Much documentation suggests that the slowest link speed within a site should be no less than 512 kilobits per second (kbps). However, this guidance is not immutable. Some organizations have links as slow as 56 or even 28 kbps within a site.

Service Placement

Because Active Directory sites manage Active Directory replication and service localization, it is not useful to create a site for a network location that does not host a domain controller or other Active Directory–aware service such as a replicated DFS resource.

NOTE Sites where there are no domain controllers

Domain controllers are only one distributed service in a Windows enterprise. Other services, such as replicated DFS resources, are site-aware as well. You might configure sites to localize services other than authentication, in which case you will have sites without domain controllers.

User Population

Concentrations of users can also influence your site design, although indirectly. If a network location has a sufficient number of users for whom the inability to authenticate would be problematic, place a domain controller in the location to support authentication within the location. After a domain controller or other distributed service is placed in the location to support those users, you might want to manage Active Directory replication to the location or localize service use by configuring an Active Directory site to represent the location.

Summarizing Site Planning Criteria

Every Active Directory forest includes at least one site. The default site created when you instantiate a forest with the first domain controller is creatively named *Default-First-Site-Name*. You should create additional sites when:

- A part of the network is separated by a slow link.
- A part of the network has enough users to warrant hosting domain controllers or other services in that location.
- Directory query traffic warrants a local domain controller.
- You want to control service localization.
- You want to control replication between domain controllers.

Server Placement

Network administrators often want to know when placing a domain controller in a remote site is recommended. The answer is, "It depends." Specifically, it depends on the resources required by users in the site and the tolerance for downtime. If users in a remote site perform all work tasks by accessing resources in the data center, for example, then if the link to the remote site fails, the users cannot access the resources they require, and a local domain controller would not improve the situation. However, if users access resources in the remote site and the link fails, a local domain controller can continue to provide authentication for users and they can continue to work with their local resources.

In most branch office scenarios, there are resources in the branch office that users require to perform their work tasks. Those resources, if not stored on the user's own computer, require domain authentication of the user. Therefore, a domain controller is generally recommended. The introduction of read-only domain controllers (RODCs) in Windows Server 2008 reduces the risk and management burden of domain controllers in branch offices, so it will be easier for most organizations to deploy DCs in each network location.

Defining Sites

Sites and replication are managed using the Active Directory Sites and Services snap-in. To define an Active Directory site, you will create an object of class *site*. The site object is a container that manages replication for domain controllers in the site. You will also create one or more subnet objects. A subnet object defines a range of IP addresses and is linked to one site. Service localization is attained when a client's IP address can be associated with a site through the relationship between the subnet object and the site object.

You can create a site object by right-clicking the Sites node in Active Directory Sites And Services and choosing New Site. In the New Object – Site dialog box that appears, shown in Figure 11-1, enter a site name and select a site link. The default site link, DEFAULTIPSITELINK, will be the only site link available to you until you create additional site links as discussed in Lesson 2, "Configuring the Global Catalog and Application Directory Partitions."

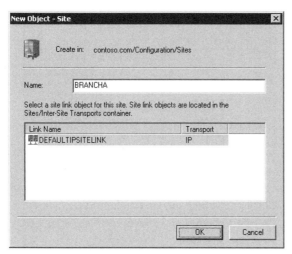

Figure 11-1   The New Object – Site dialog box

After creating a site, you can right-click it and choose Rename to rename it. It is recommended that you rename the Default-First-Site-Name site to reflect a site name that is aligned with your business and network topology.

Sites are useful only when a client or server knows the site to which it belongs. This is typically achieved by associating the system's IP address with a site, and subnet objects achieve this association. To create a subnet object, right-click the Subnets node in the Active Directory Sites And Services snap-in and choose New Subnet. The New Object – Subnet dialog box shown in Figure 11-2 appears. The subnet object is defined as a range of addresses using network prefix notation. For example, to enter a subnet representing the addresses 10.1.1.1 to 10.1.1.254 with a 24-bit subnet mask, the prefix would be 10.1.1.0/24. For more information about entering addresses, click the Learn More About Entering Address Prefixes link in the New Object – Subnet dialog box.

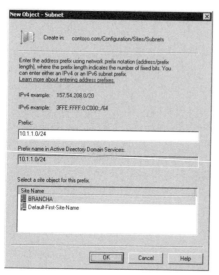

Figure 11-2   The New Object – Subnet dialog box

After entering the network prefix, select the site object with which the subnet is associated. A subnet can be associated with only one site; however, a site can have more than one subnet linked to it. The Properties dialog box of a site, shown in Figure 11-3, shows the subnets associated with the site. You cannot change the subnets in this dialog box, however; instead, you must open the properties of the subnet, shown in Figure 11-4, to change the site to which the subnet is linked.

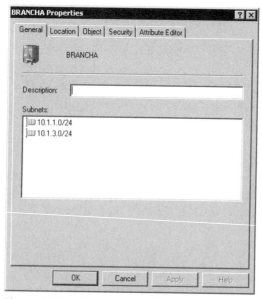

Figure 11-3   The Properties dialog box for a site

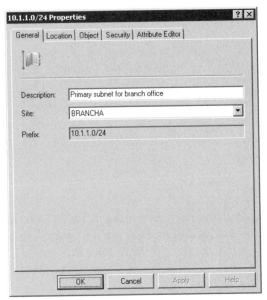

Figure 11-4   The Properties dialog box for a subnet

NOTE   Defining every IP subnet

In your production environment, be certain to define every IP subnet as an Active Directory subnet object. If a client's IP address is not included within a subnet range, the client is unable to determine which Active Directory site it belongs to, which can lead to performance and functionality problems. Don't forget backbone subnets and subnets used for remote access such as virtual private network address ranges.

Managing Domain Controllers in Sites

There are times when you might need to manage domain controllers in Active Directory sites:

- You create a new site and move an existing domain controller to it.
- You demote a domain controller.
- You promote a new domain controller.

When you create your Active Directory forest, the first domain controller is automatically placed under the site object named *Default-First-Site-Name*. You can see the domain controller SERVER01.contoso.com in Figure 11-5. Additional domain controllers will be added to sites based on their IP addresses. For example, if a server with IP address 10.1.1.17 is promoted to a domain controller in the network shown in Figure 11-4, the server will automatically be added to the BRANCHA site. Figure 11-5 shows SERVER02 in the BRANCHA site.

Figure 11-5   A domain controller in a site

Each site contains a Servers container, which itself contains an object for each domain controller in the site. The Servers container in a site should show only domain controllers, not all servers. When you promote a new domain controller, the domain controller will, by default, be placed in the site associated with its IP address. However, the Active Directory Domain Services Installation Wizard will enable you to specify another site. You can also pre-create the server object for the domain controller in the correct site by right-clicking the Servers container in the appropriate site and choosing Server from the New menu.

Finally, you can move the domain controller to the correct site after installation by right-clicking the server and choosing Move. In the Move Server dialog box, select the new site and click OK. The domain controller is moved. It is a best practice to place a domain controller in the site object that is associated with the DC's IP address. If a DC is multihomed, it can belong to only one site. If a site has no domain controllers, users will still be able to log on to the domain; their logon requests will be handled by a domain controller in an adjacent site or another domain controller in the domain.

To remove a domain controller object, right-click it and choose Delete.

Understanding Domain Controller Location

You started this lesson by examining AD DS as a distributed service, providing authentication and directory access on more than one domain controller. You learned to identify where, in your network topology, to define sites and place domain controllers. Now you are ready to examine how, exactly, service localization works—how Active Directory clients become site aware and locate the domain controller in their site. Although this level of detail is unlikely to appear on the certification examination, it can be extremely helpful when you need to troubleshoot authentication of a computer or of a user.

Service Locator Records

When a domain controller is added to the domain, it advertises its services by creating Service Locator (SRV) records, also called locator records, in DNS. Unlike host records (A records), which map host names to IP addresses, SRV records map services to host names. The domain controller advertises its ability to provide authentication and directory access by registering Kerberos and LDAP SRV records. These SRV records are added to several folders within the DNS zones for the forest. The first folder is within the domain zone. It is called _tcp and it contains the SRV records for all domain controllers in the domain. The second folder is specific to this site, in which the domain controller is located, with the path _sites*sitename*_tcp, where *sitename* is the name of the site. In Figure 11-6, you can see the Kerberos and LDAP SRV records for SERVER02.contoso.com in its site, _sites\BRANCHA_tcp. You can also see the _tcp folder at the first level beneath the zone.

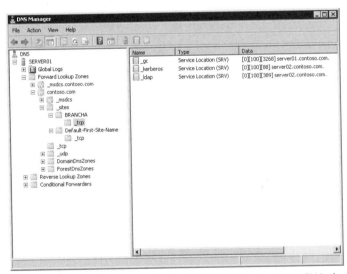

Figure 11-6   The SRV records for SERVER02 in the BRANCHA site

The same records are registered in several places in the _msdcs.*domainName* zone, for example, _msdcs.contoso.com in Figure 11-6. This zone contains records for Microsoft Domain Controller Services. The underscore characters are a requirement of RFC 2052.

Locator records contain:

- **Service name and port**   This portion of the SRV record indicates a service with a fixed port. It does not have to be a well-known port. SRV records in Windows Server 2008 include LDAP (port 389), Kerberos (port 88), Kerberos Password protocol (KPASSWD, port 464), and GC services (port 3268).

- **Protocol**   TCP or UDP will be indicated as a transport protocol for the service. The same service can use both protocols, in separate SRV records. Kerberos records, for example, are registered for both TCP and UDP. Microsoft clients use only TCP, but UNIX clients can use TCP.

- **Host name**   The name corresponds to the A (Host) record for the server hosting the service. When a client queries for a service, the DNS server returns the SRV record and associated A records, so the client does not need to submit a separate query to resolve the IP address of a service.

The service name in the SRV record follows the standard DNS hierarchy, with components separated by dots. For example, the Kerberos service of a domain controller is registered as:

```
kerberos._tcp.siteName._sites.domainName
```

Reading this SRV record name right to left like other DNS records, it translates to:

- *domainName*: the domain or zone, for example, *contoso.com*
- _sites: all sites registered with DNS
- *siteName*: the site of the domain controller registering the service
- _tcp: any TCP-based services in the site
- kerberos: a Kerberos Key Distribution Center (KDC) using TCP as its transport protocol

Domain Controller Location

Imagine a Windows client has just been joined to the domain. It restarts, receives an IP address from a DHCP server, and is ready to authenticate to the domain. How does the client know where to find a domain controller? It does not. Therefore, the client queries the domain for a domain controller by querying the _tcp folder which, you'll remember, contains the SRV records for all domain controllers in the domain. DNS returns a list of all matching DCs, and the client attempts to contact all of them on this, its first startup. The first domain controller that responds to the client examines the client's IP address, cross-references that address with subnet objects, and informs the client of the site to which the client belongs. The client stores the site name in its registry, then queries for domain controllers in the site-specific _tcp folder. DNS returns a list of all DCs in the site. The client attempts to bind with all, and the DC that responds first authenticates the client.

The client forms an affinity for this DC and will attempt to authenticate with the same DC in the future. If the DC is unavailable, the client queries the site's _tcp folder again and attempts to bind with all DCs in the site. But what happens if the client is a mobile computer—a laptop? Imagine that the computer has been authenticating in the BRANCHA site and then the user brings the computer to the BRANCHB site. When the computer starts up, it actually attempts to authenticate with its preferred DC into BRANCHA site. That DC notices the client's IP address is associated with BRANCHB and informs the client of its new site. The client then queries DNS for domain controllers in BRANCHB.

You can see how, by storing subnet and site information in Active Directory and by registering services in DNS, a client is encouraged to use services in its site—the definition of service localization.

MORE INFO   Domain controller location

For more information about domain controller location, see *http://www.microsoft.com/technet /prodtechnol/windows2000serv/reskit/distrib/dsbc_nar_jevl.mspx?mfr=true.*

Site Coverage

What happens if a site has no domain controller? Sites can be used to direct users to local copies of replicated resources such as shared folders replicated within a DFS namespace, so you might have sites without a DC. In this case, a nearby domain controller will register its SRV records in the site in a process called *site coverage*. To be precise, a site without a DC will generally be covered by a domain controller in a site with the lowest cost to the site requiring coverage. You'll learn more about site link costs in the next lesson. You can also manually configure site coverage and SRV record priority if you want to implement strict control over authentication in sites without DCs. The URL just listed contains details about the algorithm that determines which DC automatically covers a site without a DC.

PRACTICE Configuring Sites and Subnets

In this practice, you will use best practices to implement a structure of sites and subnets for the *contoso.com* domain. To perform the exercises in this practice, you must have two domain controllers, SERVER01 and SERVER02, in the domain.

▶ **Exercise 1   Configure the Default Site**

A new domain contains the Default-First-Site-Name site. In this exercise, you will rename that site and associate two subnets with the site.

1. Open the Active Directory Sites And Services snap-in.
2. Right-click Default-First-Site-Name and choose Rename.
3. Type **HEADQUARTERS** and press Enter.

    Because site names are registered in DNS, you should use DNS-compliant names that avoid special characters and spaces.
4. Right-click Subnets and choose New Subnet.
5. In the Prefix box, type **10.0.0.0/24**.
6. In the Select A Site Object For This Prefix list, select HEADQUARTERS.
7. Click OK.
8. Right-click Subnets and choose New Subnet.
9. In the Prefix box, type **10.0.1.0/24**.

10. In the Select A Site Object For This Prefix list, select HEADQUARTERS.

11. Click OK.

▶ **Exercise 2   Create an Additional Site**

Sites enable you to manage replication traffic and to localize services such as the authentication and directory access provided by domain controllers. In this exercise, you will create a second site and associate a subnet with it.

1. Open the Active Directory Sites And Services snap-in

2. Right-click Sites and choose New Site.

3. Type **BRANCHA** in the Name box.

4. Select DEFAULTIPSITELINK.

5. Click OK.

    An Active Directory Domain Services dialog box appears, explaining the steps required to complete the configuration of the site.

6. Click OK.

7. Right-click Subnets and choose New Subnet.

8. In the Prefix box, type **10.1.1.0/24**.

9. In the Select A Site Object For This Prefix list, select BRANCHA.

10. Click OK.

11. In the Active Directory Sites And Services snap-in, expand the Subnets node.

12. Right-click 10.1.1.0/24 and choose Properties.

13. In the Description box, type **Primary subnet for branch office**.

14. In the Site drop-down list, select BRANCHA.

15. Click OK.

Lesson Summary

- Sites are Active Directory objects that are used to manage directory replication and service localization.

- To configure a site, you must create a site object and associate a subnet object with the site. A site can have more than one subnet, but a subnet can belong to only one site.

- Domain controllers are placed in sites as server objects.

- Domain controllers register service locator (SRV) records to advertise their Kerberos (authentication) and directory access services. These SRV records are created in site-specific nodes within the DNS zones for the domain and forest.

- Domain members discover their site during authentication. A domain controller uses a client's IP address and the domain's site and subnet information to determine the client's site and then sends that information to the client.

Lesson Review

You can use the following questions to test your knowledge of the information in Lesson 1, "Configuring Sites and Subnets." The questions are also available on the companion CD if you prefer to review them in electronic form.

NOTE Answers

Answers to these questions and explanations of why each answer choice is right or wrong are located in the "Answers" section at the end of the book.

1. Client computers in a branch office are performing poorly during logon. You notice that the computers report that their logon server is a domain controller in a remote site rather than the domain controller in the branch office itself. Which of the following could cause this problem?

   A. The branch office domain controller is not assigned to a site.

   B. The branch office site is not assigned to a site link.

   C. The branch office IP address range is not associated with the site.

   D. The branch office subnet is assigned to two sites.

2. You are adding a read-only domain controller to a branch office location. You want to ensure that clients in the branch office are likely to authenticate with the RODC. What is required? (Choose all that apply.)

   A. A subnet object with the network prefix of the branch office IP address range

   B. An account for the domain controller in the organizational unit for the site

   C. A site link transport for the site

   D. A site object for the branch office

   E. A server object in the site object for the branch office

Lesson 2: Configuring the Global Catalog and Application Directory Partitions

As soon as you have more than one domain controller in your domain, you must consider replication of the directory database between domain controllers. In this lesson, you will learn which directory partitions are replicated to each domain controller in a forest and how to manage the replication of the GC and of application partitions.

After this lesson, you will be able to:
- Define the purpose of the global catalog.
- Configure domain controllers as global catalog servers.
- Implement universal group membership caching.
- Understand the role of application directory partitions.

Estimated lesson time: 45 minutes

Reviewing Active Directory Partitions

In Chapter 1, you learned that AD DS includes a data store for identity and management, specifically the directory database, *Ntds.dit*. Within that single file are directory partitions. Each directory partition, also called a naming context, contains objects of a particular scope and purpose. Three major naming contexts have been discussed in this training kit:

- **Domain** The domain naming context (NC) contains all the objects stored in a domain, including users, groups, computers, and Group Policy containers (GPCs).
- **Configuration** The configuration partition contains objects that represent the logical structure of the forest, including domains, as well as the physical topology, including sites, subnets, and services.
- **Schema** The schema defines the object classes and their attributes for the entire directory.

Each domain controller maintains a copy, or *replica*, of several naming contexts. The configuration is replicated to every domain controller in the forest, as is the schema. The domain naming context for a domain is replicated to all domain controllers within a domain but not to domain controllers in other domains, so each domain controller has at least three replicas: the domain NC for its domain, configuration, and schema.

Traditionally, replicas have been complete replicas, containing every object of an attribute, and replicas have been writable on all DCs. Beginning with Windows Server 2008, RODCs change the picture slightly. An RODC maintains a read-only replica of all objects in the configuration, schema, and domain NCs of its domain. However, certain attributes are not replicated to an RODC—specifically, secrets such as user passwords—unless the password policy of the RODC allows such replication. There are also attributes that are domain and forest secrets that are never replicated to an RODC.

Understanding the Global Catalog

Imagine a forest with two domains. Each domain has two domain controllers. All four domain controllers will maintain a replica of the schema and configuration for the forest. The domain controllers in Domain A have replicas of the domain NC for Domain A, and the domain controllers in Domain B have replicas of the domain NC for Domain B.

What happens if a user in Domain B is searching for a user, computer, or group in Domain A? The Domain B domain controllers do not maintain any information about objects in Domain A, so a domain controller in Domain B could not answer a query about objects in the domain NC of Domain A.

That's where the global catalog comes in. The *global catalog* (GC) is a partition that stores information about every object in the forest. When a user in Domain B looks for an object in Domain A, the GC provides the results of the query. To optimize efficiency of the GC, it does not contain every attribute of every object in the forest. Instead, it contains a subset of attributes that are useful for searching across domains. That is why the GC is also called the *partial attribute set* (PAS). In terms of its role supporting search, you can think of the GC as a kind of index for the AD DS data store.

Placing GC Servers

The GC improves efficiency of the directory service tremendously and is required for applications such as Microsoft Exchange Server and Microsoft Office Outlook. Therefore, you want a GC to be available to these and other applications. The GC can be served only by a domain controller and, in an ideal world, every domain controller would be a GC server. In fact, many organizations are now configuring their domain controllers as GC servers.

The potential downside to such a configuration relates to replication. The GC is another partition that must be replicated. In a single domain forest, very little overhead is actually added by configuring all domain controllers as GC servers because all domain controllers already maintain a full set of attributes for all domain and forest objects. In a large, multidomain forest, there will be overhead related to replication of changes to the partial attribute set of objects in other domains. However, many organizations are finding that Active Directory replication is efficient enough to replicate the GC without significant impact to their networks and that the benefits far outweigh such impact. If you choose to configure all DCs as GC servers, you no longer need to worry about the placement of the infrastructure operations master; its role is no longer necessary in a domain where all DCs are GC servers.

It is particularly recommended to configure a GC server on a domain controller in a site where one or more of the following is true:

- A commonly used application performs directory queries, using port 3268, the GC.
- The connection to a GC server is slow or unreliable.
- The site contains a computer running Exchange Server.

Configuring a Global Catalog Server

When you create the first domain in the forest, the first domain controller is configured as a GC. You must decide for each additional DC whether it should be a GC server. The Active Directory Domain Services Installation Wizard and the *Dcpromo.exe* command each enable you to configure a GC server when promoting a domain controller. You can also add or remove the GC from a domain controller by using Active Directory Sites And Services. Expand the site, the Servers container within the site, and the domain controller's server object. Right-click the NTDS Settings node and choose Properties. On the General tab, shown in Figure 11-7, select the Global Catalog check box. To remove the GC from a domain controller, perform the same steps, clearing the Global Catalog check box.

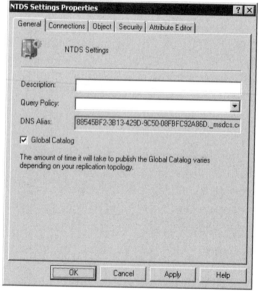

Figure 11-7   The NTDS Settings Properties dialog box, showing the Global Catalog check box

Universal Group Membership Caching

In Chapter 4, "Groups," you learned that Active Directory supports groups of universal scope. Universal groups are designed to include users and groups from multiple domains in a forest. The membership of universal groups is replicated in the GC. When a user logs on, the user's universal group membership is obtained from a GC server. If a GC is not available, universal group membership is not available. It's possible that a universal group is used to deny the user access to resources, so Windows prevents a security incident by denying domain authentication to the user. If the user has logged on to his or her computer before, he or she can log on using cached credentials, but as soon as the user attempts to access network resources, access will be denied. To summarize: if a GC server is not available, users will effectively be unable to log on and access network resources.

If every domain controller is a GC server, this problem will not arise. However, if replication is a concern, and if you have, therefore, chosen not to configure a domain controller as a GC server, you can facilitate successful logon by enabling universal group membership caching (UGMC). When you configure universal group membership caching on a domain controller in a branch office, for example, that domain controller will obtain universal group membership information from a GC for a user when the user first logs on in the site, and the domain controller will cache that information indefinitely, updating universal group membership information every eight hours. That way, if the user later logs on and a GC server is not accessible, the domain controller can use its cached membership information to permit logon by the user.

It is recommended, therefore, that in sites with unreliable connectivity to a GC server, you should configure UGMC on the site's domain controllers. To configure UGMC, open the Active Directory Sites And Services snap-in and select the site in the console tree. In the details pane, right-click NTDS Site Settings and choose Properties. The NTDS Site Settings Properties dialog box, shown in Figure 11-8, exposes the Enable Universal Group Membership Caching option. You can select the check box and specify the GC from which to refresh the membership cache.

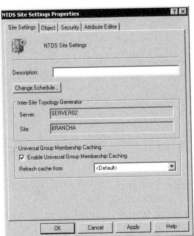

Figure 11-8   The NTDS Site Settings Properties dialog box with the option to enable Universal Group Membership Caching

Understanding Application Directory Partitions

Whereas the domain, configuration, and schema partitions of the directory are replicated to all DCs in a domain, and the configuration and schema are further replicated to all DCs in the forest, Active Directory also supports *application directory partitions*. An application directory partition is a portion of the data store that contains objects required by an application or service that is outside of the core AD DS service. Unlike other partitions, application partitions can be targeted to replicate to specific domain controllers; they are not, by default, replicated to all DCs.

Application directory partitions are designed to support directory-enabled applications and services. They can contain any type of object except security principals such as users, computers, or security groups. Because these partitions are replicated only as needed, application directory partitions provide the benefits of fault tolerance, availability, and performance while optimizing replication traffic.

The easiest way to understand application directory partitions is to examine the application directory partitions maintained by Microsoft DNS Server. When you create an Active Directory–integrated zone, DNS records are replicated between DNS servers by using an application directory partition. The partition and its DNS record objects are not replicated to every domain controller, only to those acting as DNS servers.

You can expose the application directory partitions in your forest by opening ADSI Edit. Right-click the root of the snap-in, ADSI Edit, and choose Connect To. In the Select A Well Known Naming Context drop-down list, choose Configuration and click OK. Expand Configuration and the folder representing the configuration partition, and then select the Partitions folder, CN=Partitions, in the console tree. In the details pane, you will see the partitions in your AD DS data store, as shown in Figure 11-9.

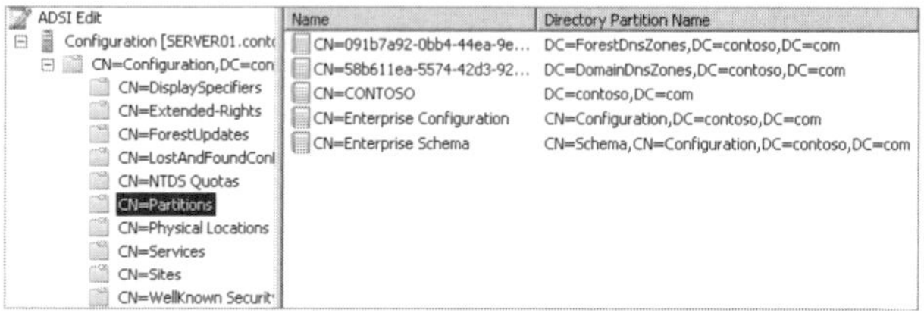

Figure 11-9   Partitions in the *contoso.com* forest

Note the two application partitions in Figure 11-9, ForestDnsZones and DomainDnsZones. Most application partitions are created by applications that require them. DNS is one example, and Telephony Application Programming Interface (TAPI) is another. Members of the Enterprise Admins group can also create application directory partitions manually by using *Ntdsutil.exe*.

An application partition can appear anywhere in the forest namespace that a domain partition can appear. The DNS partitions distinguished names—DC=DomainDnsZones,DC=contoso,DC=com, for example—place the partitions as children of the DC=contoso,DC=com domain partition. An application partition can also be a child of another application partition or a new tree in the forest.

MORE INFO **About application directory partitions**

For more information about application directory partitions, visit *http://technet2.microsoft.com /WindowsServer/en/library/ed363e83-c043-4a50-9233-763e6f4af1f21033.mspx.*

Generally speaking, you will use tools specific to the application to manage the application directory partition, its data, and its replication. For example, simply adding an Active Directory–integrated zone to a DNS server will automatically configure the domain controller to receive a replica of the DomainDns partition. With tools such as *Ntdsutil.exe* and *Ldp.exe*, you can manage application directory partitions directly.

MORE INFO **Managing application directory partitions**

To learn how to manage application directory partitions, see *http://technet2.microsoft.com /WindowsServer/en/library/920d6995-9ee9-46a7-9d1b-320e65c02d1a1033.mspx.*

It is important that you consider application partitions prior to demoting a domain controller. If a domain controller is hosting an application directory partition, you must evaluate the purpose of the partition, whether it is required by any applications, and whether the domain controller holds the last remaining replica of the partition, in which case, demoting the domain controller will result in permanently losing all information in the partition. Although the Active Directory Domain Services Installation Wizard will prompt you to remove application directory partitions, it is recommended that you manually remove application directory partitions prior to demoting a domain controller.

MORE INFO **Application directory partitions and domain controller demotion**

For more information about application directory partitions and domain controller demotion, see *http://technet2.microsoft.com/WindowsServer/en/library/1572d8a2-622c-4879-bb0b-76e26c4001291033.mspx.*

PRACTICE Replication and Directory Partitions

In this practice, you will configure replication of the GC and examine the DNS application directory partitions. To complete the exercises in this practice, you must have completed the Lesson 1 practice, "Configuring Sites and Subnets."

▶ **Exercise 1   Configure a Global Catalog Server**

The first domain controller in a forest acts as a GC server. You might want to place GC servers in additional locations to support directory queries, logon, and applications such as Exchange Server. In this exercise, you will configure SERVER02 to host a replica of the partial attribute set—the GC.

1. Log on to SERVER01 as Administrator.
2. Open the Active Directory Sites And Services snap-in.
3. Expand BRANCHA, Servers, and SERVER02.
4. Right-click NTDS Settings below SERVER02 and choose Properties.
5. Select Global Catalog and click OK.

▶ **Exercise 2   Configure Universal Group Membership Caching**

In sites without GC servers, user logon might be prevented if the site's domain controller is unable to contact a GC server in another site. To reduce the likelihood of this scenario, you can configure a site to cache the membership of universal groups. In this exercise, you will create a site to reflect a branch office and configure the site to cache universal group membership.

1. Right-click Sites and choose New Site.
2. In the Name box, type **BRANCHB**.
3. Select DEFAULTIPSITELINK.
4. Click OK.

   If this were a production environment, you would need to create at least one subnet object linked to the site and install a domain controller in BRANCHB.
5. Select BRANCHB in the console tree.
6. Right-click NTDS Site Settings in the details pane and choose Properties.
7. On the Site Settings tab, select the Enable Universal Group Membership Caching check box.
8. Click OK.

▶ **Exercise 3   Examine Application Directory Partitions**

In this exercise, you will explore the DomainDnsZone application directory partition, using ADSI Edit.

1. Open ADSI Edit from the Administrative Tools program group.
2. Right-click the root node of the snap-in, ADSI Edit, and choose Connect To.
3. In the Select A Well Known Naming Context drop-down list, choose Configuration. Click OK.
4. Select Configuration in the console tree, and then expand it.
5. Select CN=Configuration, DC=contoso, DC=com in the console tree, and then expand it.
6. Select CN=Partitions in the console tree.
7. Make a note of the Directory Partition Name of the DomainDnsZones partition: DC=DomainDnsZones,DC=contoso,DC=com.
8. Right-click ADSI Edit and choose Connect To.
9. Select the Select Or Type A Distinguished Name Or Naming Context option.
10. In the combo box, type **DC=DomainDnsZones,DC=contoso,DC=com**. Click OK.

11. Select Default Naming Context in the console tree, and then expand it.

12. Select and then expand DC=DomainDnsZones,DC=contoso,DC=com.

13. Select and then expand CN=MicrosoftDNS.

14. Select DC=contoso.com.

15. Examine the objects in this container. Compare them to the DNS records for the *contoso.com* domain.

Lesson Summary

- The global catalog (GC) contains a copy of every object in the forest but only a subset of object attributes. It is also called the partial attribute set (PAS).

- GC servers improve directory queries, support logon, and provide data for applications such as Exchange Server.

- The first domain controller in a forest is a GC server. You can configure a domain controller as a GC server by using the *Dcpromo.exe* command, the Active Directory Domain Services Installation Wizard, or the Active Directory Sites And Services snap-in after the domain controller has been installed.

- If a site does not contain a GC server, you can configure universal group membership caching (UGMC) to reduce the chance of a user's logon being denied when a GC server is not available.

- Application directory partitions are unique because they can be replicated to specific domain controllers throughout a forest. Active Directory integrated DNS zones are stored in application partitions.

Lesson Review

You can use the following questions to test your knowledge of the information in Lesson 2, "Configuring the Global Catalog and Application Directory Partitions." The questions are also available on the companion CD if you prefer to review them in electronic form.

NOTE Answers

Answers to these questions and explanations of why each answer choice is right or wrong are located in the "Answers" section at the end of the book.

1. A branch office is connected to the data center with a slow link that is not reliable. You want to ensure that the domain controller in the branch is able to authenticate users when it cannot contact a global catalog server. Which of the following should you configure?

    A. Read-only domain controller

    B. Application directory partition

    C. Intersite replication

    D. Universal group membership caching

2. You are the administrator at Contoso, Ltd. The Contoso forest consists of three domains, each with four domain controllers. You are preparing to demote a domain controller in the forest root domain. You want to be sure that you do not permanently destroy any Active Directory partitions. Which of the following Active Directory partitions might exist only on that domain controller? (Choose all that apply.)

    A. Schema

    B. Configuration

    C. Domain

    D. Partial attribute set

    E. Application directory partition

3. You want to configure all the existing domain controllers in your forest as global catalog servers. Which tools can you use to achieve this goal? (Choose all that apply.)

    A. *Dcpromo.exe*

    B. Active Directory Domain Services Installation Wizard

    C. Active Directory Sites and Services snap-in

    D. Active Directory Users and Computers snap-in

    E. Active Directory Domains and Trusts snap-in

Lesson 3: Configuring Replication

In Lesson 1, you learned how to create site and subnet objects that enable Active Directory and its clients to localize authentication and directory access; you decided *where* domain controllers should be placed. In Lesson 2, you configured GC servers and application directory partitions; you managed *what* will replicate between domain controllers. In this lesson, you will learn *how* and *when* replication occurs. You'll discover why the default configuration of Active Directory supports effective replication and why you might modify that configuration so that replication is equally effective but more efficient, based on your network topology.

After this lesson, you will be able to:
- Create connection objects to configure replication between two domain controllers.
- Implement site links and site link costs to manage replication between sites.
- Designate preferred bridgehead servers.
- Understand notification and polling.
- Report and analyze replication with *Repadmin.exe*.
- Perform Active Directory replication health checks with *Dcdiag.exe*.

Estimated lesson time: 90 minutes

Understanding Active Directory Replication

In previous lessons, you learned how to place domain controllers in network locations and how to represent those locations with site and subnet objects. You also learned about the replication of directory partitions (schema, configuration, and domain), the partial attribute set (GC), and application partitions. The most important thing to remember as you learn about Active Directory replication is that it is designed so that, in the end, each replica on a domain controller is consistent with the replicas of that partition hosted on other domain controllers. It is not likely that all domain controllers will have exactly the same information in their replicas at any one moment in time because changes are constantly being made to the directory. However, Active Directory replication ensures that all changes to a partition are transferred to all replicas of the partition. Active Directory replication balances accuracy (or *integrity*) and consistency (called *convergence*) with performance (keeping replication traffic to a reasonable level). This balancing act is described as *loose coupling*.

Key features of Active Directory replication are:
- Partitioning of the data store. Domain controllers in a domain host only the domain naming context for their domain, which helps keep replication to a minimum, particularly in multidomain forests. Other data, including application directory partitions and the partial attribute set (GC), are not replicated to every domain controller in the forest, by default.

- Automatic generation of an efficient and robust replication topology. By default, Active Directory will configure an effective, two-way replication topology so that the loss of any one domain controller does not impede replication. This topology is automatically updated as domain controllers are added, removed, or moved between sites.

- Attribute-level replication. When an attribute of an object is modified, only that attribute, and minimal metadata that describes that attribute, is replicated. The entire object is not replicated except when the object is created.

- Distinct control of intrasite replication (within a single site) and intersite replication (between sites).

- Collision detection and management. It is possible, although rare, that an attribute will have been modified on two different domain controllers during a single replication window. In such an event, the two changes will have to be reconciled. Active Directory has resolution algorithms that satisfy almost every such situation.

It is easier to understand Active Directory replication by examining each of its components. The following sections examine the components of Active Directory replication.

Connection Objects

A domain controller replicates changes from another domain controller because of AD DS connection objects, also called simply *connection objects*. Connection objects appear in the administrative tools in the Active Directory Sites and Services snap-in as objects contained in the NTDS Settings container of a domain controller's server object. Figure 11-10 shows an example: a connection object in SERVER02 configures replication from SERVER01 to SERVER02. A connection object represents a replication path from one domain controller to another.

Connection objects are one-way, representing inbound-only replication. Replication in Active Directory is always a pull technology. In the domain illustrated in Figure 11-10, SERVER02 pulls changes from SERVER01. SERVER02 is considered, in this example, a downstream replication partner of SERVER01. SERVER01 is the upstream partner. Changes from SERVER01 flow to SERVER02.

NOTE Force replication

You can force replication between two domain controllers by right-clicking the connection object and choosing Replicate Now. Remember replication is inbound only, so to replicate both domain controllers, you will need to replicate the inbound connection object of each domain controller.

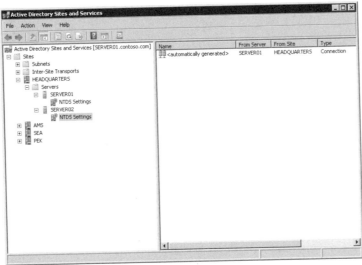

Figure 11-10   A connection object in the Active Directory Sites and Services snap-in

The Knowledge Consistency Checker

The replication paths built between domain controllers by connection objects create the replication topology for the forest. Luckily, you do not have to create the replication topology manually. By default, Active Directory creates a topology that ensures effective replication. The topology is two-way so that if any one domain controller fails, replication will continue uninterrupted. The topology also ensures that there are no more than three hops between any two domain controllers.

You'll notice in Figure 11-10 that the connection object indicates it was automatically generated. On each domain controller, a component of Active Directory called the knowledge consistency checker (KCC) helps generate and optimize the replication automatically between domain controllers within a site. The KCC evaluates the domain controllers in a site and creates connection objects to build the two-way, three-hop topology described earlier. If a domain controller is added to or removed from the site, or if a domain controller is not responsive, the KCC rearranges the topology dynamically, adding and deleting connection objects to rebuild an effective replication topology.

You can manually create connection objects to specify replication paths that should persist. Manually created connection objects are not deleted by the KCC. To create a connection object, locate the server object for the downstream replication partner—the DC that will receive changes from a source DC. Right-click the NTDS Settings container in the server object and choose New Active Directory Domain Services Connection. In the Find Active Directory Domain Controllers dialog box, select the upstream replication partner and click OK. Give the new connection object a name and click OK. Then open the properties of the connection object; use the Description field to indicate the purpose of any manually created connection object.

Within a site, there are very few scenarios that would require creating a connection object. One such scenario is standby operations masters. Operations masters are discussed in Chapter 10. It is recommended that you select domain controllers as standby operations masters to be used in the event that the operations master role must be transferred or seized. A standby operations master should be a direct replication partner with the current operations master. Thus, if a domain controller named DC01 is the RID master, and DC02 is the system that will take the RID master role if DC01 is taken offline, then a connection object should be created in DC02 so that it replicates directly from DC01.

Intrasite Replication

After connection objects between the domain controllers in a site have been established—automatically by the KCC or manually—replication can take place. Intrasite replication involves the replication of changes within a single site.

Notification

Consider the site shown in Figure 11-10. When SERVER01 makes a change to a partition, it queues the change for replication to its partners. SERVER01 waits 15 seconds, by default, to notify its first replication partner, SERVER02, of the change. *Notification* is the process by which an upstream partner informs its downstream partners that a change is available. SERVER01 waits three seconds, by default, between notifications to additional partners. These delays, called the *initial notification delay* and the *subsequent notification delay*, are designed to stagger network traffic caused by intrasite replication.

Upon receiving the notification, the downstream partner, SERVER02, requests the changes from SERVER01, and the directory replication agent (DRA) performs the transfer of the attribute from SERVER01 to SERVER02. In this example, SERVER01 made the initial change to Active Directory. It is the originating domain controller, and the change it made originates the change. When SERVER02 receives the change from SERVER01, it makes the change to its directory. The change is not called a replicated change, but it is a change nonetheless. SERVER02 queues the change for replication to its own downstream partners.

SERVER03 is a downstream replication partner of SERVER02. After 15 seconds, SERVER02 notifies SERVER03 that it has a change. SERVER03 makes the replicated change to its directory and then notifies its downstream partners. The change has made two hops, from SERVER01 to SERVER02 and from SERVER02 to SERVER03. The replication topology will ensure that there are no more than three hops before all domain controllers in the site have received the change. At approximately 15 seconds per hop, that means the change will have fully replicated in the site within one minute.

Polling

It is possible that SERVER01 might not make any changes to its replicas for quite a long time, particularly during off hours. In this case, SERVER02, its downstream replication partner, will not receive notifications from SERVER01. It is also possible that SERVER01 might be offline, which would also prevent it from sending notifications to SERVER02, so it's important for SERVER02 to know that its upstream partner is online and simply does not have any changes.

This is achieved through a process called *polling*. Polling involves the downstream replication partner contacting the upstream replication partner with a query as to whether any changes are queued for replication. By default, the polling interval for intrasite replication is once per hour. It is possible, although not recommended, to configure the polling frequency from the properties of a connection object by clicking Change Schedule.

If an upstream partner fails to respond to repeated polling queries, the downstream partner launches the KCC to check the replication topology. If the upstream server is indeed offline, the site's replication topology is rebuilt to accommodate the change.

Site Links

The KCC assumes that within a site, all domain controllers can reach each other. It builds an intrasite replication topology that is agnostic to the underlying network connectivity. Between sites, however, you can represent the network paths over which replication should occur by creating *site link* objects. A site link contains two or more sites. The intersite topology generator (ISTG), a component of the KCC, builds connection objects between servers in each of the sites to enable intersite replication—replication between sites.

Site links are greatly misunderstood, and the important thing to remember about a site link is that it represents an available path for replication. A single site link does not control the network routes that are used. When you create a site link and add sites to it, you are telling Active Directory that it can replicate between any of those sites. The ISTG will create connection objects, and those objects will determine the actual path of replication. Although the replication topology built by the ISTG will effectively replicate Active Directory, it might not be efficient, given your network topology.

An example will illustrate this concept. When you create a forest, one site link object is created: DEFAULTIPSITELINK. By default, each new site that you add is associated with the DEFAULTIPSITELINK. Consider an organization with a data center at the headquarters and three branch offices. The three branch offices are each connected to the data center with a dedicated link. You create sites for each branch office, Seattle (SEA), Amsterdam (AMS), and Beijing (PEK). The network and site topology is shown in Figure 11-11.

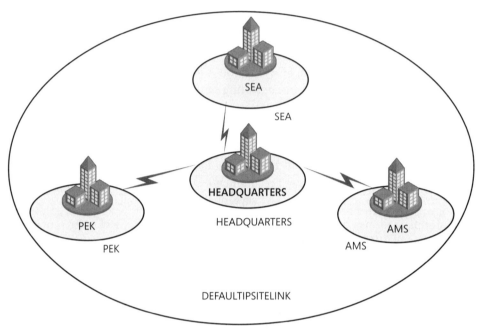

Figure 11-11 Network topology and a single site link

Because all four sites are on the same site link, you are instructing Active Directory that all four sites can replicate with each other. That means it is possible that Seattle will replicate changes from Amsterdam, Amsterdam will replicate changes from Beijing, and Beijing will replicate changes from Headquarters, which in turn replicates changes from Seattle. In several of these replication paths, the replication traffic on the network flows from one branch through the headquarters on its way to another branch. With a single site link, you have not created a hub-and-spoke replication topology even though your network topology is hub-and-spoke.

Therefore, it is recommended that you manually create site links that reflect your physical network topology. Continuing the preceding example, you would create three site links:

- HQ-AMS, including the Headquarters and Amsterdam sites
- HQ-SEA, including the Headquarters and Seattle sites
- HQ-PEK, including the Headquarters and Beijing sites

You would then delete the DEFAULTIPSITELINK. The resulting topology is shown in Figure 11-12.

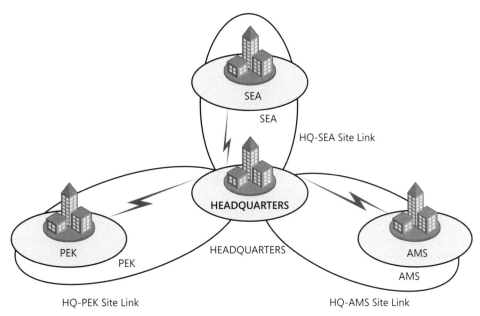

Figure 11-12   Network topology and a three-site link

After you have created site links, the ISTG will use the topology to build an intersite replication topology connecting each site. Connection objects will be built to configure the intersite replication paths. These connection objects are created automatically, and although you can create connection objects manually, few scenarios require manually creating intersite connection objects.

Replication Transport Protocols

You'll notice, in the Active Directory Sites and Services snap-in, that site links are contained within a container named IP that itself is inside the Inter-Site Transports container. Changes are replicated between domain controllers, using one of two protocols:

- **Directory Service Remote Procedure Call (DS-RPC)**   DS-RPC appears in the Active Directory Sites and Services snap-in as IP. IP is used for all intrasite replication and is the default, and preferred, protocol for intersite replication.
- **Inter-Site Messaging—Simple Mail Transport Protocol (ISM-SMTP)**   Also known simply as SMTP, this protocol is used only when network connections between sites are unreliable or are not always available.

In general, you can assume you will use IP for all intersite replication. Very few organizations use SMTP for replication because of the administrative overhead required to configure and manage a certificate authority (CA) and because SMTP replication is not supported for the domain naming context, meaning that if a site uses SMTP to replicate to the rest of the enterprise, that site must be its own domain.

Exam Tip   Although, in the production environment, you are highly unlikely to use SMTP for replication, it is possible you will encounter SMTP replication on the exam. The most important thing to remember is that if two sites can replicate only with SMTP—if IP is not an option—then those two sites must be separate domains in the forest. SMTP cannot be used to replicate the domain naming context.

Bridgehead Servers

The ISTG creates a replication topology between sites on a site link. To make replication more efficient, one domain controller is selected to be the *bridgehead server*. The bridgehead server is responsible for all replication into and out of the site for a partition. For example, if a data center site contains five DCs, one of the DCs will be the bridgehead server for the domain naming context. All changes made to the domain partition within the data center will replicate to all DCs in the site. When the changes reach the bridgehead server, those changes will be replicated to bridgehead servers in branch offices, which in turn replicate the changes to DCs in their sites. Similarly, any changes to the domain naming context in branch offices will be replicated from the branches' bridgehead servers to the bridgehead server in the data center, which in turn replicates the changes to other DCs in the data center. Figure 11-13 illustrates intrasite replication within two sites and the intersite replication using connection objects between the bridgehead servers in the sites.

To summarize, the bridgehead server is the server responsible for replicating changes to a partition from other bridgehead servers in other sites. It is also polled by bridgehead servers in other sites to determine when it has changes that they should replicate.

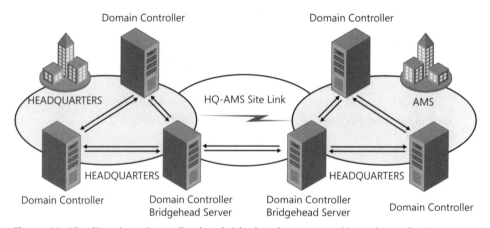

Figure 11-13   Sites, intrasite replication, bridgehead servers, and intersite replication

Bridgehead servers are selected automatically, and the ISTG creates the intersite replication topology to ensure that changes are replicated effectively between bridgeheads sharing a site link. Bridgeheads are selected per partition, so it is possible that one DC in a site might be the bridgehead server for the schema and another might be for the configuration. However, you will usually find that one domain controller is the bridgehead server for all partitions in a site unless there are domain controllers from other domains or application directory partitions, in which case bridgeheads will be chosen for those partitions.

Preferred Bridgehead Servers

You can also designate one or more *preferred bridgehead servers*. To designate a domain controller as a preferred bridgehead server, open the properties of the server object in the Active Directory Sites And Services snap-in, select the transport protocol, which will almost always be IP, and click Add.

You can configure more than one preferred bridgehead server for a site, but only one will be selected and used as the bridgehead. If that bridgehead fails, one of the other preferred bridgehead servers will be used.

It's important to understand that if you have specified one or more bridgehead servers and none of the bridgeheads is available, no other server is automatically selected, and replication does not occur for the site even if there are servers that could act as bridgehead servers. In an ideal world, you should not configure preferred bridgehead servers. However, performance considerations might suggest that you assign the bridgehead server role to domain controllers with greater system resources. Firewall considerations might also require that you assign a single server to act as a bridgehead instead of allowing Active Directory to select and possibly reassign bridgehead servers over time.

Configuring Intersite Replication

After you have created site links and the ISTG has generated connection objects to replicate partitions between bridgehead servers that share a site link, your work might be complete. In many environments, particularly those with straightforward network topologies, site links might be sufficient to manage intersite replication. In more complex networks, however, you can configure additional components and properties of replication.

Site Link Transitivity

By default, site links are transitive. That means, continuing the example from earlier, that if Amsterdam and Headquarters sites are linked, and Headquarters and Seattle sites are linked, then Amsterdam and Seattle are transitively linked. This means, theoretically, that the ISTG could create a connection object directly between a bridgehead in Seattle and a bridgehead in Amsterdam, again working around the hub-and-spoke network topology.

You can disable site link transitivity by opening the properties of the IP transport in the Inter-Site Transports container and deselecting Bridge All Site Links. Before you do this in a production environment, be sure to spend time reading the technical resources about replication in the Windows Server technical libraries on Microsoft TechNet at *http://technet.microsoft.com*.

Exam Tip   For the certification exam, you need to know that site links are transitive by default, that transitivity can be disabled, and that when transitivity is disabled, you might want to build site link bridges.

Site Link Bridges

A site link bridge connects two or more site links in a way that creates a transitive link. Site link bridges are necessary only when you have cleared the Bridge All Site Links option for the transport protocol. Remember that site link transitivity is enabled by default, in which case site link bridges have no effect.

Figure 11-14 illustrates the use of a site link bridge in a forest in which site link transitivity has been disabled. By creating a site link bridge, AMS-HQ-SEA, that includes the HQ-AMS and HQ-SEA site links, those two site links become transitive, so a replication connection can be made between a domain controller in Amsterdam and a domain controller in Seattle.

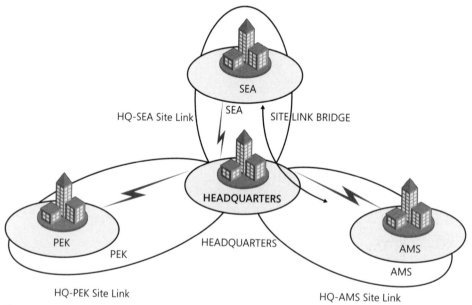

Figure 11-14   A site link bridge that includes the HQ-AMS and HQ-SEA site links

Site Link Costs

Site link costs are used to manage the flow of replication traffic when there is more than one route for replication traffic. You can configure site link cost to indicate that a link is faster, more reliable, or is preferred. Higher costs are used for slow links, and lower costs are used for fast links. Active Directory replicates using the connection with the lowest cost.

By default, all site links are configured with a cost of 100. To change the site link cost, open the properties of a site link and change the value in the Cost spin-box, shown in Figure 11-15.

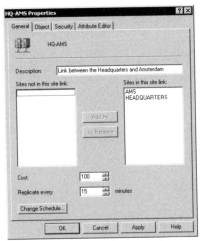

Figure 11-15 The properties of a site link

Returning to the example used earlier in the lesson, imagine if a site link was created between the Amsterdam and Beijing sites, as shown in Figure 11-16. Such a site link could be configured to allow replication between domain controllers in those two sites in the event that the links to the headquarters became unavailable. You might want to configure such a topology as part of a disaster recovery plan, for example.

With the default site link cost of 100 assigned to the AMS-PEK site link, Active Directory will replicate changes directly between Amsterdam and Beijing. If you configure the site link cost to 300, changes will replicate between Amsterdam and the Headquarters, then between the Headquarters and Beijing at a cost of 200 rather than directly over the AMS-PEK site link at a cost of 300.

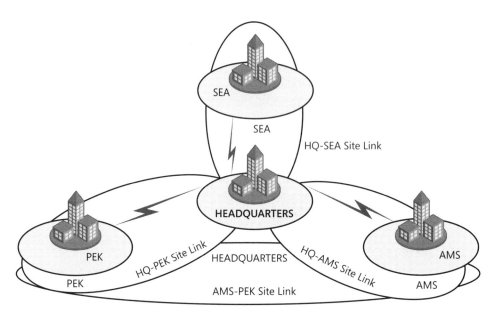

Figure 11-16 Site links and costs

Replication Frequency

Intersite replication is based only on polling; there is no notification. Every three hours, by default, a bridgehead server will poll its upstream replication partners to determine whether changes are available. This replication interval is too long for organizations that want changes to the directory to replicate more quickly. You can change the polling interval for each site link. Open the site link's properties and change the value in the Replicate Every spin-box, shown in Figure 11-15.

The minimum polling interval is 15 minutes. That means, using Active Directory's default replication configuration, a change made to the directory in one site will take several minutes before it is replicated to domain controllers in another site.

Replication Schedules

By default, replication occurs 24 hours a day. However, you can restrict intersite replication to specific times by changing the schedule attributes of a site link. Open the properties of a site link and click the Change Schedule button. Using the Schedule For dialog box shown in Figure 11-17, you can select the times during which the link is available for replication. The link shown in the figure does not replicate from 8:00 A.M. to 6:00 P.M. Monday through Friday.

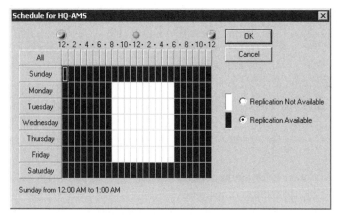

Figure 11-17   Site link schedule

You must be careful when scheduling site link availability. It is possible to schedule windows of availability that do not overlap, at which point replication will not happen. It's generally not recommended to configure link availability. If you do not require link scheduling, select the Ignore Schedules option in the properties of the IP transport protocol. This option causes any schedules for site link availability to be ignored, ensuring replication 24 hours a day over all site links.

Monitoring Replication

After you have implemented your replication configuration, you must be able to monitor replication for ongoing support, optimization, and troubleshooting. Two tools are particularly useful for reporting and analyzing replication: the Replication Diagnostics tool (*Repadmin.exe*) and Directory Server Diagnosis (*Dcdiag.exe*). This lesson introduces you to these powerful tools.

Repadmin.exe

The Replication Diagnostics tool, *Repadmin.exe*, is a command-line tool that enables you to report the status of replication on each domain controller. The information produced by *Repadmin.exe* can help you spot a potential problem before it gets out of control and troubleshoot problems with replication in the forest. You can view levels of detail down to the replication metadata for specific objects and attributes, enabling you to identify where and when a problematic change was made to Active Directory. You can even use *Repadmin.exe* to create the replication topology and force replication between domain controllers.

Like other command-line tools, you can type **repadmin /?** to see the usage information for the tool. Its basic syntax is as follows:

```
repadmin command arguments...
```

Repadmin.exe supports a number of commands that perform specific tasks. You can learn about each command by typing **repadmin /?:*command***. Most commands require arguments. Many commands take a *DSA_LIST* parameter, which is simply a network label (DNS or Net-BIOS name or IP address) of a domain controller. Some of the replication monitoring tasks you can perform with *Repadmin* are:

- **Displaying the replication partners for a domain controller**   To display the replication connections of a domain controller, type **repadmin /showrepl *DSA_LIST***. By default, *Repadmin.exe* shows only intersite connections. Add the */repsto* argument to see intersite connections as well.

- **Displaying connection objects for a domain controller**   Type **repadmin /showconn *DSA_LIST*** to show the connection objects for a domain controller.

- **Displaying metadata about an object, its attributes, and replication**   You can learn a lot about replication by examining an object on two different domain controllers to find out which attributes have or have not replicated. Type **repadmin /showobjmeta *DSA_LIST Object***, where *DSA_LIST* indicates the domain controller(s) to query. (You can use an asterisk [*] to indicate all domain controllers.) *Object* is a unique identifier for the object, its DN, or its GUID, for example.

You can also make changes to your replication infrastructure by using *Repadmin*. Some of the management tasks you can perform are:

- **Launching the KCC**   Type **repadmin /kcc** to force the KCC to recalculate the inbound replication topology for the server.

- **Forcing replication between two partners**   You can use *Repadmin* to force replication of a partition between a source and a target domain controller. Type **repadmin /replicate *Destination_DSA_LIST Source_DSA_Name Naming_Context***.

- **Synchronizing a domain controller with all replication partners**   Type **repadmin /syncall *DSA* /A /e** to synchronize a domain controller with all its partners, including those in other sites.

Dcdiag.exe

The Directory Service Diagnosis tool, *Dcdiag.exe*, performs a number of tests and reports on the overall health of replication and security for AD DS. Run by itself, *Dcdiag.exe* performs summary tests and reports the results. On the other extreme, *Dcdiag.exe /c* performs almost every test. The output of tests can be redirected to files of various types, including XML. Type **dcdiag /?** for full usage information.

You can also specify one or more tests to perform using the */test:Test Name* parameter. Tests that are directly related to replication include:

- **FrsEvent**   Reports any operation errors in the file replication system (FRS).
- **DFSREvent**   Reports any operation errors in the DFS replication (DFS-R) system.
- **Intersite**   Checks for failures that would prevent or delay intersite replication.
- **KccEvent**   Identifies errors in the knowledge consistency checker.
- **Replications**   Checks for timely replication between domain controllers.
- **Topology**   Checks that the replication topology is fully connected for all DSAs.
- **VerifyReplicas**   Verifies that all application directory partitions are fully instantiated on all domain controllers hosting replicas.

NOTE   *Repadmin.exe* and *Dcdiag.exe*

See the Help & Support Center for more information about *Repadmin.exe* and *Dcdiag.exe*.

PRACTICE **Configuring Replication**

In this practice, you will manage intrasite and intersite replication in the *contoso.com* domain. To perform the exercises in this practice, you must have completed the Lesson 1 practice as well as the Lesson 2 practice, "Replication and Directory Partitions," in this chapter.

▶ **Exercise 1   Create a Connection Object**

Configure direct replication between a domain controller that will be a standby operations master and the domain controller that is currently the operations master. Then, if the current operations master needs to be taken offline, the standby operations master is as up to date as possible with the operations master. In this exercise, you will create a connection object between SERVER01 and SERVER02, where SERVER02, the standby operations master, replicates from SERVER01, the current operations master.

1. Log on to SERVER01 as Administrator.
2. Open the Active Directory Sites And Services snap-in.
3. Expand Sites, HEADQUARTERS, Servers, and SERVER02.
4. Select the NTDS Settings node under SERVER02 in the console tree.
5. Right-click NTDS Settings and choose New Active Directory Domain Services Connection.
6. In the Find Active Directory Domain Controllers dialog box, select SERVER01 and click OK.

   Because the KCC has already created a connection from SERVER01 to SERVER02, a warning appears asking if you want to create another connection.
7. Click Yes.
8. In the New Object – Connection dialog box, type the name **SERVER01 – OPERATIONS MASTER** and click OK.

9. Right-click the new connection object in the details pane and choose Properties.

10. Examine the properties of the connection object. Do not make any changes.
    What partitions are replicated from SERVER01? Is SERVER02 a GC server?

11. Click OK to close the Properties dialog box.

12. Because the sample domain has only two DCs, and you will move the server in a later exercise, delete the connection object by right-clicking it and choosing Delete.

▶ **Exercise 2   Create Site Links**

In this exercise, you will create site links between the branch sites and the headquarters site.

1. In the Active Directory Sites And Services snap-in, expand Inter-Site Transports.

2. Select IP.

3. Right-click DEFAULTIPSITELINK and choose Rename.

4. Type **HQ-BRANCHA** and press Enter.

5. Double-click HQ-BRANCHA.

6. In the Sites In This Site Link list, select BRANCHB and click Remove. Click OK.

7. Right-click IP and choose New Site Link.

8. Type **HQ-BRANCHB** in the Name box.

9. In the Sites Not In This Site Link list, select Headquarters and click Add.

10. In the Sites Not In This Site Link list, select BRANCHB and click Add.

11. Click OK.

▶ **Exercise 3   Designate a Preferred Bridgehead Server**

You can designate a preferred bridgehead server that will handle replication to and from its site. This is useful when you want to assign the role to a domain controller in a site with greater system resources or when firewall considerations require that the role be assigned to a single, fixed system. In this exercise, you will designate a preferred bridgehead server for the site.

1. Expand Headquarters, Servers, and SERVER02.

2. Right-click SERVER02 and choose Properties.

3. In the Transports Available For Inter-Site Data Transfer list, select IP.

4. Click Add, and then click OK.

    It is recommended that if a site has a GC server, the domain controller acting as a GC server should be the preferred bridgehead server. When Active Directory designates a bridgehead server automatically, it selects a GC server if one is available.

▶ **Exercise 4   Configure Intersite Replication**

After you have created site links and, optionally, designated bridgehead servers, you can continue to refine and control replication by configuring properties of the site link. In this exercise, you will reduce the intersite replication polling frequency, and you will increase the cost of a site link.

1. Expand Inter-Site Transports.
2. Select the IP container in the console tree.
3. Double-click the HQ-BRANCHA site link.
4. In the Replicate Every spin-box, type **15** and click OK.
5. Double-click the HQ-BRANCHB site link.
6. In the Replicate Every box, type **15**.
7. Click the Change Schedule button.
8. Examine the Schedule For HQ-BRANCHB dialog box. Experiment with configuring the schedule but click Cancel when you are finished.
9. In the Cost spin-box, type **200**.
10. Click OK.

Lesson Summary

- Connection objects represent paths of replication between two domain controllers.
- Site links represent available network connectivity between two or more sites.
- Bridgehead servers in each site are responsible for replication to and from the site.
- The intersite topology generator (ISTG) creates connection objects between bridgehead servers that share a site link.
- If more than one connection is available, replication will proceed over the connection with the lowest cost.
- By default, site links are transitive. If you disable site link transitivity by clearing the Bridge All Site Links option in the properties of the intersite transport protocol, you might need to create site link bridges to create specific transitive links between two or more sites.

Lesson Review

You can use the following questions to test your knowledge of the information in Lesson 3, "Configuring Replication." The questions are also available on the companion CD if you prefer to review them in electronic form.

NOTE Answers

Answers to these questions and explanations of why each answer choice is right or wrong are located in the "Answers" section at the end of the book.

---

1. You are an administrator at Adventure Works. The Active Directory forest consists of three sites, Site A, Site B, and Site C. Site A and Site C are connected to Site B with a fast connection. Site A and Site C are connected to each other with a slow VPN connection. The Active Directory site link objects and their costs are as shown. You want to encourage replication to avoid the VPN connection. What should you do?

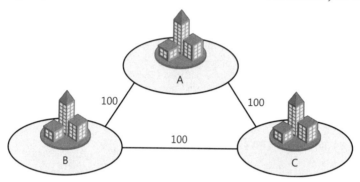

   A. Increase the cost of link A-B to 250.
   B. Increase the cost of link C-B to 250.
   C. Decrease the cost of links A-B and C-B to 75.
   D. Increase the cost of link A-C to 250.

2. You are an administrator at Adventure Works. The Active Directory forest consists of three sites, Site A, Site B, and Site C. The Active Directory site link objects and their costs are as shown. You want to ensure that all replication from Sites A and C goes to Site B before going to the other site. What should you do? (Choose all that apply. Each correct answer is part of the solution.)

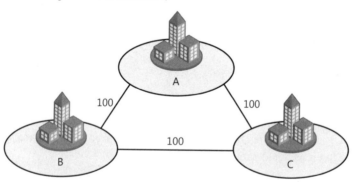

   A. Increase the cost of site link A-C to 300.
   B. Delete site link A-C.
   C. Deselect Bridge All Site Links.
   D. Reduce the costs of links A-B and B-C to 25.

3. The network infrastructure at Trey Research prevents direct IP connectivity between the data center and a research ship at sea. What must you do to support replication between the data center and the ship?

   A. Configure a separate domain in the forest for the ship.

   B. Increase the cost of the Active Directory site link containing the headquarters and the ship.

   C. Configure the domain controller on the ship as a preferred bridgehead server.

   D. Manually create a connection object between the domain controller on the ship and a domain controller at the headquarters.

4. You want to initiate replication manually between two domain controllers to verify that replication is functioning correctly. Which of the following tools can you use? (Choose all that apply.)

   A. The Active Directory Sites And Services snap-in

   B. *Repadmin.exe*

   C. *Dcdiag.exe*

   D. The Active Directory Domains And Trusts snap-in

Chapter Review

To further practice and reinforce the skills you learned in this chapter, you can perform the following tasks:

- Review the chapter summary.
- Review the list of key terms introduced in this chapter.
- Complete the case scenario. This scenario sets up a real-world situation involving the topics of this chapter and asks you to create a solution.
- Complete the suggested practices.
- Take a practice test.

Chapter Summary

- Domain controllers host replicas of Active Directory partitions: the schema, configuration, and domain naming contexts. You can configure domain controllers to host the partial attribute set (global catalog) or application directory partitions.
- Within a site, domain controllers replicate quickly, using a topology generated by the knowledge consistency checker (KCC), which is adjusted dynamically to ensure effective intersite replication.
- Between sites, the intersite topology generator (ISTG) creates a topology of connection objects between bridgehead servers in sites that share site links. Intersite replication is based on polling only, by default, with an initial frequency of every three hours.
- You can modify intersite replication behavior, including the replication frequency, site link costs, and preferred bridgehead servers.
- Advanced configuration is not generally necessary, but you can modify site link transitivity, create site link bridges, and configure site link schedules.
- The *Repadmin.exe* and *Dcdiag.exe* commands enable you to monitor and troubleshoot replication.

Key Terms

Use these key terms to understand better the concepts covered in this chapter.

- **intrasite**   Within a site.
- **intersite**   Between sites.
- **partial attribute set or global catalog (GC)**   A copy of every object from other domain naming contexts but a subset of attributes of those objects. The global catalog supports efficient forest-wide directory queries, provides universal group membership information at logon, and supports applications such as Exchange Server.
- **replica, partition, or naming context**   The top-level container of the Active Directory database. Partitions are replicated in their entirety. Every domain controller hosts a replica of the forest schema and configuration partitions. Each domain controller in a domain hosts a replica of that domain's naming context.
- **service localization**   The process by which a distributed service, available on more than one server, is provided to clients by a server in the clients' site or close to the clients' site. Domain controllers provide distributed services—authentication and directory access— and Active Directory sites and subnets localize the services so that clients use domain controllers in, or close to, their site.

Case Scenario

In the following case scenario, you will apply what you've learned about sites, subnets, partitions, and replication. You can find answers to these questions in the "Answers" section at the end of this book.

Case Scenario: Configuring Sites and Subnets

You are an administrator at Adventure Works. The Adventure Works network topology is illustrated as shown. Branch offices in Seattle, Chicago, and Miami are connected with fast, reliable links to the Denver site. Smaller branches in Portland and Fort Lauderdale are connected to Seattle and Miami, respectively. In Denver, the headquarters and the warehouse sites are connected with an extremely fast connection. There is one domain controller in each site except in the headquarters in Denver, where there are three. You are planning the Active Directory sites and replication for the domain.

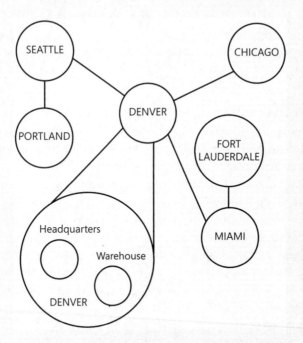

1. You want to ensure that, in Denver, any change to the directory replicates within one minute to all four domain controllers. How many Active Directory sites should you create for the Denver subnets?

2. A colleague recommends that you designate one of the domain controllers in the headquarters as a preferred bridgehead server. What are the advantages and disadvantages of doing so?

3. You want to ensure that replication follows a hub-and-spoke topology so that any change made to the directory in Denver replicates directly to all five branches and that any change made in one of the five branches replicates directly to Denver. Describe the site link changes you would make to support this goal.

4. For disaster planning purposes, you want the domain controller in the warehouse to be ready to take on forest and domain operations master roles performed by SERVER01 in the headquarters site. What change would you make to replication to support this goal?

Suggested Practices

To help you successfully master the exam objectives presented in this chapter, complete the following tasks.

Monitor and Manage Replication

In this practice, you will perform replication management and monitoring tasks, using both user interface and command-line tools. To perform these practices, you must have completed the practices in this chapter.

- **Practice 1**   Observe intersite replication by opening two instances of the Active Directory Users And Computers snap-in. In one instance, right-click the *contoso.com* domain, choose Change Domain Controller, and select SERVER01. In the other instance, right-click the *contoso.com* domain, choose Change Domain Controller, and select SERVER02. Using the SERVER01 snap-in, create an OU called People if it does not already exist. Within the People OU, create an OU called Temporary Employees. Using the SERVER02 snap-in, refresh the view to see that the objects were replicated successfully. Using the SERVER02 snap-in, create a new user named Replication Test. Confirm in the SERVER01 snap-in that the user object replicated.

- **Practice 2**   Observe the ICC and the ISTG by opening the Active Directory Sites And Services snap-in. Expand BRANCHA and Servers. Expand Headquarters and Servers. Drag SERVER02 from the HEADQUARTERS\Servers container to the BRANCHA\Servers container. In the SERVER01 Active Directory Users And Computers snap-in, create a new user object called Intersite Test 1. Examine the SERVER02 Active Directory Users And Computers snap-in. It is likely that the object replicated because the connection object between SERVER02 and SERVER01 continues to be treated as an intrasite replication connection. In the Active Directory Sites And Services snap-in, expand SERVER01, right-click NTDS Settings, choose All Tasks, and then select Check Replication Topology. Repeat the process with SERVER02. Refresh the Active Directory Sites And Services snap-in view. Select NTDS Settings in the SERVER01 container. You should see that the connection object from SERVER02 now shows that SERVER02 is in the BRANCHA site.

- **Practice 3**   Observe intersite replication and manual replication. In the SERVER01 Active Directory Users And Computers snap-in, add another user, named Intersite Test 2. In the SERVER02 snap-in, you should not see the object when you refresh the view. The servers are now replicated using intersite topology. In the Active Directory Sites And Services snap-in, select NTDS Settings under SERVER02. In the console details pane, right-click the connection object and choose Replicate Now.

Take a Practice Test

The practice tests on this book's companion CD offer many options. For example, you can test yourself on just one exam objective, or you can test yourself on all the 70-640 certification exam content. You can set up the test so that it closely simulates the experience of taking a certification exam, or you can set it up in study mode so that you can look at the correct answers and explanations after you answer each question.

MORE INFO   **Practice tests**

For details about all the practice test options available, see the "How to Use the Practice Tests" section in this book's introduction.

Chapter 12

Domains and Forests

In Chapter 1, "Installation," you learned that Active Directory Domain Services (AD DS) provides the foundation for an identity and access management solution, and you explored the creation of a simple AD DS infrastructure consisting of a single forest and a single domain. In subsequent chapters, you mastered the details of managing an AD DS environment. Now, you are ready to return to the highest level of an AD DS infrastructure and consider the model and functionality of your domains and forests. In this chapter, you will learn how to raise the domain and forest functionality levels within your environment, how to design the optimal AD DS infrastructure for your enterprise, how to migrate objects between domains and forests, and how to enable authentication and resource access across multiple domains and forests.

Exam objectives in this chapter:

- Configuring the Active Directory Infrastructure
  - ❏ Configure a forest or a domain.
  - ❏ Configure trusts.

Lessons in this chapter:

- Lesson 1: Understanding Domain and Forest Functional Levels 557
- Lesson 2: Managing Multiple Domains and Trust Relationships 567

Before You Begin

To complete the practices in this chapter, you must have created two domain controllers, named SERVER01 and SERVER02, in a domain named *contoso.com*. See Chapter 1 and Chapter 10, "Domain Controllers," for detailed steps for this task.

Real World

Dan Holme

In some organizations, there is a perception that domain controllers should be the last systems to be upgraded. My experience, however, has been that domain controllers (DCs) should be among the first systems that you should upgrade (after testing the upgrade in a lab, of course). Domain controllers are the cornerstone of identity and access management in your enterprise AD DS forest. Because of that, you should ensure that, wherever possible, DCs are dedicated—serving only the AD DS role and related core services, such as DNS. If your DCs are dedicated, the risk associated with upgrading them diminishes significantly—there are far fewer moving parts that could cause problems during an upgrade. Additionally, the sooner you upgrade your DCs, the sooner you can raise the domain and forest functional levels.

Functional levels enable the newer capabilities added by Microsoft Windows Server 2003 and Windows Server 2008. In return for added functionality, you are restricted as to the versions of Microsoft Windows that are supported for the domain controllers in the domain. (Member servers and workstations can run any version of Windows.) Some of the functionality, such as linked-value replication, last logon information, read-only domain controllers, fine-grained password policies, and Distributed File System Replication (DFS-R) of System Volume (SYSVOL), have a profound impact on the day-to-day security, management, and flexibility of AD DS. I encourage you to move with a reasonable but quick pace toward upgrading your domain controllers to Windows Server 2008 so you can raise the domain and forest functional levels to take advantage of these capabilities. They make a big difference.

Lesson 1: Understanding Domain and Forest Functional Levels

As you introduce Windows Server 2008 domain controllers into your domains and forest, you can begin to take advantage of new capabilities in Active Directory directory service. Domain and forest functional levels are operating modes of domains and forests, respectively. Functional levels determine the versions of Windows that you can use as domain controllers and the availability of Active Directory features.

After this lesson, you will be able to:
- Understand domain and forest functional levels.
- Raise domain and forest functional levels.
- Identify capabilities added by each functional level.

Estimated lesson time: 45 minutes

Understanding Functional Levels

Functional levels are like switches that enable new functionality offered by each version of Windows. Windows Server 2003 added several features to Active Directory, and Windows Server 2008 continues the evolution of AD DS. These features are not backward compatible, so if you have DCs running Windows 2000 Server, you cannot enable the functionality offered by later versions of Windows, so the newer functionality is disabled. Similarly, until all DCs are running Windows Server 2008, you cannot implement its enhancements to AD DS. Raising the functional level entails two major tasks:

- All domain controllers must be running the correct version of Windows Server.
- You must manually raise the functional level. It does not happen automatically.

NOTE Functional levels, operating system versions, and domain controllers

Remember that only domain controllers determine your ability to set a functional level. You can have member servers and workstations running any version of Windows within a domain or forest at any functional level.

Domain Functional Levels

The domain functional level affects the Active Directory features available within the domain and determines the versions of Windows that are supported for domain controllers within the domain. In previous versions of Windows, domain functional levels and modes, as they were called in Windows 2000 Server, supported domain controllers running Microsoft Windows NT 4.0. That support has ended with Windows Server 2008. All domain controllers must be running Windows 2000 Server or later before you can add the first Windows Server 2008 domain controller to the domain. Windows Server 2008 Active Directory supports three domain functional levels:

- Windows 2000 Native
- Windows Server 2003
- Windows Server 2008

Windows 2000 Native

The Windows 2000 Native domain functional level is the lowest functional level that supports a Windows Server 2008 domain controller. The following operating systems are supported for domain controllers:

- Windows 2000 Server
- Windows Server 2003
- Windows Server 2008

If you have domain controllers running Windows 2000 Server or Windows Server 2003, or if you expect that you might add one or more domain controllers running those previous versions of Windows, you should leave the domain at Windows 2000 Native functional level.

Windows Server 2003

After you have removed or upgraded all domain controllers running Windows 2000 Server, the domain functional level can be raised to Windows Server 2003. At this functional level, the domain can no longer support domain controllers running Windows 2000 Server, so all domain controllers must be running one of the following two operating systems:

- Windows Server 2003
- Windows Server 2008

Windows Server 2003 domain functional level adds a number of new features offered at the Windows 2000 Native domain functional level. These features include the following:

- **Domain controller rename**   The domain management tool, *Netdom.exe*, can be used to prepare for domain controller rename.
- **The *lastLogonTimestamp* attribute**   When a user or computer logs on to the domain, the *lastLogonTimestamp* attribute is updated with the logon time. This attribute is replicated within the domain.
- **The *userPassword* attribute**   Security principals in Active Directory include users, computers, and groups. A fourth object class, *inetOrgPerson*, is similar to a user and is used to integrate with several non-Microsoft directory services. At the Windows Server 2003 domain functional level, you can set the *userPassword* attribute as the effective password on both *inetOrgPerson* and *user* objects.

- **Default user and computer container redirection**   In Chapter 5, "Computers," you learned that you can use the *Redirusr.exe* and *Redircmp.exe* commands to redirect the default user and computer containers. Doing so causes new accounts to be created in specific organizational units rather than in the Users and Computers containers.

- **Authorization Manager policies**   Authorization Manager, a tool that can be used to provide authorization by applications, can store its authorization policies in AD DS.

- **Constrained delegation**   Applications can take advantage of the secure delegation of user credentials by means of the Kerberos authentication protocol. Delegation can be configured to be allowed only to specific destination services.

- **Selective authentication**   In Lesson 2, "Managing Multiple Domains and Trust Relationships," you will learn to create trust relationships between your domain and another domain or forest. Selective authentication enables you to specify the users and groups from the trusted domain or forest who are allowed to authenticate to servers in your forest.

Windows Server 2008

When all domain controllers are running Windows Server 2008, and you are confident that you will not need to add domain controllers running previous versions of Windows, you can raise the domain functional level to Windows Server 2008. Windows Server 2008 domain functional level supports domain controllers running only one operating system—Windows Server 2008.

Windows Server 2008 domain functional level adds four domain-wide features to AD DS:

- **DFS-R of SYSVOL**   In Chapter 10, you learned to configure SYSVOL so that it is replicated with Distributed File System Replication (DFS-R) instead of with File Replication Service (FRS). DFS-R provides a more robust and detailed replication of SYSVOL contents.

- **Advanced Encryption Services**   You can increase the security of authentication with Advanced Encryption Services (AES 128 and AES 256) support for the Kerberos protocol. AES replaces the RC4-HMAC (Hash Message Authentication Code) encryption algorithm.

- **Last interactive logon information**   When a user logs on to the domain, several attributes of the user object are updated with the time, the workstation to which the user logged on, and the number of failed logon attempts since the last logon.

- **Fine-grained password policies**   In Chapter 8, "Authentication," you learned about fine-grained password policies, which enable you to specify unique password policies for users or groups in the domain.

Raising the Domain Functional Level

You can raise the domain functional level after all domain controllers are running a supported version of Windows and when you are confident you will not have to add domain controllers running unsupported versions of Windows. To raise the domain functional level, open the Active Directory Domains And Trusts snap-in, right-click the domain, and choose Raise Domain Functional Level. The dialog box shown in Figure 12-1 enables you to select a higher domain functional level.

Figure 12-1   The Raise Domain Functional Level dialog box

IMPORTANT   One-way operation

Raising the domain functional level is a one-way operation. You cannot roll back to a previous domain functional level.

You can also raise the domain functional level by using the Active Directory Users And Computers snap-in. Right-click the domain and choose Raise Domain Functional Level, or right-click the root node of the snap-in and choose Raise Domain Functional Level from the All Tasks menu.

Forest Functional Levels

Just as domain functional levels enable certain domain-wide functionality and determine the versions of Windows that are supported for domain controllers in the domain, forest functional levels enable forest-wide functionality and determine the operating systems supported for domain controllers in the entire forest. Windows Server 2008 Active Directory supports three forest functional levels:

■   Windows 2000

- Windows Server 2003
- Windows Server 2008

Each functional level is described in the following sections.

Windows 2000

Windows 2000 forest functional level is the baseline, default functional level. At Windows 2000 functional level, domains can be running at any supported domain functional level:

- Windows 2000 Native
- Windows Server 2003
- Windows Server 2008

You can raise the forest functional level after all domains in the forest have been raised to the equivalent domain functional level.

Windows Server 2003

After all domains in the forest are at the Windows Server 2003 domain functional level, and when you do not expect to add any new domains with Windows 2000 Server domain controllers, you can raise the forest functional level to Windows Server 2003. At this forest functional level, domains can be running at the following domain functional levels:

- Windows Server 2003
- Windows Server 2008

The following features are enabled at the Windows Server 2003 forest functional level:

- **Forest trusts**   In Lesson 2, you will learn to create trust relationships between forests.
- **Domain rename**   You can rename a domain within a forest.
- **Linked-value replication**   At Windows 2000 forest functional level, a change to a group's membership results in the replication of the entire multivalued *member* attribute of the group. This can lead to increased replication traffic on the network and the potential loss of membership updates when a group is changed concurrently at different domain controllers. It also leads to a recommended cap of 5,000 members in any one group. Linked-value replication, enabled at the Windows Server 2003 forest functional level, replicates an individual membership change rather than the entire *member* attribute. This uses less bandwidth and prevents you from losing updates when a group is changed concurrently at different domain controllers.
- **Support for read-only domain controllers**   Chapter 8 discussed read-only domain controllers (RODCs). RODCs are supported at the Windows Server 2003 forest functional level. The RODC itself must be running Windows Server 2008.

> ### Quick Check
>
> - You want to add an RODC to a domain with Windows Server 2003 domain control-
>   lers. The domain is at the Windows Server 2003 functional level and already
>   includes one Windows Server 2008 domain controller. The forest is at the Windows
>   2000 functional level. Which two things must you do prior to adding the RODC?
>
> ### Quick Check Answer
>
> - You must raise the forest functional level to Windows Server 2003, and you must
>   run *Adprep /rodcprep*.

- **Improved Knowledge Consistency Checker (KCC) algorithms and scalability**   The intersite
  topology generator (ISTG) uses improved algorithms that enable AD DS to support replication in forests with more than 100 sites. At the Windows 2000 forest functional level,
  you must manually intervene to create replication topologies for forests with hundreds
  of sites. Additionally, the election of the ISTG uses an algorithm that is more efficient
  than at Windows 2000 forest functional level.

- **Conversion of *inetOrgPerson* objects to *user* objects**   You can convert an instance of an
  inetOrgPerson object, used for compatibility with certain non-Microsoft directory services, into an instance of class *user*. You can also convert a *user* object to an *inetOrgPerson*
  object.

- **Support for *dynamicObject* auxiliary class**   The schema allows instances of the dynamic
  auxiliary class in domain directory partitions. This object class can be used by certain
  applications and by developers.

- **Support for application basic groups and LDAP query groups**   Two new group types, called
  application basic groups and *LDAP query groups*, can be used to support role-based authorization in applications that use Authorization Manager.

- **Deactivation and redefinition of attributes and object classes**   Although you cannot delete
  an attribute or object class in the schema, at Windows Server 2003 for forest level, you
  can deactivate or redefine attributes or object classes.

Windows Server 2008

The Windows Server 2008 forest functional level does not add new forest-wide features. However, after the forest is configured to Windows Server 2008 forest functional level, new
domains added to the forest will operate at Windows Server 2008 domain functional level by
default. At this forest functional level, all domains must be at Windows Server 2008 domain
functional level, which means that all domain controllers must be running Windows Server
2008.

Raising the Forest Functional Level

Use the Active Directory Domains and Trusts snap-in to raise the forest functional level. Right-click the root node of the Active Directory Domains And Trusts snap-in, and choose Raise Forest Functional Level. The dialog box shown in Figure 12-2 enables you to choose a higher forest functional level.

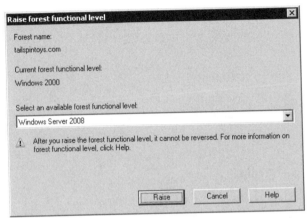

Figure 12-2   The Raise Forest Functional Level dialog box

Raise the forest functional level only when you are confident that you will not add new domains at unsupported domain functional levels. You cannot roll back to a previous forest functional level after raising it.

Exam Tip   Be sure to memorize the functionality that is enabled at each domain and forest functional level. Pay particular attention to the capabilities that affect you as an administrator.

PRACTICE Raising the Domain and Forest Functional Levels

In this practice, you will raise domain and forest functional levels. To perform the exercises in this practice, you must prepare at least one domain controller in a new domain in a new forest. Install a new full installation of Windows Server 2008.

To perform this exercise, you will need a new server running Windows Server 2008 full installation. The server must be named SERVERTST. Its configuration should be as follows:

- Computer Name: SERVERTST
- IPv4 address: 10.0.0.111
- Subnet Mask: 255.255.255.0
- Default Gateway: 10.0.0.1
- DNS Server: 10.0.0.111

Run *Dcpromo.exe* and create a new forest and a new domain named *tailspintoys.com*. Set the forest functional level to Windows 2000 and the domain functional level to Windows 2000 Native. Install DNS on the server. You will be warned that the server has a dynamic IP address. Click Yes. Also click Yes when you are informed that a DNS delegation cannot be created. Refer to Lesson 1, "Installing Active Directory Domain Services," of Chapter 1 for detailed steps to install Windows Server 2008 and to promote a domain controller as a new domain in a new forest.

In the *tailspintoys.com* domain, create two first-level organizational units (OUs) named Clients and People.

▶ **Exercise 1   Experience Disabled Functionality**

In this exercise, you will attempt to take advantage of capabilities supported at higher domain functional levels. You will see that these capabilities are not supported.

1. Log on to SERVERTST as the domain's Administrator.
2. Open a command prompt.
3. Type **redircmp.exe "ou=clients,dc=tailspintoys,dc=com"** and press Enter.

   A message appears indicating that redirection was not successful. This is because the domain functional level is not at least Windows Server 2003.
4. Type **redirusr.exe "ou=people,dc=tailspintoys,dc=com"** and press Enter.

   A message appears indicating that redirection was not successful. This is because the domain functional level is not at least Windows Server 2003.
5. Open the Active Directory Users And Computers snap-in.
6. Click the View menu, and select Advanced Features.
7. Double-click the Administrator account in the Users container.
8. Click the Attribute Editor tab.
9. Locate the *lastLogonTimestamp* attribute. Note that its value is *<not set>*.

▶ **Exercise 2   Raise the Domain Functional Level**

In this exercise, you will raise the domain functional level of the *tailspintoys.com* domain.

1. Open Active Directory Domains And Trusts.
2. Right-click the *tailspintoys.com* domain, and choose Raise Domain Functional Level.
3. Confirm that the Select An Available Domain Functional Level drop-down list indicates Windows Server 2003.
4. Click Raise. Click OK to confirm your change.

   A message appears informing you the functional level was raised successfully.
5. Click OK.

▶ **Exercise 3   Test Windows Server 2003 Domain Functional Level**

You will now discover that previously disabled functionality is now available.

1. Log off and log on as the domain Administrator.

2. Open a command prompt.

3. Type **redircmp.exe "ou=clients,dc=tailspintoys,dc=com"** and press Enter.

   A message appears indicating redirection was successful.

4. Type **redirusr.exe "ou=people,dc=tailspintoys,dc=com"** and press Enter.

   A message appears indicating redirection was successful.

5. Open the Active Directory Users And Computers snap-in.

6. Click the View menu, and ensure that Advanced Features is selected.

7. Double-click the Administrator account in the Users container.

8. Click the Attribute Editor tab.

9. Locate the *lastLogonTimestamp* attribute. Note that its value is now populated.

10. At the command prompt, type **dfsrmig /setglobalstate 0** and press Enter.

    A message appears stating that this function is available only at Windows Server 2008 domain functional level. In Chapter 10, you raised the domain functional level to Windows Server 2008 to configure DFS-R migration of SYSVOL.

Lesson Summary

■ Domain and forest functional levels determine which capabilities of Active Directory are supported and which versions of Windows are supported on domain controllers.

■ The Windows Server 2003 and Windows Server 2008 domain functional levels offer significant new functionality.

■ The Windows Server 2003 forest functional level enables linked-value replication, supports RODCs, and provides other capabilities. The Windows Server 2008 forest functional level adds no new functionality.

Lesson Review

You can use the following questions to test your knowledge of the information in Lesson 1, "Understanding Domain and Forest Functional Levels." The questions are also available on the companion CD if you prefer to review them in electronic form.

NOTE   Answers

Answers to these questions and explanations of why each answer choice is right or wrong are located in the "Answers" section at the end of the book.

---

1. You want to raise the domain functional level of a domain in the *contoso.com* forest. Which tool can you use? (Choose all that apply.)

    A. Active Directory Users And Computers

    B. Active Directory Schema

    C. Active Directory Sites And Services

    D. Active Directory Domains And Trusts

2. You are an administrator of the *contoso.com* domain. You want to add a read-only domain controller to a domain with one Windows Server 2003 domain controller and one Windows 2008 domain controller. Which of the following must be done before adding a new server as an RODC? (Choose all that apply. Each correct answer is part of the solution.)

    A. Upgrade the Windows 2003 domain controller to Windows Server 2008.

    B. Raise the domain functional level to Windows Server 2003.

    C. Raise the domain functional level to Windows Server 2008.

    D. Raise the forest functional level to Windows Server 2003.

    E. Run *Adprep /rodcprep*.

    F. Run *Adprep /forestprep*.

3. You have just finished upgrading all domain controllers in the *contoso.com* domain to Windows Server 2008. Domain controllers in the *subsidiary.contoso.com* domain will be upgraded in three months. You want to configure fine-grained password policies for several groups of users in *contoso.com*. What must you do first?

    A. Install a read-only domain controller.

    B. Run *Dfsrmig.exe*.

    C. Raise the forest functional level.

    D. Install the Group Policy Management Console (GPMC) feature.

Lesson 2: Managing Multiple Domains and Trust Relationships

Previous chapters in this training kit have prepared you to configure, administer, and manage a single domain. However, your enterprise Active Directory infrastructure might include a multidomain forest or even more than one forest. You might need to move objects between domains or restructure your domain model entirely. You might also be required to enable authentication and access to resources across domains and forests. In this lesson, you will learn the skills required to support multiple domains and forests.

> **After this lesson, you will be able to:**
> - Design an effective domain and tree structure for AD DS.
> - Identify the role of the Active Directory Migration Tool and the issues related to object migration and domain restructure.
> - Understand trust relationships.
> - Configure, administer, and secure trust relationships.
>
> **Estimated lesson time: 60 minutes**

Defining Your Forest and Domain Structure

With the perspective you have gained from the previous 11 chapters of this training kit, you are prepared to consider the design of your Active Directory forest, trees, and domains. Interestingly, the best practices guidance regarding forest and domain structure has evolved as enterprises around the world have put Active Directory into production in every conceivable configuration and as the Active Directory feature set has grown.

Dedicated Forest Root Domain

In the early days of Active Directory, it was recommended to create a dedicated forest root domain. You'll recall from Chapter 1 and Chapter 10 that the forest root domain is the first domain in the forest. A dedicated forest root domain's exclusive purpose is to administer the forest infrastructure. It contains, by default, the single master operations for the forest. It also contains highly sensitive groups, such as Enterprise Admins and Schema Admins, that can have far-reaching impact on the forest. The theory was that the dedicated forest root would enhance the security around these forest-wide functions. The dedicated forest root domain would also be less likely to become obsolete and would provide easier transfer of ownership. Underneath the dedicated forest root, according to early recommendations, would be a single global child domain with all the objects one thinks of in a domain: users, groups, computers, and so on. The structure would look something like Figure 12-3.

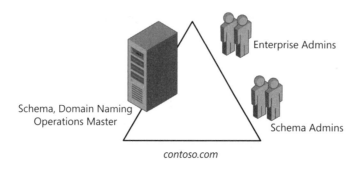

Schema, Domain Naming
Operations Master

Enterprise Admins

Schema Admins

contoso.com

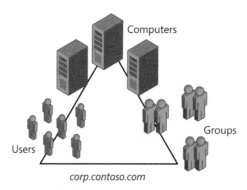

Computers

Users

Groups

corp.contoso.com

Figure 12-3   Example of a forest root domain

A Single-Domain Forest

NOTE   Single-domain forest the new recommendation

It is no longer recommended to implement a dedicated forest root domain for most enterprises. A single-domain forest is the most common design recommendation. There is no single design that is appropriate for every organization, so you must examine the characteristics of your enterprise against the design criteria presented later in this lesson.

After nine years on the market, Active Directory is better understood, and the former recommendation no longer applies. It is now recommended, for most organizations, to build a forest with a single domain. The experience and knowledge that have led to the change in guidance take into account that:

■ There are risks and costs associated with any multidomain forest, as you'll learn later in this lesson. A single domain bears the lowest hardware and support cost and reduces certain risks.

- There are not yet tools that enable an enterprise to perform pruning and grafting of Active Directory trees. In other words, you cannot break a domain off of your tree and transplant it in the forest of another enterprise. If that were possible, a dedicated forest root that you could maintain while transferring domains in and out of your forest would make more sense.

- You can implement least-privilege security within a single domain that is at least as secure, if not more secure, than in a forest with a dedicated forest root and a child domain.

Therefore, when you consider your domain design, you should begin with the assumption that you will have a single domain in your forest.

Multiple-Domain Forests

In some scenarios, a multiple-domain forest is required. The important point to remember is that you should never create a multiple-domain forest simply to reflect the organizational structure of your business. That structure—the business units, divisions, departments, and offices—will change over time. The logical structure of your directory service should not be dependent solely on organizational characteristics.

Instead, your domain model should be derived from the characteristics of domains themselves. Certain properties of a domain affect all objects within the domain, and if that consistent effect is not appropriate for your business requirements, you must create additional domains. A domain is characterized by the following:

- **A single domain partition, replicated to all domain controllers** The domain naming context contains the objects for users, computers, groups, policies, and other domain resources. It is replicated to every domain controller in the domain. If you need to partition replication for network topology considerations, you must create separate domains. Consider, however, that Active Directory replication is extremely efficient and can support large domains over connections with minimal bandwidth.

  If there are legal or business requirements that restrict replication of certain data to locations where you maintain domain controllers, you need to either avoid storing that data in the domain partition or create separate domains to segregate replication. In such cases, you should also ensure that the global catalog (GC) is not replicating that data.

- **A single Kerberos policy** The default Kerberos policy settings in AD DS are sufficient for most enterprises. If, however, you need distinct Kerberos policies, you will require distinct domains.

- **A single DNS namespace** An Active Directory domain has a single DNS domain name. If you need multiple domain names, you would need multiple domains. However, give serious consideration to the costs and risks of multiple domains before modeling your directory service domains to match arbitrary DNS name requirements.

In domains running domain functional levels lower than Windows Server 2008, a domain can support only one password and account lockout policy. Therefore, in prior versions of Windows, an organization requiring multiple password policies would need multiple domains to support that requirement. This is no longer the case in Windows Server 2008, which, at Windows Server 2008 domain functional level, can support fine-grained password policies.

Adding domains to a forest increases administrative and hardware costs. Each domain must be supported by at least two domain controllers, which must be backed up, secured, and managed. Even more domain controllers might be required to support cross-domain resource access in a geographically distributed enterprise. Additional domains can result in the need to move users between domains, which is more complicated than moving users between OUs. Group Policy objects and access control settings that are common for the enterprise will have to be duplicated for each domain.

These are just a few of the costs associated with a multiple-domain environment. There are also risks involved with having multiple domains. Most of these risks relate to the fact that a domain is not a security boundary–a forest is the security boundary. Within a forest, service administrators can cause forest-wide damage. There are several categories of vulnerability whereby a compromised administrative account, or an administrator with bad intent, could cause denial of service or damage to the integrity of the forest.

For example, an administrator in any domain can create universal groups, the membership of which is replicated to the GC. By creating multiple universal groups and overpopulating the *member* attribute, excessive replication could lead to denial of service on domain controllers acting as domain controllers in other domains. An administrator in any domain could also restore an outdated backup of the directory, which could corrupt the forest.

MORE INFO Security considerations for domain and forest design

For more information about the security considerations related to domain and forest design, see "Best Practices for Delegating Active Directory Administration" at *http://technet2.microsoft.com /windowsserver/en/library/e5274d27-88e5-4043-8f12-a8fa71cbcd521033.mspx*.

Given the costs and risks of multiple domains, it is highly recommended to construct a single-domain forest. The most common driver to multiple-domain forests is a significant requirement related to the replication of the domain naming context.

In a multidomain forest, it might make sense to create a dedicated forest root domain as an empty domain to act as the trust root for the forest. Trust roots will be discussed later in this lesson.

Multiple Trees

Remember that a tree is defined as a contiguous DNS namespace. If you have more than one domain, you can decide whether those domains share a contiguous DNS namespace and form a single tree, as shown at the top of Figure 12-4, or are in a noncontiguous DNS namespace, thus forming multiple trees, as shown on the bottom of Figure 12-4.

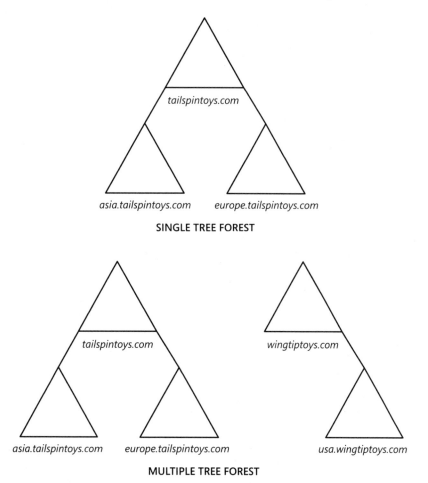

Figure 12-4   Forests with a single tree or multiple trees

Multiple Forests

A forest is an instance of Active Directory. All domains and domain controllers in a forest share replicas of the schema and configuration. Domain controllers that are GC servers host partial attribute sets for all objects in other domains in the forest. Domains in a forest share transitive, two-way trusts, meaning that all users in the domain belong to the Authenticated Users special identity in every domain. The forest's Enterprise Admins, Schema Admins, and Administrators groups in the forest root domain wield significant power over all objects in the forest.

If any of these characteristics of a forest are at odds with your business requirements, you might need multiple forests. In fact, given the market's current concerns with security, many consultants are recommending that organizations design either a single-domain forest or use multiple forests. Cross-forest trusts, discussed later in this lesson, and Active Directory Federation Services (AD FS) make it easier to manage authentication in multiple-forest enterprises.

MORE INFO   Planning the architecture

For more information about planning the architecture of an AD DS enterprise, see *http://technet2.microsoft.com/windowsserver2008/en/library/b1baa483-b2a3-4e03-90a6-d42f64b42fc31033.mspx?mfr=true*.

Moving Objects Between Domains and Forests

In multidomain scenarios, you might need to move users, groups, or computers between domains or forests to support business operations. You might need to move large quantities of users, groups, or computers between domains or forests to implement mergers and acquisitions or to restructure your domain model.

In each of these tasks, you move or copy the accounts from one domain (the *source* domain) into another domain (the *target* domain). Domain restructuring terminology, concepts, and procedures apply to *inter-forest migration* (between a Windows NT 4.0 or Active Directory source domain and an Active Directory target domain in a separate forest) and to *intra-forest migration* (that is, the restructuring or moving of accounts between domains in the same forest).

An inter-forest domain restructure preserves the existing source domain and clones (or copies) accounts into the target domain. This nondestructive method enables an enterprise to time the transition and even migrate in phases. Operations go uninterrupted because both domains are maintained in parallel to support operations for users in either domain. This method also provides a level of rollback because the original environment remains unaltered in any significant way. After the migration is complete, you can simply decommission the source domain by moving any remaining accounts, member servers, and workstations into the new domain and then taking source DCs offline, at which point, you can redeploy those DCs for roles in the new domain.

An intra-forest migration involves moving objects from the source domain to the target domain without decommissioning the source domain. After you have migrated objects, you can restructure your domains to consolidate operations and build a domain and OU structure that more accurately reflects your administrative model. Many organizations consolidate multiple domains into one Active Directory domain. This consolidation can result in cost savings and simplified administration by reducing administrative complexity and the cost of supporting your Active Directory environment.

Understanding the Active Directory Migration Tool

The Active Directory Migration Tool version 3 (ADMT v3) can perform object migration and security translation tasks. You can download ADMT v3 from *http://go.microsoft.com/fwlink/ ?LinkID=75627*. On that page, you will also find a detailed guide to the tool.

You can use ADMT to migrate objects between a source and a target domain. The migration can take place between domains in the same forest (an intra-forest migration) or between domains in different forests (an inter-forest migration). The ADMT provides wizards that automate migration tasks such as migrating users, groups, service accounts, computers, and trusts and performing security translation. You can perform these tasks, using the ADMT console or the command line, where you can simplify and automate the *Admt.exe* command with option files that specify parameters for the migration task. Then, with a simple text file, you can list objects to migrate rather than have to enter each object on the command line. ADMT also provides interfaces that enable you to script migration tasks with languages such as Microsoft VBScript. Run the ADMT console and open the online Help function for details about how to use ADMT from the command line and about scripting the ADMT.

When performing migration tasks, ADMT enables you to simulate the migration so that you can evaluate potential results and errors without making changes to the target domain. Wizards provide the Test The Migration Settings And Migrate Later option. You can then configure the migration task, test the settings, and review the log files and wizard-generated reports. After identifying and resolving any problems, you can perform the migration task. You will repeat this process of testing and analyzing results as you migrate users, groups, and computers and perform security translations.

Security Identifiers and Migration

Uninterrupted resource access is the primary concern during any migration. Further, to perform a migration, you must be comfortable with the concepts of security identifiers (SIDs), tokens, access control lists (ACLs), and *sIDHistory*.

SIDs are domain-unique values that are assigned to the accounts of security principals—users, groups, and computers, for example—when those accounts are created. When a user logs on, a token is generated that includes the primary SID of the user account and the SIDs of groups to which the user belongs. The token thus represents the user with all the SIDs associated with the user and the user's group memberships.

Resources are secured using a security descriptor (SD) that describes the permissions, ownership, extended rights, and auditing of the resource. Within the SD are two ACLs. The system ACL (SACL) describes auditing. The discretionary ACL (DACL) describes resource access permissions. Many administrators and documents refer to the DACL as the ACL. The DACL lists permissions associated with security principals. Within the list, individual access control entries (ACEs) link a specific permission with the SID of a security principal. The ACE can be an allow or deny permission.

When a user attempts to access a resource, the Local Security Authority Subsystem (LSASS) compares the SIDs in the user's token against the SIDs in the ACEs in the resource's ACL.

When you migrate accounts to a new domain, the accounts are copied or cloned from the source domain to the target domain. New SIDs are generated for the accounts in the target domain, so the SIDs of new accounts will not be the same as the SIDs of the accounts in the source domain. That is, even though the cloned accounts have the same name and many of the same properties, because the SIDs are different, the accounts are technically different and will not have access to resources in the source domain. You have two ways to address this problem: *sIDHistory* or security translation:

- **sIDHistory**   Enterprises typically prefer to take advantage of the *sIDHistory* attribute to perform effective domain restructuring. The capitalization, which appears odd, reflects the capitalization of the attribute in the AD schema. AD security principals (which include users, groups, and computers) have a principal SID and a *sIDHistory* attribute, which can contain one or more SIDs that are also associated with the account. When an account is copied to a target domain, the unique principal SID is generated by Active Directory in the target domain. Optionally, the *sIDHistory* attribute can be loaded with the SID of the account in the source domain. When a user logs on to an Active Directory domain, the user's token is populated with the principal SID and the *sIDHistory* of the user account and groups to which the user belongs. The LSASS uses the SIDs from the *sIDHistory* just like any other SID in the token to maintain the user's access to resources in the source domain.

■ **Security translation**   Security translation is the process of examining each resource's SD, including its ACLs, identifying each SID that refers to an account in the source domain and replacing that SID with the SID of the account in the target domain. The process of remapping ACLs (and other elements in the SD) to migrated accounts in the target domain is also called re-ACLing. As you can imagine, security translation or re-ACLing would be a tedious process to perform manually in anything but the simplest environment. Migration tools such as ADMT automate security translation. ADMT can translate the SDs and policies of resources in the source domain to refer to the corresponding accounts in the target domain. Specifically, ADMT can translate:

- ❏ File and folder permissions.
- ❏ Printer permissions.
- ❏ Share permissions.
- ❏ Registry permissions.
- ❏ User rights.
- ❏ Local profiles, which involves changing file, folder, and registry permissions.
- ❏ Group memberships.

In most domain restructuring and migration projects, *sIDHistory* is used to maintain access and functionality during the migration; then, security translation is performed.

MORE INFO   Domain migration

For more information about domain migration, SIDs, and SID history, see the "Domain Migration Cookbook" at *http://technet.microsoft.com/en-us/library/bb727135.aspx*.

Group Membership

The final concern related to resource access is that of group membership. Global groups can contain members only from the same domain. Therefore, if you clone a user to the target domain, the new user account cannot be a member of the global groups in the source domain to which the source user account belonged.

To address this issue in an inter-forest migration, you will first migrate global groups to the target domain. Those global groups will maintain the source groups' SIDs in their *sIDHistory* attributes, thus maintaining resource access. Then, you will migrate users. As you migrate users, ADMT evaluates the membership of the source account and adds the new account to the same group in the target domain. If the group does not yet exist in the target domain, ADMT can create it automatically. In the end, the user account in the target domain will belong to global groups in the target domain. The user and the user's groups will contain the SIDs of the source accounts in their *sIDHistory* attributes. Therefore, the user will be able to access resources in the source domain that have permissions assigned to the source accounts.

In an intra-forest migration, the process works differently. A global group is created in the target domain as a universal group so that it can contain users from both the source and the target domains. The new group gets a new SID, but its *sIDHistory* is populated with the SID of the global group in the source domain, thereby maintaining resource access for the new group. After all users have been migrated from the source to the target domain, the scope of the group is changed back to global.

Other Migration Concerns

You must address a number of issues in planning for and executing the migration of objects between domains and forests. Each of the concerns is detailed in the ADMT user guide, available from the ADMT download page listed earlier. Among the greatest concerns are:

- **Password migration**   ADMT supports migrating user passwords; however, it cannot confirm that those passwords comply with the policies of the target domain regarding password length and complexity. Nonblank passwords will migrate regardless of the target domain password policy, and users will be able to log on with those passwords until they expire, at which time a new, compliant password must be created. If you are concerned about locking down the environment at the time of migration, this might not be a satisfactory process. You might, instead, want to let ADMT configure complex passwords or script an initial password and then force the user to change the password at the first logon.

- **Service accounts**   Services on domain computers might use domain-based user accounts for authentication. As those user accounts are migrated to the target domain, services must be updated with the new service account identity. ADMT automates this process.

- **Objects that cannot be migrated**   Some objects cannot be seamlessly migrated. ADMT cannot migrate built-in groups such as Domain Admins or the domain local Administrators group. The user guide provides details for working around this limitation.

Exam Tip   For the 70-640 exam, you should recognize that the ADMT is used to copy or move accounts between domains. You should also understand that the new account in the target domain will have a new SID but that correct use of the tool can migrate group memberships and can populate *sIDHistory* with the SID of the source account.

Understanding Trust Relationships

Whenever you are implementing a scenario involving two or more AD DS domains, it is likely you will be working with *trust relationships*, or *trusts*. It is important that you understand the purpose, functionality, and configuration of trust relationships.

Trust Relationships Within a Domain

In Chapter 5, you were guided through what happens when a domain member server or workstation joins a domain. While in a workgroup, the computer maintains an identity store in the security accounts manager (SAM) database, it authenticates users against that identity store, and it secures system resources only with identities from the SAM database. When the computer joins a domain, it forms a trust relationship with the domain. The effect of that trust is that the computer allows users to be authenticated not by the local system and its local identity store but by the authentication services and identity store of the domain: AD DS. The domain member also allows domain identities to be used to secure system resources. For example, Domain Users is added to the local Users group, giving Domain Users the right to log on locally to the system. Also, domain user and group accounts can be added to ACLs on files, folders, registry keys, and printers on the system. All domain members have similar trust relationships with the domain, enabling the domain to be a central store of identity and a centralized service providing authentication.

Trust Relationships Between Domains

With that foundation, you can extend the concept of trust relationships to other domains. A trust relationship between two domains enables one domain to trust the authentication service and the identity store of another domain and to use those identities to secure resources. In effect, a trust relationship is a logical link established between domains to enable pass-through authentication.

There are two domains in every trust relationship: a trusting domain and a trusted domain. The trusted domain holds the identity store and provides authentication for users in that identity store. When a user in the directory of the trusted domain logs on to or connects to a system in the trusting domain, the trusting domain cannot authenticate that user because the user is not in its data store, so it passes the authentication to a domain controller in the trusted domain. The trusting domain, therefore, *trusts* the trusted domain to authenticate the identity of the user. The trusting domain *extends trust* to the authentication services and the identity store of the trusted domain.

Because the trusting domain trusts the identities in the trusted domain, the trusting domain can use the trusted identities to grant access to resources. Users in a trusted domain can be given user rights such as the right to log on to workstations in the trusting domain. Users or global groups in the trusted domain can be added to domain local groups in the trusting domain. Users or global groups in the trusted domain can be given permissions to shared folders by adding the identities to ACLs in the trusting domain.

The terminology can be confusing, and it is often easier to understand trust relationships with a figure. Figure 12-5 shows a simple diagram of a trust relationship. Domain A trusts Domain B. That makes Domain A the trusting domain and Domain B the trusted domain. If a user in Domain B connects to or logs on to a computer in Domain A, Domain A will pass the authentication request to a domain controller in Domain B. Domain A can also use the identities from Domain B–users and groups, for example–to grant user rights and resource access in Domain A. A user or group in Domain B can, therefore, be added to an ACL on a shared folder in Domain A. A user or group in Domain B can also be added to a domain local group in Domain A.

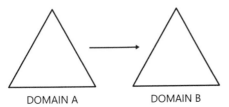

DOMAIN A   DOMAIN B

Figure 12-5   Diagram of a simple trust relationship

Exam Tip   Trust relationships are highly likely to appear on the 70-640 exam. Be certain that you completely understand the terms *trusted*, *trusting*, and *trust*. It is helpful when taking the exam to draw trust relationships so that you can more easily analyze which domain is trusted and has users and groups that the trusting domain can use to grant access to resources. Always make sure that the trust is extended from the domain with resources, such as computers and shared folders, to the domain with users.

Characteristics of Trust Relationships

Trust relationships between domains can be characterized by two attributes of the trust:

- **Transitivity**   Some trusts are not transitive, and others are transitive. In Figure 12-6, Domain A trusts Domain B, and Domain B trusts Domain C. If the trusts are transitive, then Domain A trusts Domain C. If they are not transitive, then Domain A does not trust Domain C. In most cases, you could create a third trust relationship, specifying that Domain A trusts Domain C. With transitive trusts, that third relationship is not necessary; it is implied.

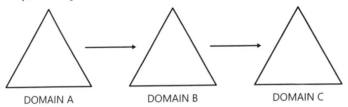

DOMAIN A   DOMAIN B   DOMAIN C

Figure 12-6   A trust relationship example

- **Direction** A trust relationship can be one-way or two-way. In a one-way trust, such as the trust illustrated in Figure 12-5, users in the trusted domain can be given access to resources in the trusting domain, but users in the trusting domain cannot be given access to resources in the trusted domain. In most cases, you can create a second, one-way trust in the opposite direction to achieve that goal. For example, you can create a second trust relationship in which Domain B trusts Domain A. Some trust relationships are by nature two-way. In a two-way trust, both domains trust the identities and authentication services of the other domain.

- **Automatic or Manual** Some trusts are created automatically. Other trusts must be created manually.

Within a forest, all domains trust each other. That is because the root domain of each tree in a forest trusts the forest root domain—the first domain installed in the forest—and each child domain trusts its parent domain. All trusts automatically created should never be deleted and are transitive and two-way. The net result is that a domain trusts the identity stores and authentication services of all other domains in its forest. Users and global groups from any domain in the forest can be added to domain local groups, can be given user rights, and can be added to ACLs on resources in any other domain in the forest. Trusts to other forests and to domains outside the forest must be manually established. With that summary, you can look at the details of trusts within and outside of an Active Directory forest.

Authentication Protocols and Trust Relationships

Windows Server 2003 Active Directory authenticates users with one of two protocols—Kerberos v5 or NT LAN Manager (NTLM). Kerberos v5 is the default protocol used by computers running Windows Server 2008, Windows Vista, Windows Server 2003, Windows XP, and Windows 2000 Server. If a computer involved in an authentication transaction does not support Kerberos v5, the NTLM protocol is used instead.

Kerberos Authentication Within a Domain

When a user logs on to a client running Kerberos v5, the authentication request is forwarded to a domain controller. Each Active Directory domain controller acts as a key distribution center (KDC), a core component of Kerberos. After validating the identity of the user, the KDC on the domain controller gives the authenticated user what is known as a ticket-granting ticket (TGT).

When the user needs to access resources on a computer in the same domain, the user must first obtain a valid session ticket for the computer. Session tickets are provided by the KDC of a domain controller, so the user returns to a domain controller to request a session ticket. The user presents the TGT as proof that he or she has already been authenticated. This enables the KDC to respond to the user's session ticket request without having to re-authenticate the user's identity. The user's session ticket request specifies the computer and the service the user wants to access. The KDC identifies that the service is in the same domain based on the service principal name (SPN) of the requested server. The KDC then provides the user with a session ticket for the service.

The user then connects to the service and presents the session ticket. The server is able to determine that the ticket is valid and that the user has been authenticated by the domain. This happens through private keys, a topic that is beyond the scope of this lesson. The server, therefore, does not need to authenticate the user; it accepts the authentication and identity provided by the domain with which the computer has a trust relationship.

All these Kerberos transactions are handled by Windows clients and servers and are transparent to users themselves.

Kerberos Authentication Within a Forest

Each child domain in a forest trusts its parent domain with an automatic, two-way, transitive trust called a *parent-child trust*. The root domain of each tree in a domain trusts the forest root domain with an automatic, two-way, transitive trust called a *tree-root trust*.

These trust relationships create what is referred to as the *trust path* or *trust flow* in a forest. The trust path is easy to understand with a diagram, as shown in Figure 12-7. The forest consists of two trees, the *tailspintoys.com* tree and the *wingtiptoys.com* tree. The *tailspintoys.com* domain is the forest root domain. On the top of Figure 12-7 is the forest as seen from a DNS perspective. On the bottom of the figure is the trust path. It indicates that the *wingtiptoys.com* tree root domain trusts the *tailspintoys.com* domain.

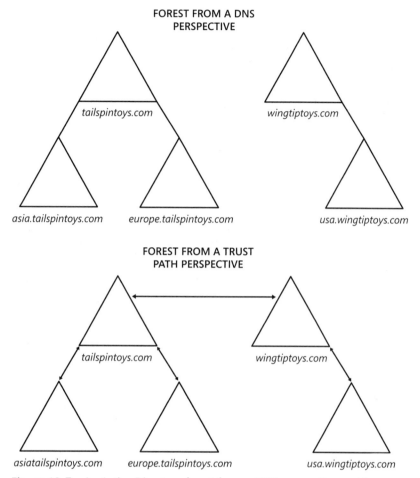

Figure 12-7   An Active Directory forest from a DNS perspective and from a trust path perspective

Kerberos authentication uses the trust path to provide a user in one domain a session ticket to a service in another domain. If a user in *usa.wingtiptoys.com* wants to access a shared folder on a server in *europe.tailspintoys.com*, the following transactions occur:

1. The user logs on to a computer in *usa.wingtiptoys.com* and is authenticated by a domain controller in *usa.wingtiptoys.com*, using the authentication process described in the previous section. The user obtains a TGT for the domain controller in *usa.wingtiptoys.com*.

   The user wants to connect to a shared folder on a server in *europe.tailspintoys.com*.

2. The user contacts the KDC of a domain controller in *usa.wingtiptoys.com* to request a session ticket for the server in *europe.tailspintoys.com*.

3. The domain controller in *usa.wingtiptoys.com* identifies, based on the SPN, that the desired service resides in *europe.tailspintoys.com*, not in the local domain.

The job of the KDC is to act as a trusted intermediary between a client and a service. If the KDC cannot provide a session ticket for the service because the service is in a trusted domain and not in the local domain, the KDC will provide the client with a *referral* to help it obtain the session ticket it is requesting.

The KDC uses a simple algorithm to determine the next step. If the KDC domain is trusted directly by the service's domain, the KDC gives the client a referral to a domain controller in the service's domain. If not, but if a transitive trust exists between the KDC and the service's domain, the KDC provides the client a referral to the next domain in the trust path.

4. The *usa.wingtiptoys.com* is not trusted directly by *europe.tailspintoys.com*, but a transitive trust exists between the two domains, so the KDC in the *usa.wingtiptoys.com* domain gives the client a referral to a domain controller in the next domain in the trust path, *wingtiptoys.com*.

5. The client contacts the KDC in the referral domain, *wingtiptoys.com*.

6. Again, the KDC determines that the service is not in the local domain and that *europe.tailspintoys.com* does not trust *wingtiptoys.com* directly, so it returns a referral to a domain controller in the next domain in the trust path, *tailspintoys.com*.

7. The client contacts the KDC in the referral domain, *tailspintoys.com*.

8. The KDC determines that the service is not in the local domain and that *europe.tailspintoys.com* trusts *tailspintoys.com* directly, so it returns a referral to a domain controller in the *europe.tailspintoys.com* domain.

9. The client contacts the KDC in the referral domain, *europe.tailspintoys.com*.

10. The KDC in *europe.tailspintoys.com* returns to the client a session ticket for the service.

11. The client contacts the server and provides the session ticket; the server provides access to the shared folder based on the permissions assigned to the user and the groups to which the user belongs.

This process might seem complicated, but recall that it is handled in a way that is completely transparent to the user.

The reverse process occurs if a user from *usa.wingtiptoys.com* logs on to a computer in the *europe.tailspintoys.com* domain. The initial authentication request must traverse the trust path to reach a KDC in the *usa.wingtiptoys.com* domain to authenticate the user.

Although it is not necessary to master the details of Kerberos authentication between domains in a forest for the 70-640 exam, it can help you in the real world to have a basic understanding that cross-domain authentication in a forest follows a trust path.

Manual Trusts

Four types of trusts must be created manually:

- Shortcut trusts
- External trusts
- Realm trusts
- Forest trusts

Each of these types of trusts will be discussed in the following sections.

Creating Manual Trust Relationships

The steps to create trusts are similar across categories of trusts. You must be a member of the Domain Admins or Enterprise Admins group to create a trust successfully.

To create a trust relationship, complete the following steps:

1. Open the Active Directory Domains And Trusts snap-in.
2. Right-click the domain that will participate in one side of the trust relationship, and choose Properties.

   You must be running Active Directory Domains And Trusts with credentials that have permissions to create trusts in this domain.
3. Click the Trusts tab.
4. Click the New Trust button.

   The New Trust Wizard guides you through the creation of the trust.
5. On the Trust Name page, type the DNS name of the other domain in the trust relationship, and then click Next.
6. If the domain you entered is not within the same forest, you will be prompted to select the type of trust, which will be one of the following:
   - Forest
   - External
   - Realm

   If the domain is in the same forest, the wizard knows it is a shortcut trust.
7. If you are creating a realm trust, you will be prompted to indicate whether the trust is transitive or nontransitive.
8. On the Direction Of Trust page, shown in Figure 12-8, select one of the following:
   - Two-Way establishes a two-way trust between the domains.
   - One-Way: Incoming establishes a one-way trust in which the domain you selected in step 2 is the trusted domain, and the domain you entered in step 5 is the trusting domain.

❑ One-Way: Outgoing establishes a one-way trust in which the domain you selected in step 2 is the trusting domain, and a domain you entered in step 5 is the trusted domain.

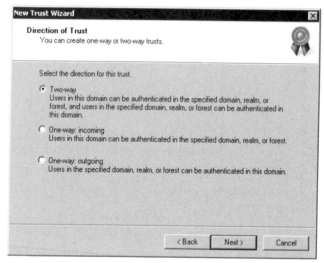

Figure 12-8 The Direction Of Trust page

9. Click Next.

10. On the Sides Of Trust page, shown in Figure 12-9, select one of the following:

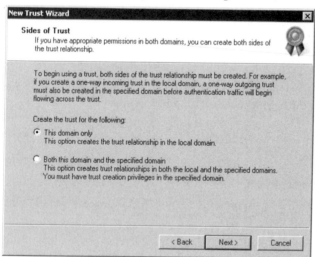

Figure 12-9 The Sides Of Trust page

❑ Both This Domain And The Specified Domain establishes both sides of the trust. This requires that you have permission to create trusts in both domains.

❑ This Domain Only creates the trust relationship in the domain you selected in step 2. An administrator with permission to create trusts in the other domain must repeat this process to complete the trust relationship.

The next steps will depend on the options you selected in steps 8 and 10. The steps will involve one of the following:

❑ If you selected Both This Domain And The Specified Domain, you must enter a user name and password with permissions to create the trust in the domain specified in step 5.

❑ If you selected This Domain Only, you must enter a trust password. A trust password is entered by administrators on each side of a trust to establish the trust. It should not be the administrators' user account passwords. Instead, it should be a unique password used only for the purpose of creating this trust. The password is used to establish the trust, and then the domains change it immediately.

11. If the trust is an outgoing trust, you are prompted to choose one of the following:

❑ Selective Authentication

❑ Domain-Wide Authentication or Forest-Wide Authentication, depending on whether the trust type is an external or forest trust, respectively.

Authentication options are discussed in the section "Securing Trust Relationships," later in this chapter.

12. The New Trust Wizard summarizes your selections on the Trust Selections Complete page. Click Next.

The Wizard creates the trust.

13. The Trust Creation Complete page appears. Verify the settings, and then click Next.

You will then have the opportunity to confirm the trust. This option is useful if you have created both sides of the trust or if you are completing the second side of a trust.

If you selected Both This Domain And The Specified Domain in step 8, the process is complete. If you selected This Domain Only in step 8, the trust relationship will not be complete until an administrator in the other domain completes the process:

■ If the trust relationship you established is a one-way, outgoing trust, then an administrator in the other domain must create a one-way, incoming trust.

■ If the trust relationship you established is a one-way, incoming trust, an administrator in the other domain must create a one-way, outgoing trust.

■ If the trust relationship you established is a two-way trust, an administrator in the other domain must create a two-way trust.

MORE INFO   **Procedures for creating trusts**

You can find detailed procedures for creating each type of trust at *http://technet2.microsoft.com /WindowsServer/en/library/f82e82fc-0700-4278-a166-4b8ab47b36db1033.mspx*.

Shortcut Trusts

In an earlier section, you followed 11 steps of the process used to grant a session ticket for a client to access a resource in another domain within a forest. Most of those steps involved referrals to domains on the trust path between the user's domain and the domain of the shared folder. When a user from one domain logs on to a computer in another domain, the authentication request must also traverse the trust path. This can affect performance, and, if a domain controller is not available in a domain along the trust path, the client will not be able to authenticate or to access the service.

Shortcut trusts are designed to overcome those problems by creating a trust relationship directly between child domains in the forest trust path. Two shortcut trusts are illustrated in Figure 12-10.

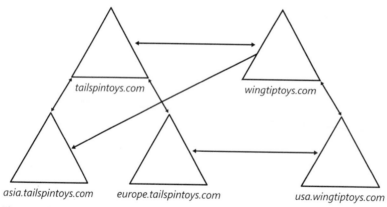

Figure 12-10   Shortcut trusts

Shortcut trusts optimize authentication and session ticket requests between domains in a multidomain forest. By eliminating the trust path, they eliminate the time required to traverse the trust path and, thereby, can significantly improve performance of session ticket requests.

Shortcut trusts can be one-way or two-way. In either case, the trust is transitive. In Figure 12-10, a one-way shortcut trust exists whereby *wingtiptoys.com* trusts *asia.tailspintoys.com*. When a user from *asia.tailspintoys.com* logs on to a computer in *wingtiptoys.com* or requests a resource in *wingtiptoys.com*, the request can be referred directly to a domain controller in the trusted domain, *asia.tailspintoys.com*. However, the reverse is not true. If a user in *wingtiptoys.com* logs on to a computer in *asia.tailspintoys.com*, the authentication request will traverse the trust path up to *tailspintoys.com* and down to *wingtiptoys.com*.

A two-way shortcut trust is illustrated between *usa.wingtiptoys.com* and *europe.tailspintoys.com*. Users in both domains can be authenticated by and can request resources from computers in the other domain, and the shortcut trust path will be used.

External Trusts

When you need to work with a domain that is not in your forest, you might need to create an external trust. An external trust is a trust relationship between a domain in your forest and a Windows domain that is not in your forest. Examples are shown in Figure 12-11.

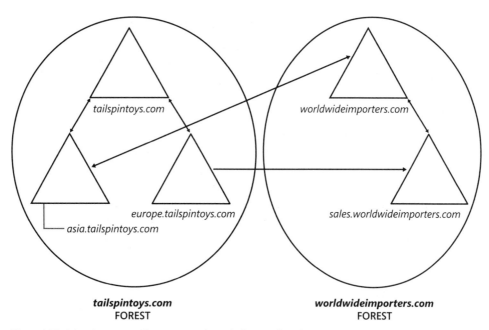

tailspintoys.com
FOREST

worldwideimporters.com
FOREST

Figure 12-11   An external trust to a domain in another forest

In Figure 12-11, you can see a one-way trust between the *sales.worldwideimporters.com* domain and the *europe.tailspintoys.com* domain. The Europe domain trusts the Sales domain, so users in the Sales domain can log on to computers in the Europe domain or connect to resources in the Europe domain.

Figure 12-11 also shows a two-way trust between the *worldwideimporters.com* domain and the *asia.tailspintoys.com* domain. Users in each domain can be given access to resources in the other domain. Technically, all external trusts are nontransitive, one-way trusts. When you create a two-way external trust, you are actually creating two one-way trusts, one in each direction.

When you create an outgoing external trust, Active Directory creates a foreign security principal object for each security principal in the trusted domain. Those users, groups, and computers can then be added to domain local groups or to ACLs on resources in the trusting domain.

To increase the security of an external trust relationship, you can choose Selective Authentication on the Outgoing Trust Authentication Level page of the New Trust Wizard. Additionally, domain quarantine, also called SID filtering, is enabled by default on all external trusts. Both of these configurations are detailed in the "Securing Trust Relationships" section, later in this chapter.

Realm Trusts

When you need cross-platform interoperability with security services based on other Kerberos v5 implementations, you can establish a realm trust between your domain and a UNIX Kerberos v5 realm. Realm trusts are one-way, but you can establish one-way trusts in each direction to create a two-way trust. By default, realm trusts are nontransitive, but they can be made transitive.

If a non-Windows Kerberos v5 realm trusts your domain, the realm trusts all security principals in your domain. If your domain trusts a non–Windows Kerberos v5 realm, users in the realm can be given access to resources in your domain; however, the process is indirect. When users are authenticated by a non–Windows Kerberos realm, Kerberos tickets do not contain all the authorization data needed for Windows. Therefore, an account mapping system is used. Security principals are created in the Windows domain and are mapped to a foreign Kerberos identity in the trusted non–Windows Kerberos realm. The Windows domain uses only these proxy accounts to evaluate access to domain objects that have security descriptors. All Windows proxy accounts can be used in groups and on ACLs to control access on behalf of the non–Windows security principal. Account mappings are managed through Active Directory Users and Computers.

Forest Trusts

When you require collaboration between two separate organizations represented by two separate forests, you can consider implementing a forest trust. A forest trust is a one-way or two-way transitive trust relationship between the forest root domains of two forests. Figure 12-12 shows an example of a forest trust between the *tailspintoys.com* forest and the *worldwideimporters.com* forest.

A single forest trust relationship allows the authentication of a user in any domain by any other domain in either forest, assuming the forest trust is two-way. If the forest trust is one-way, any user in any domain in the trusted forest can be authenticated by computers in the trusting forest. Forest trusts are significantly easier to establish, maintain, and administer than are separate trust relationships between each of the domains in the forests. Forest trusts are particularly useful in scenarios involving cross-organization collaboration, mergers and acquisitions, or within a single organization that has more than one forest, to isolate Active Directory data and services.

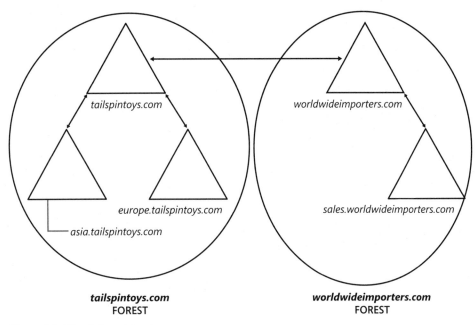

tailspintoys.com
FOREST

worldwideimporters.com
FOREST

Figure 12-12   A forest trust

When you establish a forest trust relationship, domain quarantine (also called SID filtering) is enabled by default. Domain quarantine is discussed in the "Securing Trust Relationships" section, later in this chapter. You can specify whether the forest trust is one-way, incoming or outgoing, or two-way. As mentioned earlier, a forest trust is transitive, allowing all domains in a trusting forest to trust all domains in a trusted forest. However, forest trusts are not themselves transitive. For example, if the *tailspintoys.com* forest trusts the *worldwideimporters.com* forest, and the *worldwideimporters.com* forest trusts the *northwindtraders.com* forest, those two trust relationships do not allow the *tailspintoys.com* forest to trust the *northwindtraders.com* forest. If you want those two forests to trust each other, you must create a specific forest trust between them.

Several requirements must be met before you can implement a forest trust. The forest functional level must be Windows Server 2003 or later. In addition, you must have a specific DNS infrastructure to support a forest trust.

MORE INFO   **DNS requirements for a forest trust**

You can learn about the DNS requirements for a forest trust at *http://technet2.microsoft.com /WindowsServer/en/library/f5c70774-25cd-4481-8b7a-3d65c86e69b11033.mspx*.

Administering Trusts

If you are concerned that a trust relationship is not functioning, you can validate a trust relationship between any two Windows domains. You cannot validate a trust relationship to a Kerberos v5 realm. To validate a trust relationship, complete the following steps.

1. Open Active Directory Domains And Trusts.
2. In the console tree, right-click the domain that contains the trust that you want to validate, and then click Properties.
3. Click the Trusts tab.
4. Select the trust you want to validate.
5. Click Properties.
6. Click Validate.
7. Do one of the following, and then click OK:
   - ❏ Click Yes, Validate The Incoming Trust. Enter credentials that are members of the Domain Admins or Enterprise Admins groups in the reciprocal domain.
   - ❏ Click No, Do Not Validate The Incoming Trust. It is recommended that you repeat this procedure for the reciprocal domain.

   You can also verify a trust from the command prompt by typing the following command:

   ```
   netdom trust TrustingDomainName /domain:TrustedDomainName /verify
   ```

There can also be reason to remove a manually created trust. To do so, follow these steps.

1. Open Active Directory Domains And Trusts.
2. In the console tree, right-click the domain that contains the trust you want to validate, and then click Properties.
3. Click the Trusts tab.
4. Select the trust you want to remove.
5. Click Remove.
6. Do one of the following, and then click OK:
   - ❏ Click Yes, Remove The Trust From Both The Local Domain And The Other Domain. Enter credentials that are members of the Domain Admins or Enterprise Admins groups in the reciprocal domain.
   - ❏ Click No, Remove The Trust From The Local Domain Only. It is recommended that you repeat this procedure for the reciprocal domain.
7. To delete a manually created trust from the command prompt, use the *Netdom.exe* command with the following syntax:

   ```
   netdom trust TrustingDomainName /domain:TrustedDomainName
       /remove [/force] /UserD:User /PasswordD:*
   ```

The *UserD* parameter is a user with credentials in the Enterprise Admins or Domain Admins group of the trusted domain. Specifying the *PasswordD:** parameter causes *Netdom.exe* to prompt you for the password to the account. The */force* switch is required when removing a realm trust.

NOTE **Command-line tools to manage and test trust relationships**

The Windows Domain Manager, *Netdom.exe*, and other command-line tools can be used to manage and test trust relationships. See *http://technet2.microsoft.com/windowsserver/en/library/108124dd-31b1-4c2c-9421-6adbc1ebceca1033.mspx?mfr=true* for details regarding these commands.

Securing Trust Relationships

When you configure a trust relationship that enables your domain to trust another domain, you open up the possibility for users in the trusted domain to gain access to resources in your domain. The following sections examine components related to the security of a trusting domain's resources.

Authenticated Users

A trust relationship itself does not grant access to any resources; however, it is likely that by creating a trust relationship, users in the trusted domain will have immediate access to a number of your domain's resources. This is because many resources are secured with ACLs that give permissions to the Authenticated Users group.

Membership in Domain Local Groups

As you learned in Chapter 4, "Groups," the best practice for managing access to a resource is to assign permissions to a domain local group. You can then nest users and groups from your domain into the domain local group and, thereby, grant them access to the resource. Domain local security groups can also include users and global groups from trusted domains as members. Therefore, the most manageable way to assign permissions to users in a trusted domain is to make them or their global groups members of a domain local group in your domain.

ACLs

You can also add users and global groups from a trusted domain directly to the ACLs of resources in a trusting domain. This approach is not as manageable as the previous method, using a domain local group, but it is possible.

Transitivity

When you create a realm trust, the trust is nontransitive by default. If you make it transitive, you open up the potential for users from domains and realms trusted by the Kerberos v5 realm to gain access to resources in your domain. It is recommended to use nontransitive trusts unless you have a compelling business reason for a transitive realm trust.

Domain Quarantine

By default, domain quarantine, also called SID filtering, is enabled on all external and forest trusts. When a user is authenticated in a trusted domain, the user presents authorization data that includes the SIDs of the user's account in the groups to which the user belongs. Additionally, the user's authorization data includes security identifiers from other attributes of the user and his or her groups.

Some of the SIDs presented by the user from the trusted domain might not have been created in the trusted domain. For example, if a user is migrated from one domain into another, a new SID is assigned to the migrated account. The migrated account will, therefore, lose access to any resources that had permissions assigned to the SID of the user's former account. To enable the user to continue to access such resources, an administrator performing a migration can specify that the *sIDHistory* attribute of the user's migrated account will include the former account's SID. When the user attempts to connect to the resource, the original SID in the *sIDHistory* attribute will be authorized for access.

In a trusted domain scenario, it is possible that a rogue administrator could use administrative credentials in the trusted domain to load SIDs into the *sIDHistory* attribute of a user that are the same as SIDs of privileged accounts in your domain. That user would then have inappropriate levels of access to resources in your domain.

Domain quarantine prevents this problem by enabling the trusting domain to filter out SIDs from the trusted domain that are not the primary SIDs of security principals. Each SID includes the SID of the originating domain, so when a user from a trusted domain presents the list of the user's SIDs and the SIDs of the user's groups, SID filtering instructs the trusting domain to discard all SIDs without the domain SID of the trusted domain.

Domain quarantine is enabled by default for all outgoing trusts to external domains and forests. Disable domain quarantine only if one or more of the following are true:

- You have extremely high levels of confidence in the administrators of the trusted domain.
- Users or groups have been migrated to the trusted domain with their SID histories preserved, and you want to grant those users or groups permissions to resources in the trusting domain based on the *sIDHistory* attribute.

To disable domain quarantine, type the following command:

```
netdom trust TrustingDomainName /domain:TrustedDomainName /quarantine:no
```

To re-enable domain quarantine, type this command:

```
netdom trust TrustingDomainName /domain:TrustedDomainName /quarantine:yes
```

Exam Tip   You might encounter either term—*domain quarantine* or *SID filtering*—on the 70-640 exam. Remember that this procedure is used so that users from a trusted domain are authorized using only the SIDs that originate in the trusted domain. An effect of domain quarantine is that the trusting domain ignores SIDs in the *sIDHistory* attribute, which typically contains the SIDs of accounts from a domain migration.

Selective Authentication

When you create an external trust or a forest trust, you can control the scope of authentication of trusted security principals. There are two modes of authentication for an external or forest trust:

- Selective authentication
- Domain-wide authentication (for an external trust) or forest-wide authentication (for a forest trust)

If you choose domain-wide or forest-wide authentication, all trusted users can be authenticated for access to services on all computers in the trusting domain. Trusted users can, therefore, be given permission to access resources anywhere in the trusting domain. With this authentication mode, you must have confidence in the security procedures of your enterprise and in the administrators who implement those procedures so that inappropriate access is not assigned to trusted users. Remember, for example, that users from a trusted domain or forest are considered Authenticated Users in the trusting domain, so any resource with permissions granted to Authenticated Users will be immediately accessible to trusted domain users if you choose domain-wide or forest-wide authentication.

If, however, you choose selective authentication, all users in the trusted domain are trusted identities; however, they are allowed to authenticate only for services on computers that you have specified. For example, imagine that you have an external trust with a partner organization's domain. You want to ensure that only users from the marketing group in the partner organization can access shared folders on only one of your many file servers. You can configure selective authentication for the trust relationship and then give the trusted users the right to authenticate only for that one file server.

To configure the authentication mode for a new outgoing trust, use the Outgoing Trust Authentication Level page of the New Trust Wizard. Configure the authentication level for an existing trust, open the properties of the trusting domain in Active Directory Domains And Trusts, select the trust relationship, click Properties, and then click the Authentication tab, shown in Figure 12-13.

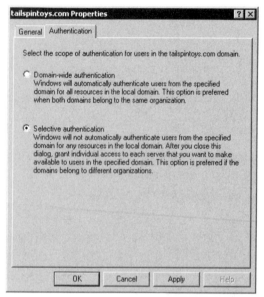

Figure 12-13   The Authentication tab of a trust relationship's Properties dialog box

After you have selected Selective Authentication for the trust, no trusted users will be able to access resources in the trusting domain, even if those users have been given permissions. The users must also be assigned the Allowed To Authenticate permission on the computer object in the domain. To assign this permission, open the Active Directory Users And Computers snap-in and make sure that Advanced Features is selected in the View menu. Open the properties of the computer to which trusted users should be allowed to authenticate—that is, the computer that trusted users will log on to or that contains resources to which trusted users have been given permissions. On the Security tab, add the trusted users or a group that contains them, and select the Allow check box for the Allowed To Authenticate permission, shown in Figure 12-14.

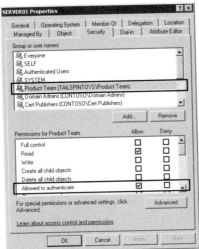

Figure 12-14   Assigning the Allowed To Authenticate permission to a trusted group

---

Quick Check

■ You have configured selective authentication for an outgoing trust to the domain of a partner organization. You want to give a group of auditors in the partner organization permission to a shared folder on SERVER32. Which two permissions must you configure?

Quick Check Answer

■ You must assign the auditors the Allowed To Authenticate permission for the SERVER32 computer object. You must also give the auditors NTFS permissions to the shared folder.

PRACTICE **Administering a Trust Relationship**

In this practice, you will create, secure, and administer a trust relationship between the *contoso.com* domain and the *tailspintoys.com* domain. In this scenario, Contoso, Ltd., is forming a partnership with Tailspin Toys. A team of product developers at Tailspin Toys require access to a shared folder in the Contoso domain. To perform this practice, you must have completed the practice in Lesson 1, "Understanding Domain and Forest Functional Levels," so that you have two domain controllers, one in the *contoso.com* domain and forest and one in the *tailspintoys.com* domain and forest.

▶ **Exercise 1   Configure DNS**

It is important for DNS to be functioning properly before creating trust relationships. Each domain must be able to resolve names in the other domain. In Chapter 9, "Integrating Domain Name System with AD DS," you learned how to configure name resolution. There are several ways to support name resolution between two forests. In this exercise, you will create a stub zone in the *contoso.com* domain for the *tailspintoys.com* domain and a conditional forwarder in the *tailspintoys.com* domain to resolve *contoso.com*.

1. Log on to SERVER01.contoso.com as Administrator.
2. Open DNS Manager from the Administrative Tools program group.
3. Expand SERVER01, and select Forward Lookup Zones.
4. Right-click Forward Lookup Zones, and choose New Zone.
   The Welcome To The New Zone Wizard page appears.
5. Click Next.
   The Zone Type page appears.
6. Select Stub Zone, and click Next.
   The Active Directory Zone Replication Scope page appears.
7. Click Next.
   The Zone Name page appears.
8. Type **tailspintoys.com**, and click Next.
   The Master DNS Servers page appears.
9. Type **10.0.0.111**, and press Tab.
10. Select the Use The Above Servers To Create A Local List Of Master Servers check box. Click Next, and then click Finish.
11. Log on to SERVERTST.tailspintoys.com as Administrator.
12. Open DNS Manager from the Administrative Tools program group.
13. Expand SERVERTST.
14. Right-click the Conditional Forwarders folder, and choose New Conditional Forwarder.
15. In the DNS Domain box, type **contoso.com**.
16. Select Click Here To Add An IP, and type **10.0.0.11**.
17. Select the Store This Conditional Forwarder In Active Directory, And Replicate It As Follows check box.
18. Click OK.

▶ **Exercise 2   Create a Trust Relationship**

In this exercise, you will create the trust relationship to enable authentication of Tailspin Toys users in the Contoso domain.

1. Users in *tailspintoys.com* require access to a shared folder in *contoso.com*. Answer the following questions:
   ❑ Which domain is the trusting domain, and which is the trusted domain?
   ❑ Which domain has an outgoing trust, and which has an incoming trust?
   Answers: The *contoso.com* domain is the trusting domain with an outgoing trust to the *tailspintoys.com* domain, which is the trusted domain with an incoming trust.

2. Log on to SERVER01 as the Administrator of the *contoso.com* domain.

3. Open Active Directory Domains And Trusts from the Administrative Tools program group.

4. Right-click *contoso.com*, and choose Properties.

5. Click the Trusts tab.

6. Click New Trust.
   The Welcome To The New Trust Wizard page appears.

7. Click Next.
   The Trust Name page appears.

8. In the Name box, type **tailspintoys**. Click Next.
   Because you did not configure DNS on SERVER01 to forward queries for the *tailspintoys.com* domain to the authoritative DNS service on SERVERTST.tailspintoys.com, you must use the NetBIOS name of the *tailspintoys.com* domain. In a production environment, it is recommended to use the DNS name of the domain in this step.
   The Trust Type page appears.

9. Select External Trust, and click Next.
   The Direction of Trust page appears.

10. Select One-way: Outgoing. Click Next.
    The Sides Of Trust page appears.

11. Select This Domain Only. Click Next.
    The Outgoing Trust Authentication Level page appears.

12. Select Domain-Wide Authentication, and click Next.
    The Trust Password page appears.

13. Enter a complex password in the Trust Password and Confirm Trust Password boxes. Remember this password because you will need it to configure the incoming trust for the *tailspintoys.com* domain. Click Next.
    The Trust Selections Complete page appears.

14. Review the settings, and click Next.

    The Trust Creation Complete page appears.

15. Review the status of changes. Click Next.

    The Confirm Outgoing Trust page appears. You should not confirm the trust until both sides of the trust have been created.

16. Click Next.

    The Completing The New Trust Wizard page appears.

17. Click Finish.

    A dialog box appears to remind you that SID filtering is enabled by default.

18. Click OK.

19. Click OK to close the *contoso.com* Properties dialog box.

    Now you will complete the incoming trust for the *tailspintoys.com* domain.

20. Log on to SERVERTST.tailspintoys.com as the Administrator of the *tailspintoys.com* domain.

21. Open Active Directory Domains And Trusts from the Administrative Tools program group.

22. Right-click *tailspintoys.com*, and choose Properties.

23. Click the Trusts tab.

24. Click New Trusts.

    The Welcome To The New Trust Wizard page appears.

25. Click Next.

    The Trust Name page appears.

26. In the Name box, type **contoso**, and click Next.

    The Trust Type page appears.

27. Select External Trust, and click Next.

    The Direction Of Trust page appears.

28. Select One-way: Incoming, and click Next.

    The Sides Of Trust page appears.

29. Select This Domain Only, and click Next.

    The Trust Password page appears.

30. Enter the password you created in step 13 in the Trust Password and Confirm Trust Password boxes. Click Next.

    The Trust Selections Complete page appears.

31. Click Next.

    The Trust Creation Complete page appears.

32. Review the status of changes, and click Next.

The Confirm Incoming Trust page appears.

33. Click Next.

The Completing The New Trust Wizard page appears.

34. Click Finish.

35. Click OK to close the *tailspintoys.com* Properties dialog box.

▶ Exercise 3   Validate the Trust

In step 33 of the previous exercise, you had the opportunity to confirm the trust relationship. You can also confirm or validate an existing trust relationship. In this exercise, you will validate the trust between *contoso.com* and *tailspintoys.com*.

1. Log on to SERVER01.contoso.com as the Administrator of the *contoso.com* domain.

2. Open Active Directory Domains And Trusts from the Administrative Tools folder.

3. Right-click *contoso.com*, and choose Properties.

4. Click the Trusts tab.

5. Select *tailspintoys.com*, and click Properties.

6. Click Validate.

A message appears indicating that the trust has been validated and that it is in place and active.

7. Click OK.

8. Click OK twice to close the Properties dialog boxes.

▶ Exercise 4   Provide Access to Trusted Users

In this exercise, you will provide access to a shared folder in the Contoso domain to the product team from Tailspin Toys.

1. Create the following objects:
   - ❏ A global group named **Product Team** in the *tailspintoys.com* domain
   - ❏ A global group named **Product Developers** in the *contoso.com* domain
   - ❏ A domain local group named **ACL_Product_Access** in the *contoso.com* domain

2. Create a folder named **Project** on the C drive of SERVER01.

3. Give the ACL_Product_Access group Modify permission to the Project folder.

4. Open the Active Directory Users And Computers snap-in for *contoso.com*.

5. Open the properties of the ACL_Product_Access group.

6. Click the Members tab.

7. Click Add.

8. Type **Product Developers**, and click OK.

9. Click Add.

10. Type **TAILSPINTOYS\Product Team**, and click OK.

A Windows Security dialog box appears. Because the trust is one-way, your user account as the administrator of *contoso.com* does not have permissions to read the directory of the *tailspintoys.com* domain. You must have an account in *tailspintoys.com* to read its directory. If the trust were a two-way trust, this message would not have appeared.

11. In the User Name box, type **TAILSPINTOYS\Administrator**.
12. In the Password box, type the password for the Administrator account in *tailspintoys.com*.
13. Click OK.
14. Note that the two global groups from the two domains are now members of the domain local group in the *contoso.com* domain that has access to the shared folder.

▶ **Exercise 5   Implement Selective Authentication**

In this exercise, you will restrict the ability of users from the *tailspintoys.com* domain to authenticate with computers in the *contoso.com* domain.

1. On SERVER01.contoso.com, open Active Directory Domains And Trusts.
2. Right-click *contoso.com*, and choose Properties.
3. Click the Trusts tab.
4. Select *tailspintoys.com*, and click Properties.
5. Click the Authentication tab.
6. Click the Selective Authentication option, and then click OK twice.

    With selective authentication enabled, users from a trusted domain cannot authenticate against computers in the trusting domain, even if they've been given permissions to a folder. Trusted users must also be given the Allow To Authenticate permission on the computer itself.

7. Open the Active Directory Users And Computers snap-in for *contoso.com*.
8. Click the View menu, and ensure that Advanced Features is selected.
9. Select the Domain Controllers OU in the console tree.
10. In the details pane, right-click SERVER01, and choose Properties.
11. Click the Security tab.
12. Click Add.
13. Type **TAILSPINTOYS\Product Team**, and click OK.

    A Windows Security dialog box appears. Because the trust is one-way, your user account as the administrator of *contoso.com* does not have permissions to read the directory of the *tailspintoys.com* domain. You must have an account in *tailspintoys.com* to read its directory. If the trust were a two-way trust, this message would not have appeared.

14. In the User Name box, type **TAILSPINTOYS\Administrator**.
15. In the Password box, type the password for the Administrator account in *tailspintoys.com*.

16. Click OK.
17. In the Permissions For Product Team list, select the check box under Allow and next to Allowed To Authenticate.
18. Click OK.

    Now the product team from *tailspintoys.com* can authenticate to SERVER01 and has been given permission to the shared folder through its membership in the ACL_Product_Access group. Those users cannot authenticate with any other computer in *contoso.com*, even if the group has been assigned permissions to folders on those computers. Also, no other users from *tailspintoys.com* can access resources on SERVER01.contoso.com

Lesson Summary

- The best practices design for an Active Directory forest is a single domain. However, there are requirements, particularly related to replication of the domain naming context, that might require multiple domains in a forest.

- The Active Directory Migration Tool (ADMT) is used to migrate objects between domains or for intra-forest or inter-forest domain restructure. When an account is moved to another domain, it receives a new SID. The SID of the source account can be added to the target account's *sIDHistory* attribute so that the new account maintains access to resources that had been assigned to the original account's SID. Group membership can also be maintained by the ADMT.

- Trust relationships allow users in a trusted domain to be authenticated by computers in a trusting domain and, therefore, to be added to domain local groups or to be given access to resources in the trusting domain.

- Within a forest, there are two-way, transitive trusts between each child and parent domain and between each tree root and the forest root domain. You can create shortcut trusts within a forest to improve authentication.

- You can create trusts to external domains, forests, and Kerberos v5 realms. Those trusts can be one-way or two-way. Kerberos v5 trusts can be transitive or nontransitive. Forest trusts are always transitive, and external trusts are always nontransitive.

- Selective authentication enables you to manage which trusted users and groups are allowed to authenticate against which computers in the trusting domain.

- Domain quarantine, also known as SID filtering, is enabled by default on all external and forest trusts. It prevents trusted users from presenting in their authorization data SIDs from domains other than the primary domain of the account.

Lesson Review

You can use the following questions to test your knowledge of the information in Lesson 2, "Managing Multiple Domains and Trust Relationships." The questions are also available on the companion CD if you prefer to review them in electronic form.

NOTE   Answers

Answers to these questions and explanations of why each answer choice is right or wrong are located in the "Answers" section at the end of the book.

---

1. You are an administrator at Wingtip Toys, which has just acquired Tailspin Toys. You plan to restructure the forests of the two companies so that all objects are in the *wingtiptoys.com* domain. Until then, you want to allow users in the *wintiptoys.com* and *europe.wingtiptoys.com* domains to log on to all computers in the *tailspintoys.com* domain. Which of the following describe the trust relationship you must configure in *wingtiptoys.com*? (Choose all that apply. Each correct answer is part of the solution.)

    A. Incoming

    B. Outgoing

    C. One-way

    D. Two-way

    E. Realm

    F. Shortcut

    G. Forest

    H. External

2. You are an administrator at Wingtip Toys, which has just acquired Tailspin Toys. You have created a one-way outgoing trust to enable users in the *tailspintoys.com* domain to access resources that have been moved into the *wingtiptoys.com* domain. Some users from *tailspintoys.com* are able to access the resources successfully, but other users are reporting that they are unable to gain access to the resources. You discover that the users having problems have worked for Tailspin Toys for eight or more years and that their accounts were migrated from a Windows NT 4.0 domain. What must you do to enable them to gain access to the resources? (Choose all that apply.)

    A. Create accounts in the *wingtiptoys.com* domain with the same user names and passwords as their accounts in the *tailspintoys.com* domain.

    B. Rebuild the Windows NT 4.0 domain and upgrade a domain controller to Windows Server 2008.

    C. Run the *Netdom* trust command with the */verify* parameter.

    D. Run the *Netdom* trust command with the */quarantine:no* parameter.

3. You are an administrator of the forest shown in the following figure. Domain controllers for the *tailspintoys.com* domain are located in Los Angeles. Domain controllers for the Asia domain are in Beijing. Domain controllers for the Europe domain are in Stockholm. Users in Europe and Asia report excessive delays when attempting to open shared folders on servers in each other's domain. Performance is reasonable for accessing resources in the users' own domains. What can you do to improve performance for these users?

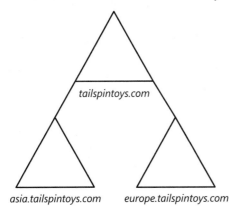

asia.tailspintoys.com   europe.tailspintoys.com

   A. Reinstall the operating systems on the users' computers.

   B. Change the IP address to a static address.

   C. Disable dynamic updates in DNS.

   D. Create a trust relationship between Europe and Asia.

Chapter Review

To further practice and reinforce the skills you learned in this chapter, you can perform the following tasks:

- Review the chapter summary.
- Complete the case scenario. This scenario sets up a real-world situation involving the topics of this chapter and asks you to create a solution.
- Complete the suggested practices.
- Take a practice test.

Chapter Summary

- Domain and forest functional levels enable features of the Active Directory that have been added by each new version of the Windows operating system. Raising the domain or forest functional level is a one-way operation. After the functional level has been raised, you can no longer add domain controllers running previous versions of Windows.
- Trust relationships between domains allow users from a trusted domain to be authenticated by computers in a trusting domain. Trusted users and groups can be added to domain local groups in the trusting domain and can be given access to resources in the trusting domain.
- Within a forest, there are two-way, transitive trusts between each child domain and its parent, and between each domain tree root domain and the forest root domain. Those trusts result in each domain in a forest trusting each other domain in the forest. You can create shortcut trusts to improve the performance and reliability of authentication within a forest.
- An external trust is created between a domain in a forest and another Windows domain. You can also create a trust with a Kerberos v5 realm.
- A cross-forest trust is established between the forest roots of two AD DS forests. It creates a trust between all domains in the two forests.
- Selective authentication can be applied in the trusting domain to control which computers allow the authentication of trusted users.
- SID filtering, or domain quarantine, is enabled by default on all external and cross-forest trusts. It prevents users in the trusted domain from presenting SIDs that were not generated in the users' primary domain.

■ The Active Directory Migration Tool (ADMT) is used to move or copy users, computers, or groups between domains. When you migrate an account, you must consider the fact that the new object will have a new SID, which can affect the object's access to resources and group membership. Use of the *sIDHistory* attribute and the migration of both users and groups can mitigate this risk.

Case Scenario

In the following case scenario, you will apply what you've learned about domain functional levels and trust relationships. You can find answers to these questions in the "Answers" section at the end of this book.

Case Scenario: Managing Multiple Domains and Forests

You are an administrator at Tailspin Toys. Your company is partnering on new product development with Wingtip Toys. You want to establish a forest trust to allow users in the *tailspintoys.com* domain to be authenticated in the *wingtiptoys.com* domain and vice versa.

1. You upgrade your domain controllers directly from Windows 2000 Server to Windows Server 2008. What must you do with the Active Directory Domains and Trusts snap-in before creating the trust relationship?

2. What type(s) of trust relationship(s) can you create in *tailspintoys.com* to achieve this goal? What must you ask administrators in *wingtiptoys.com* to do?

3. You want to control authentication so that users from *wingtiptoys.com* can access resources on only four servers in your domain. What must you do?

Suggested Practices

To help you successfully master the exam objectives presented in this chapter, complete the following tasks.

Configure a Forest or Domain

You are an administrator at Contoso, Ltd., which is expanding its operations to Europe and Asia. In this exercise, you will perform trust management tasks within a multidomain forest. These exercises require multiple domains and domain controllers. To begin the practice, you will also need two new servers, named SERVEREU.contoso.com and SERVERAS.contoso.com, with full installations of Windows Server 2008, each a member of the *contoso.com* domain.

- **Practice 1** Promote SERVEREU.contoso.com to a domain controller in a new domain named *europe.contoso.com* in the existing *contoso.com* forest. Promote SERVERAS.contoso.com to a domain controller in a new domain named *asia.contoso.com* in the existing *contoso.com* forest. Install DNS on all servers and make sure that all forest zones are replicated to both new domain controllers. Ensure also that both domain controllers use their own DNS service to resolve names—that is, configure the DC DNS server address to point to its own IP address.

- **Practice 2** Create a user account in the *europe.contoso.com* domain. Add the user to the Print Operators group in the Europe domain and in the Asia domain so that the user can log on to the domain controllers for the purposes of this practice. Create a shared folder on SERVERAS.asia.contoso.com and give the Europe user permission to the folder. Log on to SERVEREU.europe.contoso.com as the user and connect to the shared folder on SERVERAS.asia.contoso.com.

- **Practice 3** Shut down SERVER01.contoso.com. Log on to SERVEREU.europe.contoso.com as the Europe user. Ping SERVERAS.asia.contoso.com. If you cannot ping the server, DNS or networking is not configured correctly. Troubleshoot the problem. When you can ping SERVERAS, attempt to connect to the shared folder. It should fail because a domain controller in the trust path is not available.

- **Practice 4** Power on SERVER01.contoso.com. Log on to SERVEREU as the Europe administrator. Create a trust relationship with the Asia domain.

- **Practice 5** Power down SERVER01. Log on to SERVEREU.europe.contoso.com as the Europe user. Ping SERVERAS.asia.contoso.com. If you cannot ping the server, DNS or networking is not configured correctly. Troubleshoot the problem. When you can ping SERVERAS, attempt to connect to the shared folder. The connection should succeed because the shortcut trust is in place.

Take a Practice Test

The practice tests on this book's companion CD offer many options. For example, you can test yourself on just one exam objective, or you can test yourself on all the 70-640 certification exam content. You can set up the test so that it closely simulates the experience of taking a certification exam, or you can set it up in study mode so that you can look at the correct answers and explanations after you answer each question.

MORE INFO Practice tests

For details about all the practice test options available, see the "How to Use the Practice Tests" section in this book's introduction.

Chapter 13
Directory Business Continuity

Business continuity is a very hot topic today, especially since the recent disasters many organizations have faced all over the world. Hurricanes, tidal waves, and earthquakes are disasters on a catastrophic scale and have far-reaching impacts on organizations. Several studies have shown that up to 40 percent of small to medium-sized organizations that face a significant disaster and have no business continuity plan will fail. Don't let this happen to you. Prepare in advance and make sure you are ready for any eventuality.

Disasters don't have to be on a catastrophic scale to be devastating. A user whose Active Directory Domain Services (AD DS) account has been erased by mistake will be as devastated—albeit on a smaller scale—when he or she can't log on one morning without knowing why. That's why you need proactive plans that will keep you ready at all times and make sure you can react to any situation, disastrous or not. To do so, you need to address two key areas of business continuity: maintaining and protecting the directory and data store and managing directory performance.

Each of these areas addresses a facet of directory business continuity. A third area of business continuity, availability, is built into the AD DS operational model. Every domain controller (DC) but the read-only domain controller (RODC) includes the capability to support multi-master replication. Because of this, each time you put two or more DCs in place for the same domain, you provide high availability for the service. Therefore, simple deployment rules guide the process of maintaining directory service availability.

Exam objectives in this chapter:
- Maintaining the Active Directory Environment
    - ❏ Perform offline maintenance.
    - ❏ Configure backup and recovery.
    - ❏ Monitor Active Directory.

Lessons in this chapter:
- Lesson 1: Proactive Directory Maintenance and Data Store Protection 610
- Lesson 2: Proactive Directory Performance Management. 660

Before You Begin

To complete the lessons in this chapter, you must have done the following:

■ Installed Windows Server 2008 on a physical or virtual computer, which should be named SERVER10. This computer hosts the DNS Server role as well as the Active Directory Domain Services role and is a DC for the *treyresearch.net* forest root domain. Add a second disk to this server. Make it a dynamically expanding disk of 10 GB, format it, and name it **Data**.

■ Installed Windows Server 2008 on a physical or virtual computer, which should be named SERVER11 and should be a standalone server. This computer will host the DNS Server role and the Active Directory Domain Services role you will install and create through the exercises in this chapter. Assign an IPv4 address from one of the private ranges, for example, 192.168.x.x, and map its DNS server address to the address you assigned to SERVER10.

■ Performed the practice exercises outlined in Chapter 9, "Integrating Domain Name System with AD DS." This will have set up a multidomain directory service named *treyresearch.net*. This forest includes a forest root domain, a domain tree, and a child domain. Exercises in this chapter reuse the forest root domain created in Chapter 9.

Using virtual machines (VMs) is strongly recommended in support of the exercises. The DC and Domain Name System (DNS) server roles are ideal for virtualization through either Microsoft Virtual Server 2005 R2 or Hyper-V.

Real World

Danielle Ruest and Nelson Ruest

In 2003, we were asked to write a follow-up book to *Windows Server 2003: Best Practices for Enterprise Deployments*. This book would be a pocket guide and would focus on systems administration instead of operating system deployment.

We collected and collated tasks that should be performed on Windows Server 2003 infrastructures, depending on the different features deployed. We divided the tasks according to server role and created five categories, focusing only on roles available with the default installation files for Windows Server 2003, and we divided the list according to task frequency, finding four frequencies: daily, weekly, monthly, and ad hoc. The last would include both infrequent tasks and tasks needed to perform on a schedule longer than one month. Then, we put it all together in a single spreadsheet.

Before we started writing, we wanted to validate the task list, so we asked our clients if they would help us supplement it. Twenty-five clients, with network sizes ranging from 50 to 25,000 nodes, responded. We sent the list to each one to look it over, evaluate whether the task was appropriate, validate the schedule we suggested, and suggest any missing tasks. Clients did not know how many tasks we had listed for each server role beforehand.

Responses were quite varied, but every client came back with the same general comment: "We never knew you had to do all those things in Windows!" Of all the clients, only a handful even touched on the task list, and those were in the largest networks. We were shocked, but this taught us a valuable lesson.

When clients deploy Windows, things work for the most part and, because of this, few organizations assign staff to focus on proactive network monitoring. IT professionals are mostly overworked in almost every organization. When requests come in, they are always high priority; system administrators usually don't have time to be proactive because they are almost always in reactive mode and already working overtime.

Since our *Pocket Administrator for Windows Server 2003* has been published, we have been giving one-day Windows Server 2003 administration classes, updating them each time a new version would be released. In every case, attendees have come back to us to say that when they use our schedule, they no longer have to work overtime on a constant basis. Our new book, *Windows Server 2008: The Complete Reference*, contains the task list and has been updated accordingly.

Monitoring—especially proactive monitoring—is a very important part of any Windows Server deployment, especially in terms of AD DS or DNS, which supports it. Every organization that relies on the identity and access solution AD DS provides should take measures to verify the system's proper operation at regular intervals. Running Microsoft Windows technologies while not performing proactive management for them is not practical. They will work, but users can often leave themselves exposed to potential issues and, perhaps worse, potential security holes. This is why this might be the most important chapter in this book for you.

Lesson 1: Proactive Directory Maintenance and Data Store Protection

One of the most important concepts administrators need to understand when working with a directory service such as AD DS is the division of responsibilities they face. A directory service is very much like a Web service. IT administrators of a Web service are responsible for the management of Microsoft Internet Information Services (IIS) and the underlying operating system, not for the maintenance of the content included in the Web sites the server will host. Imagine having to change a comma here, a word there, a picture here, or a phrase there in addition to having to perform all the other work required to maintain a network environment. You would never have time to do anything else but work!

In a Web service, you must divide responsibilities based on data and service management. IT is responsible for service management whereas the users are responsible for data or content management. The same applies to the directory service. AD DS is a distributed database that contains information about the users, the computers, the servers, the services, and more that run in your network, hence its categorization as a network operating system (NOS) as well as a lightweight access directory protocol (LDAP) directory service. Because of this, administration activities are shared among several members of your organization:

■ Users can update their own records. If a user uses the Search Active Directory feature to locate his or her own account record, he or she will be allowed to change information such as phone number, location, and so on.

■ Security and distribution group managers, when assigned the role in AD DS, can automatically manage group content if you assign this user right to them. This is a good approach for reducing the workload system administrators face when managing a NOS directory service. How would you know whether a user should be a member of a group?

In every case, when you change group ownership, you respond to a request that was initiated by someone else. Why not cut out the middle person and make group managers directly responsible?

- Password resets are managed by the help desk. Each time a password needs to be reset, the help desk needs to get involved.
- Directory and DNS service availability is the core of the system administrator's responsibilities and should be the focus of most of his or her efforts. After all, system administrators are there to manage the availability of services and the data the directory contains, not to manage the data itself.

When you plan your proactive management strategy, focus on the service aspect of operations management and delegate data management as much as possible. AD DS delegation capabilities further enhance this model by enabling you to assign object control to others in your organization discretely. This is the approach of this chapter and the focus of this lesson.

After this lesson, you will be able to:
- Understand which administrative tasks need to be performed to maintain AD DS and DNS.
- Understand the difference between online and offline maintenance tasks.
- Perform offline maintenance tasks.
- Recover data while online.
- Recover data while offline.

Estimated lesson time: 90 minutes

Twelve Categories of AD DS Administration

When you consider it, Active Directory administration or management covers twelve major activities. These activities and their breadth of coverage are outlined in Table 13-1, which also outlines which tasks focus on data or content management and which are concentrated on service administration.

Table 13-1 AD DS Administration Activities

Task	Description	Service	Data
User and Group Account Administration	This includes user password resets, user creation and deactivation, user group creation, and membership management. Should be delegated to the help desk.	☐	☑
Endpoint Device Administration	All computers in a Windows network environment must have a computer account. This is how they interact with the directory and how the directory interacts with them. Should be delegated to technicians.	☐	☑
Networked Service Administration	This includes publication of network file shares, printers, distributed file shares (DFS), application directory partitions, and so on. Should be delegated to the administrator of each service type.	☑	☑
Group Policy Object (GPO) Management	GPOs provide the most powerful model for object management in Windows Server 2008. Should be delegated to appropriate technicians, but a central GPO steward should control GPO proliferation.	☑	☐
DNS Administration	DNS is now tied closely to the directory, and the operation is based on a properly functioning dynamic DNS service. Because DNS is integrated with the directory, DNS administration is the responsibility of the domain administrator.	☑	☐
Active Directory Topology and Replication Management	Replication is at the very core of the directory service operation. It covers the configuration of subnets, sites, site links, site link bridges, and bridgehead servers. You should rely heavily on the Knowledge Consistency Checker (KCC)—a service that automatically generates replication topologies based on the rules and guidelines you give it—to control replication. This is the responsibility of the domain administrator.	☑	☐

Table 13-1 AD DS Administration Activities

Task	Description	Service	Data
Active Directory Configuration Management	Configuration administration involves forest, domain, and organizational unit (OU) design and implementation. It also involves Flexible Single Master of Operations (FSMO) roles, global catalog servers, and DCs, including RODCs because these servers define the configuration of each forest. One last activity that is related to configuration management is time synchronization. AD DS relies on the PDC Emulator role to synchronize time in the network. These tasks are the responsibility of the forest and domain administrators.	☑	☐
Active Directory Schema Management	AD DS is a database, albeit a distributed one. As such, it includes a database schema. Schema modifications are not done lightly because added objects cannot normally be removed although they can be deactivated, renamed, and reused. This is the responsibility of the forest administrator.	☑	☐
Information Management	This refers to the population of the directory with information about the objects it contains. User objects, shared folders, and computer objects can include owners; groups can include managers; printers and computers can include location tracking information. The Active Directory Schema Management console can be used to add or remove content from the global catalog and determine whether an object should be indexed. You can also assign NTDS quotas to make sure no one adds or extracts more information than permitted in the directory. Delegate as many of the information management tasks as possible.	☐	☑
Security Administration	Security administration covers everything from setting Domain Account policies and assigning user rights to managing trusts as well as access control list (ACL) and access control entry (ACE) administration. This is the responsibility of the domain administrator or designated operators to whom it has been delegated.	☑	☐

Table 13-1   AD DS Administration Activities

Task	Description	Service	Data
Database Management	Database management involves *Ntds.dit* maintenance and AD DS object protection as well as GPO protection. Includes managing the LostandFound and LostandFoundConfig containers, which are designed to collect homeless objects in your directory. Also includes compacting the directory database on each DC. Although AD DS regularly compacts its own database automatically, it is good practice to compact it manually. This is the responsibility of the domain administrator.	☑	☐
AD Reporting	Generate reports from your directory to know how it is structured, what it contains, and how it runs. There is no default centralized reporting tool, but you can export data at several levels of the directory. You can also generate GPO reports with the Group Policy Management console. This is the responsibility of the domain administrator and the GPO steward.	☑	☑

Depending on the size of your network, each of the activities outlined in Table 13-1 can be a job by itself. This is why you need to make sure you delegate whichever part of the work you can so that you can enlist as much help as possible to ensure that the directory service is highly available at all times. A couple of tools can help in particular situations.

Using AcctInfo.dll

When you need to manage user accounts, you'll perform activities through the Active Directory Users and Computers console. This console supports enhancements, some of which are provided by Microsoft. For example, you can add an Additional Account Info tab on the user object's properties page by downloading and registering the AcctInfo.dll on a server or workstation hosting the Active Directory Users and Computers console. AcctInfo.dll is part of the Windows Server 2003 Resource Kit along with the Account Lockout and Management tools.

IMPORTANT   Additional Account Info tab

Note that this additional tab appears in the standalone Active Directory Users and Computers console only and does not appear in the Active Directory Users and Computers node of Server Manager.

To install the Additional Account Info tab, use the following procedure. You need local administrator credentials if you are on a workstation or member server but domain administrator credentials on a DC.

1. Make sure the Remote Server Administration Tools (RSAT), especially the AD DS administration tools, are installed on your system.

2. Download Account Lockout And Management Tools from the Microsoft Web site and save them to the Documents folder on the system you want to install it to.

3. Extract the tools from the executable.

4. After the tools are extracted, locate AcctInfo.dll. It should be in your Documents folder.

5. Use an elevated command prompt to run the following command:

   regsvr32 acctinfo.dll

6. Click OK when you get the successful registration message and close the command prompt.

7. If the Active Directory Users and Computers console was open, close it and reopen it. This console must be re-initialized to load the new DLL.

8. Locate a user account.

9. Open its Properties dialog box.

10. Move to the Additional Account Info tab. (See Figure 13-1.) Note the information available in this screen. In addition to this information, this screen provides the following:

    ❑ Domain PW Info displays the password policy assigned to this account. Given that AD DS supports multiple password policies in a single domain, this is a useful button.

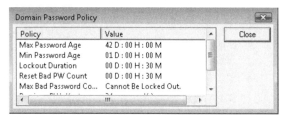

    ❑ SID History provides information on the multiple security identifiers an account might have when SID History is turned on in the domain. SID History is normally turned on when you perform a migration of accounts from one domain to the other. It enables the account object to access data from the original domain. However, in new domains, SID History is not available unless a migration occurs. It is important to turn off SID History as soon as possible after a migration occurs to avoid SID spoofing in the domain—the appropriation of an administrative SID by a malicious user. If it is turned on, you can use this button to validate that accounts have only the appropriate SIDs tied to them.

    ❑ Set PW On Site DC will enable you to reset the user's password on the user's DC to avoid replication delays and give the user immediate access to his or her new password. Use the Just Find Site button to locate the site's DC and reset the password.

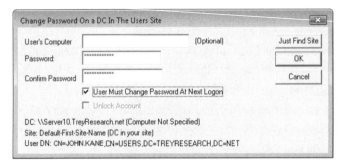

This dynamic-link library (DLL) can be quite useful to help desk staff and domain administrators alike.

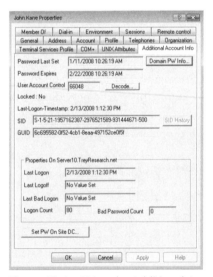

Figure 13-1 Using the Additional Account Info tab in a user's Properties dialog box

---

MORE INFO Account Lockout and Management tools

To obtain the Account Lockout and Management tools, go to *http://www.microsoft.com/Downloads /details.aspx?FamilyID=7af2e69c-91f3-4e63-8629-b999adde0b9e&displaylang=en*.

Using Specops Gpupdate

When you work with computer objects in the directory with Active Directory Users and Computers, you can right-click the object and choose Manage to launch the Computer Management console with the computer as the focus for the console, but this does not give you access to simpler functions such as remote update of GPOs or the more common *start*, *shut down*, or *restart* commands. However, you can obtain a simple and free add-on from Special Operations Software called Specops Gpupdate. Specops Gpupdate is used here only as an example and is by no means a recommendation. This tool automatically adds functionality to the Active Directory Users and Computers console and will give you control over the following activities:

- Remotely updating GPOs on an object in the directory
- Starting computers remotely, using Wake-on-LAN if enabled locally
- Remote restarting or shutting down the selected computer
- Graphically reporting the results of an operation

In addition, Gpupdate enables you to perform these tasks on single computer objects or on a collection of objects by applying them to an entire OU. This is a good tool for administrators who must manage computers and servers remotely.

NOTE   Obtaining Specops Gpupdate

To obtain the Specops Gpupdate, go to *http://www.specopssoft.com/products/specopsgpupdate /download.asp*. A one-time registration is required.

Exam Tip   Note that Specops Gpupdate, while it is quite a useful tool for object management through AD DS, is not part of the exam.

If you choose to implement Specops Gpupdate, use the following procedure. You need local administrator credentials if you are on a workstation or member server but domain administrator credentials on a DC. Also, you need to be an Enterprise Administrator for the one-time Display Specifier registration in the forest.

1. Make sure the RSAT, especially the AD DS administration tools, are installed on your system.
2. Download the Specops Gpupdate tool from the Special Operations Software Web site and save it to the Documents folder on the system you want to install it to.
3. Extract the components from the executable.
4. After the components are extracted, locate the SpecopsGpupdate.msi file. It should be in your Documents folder. Double-click .msi to launch the setup.
5. Click Run in the warning dialog box.
6. Click Next at the Welcome screen.
7. Accept the license and click Next.
8. Type your full name and organization; make sure Anyone Who Uses This Computer is selected and click Next.
9. Accept the default installation location and click Next.

10. Click Next to install the application, and then click Finish when the installation is complete.

    The installation is complete, but you must add the display specifiers to the forest. This requires Enterprise Admin credentials.

11. Launch Windows Explorer and navigate to %ProgramFiles%\Common Files\Secopssoft \SpecopsADUC Extension.

12. After the Specops files are displayed in the details pane of Windows Explorer, move to the Start menu and click Run. This displays the Run dialog box.

13. Make sure the Run dialog box is empty and move to the Windows Explorer window to click and drag SpecopsAducMenuExtensionInstaller.exe into the Run dialog box.

    The command and its path should be displayed in the Run dialog box.

14. Move to the end of the text, making sure you do not change anything, and type /**add**.

    The result should be similar to "C:\Program Files\Common Files\Secopssoft\Specops-ADUC Extension\SpecopsAducMenuExtensionInstaller.exe"/add.

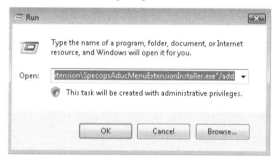

15. Press Enter to run the command.

    A command prompt will open and display command results.

16. Press any key to close the window.

Now that the display specifiers have been added, you can simply run the SpecopsGpupdate.msi file on any computer on which you want to install Specops Gpupdate by performing steps 1–10 only.

When you need to work with computer objects, you can simply use the context menu to access the new administration features on either a computer object or an organizational unit containing computer objects. (See Figure 13-2.) This tool is free and a good addition to any directory service.

Figure 13-2 The context menu commands added by Specops Gpupdate

Using AD DS Administration Tools

To perform the activities related to service administration in AD DS and DNS, you can use a series of tools. You've already seen many of these tools as you read through the previous lessons, but it is a good idea to review them here. Table 13-2 outlines which tools you can use for which task and where you can locate the tool. In this table, the focus is on service, not data administration. Many of these tools will also work with Active Directory Lightweight Directory Services (AD LDS) because it is based on the same core code as AD DS.

Table 13-2 Common Service Administration Tools

Tool	Description	Location
Active Directory Domains and Trusts	Administer trusts, domain and forest functional levels, and user principal name suffixes.	Administrative Tools program group
Active Directory Schema Snap-in	Modify the schema for AD DS directories or AD LDS instances. You must use the *Regsvr32.exe* command to register the Schmmgmt.dll first.	Custom MMC
Active Directory Sites and Services	Configure and manage replication scopes for AD DS directories and AD LDS instances.	Administrative Tools program group
Active Directory Users and Computers	Configure and manage the domain-centric FSMO roles as well as RODC features.	Administrative Tools program group
ADSI Edit	Query, view, and edit directory objects and attributes.	Administrative Tools program group
CSVDE.exe	Import data into AD DS directories or AD LDS instances.	Command line
DCDiag.exe	Diagnose AD DS directories or AD LDS instances.	Command line

Table 13-2   Common Service Administration Tools

Tool	Description	Location
Dcpromo.exe	To add or remove the DC service.	Start menu, Search
DFSRadmin.exe	Manage Distributed File System Replication, which is the system used when the forest runs in Windows Server 2008 full functional mode.	Command line
DNS Manager	Perform general maintenance of DNS servers.	Administration Tools program group or Server Manager
Dnscmd.exe	Manage all aspects of DNS servers.	Command line
DSACLS.exe	Control access control lists on directory objects.	Command line
Dsadd.exe	Add specific types of objects (users, groups, computers).	Command line
Dsamain.exe	Mount Active Directory store (.dit) backups or snapshots to identify their contents.	Command line
Dsbutil.exe (installed with AD LDS and AD DS)	Perform maintenance of the AD DS store. Configure AD LDS ports. View AD LDS instances.	Command line
Dsget.exe	View the selected properties of a specific object (user, computer).	Command line
Dsmgmt.exe	Manage application partitions and operations master roles.	Command line
Dsmod.exe	Modify an existing object of a specific type (user, computer).	Command line
Dsmove.exe	Move an object to a new location within a directory. Also rename an existing object.	Command line
Dsquery.exe	Query the directory for a specific object type according to specified criteria.	Command line
Dsrm.exe	Delete an object of a specific type or a collection of objects.	Command line
Event Viewer	Audit AD DS or AD LDS changes and log old and new values for both objects and attributes.	Administrative Tools program group
GPfixup.exe	Repair domain name dependencies in Group Policy objects. Also, relink Group Policy objects after a domain rename operation.	Command line
Group Policy Diagnostic Best Practices Analyzer	Verify the configuration of GPO as well as potential dependency errors.	Download from *microsoft.com*

Table 13-2   **Common Service Administration Tools**

Tool	Description	Location
Group Policy Management Console	Create, manage, back up, and restore GPOs.	Administrative Tools program group
Ipconfig	Display and modify IP configuration details.	Command line
Ksetup.exe	Configure a client to use a Kerberos v5 realm instead of an AD DS domain.	Command line
Ktpass.exe	Configure a non-Windows Kerberos service as a security principal in AD DS.	Command line
LDIFDE.exe	Import data into AD LDS instances.	Command line
Ldp.exe	Perform LDAP operations against the directory.	Start menu, Search
Movetree.exe	Move objects between domains in a forest.	Download from *microsoft.com*
Netdom.exe	Manage computer accounts, domains, and trust relationships.	Command line
Nltest.exe	Query replication status or verify trust relationships.	Command line
Nslookup.exe	View information on name servers to diagnose DNS infrastructure problems.	Command line
Ntdsutil.exe (installed with AD DS, not AD LDS)	Perform database maintenance on the AD DS store.	Command line
Repadmin.exe	Troubleshoot and diagnose replication between DCs that use the File Replication Service (FRS), which is the system used when the forest does not run in Windows Server 2008 full functional mode.	Command line
Server Manager	Manage existing AD DS domains or AD LDS instances.	Administrative Tools program group
System Monitor	Create charts and graphs of server performance trends. Determine performance benchmarks.	Server Manager, Diagnostics, Reliability, and Performance
Ultrasound (*Ultrasound.exe*)	Graphical tool to troubleshoot and diagnose replication between DCs that use FRS. Relies on Windows Management Instrumentation (WMI).	Download from *microsoft.com*
W32tm.exe	View settings, manage configuration or diagnose problems with Windows Time.	Command line
Windows Server Backup	Back up or restore AD DS directories or AD LDS instances and their contents.	Administrative Tools program group

---

MORE INFO   **Finding and downloading tools**

To locate the *Movetree.exe* command, go to *http://www.microsoft.com/downloads/details.aspx?Family-lyID=96a35011-fd83-419d-939b-9a772ea2df90&DisplayLang=en*. Obtain the .cab file and extract all files named movetree.* from the file. Note that not all tools contained within this file will work with Windows Server 2008; Windows Server 2003 support tools are not supported on Windows Server 2008. For example, the *ReplMon.exe* tool simply will not launch.

To obtain Ultrasound, go to *http://www.microsoft.com/Downloads/details.aspx?FamilyID=61acb9b9-c354-4f98-a823-24cc0da73b50&displaylang=en*. Note that this tool might not be immediately available for Windows Server 2008.

To obtain the GPO Diagnostic Best Practices Analyzer for x86, go to *http://www.microsoft.com /downloads/details.aspx?FamilyID=47f11b02-8ee4-450b-bf13-880b91ba4566&DisplayLang=en*. For the x64 edition, go to *http://www.microsoft.com/downloads/details.aspx?familyid=70E0EDEC-66F7-4499-83B7-4F2009DF2314&displaylang=en*.

Performing Online Maintenance

You performed many of the activities listed in Table 13-1 as you covered other lessons. Table 13-3 maps out where you locate information about each of the 12 AD DS tasks in this book.

Table 13-3   AD DS Administration Activities

Task	Location
User and Group Account Administration	Chapter 2 Chapter 3 Chapter 4
Endpoint Device Administration	Chapter 5
Networked Service Administration	Chapter 4 Chapter 7 Chapter 10 Chapter 11
Group Policy Object (GPO) Management	Chapter 6 Chapter 7
Domain Name Service Administration	Chapter 9
Active Directory Topology and Replication Management	Chapter 10 Chapter 11
Active Directory Configuration Management	Chapter 1 Chapter 2 Chapter 8 Chapter 10 Chapter 11 Chapter 12

Table 13-3   **AD DS Administration Activities**

Task	Location
Active Directory Schema Management	Chapter 14
Information Management	Chapter 2
	Chapter 3
	Chapter 4
	Chapter 5
	Chapter 11
Security Administration	Chapter 2
	Chapter 7
	Chapter 8
	Chapter 12
Database Management	Chapter 13
Active Directory Reporting	Chapter 2
	Chapter 6
	Chapter 7
	Chapter 8
	Chapter 10
	Chapter 11
	Chapter 13

Performing Offline Maintenance

One significant change in AD DS from previous versions is the transformation of the DC role into a controllable service. In previous versions of Windows Server, the DC role was monolithic: to stop the service, you needed to stop the DC as a whole. This meant that when you needed to perform maintenance on the *Ntds.dit* database—the database that contains the directory store—you needed to shut down a DC and restart it in Directory Services Repair Mode. Because of this, there was no way to automate the database maintenance operations. Consequently, most domain administrators never performed any database maintenance at all. Performing no maintenance is not a valid approach to systems management.

Every database works the same way. As new records are added, the database allocates additional space to store information associated with the record. However, when the record is deleted, the allocated space is not recovered. You need to perform database compaction activities to recover this space. The AD DS service does perform some automatic database compaction, but this compaction does not recover lost space within the database; it only rearranges data to make it easier to access. To recover lost space, you must take the database offline and run a compaction and defragmentation sequence against it.

However, with AD DS and Windows Server 2008, the AD DS service is now a manageable service that can be started and stopped like all Windows Server services. This means that to perform database maintenance activities, you no longer need to shut down the DC to restart it in Directory Services Repair Mode. It also means that because the service behaves natively, you can script the defragmentation and compaction operations through basic command-line tools.

Note that to stop the AD DS service, the DC must be able to communicate with another DC that is running the service. If not, you will not be able to stop the service. AD DS includes automatic checks and verifications that ensure that at least one DC is available at all times; otherwise, no one will be able to log on to the network.

You will work with the defragmentation and compaction operation in the practice exercises at the end of this lesson.

Exam Tip   Offline defragmentation and compaction and the restartable AD DS service are important parts of the exam.

Relying on Built-in Directory Protection Measures

Data protection is also a very important aspect of proactive systems management, and it is essential for AD DS. As you know, each account stored in the AD DS database is a unique object because it is tied to a specific and unique security identifier (SID). This means that when an account is deleted, you cannot simply re-create it. Although the account will appear the same to humans, it will be a completely different object to AD DS and, as such, will not retain the properties or attributes of the formerly deleted object. Group memberships, passwords, attribute settings, and more will be completely different for the object. This is one very good reason to reassign accounts rather than re-creating them when people change positions in your network. Reassigning them automatically grants the new person the same rights as the previous account owner. Re-creating an account means you have to dig in and identify all the access rights required by the role in your network. Re-creation is a lot more work.

It is difficult to lose data within the directory because of the multimaster replication model—when a change is performed in one location, it is automatically replicated to all other locations. However, this same replication model can also cause issues. When an operator deletes an object, especially by mistake, it will be deleted in the entire directory and might need to be restored from backup to be recovered. However, AD DS includes four features that enable you to recover information without resorting to backups:

- The new object protection option, which protects objects from deletion.
- The new AD DS Access auditing feature, which logs old and new values, enabling you to return to an original value when object properties are modified.
- The tombstone container. Each object that is removed from the directory is tombstoned for a specific period of time. While the object is still in the tombstone container, it can be recovered.
- The backup and restore feature supported by Windows Server Backup.

Each of these provides a means of protecting and recovering the information in the directory database.

Protecting AD DS Objects

By default, every new object in AD DS can be protected from deletion when it is created. In every case, you must specifically assign this feature to the object. When you create objects through batch processes or through a migration process, it will not be protected unless you assign the feature during the creation process. When you create an object interactively, you must also assign protection explicitly. Object protection is assigned or removed on the Object tab, which can be viewed only when you have Advanced Features turned on in the View menu of the Active Directory Users And Computers console. (See Figure 13-3.) Note that container objects such as OUs have this option enabled by default because they form part of your directory structure.

Figure 13-3 Protecting an object from deletion in AD DS

After object protection is assigned, you will not be able to delete the object accidentally. This also means that it cannot be moved from one location to the other.

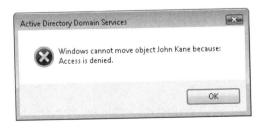

In fact, this option assigns two Deny permissions to the Everyone group: Deny Delete and Deny Delete subtree. Remember that in AD DS, deny permissions override every allow permission. The only way you can move or delete this object from this point on is if you uncheck the protection feature. This is a useful feature for organizations that delegate object administration to technical staff. In fact, you might consider making this feature part of the user account template you create to assist in the creation of user accounts in your directory.

Auditing Directory Changes

When you audit directory changes in Windows Server 2008, you automatically log old and new values of an attribute each time an object is modified. Further, because the AD DS audit policy in Windows Server 2008 now logs four subcategories of service access, you can control the assignment of this policy at a more granular level than in previous versions of Windows Server. The subcategory that controls attribute captures is Directory Service Changes. When enabled, it captures creation, modification, move, and undeletion operations on an object. Each operation is assigned a specific event ID in Directory Services Event Log.

This feature turns Event Log into a record-keeping system for directory changes, enabling you to maintain extensive records on the changes that have been made in your directory. It is also useful for fixing modifications that have been performed erroneously.

When an object is modified, at least two events are logged. The first will list the former value, and the second—most recent—will list the new value. Use the two to correct modifications that should not have been made.

Undeleting Active Directory Objects

When you mistakenly delete an Active Directory object, you can use the *Ldp.exe* command to recover it. This is performed through a procedure that exposes the deleted objects container of the directory. To undelete an object, use the following procedure on a DC. You must have domain administrator credentials to perform this operation.

1. From a command prompt, type **Ldp.exe**.
2. Click Connect from the Connection menu, type the server's fully qualified domain name (FQDN), for example, **Server10.TreyResearch.net**, and click OK.
3. Click Bind from the Connection menu, make sure the Bind As Currently Logged On User option is selected, and click OK.
4. Click Controls from the Options menu, select Return Deleted Objects from the Load Predefined drop-down list, make sure Server is selected in the Control Type section of the dialog box, and click OK.
5. Click Tree from the View menu, type the deleted object container's distinguished name (DN), and click OK.

   For example, the DN of the container in Trey Research would be cn=deleted Objects,dc =TreyResearch,dc=net.

6. In the tree pane, double-click the deleted objects container to expand its contents.
   Keep in mind that *Ldp.exe* will return only 1,000 objects by default.

7. Locate the object you want to restore in the tree pane and double-click it.
   This displays its information in the details pane. For example, if the object is a user account, it will begin with cn=username.

8. Right-click the object name in the tree pane and select Modify.

9. In the Modify dialog box, type **isDeleted** in the Edit Entry Attribute value, select Delete as the Operation, and click Enter.

10. In the Modify dialog box, type **distinguishedName** in the Edit Entry Attribute value, type the object's new DN in the Attribute value, select Replace as the Operation, and click Enter.
    For example, to restore John Kane's account to the People container in the Trey Research domain, the DN would be cn=John Kane,ou=People,dc=TreyResearch,dc=net.

11. Make sure the Synchronous and Extended check boxes are both selected in the bottom left of the dialog box, and then click Run. (See Figure 13-4.)

12. Use Active Directory Users And Computers to move to the OU you restored the object to. Use the refresh button to refresh the OU contents if the console was already opened.

13. Reset the newly restored object's password, group memberships, and any other values you need to reapply, and then click Enable.
    The object is restored. This procedure recovers the object and retains the original SID for the object as well, but it does not retain all group memberships and other values.

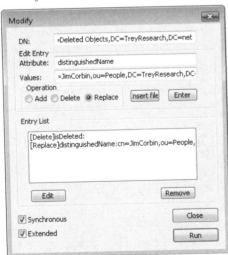

Figure 13-4   Recovering a deleted object with *Ldp.exe*

Using Quest Object Restore for Active Directory

As you can see from the previous procedure, objects are not immediately removed from the directory when they are deleted. Instead, they are tombstoned and moved to a special hidden container. You can access this container with special tools but not with the normal Active Directory consoles. You can, however, use a utility from Quest Software, Quest Object Restore for Active Directory, to access the tombstone container through a graphical console and locate objects you want to restore. This utility is free; however, it expires every six months and must be removed and reinstalled to work again. Quest Object Restore for Active Directory is used here only as an example and is by no means a recommendation.

NOTE   Obtaining Quest Object Restore

To obtain the Quest Object Restore for Active Directory, go to *http://www.quest.com/object-restore-for-active-directory/*. A one-time registration with a business e-mail address is required.

Exam Tip   Note that Quest Object Restore for Active Directory, while it is quite a useful tool for recovering deleted objects in AD DS, is not part of the exam.

Proceed as follows to download and install it. You need domain administrator credentials if you perform this on a DC or local administrator credentials if you do it on a workstation or member server.

1. Make sure the RSAT, especially the AD DS administration tools, are installed on your system.
2. Download the Quest Object Restore for Active Directory tool from the Quest Software Web site and save it to the Documents folder on the system you want to install it to.
3. Extract the components from the executable.
4. After the tools are extracted, locate the Quest Object Restore For Active Directory.msi file. It should be in your Documents folder. Double-click the .msi to launch the setup.
5. Click Run in the warning dialog box.
6. Click Next at the Welcome screen.
7. Accept the license and click Next.
8. Type your full name and organization, ensuring that Anyone Who Uses This Computer is selected, and click Next.
9. Accept the default installation location and click Next.
10. Click Next to install the application, and then click Finish when the installation is complete.

    The installation is complete.

11. To use the tool, navigate to Start\All Programs\Quest Software\Quest Object Restore For Active Directory and click Quest Object Restore For Active Directory.

    This tool runs in its own Microsoft Management console (MMC).

12. When the console is open, right-click Quest Object Restore For Active Directory and select Connect To.

13. Type the domain's FQDN or click Browse to locate it. Click OK to connect.

14. Click the domain name in the tree pane.

    This should list deleted objects in the details pane.

15. If the objects do not appear, click the Refresh button.

16. To restore an object, right-click the object name in the details pane and select Restore. (See Figure 13-5.) Click OK when the object has been restored.

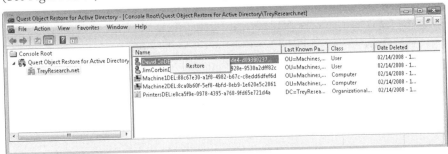

Figure 13-5   Using Quest Object Restore for Active Directory to restore objects

Basically, Quest Object Restore for Active Directory displays the tombstone container in AD DS. Because all objects are tombstoned for a period of 180 days by default, you can restore these objects any time before they are destroyed by directory database cleanup operations. However, as with the *Ldp.exe* tool, this procedure recovers the object and retains the original SID for the object as well, but it does not retain all group memberships and other values, so you must modify the object before you enable it. However, using this tool is much simpler than using the previous *Ldp.exe* procedure.

Relying on Windows Server Backup to Protect the Directory

Although you can use special tools to access the tombstone data in the directory, this does not always provide the best method for data recovery. For example, objects you restore from tombstone containers do not include all their previous attributes. Because of this, you must know ahead of time which contents and attributes were assigned to the object before deletion to be able to bring it back to its original state. However, when you restore the data from backup and reassign it to the directory, you restore all an object's attributes at once, and you do not need to reassign attributes such as group memberships and so on. This saves time after the object is restored but requires a more complex operation to perform the restore.

In addition, restoring objects in AD DS was more or less a hit-or-miss operation in previous versions of Windows Server because it was impossible to view objects within a backup data set prior to the restore. It was and continues to be impossible to restore different backup sets to different DCs and to view the data they contain. Windows Server 2008 includes a new tool, the AD DS Database mounting tool with which you can view backup data set contents prior to the restore operation. This tool can save you considerable time when you need to recover an object and help ensure that you recover the right version of the object.

When you work with Active Directory backup and restore operations, you can perform several operations:

- You can back up the entire server, including its operating system.
- You can back up only the System State Data, data that includes the server's configuration data as well as the *Ntds.dit* directory store.
- You can restore nonauthoritative data—data that will be added to the DC but updated by multimaster replication when the DC is back online.
- You can restore authoritative data—data that will be added to the DC but which will update all other DCs through multimaster replication when the DC is back online.
- You can perform Install From Media (IFM) DC setups that rely on a copy of the *Ntds.dit* from another DC to reduce the amount of replication required to create the DC during setup.

There are several ways to work with and use backup data sets when working with DCs in Windows Server 2008. However, if you are familiar with DCs from previous versions of Windows, you will find that several operations are different in Windows Server 2008.

- Backups are performed with Windows Server Backup or through its corresponding *Wbadmin.exe* command-line tool. Both are Windows Server 2008 features and must be added to the server to be made available. It is not installed by default.
- Backups are not discrete. They capture critical volumes in their entirety. On a DC, these volumes include:
  - The system volume.
  - The boot volume.
  - The volume hosting the SYSVOL share.
  - The volume that hosts the AD DS database.
  - The volume that hosts the AD DS logs.
- As with previous versions of Windows, backups can be automated or manual.
- Backups cannot be performed to tape drives or dynamic volumes, only to network drives, removable hard drives configured as basic volumes, or DVDs and CDs.
- You cannot back up individual files. Windows Server Backup supports full volume backups only.

- If you want to protect only the system state data, you must use the *Ntdsutil.exe* command-line tool. To do so, you must use the new IFM switch available in *Ntdsutil.exe* to capture this information for Install From Media installations. If the installation is for a read-only DC, this tool will automatically strip AD DS secrets from the data to create secure installation media.

- Backup operators cannot create scheduled backups; only members of the local Administrators group have this privilege in Windows Server 2008. In most cases, this means being a member of the Domain Admins group on DCs.

- If a server is down, you must use a local copy of the Windows Recovery Environment (WinRE) to restore the system. WinRE can either be installed locally or found on the Windows Server 2008 installation media.

These new capabilities affect the way you work with DCs in Windows Server 2008. Use the following recommendations when building DCs to make them easier to recover:

- Run DCs as a single-purpose server and do not add any other roles except the DNS Server role to the server.

- Run DCs as virtual machines under Windows Server 2008 Hyper-V. DCs are ideal candidates for Hyper-V because they mostly require network throughput and processing capability to manage logons. Even if your domains include thousands of users and have a high processor usage during key logon periods such as the morning and the afternoon after lunch, virtualize them and assign more resources to them.

- Do not store any other data on the DC, although you can use separate volumes for the DC database and logs if your AD DS database includes large numbers of objects.

- Transform the Windows Installation Media into an ISO file and make it available on your Hyper-V hosts so that it is readily available if you need to restore the DC. If not, install WinRE onto each DC you create. To do so, you will need access to the Windows Automated Installation Kit (WAIK).

MORE INFO Windows Automated Installation Kit (WAIK)

For more information about the Windows Automated Installation Kit, go to *http://go.microsoft.com/fwlink/?LinkId=90643*.

- Perform regular, automated backups of your DCs. These can be to a dedicated basic volume or to a mapped network drive.

- Protect the Directory Services Restore Mode password carefully. This password must be used to restore data to a DC and, because it is a highly privileged password, it must be protected at all times.

MORE INFO   **AD DS backup and recovery**

Find more information in "Step-By-Step Guide for Windows Server 2008 Active Directory Domain Services Backup and Recovery" at *http://technet2.microsoft.com/windowsserver2008/en /library/778ff4c7-623d-4475-ba70-4453f964d4911033.mspx*.

Working with the System State Only

On a server running the AD DS role, system state data includes the following data:

- Registry
- COM+ Class Registration database
- Boot files
- System files that are under Windows Resource Protection
- Active Directory Domain Services database
- SYSVOL directory

When other server roles are installed on a system, the system state will include the first four objects listed previously plus the following files:

- For the Active Directory Certificate Services role: AD CS database
- For the Failover Cluster feature: cluster service information
- For the Web Server role: IIS configuration files

System state information is important although it cannot be captured as is through Windows Server Backup. It can, however, be restored because Windows Server Backup supports three restore modes:

- Full server restore
- System state only restore
- Individual file or folder restore

Each mode enables you to recover the information you need when you need it. Keep in mind that backups generated by Windows Server Backup are always backed up to the same file and added to file content as changes are identified on the source system. However, each time a backup is generated, a new catalog file is created. This catalog file is used to locate data for a particular backup.

Exam Tip   Using Windows Server Backup, backing up volumes and system state data to removable media is an important part of the exam. Make sure you understand it fully.

Creating Installation From Media Data Sets

When you need to stage DCs in large networks, you might prefer to use removable media to create the initial directory content rather than filling up bandwidth to replicate directory contents during the DC installation process. To do this, you rely on Installation From Media, but to create the media, you must use the *Ntdsutil.exe* command with the IFM subcommand.

Ntdsutil.exe is a command interpreter and can be used either interactively or through a single command line that provides all options. Table 13-4 outlines the various options that are available in the IFM subcommand.

Table 13-4 *Ntdsutil.exe* IFM Subcommand Options

DC Type	Option	Description
Writable DC	Create Full *destination*	Create media for a normal DC or for an AD LDS instance in a destination folder.
RODC	Create RODC *destination*	Create secure media for an RODC in a destination folder.
Writable DC with SYSVOL data	Create SYSVOL Full *destination*	Create media for a normal DC, including the entire SYSVOL folder, in a destination folder.
RODC with SYSVOL data	Create SYSVOL RODC *destination*	Create media for an RODC, including the entire SYSVOL folder, in a destination folder.

Ntdsutil.exe is the only tool that supports the creation of media for installation. You will be working with this tool in the practice at the end of this lesson.

Performing a Full System Backup

Perform a full system backup in one of two ways: interactively and through a scheduled task. Each can be performed either through the graphical interface or through the command line. Begin with the graphical interface. Keep in mind that Windows Server Backup is a feature that must be installed prior to creating any backups.

Creating an Interactive Full System Backup with Windows Server Backup   Use the following procedure to protect AD DS data with Windows Server Backup. This procedure applies to both the full installation and Server Core, but when applied to Server Core, it must be performed remotely. Use the Connect To Another Computer option in the action pane to connect to a server running Server Core.

1. Log on to a DC with domain administrator credentials and launch Windows Server Backup from the Administrative Tools program group.
2. If a User Account Control dialog box appears, confirm the action and click Continue.
3. Click Backup Once in the Actions pane. This launches the Backup Once Wizard.

4. If this is the first time you run the Backup Once Wizard, choose Different Options and click Next. If not, you can also choose The Same Options.

5. Click Full Server (recommended) and click Next.

    Note that you can also check Custom, but you will not be able to omit anything other than specific volumes. You will not be able to omit folders. Remember that your DCs should be single-purpose servers and, as such, you would not need to exclude any volumes. However, if you are backing up to a local disk, you should exclude this volume from the backup operation. Note that when you use the custom option, you can select an option called Enable System Recovery, which will automatically capture all the data required to recover a full system.

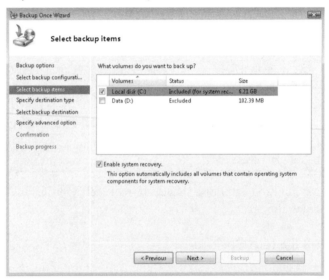

6. Choose the destination, for example, Local drives, and click Next.

    You can target DVDs, CDs, local drives, locally attached removable hard drives, or network shares.

7. If you targeted a local drive, select the drive, make sure it has enough space, and click Next.

8. On the Specify Advanced Option page, select VSS Full Backup and click Next.

    The default option, VSS copy backup, does not delete log files from the volumes and is used only if you are also using another backup product—for example, Microsoft Data Protection Manager—to back up your system. These files are then reused by the other backup tool. You select VSS Full Backup if Windows Server Backup is your only backup tool.

9. Click Backup to perform the backup.

10. Click Close.

You do not need to keep the backup window open for the backup to complete because it will continue in the background; however, it is useful to watch the progress of the backup operation.

Creating an Interactive Full System Backup with *Wbadmin.exe* You can also perform this operation at the command line through the *Wbadmin.exe* command. This procedure applies directly to either the full installation or Server Core. In the full installation, you must use an elevated command prompt—in Server Core, the command prompt is always elevated by default—and use the following command syntax:

```
wbadmin start backup -allcritical -backuptarget:location -quiet
```

where *location* is the drive letter or path to the target drive. Also, you use the –quiet option to avoid having to type **Y** for the operation to proceed.

Scheduling a Backup with Windows Server Backup Use the following procedure to protect AD DS data automatically with Windows Server Backup.

1. Log on to a DC with domain administrator credentials and launch Windows Server Backup from the Administrative Tools program group.
2. If a User Account Control dialog box appears, confirm the action and click Continue.
3. Click Backup Schedule in the Actions pane. This launches the Backup Schedule Wizard; click Next.
4. Click Full Server (Recommended) and click Next.

    Note that you can also click Custom, but this will not let you omit anything other than specific volumes, but you will not be able to omit folders. Also note that in this wizard, when you use the custom option, you will not be able to select the Enable System Recovery option.
5. On the Specify Backup Time page, choose the time of day for the backup. You can also choose to back up the system more than once a day.

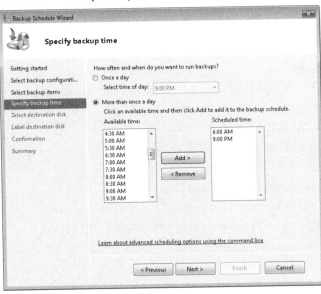

6. On the Select Destination Disk page, click Show All Available Disks, select the remote storage device, and click OK. Select the disk and click Next.

    Note that you cannot use mapped network drives with Windows Server Backup when scheduling backup tasks. It will only address rewritable media such as removable hard drives. It also supports virtual hard drives as a target for backup.

IMPORTANT   Using virtual hard disks for backup

Consider using virtual hard disk (VHD) drives as backup targets because of their portability. You can store all VHDs in a central location and place them on a single removable drive to send it to an offsite location. This enables you to combine multiple backups on one disk as opposed to using multiple removable disks, one per protected system.

---

7. When you click Next, the wizard tells you that the target disk will be reformatted. Click Yes.

    Windows Server Backup requires exclusive access to the target device and, therefore, must format it when the scheduled backup is created.

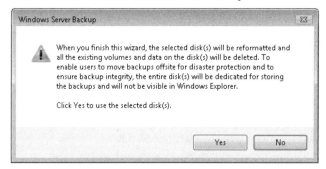

8. On the Label Destination Disk page, you must make note of the label Windows Server Backup will use for this disk before you click Next.

    When you change disks, you will need to know which disk this is to perform restores. You must, therefore, label the disk accordingly.

9. Confirm your options and click Finish.

10. Click Close to create the schedule.

    The target disk will be formatted, and the task will be added to the system's Scheduled Tasks list.

Scheduling a Backup with *Wbadmin.exe*   You can also perform this operation at the command line through the *Wbadmin.exe* command. In this case, you must use an elevated command prompt and rely on several commands. Begin by identifying the ID of the target disk:

```
wbadmin get disks >diskidentifers.txt
```

This will return a list of the disks attached to a system and place it in the Diskidentifiers.txt file. The *Wbadmin.exe* command relies on disk identifiers or globally unique identifiers (GUIDs) to locate a disk. You pipe the results of the command into a text file so that you can copy the target disk's GUID to the clipboard and reuse it in later commands.

To capture the disk GUID, type:

```
notepad diskidentifiers.txt
```

Highlight the disk identifier you need, including the brackets, and copy it to the clipboard. Close Notepad.

You are ready to create the schedule. Type the following commands:

```
wbadmin enable backup -addtarget:diskid -schedule:times -include:sourcedrives
```

where *diskid* is the GUID you copied. (Right-click and choose Paste to add it.) Times is the times when you want the backup to run in HH:MM 24-hour format. If more than one time is required, separate each with a comma. Source drives are the drive letters of the drives to protect. For example:

```
wbadmin enable backup -addtarget:{f0e2788d-0000-0000-0000-000000000000}
-schedule:21:00,06:00 -include:C:
```

will schedule a backup of drive C at 9:00 P.M. and 6:00 A.M. to the target drive identified by the GUID.

The result is a new scheduled task under the Microsoft\Windows\Backup node of the Task Scheduler. (See Figure 13-6.)

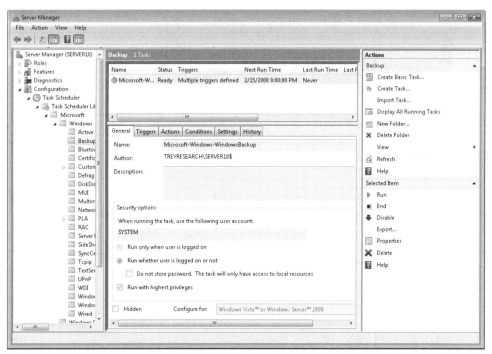

Figure 13-6 The scheduled task created by *Wbadmin.exe*

You can use this procedure to generate batch files to create these jobs, but you must pipe the results into a text file; otherwise, you will not obtain the labels for the removable disks.

Also note that the target drive will be reformatted each time the backup is run. If you need more granular schedules or if you want to change from a daily to a weekly schedule, you can modify the task in Task Scheduler after the *Wbadmin.exe* command has created it.

Performing Proactive Restores

Backup data sets are only as good as the restores and recoveries they support. This is why it is essential for you to test the restoration procedure and to test as many scenarios as possible to ensure that when you do face a disaster, you can recover the data or systems you lost by relying on your backups.

When working with a DC, there are several restoration scenarios:

■ Restoring nonauthoritative data to the directory to reduce the replication required to update a DC that has been off for some time

- Restoring authoritative data because the data in the directory has been destroyed
- Restoring a complete DC from a backup

When you need to restore data to a system, you cannot do so when the DC is running, despite the fact that in Windows Server 2008, you can control the AD DS service as you would other services. In fact, you must restart the server and run WinRE, or you must restart the server in the Directory Services Restore Mode (DSRM). Each method supports different restoration procedures. DSRM supports data restores to the directory; WinRE supports the recovery of the entire system.

Restarting in DSRM

There are two ways to launch a server into DSRM. The first relies on a server reboot and, during the reboot process, pressing F8 to view startup options. This enables you to choose the Directory Services Restore Mode. Remember that you need to have access to the DSRM password to use this mode.

```
                        Advanced Boot Options

Choose Advanced Options for: Microsoft Windows Server 2008
(Use the arrow keys to highlight your choice.)

    Safe Mode
    Safe Mode with Networking
    Safe Mode with Command Prompt

    Enable Boot Logging
    Enable low-resolution video (640x480)
    Last Known Good Configuration (advanced)
    Directory Services Restore Mode
    Debugging Mode
    Disable automatic restart on system failure
    Disable Driver Signature Enforcement

    Start Windows Normally

Description: Start Windows in Directory Services Repair Mode (for Windows
            domain controllers only).


 ENTER=Choose                                              ESC=Cancel
```

You can also force the reboot directly into DSRM by changing the boot order in the boot file of the OS. This is done with the *Bcdedit.exe* command. To use the command line to change the boot order, type the following command in an elevated command prompt:

```
bcdedit /set safeboot dsrepair
```

Then, when you need to restart the server normally, use the following command:

```
bcdedit /deletevalue safeboot
```

If you need to perform the operation only once, it might be best simply to rely on the F8 key at system startup.

IMPORTANT Resetting the DSRM password

Keep in mind that to reset the DSRM password—an activity you should perform on a regular basis—you must first boot into DSRM and then use the standard password changing methods.

Identifying the Appropriate Backup Data Set

One of the problems organizations who used AD DS in previous versions of Windows faced was the ability to identify properly whether the data they require is located in a particular backup data set. In Windows Server 2008, you can rely on the AD DS database mounting tool to view the contents of a data set before you perform a recovery operation. This avoids the previous hit-or-miss approach system administrators needed to rely on.

The mounting tool works with database snapshots. Snapshots can easily be created with the *Ntdsutil.exe* tool. For example, to generate regular snapshots of a directory, you would use the following command:

```
ntdsutil "activate instance NTDS" snapshot create quit quit
```

This will generate a snapshot on the same volume as the database. Be careful how you use this command because it will quickly fill up the disk on which the *Ntds.dit* database file is located.

Perform the following steps to view backup data set or snapshot contents.

1. Launch an elevated command prompt by right-clicking Command Prompt in the Start menu and choosing Run As Administrator.

2. Begin by listing the available snapshots. Snapshots are created each time a backup is run or through the *Ntdsutil.exe create* subcommand, but you need to have the snapshot GUID to mount it. Use the following command to pipe all snapshot GUIDs into a text file.

   ```
   ntdsutil "activate instance NTDS" snapshot "list all" quit quit >snapshot.txt
   ```

3. Now, look into the text file to locate and copy the GUID you need:

   ```
   notepad snapshot.txt
   ```

4. Locate the GUID you need and copy it to the clipboard. Remember to include the brackets in the selection. Minimize Notepad in case you need a different GUID.

5. Mount the snapshot you need to use. Remember to right-click and choose Paste to paste the GUID at the mount command.

```
ntdsutil
activate instance NTDS
snapshot
mount guid
quit
quit
```

Note the path listed for the mounted database.

6. Use the AD DS database mounting tool to load the snapshot as an LDAP server.

```
dsamain -dbpath c:\$snap_datetime_volumec$\windows\ntds\ntds.dit
-ldapport portnumber
```

Be sure to use ALL CAPS for the *dbpath* value and use any number beyond 50,000 for the *ldapport* value to make sure you do not conflict with AD DS. Also note that you can use the minus (–) sign or the slash (/) for the options in the command. The database will be mounted and will stay mounted until you have completed your operations. *Do not close the command prompt.* In fact, you might want to use two command prompts, one for mounting the snapshot in *Ntdsutil.exe* and one for the *Dsamin.exe* command. Then you can mount and dismount different snapshots until you locate the one that contains the information you need to recover.

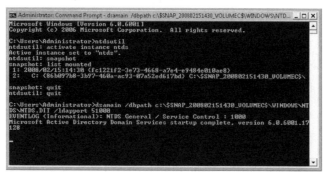

7. Now use *Ldp.exe* or Active Directory Users and Computers to access the instance. For example, launch Active Directory Users And Computers from the Administrative Tools program group.

8. Right-click Active Directory Users And Computers and select Change Domain Controller.

9. In the Change Directory Server dialog box, click <Type A Directory Server Name[:Port] Here>, type the *servername:portnumber*, for example, **Server10:51000**, and press Enter. The status should be online. Click OK.

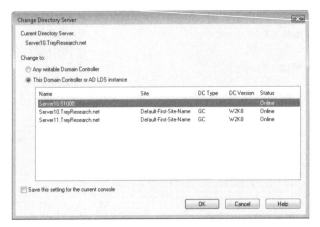

10. Search the loaded instance to locate the information you need and view its properties. If it is the instance you need, then make note of its name. Close Active Directory Users And Computers.

11. Return to the command prompt and press Ctrl+C to stop *Dsamain.exe*.

12. Unmount the database snapshot. Use the following command. Remember to paste in the GUID from the clipboard.

```
ntdsutil
activate instance NTDS
snapshot
unmount guid
quit
quit
```

13. Close the command prompt.

If the selected database snapshot was not the one you were looking for, repeat the procedure. If it was, proceed to a restore.

IMPORTANT **Using arrow keys in command prompts**

Keep in mind that you can use the up and down arrow keys when you are in a command prompt to return to previous commands. Also, note that there are different buffers in the command prompt. For example, there is a buffer in the command prompt itself and then a different buffer in the *Ntdsutil.exe* command. You can use both to return to previous commands and save typing.

Performing Nonauthoritative or Authoritative Restores

As mentioned earlier, performing a restore requires you to restart the directory in DSRM. This means shutting down the DC. Remember that you can perform either nonauthoritative or authoritative restores on both the full installation or Server Core. The first addresses a DC rebuild when no data was lost because it is still found on other DCs. The second restores data that was lost and updates the Update Sequence Number (USN) for the data to make it authoritative and ensure that it is replicated to all other servers. Both use the same procedure at first. Make sure you have connected the removable media on which you stored the backup you want to restore.

1. Repair the server, if required, and start it up. During startup, press F8 to view the startup modes.

2. Select Directory Services Restore Mode and press Enter.

3. This will boot into Windows. Log on with the DSRM account and password; this should be the account displayed at the logon screen and the DSRM password you set when you created the DC.

    You can restore the data either through the command line or with Windows Server Backup. Note, however, that when you want to restore directory data, you must perform a System State restore and, to do so, you must use the command line.

4. Launch an elevated command prompt by right-clicking Command Prompt in the Start menu and choosing Run As Administrator.

5. Type the following command:

    ```
    wbadmin get versions –backuptarget:drive –machine:servername
    ```

    For example, to list the available backups located on D drive on SERVER10, type:

    ```
    wbadmin get versions –backuptarget:d: –machine:server10
    ```

    Note the version identifier information because you need the exact name for the next command.

6. To recover system state information, type the following command:

    ```
    wbadmin start systemstaterecovery –version:datetime –backuptarget:drive
    –machine:servername -quiet
    ```

    For example, to recover the system state from a backup dated 15 February, 2008, from D drive on SERVER10, type:

    ```
    wbadmin start systemstaterecovery –version:02/15/2008-19:38
    –backuptarget:d: –machine:server10 -quiet
    ```

    You use the –quiet option to avoid having to confirm the backup operation. Note that the restore will take some time to complete.

7. Close the command prompt.

    If you were performing a nonauthoritative restore, you would be finished.

8. Restart the DC in its normal operating mode.

    When you restart the server, AD DS will automatically know that it has recovered from a restore and perform an integrity check of the database as it starts.

IMPORTANT   Using DFS replication

If your forest is in Windows Server 2008 functional mode, you will be using DFS replication. In this case, the restore will create a nonauthoritative version of the SYSVOL share. If you want to avoid additional replication, add the *–authsysvol* switch to the *Wbadmin.exe* command.

If, however, you are performing an authoritative restore, you must mark the data as authoritative. *Do not restart the server.* Use the following steps.

1. Type the following commands:

    ```
    ntdsutil
    authoritative restore
    restore database
    quit
    quit
    ```

2. Restart the server in normal mode.

    The restore database command marks all the data in the *Ntds.dit* database of this DC as authoritative.

    If you want to restore only a portion of the directory, use the following restore subcommand in *Ntdsutil.exe*:

    ```
    restore subtree ou=ouname,dc=dcname,dc=dcname
    ```

    where you must supply the distinguished name of the OU or object you want to restore.

After the server is restarted, the replication process will start, and the restored information that has been marked as authoritative will be replicated to all other DCs. However, it might restart several times as the restore operation updates system files. AD DS replication will bring it up to date when it has restarted for the last time either by replicating from this DC to others because the restore was authoritative or from other DCs to this one when the restore was nonauthoritative.

Exam Tip   Performing an authoritative or nonauthoritative Active Directory restore and working in Directory Services Recovery Mode are important parts of this topic on the exam.

Restoring from a Complete Backup

When the DC is completely down and needs to be rebuilt, but you have access to a full server backup, you can perform a complete system restore. You will need access to the full server backup files. If they are on a removable drive, make sure this drive is connected to the server before you begin the restore; otherwise, you will need to restart the server. If the files are on a network drive, make note of the path. Also, obtain the Windows Installation Media DVD or, if your new DC is a virtual machine, link its DVD drive to an ISO file containing the Windows Installation Media.

Full server recoveries can be performed through the graphical interface or through the command line.

Performing a Graphical Full Server Recovery   To perform a full server recovery with the graphical interface, use the following procedure. This procedure applies to both the full installation and Server Core.

1. Insert or connect the Windows Server 2008 installation DVD, restart the computer and, when prompted, press a key to start from the DVD.

2. On the initial Windows screen, accept or select Language options, the Time and Currency formats, and a Keyboard layout, and click Next.

3. In the Install Now window, click Repair Your Computer.

4. In the System Recovery Options dialog box, click anywhere to clear any operating systems that are selected for repair and click Next.

5. Under Choose A Recovery Tool, select Windows Complete PC Restore.

6. If the backup is stored on a remote server, click Cancel on the warning message.

7. Select Restore A Different Backup and click Next.

8. In the Select The Location Of The Backup page, perform the following steps, depending on whether the backup is stored locally or on a network share:

   a. If the backup is stored on the local computer, select the location of the backup and click Next.

   b. If the backup is stored on a network share, click Advanced and select Search For A Backup On The Network. Click Yes to confirm.

   c. In the Network Folder, type the path for the network share and click OK.

   d. Type the appropriate credentials and click OK.

   e. In the Select The Location Of The Backup page, select the location of the backup and click Next.

9. Select the backup to restore and click Next.

10. If you want to replace all data on all volumes, in the Choose How To Restore The Backup page, select Format And Repartition Disks.

11. To prevent volumes that are not included in the restore from being deleted and re-created, select Exclude Disks, select the disk(s) you want to exclude, and click OK.

12. Click Next and click Finish.

13. Select I Confirm That I Want To Format The Disks And Restore The Backup and click OK.

14. Reboot the server.

    It should start as a new image of the server you restored in the backup set you used.

Performing a Command-Line Full Server Recovery   To perform a full server recovery with the command line, use the following procedure. This procedure applies directly to either the full installation or Server Core.

1. Insert or connect the Windows Server 2008 installation DVD, restart the DC, and, when prompted, press a key to start from the DVD.

2. On the initial Windows screen, accept or select Language options, the Time and Currency formats, and a Keyboard layout, and click Next.

3. In the Install Now window, click Repair Your Computer.

4. In the System Recovery Options dialog box, click anywhere to clear any operating systems that are selected for repair and click Next.

5. Under Choose A Recovery Tool, select Command Prompt.

6. At the command prompt, type **diskpart** and press Enter.

7. At the diskpart prompt, type **list vol** and press Enter.

Identify the volume from the list that corresponds to the location of the full server backup you want to restore. The driver letters in WinRE do not necessarily match the volumes as they appeared in Windows Server 2008.

8. Type **exit** and press Enter.

9. At the Sources prompt, type the following command and press Enter:

```
wbadmin get versions –backuptarget:drive -machine:servername
```

For example, to list the available backups located on D drive on SERVER10, type:

```
wbadmin get versions –backuptarget:D: –machine:SERVER10
```

Note the version identifier information because you need the exact name for the next command.

10. At the command prompt, type the following command and press Enter:

```
wbadmin start systemstaterecovery –version:datetime –backuptarget:drive
–machine:servername -quiet
```

For example, to recover the system state from a backup dated 15 February, 2008, from D drive on SERVER10, type:

```
wbadmin start sysrecovery –version:02/15/2008-19:38 –backuptarget:d:
–machine:server10 –restoreallvolumes -quiet
```

You use the –quiet option to avoid having to confirm the backup operation.

11. After the recovery operation has completed, minimize the command window and, in the System Recovery Options dialog box, click Restart.

The server should restart and operate normally.

Quick Check

1. You are trying to move a group of objects from one location to the other in the directory, and you keep getting an access denied error. What could be the problem?

2. You look up a backup on one of your removable disks and discover to your dismay that the disk is completely blank. What could have happened?

3. Your forest is running in Windows Server 2008 full functional mode. Which tool should you rely on to manage replication between DCs?

4. What is the difference between reassigning a user account and re-creating the account?

5. You are trying to view directory changes in the event log. Specifically, you are searching for event IDs numbered 5136; but you can't seem to find them anywhere. What could be the problem?

Quick Check Answers

1. The objects have been assigned the *Protect From Accidental Deletion* attribute. Because of this, they cannot be moved from one location to another. You must use Advanced Features from the View menu to view the feature and then go to the object's Properties dialog box and the Object tab to clear the option before moving the objects. Make sure you recheck the option after the move has been performed.

2. When Windows Server Backup is run as a scheduled task, it always begins by formatting the target backup disk. If the task is interrupted after the formatting, for example, by a computer reboot, the backup operation would not occur, leaving the target disk blank.

3. When a forest runs in Windows Server 2008 full functional mode, replication no longer relies on the File Replication System. Instead, replication relies on the delta-based compression replication provided by the Distributed File System Replication engine. This means that you must use *DFSRadmin.exe* to manage replication.

4. When you reassign an account from one person to the other, the new person automatically gains all the access rights previously assigned to the account. When you re-create an account, you must first discover which rights need to be assigned and then assign them manually to the new account.

5. To enable directory object auditing, you must manually enable the event subcategory with the following command:

```
auditpol /set /subcategory:"directory service changes" /success:enable
```

Protecting DCs as Virtual Machines

When a server is created as a VM instead of being installed on a physical computer, it becomes nothing more than a set of files on a disk because the disk drives for the computer are hosted in virtual hard drives. DCs running both AD DS and DNS are ideal candidates for virtualization on either Microsoft Virtual Server R2 or on Hyper-V because they focus on providing a single, network-oriented service. When a machine is virtual, it becomes much easier to protect it, restore it, and otherwise manipulate it. If the server has a full system failure, just go back to an earlier version of the virtual machine and boot it up. In the case of a DC, multimaster replication will then automatically take care of the rest and bring it up to date. This is by far the most powerful business continuity scenario for DCs.

In addition, virtual machine protection is greatly facilitated by a single Windows Server 2008 feature: the Volume Shadow Copy Service (VSS). When configured, VSS automatically takes snapshots of the contents of a disk drive at regular intervals. If anything untoward occurs to any file on the disk drive, you simply rely on Previous Versions—a tab that appears in the Properties dialog box of any file or folder—to restore an older version of the file or folder quickly. Previous versions are enabled by default on Windows Server 2008 and Windows Vista.

On a virtual machine, you restore the virtual hard drives that make up the machine from a previous time or date, and your machine is back up and running. Overall, this procedure takes about five minutes. No other backup and restore scenario can compete with VSS and VMs.

VSS should be enabled on host servers that maintain and run the virtual machines in your data center. VSS can be added to either the full installation or Server Core. It takes about 10 minutes to enable VSS on any server; however, you must be prepared and have the proper disk structure. For example, a host system running Hyper-V should have at least three disk volumes:

- Drive C should be the system and boot drive and should host the Hyper-V role.
- Drive D should be the data drive that hosts the virtual machines. This drive should normally be stored on some form of shared storage to support continuity for the VMs it hosts.
- Drive E should be configured to host the VSS snapshots that will be created on an ongoing basis. Each VSS snapshot is 100 MB in size because it captures only disk pointers and not the entire disk structure. You can store up to 512 snapshots at a time. When you reach this maximum, VSS will automatically overwrite the oldest snapshots. Size this disk accordingly.

Enabling VSS involves the following steps:

1. Log on to the host server with local administration credentials.
2. Open Windows Explorer, locate drive D, right-click it, and select Properties.
3. In the Properties dialog box, select the Shadow Copies tab.
4. Begin by specifying VSS settings. Click the Settings button.
5. In the Settings dialog box, use the drop-down list to select D: Drive. Set the limit for the copy as appropriate (the default should be fine) and change the schedule if required. Click OK.
6. Select D: from the Select Volume list and click Enable. In the Enable Shadow Copies dialog box, click Yes.

   Begin with the default schedule at first; you can always change it later. The VSS service is now enabled.
7. Click Create Now to take the first snapshot. This generates the first protection set for the VMs.
8. Click OK to close the D drive Properties dialog box.

You can also perform this operation through the command line. If your host servers are running Server Core—as they should be to minimize host server CPU overhead—you will need to perform this operation either remotely or through the command line. Use the following commands:

```
vssadmin add shadowstorage /for=d: /on=e: /maxsize=6000mb
vssadmin create shadow /for=d:
vssadmin list shadowstorage
vssadmin list shadows
```

The first command sets up the shadow copies according to the default schedule. The second creates the first shadow copy. The next two list the associations and then available shadow copies.

Shadow copy schedules are scheduled tasks. To control the scheduled task and modify its schedule, rely on the *Schtasks.exe* command or use the Task Scheduler remotely in the Computer Management console.

To access previous versions of a file or a folder, open Windows Explorer, connect to a shared folder, in this case the default share created by the system, D$, and locate either the file or, if the file is gone, the folder in which it was stored; right-click it to select Properties, move to the Previous Versions tab, select the version you need, and click Restore. Close the Properties dialog box. You can also copy and compare files.

Monitor VSS usage to determine whether the default schedule is appropriate. Review how you use the VSS service to see whether you need to modify the default schedule. As you can see, VSS rivals any other backup and restore process for virtual machines.

MORE INFO **Providing high availability for virtual machines**

A discussion on how to provide high availability for virtual machines is beyond the scope of this book. However, if you are interested in preparing host servers running Server Core and Hyper-V, look up *Microsoft Windows Server 2008: The Complete Reference* by Ruest and Ruest (McGraw-Hill Osborne, 2008). This book outlines how to build a complete dynamic infrastructure based on Windows Server 2008.

PRACTICE **Working with the AD DS Database**

In this practice, you will work with a variety of utilities to protect and manage the AD DS database. First, you will generate a backup of directory data and then use this backup to create a new DC, using offline data to speed the process and reduce replication over the network. Then you will work with the AD DS database to perform a manual defragmentation and compaction and then automate the process. Finally, you will rely on the Group Policy Management Console (GPMC) to protect Group Policy objects. This practice relies on SERVER10 and SERVER11, which you prepared in the Before You Begin section at the beginning of this chapter.

▶ **Exercise 1   Use *Ntdsutil.exe* to Capture System State Data**

In this exercise, you will use the *Ntdsutil.exe* command to capture the data required to perform an installation from media for a DC.

   1.   Log on to SERVER 10 with the domain administrator account.

2. Verify that this server includes a formatted D drive and create a folder named **IFM** on this drive.

3. Launch an elevated command prompt by right-clicking Command Prompt in the Start menu and choosing Run As Administrator.

4. Type the following commands:

```
ntdsutil
activate instance NTDS
ifm
create sysvol full d:\ifm
```

The system should display a Creating Snapshot message while the operation is in progress and then list a series of other information as it completes the operation. Note that the system defragments the newly captured snapshot.

5. Type:

```
quit
quit
```

6. Use Windows Explorer to view the results of the snapshot you created with *Ntdusutil.exe*.

7. Share the IFM folder by right-clicking the folder and choosing Share.

8. In the drop-down list, choose Everyone, click Add, and assign the Contributor role in the Permission Level column.

9. Click Share to create the share.

10. Click Done.

Your IFM data is now ready to use to stage a new DC.

▶ **Exercise 2   Create a DC from Backup Data**

In this exercise, you will install a new DC in the *treyresearch.net* domain, using IFM data.

1. Log on to SERVER 11 with the local administrator account.

2. Launch Windows Explorer and create a new folder on the C drive, called IFM.

3. Move to the address bar in Windows Explorer, type **\\server10\ifm**, and press Enter.

4. If the credentials dialog box appears, type **TreyResearch\Administrator** or equivalent and the required password.

    If you use the same account name and password on both servers, even though SERVER11 is not a member of the domain, you will not be prompted for credentials because of pass-through authentication.

5. Copy the entire contents from the IFM folder on SERVER10 to the C:\IFM folder on SERVER11.

6. Verify that all items have been copied.

7. Install the Active Directory Domain Services role. In Server Manager, right-click the Roles node and select Add Roles.

8. Review the Before You Begin page of the wizard and click Next.

9. On the Select Server Roles page of the Add Roles Wizard, select Active Directory Domain Services and click Next.

10. Review the information on the Active Directory Domain Services page and click Next.

11. Review your choices and click Install.

12. Examine the installation results and click Close.

    Your installation is complete.

13. Click the Active Directory Domain Services node in Server Manager.

14. Click Run The Active Directory Domain Services Installation Wizard in the details pane.

    This launches the Active Directory Domain Services Installation Wizard.

15. Make sure you select the Use Advanced Mode Installation check box before you click Next.

    You need this option to install from media.

16. Review the information on the Operating System Compatibility page and click Next.

17. On the Choose A Deployment Configuration page, choose Existing Forest, select Add A Domain Controller To An Existing Domain, and click Next.

18. On the Network Credentials page, type **treyresearch.net**.

    Because you logged on locally to the server and this account does not have access rights to the *treyresearch.net* domain, you must provide alternate credentials.

19. Click Set. Type **treyresearch.net\administrator** or the equivalent account name and add the password. Click OK, and then click Next.

20. On the Select A Domain page, click *treyresearch.net* (forest root domain) and click Next.

21. On the Select A Site page, accept the default and click Next.

    This page also appears because you are running the wizard in advanced mode.

22. On the Additional Domain Controller Options page, verify that DNS Server and Global Catalog are both selected and click Next.

If you did not assign a static IP address, the AD DS Active Directory Domain Services Installation Wizard will give you a warning because you are using a dynamic IP Address.

23. Click the Yes, The Computer Will Use A Dynamically Assigned IP Address (Not Recommended) option.

The Active Directory Domain Services Installation Wizard will warn you that it cannot create a delegation for the domain.

24. Click Yes.

25. On the Install From Media page, click Replicate Data From Media At The Following Location, type **C:\IFM** or click Browse to locate the IFM folder on the C drive, and click Next.

Note that it indicates that the media must have been created from a writable DC because you did not select the RODC mode for this DC.

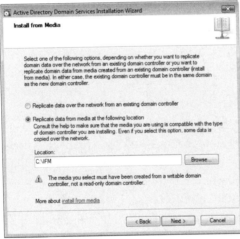

26. On the Source Domain Controller page, accept the defaults and click Next.

27. On the Location For Database, Log Files And SYSVOL page, accept the default locations and click Next.

28. Type a strong password, confirm it, and click Next.

29. Confirm your settings on the Summary page and click Next. Select Reboot On Completion and wait for the operation to complete.

Your new DC has been created from local media. This cuts down replication and then updates the data through replication after the DC has been created.

▶ **Exercise 3   Perform Database Maintenance**

In this exercise, you will perform interactive database maintenance, using the restartable Active Directory Domain Services mode. You can perform this operation now because there are two DCs in the *treyresearch.net* domain. You must have at least two DCs to be able to use restartable AD DS.

1. Log on to SERVER11 with the domain administrator account.

2. Use Windows Explorer to create a **C:\Temp** and a **C:\OrignalNTDS** folder.

   You will use these folders as temporary locations for the compacted and the original database.

3. In Server Manager, expand the Configuration node and click Services.

4. Locate the Active Directory Domain Services service (it should be first on the list) and right-click it to select Stop.

5. In the Stop Other Services dialog box, click Yes.

   The server will stop the service.

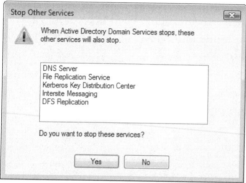

   Remember that if the service cannot contact another writable DC, it will not be able to stop; otherwise, no one would be able to log on to the domain.

6. Launch an elevated command prompt by right-clicking Command Prompt in the Start menu and choosing Run As Administrator.

7. Begin by compacting the database. Type the following commands:

   ```
   ntdsutil
   activate instance NTDS
   files
   compact to C:\temp
   ```

   The *Ntdsutil.exe* will compact the database and copy it to the new location. In very large directories, this operation can take some time.

   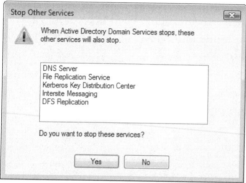

8. Type the following after the compaction operation is complete:

```
quit
quit
```

9. Now, delete all the log files. Type the following:

```
cd %systemroot%\ntds
del *.log
```

You delete the log files because you will be replacing the *Ntds.dit* file with the newly compacted file, and the existing log files will not work with the newly compacted database.

10. Now, back up the *Ntds.dit* file to protect it in case something goes wrong. Type the following:

```
copy ntds.dit \originalntds
```

11. Copy the newly compacted database to the original NTDS folder. Making sure you are still within the %SystemRoot%\NTDS folder, type the following:

```
copy c:\temp\ntds.dit
y
```

12. Finally, verify the integrity of the new *Ntds.dit* file.

After this is done, you will also perform a semantic database analysis to verify the data within the database. Type the following:

```
ntdsutil
activate instance NTDS
files
integrity
quit
semantic database analysis
go fixup
quit
quit
```

Note that if the integrity check fails, you must recopy the original *Ntds.dit* back to this folder because the newly compacted file is corrupt. If you do not do so, your DC will no longer be operational.

13. Return to Server Manager, expand the Configuration node, and click Services.

14. Locate the Active Directory Domain Services service (it should be first on the list) and right-click it to select Start.

Your server is back online and ready to deliver authentication services to the network. It can take several minutes for the dependent services to restart. Delete the Ntds.dit located in the Original NTDS folder because it is no longer valid.

▶ **Exercise 4   Automate Database Maintenance**

You can script the entire database compaction operation from the command line if you want to automate it. You should, however, make sure all the operational results are captured in a text file so that you can review them if something goes wrong.

1. Log on to SERVER11 with the domain administrator account.

2. Also, make sure both a **C:\Temp** folder and a **C:\NTDS** folder exist on your server and that both folders are empty.

   You will use this folder as a temporary location for the compacted database. You are ready to automate the compaction process.

3. Move to the C:\Temp folder and right-click in the details pane to select New; then click Text Document.

4. Name the Text document **Compaction.cmd**.

   If you cannot see the .txt extension of the file, click Folder Options from the Tools menu in Windows Explorer. On the View tab, clear Hide Extensions For Known File Types and click OK. Remove the .txt extension on your file name. Confirm the removal.

5. Right-click Compaction.cmd and choose Edit. Type the following commands:

```
del C:\temp\*.dit
del C:\originalntds\*.dit
net stop ntds /y
ntdsutil "activate instance NTDS" files "compact to C:\temp" quit quit
\cd \windows\ntds
del *.log
copy ntds.dit \originalntds
del ntds.dit
copy c:\temp\ntds.dit
ntdsutil "activate instance NTDS" files integrity quit "semantic database
analysis" "go fixup" quit quit
net start ntds
```

6. Save and close the Compaction.cmd file.

   Note that you can add a pause command after each command in your text file to verify the proper operation of the commands while testing.

7. Test the file by launching an elevated command prompt by right-clicking Command Prompt in the Start menu and choosing Run As Administrator.

8. Type:

```
cd \temp
compaction
```

9. If at any time the file does not work, use Ctrl+C to cancel the batch file and correct the errors.

   If the file works properly, you can use it to automate the compaction process.

10. Remove any pause statements you entered in the file and save it again.

    You can reuse this command file each time you want to run the compaction on your systems. It is recommended that you run this command file interactively to address any errors or issues during the process. Be very wary of putting this file into a scheduled task. You should never run compaction in unattended mode because errors could destroy your DC.

11. If a DC is nonfunctioning, you can use the following command to remove the DC role:

    `dcpromo /forceremoval`

12. Run the Active Directory Domain Services Installation Wizard again to re-create the DC. Perform the *Ntds.dit* compaction operation at least once a month.

▶ Exercise 5   Protect Group Policy Objects

In this exercise, you will use the GPMC to back up GPOs.

1. Log on to SERVER11 with the domain administrator account.
2. Verify the existence of a folder named Temp on the C drive.
3. Launch the GPMC from the Administrative Tools program group.
4. Expand Forest\Domains*domainname*\Goup Policy Objects.
5. Right-click Group Policy Objects and select Back Up All.
6. Type the location as **C:\Temp** or use the Browse button to locate the folder.
7. Type a description, in this case, **First GPO Backup** and click Back Up.
   The GPO backup tool will show the progress of the backup.
8. Click OK after the backup is complete.
   Your GPOs are now protected.
9. Back up the Temp folder.
   You can rely on this folder to copy the GPOs from one domain to another if you wish. Perform this operation at least once a week.

Exam Tip   Backing up and restoring GPOs are both important parts of the exam. Practice these operations thoroughly to prepare for this topic.

Lesson Summary

- To maintain your directory service, you must perform proactive maintenance tasks. These tasks fall into twelve categories, many of which should be delegated to others. Domain administrators are responsible for the AD DS service and should focus on core directory operations such as database administration tasks.
- Several tools are available for AD DS administration. The most commonly used tools are the three main Active Directory consoles: Active Directory Users and Computers, Active Directory Sites and Services, and Active Directory Domains and Trusts.
- With Windows Server 2008, AD DS is now a manageable service like all other servers and can be started and stopped without having to restart the server in Directory Services Restore Mode.
- When you delete an object in AD DS, you must restore the object to re-create its properties. If you simply re-create the object, it will not have the same SID and, therefore, will

not retain any of the deleted object's properties. Restoring an object restores the original SID and, therefore, will automatically restore most of the access rights associated with the object.

- There are several ways to protect information in the directory:
    - ❏ You can protect objects from deletion.
    - ❏ You can audit AD DS changes to view previous and changed values when changes are made.
    - ❏ You can rely on the tombstone container to recover deleted objects.
    - ❏ You can rely on backup and restore to recover lost information.

- To restore objects from the deleted objects container in AD DS, you must use a tool that will expose this container and enable you to modify the state of the object. Two tools are available for this operation: *Ldp.exe* and Quest Object Restore for Active Directory. After the object is restored, you must reassign its password, group memberships, and other informational attributes and then enable the object.

- When you restore an object from backup, the object is restored with all its previous attributes. No additional changes are required.

Lesson Review

You can use the following questions to test your knowledge of the information in Lesson 1, "Proactive Directory Maintenance and Data Store Protection." The questions are also available on the companion CD if you prefer to review them in electronic form.

NOTE   Answers

Answers to these questions and explanations of why each answer choice is right or wrong are located in the "Answers" section at the end of the book.

---

1. You are a systems administrator for *contoso.com*. You have been requested to compact the database on one of the two DCs for the forest root domain. However, when you try to stop the AD DS service, you find that you cannot stop it on the server you are working on. What could be the problem?

    A. You cannot stop the AD DS service on a Windows Server 2008 DC.

    B. Someone else is working on another DC in this domain.

    C. You must restart the server in Directory Services Restore Mode.

    D. You must use the *net stop* command to stop the AD DS service.

2. You are the network administrator of a large network. One of your DCs recently failed. You need to restore the DC to a working state. You have several backups of the server that were created with Windows Server Backup. Which of the following steps should you perform? (Choose all that apply.)

A. Restart the server in Directory Services Restore Mode.

B. Perform an authoritative restore using the *Ntdsutil.exe* command.

C. Reinstall Windows Server 2008.

D. Restart the server in WinRE.

E. Perform a nonauthoritative restore using the *Ntdsutil.exe* command.

F. Perform a full server recovery using the command line.

Lesson 2: Proactive Directory Performance Management

The second activity you must master to maintain your DCs proactively is performance management. When you use proper installation and creation procedures, your DCs should just work. Remember that the Domain Controller role is now in its fifth iteration since it appeared in Microsoft Windows NT, and it has evolved with the different releases of the Microsoft server operating system. This means that it is now a very solid and stable service.

However, you'll find that despite this stability, things can still go wrong, whether they are related to system or human errors. And when they do, you need to be ready to identify the issues quickly and take appropriate steps to correct the situation. When you perform proactive performance management, you are forewarned when untoward events might occur. This is the crux of this lesson.

> **After this lesson, you will be able to:**
> - Work with system performance indicators.
> - Use the Windows Server performance and reliability tools.
> - Use the Windows System Resource Monitor.
> - Generate and view performance reports.
>
> **Estimated lesson time: 45 minutes**

Managing System Resources

Windows Server includes several tools that help identify potential issues with system resources. When systems are not configured properly and are not assigned appropriate resources such as CPU, RAM, or disk space, systems monitoring will help you identify where bottlenecks occur. When you identify these bottlenecks, you then assign additional resources to the system. If the system is physical, this most often means shutting down the system; installing new resources, for example, additional memory chips; and then restarting the system. If the system is virtual, then depending on the virtualization engine you use, you might be able to allocate new resources while the virtual machine is still running. If not, shut it down; allocate new resources, for example, an additional CPU and additional RAM; and then restart it. After the system is restarted, monitor its performance again to identify whether the new resources solved the problem.

The tools you can rely on to identify performance bottlenecks in Windows Server 2008 include:

- Task Manager, which displays current system resource usage.
- Event Viewer, which logs specific events, including performance related events.

- Reliability Monitor, which tracks changes brought to the system, enabling you to identify whether a change could be the cause of a new bottleneck.
- Performance Monitor, which collects data in either real time or at specific intervals to identify potential issues.
- Windows System Resource Manager (WSRM), which can be used to profile specific applications to indicate which resources they need at which time. You can also use it to manage application resource allocation based on the profiles you generate.

You can use other tools as well, such as Microsoft System Center Operations Manager, to monitor the state of a system continuously and automatically correct well-known issues. Operations Manager relies on custom management packs to monitor specific applications.

Using Task Manager

The simplest of all tools to use is Task Manager. This tool provides real-time system status information and covers several key aspects of a system's performance, including:

- Running applications
- Running processes
- Running services
- Performance, including CPU and memory usage
- Networking, including network interface card (NIC) utilization
- Currently logged-on users

You can access Task Manager in a variety of ways, the most common of which is to right-click the taskbar and select Task Manager. Another common method is to use the Ctrl+Alt+Delete key combination and click Task Manager when the menu choices appear. For example, this is how you would access Task Manager on Server Core because it does not include a taskbar. You can also type **Taskmgr.exe** at a command prompt.

When you access information regarding system performance, the Performance tab is the most useful tab. (See Figure 13-7.) This displays complete information about your system's key resource usage. It details physical and kernel memory usage. This tab also includes a button that gives you access to Resource Monitor. Clicking this button will launch Resource Monitor while keeping Task Manager open.

Resource Monitor is a *super* Task Manager because it brings together the CPU, disk, memory, and network usage graphs in a single view. (See Figure 13-8.) In addition, it includes expandable components for each resource, displaying details of each component so that you can identify which processes might be the culprit if issues are evident. These two tools are ideal for on-the-spot verifications of resource usage. You should rely on them if you need to identify immediately whether something is wrong with a server.

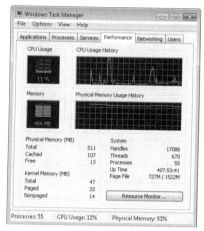

Figure 13-7   Viewing real-time performance information in Task Manager

For example, if the system does not have enough memory, you will immediately see that memory usage is constantly high. In this case, Windows will be forced to use on-disk virtual memory and will need to swap or page memory contents constantly between physical and virtual memory. Constant paging is a typical issue that servers with insufficient physical memory face and is often indicated by slow system behavior. One good indicator of insufficient memory is slow Server Manager operation.

Figure 13-8   Viewing real-time performance information in Resource Monitor

---

Working with Event Viewer

Another excellent indicator of system health is Windows Event Log. Windows maintains several event logs to collect information about each of the services running on a server. By default, these include the Application, Security, Setup, System, and Forwarded Events logs, all located in the Windows Logs folder. However, on a DC, you will also have additional logs that are specifically related to AD DS operation. These will be located in the Applications and Services Logs folder and will include:

- DFS Replication, which is available in domains and forests operating in Windows Server 2008 full functional mode. If you are running your domains or forests in one of the earlier modes, the log will be for the FRS replication service.
- Directory Service, which focuses on the operations that are specifically related to AD DS.
- DNS Server, which lists all events related to the naming service that supports AD DS operation.

However, one of the best features of Event Log is related to Server Manager. Because it acts as the central management location for each of the roles included in Windows Server 2008, Server Manager provides custom log views that percolate all the events related to a specific server role. For example, if you click the Active Directory Domain Services role, Server Manager will provide you with a log view that includes, among other things, a summary view of key events related to this service. (See Figure 13-9.)

Event Log lists three types of events: Information, Warning, and Errors. By default, the summary view displayed under the server role will list Errors with a high priority, Warnings with a medium priority, and Information messages with the lowest priority. Therefore, Errors will always appear at the top of the summary, alerting you immediately if there is an issue with your system. To drill down and see the event details, either double-click the event itself or move to the Event Viewer section under the Diagnostics node of the tree pane in Server Manager.

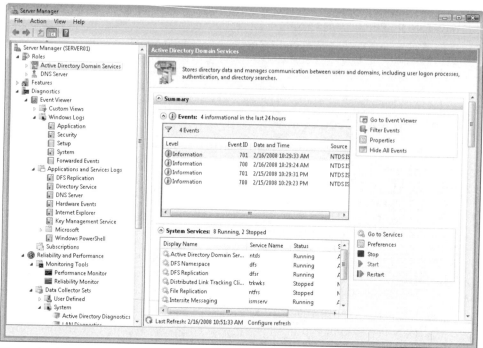

Figure 13-9   Viewing Summary Events for AD DS in Server Manager

---

MORE INFO   Active Directory Services events and errors

To learn about specific events and errors related to Active Directory Services roles go to *http://technet2.microsoft.com/windowsserver2008/en/library/67928ddc-3c01-4a4a-a924-f964908b072b1033.mspx.*

Events provide much more information in Windows Server 2008 and Windows Vista than ever before. In previous versions of Windows, events were arcane items that provided very little information about an issue. Today, you get a full explanation on an event in Event Viewer, and you can link to an online database maintained by Microsoft for each event. You can look up an event in this database by clicking the Event Log Online Help link in the event's Properties dialog box. You will be prompted to send information about the event to Microsoft. Click Yes if you want information specifically about this event.

This database does not provide information about every event in Windows, but it covers the most frequently viewed events. You can also use third-party event log databases to view information about events.

MORE INFO   Windows event IDs

To access a free database of Windows event IDs, go to *http://kb.prismmicrosys.com/index.asp.*

The more information you know about Windows events, the easier it will be to deal with the issue. You can rely on the Microsoft online event database and free third-party event databases as well as supplement this information with online searches through tools such as Windows Live Search to locate information about an issue. Searching on the event ID will return the most results.

MORE INFO   New features of Event Log

For more information on working with Event Log, download "Tracking Change" in Windows Vista, a multi-page article on the new features of Event Log and how it can be integrated with Task Manager to automate actions based on specific events as well as forward key events to a central collection system at *http://www.reso-net.com/download.asp?Fichier=A195.*

Working with Windows Reliability Monitor

Another useful tool to identify potential issues on a system is Reliability Monitor. This tool, located under the Diagnostic\Reliability and Performance\Monitoring Tools node in Server Manager, is designed to track changes that are made to a system. Each time a change is performed on the system, it is logged in Reliability Monitor. (See Figure 13-10.) Tracked changes include system changes, software installs or uninstalls, application failures, hardware failures, and Windows failures.

If an issue arises, one of the first places you should check is Reliability Monitor because it tracks every change to your system and reveals what might have happened to make your system unresponsive. For example, if the change is a new driver for a device, it might be a good idea to roll back the device installation and see whether the system becomes more responsive. Verify Reliability Monitor whenever an issue affecting performance arises on a server.

Exam Tip   Work with Task Manager, Event Viewer, and Reliability Monitor. All are important parts of the exam.

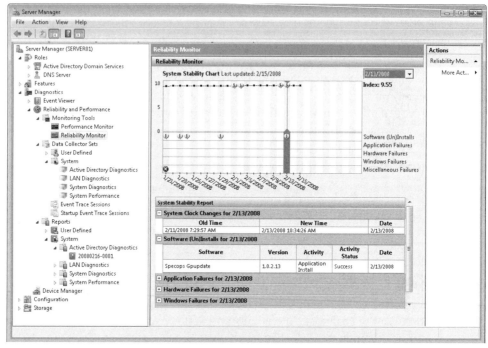

Figure 13-10   Viewing system changes in Reliability Monitor

Working with Windows Performance Monitor

Sometimes problems and issues are not immediately recognizable and require further research to identify them. In this case, you need to rely on Performance Monitor. This tool, located under the Diagnostic\ Reliability and Performance\Monitoring Tools node in Server Manager, is designed to track performance data on a system. You use Performance Monitor to track particular system components either in real time or on a scheduled basis.

If you are familiar with previous versions of Windows Server, you'll quickly note that Windows Server 2008 Performance Monitor brings together several tools you might be familiar with: Performance Logs and Alerts, Server Performance Advisor, and System Monitor. If you are new to Windows Server with the 2008 release, you'll quickly find that when it comes to performance management and analysis, Performance Monitor is the tool to use. Using Performance Monitor, you create interactive collections of system counters or create reusable data collector sets. Performance Monitor is part of Windows Reliability and Performance Monitor (WRPM). Table 13-5 outlines each of the tools in WRPM that support performance monitoring and the access rights required to work with them.

Table 13-5 **WRPM Tools and Access Rights**

Tool	Description	Required Membership
Monitoring Tools, Performance Monitor	To view performance data in real time or from log files. The performance data can be viewed in a graph, histogram, or report.	Local Performance Log Users group
Monitoring Tools, Reliability Monitor	To view the system stability and the events that affect reliability.	Local Administrators group
Data collector sets	Groups data collectors into reusable elements that can be used to review or log performance. Contains three types of data collectors: performance counts, event trace data, and system configuration information.	Local Performance Log Users group with the Log on as a batch user right
Reports	Includes preconfigured performance and diagnosis reports. Can also be used to generate reports from data collected using any data collector set.	Local Performance Log Users group with the Log on as a batch job user right

Windows Server 2008 includes a new built-in group called Performance Log Users, which allows server administrators who are not members of the local Administrators group to perform tasks related to performance monitoring and logging. For this group to be able to initiate data logging or modify data collector sets, it must have the Log On As A Batch Job user right. Note that this user right is assigned to this group by default.

In addition, Windows Server 2008 will create custom Data Collector Set templates when a role is installed. These templates are located under the System node of the Data Collector Sets node of WRPM. For example, with the AD DS role, four collector sets are created:

- The Active Directory Diagnostics set collects data from registry keys, performance counters, and trace events related to AD DS performance on a local DC.
- The LAN Diagnostics set collects data from network interface cards, registry keys, and other system hardware to identify issues related to network traffic on the local DC.
- The System Diagnostics set collects data from local hardware resources to generate data that helps streamline system performance on the local DC.
- The System Performance set focuses on the status of hardware resources and system response times and processes on the local DC.

Of the four, the most useful for AD DS is the first. This should be the data set you rely on the most. You can create your own personalized data set. If you do, focus on the items in Table 13-6 as the counters you should include in your data set.

Table 13-6 Monitor Common Counters for AD DS

Counter	Description	Reason
Network Interface: Bytes Total/Sec	Rate at which bytes are sent and received over each network adapter, including framing characters.	Track network interfaces to identify high usage rates per NIC. This helps you determine whether you need to segment the network or increase bandwidth.
Network Interface: Packets Outbound Discarded	Number of outbound packets that were chosen to be discarded even though no errors had been detected to prevent transmission.	Long queues of items indicate that the NIC is waiting for the network and is not keeping pace with the server. This is a bottleneck.
NTDS: DRA Inbound Bytes Total/Sec	Total bytes received through replication. It is the sum of both uncompressed and compressed data.	If this counter does not have any activity, it indicates that the network could be slowing down replication.
NTDS: DRA Inbound Object Updates Remaining in Packet	Number of object updates received through replication that have not yet been applied to the local server.	The value should be low on a constant basis. High values show that the server is not capable of adequately integrating data received through replication.
NTDS: DRA Outbound Bytes Total/Sec	Total bytes sent per second. It is the sum of both uncompressed and compressed data.	If this counter does not have any activity, it indicates that the network could be slowing down replication.
NTDS: DRA Pending Replication Synchronizations	The replication backlog on the server.	The value should be low on a constant basis. High values show that the server is not capable of adequately integrating data received through replication.
NTDS: DS Threads In Use	Number of threads in use by AD DS.	If there is no activity, the network might be preventing client requests from being processed.
NTDS: LDAP Bind Time	Time required for completion of the last LDAP binding.	High values indicate either hardware or network performance problems.
NTDS: LDAP Client Sessions	Number of connected LDAP client sessions.	If there is no activity, the network might be causing problems.
NTDS: LDAP Searches/Sec	Number of LDAP searches per second.	If there is no activity, the network might be causing problems.
NTDS: LDAP Successful Binds/Sec	Number of successful LDAP binds per second.	If there is no activity, the network might be causing problems.
NTDS: LDAP Writes /Sec	Number of successful LDAP writes per second.	If there is no activity, the network might be causing problems.

Table 13-6   **Monitor Common Counters for AD DS**

Counter	Description	Reason
Security System-Wide Statistics: Kerberos Authentications	Number of Kerberos authentications on the server per second.	If there is no activity, the network might be preventing authentication requests from being processed.
Security System-Wide Statistics: NTLM Authentication	Number of NTLM authentications on the server per second.	If there is no activity, the network might be preventing authentication requests from being processed.
DFS Replicated Folders: All Counters	Counters for staging and conflicting data.	If there is no activity, the network might be causing problems.
DFS Replication Connections: All Counters	Counter for incoming connections.	If there is no activity, the network might be causing problems.
DFS Replication Service Volumes: All Counters	Counters for update sequence number (USN) journal records and database processing on each volume.	If there is no activity, the processor might be causing problems.
DNS: All Counters	DNS Object Type handles the Windows NT DNS service on your system.	If there is no activity, the network might be causing problems, and clients might not be able to locate this DC.

To add counters to Performance Monitor, simply click the plus (+) sign in the toolbar at the top of the details pane. This displays the Add Counters dialog box. (See Figure 13-11.) Scroll through the counters to identify which ones you need. In some cases, you will need sub-counters under a specific heading (as shown in Table 13-6); in others, you need the entire subset of counters. When you need a subcounter, click the down arrow beside the heading, locate the subcounter, and click Add. When you need the entire counter, click the counter and click Add. This adds the counter with a star heading below it, indicating that all subcounters have been added.

IMPORTANT   The Windows Server 2008 interface

When using the classic interface in Windows Server 2008, subcounters are accessed by clicking plus signs. When using the Desktop Experience feature in Windows Server 2008, which simulates the Vista interface, subcounters are accessed through down arrows.

To obtain information about a counter, click Show Description. Then, when you click any counter or subcounter, a short description will appear at the bottom of the dialog box.

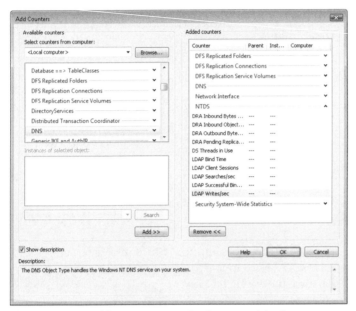

Figure 13-11 Adding counters to Performance Monitor

As soon as you are finished adding counters and you click OK, Performance Monitor will start tracking them in real time. Each counter you added will be assigned a line of a specific color. To remove a counter, click the counter, and then click the Delete button (X) on the toolbar at the top of the details pane.

You can start and stop Performance Monitor much like a media player, using the same type of buttons. When Performance Monitor runs, it automatically overwrites data as it collects more; therefore, it is more practical for real-time monitoring.

If you want to capture the counters you added into a custom data set, right-click Performance Monitor and select New; then choose New Data Collector Set. Follow the prompts to save your counter selections so that you can reuse them later.

Exam Tip Work with Performance Monitor because it is an important part of the exam. Also, note that there is no Server Performance Advisor (SPA) in Windows Server 2008. This Windows Server 2003 tool has been rolled into Windows Reliability and Performance Monitor. Don't get caught on questions regarding SPA on the exam.

Creating Baselines for AD DS and DNS

For long-term system monitoring, you must create data collector sets. These sets run automated collections at scheduled times. When you first install a system, it is a good idea to create a performance baseline for that system. Then as load increases on the system, you can compare the current load with the baseline and see what has changed. This helps you identify whether additional resources are required for your systems to provide optimal performance. For example, when working with DCs, it is a good idea to log performance at peak and nonpeak times. Peak times would be when users log on in the morning or after lunch, and nonpeak times would be periods such as mid-morning or mid-afternoon. To create a performance baseline, you need to take samples of counter values for 30 to 45 minutes for at least a week during peak, low, and normal operations. The general steps for creating a baseline include:

1. Identify resources to track.
2. Capture data at specific times.
3. Store the captured data for long-term access.

IMPORTANT Performance monitoring affects performance

Taking performance snapshots also affects system performance. The object with the worst impact on performance is the logical disk object, especially if logical disk counters are enabled. However, because this affects snapshots at any time, even with major loads on the server, the baseline is still valid.

You can create custom collector sets, but with Windows Server 2008, use the default templates that are added when the server role is installed to do so. For example, to create a baseline for a DC, simply create a user-defined data collector set that is based on the Active Directory Diagnostics template and run it on a regular basis.

Then, when you are ready to view the results of your collection, you can rely on the Reports section of the Windows Reliability and Performance node. Right-click the collector set for which you want to view the report (either User Defined or System) and select Latest Report. This will generate the report if it isn't already available and provide extensive information on the status of your DC. (See Figure 13-12.)

MORE INFO Performance Monitor scenarios

For more information on Performance Monitor, see the scenarios in the Windows Server 2008 Performance and Reliability Monitoring Step-by-Step Guide at *http://technet2.microsoft.com /windowsserver2008/en/library/7e17a3be-f24e-4fdd-9e38-a88e2c8fb4d81033.mspx?mfr=true*.

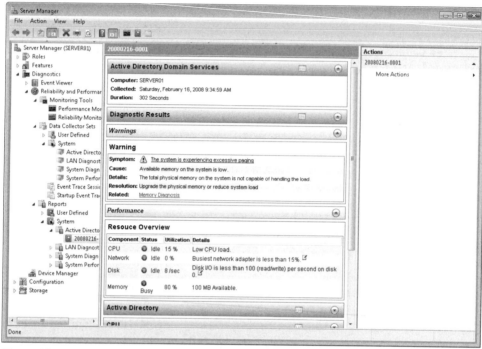

Figure 13-12   Viewing an Active Directory diagnostics report

Working with Windows System Resource Manager

Windows Server 2008 includes an additional tool for system resource management, WSRM, a feature that can be added through Add Features in Server Manager. WSRM can be used in two manners. First, it can be used to profile applications. This means that it helps identify how many resources an application requires on a regular basis. When operating in this mode, WSRM logs events in the application event log only when the application exceeds its allowed limits. This helps you fine-tune application requirements.

The second mode offered by WSRM is the manage mode. In this mode, WSRM uses its allocation policies to control how many resources applications can use on a server. If applications exceed their resource allocations, WSRM can even stop the application from executing and make sure other applications on the same server can continue to operate. However, WSRM will not affect any application if combined processor resources do not exceed 70 percent utilization. This means that when processor resources are low, WSRM does not affect any application.

WSRM also supports Alerts and Event Monitoring. This is a powerful tool that is designed to help you control processor and memory usage on large multiprocessing servers. By default, the WSRM includes four built-in management policies, but it also includes several custom resources you can use to define your own policies. Basically, WSRM will ensure that high-priority applications will always have enough resources available to them for continued operation, making it a good tool for DCs.

IMPORTANT DCs and WSRM

If you use single-purpose DCs, you will not need WSRM as much as if you use multipurpose DCs. Multipurpose DCs will usually run other workloads at the same time as they run the AD DS service. Using WSRM in this case can ensure that the AD DS service is available during peak hours by assigning it more resources than other applications. However, consider your choices carefully when deciding to create a multipurpose DC. DCs are secure servers by default and should remain this way at all times. If you add workloads to a DC, you will need to grant access rights to the DC to application administrators, administrators that do not need domain administration access rights.

Use WSRM to first evaluate how your applications are being used; then apply management policies. Make sure you thoroughly test your policies before applying them in your production environment. This way, you will be able to get a feel for WSRM before you fully implement it in your network. When you're ready, you can use WSRM Calendar to determine when which policy should be applied.

IMPORTANT WSRM resource requirements

If you are managing several servers with WSRM, you might need to dedicate resources to it because it is resource-intensive. You might consider placing it on a dedicated management server if this is the case.

Quick Check

1. You want to view potential error messages about the directory service. Where can you find this information?
2. You are using WSRM to control processor and memory resources for several applications on a server. However, after investigation, you see that none of your policies are applied. What could be the problem?
3. What are the objects you can use to allocate resources in WSRM?

Quick Check Answers

1. View potential error messages about the directory service in Event Log. You can view this information in two places. The first is by clicking the server role name in the tree pane of Server Manager. This will display a summary view of directory service events. The second is by going to the Directory Service log itself, under Event Viewer. This will display all the events related to the directory service.
2. WSRM will not apply any policies if the processor usage does not reach 70 percent.
3. WSRM resource allocations can be assigned to three objects: processes, users, or IIS application pools.

WSRM can be used for the following scenarios:

- Use predefined or user-defined policies to manage system resources. Resources can be allocated on a per-process, per-user, or per-IIS application pool basis.
- Rely on calendar rules to apply your policies at different times and dates without any manual intervention.
- Automate the resource policy selection process based on server properties, events, or even changes to available physical memory or processor count.
- Collect resource usage information in local text files or store them in a SQL database. You can also create a central WSRM collection system to collate resource usage from several systems running their own instances of WSRM.

Table 13-7 outlines the default policies included in WSRM as well as the custom resources you can use to create custom policies.

Table 13-7   WSRM Policies and Custom Resources

Built-in Policy	Description
Equal per process	Assigns each application an equal amount of resources.
Equal per user	Groups processes assigned to each user who is running them and assigns equal resources to each group.
Equal per session	Allocates resources equally to each session connected to the system.
Equal per IIS application pool	Allocates resources equally to each running IIS application pool.
Custom Resource	**Description**
Process Matching Criteria	Used to match services or applications to a policy. Can be selected by file name, command, specified users, or groups.
Resource Allocation Policies	Used to allocate processor and memory resources to the processes that match criteria you specify.
Exclusion lists	Used to exclude applications, services, users, or groups from management by WSRM. Can also use command-line paths to exclude applications from management.
Scheduling	Use a calendar interface to set time-based events to resource allocation. Supports policy-based workloads because you can set policies to be active at specific times of day, specific days, or other schedules.
Conditional policy application	Used to set conditions based on specific events to determine whether policy will run.

WSRM can completely control how applications can and should run.

PRACTICE AD DS Performance Analysis

In this practice, you will use both WRPM and WSRM to view the performance of your servers. First, you will create a custom collector set. After the collector set is created, you will run it and view the diagnostics report. In the second exercise, you will install WSRM to view the policies it provides. These exercises rely on SERVER10, but SERVER11 should also be running.

▶ **Exercise 1   Create a Data Collector Set**

A data collector set is the core building block of performance monitoring and reporting in WRPM. You can create a combination of data collectors and save them as a single data collector set.

1. Log on to SERVER10 with the domain Administrator account.

   You need to be a member only of the Performance Log Users group with the Log On As A Batch Job user right, but for the purpose of these exercises, you will use the domain administrator account.

2. In Server Manager, expand Diagnostics\Reliability and Performance\Data Collector Sets, right-click User Defined, select New, and then select Data Collector Set.

3. On the Template page, type **Custom AD DS Collector Set**, make sure Create From A Template (Recommended) is selected, and click Next.

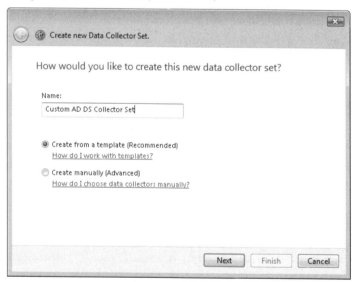

4. On the next page, select the Active Directory Diagnostics template and click Next.

5. By default, the wizard selects %systemdrive%\PerfLogs\Admin as the root directory; however, you might prefer to keep your collector sets on a separate drive if it exists. In this case, click Browse, choose drive D, and create a new folder named **AD DS Collector Sets**. Press Enter and click OK to close the dialog box, and then click Next.

6. On the Create The Data Collector Set page, in the *Run As* field, type the account name and the password to run the data collector set. Leave the defaults and click Finish.

    When you create collector sets for long-term use, use a special account that is both a member of the Performance Log Users group and has the Log On As A Batch Job user right to run your collector sets. Note that the Performance Log Users group has this right assigned to it by default.

    When you finish the New Collector Set Wizard, you are given three options:

    ❏ Open Properties Data For This Data Collector Set to view the properties of the data collector set or to make additional modifications

    ❏ Start This Data Collector Set Now to run the data collector set immediately

    ❏ Save And Close to save the data collector set without starting the collection

    Your custom data collector set has been created. Notice that it is stopped. To schedule the Start condition for your data collector set, use the following procedure.

7. Right-click Custom AD DS Collector Set and click Properties.

8. Click the Schedule tab and click Add to create a start date, time, or day schedule.

9. In the Folder Action dialog box, make sure that today's date is the beginning date, select the Expiration Date check box, and set it as one week from today. Also, make sure that the report time is set to the current time. Click OK.

    You must set the start date of the schedule to *now* for the collection set to work. If not, you will not be able to generate reports in later steps.

    Note that you can create quite a modular schedule in this dialog box. Also, note that selecting an expiration date will not stop data collection in progress on that date. It will only prevent new instances of data collection from starting after the expiration date. You must use the Stop Condition tab to configure how data collection is stopped.

10. Click the Stop Condition tab, select the Overall Duration check box, make sure it lists 5 minutes, and select the Stop When All Data Collectors Have Finished check box. Click OK.

    You select the Stop When All Data Collectors Have Finished check box to enable all data collectors to finish recording the most recent values before the data collector set is stopped if you have also configured an overall duration.

    You can also set limits on your collection. However, note that when an overall duration is configured, it will override any limits you set. If you do want to set limits, make sure the Overall Duration check box is cleared and define the following limits:

    ❏ Use When A Limit Is Reached, Restart The Data Collector Set to segment data collections into separate logs.

    ❏ To configure a time period for data collection to write to a single log file, select the Duration check box and set its value.

    ❏ To restart the data collector set or to stop collecting data when the log file reaches a specific limit, select the Maximum Size check box and set its value.

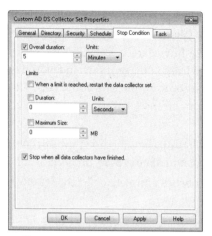

Collector sets will generate a large amount of data if you allow them to run unmonitored. To configure data management for a data collector set, use the following procedure.

11. Right-click Custom AD DS Data Collector Set and click Data Manager.

12. On the Data Manager tab, you can accept the default values or change them according to your data retention policy. Keep the defaults.

   ❑ Select the Minimum Free disk or Maximum Folders check boxes to delete previous data according to the resource policy you choose from the drop-down list (Delete Largest or Delete Oldest).

   ❑ Select the Apply Policy Before The Data Collector Set Starts check box to delete previous data sets according to your selections before the data collector set creates its next log file.

   ❑ Select the Maximum Root Path Size check box to delete previous data according to your selections when the root log folder size limit is reached.

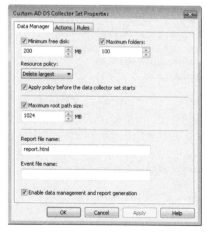

13. On the Actions tab, you can set specific data management actions for this collector set. Note that three policies already exist. Click the 1 Day(s) policy and click Edit.

    Folder actions enable you to choose how data is archived before it is permanently deleted. You can decide to disable the Data Manager limits in favor of managing all data according to these folder action rules. For example, you could copy all collection sets to a central file share before deleting them on the local server.

14. Click OK and OK again.

    Your collector set is ready to run. Wait until the scheduled time occurs for the report to run. However, if you want to view an immediate report, proceed as follows:

15. Right-click the Active Directory Diagnostics template collector set under Data Collector Sets, System and click Latest Report.

    If no report exists, this will launch the data collector set and begin the collection of information from your server. The set should run for five minutes and then stop. If a report exists, it will move you to the Reports node and display it.

16. If the report does not exist and you expand the Reports section of WRPM, you will see that the collection set is generating a report. Click the report name.

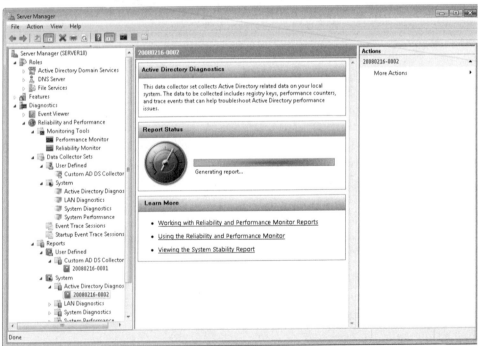

17. View the report that was generated by your collector set. Click Report Name under the collector set name in System reports.

    You can also use the other default templates to generate reports on the spot. For example, if you want to run a report from the Systems Diagnostics template, right-click the template name under the System node and select Latest Report. If no report exists, it will run the collector set and then display the report in the details pane.

▶ **Exercise 2   Install WSRM**

In this exercise, you will install the WSRM service and view how it operates. This exercise is performed on SERVER10; ensure that it is running.

1. Log on to Server10 with the domain Administrator account.

2. In Server Manager, right-click the Features node and select Add Features.

3. On the Select Features page of the Add Features Wizard, select Windows System Resource Manager and click Next.

4. Server Manager prompts you to add Windows Internal Database. Click Add Required Features. Click Next.

    Note that Windows Internal Database is a locally used database only and will not accept remote connections. To collect data from other servers, you must use Microsoft SQL Server 2005 or later.

5. Review the information on the Confirm Installation Selections page and click Install.

6. Examine the installation results and click Close.

    Your installation is complete.

7. You can now use WSRM on this system. Windows System Resource Manager is a standalone console that can be found in the Administrative Tools program group.

8. When you open the console, it will ask you which computer to connect to. Select This Computer and click Connect.

    Now you can tour the WSRM interface. (See Figure 13-13.) Note that it uses the standard Microsoft Management Console format. Explore the various features of this console.

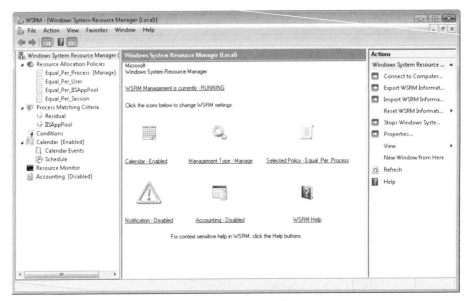

Figure 13-13   Using Windows System Resource Monitor

Lesson Summary

- In Windows Server 2008, you can use a series of tools to manage and monitor resource usage on a computer. These include Task Manager, Event Logs, Reliability Monitor, and Performance Monitor.

- Performance Monitor is now the single tool that regroups other tools used in previous versions of Windows. These tools included Performance Logs and Alerts, Server Performance Advisor, and System Monitor.

- You can use Windows System Resource Manager to control how resources behave on a scheduled basis. In fact, it provides two functions. It can monitor resource usage over time and log activity. Then, it can be used to control access to resources based on specific policies.

Lesson Review

You can use the following questions to test your knowledge of the information in Lesson 2, "Proactive Directory Performance Management." The questions are also available on the companion CD if you prefer to review them in electronic form.

NOTE   Answers

Answers to these questions and explanations of why each answer choice is right or wrong are located in the "Answers" section at the end of the book.

1. You are the systems administrator for *contoso.com*. You have been assigned the task of verifying data collector sets on a DC. You did not create the collector sets. When you check the collector sets, you find that they are continuously running and that the allocated storage area is full. What could be the problem? (Choose all that apply.)

    A. The collector sets do not have an expiration date.

    B. The collector sets have not been set to run on a schedule.

    C. The collector sets do not have a stop condition.

    D. The collector sets have been scheduled improperly.

2. You are a systems administrator at *contoso.com*. As you log on to a DC to perform maintenance, you get the impression that server response is sluggish. You want to verify what is going on. Which tool should you use? (Choose all that apply.)

    A. Reliability Monitor

    B. Event Viewer

    C. Task Manager

    D. Performance Monitor

Chapter Review

To further practice and reinforce the skills you learned in this chapter, you can perform the following tasks:

- Review the chapter summary.
- Review the list of key terms introduced in this chapter.
- Complete the case scenario. This scenario sets up a real-world situation involving the topics of this chapter and asks you to create a solution.
- Complete the suggested practices.
- Take a practice test.

Chapter Summary

- Active Directory Domain Services is a set of complex services that interact with each other to provide a highly available identity and access solution. Because of this, there are several aspects to AD DS administration. In fact, twelve activities are required to manage the environment both online and offline, although many of the twelve can be delegated to others.
- As domain administrators, operators of the directory service must concentrate on making sure the AD DS service is always available and runs at its optimum performance. Many of the operations required to do this involve offline database administration tasks. With the release of Windows Server 2008, these tasks can now be performed without having to shut down the server because the AD DS service can now be started and stopped like any other service.
- There are several ways to protect AD DS data in Windows Server 2008 and several ways to restore it. One easy way to restore data is to recover it from the Deleted Items container, but when you do so, you must update the recovered item and then enable it.
- Two tools support backups of directory data in Windows Server 2008. *Ntdsutil.exe* will support both the creation of offline installation media and the protection of the system state data required by the DC. Windows Server Backup will protect entire volumes of the system and will even protect and support the restore of an entire computer system.
- Because the DC role is one that is ideal for virtualization, you can also protect DCs by using simple services such as the Volume Shadow Copy Service on host servers. This protects the virtual hard drives that comprise the virtual machine the DC is running on.
- When performance issues arise, Windows Server 2008 provides a series of tools for analysis and problem correction. These include both real-time and scheduled analysis tools. Real-time tools include Task Manager, Resource Monitor, and Performance Monitor. Scheduled or tracking tools include Event Log, Reliability Monitor, and scheduled data collection sets in Performance Monitor.

■ Windows Server 2008 also includes a powerful tool by which you can manage policy-based workloads, Windows System Resource Manager. You must first use it to analyze running processes and then assign policies to these processes.

Key Terms

Use these key terms to understand better the concepts covered in this chapter.

■ **compaction**   The process of recovering free space from a database. When database records are created, a specific amount of space is allocated in the database—enough to contain all of the record's possible values. When the record is deleted, the space is not recovered unless a compaction operation is performed.

■ **data collector set**   A collection of values collated from the local computer, including registry values, performance counters, hardware components, and more that provides a diagnostic view into the behavior of a system.

■ *Ntds.dit*   The database that contains the directory store. This database is located on every DC and, because of multimaster replication, is updated at all times by all other DCs except RODCs.

■ **tombstone**   The container to which each deleted object in the directory is automatically moved. This container retains objects for a period of 180 days to ensure that all possible replications involving this object have been performed. You can use this container to recover objects before the end of the 180 days.

Case Scenario

In the following case scenario, you will apply what you've learned about subjects of this chapter. You can find answers to the questions in this scenario in the "Answers" section at the end of this book.

Case Scenario: Working with Lost and Found Data

You are a domain administrator with Contoso, Ltd. During a routine verification, you notice that some of the accounts that should be contained within a specific OU have disappeared. You know that a local technician was assigned to work on these accounts recently because none of them had any information tied to them. In addition, new accounts needed to be created in this OU. The technician was assigned to add information such as the user's address, manager, and office location in each of the accounts. You contact the technician and verify that he made the modifications as expected.

You examine your directory event logs to locate the answer. Fortunately, you configured a central collection server to which you forward AD DS events from all the DCs in your domain. After some time, you discover that another administrator from a remote office was working on the same OU at the same time as the technician. More examination shows that the administrator moved the OU from its original location and then moved it back at the same time as the technician was working on the accounts.

Where are the accounts you cannot find?

Suggested Practices

To help you successfully master the exam objectives presented in this chapter, complete the following tasks.

Proactive Directory Maintenance

Working with AD DS means working with a central repository that provides two key services: user authentication and object management, hence the classification of AD DS as a NOS directory service. To become even more familiar with the exam objectives covered by this chapter, perform the following additional practices.

- **Practice 1** Practice working with the various backup and restore tools found in Windows Server 2008. If you can, perform a complete server backup and then a complete server restore. Work with the DSRM and practice changing the DSRM password as well as performing nonauthoritative and authoritative restores. Make sure you examine as many of the different options available to you in each of the supported DC backup and restore scenarios as possible.

- **Practice 2** Work with the DC monitoring tools. Use Task Manager, Event Viewer, and the Windows Reliability and Performance Monitor views. Try as many of the various options as possible to become familiar with how they work. Look up the suggested article for Event Log management and apply its principles to your DCs.

- **Practice 3** Work with Windows System Resource Manager. WSRM includes many options. Examine as many as possible and test out their operation. Try assigning different policies to your DCs to see how they affect system operation. View the event logs to see how WSRM logs information about the system.

Take a Practice Test

The practice tests on this book's companion CD offer many options. For example, you can test yourself on just one exam objective, or you can test yourself on all the 70-640 certification exam content. You can set up the test so that it closely simulates the experience of taking a certification exam, or you can set it up in study mode so that you can look at the correct answers and explanations after you answer each question.

MORE INFO Practice tests

For details about all the practice test options available, see the "How to Use the Practice Tests" section in this book's introduction.

Chapter 14

Active Directory Lightweight Directory Services

Of the five different Active Directory technologies available in Windows Server 2008, the one that most resembles Active Directory Domain Services (AD DS) is Active Directory Lightweight Directory Services (AD LDS). That's because AD LDS is really nothing more than a subset of AD DS functionality. Both use the same core code, and both provide a very similar feature set.

AD LDS, formerly called Active Directory Application Mode (ADAM), is a technology that is designed to support directory-enabled applications on an application-by-application basis and without having to modify the database schema of your network operating system (NOS) directory running on AD DS. AD LDS is a boon to administrators who want to use directory-enabled applications without integrating them in their NOS directory.

Active Directory Domain Services can also support the use of directory-enabled applications. One very good example is Microsoft Exchange Server 2007. All user information in Exchange Server is provided by the directory. When you install Exchange Server into your network, it begins by extending the AD DS schema, practically doubling its size. As you know, schema modifications are not to be taken lightly because, when you add an object or an attribute to the AD DS schema, it will be added forever; it cannot be removed. You can deactivate or rename and reuse these objects, but who wants defunct objects in their NOS directory? Adding to the schema for an application such as Exchange Server is appropriate because it provides a core networking service: e-mail.

MORE INFO Best practices for Active Directory design

For a guide outlining best practices for the design of Active Directory as well as AD DS schema management guidelines, download the free "Chapter 3: Designing the Active Directory" from *Windows Server 2003: Best Practices for Enterprise Deployments*, available at *http://www.reso-net.com/Documents/007222343X_Ch03.pdf*.

For information on creating a new forest as well as migrating its contents from one forest to another, look up *Windows Server 2008: The Complete Reference* by Ruest and Ruest (McGraw-Hill Osborne, 2008). This book outlines how to build a complete infrastructure based on Microsoft Windows Server and how to migrate all of its contents from one location to another.

However, when it comes to other applications, especially applications that are provided by third-party software manufacturers, carefully consider whether you should integrate them into your AD DS directory. Remember, your production AD DS structure will be with you for a very long time. You don't want to find yourself in a situation in which you integrated a product to your directory and then, several years later when the third-party manufacturer is out of business, have to figure out what to do with the extensions this product added to your AD DS structure, increasing replication timings and adding unused content in the directory.

This is why AD LDS is such a boon. Because it can support multiple AD LDS instances on a single server (unlike AD DS, which can support only one instance of a directory on any given server), AD LDS can meet the requirements of any directory-enabled application and even provide instances on an application-by-application basis. In addition, you do not need Enterprise Administrator or Schema Administrator credentials to work with AD LDS, as you would with AD DS. No, AD LDS runs on member or standalone servers and requires only local administration access rights to manage it. Because of this, it can also be used in a perimeter network to provide application or Web authentication services. AD LDS is one of the four Active Directory technologies that enable you to extend your organization's authority beyond the firewall and into the Internet cloud. (See Figure 14-1.)

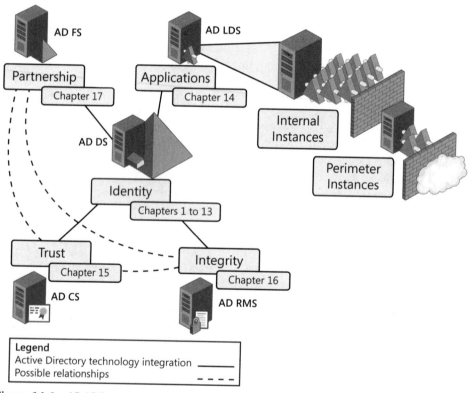

Figure 14-1   AD LDS can be used internally or externally in support of applications

Exam objectives in this chapter:

- Configuring Additional Active Directory Server Roles
  - Configure Active Directory Lightweight Directory Service (AD LDS).

Lessons in this chapter:

- Lesson 1: Understanding and Installing AD LDS 690
- Lesson 2: Configuring and Using AD LDS 701

Before You Begin

To complete the lessons in this chapter, you must have done the following:

- Installed Windows Server 2008 on a physical or virtual computer, which should be named SERVER01 and should be a domain controller in the *contoso.com* domain. The details for this setup are presented in Chapter 1, "Installation," and Chapter 2, "Administration."

- Installed Windows Server 2008 on another physical or virtual computer. The machine should be named SERVER03 and should be a member server within the *contoso.com* domain. This computer will host the AD LDS instances you will install and create through the exercises in this chapter. Make sure this computer also includes a D drive to store the data for the AD LDS instances. Ten GB is recommended for the size of this drive.

- Installed Windows Server 2008 on a third physical or virtual computer. The computer should be named SERVER04 and should be a member server within the *contoso.com* domain. This computer will be used to configure replication scopes for AD LDS. Make sure this computer also includes a D drive to store the data for the AD LDS instances. Ten GB is recommended for the size of this drive.

Real World

Danielle Ruest and Nelson Ruest

In late 2003, we were asked by Redmond Magazine (then MCP Magazine) to put together a review of the various products on the market that would assist system administrators to manage Active Directory environments. We were thrilled by the request because Active Directory was one of our favorite technologies. Besides being a true Lightweight Directory Access Protocol (LDAP) directory service, Active Directory is also a very powerful NOS directory that can manage millions of objects. In addition, Active Directory includes Group Policy, a very powerful object management platform that extends the NOS capabilities of the directory service. Finally, through Group Policy Software Delivery, you could manage the delivery of Windows Installer–based software packages throughout the entire structure of the directory. There was no doubt, for us, that Active Directory was one of the best products ever to come out of Redmond's development labs.

After scouring the Internet and polling our customers, we came up with a short list that included six products that would assist in managing Active Directory environments:

- Quest FastLane Active Roles
- Aelita Enterprise Directory Manager
- NetIQ Security Administration Suite
- Javelina ADvantage
- NetPro Active Directory Lifecycle Suite
- Bindview Secure Active Directory LifeCycle Suite

Of the six, only four were available for the article. Bindview declined to give us an evaluation copy of their product, so we had to omit this by default. NetPro, which seemed to have a great set of tools, wasn't ready to go to market yet, so we had to omit this product as well. We did, however, have a chance to write about NetPro's suite of Active Directory products later (see *http://mcpmag.com/reviews/products/article.asp?EditorialsID=454*), and it did very well indeed. So, we were left with four products to write about. The result was an article titled "The 12 Mighty Labors of Active Directory Management" (see *http://mcpmag.com/Features/article.asp?EditorialsID=359*). Readers everywhere seemed to like the article quite a bit. But we received some very biting comments from a couple of sources about one key point we made in the article.

Two of the four products we reviewed, the NetIQ and the Quest FastLane, modified the database schema for Active Directory to work. At that time, we had consulted in quite a few Active Directory implementations, and each one faced one single difficult question: how to manage schema modifications? That's because, when the schema is modified, you can't undo it. Of course, in Windows Server 2003, Microsoft allowed you to deactivate or rename and reuse schema modifications, but for our customers and for us, that was a poor second choice. It's best to leave the schema alone, if at all possible. In addition, Microsoft had just released ADAM in support of organizations that needed to integrate applications to a directory service but didn't want to modify the schema of their NOS directory.

In the end, we chose the Aelita product as the best choice for one major reason: Aelita had opted to store all of its database requirements in Microsoft SQL Server instead of modifying the Active Directory schema, yet its tool was as powerful as the other two major contenders. Javelina's tool didn't really compete with the others because it was not designed to support the same functions.

To make a long story short, about two months after we published the article, Quest bought Aelita and transformed Enterprise Directory Manager (EDM) into the next version of Active Roles. The original Active Roles, which was produced by FastLane, a small company from Ottawa, Canada, which was also bought by Quest, was rolled into EDM. The new version of Active Roles no longer required schema modifications to be implemented, yet still offered a powerful set of Active Directory management features. Did our article have anything to do with this? Who knows? One thing is sure: no one should ever take a NOS directory schema modification lightly, not when you have powerful tools like ADAM, now AD LDS, at your fingertips.

Lesson 1: Understanding and Installing AD LDS

Even though it is based on the same code as AD DS, AD LDS is much simpler to work with. For example, when you install AD LDS on a server, it does not change the configuration of the server in the same way AD DS does when you create a domain controller. AD LDS is an application and nothing more. When you install it, you are not required to reboot the server because the application installation process only adds functionality to the server and does not change its nature.

However, before you begin, you must first understand what makes up an AD LDS instance, how AD LDS instances should be used, and what their relationship is or can be with AD DS directories. Then you can proceed to the installation of the AD LDS service.

> **After this lesson, you will be able to:**
> - Understand when to use AD LDS.
> - Install AD LDS onto a member server.
> - Locate and view the AD LDS directory store.
>
> **Estimated lesson time: 30 minutes**

Understanding AD LDS

Like AD DS, AD LDS instances are based on the Lightweight Directory Access Protocol (LDAP) and provide hierarchical database services. Unlike relational databases, LDAP directories are optimized for specific purposes and should be used whenever you need to rely on fast lookups of information that will support given applications. Table 14-1 outlines the major differences between an LDAP directory and a relational database such as Microsoft SQL Server. This comparison helps you understand when to choose an LDAP directory in support of an application over a relational database.

Table 14-1   Comparing LDAP Directories to Relational Databases

LDAP Directories	Relational Databases
Fast read and searches.	Fast writes.
Hierarchical database design often based on the Domain Name System (DNS) or the X.500 naming system.	Structured data design relying on tables containing rows and columns. Tables can be linked together.
Relies on a standard schema structure, a schema that is extensible.	Does not rely on schemas.
Decentralized (distributed) and relies on replication to maintain data consistency.	Centrally located data repositories.

Table 14-1 Comparing LDAP Directories to Relational Databases

LDAP Directories	Relational Databases
Security is applied at the object level.	Security is applied at the row or column level.
Because the database is distributed, data consistency is not absolute—at least not until replication passes are complete.	Because data input is transactional, data consistency is absolute and guaranteed at all times.
Records are not locked and can be modified by two parties at once. Conflicts are managed through update sequence numbers (USNs).	Records are locked and can be modified by only one party at a time.

Table 14-1 provides guidelines for selection of the right database for an application.

In addition, AD LDS is based on AD DS, but it does not include all the features of AD DS. Table 14-2 outlines the differences in features between AD LDS and AD DS.

Table 14-2 Comparing AD LDS with AD DS

Feature	AD LDS	AD DS
Includes more than one instance on a server.	☑	☐
Includes independent schemas for each instance.	☑	☐
Runs on client operating systems such as Windows Vista or Windows Server 2008 member servers.	☑	☐
Runs on domain controllers.	☑	☑
Directory partitions can rely on X.500 naming conventions.	☑	☐
Can be installed or removed without a reboot.	☑	☐
Service can be stopped or started without reboot.	☑	☑
Supports Group Policy.	☐	☑
Includes a global catalog.	☐	☑
Manages objects such as workstations, member servers, and domain controllers.	☐	☑
Supports trusts between domains and forests.	☐	☑
Supports and integrates with public key infrastructures (PKIs) and X.509 certificates.	☐	☑
Supports DNS service (SRV) records for locating directory services.	☐	☑
Supports LDAP application programming interfaces (APIs).	☑	☑
Supports Active Directory Services Interface (ADSI) API.	☑	☑
Supports the Messaging API (MAPI).	☐	☑
Supports object-level security and delegation of administration.	☑	☑

Table 14-2 Comparing AD LDS with AD DS

Feature	AD LDS	AD DS
Relies on multimaster replication for data consistency.	☑	☑
Supports schema extensions and application directory partitions.	☑	☑
Can install a replica from removable media.	☑	☑
Can include security principals to provide access to a Windows Server network.	☐	☑
Can include security principals to provide access to applications and Web Services.	☑	☑
Is integrated into the Windows Server 2008 backup tools.	☑	☑

As you can see from the contents of Table 14-2, there are several similarities and differences between AD LDS and AD DS. For example, it is easy to see why Exchange Server must integrate with AD DS as opposed to relying on AD LDS because Exchange Server requires access to the global catalog service to run. Without it, e-mail users could not look up recipients. Because AD LDS does not support the global catalog, Exchange Server cannot rely on it. However, Exchange Server is an application that requires access to directory data in each site of the domain or forest. As such, it also relies on your domain controller positioning to ensure that each user can properly address e-mails.

AD LDS, however, provides much of the same functionality as AD DS. For example, you can create instances with replicas distributed in various locations in your network, just as with the location of domain controllers, and then use multimaster replication to ensure data consistency. In short, AD LDS is a lightweight, portable, and more malleable version of the directory service offered by AD DS.

AD LDS Scenarios

Now that you have a better understanding of AD LDS and its feature set, you can begin to identify scenarios in which you would need to work with this technology. Consider these scenarios when you decide whether to rely on AD LDS or AD DS.

- When your applications need to rely on an LDAP directory, consider using AD LDS instead of AD DS. AD LDS can often be hosted on the same server as the application, providing high-speed and local access to directory data. This would reduce replication traffic because all required data is local. In addition, you can bundle the AD LDS instance with the application when you deploy it. For example, if you have a human resources application that must rely on custom policies to ensure that users can access only specific content when their user object contains a set of particular attributes, you can store these attributes and policies within AD LDS.

■ Rely on AD LDS to provide data associated with user accounts in AD DS but requiring extensions to the AD DS schema to support it. Using AD LDS in this scenario provides the additional user data without modifying the AD DS schema. For example, if you have a centralized application that provides a photograph of each employee in your organization and associates that photograph with the user's AD DS account, you can store the photographs in an AD LDS instance. By storing the photographs in AD LDS in a central location, they are associated with the user accounts in AD DS, but because they are in AD LDS, they are not replicated with all other AD DS data, reducing bandwidth requirements for replication.

■ Rely on an AD LDS instance to provide authentication services for a Web application such as Microsoft SharePoint Portal Server in a perimeter network or extranet. AD LDS can query the internal AD DS structure through a firewall to obtain user account information and store it securely in the perimeter network. This avoids having to deploy AD DS in the perimeter or having to include domain controllers from the internal network in the perimeter. Note that you can also rely on Active Directory Federation Services (AD FS) to provide this access. AD FS is discussed in further detail in Chapter 17, "Active Directory Federation Services."

■ Consolidate various identity repositories into a single directory store. Using a metadirectory service such as Microsoft Identity Integration Server (MIIS), Microsoft Identity Lifecycle Manager (MILM), or the free Identity Integration Feature Pack (IIFP), you can obtain data from various sources and consolidate it within an AD LDS instance. MIIS and MILM support the provisioning of data from a wide variety of sources such as AD DS forests, SQL Server databases, third-party LDAP services, and much more. IIFP is a subset of MIIS and supports data integration between AD DS, AD LDS, and Exchange Server. Using these solutions reduces your identity management overhead by designating a single master source and provisioning all other repositories from this source.

MORE INFO   MIIS, MILM, and IIFP

For more information on MIIS, go to *http://www.microsoft.com/technet/miis/evaluate /overview.mspx*.

For more information on MILM, go to *http://www.microsoft.com/windowsserver/ilm2007 /default.mspx*.

For more information on and to download IIFP, go to *http://www.microsoft.com/downloads /details.aspx?familyid=d9143610-c04d-41c4-b7ea-6f56819769d5&displaylang=en*.

■ Provide support for departmental applications. In some cases, departments might require additional identity information, information that is of no relevance to any other department within the organization. By integrating this information in an AD LDS instance, the department has access to it without affecting the directory service for the entire organization.

- Provide support for distributed applications. If your application is distributed and requires access to data in several locations, you can also rely on AD LDS because AD LDS provides the same multimaster replication capabilities as AD DS.

- Migrate legacy directory applications to AD LDS. If your organization is running legacy applications that rely on an LDAP directory, you can migrate the data to an AD LDS instance and standardize it on Active Directory directory technologies.

- Provide support for local development. Because AD LDS can be installed on client workstations, you can provide your developers with portable single-instance directories they can use to develop custom applications that require access to identity data. Developing with AD LDS is much simpler and easier to manage and contain than developing with AD DS.

- In addition, when evaluating directory-enabled commercial applications, you should always give preference to an application that will rely on AD LDS or its predecessor, ADAM, before selecting one that relies on AD DS schema modifications. Deploying commercial applications with portable directories is much easier and has much less impact on your network than deploying applications that will modify your NOS directory schema forever.

Each of these scenarios represents a possible use of AD LDS. Typical applications should include white-page directories, security-oriented applications and network configuration, and policy store applications.

As you can see, AD LDS is much more portable and malleable than AD DS will ever be. Whenever you need to think about schema modifications in AD DS, think of AD LDS instead. On almost every occasion, AD LDS will provide a better choice because AD DS should always be reserved as a NOS directory and should include integration only with applications that add functionality to the NOS directory functions.

MORE INFO   AD LDS

For more information on AD LDS, go to *http://technet2.microsoft.com/windowsserver2008/en /library/b7fb96ec-3f3f-4860-a1ab-eb43e54bbefc1033.mspx.*

Exam Tip   Pay attention to the scenarios outlined previously in this chapter. Although few exam questions are about AD LDS, you can be sure that when they do arise, they will be related to choosing AD LDS over other Active Directory technologies.

Installing AD LDS

As part of Windows Server 2008, AD LDS can be installed and configured in both the full installation and in Server Core. In addition, AD LDS is an ideal candidate for virtualization through Windows Server 2008 Hyper-V. Because of its light requirements, AD LDS can easily run within a virtual instance of the Windows Server 2008 operating system and should be considered as such unless the application that is tied to the AD LDS instance has specific requirements for physical installation.

In addition, avoid installing AD LDS on domain controllers as much as possible. Although AD LDS can fully coexist with the domain controller (DC) role, and even the read-only domain controller (RODC) role, domain controllers should be considered special roles within your network and should be tied only to the DNS service and nothing else, if at all possible. Because DCs are also good candidates for virtualization, any network that can rely on host servers running Hyper-V and virtualized instances of other services should virtualize DCs as much as possible. With a virtual DC, it is much easier to ensure that no other roles are hosted on the server because all other roles can also be virtualized within their own instances of Windows Server 2008.

Also, consider running AD LDS in scenarios in which high security is required. A good example is one in which you need to run an authentication directory service in extranets or perimeter networks. Relying on Server Core installations within these environments can help reduce the attack surface of servers you expose outside of your corporate network.

Identifying AD LDS Requirements

As mentioned earlier, AD LDS has very light installation requirements. They include:

- A supported operating system such as Windows Server 2008, Standard Edition, Enterprise Edition, or Datacenter Edition.
- An account with local administration access rights.

Removing AD LDS from a server requires two activities:

- First, uninstall any instance of AD LDS you created after the role installation, using Programs And Features in Control Panel.
- Second, use Server Manager to remove the AD LDS role.

As you can see, both installation and removal requirements are straightforward. The major caveat is that you ensure that all instances have been removed from a server before you remove the role.

Exam Tip   Keep in mind that you need to remove all instances of AD LDS from a server before you can remove the role from the server.

Installing AD LDS on Server Core

Installing AD LDS is very similar to installing AD DS. First you must install the server role; then you must create the AD LDS instances you want to use. Installing AD LDS on the full installation of Windows Server 2008 is covered in the practice later in this lesson.

The installation process for AD LDS is as simple on Server Core as it is on a full installation of Windows Server 2008. Use the following process:

1. Log on with local administrative credentials to a Windows Server 2008 member or standalone server running Server Core.

2. Begin by identifying the service name for AD LDS. Use the following command:

    `oclist | more`

    Using the pipe symbol (|) followed by the *more* command enables you to view contents one screen at a time. Press the spacebar to move from one screen to the next. Use Ctrl+C to cancel the command after you have found the name of the role. This name should appear in the first screen of information and should be DirectoryServices-ADAM-ServerCore.

3. Proceed to the installation of the role. Use the following command:

    `start /w ocsetup DirectoryServices-ADAM-ServerCore`

    Role names are case-sensitive, so ensure that you type the role name exactly as displayed; otherwise, the command will not work. Also, using the *start /w* command ensures that the command prompt does not return until the role installation is complete.

If you run the *oclist* command once again, you will see that the AD LDS role has been added to this server. You can also navigate to the %SystemRoot%\ADAM folder to view the new AD LDS files. Your server is ready to host AD LDS instances.

PRACTICE Installing AD LDS

In this practice, you will install the AD LDS role on a server running the full installation of Windows Server 2008. Then you will browse the contents of the installation folder to identify which files have been installed.

▶ Exercise 1   Install AD LDS

In this exercise, you will install the AD LDS server role.

1. Make sure your Active Directory Domain Server, SERVER01.contoso.com, is running, and start your member servers, SERVER03.contoso.com and SERVER04.contoso.com.

2. Log on to SERVER03.contoso.com with the Contoso\Administrator account.

   You do not need domain administrator rights to work with AD LDS. Because each AD LDS installation is independent of AD DS, you need only local administrator rights to work with it, but using the domain administrator account is acceptable for the purpose of this exercise.

3. In Server Manager, right-click the Roles node, and then select Add Roles.

4. Review the Before You Begin screen, and then click Next.

5. In the Select Server Roles dialog box, select Active Directory Lightweight Directory Services, and then click Next.

6. Review the information in the Active Directory Lightweight Directory Services window, and then click Next.

7. Confirm your choices, and then click Install.

8. Review the installation results, and then click Close.

9. Repeat the operation on SERVER04.contoso.com.

AD LDS is installed on both member servers.

The AD LDS installation installs the service and generates a directory store called Adamntds.dit located in the %SystemRoot%\Adam folder. It also adds the tools to configure and manage AD LDS.

MORE INFO   AD LDS installation process

For a step-by-step guide to the installation of AD LDS, go to *http://technet2.microsoft.com /windowsserver2008/en/library/141900a7-445c-4bd3-9ce3-5ff53d70d10a1033.mspx?mfr=true.*

When the installation is complete, the role appears in Server Manager. (See Figure 14-2.)

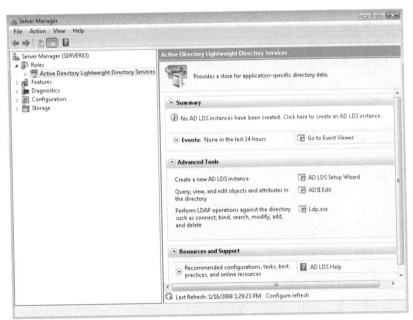

Figure 14-2   Viewing the AD LDS role within Server Manager

▶ **Exercise 2   Review the Installed AD LDS Files**

In this exercise, you will review the files AD LDS installs on servers.

1. Log on to your member server, SERVER03.contoso.com, using the Contoso\Administrator account.

2. Open a Windows Explorer window. From the Start menu, right-click Computer, and then select Explore.

3. Navigate to the %SystemRoot%\ADAM folder.

4. Review the files created by the AD LDS installation process.

   On a full installation of Windows Server 2008, AD LDS creates the ADAM folder and populates it with 20 files and two subfolders. The two subfolders include localization information. In this case, they are in U.S. English. As shown in Figure 14-3, the files contained in the ADAM folder include:

   ❑ The AD LDS program files, including .dll, .exe, .cat, .ini, and .xml files.

   ❑ The AD LDS directory store, Adamntds.dit.

   ❑ Lightweight directory format (.ldf) files that are used to populate AD LDS instances when they are created.

You will be working with these file types when you begin to configure AD LDS in the next lesson.

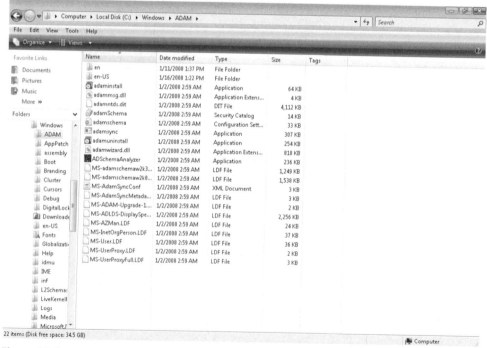

Figure 14-3   AD LDS installs into the %SystemRoot%\Adam folder and creates the AD LDS database

The installation of AD LDS on Server Core does not include the same files and folders as the installation on a full installation of Windows Server 2008. Server Core creates only one folder for localization, whereas the full installation creates two. In addition, the full installation includes an additional tool: the Active Directory Schema Analyzer, which is not installed on Server Core. (See Figure 14-4.)

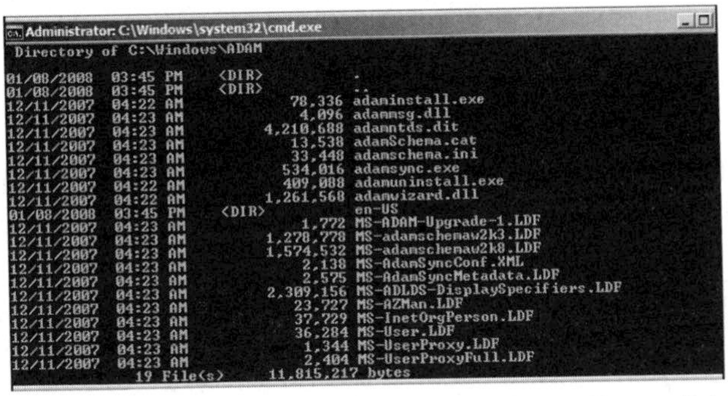

Figure 14-4   The AD LDS Installation on Server Core only includes 19 files and one single sub-folder

Lesson Summary

- As its name suggests, AD LDS is a lightweight version of AD DS. AD LDS supports all the features of AD DS except for the network operating system capabilities. As such, it is a directory service that can be tied to applications and support their need for custom configurations and authentication services in insecure environments such as perimeter networks.
- The installation requirements for AD LDS are very simple: all you need is a server running a supported version of Windows Server 2008. This server can be a member, a standalone server, or even a domain controller, although you should endeavor to keep your DCs separate from all other roles.
- To install AD LDS, you select the role in the Add Roles Wizard. The installation process is probably the most basic installation process of all the roles in Windows Server 2008.
- To remove AD LDS, you must first remove all instances through Programs And Features in Control Panel and then remove the role in Server Manager.

Lesson Review

You can use the following questions to test your knowledge of the information in Lesson 1, "Understanding and Installing AD LDS." The questions are also available on the companion CD if you prefer to review them in electronic form.

NOTE   Answers

Answers to these questions and explanations of why each answer choice is right or wrong are located in the "Answers" section at the end of the book.

1. You are a server administrator for *contoso.com*. This morning, your boss came in with a new request. You need to repurpose SERVER04 with a new role as soon as possible. SERVER04 currently hosts five AD LDS instances. You must uninstall AD LDS from this server. You log on to SERVER04 with local administrative rights and launch an elevated command prompt. You use the *ocsetup* command with the */uninstall* switch, and it does not work. Which of the following options should you use to resolve the problem?

   A. You must restart the server to make sure all running setup processes are complete and then run the *uninstall* command again.

   B. You must use Server Manager to remove all AD LDS instances and the role.

   C. You must uninstall all existing instances of AD LDS first, using Programs And Features in Control Panel, and then execute *ocsetup /uninstall* from the command prompt.

   D. You must use the *oclist* command to verify the syntax of the option you are trying to remove with the *ocsetup* command. You retry the *ocsetup* command with the correct syntax.

Lesson 2: Configuring and Using AD LDS

Now that you have installed AD LDS, you can begin to work with it to store directory-related data for various applications. The first thing you should do is become familiar with the AD LDS tool set. After you understand which tools you can use to manage AD LDS, you can begin to create your first instances. After you've created your instances, you can secure them to ensure that they are properly protected. You'll then move on to the creation of replicas for these instances so that you can install them on various other systems and control replication so that instances located on different computers can be updated through multimaster replication.

This lesson will show you the value AD LDS offers when you combine it with applications and integrate it with the other Active Directory technologies contained within Windows Server 2008.

After this lesson, you will be able to:
- Create AD LDS instances.
- Work with AD LDS tools.
- Work with application partitions.
- Manage replication between AD LDS instances.

Estimated lesson time: 30 minutes

Working with AD LDS Tools

You can work with AD LDS through a selection of tools, many of which will be familiar to you because they are the same tools you use for AD DS administration. Table 14-3 outlines each of these tools and the purpose it serves when managing the AD LDS service.

Table 14-3 AD LDS Tools and AD DS Tools

Tool Name	Usage	Location
Active Directory Schema Snap-in	Modify the schema for AD LDS instances. You must use the *Regsvr32.exe* command to register the Schmmgnt.dll first.	Custom MMC
Active Directory Sites and Services	Configure and manage replication scopes for AD LDS instances. AD LDS instances must be updated to support replication objects first.	Administrative Tools program group
AD LDS Setup	Create AD LDS instances.	Administrative Tools program group
ADAMInstall.exe	Command-line tool for the creation of AD LDS instances.	%SystemRoot% \ADAM folder

Table 14-3   **AD LDS Tools and AD DS Tools**

Tool Name	Usage	Location
ADAMSync.exe	Command-line tool for synchronizing data from AD DS forest to AD LDS instance. AD LDS instance must be updated to AD DS schema first.	%SystemRoot% \ADAM folder
ADAMUninstall.exe	Command-line tool for the removal of AD LDS instances.	%SystemRoot% \ADAM folder
ADSchemaAnalyzer.exe	Command-line tool for copying schema contents from AD DS to AD LDS or from one AD LDS instance to another. Supports third-party LDAP directory schema copies.	%SystemRoot% \ADAM folder
ADSI Edit	Interactively manage AD LDS content through ADSI.	Administrative Tools program group
CSVDE.exe	Import data into AD LDS instances.	Command line
DSACLS.exe	Control access control lists on AD LDS objects.	Command line
DSAMain.exe	Mount Active Directory store (.dit) backups or snapshots to identify their contents.	Command line
DSDBUtil.exe	Perform database maintenance, configure AD LDS ports, and view existing instances. Also, create one-step installations for transporting AD LDS instances through the Install from Media (IFM) generation process.	Command line
Dcdiag.exe	Diagnose AD LDS instances. Must use the / n:*NamingContext* switch to name the instance to diagnose.	Command line
DSMgmt.exe	Supports application partition and AD LDS policy management.	Command line
Event Viewer	To audit AD LDS changes and log old and new values for both objects and attributes.	Administrative Tools program group
LDAP Data Interchange Format (LDIF) Files	AD LDS installations can dynamically import LDIF files (.ldp) during instance creation, automatically configuring the instance.	%SystemRoot% \ADAM folder
LDIFDE.exe	Import data into AD LDS instances.	Command line
LDP.exe	Interactively modify content or AD LDS instances through LDAP.	Command line
Ntdsutil.exe	Manage AD LDS instances but only if AD DS is also installed. (Not recommended; use *DSDBUtil.exe* instead.)	Command line

Table 14-3 AD LDS Tools and AD DS Tools

Tool Name	Usage	Location
RepAdmin.exe	Analyze replication to view potential issues.	Command line
Server Manager	Manage existing AD LDS instances.	Administrative Tools program group
Windows Server Backup	Back up or restore AD LDS instances and their contents.	Administrative Tools program group

You'll use a variety of the tools listed in Table 14-3 to perform the configuration and administration operations required when you run AD LDS services.

MORE INFO   AD LDS auditing

For more information on auditing AD LDS instances or AD DS domains, go to *http://go.microsoft.com/fwlink/?LinkId=94846*.

Creating AD LDS Instances

The AD LDS role installation process is very similar to the AD DS installation process. You begin by installing the AD LDS binaries, and then, after they are installed, you create AD LDS instances to use the service. In the same way, when you deploy AD DS, you begin by installing the binaries, and then you use the Active Directory Domain Services Installation Wizard to create the AD DS instance you will use. Because of their same roots, many of the tools you use to manage them are the same.

Preparing for AD LDS Instance Creation

You create AD LDS instances by using the Active Directory Lightweight Directory Services Setup Wizard. However, you need to prepare several items before you create the instance. These items include:

- A data drive created for your server. Because this server will be hosting directory stores, place these stores on a drive that is separate from the operating system.
- The name you will use to create the instance. Use meaningful names, for example, the name of the application that will be tied to this instance, to identify instances. This name will be used to identify the instance on the local computer as well as to name the files that make up the instance and the service that supports it.
- The ports you intend to use to communicate with the instance. Both AD LDS and AD DS use the same ports for communication. These ports are the default LDAP (389) and LDAP over the Secure Sockets Layer (SSL), or Secure LDAP (636), ports. AD DS uses two additional ports, 3268, which uses LDAP to access the global catalog, and 3269, which uses Secure LDAP to access the global catalog. Because AD DS and AD LDS use the same

ports, this is another good reason for not running both roles on the same server. However, when the wizard detects that ports 389 and 636 are already in use, it proposes 50,000 and 50,001 for each port and then uses other ports in the 50,000 range for additional instances.

Quick Check

1. Which ports are used to work with AD LDS instances?
2. How do the ports in an AD LDS instance differ from ports used by AD DS?

Quick Check Answers

1. The ports used by an AD LDS instance can be the standard LDAP port, 389, or the LDAP over SSL or Secure LDAP port, 636. In addition, AD LDS can use any port over 1025. However, use ports in the 50,000 range as a best practice.
2. Both AD DS and AD LDS can use ports 389 (LDAP) or 636 (Secure LDAP). In addition, AD DS uses ports 3268 (LDAP) and 3269 (Secure LDAP) to communicate with the global catalog service. However, reserve ports 389 and 636 for AD DS as a best practice.

IMPORTANT Using ports 389 and 636

If you are creating AD LDS instances within a domain, do not use ports 389 or 636 even if you are not creating the first instance on a domain controller. AD DS uses these ports by default, and, because of this, some consoles, such as those using the Active Directory Schema snap-in, will not bind to local instances because they bind to the AD DS directory by default. As a best practice, always use ports beyond the 50,000 range for your AD LDS instances.

Exam Tip Make note of the default ports because they are sure to be on the exam even though you should avoid them in production environments.

■ The Active Directory application partition name you intend to use for the instance. You must use a distinguished name (DN) to create the partition. For example, you could use CN=AppPartition1,DC=Contoso,DC=com. Depending on how you intend to use the instance, you might or might not need the application partition. Application partitions control the replication scope for a directory store. For example, when you integrate DNS data within the directory, AD DS creates an application partition to make DNS data available to appropriate DCs. Application partitions for AD LDS can be created in one of three ways: when you create the instance, when you install the application that will be tied to the instance, or when you create the partition manually through the *LDP.exe* tool. If your application will not create application partitions automatically, create them with the wizard.

- A service account to run the instance. You can use the Network Service account, but if you intend to run multiple instances, it might be best to use named service accounts for each instance. Remember to follow the service accounts guidelines and requirements as listed here:
  - Create a domain account if you are in a domain; otherwise, use a local account (for example, in a perimeter network).
  - Name the account with the same name you gave to the instance.
  - Assign a complex password to this account.
  - Set User Cannot Change Password in the account properties. You assign this property to ensure that no one can appropriate the account.
  - Set Password Never Expires in the account properties. You assign this property to ensure that the service does not fail because of a password policy.
  - Assign the Log On As A Service User right in the Local Security Policy of each computer that will host this instance.
  - Assign the Generate Security Audits User right in the Local Security Policy of each computer that will host this instance to support account auditing.
- A group that will contain the user accounts that will administer the instance. The best practice for permission assignments is always to use groups even if only one account is a member of the group. If personnel changes, you can always add or change group members without having to add or change permissions. Create a domain group if you are in a domain; otherwise, create a local group. Name the group the same as the instance. This way, it will be easy to track the group's purpose. Add your own account to the group as well as to the service account you created earlier.
- Any additional LDIF files you need for the instance. Place these files into the %SystemRoot% \ADAM folder. These files will be imported during the creation of the instance. Importing LDIF files extends the schema of the instance you are creating to support additional operations. For example, to synchronize AD DS with AD LDS, you would import the MS-AdamSyncMetadata.ldf file. If your application requires custom schema modifications, create the LDIF file ahead of time and import it as you create the instance. Note that you can always import LDIF files after the instance is created. Default LDIF files are listed in Table 14-4.

Make note of these values because you will need them to both create and then manage the instance.

Table 14-4 Default AD LDS LDIF Files

File Name	Purpose
MS-ADAM-Upgrade-1.ldf	To upgrade the AD LDS schema to the latest version.
MS-adamschemaw2k3.ldf	Required as a prerequisite for synchronizing an instance with Active Directory in Windows Server 2003.

Table 14-4 Default AD LDS LDIF Files

File Name	Purpose
MS-adamschemaw2k8.ldf	Required as a prerequisite for synchronizing an instance with Active Directory in Windows Server 2008.
MS-AdamSyncMetadata.ldf	Required to synchronize data between an AD DS forest and an AD LDS instance through ADAMSync.
MS-ADLDS-DisplaySpecifiers.ldf	Required for the Active Directory Sites and Services snap-in operation.
MS-AZMan.ldf	Required to support the Windows Authorization Manager.
MS-InetOrgPerson.ldf	Required to create *inetOrgPerson* user classes and attributes.
MS-User.ldf	Required to create user classes and attributes.
MS-UserProxy.ldf	Required to create a simple *userProxy* class.
MS-UserProxyFull.ldf	Required to create a full *userProxy* class. MS-UserProxy.ldf must be imported first.

After you have all these items in hand, you are ready to create your instance. Make sure the account you use has local administrative rights. There are two ways to create instances. The first is through the Active Directory Lightweight Services Setup Wizard, and the second is through the command line. You will use the wizard during the practice in this lesson. Using the command line is explained in a later section.

Performing an Unattended AD LDS Instance Creation

You can also perform unattended AD LDS instance creations. For example, to create instances on Server Core installations, you must use an unattended instance creation process because there is no graphical interface to run the wizard. Unattended instance creations are also useful when you need to create an instance for a distributed application on multiple servers. Make sure you prepare all the prerequisites for the instance as outlined in the "Preparing for AD LDS Instance Creation" section earlier in this lesson.

The %SystemRoot%\ADAM folder includes an additional command, *AdamInstall.exe*, which can be run to perform unattended instance setups. As with the *Dcpromo.exe* command, this command requires a text file as input for the creation of the instance. You can run *AdamInstall.exe* on either a full installation or Server Core. Begin by creating this text file.

1. Launch Notepad
2. Type the text for the answer file. Include the following items:

```
[ADAMInstall]
InstallType=Unique
```

```
InstanceName=InstanceName
LocalLDAPPortToListenOn=PortNumber
LocalSSLPortToListenOn=PortNumber
NewApplicationPartitionToCreate=PartitionName
DataFilesPath=D:\ADAMInstances\InstanceName\Data
LogFilesPath=D:\ADAMInstances\InstanceName\Data
ServiceAccount=DomainorMachineName\AccountName
ServicePassword=Password
Administrator=DomainorMachineName\GroupName
ImportLDIFFiles="LDIFFilename1" "LDIFFilename2" "LDIFFilename3"
SourceUserName=DomainorMachineName\AccountName
SourcePassword=Password
```

Replace all names in italics with the appropriate values. Refer to the "Preparing for AD LDS Instance Creation" section earlier in this lesson to identify the required values. Use caution with this file because it includes passwords, and these passwords are displayed in clear text. The passwords are removed as soon as the file is used by the AD LDS instance creation tool.

3. Save the file in the %SystemRoot%\ADAM folder, and name it with the name of the instance you want to create.

4. Close Notepad.

MORE INFO AD LDS instance creation

For more information on AD LDS instance creation, go to *http://technet2.microsoft.com/ windowsserver2008/en/library/141900a7-445c-4bd3-9ce3-5ff53d70d10a1033.mspx?mfr=true.*

Now you're ready to create your instance. Remember that you need local administrative rights.

1. Open an elevated command prompt from the Start menu by right-clicking Command Prompt and selecting Run As Administrator.

2. In the command prompt window, move to the %SystemRoot%\ADAM folder. Type the following command, and then press Enter.

   ```
   cd windows\adam
   ```

3. Type the following command. Use quotation marks for the file name if it includes spaces.

   ```
   adaminstall /answer:filename.txt
   ```

4. Close the command prompt window.

Your instance is ready. You can verify that the instance files have been created by going to the target folder and viewing its contents.

Migrating a Previous LDAP Instance to AD LDS

You can also migrate existing LDAP directories to AD LDS or upgrade instances of ADAM to AD LDS. You can do this by importing the contents of the older instances into a new instance of AD LDS.

Importing data can be done either when you create the instance or after the instance is created. Both processes use the same approach because both rely on LDIF files or files with the .ldf extension. If you choose to import data after the instance is created, you will need to use the *LDIFDE.exe* command. Keep in mind that you must first export the data from the previous instance and place it into a file in LDIF format before you can import the data.

You can use *LDIFDE* to export contents from legacy instances. Remember that you need local administrative rights as well as administrative rights to the instance to perform these operations. Also make sure you run the command prompt with elevated credentials. Use the following command structure:

```
ldifde -f filename -s servername:portnumber -m -b username domainname password
```

In this command structure, *filename* is the name of the file to create (use quotation marks if the path includes spaces); *servername* is the name of the server hosting the instance; *portnumber* is the communications port; *username*, *domainname*, and *password* are the credentials of an instance administrator.

Use a similar command to import the data into the new instance:

```
ldifde -i -f filename -s servername:portnumber -m -b username domainname password
```

Note that to import passwords from the legacy instance, you must use the *−h* switch. This switch will encrypt all passwords, using simple authentication and security layer (SASL).

Quick Check

1. What are the three ways to create application partitions for AD LDS instances?
2. What is the purpose of the LDIF files included with AD LDS?
3. How can you debug an AD LDS instance creation process that goes awry?

Quick Check Answers

1. There are three ways to create application partitions for AD LDS instances:
   - ❏ They can be created during the creation of an instance with AD LDS Setup.
   - ❏ They can be created through the installation of the application that will be tied to an AD LDS instance.
   - ❏ They can be created manually through the *LDP.exe* tool.

2. The LDIF files included with AD LDS serve several purposes, depending on the actual file, but generally they are used to extend the schema of an instance to support specific functionality.

3. AD LDS creates log files during the creation of the instance. These files are located in the %SystemRoot%\Debug folder and are named ADAMSetup.log and ADAMSetup_loader.log. You can review them to find and resolve issues during the creation of the instance.

MORE INFO *LDIFDE*

For more information on the *LDIFDE.exe* command, go to *http://technet2.microsoft.com/windowsserver/en/library/32872283-3722-4d9b-925a-82c516a1ca141033.mspx?mfr=true*. Also, refer to Chapter 3, "Users," for additional information on *LDIFDE*.

Working with AD LDS Instances

Table 14-3, presented earlier, lists all the various tools you can use to work with AD LDS instances. Of these, the most useful are the graphical tools such as ADSI Edit, *LDP.exe*, the Schema snap-in, and Active Directory Sites and Services. They control how you view and edit content in your instances. Command-line tools are more useful for automating processes and data input for AD LDS instances.

Using ADSI Edit to Work with Instances

ADSI Edit is a general administration tool for AD LDS instances. Each time you want to work with an instance, you must first connect and bind to the instance. Remember that you must be administrator of the instance to perform administrative operations on them. Use the following procedure:

1. Launch ADSI Edit from the Administrative Tools program group.

2. In the tree pane, right-click ADSI Edit, and then select Connect To. This opens the Connection Settings dialog box. Type in the following values as shown in Figure 14-5:

    ❑ Name: should be the name of the instance to which you want to connect.

    ❑ Connection Point: choose Select Or Type A Distinguished Name Or Naming Context, and type the distinguished name of the instance.

    ❑ Computer: choose Select Or Type A Domain Or Server, and type the server name with the port number, for example, SERVER03:50000.

    ❑ Computer: select the Use SSL-Based Encryption check box if you are using a Secure LDAP port.

3. Click OK.

    This connects you to the instance. Expand all entries to view the instance contents. Explore the context menus to understand the operations you can perform with ADSI Edit on AD LDS instances.

Figure 14-5   Connecting to an AD LDS instance with ADSI Edit

Now that you are bound to the instance, you can create and manage objects within the instance. Use the following procedure:

1. Right-click the application partition distinguished name, select New, and choose Object. This opens the Create Object dialog box, which lists all the available object classes in the instance's schema.

2. Begin by creating a user group. Scroll to the Group object, select it, and then click Next.

3. Type the name of the group, for example, **AD LDS Users**, and then click Next.

4. On the next screen of the dialog box, you can click More Attributes to assign more values to this new object. For example, you can assign a description to the group. From the Select A Property To View drop-down list, select adminDescription. Type a description in the *Edit Attribute* field, for example, **Group to contain AD LDS users**, click Set, and then click OK.

5. Click Finish to create the group. By default, this creates a security group.

6. Now create a user. Right-click the application partition distinguished name, select New, and then choose Object.

7. Scroll to the User object, select it, and then click Next.

8. Type the name of the user, and then click Next.

9. Once again, you can click More Attributes to assign more values to this new object.

10. Click Finish to create the user.

11. Now add the user to the group. Locate the group in the details pane, and right-click it to select Properties.

12. In the Properties dialog box, locate the member property, and then click Edit.

13. In the Multi-Valued Distinguished Name With Security Principal Editor dialog box, click Add DN.

14. In the Add Distinguished Name dialog box, type the distinguished name of the user you created. For example, type **cn=John Kane,cn=Instance01,dc=contoso,dc=com**. Click OK. The user is now listed in the members list.

15. Click OK to complete the operation.

If you view the properties of the group again, you will see that your user has been added to the group. It is quite cumbersome to add users and groups to an instance in this manner, but you can use it for single modifications. Ideally, you will create user and group lists and then use either *CSVDE.exe* or *LDIFDE.exe* to add them in batches. Refer to Chapter 3 to review the automation of user creation and to Chapter 4, "Groups," to review the automation of group creation for more information.

Using *LDP.exe* to Work with Instances

Similarly, the *LDP.exe* console enables you to view and edit instance contents. As with the ADSI Edit tool, you must connect and then bind to the instance you need to work with. Remember that you must be administrator of the instance to perform administrative operations on it. Use the following procedure:

1. Launch *LDP.exe* from the command line or from Server Manager under the Active Directory Lightweight Directory Service, Advanced Tools section.

2. Click Connection from the Connect menu.

3. Type the name of the server you want to connect to and the port number to use. Select SSL if you are using a Secure LDAP port. Click OK.

4. Click Bind from the Connect menu.

5. If your account has the required permissions, select Bind As Currently Logged On User. If not, select Bind With Credentials, and type the appropriate credentials. Click OK.

6. Click Tree from the View menu. This will fill the tree pane.

7. In the BaseDN dialog box, click the down arrow to view the list of distinguished names, and select the name of your instance. Click OK.

    From this point, you can use the tree pane to identify where you want to work inside the instance. Explore the various menus to see which operations you can perform with *LDP.exe*, and then close *LDP.exe*.

MORE INFO   Using *LDP.exe* with AD LDS instances

For more information on using *LDP.exe* with AD LDS instances, see *http://technet2.microsoft.com/windowsserver2008/en/library/141900a7-445c-4bd3-9ce3-5ff53d70d10a1033.mspx*.

Using the Schema Snap-in to Work with Instances

You can also use the Active Directory Schema snap-in to create custom consoles to manage AD LDS instance schemas. Remember that to use this snap-in, you must first register it on the server. Use the following command in an elevated command prompt:

`regsvr32 schmmgmt.dll`

You're now ready to load the Schema snap-in and view the schema of your instances. Remember to use administrative credentials for the instance.

1. Click Start, and then type **mmc** in the Search box. Press Enter.
2. In the empty MMC, click Add/Remove Snap-in from the File menu.
3. Locate the Active Directory Schema snap-in in the Available Snap-ins list, click Add, and then click OK.
4. Save the console with an appropriate name. Make sure you save it in an appropriate location.
5. The Schema snap-in binds to the Active Directory Domain Services directory by default. To bind to an AD LDS instance, right-click Active Directory Schema in the tree pane, and select Change Active Directory Domain Controller.
6. In the Change Directory Server dialog box, select This Domain Controller Or AD LDS Instance, click <Type A Directory Server Name[:Port] Here>, type the server name with the port number separated by a colon, and then press Enter. Click OK.
7. In the warning dialog box, click Yes to change servers.

   You can now view the schema for this instance. Save this console again to save these settings. Note the similarities between the schema of an AD LDS instance and the one for an AD DS directory.

NOTE   Creating a multi-AD LDS console

If you want to create one console with multiple AD LDS instance schemas, just add additional Schema snap-ins to your console. Use one snap-in for each instance you want to connect to. When you reopen the console, it will link to each instance and save you time.

Using Active Directory Sites and Services to Work with Instances

As with the other Active Directory tools, you can manage AD LDS instances with the Active Directory Sites and Services console. However, before you can do so, you must import the MS-ADLDS-DisplaySpecifiers.ldf file to update the instance's schema to support the appropriate objects. To do so, perform the following steps:

1. Begin by adding the LDIF file to your instance if it hasn't already been done. Open an elevated command prompt.
2. Move to the %SystemRoot%\ADAM folder, cd windows\adam.
3. Import the LDIF file into the instance:

   ```
   ldifde -i -f MS-ADLDS-DisplaySpecifiers.ldf -s servername:portnumber -m -a username
   domainname password
   ```

4. Close the command prompt.
5. Launch Active Directory Sites And Services from the Administrative Tools program group.
6. The console binds to the Active Directory Domain Services directory by default. To bind to an AD LDS instance, right-click Active Directory Sites And Services in the tree pane, and select Change Domain Controller.
7. In the Change Directory Server dialog box, select This Domain Controller Or AD LDS Instance, and click <Type A Directory Server Name[:Port] Here>. Type the server name with the port number separated by a colon, and then press Enter. Click OK.
8. In the warning dialog box, click Yes to change servers.

   You can now work with the replication parameters for the instance. Note that the server name uses the Servername$InstanceName format to illustrate that it is not a domain controller.

MORE INFO   AD LDS tools and instances

For more information on AD LDS tools and instances, go to *http://technet2.microsoft.com/windowsserver2008/en/library/141900a7-445c-4bd3-9ce3-5ff53d70d10a1033.mspx*.

Exam Tip   Keep in mind that you cannot use graphical tools on Server Core. To manage instances located on Server Core installations, use the graphical tools from a full Windows installation or from a client system running Remote Server Administration Tools (RSAT) to control them remotely.

Working with AD LDS instances requires care and attention because almost every activity is performed either through the command line or by using distinguished names. As you have seen when working with AD DS, typographical errors are the bane of any administrator working with these tools. The same applies to AD LDS. Be sure to double-check all your entries before you run any command or create and manage any object by using its distinguished name.

PRACTICE Working with AD LDS Instances

In this practice, you will create your first AD LDS instance as well as a replica. Then you will manage replication between the two instances. For this, you will need the two servers listed in the "Before you Begin" section of this chapter.

▶ Exercise 1   Create an AD LDS Instance

In this exercise, you will create your first AD LDS instance. You previously installed the AD LDS service on both of the member servers mentioned in the "Before You Begin" section of this chapter. You will use the values in Table 14-5 to perform this exercise.

Table 14-5   Instance Creation Values

Item	Value
Instance Name	ADLDSInstance
Ports	50,004 for LDAP 50,005 for Secure LDAP
Application Partition Name	CN=ADLDSInstance,dc=contoso,dc=com
Data Paths	D:\ADLDS\ADLDSInstance\Data
Service Account	Network Service
Administration Account	Contoso\Administrator
LDIF Files for Import	MS-AdamSyncMetadata.ldf MS-ADLDS-DisplaySpecifiers.ldf MS-AZMan.ldf MS-InetOrgPerson.ldf MS-User.ldf MS-UserProxy.ldf MS-UserProxyFull.ldf

Make a practice of filling out a table similar to Table 14-5 each time you create a new instance of AD LDS. Because a server can host a multitude of AD LDS instances, it is a very good practice to document each one.

1. Begin by making sure your domain controller, SERVER01.contoso.com, and your member servers, SERVER03.contoso.com and SERVER04.contoso.com, are running.

2. Log on to SERVER03.contoso.com with the domain Administrator account.

   Remember that, in production, you need only local administrative rights for operations with AD LDS.

3. Launch the Active Directory Lightweight Directory Services Setup Wizard from the Administrative Tools program group.

4. Review the information on the Welcome page, and then click Next.

5. On the Setup Options page, select A Unique Instance, and then click Next.

6. On the Instance Name page, type **ADLDSInstance**, and then click Next.

    When you name the instance, you also name the service that will run that instance. Note that the service name will be ADAM_*instancename*, but the name listed in the Services console will be *instancename* alone.

7. On the Ports page, provide the ports to use to communicate with this instance. Use 50,004 for LDAP and 50,005 for the SSL port number. Click Next.

8. On the Application Directory Partition page, provide the application partition name, in this case, **CN=ADLDSInstance,dc=contoso,dc=com**, and click Next.

    You must always supply a distinguished name.

9. On the File Locations page, change the paths to D:\ADLDS\ADLDSInstance\Data, and then click Next.

    Because this is a directory store, it should be placed on a disk that is separate from the operating system, for example, on a D drive. You can also use separate subfolders for the data files and the data recovery files.

10. On the Service Account Selection page, select Network Service Account, and then click Next.

    Microsoft Windows selects the Network Service account by default. This account has limited local access rights and is a protected account. You should normally use a proper service account, but Network Service will suffice for the purpose of the exercise.

11. On the AD LDS Administrators page, select Currently Logged On User, and then click Next.

    You should normally use a predefined group, but the Administrator account will suffice for the purpose of this exercise.

12. On the Importing LDIF Files page, select all the listed LDIF files, and then click Next.

13. On the Ready To Install page, review your selections, and then click Next.

    AD LDS installs the new instance.

14. Click Finish.

    Your first instance has been created. Open Server Manager and expand the Roles\Active Directory Lightweight Directory Services node to view the results of your operation.

    AD LDS creates log files during the creation of the instance. These files are located in the %SystemRoot%\Debug folder and are named ADAMSetup.log and ADAMSetup_loader.log. You can review them if you find issues during the creation of the instance. Also, creating an instance creates a service for the instance. You can launch the Services console from the Administrative Tools program group to verify the existence of this service.

▶ **Exercise 2   Create an AD LDS Replica Instance**

In this exercise, you will create your first AD LDS replica instance, on the second member server you created.

1. Make sure your domain controller, SERVER01.contoso.com, and your member servers, SERVER03.contoso.com and SERVER04.contoso.com, are running.

2. Log on to SERVER04.contoso.com with the domain Administrator account.

3. Launch the Active Directory Lightweight Directory Services Setup Wizard from the Administrative Tools program group.

4. Review the information on the Welcome page, and then click Next.

5. Under Setup Options, select A Replica Of An Existing Instance, and then click Next.

6. On the Instance Name page, type **ADLDSInstance**, and then click Next.

7. On the Ports page, provide the ports to communicate with this instance. Use 50004 for LDAP and 50005 for the SSL port number. Click Next.

8. On the Joining A Configuration Set page, under Server, click Browse to locate Server 02. Type **SERVER03**, and then click Check Names. Click OK, and then type **50004** into the *LDAP Port* field. Click Next.

9. On the Administrative Credentials For The Configuration Set page, select Currently Logged On User, and then click Next.

    You should normally use a group, but the Administrator account will suffice for the purpose of this exercise.

10. On the Copying Application Directory Partitions page, select the CN=ADLDSInstance,dc=contoso,dc=com partition, and then click Next.

11. On the File Locations page, change the paths to D:\ADLDS\ADLDSInstance\Data, and then click Next.

12. On the Service Account Selection page, select Network Service Account, and then click Next.

    You should normally use a proper service account, but Network Service will suffice for the purpose of the exercise.

13. On the AD LDS Administrators page, select Currently Logged On User, and then click Next.

    You should normally use a group, but the Administrator account will suffice for the purpose of this exercise.

14. On the Ready to Install page, review your selections, and then click Next.

    AD LDS installs the new instance.

15. Click Finish.

    Your replica has been created.

▶ **Exercise 3   Manage Replication Between AD LDS Replicas**

In this exercise, you will view the replication parameters between your two instances. You do not need to update the instances to support Active Directory Sites and Services objects because you imported all LDIF files in the first exercise when you created the source instance.

1. Begin by making sure your domain controller, SERVER01.contoso.com, and your member servers, SERVER03.contoso.com and SERVER04.contoso.com, are running.

2. Log on to SERVER04.contoso.com with the domain Administrator account.

3. Launch Active Directory Sites And Services from the Administrative Tools program group. The console binds to the Active Directory Domain Services directory by default.

4. To bind to the AD LDS instance, right-click Active Directory Sites And Services in the tree pane, and then select Change Domain Controller.

5. In the Change Directory Server dialog box, select This Domain Controller Or AD LDS Instance, and then click <Type A Directory Server Name[:Port] Here>. Type **SERVER03:50004**, and then press Enter. Click OK.

6. In the warning dialog box, click Yes to change servers.

7. Now expand the Active Directory Sites And Services tree completely. You can do so by pressing the asterisk key (*) on your numerical keypad several times. This displays the replication structure for this instance.

    Now, you'll create a new site and move one of the instance objects into this site.

8. Right-click Sites in the tree pane, and then select New Site.

9. Name the site **Replication01**, select the DEFAULTIPSITELINK object, and click OK.

    Your new site link is created, and Active Directory Sites And Services outlines the next steps you must perform. (See Figure 14-6.)

10. Click OK to close the dialog box.

    In this case, you will not perform all activities. You will only move SERVER04 to the new site link. Expand Replication01.

11. Click SERVER04$ADLDSInstance, and drag it to the Servers container under Replication01.

12. In the Moving Objects warning box, click Yes to move the object. The object now appears under the Replication01 site.

This exercise shows you how to work with instances and control replication. In the real world, you will need to perform all the tasks listed in Figure 14-6 to create proper replication partnerships.

MORE INFO   AD LDS replication

For more information on AD LDS replication, go to *http://technet2.microsoft.com/windowsserver2008/en/library/9d4b4004-9f26-4545-a1e4-8e527102f0a71033.mspx*.

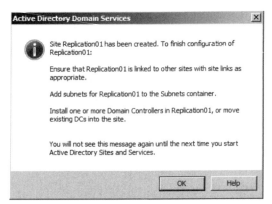

Figure 14-6   Required tasks to complete a replication partnership

Lesson Summary

- The toolset used to control AD LDS instances is very similar to the toolset used for AD DS. Refer to the tools listed in Table 14-3 for a complete list of the tools you can use with AD LDS instances.

- You can create instances both with the graphical interface through the AD LDS Setup tool and through the command line with the *ADAMInstall.exe* command. In both cases, you must plan for all the instance prerequisites beforehand. When using the *ADAMInstall.exe* tool, you will need to prepare an answer file with these values beforehand.

- Working with AD LDS instances means working with distinguished names. Distinguished names use a hierarchical structure that is similar to the hierarchical structure of AD DS forests.

- Working with AD LDS instances means working with server names and port numbers. As a best practice, note each server name and each port number for the instances you create. In fact, always document each instance you create, listing all the values you use to create it.

Lesson Review

You can use the following questions to test your knowledge of the information in Lesson 2, "Configuring and Using AD LDS." The questions are also available on the companion CD if you prefer to review them in electronic form.

NOTE Answers

Answers to these questions and explanations of why each answer choice is right or wrong are located in the "Answers" section at the end of the book.

---

1. You are a local server administrator with *contoso.com*. One of your jobs is to manage AD LDS instances on SERVER03. Recently, you had to install four instances on SERVER03. SERVER03 is a member server of your domain. You began with the default settings for the port selections of each instance. Now, you need to modify the schema of the first instance you installed, Instance01. You register the Active Directory Schema snap-in on the server and create a custom Active Directory Schema console. Yet, when you try to connect to the schema of the first instance, you keep getting an error message. Which of the following is most likely to be the problem?

   A. Instance01 does not include a schema, and you cannot edit it.

   B. You cannot modify the schema of an instance with the Active Directory Schema snap-in. You must use the *LDP.exe* command to do so.

   C. You cannot modify the schema of an instance with the Active Directory Schema snap-in. Modifying the schema of an instance is performed by importing LDIF files with the *LDIFDE.exe* command.

   D. You cannot connect to the instance with the Active Directory Schema snap-in because, by default, it uses the same port as your Active Directory Domain Services directory.

Chapter Review

To further practice and reinforce the skills you learned in this chapter, you can perform the following tasks:

- Review the chapter summary.
- Review the list of key terms introduced in this chapter.
- Complete the case scenario. This scenario sets up a real-world situation involving the topics of this chapter and asks you to create a solution.
- Complete the suggested practices.
- Take a practice test.

Chapter Summary

- As its name suggests, AD LDS is a very portable and malleable directory service. It should always be considered first when you are faced with a schema modification of your network operating system, AD DS. If it is possible to use AD LDS instead of AD DS to integrate an application, then use AD LDS. There are, however, occasions when you cannot replace AD LDS for AD DS. For example, if you implement Exchange Server, you must rely on AD DS. However, Exchange Server 2007 with Service Pack 1 also relies on AD LDS when its server roles are located in a perimeter network.

- AD LDS will run on both the full installation and the Server Core installation of Windows Server 2008. Because of its light weight, AD LDS is a prime candidate for virtualization through Hyper-V.

- AD DS and AD LDS use the same installation process. Begin by installing the role, and then create the directory service instance through a custom wizard or an unattended setup process. To remove AD LDS, you must first remove the instances you create, and then you can remove the role from the server.

- After you have installed the AD LDS service, you can begin to work with it to store directory-related data for different applications. Begin by becoming familiar with the AD LDS tool set. Then, after you understand which tools you can use to manage AD LDS, you can begin to create your first instances. When you've created your instances, you can secure them to ensure that they are properly protected. You'll then move on to the creation of replicas for these instances so that you can install them on various other systems and control replication so that instances located on different computers can be updated through multimaster replication.

Key Terms

Use these key terms to understand better the concepts covered in this chapter.

- **application partitions** Special directory partitions that control the replication scope for contents of the directory store. They can span several sites and can be assigned to either domain controllers or AD LDS instances.

- **instances** Discrete directory stores created through AD LDS. Each store is assigned to a particular application and is composed of several objects that include the store itself, the files that make it up, a service contained within the server running the instance, an optional application partition, and an optional replication scope. When created, instances become installed programs on the server.

Case Scenario

In the following case scenario, you will apply what you've learned about Active Directory Lightweight Directory Service. You can find answers to the questions in this scenario in the "Answers" section at the end of this book.

Case Scenario: Determine AD LDS Instance Prerequisites

Contoso, Ltd., has been working with several previous applications until now. Recently, Contoso managers decided to move to Active Directory Domain Services, and they have also decided to standardize on Windows Server 2008 technologies. Because of this, they want to move their former applications to Active Directory Lightweight Directory Services instances.

They turn to you as the potential administrator of AD LDS within the organization to help them address some specific questions in relation to instance prerequisites. Specifically, they want to know:

1. Where should the files for each instance be stored?
2. How should each instance be named?
3. Which ports should be used to connect to the instances?
4. Should application directory partitions be used and why?
5. How should each instance be run?

Suggested Practices

To help you successfully master the exam objectives presented in this chapter, complete the following tasks.

Work with AD LDS Instances

Because there is only one exam objective for this topic, focus on three key tasks to help you prepare for the exam:

- Installing the AD LDS server role.
- Configuring an AD LDS instance.
- Accessing the AD LDS instance through its administration tools.
- **Practice 1** On a server—virtual or physical—that is running either Windows Server 2008 Standard Edition or Windows Server 2008 Enterprise Edition, install the AD LDS server role. This server should not be a domain controller and should be a member server of an Active Directory Domain Services domain.
- **Practice 2** Create an AD LDS instance named **MyADLDSInstance**. Make sure you run through the AD LDS instance prerequisites preparation before you create the instance. Choose ports 50,010 and 50,011 for your instance. Create an application partition within the instance and assign a service account to it. Use an AD DS security group to manage the instance and make sure your account is a member of that group. Store the instance on a data drive that is separate from the operating system. Make sure you import all LDIF files into the instance when you create it.
- **Practice 3** After the instance is created, practice connecting and working with the instance. Use the following tools:
    - ❑ Active Directory Schema snap-in
    - ❑ Active Directory Sites and Services
    - ❑ *LDP.exe*
    - ❑ ADSI Edit

Use these tools to explore the instance and view its content. You can also practice creating objects within the instance. For example, create an OU and add both a group and a user within the OU.

Take a Practice Test

The practice tests on this book's companion CD offer many options. For example, you can test yourself on just one exam objective, or you can test yourself on all the 70-640 certification exam content. You can set up the test so that it closely simulates the experience of taking a certification exam, or you can set it up in study mode so that you can look at the correct answers and explanations after you answer each question.

MORE INFO   **Practice tests**

For details about all the practice test options available, see the "How to Use the Practice Tests" section in this book's introduction.

Chapter 15

Active Directory Certificate Services and Public Key Infrastructures

Public key infrastructures (PKIs) are becoming core infrastructure elements for all modern organizations. Almost every organization today has some use for public key certificates. Whether it is to secure wireless communications, to offer secure commercial services on Web sites, to integrate Secure Sockets Layer (SSL) virtual private networks, or even just to sign e-mail and identify themselves in Web environments, organizations everywhere are using PKI certificates.

With PKI certificates comes the infrastructure itself—an infrastructure you must first create and then manage. Microsoft has included the ability to generate and maintain PKIs directly in the OS for some years now. In the case of Windows Server 2008, this ability is provided by Active Directory Certificate Services (AD CS), known simply as Certificate Services in previous versions of Microsoft Windows. Because of this, organizations are now choosing to implement and manage their own infrastructures.

MORE INFO Public key infrastructures

For more information on the various aspects of a PKI, look up the PKI white paper series at *http:// www.reso-net.com/articles.asp?m=8* under the Advanced Public Key Infrastructures section.

However, the very nature of PKIs is that they are not based on software alone. Because PKI certificates are designed to prove to others that you are who you say you are, you must implement administrative processes that are designed to demonstrate effectively that each person who receives a certificate from you is really who he or she claims to be. By providing certificates to each person in your organization, you provide him or her with an undeniable tool—a tool that guarantees the identity of each person. Public key infrastructures are designed to build a world of trust in an untrustworthy environment.

In fact, PKIs can be used to extend the authority your organization has beyond the borders of the network it controls. Although Active Directory Domain Services (AD DS), as a network operating system (NOS) directory, is primarily aimed at providing authentication and authorization within the corporate network boundaries, AD CS, like the remaining three Active Directory technologies, is designed to provide these services to both internal and external networks. However, when you extend your organization's authority beyond your network boundaries with AD CS, you should rely on a third-party commercial certificate authority (CA) to support the claims you establish through the certificates you publish. (See Figure 15-1.)

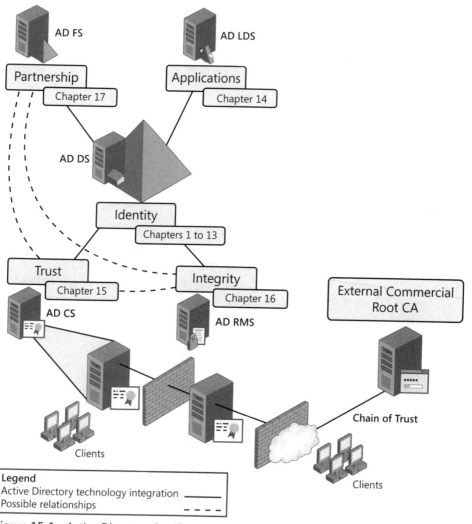

Figure 15-1   Active Directory Certificate Services can provide services both inside and outside your network

For example, when you go to a Web site using the Secure Hypertext Transfer Protocol (HTTPS) that contains an SSL certificate, this certificate proves to you that you really are where you intend to be. When you verify the certificate, you see that it includes the server name, the organization name, and the issuing certificate authority. The certificate works with your browser because browsers such as Microsoft Internet Explorer or Firefox already include a list of trusted commercial CAs that manage the certification process as a business. (See Figure 15-2.)

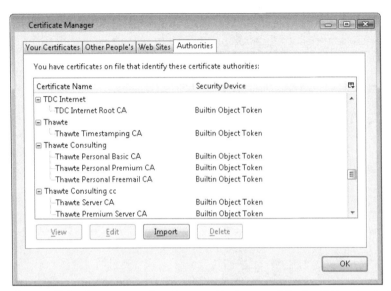

Figure 15-2   Browsers such as Internet Explorer and Firefox listing trusted CAs

The trusted CAs list is automatically updated through the update mechanisms for your selected operating system. In Windows Vista and Windows Server 2008, this update is controlled through a Group Policy setting that is turned on by default. In earlier Windows operating systems, the update of Trusted Root Certificates was a component of Windows, accessed through Control Panel.

MORE INFO   Certificate support in Windows Vista

For more information on Windows Vista certificate support, go to *http://technet2.microsoft.com /WindowsVista/en/library/5b350eae-8b08-4f2c-a09e-a17b1c93f3d01033.mspx?mfr=true*. For a list of Trusted Root Certificates in Windows, go to *http://support.microsoft.com/kb/931125*.

When you issue your own certificates—certificates that do not originate from external CAs— you must include your own organization as a trusted CA on the computers of the people who will be using these certificates. You can do this when you work with the users of your own organization because you control their computers, but when the users are people whose computers you do not control, this becomes problematic. Asking them to accept your certificate is like asking them to trust you when they don't know you.

This is one reason PKI architectures are built the way they are. Essentially, each member of a public key infrastructure is chained together in a hierarchy that ends at the topmost CA. This

CA is ultimately responsible for each of the certificates included in the chain. For example, if you obtain a certificate from your organization and your organization obtained its master certificate from a trusted commercial CA (as shown in Figure 15-3), your certificate will automatically be trusted because each browser already trusts the commercial CA. As you can imagine, this external CA must use a stringent validation program; otherwise, that certificate provider won't be in business for long.

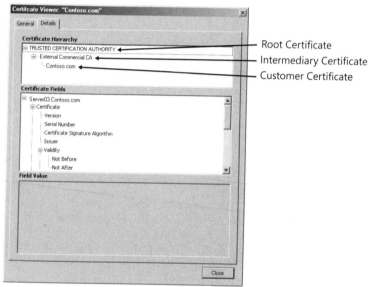

Figure 15-3   A Trusted Certificate chain

Several technologies rely on PKI certificates for operation. One very good example is Microsoft Exchange Server 2007. Because Exchange Server is divided into several roles—Hub Transport, Client Access, Mailbox, and more—and because it transports private information over TCP/IP connections, each server automatically generates a self-signed certificate at installation. Then, through the use of these certificates, e-mail is transported over secure connections. This works well for internal communications, but as soon as you open the doors to communicate with the outside world, for example, providing Microsoft Outlook Web Access (OWA) to employees outside your internal network, you must replace the self-signed certificate with one purchased from a valid vendor. Otherwise, none of your users will be able to access OWA from external Internet locations.

MORE INFO   **Learn about Exchange Server 2007**

For more information on Exchange Server 2007 and its inner workings, look up *MCITP Self-Paced Training Kit (Exam 70-238): Deploying Messaging Solutions with Microsoft Exchange Server 2007* by Ruest and Ruest (Microsoft Press, 2008).

In some cases, implementing an internal-only PKI makes sense because you are proving who you are only to yourself, but it becomes more difficult and even redundant when dealing with the Internet. How can you prove to others you are who you claim to be when you are the only one saying so? If you are the one who issues the certificates that you use for e-commerce, no one will trust you. You must always keep this in mind whenever you are considering the use of AD CS.

Exam objectives in this chapter:

- Configuring Active Directory Certificate Services
  - ❑ Install Active Directory Certificate Services.
  - ❑ Configure CA server settings.
  - ❑ Manage certificate templates.
  - ❑ Manage enrollments.
  - ❑ Manage certificate revocations.

Lessons in this chapter:

- Lesson 1: Understanding and Installing Active Directory Certificate Services 730
- Lesson 2: Configuring and Using Active Directory Certificate Services 753

Before You Begin

To complete the lessons in this chapter, you must have done the following:

- Installed Windows Server 2008 on a physical or virtual computer. The machine should be named SERVER01 and should be a domain controller in the *Contoso.com* domain. The details for this setup are presented in Chapter 1, "Installation," and Chapter 2, "Administration."

- Installed Windows Server 2008 Enterprise Edition on a physical or virtual computer that should be named SERVER03 and should be a member server within the *Contoso.com* domain. This machine will host the AD CS CAs you will install and create through the exercises in this chapter. Ideally, this computer would also include a D drive to store the data for AD CS. Ten gigabites (GB) is recommended for the size of this drive.

- Installed Windows Server 2008 Enterprise Edition on a physical or virtual computer named SERVER04 and should be a member server within the *Contoso.com* domain. This computer will be used to host an issuing CA for AD CS. Ideally, this computer would also include a D drive to store the data for AD CS. Ten GB is recommended for the size of this drive.

This setup will be sufficient to test basic AD CS installation and configuration. Testing all AD CS capabilities requires up to five computers and might be beyond the laboratory capabilities of most readers.

Real World

Danielle Ruest and Nelson Ruest

In 2003, the Canadian government issued a mandate regarding youthful offenders. Several problems and incorrect decisions had been made when judging youthful offender cases in court because some government representatives—federal, provincial, and municipal police; parole officers; and Ministry of Youth or Social Services representatives—would have information about the youth that was not available to the judging party. To resolve this issue, the government passed a law requiring all parties interacting with youthful offenders to share data among themselves so that the judging party would have all pertinent information on hand to make a more informed decision.

As infrastructure architects, we were hired to develop a system to facilitate this information sharing. Because each party affected by the law did not trust each other, the task held challenges. The police especially did not want their information to transit on the Internet nor even to leave their premises. In addition, each party used different technologies to store the data. We needed to devise a solution that would provide complete security for information transfer yet also provide absolute proof that the data was not compromised in any way.

At the same time, various Canadian governmental entities were in the process of implementing PKIs to provide a secure identity process for their employees and any vendors who interacted with them. We decided to rely on this infrastructure for our solution. In fact, our clients were among the very first to take advantage of this new PKI implementation.

We instructed the developers to use Microsoft SQL Server and the .NET Framework to create the application that would act as a central repository for all the collected information. Then, we created routines in each local data repository to extract the information on a regular basis. That's when the PKI became important. Because we wanted to create extraction files and then send them over the Internet, each partner needed two PKI certificates. The first was a personal certificate that would be used to identify each partner. The second was a server authentication certificate that would be used to identify the start and endpoints of all communication links. To obtain these certificates, each partner had, first, to undergo a training program from the governmental PKI agency to learn about its responsibilities when a certificate was assigned to it and then visit an official governmental representative for an identity verification process before it could obtain the certificates.

When everyone had certificates, we implemented them into the solution. First, we used public and private keys to sign the compressed extraction files digitally. Each partner would sign the compressed file with its private key and then the other partners would use the signing partner's public key to decrypt it. When the file was signed and encrypted, it would be transported over the Internet through an IP Security (IPSec) tunnel that would be created using the server authentication certificates. Each certificate was validated against the Certificate Revocation Lists maintained by the governmental PKI agency every time the process was used. Any invalid certificates would automatically be dropped by the application.

The result was a .NET Web-based application. Because the solution was based on PKI and the PKI agency was a trusted authority, each partner could now trust the other without reservation. This is the value of PKI and certificate services: they provide a foundation for trust in an untrustworthy world. Five years later, the application is still running.

Lesson 1: Understanding and Installing Active Directory Certificate Services

Active Directory Certificate Services provide a variety of services regarding public key infrastructures and certificate usage in general. Using Windows Server 2008 and AD CS, you can support the following certificate usage scenarios:

- You can encrypt all data files. One of the most common problems in IT today is the loss or theft of mobile computer systems. If data is encrypted, the loss is minor, but if data is unprotected, it could affect your ability to do business. With Windows Server 2008 and Windows Vista, you can encrypt all user data files automatically through Group Policy objects and enforce the strong passwords required to protect them further. The Encrypting File System (EFS) relies on certificates to lock and unlock encrypted files.

- You can encrypt all remote communications. Windows Server 2008 includes both IPSec and Secure Sockets Tunnelling Protocol (SSTP) virtual private network connections. Both rely on certificates to authenticate the start and endpoint of the communication.

- You can secure all e-mail messages. Windows Server 2008 includes support for Secure Multipurpose Internet Mail Extensions (S/MIME), the standard e-mail security protocol. Signed messages are protected from tampering and prove they originate from the correct person.

- You can secure all logons. Using smart cards, you can use certificates to support the logon process and ensure that all users, especially administrators, are who they say they are.

- You can secure all Web sites. Using Windows Server 2008 and Internet Information Services (IIS) 7.0, you can secure all communications to your Web sites, ensuring the safety of all your client transactions.

- You can secure servers to validate their authenticity. For example, when you assign certificates to servers in a Network Access Protection (NAP) infrastructure or in any other secure service, computers in your network will know they are working with your own servers and not with other servers trying to impersonate yours.

- You can secure all wireless communications. Using Windows Server 2008 and Windows Vista, you can ensure that all wireless communications originate from trusted endpoints.

- You can protect all data from tampering. Using Active Directory Rights Management Services (AD RMS), you can rely on Windows Server 2008 to protect from tampering or misuse all the information you generate.

In addition, consider issuing a certificate to all your employees to help them certify who they are in all their Internet transactions. Keep in mind that all external certificates should include a trusted CA within them to enable them to work automatically with any browser.

After this lesson, you will be able to:
- Understand when to use AD CS.
- Install AD CS.
- Install an Online Responder.
- Locate and view the AD CS installation.

Estimated lesson time: 30 minutes

Understanding AD CS

Active Directory Certificate Services is the engine Windows Server 2008 relies on to manage public key certificates. By using AD CS, you can build a comprehensive PKI hierarchy that can be used to issue and manage certificates within your organization. AD CS is composed of several components:

- **Certificate authorities**   CAs are the servers you use to issue and manage certificates. Because of the hierarchical nature of a PKI, AD CS supports both root and subordinate or child CAs. The root CA usually issues certificates to subordinate CAs, which enables them in turn to issue certificates to users, computers, and services. The subordinate CA can issue certificates only while its own certificate is valid. When this certificate expires, the subordinate CA must request a certificate renewal from its root CA. For this reason, root CAs often have certificate durations that are much longer than any of their subordinates. In turn, subordinate CAs usually have certificate durations that are longer than those they issue to users, computers, or services.

- **CA Web Enrollment**   Using Web Enrollment, users can connect to the CA through a Web browser to request certificates, perform smart card enrollments, or obtain certificate revocation lists (CRL). CRLs provide users of your public key infrastructure with a list of certificates that have been invalidated or revoked by your organization. Systems relying on PKI poll CA servers to obtain CRLs each time a certificate is presented to them. If the certificate presented to them is on this list, it is automatically refused.

- **Online responder**   This service is designed to respond to specific certificate validation requests through the Online Certificate Status Protocol (OCSP). Using an online responder (OR), the system relying on PKI does not need to obtain a full CRL and can submit a validation request for a specific certificate. The online responder decodes the validation request and determines whether the certificate is valid. When it determines the status of the requested certificate, it sends back an encrypted response containing the information to the requester. Using online responders is much faster and more efficient than using CRLs. AD CS includes online responders as a new feature in Windows Server 2008.

MORE INFO Online responders

Online responders are often an alternative to or an extension of CRLs that support the certificate revocation process. Microsoft online responders comply with request for comments (RFC) 2560 for OCSP. For more information about this RFC, go to *http://go.microsoft.com /fwlink/?LinkID=67082*.

- **Network Device Enrollment Service** Devices that use low-level operating systems, such as routers and switches, can also participate in a PKI through the Network Device Enrollment Service (NDES) by using the Simple Certificate Enrollment Protocol (SCEP), a protocol developed by Cisco Systems, Inc. These devices usually do not participate in an AD DS directory and, therefore, do not have AD DS accounts. However, through the NDES and the SCEP, they can also become part of the PKI hierarchy that is maintained and managed by your AD CS installation.

These four components form the core of the AD CS service in Windows Server 2008.

MORE INFO New features in AD CS

For more information on the new features AD CS supports in Windows Server 2008, go to *http://technet2.microsoft.com/windowsserver2008/en/library/171362c0-3773-498d-8cc3- 0ddcd8082bf51033.mspx*.

Standalone vs. Enterprise CAs

Your biggest concern when preparing to deploy an AD CS is how you will structure the four basic services AD CS offers. Initially, you will be concerned about the first role: the CAs you need to deploy. AD CS supports two CA types:

- **Standalone CA** A CA that is not necessarily integrated in an AD DS directory service. Standalone CAs are CAs running on member or standalone servers—servers in a workgroup. Standalone CAs are often used as internal root CAs and are taken offline for security purposes after they have been used to generate certificates for subordinate servers. Certificate issuing and approval are performed manually, and certificates are based on standard templates, which you cannot modify. The clients of a standalone CA can be members of an AD DS directory, but AD DS directory membership is not a requirement. Standalone CAs can run Windows Server 2008 Standard Edition, Windows Server 2008 Enterprise Edition, or Windows Server 2008 Datacenter Edition.
- **Enterprise CA** A CA that is integrated in an AD DS directory service. Enterprise CAs are usually member servers and are often used as issuing CAs—CAs that are subordinate to another CA in a hierarchy but that actually provide certificates to end users and endpoint devices. Issuing CAs are usually online at all times and must be highly available. Because they are integrated in AD DS directories, enterprise CAs automatically

issue and approve certificates when requested by members of the directory. Certificate templates are more advanced and can be edited to meet specific requirements. All encryption keys are protected through directory integration. Enterprise CAs can run only on Windows Server 2008 Enterprise Edition or Windows Server 2008 Datacenter Edition.

Table 15-1 outlines the different features supported by standalone versus enterprise CAs.

Table 15-1   Comparing Standalone and Enterprise CAs

Feature	Standalone	Enterprise
Publish CA configuration to Active Directory Domain Services directories.	Optional	Mandatory
CA certificate data integration with AD DS forests.	Optional (manual process)	Mandatory and Automatic
Certificate Revocation List publication in AD DS forests.	Optional (manual process)	Mandatory and Automatic; also includes Delta CRLs and cross certificates
AD DS forest publication assigned on a per-template level as an attribute of the template.	n/a	Supported
Web enrollment for certificate requests and validation.	Supported	Supported
Certificate Microsoft Management Console (MMC) for certificate requests and validation.	n/a	Supported
Certificate requests through HTTP or HTTPS.	Supported	Supported
Certificate requests through the remote procedure call (RPC) along with the Distributed Component Object Model (DCOM).	n/a	Default mode
V1 templates with custom object identifiers (OID) as source for certificates.	Default	n/a
V2 and V3 customizable templates as source for certificates. Templates can also be duplicated.	n/a	Default
User input during certificate requests.	Manual	Retrieved from AD DS
Supported enrollment methods.	Automatic or Pending for all templates	Automatic or Pending and applied on a template basis
Certificate approval process.	Manual	Manual or Automatic through AD DS authentication and access control

Table 15-1 Comparing Standalone and Enterprise CAs

Feature	Standalone	Enterprise
Certificate publishing.	Manually to client or CA; can be to AD DS but only through custom policy module	Depends on certificate type and template settings but can be automatically enrolled in client's certificate store and published in AD DS
Certificate publishing and management through AD DS.	n/a	Supported
Deployment options.	Domain controller (DC), member or standalone server	DC or member server only

As you can see in Table 15-1, standalone CAs are focused on delivering specific services and should be considered mostly for standalone environments where automation is not required. Good examples are root CAs or CAs located in a perimeter network and offering services to the Internet.

Enterprise CAs should be considered mostly as issuing CAs in internal networks that also include AD DS forest structures. Enterprise CAs automate the certificate allocation process and are very useful when you need to issue certificates to devices for wireless networks or to users for smart card integration. Imagine managing the entire request and approval process manually when you have thousands of users and devices. It could easily become overwhelming.

Exam Tip   Learn the differences between standalone and enterprise CAs well. These topics are an important part of the AD CS coverage in the exam.

Creating the CA Hierarchy

A second consideration when planning your CA hierarchy is security. Because a CA hierarchy is based on certificate chaining, any compromise of a top-level or root CA automatically compromises all the certificates that are based on it. This is one reason you must secure root CAs as much as possible. In fact, a common practice is to create a tiered CA hierarchy and take the top members of a tiered architecture offline. The logic is that if a server is offline, it is as secure as it can be.

However, determining the number of tiers in your AD CS architecture depends on several other factors as well. You need to consider the size and geographic distribution of your network. You also need to identify the trust relationship you will require between CAs and the certificate holders. Keep in mind that each time a certificate is presented, it must be validated through either a CRL or an online responder, so to use certificates, you must have connectivity of some sort.

Consider also the potential scenarios you intend to support with your AD CS deployment. Will you be interacting with people or partners outside your network? Will you be using smart cards? Will you be using wireless networks? Will you be using IPSec or the new SSTP? Basically, any time you need to certify the identity of a device, an application, or a user, you will need to rely on AD CS and, potentially, third-party commercial certificate authorities.

When you have the answers to these questions, you can proceed with the planning of your AD CS hierarchy. When you do so, consider the following:

- Creating a single tiered hierarchy with a single root CA only in very rare situations in which you feel the root CA cannot be compromised under any circumstance.

- Creating a two-tiered hierarchy with a root CA and issuing CAs when you need to protect the root CA but your organization size and the purpose of the hierarchy does not warrant a more complex hierarchy. In this model, you can take the root CA offline to protect it. (See Figure 15-4.)

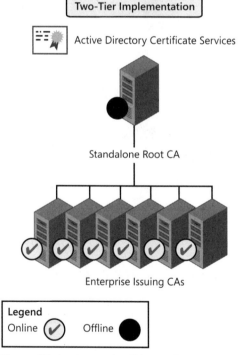

Figure 15-4 A two-tiered hierarchy

- Creating a three-tiered hierarchy with a root CA, intermediate CAs, and issuing CAs when you need higher levels of security and high availability for the issuing CAs, and your administration model, user population, and geographic scope warrant the extra cost of the additional tier. Multiple intermediate CAs are often used to support different policies in different environments in this model. If you use this model, take both the root and intermediate CAs offline to protect them, as shown in Figure 15-5.

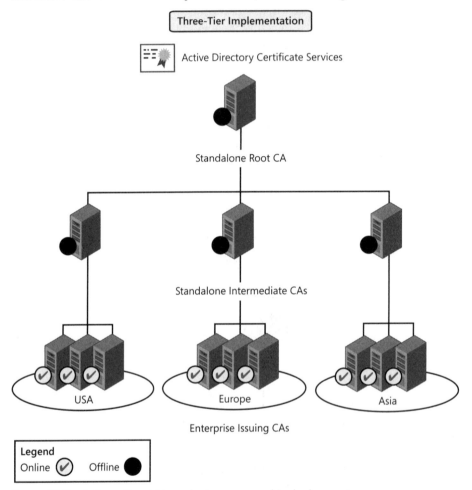

Figure 15-5   A three-tiered hierarchy in a geographic deployment

■ Creating more than three tiers only in highly complex environments that require the utmost security where the CA infrastructure must be protected at all times.

As you can see, the more tiers you create in a hierarchy, the higher the level of complexity in terms of management and administration. However, the more complex your hierarchy, the more secure it can be. In addition, consider which type of CA you need to deploy in each tier. Table 15-2 outlines the CA type based on the tier model.

Table 15-2   Assigning CA Type Based on Tier Model

CA Type	One Tier	Two Tiers	Three Tiers
Root CA	Enterprise CA (online)	Standalone CA (offline)	Standalone CA (offline)
Intermediate CA			Standalone CA (offline)
Issuing CA		Enterprise CA (online)	Enterprise CA (online)

Exam Tip   Keep these different hierarchies in mind when you take the exam. CA hierarchies are an important aspect of any AD CS deployment.

Best Practices for AD CS Deployments

Architectures using two or more tiers represent the most common deployments of AD CS. When you plan for your AD CS infrastructure, keep the following in mind:

- Avoid single-tiered hierarchies as much as possible because they are very difficult to protect.
- Root and intermediate CAs (if implemented) should be taken offline as soon as possible after the infrastructure is in place. For this reason, these CAs are excellent candidates for virtualization through Windows Server 2008 Hyper-V. Create a virtual machine (VM), install the AD CS Standalone CA role, and then save the machine state as soon as you can.
- Consider removing the VM files for the root CA from the host server as soon as it is taken offline. Store the secured VM in a vault of some type.
- If you use virtualization in support of your AD CS deployment, secure the VMs as much as possible. It is a lot easier to walk away with a VM than it is with a physical server.
- Consider creating VMs that do not have or that have disabled network connections for the root and intermediate CAs. This ensures an even higher level of protection. Certificates are transferred from these servers through either USB devices or floppy disks.
- Control the removable devices on root and intermediate CAs through device protection settings in the Local Security Policy console. This adds a further layer of protection.
- Make sure your CA administrators are highly trustworthy individuals. They control the entire CA hierarchy and, because of this, they are in a very high position of trust.
- Secure thoroughly the data center that hosts the CAs. Control access to the data center and use smart card administrative logons as much as possible.
- Consider using a single root CA but adding availability through multiple CA installations as soon as you reach the intermediate and issuing tiers of the hierarchy.
- You cannot change the name of a server after the AD CS service is installed, so plan your server names carefully and make sure you can keep them for a very long time.
- You cannot change a CA from standalone to enterprise or vice versa after AD CS is installed. Once again, plan accordingly.

■ As a general practice, do not install AD CS on a DC. Although it can be done, endeavor to keep the AD DS server role independent of all other roles except the Domain Name System (DNS) role.

These guidelines will assist you in your AD CS deployment planning phase.

MORE INFO   **Best practices for PKI deployments**

For additional information on PKI deployments with Windows infrastructures, look up "Best Practices for Implementing a Microsoft Windows Server 2003 Public Key Infrastructure" at *http://technet2.microsoft.com/windowsserver/en/library/091cda67-79ec-481d-8a96-03e0be7374ed1033.mspx?mfr=true*. It refers to Windows Server 2003 rather than to Windows Server 2008, but its practices are still valid for any version of Windows.

Additional Planning Requirements

You're almost ready to proceed. However, as mentioned earlier, planning and deploying a CA hierarchy is not only a technical activity. You need to have the appropriate administrative processes to support the use of certificates in your network. Three additional considerations need to be covered before you can move on to installing AD CS:

■ You must consider how you will support certificate enrollment.

■ You must consider how you will renew certificates.

■ You must create a certificate practice statement (CPS).

The first focuses on how you plan to support certificate requests and distribution. As mentioned earlier, a certificate is used to identify its holder thoroughly whether it is a user, a machine, or an application. Therefore, you must put in place a requester identification validation process. You don't want to issue a certificate to John Kane when you're not sure the requester is actually John Kane. Third-party certificate authorities use several types of processes for this validation, the most stringent of which will involve a visit to the person requesting the certificate by an authorized legal representative of the CA. This means a face-to-face meeting and then, after the requester is validated, you can provide him or her with a certificate in that name. To protect the certificate further, you can store it on a hardware token such as a smart card and provide that to the requester. It then becomes the responsibility of the requester to protect the certificate and the token that contains it.

However, if you plan to use automatic enrollment through enterprise CAs, you need to make sure that users are properly validated before they are given access to your network. Rely on some form of official identification such as a passport or other governmental ID mechanism. This should already be part of your human resources processes and policies.

The second consideration deals with certificate lifetimes. Certificates usually include two key pairs: a private key and a public key. When you encrypt data, you use the private key to do so.

When others decrypt the data, they usually use your public key to do so. The longer you use a certificate key pair, the more prone it is to attack or compromise. When you renew a certificate, the renewal generates a new key pair for the certificate. Therefore, you must plan certificate lifetimes and renewals carefully. In fact, you must temper key pair life with the risk of compromise.

In addition, you must ensure that your tiered hierarchy also includes tiered lifetimes. Root CAs should have the longest lifetime, then intermediate CAs if you use them, then issuing CAs, and then issued certificates. For example, you might use a gap of 10 years for each tier in your architecture; that is, assign 10 years to each tier. In a three-tier architecture, use 30 years for the root CA, 20 years for the intermediate CAs, and 10 years for issuing CAs. Then you can assign one or two years to the certificates you issue. The reason for this hierarchy of durations is that each time a certificate expires for a server, all subordinate certificates expire as well. To protect against this eventuality, you give very long durations to servers.

Finally, you must plan and prepare your certificate practice statement. CPSs are based on the certificate policies you create. Policies define the issuing organization's responsibilities in terms of each of the certificate types it issues. The issuing organization is ultimately responsible for any wrongdoing or misuse of the certificates it issued. Because of this, involve the legal, human resources, and security departments of your organization to assist you in defining the policies you use for each certificate type and then generate your CPS from that. The CPS should include several items, such as a clear definition of who you are, a list of your certificate policies; a general statement of the procedures you use to issue, assign, and revoke certificates; the way you protect your CAs; and so on.

Another important item that must be included in your CPS is the revocation policy you use. Revocation occurs when you need to cancel a certificate for any reason, usually when someone does not adhere to the policy you defined for that particular certificate type. Keep in mind that revocation is the only method you have of invalidating a certificate when it is misused.

The CPS should be publicly available to both your internal and external CA users. This usually means making it available in some form on the Internet or through intranets.

MORE INFO   Certificate practice statements

For more information on defining certificate policies and certificate practice statements, go to *http://technet2.microsoft.com/windowsserver/en/library/78c89e0f-44f8-452a-922c-5dd5b8eaa63b1033.mspx?mfr=true*.

Exam Tip   Familiarize yourself with certificate policies and certificate practice statements because they are a definite part of the exam topics for AD CS.

Quick Check

1. What are the different types of certificate authorities supported by AD CS?
2. You are planning to install a root CA in a two-tier architecture. Which type of CA should you install?
3. How is the trusted CA list updated in Windows Vista and Windows Server 2008?

Quick Check Answers

1. AD CS supports two types of certificate authorities. The standalone CA is used in environments that do not need integration with Active Directory Domain Services because it does not interact with AD DS by default. Enterprise CAs are directly integrated into the AD DS directory and can provide automated user or device enrollment.
2. You should install a standalone CA. Root CAs are usually taken offline as soon as possible after the deployment of your public key infrastructure. Therefore, it makes sense to use the simplest form of CA supported by AD CS.
3. The trusted root CA list in Windows Vista and Windows Server 2008 is updated through Group Policy settings, which are turned on by default. In previous versions of Windows, the trusted root CA list was a component of Windows controlled through Control Panel.

Installing AD CS

Installing AD CS is a much more involved process than installing Active Directory Lightweight Directory Services (AD LDS). This is because of the choice between standalone and enterprise CAs and because of the subsequent choices that ensue from this original selection.

In most cases, you will install at least a two-tiered structure, installing first a standalone, then an enterprise CA. In larger organizations, you will deploy several tiers and install several servers in each tier except for the root.

Servers hosting the AD CS role should be configured with the following capabilities whether they are physical or virtual:

- Multiple processors because they accelerate the certificate allocation process.
- Minimal amounts of RAM because RAM has little effect on certificate processing. VMs can have 512 megabytes (MB) of RAM.
- Separate disks for the certificate store. Ideally, you will have at least one data disk and store the database on it. Issuing servers for large communities should also have a separate disk for log files.

- Key lengths will have an impact on CPU and disk usage. Short keys will require more disk overhead. Long keys will require more CPU usage and lower disk usage. Keep your key lengths to medium sizes to obtain the best performance from the server.

- If using physical systems, use a redundant array of inexpensive disks (RAID) level that is balanced between reliability and improved performance.

IMPORTANT   Installation on Windows Server 2008

The AD CS role cannot be installed on Server Core and requires the full installation of Windows Server 2008 to operate. This means that if you install CAs in perimeter networks, you will have to lock down the server thoroughly through the Security Configuration Wizard. In addition, AD CS cannot be installed on Itanium-based systems.

Different editions of Windows Server 2008 will offer different features in support of AD CS. Table 15-3 outlines the supported features based on the selected edition of Windows Server 2008.

Table 15-3   AD CS Features per Windows Server 2008 Edition

Supported Components and Features	Web	Standard	Enterprise	Datacenter
Standalone certificate authority	☐	☑	☑	☑
Enterprise certificate authority	☐	☐	☑	☑
Network Device Enrollment Service (NDES)	☐	☐	☑	☑
Online responder service	☐	☐	☑	☑
Key archival	☐	☐	☑	☑
Role Separation	☐	☐	☑	☑
Certificate Manager restrictions	☐	☐	☑	☑
Delegated enrollment agent restrictions	☐	☐	☑	☑

Preparing for AD CS Installation

You must prepare your environment before installing AD CS. The prerequisites for an AD CS installation include the following:

- An AD DS forest with at least a forest root domain. Preferably, you will also have a child production domain.

- Computers to run the certificate authorities used in your hierarchy. In the simplest deployment, this will mean at least two computers: one for the root CA and one for the issuing CA. The issuing CA can also host the online responder service and NDES. The issuing CA will require the installation of IIS, but the AD CS installation process will automatically add this feature during installation. Both computers should be members of the production domain.

- ❑ Keep in mind that the root CA can run Windows Server 2008 Standard Edition. In addition, it should be disconnected from the network after the installation is complete, for security purposes.
- ❑ The enterprise issuing CA will need to run on either Windows Server 2008 Enterprise Edition or Windows Server 2008 Datacenter Edition.
- ❑ The root CA needs at least two drives, and the issuing CA should have three drives to store the certificate database and its logs.

■ You will need a special user account if you choose to install the NDES service. Create a domain account and make it a member of the local IIS_IUSRS group on each server that will host this service. For example, you could name this account NDESService.

■ Client computers, ideally running Windows Vista, to request and obtain certificates.

MORE INFO   Deploying AD CS

For more information on deploying AD CS, go to *http://technet2.microsoft.com/windowsserver2008 /en/library/a8f53a9b-f3f6-4b13-8253-dbf183a5aa621033.mspx?mfr=true.*

Now you can move on to the actual installation. To install a standalone root CA, use the procedure outlined in the following practice.

PRACTICE Installing a CA Hierarchy

In this practice, you will create a two-tier AD CS hierarchy and install the NDES feature of AD CS. To perform this practice, you must have prepared at least three virtual servers as outlined in the Before You Begin section at the beginning of this chapter.

▶ **Exercise 1   Install AD CS as a Standalone Root CA**

In this exercise, you will create a standalone root CA, which will be used as the root of your CA hierarchy. This task is performed on SERVER03. Make sure that SERVER01, your DC, is also running and that SERVER03 is a member of the domain.

1. Log on to SERVER03 with the domain Administrator account.

   You need local administrative credentials only, but for the purposes of this exercise, it is all right to use the domain administrator account. This server can be running Windows Server 2008 Standard Edition, Windows Server 2008 Enterprise Edition, or Windows Server 2008 Datacenter Edition.

2. Launch Server Manager from the Administrative Tools program group.

3. Right-click the Roles node in the tree pane and select Add Roles.

4. Review the Before You Begin information and click Next.

5. On the Select Server Roles page, select Active Directory Certificate Services and click Next.

6. On the Introduction to Active Directory Certificate Services page, review the information about the selected role and click Next.

7. On the Select Role Services page, select Certification Authority and click Next.

    Because this will be a root CA and you will take it offline as soon as you create the issuing CA, you do not assign any other role features or services.

8. On the Specify Setup Type page, select Standalone and click Next.

9. On the CA Type page, select Root CA and click Next.

10. On the Set Up Private Key page, select Create A New Private Key and click Next.

    You need to create a new private key because you are creating a new root CA. However, if you were reinstalling a CA because of a system failure, you would use an existing key, one that was generated during the initial installation of the root CA. In addition, if you were creating a root CA to be chained with an external third-party CA, you would use the last option, to use the key provided by the third-party CA. You must install the key on the server before you begin the AD CS installation for the option to be available. Use the instructions provided by your third-party CA to install the certificate.

11. On the Configure Cryptography For CA page, select the suggested cryptographic service provider (CSP). Select a key character length of 2048. Select the sha1 hash algorithm for signing certificates issued by this CA. Also select Use Strong Private Key Protection Features Provided By This CSP.

    There are several options on this page.

    ❑ CSPs are the engines the Microsoft Crypto application programming interface (API) will use to generate the key pair for this root CA. CSPs can be either software or hardware based. For example, the RSA#Microsoft Software Key Storage Provider is software based, and the RSA#Microsoft Smart Card Key Storage Provider is hardware based.

    ❑ Key character length determines the length of the keys in the pair. Four lengths are possible. Remember that the longer the key, the more processing the server will require to decode it.

    ❑ Hash algorithms are used to produce and assign a hash value on the keys in the pair. Because they are assigned to the keys, any tampering of the key will change the hash value and invalidate the key. Hash values provide further key protection. The algorithm you select will simply use a different calculation method to generate the hash value.

    ❑ The last option on the page provides further protection for the root CA because use of the CA will require administrative access and will work with only this level of access. You use this option to provide further protection for this root CA.

12. Click Next.

13. On the Configure CA Name page, type **Contoso-Root-CA**, leave the distinguished name suffix as is, and click Next.

    You use this name because it will be embedded in every subordinate certificate issued by the chain.

14. On the Set Validity Period page, change the year value to **20** and click Next.

15. On the Configure Certificate Database page, specify the storage locations for the certificate database and the certificate database log.

    Because this is a root CA that should be taken offline and should be used only to generate certificates for the issuing CAs, you can place both on the D drive.

16. For the database location, click Browse, navigate to the D drive, click Make New Folder, and name it **CertData**. Click OK. For the logs, create a folder on the D drive and name it **CertLogs**. Click Next.

17. Review the information available on the AD CS page and click Install. When the installation completes, review the installation results and click Close.

    Your root CA is installed.

    Note that you will no longer be able to change the name of this server unless you uninstall AD CS first. This is one more reason for not using a server name in the CA name in step 12.

Exam Tip   Make sure you understand these installation choices well because they are part of the exam.

Your root CA is installed. Return to Server Manager to view the results of the installation. For example, you should have an event ID 103 listed on the summary page of the AD CS role. (See Figure 15-6.) This event shows that the CA name will be added to the Certificate Authorities container in your AD DS domain. It also displays the command you can use to view the information in the directory after the name has been added.

Disconnect this CA from the network after the Group Policy cycle has been updated, to provide further protection for this server. You can now move on to installing your first issuing CA. You should install more than one issuing CA to provide high availability for your AD CS infrastructure, but each installation uses the same process.

NOTE   Review the AD CS installation process

For a step-by-step guide to the installation of AD CS, go to *http://go.microsoft.com/fwlink/?LinkId=90856*.

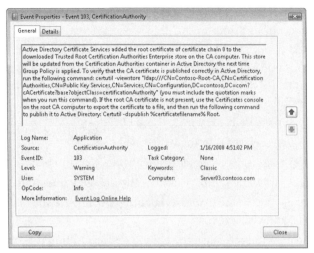

Figure 15-6 Viewing the contents of Event ID 103

▶ **Exercise 2   Install AD CS as an Enterprise Issuing CA**

You can now move on to install your issuing CA. You should normally install more than one issuing CA to provide high availability for your AD CS infrastructure, but for the purposes of this exercise, one issuing CA will be sufficient. Make sure that SERVER01, SERVER03, and SERVER04 are all running.

1. Log on to SERVER04, using the domain Administrator account.

    You need local administrative access rights only, but for the purposes of this exercise, the domain administrator account will also work. This server can be running Windows Server 2008 Enterprise Edition or Windows Server 2008 Datacenter Edition.

2. Launch Server Manager from the Administrative Tools program group.

3. Right-click the Roles node and select Add Roles.

4. Review the Before You Begin information and click Next.

5. On the Select Server Roles page, select Active Directory Certificate Services and click Next.

6. On the Introduction to Active Directory Certificate Services page, review the information about the selected role and click Next.

7. On the Select Role Services page, select Certificate Authority and Online Responder. When you select Online Responder, the wizard will ask you to add the Web Server role with the required features. Click Add Required Role Services.

8. Click Next.

    You do not select the CA Web Enrollment because this is an internal enterprise CA, and enterprise CAs rely on AD DS to distribute certificates to users and devices. If you were installing this CA in an external network, you might consider using Web Enrollment to enable users to request certificates from your CA.

You cannot choose the Network Device Enrollment Service (NDES) installation at this time because AD CS does not support installing a CA at the same time as you install NDES. If you want to install NDES, you must select Add Role Services from Server Manager after the CA installation has completed.

9. On the Specify Setup Type page, select Enterprise and click Next.

10. On the Specify CA Type page, select Subordinate CA and click Next.

11. On the Set Up Private Key page, select Create A New Private Key and click Next.

12. On the Configure Cryptography For CA page, accept the default values and click Next.

13. On the Configure CA Name page, type **Contoso-Issuing-CA01**, leave the default distinguished name suffix as is, and click Next.

    You use a valid name and a number because you should create additional issuing CAs for redundancy purposes.

14. On the Request Certificate From A Parent CA page, select Save A Certificate Request To File And Manually Send It Later To A Parent CA.

15. Select Certificate Request Name from the File Name field and copy it to the clipboard, using Ctrl + C, and then click Browse and navigate to your Documents folder. Paste the name in the *File Name* field, using Ctrl + V; click Save, and then click Next.

16. On the Configure Certificate Database page, specify the storage locations for the certificate database and the certificate database log.

    Because this is an issuing CA that will be used for testing only, you can place the data and the logs on the D drive. However, in a production environment, issuing CAs will be used heavily; this means you should place the data on the D drive and the logs on an E drive.

17. For the database location, click Browse, navigate to the D drive, click Make New Folder, and name it **CertData**. Click OK.

18. For the logs, create a folder on the D drive and name it **CertLogs**. Click Next when ready.

19. Review the installation of IIS. Click Next.

20. On the Web Server Role Services page, review the required services and click Next.

21. Review the information in the Confirm Installation Selections page and click Install. When the installation completes, review the installation results and click Close.

    The subordinate CA setup is not usable until it has been issued a root CA certificate and this certificate has been used to complete the installation of this subordinate CA.

Exam Tip   Keep in mind that you cannot install the CA and the NDES role features at the same time.

▶ **Exercise 3   Obtain and Install the Issuing CA Certificate**

Now, you will obtain the certificate to complete the installation of the issuing CA. You should normally perform this procedure offline using a removable storage device such as a floppy disk or a USB flash drive, but for the purpose of this exercise, you will use a shared folder to transfer the certificate request and the certificate after it is issued.

1. On SERVER04, launch Windows Explorer and navigate to the C drive. Create a new folder and name it **Temp**.

2. Right-click the Temp folder and select Share.

3. In the File Sharing dialog box, select Everyone in the drop-down list, and then click Add.

4. In the Permission Level column, from the drop-down list, assign the Contributor role to Everyone and click Share.

5. Copy the certificate request you generated from your Documents folder to the Temp folder.

6. On SEREVR03, launch the Certificate Authority console from the Administrative Tools program group.

7. In the Certification Authority console, right-click the root CA name in the tree pane, select All Tasks, and then choose Submit New Request.

8. In the Open Request File dialog box, move to the address bar and type **SERVER04** **Temp**. When the folder opens, select the request, and then click Open.

9. Move to the Pending Request node in the tree pane, right-click the pending request in the details pane to choose All Tasks, and then choose Issue.

10. Move to the Issued Certificates in the tree pane, right-click the issued certificate in the details pane, and choose Open.

11. In the Certificate dialog box, choose the Details tab and click Copy To File at the bottom of the dialog box.

    This launches the Certificate Export Wizard.

12. Click Next.

13. Select the Cryptographic Message Syntax Standard – PKCS #7 Certificates (P7B), select Include All Certificates In The Certification Path If Possible, and click Next.

    There are several supported formats.

    ❑ Distinguished Encoding Rules (DER) Encoded Binary X.509 is often used for computers that do not run the Windows operating system. This creates certificate files in the CER format.

❏ Base-64 Encoded X.509 supports S/MIME, which is the format used to transfer secured e-mails over the Internet. On servers, it is usually used for non-Windows operating systems. This also creates certificate files in the CER format.

❏ Cryptographic Message Syntax Standard (PKCS #7) is the format used to transfer certificates and their chained path from one computer to another. This format uses the P7B file format.

❏ Personal Information Exchange (PKCS #12) is also used to transfer certificates and their chained path from one computer to another, but in addition, this format supports the transfer of the private key as well as the public key. Use this format with caution because transporting the private key can jeopardize it. This format uses the PFX file format.

❏ Microsoft Serialized Certificate Store is a custom Microsoft format that should be used when you need to transfer root certificates from one computer to another. This uses the SST file format.

14. In the File To Export dialog box, click Browse and save the certificate in the \\SERVER04 \Temp folder. Name it **Issuing-CA01.p7b** and click Save.

15. Click Next when you return to the wizard.

16. Review your settings and click Finish.

17. Click OK when the wizard tells you that the export was successful. Return to SERVER04. Remember that, normally, you would use a removable device to transport this certificate from one server to another.

18. Go to Server Manager and select Contoso-Issuing-CA01 in the tree pane (Server Manager \Roles\Active Directory Certificate Services\Contoso-Issuing-CA01).

19. Right-click Contoso-Issuing-CA01, select All Tasks, and then choose Install CA Certificate.

20. Move to the C:\Temp folder, select the certificate, and click Open.

21. This imports the certificate and enables the server.

22. Right-click the server name, select All Tasks, and then choose Start Service.

Your issuing CA is ready to issue certificates. At this point, you should really take SERVER03 offline, but because this is a test environment and you need to conserve CPU usage and disk space, keep it running.

IMPORTANT   Protect the certificate

Now that the server is ready to work, store the transferred certificate in a safe place. You should also shut down the root CA when you have performed this task for all the issuing CAs you require in your infrastructure. If the root CA is a virtual machine, shut it down, and then remove the VM files from the host server. For example, you could copy them to a DVD and then store the DVD in a very safe place.

▶ **Exercise 4   Prepare to Install the NDES Feature**

Now, you will install the NDES feature. Again, this task is performed on SERVER04, but you must use SERVER01 to create a user account first.

1. Log on to SERVER01, using the domain Administrator account.
2. Launch Active Directory Users And Computers from the Administrative Tools program group.
3. Create the following OU structure: Contoso.com\Admins\Service Identities.
4. Right-click Service Identities, choose New, and then select User.
5. Name the user **NDESService** and use this name for both the logon and the pre-Windows 2000 logon names. Click Next.
6. Assign a strong password. Clear User Must Change Password At Next Logon and select Password Never Expires.
7. Click Next, and then Finish to create the account.
8. Return to SERVER04 and log on as the domain Administrator.
9. Launch Server Manager from the Administrative Tools program group.
10. Expand Configuration\Local Users and Groups\Groups.
11. Double-click the IIS_IUSRS group.
12. Add the NDESService account to this group and click OK.

▶ **Exercise 5   Install the NDES Feature**

Now you're ready to install the NDES service.

1. Right-click Active Directory Certificate Services in the tree pane of Server Manager and select Add Role Services.
2. On the Select Role Services page, select Network Device Enrollment Service.
   This will require the addition of Windows Authentication to your IIS installation.
3. Click Add Required Role Services and click Next.
4. On the Specify User Account page, click Select User, enter **NDESService** with its password, and click OK. Click Next.
5. On the Specify Registration Authority Information page, you need to enter the information for your registration authority or the authority that will assign and manage certificates assigned to network devices. Type **Contoso-MSCEP-RA01**, select your country from the drop-down list, and leave all other information blank. Click Next.
   Normally, you should enter all the required and optional information, but for the purpose of this exercise, leaving them blank is all right.
6. On the Configure Cryptography For Registration Authority page, keep the defaults and click Next.

Keep in mind that key length affects CPU usage; therefore, unless you have stringent security requirements, keep the 2048 key length.

7. Review the information about the installation of IIS. Click Next.

8. On the Web Server Role Services page, review the required services and click Next.

9. On the Confirm Installation Services page, click Install.

10. Review the status and progress of the installation.

11. Click Close.

Your NDES service is now installed and ready to work. Your installation of the issuing server is complete.

MORE INFO   Simple Certificate Enrollment Protocol (SCEP)

For more information on SCEP, go to *http://www3.ietf.org/proceedings/07jul/slides/pkix-3.pdf*.

Lesson Summary

- AD CS is composed of four elements: certificate authorities, CA Web Enrollment, online responders, and Network Device Enrollment Service. These are the core elements of any AD CS deployment.

- Certificate authorities are the servers you use to issue and manage certificates. Because of the hierarchical nature of a PKI, AD CS supports both root and subordinate or child CAs. The root CA usually issues certificates to subordinate CAs, which enables them in turn to issue certificates to users, computers, and services. The subordinate CA can issue certificates only while its own certificate is valid. When this certificate expires, the subordinate CA must request a certificate renewal from its root CA. For this reason, root CAs often have certificate durations that are much longer than any of their subordinates. In turn, subordinate CAs usually have certificate durations that are longer than those they issue to users, computers, or services.

- ORs are designed to respond to specific certificate validation requests through the Online Certificate Status Protocol (OCSP). Using an OR, the system relying on a PKI does not need to obtain a full CRL and can submit a validation request for a specific certificate. The OR decodes the validation request and determines whether the certificate is valid. When it determines the status of the requested certificate, it sends back an encrypted response containing the information to the requester. Using ORs is much faster and more efficient than using CRLs. AD CS includes ORs as a new feature in Windows Server 2008.

- Devices that use low-level operating systems, such as routers and switches, can also participate in a PKI through the NDES by using the SCEP, a protocol developed by Cisco Systems, Inc. These devices usually do not participate in an AD DS directory and, therefore, do not have AD DS accounts. However, through the NDES and the SCEP, they can also become part of the PKI hierarchy that is maintained and managed by your AD CS installation.

- CA server types are tied to the version of Windows Server 2008 you use. Standalone CAs can be created with Windows Server 2008 Standard Edition, Windows Server 2008 Enterprise Edition, or Windows Server 2008 Datacenter Edition. Enterprise CAs can be created with Windows Server 2008 Enterprise Edition or Windows Server 2008 Datacenter Edition only.

Lesson Review

You can use the following questions to test your knowledge of the information in Lesson 1, "Understanding and Installing Active Directory Certificate Services." The questions are also available on the companion CD if you prefer to review them in electronic form.

NOTE Answers

Answers to these questions and explanations of why each answer choice is right or wrong are located in the "Answers" section at the end of the book.

---

1. You are an administrator for the Contoso domain. Your boss has decided to deploy Active Directory Certificate Services, and he wants it done today. You tell him that you investigated AD CS and, from what you've learned, deploying a public key infrastructure is not usually done in one day. After some discussion, your boss agrees that perhaps you should install this role in a laboratory first, but he wants to be there to see how it works. He wants you to install an enterprise certificate authority. You make sure that the server you are using is running Windows Server 2008 Enterprise Edition, and you launch the installation through Server Manager. When you get to the Specify Setup Type page of the Add Roles Wizard, the Enterprise CA option is not available. (See Figure 15-7.) What could be the problem? (Choose all that apply.)

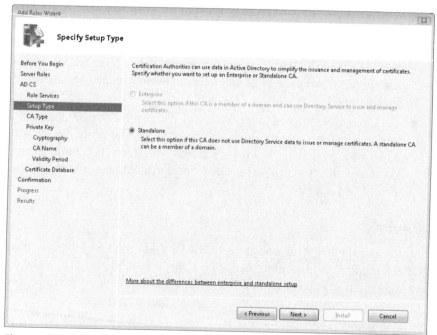

Figure 15-7   The Specify Setup Type page of the AD CS Installation Wizard

A.   Your server is not running Windows Server 2008 Enterprise Edition.

B.   You are logged on with an account that is not part of the domain.

C.   Your server is not a member of an AD DS domain.

D.   You cannot install an enterprise CA with Server Manager.

Lesson 2: Configuring and Using Active Directory Certificate Services

After you have deployed your servers, you still need to complete several configurations to begin using them to issue and manage certificates to users and devices. Several activities are required:

- To issue and maintain certificates, you must finalize the configuration of your issuing CAs.
- For your online responder to issue responses to requests, you must finalize the configuration of the online responder.
- To support network device enrollments, you must finish the configuration of the NDES on an issuing CA.
- After all of these configurations are completed, you must test your CA operations to ensure that everything is working correctly.

After this lesson, you will be able to:
- Create a revocation configuration.
- Work with CA server configuration settings.
- Work with certificate templates.
- Configure the CA to issue OCSP response signing certificates.
- Manage certificate enrollments.
- Manage certificate revocations.

Estimated lesson time: 40 minutes

Finalizing the Configuration of an Issuing CA

Finalizing the configuration of an issuing CA includes the following actions:

- Creating a certificate revocation configuration
- Configuring and personalizing certificate templates with specific attention to the following factors:
    - If you want to use the EFS to protect data, you must configure certificates for use with EFS. This also involves planning for the recovery agent or the agent that will be able to recover data if a user's EFS key is lost.
    - If you want to protect your wireless networks with certificates, you must configure wireless network certificates. This will enforce strong authentication and encrypt all communications between wireless devices.
    - If you want to use smart cards to support two-factor authentication, you must configure smart card certificates.

    ❑   If you want to protect Web sites and enable e-commerce, you must configure Web server certificates. You can also use this certificate type to protect DCs and encrypt all communications to and from them.

■   Configuring enrollment and issuance options

You perform each of these actions on the issuing CA itself or remotely through a workstation, using the Remote Server Administration Tools (RSAT).

Creating a Revocation Configuration for a CA

Revocation is one of the only vehicles available to you to control certificates when they are misused or when you need to cancel deployed certificates. This is one reason your revocation configuration should be completed before you begin to issue certificates.

To create a revocation configuration, perform the following actions:

■   Specify Certificate Revocation List (CRL) distribution points.

■   Configure CRL and Delta CRL overlap periods.

■   Schedule the publication of CRLs.

Begin with the CRL distribution point. Revocation configurations are performed in the Certification Authority console.

1.   Log on to an issuing CA with a domain account that has local administrative rights.
2.   Launch the Certification Authority console from the Administrative Tools program group.
3.   Right-click the issuing CA name and select Properties.
4.   In the Properties dialog box, click the Extensions tab and verify that the Select Extension drop-down list is set to CRL Distribution Point (CDP). Also make sure that the Publish CRLs To This Location and the Publish Delta CRLs To This Location check boxes are selected.
5.   Click OK.

    If you made any changes to the CAs configuration, you will be prompted to stop and restart the AD CS service. Click Yes to do so.

Now, move on to configuring CRL and Delta CRL overlap periods. This is performed with the *Certutil.exe* command.

1.   On the issuing CA, open an elevated command prompt and execute the following commands:

```
certutil –setreg ca\CRLOverlapUnits value
certutil –setreg ca\CRLOverlapPeriod units
certutil –setreg ca\CRLDeltaOverlapUnits value
certutil –setreg ca\CRLDeltaOverlapPeriod units
```

    Value is the value you want to use to set the overlap period, and *units* is in minutes, hours, or days. For example, you could set the CRL overlap period to 24 hours and the Delta CRL publication period to 12 hours. For this, you would use the following commands:

```
certutil -setreg ca\CRLOverlapUnits 24
certutil -setreg ca\CRLOverlapPeriod hours
certutil -setreg ca\CRLDeltaOverlapUnits 12
certutil -setreg ca\CRLDeltaOverlapPeriod hours
```

2. Go to the Certification Authority console and right-click the issuing CA server name to stop and restart the service.

Finally, configure the publication of the CRLs.

1. In the Certification Authority console, expand the console tree below the issuing CA server name.
2. Right-click Revoked Certificates and select Properties.
3. On the CRL Publishing Parameters tab, configure the CRL and Delta CRL publication periods.

   By default, both values are set to one week and one day, respectively. If you expect to have a high throughput of certificates and need to ensure high availability of the CRLs, decrease both values. If not, keep the default values.

   You can also view existing CRLs on the View CRLs tab.
4. Click OK.

Your revocation configuration is complete.

Configuring and Personalizing Certificate Templates

Certificate templates are used to generate the certificates you will use in your AD CS configuration. Enterprise CAs use version 2 and 3 templates. These templates are configurable and enable you to personalize them. To prepare templates for various uses, you must first configure each template you intend to use and, after each is configured, deploy each to your CAs. After templates are deployed, you can use them to issue certificates. Begin by identifying which templates you want to use, and then move on to the procedure.

1. Log on to an issuing CA, using domain administrative credentials.
2. Launch Server Manager from the Administrative Tools program group.
3. Expand Roles\Active Directory Certificate Services\Certificate Templates (*servername*).
4. Note that all the existing templates are listed in the details pane.

IMPORTANT   **Upgrading certificate authorities**

If you are upgrading an existing CA infrastructure to Windows Server 2008, the first time you log on to a new server running AD CS, you will be prompted to update the existing certificate templates. Answer Yes to do so. This upgrades all templates to Windows Server 2008 versions.

---

5. Note that you are connected to a DC by default.

   To work with templates, you must be connected to a DC so that the templates can be published to AD DS.

6. If you are not connected, use the *Connect To Another Writable Domain Controller* command in the Action pane to do so.

   You are ready to create the templates you require.

7. Select the source template, right-click the template to select Duplicate Template, and select the version of Windows Server to support.

   This should always be Windows Server 2008 unless you are running in a mixed PKI hierarchy.

8. Name the new template, customize it, and save the customizations.

   Customize templates according to the following guidelines:

   ❑ To create an EFS template, select the Basic EFS template as the source, duplicate it for Windows Server 2008, and name it. Use a valid name, for example, **Basic EFS WS08**, and then move through the property tabs to customize its content. Pay particular attention to key archival on the Request Handling tab and make sure you select the Archive Subject Encryption Private Key check box. Also, use encryption to send the key to the CA. Archival storage of the private key enables you to protect it if the user ever loses it. You can also use the Subject Name tab to add information such as Alternate Subject Name values. Click OK.

   ❑ If you plan to use EFS, you must also create an EFS Recovery Agent template. Duplicate it for Windows Server 2008. Name it with a valid name such as **EFS Recovery Agent WS08**. Publish the recovery agent certificate in Active Directory. Note that the recovery agent certificate is valid for a much longer period than the EFS certificate itself. Also, use the same settings on the other property tabs as you assigned to the Basic EFS duplicate.

   MORE INFO Using EFS

   For more information on the implementation of EFS, look up the "Working with the Encrypting File System" white paper at *http://www.reso-net.com/articles.asp?m=8* under the Advanced Public Key Infrastructures section.

   ❑ If you plan to use wireless networks, create a Network Policy Server (NPS) template for use with your systems. Basically, you create the template and configure it for autoenrollment. Then, the next time the NPS servers in your network update their Group Policy settings, they will be assigned new certificates. Use the RAS and IAS Server templates as the sources for your new NPS template. Duplicate it for Windows Server 2008. Name it appropriately, for example, **NPS Server WS08**. Publish it in Active Directory. Move to the Security tab to select the RAS and IAS Servers group to assign the Autoenroll as well as the Enroll permissions. Review other tabs as needed and save the new template.

❑ If you want to use smart card logons, create duplicates of the Smartcard Logon and Smartcard User templates. Set the duplicates for Windows Server 2008. Name them appropriately and publish them in Active Directory. You do not use Autoenrollment for these certificates because you need to use smart card enrollment stations to distribute the smart cards themselves to the users.

❑ If you want to protect Web servers or DCs, create duplicates of the Web Server and Domain Controller Authentication templates. Do not use the Domain Controller template; it is designed for earlier versions of the operating system. Duplicate them for Windows Server 2008, publish them in Active Directory, and verify their other properties.

NOTE   Configuring duplicate templates

The configuration of each template type often includes additional activities that are not necessarily tied to AD CS. Make sure you view the AD CS online help to review the activities associated with the publication of each certificate type.

Now that your templates are ready, you must issue the template to enable the CA to issue certificates based on these personalized templates.

9. In Server Manager, expand Roles\Active Directory Certificate Services*Issuing CA Name*\Certificate Templates.

10. To issue a template, right-click Certificate Templates, choose New, and then select Certificate Template To Issue.

11. In the Enable Certificate Templates dialog box, use Ctrl + click to select all the templates you want to issue, and then click OK. (See Figure 15-8.)

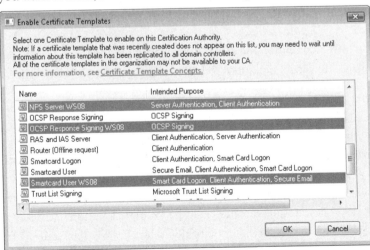

Figure 15-8   Enable Certificate Templates dialog box

Now you're ready to configure enrollment. This is done through Group Policy. You can choose either to create a new Group Policy for this purpose or to modify an existing Group Policy object. This policy must be assigned to all members of the domain; therefore, the Default Domain Policy might be your best choice or, if you do not want to modify this policy, create a new policy and assign it to the entire domain. You use the Group Policy Management Console (GPMC) to do so.

1. Log on to a DC, and then launch Group Policy Management from the Administrative Tools program group.

2. Locate or create the appropriate policy and right-click it to choose Edit.

3. To assign autoenrollment for computers, expand Computer Configuration\Policies \Windows Settings\Security Settings\Public Key Policies.

4. Double-click Certificate Services Client – Auto-Enrollment.

5. Enable the policy and select the Renew Expired Certificates, Update Pending Certificates, And Remove Revoked Certificates check box.

6. Select the Update Certificates That Use Certificate Templates check box if you have already issued some certificates manually for this purpose. Click OK to assign these settings.

7. To assign autoenrollment for users, expand User Configuration\Policies\Windows Settings\Security Settings\Public Key Policies.

8. Enable the policy and select the same options as for computers.

9. Notice that you can enable Expiration Notification for users. Enable it and set an appropriate value.

   This will notify users when their certificates are about to expire.

10. Click OK to assign these settings.

IMPORTANT   Computer and User Group Policy settings

Normally, you should not apply both user and computer settings in the same Group Policy object. This is done here only to illustrate the settings you need to apply to enable autoenrollment.

---

11. Close the GPMC.

12. Return to the issuing CA and move to Server Manager to set the default action your issuing CA will use when it receives certificate requests.

13. Right-click the issuing CA server name under AD CS and choose Properties.

14. Click the Policy Module tab and click the Properties button.

15. To have certificates issued automatically, select Follow The Settings In The Certificate Template, If Applicable. Otherwise, Automatically Issue The Certificate. Click OK.

16. Click OK once again to close the Properties dialog box.

Your issuing CA is now ready for production and will begin to issue certificates automatically when they are requested either by devices or by users.

Finalizing the Configuration of an Online Responder

If you decided to use online responders, you will need to finalize their configuration. Online responders can create an array of systems to provide high availability for the service. An array can be as simple as two CAs acting as ORs, or it can include many more servers.

To finalize the configuration of an online responder, you must configure and install an OCSP Response Signing certificate and configure an Authority Information Access extension to support it. After this is done, you must assign the template to a CA and then enroll the system to obtain the certificate. Use the following procedure to configure the OCSP Response Signing Certificate.

1. Log on to an issuing CA server, using a domain account with local administrative access rights.
2. In Server Manager, expand Roles\Active Directory Certificate Services\ Certificate Templates(*servername*).
3. Right-click the OCSP Response Signing template and click Duplicate Template. Select a Windows Server 2008 Enterprise Edition template and click OK.
4. Type a valid name for the new template, for example, **OCSP Response Signing WS08**.
5. Select the Publish Certificate in Active Directory check box.
6. On the Security tab, under Group Or User Names, click Add, click Object Types to enable the Computer object type, and click OK.
7. Type the name and click Check Names or browse to find the computer that hosts the online responder. Click OK.
8. Click the computer name and then, in the Permissions section of the dialog box, select the Allow: Read, Enroll, and Autoenroll options.
9. Click OK to create the duplicate template.

Your certificate template is ready. Now you must configure the Authority Information Access (AIA) Extension to support the OR.

IMPORTANT Assigning access rights

Normally, you should assign access rights to groups and not to individual objects in an AD DS directory. Because you will have several ORs, using a group makes sense. Ideally, you will create a group in AD DS, name it appropriately—for example, Online Responders—and add the computer accounts of each OR to this group. After you do that, you will assign the access rights of the OCSP Response Signing template to the group instead of to the individual systems. This way, you will have to do it only once.

---

1. Log on to an issuing CA, using a domain account with local administrative credentials.
2. Launch Server Manager from the Administrative Tools program group.
3. Expand Roles\Active Directory Certificate Services*Issuing CA servername.*
4. In the Actions pane, select Properties.
5. Click the Extensions tab, click the Select Extension drop-down list, and then click Authority Information Access (AIA).
6. Specify the locations to obtain certificate revocation data. In this case, select the location beginning with HTTP://.
7. Select the Include In The AIA Extension Of Issued Certificates and the Include In The Online Certificate Status Protocol (OCSP) Extension check boxes.
8. Click OK to apply the changes.

   Note that you must stop and restart the AD CS service because of the change.
9. Click Yes at the suggested dialog box.
10. Now move to the Certificate Templates node under the issuing CA name and right-click it, select New, and then choose Certificate Template To Issue.
11. In the Enable Certificate Templates dialog box, select the new OCSP Response Signing template you created earlier and click OK.

    The new template should appear in the details pane.
12. To assign the template to the server, reboot it.

    You now need to verify that the OCSP certificate has been assigned to the server. You do so with the Certificates snap-in. By default, this snap-in is not in a console. You must create a new console to use it.
13. Open the Start menu, type **mmc** in the search box, and press Enter.
14. In the MMC, select Add/Remove Snap-in from the File menu to open the Add Or Remove Snap-ins dialog box.
15. Select the Certificates snap-in and click Add.
16. Select Computer Account and click Next.
17. Select Local Computer and click Finish.
18. Click OK to close the Add Or Remove Snap-ins dialog box.
19. Select Save from the File menu to save the console and place it in your Documents folder. Name the console **Computer Certificates** and click Save.
20. Expand Certificates\Personal\Certificates and verify that it contains the new OCSP certificate.
21. If the certificate is not there, install it manually by right-clicking Certificates under Personal, choosing All Tasks, and then selecting Request New Certificate.
22. On the Certificate Enrollment page, click Next.
23. Select the new OCSP certificate and click Enroll.

24. On the next page, click the down arrow to the right of Details, and then click View Certificate. Browse through the tabs to view the certificate details. Click OK.

25. Click Finish to complete this part of the operation.

26. Right-click the Certificate, choose All Tasks, and then select Manage Private Keys.

27. On the Security tab, under User Group Or User Names, click Add.

28. In the Select Users, Computers, or Groups dialog box, click Locations and select the local server name. Click OK.

29. Type **Network Service** and click Check Names.

30. Click OK.

31. Click Network Service, and then, in the Permissions section of the dialog box, select Allow: Full Control.

32. Click OK to close the dialog box.

Your OR is ready to provide certificate validation information.

MORE INFO   Online responder

For more information on the OR service, go to *http://technet2.microsoft.com/windowsserver2008/en /library/045d2a97-1bff-43bd-8dea-f2df7e270e1f1033.mspx?mfr=true.*

You'll note that the Online Responder node in Server Manager also includes an Array Configuration node. When you add other ORs, you can add them to this array configuration to provide high availability of the OR service. Complex environments using multitiered hierarchies will have large OR arrays to ensure that all their users and devices can easily validate their certificates.

Add a Revocation Configuration for an Online Responder

When the OR is ready, add a revocation configuration. Because each CA that is an OR in an array includes its own certificate, each also requires a revocation configuration. The revocation configuration will serve requests for specific CA key pairs and certificates. In addition, you need to update the revocation configuration for a CA each time you renew its key pair. To create a Revocation Configuration, perform the following steps:

1. Log on to an issuing CA, using a domain account that has local administrative rights.

2. Launch Server Manager from the Administrative Tools program group.

3. Expand Roles\Active Directory Certificate Services\Online Responder\Revocation Configuration.

4. Right-click Revocation Configuration and choose Add Revocation Configuration.

5. Click Next at the Welcome page.

6. On the Name The Revocation Configuration page, assign a valid name.
   Because each revocation configuration is tied to a particular CA, it makes sense to include the CA's name in the name of the configuration, for example, RCSERVER04.

7. Click Next.

8. On the Select CA Certificate Location page, identify where the certificate can be loaded from.

   You can choose from Active Directory, from a local certificate store, or from a file.

9. Choose Select A Certificate For An Existing Enterprise CA and click Next.

   Now, the OR must validate that the issuer of the certificate, in this case, the root CA, has a valid certificate. Two choices are possible: Active Directory or Computer Name.

10. Because your root CA is offline, choose Active Directory and click Browse.

11. Locate the certificate for the root CA and click OK.

    After the certificate is selected, the wizard will load the Online Responder signing templates.

12. Click Next.

    On the Select A Signing Certificate page, you must select a signing method because the OR signs each response to clients before it sends it. Three choices are available:

    ❑ Automatic selection will load a certificate from the OCSP template you created earlier.

    ❑ Manually, you can choose the certificate to use.

    ❑ CA Certificate uses the certificate from the CA itself.

13. Choose Automatically Select A Signing Certificate and select Auto-Enroll for an OCSP signing certificate.

14. Browse for a CA and select the issuing CA. Click OK.

    This should automatically select the template you prepared earlier.

15. Click Next.

    Now the wizard will initialize the revocation provider. If, for some reason, it cannot find it, you will need to add the provider manually.

16. Click Provider, and then click Add under Base CRLs. For example, you could use the following HTTP address: **http://localhost/ca.crl**.

17. Click OK. Repeat this step for the Delta CRLs and use the same HTTP address. Click OK.

    However, because you are obtaining the certificate from Active Directory, the listed provider will be an address in ldap:// format and should be provided automatically by the wizard. AD CS relies on Lightweight Directory Access Protocol (LDAP) to obtain information from the AD DS directory store.

18. Click Finish to complete the revocation configuration.

You should now have a new revocation configuration listed in the details pane. Repeat this procedure for each CA that is an OR.

Exam Tip   Take note of the operations you need to enable ORs because they are part of the exam.

Considerations for the Use and Management of AD CS

Active Directory Certificate Services role services are managed by using MMC snap-ins. Table 15-4 lists the tools you have used throughout this chapter, most of which are available from within Server Manager.

Table 15-4   AD CS Management Tools

Tool	Usage	Location
Certification Authority	To manage a certificate authority.	Server Manager
Certificates	To manage certificates. This snap-in is installed by default.	Custom MMC snap-in
Certificate Templates	To manage certificate templates.	Server Manager
Online Responder	To manage an OR.	Server Manager
Enterprise PKI	To manage the entire PKI infrastructure.	Server Manager
Certutil	To manage PKI functions from the command line.	Command prompt

NOTE   Install the snap-ins without installing AD CS

The snap-ins listed in Table 15-4 can be installed by using Server Manager and selecting the AD CS tools under Remote Server Administration Tools. If the computer you want to perform remote administration tasks from is running Windows Vista Service Pack 1, you can obtain the Remote Server Administration Tools Pack from the Microsoft Download Center at *http://go.microsoft.com /fwlink/?LinkID=89361*.

As you work with AD CS, you will see that it provides a great amount of information through the Event Log. Table 15-5 lists the most common events for AD CS certificate authorities.

Table 15-5   Common Certificate Authority Event IDs

Category	Event ID	Description
AD CS Access Control	39, 60, 92	Related to insufficient or inappropriate use of permissions.
AD CS and AD DS	24, 59, 64, 91, 93, 94, 106, 107	Related to access (read or write) for AD DS objects.
AD CS Certificate Request (Enrollment) Processing	3, 7, 10, 21, 22, 23, 53, 56, 57, 79, 80, 97, 108, 109, 128, 132	One element for certificate enrollment to succeed is missing: valid CA certificate, certificate templates with proper configuration, client accounts, or certificate requests.
AD CS Certification Authority Certificate and Chain Validation	27, 31, 42, 48, 49, 51, 58, 64, 100, 103, 104, 105	Related to availability, validity, and chain validation for a CA certificate.

Table 15-5   Common Certificate Authority Event IDs

Category	Event ID	Description
AD CS Certification Authority Upgrade	111, 112, 113, 114, 115, 116, 117, 118, 119, 120, 121, 122, 123, 125, 126	Related to upgrading certificate authorities from an earlier version of Windows to Windows Server 2008 and can indicate configuration options or components that need to be reconfigured.
AD CS Cross-Certification	99, 102	Related to the cross-CA certificates created to establish relationships between the original certificate and the renewed root.
AD CS Database Availability	17	Related to CA database access issues.
AD CS Exit Module Processing	45, 46	Related to the exit module functions: publish or send e-mail notification.
AD CS Key Archival and Recovery	81, 82, 83, 84, 85, 86, 87, 88, 96, 98, 127	Related to key recovery agent certificates, exchange (XCHG) certificates and keys, or that one or all these components are missing.
AD CS Performance Counters Availability	110	Related to performance counters that cannot be started.
AD CS Policy Module Processing	9, 43, 44, 77, 78	Related to problems detected with a policy module.
AD CS Program Resource Availability	15, 16, 26, 30, 33, 34, 35, 38, 40, 61, 63, 89, 90	Related to the availability of system resources and operating system components.
AD CS Registry Settings	5, 19, 20, 28, 95	Related to the corruption or deletion of configuration settings in the registry.
AD CS Online Responder	16, 17, 18, 19, 20, 21, 22, 23, 25, 26, 27, 29, 31, 33, 34, 35	Related to Online Responder service dependencies.

Rely on the contents of Table 15-5 to identify quickly the area an issue relates to so that you can resolve it faster.

MORE INFO   AD CS event IDs

To find more information on event types, read the information at *http://technet2.microsoft.com /windowsserver2008/en/library/688d1449-3086-4a79-95e6-5a7f620681731033.mspx.*

Working with Enterprise PKI

One of the most useful tools in an AD CS infrastructure is Enterprise PKI, or *PKIView* from the command line, which is the Enterprise PKI node under Active Directory Certificate Services in Server Manager. Enterprise PKI can be used for several AD CS management activities. Basically, Enterprise PKI gives you a view of the status of your AD CS deployment and enables you to view the entire PKI hierarchy in your network and drill down into individual CAs to identify quickly issues with the configuration or operation of your AD CS infrastructure.

Enterprise PKI is mostly used as a diagnostic and health view tool because it displays operational information about the members of your PKI hierarchy. In addition, you can use Enterprise PKI to link to each CA quickly by right-clicking the CA name and selecting Manage CA. This launches the Certification Authority console for the targeted CA.

From the Actions pane, you can also gain access to the Templates console (Manage Templates) as well as to the Certificate Containers in Active Directory Domain Services (Manage AD Containers). The latter enables you to view the contents of each of the various containers in a directory that is used to store certificates for your PKI architecture. (See Figure 15-9.)

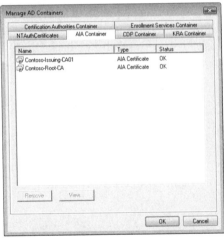

Figure 15-9   Viewing the AD containers through Enterprise PKI

Rely on Enterprise PKI to check AD CS health status visually. Its various icons give you immediate feedback on each component of your infrastructure, showing green when all is healthy, yellow when minor issues are found, and red when critical issues arise.

Quick Check

1. Name three scenarios in which you can rely on AD CS to protect your network.
2. Which certificate template versions are supported by enterprise CAs?

Quick Check Answers

1. There are several scenarios. For example, you can use AD CS to support the use of the Encrypting File System to protect data, the use of smart cards to provide two-factor authentication, or the use of the Secure Sockets Layer to protect server-to-server or server-to-client communications or even to issue certificates to end users so that they can encrypt e-mail data through S/MIME.
2. Enterprise CAs support version 2 and 3 templates. These templates can be duplicated and modified to meet your organizational requirements.

Protecting Your AD CS Configuration

Along with the security measures you must perform for your root and intermediate CAs, you must also protect each CA, especially issuing CAs through regular backups. Backing up a CA is very simple. In Server Manager, expand Roles\ Active Directory Certificate Services\CA Server Name. Right-click the server name, select All Tasks, and choose Back Up CA. When you launch the backup operation, it launches the Certification Authority Backup Wizard. To back up the CA, use the following operations.

1. Launch the Certification Authority Backup Wizard and click Next.
2. On the Items To Back Up page, select the items you want to back up.
   - ❑ The Private Key And CA Certificate option will protect the certificate for this server.
   - ❑ The Certificate Database And Certificate Database Log option will protect the certificates this CA manages. You can also perform incremental database backups.
3. Identify the location to back up to.

   For example, you could create the backup to a file share on a central server location. Keep in mind, however, that you are backing up highly sensitive data and transporting it over the network, which might not be the best solution. A better choice might be to back up to a local folder and then copy the backup to removable media.
4. Identify the location and click Next. Note that the target location must be empty.
5. Assign a strong password to the backup. Click Next.
6. Review the information and click Finish.

   The wizard performs the backup. Protect the backup media thoroughly because it contains very sensitive information.

You can also perform automated backups through the command line with the *Certutil.exe* command with the appropriate switches to back up and restore the database.

MORE INFO Using *Certutil.exe* to protect CA data

For more information on the *Certutil.exe* utility for backup and restore, go to *http://support.microsoft.com/kb/185195*.

To restore information, use the Certification Authority Restore Wizard. When you request a restore operation by right-clicking the server name, selecting All Tasks, and choosing Restore CA, the wizard will immediately prompt you to stop the CA service before the restore operation can begin. Click OK. After the service is stopped, the Welcome page of the wizard appears.

1. Click Next.
2. Select the items you want to restore. You can restore the private key and the CA certificate as well as the database and log. Choose the items to restore.
3. Type the location of the backup files or click Browse to locate the backup data. Click Next.
4. Type the password to open the backup and click Next.
5. Verify your settings and click Finish.
   After the restore operation is complete, the wizard will offer to restart the AD CS service.
6. Click Yes. Verify the operation of your CA after the restore is complete.

PRACTICE **Configuring and Using AD CS**

In this practice, you will perform four key tasks. In the first, you will work with Enterprise PKI to correct the errors in an AD CS implementation. Then you will create a custom certificate template to publish certificates. You will also enable autoenrollment for certificates to ensure that your users can obtain them automatically. Finally, you will ensure that your issuing CA will automatically enroll clients.

▶ **Exercise 1   Correct an AD CS Implementation with Enterprise PKI**

In this exercise, you will rely on Enterprise PKI to identify and then correct configuration issues with your AD CS implementation. This exercise will help you see the value of working with Enterprise PKI.

1. Make sure that SERVER01, SERVER03, and SERVER04 are running.
2. Log on to SERVER04, using the domain Administrator account.
3. Launch Server Manager from the Administrative Tools program group.
4. Expand Roles\Active Directory Certificate Services\Enterprise PKI\Contoso-Root-CA \Contoso-Issuing-CA. Click Contoso-Issuing-CA and note the errors. (See Figure 15-10.)

Errors exist in your configuration. If you navigate to the Contoso-Root-CA, you will see that this CA also includes errors according to Enterprise PKI. These errors refer to the Web-based download locations for the CRL Distribution Point and for the AIA. These errors appear because they refer to locations that do not exist. These locations must be created manually in IIS. However, because you are using an AD DS–integrated AD CS deployment, you do not need to add Web-based download locations even if they are indicated by default in the configuration of AD CS. In an AD DS–integrated deployment, the directory service is responsible for AIA and CRL distribution, and, because this service is highly available, no secondary location is required. In fact, you need to add secondary locations only if you want to make them available to mobile or external users who are outside your internal network. If you do so, your URLs will need to be available externally.

5. Click Contoso-Root-CA under the Enterprise PKI node and select Manage CA.

    This launches the Certificate Authority standalone console with a focus on the root CA. Remember that Server Manager can work with the local server only. Therefore, you need to use the standalone console.

6. Right-click Contoso-Root-CA and select Properties.

7. Click the Extensions tab and verify that CRL Distribution Point (CDP) is selected in the drop-down list.

8. Select http://<ServerDNSName>/CertEnroll/<CaName><CRLNameSuffix><DeltaCRLAllowed>.crl in the locations section of the dialog box and clear Include In CRLs, Clients Use This To Find Delta CRL Locations as well as Include in the CDP extension of issued certificates.

9. Select Authority Information Access (AIA) from the drop-down list.

10. Select http://<ServerDNSName>/CertEnroll/<ServerDNSName>_<CaName><CertificateName>.crt and clear Include in the AIA extension of issued certificates. Click OK to apply your changes.

    AD CS automatically points to a CertEnroll virtual directory under the default Web site for Web as the CDP. However, the installation process for AD CS does not create this virtual directory by default. In addition, because this is a root CA, it does not host IIS and will be taken offline. Pointing to a nonexistent Web server as a CDP location is not good practice, and this location must be removed from the CA's configuration; otherwise, it will be embedded in the certificates it issues.

11. Because you modified the configuration of the AD CS server, the console will ask you to restart AD CS on this server. Click Yes.

12. Close the Certificate Authority console and return to Enterprise PKI in Server Manager.

13. On the toolbar, click the Refresh button to update Enterprise PKI. Note that though there are no longer location errors for the root CA, there are still errors under the issuing CA.

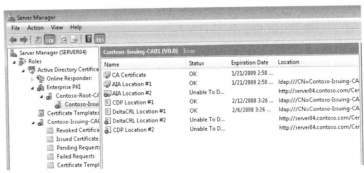

Figure 15-10   Viewing configuration errors in Enterprise PKI

You are ready to correct the errors in the issuing CA.

1. Right-click Contoso-Issuing-CA under AD CS in Server Manager and select Properties. In this case, you can use Server Manager because Contoso-Issuing-CA is the local computer.

2. Click the Extensions tab and verify that CRL Distribution Point (CDP) is selected in the drop-down list.

3. Select   http://<ServerDNSName>/CertEnroll/<CaName><CRLNameSuffix><DeltaCRL-Allowed>.crl in the locations section of the dialog box and clear Include In CRLs, Clients Use This To Find Delta CRL Locations as well as Include in the CDP extension of issued certificates.

4. Select Authority Information Access (AIA) from the drop-down list.

5. Select http://<ServerDNSName>/CertEnroll/<ServerDNSName>_<CaName><Certificate-Name>.crt and clear Include in the AIA extension of issued certificates. Click OK to apply your changes.

   Once again, AD CS automatically points to a CertEnroll virtual directory under the default Web site for Web as the CDP. However, the installation process for AD CS does not create this virtual directory by default. If you need to provide Web support for CRLs, even if this is only an internal deployment, you would need to create the virtual directory in IIS. However, in this case, it is not required. Also, as a best practice, you do not remove the HTTP location. If you need to add it later, the proper format for the URL will already be there, and you will need to recheck only the appropriate options.

6. Because you modified the configuration of the AD CS server, the console will ask you to restart AD CS on this server. Click Yes.

7. Return to Enterprise PKI in Server Manager.

8. On the toolbar, click the Refresh button to update Enterprise PKI.

   Note that there is now only one error under the issuing CA. This error stems from the original self-signed certificate that was generated during installation of this CA. This certificate is superseded by the certificate that was issued by the root CA. Because of this, you must revoke the original certificate.

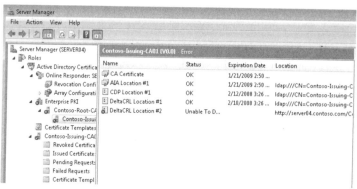

9. To finalize your configuration, move to Contoso-Issuing-CA under AD CS and select Issued Certificates.

   This will list all certificates issued by this CA in the details pane.

10. Locate the first certificate.

    It should be of a CA Exchange type. The certificate type is listed under the Certificate Template column in the details pane.

11. Right-click this certificate, select All Tasks, and then click Revoke Certificate.

12. In the Certificate Revocation dialog box, select Superseded from the drop-down list, verify the date, and click OK.

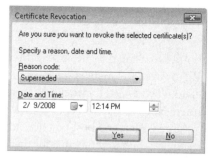

When you revoke the certificate, it is automatically moved to the Revoked Certificates folder and is no longer valid. However, because you newly revoked a certificate, you must update the revocation list.

13. Right-click the Revoked Certificates node and choose All Tasks to select Publish.

14. In the Publish CRL dialog box, select New CRL and click OK.

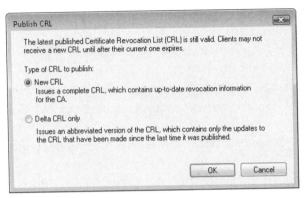

Publish CRL

The latest published Certificate Revocation List (CRL) is still valid. Clients may not receive a new CRL until after their current one expires.

Type of CRL to publish:

⦿ New CRL
Issues a complete CRL, which contains up-to-date revocation information for the CA.

◯ Delta CRL only
Issues an abbreviated version of the CRL, which contains only the updates to the CRL that have been made since the last time it was published.

[OK]   [Cancel]

15. Return to Enterprise PKI and click the Refresh button.

There should no longer be any errors in the Enterprise PKI view.

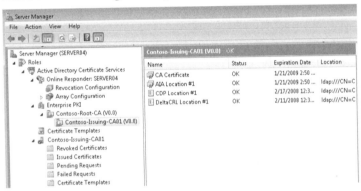

You will need to perform these activities in your network when you implement AD CS; otherwise, your Enterprise PKI views will always display errors.

▶ **Exercise 2   Create a Duplicate Certificate Template for EFS**

In this exercise, you will create a duplicate certificate to enable EFS and publish it so it can use autoenroll and use EFS to protect the system data.

1. Make sure SERVER01 and SERVER04 are both running.
2. Log on to SERVER04, using the domain Administrator account.
3. Launch Server Manager from the Administrative Tools program group.
4. Expand Roles\Active Directory Certificate Services\Certificate Templates (*servername*). Note that all the existing templates are listed in the details pane.

Note also that you are connected to a DC (SERVER01) by default. To work with templates, you must be connected to a DC so that the templates can be published to AD DS. If you are not connected, you must use the *Connect To Another Writable Domain Controller* command in the action pane to do so.

5. Select the Basic EFS template in the details pane, right-click it, and select Duplicate Template.

6. Select the version of Windows Server to support—in this case, Windows Server 2008—and click OK.

7. Name the template **Basic EFS WS08** and set the following options. Leave all other options as is.

    ❑ On the Request Handling tab, select the Archive Subject's Encryption Private Key and the Use Advanced Symmetric Algorithm To Send The Key To The CA check boxes. Archival storage of the private key enables you to protect it if the user loses it.

    ❑ On the Subject Name tab, add information to the Alternate Subject Name values. Select the E-mail Name and User Principal Name (UPN) check boxes.

8. Click OK.

9. Right-click the EFS Recovery Agent template and choose Duplicate.

10. Select the version of Windows Server to support—in this case, Windows Server 2008—and click OK.

11. Name the template **EFS Recovery Agent WS08** and set the following options. Leave all other options as is.

    ❑ On the General tab, select the Publish certificate in the Active Directory check box. Note that the recovery agent certificate is valid for a much longer period than is the EFS certificate itself.

    ❑ On the Request Handling tab, make sure you select the Archive Subject's Encryption Private Key and the Use Advanced Symmetric Algorithm To Send The Key To The CA check boxes. Archival storage of the private key enables you to protect it if the user loses it.

    ❑ On the Subject Name tab, add information to the Alternate Subject Name values. Select the E-mail Name and User Principal Name (UPN) check boxes.

12. Click OK.

13. In Server Manager, expand Roles\Active Directory Certificate Services*Issuing CA Name*\Certificate Templates.

14. To issue a template, right-click Certificate Templates, choose New, and then select Certificate Template To Issue.

15. In the Enable Certificate Templates dialog box, use Ctrl + click to select both Basic EFS WS08 and EFS Recovery Agent WS08 and click OK.

    Your templates are ready.

► Exercise 3   **Configure Autoenrollment**

In this exercise, you use Group Policy to configure autoenrollment. This exercise uses the Default Domain policy for simplicity, but in your environment, you should create a custom policy for this purpose and for all other custom settings you need to apply at the entire domain level.

1. Move to SERVER01 and log on as a domain administrator.
2. Launch Group Policy Management from the Administrative Tools program group.
3. Expand all the nodes to locate the Default Domain policy. Right-click it and choose Edit.
4. To assign autoenrollment for computers, expand Computer Configuration\Policies \Windows Settings\Security Settings\Public Key Policies.
5. Double-click Certificate Services Client – Auto-Enrollment.
6. Enable the policy and select the Renew Expired Certificates, Update Pending Certificates, And Remove Revoked Certificates check box.
7. Enable Expiration Notification For Users and leave the value at 10%.

   This will notify users when their certificates are about to expire.
8. Click OK to assign these settings.
9. Close the GPMC.

   Your policy is ready.

► Exercise 4   **Enable the CA to Issue Certificates**

Now you need to set the default action the CA will perform when it receives certificate requests.

1. Return to SERVER04 and log on, using the domain Administrator account.
2. Move to Server Manager.
3. Right-click the issuing CA server name under AD CS, Contoso-Issuing-CA01, and choose Properties.
4. Click the Policy Module tab and click the Properties button.
5. To have certificates issued automatically, select Follow The Settings In The Certificate Template, If Applicable. Otherwise, Automatically Issue The Certificate. Click OK. Click OK once again to close the Properties dialog box.

   Your issuing CA is now ready for production and will begin to issue EFS certificates automatically when they are requested either by your users or by computers.

Lesson Summary

- Revocation configurations for issuing CAs include several components. The first is a list of the Certificate Revocation List distribution points. The second is the overlap between the CRL and the Delta CRLs you send to requesters. The third is the schedule you use to publish CRLs.

- Issuing CAs should be enterprise CAs because of their capability to support autoenrollment and modify and personalize certificate templates.

- Online responders can create an array of systems to provide high availability for the service. An array can be as simple as two CAs acting as ORs, or it can include many more servers.

- ORs must rely on the Online Certificate Status Protocol (OCSP) certificates to sign the responses they send to requesters. These certificates encrypt the content of the response sent from the OR.

- ORs also require the configuration of the Authority Information Access extension before they can be fully functional. This extension is part of the properties of the certificate authority.

- Each CA that is an OR must have its own revocation configuration because each has its own certificate. To operate in an array, each of these certificates must be trusted. The revocation configuration is used to allow other array members to trust each particular CA in the array.

- Protection of every CA in your infrastructure is essential. This is why you should perform regular backups of all CA data, including the CA's certificates. Protect these backups very carefully because they contain highly sensitive data.

Lesson Review

You can use the following questions to test your knowledge of the information in Lesson 2, "Configuring and Using Active Directory Certificate Services." The questions are also available on the companion CD if you prefer to review them in electronic form.

NOTE   Answers

Answers to these questions and explanations of why each answer choice is right or wrong are located in the "Answers" section at the end of the book.

1. You are a PKI administrator for Contoso, Ltd. You want to configure your OR. You have already configured your OCSP Response Signing certificates, configured the Authority Information Access extension, and rebooted the server. Now you are ready to verify that the certificate has been automatically loaded onto the server. You create a custom console to contain the Certificates snap-in, but when you view the certificates in the Personal node of the computer, the snap-in does not appear. You decide to import the certificate manually, but when you use the Request New Certificate Wizard, you find that the certificate is not available to you. What could be the problem?

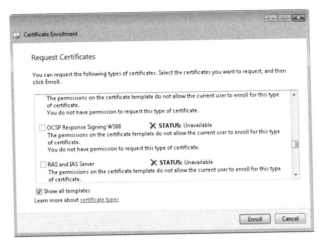

A. You cannot request this certificate through the wizard. You must use the *Certutil.exe* command.

B. The security properties of the certificate template are not set properly.

C. You cannot load an OCSP Response Signing Certificate on this server.

D. You do not need to load this certificate manually. It will be loaded automatically at the next Group Policy refresh cycle.

Chapter Review

To further practice and reinforce the skills you learned in this chapter, you can perform the following tasks:

- Review the chapter summary.
- Review the list of key terms introduced in this chapter.
- Complete the case scenario. This scenario sets up a real-world situation involving the topics of this chapter and asks you to create a solution.
- Complete the suggested practices.
- Take a practice test.

Chapter Summary

- You can use public key infrastructures to extend the authority your organization has beyond the borders of the network it controls. The role of AD DS is focused on network operating system directory services and should really be contained within the internal boundaries of your network. AD CS, however, can run both within a corporate network and outside the corporate network. When used within the network, it can be integrated with AD DS to provide automated certificate enrollment. When used outside your network, it should be installed as standalone certificate authorities and linked to a third-party trusted certificate authority to ensure that your certificates are trusted by computer systems over which you do not have control.

- You can rely on certificates for a variety of purposes, including data encryption on PCs, for communication encryption between two endpoints, for information protection, for two-factor authentications, for wireless communications, and more. All are based on the AD CS role.

- AD CS deployments are hierarchical in nature and form a chain of trust from the lowest to the topmost point of the hierarchy. If certificates are invalidated or expire at any point in the chain, every certificate that is below the invalidated certificate in the chain will be invalidated as well.

- Online Responders (ORs) can be linked to create an array configuration that will provide high availability for the OR service. The more complex your AD CS deployment becomes, the more likely you are to create these arrays to ensure that all users and devices have constant access to the certificate validation services the OR provides.

- When you deploy ORs, you must ensure that each contains its own revocation configuration. This step is necessary because each OR relies on its own certificate for validation purposes. Each revocation configuration will support a specific certificate key pair and will be published to each OR in an array. If you need to renew the OR's certificate, you will need to update its revocation configuration.

- One of the most useful management tools you have for AD CS is *Certutil.exe*. This tool supports almost every possible operation on a CA and enables you to automate maintenance and administration tasks.

Key Terms

Use these key terms to understand better the concepts covered in this chapter.

- **hierarchy**   The chain of servers that provide functionality in a PKI implementation. The chain begins with the root server and potentially extends through intermediate and issuing servers until it gets to the endpoint, the user or the endpoint device.
- **key pair**   PKI certificates usually include a key pair. The private key is used by the owner of the certificate to sign and encrypt information digitally. The public key, which is available to recipients of the information, is used to decrypt it.
- **revocation**   Certificates are issued for a specific duration of time. When the duration expires, the certificate is invalidated. If you need to deny the use of a certificate before the end of its lifetime, you must revoke it. Revoking a certificate provides immediate invalidation. All revocations are inserted into the Certificate Revocation List, which is used by all devices to validate the certificates they are presented with.

Case Scenario

In the following case scenario, you will apply what you've learned about subjects of this chapter. You can find answers to the questions in this scenario in the "Answers" section at the end of this book.

Case Scenario: Manage Certificate Revocation

You are a systems administrator for Contoso, Ltd. Contoso has deployed an AD CS infrastructure and has published certificates for a wide number of uses. One of these is to create software signing certificates for the software it distributes to its clients. These certificates are used to ensure that the software actually originates from Contoso. Contoso clients are pleased with this new approach because it guarantees that the source of the software is valid and free of malicious code.

As administrator, one of your duties is to perform weekly reviews of the event logs of your servers. Because you're using Windows Server 2008, you have configured event forwarding on each of the certificate authorities in your network. This makes administration easier, eliminating the need to log on to individual servers to view the event logs. You have to verify only one central location.

During a routine check, you notice that the root CA of your AD CS infrastructure has sent events to your central logging server. At first, you think this is very odd because the root CA should be offline at all times except for very rare maintenance operations or in the rare case when you need to issue a certificate for a new subordinate CA. As system administrator, you know that neither event has occurred in the recent past.

You look at the different events that were forwarded and you see that the CA was turned on about a week ago. During that time, it was used to generate two new root certificates under the Contoso name. Fortunately, you also included the security logs in the forwarding configuration. You look them up to see who logged on to the root CA. Because logons require smart cards, your event logs can be used to validate who used the server. You find out to your surprise that the logons belong to two employees who were fired last week. These employees should not have had access to this server.

You check on the Internet and find that the two root certificates are being used to sign software that does not originate from Contoso. In fact, it appears that the two ex-employees are currently offering software signing certificates using the Contoso name for sale on the Internet.

What do you do?

Suggested Practices

To help you successfully master the exam objectives presented in this chapter, complete the following tasks.

Working with AD CS

There are several exam objectives for this topic. Because of this, you should focus your practices on the following areas:

- Identifying the differences between standalone and enterprise CAs
- Working with the installation and configuration process for AD CS CAs
- Installing and configuring the Online Responder service
- Installing Network Device Enrollment Service
- Working with certificate templates

You should also practice using the various management tools and consoles for AD CS. Most of the consoles are available in Server Manager. The only console you need to create is the Certificates console.

Use the following instructions to perform these tasks.

- **Practice 1**   Prepare two servers—virtual or physical—as member servers of an AD DS domain. Then, install a standalone root CA and follow with the installation of an enterprise issuing CA. Run through each of the operations outlined in this chapter for the installation and configuration of both servers. For the purpose of the exercise, keep the root CA online and allow it to communicate with the issuing CA.

- **Practice 2**   Use the issuing CA to install the Online Responder service. Then run through each of the steps outlined in Lesson 2, "Configuring and Using Active Directory Certificate Services," to finalize the configuration of the Online Responder service. Pay attention to each step. ORs are new to AD CS and, therefore, will likely be on the exam.

- **Practice 3**   Follow the instructions in the practice in Lesson 1, "Understanding and Installing Active Directory Certificate Services," to install and configure the NDES. This is also a new feature of AD CS and, thus, will be on the exam.

- **Practice 4**   Modify a few template duplicates. Make sure you review the tabs of each template's property sheets thoroughly. Version 2 and 3 templates include many options and features.

- **Practice 5**   Finally, perform backups and restores and explore both Enterprise PKI and the options available through the *Certutil.exe* tool. Don't forget to study AD CS as well as PKI implementations with Windows Server 2003. The Microsoft TechNet Web site includes much more information on PKI in Windows Server 2003 than in Windows Server 2008.

Take a Practice Test

The practice tests on this book's companion CD offer many options. For example, you can test yourself on just one exam objective, or you can test yourself on all the 70-640 certification exam content. You can set up the test so that it closely simulates the experience of taking a certification exam, or you can set it up in study mode so that you can look at the correct answers and explanations after you answer each question.

MORE INFO   **Practice tests**

For details about all the practice test options available, see the "How to Use the Practice Tests" section in this book's introduction.

Chapter 16

Active Directory Rights Management Services

Active Directory Rights Management Services (AD RMS), formerly known simply as Rights Management Services, is designed to extend the reach of your internal network to the outside world. However, this time, the extension applies to intellectual property. People have been struggling with Digital Rights Management (DRM) ever since they started working with computers. In the first days of computing, software manufacturers went to great lengths to protect their software from theft. Even today, some vendors require the use of hardware keys for their software to run. Others have resorted to a Web-based approval and validation process. For example, with the release of Windows Vista, Microsoft has introduced a new licensing scheme, one option of which is a Key Management Server (KMS), to validate the licensed versions of Microsoft Windows you use.

Software creation isn't the only industry struggling with rights management. The music industry is also under pressure to determine the best way to protect digital music, sometimes even using questionable methods to do so. For instance, in 2005, Mark Russinovich, now Technical Fellow at Microsoft Corporation, discovered that Sony BMG installed a root kit with its CD player that activated when users load it onto their PCs. This root kit would send playlist information back to a central server managed by Sony through the Internet. This led to a series of articles and a flurry of activity on the Internet about the approaches music vendors were using to protect content.

MORE INFO   Mark Russinovich and Sony BMG

For more information on Mark's adventure with Sony, go to *http://blogs.technet.com/markrussinovich /archive/2005/10/31/sony-rootkits-and-digital-rights-management-gone-too-far.aspx.*

Now many record labels have decided to sell their music in MP3 format without data protection. When you buy the song, you become responsible for protecting it; however, you can play it on any device. It might or might not be related to Mark's story with Sony BMG, but the move displays just how complex DRM can become.

Music and software are not the only items that need protection. In data centers everywhere, people are starting to look to new technologies to protect their intellectual property. For example, the nice thing about e-mail is that it automatically keeps a trail of the conversations it includes. Each time you respond to a message, the original message is embedded into yours and so on. Without DRM, anyone can change the content of this embedded response at any time, changing the tone or nature of the conversation. Even worse, anyone can forward the conversation and change its content, and you won't even know about it. Implementing DRM to protect e-mail content ensures that your responses can never be modified even if they are embedded in another message.

The same applies to other intellectual property—Microsoft Office Word documents, Microsoft Office PowerPoint presentations, and other content. Many organizations rely on the value of their intellectual property. Losing this property or having it misused, copied, or stolen can cause untold damages to their operations. You don't have to be a major enterprise to profit from some form of rights management. Whenever you earn a living from the information you generate or you maintain competitive leadership through the use of internal information, consider DRM.

AD RMS enables you to protect your intellectual property through the integration of several features. In fact, in addition to a direct integration with Active Directory Domain Services (AD DS), AD RMS can also rely on both Active Directory Certificate Services (AD CS) and Active Directory Federation Services (AD FS). AD CS can generate the public key infrastructure (PKI) certificates that AD RMS can embed in documents. AD FS extends your AD RMS policies beyond the firewall and supports the protection of your intellectual property among your business partners. (See Figure 16-1.)

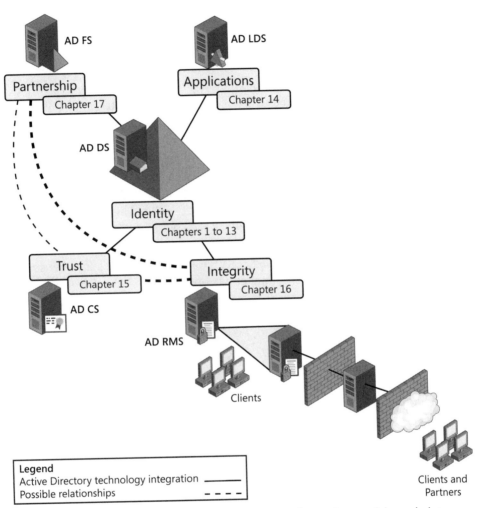

Figure 16-1   AD RMS extending the reach of authority beyond network boundaries

Exam objectives in this chapter:

■ Configuring Additional Active Directory Server Roles

  ❑ Configure Active Directory Rights Management Services (AD RMS).

Lessons in this chapter:

■ Lesson 1: Understanding and Installing Active Directory Rights
Management Services. 786

■ Lesson 2: Configuring and Using Active Directory Rights Management Services . . 809

Before You Begin

To complete the lessons in this chapter, you must have done the following:

■ Installed Windows Server 2008 on a physical or virtual computer. The computer should be named SERVER01 and should be a domain controller in the *contoso.com* domain. The details for this setup are presented in Chapter 1, "Installation," and Chapter 2, "Administration."

■ Installed Windows Server 2008 Enterprise Edition on a physical or virtual computer. The computer should be named SERVER03 and should be a member server within the *contoso.com* domain. This computer will host the AD RMS policy servers you will install and create through the exercises in this chapter. Ideally, this computer will also include a D drive to store the data for AD RMS. Forty GB will be sufficient for these exercises, although Microsoft recommends 80 GB for a working AD RMS server.

■ Installed Windows Server 2008 Enterprise Edition on a physical or virtual computer. The computer should be named SERVER04 and should be a member server within the *contoso.com* domain. This computer will host the AD RMS policy servers you will install and create through the exercises in this chapter. Ideally, this computer will also include a D drive to store the data for AD RMS. Forty GB will be sufficient for these exercises, although Microsoft recommends 80 GB for a working AD RMS server.

■ Installed Windows Server 2003 Enterprise Edition on a physical or virtual computer. The computer should be named SERVER05 and should be a member server within the *contoso.com* domain. This computer will host an installation of Microsoft SQL Server 2005, which will be used to run the configuration and logging database for AD RMS. This computer would also include a D drive to store the data for SQL Server. Ten GB is recommended for the size of this drive.

MORE INFO   **Create a SQL Server 2005 virtual appliance**

For information on how to create a virtual appliance with SQL Server 2005, go to *http://itmanagement.earthweb.com/article.php/3718566*.

If you are using Microsoft Virtual PC or Virtual Server, you can also use a preconfigured virtual machine, available in a .vhd format. More information on that at *https://www.microsoft.com/downloads/details.aspx?FamilyID=7b243252-acb7-451b-822b-df639443aeaf&DisplayLang=en*.

As you can see, a thorough test of AD RMS requires quite a few computers. For this reason, using a virtual infrastructure makes the most sense. If you can, you should also add a client computer running Windows Vista and Microsoft Office 2007 so you can use the AD RMS infrastructure after it is deployed.

Real World

Danielle Ruest and Nelson Ruest

In 2007, we were asked to create a book as part of a complete series on a specific technology, covering architectures, deployment, administration, and so on. Several author teams would participate in the project, each focusing on one book.

We rushed to prepare our table of contents (TOC) and to deliver it on the due date. Having recently installed Microsoft Office 2007, we decided to use one of the new templates in Word 2007. It gave our TOC a nice, polished look. The publisher was impressed with our format and sent it to the other teams, asking them to use the same format. When all the TOCs were in, the project was presented to the board and was approved.

The author teams started working on their copy. As it turned out, however, one of the teams was very far behind on its schedule and would not be able to complete its chapters on time. Could we help the team out and write a couple of its chapters? We agreed to look at the team's TOC.

When we received the other authors' TOC, we were not surprised to see our original format. However, as we examined the TOC to determine which chapters we could help with, we found that 33 percent of our content appeared verbatim in the other authors' TOC.

We quickly called our publisher. It was never determined whether they had performed the plagiarism on purpose or by mistake, but if we had used a digital rights management technology such as AD RMS in our own TOC, this could never have happened. Although copyrights protect content ownership, they will never be as far-reaching as DRM, which ensures that content can be used only in the manner it was intended. No other technology or principle can protect information in the same way.

Lesson 1: Understanding and Installing Active Directory Rights Management Services

Many organizations choose to implement AD RMS in stages.

- The first stage focuses on internal use of intellectual property. In this stage, you concentrate on implementing proper access rights for the documentation you produce. Employees can view, read, and manage only content they are involved with. Content cannot be copied except under strict conditions.

- The second stage involves sharing content with partners. Here you begin to provide protected content to partner firms. Partners can view and access protected documents but cannot copy or otherwise share the information.

- The third stage involves a wider audience. Your intellectual property can be distributed outside the boundaries of your network in a protected mode. Because it is protected, it cannot be copied or distributed unless you give the required authorizations.

In each case, you must be sure to communicate your document protection policy fully to the people who will be working with your data. Employees must be fully trained on the solution to understand the impact of divulging information to unauthorized audiences. Partners should be provided with policy statements so they can understand how to protect your information. Then, when you reach wider audiences, you will have to make sure they also fully understand your protection policies so they can work with your information properly.

Each stage of the implementation will require additional components to further the reach of your protection strategies.

> **After this lesson, you will be able to:**
> - Understand the components that make up AD RMS services.
> - Understand different AD RMS deployment scenarios.
> - Understand AD RMS prerequisites for deployment.
> - Install AD RMS in various scenarios.
>
> **Estimated lesson time: 40 minutes**

Understanding AD RMS

As mentioned earlier, AD RMS is an updated version of the Microsoft Windows Rights Management Services available in Microsoft Windows Server 2003. With this release, Microsoft has included several new features that extend the functionality included in AD RMS. However, the scenarios you use to deploy AD RMS remain the same.

AD RMS works with a special AD RMS client to protect sensitive information. Protection is provided through the AD RMS server role, which is designed to provide certificate and licensing management. Information—configuration and logging—is persisted in a database. In test environments, you can rely on the Windows Internal Database (WID) included in Windows Server 2008, but in production environments, you should rely on a formal database engine such as Microsoft SQL Server 2005 or Microsoft SQL Server 2008 running on a separate server. This will provide the ability to load balance AD RMS through the installation of multiple servers running this role. WID does not support remote connections; therefore, only one server can use it. Internet Information Services (IIS) 7.0 provides the Web services upon which AD RMS relies, and the Microsoft Message Queuing service ensures transaction coordination in distributed environments. The AD RMS client provides access to AD RMS features on the desktop. In addition, an AD DS directory provides integrated authentication and administration. AD RMS relies on AD DS to authenticate users and verify that they are allowed to use the service. This makes up the AD RMS infrastructure. (See Figure 16-2.)

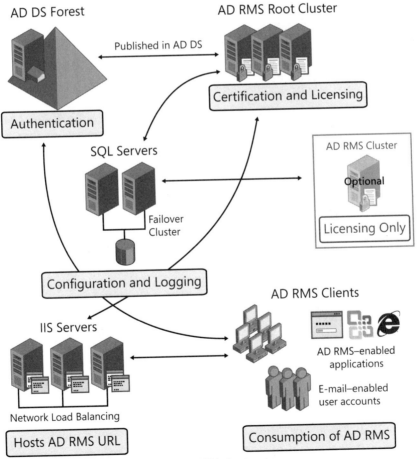

Figure 16-2   A highly available AD RMS infrastructure

The first time you install an AD RMS server, you create an AD RMS root cluster by default. A root cluster is designed to handle both certification and licensing requests. Only one root cluster can exist in an AD DS forest. You can also install licensing-only servers, which automatically form a licensing cluster. Clusters are available only if you deployed the AD RMS database on a separate server. Each time you add a new AD RMS server with either the root or the licensing role, it is automatically integrated into the corresponding existing cluster. Microsoft recommends that you rely on the root role more than on the licensing-only role for two reasons:

- Root clusters handle all AD RMS operations and are, therefore, multifunctional.
- Root and licensing-only clusters are independent; that is, they cannot share load balancing of the service. If you install all your servers as root servers, they automatically load balance each other.

After the infrastructure is in place, you can enable information-producing applications such as word processors, presentation tools, e-mail clients, and custom in-house applications to rely on AD RMS to provide information protection services. As users create the information, they define who will be able to read, write, modify, print, transfer, and otherwise manipulate the information. In addition, you can create policy templates that can apply a given configuration to documents as they are created.

Exam Tip   Keep in mind that any server installation in AD RMS automatically creates a cluster. This cluster is not to be confused with the Failover Clustering or Network Load Balancing services that are included in Windows Server 2008. The AD RMS cluster is designed to provide high availability and load balancing to ensure that the service is always available.

Usage rights are embedded directly within the documents you create so that the information remains protected even if it moves beyond your zone of authority. For example, if a protected document leaves your premises and arrives outside your network, it will remain protected because AD RMS settings are persistent. AD RMS offers a set of Web services, enabling you to extend it and integrate its features in your own information-producing applications. Because they are Web services, organizations can use them to integrate AD RMS features even in non-Windows environments.

MORE INFO   AD RMS

Find out more about AD RMS at *http://go.microsoft.com/fwlink/?LinkId=80907*.

New AD RMS Features

Active Directory Rights Management Services includes several new features:

- AD RMS is now a server role that is integrated into Windows Server 2008. In previous releases, the features supported by AD RMS were in a package that required a separate download. In addition, the Server Manager installation provides all dependencies and required component installations as well. Also, if no remote database is indicated during installation, Server Manager will automatically install Windows Internal Database.

■ As with most of the Windows Server 2008 server roles, AD RMS is administered through a Microsoft Management Console (MMC). Previous versions provided administration only through a Web interface.

■ AD RMS now also includes direct integration with Active Directory Federation Services, enabling you to extend your rights management policies beyond the firewall with your partners. This means your partners do not need their own AD RMS infrastructures and can rely on yours through AD FS to access AD RMS features. In previous releases, you could rely on only Windows Live IDs to federate RMS services. With the integration of AD RMS and AD FS, you no longer need to rely on a third party to protect information. However, to use federation, you must have an established federated trust before you install the AD RMS extension that integrates with AD FS, and you must use the latest RMS client–the Windows Vista client or the RMS client with SP2 for versions of Windows earlier than Windows Vista. For information on AD FS, see Chapter 17, "Active Directory Federation Services."

■ AD RMS servers are also self-enrolled when they are created. Enrollment creates a server licensor certificate (SLC), which grants the server the right to participate in the AD RMS structure. Earlier versions required access to the Microsoft Enrollment Center through the Internet to issue and sign the SLC. AD RMS relies on a self-enrollment certificate that is included in Windows Server 2008. Because of this, you can now run AD RMS in isolated networks without requiring Internet access of any kind.

■ Finally, AD RMS includes new administration roles so that you can delegate specific AD RMS tasks without having to grant excessive administration rights. Four local administrative roles are created:

  ❑ AD RMS Enterprise Administrators, which can manage all aspects of AD RMS. This group includes the user account used to install the role as well as the local administrators group.

  ❑ AD RMS Template Administrators, which supports the ability to read information about the AD RMS infrastructure as well as list, create, modify, and export rights policy templates.

  ❑ AD RMS Auditors, which enables members to manage logs and reports. Auditors have read-only access to AD RMS infrastructure information.

  ❑ AD RMS Service, which contains the AD RMS service account that is identified during the role installation.

Because each of these groups is local, create corresponding groups in your AD DS directory and insert these groups within the local groups on each AD RMS server. Then, when you need to grant rights to an administrative role, all you need to do is add the user's account to the group in AD DS.

> **Exam Tip**   Delegation is an important aspect of AD RMS administration. Pay close attention to the various delegation roles and the groups that support them.

> **MORE INFO**   **Features available in previous releases**
>
> For information on features released in RMS before Windows Server 2008, go to *http://go.microsoft.com/fwlink/?LinkId=68637*.

Basically, when you protect information through AD RMS, you rely on the AD RMS server to issue rights account certificates. These certificates identify the trusted entities—users, groups, computers, applications, or services—that can create and publish rights-enabled content. After a content publisher has been trusted, it can assign rights and conditions to the content it creates. Each time a user establishes a protection policy on a document, AD RMS issues a publishing license for the content. By integrating this license in the content, AD RMS binds it so that the license becomes permanently attached and no longer requires access to an AD RMS system to provide document or content protection.

Usage rights are integrated in any form of binary data that supports usage within or outside your network as well as online or offline. When content is protected, it is encrypted with special encryption keys, much like the keys created when using AD CS. To view the data, users must access it through an AD RMS–enabled browser or application. If the application is not AD RMS–enabled, users will not be able to manipulate the information because the application will not be able to read the protection policy to decrypt the data properly.

When other users access the rights-protected content, their AD RMS clients request a usage license from the server. If the user is also a trusted entity, the AD RMS server issues this use license. The use license reads the protection license for this document and applies these usage rights to the document for the duration of its lifetime.

To facilitate the publishing process, trusted users can create protection licenses from predefined templates that can be applied through the tools they are already familiar with—word processors, e-mail clients, and the like. Each template applies a specific predefined usage policy, as shown in Figure 16-3.

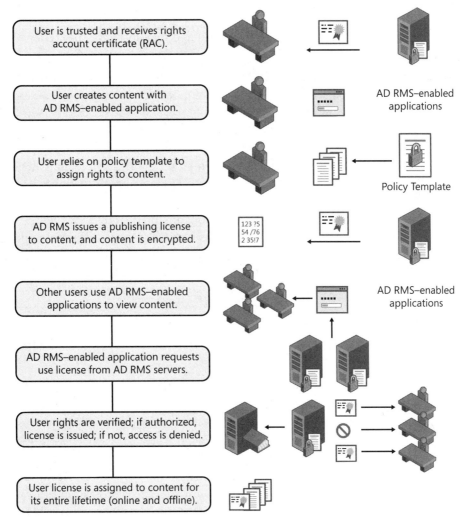

User is trusted and receives rights account certificate (RAC).

User creates content with AD RMS–enabled application.

AD RMS–enabled applications

User relies on policy template to assign rights to content.

Policy Template

AD RMS issues a publishing license to content, and content is encrypted.

Other users use AD RMS–enabled applications to view content.

AD RMS–enabled applications

AD RMS–enabled application requests use license from AD RMS servers.

User rights are verified; if authorized, license is issued; if not, access is denied.

User license is assigned to content for its entire lifetime (online and offline).

Figure 16-3 AD RMS publishing process

AD RMS Installation Scenarios

Each organization has its own needs and requirements for information protection. For this reason, AD RMS supports several deployment scenarios. These scenarios include:

- **Single server deployment** Install AD RMS on a single server. This installs the WID as the support database. Because all the components are local, you cannot scale this deployment to support high availability. Use the single server deployment only in test environments. If you want to use this deployment to test AD RMS beyond the firewall, you will have to add appropriate AD RMS exceptions.

- **Internal deployment** Install AD RMS on multiple servers tied to an AD DS directory. You must use a separate server to host the AD RMS database; otherwise, you will not be able to load balance the AD RMS role.

- **Extranet deployment** When users are mobile and do not remain within the confines of your network, you must deploy AD RMS in an extranet—a special perimeter network that provides internal services to authorized users. In this scenario, you will need to configure appropriate firewall exceptions and add a special extranet URL on an external-facing Web server to allow external client connections.

MORE INFO   AD RMS configuration in an extranet

For more information on how to configure AD RMS to collaborate outside of the organizational network, see the "Deploying Active Directory Rights Management Services in an Extranet Step-by-Step Guide" at *http://go.microsoft.com/fwlink/?LinkID=72138*.

- **Multiforest deployment** When you have existing partnerships that are based on AD DS forest trusts, you must perform a multiforest deployment. In this case, you must deploy multiple AD RMS installations, one in each forest. Then, assign a Secure Sockets Layer (SSL) certificate to each Web site that hosts the AD RMS clusters in each forest. You must also extend the AD DS forest schema to include AD RMS objects. However, if you are using Microsoft Exchange Server in each forest, the extensions will already exist. Finally, your AD RMS service account—the account that runs the service—will need to be trusted in each forest.

MORE INFO   Multiforest AD RMS deployments

For more information on this deployment model, see *http://go.microsoft.com/fwlink/?LinkId=72139*.

- **AD RMS with AD FS deployment** You can also extend the AD RMS root cluster to other forests through Active Directory Federation Services. To do so, you must prepare the following:
  1. Assign an SSL certificate to the Web site hosting the AD RMS root cluster. This will ensure secure communications between the cluster and the AD FS resource server.

2. Install the root cluster.

3. Prepare a federated trust relationship before you install the Identity Federation Support role service of AD RMS.

4. Create a claims-aware application on the AD FS resource partner server for both the certification and the licensing pipelines of AD RMS.

5. Assign the Generate Security Audits user right to the AD RMS service account.

6. Define the extranet cluster URL in AD RMS and then install the AD RMS Identity Federation Support role service through Server Manager. Have the federation URL on hand during installation.

MORE INFO   AD RMS and AD FS deployment

For more information on the AD RMS and AD FS deployment, see *http://go.microsoft.com /fwlink/?LinkId=72135.*

■ **Licensing-only server deployment**   In complex forest environments, you might want to deploy a licensing-only AD RMS cluster in addition to the root cluster. In this case, you must first assign an SSL certificate to the Web site hosting the AD RMS root cluster and then install the root cluster. After you meet these conditions, you can install licensing-only servers.

MORE INFO   Set up a licensing-only AD RMS cluster

For more information on how to set up a licensing-only AD RMS cluster, see *http:// go.microsoft.com/fwlink/?LinkId=72141.*

■ **Upgrade Windows RMS to AD RMS**   If you upgrade from an existing Windows RMS installation, you must perform the following activities:

1. Make sure your RMS systems are upgraded to RMS Service Pack 1 prior to the upgrade.

2. Back up all servers, and back up the configuration database. Store it in a secure location.

3. If you are using offline enrollment to set up your Windows RMS environment, make sure the enrollment is complete before the upgrade.

4. If you already have service connection points in Active Directory directory service, make sure you use the same URL for the upgrade.

5. If your Windows RMS database is running Microsoft SQL Server Desktop Engine (MSDE), you must upgrade to SQL Server before you upgrade to AD RMS.

6. Clear the RMS Message Queuing queue to make sure all messages are written to the RMS logging database prior to upgrade.

7. Upgrade the root cluster before upgrading the licensing-only server. This will provide the root cluster's self-signed SLC to the licensing server when you upgrade it.

8. Upgrade all other servers in the RMS cluster.

These scenarios provide the most common deployment structures for AD RMS.

Installing Active Directory Rights Management Services

A full installation of AD RMS can be quite complex. Keep in mind that a single cluster can exist within an AD DS forest and make sure you have all the prerequisites in place before you proceed. Also, because of the AD RMS dependencies, these prerequisites are comprehensive. During this preparation process, you'll be deciding how to deploy your AD RMS systems. Will you be using only root cluster members, or will you be dividing tasks between root and licensing-only clusters? Do you need interaction with outside partners? Will your deployment be internal only? Answers to each of these questions will help form the architecture of your AD RMS deployment and implementation.

After you have all the prerequisites in place, you can proceed to the actual installation. This is a multistep operation that requires care and attention.

MORE INFO AD RMS cluster installation instructions

For more information on the installation of AD RMS clusters, go to *http://technet2.microsoft.com /windowsserver2008/en/library/3f1d6d09-4e85-4ad9-83ff-a8720b5441d61033.mspx?mfr=true*.

Preparing AD RMS Installation Prerequisites

There are several prerequisites to AD RMS installation. If you are setting up only a test environment, you have few items to consider, but when you are ready to deploy AD RMS into a production environment, you will want to take the utmost care to deploy it correctly. For this reason, endeavor to make your test environment match the requirements of your production environment so that no surprises pop up when you perform the actual deployment.

IMPORTANT Additional AD RMS installation options

Note that AD RMS is not supported and does not run in Server Core installations of Windows Server 2008. However, AD RMS is a good candidate for virtualization under Hyper-V, especially in test environments. Keep this in mind when you plan and prepare your AD RMS deployment.

Begin with the prerequisites. Table 16-1 outlines the basic requirements for an AD RMS deployment. Table 16-2 outlines other considerations you need to keep in mind when preparing for AD RMS.

Table 16-1   **RMS System Requirements**

Hardware/Software	Requirement	Recommended
Processor	One Pentium, 4.3 GHz or higher	Two Pentium, 4.3 GHz or higher
RAM	512 MB	1024 MB
Hard disk space	40 GB	80 GB
Operating system	Any Windows Server 2008 edition except Windows Server Web Edition and Itanium-based systems	Windows Server Enterprise Edition or Windows Server Datacenter Edition
File system	FAT32 or NTFS	NTFS
Messaging	Message Queuing	
Web Services	IIS with ASP.NET enabled	

Table 16-2   **AD RMS Considerations**

Component	Consideration
Web Server URL	Reserve URLs that will not change and do not include a computer name nor use localhost. Also, use different URLs for internal and external connections.
Active Directory Domain Services	An AD DS domain running on Windows 2000 SP3, Windows Server 2003, or Windows Server 2008. Upgrade or run a new AD DS domain on Windows Server 2008 if possible.
Installation location	AD RMS must be installed in the same domain as its potential users. If possible, install a multidomain forest and install AD RMS in the child production domain.
Domain User accounts	E-mail address configured in AD DS.
Service Account	Standard domain user account that is a member of the local Administrators group. Domain-based service account that is assigned the Generate Security Audits user right.
Installation Account	A domain-based account. Must not be on a smart card. Must have local administrator privileges. To generate service connection points, must be a member of Enterprise Admins. To use an external database, must be a member of System Administrators role on DB server.

Table 16-2   AD RMS Considerations

Component	Consideration
Database server	Windows Internal Database or SQL Server 2005 with SP2 or later, including stored procedures to perform operations. For fault tolerance, use SQL Server 2005 with SP2 installed on a separate computer.
Database instance	Create and name the AD RMS database instance and start the SQL Server Browser service before installation.
Installation certificate	Obtain an SSL certificate for the AD RMS cluster. Use certificates only in testing environments. Obtain a trusted certificate from an external third-party commercial CA and install the certificate prior to the AD RMS installation.
Cluster key protection	Store the cluster key in the AD RMS configuration database. If possible, use a hardware protection device to store the cluster key and install it on each server before you install the AD RMS role.
DNS configuration	Create custom CNAME records for the root cluster URL and the database server. Use separate CNAME records for the AD RMS cluster URL and for the database server to protect against system loss.
Server licensor certificate name	Prepare an official name before you install. Use an official name, for example, the name of your organization.
AD RMS–enabled client	AD RMS–enabled browser or application (Word, Microsoft Office Outlook, or PowerPoint in Office 2007 Enterprise Edition, Office 2007 Professional Plus, or Office 2007 Ultimate Edition)
Smart card usage	Can be integrated in AD RMS but not for setup. Do not use a smart card for the installation account, or the account will fail.
Client OS	Windows Vista includes AD RMS client by default; XP requires Windows RMS Client with SP2.

Exam Tip   Pay attention to the installation prerequisites in Table 16-1 as well as the considerations in Table 16-2. They are complex and, because of this, will certainly appear on the exam.

NOTE   AD RMS client for Windows XP

To obtain the AD RMS client for Windows XP, go to *http://www.microsoft.com/downloads/details.aspx?FamilyId=02DA5107-2919-414B-A5A3-3102C7447838&displaylang=en.*

As you can see from Table 16-1, installing AD RMS in a production environment is not a trivial matter.

MORE INFO **Hardware and software considerations for AD RMS**

For more information, see "Pre-installation Information for Active Directory Rights Management Services" at *http://go.microsoft.com/fwlink/?LinkId=84733.*

Understanding AD RMS Certificates

Because it encrypts and signs data, AD RMS, like AD CS, relies on certificates and assigns these certificates to the various users in the AD RMS infrastructure. It also uses licenses that are in an Extensible Rights Markup Language (XrML) format. Because these licenses are embedded in the content users create, they are also a form of certificate. Like AD CS, the AD RMS hierarchy forms a chain of trust that validates the certificate or license when it is used. Table 16-3 outlines the various certificates you require in an AD RMS infrastructure.

Table 16-3 AD RMS Certificates

Certificate	Content
Server licensor certificate (SLC)	The SLC is a self-signed certificate generated during the AD RMS setup of the first server in a root cluster. Other members of the root cluster will share this SLC. If you create a licensing-only cluster, it will generate its own SLC and share it with members of its cluster. The default duration for an SLC is 250 years.
Rights account certificate (RAC)	RACs are issued to trusted users who have an e-mail-enabled account in AD DS. RACs are generated when the user first tries to open rights-protected content. Standard RACs identify users in relation to their computers and have a duration of 365 days. Temporary RACs do not tie the user to a specific computer and are valid for only 15 minutes. The RAC contains the public key of the user as well as his or her private key. The private key is encrypted with the computer's private key. (See "Machine certificate," listed later in this table.)
Client licensor certificate (CLC)	After the user has a RAC and launches an AD RMS–enabled application, the application automatically sends a request for a CLC to the AD RMS cluster. The client computer must be connected for this process to work, but after the CLC is obtained, the user can apply AD RMS policies even offline. Because the CLC is tied to the client's RAC, it is automatically invalidated if the RAC is revoked. The CLC includes the client licensor public key, the client licensor private key that is encrypted by the user's public key, and the AD RMS cluster's public key. The CLC private key is used to encrypt content.

Table 16-3   **AD RMS Certificates**

Certificate	Content
Machine certificate	The first time an AD RMS–enabled application is used, a machine certificate is created. The AD RMS client in Windows automatically manages this process with the AD RMS cluster. This certificate creates a lockbox on the computer to correlate the machine certificate with the user's profile. The machine certificate contains the public key for the activated computer. The private key is contained within the lockbox on the computer.
Publishing license	The publishing license is created when the user saves content in a rights-protected mode. This license lists which users can use the content and under which conditions as well as the rights each user has to the content. This license includes the symmetric content key for decrypting content as well as the public key of the cluster.
Use license	The use license is assigned to a user who opens rights-protected content. It is tied to the user's RAC and lists the access rights the user has to the content. If the RAC is not available, the user cannot work with rights-protected content. It contains the symmetric key for decrypting content. This key is encrypted with the public key of the user.

Exam Tip   Pay attention to the different certificates and licenses used in AD RMS. They are good candidates for exam questions.

Installation Procedure

Now that you understand the various requirements and processes that make up an AD RMS installation, you are ready to proceed. Ensure that you have prepared all the requirements listed in Table 16-1, and then perform the following steps.

Install AD RMS

1. Log on to a member server running Windows Server 2008, using Enterprise Administrative credentials.

   This server can be running Windows Server 2008 Standard Edition, Windows Server 2008 Enterprise Edition, or Windows Server 2008 Datacenter Edition.

IMPORTANT Use member servers

Do not install AD RMS on a domain controller. Use a member server only! With the advent of virtualization, aside from the operating system licensing aspect, there is no longer any reason to create multipurpose domain controllers. Each virtual machine can have its own purpose and run independently of all other services.

2. Launch Server Manager from the Administrative Tools program group.

3. Right-click the Roles node in the tree pane, and select Add Roles.

4. Review the Before You Begin information, and click Next.

5. On the Select Server Roles page, select Active Directory Rights Management Services, and click Next.

    The Add Role Wizard will ask you to add the Web Server (IIS) role with the required features, Windows Process Activation Service (WPAS), and Message Queuing.

6. Click Add Required Role Services if these services weren't installed prior to the installation of AD RMS. Click Next when you are ready.

7. On the Active Directory Rights Management Services page, review the information about the selected role, and then click Next.

8. On the Select Role Services page, make sure the Active Directory Rights Management Server check box is selected, and then click Next.

    Do not choose the Identity Federation Support option at this time. You cannot install this option until the AD FS federation relationship has been created.

9. On the Create Or Join An AD RMS Cluster page, select Create A New AD RMS Cluster option, and then click Next.

    If the cluster was already created and you were installing a second server, you would select Join An Existing AD RMS cluster because there can be only one cluster per forest.

10. On the Select Configuration Database page, select the Use A Different Database Server, and then click Next.

    If you choose to use Windows Internal Database to host the AD RMS databases for a single-server installation, steps 11 and 12 are not required. Keep in mind that when you use a WID instance, you will not be able to join other servers to this cluster. Use WID only in test environments if you do not have the resources to create a proper database server.

11. Click Select to locate the server that hosts the database, type the name, and then click Check Names. Click OK.

12. In the Database Instance drop-down list, select the appropriate instance, click Validate, and then click Next.

13. On the Specify Service Account page, click Specify, type the domain user account and password that should be used as the AD RMS service account, click OK, and then click Next.

   Remember that this account must be a member of the local Administrators group.

14. On the Configure AD RMS Cluster Key Storage page, select Use CSP Key Storage, and then click Next.

   You choose to protect the AD RMS cluster key by using a cryptographic storage provider because it is a more secure protection method. You will need to select the storage provider and then install this certificate on each new AD RMS server before you can add them to the root cluster. You can also store the key in the AD RMS database, but doing so is less secure than with a cryptographic service provider (CSP).

15. On the Specify AD RMS Cluster Key page, select the CSP to use. You can select either software or hardware cryptographic service providers. Use the one that best fits your security policy guidelines, and select Create A New Key With The Selected CSP. Click Next.

   You can also use an existing key, but do so only when you are recovering from an unrecoverable configuration database.

16. On the Select AD RMS Cluster Web Site page, select the Web site where you want to install the AD RMS Web services, and click Next. If you did not prepare the Web site beforehand, the name of the Web site will be Default Web Site.

17. On the Specify Cluster Address page, select Use An SSL-Encrypted Connection (https://).

   As a security best practice, the AD RMS cluster should be provisioned by using an SSL-encrypted connection. You should be using a certificate provided by a third-party commercial certification authority (CA) so that it can be automatically trusted by all parties. This certificate should already be installed on the server so that you can select it as you proceed through the installation.

   Do not use an unencrypted connection. You cannot rely on open connections if you intend to use Identity Federation for your AD RMS implementation.

18. In the Internal Address section of the Specify Cluster Address page, type the fully qualified domain name (FQDN) of the AD RMS cluster, and click Validate. If validation succeeds, click Next.

   This must be a valid FQDN, which cannot be changed afterward. If you want to change the default port on which AD RMS communicates, you can do it on this page of the wizard as well. You must do it now because you will not be able to change it at a later date.

19. Click Validate, and then click Next.

20. On the Choose A Server Authentication Certificate For SSL Encryption page, select Choose An Existing Certificate For SSL Encryption (Recommended), select the certificate you installed, and then click Next.

If you did not install the certificate prior to setup, you can click Import to import the certificate now. You can also use a self-signed certificate, or, if you did not obtain the certificate prior to installation, you can select the third option, to choose encryption later. Note, however, that you will not be able to complete your installation until you obtain and install this certificate if you choose the last option.

IMPORTANT **Self-signed certificates**

Self-signed certificates should be used for test environments only. In a production environment, use a proper SSL certificate issued from a commercial certification authority.

---

21. On the Name The Server Licensor Certificate page, type a valid name to identify the AD RMS cluster, and then click Next.

22. On the Register AD RMS Service Connection Point page, select Register The AD RMS Service Connection Point Now, and then click Next.

    This action will register the AD RMS service connection point (SCP) in the AD DS.

IMPORTANT **Access rights for SCP creation**

To register the AD RMS SCP, you must be logged on to the AD RMS server, using a user account with write access to the Services container in AD DS—that is, a member of the Enterprise Admins group.

If you are preparing the cluster and need to install additional cluster members before it starts servicing requests, select Register The AD RMS Service Connection Point Later. Then join the other cluster member and, when you are ready, create the SCP.

23. On the Web Server (IIS) page, review the information about IIS, and click Next.

    The pages mentioned in steps 23 and 24 are available only if IIS is not preinstalled on the server.

24. On the next page, keep the Web server default selections, and click Next.

25. On the Confirm Installation Selections page, review your choices, and click Install.

26. When the installation is complete, click Finish to close the installation wizard. Log off and log back on to update the permissions granted to the logged-on user account.

    The user account logged on when the AD RMS server role was installed is automatically made a member of the AD RMS Enterprise Administrators group. This gives you access to all AD RMS operations.

    The installation is complete. (See Figure 16-4.)

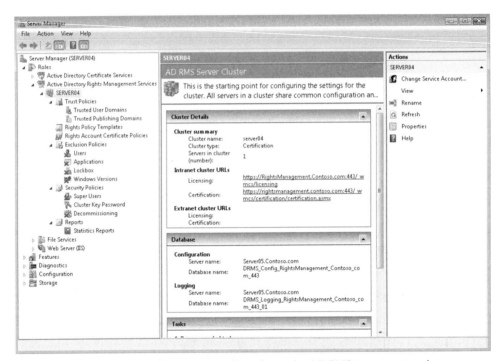

Figure 16-4 Once the installation is complete, the entire AD RMS tree structure becomes available in Service Manager

MORE INFO AD RMS cluster

For more information on how to install an AD RMS cluster, see *http://technet2.microsoft.com /windowsserver2008/en/library/74272acc-0f2d-4dc2-876f-15b156a0b4e01033.mspx?mfr=true*. For a step-by-step installation guide, see *http://go.microsoft.com/fwlink/?LinkId=72134*. To provide high availability for the cluster, you must install additional cluster members. For infor- mation on this installation, go to *http://technet2.microsoft.com/windowsserver2008/en/library /1bc393b9-5ce9-4950-acae-63a463ccfc361033.mspx?mfr=true*.

PRACTICE Installing AD RMS

In this practice, you will install AD RMS into a new cluster. First, you must add a DNS record. In the following exercises, you will create the service account and the AD RMS role groups in the directory, create and install a Web Server certificate, and then proceed to the installation. Be sure the computers listed in the "Before You Begin" section of this chapter are running before you proceed. You need SERVER01, SERVER04, and SERVER05 for this practice.

▶ **Exercise 1   Prepare the DNS Record**

In this exercise, you will create a CNAME record to prepare for the AD RMS cluster URL.

1. Log on to SERVER01, using the domain Administrator account.
2. Launch Server Manager from the Administrative Tools program group.
3. Expand Roles\DNS Server\DNS\SERVER01\Forward Lookup Zones\contoso.com.
4. Right-click in the details pane, and select New Alias (CNAME).
5. In the New Resource Record dialog box, type an alias name of **RightsManagement** and assign it to SERVER04.contoso.com in the Fully Qualified Domain Name (FQDN) For Target Host section of the dialog box. Click OK.

    You have created a new record for the AD RMS cluster URL. It will be updated to other servers as you perform the other exercises.

▶ **Exercise 2   Prepare the Directory**

In this exercise, you will create a service account and four groups for AD RMS administration delegation.

1. Log on to SERVER01, using the domain Administrator account, if you haven't done so already.
2. Launch Server Manager from the Administrative Tools program group.
3. Expand Roles\Active Directory Domain Services\Active Directory Users and Computers \contoso.com. Create the Admins\Service Identities OU structure.
4. Right-click the Service Identities OU, choose New, and then select User.
5. Name the user **ADRMSService** and use this name for both the logon and the pre–Windows 2000 logon names. Click Next.
6. Assign a complex password, clear User Must Change Password At Next Logon, and select Password Never Expires. Click Next, and then click Finish to create the account.
7. Now create the AD RMS administration groups under Contoso.com\Admins\Admin Groups\Server Delegations OU. Create these OUs if they are not already created.
8. Create four global security groups. Right-click in the details pane, select New, and then choose Group. Type the name, and click OK. Create the following four groups:
    - ❑ AD RMS Enterprise Administrators
    - ❑ AD RMS Template Administrators
    - ❑ AD RMS Auditors
    - ❑ AD RMS Service Account
9. Open the AD RMS Service Account group (right-click and choose Properties), and click the Members tab. Add the ADRMSService account to this group, and then click OK.
10. Log on to SERVER03, using the domain Administrator account, if you have not done so already.
11. Launch Server Manager from the Administrative Tools program group.

12. Expand Configuration\Local Users and Groups\Groups.

13. Select the Administrators group, and open it.

14. Add the AD RMS Service Account group to this group, and click OK.

     You are ready to proceed with the installation.

▶ Exercise 3   Prepare a Web Server Certificate

Because AD RMS requires SSL-encrypted Web connections, you must create and install a Web server certificate before you can proceed with the installation. Note that for this practice to work, you must have performed the practices in Chapter 15, "Active Directory Certificate Services and Public Key Infrastructures," first.

1. Log on to SERVER04, using the domain Administrator account.

    This will grant you Enterprise Administrator credentials, which are required to create the SCP. These rights are required for Exercise 4.

2. Launch Server Manager from the Administrative Tools program group.

3. Expand Roles\Active Directory Certificate Services\Certificate Templates (SERVER04). Note that all the existing templates are listed in the details pane.

4. Select the Web Server template in the details pane, and right-click it to select Duplicate Template.

5. Select the version of Windows Server to support, in this case, Windows Server 2008, and click OK.

6. Name the template **Web Server WS08** and set the following options. Leave all other options as is.

    a. On the General tab, make sure you select Publish Certificate In Active Directory.

    b. On the Security tab, add the computer account for SERVER04. Click Add, click Object Types, select Computers, and then click OK.

    c. Type **SERVER04**, click Check Names, click OK, and then click OK.

    d. Grant SERVER04 the Allow:Read and Enroll permissions, and click OK.

    e. Leave all other settings as is.

7. Click OK.

    Template issuance is performed in the Certification Authority console section of Server Manager.

8. Expand Roles\Active Directory Certificate Services\Contoso-*issuing-serve*\Certificate Templates.

9. To issue a template, right-click Certificate Templates, choose New, and then select Certificate Template To Issue.

10. In the Enable Certificate Templates dialog box, select Web Server WS08, and click OK.

▶ **Exercise 4   Install a Web Server Certificate**

Now, you need to request and install the certificate.

1. Move to the Start menu, type **mmc** in the Search box, and then press Enter.
2. Click Add/Remove Snap-ins from the File menu, select the Certificates snap-in, and click Add.
3. Choose Computer Account, and click Next.
4. Make sure Local Computer is selected, click Finish, and then OK.
5. Click Save As from the File menu, navigate to your Documents folder, and name it **Computer Certificates**.
6. Expand the Certificates (Local Computer)\Persona l\Certificates node.
7. Right-click Certificates, select All Tasks, and then choose Request New Certificate. Click Next.
8. Select the Web Server WS08 certificate, and then click More Information to enroll for this certificate.
9. In the Certificate Properties dialog box, on the Subject tab, add the following values:
    a. In the *Subject Name Value* field, ensure that Full DN is selected, type **CN=SERVER04,DC=Contoso,DC=com**, and then click Add.
    b. Click the Alternative Name section, select URL in the Type drop-down list, enter **RightsManagement.contoso.com** in the *Value* field, and then click Add.
    c. Click the General tab and type **Contoso DRM** in the *Friendly Name* field and **Web Server Certificate** in the *Description* field.
    d. Click the Private Key tab, expand the Key Options section, and select the Make Private Key Exportable and Allow Private Key To Be Archived check boxes.
10. Click OK, and then click Enroll. Click Finish.
11. To verify that the certificate has been issued, click Certificates, and view the certificate in the details pane.
12. Close the Certificates console.

    You are ready to install AD RMS.

▶ **Exercise 5   Install an AD RMS Root Cluster**

Ensure that you have at least SERVER01, SERVER03, and SERVER05 running, and make sure the SQL server on SERVER05 is also running. SERVER03 is the server you used to perform the practice operations in Chapter 15. Because of this, it should include AD CS and already have a certificate that you can use during this operation.

1. Log on to SERVER03, using the domain Administrator account. This will grant you Enterprise Administrator credentials, which are required to create the SCP.
2. Launch Server Manager from the Administrative Tools program group.

3. Right-click the Roles node in the tree pane, and select Add Roles.

4. Review the Before You Begin information, and click Next.

5. On the Select Server Roles page, select Active Directory Rights Management Services.

   The Add Role Wizard will ask you to add the Web Server (IIS) role with the required features, Windows Process Activation Service (WPAS), and Message Queuing.

6. Click Add Required Role Services if these services weren't installed prior to the installation of AD RMS. Click Next.

7. On the Active Directory Rights Management Services page, review the information about the selected role, and then click Next.

8. On the Select Role Services page, ensure that the Active Directory Rights Management Server is selected, and then click Next.

9. On the Create Or Join An AD RMS Cluster page, select Create A New AD RMS Cluster, and then click Next.

10. On the Select Configuration Database page, select the Use A Different Database Server, and then click Next.

    If you choose to use Windows Internal Database to host the AD RMS databases for a single-server installation, steps 11 and 12 are not required. However, using WID is valid for test purposes only.

11. Click Select to locate SERVER05, type the server name, click Check Names, and then click OK.

12. In Database Instance, select the Default instance, click Validate, and then click Next.

13. On the Specify Service Account page, click Specify, type **ADRMSService** and its password, click OK, and then click Next.

14. On the Configure AD RMS Cluster Key Storage page, select Use AD RMS Centrally Managed Key Storage, and then click Next.

    You choose to protect the AD RMS cluster key by using that database because it simplifies the exercise and does not require additional components; however, normally, you should provide the best protection for this key, through a CSP provider.

15. On the Specify AD RMS Cluster Key Password page, type a strong password, confirm it, and then click Next.

16. On the Select AD RMS Cluster Web Site page, select Default Web Site, and then click Next.

17. On the Specify Cluster Address the page, select Use An SSL-Encrypted Connection (https://).

    As a security best practice, the AD RMS cluster should be provisioned by using an SSL-encrypted connection.

18. In the Internal Address section, type **RightsManagement.contoso.com**, leave the port number as is, and click Validate. When the validation succeeds, click Next.

19. On the Choose A Server Authentication Certificate For SSL Encryption page, select Choose An Existing Certificate For SSL Encryption (Recommended), select the SERVER04 certificate, and click Next.

    If you have not run through the practice exercises in Chapter 15 yet, and the server does not include an appropriate certificate or AD CS, use a self-signed certificate.

20. On the Name The Server Licensor Certificate page, type **Contoso DRM** to identify the AD RMS cluster, and then click Next.

21. On the Register AD RMS Service Connection Point page, select Register The AD RMS Service Connection Point Now, and then click Next.

    This action will register the AD RMS service connection point (SCP) in AD DS.

22. On the Web Server (IIS) page, review the information about IIS, and then click Next.

23. On the Select Role Services page, keep the Web server default selections, and click Next.

24. On the Confirm Installation Selections page, review your choices, and then click Install.

25. When the installation is complete, click Finish to close the installation wizard.

26. Log off and log back on to update the permissions granted to the logged-on user account.

    The user account that is logged on when the AD RMS server role is installed is automatically made a member of the AD RMS Enterprise Administrators group. This gives you access to all AD RMS operations. Your installation is complete.

IMPORTANT   AD RMS administration groups

To render the administration groups you created in AD DS operational, you must add them to the respective local groups on this server. In a production environment, you need to perform this additional step to complete your setup.

Lesson Summary

- AD RMS is designed to provide support for data protection services through digital rights management. To do so, it relies on a complex infrastructure that requires additional services such as AD DS, SQL Server, Internet Information Services, and, potentially, AD FS for interforest partnerships.

- Users must have an e-mail–enabled account in an AD DS domain to use AD RMS services.

- Users must also rely on AD RMS–enabled applications to protect content. These applications can be productivity tools such as Office Word, Outlook, PowerPoint, Internet Explorer, or a custom AD RMS–enabled application. Without the application, you cannot view or work with protected content.

- Windows Vista includes the AD RMS client by default, but Windows XP does not. In Windows XP, you must download and install Windows Rights Management Client with SP2.

Lesson Review

You can use the following questions to test your knowledge of the information in Lesson 1, "Understanding and Installing Active Directory Rights Management Services." The questions are also available on the companion CD if you prefer to review them in electronic form.

NOTE Answers

Answers to these questions and explanations of why each answer choice is right or wrong are located in the "Answers" section at the end of the book.

---

1. You are an administrator for the *contoso.com* domain. You have just finished installing AD RMS, and now you want to configure AD RMS. Setup has completed without any errors. However, when you begin working with the AD RMS server, you get an error message. What could be the problem?

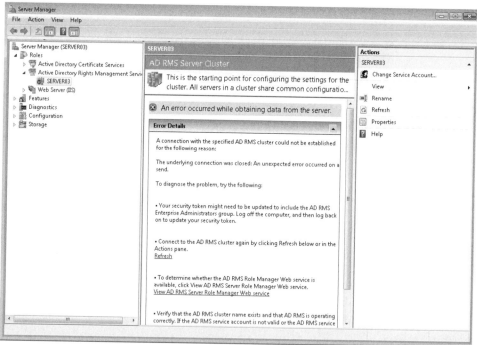

   A. Your server is not running AD RMS.

   B. The server certificate is invalid, and, because of this, the AD RMS server will not start.

   C. Your server is not a member of an AD DS domain.

   D. Your account does not have appropriate privileges to manage AD RMS.

Lesson 2: Configuring and Using Active Directory Rights Management Services

AD RMS installations can be complex to prepare, but after you have worked with the proper installation preparation process, your installations will be flawless. After your servers are installed, however, you must complete the configuration of the AD RMS cluster and prepare the usage policies you want to implement in your network. This involves several tasks:

- If you want to make AD RMS available outside your network, you must add an extranet cluster URL to your configuration.

- If you want to integrate AD RMS services with partners, you must configure proxy settings and install Identity Federation Support. Keep in mind that you must have a working AD FS implementation to add these components to your infrastructure. You must also configure trust policies for the interoperation of your AD RMS cluster with other clusters.

- You must configure the various AD RMS certificates to ensure that you set up proper validation periods.

- If your organization has decided that your rights-protection policies will not affect the entire organization and will target only a specific group of users or departments, for example, the legal department, you must configure exclusion policies.

- You must prepare user accounts for integration with AD RMS.

- You must prepare policy templates for your organization to use. These templates will facilitate the rights-protection process for your users.

- You must be familiar with the various AD RMS clients so that you can support them if your users experience problems with it.

- AD RMS relies on three databases for operation. You must be aware of these databases and maintain them for a proper AD RMS operation.

These operations will finalize the deployment of your AD RMS cluster.

After this lesson, you will be able to:
- Configure extranet URLs.
- Prepare for integration with partners.
- Work with AD RMS certificates.
- Prepare user accounts for AD RMS.
- Prepare exclusion policies.
- Work with policy templates.
- Work with the AD RMS databases.

Estimated lesson time: 30 minutes

Configuring AD RMS

AD RMS configuration, unlike Windows Rights Management Services, is performed through the MMC. This console is integrated in Server Manager but is also available as a standalone console through Remote Server Administration Tools (RSAT). Each of the tasks you need to perform to finalize your configuration is available through this console.

MORE INFO Configure AD RMS

For more information on configuring AD RMS, go to *http://technet2.microsoft.com /windowsserver2008/en/library/73829489-45f1-415b-90ab-061a263d1ef61033.mspx?mfr=true*.

Creating an Extranet URL

When you want to extend your AD RMS infrastructure to mobile users or teleworkers outside your internal network, you must configure an extranet URL. Use the following procedure.

1. Log on to a server that is a member of the root cluster, using AD RMS Enterprise Administrators credentials.
2. Launch Server Manager from the Administrative Tools program group.
3. Expand Roles\Active Directory Rights Management Services*servername*.
4. Right-click the server name, and choose Properties.
5. Click the Cluster URLs tab.
6. On the Cluster URLs page, enable Extranet URLs, and add the appropriate URL data for both Licensing and Certification.

   These URLs must point to a valid IIS installation in the extranet and should be permanent. Proper DNS registration should also be implemented for these URLs. Use SSL encryption for the communication through Secure HTTP or HTTPS connections. Finally, remember to create the appropriate virtual directories to host the AD RMS data.

7. Click OK to close the dialog box and apply the change.

   Your extranet URLs are ready.

Configuring Trust Policies

Although you can't enable federation support until you have a working AD FS infrastructure in place, you can learn about the various models AD RMS supports to provide federation of your DRM policies. AD RMS can support four trust models:

■ Trusted user domains enable your AD RMS cluster to process requests for other AD RMS clusters located in different AD DS forests. Trusted user domains are added by importing the server licensor certificate from the AD RMS cluster you want to trust into your own cluster.

- Trusted publishing domains enable your own AD RMS cluster to issue use licenses for content that was protected by another AD RMS cluster. To create a trusted publishing domain, you must import the publishing cluster's SLC as well as its private key into your own cluster.
- Windows Live ID trusts enable users who have a valid Windows Live ID (formerly known as Microsoft Passport) to use rights-protected content but not to create it.
- Federated trusts are established through AD FS and extend the operation of your AD RMS cluster to the forests with which you have established a federated trust.

Each of these trust types extends your AD RMS authority beyond the limits of your own forest.

MORE INFO Create AD RMS trusts

To learn more about working with AD RMS trusts, go to *http://technet2.microsoft.com /windowsserver2008/en/library/67d89efe-28f6-422e-b0e3-e85da40a04f01033.mspx?mfr=true.*

Exporting the Server Licensor Certificate

To work with either trusted publishing domains or trusted user domains, you must export the server licensor certificate from your root cluster or from the root cluster to be trusted. Certificates are exported to be used in establishing trusts. To perform this procedure, you need to be a member of the local AD RMS Enterprise Administrators or its equivalent.

1. Log on to a server that is a member of the root cluster, using AD RMS Enterprise Administrators credentials.
2. Launch Server Manager from the Administrative Tools program group.
3. Expand Roles\Active Directory Rights Management Services*servername.*
4. Right-click the server name, and choose Properties.
5. Click the Server Certificate Tab, and click Export Certificate.
6. In the Export Certificate As dialog box, type a valid name, for example, the name of your cluster, and select a proper location such as your Documents folder to create the .bin file. Click Save.
7. Close the Properties dialog box.
   Protect this certificate thoroughly because it controls access to your AD RMS cluster.

Preparing AD RMS Certificates

Certificates are created by default during the installation of AD RMS. However, you must configure appropriate certificate duration based on your rights-protection policies. Four activities can be performed in terms of certificate administration:

- Specify the duration of rights account certificates.
- Enable certification for mobile devices.

- Enable certification of server services.
- Authenticate clients through smart cards.

Of these, the one you must absolutely set is the validation period for the RAC. Others are optional operations that depend on your rights-protection policies. To modify the duration of the RAC, use the following procedure.

1. Log on to a server that is a member of the root cluster, using AD RMS Enterprise Administrators credentials.
2. Launch Server Manager from the Administrative Tools program group.
3. Expand Roles\Active Directory Rights Management Services*servername*.
4. Click Change Standard RAC Validity Period in the details pane.
5. Click the Standard RAC tab, and set the number of days to enable the certificate in the Standard RAC Validity Period section of the dialog box.
6. Click the Temporary RAC tab and set the number of minutes to enable the certificate in the Temporary RAC Validity Period section of the dialog box.
7. Click OK to close the dialog box.

Note that standard RACs are valid for 365 days by default, and temporary RACs last only 15 minutes. You might want to extend the duration of a temporary RAC, but be careful about extending the validity of a standard RAC because one year is already a considerable time.

Note that if you are using federated trusts, you will need to modify the RAC validity period under the Federated Identity Support node, not under the root cluster node.

MORE INFO   Managing certificates

For more information on working with the other certificate types, go to *http://technet2.microsoft.com /windowsserver2008/en/library/5eb527a9-34d8-464f-9735-e7dcd2613ffc1033.mspx*.

Preparing Exclusion Policies

When you decide the scope of your rights-protection policy implementation, you can configure exclusion policies or policies that will exclude users and computers from participating in your AD RMS implementation. You can create exclusion policies for four entities: users, applications, lockboxes, and Windows operating systems. When you do so, the list of the specified exclusion members is included in the use license for the content. You can remove an excluded entity from an exclusion list, but remember that if you remove the entity from the list, it will no longer be added to the use licenses. Existing content, however, will already contain it because use licenses are issued only once, by default. Because of this, keep three items in mind when preparing exclusion lists:

- Assign only exclusions that will be as permanent as possible.
- If you change your mind, wait until existing use licenses have expired before removing entities from an exclusion list.
- Rely on exclusion lists if the credentials of one of the supported entities, such as a user, have been compromised, and your rights protected content is at risk.

When you have decided to create an exclusion list, use the procedure that follows. In this case, you will exclude users from AD RMS.

1. Log on to a server that is a member of the root cluster, using AD RMS Enterprise Administrators credentials.
2. Launch Server Manager from the Administrative Tools program group.
3. Expand Roles\Active Directory Rights Management Services*servername*\Exclusion Policies\Users.
4. Click Enable User Exclusion in the Actions pane. This enables exclusion.
5. To exclude users, click Exclude User in the Actions pane. This launches the Exclude User Account Wizard.

   You can exclude a user either through the e-mail address or through the public key assigned to the user. The first is for users included in your AD DS directory, and the second is for external users who might not have an account in your AD DS directory. If you exclude users in your AD DS directory, make sure you exclude a group so that it is easier to manage as time goes on.
6. Select the appropriate exclusion method, either locate the user account or type in the public key string, and then click Next.
7. Click Finish to close the wizard.

Use the same node to remove the exclusion if you need to. Use the same process for other exclusion types.

Quick Check

1. How many root clusters can you deploy in an Active Directory Domain Services forest?
2. What is the difference between a root cluster and a licensing-only cluster, and which is preferable to use?
3. Which delegation roles does AD RMS support?

Quick Check Answers

1.   You can deploy only a single AD RMS root cluster per AD DS forest. This is because AD RMS creates an SCP during installation, and only one SCP can exist per forest.

2.   The root cluster offers all AD RMS, whereas the licensing-only cluster simply manages licenses. Licensing-only clusters are designed to support the root cluster role, but if you are given a choice, you should deploy only root clusters. This creates a single AD RMS cluster on your network and simplifies management while providing all the functionality you require. Use licensing-only clusters in rare occasions when root-only deployments are not practical.

3.   AD RMS supports four delegation roles:

❑   AD RMS Enterprise Administrators can manage every aspect of AD RMS.

❑   AD RMS Template Administrators can prepare and modify protection templates.

❑   AD RMS Auditors have read-only access to AD RMS logs.

❑   AD RMS Service Account is designed to grant proper access rights to the AD RMS service account.

MORE INFO   Exclusion policies

To learn more about exclusion policies, go to *http://technet2.microsoft.com/windowsserver2008/en/library/3a612201-7302-419b-86b2-3bde6d448d4e1033.mspx?mfr=true.*

Preparing Accounts and Access Rights

To ensure that your users can work with AD RMS, you must prepare their accounts. When you do so, AD RMS includes the account within its own database. However, when you remove an account, AD RMS disables the account but does not automatically remove it from its database. Because of this, the database can become large and contain obsolete data. To protect against this, either create a stored procedure in SQL Server that will automatically remove the account when you delete it or create a script that will do so on a scheduled basis.

In addition, you might need to create a special Super Users group that will contain operators that have full access to all the content protected by your AD RMS implementation. Members of this Super Users group are much like the recovery agents you would use for the Encrypting File System (EFS). These users can recover or modify any data that is managed by your AD RMS infrastructure and can, therefore, recover data from users who have left the organization. You should usually assign a Universal Group from your directory to this role. Prepare the Universal Group before enabling Super Users in AD RMS. To configure a Super User group to work with AD RMS, use the following procedure.

1. Log on to a server that is a member of the root cluster, using AD RMS Enterprise Administrators credentials.
2. Launch Server Manager from the Administrative Tools program group.
3. Expand Roles\Active Directory Rights Management Services*servername*\Security Policies.
4. Click Change Super Users Settings in the details pane.
5. In the Actions pane, click Enable Super Users.
6. Click Change Super Users Group in the details pane to view the Super User Group Property sheet.
7. Type the e-mail address of a mail-enabled universal distribution group from your forest or use the Browse button to locate it.
8. Click OK to close the Property sheet.

Members of this group will now have access to all AD RMS content. Select these members very carefully and ensure that they are completely trustworthy. In fact, you might prefer to keep the Super Users group disabled and enable it only when you need it for security purposes.

MORE INFO Account preparation

To learn more about account preparation, go to *http://technet2.microsoft.com/windowsserver2008 /en/library/5d3a2ead-319e-49e7-a1b4-e3f69a1a4f1b1033.mspx?mfr=true.*

Preparing Policy Templates

To facilitate the rights-protection application by your users, prepare policy templates. These templates will save considerable time for your users and ensure that you maintain the standards you set in your rights-protection policies. You must perform several activities with policy templates. First, you must create the template. Next, you must specify a location for the template.

Locations are usually shared folders contained within your network. However, for users to rely on the template to create content, they must have access to it. Offline users will not have access to the templates unless you configure the offline folder settings for the shared folder so that the content of the folder will automatically be available locally to the user. In addition, relying on offline folders will ensure that when you modify, add, or update templates, they will automatically be updated on the client computer the next time the user connects to the network. Offline folders, however, will not work for external users who do not have access to your internal network. You will have to consider an alternate delivery method if you choose to allow external users to create content. Users who have access only to pre-created content do not require access to the policy templates. To create a policy template, use the following procedure:

1. Log on to a server that is a member of the root cluster, using AD RMS Template Administrators credentials.
2. Launch Server Manager from the Administrative Tools program group.

3. Expand Roles\Active Directory Rights Management Services*servername*\Rights Policy Templates.

4. Under the AD RMS node of the console, select Rights Policy Templates (Server Manager \Roles\AD RMS*Servername*).

5. In the Actions pane, select Create Distributed Rights Policy Template. This launches the wizard.

6. On the Add Template Identification Information page, click Add.

7. Specify the language, type the name and description for the new template, click Add, and then click Next.

8. On the Add User Rights page, you must perform several activities:

   a. Click Add to select the user or group that will have access to the template. Selecting Anyone will enable any user to request a use license for the content. If you want to select a specific group, use the Browse button.

   b. Under Users And Rights, you must first select the user and then assign the rights to that particular user or group in the Rights For User pane. You can also create a custom right for the user.

   c. Note that the Grant Owner (Author) Full Control right with no expiration option is selected by default.

   d. In the Rights Request URL, type the appropriate URL. This will enable users to request additional rights by going to the URL.

9. Click Next.

10. On the Specify Expiration Policy page, select one of the three available options and type a value in days. If you need to ensure that content expires automatically after a number of days, select Expires After The Following Duration (Days), and type the number of days. Click Next.

11. On the Specify Extended Policy page, you can assign the following settings:

   a. Choose Enable Users to view protected content, using a browser add-on. This enables users who do not have AD RMS–enabled applications to view protected content by automatically installing the required add-on.

   b. Select Request A New Use License Every Time Content Is Consumed (Disable Client-Side Caching) if you need authentication against the AD RMS servers each time content is consumed. Note that this will not work for offline users.

   c. Select If You Would Like To Specify Additional Information For Your AD RMS-Enabled Applications, You Can Specify Them Here As Name-Value Pairs if you need to add specific data to the protected content. This option is usually reserved for developers, however.

12.   Click Next. On the Specify Revocation Policy page, you can enable revocation by selecting the Require Revocation option and then:

    a.   Selecting Location Where The Revocation List Is Published (URL or UNC) and typing the value for the location of the revocation file.

       Keep in mind that if you use a URL and you have both internal and external users, the URL should be accessible from both network locations.

    b.   Selecting Refresh Interval For Revocation List (Days) and typing the number of days the revocation list will be maintained.

       This determines when users must update their revocation list when viewing content.

    c.   Selecting File Containing Public Key Corresponding To The Signed Revocation List.

13.   Click Finish.

Note that when you implement revocation, you must be careful with its settings. To make revocation practical, you must publish the revocation list on a regular basis.

MORE INFO   **Policy templates**

To learn more about policy templates, go to *http://technet2.microsoft.com/windowsserver2008/en /library/a42680fa-2855-40d9-8e2c-74f72793ca241033.mspx?mfr=true.*

Working with AD RMS Clients

AD RMS relies on a local client to give users access to its capabilities. Two clients exist: the Windows Vista client, which is also included in Windows Server 2008, and a client that runs on Windows 2000, Windows 2003, and Windows XP. The last of these must be downloaded and installed on each client computer to work. Three versions of this client exist: x86, x64, and Itanium to support all Windows version platforms.

Clients automatically discover the AD RMS cluster through one of three methods:

■   They can rely on the AD DS Service Connection Point created during the AD RMS installation.

■   In complex, multiforest AD RMS deployments, they must rely on registry overrides, which are placed directly on the client computer. This is especially true for earlier versions of Windows operating systems.

■   They can rely on the URLs included in the issuance licenses for the content.

Each of these methods provides redundancy to ensure that clients can always access content.

MORE INFO AD RMS and Windows RMS clients

To learn more about AD RMS clients and obtain the Windows RMS clients, go to *http:// technet2.microsoft.com/windowsserver2008/en/library/3230bca4-51cb-418f-86ba-bb6539 3854181033.mspx?mfr=true.*

Quick Check
1. What is a server licensor certificate?
2. Which trust policies does AD RMS support?

Quick Check Answers
1. A server licensor certificate, or SLC, is a self-signed certificate that is generated during setup of the first server in a root cluster and assigned to the cluster as a whole. Other cluster members will share the SLC when they are installed.
2. AD RMS supports four trust policies:
   - ❑ Trusted user domains enable your AD RMS cluster to process requests for other AD RMS clusters located in different AD DS forests. Trusted user domains are added by importing the server licensor certificate from the AD RMS cluster you want to trust into your own cluster.
   - ❑ Trusted publishing domains enable your own AD RMS cluster to issue use licenses for content that was protected by another AD RMS cluster. To create a trusted publishing domain, you must import the publishing cluster's SLC as well as its private key into your own cluster.
   - ❑ Windows Live ID trusts allow users who have a valid Windows Live ID (formerly known as Microsoft Passport) to use rights-protected content but not to create it.
   - ❑ Federated trusts are established through AD FS and extend the operation of your AD RMS cluster to the forests with which you have established a federated trust.

Managing Databases

AD RMS relies on three databases to operate. Familiarize yourself with these databases and their operation to ensure the proper functioning of your AD RMS cluster. These databases include:

- ■ The configuration database, which is used to store all AD RMS configuration data. This database is accessed by AD RMS servers to provide rights-protection services and information to clients.

- The logging database, which stores data about every activity in either a root or a licensing-only cluster. This database is useful for auditing AD RMS events.
- The directory services database, which stores information about users and all their corresponding data. This information is accessed from AD DS directories through the Lightweight Directory Access Protocol (LDAP). This database requires regular maintenance if you remove users from AD RMS as mentioned earlier in this lesson.

In addition to these databases, AD RMS relies on the Message Queuing service to send events to the logging database. If you are concerned about auditing AD RMS usage, and you should be, perform regular checks and verifications of this service to ensure its proper operation.

In addition to the different functionalities available within the AD RMS console, Microsoft provides a special RMS toolkit that contains a series of utilities for AD RMS administration and operation. Download this toolkit, and add it to your AD RMS administration kit to control your deployment fully.

MORE INFO Rights Management Services administration toolkit

To download the RMS toolkit with utilities for RMS management, go to *http://www.microsoft.com /downloads/details.aspx?FamilyID=bae62cfc-d5a7-46d2-9063-0f6885c26b98&DisplayLang=en.*

MORE INFO Additional AD RMS resources

To access additional AD RMS resources, go to *http://technet2.microsoft.com/windowsserver2008/en /library/789533a5-50c5-435d-b06a-37db0ab5666e1033.mspx?mfr=true.*

PRACTICE Creating a Rights Policy Template

In this practice, you will create a customized rights policy template. You will use the AD RMS installation you created in Lesson 1 to create a new template.

▶ **Exercise 1   Create a New Template**

Templates enable users to apply rights policies in a quick, standardized manner. To create a template, you must use the AD RMS Template Administrators access right or the AD RMS Enterprise Administrators access right. To perform this exercise, you should have SERVER01, SERVER04, and SERVER05 running.

1. Log on to a server that is a member of the root cluster, using AD RMS Template Administrators credentials.
2. Launch Server Manager from the Administrative Tools program group.
3. Expand Roles\Active Directory Rights Management Services*servername*\Rights Policy Templates.

4. In the Actions pane, select Create Distributed Rights Policy Template. This launches the wizard.

5. On the Add Template Identification Information page, click Add.

6. Specify the language, type **Contoso Legal Template** for the name and **Template to protect legal documents at Contoso Ltd.** for the description for the new template, and click Add. Click Next.

7. On the Add User Rights page, you must perform several activities:

   a. Click Add to select the user or group that will have access to the template. Select Anyone.

      This will enable any user to request a use license for the content.

   b. Under Users And Rights, select Anyone, and then assign the View rights in the Rights For User pane.

   c. Make sure that the Grant Owner (Author) Full Control Right With No Expiration option is selected.

   d. In the Rights request URL, type the following URL: **https://RightsManagement .Contoso.com**.

      This will enable users to request additional rights by going to the URL.

8. Click Next. On the Specify Expiration Policy page, select Never Expires. Make sure you do not select Expires After The Following Duration (Days). Click Next.

9. On the Specify Extended Policy page, you can assign the following settings:

   ❑ Select Enable Users to view protected content, using a browser add-on. This enables users who do not have AD RMS–enabled applications to view protected content by automatically installing the required add-on.

   ❑ Do not select Request A New Use License Every Time Content Is Consumed (Disable Client-Side Caching).

   ❑ Do not select If You Would Like To Specify Additional Information For Your AD RMS-Enabled Applications, You Can Specify Them Here As Name-Value Pairs. This option is usually reserved for developers.

10. Click Next. On the Specify Revocation Policy page, do not enable revocation. Click Finish. Note that the template now appears in the details pane. It is ready for distribution.

Lesson Summary

- When you work with AD RMS, you will need to perform several configuration tasks to complete your installation. These tasks include creating an extranet URL if you want to give external users access to your DRM system. They also include configuring trust policies in support of additional external accesses.

- If you want to work with other AD RMS infrastructures, you must exchange server licensor certificates with each other. This means exporting certificates from the source cluster and importing them in the target cluster.
- If you need to exclude users from your DRM system, you must create exclusion policies.
- To facilitate user content creation, create rights policy templates. These templates will simplify users' work and ensure that your DRM strategy is used in a standard manner.

Lesson Review

You can use the following questions to test your knowledge of the information in Lesson 2, "Configuring and Using Active Directory Rights Management Services." The questions are also available on the companion CD if you prefer to review them in electronic form.

NOTE Answers

Answers to these questions and explanations of why each answer choice is right or wrong are located in the "Answers" section at the end of the book.

1. You are an administrator for the *contoso.com* domain. You have just finished installing AD RMS, and now you want to configure AD RMS. You've configured an extranet URL and tested the operation from the AD RMS server you were using to set up the URL. This URL relies on SSL to secure HTTP traffic. However, when users try to access AD RMS from outside your network, they can't. What could be the problem?
   A. Your users should be using a URL address in the HTTP:// format.
   B. The server certificate is invalid, and, because of this, users cannot access the URL.
   C. Users must have AD DS domain accounts to access the URL.
   D. The URL you provided to users is wrong.

Chapter Review

To further practice and reinforce the skills you learned in this chapter, you can perform the following tasks:

- Review the chapter summary.
- Review the list of key terms introduced in this chapter.
- Complete the case scenario. This scenario sets up a real-world situation involving the topics of this chapter and asks you to create a solution.
- Complete the suggested practices.
- Take a practice test.

Chapter Summary

- AD RMS is designed to support the extension of your organization's authority beyond the firewall. The extension applies to the protection of intellectual property.
- To protect your intellectual property, AD RMS must rely on several technologies: Active Directory Domain Services, Active Directory Certificate Services, Active Directory Federation Services, and SQL Server. AD DS provides a central authentication service, AD CS provides the public key infrastructure certificates used in AD RMS, AD FS enables you to integrate AD RMS policies with partners and external users, and SQL Server stores all AD RMS data.
- Many organizations choose to implement AD RMS in stages:
  - ❑ The first stage focuses on internal use of intellectual property.
  - ❑ The second involves sharing content with partners.
  - ❑ The third involves a wider audience where your intellectual property is distributed outside the boundaries of your network in a protected mode.
- When you install AD RMS, you create a root cluster. This cluster can supply both certification and licensing services. Each AD DS forest can host only a single root cluster; however, in large implementations, you can separate the certification and licensing roles by creating an additional licensing cluster. To consume the AD RMS services, you need AD RMS–enabled applications. These can be tools such as word processors, presentation tools, e-mail clients, or custom in-house applications. Each time a user creates new information, AD RMS templates determine usage rights for the information. These include who will be able to read, open, write, modify, print, transfer, and otherwise manipulate the information.

Key Terms

Use these key terms to understand better the concepts covered in this chapter.

- **enrollment**   Servers that must be enrolled to publish certificates. In prior releases, you needed the Microsoft Enrollment Service, but with AD RMS, servers can self-enroll through a self-enrollment certificate.
- **publishing license**   Licenses that are assigned to content when authorized users protect content. This license determines which rights are assigned to the document. When the document is opened by another authorized user, a use license is provided by the server and is permanently embedded into the content.
- **root cluster**   A root cluster that is automatically created with each AD RMS installation. The cluster provides high availability for the AD RMS service as soon as a second server is installed. Only one root cluster can be installed per AD DS forest, but you can also create licensing-only clusters to support AD RMS operations.

Case Scenario

In the following case scenario, you will apply what you've learned about Active Directory Rights Management Services. You can find answers to the questions in this scenario in the "Answers" section at the end of this book.

Case Scenario: Prepare to Work with an External AD RMS Cluster

You are a systems administrator with Contoso, Ltd. You have recently finished implementing an AD RMS deployment within your organization, and everything is running smoothly. Users both inside and outside of your network have access to your rights management policies to ensure the protection of your content.

Now your organization wants to share rights protection policies with a partner organization, but it does not want to put a federation services infrastructure in place. What are your options?

Suggested Practices

To help you successfully master the exam objectives presented in this chapter, complete the following tasks.

Work with AD RMS

There is only a single exam objective for this topic. Because of this, you should focus your practices on the following areas:

- Identifying the requirements for an AD RMS installation
- Working with the installation and configuration process for AD RMS root clusters
- Finalizing the configuration process for a root cluster
- Working with rights policy templates

You should also practice using the various console sections for AD RMS. All of these are available in Server Manager.

- **Practice 1**   Use the instructions in the "Before You Begin" section of this chapter to prepare your test environment. If at all possible, rely on an external database server to support the installation. This will enable you to configure a true root cluster. When you're ready, create the cluster and add a second server to it so that you can see how clusters operate.

- **Practice 2**   After the cluster is installed, use Server Manager to run through all the activities required to create or modify a rights policy template. These templates are an important part of the AD RMS administration process.

Don't forget to study DRM implementations with Windows Server 2008. The Microsoft TechNet Web site includes more information on AD RMS; run through as much of it as you can.

Take a Practice Test

The practice tests on this book's companion CD offer many options. For example, you can test yourself on just one exam objective, or you can test yourself on all the 70-640 certification exam content. You can set up the test so that it closely simulates the experience of taking a certification exam, or you can set it up in study mode so that you can look at the correct answers and explanations after you answer each question.

MORE INFO   Practice tests

For details about all the practice test options available, see the "How to Use the Practice Tests" section in this book's introduction.

Chapter 17

Active Directory Federation Services

Organizations have been struggling with securing their networks from the outside world ever since the Internet was invented. The basic principle is that every organization that has an interface between its network and the Internet also has a perimeter network of some sort. In many cases, organizations spend great effort implementing special security technologies such as intrusion detection systems, and yet, the basic premise of a perimeter network is to keep the firewalls it contains as secure as possible. But how does that affect potential partnerships?

In the early days of Microsoft Windows domains with Microsoft Windows NT, Microsoft provided the capability to create trusts between domains to support domain interactions. With the release of Active Directory Domain Services (AD DS) in Windows 2000, Microsoft brought forward the concept of the trust and supported inter-domain trusts. Domains within the same forest would use automatic transitive trusts, and domains from different forests would use explicit trusts when they wanted to share security contexts. With the release of Microsoft Windows Server 2003, Microsoft extended the concept of the transitive trust to forests with the introduction of forest trusts. Using a forest trust, partners could extend the security contexts of their own internal forest to trust other partner forests. However, implementing forests trusts has two significant impacts:

- First, it requires opening specific ports in a firewall to support Active Directory Domain Services (AD DS) traffic.
- Second, if the partnerships grow too large, it can become extremely cumbersome to manage multiple trusts. (See Figure 17-1.)

Using trusts might not be the best way to implement partnerships.

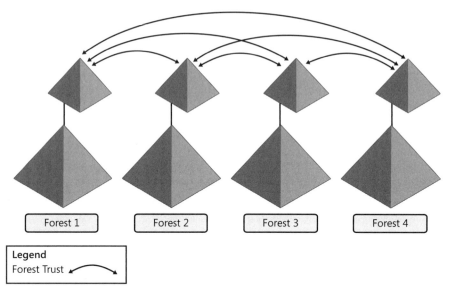

Figure 17-1   Implementing multiple forest trusts can become highly complex

The Purpose of a Firewall

Although forest trusts can become highly complex, they also have an impact on your protection mechanisms. For example, AD DS traffic will transit through the Lightweight Directory Access Protocol (LDAP) on TCP/IP port 389 or, preferably, through secure LDAP (LDAP/S) on port 636. In addition, if you need to transit global catalog (GC) traffic, you'll need to use port 3268 or, once again preferably, port 3269 on LDAP/S.

However, firewalls are designed to keep unwanted traffic out. Perforating them by opening endless numbers of TCP/IP ports is not a solution. Traditional perimeter networks will have two layers of protection. The first protects perimeter networks from external access. The second protects internal networks from the perimeter. The perimeter itself provides a series of services such as Active Directory Certificate Services (AD CS), Active Directory Rights Management Services (AD RMS), and, in some circumstances, Active Directory Lightweight Directory Services (AD LDS). AD DS is reserved exclusively for internal networks.

The ideal external firewall will use one set of key ports and this set only. These include:

- Port 53, which is used for Domain Name System (DNS) traffic. DNS traffic is usually provided in a read-only manner.
- Port 80, which is used by open Hypertext Transfer Protocol (HTTP) data. Port 80 is usually used for read-only access because it is not secured.
- Port 443 for Secure HTTP or Hypertext Transfer Protocol Secure (HTTPS). Communications on port 443 are secured through Secure Sockets Layer (SSL) or Transport Layer

Security (TLS), which both rely on Certificate Authority (CA) certificates to encrypt data. Because of this, communications on port 443 support read-write or secure data read operations.

- Port 25, which is used for Simple Mail Transfer Protocol (SMTP), a necessary risk because no one can work without access to e-mail.

All other ports should ideally be closed. The internal firewall will have a few more open ports, depending on the technologies you have running in the perimeter. (See Figure 17-2.) For example, if you are using AD LDS to provide authentication services for Web applications in the perimeter, you might want to have one-way synchronizations from your internal AD DS directory to provision your own user accounts. If you are using Internet Information Services (IIS), you might want to push and pull data to the Web sites in the perimeter. In addition, you want to get the e-mail messages from your SMTP relays in the perimeter into your internal network. This is the basis of a secure perimeter design.

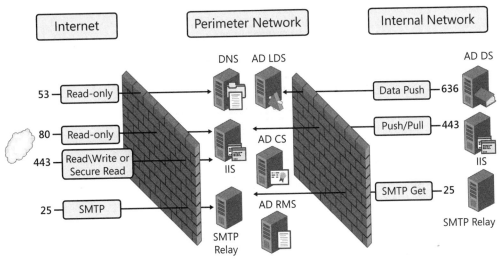

Figure 17-2   The basis of a secure perimeter is a set of secure firewalls

Active Directory Federation Services

In comes Active Directory Federation Services (AD FS), one of the Active Directory technologies included in Windows Server 2008. Once again, this Active Directory technology is designed to extend the authority of your internal network to the outside world. (See Figure 17-3.) AD FS is designed to provide similar functionality to the forest trust or the explicit trust but, this time, not through the traditional LDAP TCP/IP ports but rather through the common HTTP ports. In fact, AD FS uses port 443 because all AD FS trust communications are secured and encrypted. In this manner, it can rely on AD CS to provide certificates for each server in the AD

FS implementation. AD FS can also extend your AD RMS deployment and provide federation services for intellectual property management between partners.

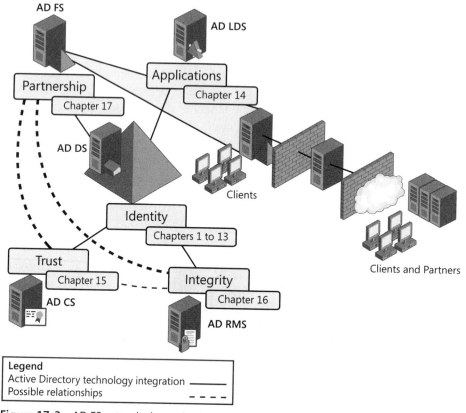

Figure 17-3 AD FS extends the authority of your internal AD DS directory

To extend your internal authority, AD FS provides extensions to internal forests and enables organizations to create partnerships without having to open any additional port on their firewalls. Basically, AD FS relies on each partner's internal AD DS directory to provide authentication for extranet or perimeter services. When a user attempts to authenticate to an application integrated to AD FS, the AD FS engine will poll the internal directory for authentication data. If the user has access provided through the internal directory, he or she will be granted access to the external application. The major advantage of this is that each partner organization needs to manage only authentication data in the internal network. The federation services of AD FS do all the rest.

In short, AD FS should be used whenever you want to implement a partnership with other organizations that also rely on internal AD DS directories. When you need to provide authentication services in your perimeter network, but the users or organizations you want to interact with do not have internal AD DS directories, or the scope of the partnership does not warrant an AD FS deployment, you should rely on AD LDS.

Exam objectives in this chapter:

■ Configuring Additional Active Directory Server Roles

❑ Configure Active Directory Federation Services (AD FS).

Lessons in this chapter:

■ Lesson 1: Understanding Active Directory Federation Services 832

■ Lesson 2: Configuring and Using Active Directory Federation Services 854

Before You Begin

To complete the lessons in this chapter, you must have performed the installations shown in the following list. It is highly recommended that you use virtual machines for this chapter because it requires access to so many computers. If you performed the exercises in the previous chapters, you will already have several of these computers in place.

■ Installed Windows Server 2008 on a physical or virtual machine. The machine should be named SERVER01 and should be a domain controller in the *contoso.com* domain. The details for this setup are presented in Chapter 1, "Installation," and Chapter 2, "Administration."

■ Installed Windows Server 2008 Enterprise Edition on a physical or virtual machine, which should be named SERVER03 and should be a member server within the *contoso.com* domain. This computer will host the internal AD FS role you will install and create through the exercises in this chapter.

■ Installed Windows Server 2008 Enterprise Edition on a physical or virtual machine, which should be named SERVER04 and should be a member server within the *contoso.com* domain. This computer will host an AD FS proxy server.

■ Installed Windows Server 2003 Enterprise Edition on a physical or virtual machine, which should be named SERVER05 and should be a member server within the *contoso.com* domain. This computer will host an installation of Microsoft SQL Server 2005, which will run the configuration and logging database for AD RMS. This computer would also include a D drive to store the data for SQL Server. 10 gigabytes (GB) should be enough for the size of this drive. You use Windows Server 2003 because it requires less RAM than Windows Server 2008. Note that this computer is not necessary for the exercises in this chapter, but having it turned on will prevent AD RMS errors from appearing on SERVER04.

■ Installed Windows Server 2008 on a physical or virtual machine, which should be named SERVER06 and should be a domain controller in the *woodgrovebank.com* domain and include the DNS server role. No special setup is required other than having a new directory named *woodgrovebank.com*.

■ Installed Windows Server 2008 Enterprise Edition on a physical or virtual machine, which should be named SERVER07 and should be a member server within the *woodgrovebank.com* domain. This computer will host the internal AD FS role you will install and create through the exercises in this chapter.

■ Installed Windows Server 2008 Enterprise Edition on a physical or virtual machine, which should be named SERVER08 and should be a member server within the *woodgrovebank.com* domain. This computer will host an AD FS proxy server.

This setup will be sufficient to test basic AD FS installation and configuration. Testing all of AD FS capabilities requires client machines as well and might be beyond the laboratory capabilities of most readers.

Note that you can create an AD FS environment with fewer computers, as outlined in the *Microsoft Step-by-Step Guide for AD FS*, which is available at *http://www.microsoft.com/downloads/details.aspx?familyid=062F7382-A82F-4428-9BBD-A103B9F27654&displaylang=en*, but it is not recommended to install AD FS on an AD DS domain controller; therefore, the recommended setup is as outlined here.

Real World

Danielle Ruest and Nelson Ruest

In 2005, one of our clients, a major health care organization, needed to put together an identity federation solution. Their goal was to have their entire health care system—doctors, pharmacists, health care workers, hospitals, social services workers, private clinics, and so on—work together through a single integrated identity and access (IDA) solution. Because most of the organizations involved used internal Active Directory for authentication and network access, this solution was to be based on Windows technologies.

The goal was to make sure that all members of the system had a verifiable identity within the system. The challenge was considerable. Although many larger partners had their own internal Active Directory forests, many of the smaller partners did not. For example, pharmacies did not have any way of linking themselves together to have a single identity authority. Private clinics or doctors did not have this capability either.

The initial solution was to create a multitude of forest trusts between each of the existing Active Directory forests. Then, to provide support for the members of the system that did not have their own directory service, a completely new directory would be created that would be located within a perimeter network hosted by a hosting firm as an outsourced service to the health care provider for a per-user fee to maintain the directory service.

The customer had several concerns about the potential solution. The first was long-term costs. When all the members of the system were tallied, they added up to over 500,000 users, more than half of them without a directory service. Maintaining an external directory for these users would become very expensive very quickly. Second, the client did not want to perforate firewalls by supporting all the ports required for forest trusts. However, the cost of a private network was prohibitive. Third, although the client wanted each of the system members to interact through a single IDA, it did not want to be responsible for all the accounts linked to the new solution.

We recommended that, although Windows Server 2008 was not available yet, Windows Server 2003 R2 was, and with it came the initial release of Microsoft Federation Services. In addition, Microsoft had released Active Directory Application Mode (ADAM) a couple of years earlier. This case seemed like a perfect candidate for the integration of the three technologies. We suggested the following:

- Use the Federation Services to link all existing directory services and make centralized applications available through the Web.
- Allow each partner to manage its own internal directory services without external intervention.
- Use ADAM instances to provide authentication services in the perimeter network. The client could even create a self-service portal that would enable members to update their own records, change passwords, and so on.
- Reduce the number of open ports on the firewall down to the most common ports that were already open.

This proposal met the customer's needs and would not cost a fortune to implement. In fact, implementation could start with a pilot project focusing on one or two key applications and then adding new system members as the solution was fleshed out. What's even better is that with the release of Windows Server 2008, Microsoft brought many of the technologies we proposed under a single banner: Active Directory.

Lesson 1: Understanding Active Directory Federation Services

In general terms, AD FS is a single sign-on (SSO) engine that allows users of your external Web-based applications to access and authenticate through a browser. That's not so different from using an external AD LDS directory store that is linked with your internal directory. However, the key feature of AD FS is that to authenticate a client, it uses the internal authentication store of the user's own domain and does not have a store of its own. It also uses the original authentication the client performed in its own network and passes this authentication to all the Web applications that are AD FS–enabled.

The advantages are clear. Organizations need to manage only a single authentication store for their own users and don't need to manage secondary stores at all. Using an AD LDS directory for extranet authentication adds administrative overhead because the organization needs to manage its own internal store and the external store or stores as well. Users also often must remember several access codes and passwords to log on to each of these stores. AD FS simplifies this because it federates the user's internal AD DS identity and projects it to the external world. Users need to authenticate only once: when they log on to their own network.

Using AD FS, you can form business-to-business (B2B) partnerships with very little overhead. In these B2B partnerships, organizations fit into two categories:

- **Resource organization**   When organizations that have exposed resources such as Web sites—e-commerce or collaboration—decide to use AD FS to simplify the authentication process to these resources, they form partnerships with other organizations—suppliers, partners, and so on. The organization that forms the partnership is deemed the resource organization because it hosts the shared resources in its perimeter network.
- **Account organization**   When organizations enter into an AD FS relationship with resource organizations, they are deemed the account organizations because they manage the accounts used to access the shared resources in SSO designs.

AD FS supports one additional authentication mode. In a Web SSO design, it will authenticate users from anywhere on the Internet. After such users have been authenticated, AD FS examines the users' attributes in AD DS or in AD LDS directories to identify which claims the users have to the application they are authenticating to.

To support this identity federation, AD FS relies on four role services.

- **Federation Service**   This service is formed by the servers that share a trust policy. The federation server will route authentication requests to the appropriate source directory to generate security tokens for the user requesting access.
- **Federation Service Proxy**   To obtain the authentication requests from the user, the federation server relies on a proxy server that is located in the perimeter network. The proxy collects authentication information from the user's browser through the WS-Federation

Passive Requestor Profile (WS-F PRP), an AD FS Web service, and passes it on to the federation service.

■ **Claims-Aware Agent**   An agent sits on the Web server and initiates queries of security token claims to the federation service. Each claim is used to grant or deny access to a given application. ASP.NET applications that can examine the various claims contained in the user's AD FS security token are deemed to be claims-aware applications. These applications can rely on the claims to determine whether the user has access to the application. Two examples of claims-aware applications are AD RMS and Microsoft Office SharePoint Server 2007.

■ **Windows Token-Based Agent**   This is an alternate agent that can convert the AD FS security token into an impersonation-level Windows NT access token for applications that rely on Windows authentication mechanisms instead of other Web-based authentication methods.

Because it is based on a standard Web service, AD FS does not need to rely on AD DS alone to support federated identities. Any directory service that adheres to the WS-Federation standard can participate in an AD FS identity federation.

Although Federation Services existed in Windows Server 2003 R2, AD FS has been improved significantly in Windows Server 2008 to facilitate the installation and administration processes. AD FS also supports more Web applications than the original release did.

MORE INFO   AD FS

For more information on AD FS, go to *http://technet2.microsoft.com/windowsserver2008/en/server-manager/activedirectoryfederationservices.mspx*

> **After this lesson, you will be able to:**
> ■ Understand the AD FS authentication process.
> ■ Understand the components that make up an AD FS implementation.
> ■ Install AD FS.
> **Estimated lesson time: 40 minutes**

The AD FS Authentication Process

After the AD FS partnerships are in place, it becomes transparent for users to log on to external Web applications that are included in the partnership. In a typical AD FS scenario, when a user logs on to a claims-aware application in an extranet, AD FS automatically provisions the user's credentials and outlines the claims included in the user's AD DS account attributes. (See Figure 17-4.)

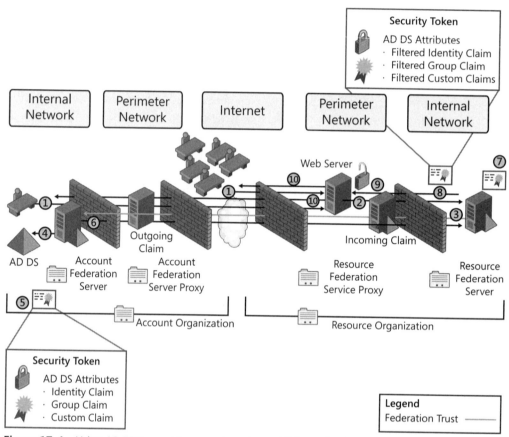

Figure 17-4   Using AD FS to provide access to extranet Web applications through Federated Web SSO

1. A user who is located within an internal network or on the Internet wants to access a claims-aware Web application in an extranet. This user belongs to one of the account organizations that is a member of the AD FS partnership.

2. The claims-aware agent on the Web server verifies with a resource federation server (RFS) in the resource organization to see whether the client is granted access. Because the request must traverse a firewall, the agent first contacts a Federation Service Proxy (FSP), who then contacts the internal federation server.

3. Because it does not have an account for the user but has a federation relationship with the directory store in the account organization—a federation trust, in fact—the federation server in the resource organization checks with an account federation server (AFS) in the account organization's internal network, once again through a proxy, to identify the user's access rights. These access rights are listed in the form of claims, which are attributes linked to the user's account object in AD DS.

4. The federation server in the account organization is directly linked to the organization's internal AD DS and obtains access rights from the directory through an LDAP query. Note that the user account can also reside in an AD LDS directory store.

5. The account organization's federation server constructs the user's AD FS security token. This token includes the user's identifier, the list of claims included in the user's AD DS account, and the digital certificate of the AFS.

6. The AFS responds to the RFS with the client's access rights contained within the signed security token, once again through the proxy server. This is an outgoing claim.

7. The RFS decrypts the token and extracts the claims for the user from the incoming claim. It then maps the claims to the organization claims it maintains and applies a filtering policy for the specific requesting Web application.

8. The filtered claims are then packaged once again into a signed security token, which is sent to the Web server in the resource organization's extranet by posting it to the URL included in the Web application's original request. In this case, the signature for the token is based either on the RFS digital certificate or on a Kerberos session key because the systems are in the same network.

9. The Web server relies on its claims-aware agent to decrypt the user's security token, looks up the user's claims, and then grants access to the application based on the claims in the token.

10. To support single sign-on, the AD FS Web agent on the Web server directs the user's browser to write a local authentication cookie for the user so that it does not need to perform this lookup again the next time it needs to authenticate during this session.

The process is simple after it is in place. However, implementing AD FS must be done with care. Each partner can use its own internal directory stores to grant users access to extranet applications. This simplifies access management, but to do so, each partner must implement federation trusts. Federation trusts rely on the partners having at least one AD FS federation server installed in their networks. The direction of the trust is always from the resource partner to the account partner.

Note that when the user is using either a public or home computer that is not part of the account organization's AD DS domain, he or she can use a special AD FS Web page, which will enable that user to select which account organization to use. This Web page also provides logon screens that can support either forms-based or Windows Integrated authentication. This enables external users to access the extranet applications even if they are not using corporate computers.

If you do not want to create a Web page that includes a list of account organizations because you do not want to publish these organization names for security reasons, you can include the account organization directly within the query string for the resource being accessed. Use the following Web query format:

```
https://webserver/appname/apppage.aspx?whr=urn:federation:accountpartner
```

In this query, you rely on the *whr* parameter to identify the account organization in the federation partnership.

Working with AD FS Designs

AD FS supports three configurations or architectural designs, depending on the type of B2B partnership you need to establish. Each includes its own particularities, and each supports a particular partnership scenario.

- **Federated Web SSO**   This model usually spans several firewalls because it links applications contained within an extranet in a resource organization to the internal directory stores of account organizations. The only trust that exists in this model is the federation trust, which is always a one-way trust from the resource organization to the account organization(s). This is the most common AD FS deployment scenario. (See Figure 17-4, presented earlier.)

- **Federated Web SSO with Forest Trust**   In this model, the organization uses two AD DS forests. One is the internal forest, but the second one is an external forest located within a perimeter network. A forest trust is established between the forest in the perimeter network and the internal forest. In addition, a federation trust is established between the resource federation server, which is located within the perimeter, and the account federation server, located in the internal network. In this scenario, external users have accounts in the perimeter forest, and internal users have accounts in the internal forest. The AD FS systems federate the access rights from the accounts in both forests to the applications in the perimeter. Because of this, internal users have access to the applications from both the internal network and the Internet, whereas external users have access to the applications only from the Internet. (See Figure 17-5.)

IMPORTANT   **Using AD DS directories in perimeter networks**

Be very wary of this design. The very function of each of the four additional Active Directory technologies—AD LDS, AD CS, AD RMS, and AD FS—is to extend the authority of your internal AD DS deployments without having to host external AD DS forests. Hosting an external AD DS forest is a risk you should avoid as much as possible. In addition, creating a forest trust between an external and an internal forest means opening up ports on a firewall—ports that should normally be closed. Instead, rely on AD LDS and AD FS to perform the same functions.

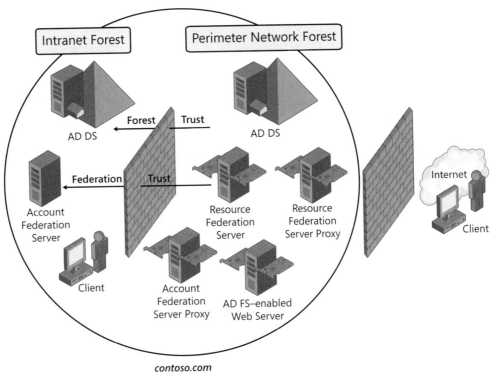

contoso.com

Figure 17-5 Relying on a forest trust as well as a federation trust to provide access to extranet applications

- ■ **Web SSO**   When all the users for an extranet application are external and do not have accounts within an AD DS domain, you must deploy Web SSO only. The Web SSO model allows the users to authenticate only once to multiple Web applications. However, this model relies on multihomed Web servers—servers that include at least two network interface cards (NICs), one that is connected to the external network and one that is connected to the internal network. The Web servers are part of the internal AD DS domain and are connected to it through the internal NIC. Clients access the applications through the external NIC. The Federation Service Proxy is also multihomed to provide access to both the external and the internal network. (See Figure 17-6.)

The most common scenarios are the first and the last but, ideally, all members of your identity federation deployment will have their own AD DS directory and will act as account organizations to simplify your deployment strategy.

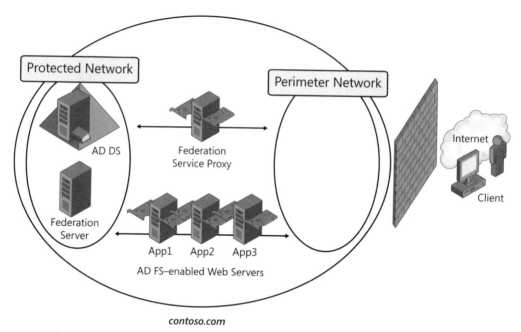

contoso.com

Figure 17-6 Using a Web SSO federation scenario

Exam Tip Pay attention to the three AD FS deployment scenarios, even the Federated Web SSO with Forest Trust scenario, although it is not recommended. Each of the exam questions will be based on one or the other.

Understanding AD FS Components

In addition to the various role services supported by AD FS, this technology relies on several components. These include:

- Claims
- Cookies
- Certificates

Each of these three components provides additional support to the AD FS process. Also, as you have seen, AD FS relies on a special terminology—a terminology of its own, in fact. To have a better grasp of the AD FS components, it is important to review and understand this terminology.

Understanding AD FS Claims

In their most basic form, claims are statements each partner in an AD FS relationship makes about its users. Claims can be based on several values, for example, user names, certificate keys, group memberships, specific privileges, or more. Claims are the basis of the authorization AD FS sends to the Web application. Claims can be obtained in three ways:

- The account federation server can query the internal directory store for the claims and provide them to a resource partner.
- The account organization can provide the claims to a resource federation server, which then passes them on to the resource application after they have been filtered.
- The federation service queries the directory store (AD DS or AD LDS) for the claims and provides them to the resource application after they have been filtered.

AD FS can support three types of claims:

- **Identity claim type**   Any claim that is based on the user's identity falls within this category. There must be at least one identity claim type in every claim for security tokens to be generated from a list of claims.
  - ❏ This can include a user principal name (UPN), which represents the user's identity in a format that resembles an e-mail address (*username@accountdomain*). Keep in mind that even if several UPNs can exist for a user account, only one can be used in an identity claim type. If other UPNs must be communicated in the claim, they must be defined as custom claim types. When included with other identity claim types, the UPN has the highest priority.
  - ❏ This can also be an e-mail address (*username@emaildomain*). Like the UPN, only one e-mail address can be communicated as the e-mail claim type. All other e-mail addresses, if they are required, must be listed as custom claim types. When included with other identity claim types, the e-mail address has the second-highest priority.
  - ❏ You can also rely on common names, which are really nothing more than arbitrary strings of characters. Note that there is no method you can use to guarantee the uniqueness of a common name; therefore, be careful when using this claim type. When included with other identity claim types, the common name has the lowest priority.
- **Group claim type**   The group memberships a user belongs to can also be used in a claim. Because a user can belong to several groups, you can provide several group claim types in a claim. For example, the same user can belong to the Tester, Developer, and User groups for an application.
- **Custom claim type**   If custom information must be provided for a user, for example, a custom identification number such as bank account number or employee number, you would put it in a custom claim type.

When claims are processed, they are filtered by the federation server. This reduces the overall number of claims an organization needs to have. If filtering was not available, then the organization would be responsible for mapping out each claim for each partner. This would greatly increase the number of claims to manage.

MORE INFO   AD FS claims and claim mapping

For more information on AD FS claims and claim mappings, go to *http://technet2.microsoft.com/ windowsserver2008/en/library/4fd78221-3d2e-4236-a971-18cdb8513d6b1033.mspx?mfr=true*.

Understanding AD FS Cookies

In addition to claims, AD FS works with cookies, which are inscribed in users' browsers during Web sessions that are authenticated through AD FS. Three types of cookies are used by AD FS.

- **Authentication cookies**   Because the first instance of an AD FS authentication can require a few transactions, AD FS generates an authentication cookie to be placed within the user's browser to support SSO for additional authentications. This cookie will include all the claims for the user. Authentication cookies are issued by both the AD FS Web agent and the federation service itself. Relying on the Web agent avoids having to place public and private key pairs on the server. When the Web agent creates an authentication cookie, it simply uses the existing security token generated by the federation server. The federation server, however, must have key pairs because it relies on these key pairs to sign security tokens.

  This cookie is signed, but it is not encrypted. This is one more reason all communications in this process are encrypted through either TLS or SSL. Also, because it is a session cookie, it is erased after the session is closed.

- **Account Partner cookies**   During the authentication process, the client must announce its account partner membership. If this announcement has a valid token, the AD FS process writes a cookie on the client so that it can rely on this cookie instead of having to perform partner discovery again the next time the client authenticates.

  This cookie is not signed or encrypted. It is a long-lived and persistent cookie.

- **Sign-out cookies**   Each time the federation service assigns a token, the resource partner or target server linked to the token is added to a sign-out cookie. The sign-out cookie is then used to facilitate an authentication artifact, for example, cached cookies, clean-up operations at the end of a user session.

  This cookie is not signed or encrypted. It is a session cookie that is deleted as part of the clean-up operations.

MORE INFO   AD FS cookies

For more information on AD FS cookies, go to *http://technet2.microsoft.com/windowsserver2008/en/library/0357bdbc-219d-4ec1-a6d0-1a3376bc1eb51033.mspx?mfr=true*.

Understanding AD FS Certificates

To ensure secure communications, the AD FS implementation uses several certificate types. In fact, AD FS can rely on your AD CS deployment to obtain the certificates it needs. Each server role within an AD FS deployment will rely on certificates. The type of certificate required by the role depends on its purpose.

- **Federation servers**   The federation server must have both a server authentication certificate and a token-signing certificate installed before it can perform any AD FS operations and become fully functional. In addition, the trust policy that forms the basic tenet of the federation relationship must rely on a verification certificate. The latter is nothing more than the public key of the token-signing certificate.

  - ❏ The server authentication certificate is an SSL authentication certificate that secures Web traffic between the federation server and the Federation Service Proxy or the Web clients. SSL certificates are usually requested and installed through IIS Manager.

  - ❏ Each time the federation server generates a security token, it must digitally sign the token with its token-signing certificate. Signing certificates ensures that it cannot be tampered with during transit. The token-signing certificate is made up of a private and public key pair.

  - ❏ When there is more than one federation server in a deployment, a verification process must take place between servers. To do this, each server must have the verification certificates for all the other servers. As mentioned previously, the verification certificate consists of the public key of the token-signing certificate for a federation server. This means the certificate is installed on the target server without its corresponding private key.

- **Federation Service proxies**   Proxies must have a server authentication certificate to support SSL-encrypted communications with Web clients.

  They must also have a client authentication certificate to authenticate the federation server during communications. This certificate can be any client authentication certificate type so long as it relies on extended key usage (EKU). Both the private and the public keys for this certificate are stored on the proxy. The public key is also stored on the federation server(s) and in the trust policy. When you work with this certificate type in the AD FS console, they are called Federation Service Proxy certificates.

■ **AD FS Web agents**   Any AD FS–enabled Web server hosting the AD FS Web agent must also have a server authentication certificate to secure its communications with Web clients.

AD FS can easily rely on AD CS to obtain and manage these certificates. Keep in mind, however, that because many of the AD FS roles are outward-facing, your certificates must be from a trusted certification authority; otherwise, you will need to modify the Trusted CA store on each Web client.

MORE INFO   AD FS certificates

For more information on AD FS certificates, go to *http://technet2.microsoft.com/windowsserver2008/en/library/505507c2-db4a-45da-ad1b-082d5484b0c91033.mspx?mfr=true*.

Exam Tip   Pay attention to AD FS certificate exchanges. Because AD FS communications must be encrypted at all times, they are a core part of this exam topic.

Understanding AD FS Terminology

Because of its reliance on several technologies, AD FS uses terminology from a wide range of sources. It is a good idea to ensure your familiarity with these terms so that you understand what is being discussed when a term arises. Table 17-1 outlines the most common terms used in AD FS. Many of these have already been covered.

Table 17-1   Common AD FS Terms

Term	Description
Account federation server	The federation server that is hosted in the account organization's internal network.
Account Federation Service Proxy	The FSP that is hosted in the account organization's perimeter network. The FSP acts as a relay between the perimeter and the federation server. The FSP is sometimes referred to as a Federation Service Proxy.
Account partner or organization	The partner that hosts the AD DS directory that contains the accounts of the users who access extranet applications.
AD FS Web Agent	An agent that is installed on a Web server running IIS. The agent is used to interpret the claims and tokens provided by the federation server. This agent can rely on claims alone or on Windows Integrated authentication to provide access to applications.
Claim	The statement the federation server makes about a user or client.
Claims-aware application	An ASP.NET application that can interpret claims to grant user access.

Table 17-1   Common AD FS Terms

Term	Description
Claim mapping	When a federation server processes an incoming claim and filters it to extract appropriate authorizations for a user, it performs claim mapping.
Client account partner discovery Web page	A Web page that lists partner organizations and allows users to identify their own organization during the logon process.
Client authentication certificate	AD FS uses two-way authentication between the federation server and the proxies. To do this, the proxy relies on a client authentication certificate, and the federation server relies on a server authentication certificate.
Client logon or logoff Web page	AD FS provides custom Web pages to give visual feedback to users when they log on or log off an AD FS session.
Federated application	The same as a claims-aware application. It can rely on federated identities for authentication.
Federated user	Any user who has been granted appropriate claims in the account directory to access applications in the resource organization.
Federation	Any two organizations that have established a federation trust.
Federation trust	The one-way trust between a resource organization and the account organization(s) it wants to partner with.
Organization claims	All claims contained within the organization's namespace.
Passive client	Any HTTP browser that can also use cookies. The client must support the WS-F PRP Web Service specification.
Resource account	If you plan to rely on Windows Integrated authentication, you must create resource accounts for each user you want to grant access to. The Windows NT authentication process requires this account to map credentials for the user.
Resource federation server	The internal server that is used to perform claims mapping and issue access security tokens for users who need to work with an application. This federation server is located within the resource organization's internal network.
Resource Federation Service Proxy	The proxy that is located in the perimeter network of the resource organization. It performs account partner discovery for Internet clients and redirects incoming requests to the internal federation server.
Resource group	Used in the resource forest to map incoming group claims. It can then be used to support Windows NT authentication.
Resource partner or organization	The organization that hosts the federated applications in its perimeter network.

Table 17-1 Common AD FS Terms

Term	Description
Security token	A digitally signed object that contains the claims for a given user. When a security token is issued, it means that the user has successfully authenticated to an account federation server.
Security Token Service (STS)	The AD FS Web Service that is used to issue tokens. To issue tokens, the STS must trust the entire chain of events that leads to the issuance. In AD FS, the federation service itself is an STS.
Server authentication certificate	AD FS uses two-way authentication between the federation server and the proxies. To do this, the proxy relies on a client authentication certificate, and the federation server relies on a server authentication certificate. AD FS–enabled Web servers also require server authentication certificates to authenticate themselves to browser clients.
Server farm	A group of federation servers that act together to provide high availability for the federation service. Server farms can be applied to any of the federation servers, proxies, or AD FS–enabled Web servers, but each farm can include only a single federation server type.
Service-oriented architecture (SOA)	SOAs are standards-based and language-agnostic architectures that rely on Web services to support distributed services on the Internet.
Single sign-on (SSO)	SSO simplifies application access by requiring a single logon from the user.
Token-signing certificate	The certificate that is used to sign the security tokens generated by the resource federation server.
Trust policy	The trust policy defines the set of parameters the federation service requires to identify partners, certificates, account stores, claims, and the various properties of the entities that are associated with the federation service. This policy is in XML file format.
Uniform Resource Identifier (URI)	AD FS relies on URIs to identify partners and account stores.
Verification certificate	The public key of a token-signing certificate loaded on all federation servers in an organization.
Web Services (WS-*)	A standards-based Internet service that forms part of an SOA. Commonly known Web services include the Simple Object Access Protocol (SOAP); the extended markup language (XML); and Universal Description, Discovery, and Integration (UDDI). Web Services are language-agnostic so they can interoperate between different IT infrastructures, for example UNIX, Linux, and Windows.

Table 17-1   Common AD FS Terms

Term	Description
Web Services Security (WS-Security)	The SOA specifications that outline how you digitally sign and encrypt SOAP messages.
Windows NT token-based application	A Windows-based application that relies in Windows NT authentication to process authorizations.
WS-Federation	The Web server specification that outlines the standards to be used when implementing federation.
WS-Federation Passive Requestor Profile (WS-F PRP)	The component of WS-Federation that outlines the standard protocol to be used when passive clients access an application through a federation service.

Installing Active Directory Federation Services

A basic installation of AD FS requires a series of computers. Ideally, you will have two AD DS domains, two perimeter networks, and AD FS servers distributed within each environment. The account organization should host AD DS and at least one federation server internally as well as a Federation Service Proxy in its perimeter network. The resource organization should have an AD DS and at least one internal federation server. Its perimeter network should include at least one AD FS–enabled Web server and one FSP. However, the full deployment you design will be based on considerations such as the number of partner organizations, the type of applications to share, the requirement for high availability and load balancing, and other considerations of this type.

Test environments can be set up with as few as four computers: one client, one AD FS–enabled Web server, and two federation servers to participate in AD FS federation between two organizations. Because of the nature of AD FS, computer clocks should be synchronized to the same time or should never have more than five minutes of difference between one and the other; otherwise, the process will not work because the token time stamps will be invalid. Because many of the computers are not part of an AD DS domain, you cannot rely on the PDC Emulator Operations Master for clock synchronization. The best way to ensure time synchronization is to use the Network Time Protocol (NTP) to link each server to an external clock server and thereby ensure that they all have the same time.

MORE INFO   **Rely on NTP for time synchronization**

For information on how to set up NTP on your servers to ensure time synchronization in the perimeter and the internal networks, look up *Windows Server 2008: The Complete Reference* by Ruest and Ruest (McGraw-Hill Osborne, 2008).

Quick Check

1. Your organization is an account organization in a federation partnership. It wants to support user access from the Internet, but it does not want to list its name within a drop-down list for privacy and security reasons. Which options are available to you to do this?
2. Which are the four role services and features that make up the AD FS server role?
3. Which are the three AD FS deployment designs?

Quick Check Answers

1. When you don't want to include your organization name in the organization drop-down list on the federation server's Web page, you can rely on the *whr* parameter to include your organization name directly within the query used to access the application. The format of the query should be as follows:

   `https://webserver/appname/apppage.aspx?whr=urn:federation:accountpartner`

2. AD FS includes four role services:
   - The Federation Service provides the core AD FS functionality managing resource access, filtering claims, and generating security tokens.
   - The Federation Service Proxy is an Internet relay that passes requests on to internal Federation Service servers.
   - The claims-aware agent supports the integration of Web applications to AD FS processes.
   - The Windows Token-based Agent supports the integration of Windows applications to AD FS processes.

3. AD FS supports three deployment designs: Federated Web Single-Sign-On, Federated Web SSO with Forest Trust, and Web SSO.

AD FS Installation Requirements

To prepare for an AD FS deployment, you must begin with its prerequisites. Table 17-2 outlines the basic requirements for an AD FS deployment. Note that the federation service was first released with Windows Server 2003 R2. Because of this, you can interoperate between Windows Server 2003 R2 and Windows Server 2008 federation systems. Table 17-2, however, lists requirements for AD FS only, which can run only on Windows Server 2008.

Table 17-2   AD FS Deployment Requirements

Hardware/Software	Requirement	Note
Processor	133 MHz for x86-based computers	Because of the low processor, memory, and disk space requirements for AD FS server roles, you can easily virtualize this role through Hyper-V.
RAM	512 MB	Recommended: 1 GB. AD FS is not a memory-intensive process, but it is always best to allocate at least 1 GB.
Hard disk space	10 MB for the AD FS installation	Recommended: a large system volume of at least 50 GB to ensure space for growth.
Operating system	Windows Server 2008 Enterprise Edition or Datacenter Edition	Federation Service, Federation Service Proxy, and AD FS Web Agent role services cannot run on earlier operating systems.
Web Services	IIS with ASP.NET enabled and .NET Framework 2.0	Use IIS 7.0 with ASP.NET 2.0 and .NET Framework 2.0.
Installation location	Default location on the system drive	The federation service and Federation Service Proxy cannot coexist on the same computer.
AD DS and AD LDS account store requirements	At least a single domain forest	Ideally, a minimum of two forests will exist. At worst, use one forest and one AD LDS store.
Installation certificate for TLS/SSL and token signing	Obtain an SSL server authentication certificate for each deployed AD FS server role	Rely on an external third-party commercial CA to obtain a trusted certificate or enterprise CAs. Use self-signed certificates only in testing environments. Each of the federation servers and the Federation Service Proxy and the Web agent servers needs an authentication certificate.
TCP/IP network connectivity	IPv4 or IPv6 connectivity, ideally static address assignments	Network connectivity must exist between client, domain controller, and computers hosting the federation service, the Federation Service Proxy and the AD FS Web agent.
DNS configuration	Create custom CNAME records of the internal server that is running the federation service	Do not use host files with DNS. Use proper DNS registrations.

Table 17-2 AD FS Deployment Requirements

Hardware/Software	Requirement	Note
Web browser	Microsoft Internet Explorer 5 or later, Mozilla Firefox, and Safari on Apple	JScript and at least trusted cookies must be enabled for the federation servers and Web applications.
Client operating system	Windows XP or Windows Vista for the AD FS client	The Vista OS is recommended.

MORE INFO   AD FS step-by-step guides

For access to AD FS step-by-step guides, go to *http://technet2.microsoft.com/windowsserver/en/technologies/featured/adfs/default.mspx.*

Exam Tip   Because of its nature, the AD FS server role is ideal for virtualization through Windows Server 2008 Hyper-V.

Quick Check
1. Which ports must be open in a firewall to support AD FS operations?
2. Which claim types are supported by AD FS?

Quick Check Answers
1. AD FS relies on a single port for all its operations: port 443, the SSL/TLS HTTP or HTTPS port.
2. AD FS supports three claim types:
   - Identity claims, which can be user principal name, e-mail address, or common name
   - Group claims, which are nothing more than membership in specific distribution or security groups in AD DS
   - Custom claims, which can include any custom information such as a bank account number for the user

Upgrade Considerations

Many organizations choose to use a specific service account when deploying services such as AD FS. If you opted to do this in your Windows Server 2003 R2 deployment of AD FS, you must make note of which account and password is assigned to which service because the AD FS upgrade process automatically resets all these services, by default, to use the Network Service account. After the upgrade is complete, you can change the service back to the named service account you had previously assigned to it.

Ideally, you will test the upgrade in a laboratory, perhaps a virtual laboratory, before you begin the process in your production networks.

PRACTICE Prepare an AD FS Deployment

In this practice, you will create a complex AD FS environment that will consist of several computers. The computers you need for this practice are outlined in the "Before You Begin" section of this chapter. Table 17-3 outlines the roles each domain and computer will play in your AD FS deployment.

Table 17-3   AD FS Computer Roles

Domain Name	Role
contoso.com	Account Domain
woodgrovebank.com	Resource Domain

Computer Name	Role
SERVER01	AD DS domain controller for contoso.com, the account domain
SERVER03	The federation server for contoso.com, the account domain
SERVER04	The Federation Service Proxy for contoso.com, the account domain
SERVER05	The SQL Server database server for the AD RMS deployment in contoso.com
SERVER06	AD DS domain controller for woodgrovebank.com, the resource domain
SERVER07	The federation server for woodgrovebank.com, the resource domain
SERVER08	The Federation Service Proxy and AD FS–enabled Web server for woodgrovebank.com, the resource domain

Begin by preparing the DNS in each forest and then move on to install the federation servers. Then install the federation service proxies in both forests and AD FS–enable the Web site in the resource forest.

IMPORTANT   Perimeter networks

Note that this layout does not include perimeter networks. Perimeter networks require a complex TCP/IP configuration, which is not required for the purpose of this practice. However, make sure that your AD FS deployments include proper server placement within perimeter networks as outlined in Lesson 1, "Understanding and Installing Active Directory Federation Services."

▶ **Exercise 1   Configure Cross-DNS References**

In this exercise, you will configure the DNS servers in each forest to refer to the servers in the other forest. Because each forest is independent of the other, their DNS servers do not know about the other. To exchange information from one forest to the other, you need to implement cross-DNS references in each forest. The easiest way to do this is to use forwarders from one domain to the other and vice versa. Make sure SERVER01 and SERVER06 are running.

1. Log on to SERVER01 with the domain Administrator account.
2. Launch Server Manager from the Administrative Tools program group.
3. Expand Roles\DNS Serve\DNS\SERVER01.
4. Right-click SERVER01 in the tree pane and select Properties.
5. Click the Forwarders tab and click Edit.
6. Type the IP address of SERVER06 and click OK twice.
7. Repeat the procedure in reverse on SERVER06; that is, add the SERVER01 IP address as a forwarder for SERVER06.
8. Test the operation by pinging each server from the other. For example, use the following command to ping SERVER01 from SERVER06:

    ```
    ping server01.contoso.com
    ```

    You should receive a response stating the IP address of SERVER01.

▶ **Exercise 2   Install the Federation Servers**

In this exercise, you will install the federation servers. This involves the installation of the server role plus the required support services for the role. Make sure SERVER01, SERVER03, SERVER06, and SERVER07 are running.

1. Log on to SERVER07 with the domain Administrator account.

    You do not need as high privileges as the domain administrator to install and work with AD FS, but using these credentials here facilitates the exercise. Local administrative privileges are all that are required to work with AD FS.
2. Launch Server Manager from the Administrative Tools program group.
3. Right-click the Roles node in the tree pane and select Add Roles.
4. Review the Before You Begin information and click Next.
5. On the Select Server Roles page, select Active Directory Federation Services and click Next.
6. Review the information about the role and click Next.
7. On the Select Role Services page, select Federation Service. Server Manager prompts you to add the required role services and features. Click Add Required Role Services. Click Next.

8. On the Choose A Server Authentication Certificate For SSL Encryption page, select Create A Self-Signed Certificate For SSL Encryption and click Next.

   In a production environment, you would need to request certificates from a trusted CA so that all your systems will work together through the Internet.

9. On the Choose A Token-Signing Certificate page, select Create A Self-Signed Token-Signing Certificate and click Next.

10. On the Select Trust Policy page, select Create A New Trust Policy and click Next.

    Make a note of the path used to save this trust policy. Your federation relationship will rely on this policy to work.

11. Review the information on the Web Server (IIS) page and click Next.

12. On the Select Role Services page, accept the default values and click Next.

13. On the Confirm Installation Selections page, review your choices and click Install.

14. When the installation is complete, click Close to close the installation wizard.

15. Repeat the same procedure for SERVER03.

    Note that because SERVER03 is a root CA, the operation is shorter. However, use the same settings as with SERVER07. This means relying on self-signed certificates wherever possible.

IMPORTANT Default Web Site

When the AD FS installation is complete, you must configure the Default Web Site in IIS with TLS/SSL security on both federation servers. This will be done in Lesson 2, "Configuring and Using Active Directory Federation Services."

You begin with SERVER07 because it does not include any role and displays all the installation pages you would see when installing the AD FS role on a new server. Note that because SERVER03 already includes some server roles, the installation process on this server is shorter.

▶ **Exercise 3 Install the Federation Service Proxies**

In this exercise, you will install the federation service proxies. This involves the installation of the server role plus the required support services for the role. Make sure SERVER01, SERVER03, SERVER04, SERVER06, SERVER07, and SERVER08 are running.

1. Log on to SERVER08 with the domain Administrator account.

2. Launch Server Manager from the Administrative Tools program group.

3. Right-click the Roles node in the tree pane and select Add Roles.

4. Review the Before You Begin information and click Next.

5. On the Select Server Roles page, select Active Directory Federation Services and click Next.

6. Review the information about the role and click Next.

7. On the Select Role Services page, select Federation Service Proxy and click Add Required Role Services. Also, select AD FS Web Agents and click Next.

    Note that although you cannot add the Federation Service Proxy on the same server as the federation server, you can combine the FSP and the AD FS Web Agents role services.

8. On the Choose A Server Authentication Certificate For SSL Encryption page, select Create A Self-Signed Certificate For SSL Encryption and click Next.

    In a production environment, you would need to request certificates from a trusted CA so that all your systems will work together through the Internet.

9. On the Specify Federation Server page, type **server07.woodgrovebank.com** and click Validate.

    The validation should fail because you have not yet set up the trust relationship between each computer. This is done by exporting and importing the SSL certificates for each server through IIS. You will perform this task in Lesson 2.

10. Click Next.

11. On the Choose A Client Authentication Certificate page, select Create A Self-Signed Client Authentication Certificate and click Next.

12. Review the information on the Web Server (IIS) page and click Next.

13. On the Select Role Services page, accept the default values and click Next.

14. On the Confirm Installation Selections page, review your choices and click Install.

15. When the installation is complete, click Close to close the installation wizard.

16. Repeat the operation on SERVER04 in the *contoso.com* domain. When asked to input the federation server, type **server03.contoso.com**. Also, use self-signed certificates when prompted and do not install AD FS Web Agents on SERVER04. Its role is only that of an FSP because it is in the account organization.

    You begin with SERVER08 because it does not include any role and displays all the installation pages you would see when installing the AD FS role on a new server. Note that because SERVER04 already includes some server roles, the installation process on this server is shorter.

Exam Tip   Pay attention to the details of each installation type; they are covered on the exam.

Lesson Summary

■ AD FS extends your internal authentication store to external environments through identity federation and federation trusts.

- Federation partnerships always involve a resource and an account organization. A resource organization can be a partner of several account organizations, but an account organization can be a partner with only a single resource organization.

- AD FS relies on secure HTTP communications by using SSL authentication certificates to verify the identity of both the server and the client during communications. Because of this, all communications occur through port 433 over HTTPS.

- AD FS is a Web Services implementation that relies on standards-based implementations to ensure that it can interact with partners using different operating systems, for example, Windows, UNIX, and Linux.

Lesson Review

You can use the following questions to test your knowledge of the information in Lesson 1, "Understanding and Installing Active Directory Federation Services." The questions are also available on the companion CD if you prefer to review them in electronic form.

NOTE Answers

Answers to these questions and explanations of why each answer choice is right or wrong are located in the "Answers" section at the end of the book.

---

1. You are a systems administrator for Contoso, Ltd. Your organization already has a federation relationship with Woodgrove Bank, which was implemented using Federation Services with Windows Server 2003 R2. To improve security, you deployed the federation service with named accounts running the service. Now you're ready to upgrade to AD FS, but when you perform the upgrade, you find out that the named account used to run the service has been removed and replaced with the Network Service account. Why did this happen?

    A. You cannot use named service accounts to run the AD FS service.

    B. The default service account used in an AD FS installation or upgrade is Network Service.

    C. Woodgrove has a policy that states that all federation services must run with the Network Service account.

    D. Microsoft prefers to use the Network Service account to run federation services and resets it as a best practice.

Lesson 2: Configuring and Using Active Directory Federation Services

As you saw in Lesson 1, servers in an AD FS relationship must rely on certificates to create a chain of trust between each other and to ensure that all traffic transported over the trust relationships is encrypted at all times. As discussed in Chapter 15, "Active Directory Certificate Services and Public Key Infrastructures," the best way to ensure that this chain of trust is valid and is trusted in all locations is either to obtain certificates from a trusted third-party CA or obtain them through the creation of a linked AD CS implementation that uses a third-party CA as its root.

This is only one aspect of the AD FS configuration that must be completed. When you deploy AD FS, you will want to configure your AD FS–aware applications, configure trust policies between partner organizations, and configure claims for your users and groups. Then, you can generally begin to run and manage AD FS.

MORE INFO   AD FS operations

For more information on AD FS operations, look up "AD FS Operations Guide" at *http:// technet2.microsoft.com/windowsserver/en/library/007d4d62-2e2e-43a9-8652-9108733cbb731033 .mspx?mfr=true*.

> **After this lesson, you will be able to:**
> - Manage AD FS certificates.
> - Finalize AD FS server configurations.
> - Work with AD FS trust policies.
>
> **Estimated lesson time: 40 minutes**

Finalize the Configuration of AD FS

When you deploy AD FS, you must perform several activities to complete the configuration. These activities include:

- Configuring the Web service on each server to use SSL/TLS encryption for the Web site that is hosting the AD FS service.
- Exporting certificates from each server and importing them into the other servers that form the relationship. For example, the federation server's token-signing certificate must be installed as a validation certificate in the other servers in the trust relationship to support the AD FS security token exchange processes.
- Configuring IIS on the servers that will host the claims-aware applications. These servers must use HTTPS for application-related communications.

- Creating and configuring the claims-aware applications you will be hosting.
- Configuring the federation servers in each partner organization. This involves several steps, which include:
    - In an account organization, configuring the trust policy, creating claims for your users, and, finally, configuring the AD DS account store for identity federation.
    - In a resource organization, configuring the trust policy creating claims for your users, configuring an AD DS account store for identity federation, and then enabling a claims-aware application.
- Creating the federation trust to enable identity federation. This also involves several steps:
    - Exporting the trust policy from the account organization and importing it into the resource organization
    - Creating and configuring a claim mapping in the resource organization
    - Exporting the partner policy from the resource organization and importing it into the account organization

Much of this effort is related to certificate mapping from one server to another. One important factor is the ability to access the roots or at least the Web sites hosting the Certificate Revocation Lists (CRL) for each certificate. As discussed in Chapter 15, CRLs are the only way you can tell a member of a trust chain whether a certificate is valid. If it is supported, you can use the Microsoft Online Responder service (OCSP) from AD CS to do this as well.

In AD FS, CRL checking is enabled by default. CRL checking is mostly performed for the security token signatures, but it is good policy to rely on it for all digital signatures.

Using and Managing AD FS

When the configuration of the identity federation is complete, you will move on to regular administration and management of the AD FS services and server roles. You will rely on the Active Directory Federation Services console in Server Manager to perform these tasks. Administration tasks will include:

- Configuring the federation service or federation server farm. Remember that you can have up to three farms in an AD FS deployment:
    - A federation server farm that includes several servers hosting the same role
    - A Federation Service Proxy farm
    - A claims-aware application server farm running IIS
- Managing the trust policy that is associated with the federation service by:
    - Administering account stores in either AD DS or AD LDS.
    - Managing the account, resource partners, or both that trust your organization.
    - Managing claims on federation servers.

❏ Managing certificates used by federation servers.

❏ Managing certificates in AD FS–protected Web applications.

Because AD FS relies so heavily on IIS, many of the federation server settings that are configured in the Active Directory Federation Services node of Server Manager are stored in the Web.config file located in the Federation Service virtual directory in IIS. Other configuration settings are stored in the trust policy file. As with other IIS settings, the Web.config file can easily be edited directly because it is nothing more than a text file. The settings you can control through the Web.config file include:

- The path to the trust policy file.
- The local certificate used for signing tokens.
- The location of the ASP.NET Web pages supporting the service.
- The debug logging level for the service as well as the path to the log files directory.
- The ability to control the access type, for example, anonymous access, to group claims you prepare for the organization.

When edited, you can publish the Web.config file to other servers requiring the same configuration settings. After IIS has been reset, the new configuration will take effect.

However, the trust policy file should never be edited manually. This file should always be edited through the controls in the AD FS console or through programmatic settings that rely on the AD FS object model.

MORE INFO AD FS object model

For more information on scripting support and the AD FS object model, see *http://msdn2.microsoft.com/en-us/library/ms674895.aspx*.

When you work with FSPs, you can rely on the AD FS console to configure:

- The federation service with which the FSP is working.
- The manner in which the FSP will collect user credential information from browsers and Web applications.

The settings configured for Federation Service proxies are also stored in a Web.config file, much like the federation server settings. However, because the FSP does not include a trust policy file, all its settings are stored within its Web.config file. These include:

- The Federation Service URL.
- The client authentication certificate to be used by the federation server proxy for TLS/SSL-encrypted communications with the federation service.
- The ASP.NET Web pages supporting the service.

Preparing and putting in place an identity federation through AD FS requires care and planning. Because of this, take the time to practice and prepare thoroughly in a laboratory before you move this technology into production.

PRACTICE Finalizing the AD FS Configuration

In this practice, you will finalize the AD FS installation you performed in Lesson 1. You will need to rely on the same computers you used in that practice. Begin by configuring the IIS server on each of the federation servers and then map certificates from one server to the other and configure the Web server. You can also create and configure the Web application that will be claims-aware. Then configure the federation servers for each partner organization. You finish the AD FS configuration by creating the federation trust.

▶ **Exercise 1   Configure SSL for the Federation Servers and the FSPs**

In this exercise, you will configure IIS to require SSL on the Default Web Site of the federation servers and the Federation Service proxies. Make sure that all servers are running. This includes SERVER01, SERVER03, SERVER04, SERVER05, SERVER06, SERVER07, and SERVER08.

1. Log on to SERVER03 with the domain Administrator account.

    You do not need domain administrative credentials; in fact, you need only local administrative credentials to perform this task, but using the domain Administrators account facilitates this exercise.

2. Launch Internet Information Services (IIS) Manager from the Administrative Tools program group.

3. Expand *Servername*\Sites\Default Web Site.

4. In the details pane, in the Features view, move to the IIS section and double-click SSL Settings.

5. On the SSL Settings page, select the Require SSL check box.

    In a production environment, you can also require 128-bit SSL, which is more secure than the default setting but requires additional processing overhead. For the purposes of this practice, the default setting is sufficient.

6. Under Client Certificates, select Accept, and then click Apply in the Actions pane.

7. Repeat this procedure on SERVER04, SERVER07, and SERVER08.

    All your AD FS servers are now configured to rely on SSL-encrypted communications.

▶ **Exercise 2   Export and Import Certificates**

One of the most important factors in setting up federation partnerships is the integration of the certificates from each server to link each server with the ones it needs to communicate with. To do so, you need to perform several tasks.

■ Create a file share that each server can access to simplify the transfer of certificate files from one server to another.

- Export the token-signing certificate from the account federation server (SERVER03) to a file.
- Export the server authentication certificate of the account federation server (SERVER03) to a file.
- Export the server authentication certificate of the resource federation server (SERVER07) to a file.
- Import the server authentication certificate for both federation servers.
- Export the client authentication certificate of the account Federation Service Proxy (SERVER04) to a file.
- Export the client authentication certificate of the resource Federation Service Proxy (SERVER08) to a file.
- Import the client authentication certificate on the respective federation servers.
- First, you need to create the file share you will use to store the certificates.

1. Log on to SERVER03 with the domain Administrator account.
2. Launch Windows Explorer and move to the C drive. Create a new folder and name it **Temp**.
3. Right-click the Temp folder and select Share.
4. In the File Sharing dialog box, select Everyone in the drop-down list, click Add, and from the Permission Level column, assign the Contributor role to Everyone.
5. Click Share.

   Your shared folder is ready. Proceed to the export of the security token signing certificate.
6. Log on to SERVER03 with the domain Administrator account.
7. Launch Active Directory Federation Services from the Administrative Tools program group.
8. Right-click Federation Service and select Properties on the General Tab. Click View.
9. Click the Details tab and click Copy To File.
10. On the Welcome To The Certificate Export Wizard page, click Next.
11. On the Export Private Key page, select No, Do Not Export The Private Key and click Next.

    You do not export the private key file because you are creating a validation certificate that consists only of the certificate's public key.
12. On the Export File Format page, ensure that DER Encoded Binary X.509 (.CER) is selected and click Next.
13. On the File To Export page, type **C:\Temp\SERVER03TokenSigning.cer** and click Next.

    This token-signing certificate will be imported to SERVER07 when the Account Partner Wizard prompts you for the Account Partner Verification Certificate. You can then use the shared TEMP folder to obtain this file over the network.
14. On the Completing The Certificate Export Wizard page, verify the information and click Finish. Click OK when you get the Certificate Export Was Successful message. Click OK twice to close the Federation Service property sheet.

So that successful communications can occur between both of the federation servers (SERVER03 and SERVER07) and their respective FSPs (SERVER04 and SERVER08) as well as with the Web server (SERVER08), each server must trust the root of the federation servers. Because you use self-signed certificates in this practice, you must export and import each certificate. Table 17-4 outlines which certificates must be exported and where they must be imported. (See also Figure 17-7.)

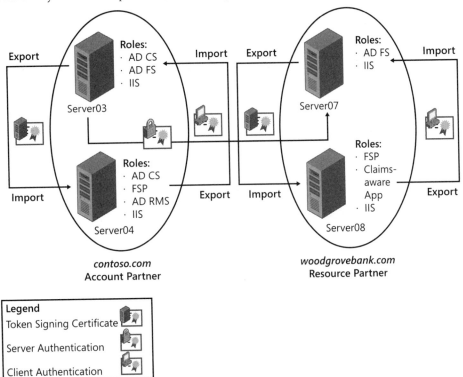

Figure 17-7   Preparing certificate mappings for AD FS

Table 17-4   AD FS Certificate Mappings

Server Name	Certificate to Export	Certificate Name	Location to Import
SERVER03	Token Signing	SERVER03TokenSigning.cer	SERVER07
SERVER03	SSL Server Authentication	SERVER03SSL.cer	SERVER04
SERVER04	SSL Client Authentication	SERVER04SSL.cer	SERVER03
SERVER07	SSL Server Authentication	SERVER07SSL.cer	SERVER08
SERVER08	SSL Client Authentication	SERVER08SSL.cer	SERVER07

▶ **Exercise 3   Export the SSL Server and Client Certificates**

Beginning with SERVER03, you will export the SSL server and client authentication certificates to a file on each server.

1. Log on to SERVER03 with domain Administrator credentials.
2. Launch Internet Information Services (IIS) Manager from the Administrative Tools program group.
3. In the details pane, click the server name.
4. In the Features view, move to the IIS section and double-click Server Certificates.
5. Double-click the Contoso-Root-CA certificate and click the Details tab.
6. On the Details tab, click Copy to File. Click Next.
7. On the Export Private Key page, select No, Do Not Export The Private Key and click Next.
8. On the Export File Format page, ensure that DER Encoded Binary X.509 (.CER) is selected and click Next.
9. On the File To Export page, click Browse and move to the C:\Temp folder. Name the certificate **SERVER03SSL.cer** and click Save. Click Next.
10. On the Completing The Certificate Export Wizard page, verify the information and click Finish. Click OK when you get the Certificate Export Was Successful message. Click OK again to close the dialog box.

Now move to SERVER04 and repeat the procedure.

1. Log on to SERVER04 with domain Administrator credentials.
2. Launch Internet Information Services (IIS) Manager from the Administrative Tools program group.
3. In the details pane, click the server name.
4. In the Features view, move to the IIS section and double-click Server Certificates.
5. Double-click the Contoso-Issuing-CA certificate and move to the Details tab.
6. On the Details tab, click Copy To File. Click Next.
7. On the Export Private Key page, click No, Do Not Export The Private Key and click Next.
8. On the Export File Format page, ensure that DER Encoded Binary X.509 (.CER) is selected and click Next.
9. On the File To Export page, click Browse and move to your Documents folder. Name the certificate **SERVER04SSL.cer**, click Save, and then click Next.
10. On the Completing The Certificate Export Wizard page, verify the information and click Finish.
11. Click OK when you get the Certificate Export Was Successful message. Click OK again to close the dialog box.

Now move to SERVER07 and repeat the procedure.

1. Log on to SERVER07 with domain Administrator credentials.
2. Launch Internet Information Services (IIS) Manager from the Administrative Tools program group.
3. In the details pane, click the server name.
4. In the Features view, move to the IIS section and double-click Server Certificates.
5. Double-click the SERVER07.WoodgroveBank.com certificate and move to the Details tab.
6. On the Details tab, click Copy To File. Click Next.
7. On the Export Private Key page, click No, Do Not Export The Private Key and click Next.
8. On the Export File Format page, ensure that DER Encoded Binary X.509 (.CER) is selected and click Next.
9. On the File To Export page, click Browse and move to your Documents folder. Name the certificate **SERVER07SSL.cer**, click Save, and then click Next.
10. On the Completing The Certificate Export Wizard page, verify the information and click Finish.
11. Click OK when you get the Certificate Export Was Successful message. Click OK again to close the dialog box.

Now move to SERVER08 and repeat the procedure.

1. Log on to SERVER08 with domain Administrator credentials.
2. Launch Internet Information Services (IIS) Manager from the Administrative Tools program group.
3. In the details pane, click the server name.
4. In the Features view, move to the IIS section and double-click Server Certificates.
5. Double-click the SERVER08.WoodgroveBank.com certificate and move to the Details tab.
6. On the Details tab, click Copy To File. Click Next.
7. On the Export Private Key page, click No, Do Not Export The Private Key and click Next.
8. On the Export File Format page, ensure that DER Encoded Binary X.509 (.CER) is selected and click Next.
9. On the File To Export page, click Browse and move to your Documents folder. Name the certificate **SERVER08SSL.cer**, click Save, and then click Next.
10. On the Completing The Certificate Export Wizard page, verify the information and click Finish.
11. Click OK when you get the Certificate Export Was Successful message. Click OK again to close the dialog box.

Because you will need to import these certificates into other servers, you need to copy them to a shared folder.

1. For SERVER04, SERVER07, and SERVER08, launch Windows Explorer and move to your Documents folder.

2. Right-click the certificate and select Copy.

3. Move to the address bar at the top of the Explorer window and type **SERVER03.Contoso.com\temp**.

4. If you used the same account name and password for the domain Administrators account in both domains, you will not be prompted for credentials. If not, type **Contoso*AdminAccount*** in the logon name box and type its corresponding password.

5. Paste the certificate into the Minimize Windows Explorer folder.

   Repeat this procedure on each server to place all the certificates in the \\SERVER03.contoso.com\TEMP folder.

▶ **Exercise 4   Import an SSL Authentication Certificate into a Server**

Beginning with SERVER03, you will import an SSL authentication certificate into a server.

1. Log on to SERVER03 with domain administrator credentials.

2. Move to the Start menu, type **mmc** in the Search box, and then press Enter.

3. In the new console, select Add/Remove Snap-in from the File menu, select the Certificate snap-in, and click Add.

4. Choose Computer Account and click Next. Ensure that Local Computer is selected, click Finish, and then click OK.

   Now you will save the console.

5. Select Save As from the File menu, browse to your Documents folder, and name it **Computer Certificates**.

6. Expand Console Root\Certificates (Local Computer) \Trusted Root Certification Authorities.

7. Right-click Trusted Root Certification Authorities, click All Tasks, and then click Import.

8. On the Welcome To The Certificate Import wizard page, click Next.

9. On the File To Import page, click Browse and move to the C:\Temp folder.

10. Select the certificate for SERVER04, SERVER04SSL.cer, and click Open. Click Next.

11. On the Certificate Store page, select Place All Certificates In The Following Store, make sure the selected store is Trusted Root Certification Authorities, and click Next.

12. On the Completing The Certificate Import Wizard page, verify the information and click Finish. Click OK to close the successful import message.

   Repeat these procedures for each certificate to import. Refer to Table 17-4 to see which certificate must be imported where. For each of the other servers, go to the shared TEMP folder on SERVER03 to obtain the certificate. Your certificate mappings are complete.

▶ **Exercise 5   Configure the Web Server**

To set up a claims-aware application on a Web server, you need to configure IIS and create a claims-aware application. To do so, perform the following steps. Make sure SERVER06 and SERVER08 are running.

1. Log on to SERVER08 with the domain Administrator account.

    You do not need domain administrative credentials; in fact, you need only local administrative credentials to perform this task, but using the domain Administrators account facilitates this exercise.

2. Launch Internet Information Services (IIS) Manager from the Administrative Tools program group.

3. In the tree, expand SERVER08\Sites\Default Web Site.

4. In the actions pane, under the Edit Site section, click Bindings.

5. In the Site Bindings dialog box, select the HTTPS binding and click Edit.

6. Verify that the SERVER08.WoodgroveBank.com certificate is bound to port 443. If not, select it and click OK.

7. Click Close to close the Site Bindings dialog box.

8. In the center pane, in the Features view, under the IIS section, double-click SSL Settings.

9. Verify that the settings require SSL and are set to accept client certificates. If not, change these settings and click Apply.

10. In the tree, double-click Default Web Site to return to the Features view.

Perform the following steps to create and configure a claims-aware application.

1. Right-click Default Web Site and select Add Application.

2. In the Add Application dialog box, in the *Alias* field, type **claimapplication01**.

3. Click Select, select Classic .NET AppPool from the drop-down list, and click OK.

4. Click the ellipse button (...) under Physical Path and select the C:\inetpub\wwwroot folder.

5. Click Make A New Folder, type **claimapplication01**, click OK, and then click OK again to close the dialog box.

    Your application has been created; however, it is an empty application. You do not need to actually create an application for the purpose of this exercise, but if you want to, you can.

MORE INFO   Create a sample claims-aware application

To create the three files that make up the sample claims-aware application, use the procedure called "Creating the Sample Claims-aware Application" from *http://207.46.196.114/ windowsserver2008/en/library/5ae6ce09-4494-480b-8816-8897bde359491033.mspx*. After these files are created, copy them into the C:\Inetpub\Wwwroot\Claimapp folder.

▶ **Exercise 6   Configure the Federation Servers**

Both federation servers need to be configured to operate properly. SERVER03, the account federation server, must have a configured trust policy. You must also create claims for your users and identify the AD DS account store. SERVER07, the resource federation server, must have a trust policy, claims for the users in the resource domain, a configured account store, and enabled claims-aware applications. Ensure that SERVER01, SERVER03, SERVER06, and SERVER07 are running.

1. Log on to SERVER03 with the domain Administrator account.

   In this case, you need to use domain administrator credentials to identify the account store.

2. Launch Active Directory Federation Services from the Administrative Tools program group.

3. Expand Federation Service\Trust Policy.

4. Right-click the trust policy to select Properties.

5. On the General tab, under Federation Service URI, type **urn:federation:Contoso**.

   Make sure you type the characters as they appear in your domain name because this value is case sensitive.

6. Ensure that the Federation Service endpoint URL lists https://SERVER03.Contoso.com /adfs/ls/.

7. Click the Display Name tab and, under Display Name For This Trust Policy, type **Contoso** to provide a name that does not depend on a single server. Click OK.

Now move to create claims for your users.

1. Expand Trust Policy\My Organization\Organization Claims.

2. Right-click Organization Claims, select New, and then choose Organization Claim.

3. In the Create A New Organization Claim dialog box, type **Woodgrove Bank Application Claim**.

4. Ensure that Group Claim is selected.

5. Click OK to create the claim.

   It should now be listed in the details pane.

Now, add the account store for *contoso.com*.

1. Move to the Account Stores node in the tree pane under My Organization.

2. Right-click Account Stores, select New, and then choose Account Store.

3. Review the information on the Welcome page and click Next.

4. On the Account Store Type page, ensure that Active Directory Domain Services (AD DS) is selected and click Next.

Note that only one AD DS store can be associated with an AD FS implementation. You can, however, add additional AD LDS stores along with the AD DS store.

5. On the Enable this Account Store page, ensure that the Enable This Account Store check box is selected and click Next. Click Finish to complete the operation.

   Note that this adds Active Directory as a valid account store under the Account Stores node.

The last item to configure in the *contoso.com* or account organization is to map a group to the group claim you created earlier.

1. Right-click Active Directory under the Account Stores node, select New, and then choose Group Claim Extraction.

2. Click Add, type **Accounting**, and then click Check Names. Click OK.

3. Ensure that Woodgrove Bank Application Claim is selected in the drop-down list and click OK.

   Note that AD FS relies on the e-mail group name to assign the group claim mapping.

The account federation server is now ready. Prepare the resource federation server, SERVER07.

1. Log on to SERVER07 with the domain Administrator account.

   In this case, you need to use domain administrator credentials to identify the account store.

2. Launch Active Directory Federation Services from the Administrative Tools program group.

3. Expand Federation Service\Trust Policy.

4. Right-click the trust policy to select Properties.

5. On the General tab, under Federation Service URI, type **urn:federation:Woodgrove-Bank**.

   Make sure you type the characters as they appear in your domain name because this value is case sensitive.

6. Make sure the Federation Service endpoint URL lists https://SERVER07.Woodgrove-Bank.com/adfs/ls/.

7. Click the Display Name tab and, under Display Name For This Trust Policy, type **Woodgrove Bank** to provide a name that does not depend on a single server. Click OK.

Now create claims for your users.

1. Expand Trust Policy\My Organization\Organization Claims.

2. Right-click Organization Claims, select New, and choose Organization Claim.

3. In the Create A New Organization Claim dialog box, type **Woodgrove Bank Application Claim**.

4. Ensure that Group Claim is selected.

5. Click OK to create the claim.

    It should now be listed in the details pane.

Now add the account store for *woodgrovebank.com*.

1. Move to the Account Stores node in the tree pane under My Organization.

2. Right-click Account Stores, select New, and choose Account Store.

3. Review the information on the Welcome page and click Next.

4. On the Account Store Type page, ensure that Active Directory Domain Services (AD DS) is selected and click Next.

5. On the Enable This Account Store page, ensure that the Enable This Account Store check box is selected and click Next. Click Finish to complete the operation.

    Note that this adds Active Directory as a valid account store under the Account Stores node.

Now add a claims-aware application to the AD FS resources.

1. Move to the Applications node under My Organization.

2. Right-click Applications, choose New, and then select Application.

3. Review the information on the Welcome page and click Next.

4. On the Application Type page, ensure that Claims-Aware Application is selected and click Next.

5. On the Application Details page, type **Claim Application 01** in the *Application Display Name* field and type the application URL as **https://SERVER08.WoodgroveBank.com/ claimapplication01**. Click Next.

6. On the Accept Identity Claims page, select User Principal Name and click Next.

    Note that you can add several identity claim types, but remember that they are processed in order, as outlined earlier.

7. Ensure that Enable This Application is selected and click Next. Click Finish to create the application.

8. Select the newly created application in the tree pane.

9. Move to the details pane and right-click Woodgrove Bank Application Claim and select Enable.

10. Verify that the new claim you created is enabled in the details pane.

    Your resource federation server is now ready to process claims.

Exam Tip   Make note of this procedure and practice the various operations several times. Configuring trust policies and user and group claim mapping is definitely part of the exam.

▶ **Exercise 7   Configure the Federation Trust**

Now that both federation servers have been configured, you can move on to the configuration of the federation trust. To do so, you must export the trust policy from the account federation server, import it into the resource federation server, create a claim mapping based on this policy, and then export the partner policy from the RFS to import it into the AFS. This will complete the AD FS implementation. Make sure that SERVER01, SERVER03, SERVER06, and SERVER07 are running.

1.   Log on to SERVER03 with the domain Administrator account.
2.   Launch Active Directory Federation Services from the Administrative Tools program group.
3.   Expand Federation Service\Trust Policy.
4.   Right-click Trust Policy and select Export Basic Partner Policy.
5.   Click Browse, move to the C:\Temp folder, and name the policy **ContosoTrustPolicy.xml**. Click Save. Click OK to close the dialog box.

   In the release of Federation Services in Windows Server 2003 R2, the export and import of polices was done manually and could lead to errors. In AD FS, this process relies on the graphical interface to perform the task, reducing the possibility of error.

Now, import the policy into the RFS in Woodgrove Bank.

1.   Log on to SERVER07 with the domain Administrator account.
2.   Launch Active Directory Federation Services from the Administrative Tools program group.
3.   Expand Federation Service\Trust Policy\Partner Organizations.
4.   Right-click Account Partners, select New, and then choose Account Partner.
5.   Review the information on the Welcome page and click Next.
6.   On the Import Policy File page, select Yes, and then click Browse.
7.   In the address bar, type **SERVER03.contoso.com\temp** and press Enter. Select the Contoso Trust Policy and click Open. Click Next.
8.   On the Account Partner Details page, review the information and click Next.

   This information should be the same information you input when you configured the Trust Policy properties for the *contoso.com* domain.

9.   On the Account Partner Verification Certificate page, ensure that Use The Verification Certificate In The Import Policy File is selected and click Next.
10.   On the Federation Scenario page, ensure that Federated Web SSO is selected and click Next.
11.   On the Account Partner Identity Claims page, ensure that the UPN Claim and the E-mail Claim check boxes are selected and click Next.

Remember that common names are very hard to validate and verify that they are unique. Therefore, avoid using them as much as possible.

12. On the Accepted UPN Suffixes page, type **Contoso.com**, click Add, and then click Next.

13. On the Accepted E-mail Suffixes page, type **Contoso.com**, click Add, and then click Next.

14. On the Enable This Account Partner page, ensure that the Enable This Account Partner check box is selected and click Next.

15. Click Finish to complete the operation.

    The account partner is now set up on the RFS. Note that it is now displayed under the Account Partners node.

Now you will create a claim mapping for this partner.

1. Right-click Contoso under the Account Partners node, select New, and then choose Incoming Group Claim Mapping.

2. In the Create A New Incoming Group Claim Mapping dialog box, type **Woodgrove Bank Application Claim**, ensure that the Woodgrove Bank Application Claim is selected in the drop-down list, and then click OK.

    Note that you must type in the uppercase and lowercase characters exactly as you typed them in the *contoso.com* domain when you created the group claim earlier. Using the same name in both the account and the resource organizations makes this easier.

You are now ready to export the partner policy from the RFS and import it into the AFS.

1. Right-click Contoso under the Account Partners node and select Export Policy.

2. In the Export Partner Policy dialog box, click Browse.

3. In the address bar, type **\\SERVER03.contoso.com\temp** and press Enter.

4. Type **ContosoPartnerPolicy** and click Save.

5. Click OK to complete the operation.

    You can now import this partner policy into the AFS.

6. Log on to SERVER03 with the domain Administrator account.

7. Launch Active Directory Federation Services from the Administrative Tools program group.

8. Expand Federation Service\Trust Policy\Partner Organizations.

9. Right-click Resource Partners, select New, and then choose Resource Partner.

10. Review the information on the Welcome page and click Next.

11. On the Import Policy File page, select Yes, and then click Browse.

12. Move to C:\Temp, select the Contoso Partner Policy and click Open. Click Next.

13. On the Resource Partner Details page, review the information and click Next.

This information should be the same information you input when you configured the trust policy properties for the Woodgrove Bank domain.

14. On the Federation Scenario page, ensure that Federated Web SSO is selected and click Next.

15. On the Resource Partner Identity Claims page, ensure that the UPN Claim and the E-mail Claim check boxes are selected and click Next.

16. On the Select UPN Suffix page, ensure that Replace All UPN Suffixes With The Following is selected and that *contoso.com* is the UPN suffix listed. Click Next.

Remember that only one UPN suffix can be used in a partnership even if you can have several in the AD DS forest.

17. On the Select E-mail Suffix page, ensure that Replace All E-Mail Suffixes With is selected and that *contoso.com* is the e-mail suffix that is listed. Click Next.

18. On the Enable This Resource Partner page, ensure that the Enable This Resource Partner check box is selected and click Next.

19. Click Finish to complete the operation.

Woodgrove Bank should now be listed as a resource partner. Your implementation is complete.

Lesson Summary

■ Because AD FS relies on secure communications, you must ensure that each server in an AD FS partnership trusts the root certificate that was used to issue certificates for each of the servers in the deployment. If you use self-signed certificates, you must export each certificate and then import it in the corresponding server's trusted CA stores.

■ When you configure a partnership, you must first create claims-aware applications and assign specific claims to each partner in the partnership.

■ After the claims have been created, you then identify which directory store will be used by each federation server in the deployment.

■ You create a federation trust between the two partners. This involves preparing the trust policy on each server, exporting the trust policy from the account federation server, and importing it in the resource federation server. Then you can use this trust policy to assign claims to the account organization. To complete the federation trust, you export the partner policy from the RFS and then import it into the AFS. At this point, your partnership has been created.

Lesson Review

You can use the following questions to test your knowledge of the information in Lesson 2, "Configuring and Using Active Directory Federation Services." The questions are also available on the companion CD if you prefer to review them in electronic form.

NOTE   Answers

Answers to these questions and explanations of why each answer choice is right or wrong are located in the "Answers" section at the end of the book.

1. You are an administrator for the *contoso.com* domain. Your organization has decided to create a federation partnership with Woodgrove Bank so that you can use identity federation to access a new application in the bank's perimeter network. The federation servers and Federation Service proxies are already in place, but you need to configure the federation trust to enable identity federation. Which steps must you perform? (Choose all that apply.)

   A. Communicate with your counterpart at Woodgrove Bank to establish how you will exchange information.

   B. Export the partner policy from Woodgrove Bank and import it into Contoso.

   C. Export the partner policy from Contoso and import it into Woodgrove Bank.

   D. Export the trust policy from Contoso and import it into Woodgrove Bank.

   E. Create and configure a claim mapping in Woodgrove Bank.

   F. Export the trust policy from the Woodgrove Bank and import it into Contoso.

Chapter Review

To further practice and reinforce the skills you learned in this chapter, you can perform the following tasks:

- Review the chapter summary.
- Review the list of key terms introduced in this chapter.
- Complete the case scenario. This scenario sets up a real-world situation involving the topics of this chapter and asks you to create a solution.
- Complete the suggested practices.
- Take a practice test.

Chapter Summary

- As a network operating system directory service, AD DS is mainly designed to work within the boundaries of your network. When you need to extend its identity and access (IDA) services to the outside world, you must rely on additional technologies. This is where AD FS comes in. The very purpose of AD FS is to provide external support for the internal IDA services you run, without having to open any special port on the firewall. Because of this, AD FS is an excellent tool for the foundation of partnerships. In the end, organizations partner through AD FS but continue to manage only their internal AD DS service.

- AD FS is composed of four role services: the Federation Service, the Federation Service Proxy, the Claims-aware Agent, and the Windows Token-based Agent. Note that the federation service and Federation Service Proxy cannot coexist on the same server.

- In addition to the basic technologies included in AD FS, the federation processes rely on claims to identify which access has been granted to users, cookies to simplify the logon process and support for single sign-on, and certificates to validate all transactions and secure all communications.

- AD FS supports three designs: Federated Web SSO, Federated Web SSO with Forest Trust, and Web SSO. Of the three, the most common deployment type is Federated Web SSO. In fact, the very existence of AD FS can help avoid the requirement for forest trusts that pass through firewalls.

Key Terms

Use these key terms to understand better the concepts covered in this chapter.

- **claim mapping**   When a federation server processes an incoming claim and filters it to extract appropriate authorizations for a user, it performs claim mapping.
- **federation trust**   The one-way trust between a resource organization and the account organization(s) it wants to partner with.
- **service-oriented architecture (SOA)**   SOAs are standards-based and language-agnostic architectures that rely on Web Services to support distributed services on the Internet.
- **Web services**   Standards-based Internet services that form part of an SOA. Commonly known Web services include the Simple Object Access Protocol (SOAP); the extended markup language (XML); and Universal Description, Discovery, and Integration (UDDI). Web services are language-agnostic, so they can interoperate between different IT infrastructures, for example, among UNIX, Linux, and Windows.
- **WS-Federation Passive Requestor Profile**   The component of WS-Federation that outlines the standard protocol to be used when passive clients access an application through a federation service.

Case Scenario

In the following case scenario, you will apply what you've learned about AD FS. You can find answers to the questions in this scenario in the "Answers" section at the end of this book.

Case Scenario: Choose the Right AD Technology

You are a systems administrator for Contoso, Ltd. Your organization has decided to deploy Windows Server 2008 and wants to implement several of its technologies. Specifically, your implementation goals are:

- To update your central authentication and authorization store.
- To ensure the protection of your intellectual property, especially when you work with partners.
- To support five applications running in the extranet.
    - ❑ Two of the applications are Windows-based and rely on Windows NT authentication.
    - ❑ Three of the applications are Web-based and rely on the authentication models supported by IIS.

- Clients for your extranet applications stem from three locations, which include the internal network, partner organizations, and the general public on the Internet.
- Because you are running applications in the extranet, you must have secure communications at all times.

Your goal is to identify which Windows Server 2008 technologies are required and how they should be implemented. What do you recommend?

Suggested Practices

To help you successfully master the exam objectives presented in this chapter, complete the following tasks.

Prepare for AD FS

The best way to practice for AD FS on the exam is to run through each of the practice exercises included in this chapter. They expose you to each of the elements required to understand the exam objective for this topic.

In addition, you can also run through the exercises outlined in the *Microsoft Step-by-Step Guide for Active Directory Federation Services*, which is available at *http://www.microsoft.com/downloads/details.aspx?familyid=062F7382-A82F-4428-9BBD-A103B9F27654&displaylang=en*.

Keep in mind that it is not recommended to install AD FS on an AD DS domain controller even though this is the method used in the step-by-step guide on the Microsoft Web site.

Take a Practice Test

The practice tests on this book's companion CD offer many options. For example, you can test yourself on just one exam objective, or you can test yourself on all the 70-640 certification exam content. You can set up the test so that it closely simulates the experience of taking a certification exam, or you can set it up in study mode so that you can look at the correct answers and explanations after you answer each question.

MORE INFO   Practice tests

For details about all the practice test options available, see the "How to Use the Practice Tests" section in this book's introduction.

Answers

Chapter 1: Lesson Review Answers

Lesson 1

1. **Correct Answers: A and B**

   A. **Correct:** A domain controller will create or join an Active Directory domain, which must have a valid DNS name.

   B. **Correct:** A domain must have a NetBIOS name to support earlier applications that use NetBIOS names.

   C. **Incorrect:** A DHCP server is not necessary. In fact, a domain controller should have statically assigned IP addresses.

   D. **Incorrect:** Although a DNS server is required for the functionality of a domain, if a DNS server does not exist, the Active Directory Installation Wizard will install and configure DNS service on the domain controller.

2. **Correct Answer: D**

   A. **Incorrect:** Windows Server 2008 forest functional level requires that all domains operate at Windows Server 2008 domain functional level. Because the Litware domain might include Windows Server 2003 domain controllers, that domain must remain at the Windows Server 2003 domain functional level. Therefore, the forest must also remain at Windows Server 2003 forest functional level.

   B. **Incorrect:** Windows Server 2008 forest functional level requires that all domains operate at Windows Server 2008 domain functional level. Because the Litware domain might include Windows Server 2003 domain controllers, that domain must remain at the Windows Server 2003 domain functional level. Therefore, the forest must also remain at Windows Server 2003 forest functional level.

   C. **Incorrect:** A domain operating at Windows Server 2008 domain functional level cannot include Windows Server 2003 domain controllers.

   D. **Correct:** The Litware domain might include Windows Server 2003 domain controllers and, therefore, must operate at Windows Server 2003 domain functional level. The forest functional level cannot be raised until all domains are operating at Windows Server 2008 domain functional level.

Lesson 2

1. **Correct Answer: A**
   A. **Correct:** A password is required so that it can be assigned to the local Administrator account on the server after AD DS is removed.
   B. **Incorrect:** SERVER02 is currently a domain controller, and you are logged on as Administrator. Therefore, you already have the credentials required to perform the demotion operation.
   C. **Incorrect:** SERVER02 is currently a domain controller, and you are logged on as Administrator. Therefore, you already have the credentials required to perform the demotion operation. The Domain Controllers group contains computer accounts for domain controllers.

2. **Correct Answer: D**
   A. **Incorrect:** AD CS is not supported on Server Core.
   B. **Incorrect:** AD FS is not supported on Server Core.
   C. **Incorrect:** AD RMS is not supported on Server Core.
   D. **Correct:** AD CS is not supported on Server Core, so you must reinstall the server with the full installation of Windows Server 2008.

Chapter 1: Case Scenario Answers

Case Scenario: Creating an Active Directory Forest

1. Yes. Server Core supports Active Directory Domain Services. You do not need a full installation of Windows Server 2008 to create a domain controller.
2. Use the *Netsh* command to configure IP addresses.
3. Use *Ocsetup.exe* to add server roles. Alternatively, there are parameters for the *Dcpromo.exe /unattend* command that can install the DNS service.
4. Use *Dcpromo.exe* to add and configure AD DS.

Chapter 2: Lesson Review Answers

Lesson 1

1. **Correct Answer: C**
   A. **Incorrect:** The Active Directory snap-in in Server Manager, if launched, will be run with the same credentials as the custom console. An Access Denied error will continue to occur.

B. **Incorrect:** Although *dsa.msc* is a shortcut to opening the Active Directory Users And Computers console, it will be run with the same credentials as the custom console. An Access Denied error will continue to occur.

C. **Correct:** An Access Denied error indicates that your credentials are not sufficient to perform the requested action. The question indicates that you are certain that you have permission. The answer introduces the assumption that you have a secondary account. Even though that account is not the Administrator, it is administrative. This is the best answer to the question.

D. **Incorrect:** *DSMOD USER* with the –*p* switch can be used to reset a user's password; however, the question is targeting the Access Denied error. There is no suggestion that the command prompt was launched with different credentials; therefore, you will continue to receive Access Denied errors.

Lesson 2

1. **Correct Answer: D**

A. **Incorrect:** An Active Directory task, whether performed using command-line commands, scripts, or remote server administration tools, can be performed by any user who has been delegated permission to the task.

B. **Incorrect:** Domain Admins are members of the Administrators group in the domain, so any permissions assigned to Administrators would also be assigned to you as a member of the Domain Admins group.

C. **Incorrect:** The ability to delete an OU or any object in Active Directory is related to permissions, not to ownership.

D. **Correct:** New organizational units are created with protection from deletion. You must remove the protection before deleting the OU. Protection can be removed using the Active Directory Users And Computers snap-in, with Advanced Features view, on the Object tab of an OU's properties dialog box.

Lesson 3

1. **Correct Answers: A, B, and D**

A. **Correct:** Assigning an administrative task requires modifying the DACL of an object such as an OU. The Advanced Security Settings dialog box provides the most direct access to the permissions in the DACL. The Delegation of Control Wizard masks the complexities of object ACEs by stepping you through the assignment of permissions to groups. DSACLS can be used to manage Active Directory permissions from the command prompt.

B. **Correct:** Assigning an administrative task requires modifying the DACL of an object such as an OU. The Advanced Security Settings dialog box provides the most direct access to the permissions in the DACL. The Delegation of Control Wizard masks the complexities of object ACEs by stepping you through the assignment of permissions to groups. DSACLS can be used to manage Active Directory permissions from the command prompt.

C. **Incorrect:** DSUTIL is used to manage the domain and directory service properties but is not used to manage object permissions.

D. **Correct:** Assigning an administrative task requires modifying the DACL of an object such as an OU. The Advanced Security Settings dialog box provides the most direct access to the permissions in the DACL. The Delegation of Control Wizard masks the complexities of object ACEs by stepping you through the assignment of permissions to groups. DSACLS can be used to manage Active Directory permissions from the command prompt.

Chapter 2: Case Scenario Answers

Case Scenario: Organizational Units and Delegation

1. The best design for computer objects at Contoso would be a single parent OU, within which child OUs would be created for each site. The support team at each site would be delegated control for computer objects in that site's OU. The parent OU would be used to delegate permissions so that the team at headquarters can manage computer objects in any site.

2. Even though each site has only one or two members of support personnel, it is always a best practice to create a group, place the users in that group, and delegate permissions to the group. As the organization and support teams grow and as users enter and leave the organization, managing permissions assigned to user accounts becomes very difficult. After the permission is assigned to a group, support personnel can simply be added to or removed from the group.

3. Because users at any site might request assistance from a support person in another site, users should remain within a single OU. There is no need to divide users into OUs by sites based on delegation or manageability. The OU containing the users would be delegated to a group that includes all support personnel. In fact, you could create a group that includes the groups of each site's support teams.

Chapter 3: Lesson Review Answers

Lesson 1

1. **Correct Answer: C**

A. **Incorrect:** Although a user account template will enable you to copy several dozen attributes of it to a new user account, you would have to copy the template 2,000 times to complete this task.

B. **Incorrect:** The *LDIFDE* command imports objects from LDIF files, which are not the format natively managed by Microsoft Office Excel.

C. **Correct:** The *CSVDE* command imports objects from comma-delimited text files. Excel can open, edit, and save these files.

D. **Incorrect:** The *Dsadd* command enables you to create a user from the command line, but you would need to run the command 2,000 times to complete your task.

2. **Correct Answer: A**

A. **Correct:** *LDIFDE* supports adding, modifying, or deleting Active Directory objects.

B. **Incorrect:** *Dsmod* modifies properties of an existing object.

C. **Incorrect:** *DEL* is a command that erases a file.

D. **Incorrect:** *CSVDE* can import users but cannot delete them.

Lesson 2

1. **Correct Answer: C**

A. **Incorrect:** There is no native cmdlet in Windows PowerShell for creating users.

B. **Incorrect:** ADSI does not provide a *NewUser* method.

C. **Correct:** A container, such as an OU or domain, provides a *Create* method to create objects of a specified class.

D. **Incorrect:** This is VBScript syntax, recognizable by its use of the Set statement.

2. **Correct Answer: D**

A. **Incorrect:** There is no native cmdlet in Windows PowerShell for creating users.

B. **Incorrect:** The *SetInfo* method commits a new user and its properties to Active Directory, but it must be used in conjunction with commands that create the object and its attributes. It cannot be used as a single command.

C. **Incorrect:** A container, such as an OU or domain, provides a *Create* method to create objects of a specified class, but until the *SetInfo* method is used, the object is not saved to Active Directory. Therefore, *Create* is not sufficient as a single command.

D. **Correct:** The *Dsadd* command can create a user with a single command.

3. **Correct Answers: A, B, and D**

A. **Correct:** An object is created by invoking the *Create* method of a container such as an OU.

B. **Correct:** The *SetInfo* method commits a new user and its properties to Active Directory. If the *SetInfo* method is not used, the new object and changes to its properties occur in your local representation of the object only.

C. **Incorrect:** This code is invalid. It is similar to code that would be used in VBScript, though not in the creation of user objects.

D. **Correct:** You must connect to the container in which the user will be created.

Lesson 3

1. **Correct Answer: C**

   A. **Incorrect:** You can use the Ctrl key to multiselect users, but they must be in a single OU. The ten users in this scenario are in different OUs.

   B. **Incorrect:** *Dsmod* will enable you to change the Office property, but *Dsget* will not locate the objects. *Dsget* is used to display attributes, not locate objects.

   C. **Correct:** You can use the *Dsquery* command to identify users whose Office property is set to *Miammi* and pipe the results to the *Dsmod* command to change the Office property.

   D. **Incorrect:** These cmdlets are not used with Active Directory objects.

2. **Correct Answers: B and C**

   A. **Incorrect:** Move-Item is a valid Windows PowerShell cmdlet that moves objects in a namespace, but Windows PowerShell does not yet expose Active Directory as a namespace.

   B. **Correct:** VBScript uses the *MoveHere* method of a container to move a user to the container.

   C. **Correct:** You can use the *Dsmove* command to move an object in Active Directory.

   D. **Incorrect:** The *Redirusr.exe* command is used to configure Active Directory so that new user objects created without specifying an OU will go to a container other than the default Users container.

   E. **Incorrect:** The Active Directory Migration Tool is used to migrate accounts between domains.

3. **Correct Answer: A**

   A. **Correct:** Computer restrictions limit the computers that a user can log on to. On the Account tab of her user account, you can click the Log On To button and add the computer by name to the list of allowed workstations.

   B. **Incorrect:** When a computer account is created, you can control who is allowed to join the computer to the domain with this button, but it has nothing to do with who can log on to the computer after it is a domain member.

   C. **Incorrect:** *Dsmove* is used to move an object in Active Directory.

   D. **Incorrect:** Although the user right to log on locally is required, the error message that she reports is not the message that would be received if she did not have the right to log on locally.

Chapter 3: Case Scenario Answers

Case Scenario: Import User Accounts

1. You should use a VBScript or Windows PowerShell script. Both of these scripting languages are capable of taking advantage of a database, such as an Excel file saved as a comma-separated values (.csv) file, as the source of data for user account creation. In the script, you can perform business logic. For example, you can construct the logon name and e-mail address attributes, using the user name information provided in the Excel file. Although *CSVDE* does enable you to import .csv files, it simply imports the attributes in the file; it cannot perform business logic or create new attributes in real time.

2. You can disable the accounts that are created until the students arrive.

3. In the Active Directory Users and Computers snap-in, you can select all users and change the *company* attribute one time. At the command prompt, you can use *Dsquery.exe* to pipe the DNs of all users to *Dsmod.exe*, which can change the company attribute.

Chapter 4: Lesson Review Answers

Lesson 1

1. **Correct Answer: B**
   A. **Incorrect:** Universal security groups cannot contain users or groups from trusted external domains. They can contain users, global groups, and other universal groups from any domain in the forest.
   B. **Correct:** Domain local security groups can contain members from trusted external domains.
   C. **Incorrect:** Global security groups cannot contain users or groups from trusted external domains. They can contain users and other global groups from the same domain only.
   D. **Incorrect:** Distribution groups cannot be assigned permissions to resources.

2. **Correct Answer: D**
   A. **Incorrect:** The group is a distribution group, which cannot be assigned permission. Changing the scope will not address that limitation.
   B. **Incorrect:** The group is a distribution group, which cannot be assigned permission. Changing the scope will not address that limitation.

C. **Incorrect:** The group is a distribution group. Adding it to the Domain Users group will not enable its members to access the shared folder.

D. **Correct:** The *−secgrp yes* switch will change the group type to a security group, after which you can add it to the ACL of the shared folder.

3. **Correct Answers: C, D, E, and F**

A. **Incorrect:** Global groups cannot contain global groups from other domains.

B. **Incorrect:** Global groups cannot contain global groups from other domains.

C. **Correct:** Global groups can contain users in the same forest.

D. **Correct:** Global groups can contain users in trusted domains.

E. **Correct:** Global groups can contain users in the same domain.

F. **Correct:** Global groups can contain global groups in the same domain.

G. **Incorrect:** Global groups cannot contain domain local groups.

H. **Incorrect:** Global groups cannot contain universal groups.

Lesson 2

1. **Correct Answers: B, C, and D**

A. **Incorrect:** The Remove-Item cmdlet in Windows PowerShell cannot be used to remove members of a group because groups are not exposed in a namespace.

B. **Correct:** *Dsrm* is used to delete a group.

C. **Correct:** *Dsmod* with the *−remmbr* option can remove members from a group.

D. **Correct:** *LDIFDE* with a change type of modify and a delete:member operation can remove members from a group.

E. **Incorrect:** *CSVDE* can import new groups. It cannot modify existing groups.

2. **Correct Answer: B**

A. **Incorrect:** *Dsrm* deletes a group. Deleting a group will not solve the problem.

B. **Correct:** You can use *Dsmod* with the *−scope* switch to change the scope of GroupA to a universal group, then to a global group. You will then be able to add GroupA to GroupB. This is a tricky question. Sometimes questions are not quite what they appear to be about on the surface. This question was not about using commands or even about adding one group to another—it was about group scope.

C. **Incorrect:** *Dsquery* searches Active Directory for objects. It cannot make a change, so it will not solve the problem.

D. **Incorrect:** *Dsget* retrieves an attribute of an object. It cannot make a change, so it will not solve the problem.

3. **Correct Answer: D**

   A. **Incorrect:** Get-Members is a Windows PowerShell cmdlet that gets the members of an programmatic object, not of a group.

   B. **Incorrect:** *Dsquery* queries Active Directory for objects matching a search filter. It does not list group membership.

   C. **Incorrect:** *LDIFDE* can be used to export a group and thereby its members, but only direct members.

   D. **Correct:** *Dsget* can return an attribute of an object, including the *member* attribute of group objects. With the *expand* option, *Dsget* can return the full membership of a group.

Lesson 3

1. **Correct Answer: D**

   A. **Incorrect:** The team members already have permission. This permission will not prevent them from accessing the folder from other computers.

   B. **Incorrect:** The team members already have permission. This permission will not prevent them from accessing the folder from other computers.

   C. **Incorrect:** This permission will not prevent users from accessing the folder from other computers.

   D. **Correct:** A Deny permission overrides Allow permissions. If a team member attempts to connect to the folder from another computer, he or she will be a member of the Network special identity group and will be denied access. If the same team member logs on locally to the conference room computer, he will be a member of Interactive and not Network, so the permissions assigned to him as a member of the team will allow access.

2. **Correct Answer: D**

   A. **Incorrect:** The Members tab of the group enables you to add and remove members but not to delegate the administration of membership.

   B. **Incorrect:** The Security tab of Mike Danseglio's user object determines who is delegated the ability to perform tasks on his object, not what Mike is able to do.

   C. **Incorrect:** The Member Of tab of Mike Danseglio's user object determines the groups to which Mike belongs, not the groups to which Mike has been delegated control.

   D. **Correct:** The Managed By tab of a group enables you to specify the group's manager and to allow the manager to update group membership.

3. **Correct Answers: B, C, and D**

    A. **Incorrect:** Account Operators does not have the right to shut down a domain controller.

    B. **Correct:** Print Operators has the right to shut down a domain controller.

    C. **Correct:** Backup Operators has the right to shut down a domain controller.

    D. **Correct:** Server Operators has the right to shut down a domain controller.

    E. **Incorrect:** The Interactive special identity group does not have the right to shut down a domain controller.

Chapter 4: Case Scenario Anwers

Case Scenario: Implementing a Group Strategy

1. Global security groups should be used to represent user roles at both Trey Research and Woodgrove Bank.

2. Domain local security groups should be used to manage Read and Write access to the Sliced Bread folders.

3. The Marketing and Research global groups will be members of the domain local group that manages Write access. The group that manages Read access will have the following members: Finance, the CEO, her assistant, and the Auditors global group from the Woodgrove Bank domain.

Chapter 5: Lesson Review Answers

Lesson 1

1. **Correct Answer: D**

    A. **Incorrect:** *Dsmove* is a command-line utility that moves existing objects in Active Directory. It does not control the default location for new objects.

    B. **Incorrect:** Move-Item is a Windows PowerShell cmdlet that moves existing objects in a namespace.

    C. **Inorrect:** *Netdom* is a command-line utility that enables you to join a domain, rename a computer, and perform other computer-related activities, but it does not control the default location for new computers.

    D. **Correct:** *Redircmp* is a command-line utility that redirects the default computer container to an alternate OU.

2. **Correct Answer: A**
   A. **Correct:** The *ms-DS-MachineAccountQuota* attribute of the domain by default allows all authenticated users the ability to join ten computers to the domain. This quota is checked when a user is joining a computer to the domain without a pre-staged account. Set this attribute to zero.
   B. **Incorrect:** This attribute configures the default quota for all Active Directory objects, not just for new computer accounts.
   C. **Incorrect:** Removing this user right does not prevent Authenticated Users from joining computers to the domain.
   D. **Incorrect:** Setting this permission will prevent all users, including administrators, from creating computer accounts.

3. **Correct Answer: B**
   A. **Incorrect:** *Dsadd* creates new objects, including computer objects, but does not join a computer to the account.
   B. **Correct:** *Netdom Join* can join the local computer or a remote computer to the domain
   C. **Incorrect:** *Dctest* tests various components of a domain controller.
   D. **Incorrect:** *System.cpl* is the System Properties control panel application. It enables you to join the local computer to a domain, but not to join a remote computer to a domain.

Lesson 2

1. **Correct Answer: C**
   A. **Incorrect:** *CSVDE* can import one or more computers but requires you first to create a comma-separated values file.
   B. **Incorrect:** *LDIFDE* can import one or more computers but requires you first to create an LDIF file.
   C. **Correct:** *Dsadd* enables you to create a computer object with a single command.
   D. **Incorrect:** Windows PowerShell enables you to use ADSI to create computers, but it takes several commands to do so.
   E. **Incorrect:** VBScript enables you to use ADSI to create computers, but it requires that you first create a script.

2. **Correct Answers: A, D, and E**
   A. **Correct:** *CSVDE* can import one or more computers from a .csv file, and Excel can save a worksheet as a .csv file.
   B. **Incorrect:** *LDIFDE* can import one or more computers, but the LDIF format cannot be created using Excel.

C. **Incorrect:** *Dsadd* enables you to create computer objects one at a time.

D. **Correct:** Windows PowerShell enables you to use ADSI to create computers and can use a .csv file as a data source.

E. **Correct:** VBScript enables you to use ADSI to create computers and can use a .csv file as a data source.

Lesson 3

1. **Correct Answer: A**

   A. **Correct:** Such events are symptomatic of a broken secure channel. Resetting the computer's account is the correct step to take to address the issue.

   B. **Incorrect:** The event does not reflect user authentication problems.

   C. **Incorrect:** Disabling the server account will prevent the server from authenticating. Enabling it will not fix the problem.

   D. **Incorrect:** The event does not reflect user authentication problems.

2. **Correct Answers: C, D, and E**

   A. **Incorrect:** Deleting the computer account will cause its SID to be removed and its group memberships to be lost. You will be forced to add the new account to the same groups and to assign permissions to the new account.

   B. **Incorrect:** Creating a new account for the new system creates a new SID. Permissions will have to be reassigned and group memberships re-created.

   C. **Correct:** Resetting the computer account makes it available for a system to join the domain using the account. The account's SID and group memberships are preserved.

   D. **Correct:** You must rename the account so that it can be joined by the new system using its name.

   E. **Correct:** After resetting and renaming the account, you must join the new system to the domain.

3. **Correct Answer: C**

   A. **Incorrect:** A down arrow indicates that computer accounts are disabled. It is not necessary to reset the accounts.

   B. **Incorrect:** A down arrow indicates that computer accounts are already disabled.

   C. **Correct:** A down arrow indicates that the accounts are disabled. You need to enable them.

   D. **Incorrect:** A down arrow indicates that computer accounts are disabled. It is not necessary to delete the accounts.

Chapter 5: Case Scenario Answers

Case Scenario 1: Creating Computer Objects and Joining the Domain

1. Computers are added to the Computers container because it is the default computer container. When a computer is joined to the domain and an account has not been pre-staged in a specific OU, Windows creates the account in the default computer container.

2. The *Redircmp.exe* command can redirect the default computer container to the Clients OU.

3. You can reduce the *ms-DS-MachineAccountQuota* attribute to zero. By default, the value is 10, which allows all authenticated users to create computers and join up to ten systems to the domain.

Case Scenario 2: Automating the Creation of Computer Objects

1. *CSVDE* can import .csv files, which can be exported from Excel.

2. *Dsquery* computer "*DN of OU*" | dsmod computer –disabled yes

3. You can select 100 systems, right-click any one system, and choose Properties. You can change the *Description* attribute for all objects at one time in the Properties For Multiple Items dialog box.

Chapter 6: Lesson Review Answers

Lesson 1

1. **Correct Answers: B and D**

   A. **Incorrect:** The central store is used to centralize administrative templates so that they do not have to be maintained on administrators' workstations.

   B. **Correct:** To create GPOs, the business unit administrators must have permission to access the Group Policy Objects container. By default, the Group Policy Creator Owners group has permission, so adding the administrators to this group will allow them to create new GPOs.

   C. **Incorrect:** Business unit administrators require permission to link GPOs only to their business unit OU, not to the entire domain. Therefore, delegating permission to link GPOs to the domain grants too much permission to the administrators.

   D. **Correct:** After creating a GPO, business unit administrators must be able to scope the GPO to users and computers in their OU; therefore, they must have the Link GPOs permission.

2. **Correct Answers: B and D**

    A. **Incorrect:** The central store is used to centralize administrative templates so that they do not have to be maintained on administrators' workstations.

    B. **Correct:** To create GPOs, the business unit administrators must have permission to access the Group Policy Objects container. By default, the Group Policy Creator Owners group has permission, so adding the administrators to this group will allow them to create new GPOs.

    C. **Incorrect:** Business unit administrators require permission to link GPOs only to their business unit OU, not to the entire domain. Therefore, delegating permission to link GPOs to the domain grants too much permission to the administrators.

    D. **Correct:** After creating a GPO, business unit administrators must be able to scope the GPO to users and computers in their OU; therefore, they must have the Link GPOs permission.

3. **Correct Answer: D**

    A. **Incorrect:** A saved report is an HTML or XML description of a GPO and its settings. It cannot be imported into another GPO.

    B. **Incorrect:** The *Restore From Backup* command is used to restore a GPO in its entirety.

    C. **Incorrect:** You cannot paste settings into a GPO.

    D. **Correct:** You can import settings to an existing GPO from the backed-up settings of another GPO.

Lesson 2

1. **Correct Answers: B and C**

    A. **Incorrect:** If you configure a domain to block inheritance, GPOs linked to sites will not be applied to users or computers in the domain. The Northwind Lockdown GPO is linked to the domain and will apply to all users, including those in the Domain Admins group.

    B. **Correct:** By blocking inheritance on the OU that contains all the users in the Domain Admins group, you prevent the policy settings from applying to those users.

    C. **Correct:** The Deny Apply Group Policy permission, assigned to Domain Admins, exempts Domain Admins from the scope of the GPO, which otherwise applies to the Authenticated Users group.

    D. **Incorrect:** All user accounts in the domain belong to the Domain Users group as their primary group. Therefore, the GPO will apply to all users, including those in the Domain Admins group.

2. **Correct Answers: A and D**

   A. **Correct:** Because the desktop restrictions are in the User Configuration node but are being applied when users log on to specific computers, loopback policy processing is required.

   B. **Incorrect:** Linking the GPO to the OU containing user accounts causes the restrictions to apply to all users at all times, not only when they log on to conference and training room systems.

   C. **Incorrect:** The Block Inheritance option is not necessary and will prevent the application of all other GPOs from parent OUs, from the domain, and from sites.

   D. **Correct:** To scope the GPO correctly, you must link it to the OU containing the computer objects of conference and training room systems.

Lesson 3

1. **Correct Answers: B and D**

   A. **Incorrect:** The Group Policy Modeling Wizard is used to simulate Group Policy application, not to report its actual application.

   B. **Correct:** The Group Policy Results Wizard can be used to report Group Policy application on a remote system.

   C. **Incorrect:** *Gpupdate.exe* is used to initiate a manual policy refresh.

   D. **Correct:** *Gpresult.exe* can be used with the */s* switch to gather RSoP information remotely.

   E. **Incorrect:** *Msconfig.exe* is used to gather system information and to control system startup.

2. **Correct Answer: A**

   A. **Correct:** *Gpresult.exe* produces an RSoP report that will indicate when the GPO was applied. Screen saver policy settings are user configuration settings, so you must run *Gpresult.exe* for user settings.

   B. **Incorrect:** There is no *–computer* option for the *Gpresult.exe* command.

   C. **Incorrect:** Screen saver settings are user, not computer, configuration.

   D. **Incorrect:** *Gpupdate.exe* is used to trigger a policy refresh, not to report policy application.

Chapter 6: Case Scenario Answers

Case Scenario: Implementing Group Policy

1. The settings that control the user's desktop environment are found in the User Configuration node.

2. Link the GPO to the OU containing the training computers. If you link the GPO to the OU containing users, the settings will affect users on all computers at Northwind Traders.

3. You must enable loopback policy processing. By linking the GPO to the OU containing training room computers and enabling loopback processing, the training room computers will apply settings in the User Configuration node of the GPO.

4. Loopback policy processing must be configured in the Replace mode. In the Replace mode, user settings in GPOs scoped to the user are ignored. Only the user settings in GPOs scoped to the computer are applied.

5. You must exclude training room computers from the scope of the screen saver GPO. You can do this in one of two ways. You can block inheritance on the training room computer OU. Alternatively, you can use the security group filtering on the domain GPO. Create a group containing training room computers and assign the Deny Apply Group Policy permission to the screen saver GPO to that group.

Chapter 7: Lesson Review Answers

Lesson 1

1. Correct Answers: A, B, C, and D

   A. **Correct:** The local Administrator account is a default member of Administrators. It cannot be removed.

   B. **Correct:** Domain Admins is added to Administrators when a computer joins the domain. The Member Of policy settings add specified groups to Administrators and do not remove existing members.

   C. **Correct:** Sydney Support is added to the Administrators group by the Sydney Support GPO. The Member Of policy settings add specified groups to Administrators and do not remove existing members.

   D. **Correct:** Help Desk is added to the Administrators group by the Corporate Help Desk GPO. The Member Of policy settings add specified groups to Administrators and do not remove existing members.

   E. **Incorrect:** The Remote Desktop Users group is not a default member of Administrators and is not added to Administrators by any of the GPOs.

2. **Correct Answers: A and C**

    A. **Correct:** The local Administrator account is a default member of Administrators. It cannot be removed.

    B. **Incorrect:** Domain Admins is added to Administrators when a computer joins the domain but is removed by the Sydney Support GPO, which specifies the authoritative membership of the group.

    C. **Correct:** Sydney Support is added to the Administrators group by the Sydney Support GPO.

    D. **Incorrect:** Help Desk is specified as a member of the Administrators group by the Corporate Help Desk GPO, but the Sydney Support GPO has higher precedence because it is linked to the OU in which DESKTOP234 exists. Therefore, the membership specified by the Sydney Support GPO's Members Of This Group setting is authoritative.

    E. **Incorrect:** The Remote Desktop Users group is not a default member of Administrators and is not added to Administrators by any of the GPOs.

3. **Correct Answers: A, C, and D**

    A. **Correct:** The local Administrator account is a default member of Administrators. It cannot be removed.

    B. **Incorrect:** Domain Admins is added to Administrators when a computer joins the domain but is removed by the Corporate Help Desk GPO, which specifies the membership of Administrators using the Members Of This Group setting.

    C. **Correct:** Sydney Support is added to the Administrators group by the Sydney Support GPO. Because the Sydney Support GPO has higher precedence than the Corporate Help Desk GPO, DESKTOP234 applies the Sydney Support GPO after applying the Corporate Help Desk GPO; thus, the Sydney Support GPO's members are added to the Administrators group.

    D. **Correct:** Help Desk is specified as a member of the Administrators group by the Corporate Help Desk GPO. When this GPO is applied, all other members of Administrators, except the Administrator account itself, are removed.

    E. **Incorrect:** The Remote Desktop Users group is not a default member of Administrators and is not added to Administrators by any of the GPOs.

Lesson 2

1. **Correct Answer: B**

    A. **Incorrect:** Local Security Policy enables you to configure the settings on a single server.

    B. **Correct:** You can use Security Configuration And Analysis to compare the test environment configuration to a template, to reconcile discrepancies, and to export the resulting settings to a security template. The security template can then be imported into a GPO.

 C. **Incorrect:** The Security Configuration Wizard does not manage user rights.

 D. **Incorrect:** The Security Templates snap-in can create a security template but cannot export the settings of the test environment server. Security Configuration And Analysis is a better answer.

2. **Correct Answer: C**

 A. **Incorrect:** Local Security Policy enables you to configure the settings on a single server.

 B. **Incorrect:** Security Configuration And Analysis enables you to create security templates that can be imported into a GPO, but the tool is not role-based. The Security Configuration Wizard is a better answer.

 C. **Correct:** The Security Configuration Wizard creates role-based security policies that manage services, firewall rules, and audit policies as well as certain registry settings.

 D. **Incorrect:** Security Templates enables you to create security templates that can be imported into a GPO, but the tool is not role-based. The Security Configuration Wizard is a better answer.

3. **Correct Answers: A and D**

 A. **Correct:** The *Scwcmd.exe /transform* command creates a GPO that includes the settings in the specified security policy.

 B. **Incorrect:** You do not need to create a GPO. The *Scwcmd.exe* command does that automatically.

 C. **Incorrect:** You do not import settings from a security policy into a GPO. You can import the settings from a security template into a GPO.

 D. **Correct:** The GPO created must be linked to an appropriate site, domain, or OU before its settings are applied to computers in that container.

Lesson 3

1. **Correct Answers: B and D**

 A. **Incorrect:** The goal is to deploy the application to computers, not to users. Therefore, the User Configuration node is not the correct place on which to create the software package.

 B. **Correct:** To deploy the application to computers, the software package must be created in the Computer Configuration node of the GPO.

 C. **Incorrect:** The software installation extension does not apply settings if a slow link is detected. Because the application is deployed to computers, not to users, configuring the connection speed in the User Configuration node does not change the default connection speed in the Computer Configuration node, 500 kbps. The connection from that branch office is less than 500 kbps, so computers in the branch office will not install the application.

D. **Correct:** The software installation extension does not apply settings if a slow link is detected. By configuring the slow link detection threshold to 256, you ensure that clients connecting over the 364 kbps connection from the branch office will detect the link as a fast link, so clients will install the application.

E. **Incorrect:** The software installation extension does not apply settings if a slow link is detected. The connection from that branch office is less than 1,000 kbps, so computers in the branch office will not install the application.

2. **Correct Answers: A and D**

A. **Correct:** You want to deploy the application to users, so you must create the package in the User Configuration policies of a GPO. The GPO must then be scoped to apply only to sales users. Because all users are in a single OU, you must create a security group with which to filter the GPO.

B. **Incorrect:** The GPO is not correctly scoped. Only computers exist in the Sales OU of each site. Computers will not process settings in the User Configuration policies under normal Group Policy processing.

C. **Incorrect:** You want to deploy the application to users. Policies in the Computer Configuration node apply to computers. Because no computers are in the sales group, the policy will not be applied by any system.

D. **Correct:** If a computer is configured to perform loopback policy processing, it applies settings in the User Configuration policies of GPOs scoped to the computer. The GPO is scoped to the sales computers by being linked to the Sales OU. Loopback processing enables the User Configuration software package to be installed by the computers.

3. **Correct Answers: A, C, D, and E**

A. **Correct:** The software deployment GPO must be scoped to apply to all users in the four branch offices. Although you could link the GPO to each of the four selected branches, that was not presented as an option.

B. **Incorrect:** The application must be fully installed before the user launches it for the first time. When you publish an application, the user must install it using Programs And Features in Control Panel on Window Server 2008 and Windows Vista or using Add/Remove Programs in Control Panel on Windows XP.

C. **Correct:** For the application to be fully installed before the user opens it the first time, you must select the Install This Application At Logon option. Otherwise, the application will be installed when the user opens the application the first time or opens a file type associated with the application.

D. **Correct:** A shadow group is a group that contains users based on a characteristic such as the OU in which the user account exists. Because the GPO is linked to the Employees OU, it must be filtered with a security group that contains the users in the four branches.

E. **Correct:** For the application to be fully installed before the user opens it the first time, you must assign the application.

F. **Incorrect:** The Required Upgrade For Existing Packages option is used only in upgrade scenarios.

Lesson 4

1. **Correct Answer: D**

    A. **Incorrect:** Logon Event auditing is used to capture local interactive and network logon to workstations and servers.

    B. **Incorrect:** Directory Service Access auditing is used to monitor changes to objects and attributes in Active Directory.

    C. **Incorrect:** Privilege Use auditing relates to program execution and termination.

    D. **Correct:** Account Logon Event auditing creates events when a user attempts to log on with a domain user account to any computer in the domain.

    E. **Incorrect:** Account Management auditing creates events related to the creation, deletion, and modification of users, computers, and groups in Active Directory.

2. **Correct Answer: B**

    A. **Incorrect:** Account Management auditing creates events related to the creation, deletion, and modification of users, computers, and groups in Active Directory, but it does not show the previous and changed values of attributes.

    B. **Correct:** The *Auditpol.exe* command can be used to enable Directory Service Changes auditing, which logs the details of changes made to attributes as defined in the SACL of Active Directory objects. The previous and changed values of the attribute are included in the event log entry.

    C. **Incorrect:** Privilege Use auditing relates to program execution and termination.

    D. **Incorrect:** Directory Service Access auditing monitors changes to objects and attributes in Active Directory, but it does not report the previous and changed values of attributes.

3. **Correct Answers: E, F, and G**

    A. **Incorrect:** You have configured permissions that prevent access by consultants. Therefore, there will be no successful access attempts to audit.

    B. **Incorrect:** File system access events will be logged on the file servers, not on the domain controllers.

C. **Incorrect:** Directory Service Access audit policy relates to changes to objects in Active Directory, not to a folder on a disk subsystem.

D. **Incorrect:** The audit policy setting must apply to the file servers, not to domain controllers.

E. **Correct:** You must enable Object Access auditing on the file servers. The Server Configuration GPO is scoped to apply to all file servers.

F. **Correct:** File system access events will appear in the Security log of each file server.

G. **Correct:** Auditing entries must be configured on the Confidential Data folder. Auditing failures to Full Control access will create audit events for any type of access that failed.

Chapter 7: Case Scenario Answers

Case Scenario 1: Software Installation with Group Policy Software Installation

1. The application package should be created in the Computer Configuration node so that it is installed on computers used by the mobile sales force. If the package is created in the User Configuration node, the application is associated with users and will be installed on any computer to which the users log on, including conference-room computers.

2. Advanced. Because the application package is created in the Computer Configuration node, Publish is not an available option. The available options are Assign and Advanced. You must choose Advanced to associate a transform with the package.

3. The GPO deploys the application in the Computer Configuration node, so the GPO must be scoped to computers. It can be linked to the domain or, better yet, to the Clients OU in which all client computers exist. The GPO must be further filtered to apply only to the computers used by the mobile sales force. This is accomplished by creating a global security group that contains the computers and using that group to filter the GPO. You must also remove the Authenticated Users group, which is given the Apply Group Policy permission by default.

Case Scenario 2: Security Configuration

1. Add an auditing entry that audits for failed attempts by the Everyone group to access the folder at the Full Control access level, which includes all other access levels. A second auditing entry must audit successful attempts by the Administrators group to access the folder at the Full Control access level, again to capture activities at any access level.

2. Restricted groups policies enable you to manage the membership of groups. A restricted groups policy setting for the Administrators group should be configured to

specify Members Of This Group are your account and the account of the VP of Human Resources. This policy setting is called the Members setting. It lists the final, authoritative membership of the specified group. The Administrator account cannot be removed from the Administrators group.

3. You must enable the Audit Object Access and Audit Privilege Use audit policies. Audit Object Access must be defined to audit Success and Failure events because the auditing entries on the Salaries folder are for both successful and failed access. Audit Privilege Use must be defined to audit Success events to log events when a member of the Administrators group takes ownership of a folder.

4. You can use security templates to manage the configuration of the seven servers. Security templates can be created on one system by using the Security Templates snap-in and imported to a database and thereafter applied to the servers by using the Security Configuration and Analysis snap-in.

5. Policy settings in Active Directory–based GPOs can override your security settings because domain-based GPOs override the configuration of local GPOs. You can monitor your server's configuration by running Resultant Set of Policy (RSoP) reports to identify settings in domain GPOs that conflict with your desired configuration or by using the Security Configuration and Analysis snap-in to compare the servers' configuration against the security template.

Chapter 8: Lesson Review Answers

Lesson 1

1. Correct Answers: C, D, and E
   A. **Incorrect:** The password policies in the Default Domain Policy GPO define policies for all users in the domain, not just for service accounts.
   B. **Incorrect:** PSOs cannot be linked to organizational units, only to groups and users.
   C. **Correct:** PSOs can be linked to groups, so you must create a group that contains the service accounts.
   D. **Correct:** The PSO must be applied to the Service Accounts group; otherwise, the settings contained in the PSO will not take effect.
   E. **Correct:** PSOs can be linked to groups, so you must create a group that contains the service accounts.
2. Correct Answer: D

A. **Incorrect:** The Account Lockout Duration policy setting is specified in minutes. This setting will lock out an account for 100 minutes, after which time the account will be unlocked automatically.

B. **Incorrect:** The Account Lockout Duration policy setting is specified in minutes. This setting will lock out an account for 1 minute, after which time, the account will be unlocked automatically.

C. **Incorrect:** The Account Lockout Threshold policy setting specifies how many invalid logon attempts result in account lockout. It does not determine the length of time for which an account is locked out.

D. **Correct:** An Account Lockout Duration policy setting of 0 locks the account indefinitely until an administrator unlocks the account.

3. **Correct Answer: C**

   A. **Incorrect:** Although PSO1 has the highest precedence value, a PSO that applies to groups is overridden by a PSO that applies directly to the user, even if the user PSO has lower precedence.

   B. **Incorrect:** A precedence value of 99 is lower than the precedence value of 1.

   C. **Correct:** Although PSO3 does not have the highest precedence value (PSO1 is higher), it is linked to the user account, so it takes precedence.

   D. **Incorrect:** PSO4 is a user-linked PSO, but its value, 200, is lower than PSO3.

Lesson 2

1. **Correct Answer: B**

   A. **Incorrect:** This setting will generate event log entries when a user successfully logs on with a domain account. A successful logon does not generate account lockout.

   B. **Correct:** Failed logons to a domain account can generate account lockout. Auditing for failed account logon events will generate event log entries that identify when the failed logons occur.

   C. **Incorrect:** Logon events generate event log entries on the computer to which a user logs on or connects over the network. Local logons are not associated with account lockout.

   D. **Incorrect:** Logon events generate event log entries on the computer to which a user logs on or connects over the network. Local logons are not associated with account lockout.

2. **Correct Answer: C**

   A. **Incorrect:** Account logon events are generated when a user logs on with a domain account to any computer in the domain.

   B. **Incorrect:** Audit policies are settings in the Computer Configuration node of a GPO. These settings do not apply to user accounts.

    C. **Correct:** Logon events are generated in the event log of a computer when a user logs on interactively to the computer or connects to the computer over the network, for example, to a shared folder on the computer.

    D. **Incorrect:** Account logon events are generated by domain controllers when they authenticate a user logging on to any computer in the domain. This GPO is not scoped to domain controllers.

Lesson 3

1. **Correct Answer: B**

    A. **Incorrect:** An RODC requires only one writable Windows Server 2008 domain controller. Such a domain controller already exists in your domain.

    B. **Correct:** You must run *Adprep /rodcprep* to configure the forest so that the RODC can replicate DNS application partitions.

    C. **Incorrect:** The *Dsmgmt* command is used to configure administrator role separation on an RODC after the RODC has been installed.

    D. **Incorrect:** You use the *Dcpromo* command to perform an installation of a domain controller, including an RODC.

2. **Correct Answer: A**

    A. **Correct:** The Policy Usage tab of the Advanced Password Replication Policy dialog box reports the accounts whose passwords are stored on an RODC.

    B. **Incorrect:** The Allowed RODC Password Replication Group specifies users whose credentials will be cached on all RODCs in the domain.

    C. **Incorrect:** The Denied RODC Password Replication Group specifies users whose credentials will not be cached on any RODC in the domain.

    D. **Incorrect:** The Resultant Policy tab evaluates the password replication policy for a user or computer; it does not indicate whether that user's or computer's credentials are yet cached on the RODC.

3. **Correct Answers: B and D**

    A. **Incorrect:** The Allowed RODC Password Replication Group specifies users whose credentials will be cached on all RODCs in the domain. The five users need to log on to only one of the branch offices.

    B. **Correct:** The Password Replication Policy tab of the branch office RODC is used to specify the credentials that can be cached by the RODC.

    C. **Incorrect:** The users do not require the right to log on locally to the branch office domain controller.

    D. **Correct:** By prepopulating the credentials of the five users, you ensure that the RODC will be able to authenticate the users without forwarding the authentication to the data center on the far side of the WAN link.

Chapter 8: Case Scenario Answers

Case Scenario 1: Increasing the Security of Administrative Accounts

1. Fine-grained password policies can be configured only in a domain at the domain functional level of Windows Server 2008. Before you can raise the domain functional level to Windows Server 2008, you must upgrade all Windows Server 2003 domain controllers to Windows Server 2008.

2. ADSI Edit.

3. You should assign a value between 1 and 9. Values closer to 1 have higher precedence. In addition, ensure that the new PSOs are not directly linked to the user account.

4. Define audit policy settings in the Default Domain Controllers GPO that configure auditing of failed account logon events.

Case Scenario 2: Increasing the Security and Reliability of Branch Office Authentication

1. Ensure that all domains are at the Windows Server 2003 domain functional level and that the forest is at the Windows Server 2003 forest functional level. On the schema master, run *Adprep /rodcprep*. Upgrade at least one Windows Server 2003 domain controller to Windows Server 2008.

2. You can delegate the installation of an RODC by pre-creating the computer accounts of the RODC in the Domain Controllers OU. When you do so, you can specify the user credentials that will be used to attach the RODC to the account, and then that user can successfully install the RODC without domain administrative privileges.

3. You can use the *Dsmgmt.exe* command to give the user local administrative privileges on the RODC.

Chapter 9: Lesson Review Answers

Lesson 1

1. **Correct Answer: C**

    A. **Incorrect:** You can use the command-line tool to create a domain tree. To do so, it is best to pre-create an answer file so that all values are passed automatically to the command during setup. However, you can also use the wizard to perform this task.

    B. **Incorrect:** Most often, you use standalone servers to create a new domain. This means you must log on with local administrative rights and then provide appropriate forest credentials to add the domain during the installation.

C. **Correct:** The option to create a domain tree is not available in the wizard unless you select the advanced mode of the wizard at the very beginning.

D. **Incorrect:** Credentials are requested by the wizard during the preparation process for the installation. Using a standalone or member server has no effect on the operation.

2. **Correct Answers: B and D**

A. **Incorrect:** You must select the advanced mode of the wizard to create the domain tree, but selecting this mode has no impact on the wizard's ability to create the delegation.

B. **Correct:** Because the delegation uses a top-level root name (.ms), you must create the delegation manually in your forest root domain. The wizard cannot create it automatically because you do not have credentials for the root DNS server that maintains this name.

C. **Incorrect:** Because you create the delegation manually, you must tell the wizard to omit the creation.

D. **Correct:** Because you created a manual delegation, you must tell the wizard to omit the delegation creation.

E. **Incorrect:** You can create the delegation manually after the domain tree has been installed; however, it is a best practice to create it beforehand and then add components to its configuration after additional domain controllers have been created in the domain tree.

Lesson 2

1. **Correct Answers: A, B, C, D, and E**

A. **Correct:** Your DNS server administrator might have already configured scavenging for all zones, but it is good practice to validate that it has been applied to your zone.

B. **Correct:** By default, replication scopes are assigned properly when you create the zone, but it is always a good practice for your zone to use the appropriate replication scope.

C. **Correct:** You might have other custom records to create, but you should create at least two: a text (TXT) record and a responsible person (RP) record. These will be used to update the Start of Authority record.

D. **Correct:** The text (TXT) record will contain the information for the DNS operating standards you will apply to the zone.

E. **Correct:** An e-mail address is assigned to a Responsible Person (RP) record to enable others to communicate with the operator in case of issues or problems with name resolution.

F. **Incorrect:** Because the zone is new, there should be no unused records in the zone.

    G. **Incorrect**: Reverse lookup zones are required only when your zone hosts secure Web applications. No information about such an application has been provided.

2. **Correct Answers: A and B**

    A. **Correct:** Because all zones are located on domain controllers, you must use domain administrator credentials to manage DNS.

    B. **Correct**: If the server is not enlisted into the partition, the partition will not be available to the server.

    C. **Incorrect**: Enterprise administrator credentials are required only to create the application directory partition, not to assign it.

    D. **Incorrect**: You can use the command line to assign zones to partitions, but it is not mandatory.

    E. **Incorrect**: You can always change the replication scope of a partition in DNS after it has been created. It is one of the basic operations DNS zone administrators must perform.

Chapter 9: Case Scenario Answers

Case Scenario: Block Specific DNS Names

Trey Research can add the two problematic names to the global query block list on their DNS servers. This is done through the command line. The corresponding command is:

```
dnscmd /config /globalqueryblocklist wpad isatap biometrics biology
```

This command ensures that the Web Proxy Automatic Discovery protocol and the Intra-site Automatic Tunneling Addressing Protocol that are blocked by default continue to be blocked as well as adding the two problematic department names. Now, even if the administrative policies are not followed, the possibility of spoofing from these departments will be greatly limited.

Remember that this command affects all the FLZs hosted on a particular DNS server. If you have other DNS servers hosting other zones, for example, a DNS server in a child domain, you must run the command on those servers as well.

Chapter 10: Lesson Review Answers

Lesson 1

1. **Correct Answer: D**

    A. **Incorrect:** Because you are upgrading the operative system of a domain controller, you must perform another step prior to the upgrade.

    B. Incorrect: The *Adprep /domainprep /gpprep* command must be run prior to upgrading the domain controller, but you must perform another step prior to running this command.

    C. Incorrect: The server is already a domain controller, so it is not necessary to run the Active Directory Domain Services Installation Wizard.

    D. Correct: You must run *Adprep /forestprep* on the schema master of the forest as the first step to prepare the forest for a Windows Server 2008 domain controller.

    E. Incorrect: The *Adprep /rodcprep* command must be run prior to installing a read-only domain controller.

2. **Correct Answers: B, C, and D**

    A. Incorrect: Because the domain was built using only Windows Server 2008 domain controllers, it is not necessary to run *Adprep /rodcprep*.

    B. Correct: To allow a nonadministrative user to attach an RODC to the domain, an account must be prestaged in the Domain Controllers OU.

    C. Correct: The UseExistingAccount option of the *Dcpromo.exe* command enables you to attach a server to a prestaged RODC account.

    D. Correct: To attach a server to a prestaged RODC account, the server must be removed from the domain prior to running *Dcpromo.exe*.

3. **Correct Answer: C**

    A. Incorrect: *NTBackup* and system state backups are not supported in Windows Server 2008.

    B. Incorrect: Adding the Windows Server Backup Features is not sufficient to create installation media.

    C. Correct: The *Ntdsutil.exe* command enables you to create installation media. The Sysvol and Full options will create installation media that include SYSVOL for a writable domain controller.

    D. Incorrect: A copy of the directory and SYSVOL is not used for installation of a domain controller.

Lesson 2

1. **Correct Answer: E**

    A. Incorrect: The infrastructure master should not be placed on a domain controller that is a GC server unless all domain controllers in the domain are GC servers.

    B. Incorrect: Although there can be benefits to transferring the RID master role, it is not the required change in this scenario.

    C. Incorrect: Although there can be benefits to transferring the schema master role, it is not the required change in this scenario.

D. **Incorrect:** Although there can be benefits to transferring the domain naming master role, it is not the required change in this scenario.

E. **Correct:** The infrastructure master should not be placed on a domain controller that is a GC server unless all domain controllers in the domain are GC servers. Because SERVER02 is not a GC server, you should transfer the infrastructure master role to SERVER02.

2. **Correct Answers: D and E**

A. **Incorrect:** The infrastructure master role is specific to each domain. You do not need to transfer it and, in fact, you cannot transfer it to a domain controller in another domain.

B. **Incorrect:** The PDC Emulator role is specific to each domain. You do not need to transfer it and, in fact, you cannot transfer it to a domain controller in another domain.

C. **Incorrect:** The RID master role is specific to each domain. You do not need to transfer it and, in fact, you cannot transfer it to a domain controller in another domain.

D. **Correct:** The schema master role is a forest role. It should be transferred to the *contoso.com* domain prior to decommissioning the domain.

E. **Correct:** The domain naming master role is a forest role. It should be transferred to the *contoso.com* domain prior to decommissioning the domain.

3. **Correct Answers: A, B, and C**

A. **Correct:** The infrastructure master is a domain operations master.

B. **Correct:** The PDC emulator is a domain operations master.

C. **Correct:** The RID master is a domain operations master.

D. **Incorrect:** The schema master is a forest operations master, not a domain operations master.

E. **Incorrect:** The domain naming master is a forest operations master, not a domain operations master.

Lesson 3

1. **Correct Answers: C and D**

A. **Incorrect:** The replication of SYSVOL by using DFS-R within a domain is dependent upon the domain controllers of that domain, not on domain controllers in other domains.

B. **Incorrect:** The replication of SYSVOL by using DFS-R within a domain is dependent upon the domain functional level of that domain, not on the forest functional level.

    C. **Correct:** All domain controllers must be running Windows Server 2008 before you can replicate SYSVOL by using DFS-R within that domain.

    D. **Correct:** The domain must be at Windows Server 2008 domain functional level before you can replicate SYSVOL by using DFS-R within that domain.

    E. **Incorrect:** The replication of SYSVOL by using DFS-R within a domain is dependent upon the domain functional level of that domain, not on the domain functional level of other domains.

2. **Correct Answer: A**

    A. **Correct:** The *Dfsrmig.exe* command is used to migrate the replication of SYSVOL from FRS to DFS-R.

    B. **Incorrect:** The *Repadmin.exe* command is used to manage Active Directory replication, not SYSVOL replication.

    C. **Incorrect:** The *Dfsutil.exe* command is used to perform administrative tasks on a DFS namespace, not to configure SYSVOL replication.

    D. **Incorrect:** The *Dfscmd.exe* command is used to perform administrative tasks on a DFS namespace, not to configure SYSVOL replication.

Chapter 10: Case Scenario Answers

Case Scenario: Upgrading a Domain

1. You must run *Adprep /forestprep* before installing any Windows Server 2008 domain controllers in a forest.

2. It is not possible for all domain controllers in a domain to be read-only. There must be at least one writable domain controller, so it is not possible to have all three branches served by read-only domain controllers. One DC must be writable. Alternatively, one writable DC could be maintained in a central location, and three RODCs could be deployed to the three branches.

3. When there is planned downtime for a server performing single master operations, you should transfer the operations to another domain controller. When the original master comes back online, you can transfer the operations back to it.

Chapter 11: Lesson Review Answers

Lesson 1

1. Correct Answer: C

A. **Incorrect:** Every domain controller is assigned to a site. It might be in the wrong site, but it is reflected as a server object in a site.

B. **Incorrect:** You cannot create a site without a site link, so the branch office site is on a site link. It might be the wrong site link, but it is assigned to a site link.

C. **Correct:** If the branch office IP address range is not represented by a subnet object, which is then associated with the site, then computers might authenticate against domain controllers in another site.

D. **Incorrect:** It is not possible to assign a subnet to two different sites.

2. **Correct Answers: A, D, and E**

A. **Correct:** A subnet object with the IP address range of the branch enables clients to be informed of their site.

B. **Incorrect:** The computer account for each domain controller should be in the Domain Controllers OU.

C. **Incorrect:** Two site link transports are supported by Active Directory: IP and SMTP. No additional site link transport is necessary.

D. **Correct:** A site object for the branch office is required to manage service localization, such as authentication, within the branch office.

E. **Correct:** A server object for the domain controller must be in the site object.

Lesson 2

1. **Correct Answer: D**

A. **Incorrect:** A read-only domain controller must still be able to contact a global catalog server.

B. **Incorrect:** Application directory partitions are not involved with user authentication.

C. **Incorrect:** Intersite replication will not address the problem caused when the branch domain controller cannot contact a global catalog server.

D. **Correct:** Universal group membership caching, implemented for the branch office site, will cause the domain controller to cache users' universal group memberships from a global catalog server, so that logon is not denied.

2. **Correct Answers: D and E**

A. **Incorrect:** The schema partition is replicated to all domain controllers in the forest. However, you should make sure that the domain controller you are demoting is not the schema operations master.

B. **Incorrect:** The configuration partition is replicated to all domain controllers in the forest.

C. **Incorrect:** The domain naming context is replicated to all domain controllers in the domain.

D. **Correct:** A global catalog is on only one domain controller, by default. It is possible that the domain controller you want to demote is the only global catalog server, in which case, you should configure another global catalog server prior to demoting the domain controller.

E. **Correct:** Application directory partitions can be hosted on one or more domain controllers. It is possible for an application directory partition to exist only on the domain controller you are planning to demote.

3. **Correct Answer: C**

A. **Incorrect:** You can use *Dcpromo.exe* to specify that a new domain controller should be a global catalog server, but you cannot use *Dcpromo.exe* to modify existing domain controllers.

B. **Incorrect:** You can use the Active Directory Domain Services Installation Wizard to specify that a new domain controller should be a global catalog server, but you cannot use the wizard to modify existing domain controllers.

C. **Correct:** Use the Active Directory Sites and Services snap-in to configure a global catalog server by opening the properties of the *NTDS Settings* object within the server object representing the domain controller.

D. **Incorrect:** The Active Directory Users and Computers snap-in cannot be used to configure global catalog servers.

E. **Incorrect:** The Active Directory Domains and Trusts snap-in cannot be used to configure global catalog servers.

Lesson 3

1. **Correct Answer: D**

A. **Incorrect:** The total cost of replication from Site A to Site C over the links to Site B would be 350. The cost of replication over link A-C is only 100. Replication will use link A-C.

B. **Incorrect:** The total cost of replication from Site A to Site C over the links to Site B would be 350. The cost of replication over link A-C is only 100. Replication will use link A-C.

C. **Incorrect:** The total cost of replication from Site A to Site C over the links to Site B would be 150. The cost of replication over link A-C is only 100. Replication will use link A-C.

D. **Correct:** The total cost of replication from Site A to Site C over the links to Site B is 200. If the cost of replication over link A-C is over 200, replication will use links A-B and C-B.

2. **Correct Answers: B and C**

  A. **Incorrect:** If there is a site link from sites A to C, it is possible that replication might occur between sites on that link. You have not prevented replication directly between Site A and Site C.

  B. **Correct:** To prevent replication between Sites A and C, you must delete the site link that contains those two sites.

  C. **Correct:** Site links are transitive by default, so Site A can replicate directly with Site C, using links A-B and B-C. You must disable site link transitivity.

  D. **Incorrect:** Reducing site link costs will encourage replication to avoid creating a connection over link A-C. However, it does not ensure that changes are sent, first, to Site B.

3. **Correct Answer: A**

  A. **Correct:** When IP connectivity is not available, SMTP must be used for replication, and SMTP cannot be used to replicate the domain naming context. Therefore, the ship must be a separate domain in the forest.

  B. **Incorrect:** Increasing the cost of the site link will not enable replication between the ship and headquarters.

  C. **Incorrect:** Designating a bridgehead server will not enable replication between the ship and headquarters.

  D. **Incorrect:** Manually creating a connection object will not enable replication between the ship and headquarters.

4. **Correct Answers: A and B**

  A. **Correct:** In the Active Directory Sites And Services snap-in, you can right-click NTDS Settings and force replication.

  B. **Correct:** The Replication Diagnostics tool, *Repadmin.exe*, enables you to force replication from the command line.

  C. **Incorrect:** The Directory Service Diagnosis tool, *Dcdiag.exe*, is a command-line tool that enables you to test the health of replication and security for Active Directory Domain Services.

  D. **Incorrect:** The Active Directory Domains And Trusts snap-in is used to create and manage user, group, and computer objects. It does not enable you to force replication.

Chapter 11: Case Scenario Answers

Case Scenario: Configuring Sites and Subnets

1. Create one Active Directory site for Denver. Intrasite replication topology, created by the KCC, generates a two-way topology with a maximum of three hops. Replication will occur within one minute. If the headquarters and the warehouse are in separate sites,

intersite replication frequency is, at best, every 15 minutes.

2. Designating a preferred bridgehead server is useful to ensure that the role is performed by a server with the most available system resources. It can also be useful if network configuration, such as firewalls, requires that replication traffic be directed to a single IP address. However, if the preferred bridgehead server is not available, the intersite topology generator (ISTG) does not automatically designate a temporary bridgehead. Therefore, replication stops if the preferred bridgehead server is offline.

3. To achieve a true hub-and-spoke topology, you must create five site links. Each site link contains the Denver site and one of the branches. Therefore, the five site links would be: Denver–Portland, Denver–Seattle, Denver–Chicago, Denver–Miami, and Denver–Fort Lauderdale. You must also disable site link transitivity so that replication cannot build connections that skip over the Denver site.

4. Create a manual connection object for the warehouse domain controller so that it receives replication from SERVER01. A manual connection object will not be deleted by the KCC when it builds the intrasite replication topology.

Chapter 12: Lesson Review Answers

Lesson 1

1. **Correct Answers: A and D**
   A. **Correct:** In Active Directory Users And Computers, you can right-click the root node of the snap-in or the domain, and you will find the Raise Domain Functional Level command.
   B. **Incorrect:** Active Directory Schema is not used to raise the domain functional level.
   C. **Incorrect:** Active Directory Sites And Services is not used to raise the domain functional level.
   D. **Correct:** You can right-click the domain in the Active Directory Domains And Trusts snap-in and choose Raise Domain Functional Level.

2. **Correct Answers: B, D, and E**
   A. **Incorrect:** You must have one writable domain controller running Windows Server 2008 before adding an RODC to a domain. You already have a Windows Server 2008 domain controller in the *contoso.com* domain.
   B. **Correct:** The domain functional level must be at least Windows Server 2003 before adding an RODC.
   C. **Incorrect:** You cannot raise the domain functional level to Windows Server 2008 because you have a domain controller running Windows Server 2003.

   D. **Correct:** The forest functional level must be at least Windows Server 2003 before adding an RODC.

   E. **Correct:** You must run *Adprep /rodcprep* before adding the first RODC to a domain.

   F. **Incorrect:** You already have a Windows Server 2008 domain controller, so you have already run *Adprep /forestprep*.

3. **Correct Answer: C**

   A. **Incorrect:** RODCs are not required to implement fine-grained password policies.

   B. **Incorrect:** The *Dfsrmig.exe* command configures DFS-R of SYSVOL.

   C. **Correct:** Windows Server 2008 forest functional level is required for fine-grained password policies.

   D. **Incorrect:** Fine-grained password policies are not managed with the GPMC.

Lesson 2

1. **Correct Answers: A, C, and G**

   A. **Correct:** The users in *wingtiptoys.com* will authenticate with computers in the *tailspintoys.com* domain. That makes *wingtiptoys.com* the trusted domain. The trust you must configure in *wingtiptoys.com* is an incoming trust.

   B. **Incorrect:** An outgoing trust would allow users in *tailspintoys.com* to authenticate with computers in *wingtiptoys.com*.

   C. **Correct:** The users in *wingtiptoys.com* are required to log on to computers in *tailspintoys.com*, but there is no requirement for users in *tailspintoys.com* to authenticate with computers in *wingtiptoys.com*.

   D. **Incorrect:** The users in *tailspintoys.com* are not required to log on to computers in *wingtiptoys.com*.

   E. **Incorrect:** Realm trusts are created with Kerberos v5 realms, not with Windows domains.

   F. **Incorrect:** A shortcut trust is used between domains in a multidomain forest.

   G. **Correct:** Because users in both the *europe.wingtiptoys.com* and *wingtiptoys.com* domains will authenticate with computers in *tailspintoys.com*, a forest trust is required. Forest trusts are transitive.

   H. **Incorrect:** An external trust would not provide the ability for users in the *europe.wingtiptoys.com* domain to authenticate with computers in the *tailspintoys.com* domain.

2. **Correct Answers: C and D**

   A. **Incorrect:** Creating duplicate accounts for the users will not enable the users to access resources.

     B. **Incorrect:** Rebuilding the Windows NT 4.0 domain will not enable the users to access resources.

     C. **Correct:** The */verify* parameter verifies the health of an existing trust relationship. Some trusted users are able to access the resources, so the trust relationship is known to be healthy.

     D. **Correct:** The fact that the problematic accounts were migrated from Windows NT 4.0 suggests that there are SIDs in the users' *sIDHistory* attributes that are being filtered out because SID filtering is enabled by default on all external trusts. The */quarantine:no* parameter will disable SID filtering.

3. **Correct Answer: D**

     A. **Incorrect:** Reinstalling the operating systems is unlikely to solve the problem because performance is reasonable for accessing resources in the users' own domains.

     B. **Incorrect:** Whether the IP address is assigned dynamically or statically is not relevant to the problem.

     C. **Incorrect:** Dynamic updates of DNS records is not relevant to the problem.

     D. **Correct:** A shortcut trust can improve performance by allowing domain controllers in one domain to refer clients to the other domain directly rather than through the forest root domain.

Chapter 12: Case Scenario Answers

Case Scenario: Managing Multiple Domains and Forests

1. You must raise the domain and forest functional level to at least Windows Server 2003. Forest trusts are allowed only at forest functional levels of Windows Server 2003 or Windows Server 2008.

2. Because you do not have an account in the *wingtiptoys.com* domain, you can create only one-way incoming and one-way outgoing trusts. Administrators in *wingtiptoys.com* must create the reciprocal one-way outgoing and one-way incoming trusts.

3. You must enable selective authentication on the outgoing trust. Then, you must give those users the Allowed To Authenticate permission on the computer objects of the four servers.

Chapter 13: Lesson Review Answers

Lesson 1

1. Correct Answer: **B**

   A. **Incorrect:** Restartable AD DS is one of the best features of Windows Server 2008.

   B. **Correct:** If someone is working on the other DC in the forest root domain and has stopped the AD DS service, you will not be able to stop it on this server because at least one DC for each domain must be operational before the service will stop.

   C. **Incorrect:** You do not need to use DSRM in Windows Server 2008 to perform database operations on a DC.

   D. **Incorrect:** You can stop the AD DS service either through the command line or through the Services console.

2. Correct Answers: **D and F**

   A. **Incorrect:** If the server has failed, you cannot restart it in DSRM.

   B. **Incorrect:** You do not need to perform an authoritative restore because there is no indication that the server contained lost data that was not found in the other DCs.

   C. **Incorrect:** You do not need to reinstall the OS if you have access to full server backups.

   D. **Correct:** You must restart the server in WinRE to launch the full server recovery operation.

   E. **Incorrect:** You cannot perform a nonauthoritative restore with *Ntdsutil.exe* in Windows Server 2008. You must use Windows Server Backup or *Wbadmin.exe*.

   F. **Correct:** You can perform a full server recovery with either the command line or the graphical interface.

Lesson 2

1. Correct Answers: **C and D**

   A. **Incorrect:** Expiration dates do not cause a collector set to stop. They stop new collections from starting when the expiration date has been reached.

   B. **Incorrect:** To be running, the collector sets must be on a schedule; otherwise, they would stop when the user who created them logged off.

   C. **Correct:** You must set a stop condition on each collector set to ensure that it stops.

   D. **Correct:** You must set a duration on the collector set when you schedule it to run; otherwise, it will not stop.

2. Correct Answers: **A, B, C, and D**

A. **Correct:** Reliability Monitor will reveal whether any changes have been made to the server recently and whether those changes could be tied to performance bottlenecks.

B. **Correct:** Event Viewer, especially the System event log, will reveal any errors or warnings about performance on the system.

C. **Correct:** Task Manager will display a real-time view into resources and enable you to identify potential bottlenecks.

D. **Correct:** Performance Monitor, especially the role-based Data Collector Set templates, will enable you to discover quickly any performance issues with the current server configuration and make recommendations on possible changes to improve performance.

Chapter 13: Case Scenario Answers

Case Scenario: Working with Lost and Found Data

Occasionally, especially in large forests, someone will delete a container at the same time someone else is creating or modifying an object in the same container. This can be on entirely different DCs, but when replication synchronizes data on the DCs, the newly created object no longer has a home. When this happens, AD DS automatically stores these objects within the LostAndFound container. This special container manages lost and found objects within the domain. Another special container, the LostAndFoundConfig container, manages lost and found objects for the entire forest. The LostAndFoundConfig container is in the forest root domain only.

Therefore, you should regularly review the LostAndFound and the LostAndFoundConfig containers for objects to determine whether these objects should be moved to new containers or simply deleted from the directory.

Use the following procedure to verify the LostAndFound container in a child domain:

1. Move to the Active Directory Users And Computers portion of Server Manager.

2. Click View, choose Advanced Features, expand the tree, and then click the LostAndFound container.

3. Identify any objects located within this container. Decide whether they need to be moved to other containers or deleted.

Be careful when deleting objects. Make sure you review the object's properties before doing so. Sometimes, it is best to move the object and deactivate it while you communicate with your peers to determine whether it is a necessary object. Remember that once deleted, SIDs cannot be recovered.

Chapter 14: Lesson Review Answers

Lesson 1

1. Correct Answer: C

   A. **Incorrect:** Existing setup processes must complete before you can initiate another setup operation. It is also difficult to tell whether setup processes have completed when you use the command line unless you use the *Start /w* command, which will return the command prompt only when an operation completes. After a reboot, you will find that there are no setup processes currently in operation, yet you still cannot uninstall AD LDS.

   B. **Incorrect:** Using Server Manager does not solve the problem because you must remove all AD LDS instances before you can remove the role.

   C. **Correct:** You must remove all existing AD LDS instances before you can remove the role from the server. After all instances have been removed, you can remove the AD LDS role. This is one more reason why AD LDS instance documentation is so important.

   D. **Incorrect:** *Oclist* will give you the name of all the roles and features to use with the *Ocsetup* command. However, this is a full installation of Windows Server 2008 because you have access to Server Manager. *Oclist* does not work on the full installation.

Lesson 2

1. Correct Answer: D

   A. **Incorrect:** All AD LDS instances have a schema, and all instance schemas can be edited. This is one reason you should use AD LDS instead of AD DS to integrate applications.

   B. **Incorrect:** You can make modifications to the instance with the *LDP.exe* command, but schema modifications should be performed through the Active Directory Schema snap-in.

   C. **Incorrect:** You can make modifications to the instance with the LDIF files and the *LDIFDE.exe* command, but schema modifications should be performed through the Active Directory Schema snap-in.

   D. **Correct:** When you use AD LDS Setup to create instances with default port numbers, the first port used on member servers is port 389. For example, to connect to the first instance, you need to use Instance01:389. However, because your Active Directory Domain Services schema also uses port 389, and your server is member of a domain, the Active Directory Schema snap-in will not connect to the instance.

This is one reason you should never use port 389 for AD LDS instances in a domain.

Chapter 14: Case Scenario Answers

Case Scenario: Determine AD LDS Instance Prerequisites

You look up the information on AD LDS on the Microsoft TechNet Center for Active Directory technologies and come up with the following answers:

1. A data drive should be created for each server that will host AD LDS instances. Because these servers will be hosting directory stores, you should place these stores on a drive that is separate from the operating system and into separate folders so that they can be easily identified.

2. You should always use meaningful names to identify instances. For example, the name of the application that will be tied to an instance is a good candidate. Instance names are used to identify the instance on the local computer as well as to identify and name the files that make up the instance and the service that supports it. Names cannot include spaces or special characters.

3. Both AD LDS and AD DS use the same ports for communication. These ports are the default LDAP (389) and LDAP over the Secure Sockets Layer (SSL), or Secure LDAP, (636) ports. AD DS uses two additional ports, 3268, which uses LDAP to access the global catalog, and 3269, which uses Secure LDAP to access the global catalog. Because AD DS and AD LDS use the same ports, you should make it a habit to use other ports, ports beyond the 50,000 range, for your AD LDS instances. This will ensure that they are segregated from AD DS services, especially if the instance is installed within a domain. In addition, you should install PKI certificates on each AD LDS instance to use Secure LDAP for communication and management. This will prevent tampering with or detection of AD LDS data.

4. Ideally, each AD LDS instance should use an application partition, even if no replication is required. Creating an application directory partition will make it easier to manage the instance through a variety of tools.

5. Instances should be run through the use of a service account. You can use the Network Service account, but if you intend to run multiple instances, it is suggested that you use named service accounts for each instance. This way, you know exactly when the instance performs operations because you can view the logon operations of the service account in the Event Viewer.

Chapter 15: Lesson Review Answers

Lesson 1

1. Correct Answers: B and C

   A. **Incorrect:** Although it is true that you cannot install enterprise CAs on Windows Server 2008 Standard Edition or Windows Server 2008 Web Edition, you are actually running the Windows Server 2008 Enterprise Edition of Windows Server because you verified this prerequisite at the beginning of the installation.

   B. **Correct:** If you are logged on with a local account, even an account with local administrative privileges, you cannot install an enterprise CA. You must use a domain account to install an enterprise CA.

   C. **Correct:** To install an enterprise CA, your server must be a member of the domain because enterprise CAs rely on the AD DS directory service to publish and issue certificates.

   D. **Incorrect:** Because of all the required components in an enterprise CA installation, you should use Server Manager to install this role.

Lesson 2

1. Correct Answer: B

   A. **Incorrect:** Although you can use *Certutil.exe* to load certificates, you should also be able to perform the same operation through the wizard.

   B. **Correct:** The certificate template access rights are not set properly. To load the certificate manually on the server, the user account must have the Allow: Enroll permission set. In addition, the server you load the certificate on should also have the Allow: Enroll permission. You must re-create the template and reissue it to correct its access rights.

   C. **Incorrect:** You should be able to load the OCSP certificate onto this server because it is an OR.

   D. **Incorrect:** Although the certificate should be able to load automatically if it has the Allow: Autoenroll permission set, there is no reason other than access rights that would stop you from loading it manually.

Chapter 15: Case Scenario Answers

Case Scenario: Manage Certificate Revocation

You go to your superiors with the information. They need to undertake a police operation immediately to stop the two ex-employees from selling certificates with the Contoso name embedded in them. In addition, your sales personnel need to initiate some damage-control operations with your clients. Having software on the market that does not originate from Contoso, yet contains Contoso certificates, can be extremely damaging to your company's reputation.

For your part, you immediately move to block the use of the certificates. To do so, you must first bring the root CA online. Then, you use the Certification Authority section of Server Manager to revoke the two stolen certificates. Fortunately, when you cancel these certificates, any certificates that were issued using these as a source will be automatically invalidated.

Then, you force publication of the Certificate Revocation List. To do so, you use the Revoked Certificates node of the Certification Authority console. Unfortunately, you realize that even if you publish this new CRL immediately, clients will not update their CRL until their next refresh cycle, which depends on the refresh configuration.

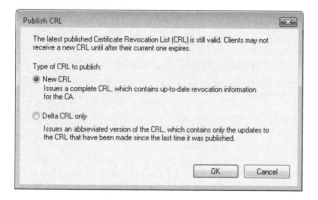

Finally, your organization should issue a public statement about the two lost certificates. All Contoso clients should know that they are at risk and must verify each certificate they receive in the Contoso name until the revocation has taken effect.

As you can see, root CA security is of the utmost importance in a PKI architecture.

Chapter 16: Lesson Review Answers

Lesson 1

1. **Correct Answer: D**

   A. **Incorrect:** The server is running AD RMS because the AD RMS node is available in Server Manager.

   B. **Incorrect:** The server certificate is validated during the installation process. At worst, you can always use a self-signed certificate. This cannot be the problem.

   C. **Incorrect:** To install AD RMS, your server must be a member of the domain because AD RMS relies on the AD DS directory service to publish and issue certificates.

   D. **Correct:** During the installation, your account is added to the AD RMS Enterprise Administrators group on the local computer. To update the privileges of your account, you must log off and then log on again. Without this procedure, your account will not have the required access rights to run AD RMS.

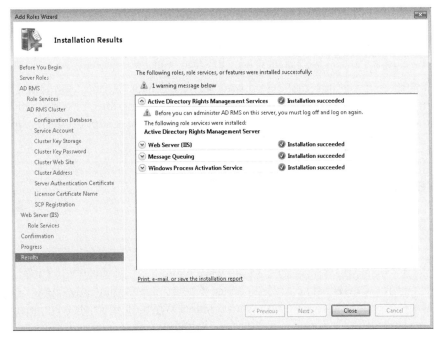

Lesson 2

1. **Correct Answer: B**

   A. **Incorrect:** To access HTTP over SSL, users must use a URL address in the HTTPS:// format.

B.   **Correct:** The server certificate is validated when users try to access the URL. If it is not from a trusted CA, it will not work. If you used a self-signed certificate, the URL would have worked when you accessed it from the server because the server trusts its own certificate, but it will not work from user browsers because they do not trust the self-signed certificate.

C.   **Incorrect:** To access AD RMS from outside the network, users do not need an AD DS account.

D.   **Incorrect:** The URL is correct because you verified it from the server you used to set it up.

Chapter 16: Case Scenario Answers

Case Scenario: Prepare to Work with an External AD RMS Cluster

The best and easiest way to share policy infrastructures without putting federation trusts in place is to rely on cross-certificate publication. This means using trusted publishing domains that enable your own AD RMS cluster to issue use licenses for content that was protected by another AD RMS cluster. To create a trusted publishing domain, you must import the publishing cluster's SLC as well as its private key into your own cluster.

To proceed, you must first export your Server Licensor Certificate and then have it imported into your partner's root cluster. Your partner must also perform the same activity. After the two certificates are imported, both environments will be able to support the issuance of publishing and use certificates for each other.

Chapter 17: Lesson Review Answers

Lesson 1

1.   **Correct Answer: B**

A.   **Incorrect:** All services can use a named service account to run.

B.   **Correct:** The named service account is automatically replaced by the Network Service account during installation. When the upgrade is complete, you must reset the service account for each AD FS service.

C.   **Incorrect:** Woodgrove's policies would affect servers in the Woodgrove network and not in your own.

D.   **Incorrect:** Although the Network Service account has limited access rights to the local computer and is a good account to use for certain services, it is by no means a best practice and Microsoft does not enforce its use.

Lesson 2

1. **Correct Answers: A, B, D, and E**

    A. **Correct:** You must communicate with your counterpart to determine how you will exchange policy files during the setup of the partnership.

    B. **Correct:** You export the partner policy from the resource organization (Woodgrove Bank) and import it into the account organization (Contoso).

    C. **Incorrect:** The partner policy must be exported from the resource organization (Woodgrove Bank) and imported into the account organization (Contoso). This option proposes the reverse.

    D. **Correct:** You export the trust policy from the account organization (Contoso) and import it into the resource organization (Woodgrove Bank).

    E. **Correct:** You must create and configure a claim mapping in the resource organization (Woodgrove Bank).

    F. **Incorrect:** The trust policy must be exported from the account organization (Contoso) and imported into the resource organization (Woodgrove Bank). This option proposes the reverse.

Chapter 17: Case Scenario Answers

Case Scenario: Choose the Right AD Technology

Answers may vary but should include all the elements presented here.

You look over the requirements and decide that it is a good opportunity to rely on the five Active Directory technologies. You decide to proceed as follows:

■   You will use AD DS to upgrade the internal directory service.

■   You will implement AD RMS to protect your intellectual property. This means that when you create a partnership, your organization will be the resource organization because you host the AD RMS installation.

■   To support the applications in the extranet, you will need to implement identity federation with AD FS. You will implement the AD FS Federated Web Single-Sign-On design, and your organization will be the resource organization. In addition, you will need to add the following elements to support each of the applications:

❑ To support the Windows-based applications in the extranet, you need access to a directory store. Because you do not want to deploy AD DS in an extranet because of the risks involved, you will deploy AD LDS. The instance of AD LDS will provide logon services for the Windows applications through AD FS. You will install the AD FS Windows Token-based Agent to support identity federation.

❑ The Web-based applications will be AD FS–enabled by installing the AD FS Claims-aware Agent.

■ The clients that access your applications will be supported by the AD FS and the AD LDS processes. Specifically, partner organizations and internal users will rely on AD FS, and the general public will rely on instances of AD LDS to gain access to the applications.

■ You will implement Active Directory Certificate Services to provide communication security. To facilitate access to all applications and ensure that all partners can validate the certificates you generate, you will rely on a third-party commercial trusted CA as the root of your AD CS deployment. This way, all your certificates will be trusted at all times because the root certificate is trusted by all.

This is a best practices implementation of the five AD technologies.

Index

Symbols and Numbers

. (dot), 102, 394
$ (dollar sign), 102, 123

A

A (host) record, 413, 517–518
AAAA (host) record, 413
access control entries. *See* ACEs (access control entries)
access control lists. *See* ACLs (access control lists)
access rights
    AD RMS considerations, 814–815
    assigning, 759
    authentication process, 835
    SCP creation, 801
account attributes, 119–121
Account Expires setting, 120
account federation server (AFS), 834, 839, 842
Account Federation Service Proxy, 842
Account Is Disabled setting, 120
Account Is Trusted For Delegation setting, 120
Account Lockout and Management tools, 614–616
Account Lockout Duration policy, 359
account lockout policies. *See* lockout policies
Account Lockout Policy node, 359
Account Lockout Threshold setting, 359
Account Operators group
    characteristics, 177–178
    creating computer objects, 192
    moving computers, 214
account organizations
    configuring AD FS, 855
    defined, 832, 842
    discovery Web page, 843
    organization claims, 843
Account Partner cookies, 840
account policies, 303, 613
Account Policy node, 361
Account property, 117
AcctInfo.dll, 614–616
ACEs (access control entries)
    AD DS administration, 613
    defined, 69
    deleted groups, 171
    effective permissions, 76
    migration considerations, 574
    viewing, 71
ACLs (access control lists)

Active Directory objects, 69–71
AD DS administration, 613, 620
AD RMS support, 7
GPO support, 262
group nesting, 153
group scope, 145
IDA support, 3–4
managing for groups, 141–143
migration considerations, 574
protected groups, 178
securing trust relationships, 591
security translation, 575
actions, 35, 100
Active Directory Application Mode (ADAM), 6, 685, 694, 831
Active Directory Certificate Services. *See* AD CS (Active Directory Certificate Services)
Active Directory data store
    AD DS administration, 620–621
    as identity store, 3
    defined, 9
    LDAP support, 8
Active Directory Diagnostics collector set, 667
Active Directory directory service
    creating computer objects, 52–54
    creating group objects, 50–52, 63–64
    creating organizational units, 46–48, 61
    creating user objects, 48–50, 61–63
    defined, 46
    finding objects, 54–67
Active Directory Domain Services. *See* AD DS (Active Directory Domain Services)
Active Directory Domain Services Installation Wizard
    child domain delegations, 405, 417
    configuring GC servers, 524
    creating domain controllers, 13
    creating instances, 703
    creating RODCs, 379, 470
    installation media, 472
    installing domain controllers, 461–463, 466–467, 474–475
    installing domain trees, 469
    managing domain controllers in sites, 516
    operations master roles, 486
    removing domain controllers, 473
    removing domains, 418
    zone delegations, 412

Active Directory Domains and Trusts snap-in
    AD DS administration, 619
    creating manual trusts, 583
    domain functional levels, 494, 560
    forest functional levels, 377, 563
    functionality, 36
    UPN suffixes, 49
Active Directory Federation Services. *See* AD FS
        (Active Directory Federation Services)
Active Directory Integrated (ADI) zone, 408
Active Directory Lightweight Directory Services. *See*
        AD LDS (Active Directory Lightweight Directory
        Services)
Active Directory Migration Tool (ADMT), 573, 575–576
Active Directory objects
    ACL support, 69
    assigning permissions, 72–73
    control access rights, 72
    creating with Windows PowerShell, 103
    delegating, 69–70
    delegating administrative tasks, 74–75
    deleting, 128, 163
    importing users with CSVDE, 90, 94–95
    importing users with LDIFDE, 90–92, 95–96
    permissions and inheritance, 73–74
    protecting from deletion, 625–626
    restoring, 626–627
    viewing ACLs, 70–71
    viewing permissions, 70–71, 75
Active Directory partitions, 523, 551
Active Directory Rights Management Service. *See* AD RMS
        (Active Directory Rights Management Service)
Active Directory schema, 37, 88
Active Directory Schema Management console, 613
Active Directory Schema snap-in
    AD DS administration, 619, 701
    AD LDS considerations, 701, 704
    working with instances, 712
Active Directory Services Interface. *See* ADSI
        (Active Directory Services Interface)
Active Directory sites. *See* sites
Active Directory Sites and Services snap-in
    AD DS administration, 619, 701
    AD LDS support, 701
    configuring GC servers, 524
    connection objects, 532
    functionality, 36, 512
    Subnets node, 513
    UGMC configuration, 525
    working with instances, 713
Active Directory Users and Computers snap-in
    AD DS administration, 619
    Additional Account Info tab, 614

assigning permissions, 73
controlling view of objects, 54
creating computer objects, 52
creating group objects, 50
creating organizational units, 46
creating RODC accounts, 470
creating user objects, 48
default containers, 11
delegating administrative tasks, 74
deleting computer accounts, 220
disabling accounts, 127, 219
domain functional levels, 560
functionality, 36
managing computers, 215
managing user accounts, 614
managing user attributes, 114–117
moving user accounts, 129
moving/renaming groups, 163
object protection, 625
resetting computer accounts, 217
Saved Queries node, 55
Specops Gpupdate tool, 616
user account hidden attributes, 88
viewing Active Directory object ACLs, 70
AD CS (Active Directory Certificate Services)
    AD RMS support, 782
    additional information, 742, 744
    CA hierarchy, 734–736
    CA Web Enrollment, 731
    certificate authorities, 6, 731
    certificate usage scenarios, 730
    deployment best practices, 737–738
    enterprise CAs, 732–734, 740
    functionality, 6, 723, 731
    installing, 740–742
    installing as enterprise issuing CA, 745–747
    installing as standalone root CA, 742–744
    installing issuing CA certificate, 747–748
    installing NDES, 749–750
    IPSec (Internet Protocol security), 6, 729
    managing, 763–764
    NDES support, 732
    new features, 732
    online responders, 731–732
    planning requirements, 738–740
    protecting configuration, 766–767
    renaming computers, 219
    standalone CAs, 732–734, 740
AD DS (Active Directory Domain Services)
    Access auditing feature, 624
    AD LDS comparison, 691–692
    adding role via Windows interface, 12
    additional information, 6, 9

administration categories, 612–614
auditing directory changes, 626
certificate authorities, 733
communication ports, 703–704
creating baselines, 671
creating domain controllers, 11–13
creating forests, 11–12, 14–21
deployment considerations, 12
DNS support, 393, 414, 417–419
domain-based GPOs, 238–239
functionality, 5, 229
IDA support, 3–7
infrastructure components, 8–11
installing, 420–422, 424–429
installing from media, 472–473
Kerberos protocol, 4
perimeter networks, 836
planning architecture, 572
policy-based administration, 8
protecting objects, 625–626
recovering information, 624–625
replication services, 8
root cluster support, 788
schema support, 8
Server Core installation, 23–29
tools supported, 36–37, 619–622, 701–703
virtual machines, 648
AD DS administration
    AcctInfo.dll, 614–616
    additional information, 622
    administration activities, 612–614
    auditing directory changes, 626
    domain controllers as virtual machines, 648–650
    offline maintenance, 623–624
    online maintenance, 622–623
    proactive restores, 638–648
    protecting objects, 625–626
    Quest Object Restore for Active Directory, 628–629
    recovering information, 624–625
    restoring objects, 626–628
    Specops Gpupdate tool, 616–619
    tools supported, 36–37, 619–622, 701–703
    Windows Server Backup, 629–638
AD FS (Active Directory Federation Services)
    AD RMS support, 782, 789, 792–793, 818
    additional information, 833, 854, 856
    authentication, 827–828, 832–836
    B2B commerce, 832
    certificates, 841–842
    claims, 839–840
    configurations supported, 836–838
    cookies, 840–841
    Federated Web SSO, 836

Federated Web SSO with Forest Trust, 836
    finalizing configuration, 854–855, 857–869
    firewalls support, 693
    functionality, 7, 825, 827–828
    installing, 845–848
    managing, 855–857
    preparing deployment, 849–852
    service roles, 832–833, 846
    terminology, 842–845
    upgrade considerations, 848–849
    Web SSO, 837
AD FS Web agent, 840, 842
AD LDS (Active Directory Lightweight Directory
        Services)
    AD DS administration, 619–621
    AD DS comparison, 691–692
    additional information, 694
    auditing support, 703
    communication ports, 703–704
    creating instances, 703–709, 714–716
    Dsbutil.exe command, 620
    functionality, 6, 685–686
    installing, 694–696
    LDAP support, 6, 690, 692
    managing replication, 692, 717–718
    migrating previous LDAP instances, 708–709
    supported scenarios, 692–694
    tools supported, 701–703
    unattended instance creation, 706–707
    working with instances, 709–717
AD LDS Setup tool, 701, 703
AD RMS (Active Directory Rights Management Service)
    AD CS support, 730
    additional information, 788, 790, 794, 810, 819
    best practices, 800
    certificate support, 797–798
    configuration preparation, 809
    configuring trust policies, 810–811
    creating extranet URLs, 810
    exporting SLCs, 811
    functionality, 7, 781–782, 786–788
    implementing in stages, 786
    installation prerequisites, 794–797
    installing, 798–807
    managing databases, 818–819
    new features, 788–790
    preparing access rights, 814–815
    preparing accounts, 814–815
    preparing certificates, 811–812
    preparing exclusion policies, 812–814
    preparing policy templates, 815–817
    RMS toolkit, 819
    system requirements, 795

working with clients, 817–818
AD RMS Auditors role, 789, 814
AD RMS Enterprise Administrators role, 789, 814
AD RMS Identity Federation Support role, 793
AD RMS Service role, 789, 814
AD RMS Template Administrators role, 789, 814
ADAM (Active Directory Application Mode), 6, 685,
    694, 831
ADAMInstall.exe command, 701, 706
ADAMSync.exe command, 702
ADAMUninstall.exe command, 702
Add Printer Wizard, 59
Add Roles Wizard, 12, 461
Add To Group command, 152
Add/Remove Columns command, 54
Add/Remove Snap-in command, 303
Address property, 117
ADI (Active Directory Integrated) zone, 408
ADM file extension, 245–246
administrative role separation, 383
administrative tasks. *See also* AD DS administration
    AD DS tools, 36–37, 619–622, 701–703
    AD RMS roles, 789
    adding to Start menu, 37
    best practices for group attributes, 169–170
    creating custom consoles, 38–41
    delegating membership management, 172–175, 181
    delegating restricted groups policies, 294–295
    deleting user accounts, 128–181
    directory service, 610–611
    disabling/enabling user accounts, 127–128
    DNS tools, 448–450
    for computer accounts, 213
    moving user accounts, 129
    protecting groups from accidental deletion, 171
    recycling user accounts, 128
    renaming user accounts, 129–130
    resetting passwords, 125–126, 132
    running with alternate credentials, 37–38
    Server Manager tools, 37
    unlocking user accounts, 126–127, 132
    VBScript support, 108–110
    Windows PowerShell support, 98–108
administrative templates
    adding, 245
    ADM file extension, 245
    ADML file extension, 245
    ADMX file extension, 245
    defined, 245
    exploring, 251–252
    filtering policy settings, 246–247
Administrative Templates node, 243–248
Administrative Tools folder, 35, 40

Administrator account
    delegation considerations, 77
    initial password, 24
    policy settings, 231
    removing domain controllers, 27
Administrators GPO, 238
Administrators role, 383
ADML file extension, 245–246
ADMT (Active Directory Migration Tool), 573, 575–576
Admt.exe command, 573
ADMX file extension, 245–246
Adprep /forestprep command, 469
Adprep /rodcprep command, 378–379, 466, 472, 562
ADSchemaAnalyzer.exe command, 702
ADSI (Active Directory Services Interface)
    AD LDS support, 691
    connecting to containers, 104
    functionality, 8
    managing user attributes, 123
    VBScript support, 109–110
ADSI Edit tool
    AD DS administration, 619, 702
    AD LDS support, 702
    application directory partitions, 526
    managing passwords, 361
    working with instances, 709–711
aDSPath attribute, 164
Advanced Encryption Services (AES), 559
Advanced Security Settings dialog box
    assigning permissions, 72–73
    delegating membership management, 174–175
    removing/resetting permissions, 75
Aelita Enterprise Directory Manager, 688–689
AES (Advanced Encryption Services), 559
AFS (account federation server), 834, 839, 842
aging, 408, 438
AIA (Authority Information Access) extension, 759–760
alias
    CNAME records, 413
    defined, 102
    single-label names, 442
Allow Apply Group Policy permission, 262
allow permissions
    ACE support, 574
    as cumulative, 76
    deny permission comparison, 76, 626
Allow Read permission, 262
Allow Write Member permission, 174
Allowed List attribute, 380–381
Allowed RODC Password Replication Group, 380
alternate credentials, 37–38, 126
Always Wait For Network At Startup And Logon policy
    setting, 236

Analyze Computer Now command, 307
Anonymous Logon group, 179
answer files
    installing child domains, 468
    installing domain trees, 469
    unattended installation, 462–464
APIPA (Automatic Private IP Addressing), 395
application basic groups, 562
application directory partitions
    AD DS administration, 612, 620
    AD LDS considerations, 704, 708–709
    additional information, 448, 527
    customized, 446–448
    defined, 408, 525, 707
    Directory Service Diagnosis tool, 545
    examining, 528–529
    overview, 445–448, 522, 525–527
    replication scope, 404, 408, 414, 445, 447
Application log, 281, 663
applications
    assigning, 323–325
    claims-aware, 842, 855, 863
    federated, 843
    maintaining, 327–329
    publishing, 323–325
    token-based, 845
    upgrading, 331–332
arrow keys, 642
assigning applications, 323–325
Asynchronous Full Transfer (AXFR), 412
Attribute Editor, 88, 116–117
attributes. *See also* specific attributes
    auditing changes, 620
    data protection measures, 624
    redefining, 562
Audit Account Logon Events setting, 336, 368
Audit Account Management setting, 336
Audit Directory Service Access setting, 336, 341–342
Audit Logon Events setting, 336
audit logs, 335, 339
Audit Object Access setting, 337, 340–341
audit policies
    auditing directory changes, 626
    balancing, 337
    configuring, 369–370
    defined, 349
    enabling, 340, 343
    functionality, 335
    scoping, 370
    Security Configuration Wizard, 312
    supported settings, 335–337
Audit Policy Change setting, 336
Audit Privilege Use setting, 336

Audit Process Tracking setting, 337
Audit System Events setting, 336
auditing
    AD DS administration, 620
    AD LDS support, 703
    AD RMS support, 789, 814
    authentication, 368–372
    configuring permissions, 343
    directory changes, 626
    file system access, 337–341
    IDA support, 4
    logging database support, 819
auditpol command, 342
Authenticated Users group
    administrative tasks, 127
    Allow Apply Group Policy permission, 262
    defined, 179
    multiple forests, 572
    securing trust relationships, 591
    selective authentication, 593
authentication
    Account Partner cookies, 840
    AD FS support, 827–828, 832–836
    AD LDS support, 693
    AD RMS support, 786
    auditing, 368–372
    authentication cookies, 840
    computer account problems, 216
    defined, 31, 355
    digital certificates, 6
    for identity, 4
    in branch offices, 374–375
    Kerberos protocol, 4, 9
    security policy support, 312
    selective, 559, 593–595, 600–601
    shortcut trusts, 586
    sign-out cookies, 840
    smart card support, 812
    special identities, 179
    trusts and, 579–582
authentication cookies, 840
authoritative restores
    deleted groups, 171
    overview, 632–645
    restoration scenario, 639
    Windows Server Backup, 630
Authority Information Access (AIA) extension, 759–760
Authorization Manager tool, 559, 562
Automatic Private IP Addressing (APIPA), 395
availability
    directory service, 611
    domain local groups, 147
    global groups, 147

group scope considerations, 146
local groups, 146
universal groups, 148
virtual machines, 650
AXFR (Asynchronous Full Transfer), 412

B

B2B commerce, 832
backlinks, 116, 184
backup functions. *See also* restore functions
    AD CS considerations, 766–767
    additional information, 632
    data protection measures, 624
    virtual hard disks, 636
    Windows Server Backup, 629–638
Backup Operators group, 178, 631
baseline settings, 310
Bcdedit.exe command, 639
Bindview Secure Active Directory LifeCycle Suite, 688
bridgehead servers
    AD DS administration, 612
    polling, 542
    preferred, 539, 546
    replication overview, 538–539
browse lists, 483
Builtin container, 11, 177
business continuity. *See* AD DS administration; backup
    functions; restore functions

C

CA (certificate authority). *See also* specific CAs
    AD CS support, 6, 731
    common event IDs, 763–764
    creating hierarchy, 734–736
    creating revocation configuration, 754–755
    defined, 731
    firewall considerations, 826
    managing, 763
    requester identification validation, 738
    SMTP considerations, 537
    trust considerations, 725, 730
    upgrading, 755, 764
    Web Enrollment process, 731
caching
    credentials, 381–382, 385–386
    DNS support, 431
    universal group membership, 524–525
canonical name (CNAME) record, 413, 803
central store, 246, 252
certificate authority. *See* CA (certificate authority)
certificate chaining, 734, 854

certificate enrollment, 738, 823
certificate practice statement (CPS), 738–739
certificate revocation
    creating configuration, 753–755
    defined, 739, 777
    online responders, 761–762
certificate revocation lists. *See* CRLs (certificate
    revocation lists)
certificate templates
    certificate authorities, 733
    configuring, 755–756
    configuring duplicate, 757
    configuring enrollment, 758–759
    customizing, 756–757
    issuing, 757
    managing, 763
    personalizing, 753–754
certificates
    AD FS support, 841–842
    AD RMS support, 797–798, 811–812
    additional information, 725, 842
    CRL support, 731
    event IDs, 764
    exporting, 854, 857–862
    Federation Server proxies, 841
    federation servers, 841
    importing, 857–859, 862
    lifetime considerations, 738–739
    managing, 763
    online responders, 731
    requester identification validation, 738
    self-signed, 801, 818
    SLC, 789, 797, 810–811, 818
    trust considerations, 725, 734
Certificates snap-in, 760–761
Certification Authority Backup Wizard, 766
Certutil command, 763, 767
CF (conditional forwarders), 417, 440–441
changeType field (LDIFDE), 161, 204
child CAs, 731
child domains
    application directory partitions, 445
    creating, 427–429
    delegations, 405, 417–418
    DNS considerations, 404–405, 414
    installing, 467–468
    replication scope, 404
    shortcut trusts, 586
child objects, 73, 77
Cisco Systems, Inc., 732
claim mapping, 843, 855, 872
claims
    additional information, 840

custom claim type, 839, 848
defined, 839, 842–843
group claim type, 839, 848
identity claim type, 839, 848
claims-aware agent, 833, 846
claims-aware applications, 842, 855, 863
CLC (client licensor certificate), 797
client authentication certificate, 843
client licensor certificate (CLC), 797
client-side extensions. *See* CSEs (client-side extensions)
cloud concept, 398
cmdlets
alias support, 102
command shell comparison, 101
defined, 98
namespace support, 103
overview, 99–101
scripting support, 99
support for variables, 102, 123
syntax, 99
CN (common name)
defined, 60
identity claim type, 839
name attributes, 118
renaming user accounts, 129–130
cn attribute, 118, 129, 144
CNAME (canonical name) record, 413, 803
collision detection and management, 532
colons (::), 395
command prompts, arrow keys, 642
command shell, 101–102
common name. *See* CN (common name)
compaction, 624, 683
computer accounts
AD DS administration, 612, 621
administrative tasks, 213
data protection measures, 624
deleting, 220
disabling/enabling, 219
logon process, 216
prestaging, 192–193, 196, 206
recycling, 220
resetting, 217, 220
RODC support, 381
secure channel, 216
troubleshooting, 216–217, 222
Computer Configuration node
Administrative Templates node, 243–248
defined, 231, 241
Policies node, 241
Preferences node, 241, 243–244
Software Installation node, 325
Software Settings node, 242

Windows Settings node, 242
Computer Management console, 35
computer objects
AD DS administration, 613, 620
checking existence, 194
configuring attributes with Dsmod, 214
configuring attributes with VBScript, 214
configuring attributes with Windows PowerShell, 214
configuring properties, 213–214
creating, 52–54, 63–64, 199–200
creating OUs, 199
creating with Dsadd, 205, 209
creating with Netdom, 205
creating with VBScript, 208, 211
creating with Windows PowerShell, 206–208, 211
delegating permissions, 192, 200
domain requirements, 190
importing with CSVDE, 203–204, 209–210
importing with LDIFDE, 204–205
managing, 215, 221–222
moving, 214–215
prestaging, 195–197
renaming, 218–219
restrictions creating, 197
Specops Gpupdate tool, 617–618
computer settings. *See* Computer Configuration node
Computers container
as default container, 11, 195
configuring, 195–196
joining computers to domains, 190
moving computers, 214
redirecting, 200, 559
conditional forwarders (CF), 417, 440–441
Conditional Forwarders node, 441
Configuration container, 509
configuration database, 310, 818
configuration management, 176, 613
configuration partition, 522
Configure Computer Now command, 307
connection objects
creating, 545–546
defined, 532
displaying for domain controllers, 544
forcing replication, 532
constructed attributes, 117
containers
connecting to, 104
default, 11
defined, 11
OUs and, 46, 190–191
permission inheritance, 73
cookies
Account Partner cookies, 840

additional information, 841
authentication cookies, 840
defined, 840
passive clients, 843
sign-out cookies, 840
Copy Object User Wizard, 87
copyrights, 785
CPS (certificate practice statement), 738–739
Create Computer Objects permission, 192
Create method, 104, 109, 206
credential caching, 381–382, 385–386
CRLs (certificate revocation lists)
AD FS configuration, 855
CA support, 733
creating revocation configuration, 754–755
defined, 731
online responders, 731
cryptographic storage providers (CSPs), 800
Cscript command, 25–26, 108
CSEs (client-side extensions)
configuring, 236
CPSI support, 322
defined, 235
GPO support, 240
policy settings, 242
CSPs (cryptographic storage providers), 800
CSV file extension
importing computers with Windows PowerShell, 208
importing groups with CSVDE, 160
importing users with CSVDE, 90
importing users with Windows PowerShell, 106
CSVDE tool
AD DS administration, 619, 702
AD LDS support, 702
importing computers, 203–204, 209–210
importing groups, 160, 165
importing users, 90, 94–95
custom claim type, 839, 848

D

DACL (discretionary ACL)
defined, 69
migration considerations, 574
property sets, 72
viewing, 71
Data Collector Set templates, 667
data collector sets
adding counters, 669
common counters, 667–669
creating, 666–667, 675–679
creating performance baselines, 671
defined, 683

tracking counters, 669
data management, 611
data protection
built-in measures, 624–625, 628
protecting objects, 625–626, 628
Windows Server Backup, 629–630
data store. See Active Directory data store
database management
AD DS administration, 614, 623–624
AD RMS support, 818–819
automating maintenance, 655–657
performing maintenance, 653–655
Dcdiag.exe (Directory Server Diagnosis), 543–545, 619, 702
DCOM (Distributed Component Object Model), 733
Dcpromo command
AD DS administration, 620
adding AD DS to Server Core, 26
additional information, 463
configuring GC servers, 524
creating RODC, 380, 470–471
demoting domain controllers, 473
installing child domains, 468
installing domain controllers, 461–463, 467
installing domain trees, 469
installing forests, 464
operation master roles, 488
promoting domain controllers, 26
removing domain controllers, 473
removing domains, 418
unattended installation, 462
DDNS (dynamic DNS) servers
defined, 398, 409
dynamic IP addresses, 443
name records, 406
server scavenging, 411
dedicated forest root domain, 567–568
Default Domain Controller GPO, 239, 301, 370
Default Domain GPO, 238
Default Domain Policy, 360–361, 758
default local groups
additional information, 179
defined, 177
example, 178
listed, 177–178
defragmentation, 624
delegation
AD RMS administration, 789–790, 814
administrative tasks, 74–75, 78–79
child domains, 405, 417–418
computer object permissions, 192
constrained, 559
defined, 81, 349

domain trees, 418
Group Policy membership, 295–298
information management tasks, 613
membership management, 172–175, 181
OU support, 77–78
overview, 69–70
permission inheritance and, 74
proactive management strategy, 611
restricted groups policies, 294–295
role-based access control, 77
zone, 412, 422–424
Delegation of Control Wizard, 74–75
Delete command, 220
Delete method (Windows PowerShell), 128
deletion
    Active Directory objects, 128, 163
    computer accounts, 220
    GPO links, 257
    groups with Dsrm, 163–164
    manual trusts, 590
    objects, 620
    organizational units, 47–48
    protecting groups, 171
    protecting objects, 625–626
    PSOs, 366
    user accounts, 128
delimiters in group names, 144
Denied List attribute, 380–381
Denied RODC Password Replication Group, 380
deny permissions
    access considerations, 171
    ACE support, 574
    allow permission comparison, 76, 626
description attribute, 162, 170, 214
DFS (distributed file shares), 612
DFS Namespaces, 510
DFS replication, 644, 663
DFS Replication log, 663
Dfscomd command, 26
DFS-R (Distributed File System Replication)
    AD DS administration, 620
    compression replication, 648
    Directory Service Diagnosis tool, 545
    domain functional level, 494–495
    GPO replication, 241
    migrating SYSVOL replication, 496
    migration stages, 495–496
    SYSVOL replication, 494–502, 559
    timestamp support, 482
DFSRadmin.exe command, 620, 648
Dfsrmig.exe command, 495–496
DHCP (Dynamic Host Configuration Protocol)
    DDNS servers, 398

DNS considerations, 443–445
IPv6 support, 395
RID master role and, 480
digital certificates. *See* certificates
Digital Rights Management (DRM), 781
digital signatures, 6, 398
Directory Replication Agent (DRA), 240
Directory Server Diagnosis (Dcdiag.exe), 543–545, 619, 702
Directory Service Access auditing category, 341
Directory Service Changes auditing category, 341–342, 345–346
Directory Service log, 663
Directory Service Remote Procedure Call (DS-RPC), 537
directory services database, 819
Directory Services Repair Mode, 623
Directory Services Restore Mode (DSRM), 639–640
Directory Services Restore Mode password, 464, 631, 639–640
diskpart command, 646
displayName attribute, 119
distinguished name. *See* DN (distinguished name)
Distributed Component Object Model (DCOM), 733
distributed file shares (DFS), 612
Distributed File System Replication. *See* DFS-R (Distributed File System Replication)
distribution groups, 51, 145
DLL (dynamic link library), 614–616
DN (distinguished name)
    AD LDS support, 704
    defined, 60
    Dsget command, 122
    Dsmod command, 121–122
    member attribute, 480–481
DNS (Domain Name System)
    AD DS administration, 417–419, 612, 620–621, 738
    AD RMS support, 810, 850
    additional information, 400, 406
    administration tools, 448–450
    application directory partitions, 408, 445–448
    configuring, 431, 596
    creating baselines, 671
    DHCP considerations, 443–445
    domain controller requirements, 12, 378
    firewall support, 826
    forest root domain, 464
    forest trusts, 589
    forwarders vs. root hints, 439–441
    functionality, 8, 393, 406
    hierarchical naming structure, 394
    IP addresses, 393
    IPv6 support, 395–396
    LDAP support, 690

name resolution process, 393, 406–408
PNRP support, 397–398
record types, 413–414
replication scope, 415
single-label names, 411, 415, 441–443, 450–451
split-brain syndrome, 400–402
TCP/IP port, 394
types of servers, 398–400
virtual machines, 648
Windows Server 2008 features, 414–416
WINS support, 442–443
zone types, 412–413
DNS Manager, 448, 620
DNS Notify process, 409
DNS records, 406, 456, 803. *See also* specific record types
DNS Server log, 663
DNS servers
   AD DS support, 417–419, 620
   administering, 448–450
   dynamic, 398, 406, 409, 411, 443
   primary, 419–420
   read-only, 399, 415
   read-write, 398
   security considerations, 431–432
   working with settings, 432–436
DNS zones. *See also* FLZ (forward lookup zones); RLZ
   (reverse lookup zones)
   ADI, 408
   background loading, 415
   configuring scavenging, 432–433
   DDNS servers, 398
   defined, 456
   domain, 409, 414
   forest, 409, 414
   primary, 410, 412
   RODC support, 399
   secondary, 411–412
   stub, 411–412
Dnscmd command
   AD DS administration, 620
   application directory partitions, 446
   functionality, 26, 448
   single-label names, 441
Dnslint command, 449
dollar sign ($), 102, 123
Domain Admins group
   auditing considerations, 341
   creating computer objects, 192, 194
   creating GPOs, 239
   creating manual trusts, 583
   default groups, 177
   deleting OUs, 48

end user support, 291
forest functional levels, 377
installing RODCs, 470
migration considerations, 576
moving computers, 214
PRP support, 380
restoring objects, 626
scheduled backups, 631
schema masters, 465
domain component, 60
Domain Controller Authentication template, 757
Domain Controller template, 757
domain controllers. *See also* operations masters; RODCs
   (read-only domain controllers)
   AD CS considerations, 738
   AD DS administration, 472–473, 613, 620–621, 623
   AD LDS considerations, 695
   application directory partitions, 527
   as virtual machines, 648–650
   auditing support, 337, 341
   build recommendations, 631–632
   certificate templates, 755
   compacting directory database, 614
   creating, 11–13
   creating from backup data, 651–653
   defined, 2, 9
   demoting, 473, 527
   Directory Service Diagnosis tool, 545
   displaying connection objects, 544
   displaying replication partners, 544
   domain-based GPOs, 238
   functional levels, 557
   functionality, 460
   global catalog, 418, 464
   GPO links, 256
   in sites, 11
   installing, 27–29, 465–466, 474–476
   installing additional, 466–467
   installing child domains, 467–468
   installing domain trees, 468–469
   installing forests, 464
   installing with Windows interface, 461–462
   Kerberos authentication, 4
   managing in sites, 515–516
   multiple-domain forests, 569
   placement in branch offices, 374–375
   placing writable, 378
   preferred bridgehead servers, 539
   recommendations, 461
   removing, 26–27, 473
   renaming, 558
   replication traffic, 510

scoping audit policies, 370
security templates, 304
service locator records, 517
synchronizing with replication partners, 544
unattended installation options, 462–464
Windows Server Backup, 630
WSRM considerations, 673
domain DNS zone, 409, 414, 527
domain functional levels
    AD DS administration, 619
    defined, 10, 557
    deploying RODCs, 377
    installing domain trees, 469
    installing forests, 464
    levels supported, 557–558
    raising, 494, 560, 563–565
    Windows 2000 Native, 558
    Windows Server 2003, 558–559, 565
    Windows Server 2008, 559
domain local groups
    characteristics, 146–147, 149
    defined, 51
    group nesting, 153
    group scope considerations, 150
    RODC support, 380
    securing trust relationships, 591
Domain Name System. See DNS (Domain Name System)
domain naming context, 522
domain naming master role
    forest-wide, 479
    functionality, 480
    identifying, 485
    placing, 483
    seizing, 487–488
domain quarantine, 592–593
domain trees
    creating, 424–426
    delegation, 418
    installing, 468–469
Domain Users group, 127, 194
domain-based GPOs, 238–239, 268
domains
    AD DS administration, 621
    authentication within, 579–580
    computers joining, 189–190, 193–195, 201
    default groups, 177–178
    defined, 9, 31
    design considerations, 570
    DFS replication, 663
    external trusts, 587
    forests and, 9
    GPO links, 234, 258

installing additional domain controllers, 465–467
installing first domain controller, 465–466
migration considerations, 575
moving objects, 163, 572–576, 621
naming considerations, 11, 118
operations master roles, 479–483
password policies, 360
removing, 418
renaming, 561
renaming objects, 163
resetting computer accounts, 217
trusts between, 577–578
trusts within, 577
domain-wide authentication, 593
dot (.), 102, 394
DRA (Directory Replication Agent), 240
DRM (Digital Rights Management), 781
DS commands. See also specific commands
    defined, 59
    managing user attributes, 132
    manipulating objects, 89
    modifiers, 89
    supported, 88–89
DSACLS.exe command, 75, 620, 702
Dsadd command
    AD DS administration, 620
    creating computers, 205, 209
    creating groups, 159–160, 165
    creating user account, 89, 94
    functionality, 88
    GroupDN parameter, 159
    optional parameters, 160
Dsamain.exe command, 620, 641, 702
Dsbutil.exe command, 620
DSDBUtil.exe command, 702
Dsget command
    AD DS administration, 620
    functionality, 88
    managing user attributes, 122
    manipulating objects, 89
    retrieving group membership, 162, 167
Dsmgmt.exe command, 383, 620, 702
Dsmod command
    AD DS administration, 620
    changing group membership, 162–163, 166
    changing group type/scope, 151
    configuring computer attributes, 214
    disabling accounts, 127
    enabling accounts, 127
    functionality, 88
    managing user attributes, 121–122
    manipulating objects, 89

renaming user accounts, 130
resetting computer accounts, 217
resetting passwords, 126
Dsmove command
AD DS administration, 620
functionality, 88
moving computers, 215
moving groups, 163
moving user accounts, 129
renaming groups, 163
Dsquery command
AD DS administration, 620
functionality, 59–60, 88
manipulating objects, 89
DSRM (Directory Services Restore Mode), 639–640
Dsrm command
AD DS administration, 620
deleting computer accounts, 220
deleting groups, 163–164
deleting user accounts, 128
functionality, 88
DSRM password, 464, 631, 639–640
DS-RPC (Directory Service Remote Procedure Call), 537
dynamic DNS servers. *See* DDNS (dynamic DNS) servers
Dynamic Host Configuration Protocol. *See* DHCP
    (Dynamic Host Configuration Protocol)
dynamic link library (DLL), 614–616
dynamic updates, 436
dynamicObject class, 562

E

e-commerce, 754
EDM (Enterprise Directory Manager), 689
EFS (Encrypting File System)
AD CS support, 6, 753
certificate templates, 756
recovery agents, 814
EKU (extended key usage), 841
e-mail, 730, 839
Encrypting File System. *See* EFS (Encrypting File
    System)
encryption
AD CS support, 730, 754
AD FS support, 827
AD RMS support, 800
certificate authorities, 826
issuing CAs, 732
Enterprise Admins group
AD RMS installation, 798
creating computer objects, 192
creating manual trusts, 583
default groups, 177

forest functional levels, 377
moving computers, 214
PRP support, 380
schema masters, 465
Specops Gpupdate tool, 617–618
enterprise CAs
automatic enrollment, 738
certificate templates, 755
defined, 732, 740
deployment best practices, 737
hierarchy considerations, 737
installation considerations, 742, 745–747
issuing CAs, 734
standalone CA comparison, 733–734
Enterprise Directory Manager (EDM), 689
Enterprise PKI, 763, 765–766
error messages, 217, 673
Errors events, 663
event IDs, 665, 763–764
event log policies, 303
event logs
auditing directory changes, 626
computer account problems, 217
examining for Group Policy, 281, 283
GPO replication errors, 241
new features, 665
Server Manager support, 663
Event Viewer
AD DS administration, 620, 702
AD LDS support, 702
DNS support, 449
functionality, 660, 663–665
location, 35
viewing Security log, 341
Everyone group, 179
Exchange Server (Microsoft). *See* Microsoft Exchange
    Server
Exclude User Account Wizard, 813
exclusion policies, 812–814
explicit permissions, 74, 198
Export Template feature, 307
exporting
certificates, 854, 857–862
information to security templates, 308
SLCs, 811
trust policy, 855
extended key usage (EKU), 841
Extensible Markup Language (XML), 349, 844
external trusts, 587–588, 593
extranets
AD RMS support, 792, 810
additional information, 792
Web SSO, 837

F

Failover Clustering service, 788
fault tolerance, 397
federated applications, 843
Federated Identity Support node, 812
federated users, 843
Federated Web SSO, 836
Federated Web SSO with Forest Trust, 836
federation, 843
Federation Server Proxy certificates, 841
federation servers
    AD FS certificates, 841
    configuring, 855, 857, 864–866
    installing, 850–851
    test environments, 845
Federation Service, 832–833, 846
Federation Service proxy. *See* FSP (Federation Service proxy)
federation trust
    configuring, 867–869
    creating, 855
    defined, 834, 843, 872
File Replication Service. *See* FRS (File Replication Service)
file systems
    auditing access, 337–341
    security templates, 303
filtering policy settings, 246–247
Find commands, 58–59
fine-grained password and lockout policy, 360–361
firewalls
    AD FS support, 693
    AD LDS support, 693
    authentication process, 834
    defined, 349
    network security, 311
    ports supported, 826–827
    purpose, 826–827
    split-brain syndrome, 401
Flexible Single Master of Operations (FSMO), 613, 619
FLZ (forward lookup zones)
    creating, 417
    creating custom records, 439
    defined, 409
    finalizing configuration, 433–435
    RLZs and, 436
    WINS support, 443
Folder Redirection node, 242
footprinting the network, 431
ForEach cmdlet, 107
forest DNS zone, 409, 414
forest functional levels

AD DS administration, 619
    defined, 10–11, 557
    deploying RODCs, 377
    installing forests, 464
    levels supported, 560–561
    raising, 563–565
    Windows 2000, 561
    Windows Server 2003, 561–562
    Windows Server 2008, 562
forest root domain
    AD CS installation, 741
    creating, 464
    dedicated, 567–568
    default groups, 177
    defined, 9, 31
    DNS considerations, 404–405, 414
    operations masters, 483
    zone placeholders, 417
forest trusts
    AD FS considerations, 825
    Federated Web SSO with Forest Trust, 836
    functionality, 588–589
    selective authentication, 593
forests
    authentication within, 580–582
    creating, 11–12, 14–21, 420–422, 685
    defined, 9, 31
    design considerations, 570
    DFS replication, 663
    installing, 464
    installing domain controllers, 465–466
    moving objects, 572–576, 621
    multiple, 572
    multiple-domain, 569–570, 586
    operations master roles, 479–480
    root cluster support, 788, 814
    SCP support, 814
    single-domain, 568–569
forest-wide authentication, 593
Format-List cmdlet, 100–101
forward lookup, 409
forward lookup zones. *See* FLZ (forward lookup zones)
Forwarded Events log, 663
forwarders
    conditional, 417, 440–441
    defined, 409
    root hints comparison, 439–441
FQDN (fully qualified domain name)
    AD RMS support, 800
    forward lookup, 409
    global query block lists, 416
    installing domain controllers, 462
    reverse lookup, 410

single-label names and, 415, 442
split-brain syndrome, 401
FRS (File Replication Service)
    AD DS administration, 621
    Directory Service Diagnosis tool, 545
    GPO replication, 241
    migrating SYSVOL replication, 496
    migration stages, 495–496
    SYSVOL replication, 494–502, 559
    timestamp support, 482
FSMO (Flexible Single Master of Operations), 613, 619
FSP (Federation Service proxy)
    Account Federation Service Proxy, 842
    authentication process, 834, 841
    configuring, 856–857
    defined, 832, 846
    federation servers, 841
    installing, 845, 851–852
    Resource Federation Service Proxy, 843
full system backups, 633–638
fully qualified domain name. *See* FQDN (fully qualified
        domain name)
functional levels. *See also* domain functional levels; forest
        functional levels
    defined, 10, 31, 557
    raising, 557

G

GC servers
    AD DS administration, 613
    configuring, 524, 527–528
    placing, 523
    UGMC considerations, 524–525
General property, 117
Get-ChildItem cmdlet, 102
Get-Help cmdlet, 101
GetInfo method, 105
GetObject statement, 109, 123
Get-Service cmdlet, 100–101
global catalog
    configuring GC servers, 524
    defined, 8, 31, 551
    domain controllers, 418, 464
    overview, 523
    placing GC servers, 523
    SRV records, 517
global cloud, 398
global groups
    characteristics, 147, 149
    defined, 51
    filtering GPOs, 263
    group nesting, 153

group scope considerations, 150
global query block lists, 415–416, 451–452
global unicast addresses, 396, 398
globally unique identifier (GUID), 240, 362, 481
GNZ (GlobalNames Zone)
    additional information, 442
    defined, 409
    single-label names, 411, 415, 441–443
    WINS comparison, 415
GPC (Group Policy Container), 240–241
GPfixup.exe command, 620
GPMC (Group Policy Management console)
    AD DS administration, 614, 621
    certificate templates, 758
    functionality, 232
    GPO precedence, 257
    Group Policy Inheritance tab, 259
    Group Policy Modeling node, 281
    Linked Group Policy Objects tab, 258
    starter GPOs, 248
GPME (Group Policy Management Editor)
    central store support, 246
    creating filters, 246–247
    editing GPOs, 232, 239, 315
    Extended tab, 243
    PDC Emulator role, 482
    Preference node support, 244
    software deployment GPO, 325
    unmanaged policy settings, 248
    WMI Filters node, 265
GPO Diagnostic Best Practices Analyzer, 620, 622
GPO Editor, 232, 238
GPO links
    defined, 234
    deleting, 257
    disabling, 257
    enforcing, 260–262
    Group Policy client, 256
    implementing Group Policy, 249–250
    joining computers to domains, 190
    managing, 255
    permissions, 239
    precedence, 260
    to domain controllers, 256
    to domains, 258
    to OUs, 234, 257–258, 269
    to sites, 234, 256, 258
GPO scope
    configuring enforced option, 272–273
    defined, 234
    enabling/disabling nodes, 266–267
    GPO inheritance/precedence, 257–262

GPO links, 255–257
Group Policy processing, 268–270
loopback policy processing, 270–271, 274–275
managing, 327
mechanisms supported, 255
password policies, 357
security filters, 234, 262–264, 273
targeting preferences, 267–268
WMI filters, 234
GPOs (Group Policy objects). *See also* local GPOs
    AD DS administration, 612, 614, 620–621
    applying to specific groups, 263
    auditing logon, 369
    creating, 232, 239, 249–250
    creating with policy settings, 272
    defined, 232, 286
    Delegation tab, 263
    Details tab, 266
    domain-based, 238–239, 268
    editing, 232, 239, 249–250, 315
    enabling/disabling, 266–267
    excluding specific groups, 263
    exploring, 250–251
    group scope, 145
    inheritance, 257–259
    managing, 232
    moving user accounts, 129
    OU support, 11, 191
    precedence, 257–259
    protecting, 657
    relinking, 620
    replicating, 240–241
    Scope tab, 263
    security templates, 304
    Specops Gpupdate tool, 617
    starter, 247–248
    storing, 240
    targeting preferences, 268
    troubleshooting status, 241
Gpotool.exe command, 241
Gpresult.exe command, 277, 279–280, 282–283
GPSI (Group Policy Software Installation)
    characteristics, 236, 322–325
    maintaining deployed applications, 327–329
    managing software, 329–332
    preparing SDPs, 325
    slow links, 329
    software deployment GPO, 325–327, 330–331
    software deployment options, 323–325
    Windows Installer packages, 322–323
GPT (Group Policy Template), 240–241, 494
GPUpdate command, 235

group accounts, 612, 624
group claim type, 839, 848
group membership
    adding members, 54, 56, 65–66
    caching for universal groups, 524–525
    changing with Dsmod, 162–163, 166
    changing with LDIFDE, 161, 166
    data protection measures, 624
    delegating management, 172–175, 181
    delegating with Group Policy, 295–298
    domain local groups, 147
    global groups, 147
    group claim type, 839
    group scope considerations, 145, 148–150
    infrastructure master role, 481
    local groups, 146
    managing, 151–153, 164
    migration considerations, 575–576
    restricted groups policy settings, 291–294
    retrieving with Dsget, 162, 167
    scripting shadow groups, 363
    taking effect quickly, 153
    universal groups, 148
group objects, 50–52, 63–64, 620
Group Policy
    AD DS support, 8
    certificate templates, 758
    defined, 231
    delegating membership, 295–298
    deploying security policies, 314–315
    examining event logs, 281
    maintaining deployed applications, 327–329
    PDC Emulator role, 482
    policy settings, 231
    processing overview, 268–270
    refreshing with GPUpdate, 235
    software installation, 236–237
    transforming security policies, 319–320
    troubleshooting, 280
Group Policy client, 235, 237, 256, 258
Group Policy Container (GPC), 240–241
Group Policy Creator Owners group, 239, 380
Group Policy Management console. *See* GPMC (Group Policy Management console)
Group Policy Management Editor. *See* GPME (Group Policy Management Editor)
Group Policy Modeling Wizard, 277, 280–281, 283–284
Group Policy Objects container, 239, 248, 257
Group Policy Operational Log, 281
Group Policy refresh, 235–236
Group Policy Results Wizard, 277–280, 282

Group Policy Software Installation. *See* GPSI (Group
    Policy Software Installation)
Group Policy Template (GPT), 240–241, 494
group scope
    converting, 149–151, 156
    membership possibilities, 145, 148–149
    overview, 145–148
    selecting, 51
groups
    administrative role separation, 383
    assigning permissions, 73
    best practices, 169–170
    computer accounts, 220
    converting types, 149–151, 156
    creating, 143–149, 155–156, 180–181
    creating with Dsadd, 159–160, 165
    defaults, 177–179
    defining naming conventions, 143–145
    deleting with Dsrm, 163–164
    group claim type, 839
    importing with CSVDE, 160, 165
    management strategies, 153–155
    managing enterprises, 141–143
    managing membership, 151–153
    managing with LDIFDE, 161
    moving with Dsmove, 163
    nesting, 153–155
    OUs and, 176
    protected, 178
    protecting from accidental deletion, 171
    renaming with Dsmove, 163
    role-based management, 141–143
    shadow, 176, 185, 362–363
    special identities, 179, 185
    types listed, 50–51, 145
GUID (globally unique identifier), 240, 362, 481

H
hash code, 358
hidden attributes, 88, 116
hierarchy
    certificate authority, 734–737, 739–740, 742–750
    defined, 777
    DNS naming structure, 394
    PKI, 731
high availability, 650, 788
HKCU PSDrive, 103
HKLM PSDrive, 103
Holme, Dan, 86, 140, 230, 290, 356, 363, 460, 508, 556
host name, 518
host (A) record, 413, 517–518

HTTP
    AD FS support, 7, 827
    certificate authorities, 733
    firewall support, 826
HTTPS (Secure HTTP)
    AD FS support, 7, 854
    certificate authorities, 733
    firewall support, 826
    SSL certificates, 724
Hyper-V
    certificate authorities, 737
    DC hardening, 444
    domain controller support, 631, 648, 695

I
IDA (identity and access) infrastructure
    AD FS support, 830
    audit trails, 4
    control access, 4
    information storage, 3
    Kerberos authentication, 4
    technologies comprising support, 5–7
identity
    authenticating, 4
    defined, 3
    group management strategies, 153
    identity claim type, 839
    special, 179, 185
identity claim type, 839, 848
Identity Integration Feature Pack (IIFP), 693
identity store, 3–4, 32, 189
IETF (Internet Engineering Task Force), 414
IFM (Install From Media), 630, 633
ifm command, 472
IIFP (Identity Integration Feature Pack), 693
IIS (Internet Information Services)
    AD CS support, 730
    AD FS support, 854, 856
    AD RMS support, 7, 786, 810
    allocating resources, 674
    firewall considerations, 827
IIS Manager, 841
importing certificates, 857–859, 862
importing computers
    CSVDE tool, 203–204, 209–210
    LDIFDE tool, 204–205, 210
    Windows PowerShell, 206–208
importing groups, 160, 165
importing security templates, 308
importing SLCs, 810
importing users

CSVDE tool, 90, 94–95
LDIFDE tool, 90–92, 95–96
Windows PowerShell, 106–108
Incremental Zone Transfer (IXFR), 412
inetOrgPerson object, 119, 562
INF file extension, 302
Information events, 663
information management, 613
infrastructure master role
    domain-wide, 479
    functionality, 480–481
    identifying, 485
    placing, 483–484
    seizing, 487
inheritance
    blocking, 260–262
    disabling, 74
    domain-linked policies, 269
    GPOs, 257–259
    permissions and, 73–74, 77
    policy, 259
initial notification delay, 534
Install From Media (IFM), 630, 633
installation media
    creating, 472–473, 476, 633
    installing AD DS, 472–473
Installing Windows Wizard, 24
instances
    Active Directory Schema snap-in, 712
    Active Directory Sites and Services snap-in, 713
    additional information, 707, 712–713
    ADSI Edit, 709–711
    creating AD LDS, 703–706, 714–716
    defined, 707
    Ldp.exe command, 711–712
    unattended AD LDS, 706–707
intellectual property
    implementing AD RMS, 786
    protecting, 782, 785
Interactive group, 179
inter-forest migration, 572
Internet Engineering Task Force (IETF), 414
Internet Explorer Maintenance node, 242
Internet Information Services. See IIS (Internet Information Services)
Internet Protocol security. See IPSec (Internet Protocol security)
intersite, 535, 551
Inter-Site MessagingSMTP (ISM-SMTP), 537
intersite replication
    bridgehead servers, 538
    configuring, 539–543, 546–547
    defined, 535

Directory Service Diagnosis tool, 545
    overview, 535–537
    replication frequency, 542
    replication schedules, 542
    replication transport protocols, 537
intersite topology generator (ISTG), 535–538, 562
Inter-Site Transports container, 537, 540
intra-forest migration, 572–573, 576
intrasite, 551
Intra-site Automatic Tunnel Addressing Protocol (ISATAP), 415–416
intrasite replication, 534–535, 537–538
IP addresses
    A records, 517
    DDNS considerations, 443
    DNS support, 393
    domain controller requirements, 12
    RLZ support, 436, 438
    round robin, 411
    subnet objects, 512
Ipconfig command, 449, 621
IPSec (Internet Protocol security)
    AD CS support, 6, 729–730
    security policies, 312
IPv4 protocol
    additional information, 397
    address types, 395–396
    APIPA support, 395
    creating RLZ, 437
    ISATAP support, 416
    security policies, 312
    WINS support, 442
IPv6 protocol
    creating RLZ, 437
    DNS support, 395–396
    ISATAP support, 416
    security policies, 312
ISATAP (Intra-site Automatic Tunnel Addressing Protocol), 415–416
ISM-SMTP (Inter-Site MessagingSMTP), 537
ISO files, 645
issuing CAs
    certificate lifetimes, 739
    certificate templates, 755
    defined, 732
    enterprise CAs, 734
    finalizing configuration, 753–759
    hierarchy considerations, 735
    installation considerations, 742, 745–748
ISTG (intersite topology generator), 535–538, 562
item-level targeting, 267–268
IXFR (Incremental Zone Transfer), 412

J

Javelina ADvantage, 688–689

K

KCC (Knowledge Consistency Checker)
  AD DS administration, 612
  Directory Service Diagnosis tool, 545
  forest functional levels, 562
  functionality, 240, 533–534
  intrasite replication, 534
  launching, 544
  site links, 535
KDC (key distribution center), 579, 582
Kerberos Password protocol (KPASSWD), 517
Kerberos protocol
  AD DS administration, 621
  AES support, 559
  authentication support, 4, 9, 579–582
  defined, 32
  multiple-domain forests, 569
  realm trusts, 588
  SRV records, 517
  validating trusts, 590
key distribution center (KDC), 579, 582
Key Management Server (KMS), 781
key pairs
  certificate lifetimes, 738
  defined, 777
  security tokens, 840
KMS (Key Management Server), 781
Ksetup.exe command, 621
Ktpass.exe command, 621

L

LAN Diagnostics collector set, 667
LAN Manager, 312
lastLogonTimestamp attribute, 558
LDAP (Lightweight Directory Access Protocol)
  AD DS administration, 610, 621
  AD LDS support, 6, 690, 692, 703
  AD RMS support, 819
  data store manipulation, 8
  defined, 349
  forest functional levels, 562
  importing computers, 203
  item-level targeting, 268
  populating user attributes, 105
  relational database comparison, 690–691
  security policy support, 312
  SRV records, 517
LDAP over SSL, 703

LDAP query groups, 562
LDIF (LDAP Data Interchange Format)
  AD LDS support, 702, 705–706
  defined, 90–91, 161
  importing computers, 204, 210
  LDIFDE support, 161
LDIFDE tool
  AD DS administration, 621, 702
  AD LDS support, 702, 708, 713
  additional information, 709
  changing group membership, 161, 166
  importing computers, 204–205, 210
  importing passwords, 126
  importing users, 90–92, 95–96
  managing groups, 161
  parameters supported, 92
Ldp.exe command
  AD DS administration, 621, 702
  AD LDS support, 702, 704
  application directory partitions, 527
  functionality, 629
  restoring objects, 626
  working with instances, 711–712
least-privilege security, 192, 569
legacy DNS, 410, 417
licensing clusters, 788, 819
Lightweight Directory Access Protocol. *See* LDAP
    (Lightweight Directory Access Protocol)
linked properties, 54, 56
linked-value replication, 561
link-local addresses, 395–396, 398
link-local cloud, 398
load balancing, 786, 788
local Administrators group
  characteristics, 146, 177
  creating computer objects, 192
  delegating membership, 295
  end user support, 291
  joining computers to domains, 190, 193–194
  migration considerations, 576
  restricted group policies, 295
  scheduled backups, 631
Local Computer GPO, 237–238
local GPOs
  configuring, 300–301
  defined, 349
  RSoP support, 237–238, 268
  security settings, 300–301
local groups, 146, 149
local security authority (LSA), 216
Local Security Authority Subsystem (LSASS), 574
local security policies, 303, 315–316
Local Security Policy console, 307, 314, 737

local Users group, 146, 194
location attribute, 214
lockout policies
    configuring, 363–366
    fine-grained, 360–361
    for domains, 360
    multiple-domain forests, 570
    overview, 359
    unlocking accounts, 126
Log On To property, 119, 121
logging database, 819
Logon Events setting, 368, 371
logon process
    AD CS support, 730
    auditing, 369
    computer accounts, 216
Logon property, 119
loopback addresses, 396
loopback policies, 270–271, 274–275
LostandFound container, 614
LostandFoundConfig container, 614
LSA (local security authority), 216
LSASS (Local Security Authority Subsystem), 574

M
MAC address, 119
machine certificate, 798
mail exchanger (MX) records, 414
maintenance. *See* AD DS administration
Manage command, 190, 193–195, 201, 215
managedBy attribute, 213
manual trusts
    additional information, 586
    creating, 583–586
    defined, 579
    deleting, 590
    external trusts, 587–588, 593
    forest trusts, 588–589, 593
    realm trusts, 583, 588
    shortcut trusts, 586–587
    types listed, 583
Maximum Password Age policy setting, 358
member attribute
    defined, 152
    deleted groups, 171
    global group replication, 147
    group membership management, 172
    importing groups with CSVDE, 160
    infrastructure master role, 480–481
    linked-value replication, 561
    multiple-domain forests, 570
    SID support, 141

Member Of restricted policy setting, 291–295
memberOf attribute, 152, 162, 481
Members attribute, 341
Members restricted policy setting, 291–294
metadata, 473, 544
methods, 100, 135
Microsoft Enrollment Center, 789
Microsoft Exchange Server
    AD LDS support, 685, 692–693
    additional information, 726
    PKI support, 726
Microsoft Federation Services, 831
Microsoft Identity Integration Server (MIIS), 693
Microsoft Identity Lifecycle Manager (MILM), 693
Microsoft Management Console. *See* MMC (Microsoft
    Management Console)
Microsoft Message Queuing service, 786, 819
Microsoft Office SharePoint Server 2007, 833
Microsoft Passport, 811, 818
Microsoft SharePoint Portal Server, 693
Microsoft SQL Server, 786
Microsoft System Center Configuration Manager, 176,
    322, 661
Microsoft Systems Management Server, 322
Microsoft Windows Update, 410
MIIS (Microsoft Identity Integration Server), 693
MILM (Microsoft Identity Lifecycle Manager), 693
Minimum Password Length policy, 358
MMC (Microsoft Management Console)
    Actions pane, 35
    AD CS role, 763
    AD RMS role, 789, 810
    Add/Remove Snap-in command, 303
    certificate authorities, 733
    console modes, 39
    creating/editing local GPOs, 238
    custom consoles, 36, 38–44
    overview, 35–36
    preconfigured consoles, 36
mobile computer systems, 730, 811
Move command, 214
MoveHere method, 129–130
MoveTo method, 129
Movetree.exe command, 621–622
MP3 format, 781
MS-adamschemaw2k3.ldf file, 705
MS-adamschemaw2k8.ldf file, 706
MS-AdamSyncMetadata.ldf file, 705–706
MS-ADAM-Upgrade-1.ldf file, 705
MS-ADLDS-DisplaySpecifiers.ldf file, 706, 713
MS-AZMan.ldf file, 706
MSC file extension, 40
ms-DS-MachineAccountQuota attribute, 197–198

MSI file extension, 322, 349
MS-InetOrgPerson.ldf file, 706
MSP file extension, 323
MST file extension, 323, 349
MS-User.ldf file, 706
MS-UserProxyFull.ldf file, 706
MS-UserProxy.ldf file, 706
Multiple Universal Naming Convention Provider (MUP), 268
multiple-domain forests, 569–570, 586
MUP (Multiple Universal Naming Convention Provider), 268
MX (mail exchanger) records, 414

N

name attribute, 118–119, 129, 144
name recursion, 410
name resolution
    application directory partitions, 445
    DNS servers, 399
    domain controller requirements, 12
    forwarders, 409, 417, 439–441
    overview, 406
    PNRP support, 397–398
    process overview, 393, 406–408
    root hints, 409–410, 439–441
namespaces
    cmdlet support, 103
    defined, 265
    DFS Namespaces, 510
    linking, 440
    multiple-domain forests, 569
    split-brain syndrome, 401–402
    trees and, 9
    zone delegations, 412
naming contexts, 522, 551
naming conventions
    best practices, 169
    for groups, 143–145
    single-label names, 442
NAS (network attached storage), 144
NDES (Network Device Enrollment Service)
    AD CS support, 741
    defined, 732
    installing, 749–750
nesting process, 153–155
net user command, 25
NetBIOS, 11
Netdom command
    AD DS administration, 621
    creating computers, 205
    deleting manual trusts, 590
    managing trusts, 591
    renaming computers, 218
    renaming domain controllers, 558
    resetting computer accounts, 217–218
netdom command, 25
NetIQ Security Administration Suite, 688–689
Netlogon service, 216–217
NetPro Active Directory LifeCycle Suite, 688
netsh command, 25
network attached storage (NAS), 144
Network Device Enrollment Service. See NDES (Network Device Enrollment Service)
Network group, 179
Network Load Balancing service, 788
network operating system (NOS), 610, 685
Network Policy Server (NPS), 756
network security, 311, 431–432
Network Service account, 705, 848
Network Time Protocol (NTP), 845
networks, footprinting, 431
New Object Computer Wizard, 192
new object protection option, 624
New Object Site dialog box, 513
New Object Subnet dialog box, 514
New Object User Wizard, 114
New Trust Wizard, 583, 585, 588
New Zone Wizard, 413
Nltest.exe command, 217–218, 621
Non-Administrators GPO, 238
nonauthoritative restores
    deleted groups, 171
    overview, 632–645
    restoration scenario, 639
    Windows Server Backup, 630
NOS (network operating system), 610, 685
notification process, 534
NPS (Network Policy Server), 756
Nslookup command, 449, 621
NT LAN Manager (NTLM), 579
Ntds.dit database
    AD DS administration, 614, 623
    defined, 522, 683
    Windows Server Backup, 630
Ntdsutil.exe command
    AD DS administration, 621, 702
    AD LDS support, 702
    application directory partitions, 527
    backup considerations, 631
    capturing system state data, 650–651
    creating snapshots, 640–641
    IFM subcommand options, 633
    installation media, 472

performing restores, 644
seizing roles, 488
NTLM (NT LAN Manager), 579
NTP (Network Time Protocol), 845

O

object class, 104, 562
object identifiers (OIDs), 733
object reference, 102
objects. *See also* specific object types
  assigning permissions, 72
  auditing changes, 620, 626
  cmdlet support, 99
  computer, 52–54, 63–64
  controlling view, 54
  creating with CSVDE, 160
  data protection measures, 624
  defined, 100, 135
  deleting, 620
  displaying metadata, 544
  DS commands, 89
  finding in Active Directory, 54–67
  finding using Dsquery command, 59–60
  group, 50–52, 63–64
  homeless, 614
  looking up, 54
  migration considerations, 576
  moving, 572–576, 620–621
  new object protection option, 624
  properties, 100
  removing permissions, 75
  renaming, 620
  resetting permissions, 75
  user, 48–50, 61–63
Oclist command, 26
Ocsetup command, 25–26
OCSP (Online Certificate Status Protocol), 731–732, 855
OCSP Response Signing certificate, 759
OIDs (object identifiers), 733
Online Certificate Status Protocol (OCSP), 731–732
online responders
  AD FS configuration, 855
  adding revocation configuration, 761–762
  additional information, 732, 761
  defined, 731–732
  event IDs, 764
  finalizing configuration, 759–762
  managing, 763
operations management, 611
operations masters
  AD DS administration, 620

defined, 478, 504
failover plans, 484
identifying, 484–485, 490
overview, 478–479
placing, 483–484
recognizing failures, 486
returning roles to original holders, 488–489
roles supported, 479
seizing roles, 487–488
transferring roles, 485–486, 489–491
Organization property, 117
organizational units. *See* OUs (organizational units)
OUs (organizational units)
  AD DS administration, 613
  assigning permissions, 73
  computer objects, 214
  containers and, 46, 190–191
  creating, 46–48, 61, 199
  defined, 11, 46
  delegating membership management, 175
  delegation support, 77–78
  deleting, 47–48
  deleting user accounts, 128
  GPO links, 234, 257–258, 269
  groups and, 176
  linking PSOs, 362–363
  permission considerations, 176
  protecting from accidental deletion, 47
  RDN requirements, 118
  shadow groups, 176
  viewing permissions, 72
Outlook Web Access (OWA), 726
OWA (Outlook Web Access), 726

P

parent objects, 73–74
parent-child trust, 580
partial attribute set (PAS), 8, 31, 523, 551
partitions, 523, 551
passive clients, 843
Password Must Meet Complexity Requirements policy, 358
Password Never Expires setting, 120, 360–361
password policies
  AD DS administration, 615
  configuring, 363–366
  domain, 360
  fine-grained, 360–361, 559, 570
  multiple-domain forests, 570
  overview, 357–359

Password Policy Basic by Special Operations Software, 361
Password Policy node, 357, 361
password replication policy. *See* PRP (password replication policy)
password settings object. *See* PSO (password settings object)
passwords
    Administrator account, 24
    alternative credentials, 126
    computer accounts, 189
    control access rights, 72
    data protection measures, 624
    Directory Services Restore Mode password, 464, 631
    for service accounts, 121
    migration considerations, 576
    PDC Emulator role, 482
    permission considerations, 73, 76
    resetting, 125–126, 132, 610
    RODC considerations, 375
    setting, 106
    trust, 585
patch files, 323
PDC Emulator role
    AD DS administration, 613
    domain-wide, 479
    functionality, 481–483
    identifying, 484
    placing, 483
    seizing, 487
PDCs (primary domain controllers), 479, 481–483
performance benchmarks, 621
performance counters, 667–670, 764
Performance Log Users group, 667
Performance Logs and Alerts tool, 666
performance management. *See also* Event Viewer
    creating performance baselines, 671
    managing system resources, 660–661
    Performance Monitor, 661, 666–671
    Reliability Monitor, 661, 665
    Task Manager, 660–663
    Windows System Resource Manager, 661, 672–674, 679–680
Performance Monitor, 661, 666–671
permissions. *See also* specific permissions
    ACE support, 69
    Advanced Security Settings dialog box, 72–73
    assigning to objects, 72
    best practice, 73
    configuring for auditing, 343
    creating AD LDS instances, 705
    creating computer objects, 197

    default groups, 177–178
    delegating, 69–70
    delegating for computer objects, 192, 200
    effective, 76–77
    explicit, 74, 198
    granting, 54, 56
    inheritance and, 73–74, 77
    least-privilege approach, 192, 569
    linking GPOs, 239
    managing for groups, 141–143
    managing with property sets, 72
    moving computers, 214
    preparing SDPs, 325
    removing from objects, 75
    reporting, 75
    resetting on objects, 75
    security templates, 303
    security translation, 575
    setting, 75
    viewing delegated, 79
    viewing for Active Directory objects, 70–71, 75
pipeline variables, 102
PKI (public key infrastructure)
    AD CS support, 6, 731, 782
    additional information, 6
    CRL support, 731
    deployment best practices, 738
    Enterprise PKI, 763, 765–766
    NDES support, 732
    online responders, 731
    trusted CAs, 725
PKIView. *See* Enterprise PKI
PNRP (Peer Name Resolution Protocol), 397–398, 417
pointer (PTR) records, 414, 436
Policies node, 241–242
policy inheritance, 259
policy settings (policy)
    applying, 235–236
    auditing, 335–337, 368
    blocking inheritance, 260
    configuring, 234
    creating GPOs with precedence, 272
    defined, 231, 241, 286
    filtering, 246–247
    GPME support, 232
    managed, 248
    modifying GPO scope, 269–270
    scoping audit policies, 370
    states supported, 234
    testing, 234
    unmanaged, 248
    viewing effects, 250

policy templates
  AD RMS configuration, 809
  creating, 788, 819–820
  manipulating, 789
  preparing, 815–817
Policy-Based QoS node, 242
polling
  bridgehead servers, 542
  defined, 535
  intersite replication, 542
  intrasite replication, 535
precedence
  GPO links, 260
  GPOs, 257–259
  PSOs, 362
Preferences node, 241, 243–244
preferred bridgehead servers, 539, 546
prestaging
  computer accounts, 192–193, 196
  computer objects, 195–197
  defined, 193
primary domain controllers (PDCs), 479, 481–483
primary zone, 410, 412, 415, 417
Print Operators group, 178
private keys, 738, 841
Profile property, 117
properties. *See also* specific properties
  for objects, 100, 116
  multiselecting user objects, 117
  object references, 102
Properties dialog box
  Account tab, 87, 115, 119
  Additional Account Info tab, 615
  Address tab, 87, 115
  Attribute Editor tab, 88, 116–117
  Authentication tab, 594
  Categories tab, 326
  COM+ tab, 116
  Deployment Options section, 326
  Deployment tab, 326
  Dial-in tab, 116
  Environment tab, 115
  Explain tab, 234, 243
  for sites, 514
  for subnets, 515
  General tab, 87, 115, 149, 433, 447, 524
  Managed By tab, 172–173, 213
  Member Of tab, 88, 115, 213
  Members tab, 151
  Modifications tab, 326
  Name Servers tab, 434
  Notes field, 170

Object tab, 171
Operating System tab, 213
Organization tab, 88, 115
Policy Module tab, 758
Previous Versions tab, 650
Profile tab, 87, 115
Remote Control tab, 115
Security tab, 70, 434
Session tab, 115
Sessions tab, 115
Shadow Copies tab, 649
SOA tab, 434
Telephones tab, 115
Terminal Services Profile tab, 115
Upgrades tab, 326
WINS tab, 434
Zone Transfers tab, 434
property sets, 72
Protect from Accidental Deletion attribute, 648
protected accounts, 178
protected groups, 178
providers, 103
PRP (password replication policy)
  configuring, 385
  defined, 380, 389
  domain-wide, 380–381
  RODC support, 375, 381
PSDrives, 103
PSO (password settings object)
  creating, 362, 364–365
  defined, 361, 389
  deleting, 366
  linking, 362–363
  managing, 361–362
  precedence, 362
  resultant, 362, 365–366, 390
PTR (pointer) records, 414, 436
public key infrastructure. *See* PKI (public key infrastructure)
public keys, 738, 841
publishing applications, 323–325
publishing license, 790, 798, 823
Put method
  computer objects, 214
  user accounts, 130
  user objects, 105, 109, 123
PutEx method, 106

Q
Quest FastLane Active Roles, 688–689
Quest Object Restore for Active Directory, 628–629

R

RAC (rights account certificate), 797, 812
RAS and IAS Server templates, 756
RC4-HMAC algorithm, 559
RDN (relative distinguished name)
  as Create method parameter, 104, 109
  defined, 60
  name attributes, 118
Read Members permission, 174–175
read-only domain controllers. *See* RODCs (read-only domain controllers)
realm trusts, 583, 588
recovery functions. *See* restore functions
Redircmp.exe command, 196, 559
Redirusr.exe command, 196, 559
registry
  adding custom settings, 304
  Administrative Template node policies, 244
  policy settings, 231
  security policy, 312
  tattooing, 248
registry permissions, 303
Regsvr32.exe command, 619, 712
relational databases, 690–691
relative distinguished name. *See* RDN (relative distinguished name)
relative identifier (RID), 479–480
Reliability Monitor, 661, 665
remote communication, 278, 730
Remote Installation Services node, 242
remote procedure call (RPC), 733
Remote Procedure Call System Service (RPCSS), 268
Remote Server Administration Tools. *See* RSAT (Remote Server Administration Tools)
renaming
  computers, 218–219
  domain controllers, 558
  domains, 561
  groups, 163
  objects, 620
  user accounts, 129–130
Repadmin.exe (Replication Diagnostics Tool), 543–544, 621, 703
replicas, 522, 551
replication. *See also* DFS-R (Distributed File System Replication); intersite replication; intrasite replication
  AD DS support, 8, 612
  AD LDS support, 692, 717–718
  configuring, 545–547
  connection objects, 532
  data protection measures, 624
  defined, 510
  DFS, 644, 663
  domain local groups, 147
  domain naming context, 522
  forcing, 532, 544
  global groups, 147
  GPOs, 240–241
  group membership changes, 153
  group scope considerations, 145
  KCC support, 533–534
  key features, 531–532
  linked-value, 561
  local groups, 146
  monitoring, 543–545
  universal groups, 148
Replication Diagnostics Tool (Repadmin.exe), 543–544, 621, 703
replication scope
  AD DS administration, 619
  application directory partitions, 404, 408, 414, 445
  best practice, 440
  changing, 447
  child domains, 404
  DNS, 415
ReplMon.exe command, 622
reporting
  AD DS administration, 614
  permissions, 75
request for comments. *See* RFC (request for comments)
Reset Account command, 218, 220
Reset Account Lockout Counter After setting, 359
Reset Password command, 127
resource accounts, 843
resource federation server (RFS), 834, 843
Resource Federation Service Proxy, 843
Resource Monitor, 661–663
resource organizations, 832, 843, 855
resource records, 410. *See also* specific records
Responsible Person (RP) records, 434–436
restore functions. *See also* backup functions
  AD CS considerations, 767
  authoritative restores, 171, 630, 632–645
  DSRM password, 464, 631, 639–640
  from complete backups, 645–648
  identifying backup data sets, 640–642
  nonauthoritative restores, 171, 630, 632–645
  Quest Object Restore for Active Directory, 628–629
  restore scenarios, 638–639
  restoring objects, 626–628
restricted groups policies
  delegating administration, 294–295
  overview, 291–294
  security templates, 303

Restricted Groups policy node, 291
resultant PSO
    defined, 362, 390
    identifying, 365–366
    overview, 362
Resultant Set of Policies. *See* RSoP (Resultant Set of
    Policies)
reverse lookup, 410
reverse lookup zones. *See* RLZ (reverse lookup zones)
revocation. *See* certificate revocation
RFC (request for comments), 410, 414
RFC 2052, 517
RFC 2560, 732
RFS (resource federation server), 834, 843
RID (relative identifier), 479–480
RID master role
    domain-wide, 479
    functionality, 480
    identifying, 485
    placing, 483
    seizing, 487–488
rights account certificate (RAC), 797, 812
RLZ (reverse lookup zones)
    creating, 417, 436–438
    defined, 410, 438
RODC accounts, 470
RODCs (read-only domain controllers)
    AD DS administration, 613, 619
    AD LDS considerations, 695
    backup considerations, 631
    configuring, 383–386
    credentials caching, 381–382
    DC hardening, 444
    defined, 375, 390
    deploying, 377–380
    DNS servers, 399
    DNS zones, 415
    forest functional levels, 561
    installing, 379–380, 384–385, 465, 469–472
    PRP support, 375, 380–381
    read-only servers, 417
    replicas, 522
role-based configuration, 304, 310
role-based management, 77, 141–143
rollback process, 314, 560
root CAs
    AD CS support, 731
    certificate lifetimes, 739
    defined, 731
    depicted, 737
    deployment best practices, 737
    hierarchy considerations, 734–735
    installation considerations, 742–744

securing, 734
    standalone CAs, 732
root clusters
    creating by default, 788
    defined, 788, 823
    deploying, 814
    installing, 805–807
    logging database, 819
root hints, 409–410, 439–441
root kits, 781
round robin, 411
RP (Responsible Person) records, 434–436
RPC (remote procedure call), 733
RPCSS (Remote Procedure Call System Service), 268
RSAT (Remote Server Administration Tools)
    AD CS support, 763
    AD RMS support, 810
    graphical tool support, 713
    installation requirements, 37, 615
    Quest Object Restore for Active Directory, 628
    Specops Gpupdate tool, 617
RSoP (Resultant Set of Policies)
    defined, 235, 277, 286
    Gpresult command support, 279–280
    Group Policy Modeling Wizard support, 280–281
    Group Policy Results Wizard support, 278–280
    local GPOs, 238
Ruest, Danielle, 404, 608, 688, 728, 785, 830
Ruest, Nelson, 404, 608, 688, 728, 785, 830
Russinovich, Mark, 781

S
SACL (system ACL)
    auditing support, 338, 340–342
    defined, 69
    migration considerations, 574
SAM (Security Accounts Manager), 146, 189, 577
sAMAccountName attribute
    computer accounts, 189, 203, 206, 216
    groups, 144, 162
    user accounts, 104, 118, 130
saved queries
    additional information, 56
    creating, 55
    customizing views, 55
    defined, 81
    saving, 55
scavenging
    removing records, 438
    server, 411
    zone, 412, 432–433
SCEP (Simple Certificate Enrollment Protocol), 732, 750

scheduling backups, 631, 635–638, 648
Schema Admins group, 177, 465
schema master role
    forest-wide, 479
    functionality, 480
    identifying, 485
    placing, 483
    seizing, 487–488
schemas
    Active Directory schema, 37, 88
    AD DS administration, 613
    AD LDS support, 694
    defined, 8, 32, 465, 522
    LDAP support, 690
Schtasks.exe command, 650
scope. *See also* GPO scope; group scope
    audit policies, 370
    defined, 234, 286
    GPO, 234
SCP (service connection point), 801, 814
scripting
    cmdlet support, 99
    importing computers, 207–208
    shadow group membership, 363
    VBScript support, 112
    Windows PowerShell support, 108, 111–112
Scripts node, 242
SCWAudit.inf template, 312
Scwcmd.exe command, 309, 314
Scw.exe command, 309
SD (security descriptor), 574
SDP (software distribution point), 323, 325
Secedit.exe utility, 308
secondary zone, 411–412, 415, 417
secure channel, 216–218, 224
Secure HTTP (HTTPS)
    AD FS support, 7, 854
    certificate authorities, 733
    firewall support, 826
    SSL certificates, 724
Secure Multipurpose Internet Mail Extensions (S/
        MIME), 730
Secure Sockets Layer. *See* SSL (Secure Sockets Layer)
Secure Sockets Tunneling Protocol (SSTP), 730
Security Accounts Manager (SAM), 146, 189, 577
Security Configuration and Analysis snap-in, 305–307,
        316–318
security configuration database, 309
Security Configuration Manager, 304
Security Configuration Wizard
    AD CS considerations, 741
    applying security policies, 313
    Audit Policy section, 312

Confirm Service Changes page, 311
    creating security policies, 309–314
    deploying security policies, 314
    editing security policies, 313
    functionality, 309, 318–319
    IPSec limitations, 312
    modifying security policy settings, 314
    Network Security section, 311
    Registry Settings section, 312
    rolling back security policies, 314
    security templates, 313
Security CSE, 236
security descriptor (SD), 574
security filters, 234, 262–264, 273
security groups, 50, 145, 380
security identifier. *See* SID (security identifier)
Security log, 341–342, 344–345, 663
security management. *See also* AD CS (Active Directory
        Certificate Services)
    AD DS administration, 613
    AD LDS considerations, 695
    best practices, 800
    CA hierarchy, 734–736
    DNS server role, 431–432
    domain/forest design, 570
    LDAP considerations, 691
    network security, 311, 431–432
security policies
    applying, 313
    configuring, 303, 315–316
    creating, 309–314
    deploying with Group Policy, 314–315
    editing, 313
    modifying settings, 314
    network security, 311
    rolling back, 314
security principals
    account properties, 119
    AD DS administration, 621
    defined, 69
    effective permissions, 76
    groups as, 141, 145
    RID master role, 480
    viewing, 70
Security Settings node, 237, 242, 304
security templates
    account policies, 303
    analyzing computer configuration, 306–307
    applying to computers, 305
    correcting discrepancies, 307
    creating, 303, 307, 316
    defined, 349
    event log policies, 303

file system permissions, 303
GPO support, 304
importing, 308
local policies, 303
managing configuration, 302–305
registry permissions, 303
restricted groups policies, 303
saving settings, 304
Secedit.exe utility, 308
Security Configuration Wizard, 313
system services, 303
Security Templates snap-in, 303–304
Security Token Service (STS), 844
security tokens
    AD FS configuration, 854
    authentication process, 835
    defined, 844
    federation servers, 841
    key pairs, 840
security translation, 575
Select dialog box, 56–57
selective authentication, 559, 593–595, 600–601
self-signed certificates, 801, 818
server authentication certificate, 844
Server Core
    AD CS considerations, 741
    adding AD DS to installation, 26
    graphical tool limitations, 713
    initial configuration tasks, 25–26
    installing, 24
    installing AD LDS, 694–699
    installing domain controllers, 27–29
    installing RODC, 380
    optional features, 24
    supported roles, 23–24
    VSS support, 649
server farms, 844, 855
server licensor certificate. See SLC (server licensor
    certificate)
Server Manager
    Active Directory Users and Computers node, 614
    AD CS support, 763
    AD DS administration, 621, 703
    AD LDS support, 703
    AD RMS support, 788
    Add Roles Wizard, 12, 461
    adding roles, 12
    administrative tools, 37
    event logs, 663
    functionality, 12
    installing Windows PowerShell, 98
    Online Responder node, 761
    performance considerations, 662

Server Operators group, 177–178
Server Performance Advisor, 666, 670
server scavenging, 411
servers. See also DNS servers
    AD CS support, 730
    AD RMS considerations, 789
    bridgehead, 538–539, 542, 546, 612
    certificate lifetimes, 739
    configuring, 863
    deployment best practices, 737
    importing certificates, 862
    placement considerations, 512
    root clusters, 788
    securing CAs, 734
    security templates, 304
Servers container, 516
service connection point (SCP), 801, 814
service localization, 508, 510, 512, 551
service principal name (SPN), 580
service records. See SRV (service) records
service-oriented architecture (SOA), 844, 872
services
    defined, 349, 361
    naming, 397
Services tool, 35
session initiation protocol (SIP), 414
Set statement, 123
SetInfo method
    committing changes, 105, 124
    computer objects, 214
    populating attributes, 105
    SetPassword method and, 106
SetPassword method, 106, 126
Setup log, 663
shadow groups
    additional information, 363
    defined, 176, 185, 362
    maintaining dynamically, 176
    overview, 176
shared folders, 613, 815
shortcut trusts, 586–587
SID (security identifier)
    AD DS administration, 615
    computer accounts, 189, 194, 219
    data protection measures, 624
    defined, 574
    deleted groups and, 171
    group support, 141, 145
    migration considerations, 574–575
    recycling accounts, 128
    RID master role, 480
    stored information, 3
    tokenGroups attribute, 117

user object support, 105
SID filtering, 592–593
sIDHistory attribute, 574–575, 592
sign-out cookies, 840
Simple Certificate Enrollment Protocol (SCEP), 732, 750
Simple Mail Transport Protocol (SMTP), 537, 827
Simple Object Access Protocol (SOAP), 844
single sign-on. *See* SSO (single sign-on)
single-domain forests, 568–569
single-label names
    creating, 451
    defined, 411
    DNS support, 415
    managing, 441–443, 450–451
SIP (session initiation protocol), 414
site link bridges, 540, 612
site links
    AD DS administration, 612
    cost considerations, 541
    creating, 546
    defined, 509, 535
    overview, 535–537
    replication schedules, 543
    transitivity, 539–540
site objects, 513–514
site planning
    connection speed, 511
    criteria summarized, 512
    server placement, 512
    service placement, 511
    user population, 511
site-local addresses, 396
sites
    AD DS administration, 612
    configuring, 519–520
    defined, 11, 32, 509
    defining, 512–515
    domain controller locations, 516–519
    GPO links, 234, 256, 258
    managing domain controllers, 515–516
    planning, 510–512
    replication traffic, 510
    service localization, 510, 512
    site coverage, 519
    UGMC considerations, 524–525
SLC (server licensor certificate)
    defined, 789, 797, 818
    exporting, 811
    importing, 810
Smart Card Is Required For Interactive Logon setting, 120
smart cards
    AD CS support, 730–731, 737–738, 753

AD RMS support, 796, 812
    certificate templates, 757
SmartCard Logon template, 757
SmartCard User template, 757
S/MIME (Secure Multipurpose Internet Mail Extensions), 730
SMTP (Simple Mail Transport Protocol), 537, 827
snap-ins, 35. *See also* specific snap-ins
snapshots
    AD DS administration, 620
    creating, 640–641
    deleted groups, 171
SOA (service-oriented architecture), 844, 872
SOA (Start of Authority) record, 411, 434–435
SOAP (Simple Object Access Protocol), 844
software deployment GPOs
    creating, 325–326, 330–331
    managing scope, 327
software distribution point (SDP), 323
Software Installation node, 325, 327
Software Settings node, 242
Sony BMG, 781
special characters in user names, 49
special identities, 179, 185
Special Operations Software, 616
Specops Gpupdate tool, 616–619
split-brain syndrome, 400–402
SPN (service principal name), 580
spoofing, 415
SRV (service) records
    contents, 517–518
    defined, 414
    domain controllers, 517
    functionality, 393, 417
    site coverage, 519
SSL (Secure Sockets Layer)
    AD DS support, 703
    AD FS configuration, 857
    AD RMS support, 792
    authentication certificates, 841
    authentication cookies, 840
    exporting certificates, 860–862
    firewall support, 826
    HTTPS support, 724
    importing certificates, 862
SSO (single sign-on)
    AD FS support, 832, 835
    defined, 7, 844
    Federated Web SSO, 836
    Federated Web SSO with Forest Trust, 836
    Web SSO, 837
SSTP (Secure Sockets Tunneling Protocol), 730
standalone CAs

defined, 732, 740
deployment best practices, 737
enterprise CA comparison, 733–734
hierarchy considerations, 737
installing AD CS, 742–744
Start of Authority (SOA) record, 411, 434–435
starter GPOs, 247–248
storage
    cryptographic storage providers, 800
    GPOs, 240
Store Passwords Using Reversible Encryption setting, 120
STS (Security Token Service), 844
stub zone, 411–412
subnets, 512, 515, 612
Subnets node, 513
subordinate CAs, 731
subsequent notification delay, 534
Super Users group, 814–815
System Diagnostics collector set, 667
System log, 281, 663
System Monitor, 449, 621, 666
System Performance collector set, 667
System Properties dialog box, 193
system resource management. *See* performance management
system services, 303
system state data, 632, 650–651
SYSVOL (system volume)
    central store, 246
    configuring DFS replication, 494–502, 559
    domain controller requirements, 12
    GPO replication, 241
    migrating replication to DFS-R, 496
    migration stages, 495–496
    raising domain functional level, 494

T

Task Manager
    Event Log support, 665
    functionality, 660–663
Task Scheduler tool, 35, 650
tattooing the registry, 248
TCP protocol, 518
TCP/IP (Transmission Control Protocol/Internet Protocol), 7, 394
templates
    administrative, 245, 251–252
    creating user accounts, 87–88, 93–94
    disabling, 87
test environments, 845
testing

Dcdiag.exe support, 544–545
    policy settings, 234
    trusts, 591
TGT (ticket granting ticket), 4, 579
ticket granting ticket (TGT), 4, 579
time synchronization, 845
Time to Live setting. *See* TTL (Time to Live) setting
timestamps, 845
TLS (Transport Layer Security), 826, 840
tokenGroups attribute, 117, 481
token-signing certificate, 844
tombstone container, 624, 628, 683
tombstone lifetime, 128, 624
transform command, 314
transitivity
    realm trusts, 588
    securing trust relationships, 592
    site links, 539–540
    trust relationships, 578
Transmission Control Protocol/Internet Protocol (TCP/IP), 7, 394
Transport Layer Security (TLS), 826, 840
tree-root trust, 580
trees, 9, 571
troubleshooting
    AD DS administration, 621
    computer accounts, 216–217, 222
    Gpotool.exe support, 241
    Group Policy, 280
    operations master roles, 486–488
    WSRM, 673
trust flow, 580–581, 586
trust passwords, 585
trust path, 580–581, 586
trust policy, 844, 855
trust relationships. *See also* forest trusts; manual trusts
    AD DS administration, 619, 621
    AD FS support, 827, 854
    AD RMS considerations, 789–790, 810–811, 818
    administering, 590–591, 595–601
    authentication protocols and, 579–582
    between domains, 577–578
    certificate authorities, 725, 730, 734
    characteristics, 578–579
    computers joining domains, 189
    creating, 597–599
    defined, 145
    managing, 591
    providing access, 599–600
    resetting computer accounts, 217
    securing relationships, 591–595
    selective authentication, 559, 593–595, 600–601
    testing, 591

validating, 590, 599
within domains, 577
Trusted Root Certificates, 725
TTL (Time to Live) setting
defined, 408, 411
false positive record results, 432
SOA records, 435
type adapter, 104, 123

U

UDDI (Universal Description, Discovery, and
Integration), 844
UDP protocol, 518
UGMC (universal group membership caching),
524–525, 528
Ultrasound.exe command, 621–622
unattended installation
answer files, 462–464
domain controllers, 462–464
listing of parameters, 26
Uniform Resource Identifier (URI), 844
Universal Description, Discovery, and Integration
(UDDI), 844
universal group membership caching (UGMC), 524–
525, 528
universal groups
AD RMS support, 814–815
characteristics, 148–149
defined, 51, 524
Universal Time Coordinate (UTC), 482
Update Sequence Number (USN), 632, 691
UPN (user principle name)
AD DS administration, 619
creating user objects, 49
identity claim type, 839
name attributes, 118
split-brain syndrome, 402
URI (Uniform Resource Identifier), 844
URLs, 810
use license, 790, 798, 812
user accounts
AD DS administration, 612
AD LDS support, 693
AD RMS considerations, 789, 809
administering, 124–130
automating creation, 93–96
certificate authorities, 742
creating with Dsadd command, 89, 94
creating with templates, 87–88, 93–94
data protection measures, 624
deleting, 128
disabling templates, 87

disabling/enabling, 127–128
group management strategies, 153
lockout policies, 126
managing, 614
migration considerations, 576
moving, 129
name attributes, 118–119
object protection, 626
recycling, 128
renaming, 129–130
resetting passwords, 125–126
unlocking, 126–127, 132
User Cannot Change Password setting, 120
User Configuration node
Administrative Templates node, 243–248
defined, 231, 241
Folder Redirection node, 242
Internet Explorer Maintenance node, 242
loopback policy processing, 270
Policies node, 241
Preferences node, 241, 243–244
Remote Installation Services node, 242
Software Settings node, 242
Windows Settings node, 242
User Must Change Password At Next Logon setting,
120, 125
user objects
account properties, 119–120
AD DS administration, 613, 620
creating, 48–50, 61–63
creating with VBScript, 109
creating with Windows PowerShell, 103–106, 110–111
hidden attributes, 88, 116–117
importing with CSVDE tool, 90, 94–95
importing with LDIFDE command, 90–92, 95–96
importing with Windows PowerShell, 106–108
managing attributes, 114–117, 121–124
multiselecting, 117, 131
name attributes, 118–119
populating attributes, 104–106
viewing attributes, 116–117, 130–131
user principle name. *See* UPN (user principle name)
user settings. *See* User Configuration node
userAccountControl attribute, 203
userPassword attribute, 558
userPrincipalName attribute, 118
Users container
as default container, 11
default groups, 177
domain local groups, 380
redirecting, 196, 559
userWorkstations attribute, 119

USN (Update Sequence Number), 632, 691
UTC (Universal Time Coordinate), 482

V

variables
  in cmdlets, 102, 123
  pipeline, 102
VBScript language
  ADMT support, 573
  configuring computer attributes, 214
  creating computers, 208, 211
  creating users, 109
  disabling accounts, 127
  enabling accounts, 128
  managing group membership, 164
  managing user attributes, 123–124
  moving computers, 215
  moving user accounts, 129
  overview, 108
  renaming user accounts, 130
  resetting passwords, 126
  unlocking user accounts, 127
  Windows PowerShell comparison, 109–110
verification certificate, 844
VHDs (virtual hard disks), 636
virtual appliances, 784
virtual machines
  AD LDS considerations, 695
  AD RMS considerations, 799
  additional information, 784
  certificate authorities, 737
  domain controllers as, 648–650
  high availability, 650
  restoring from complete backups, 645
Volume Shadow Copy Service (VSS), 648–650
VPNs (virtual private networks), 6
VSS (Volume Shadow Copy Service), 648–650
vssadmin command, 649

W

W32tm.exe command, 621
WAIK (Windows Automated Installation Kit), 631
Warning events, 663
Wbadmin.exe command
  AD DS administration, 630
  full system backup, 635
  performing restores, 643, 647
  scheduling backups, 636–638
Web browsers, 416, 731, 843
Web pages, 843

Web Proxy Automatic Discovery Protocol (WPAD), 415–416
Web server certificates, 804–805
Web Server template, 757
Web services
  AD FS support, 832, 854
  AD RMS support, 788
  defined, 844, 872
  division of responsibilities, 610
Web SSO, 837
Web.config file, 856
what-if analyses, 280–281
Where-Object cmdlet, 102
WID (Windows Internal Database), 786, 799
Win32_OperatingSystem class, 265
Windows 2000
  domain functional levels, 558
  forest functional levels, 561
Windows Automated Installation Kit (WAIK), 631
Windows Domain Manager, 591
Windows event IDs, 665
Windows Explorer, 618
Windows Installer package (.msi file), 322, 349
Windows Installer transform (.mst file), 323, 349
Windows Integrated authentication, 835
Windows Internal Database (WID), 786, 799
Windows Internet Name Service. *See* WINS (Windows Internet Name Service)
Windows Live ID, 811, 818
Windows Logs node, 281
Windows Management Interface. *See* WMI (Windows Management Interface)
Windows NT, 845
Windows Performance Monitor, 661, 666–670
  functionality, 671
Windows PowerShell
  cmdlet support, 99–103
  configuring computer attributes, 214
  console depicted, 99
  creating computers, 206–208, 211
  creating users, 103–106, 110–111
  deleting user accounts, 128
  disabling accounts, 127
  enabling accounts, 128
  importing computers, 206–208
  importing users, 106–108
  installing, 110
  managing group membership, 164
  managing user attributes, 123–124
  moving computers, 215
  moving user accounts, 129
  overview, 98–99

renaming user accounts, 130
resetting passwords, 126
script support, 108
VBScript comparison, 109–110
Windows Recovery Environment (WinRE), 631, 639
Windows Reliability and Performance Monitor (WRPM), 666
Windows Reliability and Performance node, 671
Windows Reliability Monitor, 661, 665
Windows RMS, 793–794, 818
Windows Scripting Host (WSH), 109
Windows Security log, 335
Windows Server 2003
  AD DS administration tools, 622
  domain functional levels, 558–559, 565
  forest functional levels, 561–562
Windows Server 2008
  AD DS administration tools, 622
  domain functional levels, 559
  forest functional levels, 562
  installing AD CS, 741
  system resource tools, 660–661
Windows Server Backup
  AD DS administration, 621, 703
  AD LDS support, 703
  creating installation media, 633
  data protection measures, 624, 629–630
  full system backups, 633–638
  operations supported, 630–632
  scheduling backups, 631, 635–638, 648
  system state data, 632
Windows Settings node, 242
Windows System Resource Manager (WSRM)
  functionality, 661, 672–674
  installing, 679–680
Windows Time, 621

Windows Token-Based Agent, 833, 846
Windows XP, 796
WinRE (Windows Recovery Environment), 631, 639
WINS (Windows Internet Name Service)
  DNS support, 442–443
  functionality, 409
  single-label names, 411
wireless communications, 730
wireless networks, 6, 753, 756
WMI (Windows Management Interface), 110, 264, 621
WMI filters, 234, 264–266
WMI Filters node, 265
workgroups, 189, 380, 470
WPAD (Web Proxy Automatic Discovery Protocol), 415–416
WRPM (Windows Reliability and Performance Monitor), 666
Wscript command, 108
WS-Federation Passive Requestor Profile, 832, 845, 872
WSH (Windows Scripting Host), 109
WSRM (Windows System Resource Manager)
  functionality, 661, 672–674
  installing, 679–680
WS-Security, 845

X

XML (Extensible Markup Language), 349, 844
XML Notepad tool, 327

Z

zone delegation, 412, 422–424
zone scavenging, 412, 432–433
zone transfers, 412
zones. *See* DNS zones

Windows Server 2008— Resources for Administrators

Prepare for Certification with Self-Paced Training Kits

Official Exam Prep Guides—
Plus Practice Tests

Ace your preparation for the skills measured by the MCP exams—and on the job. With official *Self-Paced Training Kits* from Microsoft, you'll work at your own pace through a system of lessons, hands-on exercises, troubleshooting labs, and review questions. Then test yourself with the Readiness Review Suite on CD, which provides hundreds of challenging questions for in-depth self-assessment and practice.

- **MCSE Self-Paced Training Kit (Exams 70-290, 70-291, 70-293, 70-294): Microsoft® Windows Server™ 2003 Core Requirements.** 4-Volume Boxed Set. ISBN: 0-7356-1953-0. (Individual volumes are available separately.)
- **MCSA/MCSE Self-Paced Training Kit (Exam 70-270): Installing, Configuring, and Administering Microsoft Windows® XP Professional, Second Edition.** ISBN: 0-7356-2152-7.
- **MCSE Self-Paced Training Kit (Exam 70-298): Designing Security for a Microsoft Windows Server 2003 Network.** ISBN: 0-7356-1969-7.
- **MCSA/MCSE Self-Paced Training Kit (Exam 70-350): Implementing Microsoft Internet Security and Acceleration Server 2004.** ISBN: 0-7356-2169-1.
- **MCSA/MCSE Self-Paced Training Kit (Exam 70-284): Implementing and Managing Microsoft Exchange Server 2003.** ISBN: 0-7356-1899-2.

For more information about Microsoft Press® books, visit: **www.microsoft.com/mspress**

For more information about learning tools such as online assessments, e-learning, and certification, visit: **www.microsoft.com/mspress** *and* **www.microsoft.com/learning**

Windows Server 2008 Resource Kit—
Your Definitive Resource!

Windows Server® 2008 Resource Kit

Microsoft® MVPs with Microsoft Windows Server Team

ISBN 9780735623613

Your definitive reference for deployment and operations—from the experts who know the technology best. Get in-depth technical information on Active Directory®, Windows PowerShell™ scripting, advanced administration, networking and network access protection, security administration, IIS, and other critical topics—plus an essential toolkit of resources on CD.

Also available as single volumes

Windows Server 2008 Security Resource Kit

Jesper M. Johansson et al. with Microsoft Security Team

ISBN 9780735625044

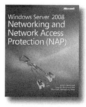

Windows Server 2008 Networking and Network Access Protection (NAP)

Joseph Davies, Tony Northrup, Microsoft Networking Team

ISBN 9780735624221

Windows Server 2008 Active Directory Resource Kit

Stan Reimer et al. with Microsoft Active Directory Team

ISBN 9780735625150

Windows® Administration Resource Kit: Productivity Solutions for IT Professionals

Dan Holme

ISBN 9780735624313

Windows Powershell Scripting Guide

Ed Wilson

ISBN 9780735622791

Internet Information Services (IIS) 7.0 Resource Kit

Mike Volodarsky et al. with Microsoft IIS Team

ISBN 9780735624412

See our complete line of books at: **microsoft.com/mspress**

System Requirements

To use the companion CD-ROM you need a computer running Microsoft Windows Server 2008, Windows Vista, Windows Server 2003, or Windows XP. The computer must meet the following minimum requirements:

- 1 GHz 32-bit (x86) or 64-bit (x64) processor (depending on the minimum requirements of the operating system)
- 1 GB of system memory (depending on the minimum requirements of the operating system)
- A hard disk partition with at least 1 GB of available space
- A monitor capable of at least 800x600 display resolution
- A keyboard
- A mouse or other pointing device
- An optical drive capable of reading CD-ROMs

The computer must also have the following software:

- A Web browser such as Internet Explorer version 6 or later
- An application that can display PDF files, such as Adobe Reader, which can be downloaded at *http://www.adobe.com/reader*

These requirements will support use of the companion CD-ROM. To perform the practice exercises in this training kit, you might require additional hardware or software. See the Introduction to the book for detailed hardware requirements.

What do you think of this book?

We want to hear from you!

Do you have a few minutes to participate in a brief online survey?

Microsoft is interested in hearing your feedback so we can continually improve our books and learning resources for you.

To participate in our survey, please visit:

www.microsoft.com/learning/booksurvey/

...and enter this book's ISBN-10 or ISBN-13 number (located above barcode on back cover*). As a thank-you to survey participants in the United States and Canada, each month we'll randomly select five respondents to win one of five $100 gift certificates from a leading online merchant. At the conclusion of the survey, you can enter the drawing by providing your e-mail address, which will be used for prize notification only.

Thanks in advance for your input. Your opinion counts!

* Where to find the ISBN on back cover

ISBN-13: 000-0-0000-0000-0
ISBN-10: 0-0000-0000-0

Example only. Each book has unique ISBN.

***Microsoft** Press*

No purchase necessary. Void where prohibited. Open only to residents of the 50 United States (includes District of Columbia) and Canada (void in Quebec). For official rules and entry dates see:

www.microsoft.com/learning/booksurvey/

Save 15%
on your Microsoft® Certification exam fee

Present this discount voucher to any participating test center worldwide, or use the discount code to register online or via telephone at participating Microsoft Certified Exam Delivery Providers. See microsoft.com/mcp/exams for locations.

Microsoft

Microsoft | Learning

Good for 15% off one exam fee in the Microsoft Certified Professional Program

Offer expires 12/31/2012

Your voucher discount code

exam voucher

Redeemable at Microsoft Certified Exam Delivery Providers worldwide. For locations, visit: www.microsoft.com/mcp/exams

Promotion Terms and Conditions

- Offer good for 15% off one exam fee in the Microsoft Certified Professional Program.
- Voucher code can be redeemed online or at Microsoft Certified Exam Delivery Providers worldwide.
- Exam purchased using this voucher code must be taken on or before December 31, 2012.
- Inform your Microsoft Certified Exam Delivery Provider that you want to use the voucher discount code at the time you register for the exam.

Voucher Terms and Conditions

- Expired vouchers will not be replaced.
- Each voucher code may only be used for one exam and must be presented at time of registration.
- This voucher may not be combined with other vouchers or discounts.
- This voucher is nontransferable and is void if altered or revised in any way.
- This voucher may not be sold or redeemed for cash, credit, or refund.

Microsoft

X13-92079